Street by Street

G000292406

ESSEX

Enlarged areas BASILDON, CHELMSFORD, CLACTON-ON-SEA, COLCHESTER, FELIXSTOWE, HARLOW, HARWICH, IPSWICH, SOUTHEND-ON-SEA, SUDBURY

Plus Bishop's Stortford, Braintree, Cheshunt, Grays, Haverhill, Hoddesdon, Ilford, Romford, Waltham Abbey, Walthamstow

2nd edition September 2005
© Automobile Association Developments Limited 2005

Original edition printed May 2001

Ordnance Survey® This product includes map data licensed from Ordnance Survey® with the permission of the Controller of Her Majesty's Stationery Office. © Crown copyright 2005. All rights reserved. Licence number 399221.

Published by AA Publishing (a trading name of Automobile Association Developments Limited, whose registered office (from 1st October 2005) will be Fanum House, Basing View, Basingstoke, Hampshire RG21 4EA. Registered number 1878835).

Mapping produced by the Cartography Department of The Automobile Association. (A02543)

A CIP Catalogue record for this book is available from the British Library.

Printed and bound by Leo, China

Ref: MX028z

Key to map pages	ii-iii
Key to map symbols	iv-1
Map pages - 1:10,000	2-21
Map pages - 1:17,500	22-339
Map pages - 1:25,000	340-399
Index – towns & villages	400-401
Index – streets	402-451
Index – featured places	451-459
Acknowledgements	460

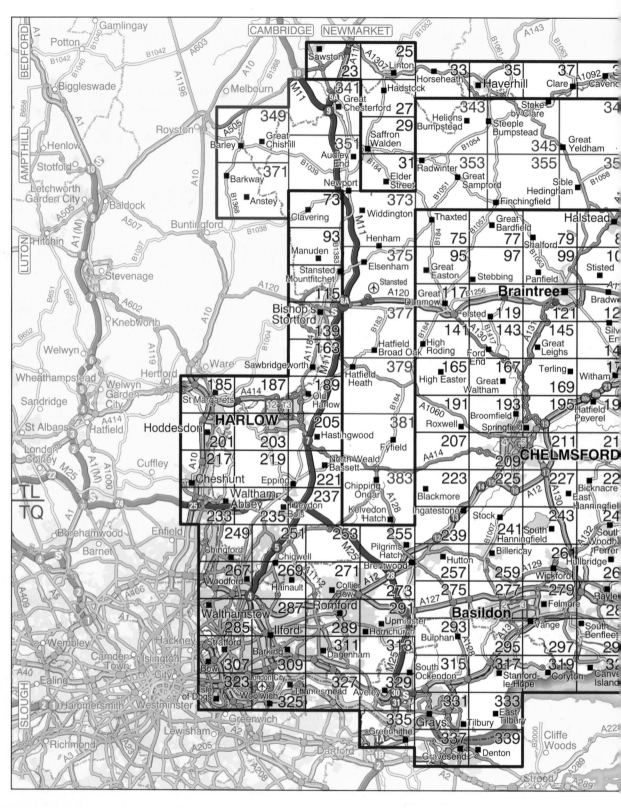

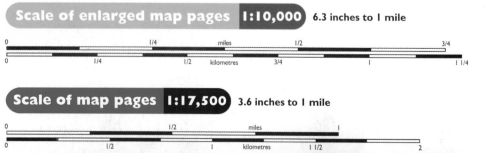

TL|TM
NEEDHAM MARKET

BURY ST EDMUNDS

A1141
A1071
B1078
B1079
A12
B1084
Woodbridge
Orford Ness

41
43
Long ford
20·21
Sudbury
45

Hadleigh
A1070

Bramford
47
49
51 Martlesham
Washbrook
16·17
IPSWICH
A14
53
55
57 Bucklesham

North Point

Hollesley Bay

Capel St Mary
59
Freston
365
61
63 Old Felixstowe
Levington
59
10·11
69 Felixstowe
65
Holbrook
Shotley Gate
67
B1080

359
Twinstead
Bures
361
Nayland
Thorington Street
Stratford St Mary
363
89
Cattawade
Harwich
14·15

83
Earls olne
85 Horkesley Heath
87
Ardleigh
91
Manningtree
Ramsey
367
Little Oakley
71
369
Fordham

103 Great Tey
Fordstreet
107
Colchester
109
111
113
Tendring Green
135
Horsey Island
The Naze

125
Coggeshall
Marks Tey
127
129 Blackheath
131 Wivenhoe
133
Great Bentley
Thorpe-le-Soken
B1034

Walton-on-the-Naze
Frinton-on-Sea

149
Tiptree
151
153
155 Brightlingsea
157 Little Clacton
St Osyth
159
137
161
Holland-on-Sea

173 Great Totham
175 Tolleshunt Knights
177 West Mersea
179 East Mersea
181 Point Clear
Jaywick
183
6·7
Clacton-on-Sea

Langenhoe
Colne Point

199 eybridge
B1026
Tollesbury
387
Bradwell Waterside

215 Maldon
385
Ramsey Island
391

231 chingdon
B1018
Maylandsea
Tillingham

247 North Fambridge
389
Southminster
395
Montsale
Burnham-on-Crouch

265 ockley
Ashingdon
393
397
Churchend

283 Rochford
Southend
Barling
399

301
18·19
303
305
SOUTHEND-ON-SEA
Shoeburyness
Shoebury Ness

Sheerness
Minster

TQ|TR
Warden Point

Margate
NORTH FORELAND

HOEK VAN HOLLAND
CUXHAVEN, ESBJERG
HOEK VAN HOLLAND

TM
TR

National Grid references are shown on the map frame of each page.
Red figures denote the 100 km square and the blue figures the 1km square.

Example, page 53 : St Josephs College 615 243

The reference can also be written using the National Grid two-letter prefix
shown on this page, where 6 and 2 are replaced by TM to give TM1543

2.5 inches to 1 mile   **Scale of map pages 1:25,000**

miles
0   1/2   1   1 1/2

kilometres
0   1/2   1   1 1/2   2

Junction 9	Motorway & junction
Services	Motorway service area
	Primary road single/dual carriageway
Services	Primary road service area
	A road single/dual carriageway
	B road single/dual carriageway
	Other road single/dual carriageway
	Minor/private road, access may be restricted
← ←	One-way street
	Pedestrian area
	Track or footpath
	Road under construction
	Road tunnel
P	Parking
P+	Park & Ride
	Bus/coach station
	Railway & main railway station
	Railway & minor railway station
⊖	Underground station

⊖	Light railway & station
+++++++++	Preserved private railway
LC	Level crossing
●—●—●—●	Tramway
- - - - - -	Ferry route
....	Airport runway
- · - · - · -	County, administrative boundary
345	Page continuation 1:25,000
93	Page continuation 1:17,500
7	Page continuation to enlarged scale 1:10,000
	River/canal, lake
	Aqueduct, lock, weir
465 ▲ Winter Hill	Peak (with height in metres)
	Beach
	Woodland
	Park
	Cemetery
	Built-up area
	Featured building
⊓⊔⊓⊔⊓⊔	City wall

A&E	Hospital with 24-hour A&E department
PO	Post Office
📖	Public library
i	Tourist Information Centre
i	Seasonal Tourist Information Centre
	Petrol station, 24 hour Major suppliers only
†	Church/chapel
	Public toilets
♿	Toilet with disabled facilities
PH	Public house AA recommended
	Restaurant AA inspected
Madeira Hotel	Hotel AA inspected
	Theatre or performing arts centre
	Cinema
⚑	Golf course
▲	Camping AA inspected
	Caravan site AA inspected
	Camping & caravan site AA inspected
	Theme park
	Abbey, cathedral or priory

	Castle
	Historic house or building
Wakehurst Place NT	National Trust property
🏛	Museum or art gallery
	Roman antiquity
	Ancient site, battlefield or monument
	Industrial interest
❋	Garden
◉	Garden Centre Garden Centre Association Member
	Garden Centre Wyevale Garden Centre
	Arboretum
	Farm or animal centre
	Zoological or wildlife collection
	Bird collection
	Nature reserve
	Aquarium
V	Visitor or heritage centre
	Country park
	Cave
	Windmill
	Distillery, brewery or vineyard

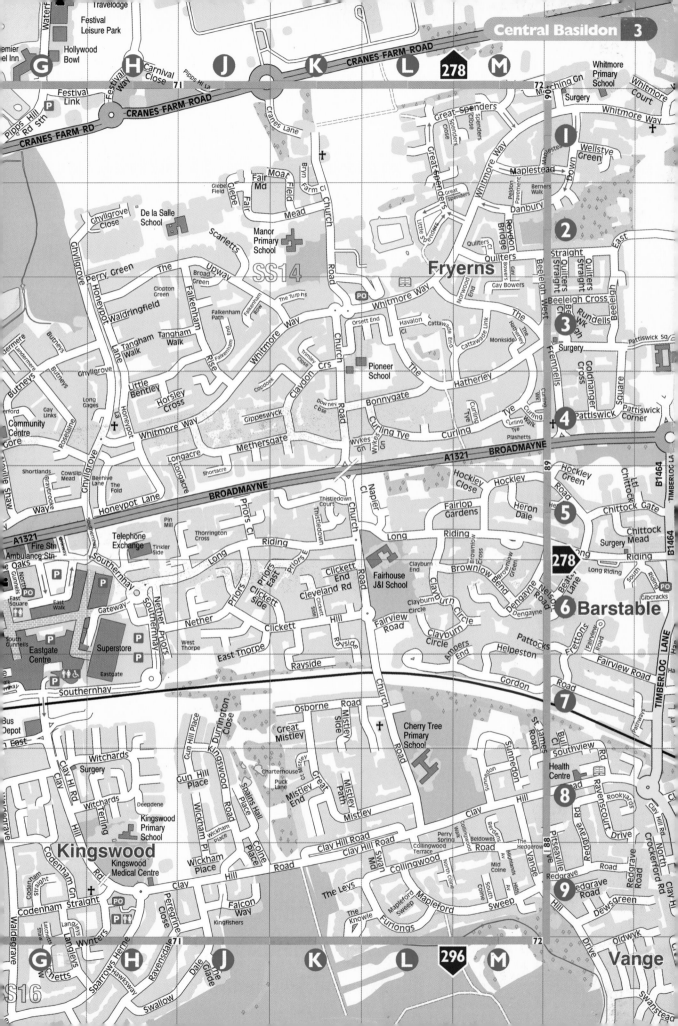

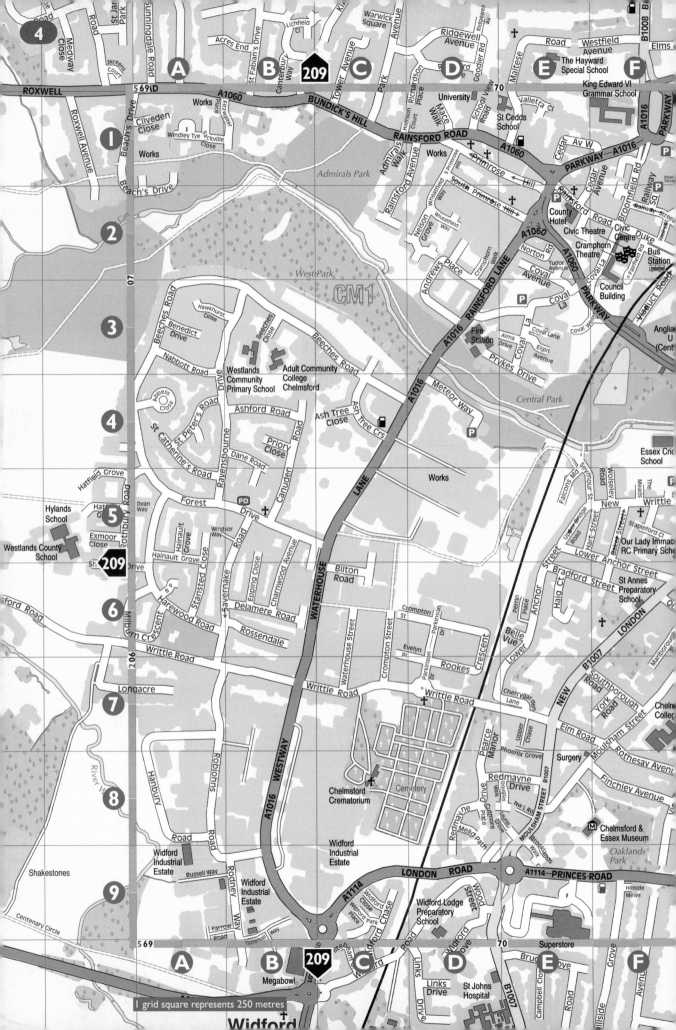

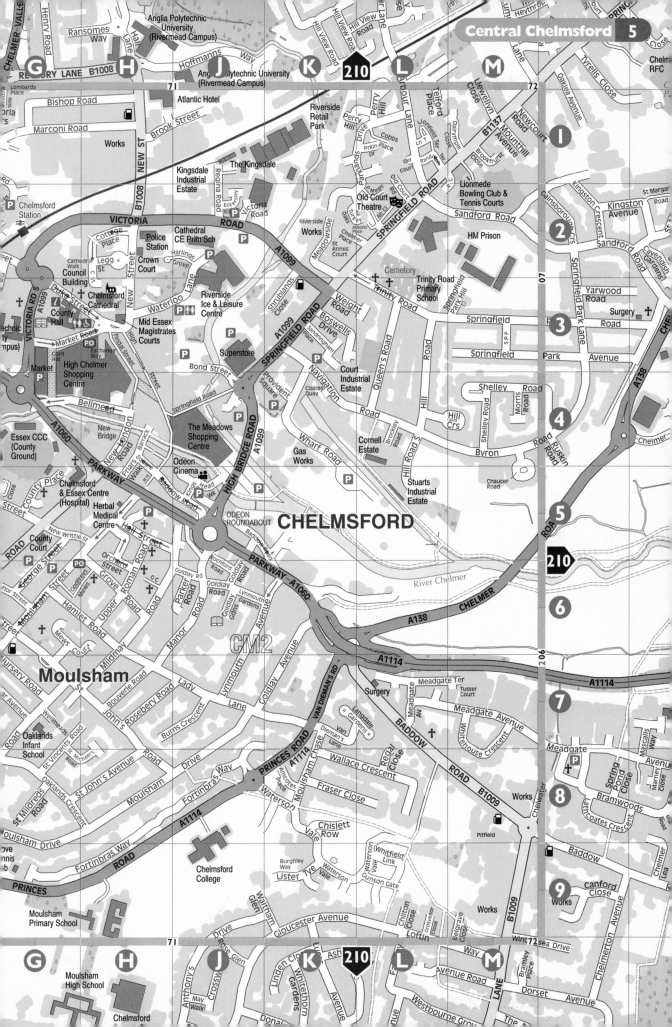

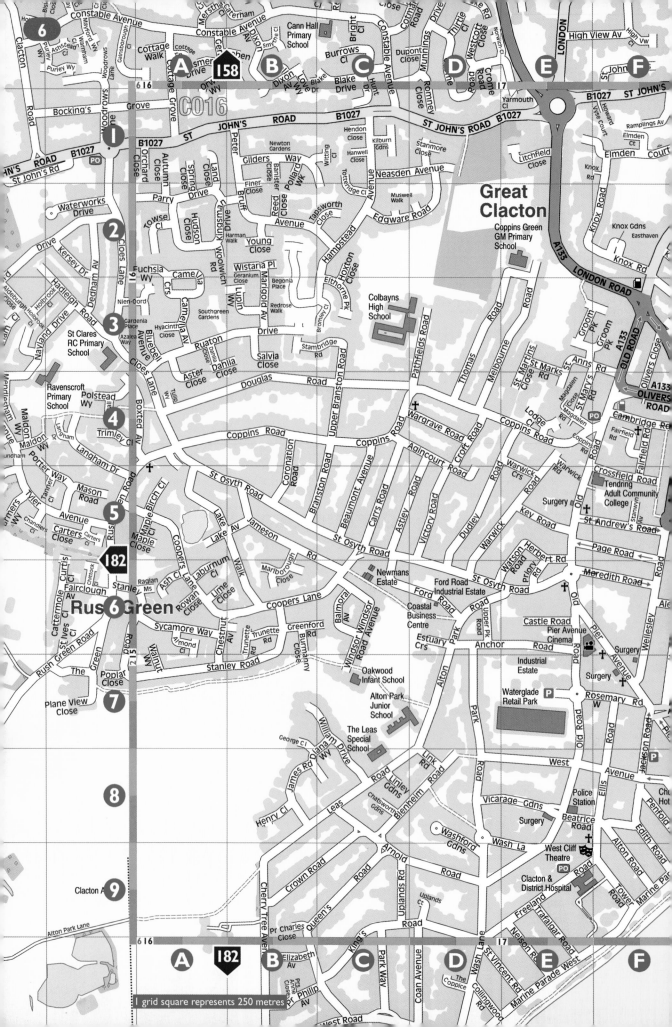

CLACTON-ON-SEA

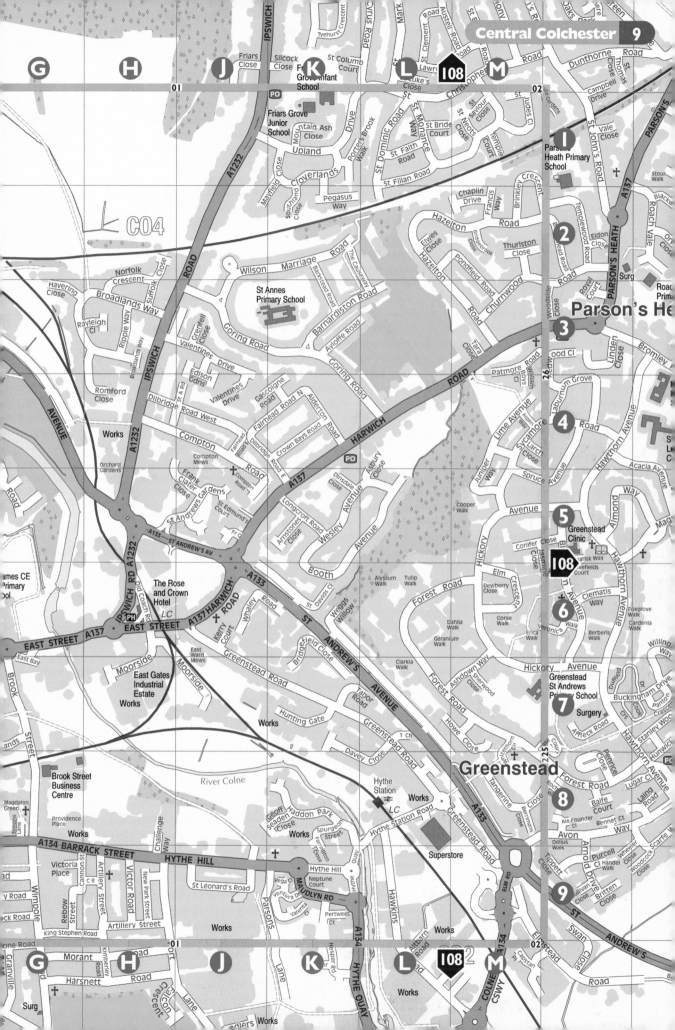

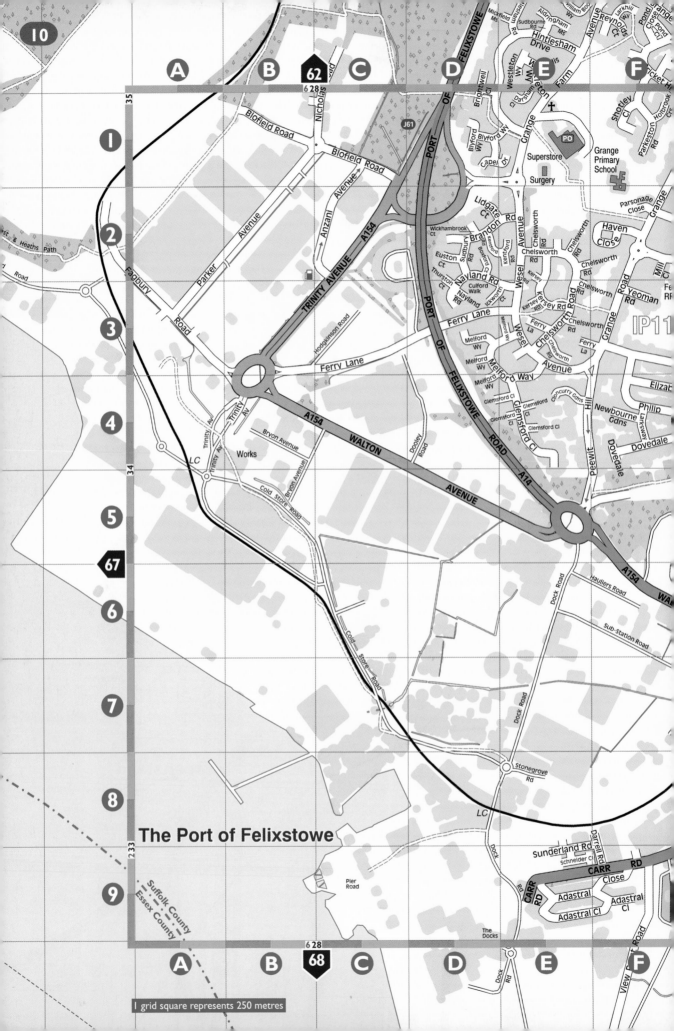

The Port of Felixstowe

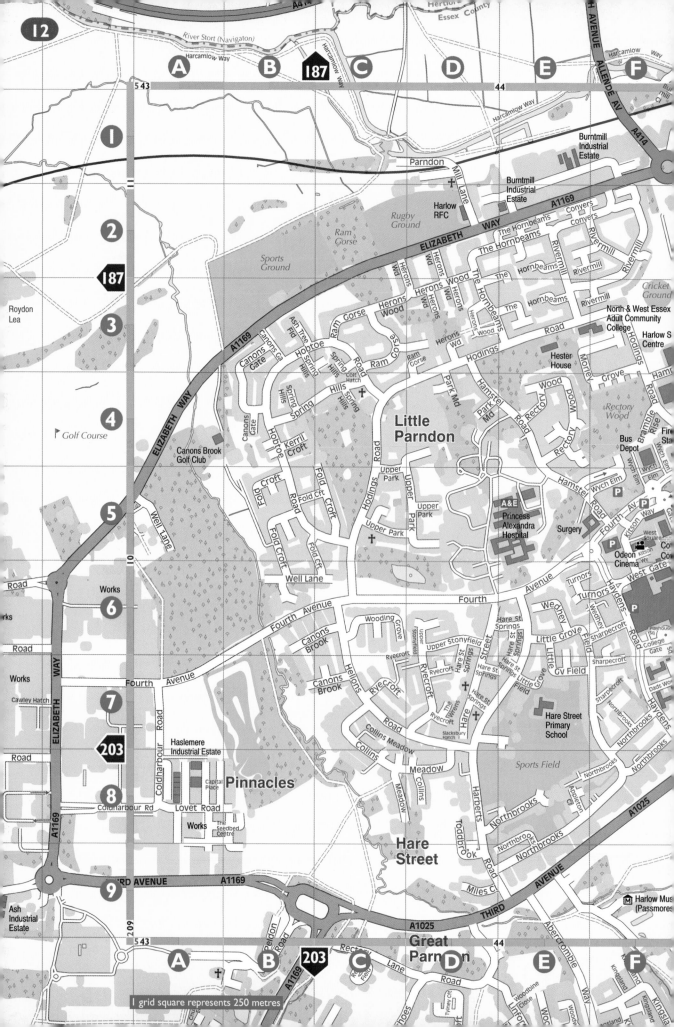

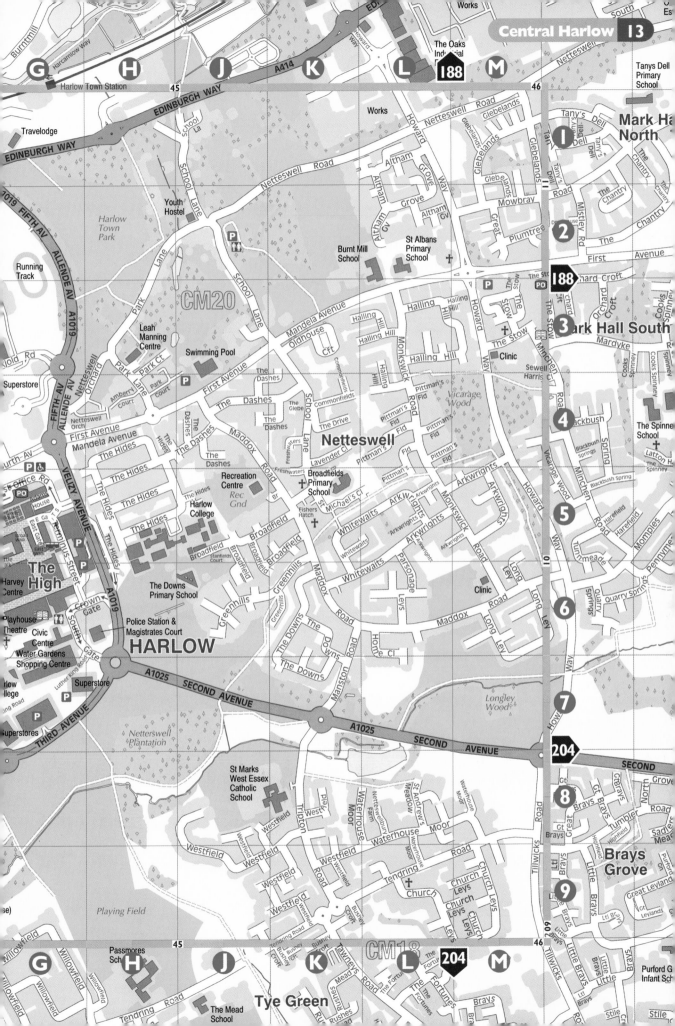

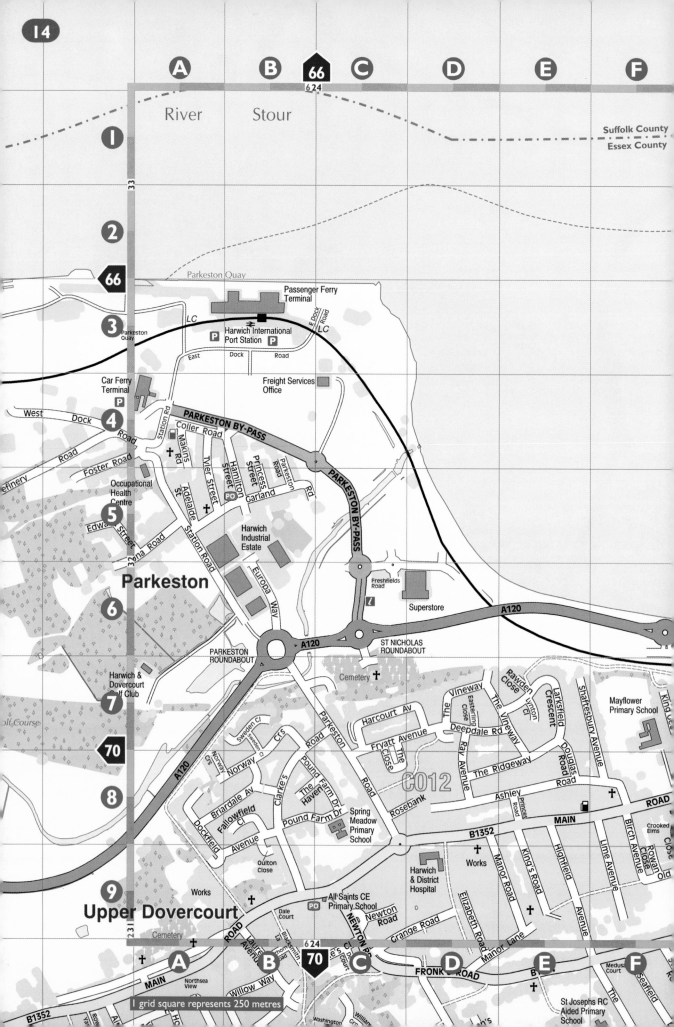

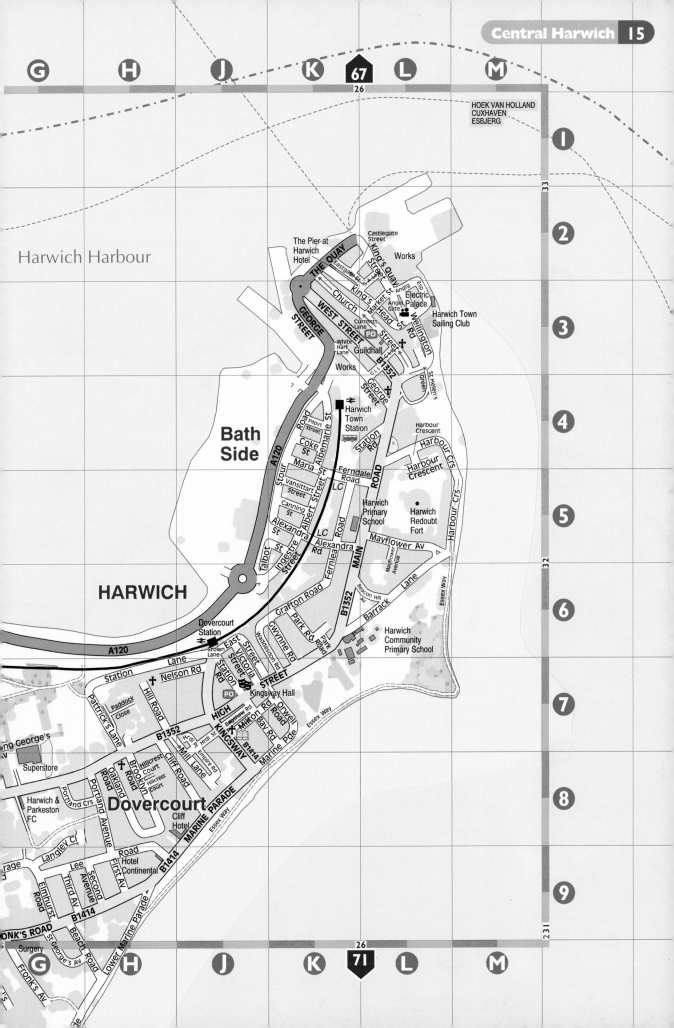

Harwich Harbour

HOEK VAN HOLLAND
CUXHAVEN
ESBJERG

The Pier at Harwich Hotel

Castlegate Street

King's Quay Street

Works

King's Head St

Market St

Anglg

Angel Gate

Electric Palace

Harwich Town Sailing Club

THE QUAY

Eastgate St

WEST STREET

Church

Wellington Rd

GEORGE STREET

Currents Lane

PO

White Hart Lane

Guildhall

Works

St Helen's Green

George Street

B1352

St Helen's Green

Bath Side

Harwich Town Station

Harbour Crescent

Harbour Crescent

Harbour Crs

Pepys Street

Coke St

Maria St

Allemarle St

Stour

Vansittart Street

Canning St

Alexandra St

Albert Street

Ferndale Road

LC

Station Rd

Ferndale Road

MAIN ROAD

A120

Talbot St

Ingestre Street

Alexandra Rd

LC

Harwich Primary School

Harwich Redoubt Fort

Harbour Crs

HARWICH

Mayflower Av

Mayflower Avenue

B1352

Beacon Hill Av

Barrack Lane

Essex Way

Dovercourt Station

A120

Crown Lane

Grafton Road

Park Rd

Gwynne Rd

Park Road

Harwich Community Primary School

Station Lane

East Street

Victoria Street

Station Rd

Waddeson Rd

Bagshaw Rd

HIGH STREET

Essex Way

Nelson Rd

Paddock Close

Hill Road

PO

Kingsway Hall

KINGSWAY

B1352

Milton Rd

Orwell Road

Bay Rd

Marine Pde

Essex Way

Patrick's Lane

Hrd Pl

Empire Rd

B1414

King George's Superstore

Hillcrest Court

Brooklyn Court

Hillcrest Court

Cliff Road

Mill Lane

Oakland Road

Portland Avenue

Portland Crs

Dovercourt

Cliff Hotel

MARINE PARADE

Essex Way

B1414

Harwich & Parkeston FC

Langley Cl

Lee Avenue

Second Av

First Av

First Road

Elmhurst Road

Third Av

Beach Road

Hotel Continental

B1414

FONK'S ROAD

MONK'S ROAD

St George's Av

Lower Marine Parade

Surgery

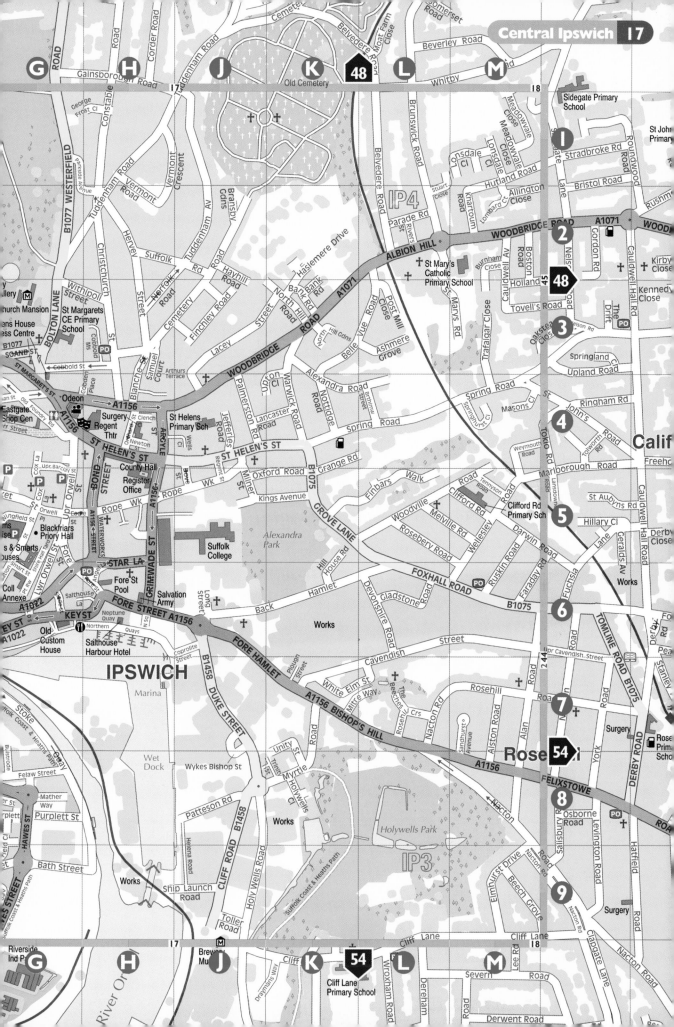

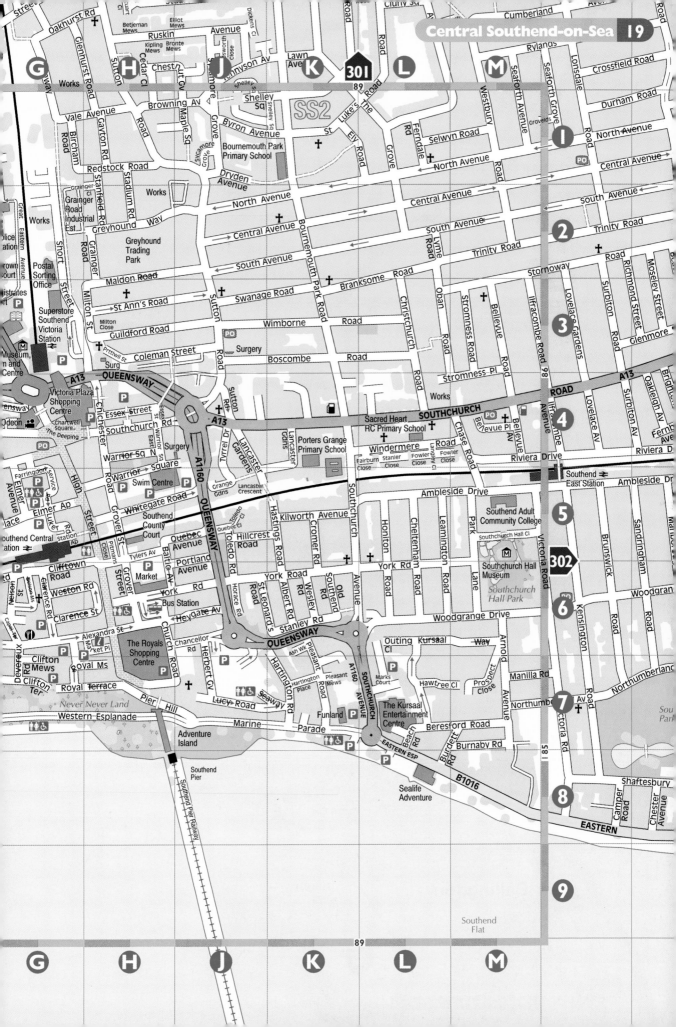

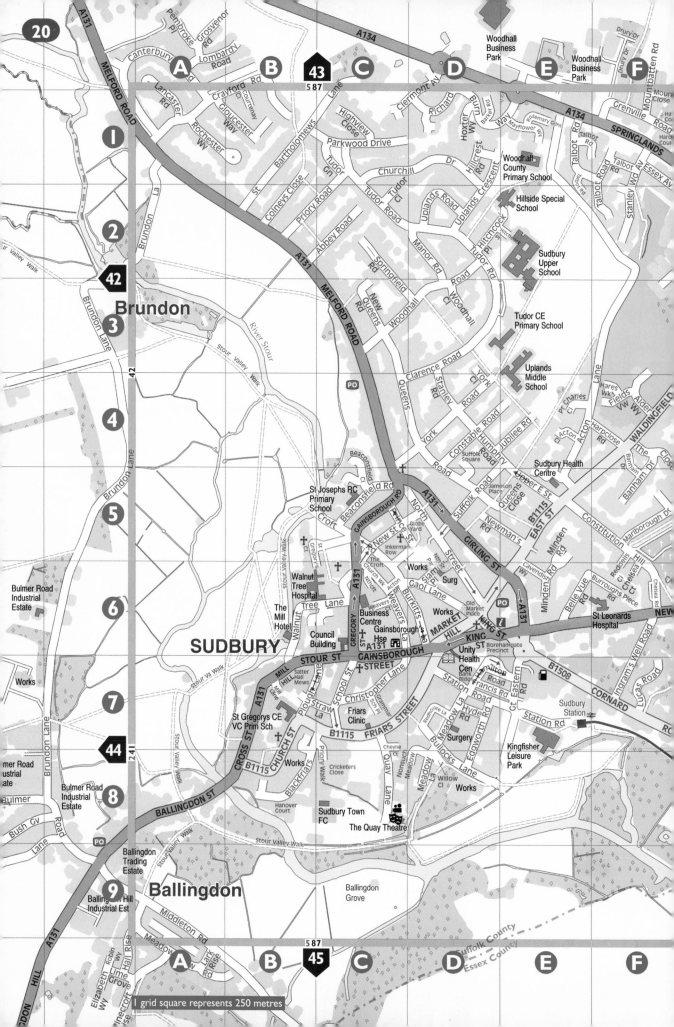

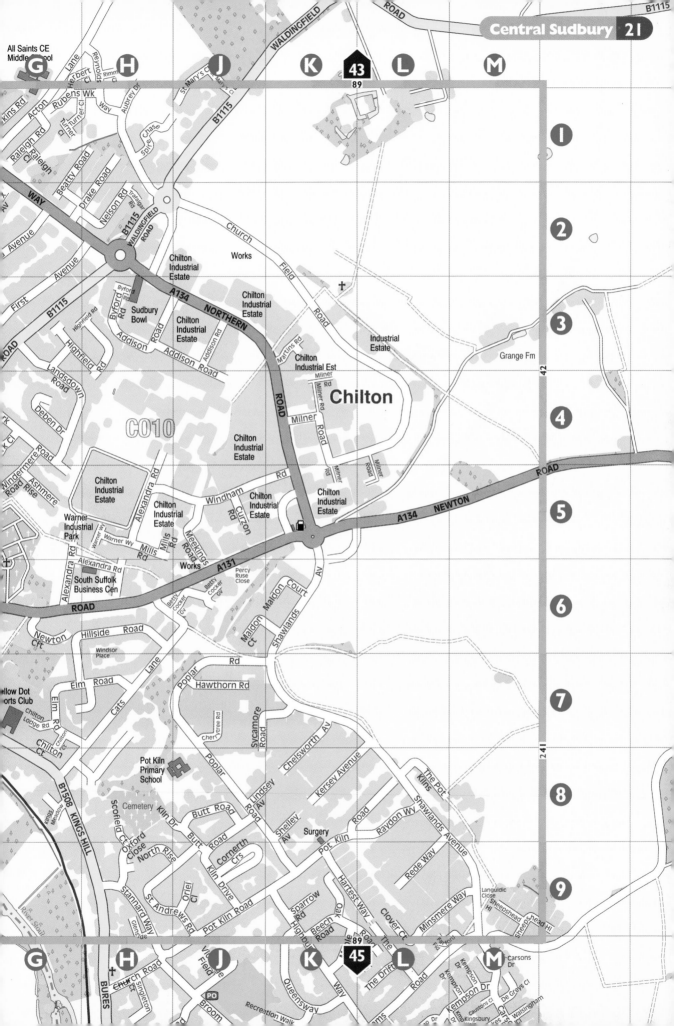

Babraham CE
Primary School

High Street

High Street

Babraham Road

G H J K L M

51 52 Fourwentways Service Area 53 50

Travelodge

Cambridge Rd

I

CAMBRIDGE ROAD A1307

Little
Abingto

Bourn Bridge Road

Bourn
Bridge

West Field

Church

The Grip
Industrial
Estate

Ivan Clark's
Corner

2

Lane

Church Close

High Street

49

A11

River Cranta

Great Abington
Primary School

PO

3

A505

Station Road

Meadow Walk

Linton Road

Great
Abington

High Street

Magna
Close

High Street

Motlock Gardens

Lewis
Crs

Lewis
Close

4

Pampisford Road

48 24

North Road

5

South Road

A11

Chalky Road

6

Hinxton
Grange

47

7

246

8

Abington Park
Farm

Cambridgeshire County
Essex County

G H J K L M

Wood Hall

57 58 59

50

1

2

49

3

4

48

5

6

A130

47 32

7

46

8

G H J K L M

57 58 59

27

Balsham Wood

Yole Farm

Balsham Road

B1052

Borley Wood

Greenditch Farm

Riveyhill Farm

Wood

Iknield Way Path

Horseheath Lodge

Heath Farm

B1052

Road

Tower View

BALSHAM

Close

Barley Way

Ballingdon Lane

Brinkman Road

Wheatsheaf Way

Howroyd's

Beautre

Crescent Way

Linton

Parsonage Way

Fairfield

Millers Close

Kent

Linton Heights Junior School

Diplin Cl

Horseheath Road

High St

Im Con Crossway

Granta Vale

Simson's Close

Bartlow

Bakers Lane

Martins Lane

Lonsdale

Harefield Rise

Kenwood Gdns

Fincham's Close

Road

The Ridgeway

A1307

A1307

1307

Barham Hall

River Bourn

Cambridgeshire County

Essex County

Iknield Way Path

Guilford Hill Vineyard

A   B   C   **24**   D   E   F

554   55   56

Linton Zoological Gardens

Lane

STOCK ROAD

B1052 LINTON ROAD

1

2

46

Cambridgeshire County

Essex County

Icknield Way Path

Icknield Way Path

45

Orch

Pightle

Moules Lane

Church Path

Back

3

Pen Farm

WALDEN ROAD

✝

Hadstock

Crave Hall Farm

B1052

4

Hadstock Common

44

341

Burtonwood Farm

Icknield Way Path

5

Icknield Way Path

B1052

6

43

Monk's Hall

Park Farm

Boy

7

B1052

Bowser's Lane

Chesterford Park

Ravenstock Green Farm

8

Mitchells

242

anuel ood

Petts Lane

554   55   56

A   B   C   **28**   D   E   F

Little Walden

B1052

1 grid square represents 500 metres

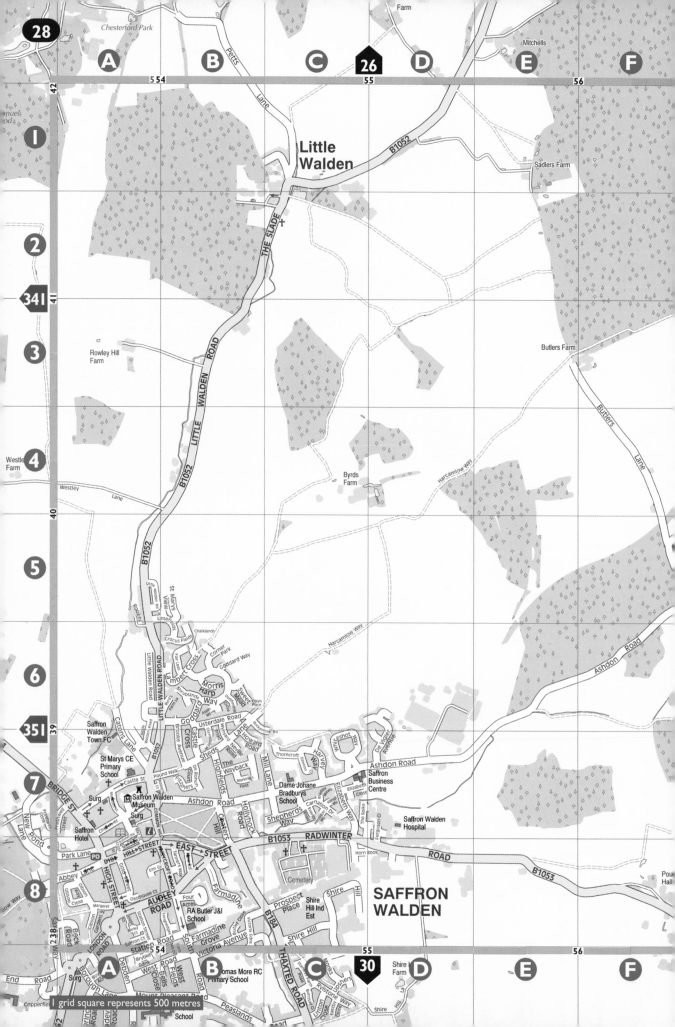

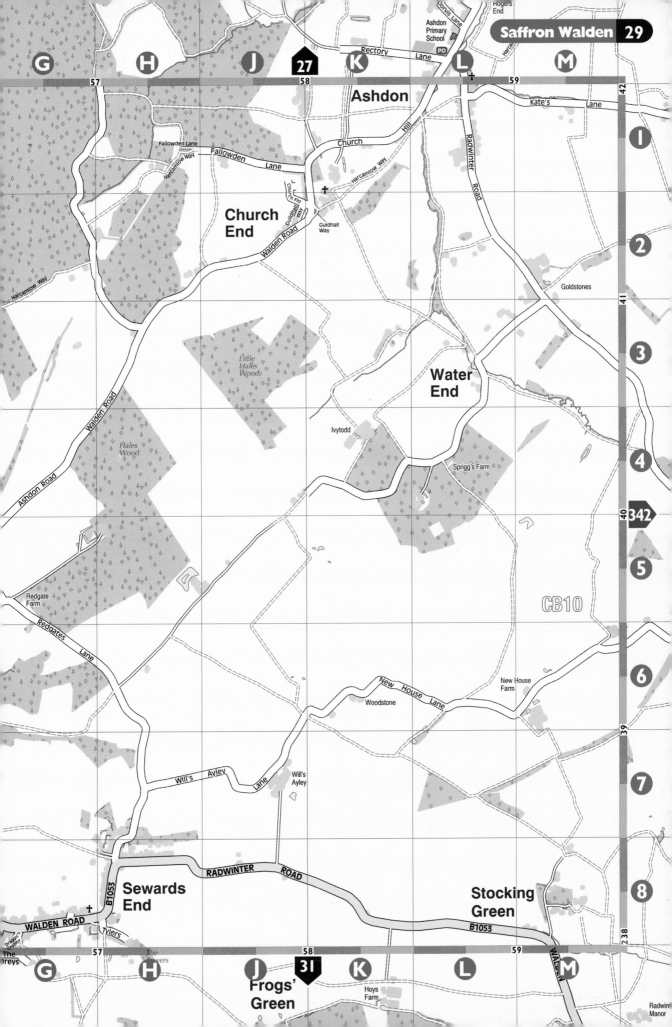

G H J **27** K L M

57 58 59 42

Ashdon

Rectory Lane

Ashdon Primary School

Jorvis Lane

Rogers End

Kate's Lane

Church Hill

Fallowden Lane

Fallowden Lane

Harcamlow Way

Church End

Walden Road

Guildhall Way

Church Fld Way

Harcamlow Way

Radwinter Road

Harcamlow way

Goldstones

Little Hales Wood

Water End

Ivytodd

Walden Road

Ashdon Road

Hales Wood

Sprigg's Farm

CB10

342

Redgate Farm

Redgates Lane

New House Lane

New House Farm

Woodstone

Will's Ayley Lane

Will's Ayley

Sewards End

B1053

RADWINTER ROAD

Stocking Green

WALDEN ROAD

Tylers

Dragon's Green

The Greys

The Tylers

B1053

G H J **31** K L M

57 58 59 38

Frogs' Green

Hoys Farm

Rogers End

WALDEN

Radwinter Manor

RADWINTER ROAD

B1053

Sewards
End

G **H** **J** 29 **K** **L** **M**
57 58 59

Tylers

W ... ROAD

The
reys

The
Towers

I Radwinter
Manor

**Frogs'
Green**

Hoys
Farm

Frogsgreen
Farm

Newhouse Farm

Tiptoft
Farm

2

Cole End Lane

**Cole
End**

+ **Wimbish**

Wimbish
Hall

3

River Pant

4

352

5

New House
Farm

Wimbish
Primary
School

Maypole
Farm

Parsonage
Farm

Mill Road

**Tye
Green**

6

Wimbish Wk

Walden Av

Rowney
Av

Broad Oaks

Debden Drive

Pinkley
Close

Close

PO

THAXTED ROAD

B184

Parsonage Lane

Mill Road

THAXTED ROAD

**Howlett
End**

Cemetery

B184

7

ver
racks

**Elder
Street**

Peppies Lane

8

G **H** **J** 373 **K** **L** **M**
57 58 59

Rowney
Wood

Peppies
Farm

Walden Road

Maple Lane

Stocki
Green

1053

38

37

36

35

234

THA

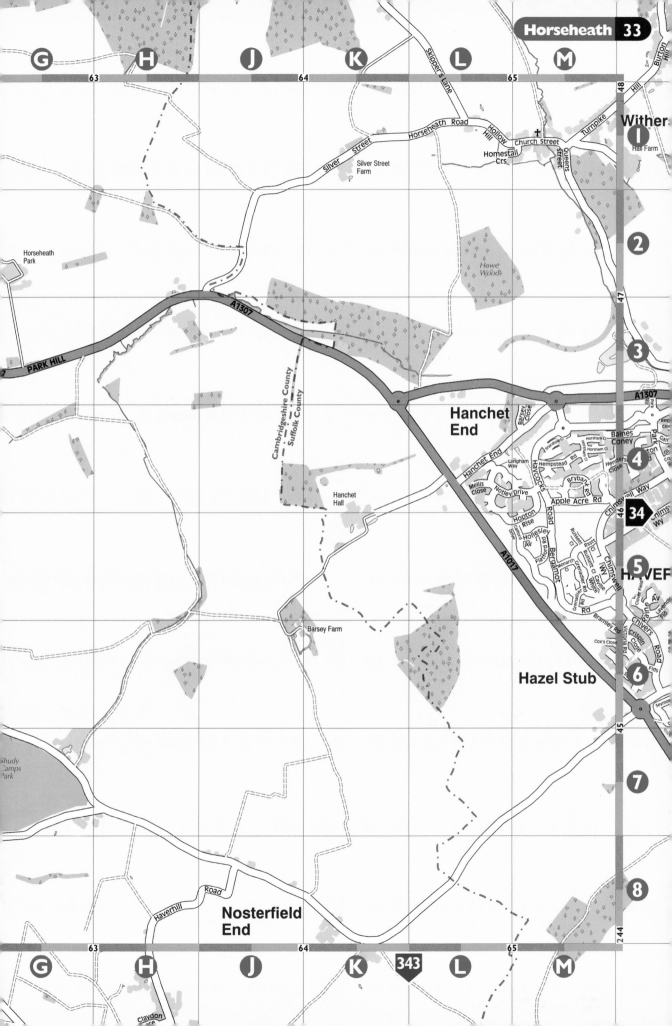

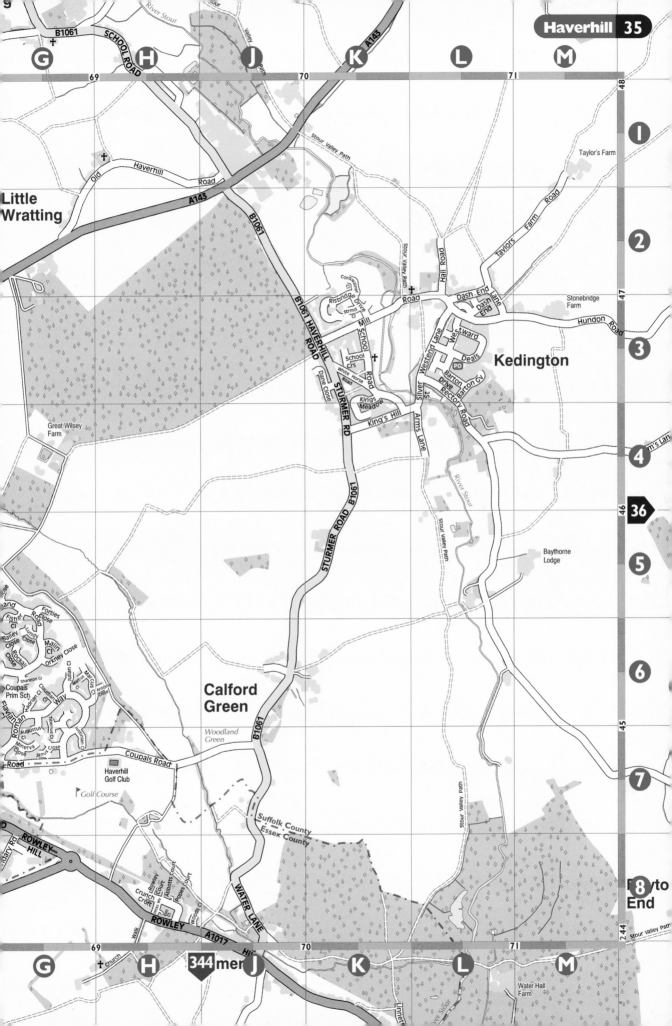

River Stour

B1061
SCHOOL ROAD

G 69 H 70 J K L 71 M

Taylor's Farm

I

Stour Valley Path

Old Haverhill Road
A143
B1061

Little Wratting

2

Taylors Farm Road

Hall Road

Stonebridge Farm

Cordwaine Drive
Risbridge Drive
Strmd Cl
Road
Dash End Lane
Dash End

Hundon Road

3

B1061 HAVERHILL ROAD
Mill
School Crs
School Road
White Horse Road
Dane Close
Kings Meadow
Westend Lane
Silver St
Westward
Deals
PO
Barton
Drive
Barton Gv

Kedington

Great Wilsey Farm

STURMER RD
King's Hill
Arms Lane
Rectory Road

m's Lan

4

River Stour

STURMER ROAD B1061

Stour Valley Path

46 **36**

Baythorne Lodge

5

Forties
Fisher Cl
Roland
Bailey Close
Close
Tundy Close
Malin Cl
Orkney Close
Rockall Close
Shannon Cl
Julian Cl
Marcus Cl
Claudian Way
Hadrian Cl
Antonia Close
Coupals Prim Sch
Flavian
Roman Way
Augustus Cl
Tiberius Cl
Janus Cl
Minerva Close
Justinian Cl

6

Calford Green

Woodland Green

B1061

7

Road
Coupals Road
Haverhill Golf Club
Golf Course
Suffolk County
Essex County

Stour Valley Path

ROWLEY HILL
Boundary Rd

to End
8

Rowley Court
Crunch Croft
Tibbotts Court
Popes Court
Woods Cl
WATER LANE
Hill

ROWLEY A1017

44
344 mer

River Stour

Water Hall Farm

Stour Valley Path

G 69 H **344** J 70 K L 71 M

Ⓐ   Ⓑ   Ⓒ   Ⓓ   Ⓔ   Ⓕ

5 72   73   74

Mount Pleasant

Clock Hall

Green Lane

Clock

Mare Hill

Clar

Ⓘ

Taylor's Farm

Buntry Lane

Brockley Green

Parsonage Farm

⓶

PH

Stonebridge Farm

Hundon Road

⓷

⓸

Sim's Lane

35

Lords Wood

⓹

⓺

Crooks Hall

Bank Lane

California Farm

Way

Stonard's Farm

⓻

Cain's Hill

Farmer's Farm

⓼

Boyton End

2 44

Stour Valley Path

5 72   73   74

Ⓐ   Ⓑ   Ⓒ   Ⓓ **345** Ⓔ   Ⓕ

Blacksmith

A1092

1 grid square represents 500 metres

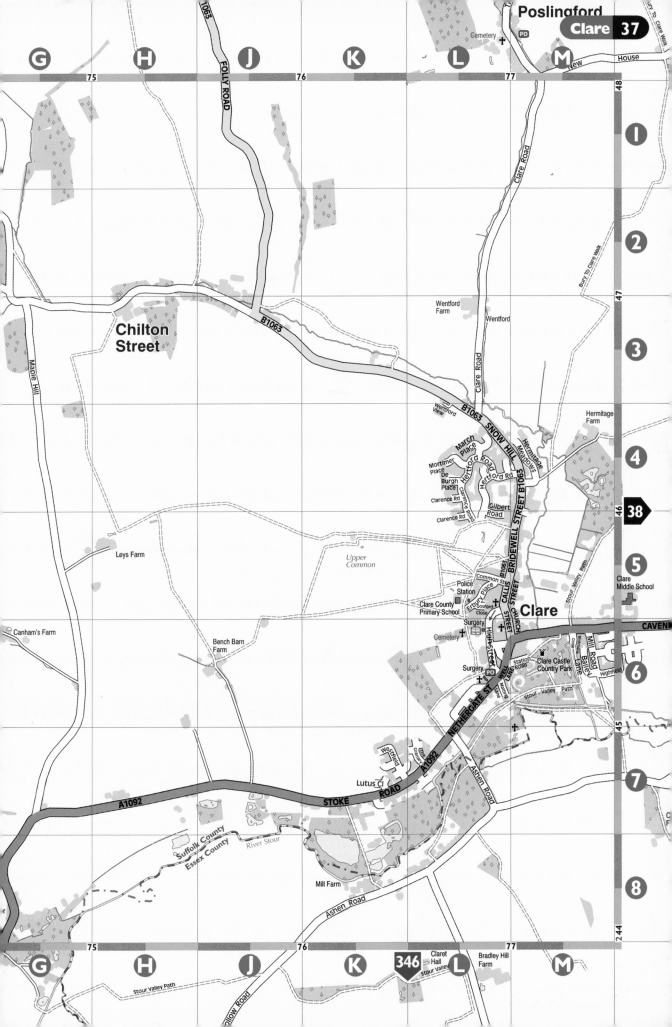

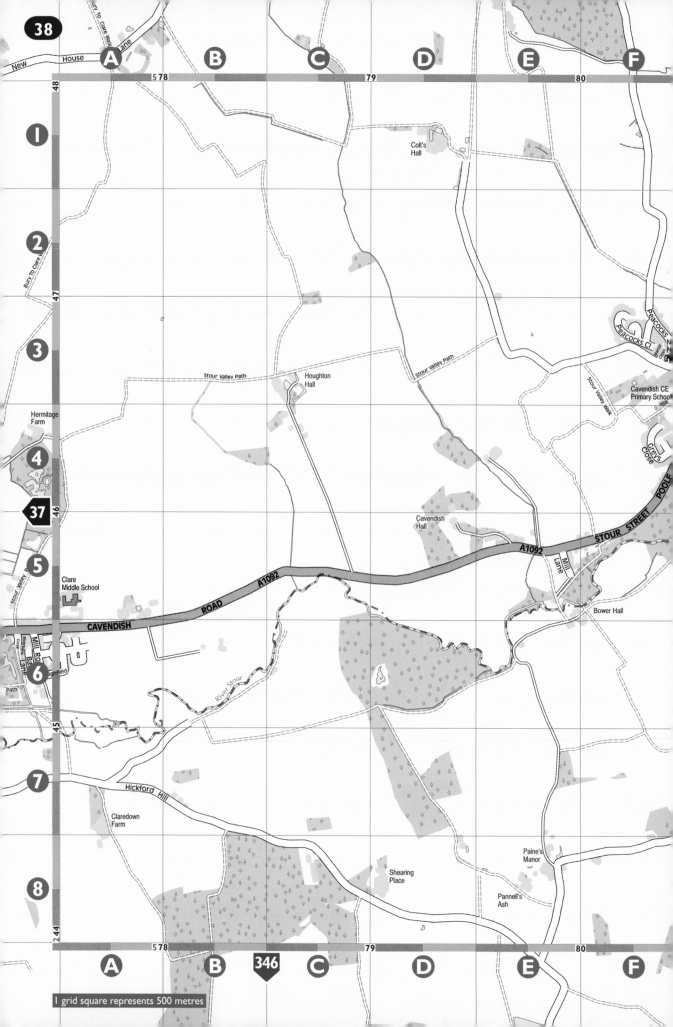

A B C D E F

New House A Lane

578 79 80

I

2

3

Bury to Clare Walk

47

Hermitage Farm

4

37 46

5

Clare Middle School

Stour Valley Path

Houghton Hall

Stour Valley Path

Stour Valley Walk

Cavendish CE Primary School

Peacocks Cl

Peacocks

Greys Close

Cavendish Hall

A1092

STOUR STREET POOLE

Mill Lane

Bower Hall

CAVENDISH ROAD A1092

Mill Road

Ba Lane

Highfield

6

Path

River Stour

45

7

Hickford Hill

Claredown Farm

8

44

Paine's Manor

Shearing Place

Pannell's Ash

578 79 80

A B 346 C D E F

I grid square represents 500 metres

A 5 84 B C Blooms Ha D E 86 F

85

I

B1066

Upper Street

Blooms Hall Lane

Stanstead

Kiln Farm

2

49

B1065

LOV EET

B1065

3

LOWER STREET

Stanstead Great Wood

CHURCHGATE

4

Windmill Road

Parkland Close

Road

Park Lane

48

B1066

Kentwell Downs

Kentw Hall

Stour Valley Walk

Stour Valley Walk

Stour Valley Walk

5

Lumpit Wood

Cranmore Green Farm

Lane

6

Park Lane

Hobbs Lane

River Glem

Cranmoregreen Lane

Parsonage Farm

Lane

39 47

7

Road

The Bl Lion H

Stour Cl

A1092

Burton's Farm

WINDMILL HILL

WESTGATE STR

8

Cranbrook Lane

School Lane

2 46

A 5 84 B C 85 D E 86 F

42 River Stour

Suffolk

PH PO

Liston

1 grid square represents 500 metres

G H J **41** K L M

87 88 89 46

I

Melford Hall (NT)

Bull Lane Industrial Estate

Acton Place

Acton Place Industrial Estate

Shaw Cordell
Chadburn Road
Middle Way
Raile Walk
Hill Cl.

Lakforth
Sampson Dr
Palmerswent

Bull Lane

King's Lane

A134

2

Barrow

Oliver's Cl
Olivers Cl
Olivers Cl

LONG MELFORD

King's Lane

Walnut Close

†

Acton

3

Sudbury Road
Coples Way
PO
High
Queensway
Browns Cl
Son Pugh
Tamage Road
Kings Cl
daniels Cl
Acton CE Primary School
Lambert
Vicarage
Acton Street
Drive
Bergh
Lane

Cuckoo Tye

4

44

Vicarage Lane

5

Acton Lane

Newman's Green

6

Chilton Grove

43

A134

Superstore

B11

Barker Road
Woodhall Business Park

Drury Dr
Drury Dr
Mountbatten Way

All Saints CE Middle School

Acton Lane

Reynolds
Rimmer Cl

St Mary's
Spire
Saint
Rubens Cl
Chase Cl

WALDINGFIELD ROAD

7

20

Grosvenor Rd
Pembroke
Lombardy Rd
erbury Road
Cranford Rd
Gloucester Way
Rochester Way
St Bartholomews Lane
Colneys Close
Parkwood Dr
Churchill Dr
Highview Way
Priory Road
Uplands
Hoxter Way
Mayflower Way
Ry Gdns
Hawkins Court
Grenville
Hacon Rd
Raleigh
Raleigh
Beatty Rd
Drake Rd
Auvrey Dr
Nelson Rd

Woodhall County Prim Sch

Springfield Rd
Talbot Rd
Stanley Wd
Essex Av
Essex Av

SPRINGLANDS WAY

Church
Works

21

8

River Stour

A131

MELFORD ROAD

A134

Tudor
Manor Road
Abbey Rd
Woodhall Road
New Queens
Clarence Rd
York Rd

Hillside Special School

Sudbury Upper School

Tudor CE Primary School

Uplands Middle School

PO

First Av
Second Av

B1115
NORTHERN ROAD
Sudbury Bowl

Byron Rd
Highfield Rd
Addison Rd
Addison Road

Church Field Road

Chilton

Chilton Industrial Estate

†

Chilton Industrial Estate

2 42

Grange Farm

87 88 89

G H J **45** K L M

St Josephs RC Prim Sch
GIRLING
Prince Charles Av
Constable Square
Suffolk Square
Jameson Place
Health Centre
WALD
Barnam Drive
The Close
Deben Dr
Park Rd
Windermere Rd
Langsdown Rd
Jubilee Rd
York Road
Humphry Rd
Fields
Alexandra Rd
Harps
Martins Rd
Windham Road
Milner Rd
Milner Rd

Chilton Road Industrial Estate

A134 ROAD A134

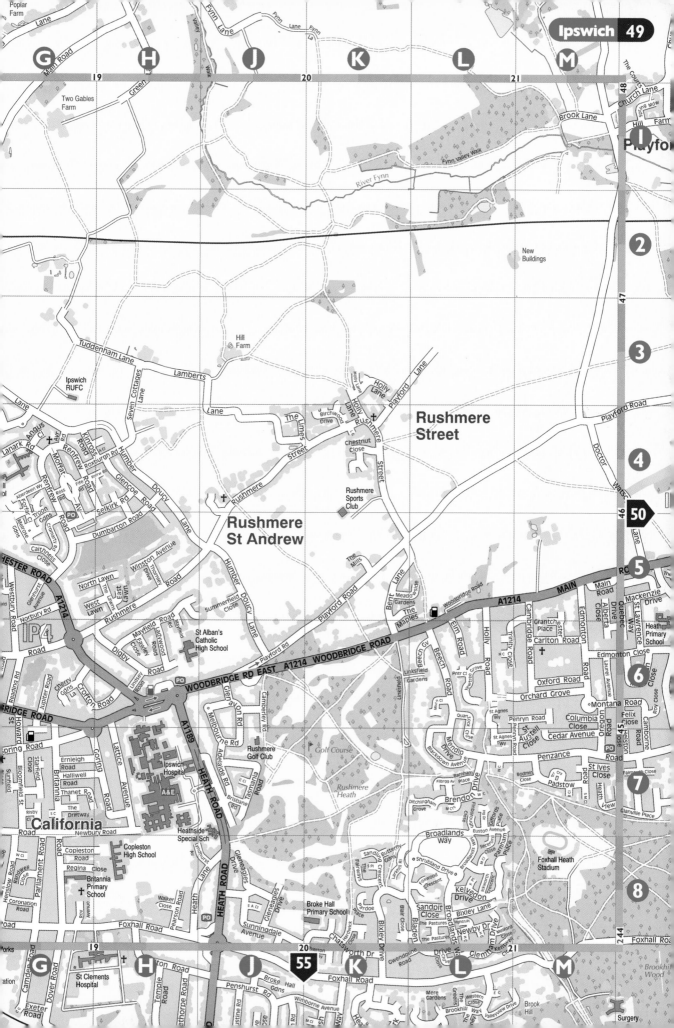

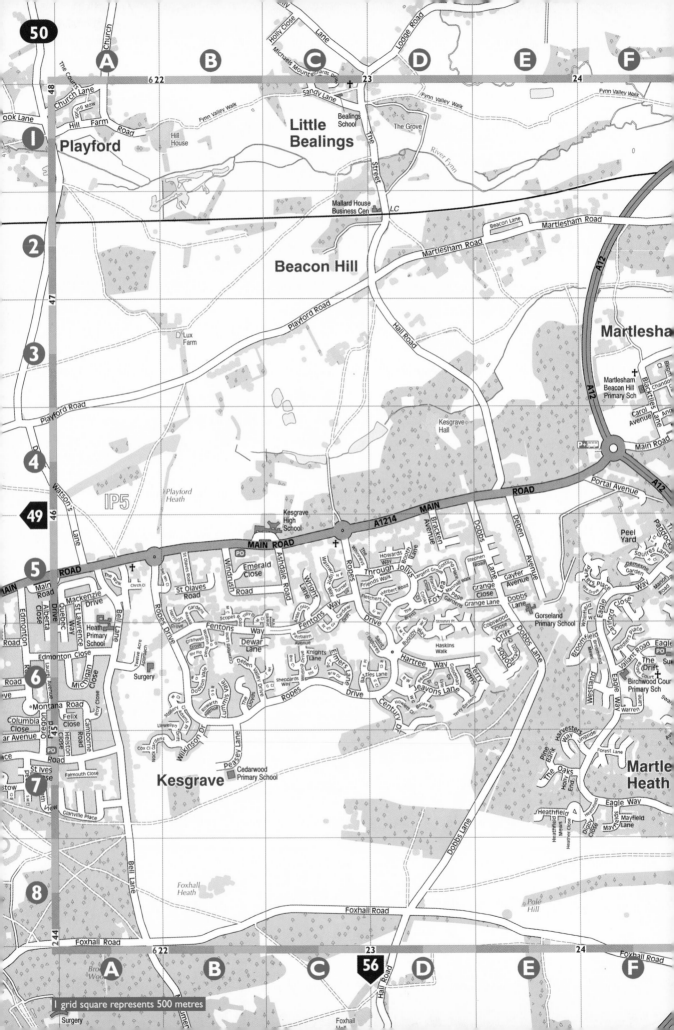

Golf Course

Seckford Hall Hotel

Seckford Hall Rd

Maidensgrave

A12

B1438

IPSWICH

California

Duke's Pk

Broom Hill

Broomheath

Kingston

Brock La

Top St

Sandy Lane

Works

Bealings Road

The Street

School Lane

Viking Cl

Viking Heights

Viking Hts

Church Lane

Holfen Close

Nunn Close

Nunn Cl

Nunn Road

Shaw Va Rd

Alban Sq

Ravens

Angela Cl

Crown

Main Road

Waldringfield Road

Waldringfield Road

Felixstowe Road

Superstore

Anson

Beardmore Park

Martinsyde

Milano Ave

Hilton Road

St Gotthards Ave

Genesta Ave

Lugano Ave

Roma Ave

Turino Ave

Moon & Sixpence

Woodbridge Road

Waldringfield Rd

A12

Closter Road

Hawker Dr

Betts Avenue

Works

PO

Barrack Square

Coopers Road

Eagle Way

Waldringfield Heath Golf Club

Golf Course

Ipswich Road

Heath Road

Woodbridge Road

Heath Road

School Rd

Woodbridge Rd

A B C **46** D E F

610 11 12

I

44

A1071 HURDLE MAKERS HILL A1071

Ivywell Farm

B1113

Fen Farm

THORPE'S HILL Burstall Bridge

A1071 R HILL

Valley Farm

Belstead Brook

2

43

Lower Barn Road

Pigeon's Lane The Grange

Washbrook Street

Pigeon's Lane

Swan Hill

3

Barn Road

Spring Road

Lower

Wood's Hill

Amor Hall

The Barvens

London Road

Whights' Corner

4

42

Chattisham

Fen Farm

Washbrook

Chapel Lane

Charlotte's

Pearsons Wy PO Mill La

The Street Pheasant Rd

Mill Lane

Junction

Copdock Primary School

School Hill

5

Chattisham Road

Church Lane

Hollow Road

Fen Vw Back

Fen Vw

Dales Vw Vw

London Road

Coles Green

Pound

6

41

Saxon Lane

Wenham Road

Mace Green

Elm Lane

Copdock

Copdock CC

County Hotel

The Avenue

Oakfield Road

A12

Rookery Farm

7

Wenham Road

The Grange Farm

8

40

58 11 **12** **59**

610 11 12

Folly Lane

Lane Farm

Redhouse Farm

Brockley Wood

Old Hall Wood

Bentley Old Hall

A12

I grid square represents 500 metres

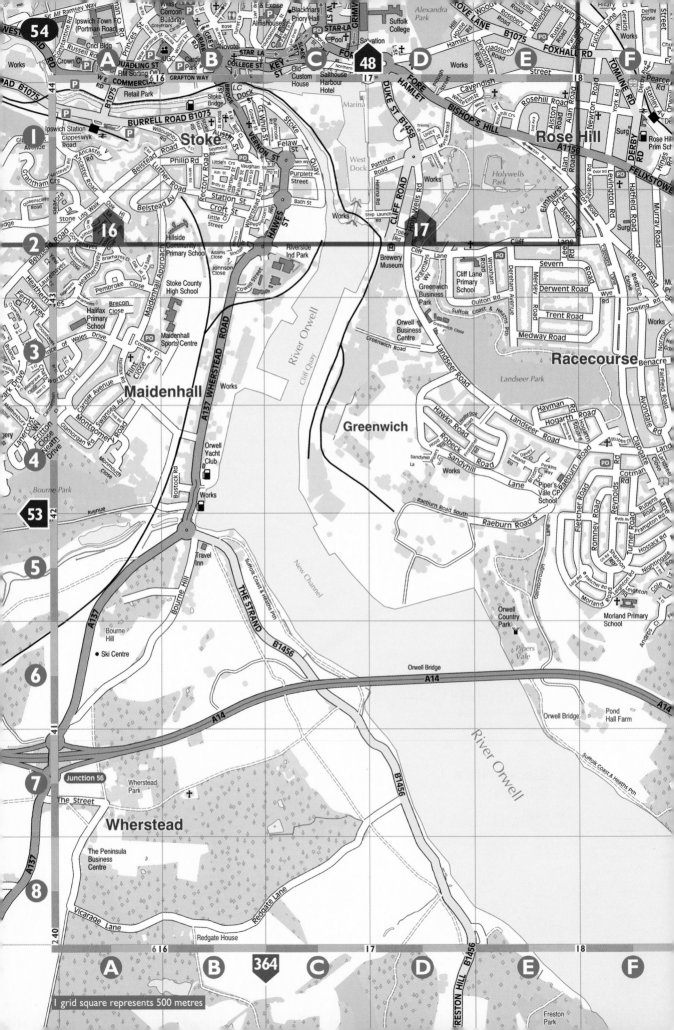

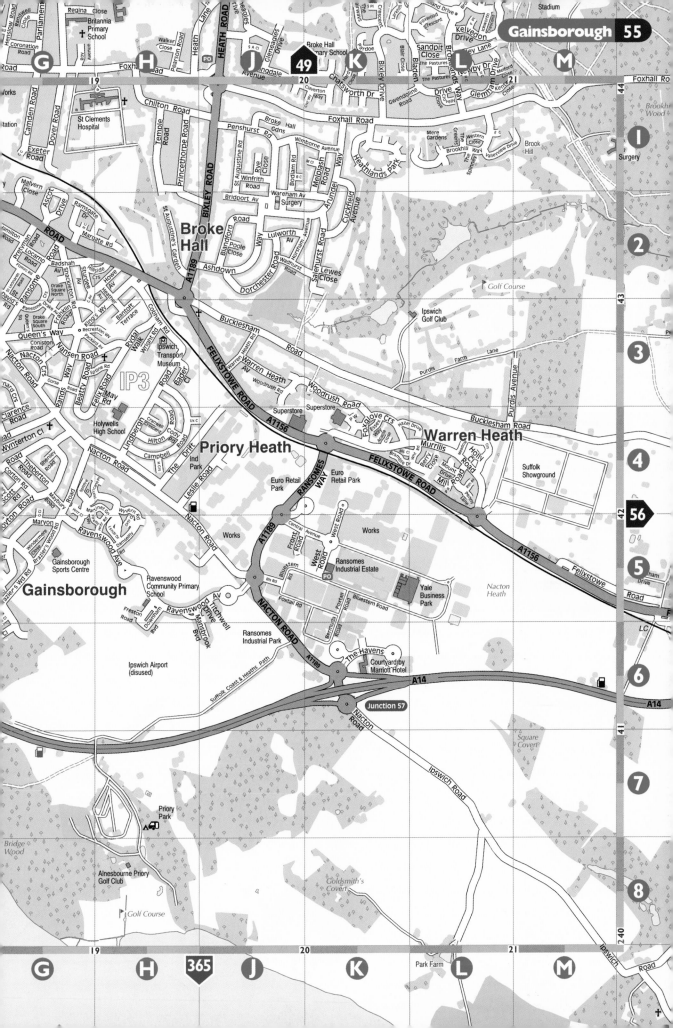

A B C **50** D E F

44 Foxhall Road 6 22 23 24 Foxhall Road

I

Surgery

Brookhill Wood

Monument Road

Foxhall Heath

Foxhall Hall

Hall Road

Pole Hill

A12

2

43

Springbank Industrial Estate

Monument Farm

Mill River

Valley Farm

Kennels Road

Lodge Farm

Purdis Farm

Purdis Farm Lane

Purdis Farm Lane

Purdis Road

Kennels Road

3

Wood House

Woodhouse Lane

Bucklesham Road

Steel's Farm

4

Low House Touring Caravan Centre

Civil Service Sports Club

A12

Main Road

Church Ct

Church La

55 42

St Mary

Lane

Green Crescent

5

Felixstowe Road

Elmham Drive

Straight Road

A14

Junction 58

Field View

PO

Levington Lane

FELIXSTOWE ROAD

LC

Felixstowe Road

6

41

A14

Seven Hills

A1156

Felixstowe Road

A14

Levington Lane

7

Amberfield School

Amberfield

Felixstowe Road

Mill Piece

Sawmill Lane

Workshop Lane

PO

Finney's Drift

8

Tomline Ct

The Street

Nacton

Bridge Road

2 40

Ipswich Road

Nacton CE VC Primary School

6 22 23 **60** 24

A B C D E F

Levington

1 grid square represents 500 metres

G H J 51 K L M

25 26 27

Newbourne Road

Brightwell

Newbourne Road

Ipswich Road

Fenn Lane

Nature Reserve

ne Street

Business Park

Newbourne Hall

Newbourne

Lower House Lane

Jackson Road

Watermill Road

Bucklesham Hall

Bucklesham

Bucklesham Primary School

Works

Newbourn Road

Kembroke Hall

IP10

Heath Cottages

Chapel Road

Tenth Road

Tenth Road

Redhouse Farm

Kirton Road

Bucklesham Road

Levington Heath

A14

Bucklesham Road

G H J 61 K L M

25 26 27

Law's

I 2 3 4 5 6 7 8

44 43 42 41 40

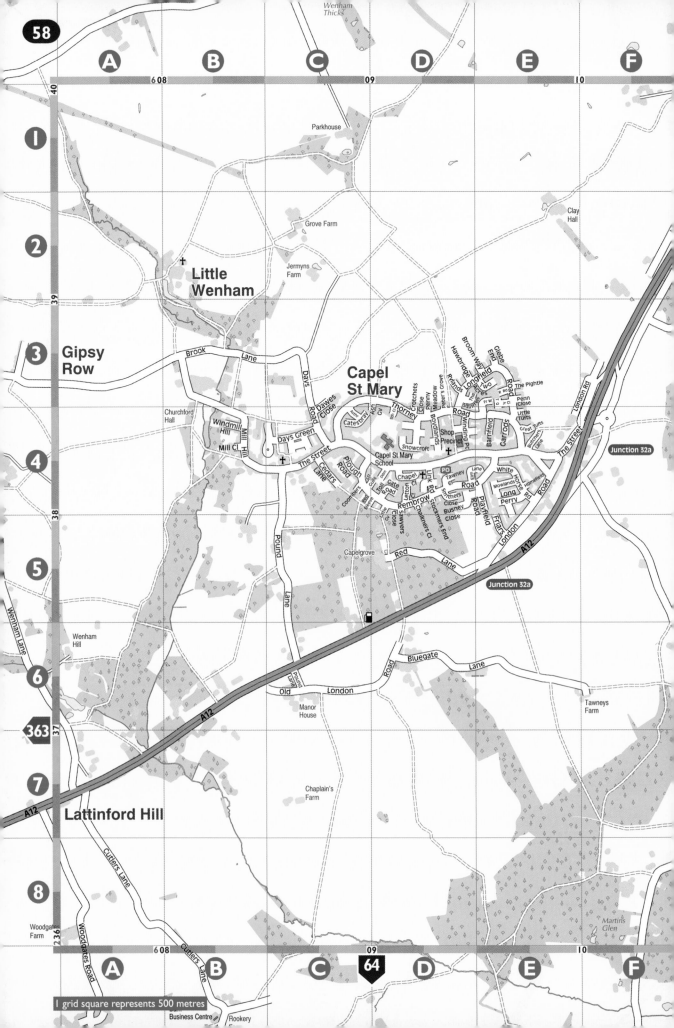

G H J 57 K L M

25 26 27

40

1

Levingham Road

Buckles

I

Law's Drift

Croft
Farm

Walk Farm

A14

LC

Croft House

Croft Lane

nley Road

Oa

2

39

Kirton Road

3

Trimley St
Primary S

Morston
Hall

Morston Hall Rd

LC

A14

**Trimley
St Martin**

Kirton

4

Mill Close Heathfields

Lane

62

Cavendish

Red House Cl

Capel
Close

Sandy
Close

Cd

5

Mill Close

Kirton Road

Old Kirton Road

Blue Barn
Close

St Martins Green Cl

Ash Cl

38

Suffolk Coast & Heaths Path

arina

Suffolk Coast & Heaths Pth

LC

**Thorpe
Common**

Thorpe Lane

Brick Kiln
Close

6

PO

High Road

Church

37

Grimston Lane

**Trimley
Lower
Street**

Grimston Lane

Garners Lane Laud

7

Grimston Hall

River

LC

J Stennetts

Orwell

8 nle
St Mar

236

25 26 27

G H J 67 K L M

rimley
arsh

P

River

G   **H**   **J** Deben   **K**   **L**   **M**

31   32   33   39

Bawdsey Ma

I

Ferry

2

P

38

Felixstowe Ferry

Felixstowe Ferry Sailing Club

Bawd and

3

Kings Fleet

Suffolk Coast & Heaths Path

Suffolk Coast & Heaths Path

Holmhill Farm

Felixstowe Marshes

Marsh Lane

Rue's Farm

Rue's Lane

4

37

Golf Course

5

Fleet House

Gulpher Road

Park Farm

Hyem's Lane

Ferry Road

Brinkley Way

Bawdsey Close

Felixstowe Ferry Golf Club

P

Cliff Road

6

36

Westmorland Road

Estuary Drive

Conway Close

Swallow Close

Hollybush Dr

Elmcroft Lane

Rydal Av

Eastcliff

The Pines

7

Upperfield

Colneis Road

Drive

Ferry Road

Kings Fleet Primary School

Kenwick Close

Western Av

Langdale Friars

Cumberland

Colneis Junior School

Avenue

Rosemary Avenue

Lansdowne

Sunray Av

Sunningdale Drive

Prestwick Avenue

Gosford Way

Church Road

St George's Road

Western Avenue

Roman Way

Castle

Monks

Earls

Dukes Close

Norman Close

Old Felixstowe

Looe Quinton's Lane

PO

Cliff Road

8

235

Lynwood Avenue

High Road

Park Avenue

East

Felixstowe International College

The Brackenbury Sports Centre

Marcus Road

Foxgrove Gardens

Lodge Farm

Golf Road

Maybush Lane

Maresllo

Croutel Road

Brook Lane

Foxgrove

Pickets Road

Thornley Rd

Allenby Park

Elizabeth Orwell

Bath Road

Roseberry

High Beach

Berners Road

Felixstowe College

Bartlet Hospital

Barton Road

Cobbold Road

Undercliff Road East

G   **H**   **J**   **K**   **L**   **M**

31   32   33

G H J **61** K L M

Trimley Marshes

Shotley Marshes

Suffolk Coast & Heaths Path

Oysterbed Road

62

Shotley Gate

PO

Ganges Museum

Gate Farm Road

Marina

Caledonia Rd

BRISTOL HILL

Shotley Sailing Club

King Edward VII Drive

68

The Port of Felixstowe

15

Suffolk County
Essex County

Harwich Harbour

The Pier at Harwich Hotel

THE QUAY

Works

King's Head

Electric Palace

Harwich Town Sailing Club

King's Quay St

Church St

WEST ST

GEORGE ST

PO

Guildhall

Harwich Town Station

Pepys St

Coke St

Maria St

Vansittart St

Canning St

Alexandra

MAIN ROAD

Harbour Crescent

Fernlea Rd

Harwich Redoubt Fort

Harwich Prim Sch

Bath Side

A120

Ingestre St

Talbot St

Mayflower Av

Suffolk County
Essex County

71

G H J K L M

A120

Dovercourt Station

Station Lane

Nelson Road

Crown

HIGH ST

Kingsway Hall

PO

Barrack La

Harwich Community Primary School

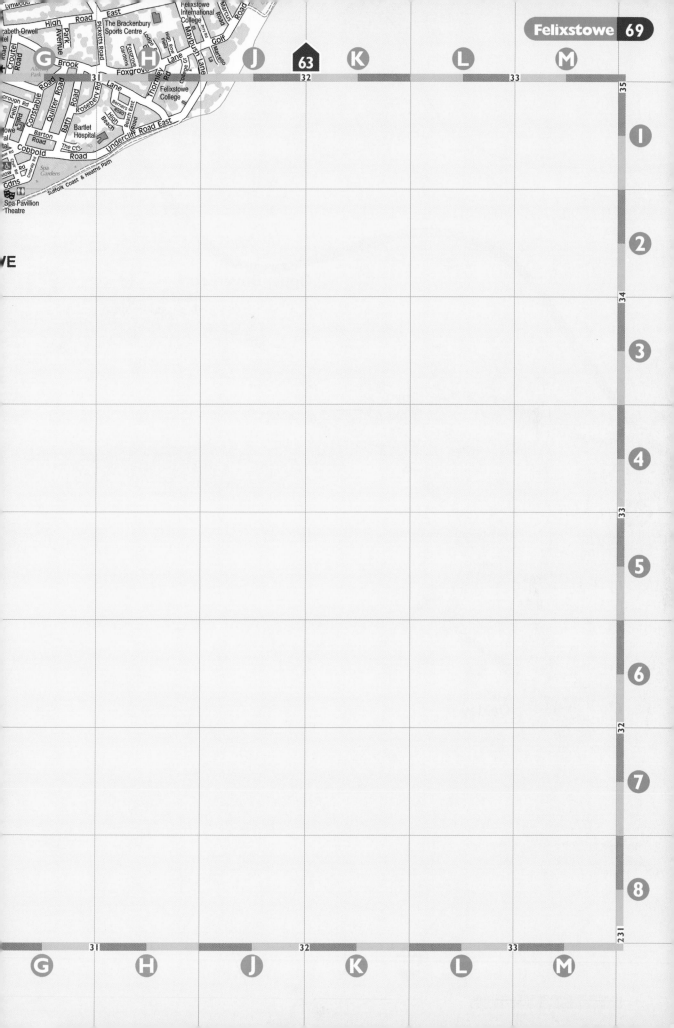

Bath Side

Dovercourt Station

HARWICH

Dovercourt

HOEK VAN HOLLAND
CUXHAVEN
ESBJERG

Mayflower
Primary
School

Superstore

Harwich &
Parkeston FC

Cliff
Hotel

Hotel Continental

St Josephs RC
Aided Primary
School

Dovercourt
Swimming Pool

Harwich
Redoubt
Fort

Harwich
Prim Sch

Harwich
Community
Primary School

Kingsway Hall

FRONK'S

G H J K L M

I
2
3
4
5
6
7
8

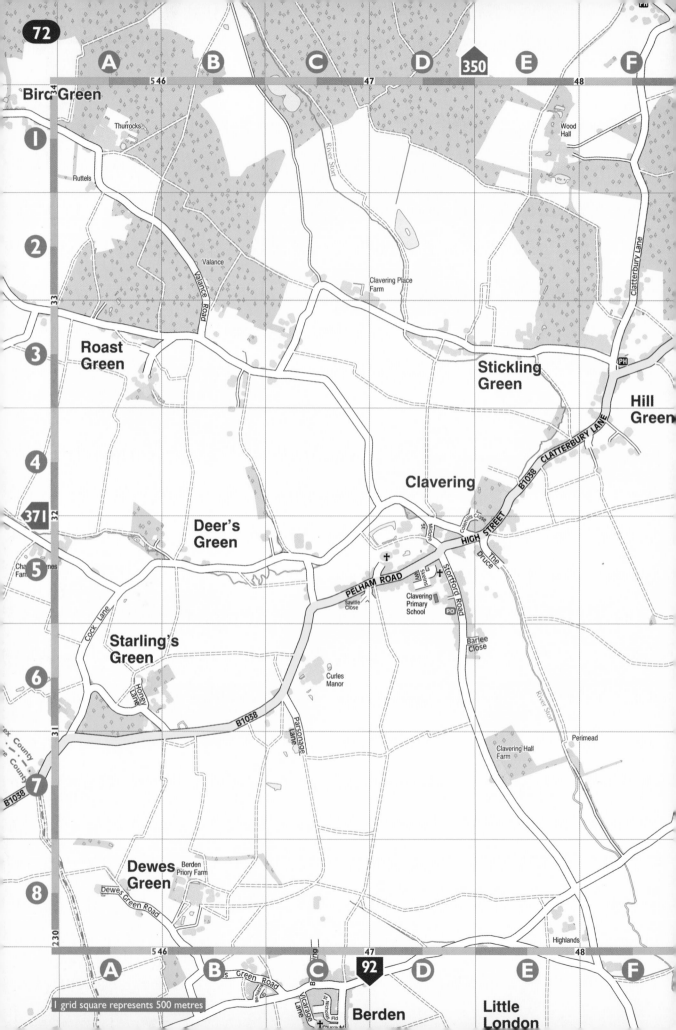

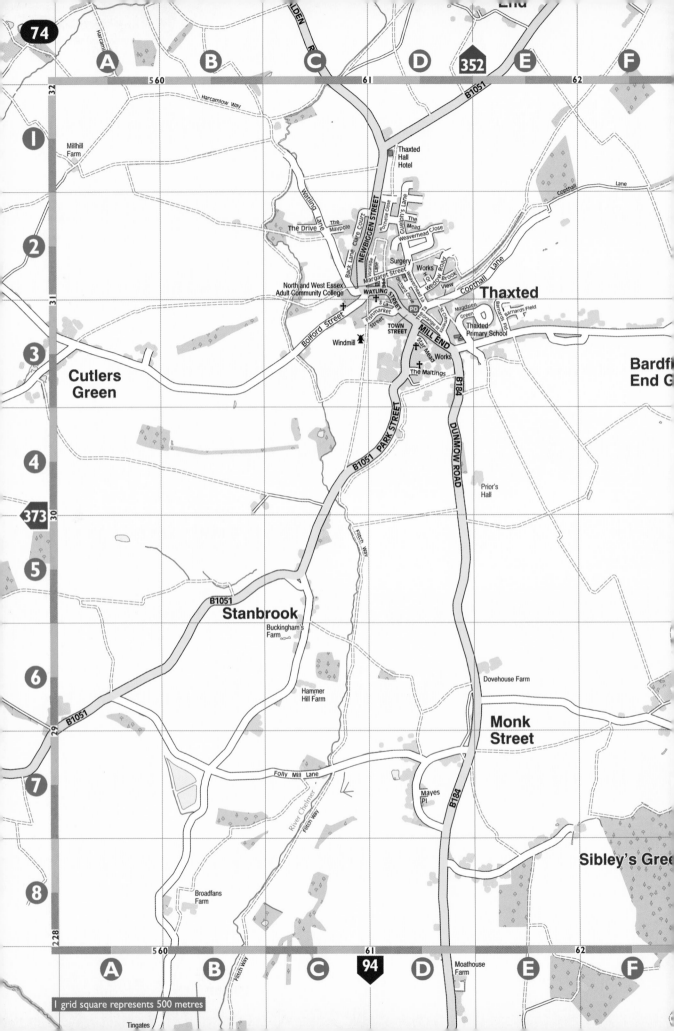

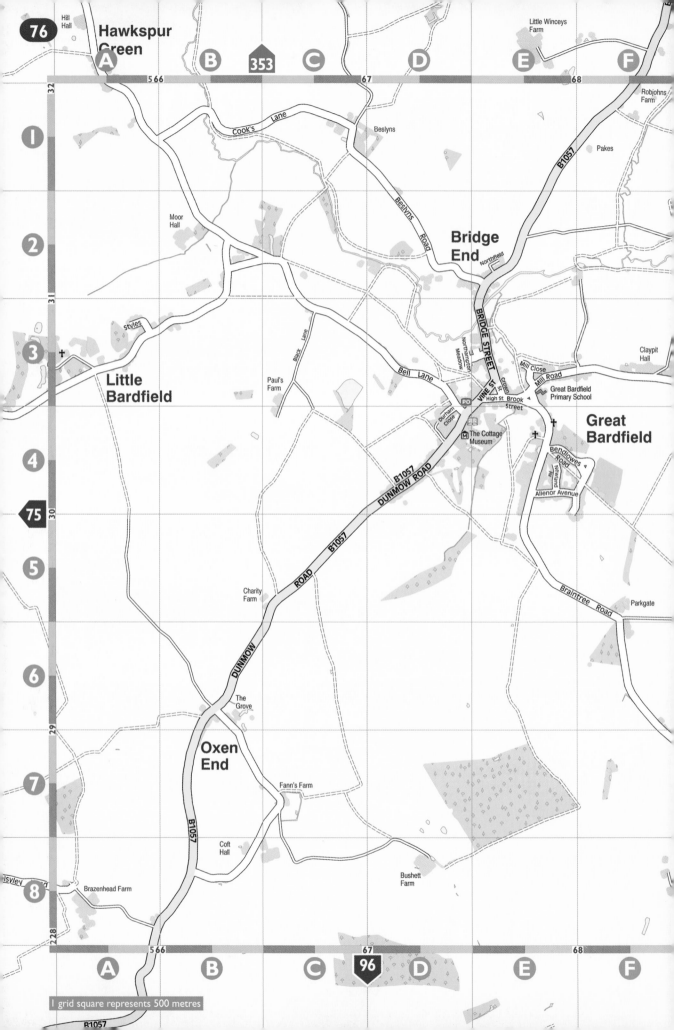

G H 354 J K M71
69 70

I

Park

Tilekiln

Petches

Daw Street
Daw Street

Nortofts

Hudson's

Saffron Gardens
Saffron Walk
Hereward Way
Saffron
Dog Chase
High Street
SILVER ST
B1053
PO
Dunkirk
Wethersfield CE Primary School
West Dr
2

Wethersfield

BRAINTREE
3

River Pant

Hawkin's Harvest

Ashwell Hall

Goll Far

Waltham's Cross

The Cross Farm

4

30 78

Bluegate Hall

Mandalay Farm

5

Redfants Manor Farm

6

S

Great Lodge

29

Hunt's Farm

7

Park Hall

Little Lodge

8

2 28

Lane

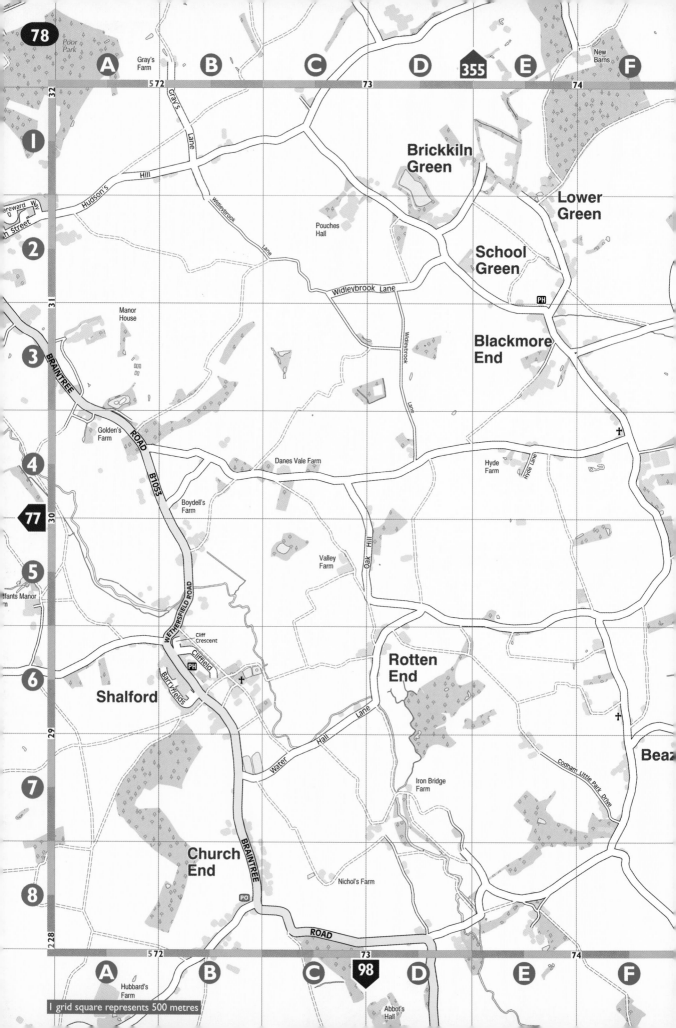

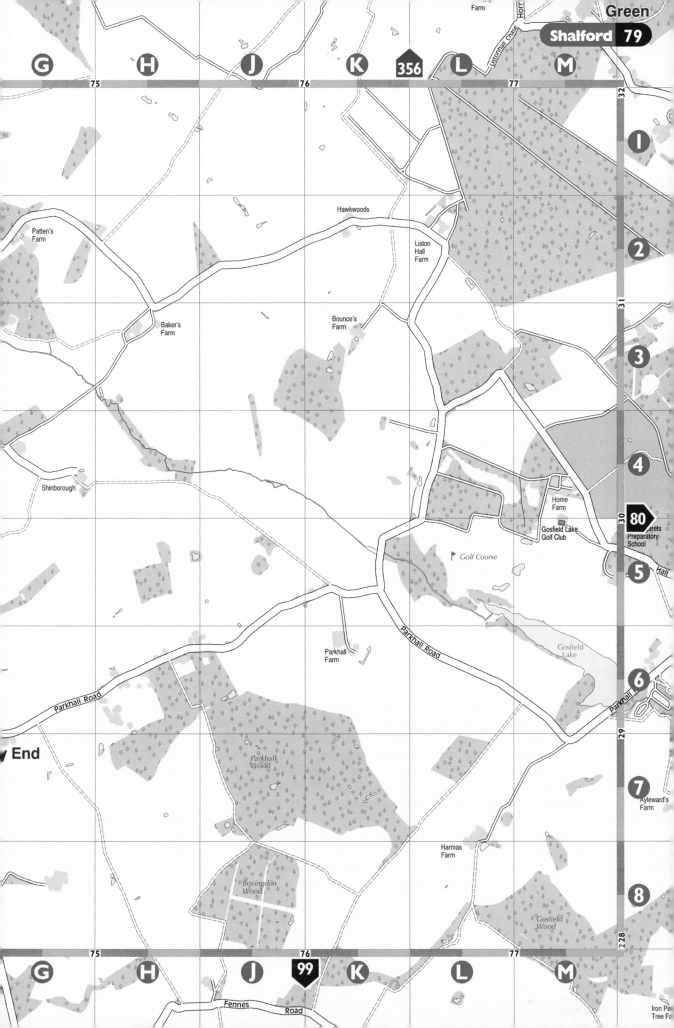

G   H   J   K   `356`   L   `Listonhall Chase`   M

75   76   77   32

`I`

Patten's
Farm

Hawkwoods

Liston
Hall
Farm

`2`

31

Baker's
Farm

Bounce's
Farm

`3`

`4`

Shinborough

Home
Farm

Gosfield Lake
Golf Club

30   `80`   `argarets`
Preparatory
School

Golf Course

`5`   Hall

Parkhall
Road

Gosfield
Lake

Parkhall
Farm

Parkhall   `6`
29

Parkhall Road

◀ **End**

Parkhall
Wood

`7`

Ayleward's
Farm

Harmas
Farm

`8`

Bovingdon
Wood

Gosfield
Wood

2 28

Fennes   Road

Iron Pe
Tree Fa

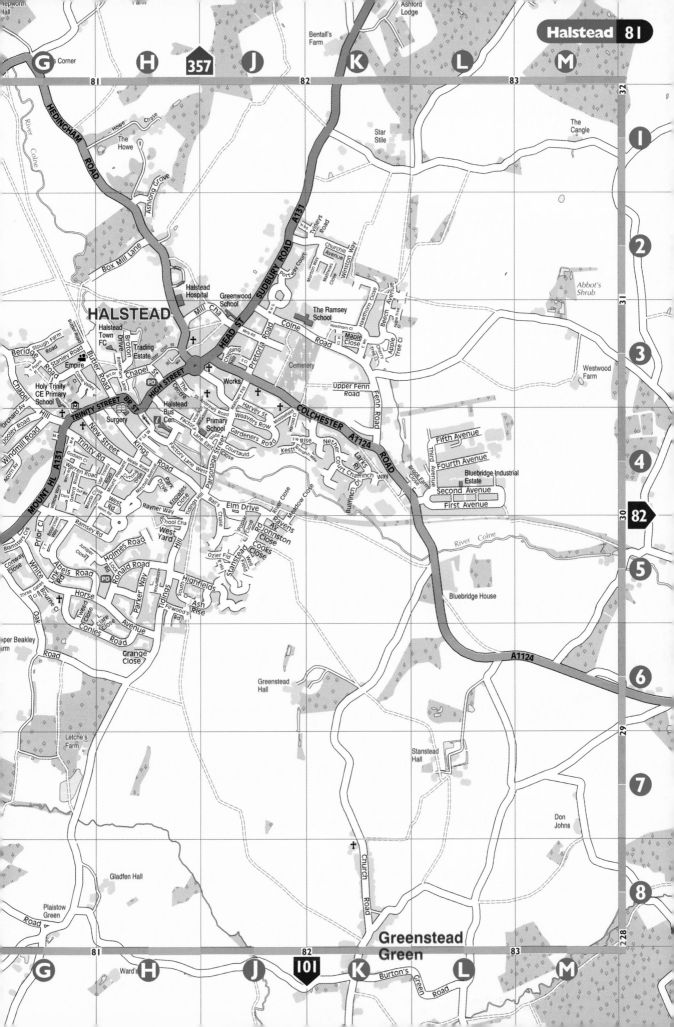

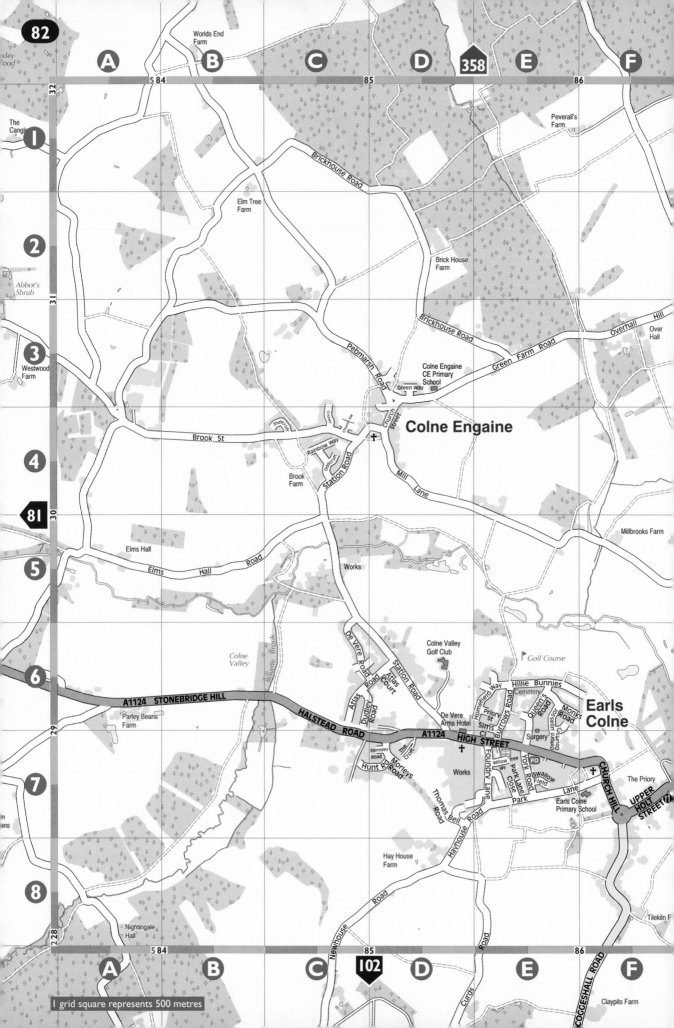

82

A   B   C   D   358   E   F
5 84   85   86

The Cangle

1

Worlds End Farm

Brickhouse Road

Elm Tree Farm

2

Abbot's Shrub

Peverall's Farm

Brick House Farm

Brickhouse Road

Overhall Hill

Over Hall

3

Westwood Farm

Pebmarsh Road

Colne Engaine CE Primary School

Green Way

Green Farm Road

Colne Engaine

Brook St

Shelley

Church View

Church Street

4

Rainbow Way

Brook Farm

Station Road

Mill Lane

81

5

Elms Hall

Elms Hall Road

Works

Millbrooks Farm

Colne Valley

Bourne Brook

Colne Valley Golf Club

Golf Course

6

A1124 STONEBRIDGE HILL

Parley Beans Farm

De Vere Road

Station Road

Atlas Court

Dudley Road

Atlas Road

De Vere Arms Hotel

Homefield Way

Priory St

Sims Cl

Burrows Road

Hillie Bunnies

Cemetery

Queen's Road

Monks Road

Surgery

Earls Colne

HALSTEAD ROAD

A1124   HIGH STREET

Kemsley Road

The Croft

Morleys Road

Hunt Rd

Willow Tree WV

Foundry Lane

York Road

PO

Park Lane Close

Oxford Mews Court

Swallow Field

Lane

7

Thomas Bell Road

Haynouse Road

Park

Works

Earls Colne Primary School

CHURCH HILL

The Priory

UPPER HOLT STREET

8

Nightingale Hall

Hay House Farm

Tilekiln F

228

A   B   C   102   D   E   F
5 84   85   86

Newhouse Road

Curds Road

COGGESHALL ROAD

Claypits Farm

1 grid square represents 500 metres

32   31   30   29

G H J K L M

359

87 88 89

32

I
2
31
Inworth
3

Wakes Colne Green
4
Lower Green
30 84
5

6

29

7

8

2 28

White's Farm

Baggarett's Farm

Catley's Farms

Moreland's

Little Loveny Hall

Weirstock Farm

Countess Cross

Middle Green

Home Farm

Berewyk Hall

Colne Park

Bart Hall

Lane Rd

Lane Farm

Lane Road

Park Road

Station Road

Boley Road

Wakes Hall

COLNEFORD HILL

COLCHESTER ROAD A1124

TYBURN HILL

Lane Road

White Colne

Chappel

WAKES STREET A1124

Station Road

Tey Road

Lowefields

Swanscomb Farm

Swanscomb Road

Wakes Colne

Chappel Hill

Swan Grove

The Street

PO
PH
COLC

Chappel Primary School

Hill House

Tey Road

Pope's

G H J K L M

87 88 89

103

Chalkney W

Oak Road

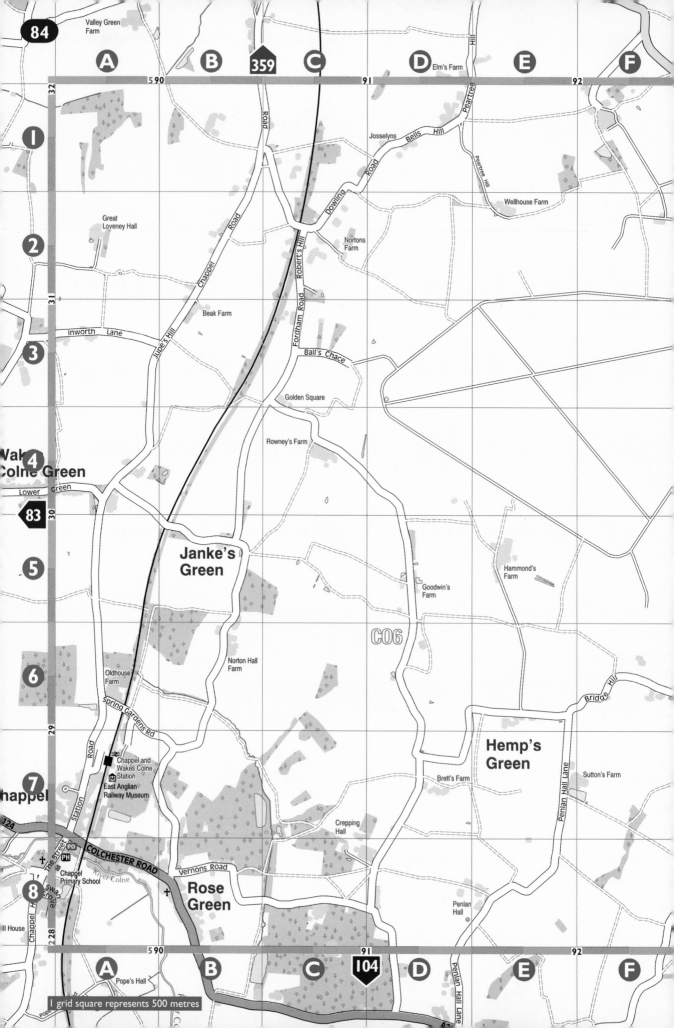

363

G H J K L M

Monk's

**Lamb
Corner**

The
Grove

GROVE HILL

B1029 ARDLEIGH ROAD

May's Lane

Louise Lane

Gull's Lane

Essex Way

CU ROAD

Castle House

East House

East Lane

Castle Hill

The Heath

The Chase

**Dedham
Heath**

Essex Way

Long Road West

Long Road East

Dedham Meade

Dedham Road

Coggeshall Road

Great Hickle House

Hunter's Chase

Goodhall

Rookery Farm

Rookery Chase

Farm Lane

Malting Farm

B1029

hhall er

DEDHAM ROAD

Fen Lane

**Ardleigh
Heath**

HARWICH ROAD

Home Farm Lane

Badliss Hall

**Foxash
Estate**

Long Road East

Hill Farm

Bargate Lane

Foxwood Close

A137 **HAR**

Tile Barn Lane

Stour House

Jupes Hill

Hungerdowns

Hungerdown Lane

Bounds Farm

I
2
3
4
90
5
6
7
8

32
31
30
29
28

THE STREET

PO

Moorhouse Green

Surgery

Ardleigh St Marys
CE Primary School

Mary Warner Road

Gernon Rd

Aveline Road

Works

Chapel Croft

B1029

Ardleigh

Cemetery

New Hall

Little Bromley Road

Lt Bromley Rd

Badley Hall

Green Lane

Green Lane

LC

Garden Centre

STATION ROAD

Martells Industrial Estate

Martells Hall

Martells Industrial Estate

Slough Lane

FRATING

Morrow Lane

Old Shields Farm

Waterhouse La

Waterhouse Farm

Chancery Farm

Park Farm

109

Burnt Heath Cottages

ROAD

**Burnt
Heath**

Back Road

B1029

Mill Lane

Briar Road

Tilley's Lane

Bromley Cross

G H J K L M

05 06 07

G H J 65 K L M

I

Mistley

Suffolk County
Essex County

BRICKMAN'S HILL

New Mistley

Mistley Heath

CO11

366 adfi Heath

B1035 CLACTON ROAD

CLACTON ROAD B1035

Dickley Hall

Horsleycross Street

New Hall

Bradfield Lodge

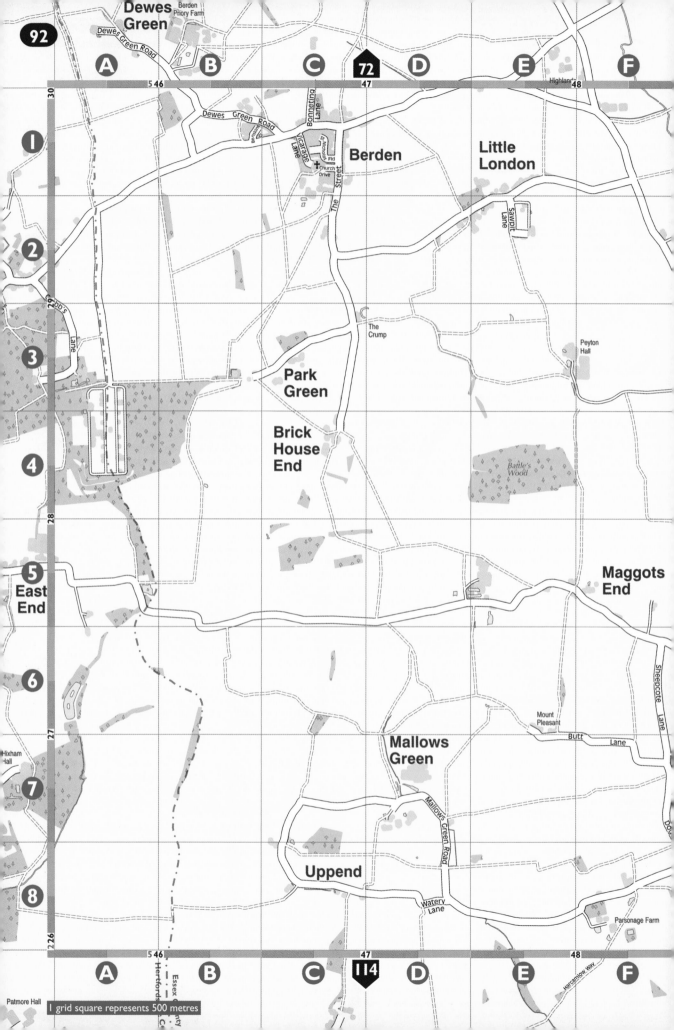

92

A   B   C   **72**   D   E   F

Dewes Green

Dewes Green Road

Berden Priory Farm

5 46

Dewes Green Road

Birchanger

Vicarage Lane

Bonneting Lane

St Nicholas Fld

Church Drive

The Street

Berden

Little London

Highland 48

Sawpit Lane

I

2

Cob's Lane

29

3

4

28

Peyton Hall

The Crump

Park Green

Brick House End

Battle's Wood

5
East End

6

27

Hixham Hall

7

8

2 26

5 46

Maggots End

Mount Pleasant

Butt Lane

Sheepcote Lane

Mallows Green

Mallows Green Road

Uppend

Watery Lane

Parsonage Farm

Haramlow Way

A   B   C   **114**   D   E   F

47

48

Patmore Hall

Hertfordshire

Essex County

I grid square represents 500 metres

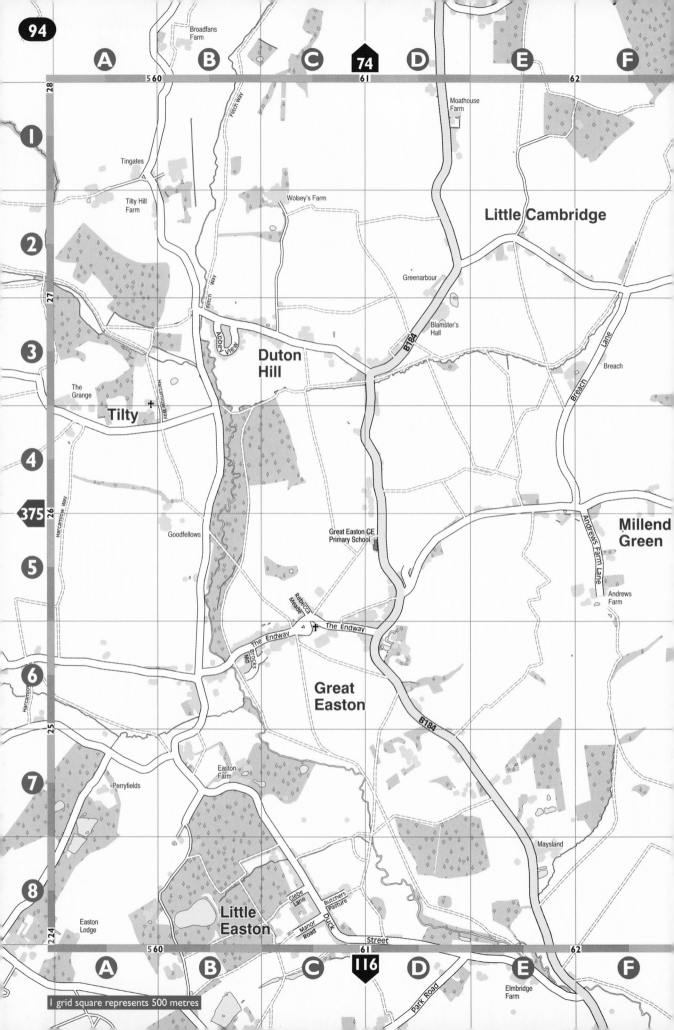

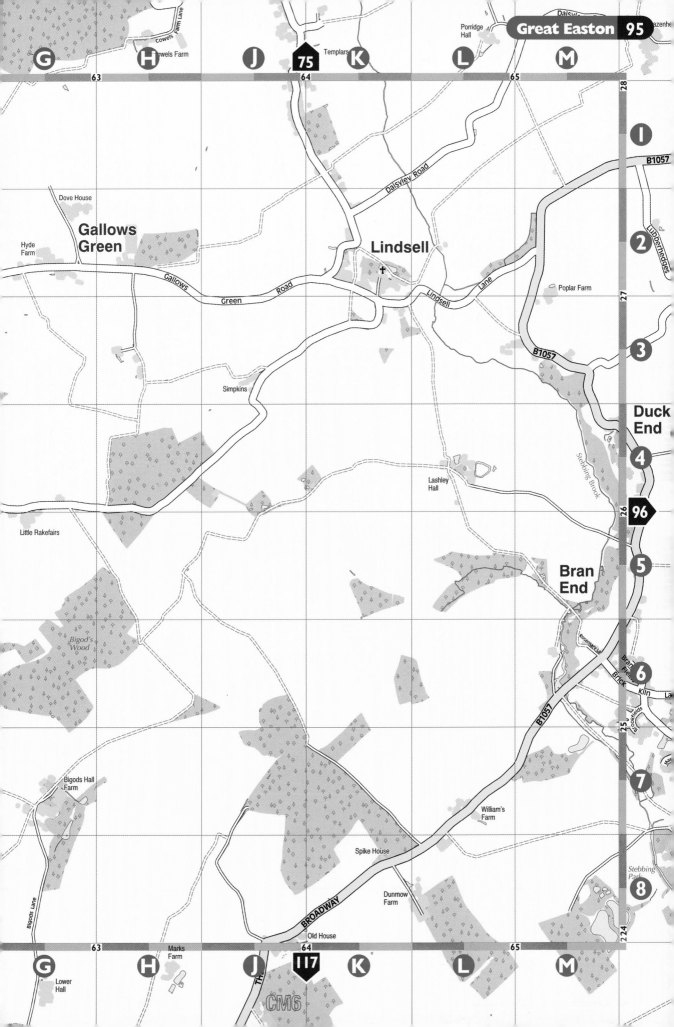

G 63
H Cowels Farm Lane
Howels Farm
J
75
64
Templars
K
65
L Porridge Hall
Daisy...hedges
M

Great Easton 95

1
B1057

Dove House

Hyde Farm

Gallows Green

Lindsell

Lubberhedges

2

Gallows Green Road

Lindsell Lane

Poplar Farm

27

Simpkins

B1057

3

Little Rakefairs

Lashley Hall

Duck End

Stebbing Brook

4

26

96

5

Bigod's Wood

Bran End

Rosemary La.

6

Bran Field

Brick

Kiln La.

Bigods Hall Farm

William's Farm

25

Lubbersheffields

7

Bigods Lane

Spike House

Stebbing Park

8

Old House

BROADWAY

Dunmow Farm

24

G 63
H Marks Farm
Lower Hall
J 117
64
Th...
K 65
CM6
L
M

G H J 77 K L M
69 70 71 28

Little Lodge

I 1

Plums Lane

New Green Farm

Elms Farm

Dynes Farm

Shalfo Green 2
27

Jaspe Greer 3

†

field g

Woolpits

Pudneys Farm

4

Woolpit's Road

98 26

Crow's Green

†

5

PO

Great Saling

Piccotts Lane

Piccotts Farm

Bett's Farm

Vicarage Close

Piccotts Lane

Saling Grove

6

Mount's Farm 25

Andrewsfield (Saling) Aerodrome

7

Onchor's Farm

Bacons Farm

8 Old Hall

Hxted Wood

A   B   C   **80**   D   E   F

578   79   80

I

Iron Pear
Tree Farm

Peterfield's
Farm

Peterfield's Lane

A1131

Penny
Pot

Highbarn Hall

Rayne Hatch
Wood

2

Foley
House

Boon's Farm

Rayne
Hatch
Farm

Boultwood's Farm

GOSFIELD ROAD

BRAINTREE

HALSTEAD

ROAD

A1017

A131

27

28

3

GARRETT

Sunnyfields
Road

Trotters'
Rest

HIGH

Church
Farm

4

Kentishes
Farm

Lordsland Lane

99

Willoughby's Lane

Willoughby's
Farm

5

Woolmer Green
Farm

Madgements Road

Lyons Hall Road

Lyons Hall

26

6

Covenbrook
Hall

Kings Lane

Stisted CE
Primary
School

RECTORY

Road

Back Lane

Stisted

A131

25

7

Golf Course

Braintree
Golf Club

The Street

sarcet

River Blackwater

8

Gilbert Way

Cavendish Gdns

Hereford Dr

Hereford

Bridport

Rayleigh Close

Stafford
Crs

A131

Jenkin's Farm

Shelborn Bridge

24

Lyons Hall
County Prim

Nelson

A   B   C   **122**   D   E   F

578   Kings Lane   79   80

Water
Lane

River Blackw

1 grid square represents 500 metres

G H J **81** K L M

82

Greenstead Green

83

1

2

27

3

4

26 **102**

5

6

25

7

8

224

G H J **123** K L M

81 82 83

Pattiswick

Gladfen Hall

Plaistow Green

Ward's Farm

Burton's Green Road

Whitings

Perces

Clavering's Farm

Burton Green

Mann's Farm

Markshal

Nunty's Lane

Great Nunty's Farm

Brookes's Farm

Folly Green

...wer's Farm

Nunty's Lane

Great Monks Wood

Bungate Wood

Woodhouse Farm

Back Lane

Potash Farm

Compasses Road

PH

Old Road

Church Road

Doghouse Road

Pattiswick Hall

Hovells Farm

A   Nightingale Hall   B   C   **82**   D   E   F   Tilekiln F

Newhouse Road

85

86

Coggeshall Road

Claypits Farm

B1024

Curds Road

I

Lodge Farm

2

Golf Course

Curds Road

Hungary Hall

27

Ame Farr

3

Markshall Wood

Industrial Estate

Lancaster Way

Marauder Way

The Essex Golf & Country Club

Works

America Road

4

Gatehouse Farm

101

26

5

Witch Lane

Hopgreen Farm

Colne Road

B1024

Markshall

Herons Farm

6

Marks Hall Arboretum

25

Palmer's Farm

Marygolds

Marks Hall Road

7

Purley Farm

Colne

Robins Brook

Marks

Hall

Maltbeg Farm

Tey Road

8

Road

Bouchier's Grange

Colne Road

2 24

5 84

Cradle House

B1024

85

124

86

A   B   C   D   E   F

A120

Monk Downs

I grid square represents 500 metres

G H J 83 K L M

87 88 89 28

I

Chappel Primary School
Chappel River
Mouse
Pope's

Oak Road

Chalkney Wood

Swanscomb Road

Holmwood Farm

Tey Road

Priory Road

Oaklands

Swan Street

Bacon's Lane

2

27

Lambert's Farm

Works
Pattock's Farm

Essex Way

Tey Road

America Road

Lambert's Road

Swan Street

Pattocks Lane

3

Cucumber Hall

Earls Colne Road

Teycross Farm

Tey Road

Burnthouse Road

Chappel Road

Belt's Farm

Essex Way

Earls Colne Road

Newbarn Road

Lower Langley

4

104

26

Florie's Farm

Great Tey CE Primary School
Chrismutte Way
Greenfield Drive
Garden Fields
Windmill
Hill Ch
Farmfield Road
Harvesters' Way
PO

Moor

Great Tey

Baldwin's Farm

Florie's Road

Brookhouse Road

The Street
The Chase

Essex Way

Brook Road

5

Baldwin's Lane

Abraham's Farm

Roman River

Walcott's Hall

Coggeshall Road

Essex Way

6

25

Coggeshall Road

Buckler's Farm

Teybrook Farm

7

Buckley's Lane

Gull's Farm

Cranmer's Lane

Dowsland Green

Trumpingtons Farm

Little Hey House

Essex Way

8

224

Roman Brook

Essex Way

Great Tey Road

G H J 125 K L M

87 East Gor 88 **East Gores** 89

Upper Hall Farm

Little Tey

Salmo

ROAD

Vernons Road

Rose Green

Chappel
Primary School

River Colne

A

B

C

84
91

D

E

F

590

92

ll House

Pope's Hall

River Colne

Penlan
Hall

Penlan Hall Lane

A1124 HALSTEAD ROAD

1

**Swan
Street**

Broom House

Essex Way

Wash Farm

A1124 FORD STREET

Fordstree

Bacon's
Farm
Way

Essex Way

Bacon's Lane

Essex Way

2

27

Essex Way

New Road

FORDSTREET HILL

3

Wick Farm

New Road

Green Lane

Belt's
Farm

Essex Way

Bourchier's
Hall

4

Tey Road

103
26

Road

Moor Farm

Tey Road

Hardings Cl

Green Lane

Great Tey

Church Gv

The Chase

5

Hoe
Farm

Rectory Road

Hines Cl

Aldham

6

Rectory Road

Brook Road

Church
House
Farm

Rectory Road

Chippetts

Chipp
Farm

Chippetts La

25

Roman River

LC

Aldham
Hall

7

Little Hey
House

Brook Road

8

Great

Tey Road

224

590

91

92

Little
ey

Works

Marks Tey
Station

North Lane

A

B

C

126
91

Church Lane

D

Station Rd

E

A12

A12

LONDON RD

PO

Surgery

F

Mill Rd

LON

1 grid square represents 500 metres

Marks Tey

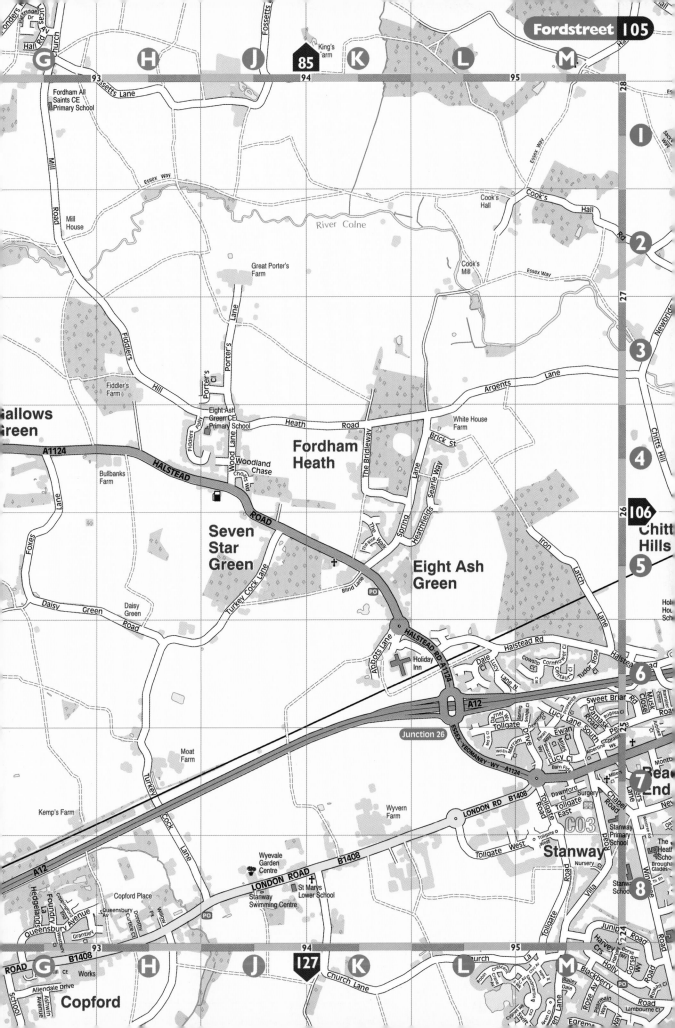

A   **B**   **C**   90   **D**   **E**   **F**

09

I

Farm

Lilley's Lane

Newhouse

2

Carringtons Road

Carringtons Farm

Little

Bromley Road

Morebarn Road

Barton Road

Little Bromley Hall

Spratts Lane

Church Lane

Mulley's Farm

Payne's Lane

B1029

HALL

Bush Farm

3

ROAD

C07

Badley Hall Road

Badley Hall

Hilliards

Great Bromley

Gt Bromley St Georges CE Primary School

St George's Close

4

Stone Road

The Chase

109

PO

BROOK STREET

Mary Lane North

Cowey Green

5

Tenpenny Brook

B1029

PARSONS HILL

Hamilton Lodge

Chase Road East

6

Back Lane West

Camp Road

Mary Lane North

A120

Cold Hall

Fairfield Cl

Chase Road West

Mary Lane South

Harwich Road

7

Cold Hall Chase

Back Lane East

Meadow Close

A133

Mill Farm

Harwich Road

Hare Green

Raven's Green

Brundells Road

8

B1029

Chapel Lane

Furze Lane

Balls Green

A   **B**   **C**   132   **D**   **E**   **F**

Morehall Hall

09

A133

1 grid square represents 500 metres

G　H　J　**91**　K　L　M

91

I1　I2　I3

CLACTON ROAD

Bradfield Lodge

Abbott's Hall

A120

Horsley Cross

Hempstall's Farm

B1035

Harwich Road

Welham's Farm

Red House Farm

Bentley Road

A120

Byes Farm

Little Bentley Road

Tendring Heath

ark Farm

Harwich Road

Little Bromley Road

Manningtree Road

The Oaks

Little Bentley

Holland Brook

112

Road

Rectory Road

Tendring Road

Mill Green

Pilcox

Clip Hedge Farm

Church Road

PO

Bentley Manor

Pilcox

Pilcox Hall

Hall Lane

Church Road

Little Bentley Hall

G　H　J　**133**　K　L　M

133

I1　I2　I3

Paynes Farm

Rowherns Lane

Gurnhams

28　27　26　25　24

1　2　3　4　**112**　5　6　7　8

Church Road

A   B   C   D   366   E   F

Crossman's Farm   614

Wix & Wrabness Primary School

Clayha

Cledie Close

Daleview Avenue

1

Colchester

A120

Cansey Lane

Colchester Rd

Goose Green

Spring Farm

Honeypot Lane

Wix Road

Den Hall

2

Hempstall's Farm

Tendring Road

Colchester Road

Frith's Farm

Block Farm   Colchester Road

3

Brocketts Hall

Stonehall Lane

Stonehall Farm

ndring ath

4

Wolves Hall Lane

Higher Barn Farm

Stonehall Lane

Skigh

HEATH

Parsonage Lane

Chapel Lane

Tendring Green

Wolves Hall Farm

PO

5

Pilcox Hall Lane

ROAD

Tendring Lodge

Hall Lane

6

Pilcox

Pilcox Hall

B1035

Goose Green

Church Farm

Lodge Lane

Tendring Primary School

B1035

7

SCHOOL ROAD

Hannam's Hall

8

THE STREET

Hollyview Close

Tendring

THORPE ROAD   B1035

Crown Lane

Hill F 614

New Hall

134

Crow Lane

Manor House

Lane

A   B   C   15   D   16   E   F

1 grid square represents 500 metres

G   H   J   K   367   L   M

I   Gre
Oak

Oakley Road   Redhouse Farm   Great Oakley Lodge

House

HARWICH RD

Oakley Road

Parkers Farm

Holt Farm

HIGH STREET

Back Lane

Farm Road

Lane

The Avenue

Wix Road

Great Oakley CE Primary School

Orchard Close

Hamford Drive

B1414

SCHOOL RD

Pesthouse

Woodlands

Red Barn Lane

Stones Green Road

Houbridge Hall

Brooklands

Marden's Farm

Stones Green Road

BEAUMONT ROAD

CROSS HILL

Moze C

Stones Green

Clacton Road

Ratcliff's Farm

B1414

368

Wix Road

Potland

Wix Road

Goff's Lane

The Oak

HARWICH ROAD   Oldhouse Farm

Beaumont

Chapel Road

Lucas's Lane

Church Lane   B1414

HARWICH ROAD

Road

Swan

Pond Farm

Beaumont Hall

Barker's Farm

Beaumont Quay

Quay Lane

G   H   J   135   K   L   M

TENDRING

**Thorpe
Green**

17   18   19   28   27   26   25   224

1   2   3   4   5   6   7   8

Uppend

Watery Lane

92
47

Patmore

Harcamlow Way

Essex County
Hertfordshire County

Farnham Green

Chatter End

Harcamlow Way

Watersi
School

Bourne Brook

The Common

Farnham CE
Primary School

Rectory Lane

Globe
Crescent

Farnham

Upwick Green

Level's Green

Upwick Hall

Mill Hill

Hertfordshire Way

Walnuttree Green

A120

Wickham Hall

A120

Hertfordshire Way

Hadham Park

Dane O'Coys Road

MSF
Whitehall
College

HADHAM

ROAD

Rugby Club

Northgate
Primary
School

Cricketfield

A120

138

Hadham
Gv

Stortford
Park

Patmore

Dane O'Coys Rd

Carters
Leys

Crailand

Willow
Springs

Hadham ct

HADHAM_ROAD

Westfield Rd

Willow

1 grid square represents 500 metres

A B C D E F

Easton Lodge

Little Easton

Glebe Lane

Butchers Pasture

Duck

94

Street

Park Road

Elmbridge Farm

I

62

B184

Park Road

†

2

375 23

Ravens Farm

Newton Hall

Dunmow Sports Centre

Helena Romanes School

The Mead

Emblems

Godfr

The Pop

W Cl

3

Toowns

R Cl

Rosemary Crs

enry

4

Woodside Way

Woodlands Pk Dr

Larch Way

L Dr

Cypress

Pine Av

Spruce Av

Newton Gn

Green Lane

Woodlands Park Drive

Jubilee Ct

Wadgrooms Ct

Rd

R Cr

stone all

High Wood

Superstore

Stortford Road

Stortford

High Stile

South Vw

C

Be

Du

St

Pri

STORTFORD ROAD

B1256

Folly Farm

High Meadow

South Vw

5

Flitch Way

Strood Hall

Flitch Way

Buttleys Lane

22

B1256

Stortford Road

East Lane

Hale's Farm

Flitch Way

A120

Minchins

Olives or Shingle Hall

G D

ROAD

6

377 21

angthorns

7

ONG

High Cross Lane

Newlands

B184

Trutons

8

Great Oddyns

20

Lane

560

61

Pharisee House

62

Tanners

Bedfords

Pharisee Green

A B C D E F

140

Puttoc

Lane

Mountain's

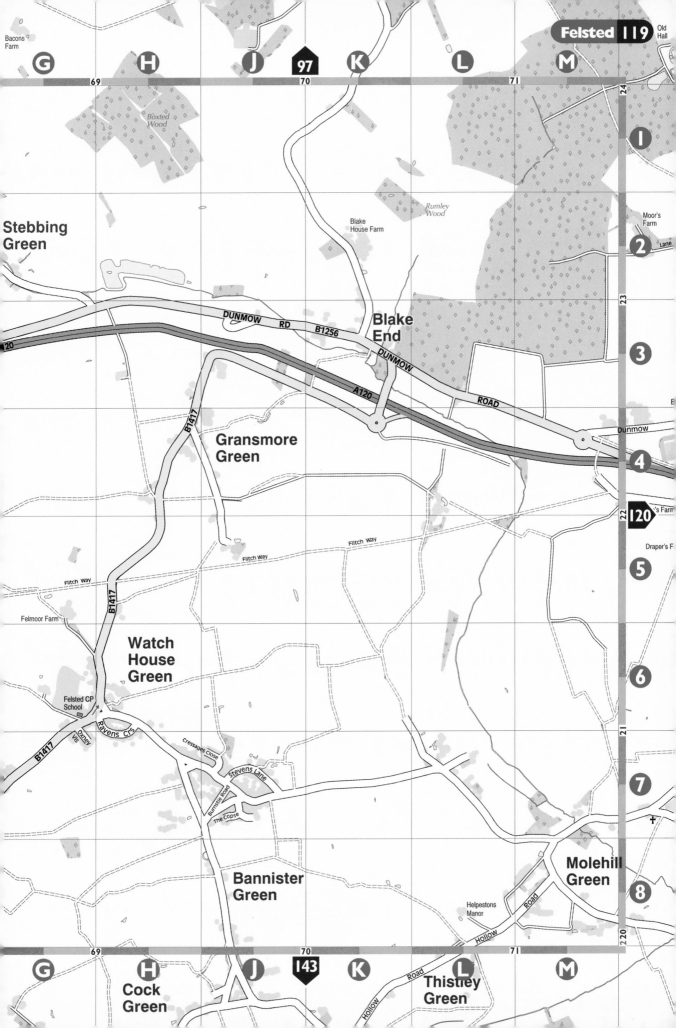

Bacons Farm

Old Hall

G

H

J

97

K

L

M

69

70

71

24

I

Boxted Wood

Moor's Farm

2

Lane

Rumley Wood

23

3

Stebbing Green

Blake House Farm

Blake End

DUNMOW RD B1256

DUNMOW

A120

A120

ROAD

Dunmow

4

B1417

Gransmore Green

120

22

Draper's F

5

Flitch Way

Flitch Way

Flitch Way

Felmoor Farm

B1417

6

Watch House Green

Felsted CP School

Ravens Crs

Oxney Vw

Cressages Close

Stevens Lane

21

7

B1417

Burnetts Road

The Copse

Molehill Green

Molehill Green

8

Bannister Green

Helpestons Manor

Hollow Road

220

69

70

71

G

H

J

143

K

L

M

Cock Green

Hollow Road

Thistley Green

G H J 101 K L M
82

Pattiswick Hall
Pattiswick
81

Doghouse Road
Church Road
Old Road

Hovells Farm

Holfield Grange

1
2
3

A120

The Street

+ Bradwell

Black Notley Hospital

Coggeshall Road

Whiteshill Farm

COGGESHALL ROAD A120

Grigg's Far

Church Road

Park House

Church Road

Perry Green

Fiveash Lane

Bradwell Hall

Essex Way

River Blackwater

Watery Lane

4

124
22

Essex Way

Essex Way

Curd Hall Farm

5

Links Road

Essex Way

Gosling's Farm

Herons Farm

Cuthedge Lane

Haywards

6

21

7

Rolphs Farmhouse

Sheepcotes Farm

Woodhouse Farm

Allshot's Farm

8

20

Works

Broadway

Broadway Court

Sheepcotes Lane

Boars Tye Road

Abraham

Daniel Way

SILVER HD

Storey's Wood

G H J 147 K L M
81 82 83

Police Str

PO

24
23

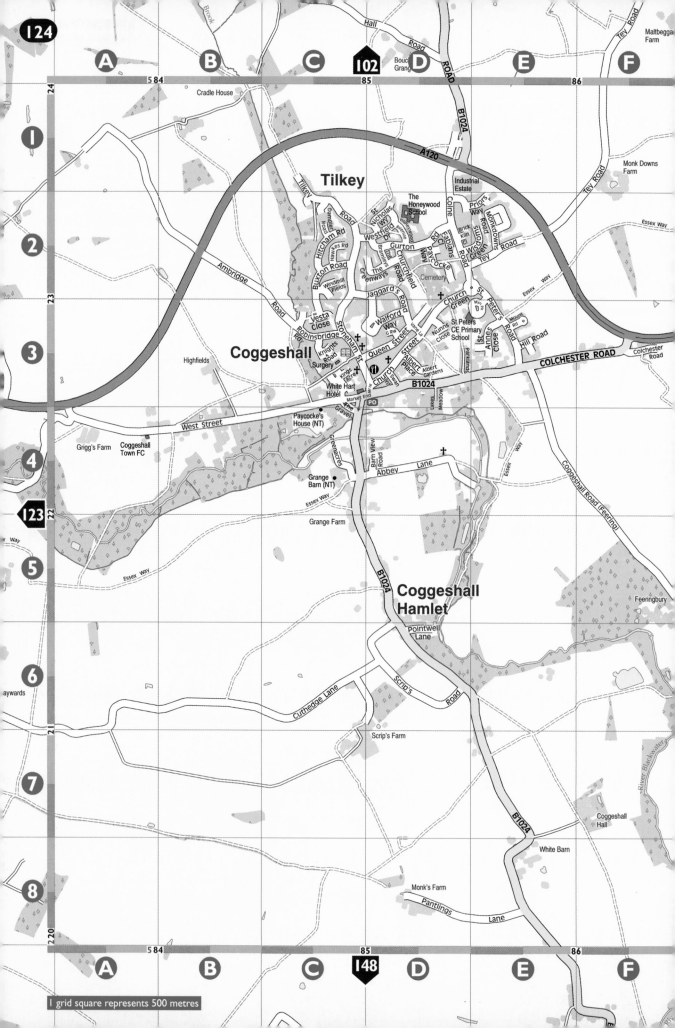

G　H　J　103　K　L　M

87　88　89

24

East Gores Road

East Gores

Upper Hall Farm

Little Tey

Godbolt's

Houchin's Farm

Essex Way

Salmon's Lane

Bracks Lane

Church Lane

COGGESHALL ROAD

Broad Green

Elm Farm

Elm Lane

23

COLCHESTER ROAD

A120

Surrex

2

Old Road

Mill Lane

Lane

Skye Green

Hornigals

3

Mill Lane

Old Road

4

Elm Lane

22　126

Langley Green

Domsey Chase

Great Domsey

A12

LONDON ROAD

5

Old Will's Farm

Little Tey Road

Hill House Farm

Easthorpe Road

21

Frame Farm

Old Mill Lane

Coggeshall Road

6

Gypsy Lane

Scott

7

Travelodge

Long Acres

Hanover Bridge

New Lane

Glebe Gdns (Feering)

PO

The Street

B1024

8

20

Deering Primary School

Watermill Rd

Millers Mead

Cemetery

LONDON RD

Rye Mill Lane

Sherwood Way

Hall Lane

B1024

Blackwater

A12

Prested Hall

Domsey Brook

G　H　J　149　K　L　M

87　88　89

1

2

3

4

5

6

7

8

I

A   B   C   **104**   D   E   F

590   91   92

24

ittle
ey **1**

Godbolt's Farm

Marks Tey

Works
Marks Tey
Station

Station Rd

North

A12

A12

LONDON RD

Surgery
PO

Junction 25

A120

Godmans
Stane Fld
St Andrews
CE Prim Sch
Mandeville
Rd
Wilson's
Lane

Hawkmark End
Domsey
Bank
Proctor W.
Pinants Crs

Patten
Cl
Bagers
Lane
Keable
Road
Jays Lane

Bury Cl

LC

Dobbies La

The Crescent

London Road

Hall Chase

23

2

3

Potts
Green

Doggetts Lane

**Copfore
Green**

22

125

4

Damyon's Farm

Little Birch
Holt Farm

Rectory Road

Easthorpegreen
Farm

LONDON ROAD

A12

5

Easthorpe Road

Easthorpe

21

6

horpe   Road

Badcock's
Farm

Churchwell
Avenue

Well Lane

Whitehouse Farm

7

Scottie's Farm

Winterflood's
Farm

Shemmir
Farm

220

8

Cantfield's
Farm

Easthorpe   Road

590   91   92

A   B   C   **150**   D   E   F

Blind Lane

A12

Garden Centre

LONDON ROAD

Nursery Cl

Brough Glades

Copford Place

Queensbury Av

St Marys Lower School

Stanway Swimming Centre

G **H** **J** **105** **K** **L** **M**

94 95

Tollgate

Juniper Road

Harvey Crs

Holly

Gorse Wy

ROAD B1408

Windmill Ct Works

Allendale Drive

Astwin Avenue

School Road

Copford

Church Lane

Church

Blackberry

Rose Av

PO

I

Lambourne Cl

Warren Lane

Egremont

Dyer's

Star Green

2

23

Hall Road

Bellhouse Farm

3

ICE School

School Road

St Michael's Cha

Orchard

Church Road

Copford Hall

Roman River

Aldercar Road

Warren Lane

MA

4

Colchester Zoo

22 **128**

Upper Hill Farm

Fountain Lane

Fountain Lane

5

Fountain Lane

Heckfordbridge

Bockingham Hall Farm

Lukes Farm

Birch Business Centre

ROAD

6

21

Hardy's Green

Hellen's

Beckingham Hall

MALDON

Orpen's

Leas Lane

Birch Hall

7

Conduit Farm

B1022

Hill

8

Lower Road

Birch

B1022

Caper

ROAD

G **H** **J** **151** **K** **L** **M**

93 94 95

Brake's Farm

Birch Primary School

220

Tye Farm

Fen Farm

Market Field School

The Beth Chatto Gardens

CLACTON

ROAD

A133

G 05 **H** **J** **109** 06 School Road **K** **L** 07 **M**

I

Grove Farm

Park Farm

FRATING HILL

2

23

Keelars Tye

B1027

3

B1027

Tye Lane

Elmstead Heath

Blue Gates

4

Keelars Lane

Cockaynes Lane

132

22

Millfields Primary School

Alresford Road

Cockaynes

B1027

Elmstead Row

Alresford Business Centre

Tenpenny Farm

5

Heath Road

Orchard Road

Oak Tree

Worcester

Elm

Alresford

Station Road

Cox Road

Laxton Road

Newkins Road

Coast Road

Crestlands

Alresford Station PO

LC

Poplars Cs

LC

6

B1027

ST OSYTH RD

Confer

Furze Crs

Wivenhoe Road

Church Road

Tenpenny Brook

21

Marsh Farm

Alresford Grange

St. Andrews

Alresford Primary School

7

River Colne

Ford Lane

Sixpenny Brook

Alresford Hall

8

220

Alresford Lodge

G 05 **H** **J** **155** 06 **K** **L** 07 **M**

The Ford

Ford Lane

Plumpton's Farm

G H J K L M

I
2
3
4
134
5
6
7
8

Paynes Farm
Rowherns Lane
Gurnhams
Crown Lane
Br Ha

A133 COLCHESTER ROAD
Rowherns Lane
Warren's Farm

Crabtree Farm

The Grange

A133 COLCHESTER ROAD
Fisher's Farm

Heckford's Road

Admiral's Farm

Moors Lane

Shair Lane

Sturrick Farm
Swallow's Row

Finch Dr
Larkfield Road
Robin Close
Linnet Way
Cherrywoods

Moors Close

Surgery

Weeley Road

Weeley Road
Risby's Farm

Sturrick Lane
Road

Great Bentley

Weeley Road

Avenue
Cedar Way
Birch
Pine Close

Plough Road
PO
New Cut
Morella Close
Station Road

The Tye Road

LC Great Bentley Station
Industrial Estate

Great Bentley Primary School
Hall VW Road
Keeble Court

St Mary's Farm
Lover's Lane

Plough Road

Tye Homestead

Coppice Farm

Weeley Rd
Aingers Green Road
Aingers Green
Colles Brook Road
St Mary's Rd
Pfd
Wick Road
Moynes Farm
Bentley Rd

College Farm

Plough Road
Colles Brook Road

A133

The Lodge

A · B · C · D · E · F

Tendring **112**

THE STREET
Hollyview Close
THORPE
B1035

Hill Farm
Crown Lane
New Hall
The Mill
Crow Lane
Manor House
Whitehall Lane
Bradley Hall
Hannam's Hall

Crown Lane
Brett's Hall
Pestles Hall
Hillhouse Lane
White Hall

Hawk Farm
Crow Lane
Holland Brook
COLCHES

B1033
COLCHESTER ROAD
THORPE ROAD B1033
Wdln Rd Hilltop Crs
Hilltop Rise
Weeley
Street
PO
St Andrew's Rd
Fr Av
Thornberry Avenue
Alexandra Road
Second Avenue

133

A133
WEELEY BY-PASS ROAD
Weeley Station
St Andrews BA CE Primary School
B1441
Weeley Brook

Hall Lane
Gutteridge Hall
Gutteridge

Church Lane
Weeleyhall Wood

A133
Weeley Heath
Flds Road
Clacton Road
Mill Lane

Bentley Roxburghe Road
Wenlock Road
Green Lane
Mill Road
ROAD
Connaught Road

Norwood Lodge
A133
Victoria Road
Botany Lane

Bentley Road
Highbirch Road
Rectory Road
Kempston Park
B1441
HARWIC

College Farm
158
B1441
Batemans Road
Talbot Rd
Honing Rd
Ame
Honeypot Farm

1 grid square represents 500 metres

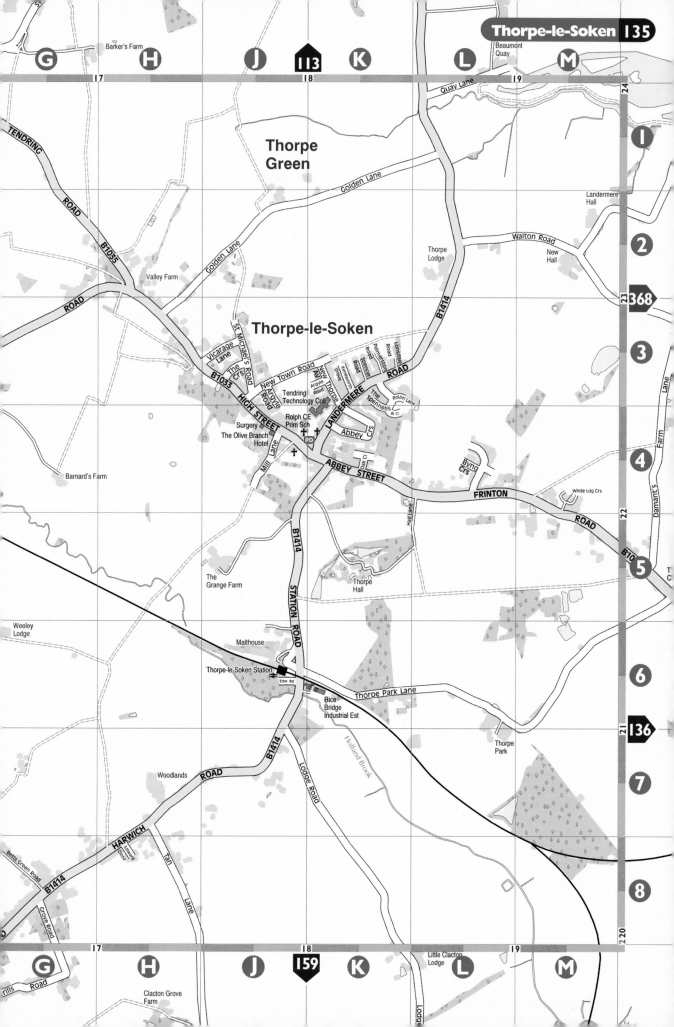

G H J 113 K L M

Thorpe Green

Barker's Farm

Beaumont Quay

Quay Lane

TENDRING ROAD B1035

Golden Lane

Landermere Hall

Thorpe Lodge

Walton Road

New Hall

368

Valley Farm

Golden Lane

Thorpe-le-Soken

St Michael's Road

Vicarage Lane

The Crs

B1035

HIGH STREET

Argyle Road

New Town Road

New Thorpe Av

Argyle Road

Kenilworth Grove

Spencer Road

Palmerston Road

Lonsdale Road

B1414

LANDERMERE ROAD

The Spennells

Rolph Lane

Tendring Technology Coll

Rolph CE Prim Sch

Surgery

The Olive Branch Hotel

PO

Mill Lane

Abbey

Cls

Byng Crs

White Ldg Crs

ABBEY STREET

Hall Lane

FRINTON ROAD B10

Barnard's Farm

B1414 STATION ROAD

The Grange Farm

Thorpe Hall

Thorpe Park Lane

Damant's Farm Lane

TC

Weeley Lodge

Malthouse

Thorpe-le-Soken Station

Edw Rd

Rice Bridge Industrial Est

Holland Brook

Thorpe Park

136

Woodlands

ROAD

B1414

Lodge Road

HARWICH ROAD

Leonard Close

Tan Lane

Betts Green Road

B1414

Grove Road

rills Road

Clacton Grove Farm

Little Clacton Lodge

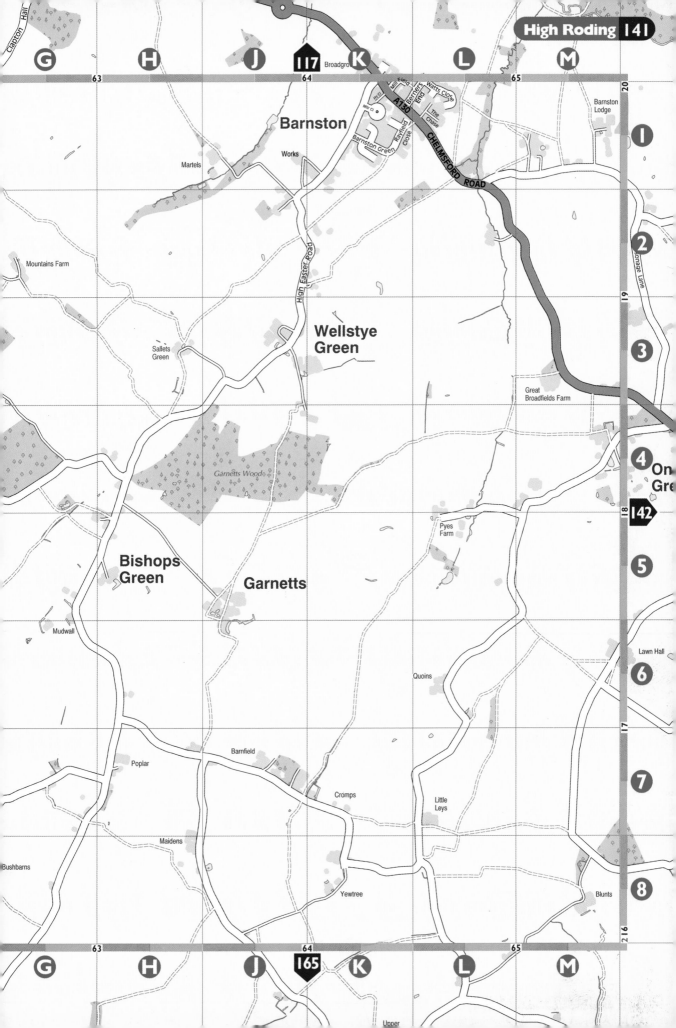

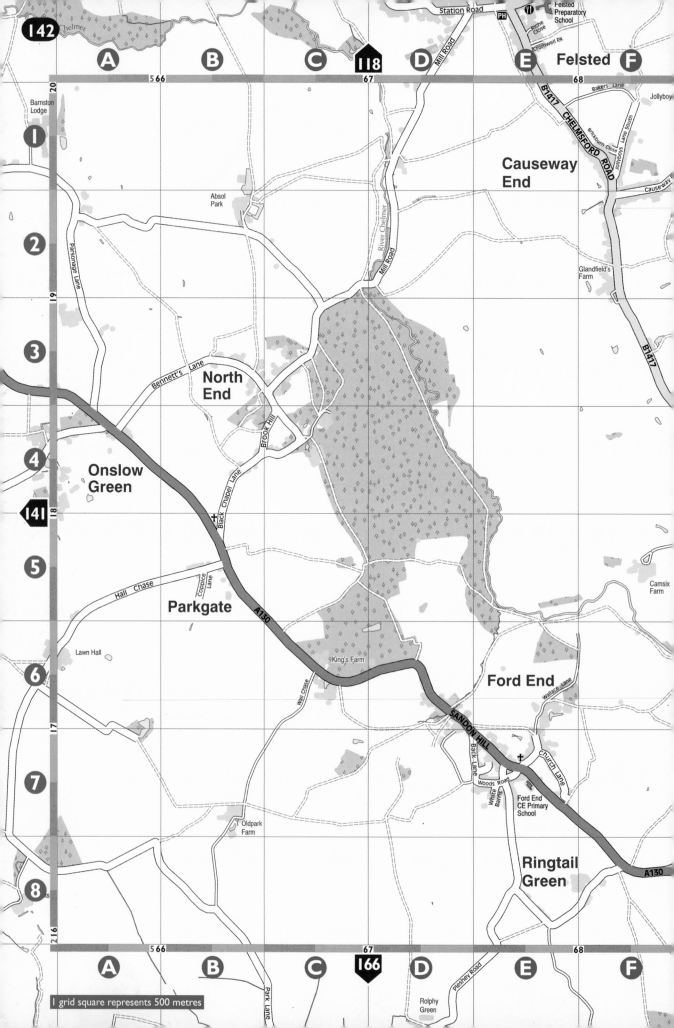

Bannister
Green

G H J 119 K L M

Cock
Green

Thistley
Green

Cobler's
Green

Pondpark Farm

Rutlands

Howletts

Dunney
Lane

Leighs
Lodge

Dunney Lane

Leez Lane

Lodge Lake

Lavender
Lake

River Ter

Warre
Farm

Causeway

144

Church Lane

Littleypark

Mattock's
Farm

Works

Hartford
End

Ridleys
Brewery

Mill Lane

River Chelmer

Littley
Green

Mabb's
Farm

Old Shaw's
Farm

G H J 167 K L M

Warner's
Farm

Essex Way

I

2

3

4

5

6

7

8

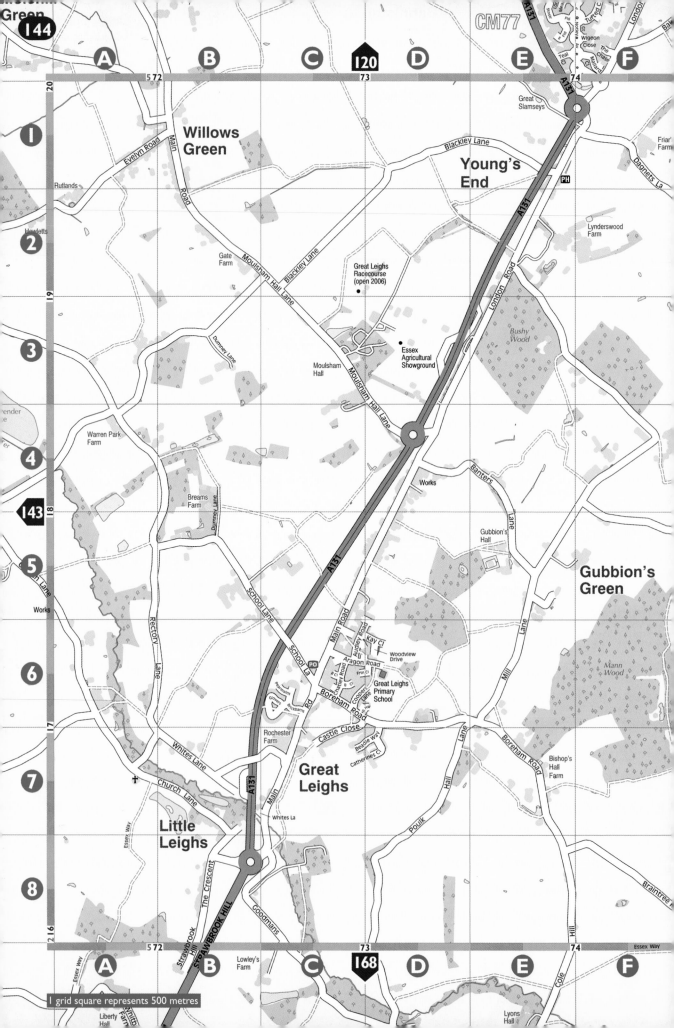

The
Green

G   H   J   **121**   K   L   M

75   76   77   20

Cards Farm

Wren
Park

Dagnets Lane
Dagnets
Farm

Green   Lane

Elms
Farm

Pole   Lane

Webb's
Farm

Littlebury
Farm

Hazelton
Wood

North
Whitehouse

Great
Walley Hall

Westock's
Farm

146

Rank's
Green

Blixe's
Farm

Dines
Hall

Beauchamps

Troys Hall

Fairstead

Troys   Chase

Fairstead
Lodge

Fairstead Hall Road

Fairstead Road

Peg Millar's Lane

Hal
Farm

Essex   Way

Braintree Road

Ful G
Street   H   J   **169**   K   L   M

Three
Ashes
Farm

Great
Loyes

Penr
Farm

I

2

3

4

5

6

7

8

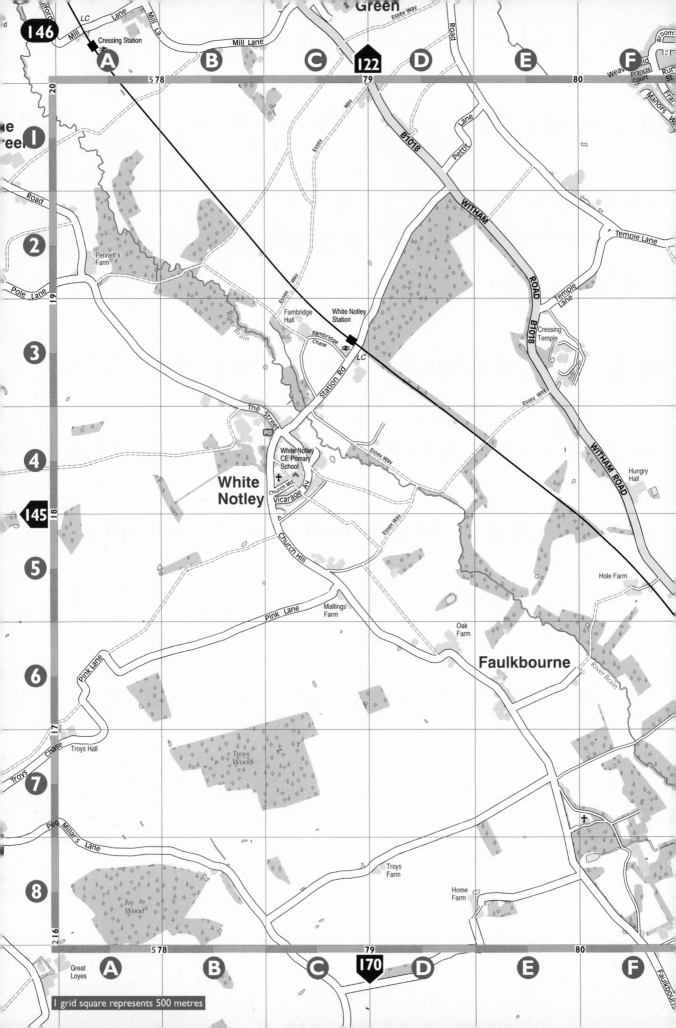

A   B   C   D   E   F

Cantfield's Farm

Easthorpe Road

126

91   92

I

Messing Lodge

Blind Lane

Easthorpe Road

Lodge Road

2

Blind Lane

Palmer's Farm

B1022

The Street

Birch Holt

Harborough Hall Road

Smythe'

3   Messing

Messing cum Inworth Comm Prim Sch

School Road

Messing Gn

Harborough Hall Farm

Road

4

Layer Wood

149

B1022

5   Pods Wood

Haynes Green

Haynes

Green

Road

Stockhouse Road

COLCHESTER ROAD

6

Road

Cedar Aven

Newbridge Road

Tiptree Sports Centre

MAYPOLE ROAD

Thurstable School

Spinneyfields

Heaton Way

Milldene Primary School

Viners Farm

Barbrook

7

Lane

Green Lane

Millwrights Lane

Brassingham Crescent

Grove Road

Works

Mill Close

Heycroft Way

Grove Road

Wilkin Dr

Tawell

Southgate Crescent

Ransom Road

The Medical Centre

Rockingham Farm

Holly Way

Anchor Press Social & Sports Club

Grosvenor

Grove Road

CHURCH

8   Rosemary Cl

Glebe

PO

Winston Avenue

Churchill Road

Newbridge Road

Works

Elwin Road

Keeble Close

Gager

ROAD

New Road

St Lukes Church Primary School

Bird Lane

Chapel Road

Birchwood Close

Birchwood Way

Long Wood

Anchor

Saffron Wy

Morley Road

B1023

Gladstone Road

Caxton

A   B   C   D   E   F

90   91   174   92

Station

Tiptree

1 grid square represents 500 metres

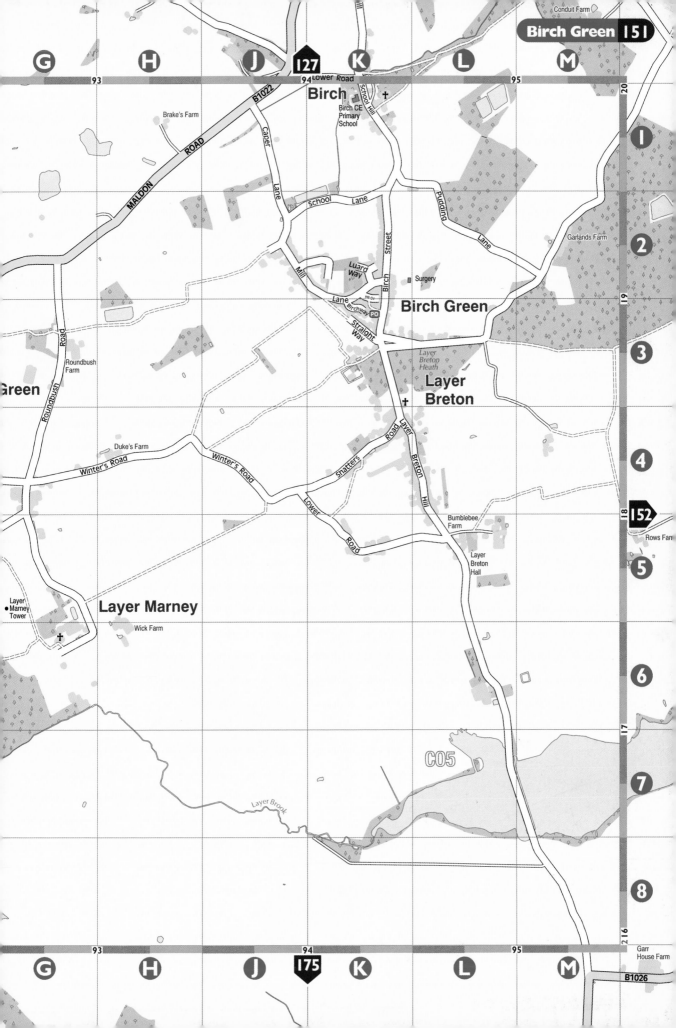

G   H   J   **127**   K   L   M

93   94 Lower Road   95   20

Birch

Conduit Farm

Brake's Farm

B1022

MALDON   ROAD

Caper   Lane

School   Lane

Birch CE Primary School

School Hill

Birch   Street

Pudding   Lane

Garlands Farm

1

2

19

Luard Way

Mill   Lane

Birchway

Hill Dr

PO

Surgery

Straight   Way

Birch Green

Layer Breton Heath

3

Roundbush Farm

Roundbush   Road

Green

Layer   Breton   Hill

Layer Breton

Duke's Farm

Winter's Road   Winter's Road

Shatters   Layer   Road

Lower   Road

Bumblebee Farm

Rows Farm

18 **152**

4

5

Layer Marney Tower

Layer Marney

Wick Farm

Layer Breton Hall

6

17

Layer Brook

C05

7

216

Garr House Farm

8

G   H   J   **175**   K   L   M

93   94   95

B1026

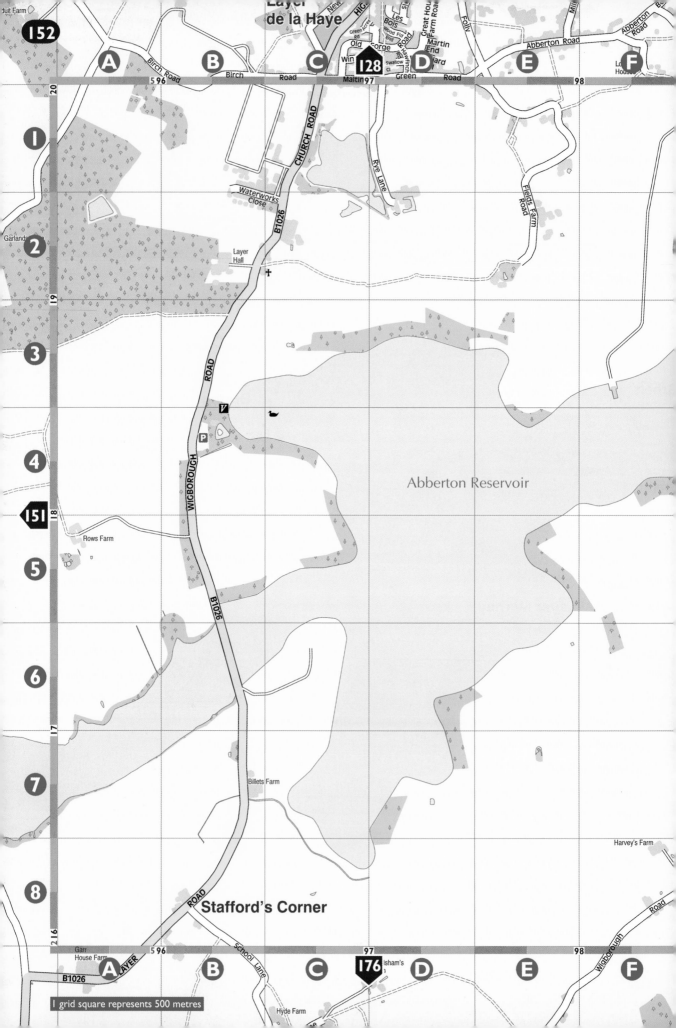

152

A   Birch Road   B   Birch   Road   C   Old Forge   D   Abberton Road   E   F

Layer de la Haye

128

Win   Maltin 97   Green   Road

5 96   97   98

1

Juit Farm

Church Road

Waterworks Close

Rye Lane

Fields Farm Road

2

Garland's

Layer Hall

B1026

3

Wigborough   Road

4

V

P

Abberton Reservoir

151

Rows Farm

5

6

B1026

7

Billets Farm

Harvey's Farm

8

Layer   Road

Stafford's Corner

2 16   Garr House Farm   A   Layer 5 96   School Lane   B   C   **176**   D   E   98 Wigborough Road   F

B1026   Isham's

Hyde Farm

1 grid square represents 500 metres

G   H   J   **131**   K   L   M

I

2

3

4

156

5

6

7

8

05   06   07

20
19
18
17
216

Sixpenny Brook

Alresford Lodge

The Ford

Ford Lane

Ford Lane

Ford Lane

Plumpton's Farm

Alresford Creek

Nature Reserve

Wick Lane

V
P

Aldboro Point

Moverons Lane

Moverons

Moverons Lane

Wareing Lane

Moverons Lane

BRIG

Geedon Saltings

River Colne

Rat Island

Pewit Island

Westmarsh Point

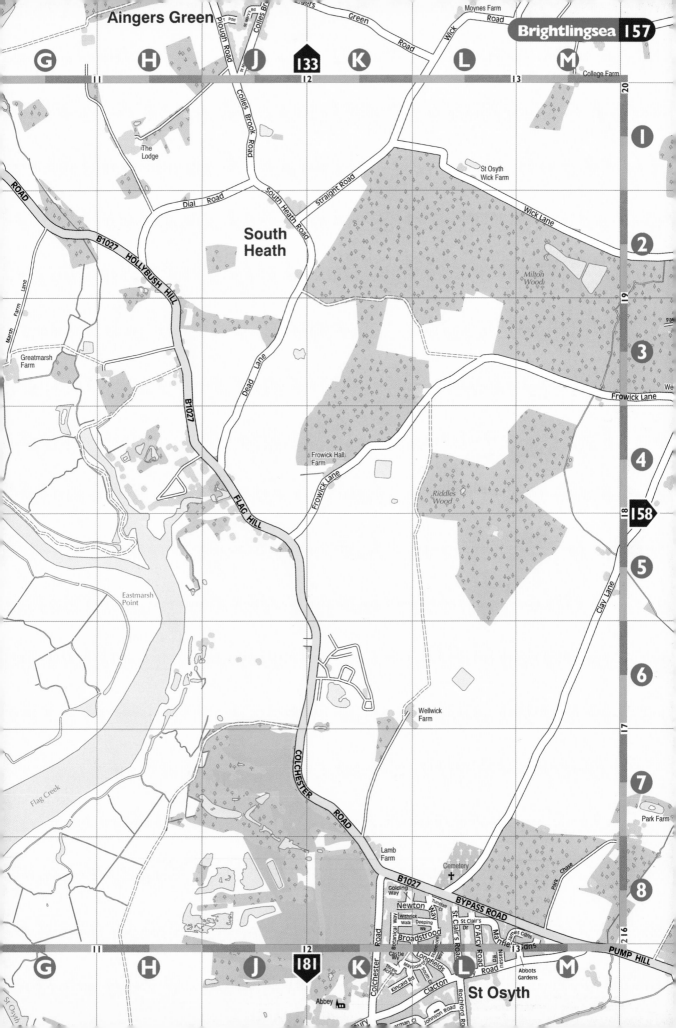

G **H** **J** ⬢**133** **K** **L** **M**

11 12 13

College Farm

I

The Lodge

2

Colles Brook Road

Moynes Farm Road

Wick Road

St Osyth Wick Farm

Wick Lane

Dial Road

South Heath Road

Straight Road

South Heath

ROAD

B1027 HOLLYBUSH HILL

Marsh Farm Lane

Greatmarsh Farm

B1027

Milton Wood

3

Frowick Lane

We

Dead Lane

Frowick Hall Farm

Frowick Lane

Riddles Wood

4

FLAG HILL

158

Eastmarsh Point

Clay Lane

5

6

Flag Creek

Wellwick Farm

7

Park Farm

COLCHESTER ROAD

8

Lamb Farm

Cemetery

Park Chase

B1027

BYPASS ROAD

Golding Way

PUMP HILL

Newton Way

Broadstrood

St Clair's Road

D'Arcy Road

Manfield Gdns

Abbots Gardens

216

St Osyth

Abbey

A **B** **C** **D** **E** **F**

136

Holland Brook

CLACTON

B1032

Sladbury's Old House

Pond House

Sladbury's Lane

Holland Haven

159

Picker's Ditch

Pickers Way

Fleetwood

Hicks Av

Elmfield

Suffolk Cl

Broadmere Cl

Kent's Av

Norfolk

Grenfell

Oakwood Avenue

Avenue

Avenue

Park Blvd

Briarwood

Av

Aylesbury Drive

Frinton Road

Way

Manor

The Cape

Haven Av

The Esplanade

Nansen Rd

Merrilees Crs

Norman Road

Pembroke Gdns

Av

Sussex Cl

Holland Haven Prim Sch

Ingatfield Rd

Edison Road

Surgery

Saxon Wk

Grendel

Way

Viking

B1032

Snd Cl

Brentwood

Ipswich Road

Stratford Road

Road

Surgery

PO

FRINTON ROAD

Manchester Rd

Nottingham Rd

Primrose

Hereford

Kenilworth Rd

Brighton

Road

Bramsuen Rd

The

Chelmsford

Road

Colchester

Road

FRINTON ROAD

Frinton Road Medical Cen

Surgery

York

Road

HG Ct

Canterbury Road

The Parade

Chase

Fernwood Av

Windermere Rd

Preston

Road

Bedford

Road

Salisbury

Road

Dulwich Rd

Cliff Road

Madeira Rd

Kings

Holland-on-Sea

Turpins Av

Kings

Avenue

Dulwich Road

Queensway

Road

PO

Madeira

Kings

Parade

Lyndhurst Rd

Hazlem

183

6

7

8

1 grid square represents 500 metres

A **B** **C** **D** **E** **F**

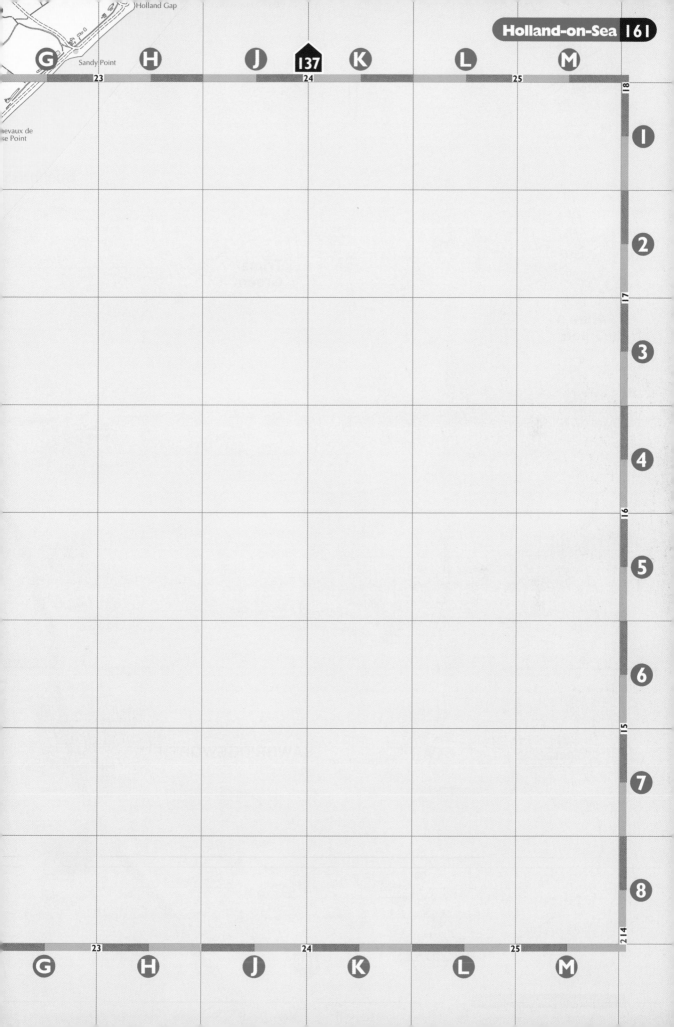

G   H   J   137   K   L   M

Holland Gap

Sandy Point

nevaux de
se Point

23   24   25

18

1

2

17

3

4

16

5

6

15

7

8

214

G   H   J   24   K   L   M

23   24   25

G   H   J   141   K   L   M

I

2

Pleshey
Grange

Bushbarns

Yewtree

Upper
Harveys

Essex Way

Close
PO

The street   The street

**Stagden
Cross**

Haydens

Acreland
Green

Raylands

166

Linsteads

Essex Way

Baileys

Ducker's Lane

Elbows

Havron's Lane

Armours   Bedfords

Bedfords Hl

Fridays

Essex Way

Tye Green

Barrack Road

Mashbury Rd

Smallshoes

Mill Road

Barrack
Road

Gatehouse

**Good
Easter**

Souther   Cross   Road

Wares Rd 64

Wares

Little
Newarks

Mashbury

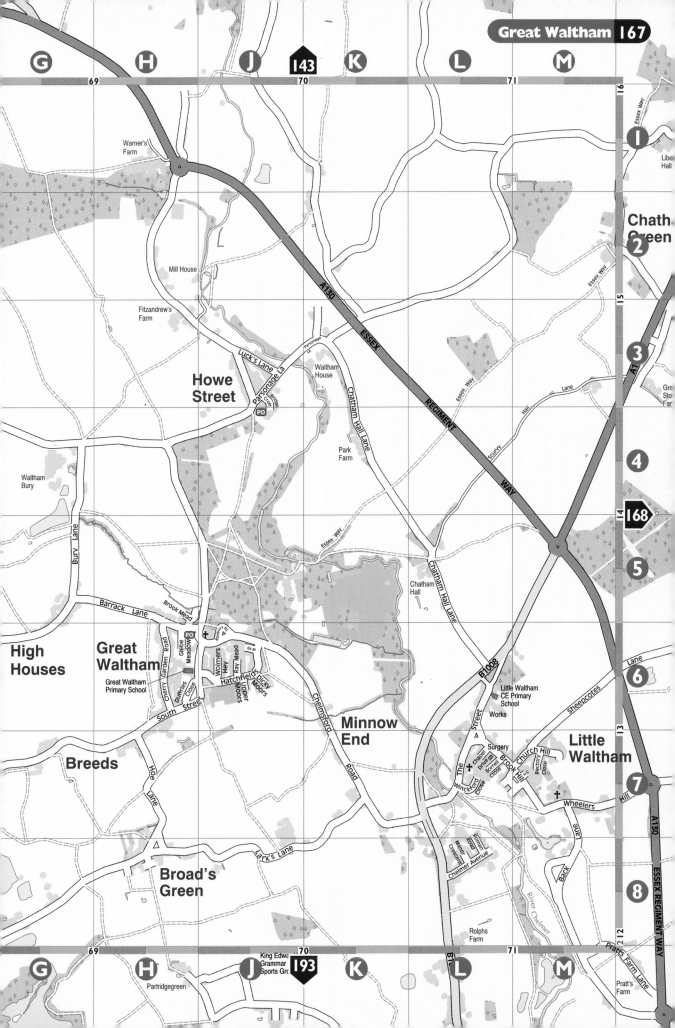

G H J 143 K L M

69 70 71 16

1

Warner's Farm

Libe Hall

2

15

Mill House

3

A1

Gre Sto Far

Fitzandrew's Farm

Luck's Lane

Parsonage La

Waltham House

Howe Street

Parsonage La

PO

Chatham Hall Lane

Essex Way

Lane

Park Farm

REGIMENT

Scurvy

Hall

4

Waltham Bury

168

14

Essex Way

WAY

5

Chatham Hall

Chatham Hall Lane

Bury Lane

Barrack Lane

Brook Mead

High Houses

Great Waltham

Glebe Meadow

PO

Wolmers

Ray Mead

Bk M

B1008

Little Waltham CE Primary School

Lane

Sheepcotes

6

13

Cherry Garden Road

Great Waltham Primary School

Dunfries Close

Hatchfields

Dicky Moors

Upper Moors

Works

Church Hill

Little Waltham

South Street

Chelmsford Road

Minnow End

The Street

Chapel

Surgery

Drive

Sorrell Close

Brook

Rectory Close

7

A130

Breeds

Hoe Lane

Winckford Close

Wheelers

Lark's Lane

Roman Road

Manor Crescent

Chelmer Avenue

Back Lane

Hill

ESSEX REGIMENT WAY

8

Broad's Green

River Chelmer

212

Pratts Farm Lane

Rolphs Farm

Pratt's Farm

69 70 71

G H J 193 K L M

Partridgegreen

King Edwa Grammar Sports Gro

A   B   C   144   D   E   F
73

5 72   74

Essex Way

Braintree

I   Liberty Hall

Whitbreads Farm Lane

A131

Strawbrook

STRAWBROOK HILL

The Crescent

Goodmans Lane

Lowley's Farm

Lyons Hall

Cole

River Ter

Essex Way

Chatham Green

2   Essex Way

A131

3   Lane

Great Stonage Farm

Daisleys Lane

Lyonshall Wood

Wakering's Farm

White House Farm

Boreham Road

4   Long's Farm

Longs Lane

167   14

Noak Farm

5

Boreham Road

Sheepcotes Farm

Lane

6   Sheepcotes

Alstead's Farm

Drakes Lane

Drake's Farm

Drakes Lane

Lawns Farm

Drakes Lane Industrial Estate

Boreham Rd

Little Waltham

13

Leighs Road

Wheelers Hill

Power's Farm

7   Wheelers Hill

A130

Back Lane

Domsey Lane

Peverel's Farm

8

A130 ESSEX REGIMENT WAY

212

Pratts Farm Lane

Pratt's Farm

A   B   C   194   D   E   F

5 72   73   74

Boreham Airfield

1 grid square represents 500 metres

172

A B C 148 D E F
85
584 86

I

tion 22

Coleman's
Farm
2

15

3
Little Braxted

Hall Broad
Farm

Church Chase

Golf Course

Braxted Park
Golf Club

Braxted Park
House

The Avenue

Great Braxted
Hall

Braxted Park Road

Noak's
Cross

Sextons
Lane

Broomfield's
Farm

4

171 14

Sewells
Farm

Lea Lane

Threadgold's
Farm

PH
PO
Gre

Bung Row

Braxted La

5

Hale's Farm

Chase
Glen
Acres
6
Blue
Mills

13

Chantry
Wood

Green Man Lane

Carters Lane

Mountains Road

Mountains

Road

Braxted

Maclarens

Beacon Hill

7
Glebe Farm

Witham Road

Birch Rise

Heathgate

Wellands Close

Wellands

Holt Dr

Byron Dr

Road

Handley's Lane

Surgery
Finch's

Beacon

Hill

Goat Lodge Road

Stapleford

B1022

8
Wickham
Bishops

Mope Lane

Leigh Drive

Church
Road

Tiptree
The Warrens
PH
Beech
Green
Poney Chase
PO

Handley's Lane

Kelvedon

Great Totham
County Primary
School

Forre
Park
Tenn

212

Station Road

Church
Close
Hill
Place

A

584

Blacksmiths Lane

Roots Lane

Long Meads

Grange
Road

Back

School
Road

B

Great Totham Road

Maypole

Lane

Prince

C

198

Gre
Totham

85

Walden

House Road

Crabb's Farm

Catchpole Lane

D

Staplers Heath

Walden
Close

Stanle

Main Rd

E

ROAD
86

seagers

F

1 grid square represents 500 metres

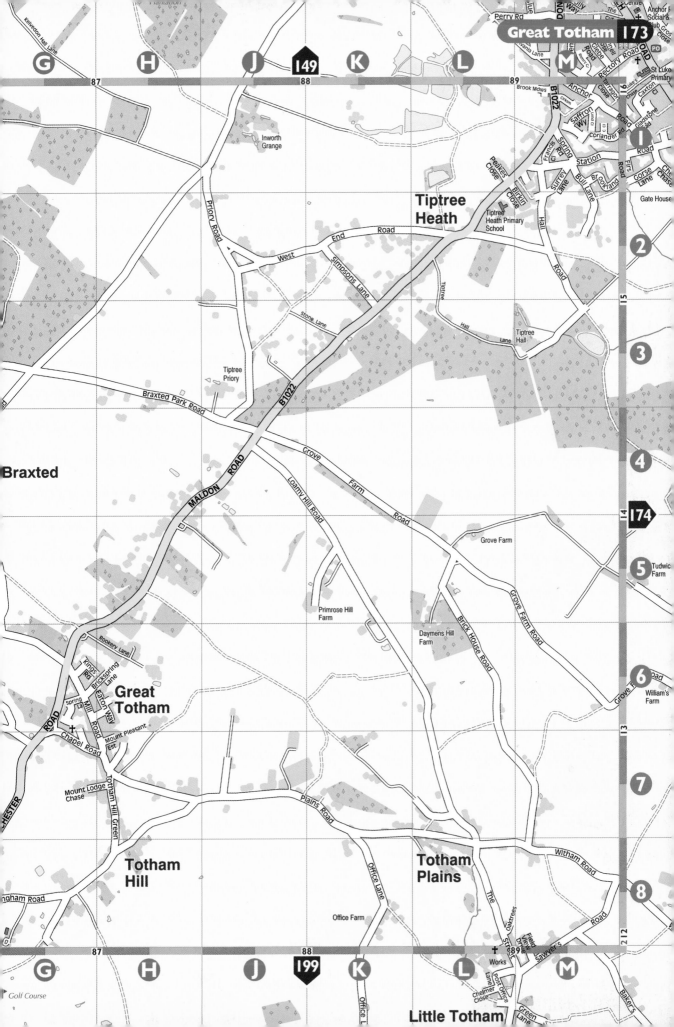

G | H | J | K | L | M

149

199

174

Great Totham

Braxted

Tiptree Heath

Tiptree Priory

Inworth Grange

Totham Hill

Totham Plains

Little Totham

Golf Course

West End Road

Simpsons Lane

Stone Lane

Braxted Park Road

MALDON ROAD

B1022

Grove Farm Road

Loamy Hill Road

Primrose Hill Farm

Daymens Hill Farm

Grove Farm

Tudwic Farm

William's Farm

Brick House Road

Plains Road

Office Lane

Office Farm

Mount Lodge Chase

Totham Hill Green

Chapel Road

Rookery Lane

Brickspring Lane

Kings Rd

Eaton Way

Mill Road

Spring La

Mount Pleasant Est

Priory Road

Tiptree Heath Primary School

Peakes Close

Birkin Close

Spring Rd

Surrey Lane

Bull Lane

Hall Road

Francis

Saffron Wy

Anchor

B1022

Perry Rd

Brook Mdws

Coriander Rd

Rectory Road

St Luke's Primary

Gate House

Firs Road

Gorse Lane

Witham Road

Sawyer's Road

The Oaktrees

Field View Dr

Chelmer Close

Green Lane

Grove Farm Road

87 | 88 | 89

I5 | I4 | I3 | 2I2

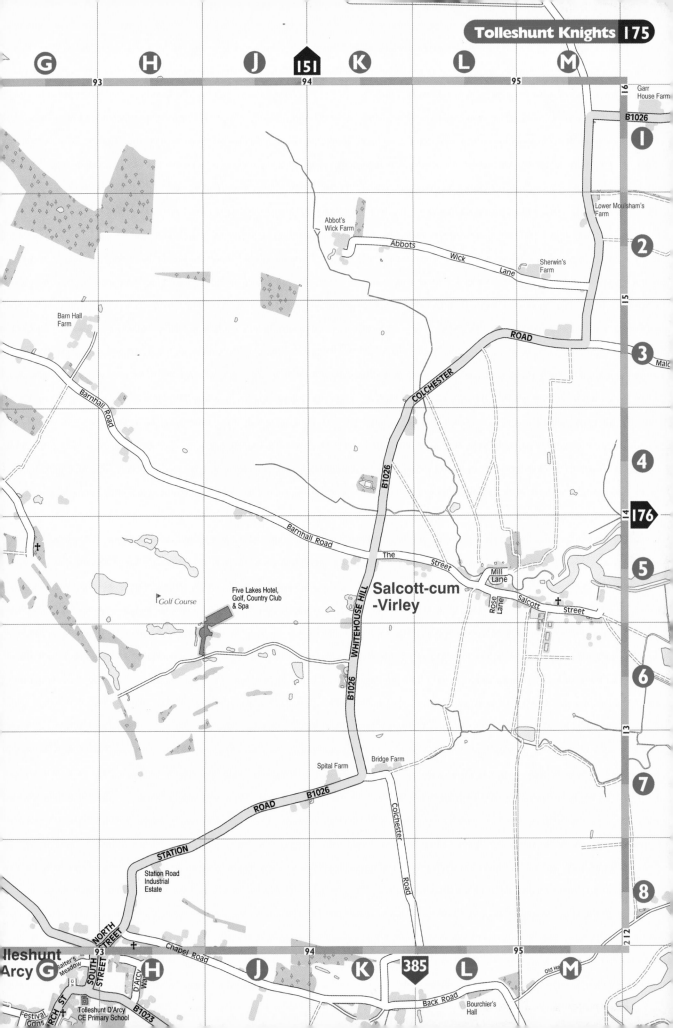

G H J **151** K L M
93 94 95 16

Garr House Farm

B1026

1

Lower Moulsham's Farm

2

Abbot's Wick Farm

Abbots Wick Lane

Sherwin's Farm

15

Barn Hall Farm

COLCHESTER ROAD

3 Malc

Barnhall Road

B1026

4

176 14

The Street

Mill Lane

Salcott

5

Golf Course

Five Lakes Hotel, Golf, Country Club & Spa

Salcott-cum -Virley

WHITEHOUSE HILL

B1026

Rose Lane

Salcott Street

6

B1026

13

Spital Farm

Bridge Farm

Colchester Road

7

STATION ROAD B1026

Station Road Industrial Estate

212

8

lleshunt Arcy **G**

NORTH STREET

SOUTH STREET

Salter's Meadow

D'Arcy Wa

B1023

Chapel Road

Festival Gdns

Tolleshunt D'Arcy CE Primary School

RCH ST

93 **H** 94 **J** 95 **K** **385** **L** **M**

Back Road

Bourchier's Hall

Old Ha

G H J **153** K L M

Lower Newpots Close Mersea Kemps Farm Mersea Road Road

99 600 01 191

I

Copthall Grove

Sampson's Farm Sampson's Lane Newpots

THE STROOD

2

Bonner's Saltings

115

3

B1025

Ray Island Nature Reserve

COLCHEST 4

PI4 **178** Wellh Farm

Strood Channel

ROAD 5

Sampsons Creek

Constable Close

Colchester Road Trinity Close Windsor 6

B1025

Feldy Marshes

Dabchicks Sailing Club Whittaker Wy Woodfield Drive Woodstock Chatsworth Lawns Close MILL ROAD

Carriers Cl Spruce Cl Upland Crescent Upland Road

The Lane Pine Grove Cemetery Ms Reymead Close Vince Close Surgery Elmwood Qu Anne Rd

City Road Stonehill Way Firs Road High Street North Grays Close KINGSLAN Rainbow Road Qu Anne Rd

P Firs Chase Mersea Avenue Vince Close **BARFIELD RD** 7

Little Ditch Firs Hamlet Blackwater New Captains Road B1025 Vince Close Atorick Avenue Mersea Island School Rushmere Prince Albert

Works. The Seafield Rd Captains Rd HIGH ST Melrose Road Close Rd Coverts

Thorn Fleet Victory St Peter's Road Churchfields Mersea Community & Sports Centre Beach Rd

Mersea Fleet Road PO Church Rd Yorick Road Grove Avenue Kingsland Beach

WEST MERSEA Pharos Lane Meadow Lane

Coast Road West Mersea Museum 8

Besom Fleet

Cobmarsh Island

99 600 01 212

G H **386** J K L M

Mersea Quarters

A   B   C   154   D   E   F
03

602   15   03   04

I

Reeveshall
Marsh

Maydays
Marsh

Broad Fleet

2

STROOD

15

Maydays Farm

Reeves
Hall

3

B1025

Mersea Island

Haycocks

Bocking
Hall

Meeting Lane

Bower
Hall

East Mersea Road

CO5

4

COLCHESTER

Bower Hall Lane

Blue
Row

Haycocks Lane

Chapmans Lane

177   14

Wellhouse
Farm

Weathercock

East   Mersea   Road

Rewsalls
Farm

Mersea Island
Vineyard

5

ROAD

B1025

Dawes Lane

East Road

Waldegraves Lane

Essex County Council
Youth Camp

6

Constable
Close

Gdn Farm

Garden
Farm

Oakwood Road

Windsor

Suffolk Av

Brierley
Avenue

Stable
Mews

Cross
Way

The Cross

Cross Lane

Waldegraves
Farm

Trinity Close

Lawns
Close

MILL

East   Road

Norfolk Avenue

Beverley
Avenue

Oakwood
Dr

Farthings
Chase

Fairhaven

Seaview

7

RFIELD RD

KINGSLAND

Surgery

Ou Anne Rd

Empress
Dr

King
Charles
Rd

Estuary Park Rd

Waldegraves
Holiday Park

Mer
Island
School

Rushmere
Close

Prince Albert

The Coverts

Alexandra Av

Esplanade

13

Road

Broomhills

Willoughby Av

Victoria

Avenue

Kingsland Road

8

212

602   03   04

A   B   C   D   E   F

Westmarsh Point

G H J 155 K L M

05 06 07 116

1

Nature Reserve

Ivy House

Mersea Stone

2

East Road

North Barn

Ivy Lane

115

3

Broman's Farm

East Road

Shop Lane

East Road

Broman's Lane

P

Cudmore Grove Country Park

East Road

Fen Farm

PO

East Mersea

Church Lane

Road

4

114 180

5

Works

6

Mersea Flats

113

7

112

8

G   H   J   157   K   L   M

B1027

BYPASS ROAD

Golding Way

Newton

Withrick Walk

Deeping Wk

Tunstall Way

James Gdns

Broadstrood

Castle Wy

Botanical Way

Maypole Rd

Three Acres

Longfields

South Rd

Stammore

D'ARCY Road

Manfield Rd

Nassau Rd

Manfield Gdns

PULP HILL

Surgery Road

Abbots Gardens

Colchester Road

Kincaid Rd

Clacton

Johnson Road

Rochford Road

St Osyth

PO Norman Cl

Abbey

The Bury

church sq

Chapel La

St Osyth CE Primary School

Mill street

Spring Road

School La

King's

Brook Vale

St Osy

Warren Farm

Daltes Lane

St Os

Point Clear Road

Mill Dam Lake

St Clere's Hall Lane

Brazier's Farm

Dalte Farm

Point Clear Road

Wigboro Wick Lane

St Clare's Hall

Beach Road

Lee Wick Farm

Wigboro Wick Farm

Whyers Hall Farm

Cockett Wick Lane

182

ck Farm

Beach Road

St Osyth Marsh

Seawick

PO Holiday Park

Seawick Road

Priory Cl

Bishops Dr

Lilac Av

Willow Av

Links Rd

Club

Parade

Rose Gdns

Fourth Av

Third Av

Second Av

First Avenue

ver-Sands

street

Promenade

St Osyth Creek

G   H   J   K   L   M

I 2 3 4 5 6 7 8

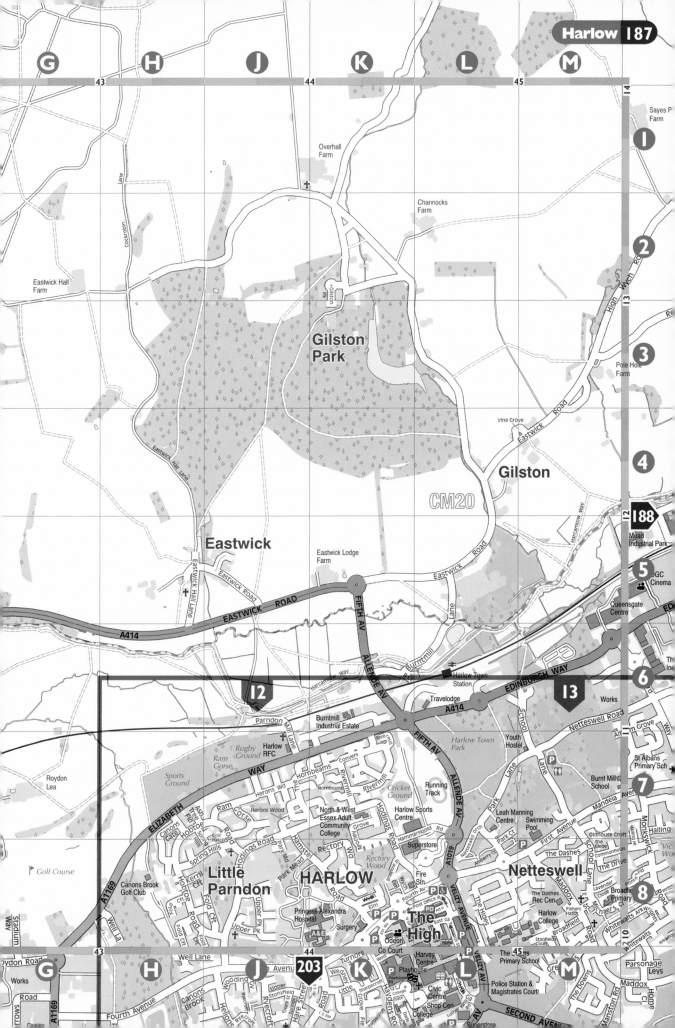

G H J 163 K L M

Sheering

Newhouse

Plashets

Primley CI

Crown CI

Orchard Close

THE STREET

Sheering

Sheering CE Primary School

PO

B183

Stort Valley Way

1

2

3

4

378

5

6

7

8

River Stort (Navi...)

Luxford Place

Sheering Lower Road

Durrington Hall

Aylmers Farm

B183 HARLOW ROAD

ROAD

Sheering Hall

M11

SHEERING

Campions

Wheelers Farm

High Lane

Harlow Road

Housham Hall

Harlow Road

N
E

Harlow Road

Churchgate Street

Wetherly Close

Boden CI

Feltimores

Moor

Hall

Road

Matching Road

Harlow Road

Rainbow Road

Mat...
ye

Nicholas
...ool

Harlow Tye

Carter's Green

Matching Park

Matching
Tye

Franklins Farm

Chalk Lane

Forest Way

Housham Tye

Stort Valley Way

bridge

M11

Hobbs Cross Road

Forest Way

Way

Lane

New Way

Faggotters
Lane

...yte...
Green

Roffey Hall

New Way

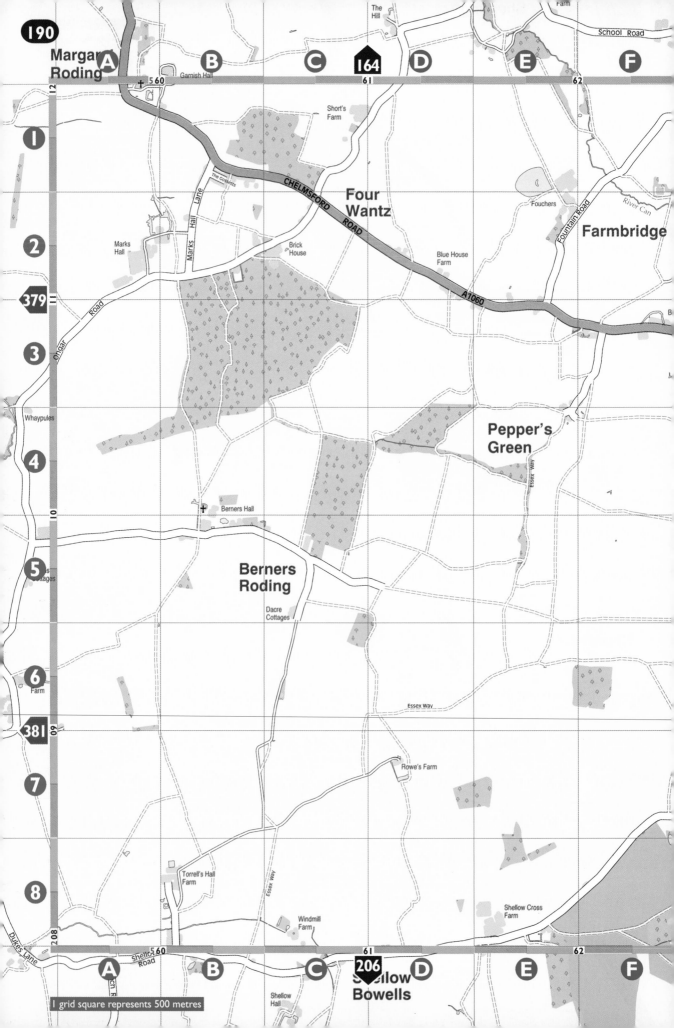

Good
Easter

G ther Cross Road **H** **J** **165** **K** **L** **M**

63 Wares Road 64 65 12

Essex Way

Wares

Little Newarks

Mashbury **I**

Farmbridge End Road

Fortescues

Ladyland

Great Newarks

2

Chalk End

ALT'S GREEN

3

Little Boyton Hall

4

A1060

Hill Farm

192 10

Newland Hall

Mountneys

5

Newland Brook

Boyton Cross

6

09

Dukes

Elms Farm

7

Elms Road

Lightfoots

Roxwell CE Primary School

Elms Rd

The Street

PO

Roxwell

Skreens Park Farm

Mill Close

Stonehill Road

St Michael's Drive

Church Green

Vicarage Rd

Green Lane

Galleons Hill

Thatcher's Farm

8

Vicarage

Tye Hall

208 Road

G **H** **J** **207** **K** **L** **M**

63 64 65 Hoestreet

Skreens Park

Stonehill Rd

Roxwell Br

Toppinghoehall Wood

G Works

H Farm

J 169

K

L

M

75 76 77

Berwick Place

1

Toppinghoe Hall

Wallace's Lane

Waltham Road

Industrial Estate

A12 MAIN ROAD 2

Chantry Farm

Works

Chantry Lane

Mowden Hall Lane

3 Hogwells

A12

Damases Lane

Boreham Industrial Est

Porter's Park

MAIN ROAD

4 196

M

Brick House Farm

Boleyn Way

B1137

A12

Allens Close

St Andrews Road

Plantation Road

Claypits Road

Villiers Place

Elm Way

Dudley Close

Hutton Cl

Seabrook

Essex Close

Butterfield Road

Fitzwalter

Haselfoot Road

5 Brakey Wood

Old Forge Road

Boons

Juniper Road

Boreham Primary School

Church Road

PO

Tyssen Mead

Lewis Place

The Willows

Surgery

MAIN ROAD

Boreham

The Chase

Lodge Crs

The Chase

Old Hall

Culvert's Farm

6

Boreham Hall

Church Road

7

River Chelmer

Hammonds Road

8

G

H llow's Farm

J

K

L

M

75 76 77

211

Holybreds Farm

Holybread Lane

Little Badde

WIC
ish

G H J 171 K L M

81 82 83

Sandford's Farm

Lane's Farm

Wickham

Bishop   Road   Hatfield   Road

Wickham
Place

B1018

Station Road

Hill
Place

Whiteho

1

Wickham

2

Smallands
Hall Farm

River Blackwater

Langford

Wickham
Hall

Road

3

Gray's
Farm

Spring Lane

Lea Grove

Works

utlers

4

198

The Elms

5

Ulting Grove

Road

Farm

MALDON ROAD

B1019

Stock Hall
Farm

Ashfield

Ulting Lane

HATFIELD ROAD

6

B1019

Works

Ulting Hall Road

Stammer's Farm

7

Ulting Lane

Chelmer & Blackwater Navigation

8

208

Manor Road

Hoe Mill
Barns

Manor
Farm

Causeway

The

G H J 213 K L M

81 82 83

Hoe Mill Road

Gardens Lane

Manor Lane

Woodlands

Be
Gra
Far

Wickham
Bishops

Great
Totham

Maldon

Broad Street
Green

Heybridge

Langford

1 grid square represents 500 metres

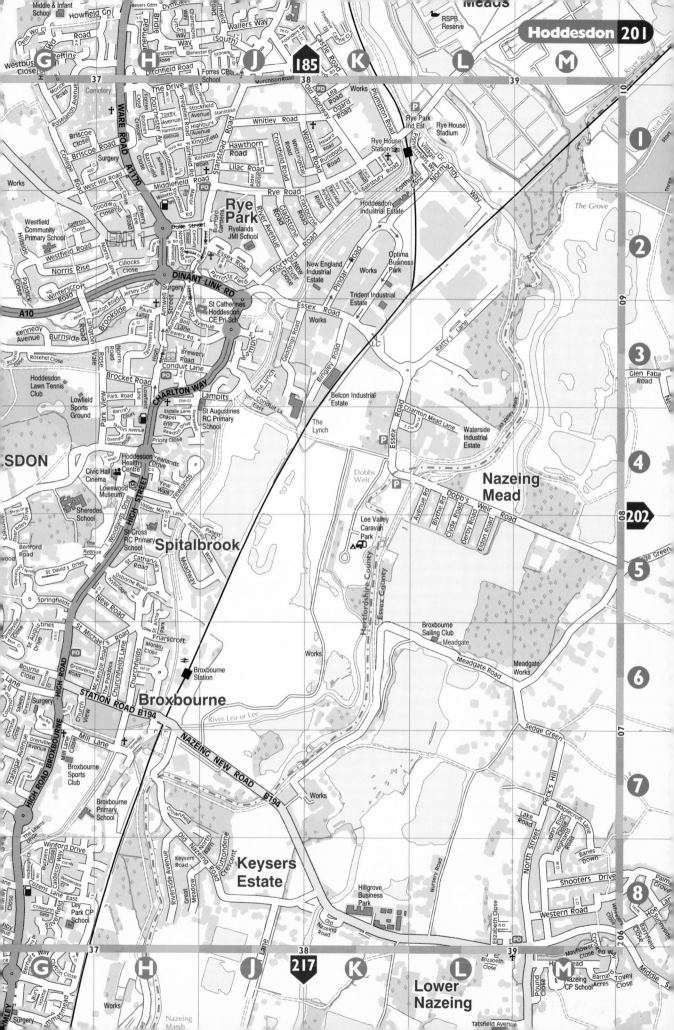

A　　**B**　　**C**　　**186** **Roydon** **D**　　**E**　　**Eas F nd**

5 40　　　　　　　　　　41　　　　　　　　　　42

Hoydon Mill
Leisure Park

The Granary

HIGH STREET

Harlow Road

Roydon Road

River Stort

Stort Valley Way

Three Forests Way

Forests

Way

Temple Mead

Md

PO

41

The Brook

The
Brook

Greenway

Sandringham Avenue

Horsecroft

Harlow
Business
Park

Pkwy

I

The Grove

Roydon
CP School

Lightfoots

Hansells Mead

Park

Fields

B181

Beaumont Dr

Orange La

Bakery
Close

Kingsmead
Close

W Cl

The Spire
Green Centre

2

60

EPPING ROAD

Whitehall
Estate

Downe
Hall

Didgemere
Hall

3

Glen Faba
Road

Low Hill Road

Stort

Valley

Way

Halls
Green

CM19

Old House Lane

Netherhall Road

B181

EPPING ROAD

Kat

4

80

201

Sedge Green

Stort Valley Way

Reeves Lane

5

Barn Hill

Hamlet Hill

**Roydon
Hamlet**

Tylers

Road

Stort Valley Way

B1133

WAT

6

07

Stoneshot Common

**Broadley
Common**

7

Maplecroft Lane

Banes
down

Shooters Drive

Hoe Lane

Betts

Lane

Three Forests Way

Nazeing Common

Common Road

8

Palmers
Grove

Hoe
Lane

Barnfield
Close

Hoe

Sunnyside

rn Road

Wheelers Close

Nazeing

Back

Lane

Nazeing
Park School

Nazeing Common

90

Mayflower
ed Way

Mead

Barnar
Acres

Tovey
Close

Middle
Street

Nazeing
CP School

A　　**B**　　**C**　　**218**　　**D**　　**E**　　**F**

5 40　　　　　　　　　　41　　　　　　　　　　42

Golf Course

1 grid square represents 500 metres

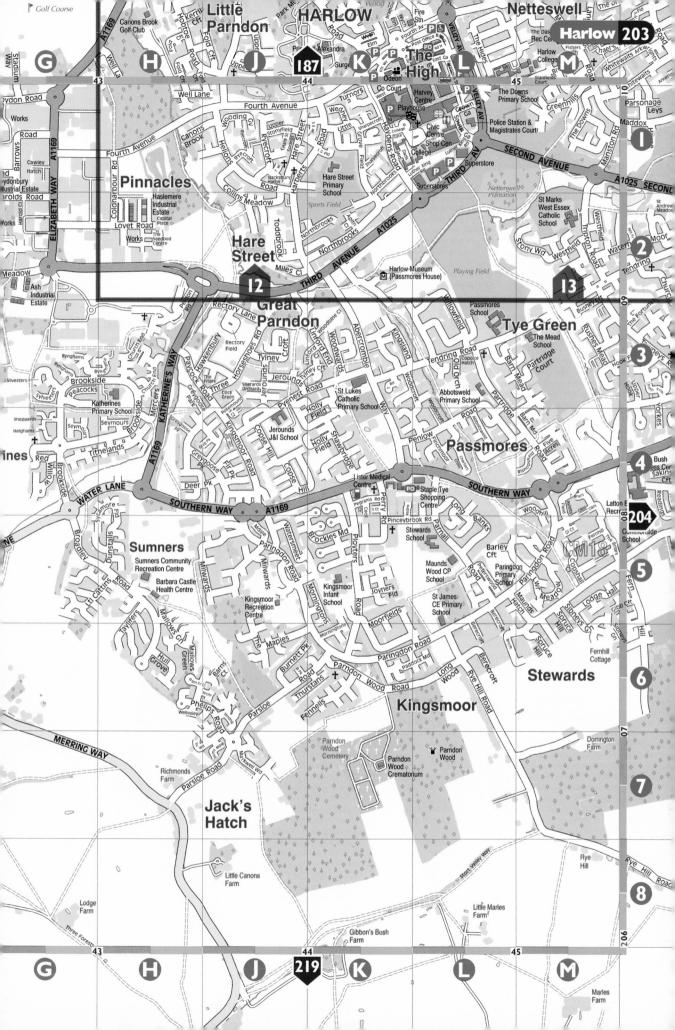

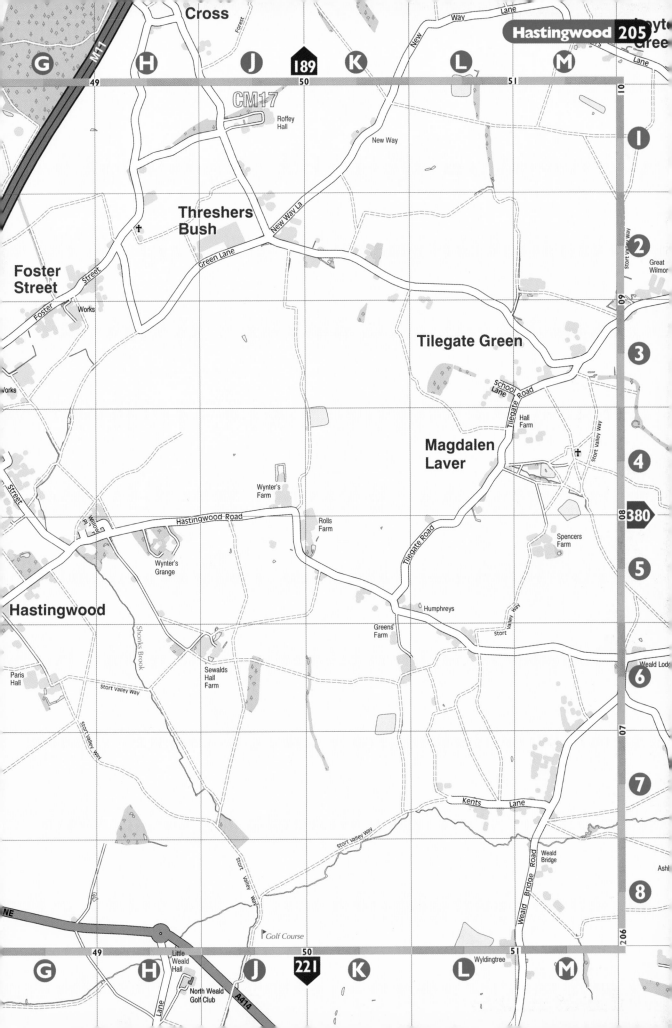

Dukes Lane

A 560 **B** Wi Fa **C** **190** 61 **D** Shellow Cross Farm **E** 62 **F**

Shellow Road

Beech Road

08

I

Shellow Hall

Shellow Bowells

Sawyer's Farm

M Yd

The Street

Road

PO

Wood Lane

Stays Lane

Quires Green

Butt Hatc Farm

2 Wood Lane

Warden's Hall

Spains Hall Road

Spains Wood

Silver Lane

07

3 Spains Hall Road

Wall's Green

Pooty Pools

Spains Hall

Bridge Farm

4

Pigstye Green

381 06

Rockhills

Norton Heath Road

Pigstye Green Road

Bassett's Lane

5

Norton Heath

Telfords

Willingale Road

6 Offin's Cottages

Hulke's Farm

Bassett's Farm

Radl Gree

Radley Green Road

05

Hand's Farm

7 Spriggs

Willingale Road

Dodd's Farm

A414

Norton Heath

Norton Manor

Horsfrith Park Farm

Readings

Ladylands

Old Barns Lane

8

04

Spurriers

560

61

222 62

A **B** **C** **D** **E** **F**

D ROAD A414

The Orchard

ngrith

1 grid square represents 500 metres

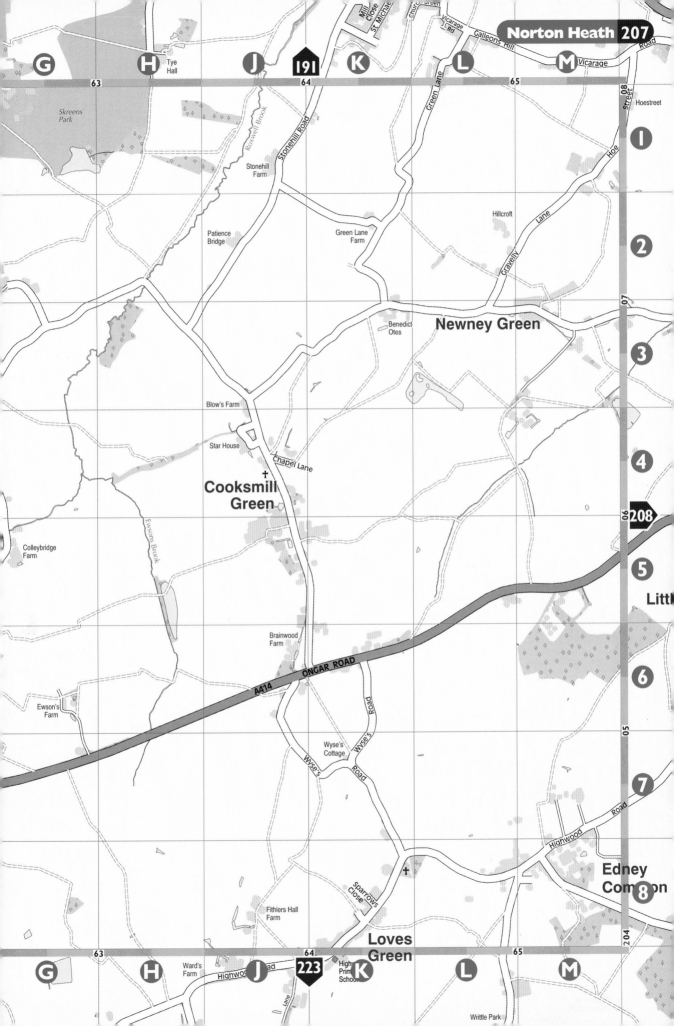

G H J 191 K L M

Mill Close

St Michael

Church Green

Vicarage Rd

Galleons Hill

Vicarage

Street

Hoestreet

Hoe Lane

63 64 65 08

Skreens Park

Roawell Brook

Stonehill Farm

Patience Bridge

Stonehill Road

Green Lane Farm

Hillcroft

Gravelly Lane

Green Lane

07

Newney Green

Benedict Otes

Blow's Farm

Star House

Chapel Lane

Cooksmill Green

Colleybridge Farm

Ewsons Brook

06 **208**

Littl

Brainwood Farm

Ewson's Farm

A414 ONGAR ROAD

Wyse's Cottage

Wyse's Road

Wyse's Road

05

Highwood Road

Edney Common

Sparrows Close

Fithlers Hall Farm

Ward's Farm

Highwood Road

High Prim School

Loves Green

Writtle Park

63 64 223 65

G H J K L M

I 1
2
3
4
5
6
7
8

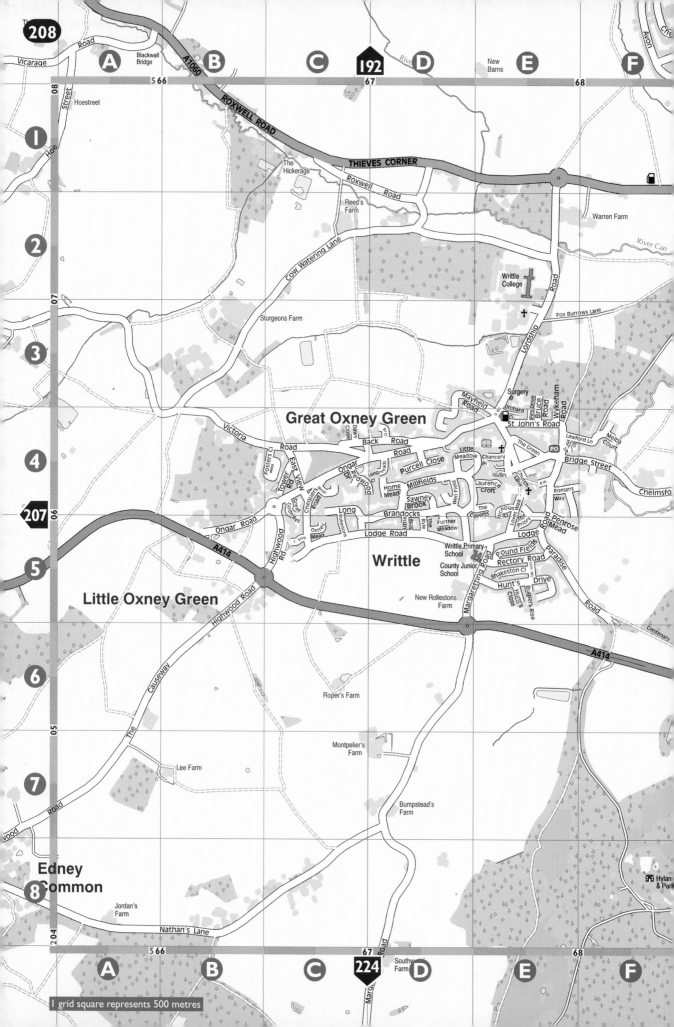

G   H   J   **195**   K   L   M

Little Ldd

75   76   77   08

Phillow's Farm

Holybreds Farm

Holybread

Colam Lane

1

Hurrells Lane

Chapel Lane

New Lodge

New Lodge

Blake's Wood

2

07

Hammond's Farm

Grace's Walk

Chase

3

Rumbold's Farm

Hammonds Road

Graces Lane

Riffhams

4

Riffhams

Great Graces Farm

Riffhams Lane

Hall Wood

06   **212**

CM3

5

Lingw Comn

A12

Sandon Brook Pl

St Clere's Hall

Elm Green Lane

Colemans

Mildmays

Parkdale

MALDON ROAD

Sandon Bridge

A414 **MAIN** **ROAD**

A414 **BELL** **HILL**

Well Lane Industrial Estate

Danbury Park Primary School

Woodford Medical Clinic

The Heights

6

05

Junction 18

Hull's Lane

Danbury Country Park

Danbury Palace

Well Lane

Beaumont

St Cleres

Woodview Rd

7

Horne Row

Woodhill

Fitzwalter Lane

Lu

Mayes Lane

Garrettlands

Woodhill Road

Paternoster Farm

8

Mayes Farm

Woodhill Common Road

Sporehams Lane

04

Blind Lane

Sporeham

Butt

Sporehams

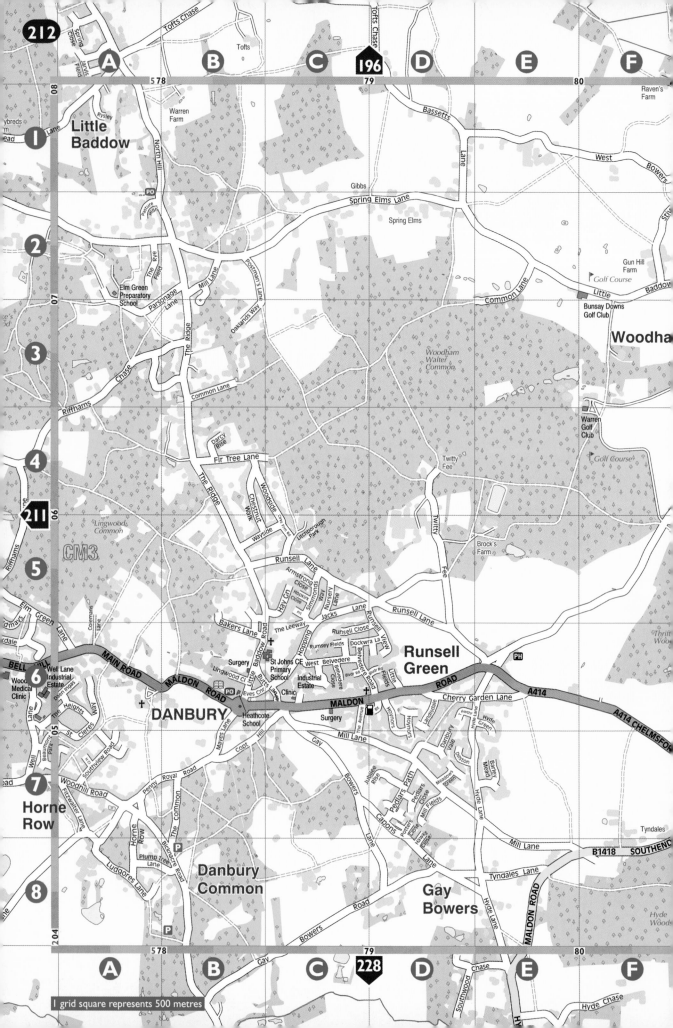

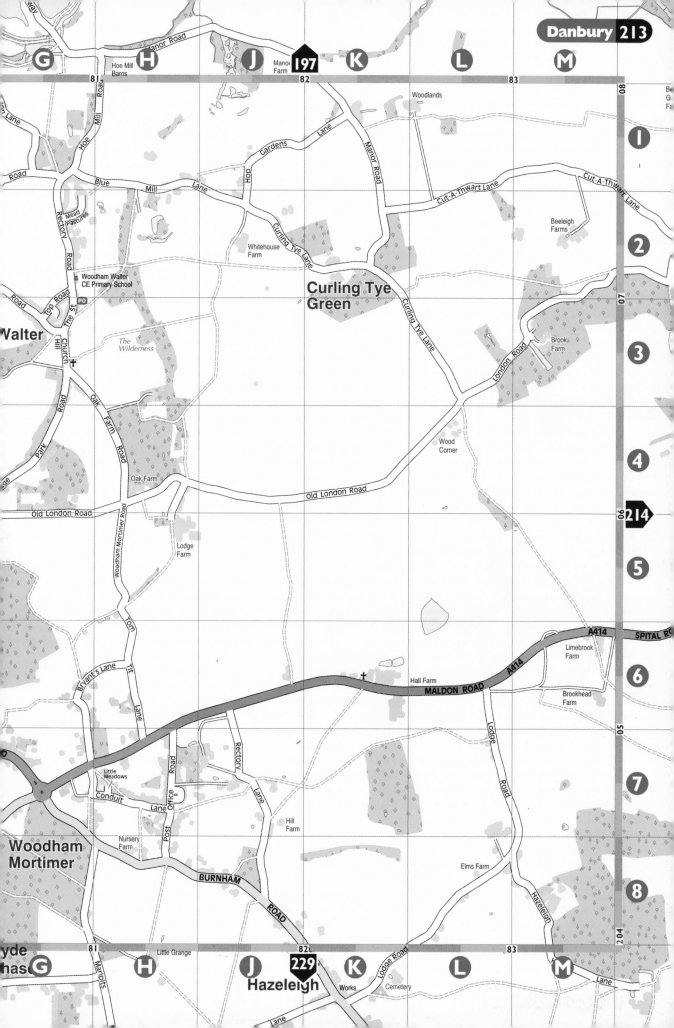

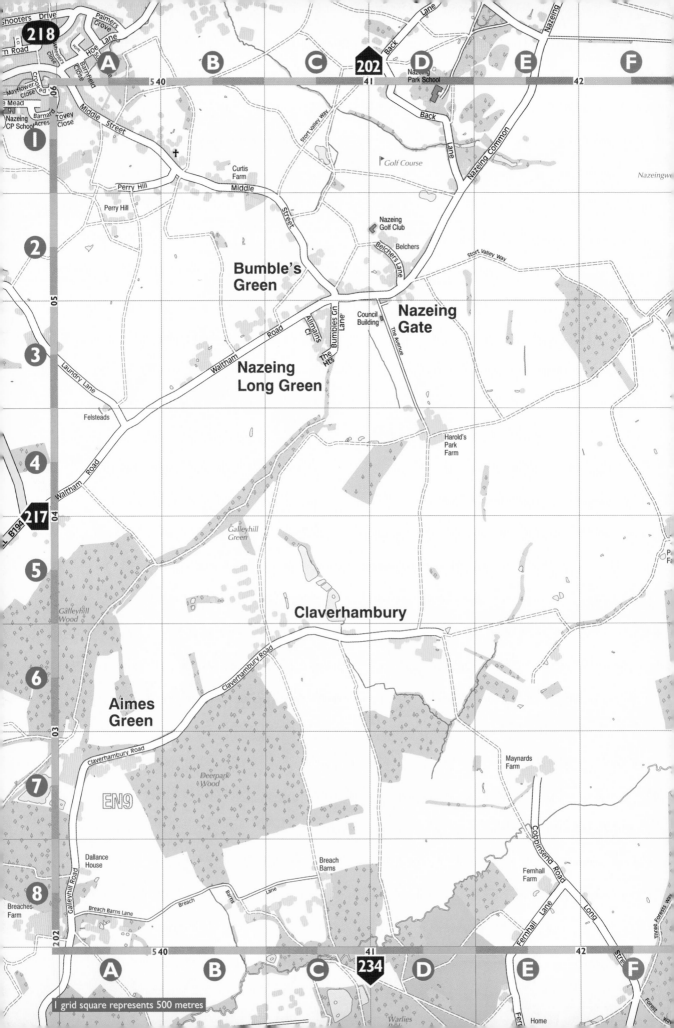

Shooters Drive
Palmers Grove
Hoe Lane
n Road
Wheelers Close
Barnfield Close
Mayflower Close
e Mead
Nazeing CP School
Barnard Acres
Tovey Close
Crooked Mile
90

A 5 40 **B** **C** **202** 41 **D** Nazeing Park School **E** 42 **F**

Back Lane
Nazeing
Back Lane
Nazeing Common
Nazeingwe

I
Middle Street
†
Curtis Farm
Golf Course
Nazeingwe

Perry Hill
Perry Hill
Middle Street
Nazeing Golf Club

2
05
Belchers Lane
Belchers
Stort Valley Way

Bumble's Green

Nazeing Gn Lane
Council Building
Nazeing Gate

3
Laundry Lane
Waltham Road
Allmains Ct
The Hts
Bumbles Gn Lane
The Avenue
Nazeing Long Green

Felsteads

Harold's Park Farm

4
Waltham Road
217
04

Galleyhill Green

5
Galleyhill Wood
P Fa

Claverhambury

6
03
Claverhambury Road
Maynards Farm

Aimes Green
Claverhambury Road

7
EN9
Deerpark Wood

Dallance House
Breach Barns
Fernhall Farm
Cobbinsend Road

8
Galleyhill Road
202
Breaches Farm
Breach Barns Lane
Breach Barns Lane
Fernhall Lane
Long St
Three Forests Way

A 5 40 **B** **C** 41 **234** **D** **E** 42 **F** Fern Home

B194
B194
217
Nazeing

1 grid square represents 500 metres

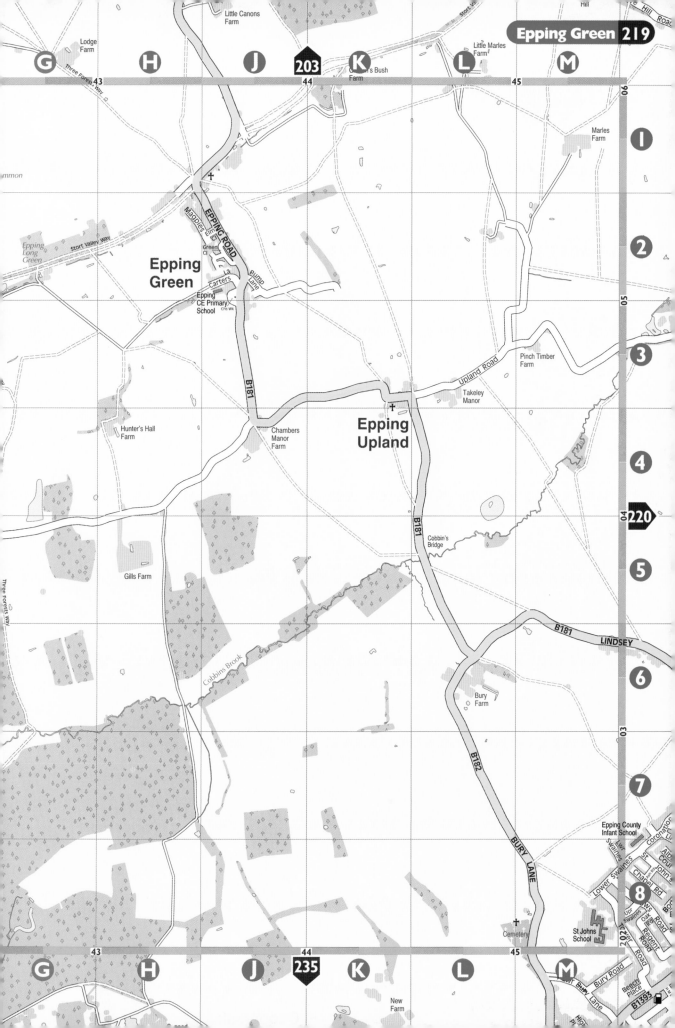

G H J 203 K L M

43 44 45

Three Forest Way

Little Canons Farm

Lodge Farm

Camon's Bush Farm

Little Marles Farm

Marles Farm

I

Epping Long Green

Stort Valley Way

Epping Green

Magpies

Elm Cl

Green Cl

EPPING ROAD

La

Carters

Pump Lane

Epping CE Primary School Chu Wk

2

05

Upland Road

Pinch Timber Farm

Takeley Manor

3

B181

Hunter's Hall Farm

Chambers Manor Farm

Epping Upland

4

04 220

Three Forests Way

Gills Farm

Cobbin's Bridge

5

Cobbins Brook

B181 LINDSEY

6

Bury Farm

03

B182

7

Epping County Infant School

Bury Lane

Lower Swaines Upr Swaines

Chapel Rd

8

Cemetery

St Johns School

Regent Road

Beech Place

B1393

A B C **204** D E F

5 46   47   48

I

2

Horseshoes
Farm

Rivetts Farm

Hill Road

Hill

B1393

Rye Hill Road

Orchard
Farm

Cripsey Brook

M11

Weald

HIGH ROAD

Esgors

West Pl

Blake
Hall

Upland Road

Upper
Clapton RFC

**Thornwood
Common**

3

Hayleys
Manor
Farm

Upland Road

Weald Hall Lane

Brookfield

Carpenters
Arms Lane

Industrial Estate

Rowley Md

Duck Lane

4

219

5

HIGH ROAD

B1393

Woodside Road

Woodside

The
Lower
Forest

Silver Birch Ave

Forest Glade

04

05

06

6

7

8

LINDSEY

STREET

James St

Frampton Rd

Barnfield

Woodberry Down

Meadow Road

Shaftesbury Rd

Works

Beaconfield Rd

Clover Leas

Lincolns Fld

Coronation Hill

Beaconfield Road

Ingels Md

Rayfield

Albany
Court

John's
Rd

Baxters

Chapel Rd

Bodley Rd

Epping County
Infant School

St Johns
School

Crows Oak

Upr Swaines

Regent Rd

Tower Road

Lwr Bur Lane

Beech
Place

Council
Building

High

NICHOLL

Epping
Junior
School

Kendal

Hartland Road

Station Road

Beulah Rd

PALMERS HILL

Lindsey St

Church Hill

Severns Fld

Wheatley

Theydon Gv

Surgery

PO

Council
Building

Police Station

Wedgewood Cl

STREET

Wood
Meads

Winch
View

Tidy's
Lane

Granville
Rd

Fairfield
Road

Works

THE PLAIN

The Plain

The Limes
Medical Centre

St Margarets
Hospital

CM16

Epping Ongar Railway

Ravensmere

Thornwood Road

B181

Coopersale
Common Road

LC

Garnon Mead

Chevely
Close

Institute
Rd

Laburnum Rd

St Albans Rd

Brickfield Rd.

Vicarage
Rd

Gernon
Bushes

Woodlands

Essex Way

Coopersale
& Theydon
Garnon CE Sch

**Coopersale
Common**

Houblons Hill

Essex Way

Stonards

Stonards Hill

Gayne
Park

EPPING

Coopersale

A B C **236** D E F

5 46   47   48

03

02

1 grid square represents 500 metres

G H J 205 K L M

49 50 51 06

I

New House Farm

Little Weald Hall

North Weald Golf Club

A414

Bluemans End

Tower Close

St Andrews Close

Hows Mead

Tyler's Green 2

Travelodge

HIGH ROAD A414

380

05

Weald Hall

Merlin Way

Vicarage Lane

Ravley Lane

Church Lane

St Andrews CE Primary School

The Pavilions

B181

3

Oak Piece

School Green Lane

Beamish Close

Princes Close

Queens Road

HIGH

Church Lane

HIGH ROAD

North Weald Airfield

The Limes Medical Centre

Higham View

Emerson View

Thornhill

PO

4

NORTH WEALD BASSETT

Lancaster Road

George Avey Cft

ROAD

Elm Gdns

Bassett Gardens

The Birchers

04

Merlin Way

Hampden Cl

Wellington Rd

Blenheim Way

York Road

B181

HIGH

Dukes Cl

PH

Station Road

Ongar Park Hall

5

Roughtallys

Park Cl

Watermans Wy

Tempest Md

Kiln Road

North Weald Station

Epping Ongar Railway

Pike Way

Hawks Hl

'Roughtalley's Wood'

6

Cold Hall Farm

03 382

Mill Lane

7

Essex Way

Essex Way

Essex Way

Colliers Hatch

Does Farm

Hill Crest Road

Curnley Road

Epping Road

8

Epping Road

Freemans Farm

School Road

202

G H J 237 K L M

49 50 51

Mount Farm

Toot Hill Golf Club

Blakes

206

I grid square represents 500 metres

Spurriers

A414

The Orchard

Fingrith Hall Lane

Fingrith Hall

Old Barns

Rookery Farm

Rook Road

Spriggs

Saybridge Lodge

Lane

Nine Ashes

Nine Ashes

Nine Ashes Road

Sprigg's Farm

Well's Farm

Redrose

Red Rose Farm

Chelmsford Road

Howlett's Hall

383

Woollard Way

Blackmore CP School

Jericho Place

PO

Orchard Piece

Lane

Elkins Green

Poplar Close

Meadow Rise

Blackmore Road

The Gn

Church Street

Blacksmiths Alley

St. Peter's Way

's Way

Jericho Priory

Blackmore

St. Peter's Way

Copyhold Farm

Ingatestone Road

Fryerning Wood

Wenlocks Lane

Wenlock's Farm

Blackmore Road

The Hyde

Wood Barns Farm

Furze Hall

Blackmore Road

Park Farm Lane

Green Lane

Stubbers Farm

Green Street

Avenue

Spring Pond Meadow

8

Little Woodbarns

Hay Green

Hay Green

Hay Green Lane

238

The Robins

Road

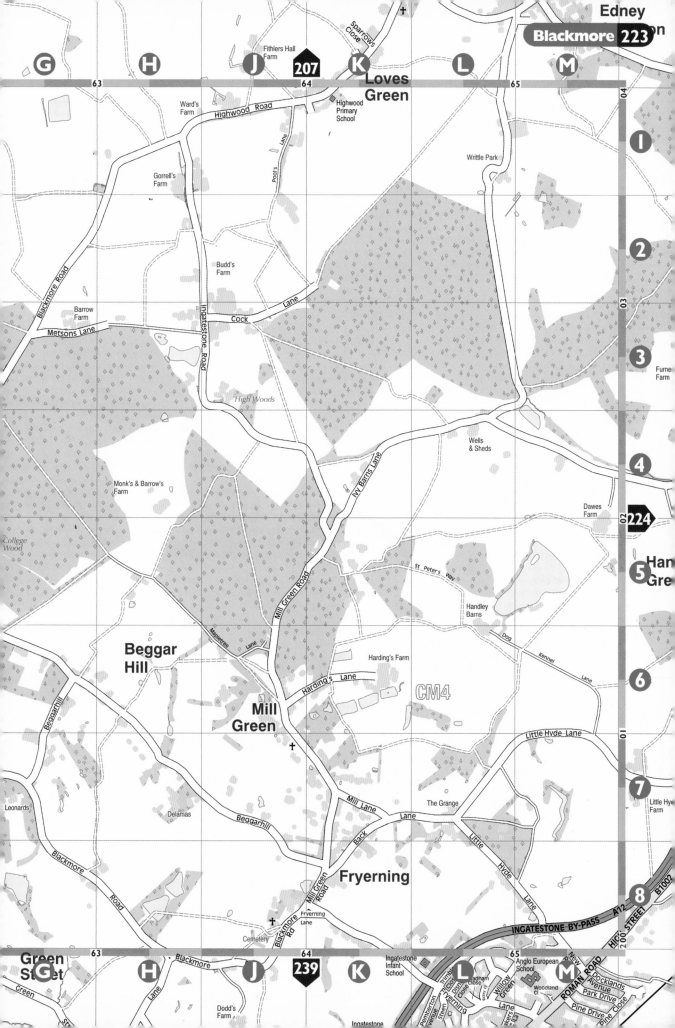

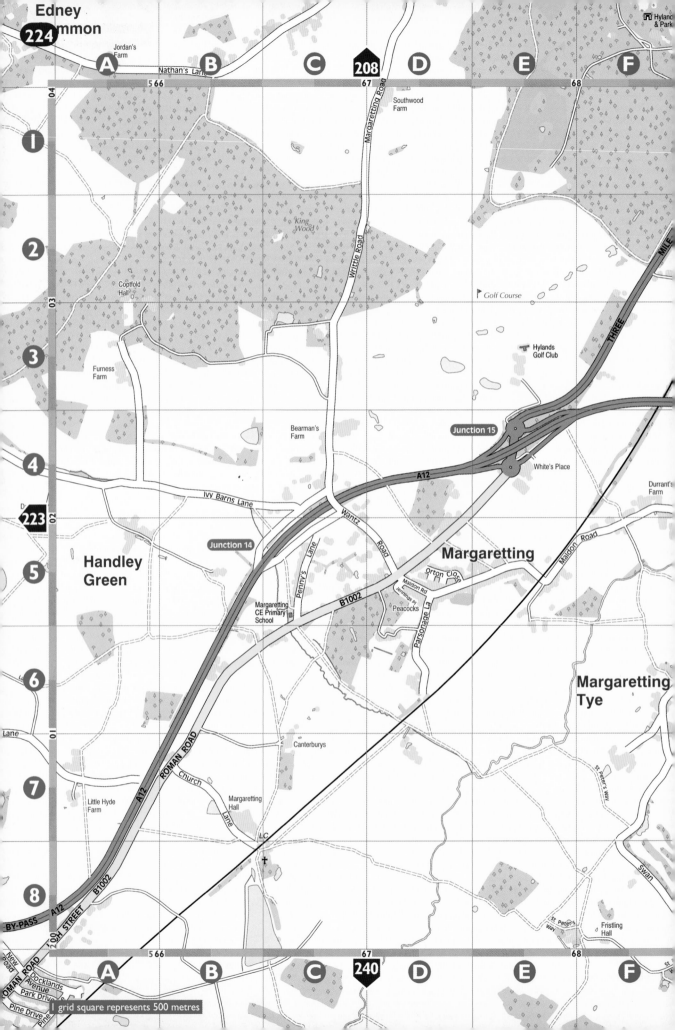

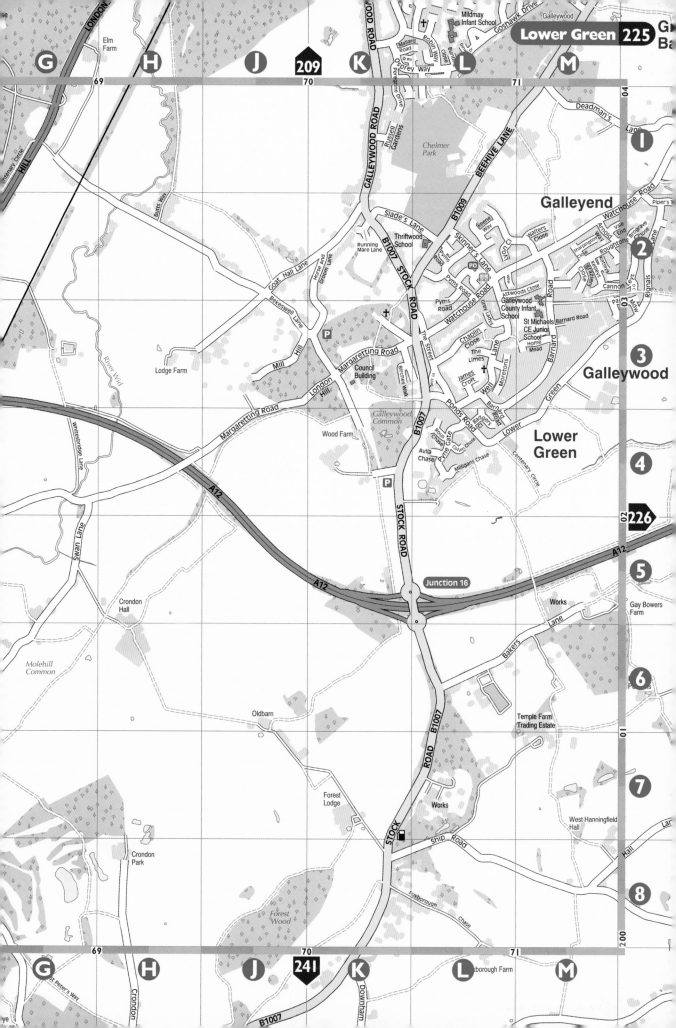

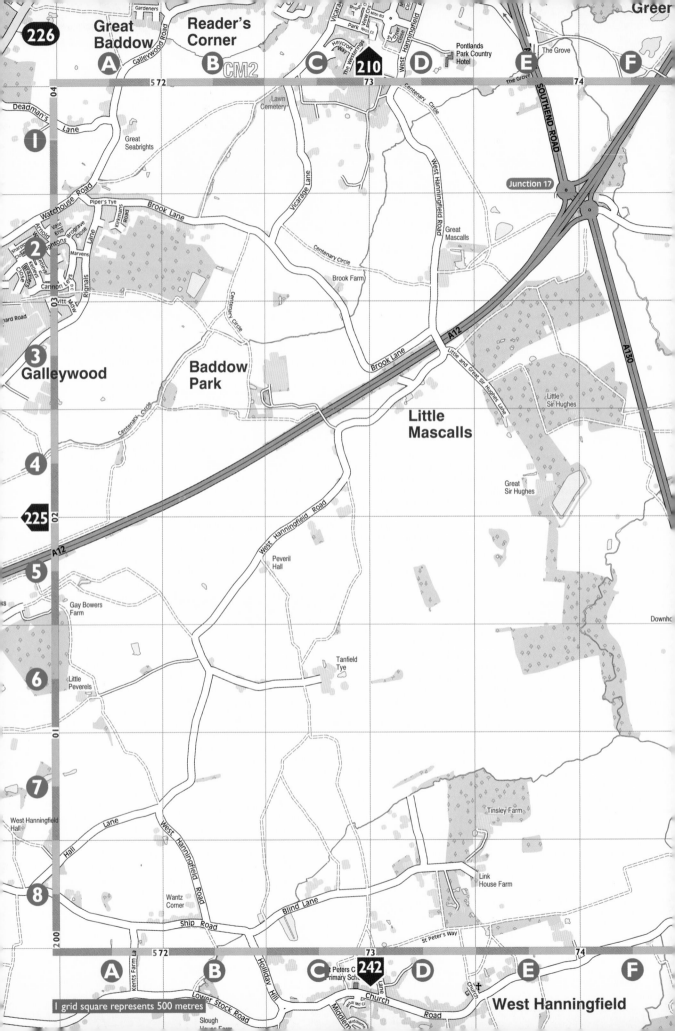

G   H   J   211   K   L   M

75   76   77   04

I

Sandon
Hall Farm

Blind
Lane

Sporehams Lane

Sporehams

2

Little
Gibcrack

Butt's
Green

Howe
Green

Sandon Hall Bridleway

Alexander Mews

East Hanningfield Road

chalklands

Southlands Chase

Grove Farm

Great Gibcracks Chase

Works

3

South
Gibcracks

Southlands
Farm

Old Southend Road

Southend Road

Great
Claydons

4

Bickacre Road

228

Salesfrith
Farm

5

Little Claydons
Farm

Highfields Mead

The
Gables

The Common

East
Hanningfield

Claydons Farm

Back Lane

Abbey Fields

6

Bushy
Wood

East Hanningfield
CE Primary School

St Peter's Way

St Peter's Way

St Peter's Way

Ashley Green

Nicholson Place

Payne
Pl
Pease
Pl

PO

The

East Hanningfield
Industrial Estate

Patten's Farm

A130

Hill Farm

Back Lane

Old Church Road

Main Road

7

Pan Lane

Paprill's Farm

8

Southend Road

200

G   H   J   243   K   L   M

75   76   77

B...s Farm

Main Road

Cre...

A **B** **C** 212 **D** **E** **F**

Danbury Common

Gay Bowers

Hyde Woods

5 78   79   80

1

Overshot Bridge

2

Little Gibcracks

Moor Hall Lane

Bicknacre Road

Peartree Lane

White Elm Farm

Slough

Hyde Chase

Hyde Lane

Southdowns Chase

B1418

Jacklett's Farm

Cemetery

WHITE ELM ROAD

3

St Giles

Bicknacre

Wickhams

4

South Gibcracks

Priory Road

Thrift Wood

Hill View

St Peter's Way

St Peter's Way

Bicknacre Road

Barbrook Way

Thrift Wood

Priory Lane

New England

The Grove

Deerhurst Chase

Lyndhurst Drive

Brockenhurst Way

5

St Peter's Way

Leighams Road

Leigham's Farm

MAIN ROAD

Thrift Wood

Woodham Hall

6

Peter's Way

01

Quilters' Farm

Lodge Road

7

Leighams Road

Woodham Lodge

Fultons Farm

B1418 MAIN ROAD

Hobclerk's Farm

Crows Lane

Lodge Road

8

Creephedge Lane

Creephedge House

Chapel Row

Bucknatch Lane

Main Road

2 00   5 78   79 244   80

A **B** **C** 244 **D** **E** **F**

Ormonds Crs

St Marys CE Primary School

Woodham Ferrers

G H J **213** K L M

Mortimer

BURNHAM ROAD B1010

Elms Farm

1

Hyde Chase

Little Grange

Marlpits Road

Hazeleigh

House Lane

Works

Lodge Road

Cemetery

Goat

Chimney Pot Lane

Hackmans Lane

+

Cock Clarks

Birchwood Road

Rudley Green

CHELMSFORD

Mosklyns

Hazeleigh Hall

Spar Lane

Hazeleigh Hall Lane

2

ROAD B1010

3 New Ha Vineyar

Scotts Farm

Lodge Lane

St Peter's Way

St Peter's Way

Purleigh CP School

Westerings

4

Pump

Wickham's Farm

Corporation Farm

Birchwood Road

Walton Hall

Mill Lane

Mill Hill

Callowood The C **230**

5 Chapel Lane

Howegreen

6

Seven Acre Farm

Chase

Flambird's

Hackmans Lane

Great Whitmans

7

Flambirds Farm

Great Canney

8

Haggs Hill

zils

Crows Lane

Charity Farm

Stow Road

The Street

G H J **245** K L M

Crows Lane

Stow

230

A B C **214** D E F

5 84 85 86

1

Lane

Copkitchen's
Farm

Stud
Farm

2
Spar
Lane

eleigh

3
ROAD
B1010

New Hall
Vineyard

Purleigh
Wash Farm

Bli

Blind Lane

St. Peter's Way

BARON'S LANE B1010

Eastcroft

4
St. Peter's Way

Purleigh CP
School

Hawthornes

Westerings

Pump Lane

Purleigh

Simmonds Lane

B1010

Clock
House

Mill La

Callowood Croft
PO

Church Hill

Purleigh Street

229
The Glebe

The Street

St. Peter's Way

Roundbush Road

FAMBRIDGE

5
Chapel
Lane

Howegreen

Roundbush

Burnham Road

6

**Farther
Howegreen**

Great
Whitmans

Old
Redgate Farm

7
Howe Green Road

Cherry Blossom Lane

Crown Road

Victoria Road

Junction Road

Green Trees Avenue

Station Road

Hackmans Lane

Great Canney

Clarke Rise

Latchingdon Road

Cold Norton
County Primary
School

Ferris Avenue
Station
Crescent

Purleigh
Grove

PO

B1010

Works

Hagg
Hill

Three Rivers
Golf & Country Club

The Fairways

8
Burnham Avenue

B1018

Newport
Avenue

Stow Road

**Cold
Norton**

Golf Course

Norton

FAMBRIDGE ROAD

A B C St Step **246** D E F

5 84 85 86

1 grid square represents 500 metres

G   H   J   **215**   K   L   M

Garlands

Blackwater
Farm

White
House
Farm

Brookmead
Farm

New Hall Lane

Mundon Wash

Vicarage Lane

Mundon

Mundon
Hall

St Peter's Way

Sparrow
Wycke

West Chase

St. Peter's Way

Parsonage Chase   Wood Lane

Limbourne
Park Farm

Parsonage
Farm

388

Works

Maldon Road

Butterfields

St Andrew's
Farm

Mayfair
Industrial
Estate

Thatchers
Croft

Steeple Road

Ramsey
Chase
Ludgrove

Meadow Way

Latchingdon
Primary
School

Bridgemans
Green

PO

B1018

Buchanan
Way

Granary Way

Good
Hares

Crofton

St Michaels
Close

Snoreham
Gardens

Lawling Road

Heritage
Way

COLD   NORTON   ROAD

THE STREET

Latchingdon

BURNHAM

B1018

Purleigh
Barns

Snoreham
Hall

Redmans

G   H   J   **247**   K   L   M

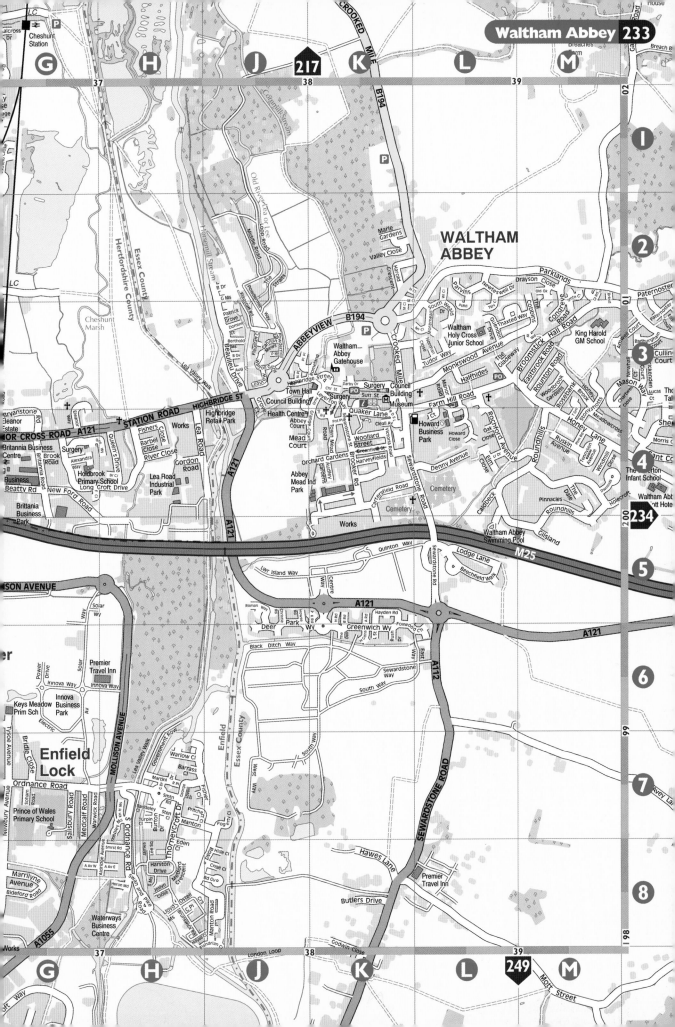

G · H · J · **219** · K · L · M

43 · 44 · 45

I

New Farm

Copped Hall

St Johns School

Cemetery

Upr Swaines
Oak
Regent
Chapel Rd
Uppr Swaines

Beech Place

Lwr Bury Lane

Bury Road

Bell Common

Highfield
Highfield Pl

Ivy Chimneys

2

Centenary Wk

Bell Common

Ivy Chimneys Primary School

ROAD

HIGH

M25

Ivy Chimneys Road

Forest Side

Great Gregories Lane

3

The Warren

Crown Hill

Crown Hill

Centenary Walk

Great Gregories Farm

Theydon Road

Theydon Bois Golf Club

Golf Course

4

Lodge Road

Ambresbury Banks Fort

Little Gregories

236

Lti Gregories Lane

Piercing Hill

Dukes

5

EPPING ROAD B1393

Wansfell College

Harewood Hill
Woodland Way
Purlieu Way
Baldocks Rd
Heath Rd

Avenue

B172

B172

Piercing Hill

Theydon Bois Primary School

Orchard Drive
Morgan Crescent
Elizabeth Drive
Buxton Road
Mead Barn

Forest Drive

Slade End

6

A121 GOLDING'S HILL

College of Teachers

COPPICE ROW

Sidney Road

The Gn

PO

Thrifts

B172

Theydon B Station

Surgery

Birch Hall

Theydon Bois

Avenue Rd

Council Building

The Green

Green Old
Poplar Wk
Green Cld
Oakes Wy

7

Centenary Walk

Hornbeam Road
The Green
Woburn Ave
Hornbeam Close

Loughton Lane

Hmbm Rd

Blackacre Road

Green Glade

Thrifts Hall Fa

Ripley Grange

Hill Road

8

Debden Road

Ripley View

Debden Green

Davenant Foundation School

Theydon Road

Lane

Broadstrood

Campions
The Beacons

Stanmore Way

Golf Course

Loug Golf Club

Wren Ter
Clay's La
Bracken Close
Cleland Path

Drive

Hereward Green
Chester Road
Russell Road
Willingale Road

The Hereward County School

G · **250** · H · J · **251** · K · L · M · **251**

43 · 44 · 45

The Summit
Whitaker's Way
Woodcroft
Hill Way
Goldings Rise
Goldings

Colliers Hatch

Epping Road

School Road

G | H | J | K | L | M

221

49 | 50 | 51

Golf Course

Toot Hill Golf Club

Blakes

1

Mount Farm

Banks Lane

Tawney Common

Tawney Lane

Nickerlands

2

Woodhatch

Mount End

Tawney Common

Berwick Lane

3

Beachet Wood

Tawney Lane

4

Berwick

200 | 382

Howfields

5

Little Tawney Hall

Coleman's Farm

eakes arm

Three Forests Way

6

+ **Theydon Mount**

Stapleford Tawney

M25

+

Three Forests Way

7

Great Tawney Hall

Abridge Golf & Country Club

Golf Course

Shales More

kinners Farm

8

Epping Lane

49 | 50 | 51

G | 252 | H | J | K | Tawney Lane | L | 253 | M

Londoners

Suttons

Suttons Clinic

Passingford Bridge

Arnolds Farm

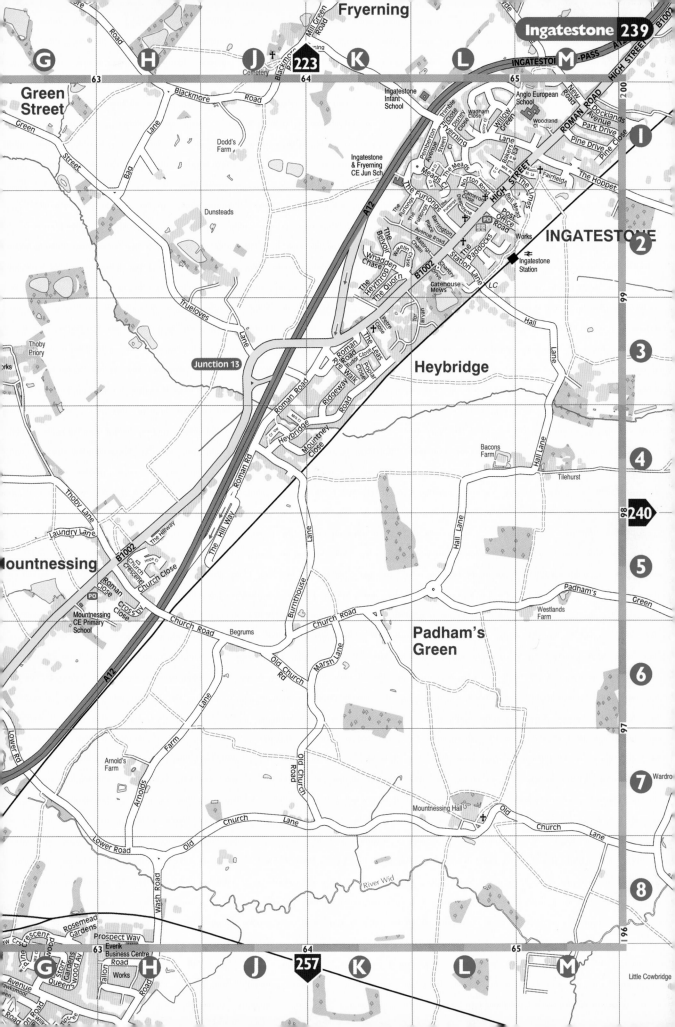

G H J **225** K L M

69 70 71 200

Stock Road

St Peter's Way

Crondon Park Lane

Foxborough

Foxborough Farm

Downham Road

Keelings

Lower Stock Road

B1007 STOCK ROAD

I

2

99

Swan Lane

Dakyn Drive

Stock CE
Primary School

Brookmans
Road
Lane

B1007

Hightrees

Rectory
Close

Stock

Greenwoods
Estate Health
Spa & Retreat

Greenwoods
Stock

Falkner
Close

Birch Lane

PO

PH

The
Paddock

HIGH STREET

Common Road

Myin
Meadow

Garden
End

The Square

Bakers
Field

Mill Road

Valentines

Thornton
Place

The
Lindens

Whites

Wells Lane

Madles Lane

Whites
Hill

Marigold Lane

Peter Street

Brittons Lane

Furze
Lane

Furze Lane

Smallgains Lane

Greenacre
Lane

Small Gains Lane

Greenacre
Farm

Goatsmoor Lane

Lilystone
Hall

STOCK ROAD

Vale

Potash

Penwood
Cl

Broome Road

Bridleway

Meade Road

Derby
Close

Martingale Road

Chepstow
Close

Sadlers
Close

Carson
Road

Smythe
Road

Shire Close

Norsey Road

Oaklands Farm
Industrial Estate

Forty
Acre
Plantn

Goatsmoor Lane

Meadowgate

Mill Lane

St Peter's Way

Leatherbottle Hill

Steel's Farm

Seamans Lane

St Peter's Way

Mill Road

Great
Prestons

Downham Road

Broomwood Lane

Dowsett Lane

Downham Road

Whitelilies Farm

Common Farm

Mill Lane

Dowsett Lane

Crowsheath Farm

3

4

242 98

5

6

97

7

8

196

G H J **259** K L M

69 70 71

Heath Road

Hunts Farm

Mill Lane

Johns Pl

Stoney Hills

Tipiers
Bridge

Allens Road

Birds

Swimming Pool
Centre

Willowmead

Heath Road

Downham Road

Carsey Cl

Downham CE
Primary School

Norsey Wood

P

242

A **B** **C** **226** **D** **E** **F**

5 72 73 74

2 00

Wantz
Corner

Field Road

Ship Rd

Blind Lane

St Peter's Way

Link
House Farm

Lower Stock Road

Holliday Hill

St Peters CE
Primary School

Helmons Lane

Church

church

West Hanningfield

I

Slough
House Farm

Kents Farm La

Middlemead

Church

Road

98

St. Peter's Way

2

3

Seamans Lane

Great
Prestons

Middlemead

4

241 98

Hanningfield
Reservoir

5

Downham
ilies Farm

Road

P

South Hannir

Middlemead

6

Hawkswood Road

97

Crowsheath Farm

Hawkswood

Road

Warren Road

7

Crowsheath Lane

8

Brock
Hill

Flemings Farm

Willowmead

Downham

Road

Windsor
Road

Oak Road

School
Road

Sudbury

Brock Hill

Road

Carsey Cl

Brabner
Gdns

Downham
Road

5 72

Downham

73

260

74

Sudbury's Farm

The
Grange

A **B** **C** **D** **E** **F**

Windsor
Trading

Downham CE
Primary School

I grid square represents 500 metres

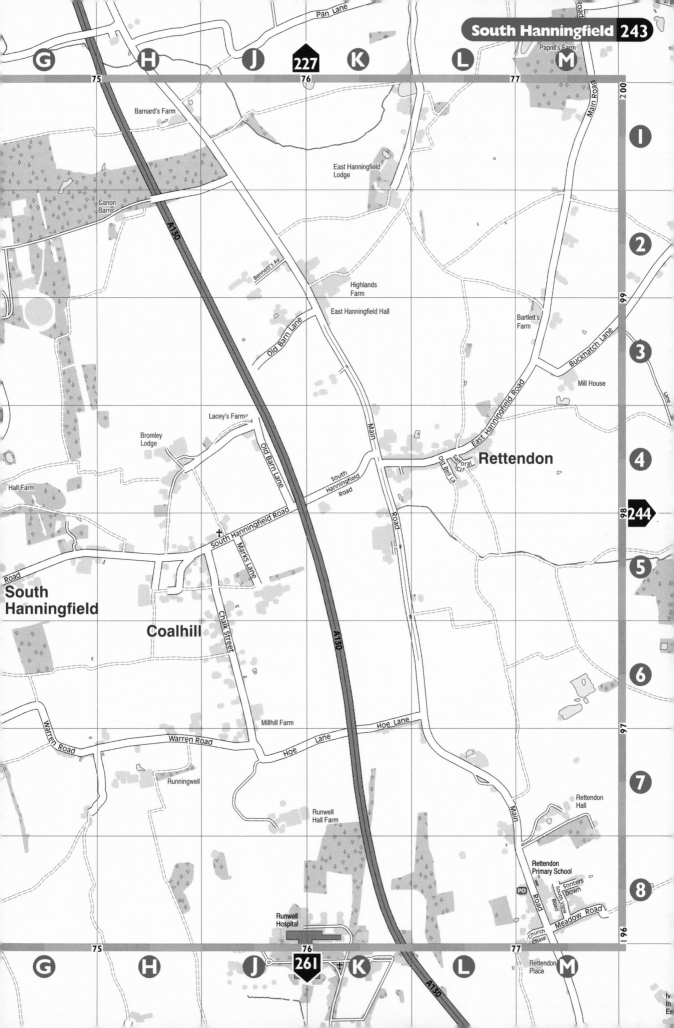

G   H   J   227   K   L   M

South Hanningfield

Coalhill

Rettendon

Pan Lane

Barnard's Farm

Canon Barns

A130

Bennett's Av

Highlands Farm

East Hanningfield Lodge

East Hanningfield Hall

Old Barn Lane

Lacey's Farm

Bromley Lodge

Hall Farm

South Hanningfield Road

Marks Lane

Chalk Street

Road

Millhill Farm

Warren Road

Hoe Lane

Runningwell

Runwell Hall Farm

Runwell Hospital

Main Road

South Hanningfield Road

Old Bell La

Sal oral Cl

Main Road

Paprill's Farm

Main Road

Bartlett's Farm

Buckhatch Lane

Lane

Mill House

East Hanningfield Road

244

Rettendon Hall

Rettendon Primary School

PO

South View Road

Sonters Down

Church Chase

Meadow Road

Rettendon Place

Hoe Lane

G   H   J   261   K   L   M

75   76   77

I
2
3
4
5
6
7
8

200
99
98
97
96

Chapel
Row

228

Woodham
Ferrers

A **B** **C** **D** **E** **F**

I

2

3

4

243

5

6

7

8

Creephedge
Lane

Creephedge
House

Buckhatch Lane

578

Ormonds Crs

St Marys CE
Primary School

B1418

MAIN ROAD

THE STREET

RHS Garden
Hyde Hall

Garden
Centre

Hyde
Hall

Buckhatch
Farm

Buckh Lane

Potters Lane

Mill House

Potter's Farm

Creephedge Lane

Edwin's Hall Road

Workhouse Lane

Ilgar's
Manor

Willow Grove

Shaw's Farm

B1418

Woodve
Primary

Edwin
Hall
Vnew
King's
Way

Surgery

BURNHAM ROAD

Old Wickford Rd
Fenn Cl
Cornfields
Elm Road

The Chase
Chase
PO
Manor

LC

Wickford Road

BURNHAM ROAD A132

Ferrers Road

Woodham
Ferrers Stn.
Station
Approach

LC

Woodham
Halt

Surg
Pe

Woodham
Fenn

A132

Tabrum's
La
Tabrum's
Farm

Ferrers Road

Hartwhistle
Bres Brunel
Way

Mark's
Farm

Rettendon
Grange Farm

Tabrum's Lane

Woodham Road

Celeborn
Street
Lorien
Gdns
Hill
Thorn's
Gladden Fields
Arwen Gv
Celeborn St

Rettendon
Hall

BURNHAM ROAD

A132

Eyott's
Farm

Fenn Creek

onters
Down

Meadow Road

Rettendon
Lodge

Hayes Chase

Long Reach

A **B** **C** **D** **E** **F**

578

Farm Crs

79

262

Hayes Chase

A132

80

Sta

Estate

I grid square represents 500 metres

G H J 229 K L M

81 82 83 200

Stow Maries

Charity Farm

Hawe's Wood

Crows Lane

I

2

Church

Woodham Road

PH

3

Wellinditch

B1012

Great Hayes

Woodham Road

4

Morris Farm

LOWER BURNHAM ROAD

Little Hayes Chase

Hamberts Farm

BURNHAM ROAD

SOUTH WOODHAM FERRERS

Blackall Industrial Estate

B1012 WOODHAM ROAD

Hogwell Chase

98 246

Brent
Dunlin Cl
Barton Hamberts
Paston Cl
Bankside Cl
Hawkwood
Road
Hawthorn Walk
Glendale
King Edward's
Mitchell Wy
East Bridge Rd
Whitehouse Road
Drapers Road
Bancrofts
Redhills Rd
Saltcoats

LC LC

Hogwell Farm

5

Longfield
Bandhills Close
Clements
Coxs Cl
Downs Cl
Cutlers Rd

Saltcoats

Compass Gardens & Saltcoats Park

6

Saltcoats Road
Guys Farm
Overmead Dr
Lane
Ferrers Road
South Woodham Ferrers Leisure Cen
Oakland Business Cen
Surgery
William De Ferrers School

Elmwood Primary School
PO
Flix Cinema
Reeves Wy
Brickfields
Creekview Road
Cornwells

Surgery Surgery
Leigh La
Inchbonnie Road
Squire Street
Tallow Ga
Cutler Rd
Cornwells Drive

Thornborough Av
Spencer Close
Troubridge
Bickerton Point
Beatty Rise

7

Helena Ct
Victoria Rd
Abbotsleigh
Ferrers
Benbow Dr
Nelson Place
Melville
Heath
Merton Place
Collingwood Road

Cimli Watch
Hullbridge Road
Littlecroft
Hallowell Down
Blackwood Chine
Collingwood Primary School

Clementsgreek Creek

Chetwood Primary School
Broughton Road
Carron Mead
Windward Wy

Taffrail Gdns
The Spinnaker
Leeward Rd
Becket Rd
The Bight

8

Marsh Farm
Holkham Avenue
Haddon Md
Marsh Farm Road
Halyard Reach
Cringle Lock
Brace Walk
Anchor Reach
Clevis Drive

Marsh Farm Country Park

81 82 263 83

G H J K L M

River

Brandy Hole Yacht Club

246

Hagg Hill

A

Cold B ton

Three Rivers Golf & Country Club

Cold Norton County Primary School

Ferris Avenue

Station Crescent

Burnham Avenue

Purleigh Grove

Newport Avenue

C **230** **D** **E** **F**

Golf Course

St Stephens Road

Norton Hall

B1018

PO

Fambridge Road

The Street

Stow Road

1

Church Lane

Golf Course

Honey Pot Lane

2

3 B1012 LOWER BURNHAM ROAD

Little Cooks

Fambridge Road

B1010

B1012

Great Hayes

Rookery Farm

Rookery Lane

Hainault Road

Kitchener Road

Wild Farm

B1012 ROAD

4

245

Rookery Lane

Buller Road

Russell Road

Rectory Road

Franklin Road

Fambridge Station

5

Stephenson Road

Station Approach

Strathmore Rd

Stow Creek

North Fambridge

North Fambridge Yacht Club

Church Road

The Avenue

Blue House Farm Chase

6

Ferry Rd

Brabant Rd

Roberts Rd

PO

Fambridge Road

7

PH

8

Works

Pemberton Field

A **B** **C** **264** **D** **So Eh E Fambridge** **F**

Brickhouse Farm

Church Rd

1 grid square represents 500 metres

Crofton

COLD NORTON ROAD

G 87 H J K 231 88 L 89 M 200 BURNHAM B101

Latchingdon

St Michaels Close
snorenam Gardens
Heritage Way
Road

Red Lyons Farm

I

Purleigh Barns

Snoreham Hall

Rosedale Farm

99 2

London Hayes

Scatterbrook Farm

Tyle Hall

3

Marsh House Farm

LOWER BURNHAM ROAD

Ulehams Farm

†

Stamfords Farm

4

98 392

LC

5

Bridgemarsh Creek

6

97

Bridgemarsh Island

7

Landsend Point

8

196

River Crouch

G 87 H J 265 88 K L 89 M

Upper Raypitts Farm

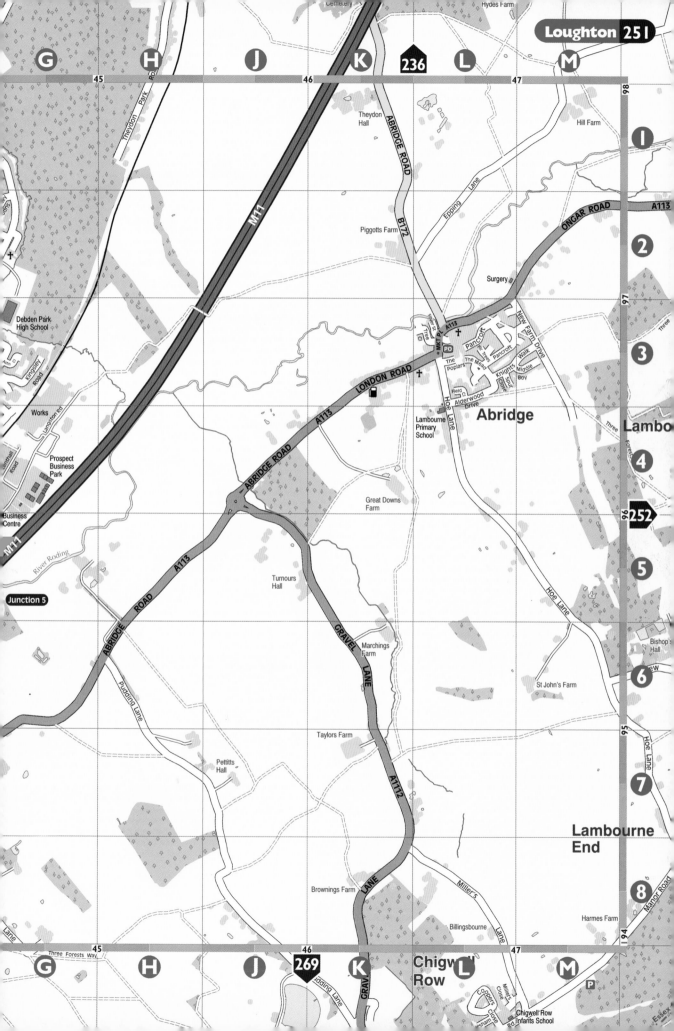

G H J K L M

236

98

1

ONGAR ROAD A113

2

97

3

Hill Farm

Theydon Hall

ABRIDGE ROAD

B172

Piggotts Farm

Epping Lane

Surgery

New Farm Drive

M11

Silver St.

MKT PL.

A113

PO

Pancroft

Pancroft

The Poplars

The Mead

Knights Spur Close

Middle Boy

Alderwood Drive

London Road

A113

Abridge

Lambo

Lambourne Primary School

Hoe Lane

Three Forests

4

96

252

5

Hoe Lane

Bishop's Hall

6

Debden Park High School

Kingsley Road

Ash

Works

Langston Rd.

Prospect Business Park

Business Centre

M11

River Roding

Junction 5

ABRIDGE ROAD

A113

Great Downs Farm

Turnours Hall

GRAVEL LANE

Marchings Farm

St John's Farm

95

7

Pudding Lane

Taylors Farm

A1112

Lambourne End

Pettitts Hall

8

Harmes Farm

Brownings Farm

GRAVEL LANE

Millers Lane

Billingsbourne

94

Manor Road

Essex

G H J K L M

45 46 47

269

Three Forests Way

dding Lane

GRAV

Chigwell Row

Millers Close

Copers Close

rsham Close

P

Chigwell Row Infants School

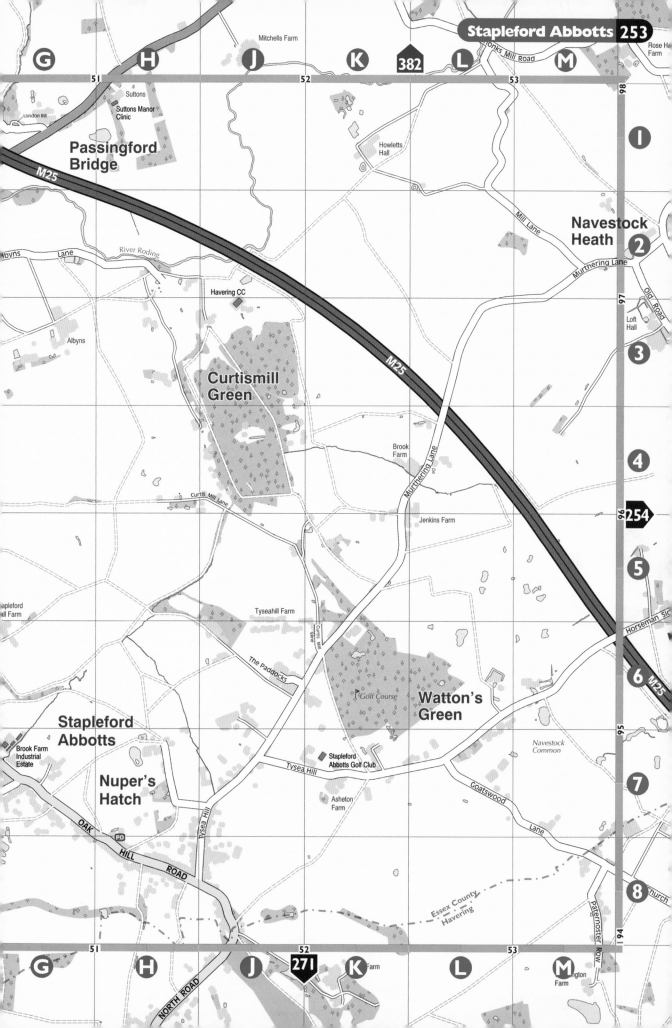

G   H   J   K   382   L   M

Mitchells Farm

51   52   53   98

I

Suttons

London Rd

Suttons Manor
Clinic

**Passingford
Bridge**

Howletts
Hall

M25

Mill Lane

**Navestock
Heath**

2

Murthering Lane

Albyns   Lane

River Roding

Old Road

Loft
Hall

97

Havering CC

3

Albyns

**Curtismill
Green**

M25

Brook
Farm

Murthering Lane

4

Curtis Mill Lane

Jenkins Farm

96   254

Stapleford
Hall Farm

Tyseahill Farm

5

Curtis Mill
Lane

The Paddocks

Horseman Sic

6   M25

Golf Course

**Watton's
Green**

**Stapleford
Abbotts**

Navestock
Common

95

Brook Farm
Industrial
Estate

Tysea Hill

Stapleford
Abbotts Golf Club

**Nuper's
Hatch**

7

OAK

PO

HILL

ROAD

Tysea Hill

Asheton
Farm

Goatswood

Lane

Essex County
Havering

8   Church

Paternoster Row

94

51   52   271   53

G   H   J   K   Farm   L   M   ngton
Farm

NORTH ROAD

254

382

554

A · B · C · D · E · F

98

97

96

95

94

I · 2 · 3 · 4 · 253 · 5 · 6 · 7 · 8

55

56

Rose Hall Farm

Navestock Hall Farm

Navestock Health

Murthering Lane

Loft Hall

Old Road

Sabine's Green

Church Road

Sabines Road

Tan House Lane

Prince's Road

Princes Gate

Wheelers Lane

The Mores

Snakes

Navestock Side

Bower Farm

South Weald Common

Old Road

Horseman Side

Dytchleys Road

Horseman Side

Coxtie Green Road

Warwick Place

Weald Park Hotel (Golf & Country Club)

Dytchleys

Gilstead Hall

Golf Course

Lincolns Lane

Lincolns

253

Waterhales

Horseman Side

Weald Brook

Frieze Hall

CM

M25

Havering Plain

Coxtie Green Road

Hou Hatch

Lane

Church Road

Paternoster Row

Becketts

Wrightsbridge Road

Weald Road

Wealdside

St Vincent's Hamlet

Chequers Road

554

Noak Hill School

Close

Noke

Lower

272

M25

A · B · C · D · E · F

Hill

ddrington rm

1 grid square represents 500 metres

Norsey Wood
(Nature Reserve)

CAY

Sunnymede

Sunnymede
Primary School

South
Green

SOUTHEND ROAD

Lodge
Farm

Hunts Farm

Heath Road

St Johns

Swimming Pool
Centre

Downham CE
Primary School

Ran
Hea

Cox
Greer

The Ramsden Hall
Special School

Meepshole
Wood

Park Lane

Church Road

Short La

Moat Cl

CM11

Ramsden
Park Farm

Ramsden Park

Outwood
Farm

Outwood Farm Road

Browns
Farm

Common Road

Highfield Road

Farm Road

260

Crays
Hall Farm

Coxes

Works

St Peters RC
Primary School

Kings
Way

Tyrrels
Road

Gurnard's
Farm

Grantes
Chase

River Crouch

Church Lane

Stacey's

CRAYS

A129

SOUTHEND ROAD

Mathews
Md

Bromfelde Rd

Crays
Hill

Hope Rd

A129

Grays
Hill

at
stead

A129

241

277

Harleylands

Council

262
ponters Down
adow Road

A   5 78   **B**   **C**   79   **244**   **D**   **E**   80   **F**
nile Ro
Mereworth
Stn

I

Ivanhurst
Industrial
Estate

Hayes Chase

Crittenden
idge

Hayes   Chase

Long Reach

Esp

Woodham Road

High House

2

ell

A132

BURNHAM   ROAD   A132

River
Gdns

Cre

Hawk Hill

95

Gosse's Farm

Battlesbridge Road

River Crouch

3

Battlesbridge Station

Battlesbridge

Battlesbridge
Motorcycle
Museum

Maltings

Highlands Road

Watery Lane

Hawk Hill

Hawk La

Beeches Road

Beeches Road

Watery
La

Chelmsford Rd

Beeches
Farm

4

A1245

SS11

Chelmsford Road

chelmsford Rd

Watery
Lane

261   94

Vanderbilt Av

Me

5

A130

Burrells
Farm

Goldsmith Drive

Golds

Church Road

Chelmsford
Road

Tryndehayes

Avenue

McCalmont Drive

Maple

6

93

St Nicholas
CE Primary
School

Bedfords Av

CHELMSFORD   ROAD

Rawreth

Rawreth Lane

Hayes Farm

Madrid Avenue

Havana Drive

Trenders

Cheshunt Dr Drive

Cheshunt
Dr

Rutland
Dr

Parkhurst

Hooley Drive

Lubai
Lodge

ndon

Old London Road

Chelmsford Rd

Rawreth
Hall

Lenm Wy

Rawreth
Cl

Kelso
Cl

Mann
Way

7

ROAD

Old London Road

A1245

Chichester Hotel

Laburnum Wy

Park
School

Lincoln

Rawreth Industrial Estate

Superstore

Westfield
Cl

Deepdene
Avenue

Park

Canterbury
Close

Norwich
Crs

Bristol

8

92

Doublegate
Lane

Doublegate
Lane

mans

Rawreth
Industrial
Estate

Victoria Av

Arune
Gdns

Grosvenor Rd

Cl

Downhill

A   5 78   **B**   79   **280**   **D**   **E**   80   **F**

Lower
Barn Farm

LONDON   ROAD

Cheap

Boston AV

West

Wimarc Crs

Fairmead

Canterbury
Close

Ce

Downhill

I grid square represents 500 metres

Hartford
Ce Crs

sons Av

The Sweyne
Park School

G H J **245** K L M

82

96

I

River Crouch

Brandy Hole
Yacht Club

2

**Brandy
Hole**

Marsh Farm
Country P

95

Pooles Lane

Long Lane

Kingsmans Farm Road

HULLBRIDGE

Riverside
Primary
School

Crouch View Grove

The Drive

Alfreda Av
The Av
The Walk
Tyndale Close
Birchdale
Haddon
Chine
Marsh Farm Road
Halyard Reach
Inch
The Spinnaker
Anchor Reach
Clevis Drive
Brace Walk
Cringle Lo

3

Surgery PO

Sheepcotes
Farm

Avenue

Windermere Avenue

Keswick Avenue

Mayfield Avenue

Clinic

Hullbridge Clinic

Ambleside Gdns

Elm Cv

PO

Council Building

Malyons Lane

Harrison Gdns

Ferry Road

Cedar Drive

Beech Rd

Cherrydene Close

Pinewood Close

Cracknell's
Farm

Mapledene
Avenue

Thorpedene
Avenue

Broom Rd

Burnham Road

Waxwell Road

Long Lane

Rosilian Drive

4

Lower Road

264

Oakleigh Av

Meadow Rd

Coventry Close

Pevensey Gardens

Wacham Park Avenue

The Priories

Abbey Road

High Elms Road

South Av

Hillcrest Avenue

Crouch Avenue

Hilltop Avenue

Coventry Hill

Lower Road

Central Avenue

First Av

Hullbridge
Sports Club

5

Kendal Close

Lower Road

Kingsway

Wellington Avenue

Qu Anns Cv

Second Av

Pevensey Gdns

Merton
Road

Wadham Park Avenue

Church Road

Mill
Hill

SS5

6

Hullbridge Road

The Avenue

Blountswood Rd

Murrels Lane

Church Rd

St Peters Road

HOCKLE

93

Westminster

Blounts
Farm

Hockley
Primary School

7

Folly Chase

Folly Lane

Manor Road

Osbourne Avenue

Buckingham

Well Dri

MAIN R

Home Farm

Bowers
Gav
Hawthorne
Gardens
Sunnyfield
Gdns
Laburnum
Grove

Police
Station

Badgers Mount

Bullwood Road

Ferndale Rd

Mortimer Road

Saxon Cl
Kings Cl
Eastview Drive
Fairland Cl

Works

Brooklyn Drive

Teignmouth Drive

PO

High Road

Fountain La

ALDERMAN'S HILL B1013

Hillside Road

Woodside Road

Crown Road

Bullwood Approach

Wood Cl

8

The Hyl

G H J **281** K L M

81 82 83

The Gat

Hockley
Woods

92

G   H   J   247   K   L   M

87   88   89   96

Upper
Raypitts
Farm

1

2

95 392

Pudsey
Hall

Bolt
Hall

Canewdon

3

Butts

Roach Valley Way

Canewdon Hall Cl

Scaldhurst
Farm

Larkhill Avenue

Pudsey Hall Lane

Lark Hill Road

4

White House
Farm

Ar

Lark Hill Road

Moon's
Farm

94

s Hall Road

Road

5

Roach Valley Way

Mink
Farm

6

ASHINGDON

Little
Doggetts

Scott's
Hall

93 396

Moons
Close

Apton
Hall Farm

7

Ashingdon Road

Newton Hall
Gdns

Canewdon View Road

Hyde Wood Lane

Way

Victory
La

Golden Cross Road

Nelson
Rd

Nansen
Avenue

Apton Hall Road

Golden Cross Ms

Doggetts Chase

Becket
Close

Brays

8

Central Avenue

Brays Lane

92

Little
Stambridge Hall

S
E
Far

dens

The Brambles

Doric Avenue

Manstead
Gardens

Craven
Close

Johnson
Close

Hilary
Close

Spencer Gardens

Vaughan
Close

The
King Edmund
School

87   88   283   89

G   PO   H   J   283   K   L   M

Silve

Eastbury
Avenue

Oxford Rd

Holt

Ashi

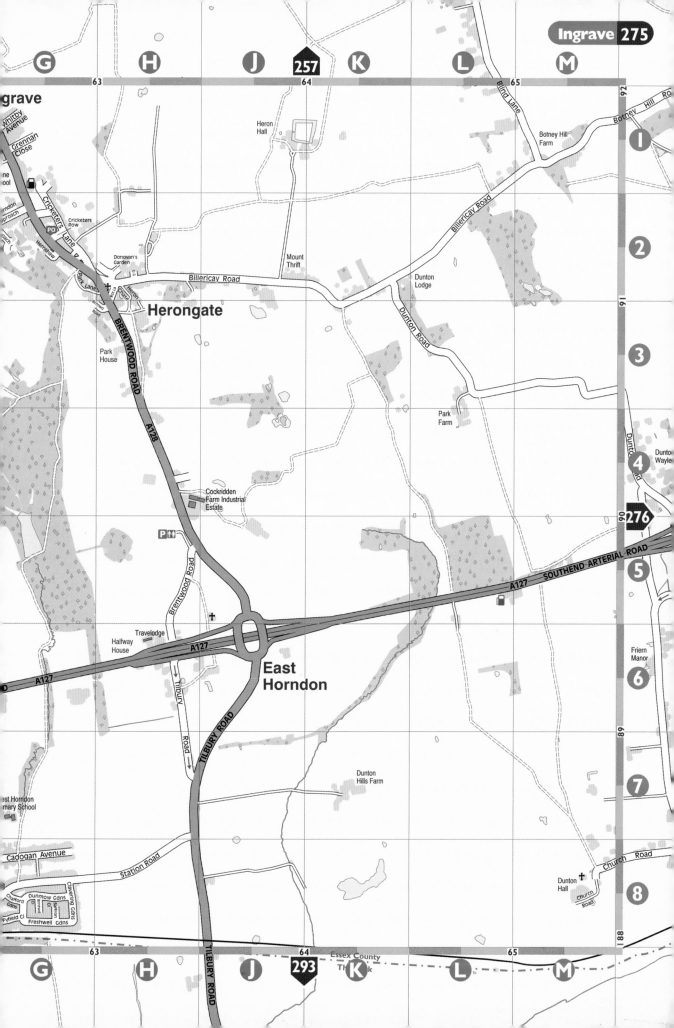

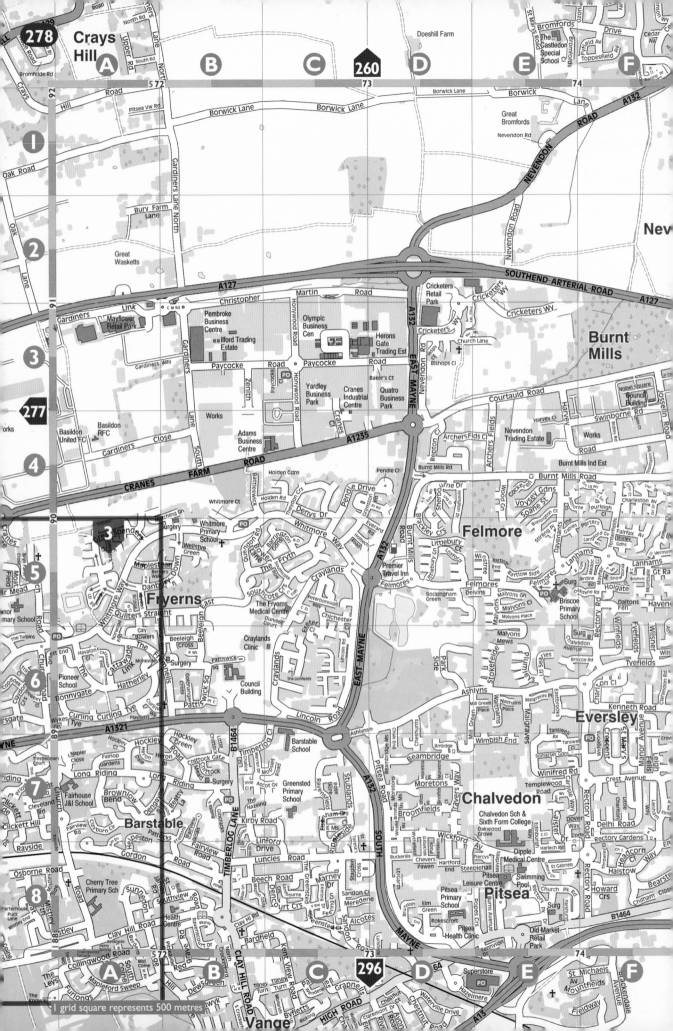

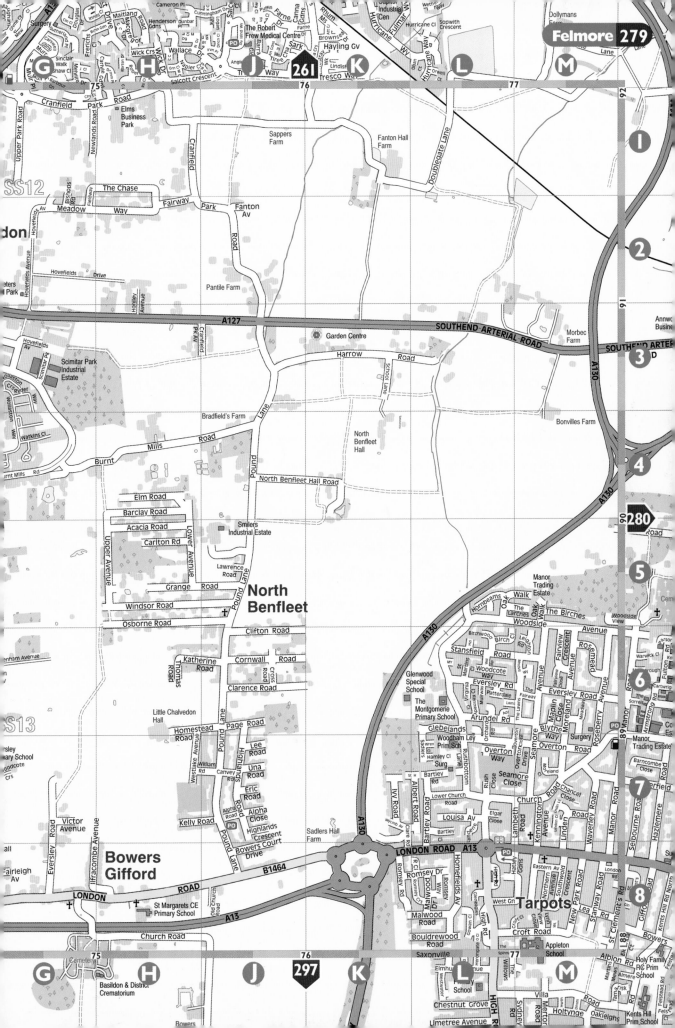

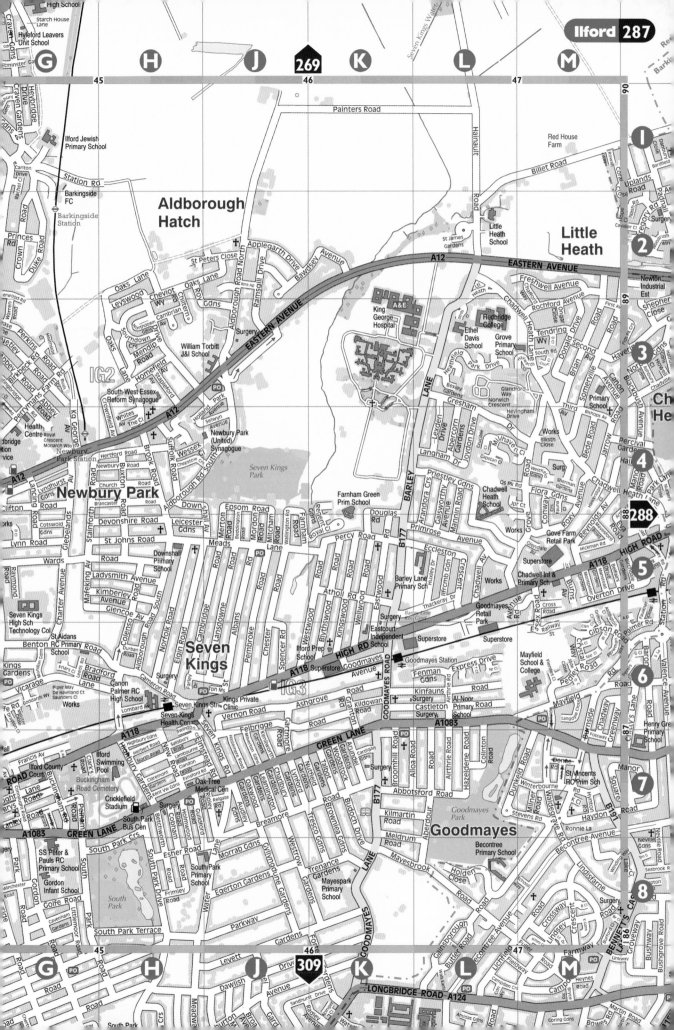

Dunton

Chafford Gdns
Dunmow Gdns
Saffron Gdns
Clavering Gdns
Fyfield Cl
Gdns

G 63 **H** Station **J** **275** **K** **L** 65 **M** 88

Essex County
Thurrock

I

TILBURY ROAD

Blue
House Farm

2

87

Field House

Brentwood Road

A128

3

BULPHAN

Peartree Lane

Noke
Hall Farm

Doesgate

Slose

Brentwood

4

BY-PASS

Doesgate Lane

86 294

Bulphan CE
Primary School

Bulphan

China La

Fen Lane

Church   Road

PO

Church   Road

Manor
House

5

Hatch Farm

Stanley Road

Albert Road

Victoria   Road

Fen Cl

6

85

Church

Lane

The
Elms Farm

7

Ongar
Hall Farm

BRENTWOOD ROAD

A128

8

84

Parker's Farm Road

G 63 **H** **J** **315** **K** **L** 65 **M**

Parker's Farm

Lorkins
Farm

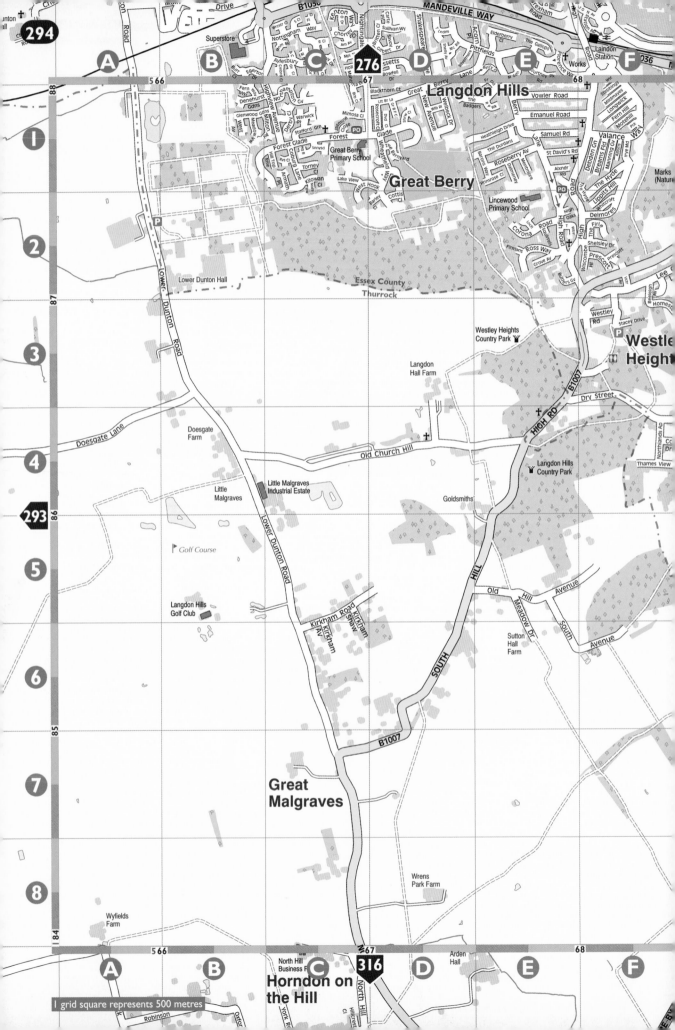

A **B** **C** **D** **E** **F**

5 66 67 68 036

Laindon
Station

Works

Langdon Hills

Vowler Road

Great Berry

Emanuel Road

Samuel Rd

Valance

St David's Rd

Roseberry AV

Great Berry
Primary School

Forest Glade

Lincewood
Primary School

Corona

Road

Ross Way

Grove Av

Westley
Rd

Stacey Drive

Lower Dunton Hall

Essex County
Thurrock

Westley Heights
Country Park

Westley
Heights

Langdon
Hall Farm

HIGH RD

Dry Street

B1007

Doesgate Lane

Doesgate
Farm

Old Church Hill

Langdon Hills
Country Park

Thames View

293

Little
Malgraves

Little Malgraves
Industrial Estate

Goldsmiths

Golf Course

Langdon Hills
Golf Club

Old Hill Avenue

Meadow Dr

South Avenue

Sutton
Hall
Farm

Kirkham Road

Kirkham Shaw

Kirkham AV

SOUTH HILL

B1007

**Great
Malgraves**

Wrens
Park Farm

Wyfields
Farm

North Hill
Business P

316

Horndon on
the Hill

North Hill

Arden
Hall

A **B** **C** **D** **E** **F**

5 66 67 68

I grid square represents 500 metres

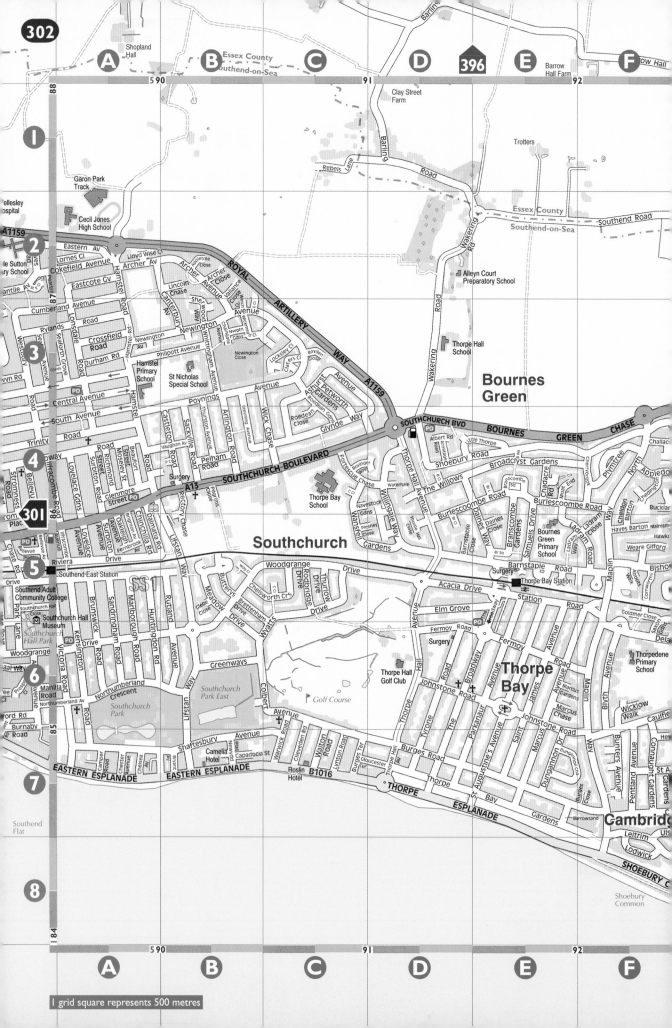

Grid references (top): G 93 H 94 J K 397 L 95 M

Grid references (right, top to bottom): I 88, 2 87, 3, 4 86 304, 5, 6 85, 7, 84, 8

Samuel Corner

The Crofts

Oldbury Farm

Coronation Close
The Great Wakering Health Centre
Great Wakering Sports Centre

SOUTHEND RD
B1017 HIGH STREET

Twyford Avenue
Lee Lotts
Rushley Close
Olvers
North Street
Chapel Lane
Lindsey Road
Havering Close
Newstead
Wedds Way
Common

Exhibition Lane
Star Lane Industrial Estate
Alexandra Road
STAR LANE B1017

Mercer Av
Northfield Crescent
Orchard Close
White Hall
M Cl
The Anchorage

Great Wakering Primary School
PO Fairfield
Conway Avenue
St John's Road
Shoebury Road

Great Wakering

Works
Milton Hall Close

Glebe Close
Morrins Cl

Mariners Court
Seaview Avenue
Brookside Avenue
Estuary Gardens
Goldsworthy Drive
Victoria Drive
Cupids Chase
Beach Court
Broomways

POYNTERS LANE B1017
Poynters Lane
Crouchmans

Churchfields
Keighley Cl
Mews
Datchet
Eton Wk
Chertsey
Walk
Weybridge
Sunbury
Maitland Place
M Cl

Ravendale Way
Mountbatten Drive
Frobisher
Colne Drive
Camellia Close
Exeter Close
Picasso Way

North Shoebury

Cherrytree Chase
LC

A13 NORTH SHOEBURY RD
Surgery
Superstore
Eagle
Wellings Way
Boxbank
Peregrine
Raphael Drive
Constable
Goya Rise
Wakering Road
Goya Way
Rubens Close
Whistler
Hobarth Drive

Brodie Road
Sandpit Road
I Butts Rd
LC
LC

Surgery
Drewsteignton
The Drakes
Jacana Way
Sandpiper Close
Friars Primary School
Ashanti Close
Turner Cl
Newell Avenue
Castle Cl
Peel Avenue

Pigs Bay

St Georges RC Primary School
Shoebury Park
Bulwark Road
Elm Road
Vanstone Way
Works
Seedbed Business Centre
Blackgate Road
LC
The Goslings

Sutton Road
Rosshill Road
Ness Road A13
Bridge
Elm
Works
The Vanguards
Friars St Works
Shoebury Av
Wakering Avenue
High Street
Gunners Road
P

East Beach

Richmond Avenue Primary School
Waterloo Road
Cheimer Cl
West Way
Seaview Rd
Towerfield Close
Towerfield Rd
Terminal Close
Primary School
Hingular St
Shoeburyness Station
PO

Shoeburyness

Antrim Road
Tudor Gardens
The Eye Clinic
Linton Road
Richmond Road
Campfield Road
Horseshoe Crs
Chapel Road
Smith Street
Rampart Street

Town Avenue
Fremantle
Admirals Walk
Waterford Road
B1016 NESS ROAD
Gunners Park
Magazine Road
Dane's Av
Beach Rd
Ness Road
Pier
Barge
Warrior

304

A   B   397   C   Bridge Road   D   E   398   F   Havengo Head

5 96   97   98

Haven Point

1

Samuel's Corner   Stairs Road

Stairs Rd

Road   Stairs
Rd

Glebe
Close   Morrin's
Close

2

Beach   Broomways   LC   Morrin's   Chase   Wakering Stairs

Drive

Estuary
Gardens

Idsworthy
Drive

aria Drive

3   Cherrytree Chase

LC

ds
e

Road

LC

Black
Grounds

4

utts Rd

303   Essex County
Southend-on-Sea

5   Pigs
Bay

6

85

7

8

I 84

5 96   97   98

A   B   C   D   E   F

I grid square represents 500 metres

G H J K L M

99 600 01

88

1

2

87

3

4

86

5

6

85

7

8

84

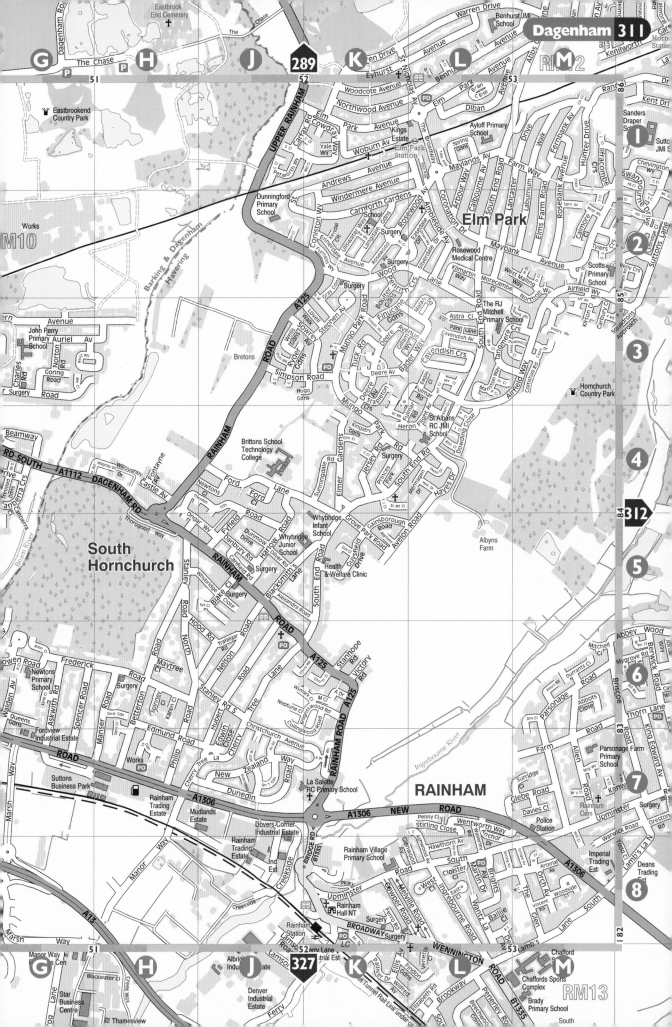

G H J 293 K L M

Orsett Fen

Hobletts

Lorkins Farm

CONWAY'S ROAD

B188

Home Farm

Orsett Hall

Orsett Avenue

Prince Charles

RECTORY ROAD

Malting Lane

Ridgwell Av

T Spnn

Penn Cl

Orsett

Lofthall Farm

Fen Lane

Poplars Farm

Orsett House

Pound Lane

PO

Surgery

Fordhams Rw

South Vw

Fen Lane

Orsett Hospital

The Green

PKWY

Herga Hyll

A128 BRENTWOOD ROAD

Baker Street

ROAD

Rowley Road

School

Mill La

Orsett CE Primary School

Rectory Lane

Barrington's Farm

STANFORD-LE-HOPE

Springfield

HIGH

B188

BAKER STREET

RM16

Mill Lane

A1013

ROAD

A1089

A13

STANFORD

Hornsby Lane

Welling Road

Sout

Golf Course

Grey Goose Farm

DOCK APPROACH ROAD

White Crofts

Heath Place

Golf Co

Long Lane

Kerry Rd

Milford Road

Jesmond Road

Highfield Gardens

Heath Rd

Chasefield Rd

Rushley Cl

Tyrdown

Bedfords Mount

Foxes Gn

Heath Road

Brentwood Road

Brook Farm

G H Orsett Heath J 331 K L M

Thurrock Athletics Stadium

Springfield Road

Blackshots Leisure

Broadview Avenue

316

I 2 3 4 5 6 7 8

316

294

Horndon on the Hill

North Hill
Business Park

Arden
Hall

Wrens
Park Farm

Horndon on the Hill
CE Prim School

Home
Farm

315

Horndon
House

Saffron
Gardens

Cholley's
Farm

St Cleres
Hall Golf Club

St Cleres
Hall

Golf Course

Stanford
Industrial
Estate

Lingwood Clin

Stanford-le-
Hope Station

Surge

Stanford le Hope By Pass

Barrington's
Farm

Orsett Industrial
Estate

Criton Industrial
Estate

St Cleres
School

Bluehouse
Farm

Southfields

Golf Course Road

Golf Course

Orsett
Golf Club

Collingwood
Farm

Brook Farm

1 grid square represents 500 metres

332

G · H · J · K · L · M

75 · 76 · 77

297

Northwick

Works

Northwick Road

Roscommon Way

CANVEY ROAD A130

1

St Marks Road

Holland Av

Harlem Road

Batavia

Limburg Road

2

Mulberry Rd

Pickett's Av

Charfleet Service Rd

Vikings Way

Charfleet Rd

Runwood Road

Charfleet Industrial Estate

St. Paul's

St. M

International Business Park

Cannon Cl

Kings Road

International Business Centre

3

Holehaven Creek

Romainville Way

Koin Cl

M Pool

Kings

St Mur

Fullmen Industrial Park

Ormiston Road

H H

4

Lower Horse

Shellhaven Point

Hole Haven

320

84

83

82

5

Oil Refinery

Shell Haven

Coryton Wharves

6

Thurrock

Medway Towns

Sea Reach

81

7

River Thames

8

Blythe Sands

80

G · H · J · K · L · M

75 · 76 · 77

I

2

3

4

328

5

6

7

8

RM13

Manor Way Business Cen

Star Business Centre

Blackwater Cl

Thamesview Business Centre

Lorimar Business Cen

Fairview Industrial Centre

Marsh Way

Frog Lane

Barlow Way S

Barlow Wy

Barlow Way South

Creek Way

Salamons Wy

Ferry Lane

Ferry Lane

Denver Industrial Estate

Albright Industrial Estate

Denver Industrial Estate

Lamson Rd

Lamson Road

Ferry Lane Industrial Est

Channel Tunnel Rail Link under construction

Rainham Hall

Upminster

Cowper Road

Melville Road

Ingrebourne Road

West

Cloister Cl

Brights Cl

Martin Dr

The Glen

Deans Trading Est

A1306

A13

Way

51

52

53

WENNINGTON

ROAD

B1335

Chafford School

Chaffords Sports Complex

Brady Primary School

South Hall Farm

Penerley Road

Rothbury Av

Beechwood Gdns

Eastwood Drive

South Hall Drive

Brookway

Elizabeth Rd

Pallister Dr

Ellis Av

Wilfred

Findon

Venette

Surgery

Surgery

PO

LC

A13

A13

A13

Rainham Marshes

Wenning Marshe

Industrial Estate Annexe

KP Estate

Frog Island

Ferry Lane

Coldharbour Lane

Coldharbour Lane

Coldharbour Lane

Wenningtree Point

Belvedere Industrial Estate

Works

Works

Erith Reach

Coldharbour

Erith Rands

Havering

Bexley

Crayford Ness

Darent Industria Park

Lower Rd

Church Manorway

Corinthian Manorway

Galleon Close

West Street

St Fidelis Rd

Victors Rd

Chichester Whf

Riverside Swimming Centre

Europa Trading Estate

Hamlet International Industrial Estate

Erith

Erith Playhouse

Erith Station

Library & Mus

Christ Church Av

Christ Church Primary School

Debrabant Close

Lesley Park Crescent

West Park Road

Pier Road

Queens Road

Erith High St

Health Centre

Crescent Road

Manor Road

Wharfside Cl

Business Centre

Superstore

Watt

Wheatley Ter

Works

Manford Industrial Estate

A206

A2016

A220

A206

B252

51

52

53

328

A   B   C   **312**   D   E   F

554   55   56

RM13

82

Deans Trading Est

Trading Est

NEW ROAD

Launder's Lane

Bretts Farm

Kenningtons

Usk

2

Hall Lane

East

Church Lane

A1306

Wennington Hall Farm Business Centre

Premier Travel Inn

Moor Hall

81

WENNINGTON ROAD B1335

The Gn

Wennington

Romford Road

Surgery

Ravel

Usk

PO

Tamar Drive

Kenni Prima

Shannon Way

Perry Wy

Nethan

Monnow

Driv

3

RM13

SANDY LANE B1335

AVELE

Ave FC

St Mich

Rowan Grove

Mill

A13

Sandy Lane Farm

Toplands Av

Orange Road

Manor Close

Grange Road

Lowlands Road

Blenheim Gdns

Field Rd

Manning Road

4

Wennington Marshes

LONDON RD

A1306

Purfleet Ind Park

A13

Purfleet

Arnhem Avenue

Myrtie Grove

Beech

Love Lane

Central AV

Crs

327

80

Havering Thurrock

Channel Tunnel Rail Link under construction

Juliette Wy

Kerry Avenue

Juliette Way

Purfleet Ind Park

Kent View Lane

Hall Road

Crescent

Walk

5

Aveley Marshes

LONDON ROAD

A13

Fanns Farm

79

6

Mar Dyke

LC

Milehams Industrial Estate

RM19

7

River

Water Surgery Lane

Marlow AV

Fanns Rise

Thamley

Centurion Way

TANK HILL RD

Chieftan Drive

Council Building

Marine Court

Purfleet Primary School

Tank Lane

Beacon Hill Industrial Estate

A1306 ARTERIAL ROAD

Wood AV

North Road

Channel Tunnel Rail Link un

Crayford Ness

Premier Travel Inn

HIGH ST

Church Lane

A1090

Purfleet

Harrisons Wharf

Works

8

78

Landau Way

Darent Industrial Park

Purfleet Station

LC

A1090

Botany Way

Beacon Hill Industrial Estate

Wingrove Drive

Beacon Hill

Linnet Way

Oakhill Rd

Works

LONDON

Mill Road

Linden Cl

ROAD

River Thames

A   B   C   **334**   D   E   F

554   55   56

1 grid square represents 500 metres

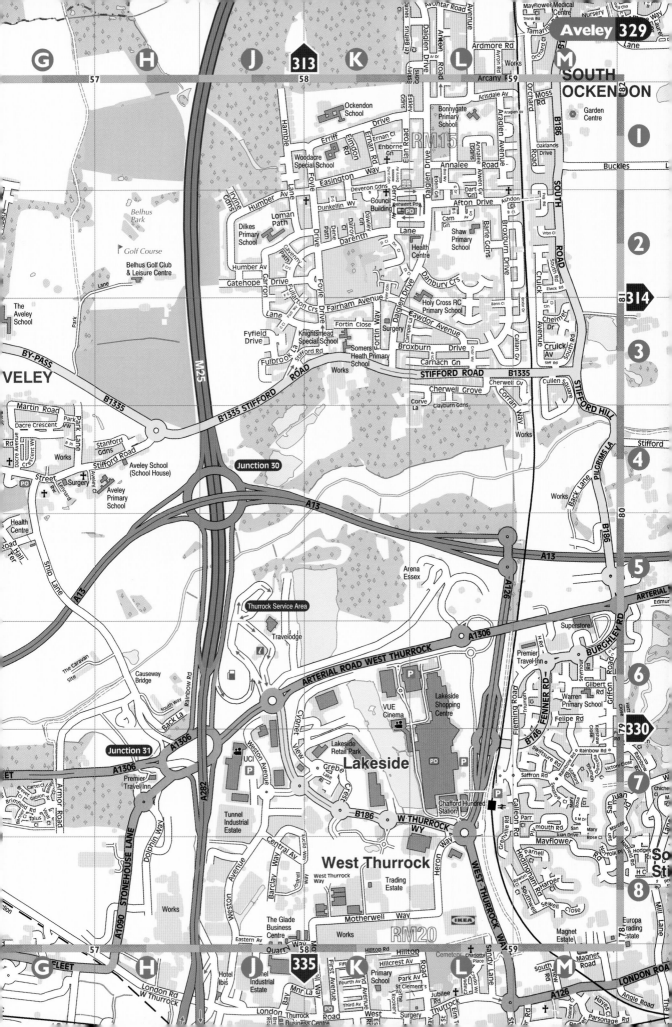

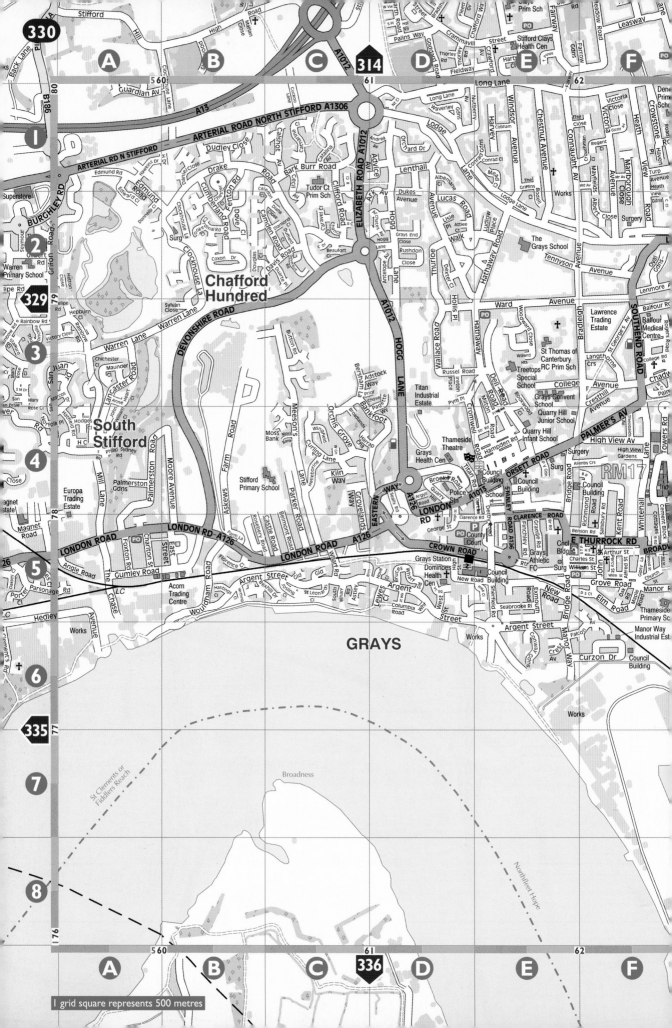

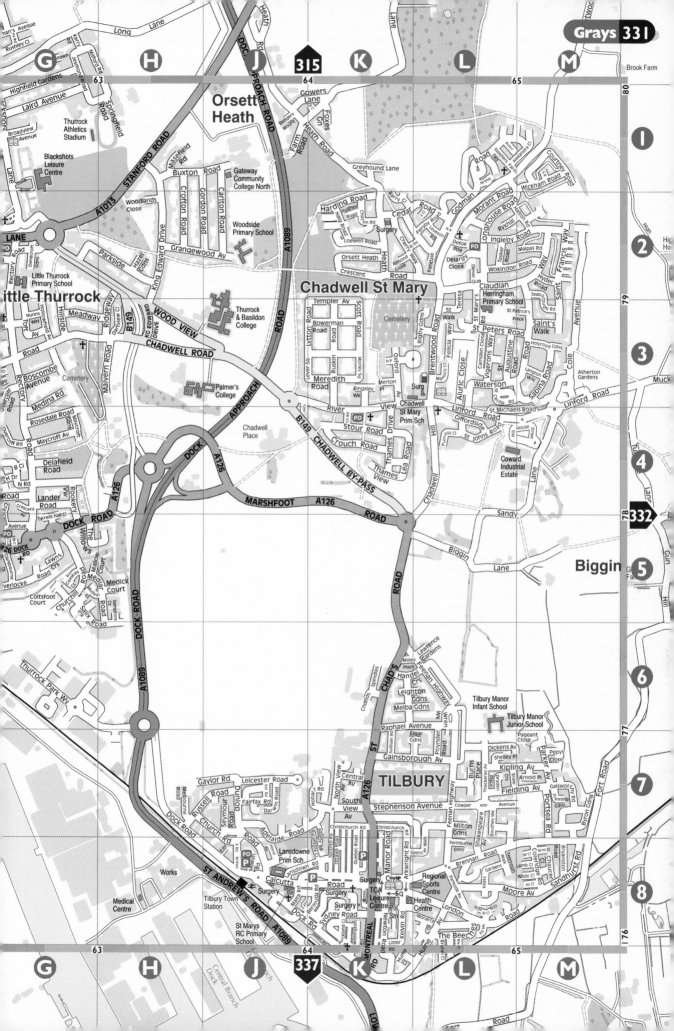

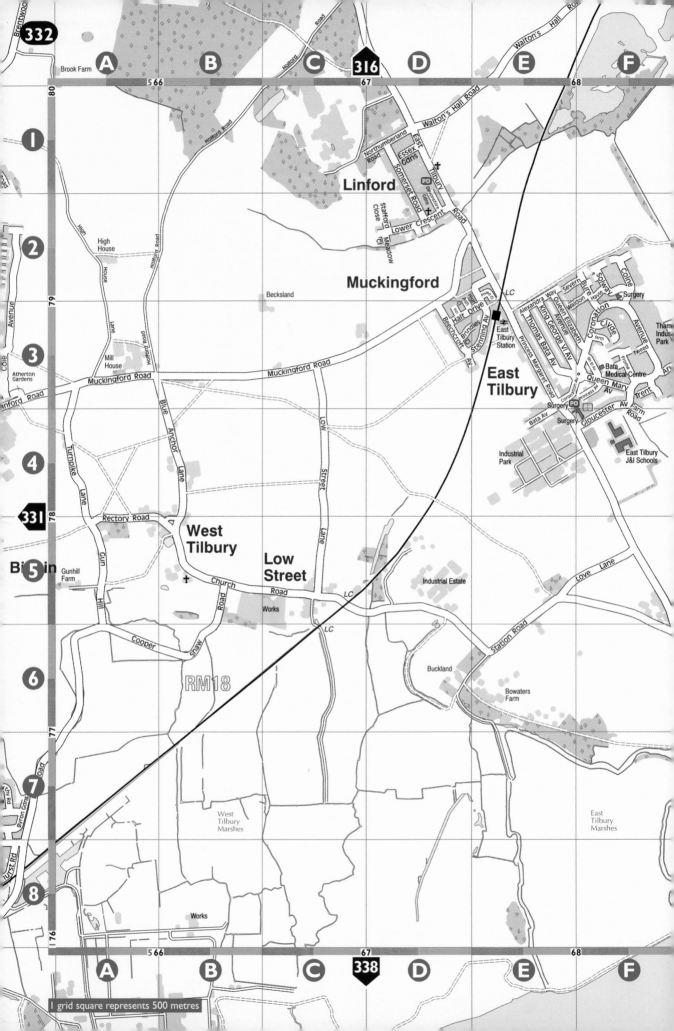

G H J **317** K L M

69 70 71 80

I

2

79

Lower
Hope Point

3

4

78

5 Mead W

6

77

Saxon Shore Way

7

8

176

king
Marshes

Thurrock
Medway Towns

✝
Linley
Gordon
Close

Princess Margaret Road

✝

P

Coalhouse Fort

Thurrock

Medway Towns
Kent County

Coalhouse
Point

G 69 H J **339** K L M

70 71

G H J 333 K L M

Coalhouse
Point

I

2

Saxon Shore Way

Higham Marshes

3

Shorne Marshes

4

Beckley
Hill
Works

Nuralite
Industrial
Centre

Canal Road

5

Bull

6

Queen's
Farm

P

Queen's Farm Road

King's Farm

Church Street

Cliffe Street

Core Green Rd

Lower Higham Road

Lower Road

Lower Road

Chalk Road

PO

Martins Cl

7

Lake Drive

Higham
Station

Green Farm Lane

Green
Farm

Higham Hall

Steadman Close

School Lane

Higham
Primary
School

Hill Farm

Taylors Lane

8

G H J K L M

Burdett Av

Coutts
Avenue

The
Knowle

High
View

GRAVESEND ROAD

A226

Higham

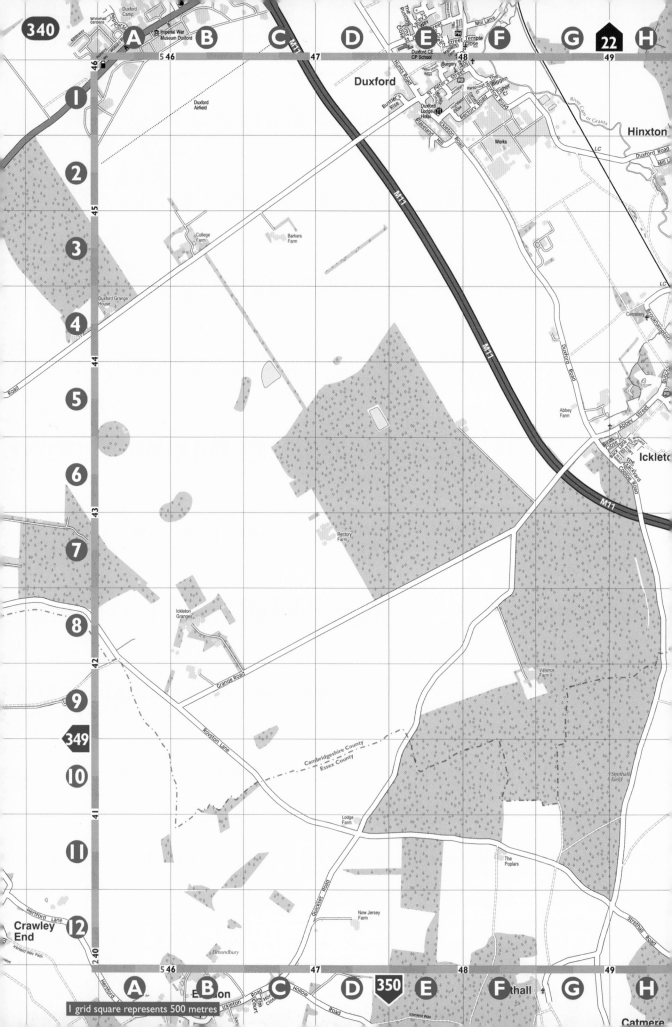

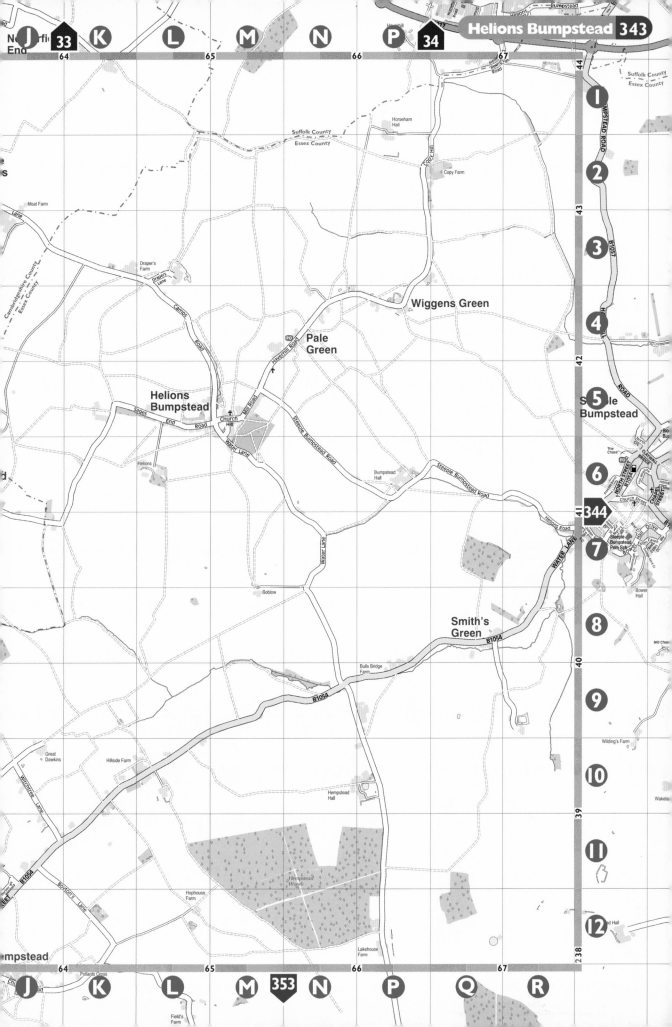

J K L M N P
34
33
64 65 66 67

1
2
3
4
5
6
7
8
9
10
11
12

MPSTEAD ROAD
B1057

Suffolk County
Essex County

Moat Farm
Lane

Cambridgeshire County
Essex County

Draper's Farm
Drapers Lane

Camps Road

Copy Farm

Horseham Hall

Cock Hill

Suffolk County
Essex County

Wiggens Green

Pale Green

Havernill Road

Helions Bumpstead

Sages End Road

Church Hill

Mill Road

Water Lane

Helions

Steeple Bumpstead Road

Bumpstead Hall

Steeple Bumpstead Road

Helions Road

Steeple Bumpstead

The Chase

NORTH STREET
CHAPEL STREET
B1054
Church Street

344

Steeple Bumpstead Prim Sch

WATER LANE

Bower Hall

Boblow

Water Lane

Smith's Green
B1054

Bulls Bridge Farm

B1054

Wilding's Farm

Great Dawkins

Hillside Farm

Wichtree Lane

Hempstead Hall

Hophouse Farm

Hempstead Wood

Lakehouse Farm

Hall

mpstead

B1054

BOYTON'S Lane

Pollards Cross

Field's Farm

A B C D 35 E F G H

5 68 69 70 71

44

Suffolk County
Essex County

I

2

43

3

BUMPSTEAD ROAD
B1057

4

42

Garland's Farm

5 Steeple
Bumpstead

HAVERHILL ROAD
BLOIS ROAD

The Endway
Blois Meadow
Business Centre
Blois Farm

6

The Chase
NORTH STREET
B1054
PO
Home
Close
CHAPEL STREET
CLAYHALL BRIDGE
Church Street

41

Freshfield

Steeple
Bumpstead
Prim Sch
Cavell Wy

B1054

B1057

Cemetery

7

WATTLE LANE

FINCHINGFIELD ROAD

Bower
Hall

8

B1054

40

Mill Chase

Mill Chase

Old Hall

9

Wilding's Farm

B1057

10

39

Wakeland's Farm

II

12

Herkstead Hall
Farm

Martin's Farm

2 38

5 68 69 70 71

A B C 354 D E F G H

Sturmer

Hill Lane
A1017
SWLE
HILL

Roost
End

Water Hall
Farm

New
England

A1017

Upper House
Farm

B1054

B1054

Fell Road

Rylands
Farm

Birdbrook

Moat House

Moat Road

Line Street

Stud Farm

Daw Street

Frinkle
Green

Whitehouse
Farm

Park
Wood

Egypt End Lane

Birdbrook Road

Stambourne
Green

Cornish Hall End Road

Chapel End

PO Way

Mill

Stam

Revels Farm

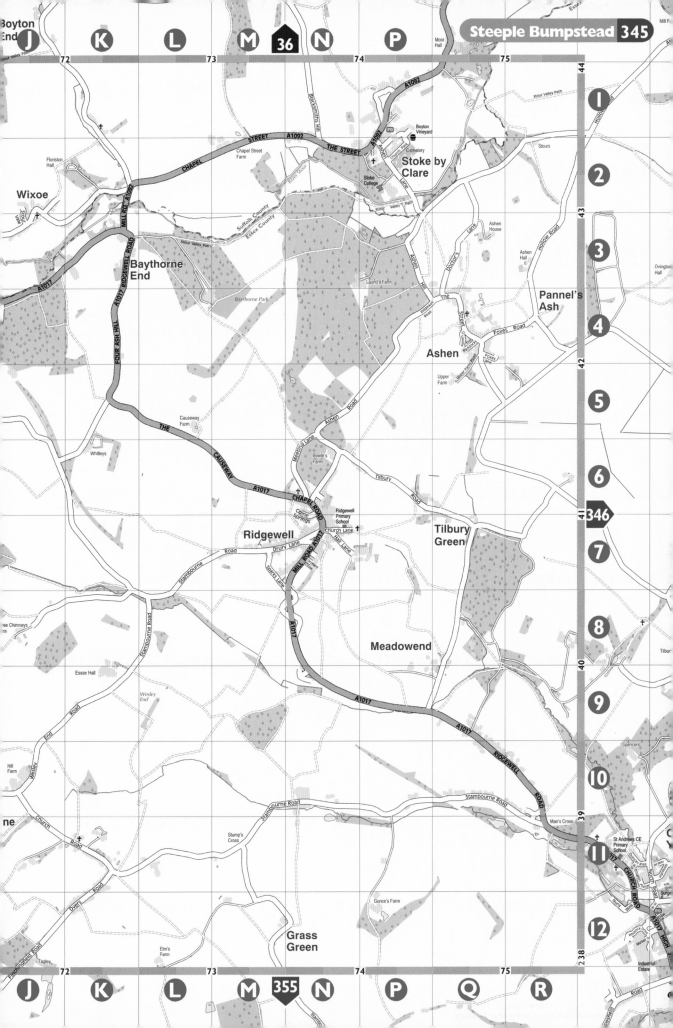

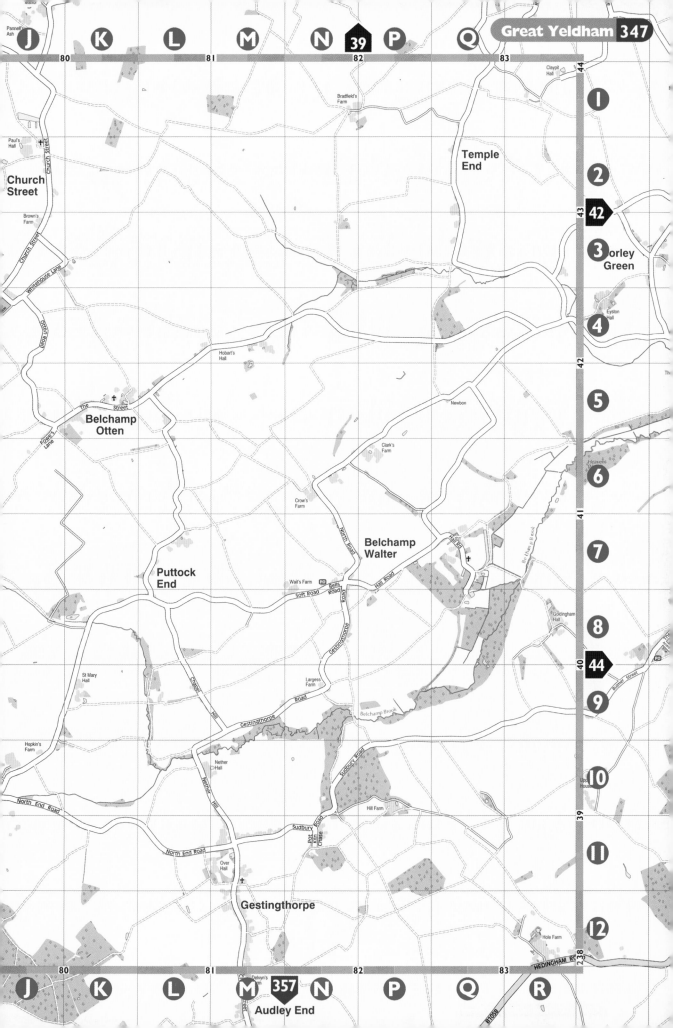

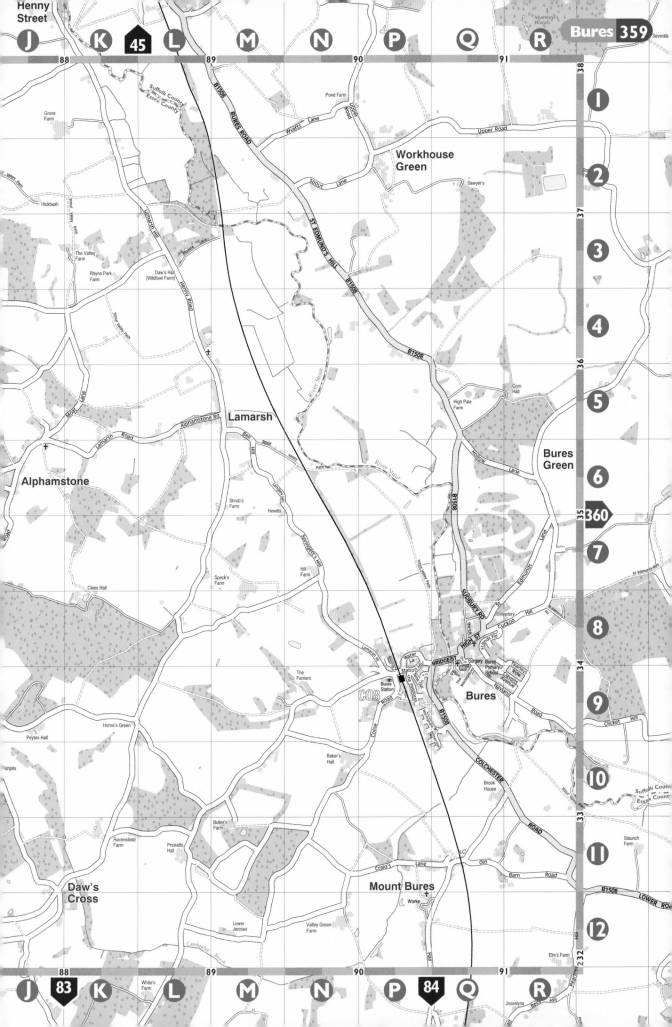

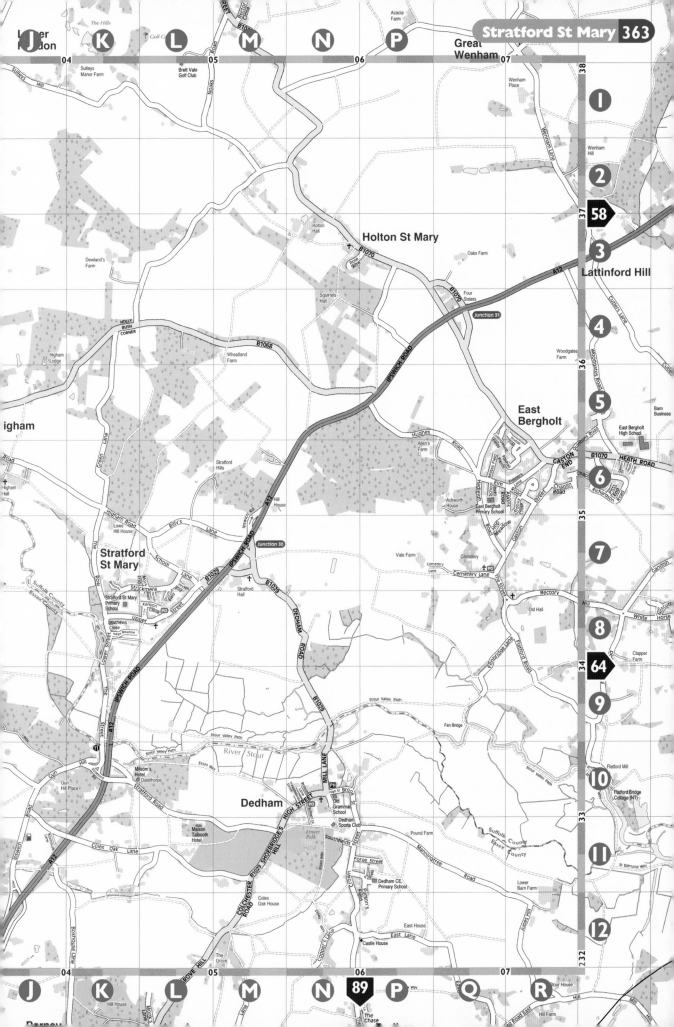

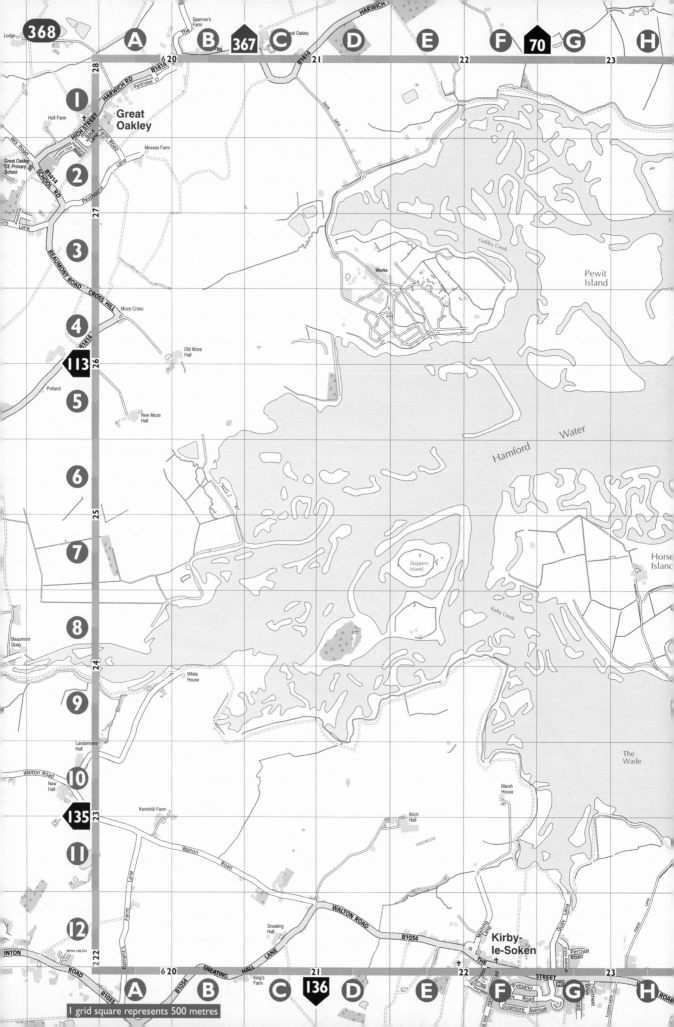

Pennyhole
Bay

Stone
Marsh

Hedge-end
Island

Walton Channel

The Twizzle

Marina

Nature
Reserve

The
Naze

Walton
Hall

Old Hill Lane

Naze Park Road

Second Avenue

Third Avenue

First Avenue

Louise Close

Florence Rd

Greville

Beatrice Road

Percival Rd

Green Lane

Hall

East Terrace

The Frinton &
Walton Heritage Museum

Walton &
Frinton
Yacht Club

Frinton & Walton
Swimming Pool

Walton
Primary
Sch

Standley
Rd

PRINCE'S ESP

CO14

Coles Lane

Mill Lane

Saville Street

Suffolk Street

High Street

Wade

ROAD

Clays

B1034

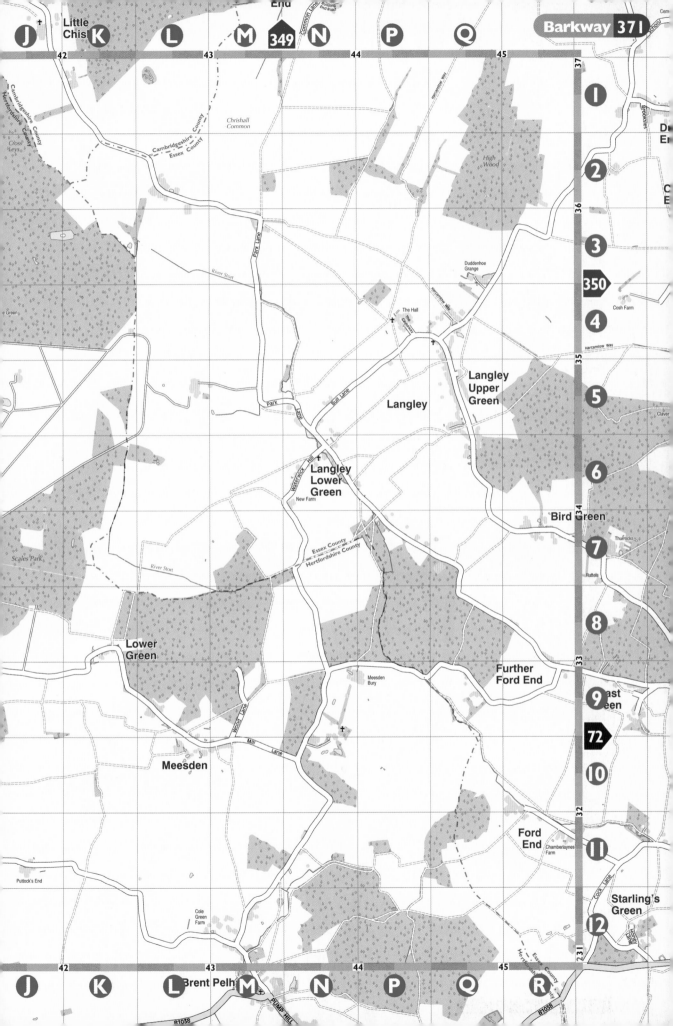

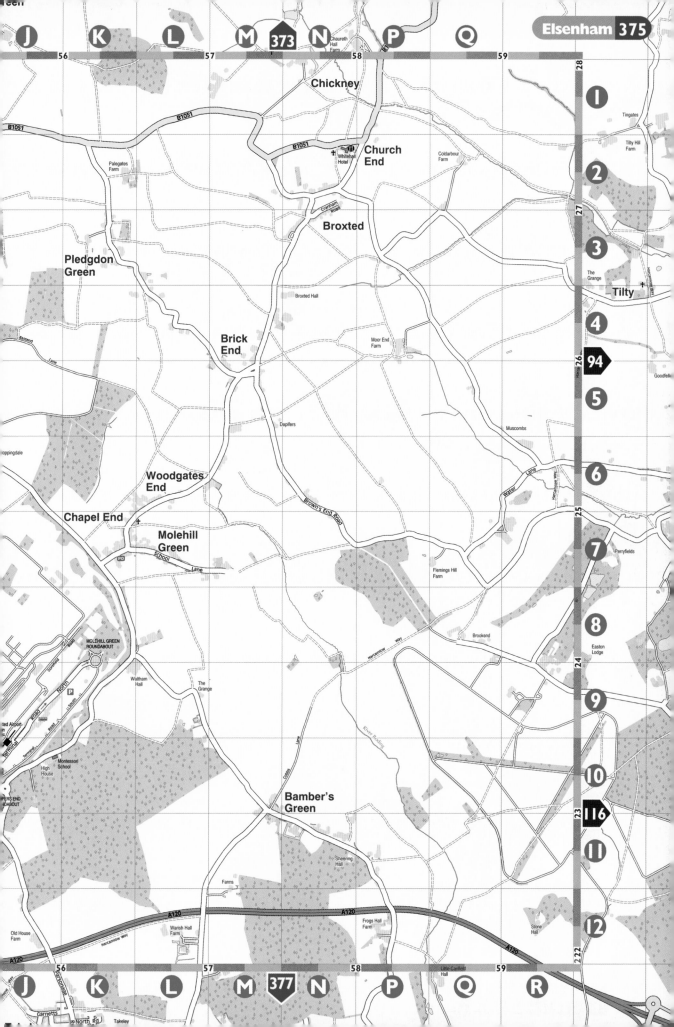

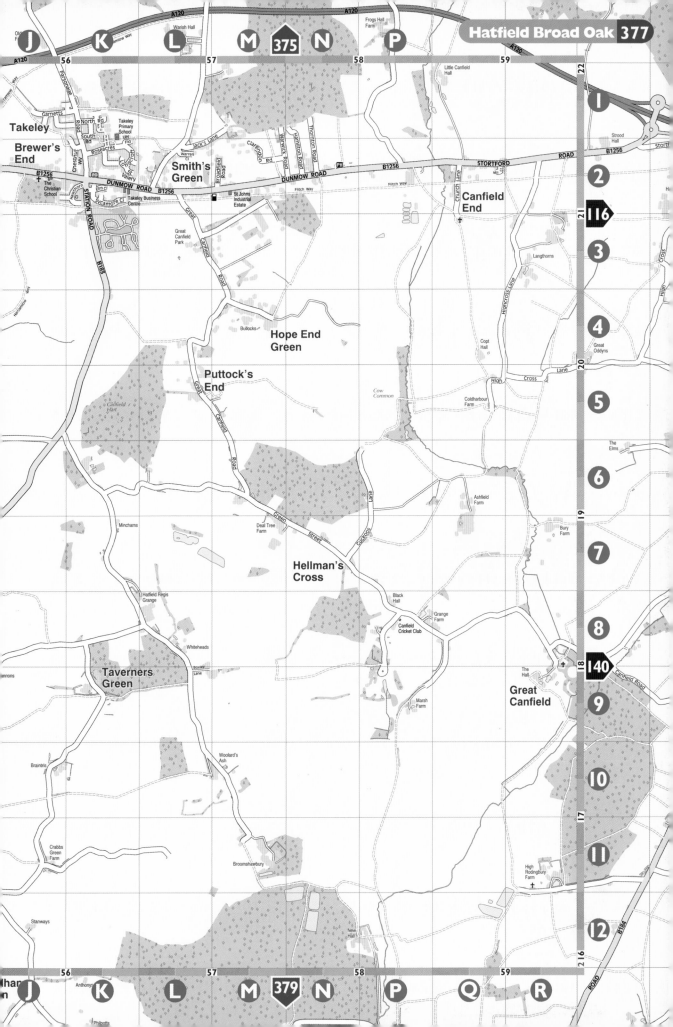

J K L M **377** N P Q

56 57 58 59

1
2
3
4
164
5
6
7
8
9
10
190
11
12

Stanways

dham
en

Anthonys

Philpotts

Poplars
Farm

Aythorpe
Roding

Highhams

Roundbush
Green

Wycomb
Meadows

Drury
Lane

B184

Keeres
Green

Wood Lane

Prows
Farm

Walkers
Farm

Langlands

Rodings
Primary School

Leaden
Roding

Marks
Hall

Three Forests Way

Lucas
Farm

The
Rodings

Holmans
Crescent

Leaden Gdns

Lordship Lane

White Roding or
White Roothing

St Martin's
Close

Church Lane

A1060

New House
Farm

A1060

Brownlows
Close

Works

Stortford Road

Thomsett

White
Hall

A1060

Kingstons

Matching Lane

Mascallsbury
Farm

Three Forests Way

B184

Hales
Farm

Megs

Margaret
Roding

Waterloo
Farmhouse

Snows
Farm

Nether
Street

Fairlands

Anchor Lane

Green Hill
Farm

Berwick
Hall

Marks
Hall

Abbess
Roding

Anchor Lane

Abbess
End

School Lane

Fraves
Chase

Fraves

190

Rookwood
Hall

Works Lane

B184

Longbarns

Dunmow Road

River Roding

Orimar

Whaypules

Cobbler's
Pieces

Beauchamp
Roding

School
Lane

Flands
Cottages

Woodend

56 57 58 59

J K L M **381** N P Q R

Slades
Farm

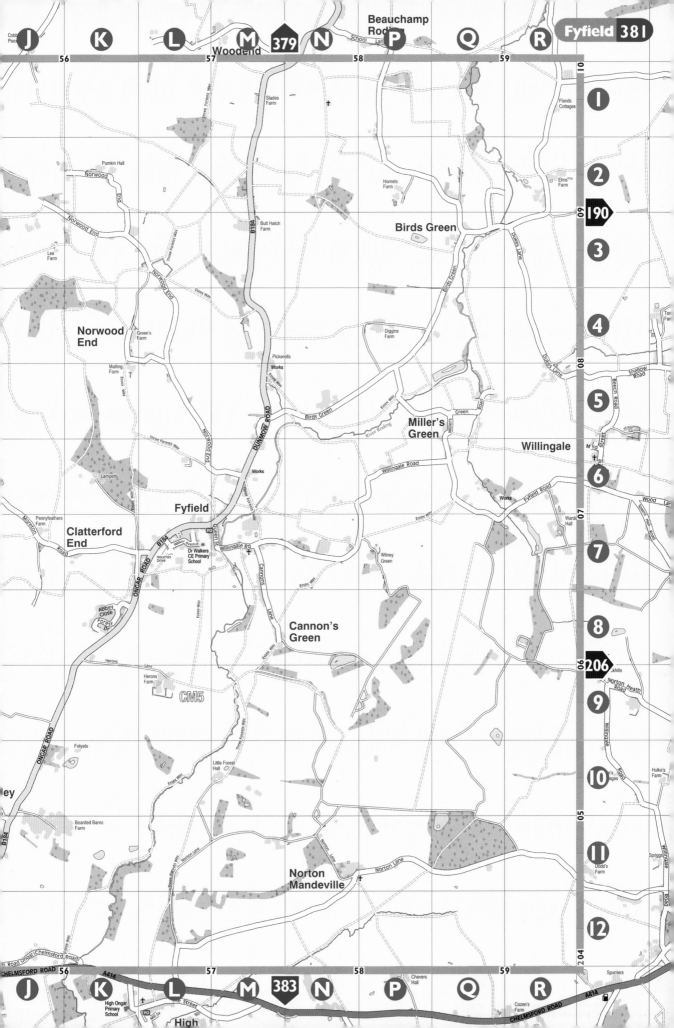

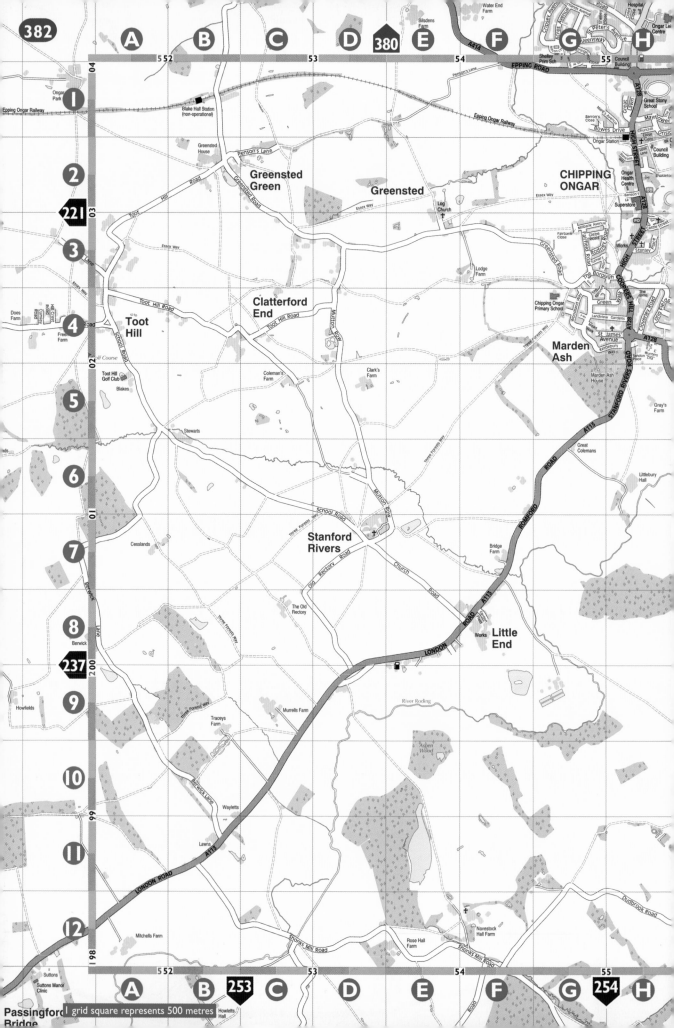

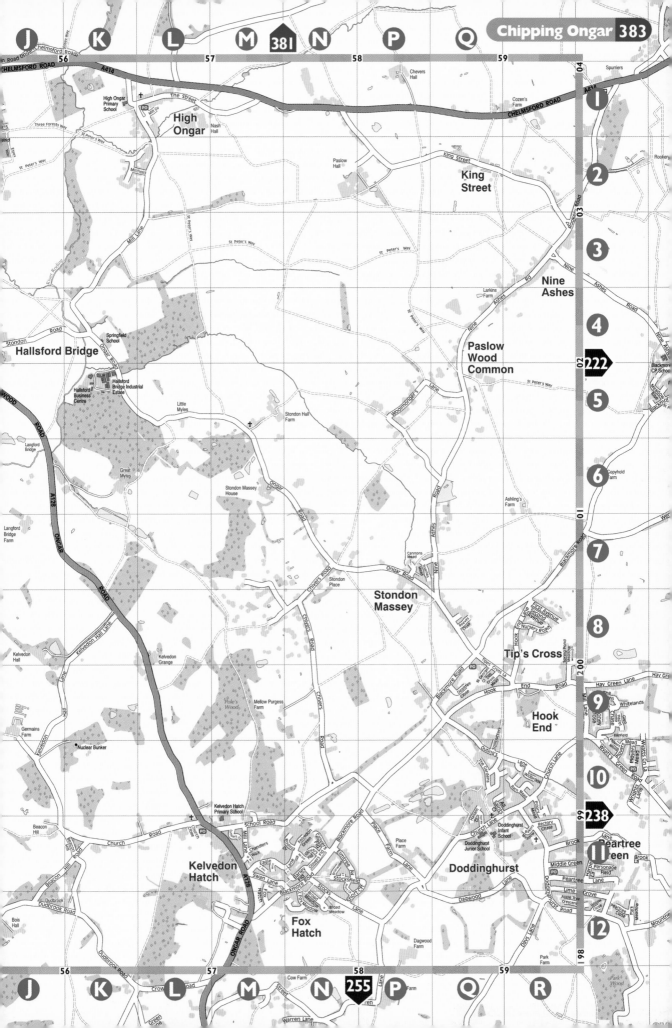

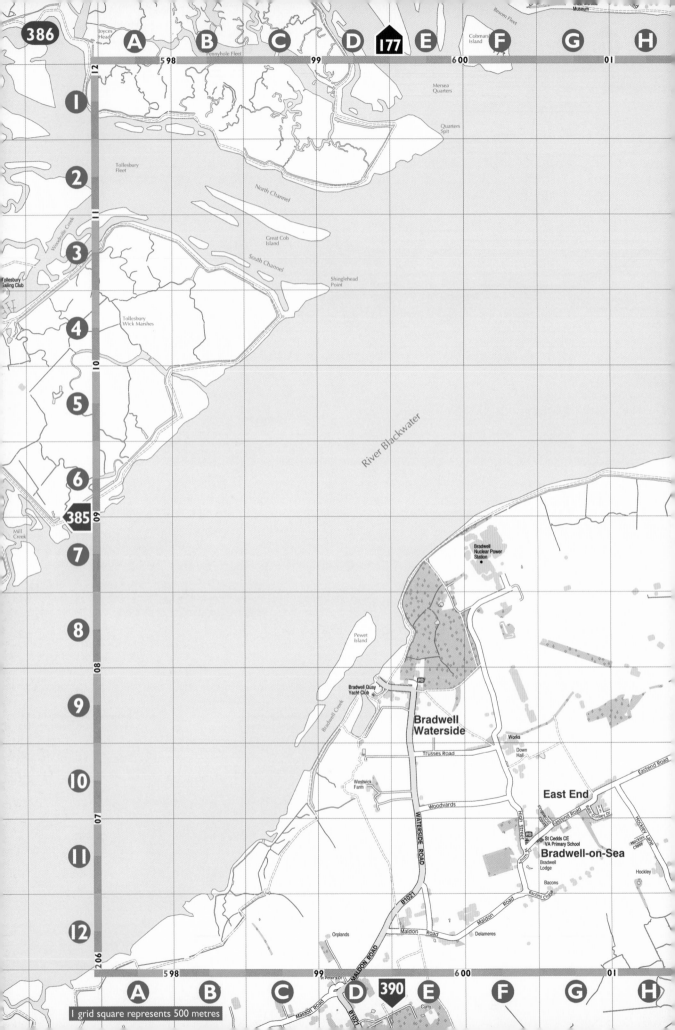

A   B   C   D   **177**   E   F   G   H

Joyces Head

598   99   600   01

Cobmarsh Island

West Mersea Museum

1

Pennyhole Fleet

Blooms Fleet

Mersea Quarters

Quarters Spit

2

Tollesbury Fleet

North Channel

3

Tollesbury Sailing Club

Great Cob Island

South Channel

Shinglehead Point

Woodrolfe Creek

4

Tollesbury Wick Marshes

5

11

10

River Blackwater

6

385

09

Mill Creek

Bradwell Nuclear Power Station

7

8

Pewet Island

9

Bradwell Quay Yacht Club

Bradwell Waterside

Works

08

10

Trusses Road

Down Hall

East End

Eastend Road

Westwick Farm

Woodyards

WATERSIDE ROAD

High Street

St Cedds CE VA Primary School

Eastend Road

Hockley Lane

07

11

Bradwell-on-Sea

Bradwell Lodge

Hockley

South St

Bacons

Hockley Close

12

B1021

Maldon Road

Bacons Creek

Orplands

Maldon Road

Maldon Road

Delameres

206

598   99   600   01

St Peter's Cr

MALDON ROAD

B1021

Curry

A   B   C   D   **390**   E   F   G   H

1 grid square represents 500 metres

J K L M N P

02 03 04 05 12

1

11

2

3

10

4

5

6

09

7

8

08

9

10

07

11

12

206

Sales
Point

Tip
Head

East Hall
Farm

Eastend Road

Eastlands

Eastend Road

East Hall

Munkins
Farm

St Peter's Way

St Peter's Way

Bradwell Marshes

Key Lane

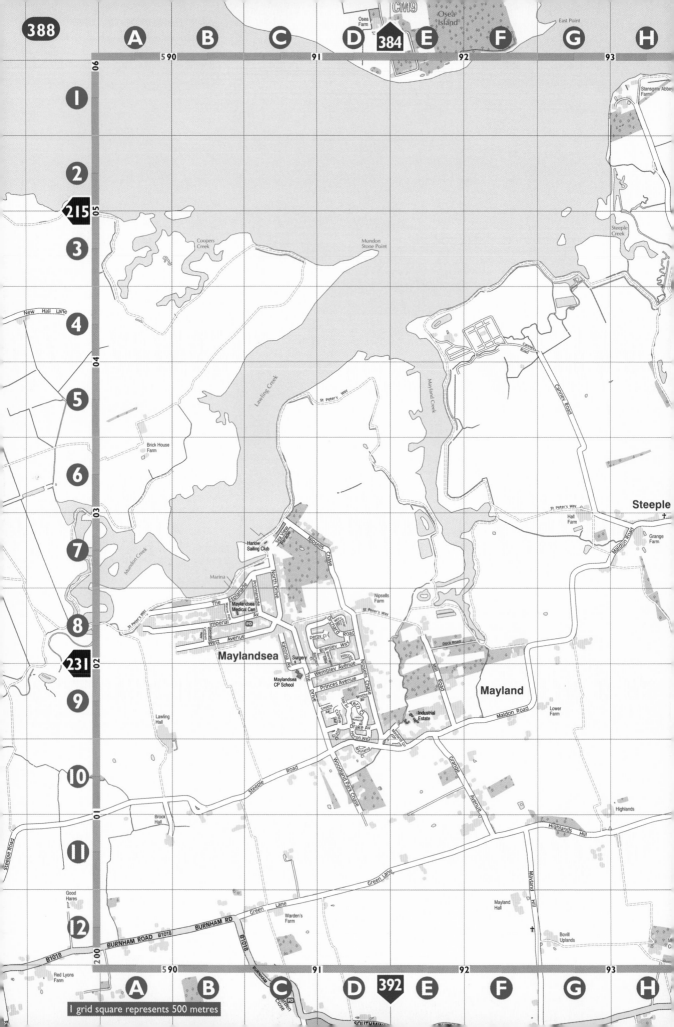

CM9

Osea
Farm

Osea
Island

East Point

A   B   C   D   E   F   G   H

5 90   91   92   93

06

Stansgate Abbey
Farm

1

2

215

Steeple
Creek

3

Coopers
Creek

Mundon
Stone Point

Cennen
Road

Cennen Road

4

New Hall Lane

05

04

5

Lawling Creek

St Peter's Way

Mayland Creek

Brick House
Farm

03

Steeple

6

Hall
Farm

Grange
Farm

St Peter's Way

7

Mundon Creek

Harlow
Sailing Club

Sea View
Parade

Nipsells
Farm

Nipsells Chase

North Drive

Maldon Road

8

Marina

The
Esplanade

Promenade

Maylandsea
Medical Cen

St Peter's Way

Dock Road

231

PD

Imperial
Av

Orchard Road

Nipsells Chase

Mill Road

West   Avenue

Derby Cl

Bramley Way

9

Maylandsea

Surgery

Mayland

02

Lawling
Hall

Maylandsea
CP School

Wembley Avenue

Princes Avenue

Industrial
Estate

Lower
Farm

Maldon Road

Drake Av

10

Steeple   Road

Woodland Park Chase

Grange   Avenue

01

Highlands

Brook
Hall

Highlands Hill

11

Green Lane

Mayland Hill

Good
Hares

Green Lane

12

BURNHAM RD

Warden's
Farm

Mayland
Hall

Bovill
Uplands

BURNHAM ROAD B1018

B1018

B1018

Red Lyons
Farm

2 00

5 90   91   92   93

Holden
Close

SOUTHMIN

1 grid square represents 500 metres

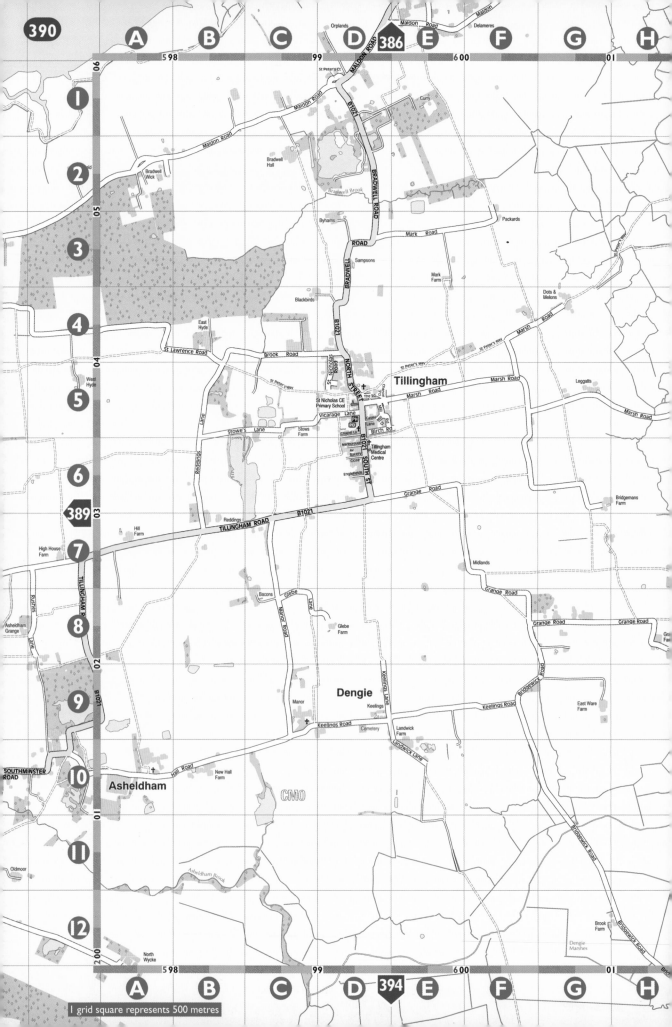

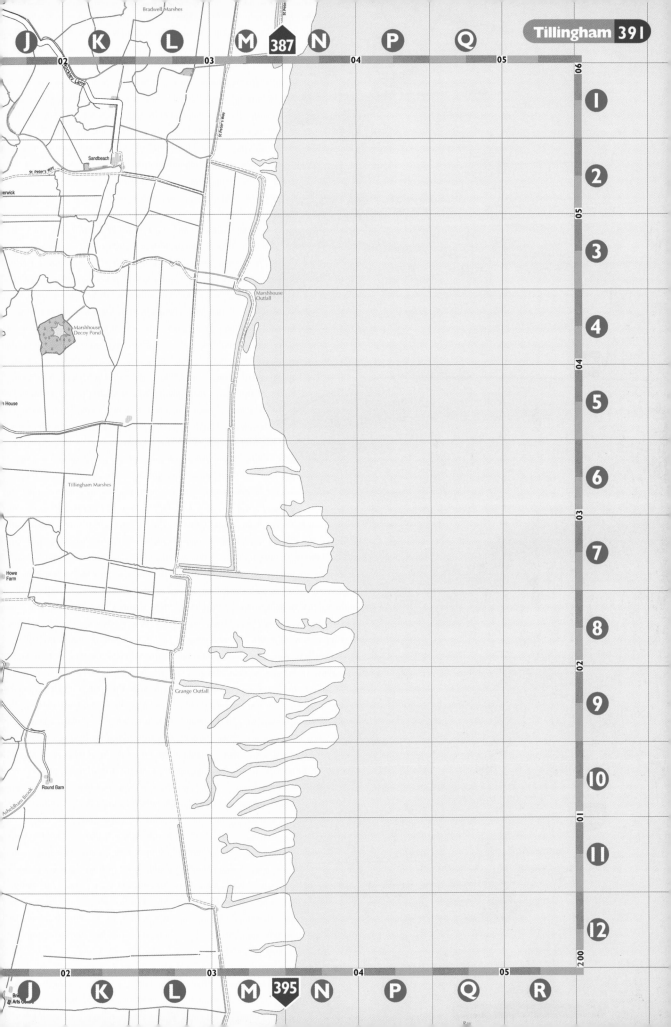

Bradwell Marshes

Rockley Lane

Sandbeach

St. Peter's Way

erwick

St. Peter's Way

Marshhouse
Outfall

Marshhouse
Decoy Pond

h House

Tillingham Marshes

Howe
Farm

Grange Outfall

Round Barn

Asheldham Brook

Bradwell Marshes

Bri
& Arts Centre

Ray

1 2 3 4 5 6 7 8 9 10 11 12

06 05 04 03 02 01 00

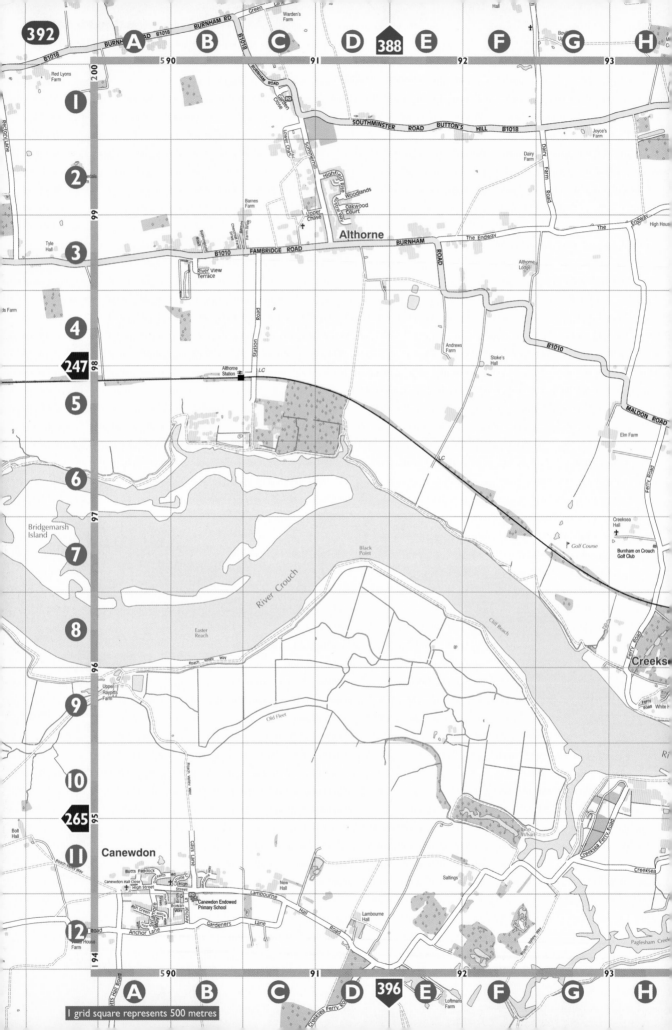

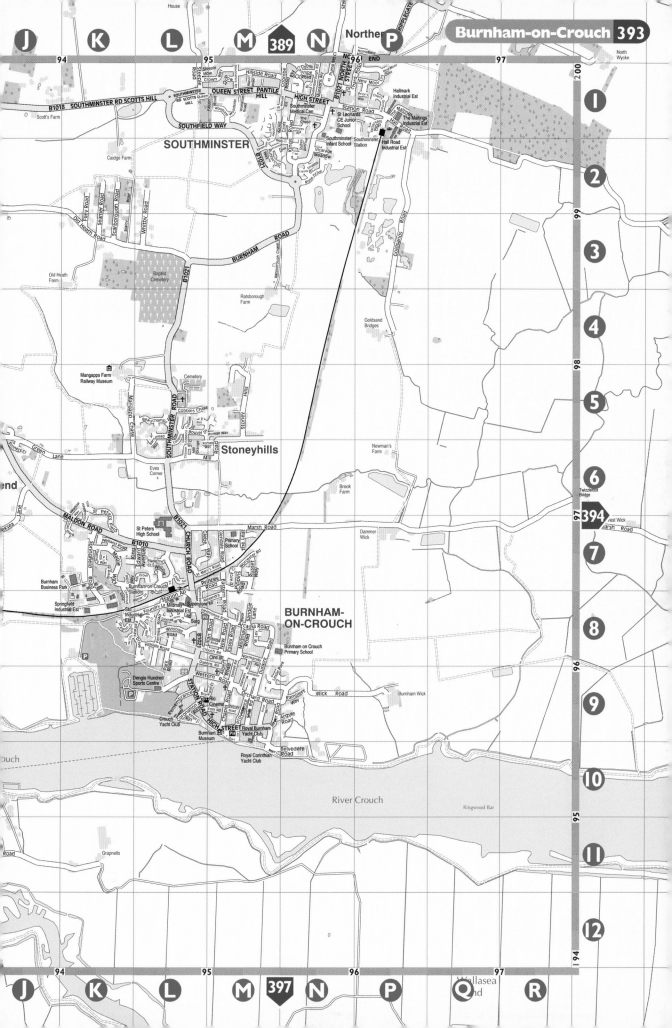

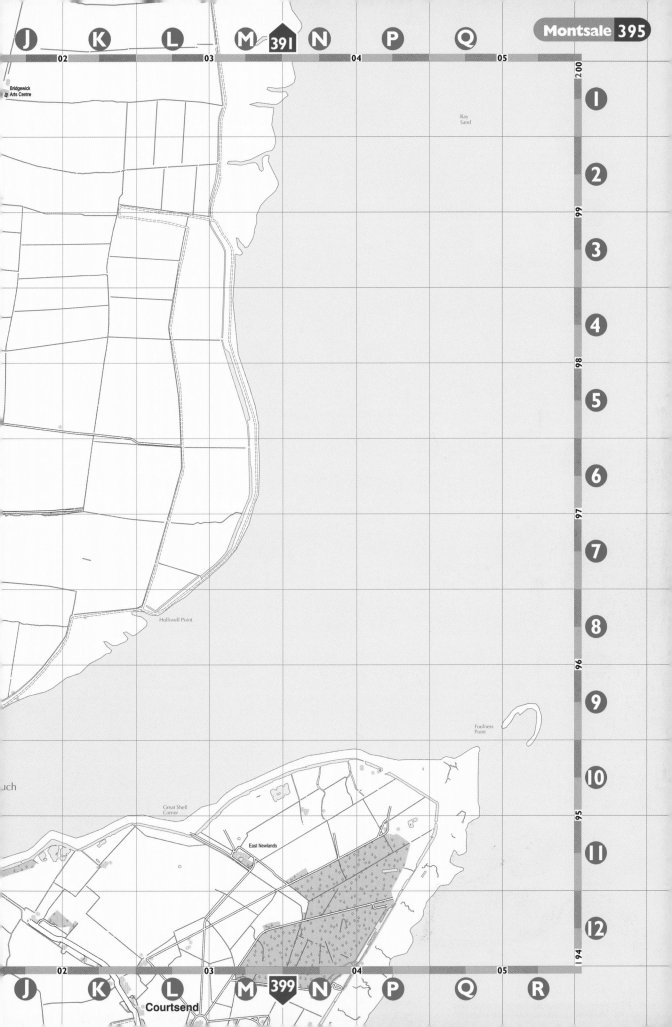

Bridgewick
Arts Centre

Ray
Sand

Holliwell Point

Foulness
Point

uch

Great Shell
Corner

East Newlands

Courtsend

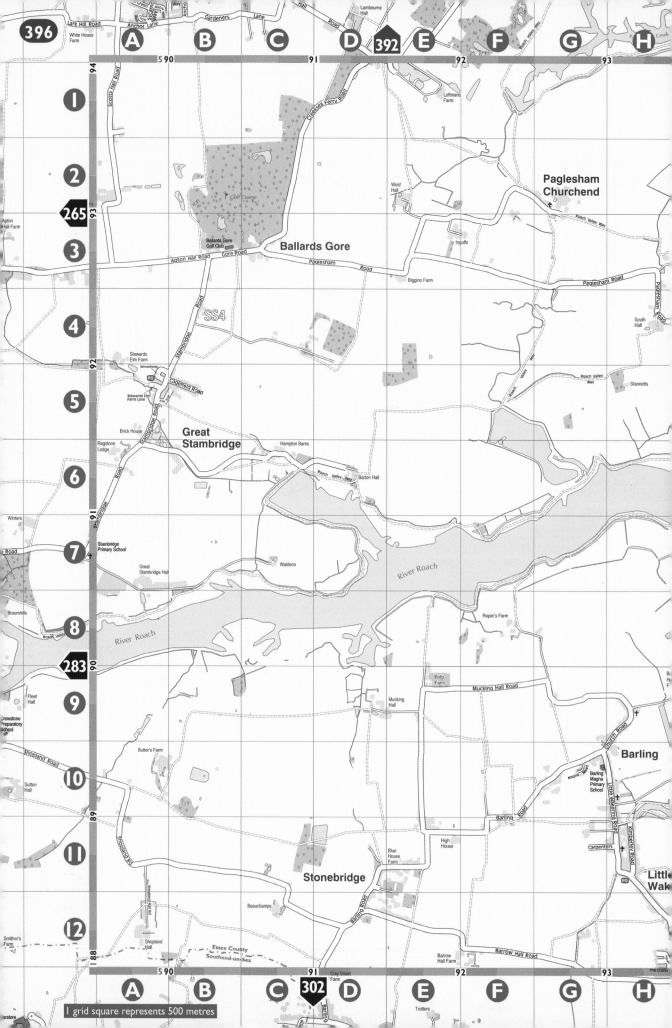

Ballards Gore

Paglesham
Churchend

Great
Stambridge

River Roach

Barling

Stonebridge

Little
Wak

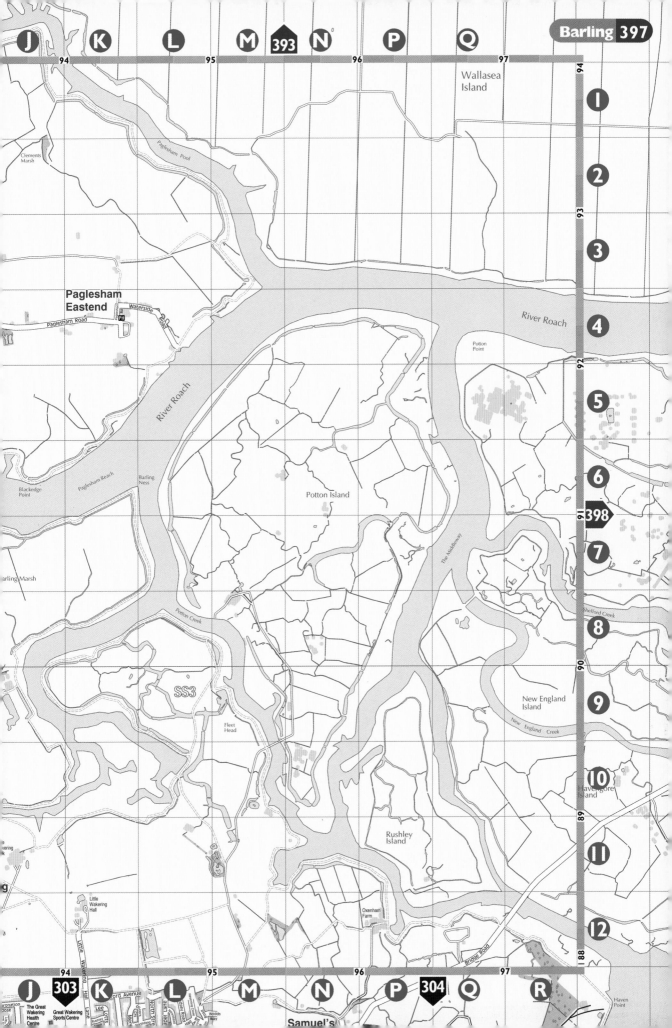

J K L M 393 N P Q

94 95 96 97

1
2
3
4
5
398
6
7
8
9
10
11
12

94 93 92 91 90 89 88

Wallasea Island

Clements Marsh

Paglesham Pool

Paglesham Eastend

Waterside Road
Paglesham Road
PH

River Roach

River Roach

Potton Point

Blackedge Point

Paglesham Reach

Barling Ness

Barling Marsh

Potton Island

Potton Creek

SS3

Fleet Head

The Middleway

Shelford Creek

New England Island

New England Creek

Havengore Island

Rushley Island

Little Wakering Hall

Oxenham Farm

Haven Point

J 303 K L M N P 304 Q R

94 95 96 97

The Great Wakering Health Centre

Great Wakering Sports Centre

Bridge Road

Samuel's

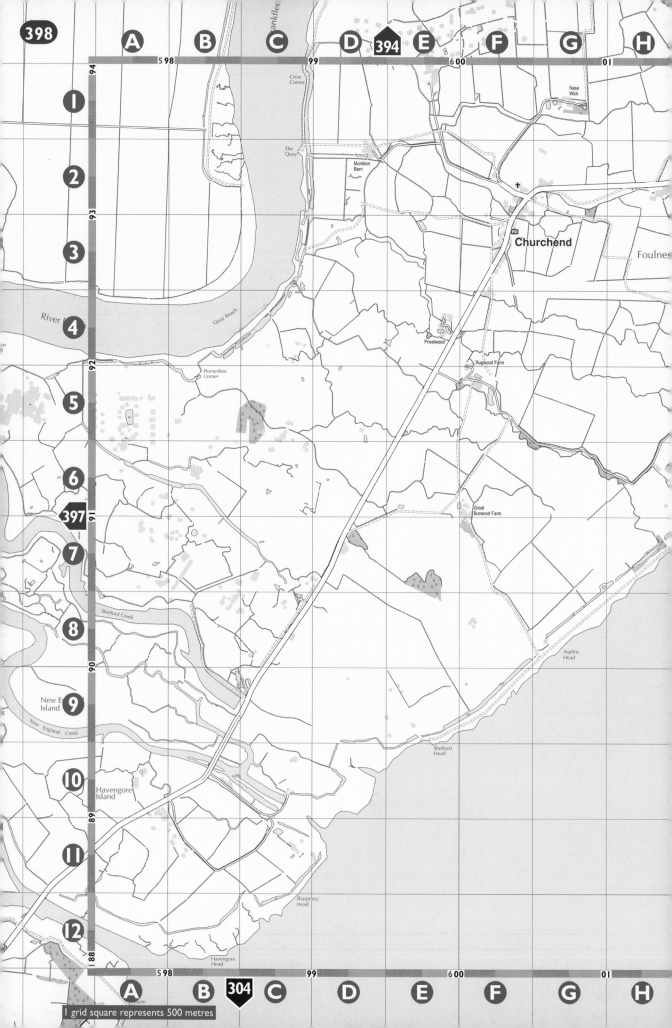

A   B   C   D   E   F   G   H

5 98   99   6 00   01

I

2

3

River

4

5

6

397

7

8

9

10

11

12

Crow
Corner

The Quay

Monkton
Barn

Churchend   Foulnes

Priestwood

Rugwood Farm

Horseshoe
Corner

Great
Burwood Farm

Asplins
Head

Shelford Creek

New E
Island

New England Creek

Havengore
Island

Shelford
Head

Sharpness
Head

Havengore
Head

188

5 98   99   6 00   01

A   B   C   D   E   F   G   H

Nase
Wick

1 grid square represents 500 metres

Courtsend

The Chase

New House Farm

Fishermans Head

East Wick

Eastwick Head

gwood Head

Abberton 153 K2
Abbess End 379 M10
Abbess Roding 379 L9
Abbey Field 107 H8
Abbey Wood 325 L7
Abridge 251 L4
Acton Place 43 K1
Aimes Green 218 A6
Aingers Green 133 H8
Aldborough Hatch 287 H2
Aldbrook 285 M6
Aldham 104 E5
Allen's Green 162 A3
Alphamstone 359 J6
Alresford 131 K5
Althorne 392 D3
Anstey 370 C9
Ardleigh 89 J6
Ardleigh Green 289 M1
Ardleigh Heath 89 H4
Ardley End 378 C4
Arkesden 350 F11
Armigers 373 R11
Ashdon 29 K1
Asheldham 390 A10
Ashen 345 P4
Ashingdon 265 G6
Audley End 351 Q5
Audley End 357 M1
Aveley 329 C5
Aythorpe Roding 379 Q2
Bacon End 140 B3
Baconend Green 140 B1
Baddow Park 226 B3
Baker Street 315 J6
Ballards Gore 396 C3
Ballingdon 20 A9
Balls Green 110 D8
Bamber's Green 375 N10
Bannister Green 119 J8
Bardfield End Green 74 F3
Bardfield Saling 97 K5
Barking 309 G4
Barkingside 286 E1
Barkway 370 C3
Barley 348 F9
Barling 396 H10
Barnston 141 J1
Barstable 278 A7
Bartholomew Green 120 B6
Bartlow 27 K2
Basildon 2
Bath Side 15 J4
Battlesbridge 262 A3
Baythorne End 345 K3
Beacon End 106 A7
Beacon Hill 50 C2
Beacon Hill 172 E7
Beauchamp Roding 379 P12
Beaumont 113 J6
Beazley End 78 F7
Beckton 324 C2
Becontree 310 A2
Bedlar's Green 376 B4
Beggar Hill 223 H6
Belchamp Otten 347 K5
Belchamp St Paul 346 G4
Belchamp Walter 347 P7
Bell Common 235 L2
Belstead 53 H6
Belvedere 326 E8
Bentfield Bury 115 J1
Bentfield Green 115 K1
Bentley 59 H6
Bentley 255 H5
Berden 92 C1
Berechurch 129 H4
Berners Roding 190 B5
Bicknacre 228 C3
Biggin 331 M5
Billericay 258 F2
Birch 151 K1
Birchanger 115 M7
Birch Green 151 K3
Birchall Corner 88 F3
Birdbrook 344 F6
Bird Green 371 R7
Birds Green 381 P5
Bishops Green 141 H5
Bishop's Stortford 138 D2
Blackheath 129 L5
Blackmore 222 C5
Blackmore End 78 E3
Black Notley 121 L8
Blacksmith's Corner 53 H7
Blackwall 323 G4
Blake End 119 K3
Blasford Hill 193 L2
Bobbingworth 380 E9
Bocking 121 J1
Bocking Churchstreet 99 J5
Bocking's Elm 158 D8
Boreham 195 H5
Borley 42 C6
Borley Green 42 A7
Bournes Green 302 E3
Bovinger 380 A10
Bow 306 D6
Bow Common 322 D1
Bowers Gifford 279 H8
Boxted 87 K1
Boxted Cross 362 C12
Boyton Cross 191 L6
Boyton End 36 A8
Boyton End 352 E12
Bradfield 366 C7
Bradfield Heath 366 A9
Bradwell 123 G3
Bradwell-on-Sea 386 G11
Bradwell Waterside 386 E9
Braintree 171 J2
Braiswick 106 E3
Bramford 46 F3
Brandy Hole 263 K1
Bran End 95 M5
Brantham 65 G4
Brays Grove 204 B2
Breeds 167 G7
Brentwood 273 L1
Brewer's End 377 J2
Brick End 375 M4
Brick House End 92 C4
Bricklin Green 92 E6
Bridge End 76 D2
Bridge Green 350 C7
Bridge Street 41 H2
Brightlingsea 156 F3
Brightwell 57 H2
Brimsdown 248 B2
Broad Green 125 H2
Broad Green 349 N8
Broadley Common 202 E6
Broad's Green 167 H8
Broad Street Green 198 F5
Brock Hill 242 E8
Brockley Green 36 B2
Broke Hall 55 H2
Bromley 306 D7
Bromley Cross 109 M1

Brook Street 273 H3
Broomfield 193 L3
Broom Hill 51 K1
Broxbourne 201 H6
Broxted 375 N3
Brundon 42 F8
Buckhurst Hill 267 K2
Buckingham 57 G5
Building End 349 M12
Bulls Cross 232 B6
Bulmer 44 C4
Bulmer Tye 44 C6
Bulphan 293 J4
Bumble's Green 218 A2
Bures 359 Q9
Bures Green 359 R6
Burnham-on-Crouch 393 N8
Burnt Heath 89 L8
Burnt Mills 278 F3
Bursville Park 159 K6
Burton End 374 D9
Burton Green 101 L3
Bury Green 232 C1
Bush End 376 H5
Buttsbury 240 B3
Butt's Green 227 J2
Calford Green 35 L8
California 49 G7
Cambridge Town 302 F7
Campions 189 M7
Camps End 342 D4
Canary Wharf 322 D4
Canewdon 392 A11
Canfield End 377 Q2
Canning Town 323 L1
Cannon's Green 381 N8
Canvey Island 320 B3
Carter's Green 189 M7
Cardinal's Green 32 E3
Carter's Green 189 M7
Castle Camps 343 J6
Castle Green 309 M5
Castle Hedingham 356 F5
Castle Hill 47 M2
Catmere End 350 H1
Cattawade 65 G6
Causeway End 142 E1
Cavendish 39 G3
Chadwell Heath 288 A3
Chadwell St Mary 331 J2
Chafford Hundred 330 B2
Chalk 338 D6
Chalk End 191 H5
Chalkwell 300 D5
Chalvedon 278 D7
Chantry 53 K2
Chapel End 375 K7
Chapel Row 228 D8
Chappel 83 M7
Charlton 324 A4
Chase Cross 271 H5
Chatham Green 168 A2
Chatter End 114 J2
Cheapside 370 C8
Chelmer Village 210 G2
Chelmondiston 365 Q6
Chelmsford 5 K5
Cherry Green 373 M9
Cheshunt 216 C3
Chickney 375 N1
Chignall St James 192 C5
Chignall Smealy 192 C2
Chigwell 268 E1
Chigwell Row 269 L1
Childerditch 274 C6
Chilton 21 K4
Chilton Street 37 H3
Chingford 249 G8
Chingford Green 248 F8
Chingford Hatch 267 H3
Chipping Hill 171 H2
Chipping Ongar 382 H2
Chitts Hills 106 A5
Chrishall 349 Q8
Church End 29 J2
Church End 60 E8
Church End 78 B8
Church End 375 P2
Churchend 117 H2
Churchend 398 F3
Church End 216 C7
Churchgate Street 189 C6
Church Langley 204 E3
Church Street 347 J2
Clacton-on-Sea 7 J3
Clapton Park 306 C1
Clare 37 M5
Clatterford End 164 E6
Clatterford End 381 K7
Clatterford End 382 C4
Claverhambury 218 C5
Clavering 72 D4
Clayhall 268 C8
Clifftown 18 E7
Coalhill 243 H6
Cobbs Fenn 356 E10
Cobler's Green 143 G2
Cock Clarks 229 J3
Cock Green 143 H1
Coggeshall 124 B5
Coggeshall Hamlet 124 B7
Cokenach 370 D2
Colchester 8 A7
Coldharbour 327 A7
Cold Norton 230 B8
Cole End 31 G3
Coles Green 52 A5
Collier Row 270 F7
Colliers Hatch 221 K8
Colne Engaine 82 D4
Cook's Green 159 L4
Cooksmill Green 207 J4
Coopersale Common 220 D7
Coopersale Street 236 D5
Cooper's End 350 B8
Copdock 52 E6
Copford 127 G1
Copford Green 126 F3
Copthall Green 234 E3
Corbets Tey 312 E2
Cornish Hall End 354 A4
Corringham 317 K1
Coryton 318 F4
Countess Cross 83 C3
Courtsend 399 L1
Coxtie Green 255 G3
Cradle End 138 A1
Craig's End 354 A2
Cranbrook 286 D2
Cranham 291 H5
Crawley End 349 Q6
Crays Hill 260 A8
Creekmouth 325 K7
Creeksea 392 H4
Cressing 122 D7
Cripple Corner 358 F2
Crockleford Heath 108 F3
Crockleford Hill 108 D4
Cross End 358 F9

Crow Green 255 K3
Crow's Green 97 H5
Cubitt Town 322 F7
Cuckoo Tye 43 G5
Curling Tye Green 213 K2
Curtismill Green 253 K2
Custom House 324 B3
Cutlers Green 74 A5
Dagenham 310 A4
Danbury 212 A6
Danbury Common 212 B8
Daw's Cross 359 K11
Daws Heath 281 G8
Debden 373 J2
Debden Green 235 K8
Debden Green 373 N4
Dedham 363 M10
Dedham Heath 89 K1
Deer's Green 72 B5
Delvin End 356 A6
Dengie 390 D9
Denton 338 B5
Dewes Green 72 A8
Doddinghurst 383 Q11
Dorking Tye 360 B3
Dovercourt 15 H8
Downham 260 B1
Dry Street 295 J3
Duck End 96 A4
Duck End 115 M8
Duck End 354 B10
Duckend Green 203 J3
Duddenhoe End 350 B7
Dutch Village 320 A1
Duton Hill 94 B3
Duxford 340 D1
Earls Colne 82 F6
East Bergholt 363 R5
East End 65 G3
East End 186 F8
East End 386 G10
East Gores 125 K1
East Ham 325 K4
East Hanningfield 227 M6
East Horndon 275 J4
Easthorpe 126 E6
East Mersea 179 G4
East Tilbury 332 E3
Eastwick 187 J5
Eastwood 282 B8
Edney Common 207 M8
Eight Ash Green 105 L5
Elder Street 222 C5
Elkins Green 222 C5
Elmdon 350 B1
Elm Park 311 L2
Elmstead 109 K5
Elmstead Heath 131 K3
Elmstead Market 109 L7
Elmstead Row 131 L5
Elsenham 374 C3
Emerson Park 290 B4
Enfield Lock 233 G7
Enfield Wash 232 F8
Epping 220 B8
Epping Green 219 H2
Epping Upland 219 K4
Erith 327 J8
Erwarton 66 A3
Eversley 278 E6
Fair Cross 309 J2
Fairlop 269 H7
Fairstead 145 L7
Fanner's Green 166 E8
Farmbridge End 190 F2
Farnham 131 D3
Farnham Green 114 C2
Farther Howegreen 230 B6
Faulkbourne 146 E6
Feering 148 F2
Felixstowe 11 L4
Felixstowe Ferry 63 L3
Felmore 278 D5
Felsted 118 E8
Fiddlers Hamlet 236 D2
Finchingfield 354 A11
Fingringhoe 130 D8
Flack's Green 169 L3
Flamstead End 216 C6
Flint Cross 348 H1
Fobbing 296 A8
Ford End 142 E6
Ford End 371 R11
Fordham 84 F7
Fordham Heath 105 J4
Fordstreet 104 F2
Forest Gate 307 K2
Forry's Green 356 B11
Foster Street 205 G2
Four Wartz 39 M7
Foxash Estate 89 M4
Foxearth 39 M7
Fox Hatch 383 N12
Fox Street 108 D1
Frating 132 B4
Frating Green 132 D2
Freezy Water 232 F6
Freston 364 H2
Friday Hill 267 G2
Frinkle Green 344 F6
Frinton-on-Sea 137 L5
Frogs' Green 31 J1
Fryerning 223 K8
Fryerns 3 L2
Fuller's End 374 D5
Fuller Street 169 G1
Fullwell Cross 269 G7
Further Ford End 371 Q9
Fyfield 381 L6
Gainsborough 55 G5
Gainsford End 355 K5
Galleyend 189 G4
Galleywood 225 M3
Gallows Corner 272 A7
Gallows Green 95 G2
Gallows Green 105 G4
Gamble's Green 169 J3
Gants Hill 286 C4
Gaston Green 163 J3
Garnetts 141 J5
Gaunt's End 374 H6
Gay Bowers 212 D8
Gestingthorpe 357 M12
Gidea Park 271 J8
Gilston 187 L4
Gilston Park 187 K3
Gilwell Park 248 F3
Gipsy Row 58 A3
Glemsford 39 M1
Globe Town 306 A7
Goldhanger 384 C6
Good Easter 165 G8
Goodmans 287 L7
Gooseberry Green 225 J5
Goose Green 112 A2
Goose Green 112 A6
Goose Green 200 D2
Gore Pit 149 H1
Gosfield 80 B5

Grange Hill 269 G5
Gransmore Green 119 J4
Grass Green 345 N12
Gravesend 337 L3
Grays 330 C6
Great Abington 23 L3
Great Amwell 184 F4
Great Baddow 210 A8
Great Bardfield 76 F4
Great Bentley 133 G5
Great Berry 294 D1
Great Braxted 172 F4
Great Bromley 110 B4
Great Burstead 258 F6
Great Canfield 377 R9
Great Chesterford 341 M7
Great Chishill 349 K9
Great Clacton 6 D2
Great Claydons 227 K4
Great Dunmow 116 F6
Great Easton 94 C6
Great Hallingbury 139 L5
Great Henny 358 F1
Great Holland 136 C6
Great Horkesley 86 D4
Great Leighs 144 C7
Great Malgraves 294 C2
Great Maplestead 357 K7
Great Notley 120 E7
Great Oakley 368 A1
Great Oxney Green 208 C4
Great Parndon 203 J3
Great Saling 97 K5
Great Sampford 353 K5
Great Stambridge 396 C6
Great Tey 103 M5
Great Totham 173 G6
Great Wakering 303 K2
Great Waltham 167 H6
Great Warley 273 K7
Great Wigborough 176 B2
Great Yeldham 346 B11
Greenhithe 335 J6
Greenstead 9 M8
Greenstead Green 81 K8
Greensted 382 D2
Greensted Green 382 C2
Green Street 239 G1
The Green 145 M1
Greenwich 54 C4
Greenwich 323 G8
Gubbion's Green 144 F5
Hackney Wick 306 D3
Hacton 312 B2
Hadleigh 299 H2
Hadstock 26 F3
Hailey 185 G7
Hainault 269 J6
Hale End 267 G5
Hallingbury Street 376 C5
Hallsford Bridge 383 J4
Halls Green 202 D3
Halstead 81 G3
Hamperden End 373 M7
Hanchet End 33 L4
Handley Green 224 A5
Hardy's Green 127 G7
Hare Green 110 D3
Hare Street 12 C9
Harkstead 365 L11
Harlow 11 H6
Harold Hill 272 B4
Harold Park 272 E5
Harold Wood 272 D7
Hartford End 143 G5
Harwich 15 H4
Hastingwood 205 G5
Hatfield Broad Oak 376 G12
Hatfield Heath 378 C2
Hatfield Peverel 196 E1
Haverhill 34 A5
Havering-atte-Bower 271 H2
Hawbush Green 122 C8
Hawkin's Hill 353 P9
Hawkspur Green 353 N12
Hawkwell 264 D8
Hay Green 222 C8
Hazeleigh 229 J1
Hazel End 115 H5
Hazel Stub 33 M6
Heath Park 289 L4
The Heath 59 L7
Heckfordbridge 127 L5
Helions Bumpstead 343 L5
Hellman's Cross 377 N7
Hemp's Green 84 E7
Hempstead 343 J12
Henham 372 F12
Henny Street 45 J8
Herongate 275 H3
Hertford Heath 184 C6
Heybridge 198 F2
Heybridge 239 L3
Heybridge Basin 215 G2
Heydon 349 M6
Higham 363 J5
Higham Hill 266 B8
Highams Park 249 E6
High Beach 249 L1
High Easter 164 F3
Highfields 149 G5
High Garrett 99 M3
High Houses 167 G6
High Laver 380 C3
High Ongar 383 L1
High Park Corner 130 F7
High Roding 140 B6
Highstreet Green 356 B7
The High 13 G6
High Wych 162 C8
Hildersham 24 C4
Hill Green 341 G4
Hinxton 340 H1
Hobbs Cross 189 H8
Hobbs Cross 236 E6
Hockerill 139 J3
Hockley 263 M6
Hoddesdon 200 F4
Holbrook 364 G7
Holder's Green 75 H7
Holland-on-Sea 160 B4
Holton St Mary 363 P3
Holyfield 217 K6
Homerton 306 A3
Honey Tye 361 J5
Hook End 383 R9
Hope End Green 377 M4
Hope's Green 297 M3
Horkesley Heath 86 D6
Hornchurch 290 C4
Horndon on the Hill 316 C10
Horne Row 211 M7
Hornestreet 362 E12
Horns Cross 335 J8
Horseheath 32 E2
Horseman Side 254 B4
Horsley Cross 111 K2
Horsleycross Street 91 K7
Housham Tye 189 L7

Howe Green 139 M7
Howe Green 226 F2
Howegreen 229 M5
Howe Street 167 H5
Howe Street 354 E8
Howlett End 31 K7
Hullbridge 263 H2
Hunsdonbury 186 D5
Hurst Green 156 D7
Hutton 256 F2
Hutton Mount 256 F4
Hyde Chase 229 C1
The Hythe 130 A1
Ickleton 340 H6
Ilford 286 E8
Ingatestone 239 M2
Ingrave 274 F1
Inworth 149 G5
Ipswich 17 H7
Isle of Dogs 322 F7
Ivy Chimneys 235 M2
Jack's Hatch 203 J7
Janke's Green 84 A3
Jasper's Green 98 A3
Jaywick 182 G5
Katherines 202 F4
Kedington 35 L3
Keelars Tye 131 K2
Keeres Green 164 K4
Kelvedon 149 G4
Kelvedon Hatch 383 L11
Kesgrave 201 J8
Keysers Estate 201 J8
Kings Farm 337 M8
Kingsmoor 203 K6
Kingston 51 L2
King Street 383 G2
Kingswood 3
Kirby Cross 136 E2
Kirby-le-Soken 368 F12
Knockhall 335 L5
Knowl Green 346 C6
Laindon 277 C6
Lakeside 329 K7
Lamarsh 359 M5
Lamb Corner 89 C1
Lambourne 252 A4
Lambourne End 251 M7
Langdon Hills 294 D1
Langenhoe 153 K3
Langford 198 A6
Langham 88 C3
Langley 371 P5
Langley Green 125 J3
Langley Lower Green 371 N6
Langley Upper Green 371 N6
Latchingdon 231 K8
Latchmore Bank 139 H7
Lattinford Hill 58 F7
Latton Bush 204 B5
Lawford 90 D2
Layer Breton 151 L3
Layer de la Haye 128 C3
Layer Marney 151 H5
Lea Bridge 284 A4
Leaden Roding 379 G4
Leavenheath 361 L4
Lee Chapel 2
Lee-over-Sands 180 F7
Leigh Beck 321 G4
Leigh-on-Sea 300 A4
Level's Green 114 D4
Levington 60 D2
Lexden 106 C7
Leyton 285 G8
Leytonstone 285 H4
Limehouse 322 B3
Lindsell 95 J2
Linford 332 C1
Linton 332 C1
Lippitts Hill 249 J2
Liston 42 D3
Liston Garden 42 B1
Little Abington 24 A1
Little Baddow 212 A1
Little Bardfield 76 A3
Little Bealings 50 C1
Little Bentley 111 K5
Little Braxted 171 M3
Little Bromley 90 E7
Little Burstead 276 D1
Littlebury 351 M1
Littlebury Green 350 H4
Little Cambridge 94 E2
Little Chesterford 341 M9
Little Chishill 349 K12
Little Clacton 159 G2
Little Dunmow 118 B6
Little Easton 94 D6
Little End 382 F2
Little Hallingbury 163 K1
Little Heath 287 A2
Little Henham 372 E9
Little Horkesley 86 B2
Little Ilford 308 C2
Little Laver 380 C1
Little Leighs 144 F3
Little Linton 24 D6
Little London 92 E1
Little London 354 A6
Little Maplestead 357 P6
Little Mascals 226 D4
Little Oakley 70 B6
Little Oxney Green 208 A5
Little Pardon 12 C4
Little Sampford 353 M9
Little Tey 125 M1
Little Thurrock 330 D4
Little Totham 199 K5
Little Wakering 396 H11
Little Walden 28 C1
Little Waltham 167 M7
Little Warley 274 C4
Little Wenham 58 B2
Little Wigborough 176 B2
Little Wratting 35 G2
Little Yeldham 346 F9
Littley Green 143 J6
Long Gardens 358 C4
Long Melford 43 G2
Loughton 250 C4
Loves Green 207 K8
Lower Bobbingworth Green 380 C10
Lower Falkenham 62 D1
Lower Green 104 C6
Lower Green 210 F8
Lower Green 355 M4
Lower Green 371 K8
Lower Holbrook 365 K10
Lower Nazeing 217 L2
Lower Sheering 163 H8
Lower Street 364 C12
Lower Street 308 G3
Loxford 308 C3
Loyter's Green 205 J4
Lucking Street 357 M1
Mace Green 52 C6
Magdalen Laver 205 L4
Maggots End 92 F5

Maidenhall 54 A3
Maldon 214 E2
Mallows Green 92 D7
Manningtree 90 E1
Manor Park 308 B1
Manuden 93 G7
Manwood Green 378 F8
Maple End 352 A2
Marden Ash 382 G4
Margaret Roding 379 E8
Margaretting 224 D5
Margaretting Tye 224 F6
Mark Hall North 188 B6
Mark Hall South 188 B7
Marks Gate 270 B8
Marks Tey 126 C1
Martlesham 50 F3
Martlesham Heath 50 F7
Mashbury 191 M1
Matching 378 B9
Matching Green 378 E10
Matching Tye 378 A10
Mayland 388 F9
Maylandsea 388 B8
Maypole Green 129 G4
Meadowend 345 P8
Meesden 371 L10
Messing 149 M3
Middleton 45 H5
Mile End 87 K8
Mile End 306 B8
Milend Green 94 F5
Miller's Green 381 F5
Mill Green 32 F6
Mill Green 223 J6
Mill Hill 263 L6
Mill Meads 307 G6
Millwall 322 D6
Milton 338 A4
Minnow End 167 K6
Mistley 91 K1
Mistley Heath 91 L3
Molehill Green 119 M8
Molehill Green 375 L7
Monk Street 74 E6
Montsale 394 G5
Moreton 380 D7
Mott's Green 163 L3
Moulsham 5 G7
Mount Bovers 282 A2
Mount Bures 359 P11
Mount End 237 G2
Mountnessing 239 G5
Mount Pleasant 36 E1
Mowden 196 A4
Mucking 317 G6
Muckingford 332 C2
Mundon 231 H3
Nacton 56 B8
Navestock Heath 253 M2
Navestock Side 254 F2
Nayland 361 N8
Nazeing 202 C8
Nazeing Gate 218 D3
Nazeing Long Green 218 B3
Nazeing Mead 201 L4
Needham Green 378 H1
Nether Street 379 P9
Netteswell 13 K4
Nevendon 278 F2
Newbourne 57 L3
Newbury Park 287 G4
New Charlton 324 A7
New England 344 H3
New House 337 H7
Newman's End 378 A8
Newman's Green 43 K5
New Mistley 91 K2
Newney Green 207 L3
Newport 372 B1
Newsells 348 C12
New Thundersley 280 A6
New Town 334 C8
Nine Ashes 383 R3
Noak Bridge 277 J4
Noak Hill 272 B1
Noak Hill 276 F1
North Benfleet 279 J5
North End 142 B3
North End 346 C10
Northend 351 P1
Northend 389 N12
North Fambridge 246 D6
Northfleet 336 F3
North Ockendon 313 L2
North Shoebury 303 J4
North Stifford 314 B7
North Weald Bassett 221 G4
North Woolwich 324 B5
Norton Heath 206 B7
Norton Mandeville 381 N11
Norwood End 381 K4
Nosterfield End 33 J8
Nounsley 196 D3
Nuper's Hatch 253 H7
Nuthampstead 370 G5
Old Felixstowe 63 J8

Old Ford 306 B5
Old Harlow 188 E5
Old Heath 129 M2
Old Mead 374 E1
Olmstead Green 342 H6
Onslow Green 142 A4
Orsett 315 L5
Orsett Heath 331 J1
Ostend 392 H6
Ovington 346 C4
Oxen End 76 B7
Oxley Green 174 D4
Padham's Green 239 L6
Paglesham Churchend 396 G2
Paglesham Eastend 397 K4
Pale Green 343 N4
Pampisford 22 D4
Panfield 98 D6
Pannel's Ash 345 R4
Parkeston 70 D1
Parkgate 142 B5
Park Green 92 C3
Parney Heath 88 E1
Parrock Farm 338 A8
Parsonage Green 193 K5
Parson's Heath 108 A4
Paslow Wood Common 383 Q4
Passingford Bridge 253 C1
Passmores 203 L4
Paternoster Heath 174 D2
Pattiswick 101 H8
Peartree Green 238 A3
Pebmarsh 358 C10
Pedlars End 153 G7
Peldon 153 G7
Pentlow 39 H7
Pentlow Street 39 K5
Pepper's Green 190 E4
Perry Green 123 G4
Perry Street 337 J5
Pharisee Green 116 D8
Philpot End 140 D3
Piercing Hill 235 L5
Pigstye Green 206 C4
Pilgrims Hatch 255 L4
Pin Mill 365 Q4
Pinnacles 12 B8
Pipps Hill 2 D1
Pitsea 278 E8
Plaistow 307 J7
Plashet 308 A3
Pledgdon Green 375 K5
Pleshey 166 B3
Plumstead 324 F8
Point Clear 180 E5
Pond Street 350 A6
Poplar 322 D3
The Port of Felixstowe 10 A8
Potash 59 H6
Potter Street 204 E3
Powers Hall End 170 F2
Presdales 184 F7
Priory Heath 55 J4
Prittlewell 301 H2
Purfleet 328 D8
Purleigh 230 B4
Puttock End 347 L7
Puttock's End 377 L5
Queen's Park 240 D7
Quendon 372 A7
Racecourse 54 E7
Radley Green 206 F6
Radwinter 352 B2
Radwinter End 342 D9
Rainham 311 L7
Ramsden Bellhouse 260 B4
Ramsden Heath 260 A1
Ramsey 367 Q7
Ramsey Island 389 L1
Rank's Green 145 G5
Raven's Green 110 F8
Rawreth 262 B6
Rawreth Shot 261 M6
Rayleigh 281 G2
Rayne 120 B3
Reader's Corner 210 B8
Redbridge 285 M3
Rettendon 243 L4
Richmond's Green 75 G6
Rickling 73 J5
Rickling Green 93 L1
Ridgewell 345 M7
Ringtail Green 142 B8
Rise Park 271 H7
Rivenhall 147 L6
Rivenhall End 148 B7
Roast Green 72 A3
Robinhood End 354 C4
Rochford 283 K3
Rodbridge Corner 42 F5
Romford 208 B3
Rook End 372 H4
Roost End 344 F1
Rosedale 216 A6
Rose Green 84 B8
Rose Green 360 D1

Rose Hill 17 M8
Rosherville 337 J3
Rotherhithe 322 A6
Rotten End 78 D6
Roundbush 230 D5
Roundbush Green 379 R3
Row Green 121 G7
Row Heath 158 D2
Rowhedge 130 B5
Roxwell 191 G7
Roydon 186 C8
Roydon Hamlet 202 D5
Rudley Green 229 M2
Runsell Green 212 D6
Runwell 261 H4
Rush Green 182 E2
Rush Green 184 D3
Rush Green 289 H5
Rushley Green 356 G3
Rushmere St Andrew 49 J5
Rushmere Street 156 B4
Rye Meads 185 L8
Rye Park 201 J2
Sabine's Green 254 A2
Saffron Walden 28 D8
St Lawrence 389 Q4
St Margarets 185 H5
St Osyth 181 L1
St Osyth Heath 158 B4
St Vincent's Hamlet 254 D8
Salcott-cum-Virley 175 K5
Samson's Corner 156 B4
Samuel's Corner 304 A1
Sandon 210 F7
Sawbridgeworth 162 C7
Sawston 22 D2
School Green 78 E2
Scotland Street 361 R4
Seawick 181 M6
Seven Kings 287 H6
Seven Star Green 105 J5
Sewards End 29 H8
Sewardstone 248 F2
Sewardstonebury 249 H5
Shaftenhoe End 348 G11
Shalford 78 A6
Shalford Green 97 M2
Sheering 189 L1
Shelley 380 H10
Shellow Bowells 206 C1
Shenfield 256 B3
Shoeburyness 303 K7
Shop Corner 365 R12
Shotgate 261 L7
Shotley 66 D2
Shotley Gate 67 G4
Shrub End 128 E1
Shudy Camps 32 E7
Sible Hedingham 356 F7
Sibley's Green 74 E8
Silver End 147 H1
Silvertown 323 M5
Skye Green 125 H4
Smith's End 348 F11
Smith's Green 343 Q8
Smith's Green 377 L2
Smythe's Green 150 F3
Snow End 370 F10
South Benfleet 298 B2
South Bromley 323 G2
Southchurch 302 B5
Southend-on-Sea 18 E3
Southey Green 356 D12
South Fambridge 264 E1
Southfields 276 B6
Southfields 316 A7
South Green 154 D2
South Green 259 G6
South Hanningfield 243 G5
South Heath 157 J2
South Hornchurch 311 G5
Southminster 393 L2
South Ockendon 313 M8
South Stifford 330 A4
South Weald 273 H1
South Woodford 267 K8
South Woodham Ferrers 245 J4
Spellbrook 162 F1
Spitalbrook 201 H5
Springfield 194 A7
Springwell 341 P10
Sproughton 47 G7
Stafford's Corner 152 B8
Stagden Cross 165 J3
Stambourne 344 H11
Stambourne Green 344 F12
Stanway 105 M8
Stanway Green 128 A2
Stapleford Abbotts 253 G6
Stapleford Tawney 237 K6
Starling's Green 72 A6

Start Hill 376 B2
Stebbing 96 B8
Stebbing Green 119 G2
Steeple 388 H6
Steeple Bumpstead 344 A5
Steventon End 27 M7
Stewards 203 M6
Steward's Green 236 C2
Stickling Green 72 E3
Stisted 100 F7
Stock 241 J2
Stocking Green 29 L8
Stoke 16 D8
Stoke by Clare 345 P2
Stoke-by-Nayland 361 N4
Stoke Park 53 L4
Stoke Tye 361 N1
Stondon Massey 383 P8
Stone 335 J7
Stonebridge 396 C11
Stones Green 113 G3
Stonewood 336 A8
Stoneyhills 393 M6
Stow Maries 245 M1
Stratford 306 F4
Stratford Marsh 306 E5
Stratford New Town 306 F3
Stratford St Mary 363 K7
Strethall 350 F1
Stroud Green 282 F3
Sturmer 344 D1
Stutton 364 C11
Sucksted Green 373 Q11
Sudbury 20 A6
Sumners 203 H5
Sunken Marsh 298 F8
Sunnymede 259 C3
Surrex 125 H3
Swallows Cross 238 C3
Swanscombe 336 C3
Swan Street 103 M2
Takeley 377 J1
Takeley Street 376 G2
Tarpots 279 N8
Tattingstone 59 M6
Tattingstone White Horse 364 A4
Taverners Green 377 K9
Temple End 347 Q2
Temple Fields 188 B5
Temple Hill 334 A6
Temple Mills 306 E2
Tendring 112 C8
Tendring Green 112 B5
Tendring Heath 111 M4
Terling 169 M2
Thamesmead 325 J3
Thaxted 74 E2
Theydon Bois 235 L7
Theydon Garnon 236 D6
Theydon Mount 237 H6
Thistley Green 143 L1
Thorington Street 362 D6
Thorley 138 D7
Thorley Houses 138 B4
Thorley Street 138 F6
Thornwood Common 220 C3
Thorpe Bay 302 E6
Thorpe Common 61 K5
Thorpe Green 135 J1
Thorpe-le-Soken 135 J3
Thorrington 132 E8
Thresher's Bush 205 H2
Thundersley 280 B7
Tilbury 331 K7
Tilbury Green 345 Q7
Tilbury Juxta Clare 346 D2
Tilegate Green 205 L3
Tilekiln Green 376 A3
Tilkey 124 C1
Tillingham 390 E5
Tilty 94 A4
Tindon End 352 E8
Tip's Cross 383 R8
Tiptree 149 L2
Tiptree Heath 173 L2
Tolleshunt D'Arcy 384 F1
Tolleshunt Knights 174 D3
Tolleshunt Major 384 B1
Toot Hill 382 A4
Toppesfield 355 N2
Totham Hill 173 H8
Totham Plains 173 L8
Trimley Lower Street 61 K7
Trimley St Martin 61 M4
Trimley St Mary 62 B7
Trims Green 162 D2
Turnford 216 E3
Twinstead 358 F3
Twinstead Green 358 D4
Tye Common 258 C6
Tye Green 31 M6
Tye Green 122 B7
Tye Green 165 H7
Tye Green 203 L3
Tye Green 374 F7
Tyler's Green 221 L2

Ugley 372 A11
Ugley Green 374 B2
Ulting 196 F6
Upminster 290 F7
Uppend 92 C8
Upper Dovercourt 70 C2
Upper Street 364 B12
Upper Walthamstow 284 C2
Upshire 234 D2
Upton 307 L4
Upton Park 307 M5
Vange 296 B1
Wakes Colne 83 L7
Wakes Colne Green 83 M4
Wallend 308 D5
Waltham Abbey 233 L2
Waltham Cross 232 D3
Waltham's Cross 77 H4
Walthamstow 284 C2
Walton 62 E8
Walton-on-the-Naze 369 J12
Wanstead 285 L5
Warley 273 L4
Warren Heath 55 L4
Washbrook 52 D4
Washbrook Street 52 D3
Watch House Green 119 H6
Water End 29 L3
Waterhales 254 A6
Watton's Green 253 L6
Weeley 134 C4
Weeley Heath 134 C7
Weir 280 F5
Wellstye Green 141 K3
Welshwood Park 108 C4
Wendens Ambo 351 M8
Wennington 328 B3
West Bergholt 106 B2
Westbourne 47 K4
West Court 338 B7
Westerfield 48 D1
West Hanningfield 242 E1
West Horndon 274 F8
Westley Heights 294 F3
West Mersea 177 K7
West Thurrock 329 K8
West Tilbury 332 B5
Westwood Park 86 B4
Wethersfield 77 L2
Wherstead 54 A7
Whiteash Green 80 C2
White Colne 83 H7
White House 47 K3
White Notley 146 B4
White Roding or
White Roothing 379 K6
Whitton 47 J2
Wicken Bonhunt 73 J1
Wickford 260 E5
Wickham Bishops 172 A8
Wickham St Paul 357 R4
Widdington 372 G5
Widford 209 H7
Wiggens Green 343 P4
Willingale 381 R6
Willows Green 144 B1
Wimbish 31 M3
Wimbish Green 352 B6
Winter Gardens 298 B8
Witham 171 K4
Withermarsh Green 362 C2
Withersfield 34 A1
Wivenhoe 130 A1
Wix 366 F12
Wixoe 345 J2
Woodend 379 M12
Woodend Green 373 J2
Woodford 267 L5
Woodford Bridge 268 C6
Woodford Green 267 K6
Woodford Wells 267 L2
Woodgates End 375 L6
Wood Green 234 D4
Woodham Ferrers 244 E1
Woodham Mortimer 213 G8
Woodham Walter 212 F3
Woodhill 211 L7
The Woodlands 360 E6
Woodside 220 E4
Woodside Green 376 A8
Woollensbrook 184 B8
Woolverstone 365 K4
Workhouse Green 359 P2
Workhouse Hill 87 H1
Wormingford 360 C12
Wormley 216 F2
Wormleybury 216 C1
Wormley West End 200 B8
Wrabness 367 J6
Wright's Green 163 L2
Writtle 208 D5
Young's End 144 D1

USING THE STREET INDEX

Street names are listed alphabetically. Each street name is followed by its postal town or area locality, the Postcode District, the page number, and the reference to the square in which the name is found.

Standard index entries are shown as follows:

Aalten Av *CVI* SS8...................**321**   J2

Street names and selected addresses not shown on the map due to scale restrictions are shown in the index with an asterisk:

Abbey Pl *DART* DA1 * ....**334**   A

GENERAL ABBREVIATIONS

ACC	ACCESS
ALY	ALLEY
AP	APPROACH
AR	ARCADE
ASS	ASSOCIATION
AV	AVENUE
BCH	BEACH
BLDS	BUILDINGS
BND	BEND
BNK	BANK
BR	BRIDGE
BRK	BROOK
BTM	BOTTOM
BUS	BUSINESS
BVD	BOULEVARD
BY	BYPASS
CATH	CATHEDRAL
CEM	CEMETERY
CEN	CENTRE
CFT	CROFT
CH	CHURCH
CHA	CHASE
CHYD	CHURCHYARD
CIR	CIRCLE
CIRC	CIRCUS
CL	CLOSE
CLFS	CLIFFS
CMP	CAMP
CNR	CORNER
CO	COUNTY
COLL	COLLEGE
COM	COMMON
COMM	COMMISSION
CON	CONVENT
COT	COTTAGE
COTS	COTTAGES
CP	CAPE
CPS	COPSE
CR	CREEK
CREM	CREMATORIUM
CRS	CRESCENT
CSWY	CAUSEWAY
CT	COURT
CTRL	CENTRAL
CTS	COURTS
CTYD	COURTYARD
CUTT	CUTTINGS
CV	COVE
CYN	CANYON
DEPT	DEPARTMENT
DL	DALE
DM	DAM
DR	DRIVE
DRO	DROVE
DRY	DRIVEWAY
DWGS	DWELLINGS
E	EAST
EMB	EMBANKMENT
EMBY	EMBASSY
ESP	ESPLANADE
EST	ESTATE
EX	EXCHANGE
EXPY	EXPRESSWAY
EXT	EXTENSION
F/O	FLYOVER
FC	FOOTBALL CLUB
FK	FORK
FLD	FIELD
FLDS	FIELDS
FLS	FALLS
FLS	FLATS
FM	FARM
FT	FORT
FWY	FREEWAY
FY	FERRY
GA	GATE
GAL	GALLERY
GDN	GARDEN
GDNS	GARDENS
GLD	GLADE
GLN	GLEN
GN	GREEN
GND	GROUND
GRA	GRANGE
GRG	GARAGE
GT	GREAT
GTWY	GATEWAY
GV	GROVE
HGR	HIGHER
HL	HILL
HLS	HILLS
HO	HOUSE
HOL	HOLLOW
HOSP	HOSPITAL
HRB	HARBOUR
HTH	HEATH
HTS	HEIGHTS
HVN	HAVEN
HWY	HIGHWAY
IMP	IMPERIAL
IN	INLET
IND EST	INDUSTRIAL ESTATE
INF	INFIRMARY
INFO	INFORMATION
INT	INTERCHANGE
IS	ISLAND
JCT	JUNCTION
JTY	JETTY
KG	KING
KNL	KNOLL
L	LAKE
LA	LANE
LDG	LODGE
LGT	LIGHT
LK	LOCK
LKS	LAKES
LNDG	LANDING
LTL	LITTLE
LWR	LOWER
MAG	MAGISTRATE
MAN	MANSIONS
MD	MEAD
MDW	MEADOWS
MEM	MEMORIAL
MKT	MARKET
MKTS	MARKETS
ML	MALL
ML	MILL
MNR	MANOR
MS	MEWS
MSN	MISSION
MT	MOUNT
MTN	MOUNTAIN
MTS	MOUNTAINS
MUS	MUSEUM
MWY	MOTORWAY
N	NORTH
NE	NORTH EAST
NW	NORTH WEST
O/P	OVERPASS
OFF	OFFICE
ORCH	ORCHARD
OV	OVAL
PAL	PALACE
PAS	PASSAGE
PAV	PAVILION
PDE	PARADE
PH	PUBLIC HOUSE
PK	PARK
PKWY	PARKWAY
PL	PLACE
PLN	PLAIN
PLNS	PLAINS
PLZ	PLAZA
POL	POLICE STATION
PR	PRINCE
PREC	PRECINCT
PREP	PREPARATORY
PRIM	PRIMARY
PROM	PROMENADE
PRS	PRINCESS
PRT	PORT
PT	POINT
PTH	PATH
PZ	PIAZZA
QD	QUADRANT
QU	QUEEN
QY	QUAY
R	RIVER
RBT	ROUNDABOUT
RD	ROAD
RDG	RIDGE
REP	REPUBLIC
RES	RESERVOIR
RFC	RUGBY FOOTBALL CLUB
RI	RISE
RP	RAMP
RW	ROW
S	SOUTH
SCH	SCHOOL
SE	SOUTH EAST
SER	SERVICE AREA
SH	SHORE
SHOP	SHOPPING
SKWY	SKYWAY
SMT	SUMMIT
SOC	SOCIETY
SP	SPUR
SPR	SPRING
SQ	SQUARE
ST	STREET
STN	STATION
STR	STREAM
STRD	STRAND
SW	SOUTH WEST
TDG	TRADING
TER	TERRACE
THWY	THROUGHWAY
TNL	TUNNEL
TOLL	TOLLWAY
TPK	TURNPIKE
TR	TRACK
TRL	TRAIL
TWR	TOWER
U/P	UNDERPASS
UNI	UNIVERSITY
UPR	UPPER
V	VALE
VA	VALLEY
VIAD	VIADUCT
VIL	VILLA
VIS	VISTA
VLG	VILLAGE
VLS	VILLAS
VW	VIEW
W	WEST
WD	WOOD
WHF	WHARF
WK	WALK
WKS	WALKS
WLS	WELLS
WY	WAY
YD	YARD
YHA	YOUTH HOSTEL

POSTCODE TOWNS AND AREA ABBREVIATIONS

ABR/ST	Abridge/Stapleford Abbotts
ABYW	Abbey Wood
BARK	Barking
BARK/HLT	Barkingside/Hainault
BCAYE	Billericay east
BCAYW	Billericay west
BCTR	Becontree
BELV	Belvedere
BERM/RHTH	Bermondsey/Rotherhithe
BETH	Bethnal Green
BKHH	Buckhurst Hill
BKHTH/KID	Blackheath/Kidbrooke
BOC	Burnham-on-Crouch
BOW	Bow
BROX	Broxbourne
BRTR	Braintree
BRW	Brentwood
BRWN	Brentwood north
BSDN	Basildon
BSF	Bishop's Stortford
BUNT	Buntingford
BURES	Bures
CAN/RD	Canning Town/Royal Docks
CBE/LIN	Cambridge east/Linton
CBS	Cambridge south
CDW/CHF	Chadwell St Mary/Chafford Hundred
CHARL	Charlton
CHDH	Chadwell Heath
CHES/WCR	Cheshunt/Waltham Cross
CHESW	Cheshunt west
CHIG	Chigwell
CHING	Chingford
CHLM/GWD	Chelmsford/Galleywood
CHLM/WR	Chelmsford/Writtle
CHONG	Chipping Ongar
CHTY	Chantry
CLAY	Clayhall
CLPT	Clapton
COL	Colchester
COLN	Colchester north
COLS	Colchester south
COLW	Colchester west
COS	Clacton-on-Sea
CRW	Collier Row
CVI	Canvey Island
DAGE	Dagenham east
DAGW	Dagenham west
DART	Dartford
DEPT	Deptford
ED	Edmonton
EHAM	East Ham
EMPK	Emerson Park
EN	Enfield
ENC/FH	Enfield Chase/Forty Hill
EPP	Epping
ERITH	Erith
ERITHM	Erith Marshes
FOS	Frinton-on-Sea
FRAM/WMKT	Framlingham/Wickham Market
FSTGT	Forest Gate
FX	Felixstowe
GDMY/SEVK	Goodmayes/Seven Kings
GNTH/NBYPK	Gants Hill/Newbury Park
GNWCH	Greenwich
GPK	Gidea Park
GRAYS	Grays
GRH	Greenhithe
GTDUN	Great Dunmow
GVE	Gravesend east
GVW	Gravesend west
HADL	Hadleigh
HAR	Harwich
HARH	Harold Hill
HCH	Hornchurch
HERT/BAY	Hertford/Bayford
HLW	Harlow
HLWE	Harlow east
HLWS	Harlow south
HLWW/ROY	Harlow west/Roydon
HOC/HUL	Hockley/Hullbridge
HOD	Hoddesdon
HOM	Homerton
HOO/HM	Hoo St Werburgh/Higham
HSTD	Halstead
HVHL	Haverhill
IL	Ilford
ING	Ingatestone
IP	Ipswich
IPNE	Ipswich northeast
IPSE	Ipswich southeast
K/T/MI	Kelvedon/Tiptree/Mersea Island
KESG	Kesgrave
KIR/NAC	Kirton/Nacton
LAIN	Laindon
LEY	Leyton
LOS	Leigh-on-Sea
LOU	Loughton
MAL	Maldon
MEO	Meopham
MGTR	Manningtree
MHAD	Much Hadham
MNPK	Manor Park
NHMKT	Needham Market
NWCR	New Cross
PEND	Ponders End
PIT	Pitsea
PLSTW	Plaistow
POP/IOD	Poplar/Isle of Dogs
PUR	Purfleet
RAIN	Rainham (Gt Lon)
RAYL	Rayleigh
RBRTR	Rural Braintree
RBRW/HUT	Rural Brentwood/Hutton
RBSEDS	Rural Bury St Edmunds south
RBSF	Rural Bishop's Stortford
RCFD	Rochford
RCHLM	Rural Chelmsford
RCOLE	Rural Colchester east
RCOLW	Rural Colchester west
RCOS	Rural Clacton-on-Sea
RDART	Rural Dartford
REDBR	Redbridge
RIPS/CAP	Rural Ipswich south/Capel St Mary
RIPW	Rural Ipswich west
ROM	Romford
ROMW/RG	Romford west/Rush Green
ROY	Royston
SAFWN	Saffron Walden north
SAFWS	Saffron Walden south
SBF/HAD	South Benfleet/Hadleigh
SBN/FI	Shoeburyness/Foulness Island
SBW	Sawbridgeworth
SLH/COR	Stanford-le-Hope/Corringham
SOCK/AV	South Ockendon/Aveley
SOS	Southend-on-Sea
SOSN	Southend-on-Sea north
SRTFD	Stratford
STDN	Standon
STSD	Stansted
SUD	Sudbury
SWCM	Swanscombe
SWFD	South Woodford
THMD	Thamesmead
TIL	Tilbury
TOTM	Tottenham
UED	Upper Edmonton
UPMR	Upminster
VGE	Vange
WAB	Waltham Abbey
WALTH	Walthamstow
WAN	Wanstead
WAP	Wapping
WARE	Ware
WCHPL	Whitechapel
WDBR	Woodbridge
WFD	Woodford
WICKE	Wickford east
WICKW	Wickford west
WIT	Witham
WOOL/PLUM	Woolwich/Plumstead
WOS/PRIT	Westcliff-on-Sea/Prittlewell
WOTN	Walton-on-the-Naze
WTHK	West Thurrock

1

1 Av *WOOL/PLUM* SE18 ... **324** E6

A

Aalten Av *CVI* SS8 ... **321** J2
Aaron Hill Rd *EHAM* E6 ... **324** D1
Abbas Wk *SUD* CO10 ... **45** M4
Abberton Rd *COLS* CO2 ... **128** F8
K/T/MI CO5 ... **153** M2
Abbess Cl *CHLM/WR* CM1 ... **4** A4
Abbey Cl *CHONG* CM5 ... **381** K8
HOC/HUL SS5 ... **263** G3
ROM RM1 ... **289** J4
Abbey Ct *WAB* EN9 ... **233** J4
Abbey Crs *BELV* DA17 ... **326** D7
RCOS CO16 ... **135** K4
Abbey Dale Cl *HLWE* CM17 ... **204** D2
Abbey Flds *RCHLM* CM3 ... **227** L6
Abbey Gate St *COL* CO1 ... **8** C8
Abbey Gv *ABYW* SE2 ... **325** L7
Abbey La *RCOLW* CO6 ... **124** D4
SAFWN CB10 ... **28** A8
SRTFD E15 ... **306** F6
Abbey Meadow *HSTD* CO9 ... **356** E7
Abbey Ms *WALTH* E17 ... **284** D3
Abbey Mt *BELV* DA17 ... **326** C8
Abbey Pl *DART* DA1 * ... **334** A7
Abbey Rd *BARK* IG11 ... **308** F5
BCAYW CM12 ... **258** C4
BELV DA17 ... **326** A7
CHES/WCR EN8 ... **232** F4
GNTH/NBYPK IG2 ... **287** G3
GRH DA9 ... **335** M7
GVE DA12 ... **338** B6
HOC/HUL SS5 ... **263** G4
SRTFD E15 ... **307** G6
SUD CO10 ... **20** C2
Abbey St *PLSTW* E13 ... **307** K8
RCOS CO16 ... **135** K4
SAFWN CB10 ... **340** H5
Abbey Ter *ABYW* SE2 ... **325** M6
Abbey Turning *MAL* CM9 ... **214** A2
Abbey Vw *GTDUN* CM6 ... **94** B3
Abbeyview *WAB* EN9 ... **233** K3
Abbey Wood La *RAIN* RM13 ... **312** A6
Abbey Wood Rd *ABYW* SE2 ... **325** L7
Abbotsbury Cl *CHTY* IP2 ... **53** M4
SRTFD E15 ... **306** F6
Abbots Cl *BRWN* CM15 ... **256** D4
COS CO15 ... **159** H7
MGTR CO11 ... **366** F12
RAIN RM13 ... **311** M6
Abbots Ct *LAIN* SS15 ... **277** H4
Abbotsford Gdns *WFD* IG8 ... **267** K6
Abbotsford Rd
GDMY/SEVK IG3 ... **287** K7
Abbots Gdns *RCOS* CO16 ... **181** M1
Abbotshade Rd
BERM/RHTH SE16 * ... **322** A4
Abbots La *RCOLW* CO6 ... **105** K6
Abbotsleigh Rd *RCHLM* CM3 ... **245** G6
Abbotsmead *MAL* CM9 ... **198** C8
Abbots Ride *BCAYE* CM11 ... **258** F3
Abbot's Rd *COLS* CO2 ... **129** M2
EHAM E6 ... **308** A5
Abbots Wk *SBN/FI* SS3 ... **302** F5
Abbotsweld *HLWS* CM18 ... **203** L4
Abbots Wick La *K/T/MI* CO5 ... **175** K2
Abbotswood *SBF/HAD* SS7 ... **280** F8
Abbotswood Cl *BELV* DA17 ... **326** B6
Abbotswood Gdns *CLAY* IG5 ... **286** C1
Abbott Rd *HAR* CO12 ... **70** E3
POP/IOD E14 ... **322** F1
Abbotts Cl *CHLM/WR* CM1 ... **5** L2
LOS SS9 ... **282** B8
ROMW/RG RM7 ... **288** E1
THMD SE28 ... **325** M3
Abbotts Ct *HVHL* CB9 ... **35** H8
Abbotts Crs *CHING* E4 ... **267** G3
Abbotts Dr *SLH/COR* SS17 ... **317** H3
WAB EN9 ... **234** B4
Abbotts Hall Cha
SLH/COR SS17 ... **317** H3
Abbotts Park Rd *LEY* E10 ... **284** F5
Abbotts Pl *CHLM/WR* CM1 ... **5** K2
Abbotts Ri *WARE* SG12 ... **185** L5
Abbotts Rd *HVHL* CB9 ... **34** D4
Abbotts Wy *BSF* CM23 ... **138** F6
WARE SG12 ... **185** L5
Abbs Cross Gdns *HCH* RM12 ... **289** M6
Abbs Cross La *HCH* RM12 ... **289** M8
Abdy Av *HAR* CO12 ... **70** D3
Abell Wy *CHLM/GWD* CM2 ... **210** E1
Abels Rd *HSTD* CO9 ... **81** G5
Abenberg Wy
RBRW/HUT CM13 ... **256** D5
Abensburg Rd *CVI* SS8 ... **299** G8
Aberavon Rd *BOW* E3 ... **306** B7
Abercorn Gdns *CHDH* RM6 ... **287** L4
Abercorn Wy *WIT* CM8 ... **171** K3
Abercrombie Wy
HLWW/ROY CM19 ... **12** E9
Aberdeen Gdns *LOS* SS9 ... **299** K3
Aberdeen Wy *IPNE* IP4 ... **49** G4
Aberdour Rd *BCTR* RM8 ... **287** L8
Aberfeldy St *POP/IOD* E14 ... **322** F2
Aberfoyle Cl *IPNE* IP4 ... **49** H4
Abery St *WOOL/PLUM* SE18 ... **325** H7
Abingdon Ct *PIT* SS13 ... **278** D4
Abinger Cl *GDMY/SEVK* IG3 ... **309** K1
RCOS CO16 ... **158** F7
Abraham Ct *UPMR* RM14 ... **290** D7
Abraham Dr *WIT* CM8 ... **147** H1
Abram's La *ROY* SG8 ... **349** P6
Abreys *SBF/HAD* SS7 ... **280** D6
Abridge Cl *CHES/WCR* EN8 ... **232** E5
Abridge Gdns *CRW* RM5 ... **270** D5
Abridge Rd *CHIG* IG7 ... **251** H6
EPP CM16 ... **236** B7
Abridge Wy *BARK* IG11 ... **309** L6
Acacia Av *COLN* CO4 ... **108** B5
HCH RM12 ... **289** J7
Acacia Cl *DEPT* SE8 ... **322** B7
IPSE IP3 ... **55** K4
Acacia Dr *MAL* CM9 ... **214** B3
SOS SS1 ... **302** D5
UPMR RM14 ... **312** D1
Acacia Gdns *UPMR* RM14 ... **291** J5
WIT CM8 ... **171** L1
Acacia Rd *GRH* DA9 ... **335** H8
PIT SS13 ... **279** H5
WALTH E17 ... **284** B4
WAN E11 ... **285** H7
Accommodation Rd *COLN* CO4 ... **87** G6
Acer Av *RAIN* RM13 ... **312** A7
Acer Gv *RIPW* IP8 ... **53** H4
Achilles Wy *BRTR* CM7 ... **99** L8
Achnacone Dr *COLN* CO4 ... **106** F2
Ackroyd Dr *BOW* E3 ... **322** D1
Acland Av *COLW* CO3 ... **106** D6
Acorn Av *BRTR* CM7 ... **121** G3
HSTD CO9 ... **81** G4
Acorn Cl *CHING* E4 ... **266** E4
COLN CO4 ... **108** A1
HAR CO12 ... **70** E4
MAL CM9 ... **198** C8
RIPW IP8 ... **53** H3
Acorn Pl *VGE* SS16 ... **276** D8
The Acorns *HOC/HUL* SS5 ... **264** B6
Acorn St *WARE* SG12 ... **186** E2
Acre Rd *DAGE* RM10 ... **310** E4
Acres Av *CHONG* CM5 ... **380** G12
Acres End *CHLM/WR* CM1 ... **209** H1
The Acres *SLH/COR* SS17 ... **317** J2
Acton Cl *CHES/WCR* EN8 ... **232** F1
RIPW IP8 ... **46** F3
SUD CO10 ... **20** E4
Acton Gdns *RIPW* IP8 ... **46** F2
Acton Gn *SUD* CO10 ... **20** C6
Acton La *SUD* CO10 ... **20** E4
Acton Pl *SUD* CO10 * ... **20** C6
Acton Rd *RIPW* IP8 ... **46** F3
Ada Gdns *POP/IOD* E14 ... **323** G2
SRTFD E15 ... **307** J5
Adair Rd *IP* IP1 ... **47** J5
Adalia Crs *LOS* SS9 ... **299** L3
Adalia Wy *LOS* SS9 ... **299** L3
Adam Rd *CHING* E4 ... **266** C5
Adams Cl *CHTY* IP2 ... **54** B2
Adams Ct *SAFWS* CB11 ... **351** R5
Adamsfield *CHESW* EN7 ... **216** A4
Adams Gld *RCFD* SS4 ... **265** G7
Adams House *HLW* CM20 ... **13** G5
Adamson Rd *CAN/RD* E16 ... **323** K2
Adams Pl *KESG* IP5 ... **50** B6
Adams Rd *SLH/COR* SS17 ... **317** H4
Adam Wy *WICKE* SS11 ... **261** H5
Adastral Cl *FX* IP11 ... **10** F9
Adderley St *POP/IOD* E14 ... **322** F2
Addington Rd *BOW* E3 ... **306** D7
CAN/RD E16 ... **307** H8
FX IP11 ... **62** B6
Addis Cl *PEND* EN3 ... **248** A1
Addison Ct *EPP* CM16 ... **236** B1
Addison Gdns *GRAYS* RM17 ... **330** F3
Addison Rd *BARK/HLT* IG6 ... **268** F7
FOS CO13 ... **136** D4
SUD CO10 ... **21** J3
WALTH E17 ... **284** E3
WAN E11 ... **285** K4
Adelaide Dr *COLS* CO2 ... **129** K4
Adelaide Gdns *CHDH* RM6 ... **288** B3
SBF/HAD SS7 ... **298** A4
Adelaide Rd *IL* IG1 ... **286** E7
IPNE IP4 ... **49** J7
LEY E10 ... **284** F8
TIL RM18 ... **331** J7
Adelaide St *HAR* CO12 ... **14** A5
The Adelaide *HOO/HM* ME3 ... **339** M7
Adeliza Cl *BARK* IG11 ... **308** F4
Adelphi Crs *HCH* RM12 ... **289** K7
Adelsburg Rd *CVI* SS8 ... **320** F1
Aden Rd *IL* IG1 ... **286** E5
PEND EN3 ... **248** B4
Adine Rd *PLSTW* E13 ... **307** K8
Adley St *HOM* E9 ... **306** B2
Admiral Pl *BERM/RHTH* SE16 ... **322** B4
Admirals Cl *SWFD* E18 ... **285** L2
Admiral St *HERT/BAY* SG13 ... **184** B3
Admirals Wk *CHLM/WR* CM1 ... **4** C1
GRH DA9 ... **335** L7
HOD EN11 ... **201** J5
RCOLE CO7 ... **130** E5
SBN/FI SS3 ... **303** G8
Admirals Wy *POP/IOD* E14 ... **322** E5
Admiral Ms *WOS/PRIT* SS0 ... **300** F6
Adnams Wk *RAIN* RM13 ... **311** K2
Adomar Rd *BCTR* RM8 ... **288** A8

Adstock Wy GRAYS RM17 ....330 C3
Advent Wy UED N18 ....266 A4
Aetheric Rd BCTR CM7 ....121 H2
Affeck Rd COLN CO4 ....108 H8
Afton Dr CHIG IG7 ....329 L2
Agar Road Ap WOTN CO14 ....137 M1
Agate CI CAN/RD E16 ....324 A2
  IP IP1 ....47 J4
Agate Rd COS CO15 ....6 FB
Agincourt Rd COS CO15 ....6 FB
Agister CI CHIG IG7 ....269 K4
Agnes Av CHING E4 ....308 D1
  LOS SS9 ....299 L3
Agnes CI EHAM E6 ....324 D5
Agnes Gdns BCTR RM8 ....310 B4
Agnes St POP/IOD E14 ....322 C2
Aidan CI DAGW RM9 ....310 B1
Ailsa Rd WDOW/PRIT SS0 ....300 F5
Ailsa St POP/IOD E14 ....322 F1
Ainger Rd HAR CO12 ....70 J3
Aingers Green Rd RCOLE CO7 ....133 M1
Ainslie Av UPMR RM7 ....288 F4
Ainslie Rd IP IP1 16
Ainslie Wood Crs CHING E4 ....266 E6
Ainslie Wood Gdns CHING E4 ....266 E6
Ainslie Wood Rd CHING E4 ....266 E6
Aintree Av EHAM E6 ....308 B5
Aintree CI GVE DA12 337
Aintree Crs BARK/HLT IG6 ....268 F8
Aintree Gv UPMR RM14 ....290 D7
Airborne CI LOS SS9 ....282 B8
Aire Dr SOCK/AV RM15 ....313 G4
Airfield Wy HCH RM12 ....311 L3
Airlie Gdns IL IG1 ....286 B7
Airthrie Rd CDMY/SEVK IG3 ....287 L6
Aisher Rd THMD SE28 ....325 M3
Aisne Rd COLS CO2 ....129 G1
Aisthorpe RIPS/CAP IP9 ....58 C4
Ajax CI BRTR CM7 ....99 J3
Akenfield CI RCHLM CM3 ....245 K6
Alafin Vls MGTR CO11 * 65 G7
Alamein CI BROX EN10 ....200 A4
Alamein Rd BOC CM0 ....393 M9
  CHLM/WR CM1 ....194 J7
  COLS CO2 ....128 F3
  SWCM DA10 ....336 A4
Alanbrooke GVE DA12 337
Alanbrooke Rd COLS CO2 ....130 A3
Alan CI COS CO15 ....282 B7
Alan Dr RCOS CO16 ....159 G4
Alan Gv LOS SS9 ....282 C8
Alan Hockern Wy SRTFD E15 ....307 L6
Alan Rd IPSE IP3 17
  WIT CM8 ....171 H4
Alan Wy COLW CO3 ....128 C1
Alban Sq WDBR IP12 ....51 L3
Albany Av WOS/PRIT SS0 ....18 D3
Albany Cha COS CO15 * 7 K7
Albany CI CHLM/WR CM1 ....193 M8
  RCOLW CO6 ....106 B1
Albany Ct EPP CM16 ....220 A8
Albany Gdns East COS CO15 ....7 L4
Albany Gdns West COS CO15 ....7 L4
Albany Pde PEND EN3 232
Albany Pk PEND EN3 * 232 E7
Albany Rd BRWN CM15 255
  CHDH RM6 ....289 C4
  HCH RM12 ....308 A1
  MNPK E12 ....308 A1
  PEND EN3 ....232 E7
  RAYL SS6 ....281 K4
  RCOLW CO6 ....106 C1
  TIL RM18 ....331 H1
  WALTH E17 ....284 B4
  WICKW SS12 ....261 G1
The Albany IPNE IP4 48
Albany Vw BKHH IG9 ....249 K8
Alba Rd HLWE CM17 ....188 D8
Albatross CI EHAM E6 ....308 C8
Albemarle Ap GNTH/NBYPK IG2 ....286 E4
Albemarle Av CHES/WCR EN8 ....216 D6
Albemarle CI GRAYS RM17 ....330 D1
Albemarle Gdns BRTR CM7 99
  GNTH/NBYPK IG2 ....286 E4
Albemarle Link CHLM/WR CM1 ....194 C5
Albemarle St HAR CO12 ....15 K4
Alberta CI KESC IP5 ....49 M5
Albert Av CHING E4 ....266 D3
Albert CI CDW/CHF RM16 ....330 F2
  RAYL SS6 281
  RCFD SS4 ....264 F6
Albert Crs CHING E4 ....266 D3
Albert Dr LAIN SS15 ....276 F7
Albert Gdns COS CO15 ....7 K5
  HLWE CM17 204
  RCOLW CO6 ....124 D3
  WCHPL E1 322
Albertine CI COLW CO3 ....105 M7
Albert Ms POP/IOD E14 * 322 B2
  WOS/PRIT SS0 ....18 D5
Albert Murray CI GVE DA12 337
Albert PI RCTW RM6 124
Albert Rd BCTR RM8 ....288 C6
  BELV DA17 ....326 C8
  BKHH IG9 ....268 A1
  BOC CM0 ....393 M9
  BRTR CM7 121
  CAN/RD E16 ....324 B4
  IL IG1 ....286 F8
  LEY E10 284
  RAYL SS6 ....281 J3
  RCFD SS4 ....264 F6
  RCOLE CO7 134
  RCOLE CO7 ....156 D7
  ROM RM1 289
  SBF/HAD SS7 ....279 L7
  SOS SS1 ....19 K6
  SOS SS1 302
  SWCM DA10 ....336 C4
  SWFD E18 ....285 L1
  UPMR RM14 293
  WALTH E17 ....284 D3
  WIT CM8 ....171 H4
Albert Sq SRTFD E15 ....307 H2
Albert St BRW CM14 ....273 M4
  COL CO1 15
  HAR CO12 ....15 K5
Albert Wk FX IP11 11
Albion CI ROMW/RG RM7 289
Albion Ct BCAYW CM12 * 258
Albion Gv COLS CO2 107
Albion HI IPNE IP4 17
Albion Pk LOU IG10 250
Albion Rd GVE DA12 337
  SBF/HAD SS7 297
  WALTH E17 284
  WOS/PRIT SS0 18
Albion St K/T/MI CO5 ....130 D6
  GVE DA12 337
Albion Ter CHING E4 * 308 E4
  GVW DA11 337
Albion Vls SOS SS1 * 19 K7
Albrighton Cft COLN CO4 ....107 M1
Albury Grove Rd CHES/WCR EN8 ....216 E8

Albury Ms MNPK E12 ....285 M6
Albury Ride CHES/WCR EN8 ....232 E1
Albury Wk CHES/WCR EN8 ....216 E8
Albyns CI WIT CM8 ....294 H1
Albyns La ABR/ST RM4 ....253 L2
Alconbury BSF CM23 ....115 J3
Alcotes BSDN SS14 ....278 A4
Aldborough Ct GTDUN CM6 * 74
  UPMR RM14 ....290 D7
Aldborough Rd DAGE RM10 ....310 D2
Aldborough Rd North GNTH/NBYPK IG2 ....287 J2
Aldborough Rd South GNTH/NBYPK IG2 ....287 H6
Aldburgh PI WFD IG8 ....267 K3
Aldeburgh CI RCOLN CO4 ....107 L1
Aldeburgh Gdns COLN CO4 ....107 L1
Aldeburgh PI WFD IG8 ....267 K3
Aldeburgh St GNWCH SE10 ....323 K3
Aldeburgh Wy CHLM/WR CM1 ....194 A8
Alden Av SRTFD E15 ....307 J7
Alder Av UPMR RM14 ....312 C1
Alderbury Lea RCHLM CM3 ....228 C4
Alderbury Rd STSD CM24 ....115 M1
Aldercar Rd RCOLW CO6 ....127 J4
Alder CI BSF CM23 138
  HOD EN11 ....201 J1
  LAIN SS15 ....277 G4
Aldercroft CI IP IP1 ....48 A3
Aldercroft Rd IP IP1 ....48 A3
Alder Dr CHLM/GWD CM2 ....209 L2
  SOCK/AV RM15 ....313 M8
Alderford Maltings HSTD CO9 * 356 B9
Alderford St HSTD CO9 ....356 F9
Alderlee CHTY IP7 ....53 L5
Alderleys SBF/HAD SS7 ....280 A6
Alderman Av BARK IG11 ....309 K7
Alderman CI COLN CO4 * 107 L1
Alderman's HI HOC/HUL SS5 ....263 L8
Alderman Wk SLH/COR SS17 ....295 L2
Aldermary Gdns WICKE SS11 ....260 F3
Alderney Rd WCHPL E1 ....306 F4
Alde Rd HVHL CB9 ....34 D5
Alders Av WFD IG8 ....267 H5
Aldersbrook La MNPK E12 ....285 M7
Aldersbrook Rd MNPK E12 ....285 M7
Alders CI WAN E11 ....285 L1
Aldersey Gdns BARK IG11 ....309 G3
Alders Wk SBW CM21 ....162 F4
Alderton CI BRWN CM15 255
  GTDUN CM6 118
  LOU IG10 250
Alderton Hall La LOU IG10 ....250 C5
Alderton HI LOU IG10 ....250 C5
Alderton Ri LOU IG10 ....250 C5
Alderton Rd CDW/CHF RM16 ....316 D6
  COLN CO4 ....107 K2
Alderton Wy LOU IG10 ....250 C5
Alderwood Av SUD CO10 ....20 F4
Alderwood Dr ABR/ST RM4 ....251 L3
Alderwood Wy SBF/HAD SS7 ....298 C3
Aldham Gdns RAYL SS6 ....280 C3
Aldingham Gdns HCH RM12 ....311 K2
Aldington Rd WOOL/PLUM SE18 ....324 A6
Aldon CI HAR CO12 ....70 A4
Aldous CI RCOLE CO7 ....363 H6
Aldreath Dr SLH/COR SS17 ....295 H8
Aldriche Wy CHING E4 ....266 F5
Aldria Rd SLH/COR SS17 ....295 H8
Aldridge Av PEND EN3 ....233 H8
Aldridge CI CHLM/GWD CM2 ....210 D1
Aldrin PI SLH/COR SS17 ....317 J1
Aldringham Ms FX IP11 ....62 C8
Aldrin Wy LOS SS9 ....282 C8
Aldworth Rd SRTFD E15 ....307 H4
Aldwyth Av BARK/HLT IG6 ....286 F5
Aldwych CI HCH RM12 ....289 K7
Ale Founder CI COLN CO4 ....108 B7
Alestan Beck Rd CAN/RD E16 ....324 B2
Alethea Farm PI HSTD CO9 * 345 G7
  HSTD CO9 ....346 B10
Alexander La BRWN CM15 ....256 D1
Alexander Ms CHLM/GWD CM2 ....227 J3
  GRH DA9 ....335 M7
  VGE SS16 ....294 E1
Alexander Ter SRTFD E15 * 325 L1
Alexandra Av K/T/MI CO5 ....178 A7
Alexandra CI RCOLE CO7 ....130 F2
Alexandra Rd BOC CM0 ....393 L8
  CHDH RM6 ....288 A4
  COLW CO3 8
  COS CO15 6
  EHAM E6 ....308 D7
  FX IP11 ....62 D7
  GVE DA12 ....338 B5
  HAR CO12 15
  HSTD CO9 ....356 F8
  IPNE IP4 17
  LEY E10 ....284 A1
  LOS SS9 ....300 B5
  PEND EN3 ....248 A4
  RAIN RM13 ....311 J1
  RAYL SS6 ....281 J3
  RCFD SS4 ....264 F6
  RCOS CO16 ....134 C5
  ROM RM1 289
  SBF/HAD SS7 ....298 D3
  SBN/FI SS3 ....303 K2
  SUD CO10 39
  SWFD E18 ....285 L1
  TIL RM18 ....331 J8
  WALTH E17 ....284 C7
Alexandra St CAN/RD E16 ....323 K1
  HAR CO12 15
  JOS SS1 ....19 H6
Alexandra Ter COLW CO3 ....8 A9
Alexandra Wy CHES/WCR EN8 ....233 L4
Alexandria Dr RAYL SS6 ....280 D1
Alfells Rd RCOLE CO7 ....109 J7
Alford Rd ERITH DA8 ....326 H6
Alfreda Av HOC/HUL SS5 ....263 K5
Alfred CI WAB EN9 ....234 B3
Alfred PI GVW DA11 ....337 M7
Alfred Rd BELV DA17 ....326 C1
  BKHH IG9 ....268 A1
  BRW CM14 ....256 A5
  GVW DA11 ....337 M7
  SOCK/AV RM15 ....328 F4
  SRTFD E15 ....307 J2
Alfred's Gdns BARK IG11 ....309 H6
Alfred St BOW E3 ....306 C5
  GRAYS RM17 ....330 F5
Alfred's Wy (East Ham & Barking By-Pass) BARK IG11 ....309 H6
Algars Wy RCHLM CM3 245

Algers CI LOU IG10 ....250 A5
Algers Rd LOU IG10 ....250 A5
Algers Md LOU IG10 ....250 A5
Alibon Gdns DAGE RM10 ....310 D2
Alibon Rd DAGE RM10 ....310 D2
Alice La BOW E3 ....306 C5
Alicia Av WICKE SS11 ....261 K6
Alicia CI WICKE SS11 ....261 K6
Alicia Wk WICKE SS11 ....261 K6
Alicia Wy WICKE SS11 ....261 K6
Alienor Av BRTR CM7 ....76 E4
Alkerden La GRH DA9 ....335 M8
Allard CI CHESW EN7 ....216 A5
Allard Wy BROX EN10 ....200 F7
Allectus Wy WIT CM8 ....171 G5
Allenby Crs GRAYS RM17 ....330 E4
Allenby Dr EMPK RM11 ....290 B6
Allendale Dr RCOLW CO6 ....127 G1
Allendale Rd EMPK RM11 ....289 J5
  PEND EN3 ....232 E6
Allens CI RCHLM CM3 ....195 L4
Allens Rd BCAYE CM11 ....241 M8
Allensway SLH/COR SS17 ....317 J2
Allen Wy RCOS CO16 ....180 D2
Allerton CI RCFD SS4 ....264 F7
Alley Dock LOS SS9 ....300 A5
Alleyndale Rd BCTR RM8 ....287 M7
Alleyne Wy COS CO15 ....182 D5
Alleyn PI WOS/PRIT SS0 ....300 F4
Allfields HAR CO12 ....70 E5
Allhallows Rd EHAM E6 ....324 A2
Alliance Rd PLSTW E13 ....307 M8
Allington CI IPNE IP4 17
Allington Ct BCAYE CM11 * 259 G6
Allington Wy HVHL CB9 ....34 B8
Allis Ms HLWE CM17 ....188 D8
Allison CI WAB EN9 ....234 B3
Allistonway SLH/COR SS17 ....317 J2
Allmains CI WAB EN9 ....218 C3
Allnutts Rd EPP CM16 ....236 B3
Alloa Rd DEPT SE8 ....322 A8
  GDMY/SEVK IG3 ....287 M3
All Saints Av CDW/CHF RM16 ....331 H5
All Saints CI BRWN CM15 ....383 Q10
  BSF CM23 ....139 H1
  CHIC IG7 ....269 J5
  CHLM/WR CM1 ....210 B1
  SWCM DA10 ....336 C3
All Saints' Rd GVW DA11 ....337 J6
  IP IP1 ....16 A1
Allwood Rd CHESW EN7 ....216 A5
Alma Av CHING E4 ....266 F6
Alma CI IPNE IP4 48
  SBF/HAD SS7 ....299 J3
  WICKW SS12 ....260 D7
Alma Dr CHLM/WR CM1 4
Alma Rd PEND EN3 ....248 B5
  SBF/HAD SS7 ....299 K3
  SWCM DA10 ....336 B3
Alma Sq RCOLE CO7 ....130 E5
Alma St RCOLE CO7 ....130 E5
  SRTFD E15 ....307 G3
Alma Ter HAR CO12 15
  SBF/HAD SS7 ....297 H4
Almond Av HOC/HUL SS5 * 264 H2
  WICKW SS12 ....260 F6
Almond CI CDW/CHF RM16 ....331 K2
  COS CO15 ....6 A6
  K/T/MI CO5 ....149 M7
  RCOLE CO7 ....130 E5
Almondhayes CHTY IP2 16
Almonds Av BKHH IG9 ....267 K1
Almond Wk COLN CO4 ....108 B5
Almond Wy COLN CO4 ....108 B5
Almshouse La EN EN1 ....232 C7
Alnwick CI VGE SS16 ....270 B8
Alnwick Rd CAN/RD E16 ....323 M2
Alpe St IP IP1 16
Alpha CI BRTR CM7 ....121 K3
  PIT SS13 ....279 J7
Alpha Gv POP/IOD E14 ....322 F2
Alphamstone Rd BURES CO8 ....359 L5
Alpha PI BSF CM23 ....139 L1
Alpha Rd BOC CM0 ....393 M8
  CHING E4 266
  PEND EN3 ....248 B4
  RCOS CO16 ....180 E2
Alpha Ter CBE/LIN CB1 * 342 H2
Alpine Wy EHAM E6 ....324 D1
Alport Av COLS CO2 ....128 E1
Alracks LAIN SS15 ....2 B5
Alresford Gn WICKW SS12 ....261 H7
Alresford Rd RCOLE CO7 ....131 H5
Alsa Gdns RBSF CM22 ....374 D3
Alsa Leys RBSF CM22 ....374 D3
Alsa St STSD CM24 ....374 A4
Alsike Rd BELV DA17 ....326 A6
Altair CI LAIN SS15 ....276 F6
Altar PI LAIN SS15 276
Altbarn CI COLS CO2 ....108 A8
Altbarn Rd COLS CO2 13
Altham CI PIT SS13 ....278 A4
Althorne CI PIT SS13 ....285 J2
Althorne Gdns SWFD E18 ....285 J2
Althorne Wy DAGE RM10 ....288 D7
  RCFD SS4 ....392 B11
Althorpe CI HOC/HUL SS5 ....264 H4
Altmore Av EHAM E6 ....308 C4
Alton Dr COLW CO3 ....106 E7
Alton Gdns SOSN SS2 ....302 B2
Alton Hall La RIPS/CAP IP9 ....364 C9
Alton Park La COS CO15 ....182 C5
Alton Park Rd COS CO15 6
Alton Rd COS CO15 6
Aluric CI CDW/CHF RM16 ....331 L3
Alverstoke Rd HARH RM3 ....272 B6
Alverstone Rd MNPK E12 ....308 D1
Alverton CI BSF CM23 ....138 C2
Alverton St DEPT SE8 ....322 F8
Alverton Wy COLN CO4 ....107 L2
Alveston Sq SWFD E18 ....267 K8
Alvin CI COS CO15 182
Alvis Av COS CO15 ....182 D5
Alwen Gv SOCK/AV RM15 ....329 L1
Alwyne Av BRWN CM15 256
Alyssum CI CHLM/WR CM1 ....194 D7
Alyssum Wk COLN CO4 9
Amanda CI CHIG IG7 ....269 K8
Amanda Ms ROMW/RG RM7 ....288 F5
Amardeep Ct WOOL/PLUM SE18 ....325 J8
Ambassador Gdns EHAM E6 324
Ambassador Sq POP/IOD E14 ....322 E3
Amberley CI RCOLE CO7 ....130 F4
Amberley Gdns SOCK/AV RM15 ....329 M1
Amberley Rd WALTH E17 266
Amberry Ct HLW CM20 13

Amber St SRTFD E15 * 307 G3
  WICKE SS11 ....261 L6
Ambleside EPP CM16 ....236 B3
Ambleside Av HCH RM12 ....311 L2
Ambleside CI LEY E10 ....284 A1
Ambleside Ct SOS SS1 7
Ambleside Crs PEND EN3 ....248 F1
Ambleside Dr SOS SS1 ....19 L5
Ambleside Gdns HOC/HUL SS5 ....263 G3
  REDBR IG4 286
Ambleside Wk COS CO15 ....320 C1
Ambrook Rd BELV DA17 ....326 D6
Ambrose Av COLW CO3 ....128 C1
Amcotes PI CHLM/GWD CM2 5
Ameland Rd CVI SS8 ....298 D2
Amerells Rd RCOS CO16 ....158 C5
America Rd RCOLW CO6 ....102 A4
America St MAL CM9 214
Amersham CI HARH RM3 ....272 C8
Amersham Rd HARH RM3 ....272 B5
Amersham Wk HARH RM3 ....272 C5
Amery Gdns GPK RM2 ....272 A8
Amesbury WAB EN9 ....234 B2
Amesbury Dr CHING E4 ....248 E6
Amesbury Rd DAGW RM9 ....310 A4
  EPP CM16 ....236 A3
Amethyst CI WAN E11 ....307 L7
Amidas Gdns BCTR RM8 ....309 L1
Amid Rd CVI SS8 ....298 E8
Amoss Rd CHLM/GWD CM2 ....210 C5
Ampers End BSDN SS14 3
Ampleforth Rd ABYW SE2 ....325 L1
Amsterdam Rd POP/IOD E14 ....322 F6
Amwell Ct HOD EN11 ....201 J1
  WAB EN9 ....233 M3
Amwell End WARE SG12 ....184 A2
Amwell HI WARE SG12 ....185 G3
Amwell La WARE SG12 ....185 H3
Amwell St HOD EN11 ....201 H3
Amy Warne CI EHAM E6 ....324 B1
Ancaster Rd IP IP1 16
Anchorage HI MAL CM9 ....214 C8
The Anchorage SBN/FI SS3 ....303 H5
Anchor Bvd GRH DA9 ....334 F6
Anchor CI BARK IG11 ....309 L1
  CHES/WCR EN8 ....216 E6
Anchor Rd RAIN RM13 ....311 H3
Anchor End MGTR CO11 * 91 K1
Anchor HI RCOLE CO7 130
Anchor & Hope La CHARL SE7 ....323 M7
Anchor La CHONG CM5 * 379 J9
  MAL CM9 ....198 D8
  MGTR CO11 ....91 K1
Anchor Reach RCHLM CM3 ....245 H8
Anchor Rd COS CO15 6
  K/T/MI CO5 ....173 H1
Anchor St BSF CM23 ....139 H1
  CHLM/GWD CM2 5
Ancona Rd WOOL/PLUM SE18 ....325 J8
Anders Fall LOS SS9 ....282 D7
Anderson CI BSF CM23 ....93 G7
Anderson Rd HOM E9 ....306 A3
Andersons SLH/COR SS17 ....317 J3
Anderson Wy BELV DA17 ....326 F3
Andover Av CAN/RD E16 ....324 C2
Andover CI COS CO15 ....159 K7
Andrea Av CDW/CHF RM16 ....330 F2
Andrew CI BARK/HLT IG6 ....269 G6
  BRTR CM7 99
  FX IP11 11
  SLH/COR SS17 ....317 G1
Andrew St POP/IOD E14 ....322 F2
Andrewes Gdns EHAM E6 ....324 B2
Andrews CI BKHH IG9 ....267 M1
Andrews Farm La CHESW EN7 ....216 C6
Andrews La CHESW EN7 ....216 C6
Andrews PI CHLM/WR CM1 4
Andros CI IPSE IP3 54
Andwell CI ABYW SE2 ....325 L1
Andyk CI CVI SS8 ....321 H5
Anemone CI COLN CO4 106
Anerley Rd WOS/PRIT SS0 ....18 B4
Angela CI WDBR IP12 ....50 F4
Angel CI VGE SS16 ....296 A2
Angel Ga HAR CO12 ....15 L3
Angelgate Rd HAR CO12 ....15 L3
Angelica Dr EHAM E6 ....324 D1
Angel La GTDUN CM6 117
  IPNE IP4 17
  SRTFD E15 ....307 G3
  SUD CO10 ....39 L1
Angel Meadow SUD CO10 * 39 L1
Angel Rd RIPW IP8 ....46 F3
Angel Wy ROM RM1 ....289 H4
Angle Rd WTHK RM20 ....330 A5
Angle Side BRTR CM7 ....121 L3
Anglesea PI GVW DA11 ....337 J4
Anglesea Rd IP IP1 16
  RCOLE CO7 130
  WOOL/PLUM SE18 ....324 C6
Anglesey CI BSF CM23 ....138 D2
Anglesey Dr RAIN RM13 ....311 K8
Anglesey Gdns WICKW SS12 ....261 J7
Anglia CI COLS CO2 ....128 D2
Anglian Rd WAN E11 ....285 G6
Anglian Wy BRTR CM7 ....121 L3
Anglo Rd BOW E3 ....306 C8
Angus CI IPNE IP4 49
Angus Dr LOS SS9 ....282 C7
Anita CI East CHTY IP2 ....47 K8
Anita CI West CHTY IP2 ....47 K8
Anjou Gn CHLM/WR CM1 ....194 D6
Annabel CI POP/IOD E14 322
Annabel Av CDW/CHF RM16 ....316 A8
Annalee Gdns SOCK/AV RM15 ....329 L2
Annalee Rd SOCK/AV RM15 ....329 L2
Annandale Rd GNWCH SE10 ....323 J8
Anna Neagle CI FSTGT E7 ....307 K1
Annan Wy ROM RM1 271
Anne CI RCFD SS4 283
Anne Boleyn Dr RCFD SS4 ....283 L1
Anne Boleyn Man PIT SS13 * 278
Anne Heart CI WTHK RM20 ....330 A5
Anne of Cleves Rd DART DA1 334
Anne St IP IP1 16
  PLSTW E13 307
Annett CI WICKW SS12 ....261 K6
Anne Wy BARK/HLT IG6 268
Annie Besant CI BOW E3 * 306 C5
Annis Rd HOM E9 306
Ann St IP IP1 16
  WOOL/PLUM SE18 ....325 G8
Ann Suckling Rd HVHL CB9 ....34 B5
Ansar Gdns WALTH E17 ....284 B3
Ansgar CI SAFWS CB11 ....30 B2

Anson Cha SBN/FI SS3 ....303 H5
Anson CI HAR CO12 ....70 F3
  ROMW/RG RM7 ....245 H7
  ROMW/RG RM7 ....270 E8
Anson Wy BRTR CM7 ....121 H1
Anstead Dr RAIN RM13 ....311 K6
Anstey CI LOS SS9 ....282 A6
Antelope Av CDW/CHF RM16 ....330 C6
Antelope Rd WOOL/PLUM SE18 ....324 C6
Anthony CI BCAYE CM11 ....259 G7
  COLN CO4 ....108 A2
Anthony Dr SLH/COR SS17 ....317 H1
Antill Rd BOW E3 ....306 D7
Antill Ter WCHPL E1 ....322 F4
Antlers CVI SS8 ....320 C3
Antlers HI CHING E4 ....248 F6
Antonia CI HLWE CM17 ....35 H6
Antonius St COLN CO4 ....87 L7
Anton Rd SOCK/AV RM15 ....313 L6
Antony CI CVI SS8 ....298 E8
Antrim PI IP IP1 ....47 J4
  SBN/FI SS3 ....303 J4
Anvil Wy BCAYW CM12 240
  CHLM/WR CM1 ....194 B5
Anworth CI WFD IG8 ....267 L5
Anzani Av CI IP1 ....10 C2
Anzio Crs COLS CO2 ....128 F3
Apeldoorn SBF/HAD SS7 ....279 L6
Apollo CI EMPK RM11 ....289 L7
Apollo PI WAN E11 ....285 M8
Apollo Wy WOOL/PLUM SE18 ....325 G6
Apple Acre Rd HVHL CB9 ....33 M4
Appleby CI CHING E4 ....266 F6
  RIPW IP8 ....53 H4
Appleby Dr HARH RM3 ....271 M4
  VGE SS16 295
Appleby Rd CAN/RD E16 ....323 K2
Appledene CI RAYL SS6 ....281 G1
Appledore SBN/FI SS3 ....302 F4
Appledore CI HARH RM3 ....271 M7
Appleford Ct PIT SS13 ....278 F3
Appleford's CI HOD EN11 ....201 H3
Applegarth Dr GNTH/NBYPK IG2 ....287 J2
Applegarth Rd THMD SE28 ....325 L4
Apple Ga BRW CM14 ....255 J5
Apple Rd WAN E11 ....285 G7
Appleton CI HLWW/ROY CM19 ....12 C2
Appleton Flds BSF CM23 ....138 D5
Appleton Rd LOU IG10 ....250 A5
  SBF/HAD SS7 ....297 L2
Appleton Wy HCH RM12 ....290 A6
Apple Tree CI LOS SS9 ....81 K3
Appletree CI BRTR CM7 ....122 F5
  SOSN SS2 ....302 B2
Apple Tree Crs BRWN CM15 ....383 R12
Apton CI BSF CM23 ....139 G2
Apton Flds BSF CM23 ....139 G2
Apton Hall Rd RCFD SS4 ....265 K7
Apton Rd BSF CM23 ....139 G2
Arabia CI CHING E4 ....248 F7
Araglen Av SOCK/AV RM15 ....329 L1
Aragon CI COS CO15 ....182 C5
  LOU IG10 ....250 B6
  SOSN SS2 ....301 K7
Aragon Dr BARK/HLT IG6 ....268 F4
Aragon Rd HVHL CB9 ....34 D6
  RCHLM CM3 ....144 C6
Arakan CI COLS CO2 ....128 E4
Arandora Crs CHDH RM6 ....287 L5
Arbery Rd BOW E3 ....306 B7
Arbor CI CHING E4 ....267 G4
Arbour CI BRW CM14 ....256 A6
Arbour La CHLM/WR CM1 ....210 A6
  WIT CM8 ....172 B8
Arbour Rd PEND EN3 ....248 A4
Arbour Wy COLN CO4 ....107 M1
  HCH RM12 ....311 L2
Arcade Buildings COS CO15 * 7
Arcade Chambers COS CO15 * 7
Arcade CI COS CO15 * 7
Arcade PI ROM RM1 ....289 H5
Arcade St IP IP1 16
The Arcade WALTH E17 * 284 C4
  WICKE SS11 * 261
Arcadian Gdns SBF/HAD SS7 298
Arcadia Rd BOC CM0 393
  CVI SS8 321
Arcadia St POP/IOD E14 322
Archangel Gdns CHTY IP2 * 53 K1
Archangel St WOOL/PLUM SE18 ....322 A5
Archates Av CDW/CHF RM16 ....330 C6
Archer CI SOSN SS2 ....302 B2
Archer Crs K/T/MI CO5 150
Archer Rd LAIN SS15 276
Archers EPP CM16 ....236 H6
Archers Fld IP IP1 16
Archers CI BCAYW CM12 258
Archery Flds COS CO15 182
The Arches SAFWN CB10 * 28
Archibald Rd HARH RM3 272
Archway HARH RM3 271
Arden CI COLN CO4 ....107 M2
  THMD SE28 326
Arden Crs DAGW RM9 310
  POP/IOD E14 322
Arderne CI HAR CO12 70
Ardleigh VGE SS16 296
Ardleigh CI EMPK RM11 ....290 A1
Ardleigh Ct BRWN CM15 ....256 C5
Ardleigh Gdns BRBW/HLT CM13 ....257 H2
Ardleigh Green Rd EMPK RM11 ....290 A3
Ardleigh Rd MGTR CO11 * 90
  RCOLE CO7 89
  RCOLE CO7 ....109 L1
  WALTH E17 266
Ardleigh Ter WALTH E17 266
Ardley CI RBSF CM22 378
Ardley Crs DAGW RM9 310
  RAYL SS6 ....
Ardmore La BKHH IG9 249
Ardmore PI BKHH IG9 249
Ardmore Rd SOCK/AV RM15 313
Ardra Rd ED N9 266
Ardwell Av BARK/HLT IG6 286
Arethusa Rd GRH DA9 335
Argall Av LEY E10 284
Argall Wy LEY E10 284
Argents La COLW CO3 105
Argent St WTHK RM20 330

Argles Cl GRH DA9 ...335 K7
Argus Cl ROMW/RG RM7 ...270 E7
Argyle Gdns UPMR RM14 ...291 C8
Argyle Rd BOC CM0 ...393 N9
  CAN/RD E16 ...323 L2
  IL IG1 ...286 D7
  RCOS CO16 ...135 K3
  SRTFD E15 ...307 H4
  WCHPL E1 * ...306 H4
Argyle St IPNE IP4 ...17 H4
Argyll Rd CHLM/GWD CM2 ...194 D8
  GRAYS RM17 ...330 D4
  WOOL/PLUM SE18 ...324 F6
  WOS/PRIT SS0 ...18 B4
Ariel Cl COLN CO4 ...108 B6
Arisdale Av SOCK/AV RM15 ...313 L1
Arjan Wy CVI SS8 ...319 M2
Ark Av CDW/CHF RM16 ...330 D2
Ark La RCFD SS4 ...282 C4
Arkle Ct KESG IP5 ...50 C6
Arkley Crs WALTH E17 ...284 C3
Arkley Rd WALTH E17 ...284 C3
  TIL RM18 ...331 K8
Arkwrights HLW CM20 ...13 M5
Arlington Crs CHES/WCR EN8 ...232 C3
Arlington Gdns HARH RM3 ...272 C5
  IL IG1 ...286 C5
Arlington Rd SOSN SS2 ...302 B4
  WFD IG8 ...267 K7
Arlington Wy BCAYW CM12 ...240 C8
Armada Cl LAIN SS15 ...277 C8
Armadale CVI SS8 ...320 C1
Armada Wy EHAM E6 ...324 F2
Armagh Rd BOW E3 ...306 C5
  SBN/FI SS3 ...303 C6
Armagh Ter MGTR CO11 * ...91 K7
Armath Pl VGE SS16 ...294 C1
Armidale Wk COLS CO2 ...129 K3
Armiger Wy WIT CM8 ...171 G7
Armitage Rd GNWCH SE10 ...323 J8
  SOS SS1 ...302 D4
Armonde Cl RCHLM CM3 ...195 H4
Armond Rd WIT CM8 ...171 H7
Armond Rd PUR RM19 ...329 G7
Armourers Cl BSF CM23 ...138 C2
Armoury Dr GVE DA12 ...337 M5
Armoury Rd RCOLW CO6 ...106 C1
Arms La HVHL CB9 ...35 L4
Armstead Wk DAGE RM10 ...310 H4
Armstrong Av WFD IG8 ...267 H5
  EHAM E6 ...324 C2
  RCHLM CM3 ...212 C4
  SLH/COR SS17 ...317 H3
Armstrong Rd SBF/HAD SS7 ...280 A6
  WOOL/PLUM SE18 ...324 F6
Armstrong Wy HSTD CO9 ...346 B11
Arne Cl SLH/COR SS17 ...317 G2
Arne Ct LAIN SS15 ...276 C5
Arne Ms LAIN SS15 ...276 C5
Arnett Sq CHTY IP2 ...266 C5
Arneways Av CHDH RM6 ...288 C2
Arnheim Pl POP/IOD E14 ...322 C6
Arnheim Rd BOC CM0 ...393 M9
Arnhem Av SOCK/AV RM15 ...328 F4
Arnhem Gv RTR CM7 ...99 H8
Arnhem Rd CHLM/GWD CM1 ...193 H7
Arnold Av SOS SS1 ...19 M6
Arnold Av East PEND EN3 ...233 G8
Arnold Av West PEND EN3 ...233 G8
Arnold Cl IP IP1 ...47 L2
Arnold Dr COLN CO4 ...108 B7
Arnold Pl TIL RM18 ...331 M7
Arnold Rd BOW E3 ...306 C7
  COS CO15 ...6 C9
  DAGW RM9 ...310 C4
  GVE DA12 ...337 H2
  WAB EN9 ...233 K5
Arnolds Av RBRW/HUT RM13 ...256 F1
Arnolds Cl RBRW/HUT RM13 ...256 F1
Arnolds Farm La
  RBRW/HUT RM13 ...239 H7
Arnolds Wy RCFD SS4 ...264 F6
Arnold Vls K/T/MI CO5 ...149 M1
Arnold Wy CHLM/GWD CM2 ...225 M2
Arnott St THMD SE28 ...325 H4
Arnstones Cl COLN CO4 ...9 M5
Arragon Rd EHAM E6 ...308 A5
Arran Ct WICKW SS12 ...261 J7
Arran Dr MNPK E12 ...286 A6
Arras Rd COLS CO2 ...129 C1
Arrendene Rd HVHL CB9 ...34 C4
  COLN CO4 ...108 C6
Arrow Rd BOW E3 ...306 E7
Arrowsmith Rd CHIG IG7 ...269 J4
Arsenal Wy CAN/RD E16 ...324 C3
Artemis Cl GVE DA12 ...338 C5
Arterial Av RAIN RM13 ...311 M8
Arterial Rd SBF/HAD SS7 ...280 E5
Arterial Rd North Stifford
  CDW/CHF RM16 ...330 B1
Arterial Rd Purfleet
  PUR RM19 ...329 F7
Arterial Rd West Thurrock
  WTHK RM20 ...329 J1
Artesian Cl ROM RM1 ...289 G2
Arthingworth St SRTFD E15 ...307 H5
Arthur Ct CHLM/GWD CM1 ...193 J7
Arthur Gv WOOL/PLUM SE18 ...324 F7
Arthur Rd CHDH RM6 ...287 M5
  EHAM E6 ...308 C6
Arthurs Ter IPNE IP4 ...17 H3
Arthur St COL CO1 ...8 E8
  GRAYS RM17 ...330 D5
  GVW DA11 ...337 G5
Arthy Cl RCHLM CM3 ...196 D1
Artillery Cl GNTH/NBYPK IG2 ...286 C3
Artillery Dr HAR CO12 ...70 E4
Artillery Pl WOOL/PLUM SE18 ...324 C8
Artillery Rw GVE DA12 ...337 M5
Artillery St COL CO1 ...9 H9
Arun TIL RM18 ...332 F3
Arun Cl CHLM/WR CM1 ...193 M8
Arundel Cl CHMD RM6 ...216 C6
  SRTFD E15 ...307 H1
  WFD IG8 ...267 H2
Arundel Dr SLH/COR SS17 ...317 H1
Arundel Gdns GDMY/SEVK IG3...287 K7
  RAYL SS6 ...262 E8
  WOS/PRIT SS0 ...300 D2
Arundel Rd HARH RM3 ...272 C6
  SBF/HAD SS7 ...279 C4
  WICKE SS11 ...260 F4
Arundel Wy BCAYW CM12 ...258 D3
  IPSE IP3 ...55 K2
Arwela Rd FX IP11 * ...11 J5
Arwen Gv RCHLM CM3 ...244 D7
Asbaston Ter UPMR RM14 ...291 H4
Asbury Cl COLN CO4 ...9 L5
Asbury Dr RCOLW CO6 ...126 C2
Ascension Rd CRW RM5 ...270 C4
Ascham Dr WALTH E17 ...266 C6
Ascham End WALTH E17 ...266 B7
Ascot Cl BARK/HLT IG6 ...269 H5
  BSF CM23 ...139 K1
  SBF/HAD SS7 ...280 E6
Ascot Dr FX IP11 ...62 D7
  IPSE IP3 ...55 G2

Ascot Gdns HCH RM12 ...312 B1
  PEND EN3 ...232 D7
Ascot Gv BSDN SS14 ...278 B3
Ascot Rd EHAM E6 ...308 C7
  WIT CM8 ...337 L8
Ashanti Cl SBN/FI SS3 ...303 J5
Ashbeam Cl RBRW/HUT CM13 ...273 M5
Ashbourne Av SWFD E18 ...285 L2
  BROX EN10 ...201 D7
  HARH RM3 ...271 L1
Ashbridge Rd WAN E11 ...285 H5
Ashbrook Rd DAGE RM10 ...288 D8
Ash Bungalows BRTR CM7 ...121 H2
Ashburnham Gdns
  UPMR RM14 ...290 E6
Ashburnham Rd BELV DA17 ...326 F7
  SOS SS1 ...18 F4
Ashburton Av
  GDMY/SEVK IG3 ...309 J1
Ashburton Rd CAN/RD E16 ...323 K2
Ashbury Gdns CHDH RM6 ...288 A5
Ashby Cl CDW/CHF RM16 ...316 B6
  EMPK RM11 ...290 D6
Ashby Ri BSF CM23 ...115 J8
Ashby Rd WIT CM8 ...171 K6
Ash Cl BRWN CM15 ...255 J5
  COS CO15 ...7
  RCHLM CM3 ...196 D1
  RCOLE CO7 ...156 B6
  ROMW/RG RM7 ...270 E6
Ashcombe RCFD SS4 ...283 C2
Ashcombe Cl LOS SS9 ...281 L7
Ashcombe Wy RAYL SS6 ...281 J3
Ashcroft Rd BSF CM23 ...138 E3
  IP IP1 ...47 L4
Ashdale BSF CM23 ...138 C5
Ashdale Rd KESG IP5 ...50 C5
Ashdene Cl HOC/HUL SS5 ...263 H3
Ashdon Cl RBRW/HUT CM13 ...256 F2
  SOCK/AV RM15 ...329 L2
  WFD IG8 ...267 L5
Ashdon Rd SAFWN SS16 ...28 B7
  SAFWN LOU ...342 A9
Ashdown Cl BRTR CM77 ...120 D3
  SLH/COR SS17 ...295 J8
  SBF/HAD SS7 ...299 H1
Ashdown Crs CHES/WCR EN8 ...216 C7
Ashdown Rd SAFWN SS16 ...28 C11
Ashdown Wk ROMW/RG RM7 ...270 D3
Ashdown Wy COLN CO4 ...9 M4
  IPSE IP3 ...55 J2
Ashen Cl SUD CO10 ...345 L2
Ashenden Rd CLPT E5 ...306 B2
Ashen Hi SUD CO10 ...345 P3
Ashen La SUD CO10 ...345 P4
Ashen Rd HSTD CO9 ...345 N5
  SUD CO10 ...345 L7
Ashes Cl WOTN CO14 ...137 J1
Ashes Rd BRTR CM77 ...122 C6
Ash Fall WIT CM8 ...147 K8
Ashfield RAYL SS6 ...280 C2
Ashfield Farm Rd MAL CM9 ...197 G5
Ashfield La LOU IG10 ...250 C3
  PIT SS13 ...278 F6
Ashford Av BRW CM14 ...273 L2
Ashford Cl WALTH E17 ...284 C4
Ashford Rd CHLM/WR CM1 * ...4 B4
  EHAM E6 ...308 C3
  SWFD E18 ...267 L8
Ash Gn RCFD SS4 ...392 A12
  SAFWN CB10 ...341 L8
Ash Ground Cl FX IP11 ...62 A3
  MGTR CO11 ...65 C5
Ash Gv BOC CM0 ...393 L7
  CHLM/GWD CM2 ...209 M6
  COLS CO2 ...129 K5
  GTDUN CM6 ...150 G6
  HVHL CB9 ...34
  MAL CM9 ...198 E7
  RCOLE CO7 ...130 F2
  RIPS/CAP IP9 ...58 D4
  SUD CO10 ...45 L4
Ashgrove Rd GDMY/SEVK IG3 ...287 J6
Ash Groves SBW CM21 ...163 H4
Ashingdale Cl CVI SS8 ...320 F3
Ashingdon Rd CHING E4 ...266 F3
Ashingdon Hts RCFD SS4 ...264 C6
Ashingdon Rd HOC/HUL SS5 ...264 E7
Altar Pl WOOL/PLUM SE18 ...324 E7
Ashlea Cl HVHL CB9 ...34 E7
Ashlea Rd HVHL CB9 ...34 E7
Ashleigh Cl CVI SS8 ...298 D7
Ashleigh Dr LOS SS9 ...300 C7
Ashleigh Gdns UPMR RM14 ...291 G8
Ashley Av BARK/HLT IG6 ...268 E8
Ashley Cl SLH/COR SS17 ...317 K1
Ashley Gdns CDW/CHF RM16 ...314 E8
  COLW CO3 ...106 F7
Ashley Gn RCHLM CM3 ...227 L6
Ashley Rd CHING E4 ...266 D4
  FSTGT E7 ...307 M4
  HAR CO12 ...14 D8
Ashley St CHTY IP2 ...16 F9
Ashlin Rd SRTFD E15 ...307 G1
Ashlong Gv HSTD CO9 ...81 K12
Ashlyn Gv EMPK RM11 ...290 A1
Ashlyns PIT SS13 ...278 D6
Ashlyns Rd EPP CM16 ...220 A8
  FOS CO13 ...137 H5
Ashmans Rw RCHLM CM3 ...245 G7
Ashmere Gv IPNE IP4 ...17 L3
Ashmere Ri SUD CO10 ...21 L5
Ash Mi ROY SG8 ...370 B4
Ashmole Dr FOS CO13 ...137 J3
Ashmour Gdns ROM RM1 ...271 G8
Ashpole Rd BRTR CM7 ...99 L4
Ash Ri HSTD CO9 ...81 K5
  RCOLW CO6 ...361
Ash Rd CVI SS8 ...320 F2
  RCOLE CO7 ...131 K5
  SBF/HAD SS7 ...299 H4
  SRTFD E15 ...307 H2
Ashstead Rd RCOS CO16 ...158 D7
Ashton Cl CHTY IP2 ...16 A8
Ashton Gdns CHDH RM6 ...288 B4
Ashton Pl CHLM/GWD CM2 ...210 D7
Ashton Rd HARH RM3 ...272 A6
  PEND EN3 ...232 F6
  SRTFD E15 ...307 G1
Ashton St POP/IOD E14 ...322 F1
Ash Tree Cl CHLM/WR CM1 ...4 B4
Ash Tree Crs CHLM/WR CM1 ...4 B3
Ash Tree Fld HLW CM20 ...12 B3
Ashurst Av SOSN SS2 ...302 C5
Ashurst Cl K/T/MI CO5 ...150 C5
  CHLM/WR CM1 ...194 A6
  GNTH/NBYPK IG2 ...286 E4
Ashvale Gdns CRW RM5 ...271 G4
  UPMR RM14 ...291 H4
Ashville Rd WAN E11 ...285 G7
Ash Wk SOCK/AV RM15 ...314 A5
  SOS SS1 ...19 K6
Ash Wy COLW CO3 ...128 C2
  HOC/HUL SS5 ...264 B5
Ashway SLH/COR SS17 ...295 H3

Ashwells Rd BRWN CM15 ...255 J3
Ashwin Av RCOLW CO6 ...127 G1
Ashwood Av RAIN RM13 ...311 L7
Ashwood Rd CHING E4 ...267 C4
Ashworth Pl HLWE CM17 ...204 E5
Ashworths CVI SS8 * ...298 F7
  BSF CM23 ...264 F7
Askews Farm Rd
  GRAYS RM17 ...330 B4
Askin Rd RCOLE CO7 ...363 R6
Askwith Rd RAIN RM13 ...311 G6
Asland Rd SRTFD E15 ...307 G3
Aspdin Rd GVW DA11 ...337 G8
Aspen Cl CVI SS8 ...320 B1
  HVHL CB9 ...34
Aspen Ct LAIN SS15 ...276 E4
  RBRW/HUT CM13 ...256 D6
Aspen Gn ERITHM DA18 ...326 C6
Aspen Gv UPMR RM14 ...312 D1
The Aspens BSF CM23 ...115 J3
Aspen Wy COLN CO4 ...9 M4
  PEND EN3 ...232 E5
  POP/IOD E14 ...322 F3
  SOCK/AV RM15 ...314 A3
Aspin Ms SAFWN CB10 ...28 A6
Asquith Av SBF/HAD SS7 ...280 F7
Asquith Cl BCTR RM8 ...287 M6
Asquith Rd COLN CO4 ...87 M8
Asquith Gdns SBF/HAD SS7 ...280 F7
Assandune Cl RCFD SS4 ...265 G7
Assington St SUD CO10 ...360 D1
Astell Ct FOS CO13 * ...137 J5
Aster Cl BSF CM23 ...138 E3
  RCOS CO16 ...135
Aster Ct CHLM/WR CM1 ...194 C7
Aster Rd CHTY IP2 ...53 K1
Astley GRAYS RM17 ...330 C5
Astley Rd COS CO15 ...6 C5
Aston Rd LAIN SS15 ...276 E7
Aston St WCHPL E1 ...322 B2
Astra Cl HCH RM12 ...311 L3
Astra Rd ROMW/RG RM7 ...288 E4
Ataka Rd FX IP11 * ...62 F7
Atcost Rd BARK IG11 ...325 K1
Athelstan Cl HARH RM3 ...272 C1
Athelstane Gv BOW E3 ...306 C6
Athelstan Gdns WICKE SS11 ...261 G4
Athelstan Rd COLW CO3 ...106 D7
  HARH RM3 ...272 C7
Atherstone Cl CVI SS8 ...320 F3
Atherstone Rd CVI SS8 ...320 F3
Atherton End SBW CM21 ...162 F6
Atherton Gdns
  CDW/CHF RM16 ...331 M3
Atherton Ms FSTGT E7 ...307 L3
Atherton Rd CHTY IP2 ...53 J1
  CLAY IG5 ...268 B2
  FSTGT E7 ...307 L2
Athlone Ct WALTH E17 ...285 G1
Atholl Rd CHLM/GWD CM2 ...194 C8
  GDMY/SEVK IG3 ...287 K5
Athol Rd ERITH DA8 ...326 F5
Athol Sq POP/IOD E14 ...322 F2
Athos Rd CVI SS8 ...298 F8
Atkinson Rd CAN/RD E16 ...323 M1
Atlanta Bvd ROM RM1 ...289 H4
Atlantic Cl SWCM DA10 ...336 B3
Atlantis Cl BARK IG11 ...309 L7
Atlas Ct WICKW SS12 ...261 J7
Atlas Gdns CHARL SE7 ...323 M7
Atlas Rd DART DA1 ...334 C5
  PLSTW E13 ...307 K6
Atley Rd BOW E3 ...306 D5
Atridge Cha BCAYW CM12 ...258 D1
Atterton Rd HVHL CB9 ...34
Attlee Ct GRAYS RM17 ...330 D2
Attlee Dr DART DA1 ...334 D7
Attlee Gdns COL CO1 ...8
Attlee Rd THMD SE28 ...325 L3
Attlee Ter WALTH E17 ...284 E2
Attwood Cl COLN CO4 ...87 L8
Attwoods Cl CHLM/GWD CM2 ...225 L2
Aubrey Cl CHLM/WR CM1 ...193 L6
Aubrey Dr SUD CO10 ...21 H1
Aubrey Rd WALTH E17 ...284 D1
Aubrietia Cl HARH RM3 ...272 A7
Auckland Av RAIN RM13 ...311 J7
Auckland Cl CHLM/WR CM1 ...193 H8
  EN EN1 ...232 C7
  TIL RM18 ...331 K8
Auckland Rd IL IG1 ...286 E6
  LEY E10 ...284 E6
Audleigh Pl CHIG IG7 ...268 D5
Audley Cl BRTR CM77 ...120 E6
Audley Ct SWFD E18 ...285 J2
Audley Dr CAN/RD E16 ...323 L6
Audley End Rd SAFWS SS11 ...351 P4
Audley Gdns GDMY/SEVK IG3 ...287 J7
  LOU IG10 ...250 C5
  WAB EN9 ...233 K4
Audley Rd COLW CO3 ...144 C6
  RCHLM CM3 ...144 C6
  SAFWS SS11 ...350
Audleys Cl SOSN SS2 ...283 H1
Audley Wy BSDN SS14 ...277
  CBE/LIN CB1 ...32 D2
  FOS CO13 ...137 K3
Audrey Gdns BSF CM23 ...139 G1
Audrey Rd IL IG1 ...286 E8
Audwick Cl CHES/WCR EN8 ...216 E6
Augurs La PLSTW E15 ...307 L1
Augustine Ct WAB EN9 ...233 J3
Augustine Rd GVE DA12 ...337 M5
Augustus Cl COLN CO4 ...87 L7
  HVHL CB9 ...35 G7
Augustus Wy WIT CM8 ...171 H5
Aukingford Gn CHONG SM5...380 G12
Aukingford Gn CHONG CM5...382 C1
Auriel Av DAGE RM10 ...311 G3
Austen Cl BRTR CM7 ...121 G1
  CRH DA9 * ...335 M8
  LOU IG10 ...251 J4
  THMD SE28 ...325 L4
  TIL RM18 ...331 M8
Austen Dr ING CM4 ...241 G7
Austin Av COS CO15 ...182 B7
Austin Gd GVW DA11 ...337 J6
Austin St CHTY IP2 ...16 F7
Austral Dr EMPK RM11 ...290 A5
Austral Wy RCHLM CM3 ...392 C2
Auton Cft SAFWS CB11 ...30 A7
Autoway COLN CO4 ...107 M1
Autumn Cl RCOS CO16 ...6 A1
Autumn St BOW E3 ...306 D5
Avebury Rd WAN E11 ...285 H1
  WOS/PRIT SS0 ...18 D2
Aveley By-Pass
  SOCK/AV RM15 ...328 F3
Aveley Cl RCOS CO16 ...158 F3
Aveley La SUD CO10 ...41 H1
Aveley Rd UPMR RM14 ...312 A4
  CDW/CHF RM16 ...329 M4
  CHDH RM6 ...288
  COLW CO3 ...106 D6
  FX IP11 ...62 D7
  GTDUN CM6 ...74 C7

  RAIN RM13 ...311 K5
Avenons Rd PLSTW E13 ...323 K1
Avenue Cl HARH RM3 ...272 C6
Avenue Ga LOU IG10 ...249 M6
Avenue Ldg BRW CM14 * ...330 E2
Avenue Rd BRW CM14 ...273 M3
  BSF CM23 ...139 A3
  CHLM/GWD CM2 ...210 A6
  EPP CM16 ...235 L6
  FSTGT E7 ...307 L2
  GDMY/SEVK IG3 ...287 H3
  HARH RM3 ...272 C6
  HOD EN11 ...201 L5
  ING CM4 ...239 L2
  LOS SS9 ...300 B5
  SBF/HAD SS7 ...298 A4
  WFD IG8 ...267 M5
  WIT CM8 ...171 K2
  WOS/PRIT SS0 ...18 D5
Avenue Ter WOS/PRIT SS0 ...18 D5
The Avenue BCAYW CM12 ...258 D3
  CHLM/GWD CM1 ...208 C4
  CHING E4 ...267 C5
  COLW CO3 ...106 F9
  COS CO15 ...159 L6
  CVI SS8 ...320 C1
  FX IP11 ...62 A6
  GRH DA9 ...335 M6
  GTDUN CM6 ...117 H5
  HCH RM12 ...290 A7
  HOD EN11 ...201 G5
  IP IP1 ...48 B4
  LOU IG10 ...250 B6
  RBRW/HUT CM13 ...274 C7
  RCHLM CM3 ...212 C7
  RCHLM CM3 ...246 C6
  RCOLE CO7 ...130 E4
  RCOLW CO6 ...106 E4
  RIPW IP8 ...52 E5
  ROM RM1 ...289 C2
  SBF/HAD SS7 ...299 H4
  SLH/COR SS17 ...296 A6
  WAB EN9 ...285 L4
  WIT CM8 ...171 K4
  WOS/PRIT SS0 ...18 D5
Avery Gdns GNTH/NBYPK IG2 ...286 C3
Avey La LOU IG10 ...234 B8
Aviary Cl CAN/RD E16 ...323 J1
Aviation Wy SOSN SS2 ...282 F6
Avignon Cl COLS CO2 ...129 L1
Avila Cha CHLM/GWD CM2 ...225 L4
Avis Sq WCHPL E1 ...322 A2
Avocet Cl FOS CO13 * ...137 H3
  K/T/MI CO5 ...149 G3
  K/T/MI CO5 ...178 A1
Avocet La FX IP11 * ...11 J7
Avocet Ms THMD SE28 ...325 G6
Avocet Wy MAL CM9 ...198 A6
Avon Cl GVE DA12 ...338 A7
  RCFD SS4 ...264 C7
Avondale Cl LOU IG10 ...250 C7
  RAYL SS6 ...281 J3
Avondale Dr LOS SS9 ...300 C1
Avondale Gdns SLH/COR SS17...295 J7
Avondale Rd CAN/RD E16 ...323 H1
  COS CO15 ...7 J5
  IPSE IP3 ...54 F3
  RAYL SS6 ...281 J3
  SBF/HAD SS7 ...298 A4
  WFD IG8 ...267 M5
Avon Gn SOCK/AV RM15 ...329 L4
Avonmouth Rd DART DA1 ...334 A7
Avon Rd CHLM/WR CM1 ...192 M7
  CVI SS8 ...320 D2
  UPMR RM14 ...290 C1
  WALTH E17 ...285 C1
Avontar Rd SOCK/AV RM15 ...313 G6
Avon Wy COLN CO4 ...108 C6
  SBN/FI SS3 ...303 C1
  SWFD E18 ...285 K3
Avril Wy CHING E4 ...266 F6
Avro Rd SOSN SS2 ...283 C1
Axe St BARK IG11 ...308 F5
Axon Pl IL IG1 ...286 D1
Aylands Rd PEND EN3 ...232 E6
Aylesbeare SBN/FI SS3 ...303 C3
Aylesbury Cl FSTGT E7 ...307 L3
Aylesbury Dr COS CO15 ...160 C5
  VGE SS16 ...276 D8
Aylets Fld HLWS CM18 ...203 M4
Aylett Cl CVI SS8 ...320 F1
Aylett Rd UPMR RM14 ...290 D7
Ayletts CHLM/WR CM1 ...193 L2
Aylmer Rd BCTR RM8 ...288 B5
  WAN E11 ...285 J5
Ayloffe Rd DAGW RM9 ...310 C4
Ayloffs Cl EMPK RM11 ...290 B2
Ayloff's Wk EMPK RM11 ...290 B2
Aylsham La HARH RM3 ...271 M3
Aylsham Rd HOD EN11 ...201 K1
Aylward Rd WFD IG8 ...267 M3
Aylward St WCHPL E1 ...322 A2
Aynsley Gdns HLWE CM17 ...204 D4
Aynsworth Av BSF CM23 ...115 H7
Ayres Cl PLSTW E13 ...307 K7
Ayr Gn ROM RM1 ...271 J4
Ayron Rd SOCK/AV RM15 ...313 L6
Ayr Rd IPNE IP4 ...49 G4
Ayr Wy ROM RM1 ...271 H7
Azalea Av WICKW SS12 ...260 F6
Azalea Cl IL IG1 ...308 C2
Azalea Cl WFD IG8 * ...267 G6
Azalea Ct CVI SS8 ...320 D3
Azalea Wy RCOS CO16 ...182 C1
Azof St GNWCH SE10 ...323 H7

B

Baardwyk Av CVI SS8 ...321 H2
Baas Hl BROX EN10 ...200 F7
Baas Hill Cl BROX EN10 ...200 F7
Baas La BROX EN10 ...200 F7
Babbacombe Gdns
  REDBR IG4 ...286 B2
Babington Rd BCTR RM8 ...309 M1
  HCH RM12 ...289 M6
Babraham Rd CBS CB2 ...22 F1
Back Hamlet IPSE IP3 ...17 H8
Back Hl CBE/LIN CB1 ...26 A5
Back La BRTR CM77 ...100 F1
  CDW/CHF RM16 ...329 M4
  CHDH RM6 ...288 A5
  COLW CO3 ...106 D6
  FX IP11 ...62 D7
  GTDUN CM6 ...74 C7

Back La East RCOLE CO7 ...110 D7
Back La West RCOLE CO7 ...110 C6
Back Rd CBE/LIN CB1 ...24 E5
  CHLM/GWD CM1 ...208 C4
  WAN E11 ...385 L8
  RCOLE CO7 ...89 L8
Back Waterside La
  RCOLE CO7 ...156 C8
Bacon Link CRW RM5 ...270 E5
Bacons Cha BOC CM0 ...386 F12
Bacon's La RCOLW CO6 ...103 H8
Bacton Rd FX IP11 ...11 J3
Badburgham Ct WAB EN9 ...234 A3
Baddeley Cl PEND EN3 ...233 H7
Baddow Cl DAGE RM10 ...310 D5
  WFD IG8 ...268 A5
Baddow Hall Av
  CHLM/GWD CM2 ...210 D6
Baddow Hall Crs
  CHLM/GWD CM2 ...210 D6
Baddow Place Av
  CHLM/GWD CM2 ...210 D7
Baddow Rd CHLM/GWD CM2 ...5 J5
Baden Powell Cl DAGW RM9 ...310 B5
Baden Powell Dr COLW CO3 ...128 D2
Baden Rd IL IG1 ...308 E2
Bader Cl IPSE IP3 ...55 H5
Bader Ct KESG IP5 ...50 C5
Bader Wk GVW DA11 ...337 H8
Bader Wy HCH RM12 ...311 K3
Badger Gv BRTR CM7 ...121 L2
Badger Hall Av SBF/HAD SS7 ...298 C1
Badgers BSF CM23 ...138 F4
Badgers Bank CHTY IP2 ...53 K4
Badgers Cl CHLM/GWD CM2 ...225 L4
  HERT/BAY SG13 ...184 C3
  WOS/PRIT SS0 ...300 E1
Badgers Cft BROX EN10 ...200 F7
Badgers Gn RCOLW CO6 ...86 E4
Badgers Gv RCOLW CO6 ...86 E4
Badgers Keep BOC CM0 ...393 L5
  HOC/HUL SS5 ...263 M8
The Badgers VGE SS16 ...294 C3
Badgers Wy SBF/HAD SS7 ...298 D5
Badley Hall Rd RCOLE CO7 ...110 C5
Badlis Rd WALTH E17 ...266 D8
Badminton Ms CAN/RD E16...323 K4
Badminton Pl BROX EN10 ...200 F6
Badminton Rd COS CO15 ...182 D6
Badsham Av IPSE IP3 ...55 K6
Bag La ING CM4 ...239 H1
Bagleys Spring CHDH RM6 ...288 B2
Bagshaw Rd HAR CO12 ...15 J7
Bailey Av KESG IP5 ...50 C5
Bailey Bridge Rd BRTR CM7 ...99 H8
Bailey Cl CHTY IP2 ...47 K7
  HVHL CB9 ...35 G6
  PUR RM19 ...329 G7
Bailey Dl COLW CO3 ...127 M1
Bailey La SUD CO10 ...37 M6
Bailey Rd LOS SS9 ...299 L3
The Bailey RAYL SS6 ...281 H3
Baillie Rd RAIN RM13 ...311 L8
Bainbridge Dr K/T/MI CO5 ...174 A1
Bainbridge Rd DAGW RM9 ...310 A1
Baines Cl COLW CO3 ...106 C8
Baines Coney HVHL CB9 ...33 M4
Baird Cl CHTY IP2 ...47 L6
Bakehouse Ct SAFWN CB10 * ...28 A7
Baker Md RCHLM CM3 ...196 D2
Baker Ms MAL CM9 ...214 E8
Baker Rd RIPS/CAP IP9 ...66 E5
Baker Av WALTH E17 ...284 L4
Bakers Cl BSDN SS14 ...278 D3
  COL CO1 ...8
Bakerscroft CHES/WCR EN8 * ...216 E4
Bakers Farm Cl WICKE SS11 ...261 K6
Bakers Fld ING CM4 ...241 G8
Baker's La BRTR CM77 ...120 F8
  CBE/LIN CB1 ...25 G7
  CHLM/GWD CM2 ...4
  COLN CO4 ...108
  EPP CM16 ...220 A8
  GTDUN CM6 ...142 F1
  ING CM4 ...239 L1
  MAL CM9 ...199 M1
  RCHLM CM3 ...212 B6
  ROY SG8 ...348 E8
Bakers Md RCHLM CM3 ...167 L8
Bakers Meadow BRWN CM15 ...383 R11
Bakers Ms ING CM4 ...239 L1
Bakers Rd CHESW EN7 ...216 C8
  SUD CO10 ...346 G4
Bakers Rw SRTFD E15 ...307 H4
Baker St CDW/CHF RM16 ...315 H6
  CHLM/GWD CM2 ...4 F5
Bakery Cl BOC CM0 ...390 D1
  HLWW/ROY CM19 ...202 F4
Bakery Ms WOS/PRIT SS0 * ...18 D5
Balaam St PLSTW E13 ...307 K2
Baldocks Rd EPP CM16 ...235 M5
Baldry Cl RIPW IP8 ...53 H4
Baldwin's Hi LOU IG10 ...250 C1
Baldwin's La RCOLW CO6 ...103 H5
Bale Cl COLW CO3 ...
Bale Rd WCHPL E1 ...322 B1
Balfe Ct COLN CO4 ...108 B7
Balfour Cl WICKW SS12 * ...261 H8
Balfour Rd GRAYS RM17 ...330 E3
  IL IG1 ...286 E3
Balgonie Rd CHING E4 ...249 G5
Balgores Crs GPK RM2 ...289 L1
Balgores La GPK RM2 ...289 L2
Balgores Sq GPK RM2 ...289 L2
Balgowan St
  WOOL/PLUM SE18 ...325 J7
Balingdon La CBE/LIN CB1 ...25 J6
Balkerne Hl COL CO1 ...8 B7
Balkerne Pas COL CO1 ...8 B7
Ball Aly COL CO1 ...8
Ballance Rd HOM E9 ...306 D1
Ballards Rd DAGE RM10 ...310 D4
Ballards Wk LAIN SS15 ...277
Ballast Quay GNWCH SE10 ...323 C8
Ballast Quay Rd RCOLE CO7 ...130

Ballater Cl IP IP1 ...47 K1
Ballingdon Hl SUD CO10 ...44 F4
Ballingdon St SUD CO10 ...20 A8
Balliol Av CHING E4 ...267 G3
Ball's Cha COLS CO2 ...129 K8
Ball's Chace RCOLW CO6 ...84 J4
Balmerino Av SBF/HAD SS7 ...280 F7
Balmer Rd BOW E3 ...306 E4
Balmoral Av COS CO15 ...6
  SLH/COR SS17 ...317 H2
Balmoral Ct BCAYE CM11 ...259 H4
  CHES/WCR EN8 ...232 E4
  CHTY IP2 ...53 L8
Balmoral Gdns HOC/HUL SS5 ...263 M7
Balmoral Rd BRWN CM15 ...255 M1
  FSTGT E7 ...307 M1
  GPK RM2 ...289 J2
  HCH RM12 ...290 A8
  LEY E10 ...284 E7
  PEND EN3 ...232 E6
  WOS/PRIT SS0 ...18 D4
Balsham Rd CBE/LIN CB1 ...25 J6
Balstonia Dr SLH/COR SS17 ...295 H8
Baltic Av WICKW SS12 ...19 H5
Baton Wy HAR CO12 ...70 E3
Bamford Wy GRW RM5 ...270 E4
  WALTH E17 ...266 E8
Banbury Rd HOM E9 ...306 A4
Banbury Sq RCHLM CM3 ...167 J6
Bancroft Cha RCHLM CM3 ...289 J7
Bancroft Rd WCHPL E1 ...306 A7
Bancrofts Rd RCHLM CM3 ...245 H5
Bandhills Cl RCHLM CM3 ...245 H5
Banes Down WAB EN9 ...201 M8
Banham Dr SUD CO10 ...20 C7
Banister Cl RCOS CO16 ...6 B1
Bankart La CHLM/GWD CM2 ...210 C1
Bank Buildings CHING E4 * ...267 G5
  SUD CO10 ...20 D7
Bankes Md CBS CB2 ...22 A7
Bankfoot GRAYS RM17 ...330 C5
Bank Rd IPNE IP4 ...17 K3
Bankside GVW DA11 ...336 F4
Bankside Cl RCHLM CM3 ...245 H4
Bankside Rd IL IG1 ...308 F2
Banks La EPP CM16 ...236 F2
Bank St BRTR CM7 ...121 J2
  GVE DA12 ...337 G4
Bann Cl SOCK/AV RM15 ...329 L3
Banner Cl PUR RM19 ...329 G7
Banning St GNWCH SE10 ...323 H8
Bannister Dr
  RBRW/HUT CM13 ...256 F2
Bannister Gn WICKW SS12 ...261 H7
Bannockburn Rd
  WOOL/PLUM SE18 ...325 H7
Bansons La CHONG CM5 ...382 A2
Bansons Wy CHONG CM5 ...382 A2
Banters La RCHLM CM3 ...144 D4
Bantoft Ter IPSE IP3 ...55 H3
Banyard Cl KESG IP5 ...50 C6
Banyards EMPK RM11 ...290 B3
Banyardway RCFD SS4 ...282 A2
Barbara Av CVI SS8 ...320 C2
Barbara Cl RCFD SS4 ...283 G2
Barbara Ville RCOS CO16 * ...134 D7
Barbel Cl CHES/WCR EN8 ...233 H4
Barberry Rd COLN CO4 ...108 C4
Barberry Cl HARH RM3 ...271 M5
Barbers Rd SRTFD E15 ...306 E6
Barbour Gdns COLS CO2 ...128 C3
Barbour Gn WICKW SS12 ...261 G8
Barbrook Wy RCHLM CM3 ...228 F3
Barchester St POP/IOD E14 ...322 E1
Barclay Cl CHLM/GWD CM2 ...210 C2
  HERT/BAY SG13 ...184 C5
Barclay Ct HOD EN11 ...201 H4
Barclay Ov WFD IG8 ...267 K3
Barclay Rd PIT SS13 ...279 H4
  PLSTW E13 ...307 M8
  WALTH E17 ...284 F3
  WAN E11 ...285 J6
Barclay Wy WTHK WM20 ...329 J8
Bardell Cl CHLM/GWD CM2 ...193 J7
Bardenville Rd CVI SS8 ...321 H2
Bardfield VGE SS16 ...278 B8
Bardfield Rd CHDH RM6 ...288 A1
Bardfield Rd BRTR CM7 ...97 J4
  COLS CO2 ...121 K4
  GTDUN CM6 ...75 J1
Bardfield Wy FOS CO13 ...137 J3
  RAYL SS6 ...280 D2
Bardwells Yd RCHLM CM3 * ...230 B7
Barfield Rd K/T/MI CO5 ...177 M7
  WAN E11 * ...285 J2
Barfields LOU IG10 ...250 D4
Barfields Gdns LOU IG10 ...250 D4
Barfields Pth LOU IG10 ...250 D4
Barfleur Cl WOOL/PLUM SE18 ...325 K3
Bargate Cl RCOLE CO7 ...89 L2
Barge House Rd CAN/RD E16 ...324 E5
Barge Pier Rd SBN/FI SS3 ...303 H4
Barham Cl GVE DA12 ...338 C6
  ROMW/RG RM7 ...270 E8
Barington Ct
  RBRW/HUT CM13 ...256 F2
Bark Burr Rd CDW/CHF RM16 ...331 G7
Barker Cl CHTY IP2 ...47 J8
  HVHL CB9 ...344 E7
  MGTR CO11 ...90 E1
Barker Rd SUD CO10 ...9 G9
Barking Rd EHAM E6 ...308 C5
  PLSTW E13 ...307 L2
  POP/IOD E14 ...323 H2
Barkis Cl CHLM/WR CM1 ...193 J6
Barkstead Rd COLN CO4 ...9 G1
Barkway Hl ROY SG8 ...370 D1
Barkwood Cl ROMW/RG RM7 ...288 B3
Barlee Cl SAFWS CB11 ...72 D6
Barle Gdns SOCK/AV RM15 ...329 L2
Barley Cl RBSF CM22 ...378 E3
  VGE SS16 ...
Barleycorn Wy EMPK RM11 ...290 C4
Barley Ct SAFWS CB11 ...28 A8
Barley Cft SAFWS CB11 ...203 L5
Barley Fld BRWN CM15 ...383 N11
Barley Flds WIT CM8 ...171 K4
Barley Hills BSF CM23 ...138 C3
Barleylands Rd LAIN SS15 ...277 J2
Barley La GDMY/SEVK IG3 ...287 K4
Barley Md RCHLM CM3 ...212 C4
Barley Rd ROY SG8 ...348 F5
  CBE/LIN CB1 ...106 A3
  COLW CO3 ...
Barling Rd SBN/FI SS3 ...302 D1
Barlon Rd RCOS CO16 ...110 C1
Barlow's Reach
  CHLM/GWD CM2 ...210 D1
Barlow Wy DAGW RM9 ...327 G3
Barlow Wy South DAGW RM9 ...327 G3
Barnabas Rd HOM E9 ...306 A3
Barnaby Rudge
  CHLM/WR CM1 ...193 J6

Barnaby Wy CHIG IG7 ...268 D2
Barnard Acres WAB EN9 ...217 M1
Barnard Cl SAFWS CB11 ...351 N12
Barnardiston Rd COLN CO4 ...296 B2
Barnardiston Wr MAL 171 J3
Barnardo Dr BARK/HLT IG6 ...286 D1
Barnardo Gdns WCHPL E1 * ...322 E4
Barnardo St WCHPL E1 ...322 E4
Barnard Rd CHLM/GWD CM2 ...225 M3
  LOS SS9 ...299 J3
  SBW CM21 ...162 F6
Barnards Av CVI SS8 ...321 G1
Barnards Fld GTDUN CM6 ...74 E3
Barnby St SRTFD E15 ...307 H5
Barncombe Cl SBF/HAD SS7 ...280 A7
Barncroft Cl COLN CO4 ...107 L2
  LOU IG10 ...250 D5
Barncroft Gn LOU IG10 ...250 D5
Barncroft Wy LOU IG10 ...250 D5
Barnes Cl BRW CM14 ...308 L1
Barnes Farm Dr RCHLM CM3 ...392 H4
Barnes Rd IL IG1 ...308 F2
Barnes St POP/IOD E14 ...322 C8
Barnet Park Rd WICKE SS11 ...261 J3
Barney Cl CHARL SE7 ...323 M8
Barnfield EPP CM16 ...220 B6
  FX IP11 ...62 D1
  GVW DA11 ...337 K7
  K/T/MI CO5 ...149 G2
  MGTR CO11 ...91 G1
  RBSF CM22 ...376 B11
  RIPS/CAP IP9 ...58 E4
Barnfield Av CVI SS8 ...321 G1
Barnfield Ms CHLM/WR CM1 ...193 K7
Barnfield Pl WIT CM8 ...171 J4
Barnfield Rd RCOLW CO6 ...86 K7
Barn Flds COLW CO3 ...105 M7
Barnfield Ter MGTR CO11 * ...91 G1
Barn Gn CHLM/WR CM1 ...194 B5
Barn Hall Av COLS CO2 ...129 L5
Barnhall Rd MAL CM9 ...174 A3
Barnham Dr THMD SE28 ...325 J4
Barnham Pl KESG IP5 ...49 L7
Barn Hl HLWW/ROY CM19 ...202 F5
Barn Mead BRTR CM7 ...122 A5
  BRWN CM15 ...383 R10
  HLWS CM18 ...203 M4
Barnmead Gdns DAGW RM9 ...310 A5
Barnmead Rd DAGW RM9 ...310 C2
Barnmead Wy BOC CM0 ...393 L6
Barn Rw RCFD SS4 * ...397 K4
Barns Ct EPP CM16 ...203 H4
Barnsdale Av POP/IOD E14 ...322 E7
Barnsley Rd HARH RM3 ...272 C6
Barnstable Cl SOS SS1 ...303 M1
Barnstaple Rd HARH RM3 ...271 M4
  SOS SS1 ...302 E5
Barnston Gn GTDUN CM6 ...141 K1
Barnston Wy
  RBRW/HUT CM13 ...256 F1
Barn View Rd RCOLW CO6 ...124 D4
Barnwell Dr HOC/HUL SS5 ...264 C1
Barnwell Rd DART DA1 ...334 C5
Baron Gdns BARK/HLT IG6 ...286 F1
Baronia Cft COLN CO4 ...107 M2
Baron Rd BCTR RM8 ...288 A6
  RCHLM CM3 ...245 H6
Barons Cl FX IP11 ...63 J7
Baronsdale Cl IP IP1 ...48 E1
Baron's La RCHLM CM3 ...230 A1
The Barons BSF CM23 ...138 E4
Barons Wy VGE SS16 ...294 E1
Baronswood Wy COLS CO2 ...129 G3
Barrack La HAR CO12 ...15 L1
  IP IP1 ...16 D1
  RCHLM CM3 ...167 H5
Barrack Rd CHLM/WR CM1 ...165 L5
Barrack Rw GVW DA11 ...337 L4
Barrack Sq CHLM/GWD CM2 ...5 H4
  KESG IP5 ...51 G6
Barrack St SUD CO10 ...360 C2
  COL CO1 ...9 G4
  MGTR CO11 ...366 E9
Barra Gld WICKW SS12 ...261 J4
Barrass Cl CAN/RD E16 ...308 E1
Barr Cl RCOLE CO7 ...132 D2
Barrel Cl RCOLE CO7 ...132 D2
Barrells Down Rd BSF CM23 ...114 F8
Barrett La BSF CM23 ...139 G2
Barrett Rd WALTH E17 ...284 F2
Barrier Point Rd CAN/RD E16 ...323 M5
Barrington Cl BSDN SS14 ...278 F5
  CHLM/GWD CM2 ...210 A7
  CLAY IG5 ...268 A3
  RCOS CO16 ...158 F3
  SBN/FI SS3 ...303 H4
Barrington Gdns BSDN SS14 ...278 C5
  COS CO15 ...159 J4
Barrington Gn LOU IG10 ...250 D4
Barrington On MAL CM9 ...239 L2
Barrington Rd COLS CO2 ...107 K8
  LOU IG10 ...250 D4
  MNPK E12 ...308 D1
Barringtons Dr RAYL SS6 ...281 G2
Barron's Cl CHONG CM5 ...382 A3
Barrow Hall Farm
  SBN/FI SS3 * ...396 F12
Barrow Hall Rd SBN/FI SS3 ...396 F12
Barrow La CHESW EN7 ...232 A1
Barrowsand SOS SS1 ...302 E7
Barrows Rd
  HLWW/ROY CM19 ...203 G1
Barr Rd GVE DA12 ...338 C7
Barry Cl CDW/CHF RM16 ...331 G2
Barryfields BRTR CM7 ...78 B6
Barry Rd EHAM E6 ...324 B2
Barsey Cl HVHL CB9 ...33 M4
Barstable Rd SLH/COR SS17 ...317 G6
Barth Ms WOOL/PLUM SE18 ...325 H7
Bartholomew Cl SAFWN CB10 ...341 M7
Bartholomew Dr HARH RM3 ...272 A8
Bartholomew Rd BSF CM23 ...139 G3
Bartholomew St IPNE IP4 ...17 L4
Barth Rd WOOL/PLUM SE18 ...325 H7
Bartle Av EHAM E6 ...308 B6
Bartlett Cl POP/IOD E14 * ...322 E1
  RCHLM CM3 ...388 D1
Bartlett Rd GVW DA11 ...337 K6
Bartletts RAYL SS6 ...281 K5
Bartley Cl SBF/HAD SS7 ...279 L7
Bartlow End FX IP11 ...278 B5
Bartlow Gdns CRW RM5 ...271 G2
Bartlow Rd CBE/LIN CB1 ...26 B8
  CBE/LIN CB1 ...342 F11
Bartlow Side PIT SS13 ...278 B5
Barton Av DAGE RM10 ...268 F6
Barton Cl CHIG IG7 ...268 D2
  CHTY IP2 ...53 K8
  RCHLM CM3 ...245 J8
Barton Gv HVHL CB9 ...35 J3
  HVHL CB9 ...35 L3

Barton Mdw BARK/HLT IG6 ...286 E2
Barton Rd FX IP11 ...69 G1
  HCH RM12 ...289 K6
Bartrip St HOM E9 ...306 B3
Bartram Av BRTR CM7 ...121 M2
The Barvens RIPW IP8 ...52 F4
Barward Cl WOOL/PLUM SE18...324 D4
Barwell Wy WIT CM8 ...171 J3
Barwick Rd FSTGT E7 ...307 L1
Baryta Cl SLH/COR SS17 ...316 F4
Basbow La BSF CM23 ...139 G2
Basedale Rd DAGW RM9 ...309 L4
Baseing Cl EHAM E6 ...324 D3
Basil Av EHAM E6 ...308 B7
Basildon Av CLAY IG5 ...268 A2
Basildon Dr LAIN SS15 ...276 F6
Basildon Rd ABYW SE2 ...325 K8
  LAIN SS15 ...2 A2
Basil Ms HLWE CM17 ...188 A6
Basin Ap POP/IOD E14 ...322 D2
Basin Rd MAL CM9 ...215 H5
Baslow Wk CLPT E5 ...306 A1
Bassenthwaite Rd
  SBF/HAD SS7 ...280 B7
Bassett Gdns EPP CM16 ...221 J4
Bassett's La CHONG CM5 ...206 C5
  MAL CM9 ...212 D1
Bassingbourne Cl BROX EN10...201 L5
Bassingbourn Rd STSD CM24 ...374 G11
Bastable Av BARK IG11 ...309 K6
Bastion Av ABYW SE2 ...325 K8
Bata Av TIL RM18 ...332 E4
Batavia Cl CVI SS8 ...320 A1
Bate-Dudley Dr BOC CM0 ...386 G10
Bateman Cl BARK IG11 ...308 F3
Bateman Rd CHING E4 ...266 D5
  RCOLE CO7 ...130 E6
Batemans Rd RCOS CO16 ...158 E5
Bates Rd HARH RM3 ...272 D6
  MAL CM9 ...214 A1
Bate St POP/IOD E14 ...322 C2
Bath Rd FSTGT E7 ...308 A3
  FX IP11 ...69 G1
Bath St CHTY IP2 ...17 L5
  GVW DA11 ...337 L4
Bathurst Cl COLS CO2 ...130 E6
Bathurst Rd IL IG1 ...286 E5
Bathway WOOL/PLUM SE18 ...324 D7
Baton Cl PUR RM19 ...329 G2
Battery La RIPS/CAP IP9 ...67 G5
Battery Rd THMD SE28 ...325 J3
Battisford Dr RCOS CO16 ...182 D1
Battle Rd ERITH DA8 ...326 F7
Battlesbrook Rd COLS CO2 ...130 A1
Battles La MAL CM9 ...50 C6
Battleswick BSDN SS14 ...278 B6
Batt's Rd BOC CM0 ...389 J3
The Baulks CBS CB2 ...22 B2
Bawdsey Av GNTH/NBYPK IG2...287 J2
Bawdsey Cl FX IP11 ...63 J7
  RCOS CO16 ...182 E1
Bawn Cl BRTR CM7 ...121 J1
Bawtree Crs CBE/LIN CB1 ...25 H6
Bawtree Wy COLW CO3 ...106 D8
Baxter Av SOSN SS2 ...18 C5
Baxter Cl CAN/RD E16 ...323 M2
  IL IG1 ...308 E2
Baxters RCHLM CM3 ...212 D6
Bayard Av RCOLE CO7 ...156 D5
Bayley's Md RBRW/HUT CM13...256 F5
Bayley St HSTD CO9 ...356 C5
Bayliss Av ROM SE28 ...326 A3
Bayly Rd DART DA1 ...334 D8
Bay Manor La WTHK RM20 ...335 J1
Baymans Wd BRWN CM15 ...256 J5
Baynard Av GTDUN CM6 ...118 B7
Baynards Crs FOS CO13 ...137 H3
Bayne Cl EHAM E6 ...324 C2
Bay Rd HAR CO12 ...15 L1
Baythorne St BOW E3 ...322 C1
Bay Tree Ct BRTR CM77 * ...120 C5
  CHESW EN7 ...216 A5
Bay Vw BOC CM0 ...389 M1
Bay View Crs HAR CO12 ...70 E3
Baywood Sq CHIG IG7 ...269 L3
Bazely St POP/IOD E14 ...322 F2
Beach Ap RCOS CO16 * ...181 L7
Beach Hl LOS SS9 ...300 D5
Beach Crs COS CO15 ...182 C7
Beachcroft Av FOS CO13 ...137 J3
Beachcroft Rd WAN E11 ...285 H8
Beaches Rd HOC/HUL SS5 ...264 C1
Beach House Gdns CVI SS8 ...321 H3
Beach Rd COS CO15 ...7 H1
  CVI SS8 ...321 G1
  HAR CO12 ...15 G3
  K/T/MI CO5 ...177 M7
  RCOS CO16 ...180 B5
  SBN/FI SS3 ...303 J4
  SOS SS1 ...19 L1
Beach's Dr CHLM/WR CM1 ...209 G4
Beach Station Rd FX IP11 ...11 H7
Beach Wy COS CO15 ...182 C7
Beachway RCOS CO16 ...320 E3
Beachy Dr BOC CM0 ...389 M4
Beachy Rd BOW E3 ...306 D4
Beacon Cl RCOLE CO7 ...156 D7
Beacon Fld FX IP11 ...62 D3
Beaconfield Av EPP CM16 ...220 A7
Beaconfield Rd EPP CM16 ...220 A7
Beaconfield Ms EPP CM16 ...220 A7
Beacon Hts RCOS CO16 ...180 E3
Beacon Hl BRW CM14 ...383 K11
  MAL CM9 ...214 A1
  PUR RM19 ...328 E4
  WIT CM8 ...172 A7
Beacon Hill Av HAR CO12 ...15 M3
Beacon Hill Rd BRW CM14 ...383 J11
Beaconsfield Cl SUD CO10 ...20 C4
Beacon La FRAM/WMKT IP13 ...50 C1
Beaconsfield Rd CAN/RD E16 ...307 J3
  COS CO15 ...7 H1
  IP IP1 ...47 L8
  LEY E10 * ...284 F7
  PEND EN3 ...232 E7
  SUD CO10 ...20 C5
  WALTH E17 ...284 C1
The Beacons LOU IG10 ...235 J4
Beacontree Av WALTH E17 ...267 L6
Beacontree Rd WAN E11 ...285 J5
Beacon Wy COLW CO3 ...105 M7
Beadles Av BRTR CM7 ...121 J4
Beadon Dr BRTR CM7 ...121 J4
Beads Hall La BRWN CM15 ...255 L4
Beale Pl BOW E3 ...306 C4
Beale Rd BOW E3 ...306 C4
Bealings Rd WDBR IP12 ...51 G2
Beal Rd IL IG1 ...286 D6

Beam Av DAGE RM10 ...310 F6
Beambridge PIT SS13 ...278 D7
Beambridge Ct PIT SS13 ...278 D7
Beambridge Ms PIT SS13 ...278 D7
Beaminster Gdns
  BARK/HLT IG6 ...286 E1
Beamish Cl EPP CM16 ...221 K3
Beams Wy BCAYE CM11 ...258 F6
Beamway DAGE RM10 ...311 G4
Beanacre Cl HOM E9 ...306 C3
Beane Cft GVE DA12 ...338 C6
Beanfield Rd SBW CM21 ...162 B5
Bean Rd GRH DA9 ...335 L8
Beansland Gv CHDH RM6 ...270 A6
Bear Cl ROMW/RG RM7 ...288 D2
Beardmore Pk KESG IP5 ...51 G5
Beardsfield PLSTW E13 ...307 K5
Beard's La SAFWS CB11 ...350 C3
Bearing Cl CHIG IG7 ...269 K3
Bearing Wy CHIG IG7 ...269 K3
Bear St RCOLW CO6 ...361 M8
Beaton Cl GRH DA9 ...335 L6
Beatrice Av CVI SS8 ...320 E1
  FX IP11 ...62 F7
Beatrice Cl HOC/HUL SS5 ...264 A7
  PLSTW E13 ...307 K8
Beatrice Gdns GVW DA11 ...337 K9
  WALTH E17 ...284 D3
  WOTN CO14 ...369 N11
Beatty Gdns BRTR CM7 ...121 J4
Beatty La BSDN SS14 ...278 B3
Beatty Ri RCHLM CM3 ...245 J7
Beatty Rd CHES/WCR EN8 ...233 G4
  IPSE IP3 ...55 G3
Beattyville Gdns CLAY IG5 ...286 D1
Beauchamp Rd FSTGT E7 ...307 L4
Beauchamps BOC CM0 ...393 L5
Beauchamps Cl
  CHLM/WR CM1 ...194 D6
Beauchamps Dr WICKE SS11 ...261 K6
Beaufort Cl CDW/CHF RM16 ...330 C2
  CHING E4 ...266 E5
  EPP CM16 ...221 H5
  ROMW/RG RM7 ...288 F2
Beaufort Gdns BRTR CM7 ...121 D6
  CHLM/GWD CM2 ...210 D1
Beaufort St IP IP1 ...16 B7
  SOSN SS2 ...302 A4
Beaulieu Av CAN/RD E16 ...323 L4
Beaulieu Bvd
  CHLM/WR CM1 ...194 D6
Beaulieu Dr WAB EN9 ...233 J3
Beauly Wy ROM RM1 ...271 H7
Beaumont Av COS CO15 ...7 H6
  RCOLE CO7 ...156 D6
Beaumont Cl COLN CO4 ...107 H1
  GPK RM2 ...271 M8
  WOTN CO14 ...137 J2
Beaumont Ct HVHL CB9 ...34 E7
Beaumont Dr GVW DA11 ...337 J5
Beaumont Gdns
  HLWW/ROY CM19 ...202 C1
Beaumont Pl BRTR CM7 ...121 C2
Beaumont V HVHL CB9 ...34 E7
Beaumont Wy MAL CM9 ...214 E5
Beaumont Park Dr
  HLWW/ROY CM19 ...202 C1
Beaumont Sq WCHPL E1 ...322 A1
Beaver Cl COLW CO3 ...106 B6
Beaver Bet BARK/HLT IG6 ...269 M4
Beazley End WICKW SS12 ...261 H7
Bebbington Rd
  WOOL/PLUM SE18 * ...325 H7
Bebington Cl BCAYW CM12 ...258 C2
Beccles Ct WICKE SS11 ...261 J3
Beccles Dr BARK IG11 ...309 J3
Beccles St POP/IOD E14 ...322 C3
Beche Rd COL CO1 ...107 L8
Becker Rd COLW CO3 ...122 A4
Beckers Green Rd BRTR CM7 ...122 B3
Becket Av EHAM E6 ...308 D3
Becket Cl RBRW/HUT CM13 ...273 M5
  RCFD SS4 ...265 G8
Beckett Cl BELV DA17 ...326 B6
Beckett Dr SLH/COR SS17 ...317 G1
Becketts LAIN SS15 * ...276 D7
Becketts La HADL IP7 ...362 C1
Becket Wy RCHLM CM3 ...245 H8
Beck Farm Cl CVI SS8 * ...321 J2
Beckford Rd MGTR CO11 ...91 K1
Beckingham Rd MAL CM9 ...172 E8
Beckingham St MAL CM9 ...189 M3
Beckley Ct GVE DA12 ...338 E7
Beck Rd CVI SS8 ...321 J2
  SAFWN CB10 ...28 A8
Becontree Av BCTR RM8 ...309 L1
Becontree Cl COS CO15 ...159 J5
Bective Rd FSTGT E7 ...307 K1
Bedale Rd HARH RM3 ...272 D4
Beddington Rd
  GDMY/SEVK IG3 ...287 J5
Bedells Av BRTR CM77 ...121 L4
Bede Rd CHDH RM6 ...288 M4
Bedford Ct BRTR CM7 ...121 L1
  K/T/MI CO5 ...150 A8
  RAYL SS6 ...281 G4
Bedford Crs PEND EN3 ...232 F5
Bedford Gdns HCH RM12 ...289 M7
Bedford Rd COLN CO4 ...87 J8
  COS CO15 ...160 A4
  EHAM E6 ...308 D5
  GRAYS RM17 ...330 E4
  GVW DA11 ...337 J7
  IL IG1 ...286 E8
  LAIN SS15 ...276 E7
  SWFD E18 ...267 K8
  WALTH E17 ...266 D8
Bedfords Rd HARH RM3 ...271 K1
Bedloes Av WICKE SS11 ...262 B8
Bedwell Rd BELV DA17 ...326 B5
Bedwell Av BKHH IG9 ...267 J1
  BRTR CM7 ...121 J8
  HSTD CO9 ...356 C4
  RAYL SS6 ...281 G2
  RBRW/HUT CM13 ...256 F5
  RCOLE CO7 ...130 E4
  UPMR RM14 ...331 G1
Beeby Rd CAN/RD E16 ...323 L1
Beecham Ct LAIN SS15 ...276 D7
Beech Av BKHH IG9 ...267 J1

RBSF CM22 ...377 K1
RIPW IP8 ...46 F7
Beechcombe SLH/COR SS17 ...295 L8
Beechcroft Av TIL RM18 ...332 B3
Beechcroft Rd CVI SS8 ...320 B2
  IP IP1 ...47 L8
  SWFD E18 ...267 L8
Beech Dr SBW CM21 ...188 D3
Beeches Cl CHLM/WR CM1 ...4
  SAFWS CB11 ...351 N6
Beeches Rd CHLM/WR CM1 ...4
  MAL CM9 ...198 C8
  WICKE SS11 ...262 B8
The Beeches BRW CM14 ...262 B3
  CHING E4 * ...249 G8
  IPSE IP3 ...17 L7
  MGTR CO11 ...91 G1
  SAFWS CB11 * ...351 M8
  TIL RM18 ...331 L8
Beechfield HOD EN11 ...185 K7
  SBW CM21 ...163 G7
Beechfield Gdns
  ROMW/RG RM7 ...288 F5
Beechfield Wk WAB EN9 ...233 H3
Beech Gdns DAGE RM10 ...310 E4
Beech Gn WIT CM8 ...172 C8
Beech Gv BARK/HLT IG6 ...269 H5
  HAR CO12 ...70 A6
  HSTD CO9 ...356 C6
  HVHL CB9 ...34 A4
  IPSE IP3 ...17 M9
  KESG IP5 ...51 L6
  SOCK/AV RM15 ...328 F5
Beech Hall Crs CHING E4 ...267 G6
Beech Hall Rd CHING E4 ...266 F6
Beech Hl COLW CO3 ...106 D8
Beech Hill Gdns WAB EN9 ...234 C5
Beechlands BSF CM23 ...139 G4
Beech La CBS CB2 ...22 F4
Beech Ms WARE SG12 ...184 C2
Beechmont Gdns SOSN SS2 ...301 H1
Beech Pl EPP CM16 ...236 A1
Beech Ri RCHLM CM3 ...196 D1
  CHONG CM5 ...206 A1
  HOC/HUL SS5 ...263 H3
  KESG IP5 ...51 G5
  SBF/HAD SS7 ...299 C5
  SUD CO10 ...20 D4
Beech St ROMW/RG RM7 ...288 F5
Beech Tree Gld CHING E4 ...249 J8
Beech Wy CBE/LIN CB1 ...24 F7
Beechwood Cl COLS CO2 ...129 G3
  HERT/BAY SG13 ...184 A3
Beechwood Dr WFD IG8 ...267 J4
Beechwood Gdns CLAY IG5 ...286 C1
  RAIN RM13 ...327 L1
Beechwood Pk SWFD E18 ...285 K7
Beecroft Cl CVI SS8 ...320 B2
Beechwood Av WICKE SS11 ...261 J7
  WOS/PRIT SS0 ...18 A2
Beehive Cha BRWN CM15 ...238 A4
Beehive Ct COL CO1 ...8 F9
  RBSF CM22 ...378 B2
Beehive La BSDN SS14 ...278 H5
  CHLM/GWD CM2 ...210 C5
  REDBR IG4 ...286 C3
Beeleigh Av MAL CM9 ...214 A4
Beeleigh Cl COLS CO2 * ...129 K4
  SOSN SS2 ...301 H2
Beeleigh Cross BSDN SS14 ...278 B6
Beeleigh East BSDN SS14 ...278 B6
Beeleigh Link
  CHLM/GWD CM2 ...210 C2
Beeleigh Rd MAL CM9 ...214 C2
Beeleigh West BSDN SS14 ...3 M2
Beeston Dr CHES/WCR EN8 ...216 E5
Beggarhill INC CM4 ...223 G6
Begonia Cl CHLM/WR CM1 ...194 D7
  EHAM E6 ...308 B8
Begonia Pl RCOS CO16 ...6 B3
Beke Hall Cha North
  RAYL SS6 ...280 B1
Beke Hall Cha South
  RAYL SS6 ...280 B2
Bekesbourne St
  POP/IOD E14 * ...322 B2
Bekeswell La
  CHLM/GWD CM2 ...J2
Belbin Wy CBS CB2 ...22 J1
Belchamp Rd WICKE SS11 ...261 J5
Belchamps Rd WICKE SS11 ...264 B8
Belcham's La SAFWS CB11 ...93 M8
Belcher Rd HOD EN11 ...201 J4
Belchers La WAB EN9 ...218 G2
Beldams Cl RCOS CO16 ...135 K4
Beldams Ga BSF CM23 ...139 K3
Beldams La BSF CM23 ...139 K3
Beldowes VGE SS16 ...3 M8
Belfairs Cl LOS SS9 ...300 A3
Belfairs Dr CHDH RM6 ...287 M5
  LOS SS9 ...300 A3
Belfairs Park Cl LOS SS9 ...281 M8
Belfairs Park Dr LOS SS9 ...281 M8
Belford Gv WOOL/PLUM SE18 ...324 D7
Belgrave Av GPK RM2 ...289 M1
Belgrave Cl IPNE IP4 ...48 D1
  LOS SS9 ...300 A3
  RAYL SS6 ...280 C1
Belgrave Cl BCAYW CM12 ...258 C7
  IL IG1 ...286 D7
  LOS SS9 ...307 M8
  PLSTW E13 ...307 M8
  WALTH E17 ...266 C8
Belgrave St WCHPL E1 ...322 A2
Beliamaine Cl THMD SE28 ...325 J5
Bellamy Cl FOS CO13 ...137 G3
  POP/IOD E14 ...322 D5
Bellamy Rd CHES/WCR EN8 ...216 F7
  CHING E4 ...249 M8
Bell Av HARH RM3 ...271 L7
Bell Cl CHTY IP2 ...54 C8
  COLS CO2 ...130 A3
  GRH DA9 ...335 J7
Bell Common EPP CM16 ...235 M2
Bell Ct RCHLM CM3 ...243 M4
Bellcroft WIT CM8 ...171 K2
Belle Staines Pleasaunce
  CHING E4 ...266 D1
Belle Vue CHLM/GWD CM2 ...5 E6
Bellevue Av SOS SS1 ...19 M4
Bellevue Pl SOS SS1 ...19 M4
Belle Vue Rd COL CO1 ...270 C3
  CRW RM5 ...270 C3
  IPNE IP4 ...17 M6
  SOS SS1 ...20 C6
  WALTH E17 ...267 G8
Bellevue Rd BCAYW CM12 ...258 C5
  EMPK RM11 ...290 B1
  SOSN SS2 ...19 M3
Bell Farm Av DAGE RM10 ...310 E5
Bell Farm Gn BCAYW CM12 ...258 E5
Bellfield VGE SS16 ...3 M8
Bellfield Av RCOLE CO7 * ...156 C5

Bellfield Cl RCOLE CO7 156 D6
Bellfield Gdns HLWE CM17 204 D2
Bellfiled Cl RCOLE CO7 156 D6
Bell Gdns LEY E10 * 284 D6
Bell Hl BURES CO8 359 M5
RCHLM CM3 211 M6
Bell Hill Cl BCAYW CM12 258 E5
Bellhouse Crs LOS SS9 282 A8
Bellhouse La BRW CM14 255 H5
LOS SS9 300 A1
Bellhouse Rd LOS SS9 282 A7
Bell House Rd
ROMW/RG RM7 288 F6
Bellingham La RAYL SS6 281 G3
Bellingham Pl K/T/MI CO5 148 F2
Bell La BROX EN10 200 F7
BRTR CM7 76 D3
BRTR CM7 98 D6
CAN/RD E16 323 K4
CHTY IP2 16 F7
GTDUN CM6 74 D2
HOD EN11 201 H3
KESG IP5 50 A5
PEND EN3 232 E8
ROY SG8 370 G5
Bellmaine Av SLH/COR SS17 317 J1
Bellman Av GVE DA12 338 B6
Bellmead CHLM/GWD CM2 5 G4
Bell Md ING CM4 239 L2
SBW CM21 162 F7
Bellot St GNWCH SE10 323 H8
Bell-Reeves Cl SLH/COR SS17 316 F3
Bells Cha CHLM/GWD CM2 210 B7
Bells Cl SAFWS CB11 30 A1
Bells Hl BSF CM23 138 F2
BURES CO8 84 D1
Bells Hill Rd VGE SS16 295 L3
Bells Rd SUD CO10 347 N7
Bell St CHLM/GWD CM2 210 C7
SBW CM21 162 F7
Bell Wk WOS/PRIT SS0 301 G1
Bell Water Ga
WOOL/PLUM SE18 324 D6
Bell Whf LOS SS9 * 300 B5
Belmer Rd STSD CM24 374 E9
Belmonde Dr CHLM/WR CM1 194 A6
Belmont Av UPMR RM14 290 C7
WICKW SS12 260 D7
Belmont Cl CHING E4 267 G4
CHLM/WR CM1 194 B6
WFD IG8 267 L3
WICKW SS12 260 E6
Belmont Crs COLN CO4 107 M2
Belmont Hl SAFWS CB11 351 P12
Belmont Park Rd LEY E10 284 E4
Belmont Pl COL CO1 129 M1
Belmont Rd GRAYS RM17 330 C4
HCH RM12 290 A8
IL IG1 286 F8
RIPW IP8 53 H4
Belsize Av COS CO15 182 A7
Belson Rd WOOL/PLUM SE18 324 C7
Belstead Av CHTY IP2 16 D9
Belstead Rd CHTY IP2 53 L4
Belsteads Farm La
CHLM/WR CM1 194 A3
Belstedes LAIN SS15 277 G7
Beltinge Rd HARH RM3 290 C1
Beltona Gdns CHES/WCR EN8 216 E5
Belton Br LOS SS9 300 A5
Belton Cnr LOS SS9 * 300 A5
Belton Gdns LOS SS9 299 M5
Belton Rd WAN E11 307 H1
Belton Wy BOW E3 322 D1
Belton Wy East LOS SS9 299 M5
Belton Wy West LOS SS9 299 L5
Beltwood Rd BELV DA17 326 F7
Belvawney Cl CHLM/WR CM1 193 H7
Belvedere Av CLAY IG5 268 E8
HOC/HUL SS5 263 M7
Belvedere Cl GVE DA12 337 M6
RCHLM CM3 212 C6
Belvedere Ct BELV DA17 326 C6
Belvedere Pl MAL CM9 214 C5
Belvedere Rd BOC CM0 393 M10
BRW CM14 273 J2
IPNE IP4 48 E5
LEY E10 284 B6
RCHLM CM3 212 C6
THMD SE28 326 A4
The Belvoir ING CM4 239 K2
Bembridge Cl COS CO15 159 J5
Bemerton Gdns FOS CO13 136 F3
Bemsted Rd WALTH E17 284 C1
Benacre Rd IPSE IP3 54 F3
Benares Rd
WOOL/PLUM SE18 325 J7
Benbow Dr RCHLM CM3 245 H7
Bencroft CHESW EN7 216 B4
Benderloch CVI SS8 320 B1
Bendish Rd EHAM E6 308 B4
Bendlowes Rd BRTR CM7 76 E4
Bendmore Av ABYW SE2 325 K8
Benedict Dr CHLM/WR CM1 4 A3
Benedictine Ga
CHES/WCR EN8 216 F5
Benets Rd EMPK RM11 290 D6
Benezet St IP IP1 16 C2
Benfield Wy BRTR CM7 121 L3
Benfleet Park Rd
SBF/HAD SS7 297 L2
Benfleet Rd SBF/HAD SS7 298 D3
Benford Rd HOD EN11 201 G5
Bengal Rd IL IG1 308 E1
Benhall Cl RCOS CO16 182 D1
Benhooks Av BSF CM23 138 F4
Benhurst Av HCH RM12 311 L1
Benjamin Cl EMPK RM11 289 K4
Ben Jonson Rd WCHPL E1 322 B1
Benledi St POP/IOD E14 323 G2
Bennet Ct COLN CO4 108 B7
Bennett Cl BRTR CM7 121 K5
WOTN CO14 137 K1
Bennett Rd CHDH RM6 288 B4
IP IP1 47 J5
PLSTW E13 307 M8
Bennett's Av RCHLM CM3 243 J2
Bennett's Castle La
BCTR RM8 309 M1
Bennett's La GTDUN CM6 142 A3
Bennett Wy RCHLM CM3 196 D1
Bennington Rd WFD IG8 * 267 H6
Bennions Cl HCH RM12 312 A3
Bennison Dr HARH RM3 272 A8
Benn St HOM E9 306 B3
Benrek Cl BARK/HLT IG6 268 F6
Benskins Cl BSF CM23 92 B1
Benskins La ABR/ST RM4 254 A8
Benson Av PLSTW E13 307 M6
Benson Rd GRAYS RM17 330 E5
Bentall Cl HSTD CO9 * 81 J5
Bentalls BSDN SS14 2 F1
Bentalls Cl SOSN SS2 301 K1
Bentfield End Cswy
STSD CM24 115 L2
Bentfield Gdns STSD CM24 115 L2
Bentfield Rd STSD CM24 115 L2
Bentham Rd HOM E9 306 A3
THMD SE28 325 L4
Bent Hl FX IP11 11 M3
Ben Tillet Cl BARK IG11 309 K4
CAN/RD E16 * 324 C4
Bent La IPNE IP4 49 K5
Bentley Av COS CO15 182 B7
Bentley Cl BSF CM23 139 G4
Bentley Dr GNTH/NBYPK IG2 286 F4
HLWE CM17 204 D2
Bentley La RIPS/CAP IP9 364 A9
RIPW IP8 53 H8
Bentley Rd IP IP1 47 H4
MGTR CO11 110 F1
RCOS CO16 133 M8
WIT CM8 171 H1
The Bentleys SOSN SS2 282 C6
Bentley St GVE DA12 337 M4
Bentley Wy WFD IG8 267 K2
Benton Cl BRTR CM77 122 B7
WIT CM8 171 K6
Benton Gdns SLH/COR SS17 295 J8
Benton Rd IL IG1 287 G6
Bentons WAB EN9 * 201 M8
Bentonwood SBF/HAD SS7 280 F8
Bentry Cl BCTR RM8 288 B7
Bentry Rd BCTR RM8 288 B7
Benvenue Av LOS SS9 282 C6
Benworth St BOW E3 306 C7
Benyon Pth SOCK/AV RM15 313 M6
Berberis Cl VGE SS16 294 C1
Berberis Wk COLN CO4 * 108 B6
Berbice La GTDUN CM6 116 F3
Berdens VGE SS16 3 M8
Berechurch Hall Rd COLS CO2 128 F4
Berechurch Rd COLS CO2 129 G4
Berecroft HLWS CM18 203 L6
Beredens La RBRW/HUT CM13 273 J8
Berens Cl WICKE SS11 261 J4
Beresford Cl SBF/HAD SS7 299 G1
Beresford Ct BCAYW CM12 240 C8
Beresford Dr WFD IG8 267 M3
Beresford Gdns CHDH RM6 288 B3
SBF/HAD SS7 298 F1
Beresford Rd CHING E4 249 H8
GVW DA11 337 H5
SOS SS1 19 L7
WALTH E17 266 E7
Beresford Sq
WOOL/PLUM SE18 324 E7
Beresford St
WOOL/PLUM SE18 324 F6
Bere St WAP E1W 322 A3
Bergamot Rd HVHL CB9 33 M5
Berg Av CVI SS8 299 G8
Berger Rd HOM E9 306 A3
Bergholt Av REDBR IG4 286 B3
Bergholt Rd COLN CO4 107 G3
MGTR CO11 64 E6
Beridge Rd HSTD CO9 81 G3
Beriffe Pl RCOLE CO7 * 156 C6
Bering Wk CAN/RD E16 324 A2
Berkeley Av CLAY IG5 268 D8
CRW RM5 270 F6
Berkeley Cl IPNE IP4 48 D4
UPMR RM14 290 E7
Berkeley Dr BCAYW CM12 240 D8
EMPK RM11 290 D6
Berkeley Gdns K/T/MI CO5 * 130 C6
LOS SS9 299 K4
Berkeley La CVI SS8 320 D3
Berkeley Rd COS CO15 7 G3
MNPK E12 308 B2
Berkeley Ter TIL RM18 * 331 K6
Berkely Dr CHLM/GWD CM2 210 C3
Berkhampstead Rd
BELV DA17 326 D8
Berkley Av CHES/WCR EN8 232 E4
Berkley Cl COLN CO4 107 M1
Berkley Hl SLH/COR SS17 317 H1
Berkley Pl CHES/WCR EN8 * 232 E4
Berkley Rd GVE DA12 337 L4
Berkley Rw GVE DA12 * 337 L4
Berkshire Cl LOS SS9 281 M8
Berkshire Rd HOM E9 306 C3
Berkshire Wy EMPK RM11 290 D3
Bermuda Rd KIR/NAC IP10 55 K6
TIL RM18 331 K8
Bernal Cl THMD SE28 326 A3
Bernard Ashley Dr CHARL SE7 323 L8
Bernard Cassidy St
CAN/RD E16 * 323 J1
Bernard Cl FOS CO13 137 H3
Bernard Crs IPSE IP3 55 G3
Bernard Gv WAB EN9 233 J3
Bernard Rd ROMW/RG RM7 288 F5
Bernards Cl BARK/HLT IG6 268 F6
Bernard St GVE DA12 337 L4
Berners End GTDUN CM6 141 K1
Berners Rd FX IP11 69 H1
Berners St IP IP1 16 D3
Berners Wk BSDN SS14 3 M2
Berners Wy BROX EN10 217 G1
Bernice Cl RAIN RM13 311 M8
Bernside BRTR CM7 121 J3
Bernwell Rd CHING E4 267 H2
Berrimans Cl COLN CO4 9 M8
Berrybank Cl CHING E4 266 F1
Berry Cl DAGE RM10 310 D2
HCH RM12 311 M2
IPSE IP3 55 L4
VGE SS16 276 E8
WICKW SS12 260 F7
Berry Field Cl WALTH E17 284 E2
Berry La VGE SS16 294 E1
Berryman Cl BCTR RM8 287 M8
Berrys Ar RAYL SS6 * 281 G3
Berry Ter SUD CO10 * 20 E6
Berry V RCHLM CM3 245 H7
Bersham La CDW/CHF RM16 330 C3
Berther Rd EMPK RM11 290 B5
Berthold Ms WAB EN9 233 J3
Berthons Gdns WALTH E17 * 285 G3
Bertram Av RCOS CO16 159 G4
Bertrand Wy THMD SE28 325 L3
Berwick Av CHLM/WR CM1 193 K5
Berwick Cl CHES/WCR EN8 233 H4
Berwick La CHONG CM5 237 M3
Berwick Pond Cl RAIN RM13 312 A6
Berwick Pond Rd
UPMR RM14 312 C4
Berwick Rd CAN/RD E16 323 L2
RAIN RM13 312 A6
Berwood Rd SLH/COR SS17 317 J2
Beryl Av EHAM E6 324 B1
Beryl Rd HAR CO12 70 C4
Beslyns Rd BRTR CM7 76 D2
Bessie Lansbury Cl EHAM E6 324 D2
Bestwood St DEPT SE8 322 A7
Betchworth Rd
GDMY/SEVK IG3 287 H7
Bethany St RCOLE CO7 130 E6
Bethell Av CAN/RD E16 307 J8
IL IG1 286 D5
Betjeman Cl BRTR CM7 121 K5
CHESW EN7 216 B6
RAYL SS6 281 J2
Betjeman Ms SOSN SS2 301 K2
Betjeman Wy CHONG CM5 380 G12
Betony Crs BCAYW CM12 240 C8
Betoyne Av CHING E4 267 H3
Betoyne Cl BCAYE CM11 259 G3
Betsham Rd SWCM DA10 336 B5
Betterton Rd RAIN RM13 311 H6
Bettons Pk SRTFD E15 307 H5
Betts Av KESG IP5 51 G6
Betts Green Rd RCOS CO16 135 G8
Bett's La HOC/HUL SS5 264 A7
WAB EN9 202 D7
Betts Rd CAN/RD E16 323 L2
Betty Cocker Gv SUD CO10 21 H6
Betula Ter CHES/WCR EN8 * 232 F2
Beulah Rd EPP CM16 220 B7
HCH RM12 289 M8
WALTH E17 284 E3
Bevan Av BARK IG11 309 K4
Bevan Rd ABYW SE2 325 L8
Bevans Cl GRH DA9 335 M8
Bevan Wy HCH RM12 290 C8
Beveland Rd CVI SS8 321 K2
Beverley Av CVI SS8 320 C2
K/T/MI CO5 178 A6
Beverley Cl CDW/CHF RM16 * 316 A6
EMPK RM11 290 C5
Beverley Crs WFD IG8 267 L7
Beverley Dr FOS CO13 137 H2
Beverley Gdns CHESW EN7 232 A1
EMPK RM11 290 C5
SOSN SS2 301 H1
Beverley Ri BCAYE CM11 258 F4
Beverley Rd CHING E4 267 G5
COLW CO3 107 G7
DAGW RM9 310 B1
EHAM E6 308 A7
IPNE IP4 48 E5
Beverly Cl BROX EN10 200 F7
Bevin Cl BERM/RHTH SE16 322 B4
Bevington Ms WIT CM8 171 L3
Bewick Ct HSTD CO9 356 F7
Bewley Cl CHES/WCR EN8 232 E1
Bexhill Cl COS CO15 182 F5
Bexhill Dr GRAYS RM17 330 B5
Bexley Av HAR CO12 70 E4
Bexley Gdns CHDH RM6 287 L3
Bexley Rd ERITH DA8 * 327 J8
Beyers Gdns HOD EN11 185 H8
Beyers Prospect HOD EN11 185 H8
Beyers Ride HOD EN11 185 H8
Bibb Wy IP IP1 16 B5
Bibby Cl SLH/COR SS17 317 K2
Bickenhall SBN/FI SS3 303 G5
Bickerton Point RCHLM CM3 245 J7
Bickley Rd LEY E10 284 E5
Bicknacre Rd RCHLM CM3 227 M4
Biddenden Ct PIT SS13 278 F7
Bidder St CAN/RD E16 323 H1
Bideford Cl HARH RM3 271 M7
WOS/PRIT SS0 282 D8
Bideford Rd PEND EN3 233 G8
The Biggen CBS CB2 340 F1
Biggerstaff Rd SRTFD E15 306 F5
Biggin Hl BUNT SG9 370 C8
Biggin La GRAYS RM17 331 L5
The Bight RCHLM CM3 245 J8
Bignalls Cft COLN CO4 107 M1
Bignell Rd WOOL/PLUM SE18 324 E8
Bignold Rd FSTGT E7 307 K1
Bigods La GTDUN CM6 95 G8
Bijou Cl K/T/MI CO5 150 A7
Bilberry End CBE/LIN CB1 26 F2
Billericay Rd
RBRW/HUT CM13 275 H2
Billers Cha CHLM/WR CM1 194 D6
Billet La EMPK RM11 290 A6
SLH/COR SS17 317 H4
Billet Rd CHDH RM6 287 M1
WALTH E17 266 A7
The Billett SLH/COR SS17 * 317 J4
Billings Cl DAGW RM9 309 M4
Billson St POP/IOD E14 322 F7
Billy's La RCOLE CO7 363 L7
Bilsdale Cl COLN CO4 107 M1
Bilton Rd CHLM/WR CM1 4 C6
SBF/HAD SS7 299 H2
Bilton Wy PEND EN3 248 C1
Bingham Cl SOCK/AV RM15 329 L2
Bingley Rd CAN/RD E16 323 M2
HOD EN11 201 K3
Binley Rd CHLM/GWD CM2 210 B3
Binsey Wk ABYW SE2 325 M5
Birchalls STSD CM24 115 M1
Bircham Rd SOSN SS2 19 G1
Birchanger La BSF CM23 115 L7
Birch Av HAR CO12 14 F8
RCOLE CO7 133 H5
Birch Cl BKHH IG9 268 A2
BRTR CM7 120 F3
CAN/RD E16 323 H1
COS CO15 6 A5
CVI SS8 320 D3
RAYL SS6 280 F2
RCFD SS4 392 B12
RCOLE CO7 156 B7
ROMW/RG RM7 288 E1
SBF/HAD SS7 279 L6
SOCK/AV RM15 314 A4
Birch Crs EMPK RM11 290 B2
SOCK/AV RM15 314 B3
Birchcroft Rd IP IP1 48 A3
Birchdale HOC/HUL SS5 263 G2
Birchdale Gdns CHDH RM6 288 A5
Birchdale Rd FSTGT E7 307 M2
Birchdene Dr THMD SE28 325 K4
Birch Dr MGTR CO11 65 G4
Birche Cl LOS SS9 300 B1
The Birches EPP CM16 221 J4
FOS CO13 137 H3
RBRW/HUT CM13 256 B6
SBF/HAD SS7 279 M5
Birches Wk CHLM/GWD CM2 225 K5
Birch Fall RCOLW CO6 361 L8
Birchfield Rd CHES/WCR EN8 216 C7
Birchfield St POP/IOD E14 322 D3
Birch Gdns DAGE RM10 288 F8
Birch Gn WICKW SS12 261 G6
Birch Gv KESG IP5 51 G7
WAN E11 285 H8
Birch La ING CM4 241 J2
Birch Pl GRH DA9 335 H8
Birch Ri WIT CM8 172 B7
Birch Rd BOC CM0 390 D5
COLS CO2 128 B8
ROMW/RG RM7 288 E1
Birch St COLS CO2 151 K2
RCOLW CO6 361 M8
Birchway COLS CO2 151 K3
Birchwood BSF CM23 115 L7
SBF/HAD SS7 279 L6
Birchwood Cl K/T/MI CO5 174 B1
Birch Wood Cl K/T/MI CO5 * 178 A7
Birchwood Cl
RBRW/HUT CM13 * 273 M5
Birchwood Dr KESG IP5 49 K4
LOS SS9 300 D3
Birchwood Rd COLN CO4 88 D1
RCHLM CM3 229 J3
SLH/COR SS17 295 L8
Birchwood Wy K/T/MI CO5 150 C8
Birdbrook Cl DAGE RM10 310 F4
RBRW/HUT CM13 256 E2
Birdbrook Rd HSTD CO9 344 F10
Birdbush Av SAFWS CB11 30 A2
Birdie Wy HERT/BAY SG13 184 C2
Bird La K/T/MI CO5 174 B1
RBRW/HUT CM13 273 M8
UPMR RM14 291 G3
Birds Cl BCAYE CM11 241 M8
SAFWN CB10 340 G6
Birds Farm Av
ROMW/RG RM7 270 E7
Birdsfield La HOM E9 306 C5
Birds Gn CHONG CM5 381 N5
Birkbeck Rd GNTH/NBYPK IG2 287 G3
RBRW/HUT CM13 257 G2
ROMW/RG RM7 289 G6
Birkdale Av HARH RM3 272 D6
Birkdale Ri RCHLM CM3 196 E1
Birkdale Rd ABYW SE2 325 K7
Birkfield Cl CHTY IP2 16 A8
Birkfield Dr CHTY IP2 53 L3
Birkin Cl K/T/MI CO5 173 L1
Birs Cl WICKE SS11 261 G4
Biscay SOSN SS2 282 D6
Biscay Cl HVHL CB9 34 F6
Bishop Rd CHLM/WR CM1 5 G1
COLS CO2 128 D2
Bishops Av BRTR CM7 121 L2
BSF CM23 139 G6
CHDH RM6 287 M4
PLSTW E13 307 L5
Bishops Cl FX IP11 63 J7
PIT SS13 278 D3
WALTH E17 284 E2
Bishops Ct CHES/WCR EN8 * 216 C8
GRH DA9 335 J7
Bishopscourt Gdns
CHLM/WR CM1 210 B1
Bishops Dr RCOS CO16 181 L7
Bishopsfield HLWS CM18 203 M4
Bishop's Hall Rd BRWN CM15 255 L6
Bishop's Hl IPSE IP3 17 K7
Bishop's La HSTD CO9 358 E6
K/T/MI CO5 149 M6
Bishops Park Wy BSF CM23 138 C3
Bishops Pl WIT CM8 * 172 C8
Bishops Rd SLH/COR SS17 317 J2
WICKW SS12 279 G2
Bishopsteignton SBN/FI SS3 302 F5
Bishops Wk BRWN CM15 256 C5
Bisley Cl CHES/WCR EN8 232 E3
RCOS CO16 * 158 E7
Bisson Rd SRTFD E15 306 F6
Bistern Av WALTH E17 285 G1
Bittern Cl CHTY IP2 53 K2
K/T/MI CO5 149 G3
Bixley Dr IPNE IP4 49 K8
Bixley La IPNE IP4 49 L8
Bixley Rd IPSE IP3 55 J2
Blackacre Rd EPP CM16 235 M7
Black Barns FX IP11 62 B6
Blackberry Rd COLW CO3 127 M1
Blackborne Rd DAGE RM10 310 D3
Black Boy La MGTR CO11 367 K5
Blackbrook Rd RCOLW CO6 86 F6
Blackbush Av CHDH RM6 288 A3
Blackbushe BSF CM23 115 K8
Black Bush La
CDW/CHF RM16 316 A1
Blackbush Spring HLW CM20 188 B8
Black Chapel La GTDUN CM6 142 B5
Blackdale CHESW EN7 216 B5
Black Ditch Rd WAB EN9 * 233 K6
Black Ditch Wy WAB EN9 233 J6
Blackdown Av KESG IP5 49 L7
Blackfriars SUD CO10 20 B8
Blackfriars Ct IPNE IP4 * 17 G5
Blackgate Rd SBN/FI SS3 303 K6
Blackheath COLS CO2 129 K5
Black Horse La IP IP1 16 E4
Blackhorse La EPP CM16 221 L3
WALTH E17 266 A8
Blackhorse Rd WALTH E17 284 A1
Blackhouse La SUD CO10 45 L6
Blacklands Cl SAFWS CB11 351 R6
Black La BRTR CM7 76 C3
Blackley La RCHLM CM3 144 C2
Black Lion Ct HLWE CM17 * 188 D5
Blacklock CHLM/GWD CM2 210 D2
Blackman Wy WIT CM8 171 K4
Blackmore Av CVI SS8 320 E3
Blackmore Cl HVHL CB9 34 C4
Blackmore Ct WAB EN9 234 B3
Blackmore Md ING CM4 222 C5
Blackmore Rd BKHH IG9 250 B7
BRWN CM15 383 M12
GRAYS RM17 330 F4
ING CM4 222 B5
ING CM4 222 C7
Blackmores LAIN SS15 276 B7
Blackshots La
CDW/CHF RM16 314 F7
Blacksmith Cl BCAYW CM12 240 E8
CHDH RM6 287 M4
CHLM/WR CM1 194 B5
Blacksmiths Aly ING CM4 222 B5
Blacksmiths Cl BSF CM23 138 C4
Black Smiths Cl WARE SG12 185 H2
Blacksmiths Hl SUD CO10 345 N1
Blacksmiths La CBE/LIN CB1 32 F8
HAR CO12 14 B9
RAIN RM13 311 J5
SUD CO10 44 C7
WIT CM8 172 B8
Blacksmiths Wy SBW CM21 162 C8
Blackthorn Av COLN CO4 108 B5
Blackthorn Cl CHLM/WR CM1 208 D4
IPSE IP3 55 K4
Blackthorn Ct VGE SS16 294 D1
Blackthorne Dr CHING E4 267 G3
Blackthorne Rd CVI SS8 320 F2
Blackthorn Rd
CDW/CHF RM16 314 E8
HAR CO12 70 E3
HOC/HUL SS5 264 C5
IL IG1 309 G2
WIT CM8 171 H1
Blackthorn St BOW E3 306 D8
Blackthorn Wy BRW CM14 256 A8
MAL CM9 174 D3
RCOLW CO6 360 H4
Blacktiles La WDBR IP12 50 F3
Blackwall Br CHLM/WR CM1 192 A8
Blackwall La GNWCH SE10 323 H8
Blackwall Tunnel Ap
POP/IOD E14 322 F3
Blackwall Tunnel Northern Ap
BOW E3 306 E7
Blackwall Wy POP/IOD E14 322 F3
Blackwater SBF/HAD SS7 298 C1
Blackwater Av COLN CO4 108 B4
Blackwater Cl BOC CM0 393 M8
CHLM/WR CM1 193 M7
MAL CM9 215 H2
RAIN RM13 327 G1
SBN/FI SS3 303 H4
Blackwater Dr K/T/MI CO5 177 K7
Blackwater La WIT CM8 171 L5
Blackwater Wy BRTR CM7 121 K1
Blackwell Cl CLPT E5 306 B1
Blackwell Dr BRTR CM7 120 F1
Blackwood Chine
RCHLM CM3 245 H7
Bladen Dr IPNE IP4 49 L8
Bladon Cl BRTR CM7 99 H6
K/T/MI CO5 150 B8
Bladon Wy HVHL CB9 34 E4
Blaine Dr FOS CO13 137 H2
Blair Cl BSF CM23 138 D2
IPNE IP4 49 K8
Blair St POP/IOD E14 322 F2
Blake Av BARK IG11 309 H5
RIPS/CAP IP9 66 F4
Blake Cl MGTR CO11 90 E1
RAIN RM13 311 J5
Blake Dr BRTR CM7 121 M1
RCOS CO16 159 G7
Blake Gdns DART DA1 334 C6
Blake Hall Dr WICKE SS11 261 K7
Blake Hall Rd CHONG CM5 380 B12
WAN E11 285 K6
Blakeland Hl CBS CB2 340 E1
Blakemore Wy BELV DA17 326 B6
Blake Rd CAN/RD E16 307 J8
IP IP1 47 L2
WIT CM8 147 J8
Blaker Rd SRTFD E15 306 F5
Blamsters Crs HSTD CO9 81 G5
Blanchard Cl FOS CO13 136 D2
Blanchard Gv PEND EN3 233 H8
Blanchard Ms HARH RM3 272 C6
Blanche St CAN/RD E16 307 J8
IPNE IP4 17 H4
Blandford Cl ROMW/RG RM7 288 E2
Blandford Crs CHING E4 248 F7
Blandford Rd IPSE IP3 55 J2
Blaney Crs EHAM E6 308 F7
Blatches Cha LOS SS9 282 C7
Bledlow Cl THMD SE28 325 M3
Blendon Ter
WOOL/PLUM SE18 324 F8
Blenheim Av
GNTH/NBYPK IG2 286 D4
Blenheim Cha LOS SS9 300 A2
Blenheim Cl BRTR CM7 99 H6
HOC/HUL SS5 264 B5
HVHL CB9 34 E4
MGTR CO11 65 G4
RCHLM CM3 228 C3
ROMW/RG RM7 288 F2
SBW CM21 188 C1
UPMR RM14 291 H6
Blenheim Ct BSF CM23 138 D2
WFD IG8 267 L6
WICKE SS11 * 261 K8
Blenheim Crs LOS SS9 300 B2
Blenheim Dr COLS CO2 129 K5
Blenheim Gdns RCHLM CM3 388 D8
SOCK/AV RM15 328 E4
Blenheim Gv GVE DA12 337 M5
Blenheim Ms LOS SS9 300 B2
Blenheim Park Cl LOS SS9 300 C1
Blenheim Rd BRWN CM15 255 K6
COS CO15 6 C8
EHAM E6 308 A7
IP IP1 16 A1
WALTH E17 284 A1
WAN E11 307 H1
Blenheim Wy EPP CM16 221 H5
K/T/MI CO5 150 B8
Blessing Wy BARK IG11 309 M6
Blickling Cl CHTY IP2 54 A3
Blickling Rd BRTR CM77 120 F5
Bligh Rd GVW DA11 337 K4
Blind La BCAYW CM12 257 L7
CHLM/GWD CM2 226 C8
CHLM/GWD CM2 227 H8
K/T/MI CO5 150 E2
MAL CM9 174 E4
MAL CM9 199 M6
MAL CM9 230 E3
RCOLW CO6 105 K5
Blindman's La
CHES/WCR EN8 216 E8
Blithbury Rd DAGW RM9 309 L3
Blithdale Rd ABYW SE2 325 K7
Blockhouse Rd GRAYS RM17 330 F5
Blofield Rd FX IP11 10 C1
Blois Rd HVHL CB9 344 C5
Blomville Rd BCTR RM8 288 B7
Blondin St BOW E3 306 D6
Bloom Cl FOS CO13 137 J3
Bloomfield Av FOS CO13 137 H2
Bloomfield Crs
GNTH/NBYPK IG2 286 E4
Bloomfield Rd
WOOL/PLUM SE18 324 E8
Bloomfield St IPNE IP4 49 G7
Blooms Hall La SUD CO10 20 C2
Blossom Cl DAGW RM9 310 C5
Blount St POP/IOD E14 322 B2
Blountswood Rd
HOC/HUL SS5 263 K6
Blower Cl RAYL SS6 281 J2
Bloxhall Rd LEY E10 284 C6
Blue Anchor La TIL RM18 332 B3
Blue Barn Cl FX IP11 61 M5
Bluebell Av FSTGT E7 308 A2
RCOS CO16 6 A3
Bluebell Cl CHTY IP2 53 K1
HERT/BAY SG13 184 B3
ROMW/RG RM7 289 H7
WIT CM8 171 H2
Bluebell Wy IL IG1 308 E3
Bluebell Wd BCAYW CM12 258 A1
Blueberry Cl WFD IG8 267 K5
Bluebird La DAGE RM10 310 D4
Bluebird Wy THMD SE28 325 G5
Bluegate La RIPS/CAP IP9 58 D6
Bluehouse Av RCOS CO16 182 D1
Blue House Farm Cha
RCHLM CM3 246 E6
Bluehouse Rd CHING E4 267 H2
Bluehouses VGE SS16 2 E7
Bluemans EPP CM16 221 L2
Bluemans End EPP CM16 221 L2
Blue Mill La MAL CM9 213 G1
Blue Mills Hl WIT CM8 171 L6
Blue Rd K/T/MI CO5 149 M8
Bluestem Rd IPSE IP3 55 K5
Blunden Cl BCTR RM8 287 M6
The Blundens RCOLW CO6 361 P3
Blunts Hall Rd WIT CM8 170 F4
Blunts Wall Rd BCAYW CM12 258 B4
Blurton Rd CLPT E5 306 A1
Blyford Rd RCOS CO16 182 D1
Blyford Wy FX IP11 10 D1
Blyth Av SBN/FI SS3 302 F6
Blyth Cl CHTY IP2 53 M4
Blythe La RCOLE CO7 * 130 E5
Blythe Rd HOD EN11 201 L5
SLH/COR SS17 317 H1
Blythe Wy MAL CM9 214 D6
SBF/HAD SS7 279 M6
Blyth Rd THMD SE28 325 M3
Blyth's Meadow BRTR CM7 121 J2
Blyth's Wy BRTR CM77 120 C3
Blyth's Whf POP/IOD E14 * 322 B3

Blythswood Rd GDMY/SEVK IG3 ....287 K6
Blyth Wk UPMR RM14 ....115 H5
Blythwood Gdns STSD SM24 ....115 G8
Blyton Cl WICKW SS12 ....261 G2
Boadicea Wy COLS CO2 ....128 F1
Boarded Rw RCFD SS4 * 397 K4
Boardman Av CHING E4 ....285 E5
Boardwalk Pl POP/IOD E14 ....322 F4
Boars Tye WIT CM8 ....122 F7
Boat Lifter Wy
BERM/RHTH SE16 ....322 E7
Boat Quay CAN/RD E16 ....323 M3
Bob Anker Cl IS * 307 K7
Bobbing Cl RCFD SS4 ....283 J4
Bobbingworth Ml
CHONG CM5 ....380 B10
Bobbits La RIPS/CAP IP9 ....53 L5
Bobbits Wy RCOLE CO7 ....130 F6
Bober Ct COLS CO2 ....129 L6
Bocking End BRTR CM7 ....121 J2
Bocking Pl BRTR CM7 * 121 K1
Bodell Cl CDW/CHF RM16 ....330 E1
Bodiam Cl IPSE IP3 ....55 L1
Bodiam Rd BI IPSE IP3 ....55 J1
Bodle Av SWCM DA10 ....336 A5
Bodley Cl EPP CM16 ....220 A8
Bodmin Gn KESG IP5 ....49 M7
Bodmin Rd CHLM/WR CM1 ....194 A8
Bogmoor Rd ROY SO8 ....370 E1
Bohemia Cha LOS SS9 ....281 H6
Bohn Rd WCHPL E1 * 322 B1
Bohun Cl RCHLM CM3 * 144 C6
Bois Hall Gdns HSTD CO9 ....81 J3
Boley Dr COS CO15 ....7 K3
Boleyn Av BCAYW CM12 ....240 C8
CDW/CHF RM16 ....330 C8
LOS SS9 ....281 M6
LOU IG10 ....250 B6
WALTH E17 ....284 D2
Boleyn Ct BKHH IG9 ....249 L8
BROX EN10 ....200 F9
Boleyn Gdns DAGE RM10 ....310 F4
RBRW/HUT RM13 ....256 B6
Boleyn Rd EHAM E6 ....308 A4
FSTGT E7 ....307 K4
Boleyns Av BRTR CM7 ....99 J7
Boleyn Wy BARK/HLT IG6 ....268 F5
COS CO15 ....182 C5
HVHL CB9 ....34 A6
RCHLM CM3 ....195 J4
SWCM DA10 ....336 B5
Boley Rd RCOLW CO6 ....83 J6
Bolford St GTDUN CM6 ....74 D3
Bolingbroke Cl RCHLM CM3 ....144 C6
Bolney Dr LOS SS9 ....281 M6
Bolton La IPNE IP4 ....17 G3
Bolton Rd FSTGT E7 ....307 J3
The Boltons WFD IG8 * 267 L4
Bommel Av LOS SS9 ....321 K4
Bonchurch Av LOS SS9 ....300 A3
Bond St CHLM/GWD CM2 ....5 H7
IPNE IP4 ....17 G5
SRTFD E15 ....307 H2
Boneta Rd WOOL/PLUM SE18 ....324 A6
Bonham Cl COS CO15 ....7 J4
Bonham Gdns BCTR RM8 ....288 A8
Bonham Rd BCTR RM8 ....288 B7
Bonington Cha
CHLM/WR CM1 ....194 B7
Bonington Rd HCH RM12 ....312 A2
Bonks Hi SBW CM21 ....162 G8
Bonner Wk CDW/CHF RM16 * 330 C2
Bonnetting La BSF CM23 ....92 C1
Bonney Gv CHESW EN7 ....216 A8
Bonnington Av IPSE IP3 ....54 E4
Bonningtons
RBRW/HUT RM13 ....256 C6
Bonnygate BSDN SS14 ....3 J1
Boone Pl WIT CM8 ....171 K8
Boons Cl RCHLM CM3 ....195 H5
Boord St GNWCH SE10 ....323 H5
Boot Drift RIPS/CAP IP9 ....60 D8
Bootham Av BCAYW CM12 ....258 C4
Bootham Rd BCAYW CM12 ....258 C4
Booth Av COLN CO4 ....9 A4
Booth Cl THMD SE28 ....325 L4
Booth La KESG IP5 ....50 D5
Booth Pl BOC CM0 ....393 M4
Borda Cl CHLM/WR CM1 ....193 K8
Border's La LOU IG10 ....250 D4
Boreham Av CAN/RD E16 ....323 K2
Boreham St WICKE SS11 ....261 L9
Borehamgate SUD CO10 * 20 C6
Borehamgate Prec SUD CO10 ....20 D6
Boreham Rd RCHLM CM3 ....144 C6
Borgard Rd
WOOL/PLUM SE18 ....324 C7
Borland Cl GRH DA9 ....337 K7
Borley Rd SUD CO10 ....42 D1
Borman Cl LOS SS9 ....282 D7
Borough La SAFWS CB11 ....30 A1
The Borough CHLM CM5 ....382 C3
Borradale Ct HVHL CB9 ....344 A7
Borrell Cl BROX EN10 ....200 F6
Borrett Av CVI SS8 ....320 D1
Borrowdale Av IPNE IP4 ....48 C4
Borrowdale Cl REDBR IG4 ....286 B2
SBF/HAD SS7 ....280 C4
Borrowdale Rd SBF/HAD SS7 ....280 C4
Borthwick Ms WAN E11 * 307 H1
Borthwick Rd SRTFD E15 ....307 H1
Borthwick St DEPT SE8 ....322 H1
Borwick Av WALTH E17 ....284 C1
Borwick La BCAYE CM11 ....278 C6
Bosanquet Rd HOD EN11 ....201 L4
Boscombe Av EMPK RM11 ....290 A5
Boscombe Rd EMPK RM11 ....331 C8
LEY E10 ....285 G5
WICKW SS12 ....261 C5
Boscombe Cl CLPT E5 ....306 F2
Boscombe Rd SOSN SS2 ....302 K3
Bosgrove CHING E4 ....248 B8
Boss Hall Rd IP IP1 ....47 K6
Bostall Heath ABYW SE2 * 325 J8
Bostall Hi ABYW SE2 ....325 L8
Bostall La ABYW SE2 ....325 L8
Bostall Manorway ABYW SE2 * 325 J8
Bostock Rd CHTY IP2 ....54 A1
Boston Av RAYL SS6 ....280 C1
SOSN SS2 ....18 D2
Boston Rd EHAM E6 ....308 D4
IPNE IP4 ....17 M2
Boswell Av RCFD SS4 ....265 C4
Boswells Dr CHLM/GWD CM2 ....5 D4
Bosworth Cl HOC/HUL SS5 ....282 C1
WALTH E17 ....266 C7
Bosworth Crs HARH RM3 ....271 M5
Bosworth Rd DAGE RM10 ....310 D1
LOS SS9 ....281 M6
Botanical Wy RCOS CO16 ....181 K9
Botany Dr BRTR CM7 ....122 A2
Botany La RCOS CO16 ....134 C3
Botany Ter RM19 * 328 B8
Botany Wy PUR RM19 ....328 B8

Botelers VGE SS16 ....2 B9
Boteley Cl CHING E4 ....267 G1
Botha Av PLSTW E13 ....323 L1
Bothwell Cl CAN/RD E16 ....323 K1
Botney Hill Rd BCAYW CM12 ....275 M1
Boucher Dr GVW DA11 ....337 J8
Bouchers Md CHLM/WR CM1 ....194 C3
Boughton Rd THMD SE28 ....325 H6
Boulcott St WCHPL E1 ....322 C2
Bouldrewood Rd
SBF/HAD SS7 ....279 L1
The Boulevard RCFD SS4 ....283 J2
WFD IG8 ....268 D6
Boulter Gdns RAIN RM13 ....311 K3
Boulton Rd BCTR RM8 ....288 B7
Boult Rd LAIN SS15 ....276 F5
Boultwood Rd EHAM E6 ....324 C2
Boundary Dr
RBRW/HUT CM13 ....257 H3
Boundary La PLSTW E13 ....308 A8
Boundary Rd BARK IG11 ....308 F6
BSF CM23 ....139 H4
COLN CO4 ....130 D1
HVHL CB9 ....35 L6
LOS SS9 ....281 L5
PLSTW E13 ....307 M6
ROM RM1 ....289 K4
UPMR RM14 ....290 D1
WALTH E17 ....284 C1
Bounderby Gv
CHLM/WR CM1 ....193 H7
Bounstead Hill COLS CO2 ....128 F8
Bounstead Rd COLS CO2 ....129 F8
Bourchier Av BRTR CM7 ....100 A8
Bourchier Wy HSTD CO9 ....81 G5
Bourn Bridge Rd CBE/LIN CB1 ....23 J4
Bourne Av LAIN SS15 ....276 D5
Bournebridge Cl
RBRW/HUT CM13 ....257 H3
Bournebridge HI HSTD CO9 ....80 F7
Bournebridge La ABR/ST RM4 ....252 E7
Bourne Cl BROX EN10 ....201 L6
HSTD CO9 ....81 G5
LAIN SS15 ....276 D5
Bourne End EMPK RM11 ....290 D6
Bourne Gdns CHING E4 ....266 F3
Bourne Hi CHTY IP2 ....54 B5
Bournemouth Park Rd
SOSN SS2 ....301 L2
Bournemouth Rd COS CO15 ....160 K1
Bournes Gn SBN/FI SS3 * 302 D3
Bournes Green Cha
SBN/FI SS3 ....302 E3
The Bourne BSF CM23 ....139 J1
Bouvel Dr BOC CM0 ....393 J4
Bouverie Rd CHLM/GWD CM2 ....5 H7
Bouverie Rd WEST PEND EN3 ....329 L1
Bovey Wy SOCK/AV RM15 ....329 L1
Bovingdon Rd BRTR CM7 ....99 K6
Bovinger Wy SOS SS1 ....302 C4
Bow Arrow La DART DA1 ....334 D8
Bowater Rd
WOOL/PLUM SE18 ....324 A6
Bowbank Cl SBN/FI SS3 ....303 J4
Bow Bridge Est BOW E3 ....306 E7
Bow Common La BOW E3 ....306 C8
Bowden Dr EMPK RM11 ....290 F4
Bowden Rd BCAYW CM12 ....258 D4
Bowditch DEPT SE8 ....322 C8
Bowdon Rd LEY E10 ....284 D5
Bowen St POP/IOD E14 ....322 E2
Bower Cl CRW RM5 ....271 F4
Bower Farm Rd ABR/ST RM4 ....270 F2
Bower Gdns MAL CM9 ....214 C8
Bower Hall Dr HVHL CB9 ....344 A7
Bower Hall La K/T/MI CO5 ....178 F5
Bower HI EPP CM16 ....236 B2
Bower La BSDN SS14 ....278 B5
Bowerman Rd
CDW/CHF RM16 ....331 K3
Bowers Cl WIT CM8 ....147 K1
Bowers Court Dr PIT SS13 ....279 J8
Bowers Rd SBF/HAD SS7 ....280 A4
Bower St WCHPL E1 * 322 C2
Bower V EPP CM16 ....236 D2
Bowes Dr CHONG CM5 ....382 C1
Bowes Rd BCTR RM8 ....309 M1
RCOLE CO7 ....130 F4
Bowfell Dr VGE SS16 ....276 D4
Bowhay RBRW/HUT CM13 ....256 E5
Bowland Dr RBRW/HUT 53 H4
Bowland Rd WFD IG8 ....267 M5
Bowles Gdn EN EN1 ....232 C6
Bowley St POP/IOD E14 ....322 C3
Bowling Green Rw
WOOL/PLUM SE18 * 324 C7
Bow Locks BOW E3 * 306 F8
Bowman Av CAN/RD E16 ....323 K3
LOS SS9 ....281 L7
Bowmans Pk HSTD CO9 ....356 F9
Bowmont Cl
RBRW/HUT CM13 ....256 E2
Bown Cl TIL RM18 ....331 H4
Bowness Wy HCH RM12 ....311 K2
Bowood Rd PEND EN3 ....248 A2
Bow Rd BOW E3 ....306 D7
Bowsers La SAFWN CB10 ....26 A5
Bow St SRTFD E15 ....307 H2
Bowthorpe Cl IP IP1 ....16 C7
Bowyer Cl EHAM E6 ....324 C1
Box Cl LAIN SS15 * 277 G4
Boxford Cl RAYL SS6 ....280 C2
Boxford Ct FX IP11 ....10 C7
Boxgrove Rd ABYW SE2 ....325 K2
Boxhouse La RCOLE CO7 ....363 K12
Box La BARK IG11 ....309 M6
HOD EN11 ....200 F4
Boxley La RBSF CM22 ....377 J2
Boxley St CAN/RD E16 ....323 L4
Box Mill La HSTD CO9 ....81 H2
Boxmoor Rd CRW RM5 ....270 F4
Boxoll Rd DAGW RM9 ....310 C2
Boxted Av RCOS CO16 ....182 C1
Boxted Church Rd
RCOLW CO6 ....361 P12
Boxted Cl BKHH IG9 ....250 B8
Boxted Rd COLN CO4 ....87 D4
RCOLW CO6 ....86 D7
Boxted Straight Rd
COLN CO4 ....362 B12
Boyard Rd WOOL/PLUM SE18 ....324 A6
Boyce Gn SBF/HAD SS7 ....298 D3
Boyce Hill Cl LOS SS9 ....281 H4
Boyce Rd SBN/FI SS3 ....303 L5
SLH/COR SS17 ....316 F7
Boyce Wy PLSTW E13 ....307 M3
Boyd Cl BSF CM23 ....139 J3
Boyd St WICKW SS12 ....261 J3
Boyden Cl SOSN SS2 ....302 A3
Boydlands RIPS/CAP IP9 ....58 D4
Boyles Ct COLS CO2 ....129 L6

Boyne Dr CHLM/WR CM1 ....194 A7
Boyne Rd DAGE RM10 ....288 D9
Boyton Cl HAD CM8 ....34 D3
Boyton Rd IPSE IP3 ....55 J1
Boytons LAIN SS15 ....2 B5
Boytons Acre SAFWS CB11 ....30 A1
Boyton's La SAFWN CB10 ....343 J11
Brabant Rd DAGE RM10 ....246 D6
Brabazon St POP/IOD E14 ....322 E2
Brabner Gdns HARH RM3 ....259 M1
Bracelet Cl SLH/COR SS17 ....295 J8
Brace Wk RCHLM CM3 ....245 H5
Brackenbury Cl IP IP1 ....48 A5
Bracken Cl EHAM E6 ....324 C1
LOU IG10 ....250 E2
Brackendale BCAYE CM11 ....259 G2
Brackendale Av PIT SS13 ....296 F1
Brackendale Gv HOC/HUL SS5 ....264 B6
Brackendale Gdns
UPMR RM14 ....312 F1
Bracken Dell RAYL SS6 ....281 H3
Brackenden Dr
CHLM/WR CM1 ....194 A6
Bracken Dr CHIG IG7 ....268 A5
Brackenhayes Cl CHTY IP2 ....54 D4
Bracken Ms ROMW/RG RM7 ....288 D4
Brackens Dr BRW CM14 ....256 A6
The Brackens CHING E4 ....107 L2
Bracken Wy K/T/MI CO5 ....153 K3
SBF/HAD SS7 ....280 D6
Brackley Cl K/T/MI CO5 ....153 L2
Brackley Crs PIT SS13 ....278 F8
Brackley Sq WFD IG8 ....268 A6
Bracks La RCOLW CO6 ....125 J2
Bracondale Rd GRAYS RM17 ....330 C6
Bradbourne Rd GRAYS RM17 ....330 C6
Bradbourne Wy PIT SS13 ....278 F8
Bradbury Dr BRTR CM7 ....121 J2
Bradd Cl SOCK/AV RM15 ....313 M7
Braddock Cl CRW RM5 ....270 C1
Braddfield St ABR/ST RM4 ....252 B1
Bradfield Dr BARK IG11 ....309 L4
Bradfield Rd CAN/RD E16 ....323 K5
MGTR CO11 ....366 E10
Bradford Bury LOS SS9 ....281 M7
Bradford Cl IL IG1 ....287 G6
Bradfords Ct BRTR CM7 ....121 K1
Bradford St BRTR CM7 ....121 J2
CHLM/GWD CM2 ....4 E6
Brading Av COS CO15 ....159 K6
Bradleigh Av GRAYS RM17 ....330 F3
Bradley Common BSF CM23 ....115 K6
Bradley Link SBF/HAD SS7 ....280 C8
Bradley Ms SAFWN CB10 ....14 C2
Bradley Rd PEND EN3 ....232 F5
WAB EN9 ....233 K5
Bradley Stone Rd EHAM E6 ....324 C2
Bradley St CHTY IP2 ....16 C4
Bradley Wy RCFD SS4 ....283 H4
Bradshaw Rd CDW/CHF RM16 ....314 M2
Bradstock Rd HOM E9 ....306 A3
Bradwell Cl HCH RM12 ....311 L3
Bradwell Av DAGE RM10 ....288 D7
Bradwell Gn
RBRW/HUT CM13 ....256 F2
Bradwell Rd BKHH IG9 ....250 B8
BOC CM0 ....389 K6
BOC CM0 ....389 P3
Brady Av LOU IG10 ....250 F1
Bradymead EHAM E6 ....324 C2
Braemar Av CHLM/GWD CM2 ....4 F7
Braemar Cl LOS SS9 ....299 K3
Braemar Gdns EMPK RM11 ....290 A5
Braemar Rd PLSTW E13 ....307 J8
Braemore CVI SS8 ....298 C8
Braesyde Cl BELV DA17 ....326 C7
Braganza Wy CHLM/GWD CM2 ....194 D3
Brain Rd WIT CM8 ....171 J2
Braintree Av REDBR IG4 ....286 B3
Braintree Rd BRTR CM7 ....76 A3
BRTR CM7 ....78 F7
BRTR CM77 ....122 A6
DAGE RM10 ....288 D7
GTDUN CM6 ....117 J4
GTDUN CM6 ....118 J4
HSTD CO9 ....81 G2
RCHLM CM3 ....144 F6
WIT CM8 ....171 K2
Brain Valley Av BRTR CM77 ....121 L7
Braiswick COLN CO4 ....106 C3
Braiswick La COLN CO4 ....107 C1
Braiswick Pl LAIN SS15 ....276 E5
Braithwaite Av
ROMW/RG RM7 ....288 D5
Braithwaite Dr COLN CO4 ....8 B1
Braithwaite Rd PEND EN3 ....248 A1
Bramall Cl SRTFD E15 ....307 J2
Brambledown
WOOL/PLUM SE18 ....325 C8
Bramble Cl HVHL CB9 ....34 A4
LOS SS9 ....281 L6
Bramble Cft ERITH DA8 ....326 E1
Bramble Dr IPSE IP3 ....55 K4
Bramble La GTDUN CM6 ....118 B4
Bramble Ri HLW CM20 ....12 F4
Bramble Rd CVI SS8 ....320 E1
SBF/HAD SS7 ....281 J4
WIT CM8 ....171 H1
Brambles WOTN CO14 ....171 M5
The Brambles BOC CM0 ....393 N2
BRTR CM7 * 121 H2
BSF CM23 ....138 D3
CHES/WCR EN8 ....232 E1
CHIG IG7 ....268 E1
COLW CO3 ....128 C2
LAIN SS15 * 276 D5
Bramble Tye RCOLW CO6 ....277 J4
Bramble Rd RCOLW CO6 ....360 H4
Brambledown RIPW IP9 ....53 H3
The Bramblings CHING E4 ....267 G3
Bramerton Rd HOC/HUL SS5 ....264 A7
Bramfield Rd East RAYL SS6 ....281 K3
Bramfield Rd West RAYL SS6 ....281 J3
Bramford La IP IP1 ....47 H5
Bramford Rd IP IP1 ....16 B2
Bramhall Cl CHTY IP2 ....53 M2
Bramley Cl BRTR CM7 ....121 K4
COLW CO3 ....106 C6
COLW CO3 ....128 B6
LAIN SS15 * 276 D5
WFD IG8 ....268 B6
Bramley Crs GNTH/NBYPK IG2 ....286 D4
Bramley Gdns LAIN SS15 ....276 D5
Bramley Pl CHLM/GWD CM2 ....210 A6
Bramley Rd HVHL CB9 ....33 H5
Bramleys SLH/COR SS17 ....317 G5

Bramley Shaw WAB EN9 ....234 A3
The Bramleys RCFD SS4 ....265 G8
RCOLW CO6 ....124 D8
Bramley Wy RCHLM CM3 ....388 D8
Brampstead LAIN SS15 ....276 C7
Brampton Cl CHESW EN7 ....295 K8
WOS/PRIT SS0 ....46 D5
Brampton Rd EHAM E6 ....308 D4
Bramshaw Rd HOM E9 ....306 A3
Bramston Cl BARK/HLT IG6 ....269 J5
CHLM/GWD CM2 ....210 C5
Bramston Link LAIN SS15 ....276 B6
Bramston Vw WIT CM8 * 171 J3
Bramston Wy LAIN SS15 ....276 B7
Bramwoods Rd
CHLM/GWD CM2 ....210 B5
Brancaster Br
GNTH/NBYPK IG2 ....287 H4
Brancepeth Gdns BKHH IG9 ....267 K1
Branch La BARK/HLT IG6 ....269 C4
POP/IOD E14 ....322 B3
SBF/HAD SS7 ....299 H3
Brancroft Wy PEND EN3 ....248 B1
Brand Ct BRTR CM7 ....99 J3
Brand Dr K/T/MI CO5 ....153 L2
Brandenburg Rd CVI SS8 ....299 D8
Brandesbury Sq WFD IG8 ....268 D5
Brandon Cl BCAYW CM12 ....240 D5
Brandon Groves Av
SOCK/AV RM15 ....313 M7
Brandon Rd BRTR CM7 ....121 J7
FX IP11 ....11 D2
WALTH E17 ....284 F1
Brandon St GVW DA11 ....337 J8
Brandreth Rd EHAM E6 ....324 C2
Brands Cl SUD CO10 ....45 M4
Brandville Gdns
BARK/HLT IG6 ....286 E2
Bran End Flds GTDUN CM6 ....96 A3
Branfill Rd UPMR RM14 ....290 D1
Branksome Av HOC/HUL SS5 ....264 B6
SLH/COR SS17 ....317 G1
WICKW SS12 ....261 K6
Branksome St GNAL SS14 ....198 M6
Bransby Gdns IPNE IP4 ....17 J4
Bransdale Cl FOS CO13 ....136 F2
Bransford Cl FOS CO13 ....136 F2
Bransom Cl COS CO15 ....182 B3
Branston Rd COS CO15 ....160 B3
Brantham HI MGTR CO11 ....4 B5
Branton Rd GRH DA9 ....335 J8
Brantwood Cl WALTH E17 ....284 C1
Brantwood Gdns REDBR IG4 ....286 B3
Brassington Crs K/T/MI CO5 ....150 B7
Braxted Cl RCFD SS4 ....282 F1
Braxted La WIT CM8 ....172 D3
Braxted Park WIT CM8 ....172 D7
Braxted Rd WIT CM8 ....172 D7
Braxted LAIN SS15 ....276 D7
Braybrooke BSDN SS14 ....3 J1
Braybrooke Gdns SAFWS CB11 ....30 A1
Bray Ct RCOLW CO6 ....106 C1
SBN/FI SS3 ....303 H3
Bray Crs BERM/RHTH SE16 ....322 A5
Bray Dr CAN/RD E16 ....323 J4
Brayers Ms RCFD SS4 ....283 J4
Bray Ldg CHING E4 ....248 A8
Brays La RCFD SS4 ....265 H8
Brays Md HLWS CM18 ....204 A3
Braziers Cl CHLM/GWD CM2 ....245 J6
Braziers Fld HERT/BAY SG13 ....184 A3
Braziers Quay BSF CM23 ....139 J1
Brazier's Wood Rd IPSE IP3 ....55 G5
Breach Barns La WAB EN9 ....218 B4
Breachfield Rd COLS CO2 ....128 E3
Breach La DAGW RM9 ....310 D7
GTDUN CM6 ....94 E3
Breach Rd WTHK RM20 ....335 J1
Break Egg HI BCAYE CM11 ....259 G4
Breakneck HI GRH DA9 ....335 H8
Bream Gdns EHAM E6 ....308 D7
Breams Fld VGE SS16 ....294 F5
Bream St BOW E3 ....306 D4
Brecon Cl CHTY IP2 ....54 A3
PIT SS13 ....278 F4
Brede Cl RCOLW CO6 ....126 D2
Bredfield Cl FX IP11 ....62 D9
Bree Av RCOLW CO6 ....126 B2
Bree HI RCHLM CM3 ....244 B2
Bremer Ms WALTH E17 ....284 F2
Brempsons BSDN SS14 ....2 H1
Brendans Cl EMPK RM11 ....290 A4
Brendon Pl CHLM/WR CM1 ....210 A4
Brendon Rd BCTR RM8 ....288 A5
WOS/PRIT SS0 ....282 D6
Brennan Rd TIL RM18 ....331 L8
Brent Av RCHLM CM3 ....245 G4
Brent Cl FOS CO13 ....137 J2
RDART DA2 ....334 F7
WIT CM8 ....171 H3
Brentfield Rd DART DA1 ....334 D8
Brent Hall Rd BRTR CM7 ....354 M1
Brenton St POP/IOD E14 ....322 B2
Brent Rd CAN/RD E16 ....323 K2
Brent Wy DART DA1 ....334 E7
Brentwood Pl BRWN CM15 ....256 A4
Brentwood Rd
CDW/CHF RM16 ....331 L3
CHONG CM5 ....380 C7
COS CO15 ....159 M7
RBRW/HUT CM13 ....256 B6
RBRW/HUT CM13 ....293 J3
ROM RM1 ....289 J4
RRM RM4 ....293 K4
Bressey Gv SWFD E18 ....267 J2
Bressingham Gdns
RCHLM CM3 ....244 F6
Bretons LAIN SS15 ....277 J2
Brett Cl IP IP1 ....47 K5
Bretten Rd RCOS CO16 ....182 C1
Brettenham Av WALTH E17 ....266 E5
Brettenham Dr SOS SS1 ....302 C5
Brett Gdns DAGW RM9 ....310 B2
The Bretts KESG IP5 ....50 D6
Brevet Cl PUR RM19 ....329 G7
Brewers Cl BSF CM23 ....138 D4
Brewery Rd CBS CB2 ....20 E2
HOD EN11 ....201 L4
WOOL/PLUM SE18 ....325 G8
Brewhouse Rd
WOOL/PLUM SE18 ....324 C7
Brewhouse Wk
BERM/RHTH SE16 ....322 E4
Brewhouse Yd GVE DA12 ....337 L7
Brewood Rd BCTR RM8 ....309 M8
Brewster Cl CVI SS8 ....320 D1
Brewster Rd LEY E10 ....285 L1
Brian Bishop Cl WOTN CO14 ....137 L1
Brian Cl CHLM/GWD CM2 ....5 J3
HCH RM12 ....311 L1

Brian Rd CHDH RM6 ....287 M3
Briar Cl BCAYE CM11 ....259 G3
BKHH IG9 ....268 A3
CHES/WCR EN8 ....216 D7
HOC/HUL SS5 ....282 B1
Briardale Av HAR CO12 ....14 A8
Briarfields FOS CO13 ....136 F1
Briarhayes CHTY IP2 ....54 A3
Briarhayes Av CHTY IP2 ....54 A3
Briarleas Gdns UPMR RM14 ....291 H5
Briarley Cl BROX EN10 ....201 G8
Briar Md LAIN SS15 ....276 E6
Briar Rd HARH RM3 ....271 J4
RCOLE CO7 ....109 L1
Briarsford WIT CM8 * 171 L4
The Briars CHES/WCR EN8 ....232 F1
HERT/BAY SG13 ....184 B5
HLWS CM18 ....235 M4
Briars Wk HARH RM3 ....272 B8
Briarswood CHLM/WR CM1 ....194 A6
CVI SS8 ....298 D8
Briar Vw BCAYE CM11 ....259 G3
Briarwood BRWN CM15 ....383 N11
Briarwood Av COS CO15 ....160 B3
Briarwood Cl LOS SS9 ....282 A8
Briarwood Dr LOS SS9 ....282 A8
Briarwood End COLN CO4 ....107 L2
The Briary WICKW SS12 ....260 F6
Briceway SLH/COR SS17 ....317 G1
Brickbarns RCHLM CM3 ....144 G6
Brickburn Cl GTDUN CM6 ....142 F1
Brick Ct GRAYS RM17 * 330 D5
Brickenden Ct WAB EN9 ....234 A3
Brickfield Cl CHTY IP2 ....16 A6
VGE SS16 ....296 A3
Brickfield Rd BOW E3 ....306 F8
EPP CM16 ....220 B8
VGE SS16 ....296 A3
Brickfields Rd RCHLM CM3 ....245 K6
Brickfields Wy RCFD SS4 ....283 K4
Brickfield Ter RIPS/CAP IP9 * 60 C1
Brickhouse Cl K/T/MI CO5 ....177 L6
Brick House Rd RCHLM CM3 ....195 H4
Brick House Rd MAL CM9 ....173 L5
Brickhouse Rd RCOLW CO6 ....82 C5
RCOLW CO6 ....124 C2
Brick Kiln Cl FX IP11 ....61 M6
RCOLW CO6 ....124 D2
Brick Kiln La GTDUN CM6 ....95 M6
RCOLW CO6 ....88 B8
RCOLE CO7 ....132 B6
SAFWS CB11 ....73 L4
Brick Kiln Rd CHLM/GWD CM2 ....210 F6
COL CO1 ....8 B2
RIPS/CAP IP9 ....365 L12
Brick Kiln Wy BRTR CM7 ....122 A3
Brickmakers La COLN CO4 ....107 J3
Brickman's HI MGTR CO11 ....91 M2
Brick Rw RCFD SS4 * 396 G2
Brickspring La MAL CM9 ....173 G6
Brickstock Furze
BRWN CM15 ....256 F6
Brick St COLW CO3 ....105 L4
Brickwall Cl BOC CM0 ....393 M2
Bridewell St SUD CO10 ....37 M5
Bridge Av UPMR RM14 ....290 D1
Bridgebrook Cl COLN CO4 ....9 M2
Bridge Cl GRH DA9 ....335 G5
RBRW/HUT RM13 ....256 B6
ROM RM1 ....289 J3
SBN/FI SS3 ....303 H6
Bridgecote La LAIN SS15 ....277 J2
Bridge Ct GRAYS RM17 * 330 D5
Bridge Cft RCHLM CM3 ....167 J3
Bridge End WALTH E17 ....266 F7
Bridge End La BRTR CM77 ....120 F5
Bridgefield Cl COL CO1 ....9 J7
Bridge Hi EPP CM16 ....236 A3
RCOLW CO6 ....84 F6
Bridge House Cl
WICKW SS12 * 260 F6
Bridge House Quay
POP/IOD E14 ....322 F4
Bridgemans Rd CAN/RD E16 ....323 K7
Bridgemans Gn RCHLM CM3 ....231 H7
Bridgend Cl RCHLM CM3 ....245 H5
Bridgend Rd EN EN1 ....232 D7
Bridge Pde BCAYW CM12 * 258 C2
Bridge Rd CHONG CM5 ....380 D7
EHAM E6 ....308 C4
FX IP11 ....62 D9
GRAYS RM17 ....330 E5
KIR/NAC IP10 ....60 C2
RAIN RM13 ....311 K8
SBN/FI SS3 ....397 G12
SRTFD E15 ....307 J2
WALTH E17 ....284 C5
WICKE SS11 ....261 K6
Bridges Dr DART DA1 ....334 E7
Bridge St BRTR CM7 ....354 E11
BSF CM23 ....139 G2
BURES CO8 ....359 G9
CHLM/WR CM1 ....208 A4
HSTD CO9 ....81 H3
HSTD CO9 ....346 B12
IP IP1 ....16 F7
LAIN SS15 ....277 M3
SAFWN CB10 ....351 R3
WIT CM8 ....171 J4
Bridge Street Rd SUD CO10 ....41 K2
Bridge Ter MAL CM9 ....198 D8
SRTFD E15 ....307 L2
SUD CO10 ....20 D7
Bridge Vw GRH DA9 ....335 G6
Bridgewater Rd SRTFD E15 ....306 D3
Bridgeway BARK IG11 ....309 J4
Bridgewick Rd BOC CM0 ....390 F9
Bridgwater Dr LOS SS9 ....282 C8
WOS/PRIT SS0 ....300 D9
Bridgwater Rd CHTY IP2 ....53 J5
HARH RM3 ....271 J4
Bridgwater Wk HARH RM3 ....272 A4
Bridle Cl HOD EN11 ....185 H7
PEND EN3 ....233 J7
The Bridle Pth WFD IG8 ....267 G8
Bridleway BCAYE CM11 ....241 G8
Bridle Wy WARE SG12 ....185 H3
Bridle Wy North HOD EN11 ....185 H6
Bridle Wy South HOD EN11 ....185 H6
The Bridleway COLN CO3 ....105 K4
Bridon Cl RCHLM CM3 ....227 L7
Bridport Av IPSE IP3 ....55 J2
ROMW/RG RM7 ....288 E4
Bridport Rd CHLM/WR CM1 ....194 A8
Bridport Wy BRTR CM7 ....100 A8
Brierley Av K/T/MI CO5 ....150 A7
Brierley Cl EMPK RM11 ....289 M4
Brierley Rd WAN E11 ....311 G1
Brigadier Wy SBN/FI SS3 ....303 G11
Bright Cl BELV DA17 ....326 A7
RCOS CO16 ....159 G2
Brightside Wk WOS/PRIT SS0 ....300 B2
Brightingsea Pl POP/IOD E14 ....322 C3
Brightlingsea Rd RCOLE CO7 ....130 F7
RCOLE CO7 ....156 A3
Brighton Av SOS SS1 ....302 A4
WALTH E17 ....284 C3
Brighton Rd COS CO15 ....160 C3

EHAM E6 ...308 D7
Brights Av RAIN RM13 ...311 L8
Brightside BCAYW CM12 ...258 B1
  FOS CO13 ...137 H2
Brightside CI BCAYW CM12 ...258 B1
Bright St POP/IOD E14 ...322 E2
Brights Wk KESG IP5 ...50 D6
Brightwell Av WOS/PRIT SS0 ...18 B2
Brightwell CI FX IP11 ...10 D1
Brigstock Rd BELV DA17 ...326 F1
Brimfield Rd PUR RM19 ...329 D7
Brimpsfield CI ABYW SE2 ...325 L6
Brimsdown Av LAIN SS15 ...276 B2
  PEND EN3 ...248 B1
Brimstone Ct BRTR CM7 ...121 H5
Brimstone Rd RIPW IP8 ...53 K5
Brindles CVI SS8 ...320 C1
  EMPK RM11 ...290 B2
Brindles La RBRW/HUT CM13 ...256 F5
  TIL RM18 ...332 D3
Brindley Rd COS CO15 ...159 L5
Brindwood Rd CHING E4 ...266 D7
The Bringey CHLM/GWD CM2 ...210 D7
Brinkburn CI ABYW SE2 ...325 K7
Brinkley Crs COLN CO4 ...9 M2
Brinkley Grove Rd COLN CO4 ...87 K8
Brinkley La COLN CO4 ...87 M8
Brinkley PI COLN CO4 ...107 J2
Brinkley Wy FX IP11 ...63 J6
Brinkman Rd CBE/LIN CB11 ...25 G6
Brinkworth CI HOC/HUL SS5 ...264 A7
Brinkworth Wy HOM E9 ...306 C3
Brinley CI CHES/WCR EN8 ...232 E1
Brinsmead Rd HARH RM3 ...272 D8
Brion PI POP/IOD E14 ...322 F1
Brisbane Rd IL IG1 ...286 F5
  IPNE IP4 ...49 J7
  LEY E10 ...284 E7
Brisbane Wy COLS CO2 ...129 K4
Briscoe CI HOD EN11 ...201 G1
  WAN E11 ...285 J7
Briscoe Rd HOD EN11 ...201 G1
  PIT SS13 ...278 E6
  RAIN RM13 ...311 M6
Brise CI BRTR CM7 ...121 K4
Bristol CI RAYL SS6 ...262 F8
Bristol Ct WIT CM8 ...147 H2
Bristol HI RIPS/CAP IP9 ...67 G5
Bristol Hill Pk RIPS/CAP IP9 ...67 G5
Bristol Park Rd WALTH E17 * ...284 B2
Bristol Rd COL CO1 ...8 F5
  FSTGT E7 ...307 M3
  GVE DA12 ...338 A4
  IPNE IP4 ...48 H7
  SOSN SS2 ...283 G7
Bristowe CI CHLM/GWD CM2 ...210 D8
Bristowe Dr CDW/CHF RM16 ...316 A6
Britannia CI BCOLE CO7 ...130 E4
Britannia Crs RCOLE CO7 ...130 E4
Britannia Ga CAN/RD E16 ...323 K4
Britannia Rd BRW CM14 ...273 M4
  CHES/WCR EN8 ...233 G1
  IL IG1 ...286 E8
  IPNE IP4 ...49 G7
  POP/IOD E14 ...322 D7
  WOS/PRIT SS0 ...300 F5
British Est BOW E3 ...306 C7
British Legion Rd CHING E4 ...267 J1
British St BOW E3 ...306 C7
Britric CI GTDUN CM6 ...118 C7
Brittain Rd BCTR RM8 ...288 B8
Brittany Wy COLS CO2 ...129 L1
Britten CI COLN CO4 ...108 B7
  GVE SS16 ...276 D8
Britten Crs CHLM/GWD CM2 ...210 C5
Britton Ct RAYL SS6 ...281 C4
Brittons La ING CM4 ...241 J5
Brixham CI COS CO15 ...182 C4
  RAYL SS6 ...263 C4
Brixham Gdns
  GDMY/SEVK IG3 ...309 H2
Brixham Rd CAN/RD E16 ...324 C4
Brixton La GRH CM23 ...93 H4
Broad CI HOC/HUL SS5 ...264 B7
Broadclyst Av LOS SS9 ...282 A4
Broadclyst Ct SOS SS1 ...302 D4
Broadclyst Gdns SOS SS1 ...302 C4
Broadcroft Crs HVHL CB9 ...34 B5
Broadfield BSF CM23 ...115 J4
  GTDUN CM6 ...140 B6
  HLW CM20 ...13 K6
Broadfield Rd RBSF CM22 ...377 M2
Broadfields RCOLE CO7 ...130 F1
  SBW CM21 ...162 E7
Broadfield Wy BKHH IG9 ...267 M1
Broadgate WAB EN9 ...234 A3
Broad Gn BSDN SS14 ...3 J2
Broadhope Rd SLH/COR SS17 ...316 F5
Broadhurst Av
  GDMY/SEVK IG3 ...309 J1
Broadlands GRAYS RM17 ...330 F4
  SBF/HAD SS7 ...280 C7
Broadlands Rd HOC/HUL SS5 ...264 C7
Broadlands Wy COLN CO4 ...9 H4
  IPNE IP4 ...49 J8
Broad La RCOLW CO6 ...86 F3
Broadlawn LOS SS9 ...299 M1
Broadleaf Av BSF CM23 ...138 E5
Broadley Rd
  HLWW/ROY CM19 ...203 G5
Broadmayne BSDN SS14 ...3 F6
Broad Meadow BRWN CM15 ...383 N12
  RIPW IP8 ...53 L8
Broadmead Rd COLN CO4 ...108 B4
  WFD IG8 ...267 K5
Broadmere CI COS CO15 ...160 D8
Broadmere Rd IP IP1 ...47 K5
Broad Oak WFD IG8 ...267 L4
Broadoak Av PEND EN3 ...232 E5
Broadoak Cha MAL CM9 * ...173 H7
Broad Oak CI CHING E4 ...266 D4
Broadoaks EPP CM16 ...236 A2
Broad Oaks RCOLW CO6 ...361 J1
  WICKW SS12 ...261 H7
Broad Oaks CI SAFWN CB10 ...31 H7
Broadoaks Crs BRTR CM7 ...122 A4
Broad Oaks Pk COLN CO4 ...108 A4
Broad Oak Wy RAYL SS6 ...281 H5
Broad Pde HOC/HUL SS5 ...264 B7
Broad Rd HCH RM12 ...99 D4
  SWCM DA10 ...336 B4
Broadstone Rd HCH RM12 ...289 K7
Broad St DAGE RM10 ...310 D4
  HVHL CB9 ...34 C5
  RBSF CM22 ...376 G11
Broad Street Green Rd
  MAL CM9 ...198 A4
Broadstrood LOU IG10 ...235 H3
  RCOS CO16 ...157 H9
Broadview Av CDW/CHF RM16 ...316 C5
Broadwalk HLW CM20 ...13 G5
  HOC/HUL SS5 ...264 C7
Broadwalk SWFD E18 ...285 K1

The Broad Wk North
  RBRW/HUT CM13 ...256 D6
The Broadwalk South
  RBRW/HUT CM13 ...256 D7
Broadwater Gdns
  RIPS/CAP IP9 ...66 F5
Broadwater Gn LAIN SS15 ...276 D7
Broadwater Rd
  WOOL/PLUM SE18 ...325 C6
Broad Wy HOC/HUL SS5 ...264 C6
Broadway BARK IG11 ...308 F5
  COS CO15 ...182 D7
  GPK RM2 ...289 K1
  GRAYS RM17 ...330 F5
  LOS SS9 ...300 B5
  PIT SS13 * ...278 E8
  RAIN RM13 ...311 K8
  SRTFD E15 ...307 C4
  SUD CO10 * ...37 L6
  TIL RM18 ...331 J8
Broadway Av HLWE CM17 ...188 C3
Broadway Ct WFD IG8 ...267 L5
Broadway Ct WIT CM8 ...123 G8
Broadway Pde FX IP11 * ...266 F5
The Broadway BCTR RM8 ...288 C7
  GTDUN CM6 ...117 J1
  HCH RM12 ...311 L1
  LOU IG10 ...250 F3
  PIT SS13 * ...278 E8
  PLSTW E13 ...307 K6
  SOS SS1 * ...9 J4
  SOS SS1 ...302 D7
  WFD IG8 ...267 L5
  WICKW SS12 ...261 L5
Broadway West LOS SS9 ...300 A5
Brock CI K/T/MI CO5 ...150 B7
  WIT CM8 ...171 H5
Brockdish Av BARK IG11 ...309 J2
Brockenhurst Dr
  SLH/COR SS17 ...316 F5
Brockenhurst Gdns IL IG1 ...308 F2
Brockenhurst Wy
  RCHLM CM3 ...228 C4
Brocket CI CHIG IG7 ...269 J3
Brocket Rd HOD EN11 ...201 H3
Brockett Rd CDW/CHF RM16 ...331 K2
Brockett Wy CHIG IG7 ...269 J6
Brock Gn SOCK/AV RM15 ...329 L2
Brockham CI RCOS CO16 ...158 E7
Brockham Dr
  GNTH/NBYPK IG2 ...286 F4
Brock HI WICKE SS11 ...242 F8
Brock Hill Dr WICKE SS11 ...260 F2
Brockhill Rd FRAM/WMKT IP13 ...51 H1
Brockiebank Rd CHARL SE7 ...323 L7
Brockles Md
  HLWW/ROY CM19 ...203 K5
Brockley Crs CRW RM5 ...270 F2
  IP IP1 ...47 J1
Brockley Gv RBRW/HUT CM13 ...256 D4
Brockley Gv CHLM/GWD CM2 ...5 L1
Brock PI BOW E3 ...306 E8
Brock St BOW E3 ...323 L1
Brocksford Av RAYL SS6 ...281 J4
Brocks Md GTDUN CM6 ...94 B6
Brocksparkwood
  RBRW/HUT CM13 ...256 E6
Brockton CI ROM RM1 ...289 J2
Brockway CI WAN E11 ...285 H7
Brockwell La K/T/MI CO5 ...148 F4
Brodie Rd CHING E4 ...248 F8
  SBN/FI SS3 ...303 L4
Brodie Wk WICKW SS12 ...261 J8
Brodlove La WAP E1W ...322 A3
Brodrick Gv ABYW SE2 ...325 L7
Brograve CI CHLM/GWD CM2 ...226 A2
Broke Av RIPW IP8 ...47 G3
Broke Hall Gdns IPSE IP3 ...55 J1
Brokesley St BOW E3 ...306 C8
Broman's La K/T/MI CO5 ...179 K3
Bromefield Ct WAB EN9 ...234 B3
Bromeswell Rd IPNE IP4 ...48 D4
Bromfelde Rd BCAYE CM11 ...258 M8
Bromfords CI WICKW SS12 ...260 D5
Bromfords Dr WICKW SS12 ...260 D5
Bromhall Rd DAGW RM9 ...309 L3
Bromholm Rd ABYW SE2 ...325 L6
Bromleigh CI CHES/WCR EN8 ...216 F7
Bromley GRAYS RM17 ...330 C5
Bromley CI CHTY IP2 ...47 J7
  RCOS CO16 ...6 C3
Bromley Hall Rd
  POP/IOD E14 ...322 F1
Bromley High St BOW E3 ...306 F7
Bromley La SAFWS CB11 ...351 Q12
Bromley Ms RAYL SS6 ...280 C2
Bromley Rd COLN CO4 ...108 B4
  MGTR CO11 ...90 D3
  RCOLE CO7 ...109 L8
  WALTH E17 ...284 D1
Bromley St WCHPL E1 ...322 A1
Brompton CI BCAYW CM12 ...240 D8
Brompton Gdns MAL CM9 ...214 D5
Bronte CI BRTR CM7 ...121 K5
  FSTGT E7 ...307 K1
  GNTH/NBYPK IG2 ...286 D3
  TIL RM18 ...331 M8
Bronte Gv DART DA1 ...334 C6
Bronte Ms SOSN SS2 ...301 K2
Bronte Rd WIT CM8 ...123 G8
Bronte Vw GVE DA12 ...337 M6
Bronze Age Wy BELV DA17 ...326 F6
Brook Av DAGE RM10 ...310 E4
Brook CI BRTR CM7 ...120 F3
  GPK RM2 ...271 J7
  K/T/MI CO5 ...173 L1
  MAL CM9 ...198 D2
  MAL CM9 ...213 C3
  RCFD SS4 ...283 K5
Brook Crs CHING E4 ...266 C3
Brookdale IP UPMR RM14 ...290 D8
Brookdale Av UPMR RM14 ...290 E8
Brookdale Rd WALTH E17 ...284 D1
Brookdene Rd
  WOOL/PLUM SE18 ...325 H7
  WICKW SS12 ...261 H7
Brook Dr SLH/COR SS17 ...295 M4
Brooke Av SAFWN CB10 ...28 B6
Brooke Dr GVE DA12 ...338 E6
Brooke Gdns BSF CM23 ...139 G4
Brooke End SBW CM21 ...162 E7
Brook End Rd
  CHLM/GWD CM2 ...210 C2
Brook End Rd North
  CHLM/GWD CM2 ...210 D1
Brook End Rd South
  CHLM/GWD CM2 ...210 D2
Brooker CI POP/IOD E14 ...322 C1
Brooker Rd GRAYS RM17 ...330 D4
  WALTH E17 ...284 C2
Brooke Sq WAB EN9 ...214 D4
Brook Farm CI HSTD CO9 ...81 K4
Brook Farm La RIPS/CAP IP9 ...364 F12
Brookfield EPP CM16 ...236 D3
Brookfield Av WALTH E17 ...284 D1
Brookfield CI CBS CB2 ...22 C4

Brookfield Gdns
  CHES/WCR EN8 ...216 E5
Brookfield La
  CHES/WCR EN8 ...216 C6
Brookfield La East
  CHES/WCR EN8 ...216 E5
Brookfield La West
  CHES/WCR EN8 ...216 D6
Brookfield Pth CHING E4 ...267 C5
Brookfield Rd CBS CB2 ...22 C4
  HOM E9 ...306 D3
  IP IP1 ...47 L5
Brookfields CHONG CM5 ...380 G12
  GTDUN CM6 ...96 A7
  LOS SS9 ...282 A8
  PEND EN3 ...248 A4
  SBW CM21 ...162 E7
Brookfields CI LOS SS9 ...282 A8
Brook Gdns CHING E4 ...266 E3
Brook Hall Rd K/T/MI CO5 ...130 E7
Brookhampton St
  SAFWN CB10 ...340 H4
Brook HI GTDUN CM6 ...142 C4
  RCHLM CM3 ...167 L7
Brook Hill Rd IP IP1 ...47 M5
Brookhill Rd GDMY/SEVK IG3 ...287 K7
  WFD IG8 ...267 K5
Brookhouse Gdns CHING E4 ...267 H3
Brookhouse Rd RCOLW CO6 ...103 K5
Brookhurst CI CHLM/GWD CM2 ...5 M1
Brooking Ct BCTR RM8 ...287 M3
Broking Rd FSTGT E7 ...307 K2
Brookland K/T/MI CO5 ...173 M1
Brooklands COL CO1 ...8 F8
  COS CO15 ...182 D7
  WICKW SS12 ...260 E6
Brooklands Ap ROM RM1 ...289 G2
Brooklands Av LOS SS9 ...282 B7
Brooklands CI
  ROMW/RG RM7 ...289 G2
Brooklands Gdns COS CO15 ...182 B7
  EMPK RM11 ...290 M3
Brooklands La
  ROMW/RG RM7 ...289 G2
Brooklands Pk LAIN SS15 ...276 C7
Brooklands Ri MGTR CO11 ...65 C7
Brooklands Rd MGTR CO11 ...64 F6
  ROMW/RG RM7 ...289 G2
Brooklands Sq CVI SS8 ...320 B3
Brooklands Wk
  CHLM/GWD CM2 ...4 E8
Brook La BRWN CM15 ...383 R11
  CHLM/GWD CM2 ...210 E3
  CHLM/GWD CM2 ...226 A2
  FX IP11 ...65 G3
  KIR/NAC IP10 ...62 C3
  NHMKT IP6 ...49 M1
  RIPS/CAP IP9 ...58 D7
  SBW CM21 ...162 E7
Brooklane Fld HLWS CM18 ...204 C4
Brooklyn Av LOU IG10 ...250 B4
Brooklyn Dr RAYL SS6 ...263 G8
Brooklyn Ms HAR CO12 * ...15 H5
Brookman's Av CDW/CHF RM16 ...314 A7
Brookmans CI UPMR RM14 ...291 H5
Brookmans Ct ING CM4 ...241 H5
Brook Md LAIN SS15 ...276 A6
  RCHLM CM3 ...167 M1
Brook Meadow HSTD CO9 ...356 H8
Brook Meadow CI WFD IG8 ...267 M4
Brook Mdw Wy K/T/MI CO5 ...173 M1
Brook Ri CHIG IG7 ...268 D2
Brook Rd BKHH IG9 ...267 G8
  BOC CM0 ...390 C4
  BRW CM14 ...273 J2
  CHES/WCR EN8 ...233 G4
  EPP CM16 ...236 D3
  GNTH/NBYPK IG2 ...287 H4
  GPK RM2 ...271 J8
  GVW DA11 ...337 H6
  K/T/MI CO5 ...174 C2
  LOU IG10 ...250 B5
  RAYL SS6 ...280 C5
  RCOLW CO6 ...103 H6
  RCOLW CO6 ...104 E8
  SBF/HAD SS7 ...297 M4
  SBW CM21 ...162 E8
  STSD CM24 ...115 M3
Brooks Av EHAM E6 ...308 C8
Brooksbank CI HOM E9 * ...306 C4
Brooksby's Wk HOM E9 ...306 A4
Brookscroft Rd WALTH E17 ...266 F7
Brook Service Rd HVHL CB9 ...34 D5
Brookside BARK/HLT IG6 ...268 F5
  BCAYE CM11 ...240 F7
  CVI SS8 ...298 D8
  EMPK RM11 ...290 B8
  HLWW/ROY CM19 ...203 G4
  HOC/HUL SS5 ...282 C1
  HOD EN11 ...201 H4
  WAB EN9 ...233 M4
Brookside Av SBN/FI SS3 ...303 M4
Brookside CI COLS CO2 ...129 L1
Brookside Gdns EN EN1 ...232 C1
Brooksies SAFWS CB11 ...350 A7
Brooks Malting MGTR CO11 * ...91 J7
Brooks's Rd PLSTW E13 ...307 K5
Brook St BELV DA17 ...326 E8
  BRTR CM7 ...76 D3
  BRW CM14 ...273 H3
  CHLM/WR CM1 ...5 H1
  COL CO1 ...9 G7
  GTDUN CM6 ...118 D4
  MGTR CO11 ...91 C1
  RCOLE CO7 ...110 C4
  RCOLE CO7 ...130 C5
  RCOLW CO6 ...82 E4
Brook Ter HSTD CO9 ...356 H9
Brook V RCOS CO16 ...181 H1
Brook Vw CHLM/GWD CM2 ...210 D7
  GTDUN CM6 ...74 D1
Brookview CHTY IP2 ...53 M4
Brook Wy CHIG IG7 ...268 D2
Brookway RAIN RM13 ...327 L1
Broom CI CHESW EN7 ...216 B5
Brooms CI IPSE IP3 ...54 E4
Broome Gv RCOLE CO7 ...130 C5
Broome PI SOCK/AV RM15 ...329 G4
Broome Rd BCAYE CM11 ...241 G8
Broomer PI CHES/WCR EN8 ...216 E7
Broom Farm Rd RBSF CM22 ...374 D3
Broom Fld FX IP11 ...62 D7
Broomfield HLWE CM20 ...188 D6
  KESG IP5 ...50 D6
  SBF/HAD SS7 ...297 L4
  WALTH E17 ...284 C5
  WIT CM8 ...122 F4
Broomfield Av BROX EN10 ...216 H4
  LOS SS9 ...282 B8
  LOU IG10 ...250 D4
  RAYL SS6 ...280 D2
Broomfield CI CRW RM5 ...271 G5
Broomfield Common RIPW IP8 ...47 G7

Broomfield Crs RCOLE CO7 ...130 E3
Broomfield Gn CVI SS8 ...298 C8
Broomfield Ms KESG IP5 ...50 F6
Broomfield Rd CHDH RM6 ...288 A5
  CHLM/WR CM1 ...4 F2
  SWCM DA10 ...336 A5
Broomfields PIT SS13 ...278 D7
  RBSF CM22 ...378 B2
Broomfields Ct PIT SS13 ...278 D7
Broomfields Ms PIT SS13 ...278 D7
Broomfields PI PIT SS13 ...278 D7
Broomfield St POP/IOD E14 ...322 D1
Broomhall CI CHLM/WR CM1 ...193 L3
Broomhall Rd CHLM/WR CM1 ...193 K3
Broomhayes CHTY IP2 ...53 M8
Broomhill RIPS/CAP IP9 * ...364 G12
Broom Hill Rd IP IP1 ...47 M5
Broomhill Rd GDMY/SEVK IG3 ...287 K7
  WFD IG8 ...267 K5
Broomhills Cha BCAYW CM12 ...258 D8
Broomhills Rd K/T/MI CO5 ...178 A7
Broom Knoll MGTR CO11 ...64 C7
Broom Rd HOC/HUL SS5 ...263 H5
Broom St SUD CO10 ...45 L8
Broom Wy K/T/MI CO5 ...153 L3
Broomways SBN/FI SS3 ...303 M2
Broomwood Gdns
  BRWN CM15 ...255 K6
Broseley Gdns HARH RM3 ...272 B3
Broseley Rd HARH RM3 ...272 B3
Brotherton Av FX IP11 ...62 A5
Broton Dr HSTD CO9 ...81 H3
Brougham CI WICKW SS12 ...303 K1
Brougham Glades COLW CO3 ...106 A8
Broughton CI COLS CO2 ...128 F2
  RCHLM CM3 ...245 H7
  SBF/HAD SS7 ...297 M4
Broughton Dr IP IP1 ...16 D1
Browell Rd CHING E4 ...266 E6
Brown Av WICKE SS11 ...261 G1
Browning Av CHLM/WR CM1 ...193 K8
  SOSN SS2 ...19 H1
  WALTH E17 ...284 F3
Browning CI COLW CO3 ...106 C7
  DART DA1 ...334 C6
  IP IP1 ...47 L2
  MGTR CO11 ...64 D5
  WAN E11 ...285 J5
Brownings Av CHLM/WR CM1 ...193 K8
Brownlea Gdns
  GDMY/SEVK IG3 ...287 K7
Brownlow Bend BSDN SS14 ...3 J3
Brownlow Cross BSDN SS14 ...3 M6
Brownlow Gn BSDN SS14 ...3 M6
Brownlow Rd CHLM/WR CM1 ...208 E5
  FX IP11 ...68 F1
Brownlows CI GTDUN CM6 ...379 P4
Brown Rd GVE DA12 ...338 B7
Browns Av WICKE SS11 ...261 K8
Browns CI SUD CO10 ...43 M3
Brownsea Wy COLW CO3 ...128 K8
Brown's End Rd GTDUN CM6 ...375 N6
Browns Gv KESG IP5 ...50 D5
Brown's Rd WALTH E17 ...284 D1
Broxbourne Av WAN E11 ...285 L4
Broxbourne House BOW E3 ...306 A8
Broxbourne Rd FSTGT E7 ...285 K8
Broxburn Dr SOCK/AV RM15 ...329 K3
Broxhill Rd ABR/ST RM4 ...271 K2
Broxted Dr WICKE SS11 ...261 H7
Broxted End WICKW SS12 * ...261 H7
Bruce Av HCH RM12 ...289 D8
  HCH RM12 ...290 A7
Bruce Gv CHLM/GWD CM2 ...209 K6
  WICKE SS11 ...261 K7
Bruce Rd BOW E3 ...306 E7
  CHLM/WR CM1 ...208 G4
Bruces Wharf Rd
  GRAYS RM17 ...330 D5
Bruce Wy CHES/WCR EN8 ...232 E4
Bruff CI COLN CO4 ...8 B1
Bruff Dr WOTN CO14 ...137 K2
Bruges CI HAR CO12 ...70 D4
Bruges Rd CVI SS8 ...320 E3
Brundells Rd RCOLE CO7 ...110 C3
Brundish PIT SS13 ...278 C8
Brundon La SUD CO10 ...20 A5
Brunel CI ROM RM1 ...289 H2
  TIL RM18 ...331 L8
Brunel Ct COLN CO4 ...87 M7
Brunel Rd BRTR CM7 ...121 K4
  CHTY IP2 ...47 K7
  COS CO15 ...159 L5
  LOS SS9 ...281 M6
  SBF/HAD SS7 ...280 A6
  WALTH E17 ...284 A4
  WFD IG8 ...268 C4
Brunel St CAN/RD E16 ...323 J2
Brunel Wy COLN CO4 ...87 M7
  RCHLM CM3 ...244 M7
Brunner Rd WALTH E17 ...284 C1
Brunswick Av UPMR RM14 ...291 H4
Brunswick Gdns
  BARK/HLT IG6 ...268 F6
Brunswick House Cut
  MGTR CO11 ...91 K2
Brunswick PI RAYL SS6 ...280 E1
Brunswick Quay
  BERM/RHTH SE16 ...322 A6
Brunswick Rd IPNE IP4 ...17 J1
  LEY E10 ...284 E1
  PEND EN3 ...233 H8
  SOS SS1 ...302 A5
Brunswick St WALTH E17 ...284 F3
Brunswick Wk GVE DA12 ...338 A4
Brunton PI POP/IOD E14 ...322 B2
Brunwin Rd BRTR CM7 ...120 D4
Brunwins CI WICKE SS11 ...261 K8
Brushwood CI POP/IOD E14 ...322 C1
Brussels CI HAR CO12 ...71 G4
Brussum Rd CVI SS8 ...321 G3
Bruton Av WOS/PRIT SS0 ...282 C4
Bryan Rd BERM/RHTH SE16 ...322 C5
Bryanstone Mews
  COLW CO3 ...106 B8
Bryanstone Rd
  CHES/WCR EN8 ...233 G4
Bryant Av HARH RM3 ...272 A3
  SOS SS1 ...302 A5
Bryant Link CHLM/GWD CM2 ...210 G1
Bryant's La MAL CM9 ...213 G6
Bryant St SRTFD E15 ...307 H4
Brybank Rd HVHL CB9 ...33 M4
Bryce Rd BCTR RM8 ...309 H1
Brydges Rd SRTFD E15 ...307 G2
Brymay CI BOW E3 ...306 D6
Bryn Farm CI BSDN SS14 ...3 K1
Bryon Av FX IP11 ...10 B5

Bryony CI HVHL CB9 ...34 B4
Buchanan CI SOCK/AV RM15 ...328 E3
Buchanan Gdns WICKW SS12 ...261 G8
Buchanan Wy RCHLM CM3 ...231 M3
Buchan Ct BRTR CM7 ...121 K5
Buckenhoe Rd SAFWN CB10 ...28 B6
Buckeridge Wy BOC CM0 ...386 C10
Buckerills PIT SS13 ...278 C10
Buckfast Av FOS CO13 ...137 G5
Buckfast CI CHTY IP2 ...54 B4
Buckhatch La RCHLM CM3 ...243 M3
Buck HI BRTR CM7 ...121 J7
Buckhurst Wy BKHH IG9 ...268 A4
Buckingham CI EMPK RM11 ...290 A3
  WDBR IP12 ...50 F3
Buckingham Ct
  CHLM/GWD CM2 ...210 C1
  GTDUN CM6 * ...117 H6
Buckingham Dr COLN CO4 ...108 B6
Buckingham Hill Rd
  CDW/CHF RM16 ...316 D7
Buckingham Rd GVW DA11 ...337 D5
  HOC/HUL SS5 ...264 A7
  HVHL CB9 ...34 B7
  IL IG1 ...287 G2
  LAIN SS15 ...2 A1
  LEY E10 ...284 D5
  SRTFD E15 ...307 J2
  SWFD E18 ...285 L2
  WAN E11 ...285 L2
Buckingham Sq WICKE SS11 * ...261 H7
Buckland CI SBN/FI SS3 ...302 F4
Buckland Rd LEY E10 ...284 F7
Bucklebury Heath
  RCHLM CM3 ...245 G7
Bucklers CI BROX EN10 ...201 G8
Bucklers Ct HARH RM3 ...273 M4
Bucklesham Rd IPSE IP3 ...55 J3
  KIR/NAC IP10 ...57 L1
Buckles La SOCK/AV RM15 ...329 M4
Buckley CI SLH/COR SS17 ...295 H4
Buckleys CHLM/GWD CM2 ...210 C6
Buckleys La WIT CM8 ...172 B6
Buckley's La BRTR CM7 * ...121 J6
Buckrell Rd CHING E4 ...266 D7
Bucks Cross Rd GVW DA11 ...337 D8
Buck's Horns La RIPW IP8 ...53 G8
Buckters Rents
  BERM/RHTH SE16 ...322 B4
Buckwoods Rd BRTR CM7 ...121 K5
Buckwyns Cha BCAYW CM12 ...258 C1
Buckwyns Ct BCAYW CM12 * ...258 C1
Buddleia CI CHTY IP2 ...53 K1
Buddleia Ct RCOLE CO7 ...130 D3
Bude Ct KESG IP5 ...49 M7
Budna Rd CVI SS8 ...298 C8
Budoch Dr GDMY/SEVK IG3 ...287 K7
Buffett Wy COLN CO4 ...108 A7
Buglers Ri CHLM/WR CM1 ...208 E5
Bugsbys Wy GNWCH SE10 ...323 H1
Buick Av COS CO15 ...182 A7
Building End Rd ROY SG8 ...349 N12
Bulbecks Wk RCHLM CM3 ...245 L8
Bulford La BRTR CM7 * ...121 M8
Bulford Mill La BRTR CM7 ...121 M8
Bulace CI COLN CO4 ...108 A2
Bullards PI BETH E2 ...306 A7
Bullbanks Rd BELV DA17 ...326 F7
Bull CI CDW/CHF RM16 ...316 A4
  VGE SS16 ...278 B7
Bullen CI RIPW IP8 ...46 E3
Bullen La RIPW IP8 ...46 E3
Buller Rd BARK IG11 ...309 H4
  LAIN SS15 ...276 E6
  RCHLM CM3 ...246 D4
Bullfields SAFWS CB11 ...372 B7
  SBW CM21 ...162 F6
Bullfinch CI COLN CO4 ...108 C5
  HAR CO12 ...70 D4
Bullfinch Dr HSTD CO9 ...81 K4
Bull Hill Rd COS CO15 ...7 J5
Bullivant CI GRH CM23 ...335 K7
Bullivant St POP/IOD E14 ...322 F3
Bull La CDW/CHF RM16 ...316 A4
  HOC/HUL SS5 ...263 M7
  K/T/MI CO5 ...173 M1
  RAYL SS6 ...281 H4
  SAFWS CB11 ...371 K5
  SUD CO10 ...43 H1
Bullocks La SUD CO10 ...20 A7
Bullock Wood CI COLN CO4 ...108 A4
Bull Rd SRTFD E15 ...307 J6
Bulls Cliff FX IP11 * ...11 H4
Bull's Cross EN EN1 ...232 B6
Bulls Cross Ride CHESW EN7 ...232 B4
Bullsmoor CI CHES/WCR EN8 ...232 B5
Bullsmoor Gdns
  CHES/WCR EN8 ...232 B5
Bullsmoor La EN EN1 ...232 C5
Bullsmoor Ride
  CHES/WCR EN8 ...232 B5
Bullsmoor Wy
  CHES/WCR EN8 ...232 C5
Bullwood Hall La
  HOC/HUL SS5 ...281 K1
Bullwood Rd HOC/HUL SS5 ...264 A8
Bull Yd GVE DA12 * ...337 M4
Bulmer Rd SUD CO10 ...44 A5
Bulmer St SUD CO10 * ...44 A3
Bulmer Ter SUD CO10 * ...44 A4
Bulow Av CVI SS8 ...320 E2
Bulphan By-Pass UPMR RM14 ...293 K3
Bulphan CI WICKW SS12 ...261 H7
Bulrush CI BRTR CM7 ...121 L4
Bulstrode Rd CHTY IP2 ...17 G7
Bulwark Rd SBN/FI SS3 ...303 H5
Bulwer Court Rd WAN E11 ...285 G4
Bulwer Rd WAN E11 ...16 B3
  WAN E11 ...285 G5
Bumbles Green La WAB EN9 ...218 C3
Bumfords La RCHLM CM3 ...196 D6
Bumpstead Rd HVHL CB9 ...33 M2
Bunces La WFD IG8 ...267 J4
Bundick's HI CHLM/WR CM1 ...5 J1
Bung Rw WIT CM8 ...172 E4
Bunsen St BOW E3 ...306 C6
Bunters Av SBN/FI SS3 ...302 F7
Buntingbridge Rd
  GNTH/NBYPK IG2 ...287 D3
Bunting CI CHLM/GWD CM2 ...209 D8
  ED N9 ...248 A8
Bunting La CHTY IP2 ...53 K3
Bunting Rd CHTY IP2 ...53 J3
Bunting Ter SBF/HAD SS7 ...280 B3
Bunton St WOOL/PLUM SE18 ...324 D4
Buntry La SUD CO10 ...36 B1
Bunyan Av IP IP1 ...47 L2
Bunyan Rd BRTR CM7 ...121 H7
  WALTH E17 ...284 B1
Burbage CI CHES/WCR EN8 ...232 F4
Burcham St POP/IOD E14 ...322 E2
Burchell Rd LEY E10 ...284 E6
Burches LAIN SS15 ...277 H4
Burches Md SBF/HAD SS7 ...280 B3

Burches Rd SBF/HAD SS7 ....280 A4
Burchwall Cl CRW RM5 ....270 F6
Burden Wy WAN E11 ....285 L7
Burdett Av WOS/PRIT SS0 ....18 C4
Burdett Rd DAGW RM9 ....310 C5
  POP/IOD E14 ....322 C2
  SOS SS1 ....19 L8
Burdetts Rd DAGW RM9 ....310 C5
Bure TIL RM18 ....332 F2
Bure Dr WIT CM8 ....171 G2
Buregate Rd FX IP11 ....11 D3
Buren Av CVI SS8 ....321 J1
Bures Rd RCOLW CO6 ....360 E9
  SUD CO10 ....45 K4
Burfield Cl LOS SS9 ....282 C7
Burfield Rd LOS SS9 ....282 C7
Burford Cl BARK/HLT IG6 ....286 F2
  BCTR RM8 ....287 M8
Burford Gdns HOD EN11 ....201 H3
Burford Rd EHAM E6 ....308 D2
  SRTFD E15 ....307 G4
Burford St HOD EN11 ....201 H3
Burgate Cl RCOS CO16 ....182 C3
Burges Cl EMPK RM11 ....290 C4
  SOS SS1 ....302 F2
Burges Rd SRTFD E15 ....307 H1
Burgess Av SLH/COR SS17 ....317 H6
Burgess Fld CHLM/GWD CM2 ....210 C1
Burgess Leas IG5 ....281 H1
Burgess Rd SRTFD E15 ....307 H1
Burgess St POP/IOD E14 ....322 D1
Burges Ter SOS SS1 ....302 C7
Burghley Av BCAYW CM12 ....240 E8
Burghley Cl BRTR CM77 ....120 B1
  CHTY IP2 ....53 J3
Burghley Rd CDW/CHF RM16 ....329 M6
  WAN E11 * 285 L1
Burghstead Cl CHLM/GWD CM2 ....5 K9
Burgundy Gdns PIT SS13 ....278 E5
Burke Cl IP IP1 ....47 L2
Burke Rd IP IP1 ....47 M2
Burke St CAN/RD E16 ....323 G4
Burkitts La SUD CO10 ....20 C6
Burland Rd BRWN CM15 ....256 A6
  CRW RM5 ....270 F6
Burleigh Cl BCAYW CM12 ....240 E8
Burleigh Rd CHES/WCR EN8 * 232 F2
  HERT/BAY SG 184 B2
Burleigh Sq SOS SS1 ....302 E5
Burlescoombe Cl SOS SS1 ....302 D5
Burlescoombe Leas SOS SS1 ....302 L4
Burlescoombe Rd SOS SS1 ....302 L4
Burley Cl CHING E4 ....266 C4
Burley HI HLWE CM17 ....204 E2
Burley Rd BSF CM23 ....139 H5
  CAN/RD E16 ....323 M2
Burlington Av ROMW/RG RM7 ....288 E4
Burlington Cl EHAM E6 ....324 D1
Burlington Ct PIT SS13 ....278 E5
Burlington Gdns CHDH RM6 ....288 B5
  SBF/HAD SS7 ....299 J2
Burlington Pl WFD IG8 ....267 K2
Burlington Rd COLW CO3 ....A8
  IP IP1 ....16 C4
Burmanny Cl COS CO15 ....6 B6
Burnaby Rd GVW DA11 ....337 H6
  SOS SS1 ....19 M7
Burncroft Av PEND EN3 ....248 A1
Burne Av WICKW SS12 ....260 D7
Burnell Ga CHLM/WR CM1 ....194 D6
Burnells Wy STSD CM24 ....115 M2
Burnell Wk RBRW/HUT CM13 ....274 F3
Burnels Av EHAM E6 ....308 D7
Burnet Cl RIPW IP8 ....53 J5
Burnett La WFD IG8 ....268 A6
Burnett Pk HLWW/ROY CM19 ....203 K8
Burnett Rd ERITH DA8 ....334 A1
Burney Dr LOU IG10 ....250 F3
Burnham Av BRWN CM15 ....256 A6
Burnham Cl FX IP11 ....62 B6
  IPNE IP4 ....17 M2
  WOTN OC14 ....137 L1
Burnham Ct COS CO15 ....182 F5
Burnham Crs WAN E11 ....285 M1
Burnham Rd BOC CM0 ....393 M3
  CHING E4 ....266 C4
  CHLM/WR CM1 ....194 A8
  DAGW RM9 ....309 L4
  DART DA1 ....334 A7
  HOC/HUL SS5 ....263 H3
  LOS SS9 ....299 M4
  MAL CM9 ....213 J8
  MAL CM9 ....230 F5
  RCHLM CM3 ....244 E6
  RCHLM CM3 ....388 B12
  ROMW/RG RM7 ....289 M1
  WICKE SS11 ....262 B2
Burnham Rd Summerhill
  RCHLM CM3 ....392 C2
Burnham Ter DART DA1 * 334 A7
Burnley Rd WTHK RM20 ....335 J3
Burnsall Cl SBF CM23 ....30 C1
Burns Av CHDH RM6 ....287 M5
  COLW CO3 ....106 C8
  PIT SS13 ....278 E9
Burns Cl BCAYE CM11 ....258 E2
  MAL CM9 ....214 D4
  WALTH E17 ....284 F2
Burns Crs CHLM/GWD CM2 ....5 H7
  HOD EN11 ....201 G3
  SBW CM21 ....162 E7
Burnside Av CHING E4 ....266 B4
Burnside Cl BERM/RHTH SE16 ....322 A4
Burnside Crs CHLM/WR CM1 ....193 L6
Burnside Rd BCTR RM8 ....287 M7
Burns Rd RTI RM18 ....331 L7
Burns Rd IP IP1 ....47 K2
Burnstie Rd GTDUN CM6 ....119 J7
Burns Wy RBRW/HUT CM13 ....275 G3
Burnt Dick HI COLN CO4 ....361 Q10
Burnt Heath Cottages
  RCOLE CO7 ....89 K8
Burnthouse La
  RBRW/HUT CM13 ....239 J5
Burnthouse Rd RCOLW CO6 ....103 H4
Burntmill Cl HLW CM20 ....187 K6
Burntmill La HLW CM20 ....187 K6
Burnt Mills Rd PIT SS13 ....278 C3
Burntwood Av EMPK RM11 ....290 A4
Burntwood Cl BCAYW CM12 ....258 C3
  RBRW/HUT CM13 ....275 G3
Burnway EMPK RM11 ....290 C3
Burrage Gv
  WOOL/PLUM SE18 ....324 E7
Burrage Pl
  WOOL/PLUM SE18 ....324 E7
Burrage Rd
  WOOL/PLUM SE18 ....324 E7
Burrard Rd CAN/RD E16 ....323 K2
Burr Cl HAR CO12 ....70 D4
  VGE SS16 ....276 B8
Burrell Rd CHTY IP2 ....16 D7
Burrels Whf POP/IOD E14 ....322 E8
Burr Hill Cha SOSN SS2 ....301 H2

Burroughs Piece Rd SUD CO10 ....20 E6
Burrow Gn CHIG IG7 ....269 J4
Burrow Rd CHIG IG7 ....269 J4
Burrows Cl MGTR CO11 ....90 C2
  RCOS CO16 ....159 L4
Burrows Rd RCOLW CO6 ....82 F4
Burrows Wy RAYL SS6 ....280 C4
Burrs La ROY SG8 ....370 B4
Burrs Rd COS CO15 ....182 E1
Burr's Wy SLH/COR SS17 ....317 L1
Burrswood Pl MAL CM9 ....215 H4
Burses Wy RBRW/HUT CM13 ....256 C8
Bursland Rd PEND EN3 ....248 A1
Burslem Av BARK/HLT IG6 ....269 K5
Burstall Cl RCOS CO16 ....182 B3
Burstall Hall La RIPW IP8 ....46 A4
Burstall La RIPW IP8 ....46 A4
Burstead Dr BCAYE CM11 ....259 G4
Burstead Gra BCAYE CM11 ....259 G4
Burton Cl HVHL CB9 ....34 A4
  SLH/COR SS17 ....295 J8
Burton Dr PEND EN3 ....233 J7
Burton End HVHL CB9 ....34 A4
Burton Pl CHLM/GWD CM2 ....210 A3
Burton Rd LOU IG10 ....250 F4
  SWFD E18 ....285 J1
Burtons Ct SRTFD E15 ....307 L4
Burton's Green Rd HSTD CO9 ....101 H3
Burwash Rd
  WOOL/PLUM SE18 ....325 G5
Burwell Av CVI SS8 ....298 C8
Burwell Rd LEY E10 ....284 A6
Burwood Gdns RAIN RM13 ....311 H3
Burwood Pl BERM/RHTH SE16 ....322 A4
  COL CO1 ....8 F3
  RCOLW CO6 ....126 C2
Bury Farm La BCAYE CM11 ....278 A2
Bury Flds GTDUN CM6 ....118 D3
Bury Green Rd CHES/WCR EN7 ....232 B1
Bury Holme BROX EN10 ....217 G1
Bury La EPP CM16 ....219 L8
  RCHLM CM3 ....167 G5
  ROY SG8 ....349 Q10
Bury Lodge La RBSF CM22 ....376 B2
  STSD CM24 ....374 B10
Bury Rd CHING E4 ....249 G4
  DAGE RM10 ....310 F2
  EPP CM16 ....235 M1
  HAR CO12 ....70 D4
  IP IP1 ....47 J5
The Bury RCOS CO16 ....181 L1
Bury to Clare Wk SUD CO10 ....37 M2
Bury Water La SAFWS CB11 ....351 M12
Burywoods COLN CO4 ....106 E3
Bushbarns CHESW EN7 ....216 C3
Bushberry Rd HOM E9 ....306 B3
Bushby Av BROX EN10 ....201 M8
Bush Cl GNTH/NBYPK IG2 ....287 G3
Bush Elms Rd EMPK RM11 ....289 K5
Bushell Wy FOS CO13 ....137 H5
Bushey Av SWFD E18 ....285 J1
Bushey Cl CHING E4 ....266 F2
  RCHLM CM3 ....245 H5
  RIPS/CAP IP9 ....58 D4
Bushey Cft HLWS CM18 ....13 K9
Bushey Ley BRTR CM7 ....122 A3
Bushey Rd PLSTW E13 ....307 M6
Bushfields LOU IG10 ....250 D5
Bush Gv SUD CO10 ....44 D1
Bushgrove Rd BCTR RM8 ....310 A1
Bush Hall Rd BCAYW CM12 ....240 F8
Bushman Gdns RIPW IP8 ....46 F3
Bush Rd BERM/RHTH SE16 ....322 F1
  BKHH IG9 ....268 A5
  SAFWN CB10 ....352 H7
  WAN E11 ....285 J1
Bushway BCTR RM8 ....310 A1
Bushwood WAN E11 ....285 J1
Bushy Md LAIN SS15 ....276 E5
Bustler's Ri CBS CB2 ....340 C1
Butcher Rw POP/IOD E14 ....322 A3
  SAFWN CB10 ....28 A1
Butcher's HI SAFWN CB10 ....340 H5
Butchers La RIPS/CAP IP9 ....58 F4
  WOTN OC14 ....137 H5
Butchers Pasture GTDUN CM6 ....94 D3
Bute Rd BARK/HLT IG6 ....286 E3
Butler Rd BCTR RM8 ....309 L1
  HSTD CO9 ....81 F3
Butlers Cl CHLM/WR CM1 ....193 G2
Butlers Dr CHING E4 ....233 F8
Butlers Gv VGE SS16 ....294 E2
Butler's La MGTR CO11 ....366 F4
  SAFWN CB10 ....28 A1
Butler Smith Gdns KESG IP5 ....50 B6
Butlers Wy CBS CB2 ....22 C7
  HSTD CO9 ....346 B12
Butley Cl CHTY IP2 ....53 J5
Butley Rd FX IP11 ....11 J1
Butneys BSDN SS14 ....3 C3
Butteill Cl GRAYS RM17 ....331 G4
Butterbur Cha RCHLM CM3 ....244 A5
Buttercross La EPP CM16 * 220 B8
Buttercup La BCAYW CM12 * 258 D1
Buttercup Wk WIT CM8 ....171 G1
Buttercup Wy BOC CM0 ....393 M4
Butterfield Rd RCHLM CM3 ....195 H4
Butterfields WALTH E17 ....284 F1
Butterfield Sq EHAM E6 ....324 C1
Butterfly Gdns IPNE IP4 ....49 K6
Butteridges Cl DAGW RM9 ....310 C5
Buttermarket IP IP1 ....16 F4
Buttermere BRTR CM77 ....120 F6
Buttermere Cl WAN E11 ....307 L3
Buttersweet Ri SBW CM21 ....162 F6
Butterworth Gdns WFD IG8 ....267 K5
Butterys SOS SS1 ....302 B5
Buttfield Cl DAGE RM10 ....310 F4
Butt La BSF CM23 ....92 E7
  MAL CM9 ....214 D3
Buttleys La GTDUN CM6 ....116 C5
Butt's Green Rd
  CHLM/GWD CM2 ....227 J1
  EMPK RM11 ....290 A4
Butts La RCHLM CM3 ....212 D5
Butts Paddock RCFD SS4 ....392 A11
Butts Rd SLH/COR SS17 ....316 F4
The Butts BROX EN10 ....216 F2
Butts Wy CHLM/GWD CM2 ....225 H2
Buxey Cl K/T/MI CO5 ....177 L6
Buxhall Crs HOM E9 ....306 C3

Buxton Av LOS SS9 ....299 K2
Buxton Cl LOS SS9 ....299 K2
  WFD IG8 ....268 A5
Buxton Dr WAN E11 ....285 J1
Buxton Rd CDW/CHF RM16 ....331 H1
  CHING E4 ....249 K5
  COLS CO2 ....129 K3
  EHAM E6 ....308 A2
  EPP CM16 ....235 M6
  GNTH/NBYPK IG2 ....287 H4
  RCOLW CO6 ....124 C7
  SRTFD E15 ....307 J3
  WAB EN9 ....234 B2
  WALTH E17 ....284 B2
Buxton Sq LOS SS9 ....299 K2
Buyl Av CVI SS8 ....298 E8
Bycliffe Ms GVW DA11 * 337 J5
Bycliffe Ter GVW DA11 * 337 J5
Byefield Cl BERM/RHTH SE16 ....322 A4
Byelands Cl BERM/RHTH SE16 ....322 A4
Byfield LOS SS9 ....282 C6
Byfield Cl BERM/RHTH SE16 ....322 B5
Byfield Rd RBRW/HUT CM13 * 274 F3
Byfletts VGE SS16 ....296 C1
Byford Cl SRTFD E15 ....307 H4
Byford Rd RAYL SS6 ....281 H3
Bygrove St POP/IOD E14 ....322 F2
Bylam La RIPS/CAP IP9 ....365 M6
Byland Cl ABYW SE2 ....325 L6
  CHTY IP2 ....53 M3
Bylands Cl BSF CM23 ....138 E5
Byng Crs RCOS CO16 ....135 L4
Byng Gdns BRTR CM7 ....121 M1
Bynghams HLWW/ROY CM19 ....203 M3
Byng St POP/IOD E14 ....322 D5
Bypass Rd RCOS CO16 ....157 L8
By-Pass Rd SLH/COR SS17 ....316 D3
Byrd Cl LAIN SS15 ....276 F5
Byrd Md BRWN CM15 * 383 P7
Byrd's Farm La SAFWN CB10 ....28 A3
Byrne Dr SOSN SS2 ....302 A1
Byron Av COLW CO3 ....205 G5
  MNPK E12 ....308 B3
  SOSN SS2 ....19 J1
  SWFD E18 ....285 J1
Byron Ct BRTR CM7 ....121 K5
  CVI SS8 ....320 F1
  THMD SE28 ....325 M4
Byron Dr WIT CM8 ....171 G2
Byron Gdns TIL RM18 ....331 M7
Byron Rd CHLM/GWD CM2 ....216 D7
  DART DA1 ....334 E6
  IP IP1 ....47 H1
  LEY E10 ....284 L6
  RBRW/HUT CM13 ....257 H7
  WALTH E17 ....284 D1
Byron St POP/IOD E14 ....322 F2
Byron Wy HARH RM3 ....271 M4
Byrony Cl WIT CM8 ....171 G1
Bysouth Cl CLAY IG5 ....268 C2
Bywater Pl BERM/RHTH SE16 ....322 B4
Bywater Rd RCHLM CM3 ....244 A5

C

Cabborns Crs SLH/COR SS17 ....317 G5
Cabinet Wy CHING E4 ....266 C5
  LOS SS9 ....281 M7
Cables Cl BELV DA17 ....326 A3
Cabot Sq POP/IOD E14 ....322 D4
Cabot Wy EHAM E6 ....308 A5
Cadenhouse Ms COLW CO3 ....106 B6
Cadet Pl GNWCH SE10 ....323 H8
Cadges Ct SUD CO10 * 42 F2
Cadiz Rd DAGE RM10 ....310 F4
Cadmore La CHES/WCR EN8 ....216 F8
Cadmus Rd IP IP1 ....47 J6
Cadogan Av
  RBRW/HUT CM13 ....275 G3
Cadogan Cl HOM E9 * 306 C4
Cadogan Gdns SWFD E18 ....285 L1
Cadogan Rd
  WOOL/PLUM SE18 ....324 C7
Cadogan Ter HOM E9 ....306 C3
Caernarvon Cl EMPK RM11 ....290 D6
  HOC/HUL SS5 ....264 A7
Caernarvon Dr CLAY IG5 ....268 C2
Cage End RBSF CM22 ....376 G12
Cage End RBSF CM22 ....376 G12
Cagefield Rd RCFD SS4 ....396 B5
Cage La COLN CO4 ....362 C12
  FX IP11 ....62 D8
Cahir St POP/IOD E14 ....322 E7
Cairns Av WFD IG8 ....268 C5
Cairns Cl DART DA1 ....334 A7
Cairns Rd COLS CO2 ....129 K3
Cairo Rd WALTH E17 * 284 C2
Caister Dr PIT SS13 ....278 C4
Caister Park Rd SRTFD E15 ....307 L5
Caithness Cl IPNE IP4 ....49 J3
Caladonia La WICKW SS12 ....261 H8
Calamint Rd WIT CM8 ....171 G1
Calbourne Av HCH RM12 ....311 L2
Calcott Cl BRW CM14 ....255 J8
Calcott Rd COLS CO2 ....129 L4
Calcutta Rd TIL RM18 ....331 J8
Caldbeck WAB EN9 ....233 L4
Caldecot Av CHESW EN7 ....216 A4
Caldecott Wy CLPT E5 ....284 A4
Caldecott Wy BROX EN10 ....201 L4
Calderon Rd WAN E11 ....306 F1
Calderwood St
  WOOL/PLUM SE18 ....324 D7
Caldwell Rd SLH/COR SS17 ....316 L4
Caldy Rd BELV DA17 ....326 A3
Caledonian St
  SOCK/AV RM15 * 287 L6
Caledonia Rd RIPS/CAP IP9 ....67 G7
Caledon Rd EHAM E6 ....308 C1
Calford Dr HVHL CB9 ....33 M5
California Cl COLN CO4 ....107 G1
California Rd MGTR CO11 ....91 H7
Caliph Cl GVE DA12 ....338 C7
Callan Gv SOCK/AV RM15 ....329 M3
Callingham Cl POP/IOD E14 ....322 C1
Callis Rd WALTH E17 ....307 J3
Callis St CLAY IG5 ....37 L5
Callowood Cft HCH RM12 ....230 A4
Calmore Cl HCH RM12 ....311 J4
Calne Av CLAY IG5 ....268 C2
Calshot Av CDW/CHF RM16 ....330 C6
Calverley Cl CHES/WCR EN8 ....138 G5
Calverley Crs DAGE RM10 ....288 D1
Calvert Cl BELV DA17 ....326 A3
Calvert Dr PIT SS13 ....278 C4
Calvert Rd GNWCH SE10 ....323 J8
Calverton Rd EHAM E6 ....308 D2
Calvert Rd GNWCH SE10 ....323 J8
Calvin Cl LAIN SS15 ....277 J3
Calydon Rd CHARL SE7 ....323 L8
Calypso Wy
  BERM/RHTH SE16 ....322 C4
Camberley Rd IPNE IP4 ....49 J4

Camberton Rd BRTR CM7 ....99 H7
Cambeys Rd DAGE RM10 ....310 F2
Camborne Av HARH RM3 ....272 A6
Camborne Ms HARH RM3 ....272 A6
Camborne Rd KESG IP5 ....50 A6
Cambrai Cl COLS CO2 ....107 G8
Cambria Cl CVI SS8 ....319 M2
Cambrian Av
  GNTH/NBYPK IG2 ....287 H3
Cambrian Gv GVW DA11 * 337 G5
Cambrian Rd LEY E10 ....284 D5
Cambridge Av GPK RM2 ....271 M8
  HSTD CO9 ....356 F9
Cambridge Barracks Rd
  WOOL/PLUM SE18 ....324 C7
Cambridge Cl CHES/WCR EN8 ....216 D7
  RCFD SS4 ....264 F8
Cambridge Ct CHTY IP2 ....53 K4
Cambridge Dr CHTY IP2 ....53 K4
Cambridge Gdns
  CDW/CHF RM16 ....331 K3
  RCFD SS4 ....264 F8
Cambridge Pk WAN E11 ....285 F8
Cambridge Park Rd WAN E11 ....285 K5
Cambridge Rd BARK IG11 ....308 C3
  CBE/LIN CB1 ....23 L1
  CBE/LIN CB1 ....24 C5
  CHING E4 ....249 G8
  COLW CO3 ....106 F8
  COS CO15 ....6 C1
  CVI SS8 ....320 C2
  FOS CO13 ....137 K4
  FX IP11 ....69 G3
  GDMY/SEVK IG3 ....287 H6
  HLW CM20 ....188 D3
  KESG IP5 ....49 M5
  RAYL SS6 ....281 N11
  SBW CM21 ....162 F4
  STSD CM24 ....115 M3
  WAN E11 ....285 K3
  WOS/PRIT SS0 ....18 E6
Cambridge Rw
  WOOL/PLUM SE18 ....324 D7
Cambridge Wy BURES CO8 ....359 Q9
  HVHL CB9 ....34 B4
Cambus Rd CAN/RD E16 ....323 K1
Camden Cl CDW/CHF RM16 ....331 L3
Camden Rd CDW/CHF RM16 ....330 F6
  IPSE IP3 ....55 H4
  WALTH E17 ....284 C4
Camden St
  POP/IOD E14 ....322 D2
Camden Wy CDW/CHF RM16 ....330 F6
Camdenhurst St
  POP/IOD E14 ....322 D2
  IPSE IP3 ....55 H4
  WALTH E17 ....284 C4
  WAN E11 ....285 L4
Camelia Av RCOS CO16 ....6 A3
Camelia Cl CHLM/WR CM1 * 193 G2
  HARH RM3 ....272 B7
Camelia Crs RCOS CO16 ....6 A3
Camelot Cl CHLM/WR CM1 ....193 G2
  WOOL/PLUM SE18 ....325 G5
Camelot Gdns PIT SS13 ....278 F5
Cameron Cl BRTR CM7 ....99 H5
  BRW CM14 ....273 M3
  ING CM4 ....239 L2
  LOS SS9 ....299 H5
  SLH/COR SS17 ....295 H7
  SUD CO10 * 42 F3
Cameron Pl WICKW SS12 ....261 H8
Cameron Rd GDMY/SEVK IG3 ....287 H6
Cam Gn SOCK/AV RM15 ....329 L3
Camoise Cl HSTD CO9 ....355 N2
Camomile Av IL IG1 ....287 H1
Camomile Rd ROMW/RG RM7 ....289 L1
Camomile Wy COLN CO4 ....106 E3
Campbell Av BARK/HLT IG6 ....286 F2
Campbell Cl CHLM/GWD CM2 ....210 K6
  HLWE CM17 ....204 C2
  ROM RM1 ....271 H5
  WICKW SS12 ....261 H8
Campbell Dr COLN CO4 ....108 B3
Campbell Rd BOW E3 ....306 F8
  EHAM E6 ....308 B5
  GVW DA11 ....337 J6
  IPSE IP3 ....55 H4
  SRTFD E15 ....307 H1
  WALTH E17 ....284 C2
  WIT CM8 ....147 J8
Campden Crs BCTR RM8 ....309 M1
Campden Wy BCTR RM8 ....309 L1
Camperdown Rd CVI SS8 ....298 F8
Camper Ms SOS SS1 ....302 C3
Campernell Cl RCOLE CO7 ....156 C5
Camper Rd SOS SS1 ....302 A7
Campfield Rd SBN/FI SS3 ....303 H1
Campine Cl CHES/WCR EN8 ....216 C3
Campion Av EHAM E6 ....308 C3
  ROMW/RG RM7 ....289 G4
Campion Gdns WFD IG8 ....267 K4
Campion Pl THMD SE28 ....325 L4
Campion Pl CHTY IP2 ....53 J5
  COLS CO2 ....107 K9
Campions LOU IG10 ....235 J7
Campions HI RCOLW CO6 ....361 Q9
The Campions SBN/FI SS3 * 302 C3
  STSD CM24 ....115 M2
Campion Wy SOCK/AV RM15 ....360 H4
  WIT CM8 ....171 G1
Cample La SOCK/AV RM15 ....329 K3
Camp Rd RCOLE CO7 ....110 C6
Campsey Rd DAGW RM9 ....309 L4
Camps Rd CBE/LIN CB1 ....27 L2
  HVHL CB9 ....34 C6
Camrose St ABYW SE2 ....325 J1
Camulodunum Wy COLS CO2 ....128 D3
Camulus Cl BRTR CM7 ....121 K3
  COLS CO2 ....128 D3
Cam Wy WIT CM8 ....171 G3
Camwood Gdns IPSE IP3 ....55 H4
Canada Av BROX EN10 ....216 E1
The Canadas BROX EN10 ....216 E1
Canada St BERM/RHTH SE16 ....322 A5
Canal Basin GVE DA12 ....338 A4
Canal Cl COLN CO1 ....8 ....
  WCHPL E1 ....306 E8
Canberra Cl CHLM/WR CM1 ....193 H4
  COLS CO2 ....129 K3
  DAGE RM10 ....311 L4
Canberra Gdns DAGE RM10 ....311 G4
Canberra Rd EHAM E6 ....308 C1
Canberra Sq TIL RM18 ....331 K8
Cander Wy SOCK/AV RM15 ....329 L3
Candlelight Ct SRTFD E15 * 307 K8
The Candlemakers SOSN SS2 ....283 H7

Candlet Gv FX IP11 ....62 E8
Candlet Rd FX IP11 ....62 D6
Candover Rd EMPK RM11 ....289 K8
Candy Cl BOW E3 ....306 F9
Candytuft Rd CHLM/WR CM1 ....194 C7
Cane HI HARH RM3 ....272 A4
Canes La HLWE CM17 ....204 F8
Canewdon Cl WICKE SS11 ....261 J5
Canewdon Gdns WICKE SS11 ....261 J5
Canewdon Hall Cl RCFD SS4 ....392 A11
Canewdon Rd RCFD SS4 ....264 E5
  WOS/PRIT SS0 ....18 B5
Canewdon View Rd RCFD SS4 ....265 J7
Canfield BSF CM23 ....138 F5
Canfield Rd GTDUN CM6 ....140 A2
  RAIN RM13 ....311 J5
  WFD IG8 ....268 A5
Canford Av WICKW SS12 ....260 C5
Canford Cl CHLM/GWD CM2 ....210 B6
Canhams Rd SUD CO10 ....45 G6
Canham St IP IP1 ....16 C4
Canna Gdns WICKW SS12 ....261 L8
Canney Rd BOC CM0 ....388 G5
Cann Hall Rd WAN E11 ....307 J1
Canning Rd SRTFD E15 ....307 H6
  WALTH E17 ....284 C1
Canning St HAR CO12 ....15 K5
Cannington Rd DAGW RM9 ....309 M1
Cannon Cir BRTR CM7 ....355 J11
Cannon Cl POP/IOD E14 ....322 C5
Cannon Leys CHLM/GWD CM2 ....210 C5
Cannon Ms WAB EN9 ....233 J4
Cannon Pl CHARL SE7 ....324 B8
Cannon Rd BOC CO1 ....9 H9
  COLS CO2 ....115 H9
Cannon St COL CO1 ....9 G1
Cannon Av CHDH RM6 ....287 M3
Cannon Cl HVHL CB9 ....34 C4
  SLH/COR SS17 ....317 J3
Canonium Ms K/T/MI CO5 ....148 F3
Canon Pugh Dr SUD CO10 ....43 M3
Canons Brook
  HLWW/ROY CM19 ....B7
Canons Cl RCHLM CM3 ....228 B4
Canons Ga CHES/WCR EN8 ....217 G4
  HLW CM20 ....12 B4
Canonsleigh Rd DAGW RM9 ....309 L4
Canonsleigh Crs LOS SS9 ....300 B4
Canopy La HLWE CM17 ....189 G4
Cansey La BRTR CM7 ....255 L3
Cansey La MGTR CO11 ....366 A9
Canterbury Av IL IG1 ....286 B5
  SOSN SS2 ....302 B2
  UPMR RM14 ....291 G4
Canterbury Cl BSDN SS14 ....278 C5
  CHIG IG7 ....269 J3
  CHTY IP2 ....53 L5
  EHAM E6 ....324 C2
  RAYL SS6 ....281 J8
Canterbury Gra BRTR CM7 ....99 J5
Canterbury Rd COLS CO2 ....107 K8
  COS CO15 ....160 B4
  GVE DA12 ....337 J5
  LEY E10 ....284 E5
  SUD CO10 ....42 F7
Canterbury Wy CHLM/WR CM1 ....4 A3
  DART DA1 ....334 C4
  RBRW/HUT CM13 ....257 M5
  WTHK RM20 ....335 H3
The Canters SBF/HAD SS7 ....280 E8
Cantley Gdns
  GNTH/NBYPK IG2 ....286 F5
Canton St POP/IOD E14 ....322 D2
Cantrell Rd BOW E3 ....306 D8
Canuden Rd CHLM/WR CM1 ....4 A8
Canute Cl RCFD SS4 ....392 B11
Canvey Rd CVI SS8 ....298 A7
  LOS SS9 ....299 L4
  PIT SS13 ....278 J7
Canvey Wk CHLM/WR CM1 ....194 D6
Canvey Wy SBF/HAD SS7 ....297 K2
Canwick Gv COLS CO2 ....129 M1
Capadocia St SOS SS1 ....302 E2
Cape Cl BARK IG11 ....308 A3
  COLW CO3 ....106 C8
Capel Cl BRTR CM77 ....120 C3
  CHLM/WR CM1 ....193 G2
  FX IP11 ....63 A3
  SLH/COR SS17 ....317 J3
Capel Dr RCOLE CO7 ....156 F8
Capel Gdns GDMY/SEVK IG3 ....309 H1
Capel Hall La FX IP11 ....62 C3
Capel Pk FOS CO13 ....137 H2
Capel Rd BRTR CM77 ....120 C3
  COLW CO3 ....106 C6
  EN EN1 ....232 C6
  FSTGT E7 ....307 L1
Capelston LAIN SS15 ....276 ....
Capel Ter SOS SS1 * 19 G6
Caper La COLS CO2 ....151 J3
Capital Pl HLWW/ROY CM19 ....B7
Capon Cl BRW CM14 ....255 L8
Capons La BCAYW CM12 ....258 C3
Cappell La WARE SG12 ....185 K4
Cap Pillar Cl RCOLE CO7 ....130 E3
Capstan Cl CHDH RM6 ....287 L4
Capstan Ct CRH CM3 ....334 F6
Capstan Pl COLN CO4 ....108 A3
Capstan Rd DEPT SE8 ....322 E2
Capstan Sq POP/IOD E14 ....322 F5
Capstan Wy
  BERM/RHTH SE16 ....322 B4
Captains Ga K/T/MI CO5 ....177 J7
Captains Wood Rd MAL CM9 ....198 D3
Capulet Ms CAN/RD E16 ....323 G4
Capworth St LEY E10 ....284 E5
Caracalla Wy COLN CO4 ....107 G1
Caradoc St GNWCH SE10 ....323 H8
Caradon Ct WAN E11 ....285 H4
The Caravan Site
  SOCK/AV RM15 ....329 G6
Caravel Cl CDW/CHF RM16 ....330 C6
Caraway Cl PLSTW E13 ....323 G1
Carbis Cl CHING E4 ....249 G6
Carbis Rd POP/IOD E14 ....322 C2
Carbury Cl HCH RM12 ....311 M3
Cardale St POP/IOD E14 ....322 F5
Cardew Brft KESG IP5 ....50 C5
Cardiff Av CHTY IP2 ....54 A4
Cardigan Av WOS/PRIT SS0 ....300 F2
Cardigan Gdns
  GDMY/SEVK IG3 ....287 K7
Cardigan Rd BOW E3 ....306 C6
Cardinal Cl CHESW EN7 ....216 A4
  COLN CO4 ....108 C2
Cardinal Dr BARK/HLT IG6 ....268 F5
Cardinal Rd CDW/CHF RM16 ....330 B6
Cardinal Wy RAIN RM13 ....311 J6
  RAIN RM13 ....16 A6
Card's Rd CHLM/GWD CM2 ....210 F2
Carey Rd DAGW RM9 ....310 B1
Carfax Rd HCH RM12 ....311 J4

Carisbrooke Av COS CO15 .....159 K6
Carisbrooke Cl EMPK RM11 ...290 D6
 PIT SS13 ....278 E7
Carisbrooke Dr RCHLM CM3 ...244 A6
 SLH/COR SS17 ....317 K1
Carisbrooke Rd BRWN CM15 ...255 F6
 WALTH E17 * 284 B2
 WOS/PRIT SS0 ....18 C2
Carleton Rd CHES/WCR EN8 ...216 E5
Carlford Cl KESG IP5 ....50 F6
Carlile Cl BOW E3 ....306 C6
Carlina Gdns WFD IG8 ....267 L4
Carlingford Dr WOS/PRIT SS0 ...300 F2
Carlisle Cl COL CO1 ....8 F4
Carlisle Gdns IL IG1 ....286 F4
Carlisle Rd DART DA1 ....334 D6
 LEY E10 ....284 D6
 ROM RM1 ....289 J3
Carlisle Wy PIT SS13 ....278 E7
Carlton Av GRH DA9 ....335 H6
 WOS/PRIT SS0 ....300 F1
Carlton Cl HSTD CO9 ....346 E8
 HVHL CB9 ....34 C5
 UPMR RM14 ....290 E7
Carlton Dr BARK/HLT IG6 ....287 C1
 LOS SS9 ....300 C4
 SBF/HAD SS7 ....298 F1
Carlton Rd CDW/CHF RM16 ...331 J1
 COS CO15 ....7 J3
 GPK RM2 ....289 K3
 KESG IP5 ....49 M6
 MNPK E12 ....308 A1
 PIT SS13 ....278 F7
 WALTH E17 ....266 B7
 WAN E11 ....285 J6
 WICKE SS11 ....260 F3
Carlton Sq WCHPL E1 * 306 A8
Carlton Ter WAN E11 ....285 L3
Carlton Vls SOSN SS2 * 19 H3
Carlton Wy IPNE IP4 ....48 B5
Carlyle Cl IP IP1 ....47 L1
Carlyle Rd BCAYW CM12 ....240 C8
 WICKW SS12 ....261 H6
Carlyle Rd MNPK E12 ....308 B1
 THMD SE28 ....325 L3
Carmania Cl SBN/FI SS3 ....303 M4
Carmarthen Cl CHTY IP2 ....53 M4
Carmel St SAFWN CB10 ....341 L7
Carmen St POP/IOD E14 ....322 E2
 SAFWN CB10 ....341 L6
Carnaby Rd BROX EN10 ....200 F6
Carnach Gn SOCK/AV RM15 ...329 L3
Carnanton Rd WALTH E17 ...267 G7
Carnarvon Rd COS CO15 ....7 G6
 LEY E10 ....284 F4
 SOSN SS2 ....19 H3
 SRTFD E15 ....307 J3
 SWFD E18 ....267 J7
Carnation Cl CHLM/WR CM1 ...194 C8
 ROMW/RG RM7 ....289 H7
Carnation St ABYW SE2 ....325 L8
Carnegie Cl PEND EN3 ....233 J8
Carnforth Gdns HCH RM12 ...311 K2
Carnoustie Cl THMD SE28 ...326 A2
Car Av WDBR IP12 ....50 G4
Carolbrook Rd CHTY IP2 ....53 K4
Carol Cl FX IP11 ....63 H8
 LAIN SS15 ....277 G6
Carolina Cl SRTFD E15 ....307 H2
Caroline Cl RCOLE CO7 ....130 C2
 COLS CO2 * 128 D2
Caroline's Cl SOSN SS2 * 283 H8
Caroline St WCHPL E1 ....322 F2
Caro Rd CVI SS8 ....320 F2
Carpenter Cl BCAYW CM12 ....258 C1
Carpenter Pth
 RBRW/HUT CM13 * 257 G1
Carpenters Arms La
 EPP CM16 ....220 C3
Carpenters Rd BRTR CM77 ...120 E6
Carpenters Rd EN EN1 ....232 D6
 SRTFD E15 ....306 E4
The Carpenters BSF CM23 ...138 C5
Carraways WIT CM8 ....171 L5
Carriage Cl FX IP11 ....62 B5
Carriage Dr CHLM/WR CM1 ...194 B5
Carriage Ms IL IG1 ....286 F7
Carrick Dr BARK/HLT IG6 ....268 F7
Carriers Cl K/T/MI CO5 ....177 K6
Carriers Ct RCOLE CO7 ....64 C2
Carrigans BSF CM23 ....138 F1
Carrill Wy BELV DA17 ....326 A4
Carrington Cl K/T/MI CO5 ....178 A6
Carrington Gdns FSTGT E7 ...307 K1
Carrington Rd DART DA1 ....334 C8
Carringtons Rd RCOLE CO7 ...109 L1
Carrington Wy BRTR CM7 ....289 J5
Carroll Cl SRTFD E15 ....307 L2
Carroll Hl LOU IG10 ....250 D1

Carvers Wd BCAYE CM11 ....258 F6
Cary Rd WAN E11 ....307 H1
Cascade Rd BKHH IG9 ....268 A1
Case La RIPS/CAP IP9 ....59 G7
Casey La BOC CM0 ....390 D6
Cashiobury Ter SOS SS1 ....18 F6
Cashmere Wy VGE SS16 ....296 A2
Caspian Wk CAN/RD E16 ....324 A2
Cassandra Ga CHES/WCR EN8 ...217 C5
Cassel Av CVI SS8 ....298 F8
Cassida Rd HOM E9 ....325 K7
Cassino Rd CHLM/WR CM1 ...193 H7
 COLS CO2 ....128 F2
Cassiobury Rd WALTH E17 ...284 A3
Cassland Rd HOM E9 ....306 B1
Castellan Av GPK RM2 ....289 L1
Castell Rd LOU IG10 ....250 F1
Castle Av CHING E4 ....267 G5
 RAIN RM13 ....311 H4
Castle Cl FX IP11 ....63 J7
 HARH RM3 ....271 M2
 HOD EN11 ....185 K8
 HSTD CO9 ....356 F6
 RAYL SS6 ....280 F4
 RCHLM CM3 ....144 F7
 SBN/FI SS3 ....303 K5
Castle Ct RAYL SS6 ....280 F4
Castle Cross SAFWN CB10 ...28 B6
Castle Dr BCAYE CM11 ....260 D5
Castle Dr LOS SS9 ....299 L5
 RAYL SS6 ....280 F2
 REDBR IG4 ....286 B4
Castlegate St HAR CO12 ....15 L2
Castle Hl RCOLE CO7 ....89 J1
Castle Hill Pk COS CO15 * 159 A6
Castle La GVE DA12 ....338 C2
 HSTD CO9 ....356 G5
 HVHL CB9 ....34 B5
 SBF/HAD SS7 ....299 H3
Castle Meadow HSTD CO9 ....356 E7
Castle Rd COL CO1 ....6 C8
 COS CO15 ....8 D5
 DAGW RM9 ....309 L5
 GRAYS RM17 ....330 B5
 HOD EN11 ....185 K8
 IP IP1 ....47 K4
 PEND EN3 ....248 B1
 RAYL SS6 ....280 F4
 SBF/HAD SS7 ....299 H3
 SWCM DA10 ....336 C4
Castle St BSF CM23 ....139 G5
 COLN CM5 ....382 H6
 EHAM E6 ....307 J2
 GRH DA9 ....335 K7
 SAFWN CB10 ....28 A7
 SWCM DA10 ....336 C4
Castle Ter RAYL SS6 ....280 F4
Castleton Rd GDMY/SEVK IG3 ...287 L6
 SOSN SS2 ....302 A4
 WALTH E17 ....267 G8
Castle Vw BSF CM23 ....139 H2
Castle View Gdns IL IG1 ....286 B4
Castle View Rd CVI SS8 ....298 D7
Castle Wk HVHL CB9 ....34 B5
Castleward Cl RCOLE CO7 ....130 F5
Castle Wy RCOS CO16 ....181 K1
Castor La POP/IOD E14 ....322 E2
Caswell Cl SLH/COR SS17 ....317 K1
Caswell Ms CHLM/GWD CM2 ...210 C3
Catalina Gv CDW/CHF RM16 ...330 C1
Catchpole La MAL CM9 ....198 D1
Catchpool Rd COL CO1 ....8 A2
Caterham Av CLAY IG5 ....268 D8
Caterham Ct RCOS CO16 ....158 F7
Caterham St WAB EN9 ....234 A4
Cater Wd BCAYW CM12 ....258 C2
Catesbray RIPS/CAP IP9 ....58 C4
Cathall Rd WAN E11 ....285 H8
Catharine Cl CDW/CHF RM16 ...330 D1
Cathedral Dr LAIN SS15 ....276 F6
Cathedral Wk CHLM/WR CM1 ...5 J2
Catherine Cl BRWN CM15 ....255 K5
 COS CO15 ....7 J1
Catherine Hunt Wy COLS CO2 ...128 C1
Catherine Rd GPK RM2 ....289 L1
 PEND EN3 ....248 B2
 SBF/HAD SS7 ....298 A1
Catherines Cl RCHLM CM3 ....144 C7
Catisfield Rd PEND EN3 ....232 F7
Catkin Cl HVHL CB9 ....34 A4
Catons La SAFWN CB10 ....28 A7
Cats La SUD CO10 ....77 J3
Cattawade End BSDN SS14 ....3 L3
Cattawade Link BSDN SS14 ....3 M3
Cattawade St MGTR CO11 ....64 E8
Cattermole Cl RCOS CO16 ....182 E2
Catts Cl RIPS/CAP IP9 ....364 C11
Catsfield RIPS/CAP IP9 ....364 C11
Cauldwell Av IPNE IP4 ....17 M3
Cauldwell Hall Rd IPNE IP4 ...48 F1
Caulfield Rd EHAM E6 ....308 C4
 SBN/FI SS3 ....302 F6
Causeway CBS CM23 ....22 F4
 RCHLM CM3 ....143 J4
Causeway Br SOCK/AV RM15 ...329 L6
Causeway End MGTR CO11 * ...64 E8
Causeway End Rd
 GTDUN CM6 ....142 F2
Causeway Reach RCOS CO16 ...159 H6
The Causeway BRTR CM7 ....121 J2
 BRTR CM7 ....354 B11
 BSF CM23 ....139 G2
 CHLM/GWD CM2 ....210 D3
 CHLM/WR CM1 ....208 A2
 COLN CO4 ....9 K2
 GTDUN CM6 ....117 G3
 HSTD CO9 ....81 H4
 HSTD CO9 ....345 L5
 HSTD CO9 ....355 N5
 HVHL CB9 ....34 B6
 MAL CM9 ....197 G7
 MAL CM9 ....214 D1
 RCOLW CO6 ....86 D2
 SAFWS CB11 ....371 P4
 SAFWS CB11 ....373 J2
Causton Rd COL CO1 ....8 B3
Caustons Cl SUD CO10 ....45 M4
Causton Sq DAGE RM10 ....310 D4
Caustonway RAYL SS6 ....281 G1
Cautherly La WARE SG12 ....185 G1
Cavalier Cl CHDH RM6 ....287 M2
Cavalry Barracks COLS CO2 * ...107 G8
Cavan Rd IP IP1 ....47 J3
Cavell Crs DART DA1 ....334 D6
Cavell Rd BCAYE CM11 ....258 F4
 CHESW EN7 ....216 B5
Cavendish Av COLS CO2 ....129 M1
 HCH RM12 ....311 J3
 WFD IG8 ....267 L6
Cavendish Crs HCH RM12 ....311 J3
Cavendish Dr MGTR CO11 ....90 E2
Cavendish Gdns BARK IG11 ...309 J2
 BRTR CM7 ....99 M8
 CHDH RM6 ....288 B1

 CHLM/GWD CM2 ....210 B2
 IL IG1 ....286 D5
 WOS/PRIT SS0 ....300 D3
 FX IP11 ....11 J7
 HOC/HUL SS5 ....264 C8
 SUD CO10 ....38 A6
Cavendish St IPSE IP3 ....17 L1
Cavendish Ter BOW E3 * 306 C7
Cavendish Wy SS15 ....277 G4
 SUD CO10 ....20 E8
Cave Rd PLSTW E13 ....307 G2
Caversham Av SBN/FI SS3 ....303 H4
Caversham Park Av RAYL SS6 ...262 F4
Caversham Vls
 SBF/HAD SS7 * 280 C5
Caville White CHLM/WR CB9 ...3 K8
Cawdor Av SOCK/AV RM15 ....329 K8
Cawkell Ct STSD CM24 ....115 L2
Cawkell Cl CHLM/GWD CM2 ...210 C1
Cawley Hatch
 HLWW/ROY CM19 ....203 G1
Caxton Cl K/T/MI CO5 ....174 A1
Caxton Ct COLN CO4 ....87 M7
Caxton Gv BOW E3 ....306 C6
Caxton Hl HERT/BAY SG14 ...184 A3
Caxton Rd HOD EN11 ....185 J7
Caxton St North CAN/RD E16 ...307 G5
Caxton Wy ROM RM1 ....289 H2
Cazenove Rd WALTH E17 ....266 D7
Cecil Av BARK IG11 ....309 G4
 CDW/CHF RM16 ....330 C6
 EMPK RM11 ....290 B1
Cecil Cl BSF CM23 ....139 G1
Cecil Ct HLWS CM18 ....203 M6
Cecilia St IP IP1 ....16 C4
Cecil Rd CHDH RM6 ....288 A5
 CHES/WCR EN8 ....232 A4
 GVW DA11 ....337 J6
 HOD EN11 ....201 H1
 IL IG1 ....308 E1
 IP IP1 ....16 B3
 PLSTW E13 ....307 G5
 WALTH E17 ....266 D7
 WAN E11 ....285 D7
Cecil Wy RAYL SS6 ....281 J3
Cedar Av CHDH RM6 ....288 B1
 CHES/WCR EN8 ....232 E5
 CHLM/WR CM1 ....4 F2
 K/T/MI CO5 ....149 M6
 KESG IP5 ....49 M7
 RCOLE CO7 ....156 A6
 UPMR RM14 ....312 D1
 WICKW SS12 ....260 F3
Cedar Av West CHLM/WR CM1 ...4 F2
Cedar Cl BKHH IG9 ....249 A1
 BOW E3 ....306 C6
 IL IG1 ....309 G2
 MGTR CO11 ....65 G4
 RAYL SS6 ....281 J5
 RBRW/HUT CM13 ....257 G5
 ROMW/RG RM7 ....288 F2
 SBW CM21 ....162 F8
 SOSN SS2 ....301 K2
 WARE SG12 ....184 E1
 WOTN CO14 ....137 K2
Cedar Ct SBF CM23 ....115 G8
 RCOLW CO6 ....86 F2
Cedar Crs RBRW/HUT CM13 ...275 E8
Cedarcroft Rd IP IP1 ....47 M3
Cedar Dr HOC/HUL SS5 ....263 H3
 LOU IG10 ....250 F2
 WFD IG8 ....267 K5
Cedar Gv UPMR RM14 ....290 F8
Cedar Gv HOD EN11 ....201 H1
Cedar Hall Gdns SBF/HAD SS7 ...280 C5
Cedar Ldg CHES/WCR EN8 ...216 B6
Cedar Ms HOC/HUL SS5 ....263 H3
Cedar Pk BSF CM23 ....138 E5
Cedar Park Cl SBF/HAD SS7 ...280 C5
Cedar Park Gdns CHDH RM6 ...288 A5
Cedar Pl CHARL SE7 ....323 J8
Cedar Rd SOCK/AV RM15 ....314 A4
Cedar Rd CDW/CHF RM16 ...331 K2
 CVI SS8 ....320 C1
 HCH RM12 ....289 H4
 RBRW/HUT CM13 ....257 F2
 ROMW/RG RM7 ....280 F2
 SBF/HAD SS7 ....280 C5
Cedars SLH/COR SS17 ....317 H5
Cedars Av WALTH E17 ....284 A2
Cedars La RIPS/CAP IP9 ....58 C4
Cedars Rd COLS CO2 ....8 C5
 SRTFD E15 * 307 H3
The Cedars BKHH IG9 ....249 K8
 HOM E9 * 306 A4
 RCHLM CM3 ....245 G5
 SBN/FI SS3 ....303 L1
 SRTFD E15 * 307 J1
Cedar Wk RCFD SS4 ....392 A12
Cedar Wy ROLE CO7 ....133 H6
Cedric Av ROM RM1 ....289 H1
Celadon Cl PEND EN3 ....248 B3
Celandine Cl BCAYW CM12 ...240 C6
 POP/IOD E14 * 322 D1
 SOCK/AV RM15 ....313 M8
Celandine Ct COLN CO4 ....106 D5
Celandine Dr THMD SE28 ....325 L4
Celandine Wy SRTFD E15 ....307 H7
Celeborn St BSDN SS14 ....244 F7
Celedon Cl CDW/CHF RM16 ...330 D5
Celtic St POP/IOD E14 ....322 E1
Cement Block Cottages
 GRAYS RM17 ....330 F2
Cemetery La IPNE IP4 ....48 D1
 RCOLE CO7 ....363 Q7
Cemetery Rd BSF CM23 ....139 G4
 FSTGT E7 ....307 J2
 IPNE IP4 ....17 H3
Centaur Wy MAL CM9 ....214 D1
Centaury Cl COLW CO3 ....105 M9
Centenary Cir
 CHLM/GWD CM2 ....210 L4
 CHLM/WR CM1 ....192 H4
 RCHLM CM3 ....194 D4
Centenary Rd PEND EN3 ....248 D4
Centenary Wk EPP CM16 ....235 K4
Centenary Wk
 LOU IG10 ....249 L6
 WALTH E17 * 285 K7
 WAN E11 ....285 K7
 WFD IG8 ....267 K5
Central Av RCOS CO16 ....159 H4
Central Av BCAYW CM12 ....240 C6
 CHES/WCR EN8 ....232 F3
 CVI SS8 ....298 B8
 GVE DA12 ....338 B3
 HOC/HUL SS5 ....263 J4
 IPSE IP3 ....55 G5
 RCFD SS4 ....392 D7
 SBN/FI SS3 ....281 H8
 SLH/COR SS17 ....295 K8
 SOCK/AV RM15 ....328 E5
 SOSN SS2 ....19 J2
 TIL RM18 ....331 K7

 WAN E11 ....285 G7
 WOTN CO14 ....137 K3
 WTHK RM20 ....329 J8
Central Cl SBF/HAD SS7 ....299 H1
Central Ct CHIG IG7 ....269 H4
Central Dr HCH RM12 ....290 C8
Central Maltings MGTR CO11 * ...91 G7
Central Pde COS CO15 * 6 C7
 WALTH E17 * 284 C2
Central Park Av DAGE RM10 ...288 B6
Central Park Rd EHAM E6 ....308 B6
Central Rd DART DA1 ....334 B7
 HLW CM20 ....188 B3
 SLH/COR SS17 ....317 G4
 WAN E11 ....285 K7
The Centre HSTD CO9 ....81 H5
Centre Wy WAB EN9 ....233 K5
Centurian Wy ERITHM DA18 ...326 C6
Centurion Cl SBN/FI SS3 ....303 J5
Centurion La BOW E3 ....306 C6
Centurion Wy COLS CO2 ....128 C2
 PUR RM19 ....328 Z2
Century Dr KESG IP5 ....50 F7
Century Rd HOD EN11 ....201 H2
 WALTH E17 ....284 C1
Ceres Rd WOOL/PLUM SE18 ...325 J7
Cervia Wy GVE DA12 ....338 C8
Ceylon Rd WOS/PRIT SS0 ....18 C4
Chadacre Av CLAY IG5 ....286 C1
Chadacre Rd SOS SS1 ....302 A4
Chadburn St SUD CO10 ....43 G1
Chadfields TIL RM18 ....331 K6
Chadville Gdns CHDH RM6 ...288 A3
Chadway BCTR RM8 ....287 M7
Chadwell Av CHDH RM6 ....287 M1
 CHES/WCR EN8 ....216 D6
Chadwell By-Pass
 GRAYS RM17 ....331 K4
Chadwell Heath La
 CHDH RM6 ....287 G2
Chadwell Hl CDW/CHF RM16 ...331 G4
Chadwell Ri WARE SG12 ....184 D1
Chadwell Rd GRAYS RM17 ....330 F3
Chadwick Av CHING E4 ....267 G3
Chadwick Cl GVW DA11 ....337 H7
Chadwick Dr HARH RM3 ....272 A2
Chadwick Rd IL IG1 ....286 E8
 RCHLM CM3 ....245 H4
 WAN E11 ....285 H5
 WOS/PRIT SS0 ....300 D1
Chadwick Wy THMD SE28 ....326 A3
Chadwin Rd PLSTW E13 ....323 L1
Chaffinch Cl ED N9 ....248 A3
 SBN/FI SS3 ....303 H5
Chaffinch Dr HAR CO12 ....70 D2
Chaffinch Gdns COLN CO4 ...108 C5
Chaffinch Wy HSTD CO9 ....81 K4
Chafford Gdns
 RBRW/HUT CM13 ....275 C8
 CHDH RM6 ....287 M2
Chaingate Av SOSN SS2 ....302 B3
Chalcombe Av ABYW SS2 ....325 L3
Chalfont Cl LOS SS9 ....300 A1
Chalfont Rd COLN CO4 ....107 J5
Chalforde Gdns GPK RM2 ....289 L2
Chalgrove Crs CLAY IG5 ....268 A7
Chalice Cl BSDN SS14 ....278 E7
Chalice Wy GRH DA9 ....335 H5
Chalk Ct GRAYS RM17 ....330 F5
Chalk End PIT SS13 ....278 E5
Chalklands CBE/LIN CB1 ....24 C7
 CHLM/GWD CM2 ....227 G3
 SAFWN CB10 ....28 B8
Chalk La HLWE CM17 ....189 H7
Chalkners Cl RIPS/CAP IP9 ...58 F2
Chalk Rd CVI SS8 ....298 D7
 GVE DA12 ....338 D6
 HOC/HM ME3 ....339 M7
 PLSTW E13 ....323 L3
Chalks Av SBW CM21 ....162 G6
Chalks Rd WIT CM8 ....171 J3
Chalkstone Wy HVHL CB9 ....34 D4
Chalk St RCHLM CM3 ....243 H5
Chalkwell Av WOS/PRIT SS0 ...300 A1
Chalkwell Esp WOS/PRIT SS0 ...300 C3
Chalkwell Park Dr LOS SS9 ...300 C3
Chalky La ROY SS6 * 349 G9
Chalky Rd CBE/LIN CB1 ....23 L3
Challacombe SBN/FI SS3 ....302 F4
Challacombe Cl
 RBRW/HUT CM13 ....256 C4
Challenge Wy COL CO1 ....9 J4
Challinor HLWE CM17 ....204 F1
Challis La BRTR CM7 ....121 K5
Challock Lees PIT SS13 ....278 F7
Chalon St IP IP1 ....16 B3
Chalvedon Av PIT SS13 ....278 E6
Chamberlain Av CVI SS8 ....320 F1
 SLH/COR SS17 ....295 H6
 WOTN CO14 ....137 L2
Chamberlain Cl HLWE CM17 ...204 D1
 IL IG1 ....286 E6
 WOOL/PLUM SE18 ....325 G2
Chamberlain Pl WALTH E17 * ...284 D1
Chamberlains Ride
 RCHLM CM3 ....245 G2
Chamberlain Wy RIPW IP8 ....53 H3
Chambers Cl GRH DA9 ....335 K7
Chamois Cl CBS CM23 ....22 C7
Champion Cl SLH/COR SS17 ...317 H1
 WICKW SS12 ....261 G7
Champion Rd UPMR RM14 ....290 F7
Champions Wy HOD EN11 ....185 H6
 RCHLM CM3 ....244 N7
Champlain Av CVI SS8 ....298 C8
Champness Rd BARK IG11 ....309 J4
Chance Cl CDW/CHF RM16 ...330 C3
Chancel Cl BOC CM0 ....390 D4
 LAIN SS15 ....276 F7
 SBF/HAD SS7 ....279 M7
Chancellor Av
 CHLM/GWD CM2 ....210 A1
Chancellor Rd SOS SS1 ....19 M4
Chancelot Rd ABYW SE2 ....325 L3
Chancery Gv COLS CO2 ....129 K5
Chancery Pl CHLM/WR CM1 ...208 C4
Chandler Av CAN/RD E16 ....323 K5
Chandlers BOC CM0 ....393 K7
Chandlers Cl BSF CM23 ....138 D5
 RCOS CO16 ....182 E2
Chandlers Cha CHLM/WR CM12 * ...258 B1
Chandlers Dr ERITH DA8 ....314 D6
Chandlers Quay MAL CM9 ...214 D2
Chandlers Rw COL CO1 ....107 M8
Chandlers Wk BRWN CM15 ...383 M11
Chandlers Wy ROM RM1 ....289 H3

 SOSN SS2 ....283 J8
Chandos Av WALTH E17 * 266 C5
Chandos Cl BKHH IG9 ....267 L1
Chandos Ct WDBR IP12 ....50 E7
Chandos Pde SBF/HAD SS7 ...299 G5
Chaney Rd RCOLE CO7 ....307 G2
Chanlock Pth SOCK/AV RM15 ...325 J8
Chanmelsea Rd SRTFD E15 ...307 H5
Channing Cl EMPK RM11 ....290 C5
Chanterelle COLN CO4 ....107 L2
Chanton Cl LOS SS9 ....282 A6
Chantrees Cl DAGE RM10 ....310 D7
Chantreywood
 RBRW/HUT CM13 ....256 D6
Chantry Cl BSF CM23 ....138 F1
 COS CO15 ....159 H6
Chantry Crs SLH/COR SS17 ...316 F4
Chantry Dr ING CM4 ....239 L2
 LAIN SS15 ....276 F6
 RCOLW CO6 ....85 H1
Chantry Gn CHTY IP2 ....53 M3
Chantry La RCHLM CM3 ....195 K2
Chantry Pk CHTY IP2 * 47 L8
Chantry Rd BSF CM23 ....138 F1
The Chantry CHING E4 * 248 F6
 COLW CO3 ....106 F6
 DAGE RM10 ....188 B7
Chantry Wy BCAYE CM11 ....258 E3
 SRTFD E15 * 307 G4
Chant St SRTFD E15 ....307 H4
Chanute Rd BRTR CM7 ....354 H10
Chapel Cl RIPS/CAP IP9 ....58 D4
 WTHK RM20 ....335 L1
Chapel Ct BCAYE CM11 ....258 E3
Chapel Cft ING CM4 ....239 L1
 RCOLE CO7 ....89 H6
Chapel Cut MGTR CO11 ....91 G7
Chapel Dr RCHLM CM3 ....167 L2
Chapel End HOD EN11 ....201 H4
Chapel Fld HSTD CO9 ....344 D11
Chapel Fld RIPW IP8 ....46 F3
Chapel Flds HLWE CM17 ....204 D3
Chapelfields FOS CO13 ....137 L8
 WARE SG12 ....185 L4
Chapelfield Wy CBS CM23 ...22 C1
Chapel Gn HSTD CO9 ....345 N6
 HSTD CO9 ....81 H3
 STSD CM24 ....115 L2
 SUD CO10 ....347 L9
Chapel House St
 POP/IOD E14 ....322 E8
Chapel La BOC CM0 ....390 D6
 CHIG IG7 ....269 J2
 CHLM/WR CM1 ....207 H4
 FOS CO13 ....136 D3
 HLWE CM17 ....204 D3
 MAL CM9 ....213 K1
 RCHLM CM3 ....211 L2
 RCHLM CM3 ....230 A5
 RCOLE CO7 ....108 E4
 RCOLE CO7 ....109 K7
 RCOLE CO7 ....110 D8
 RCOLW CO6 ....132 D8
 RCOLW CO6 ....106 B2
 RCOS CO16 ....181 K1
 RIPW IP8 ....46 D2
 SAFWS CB11 ....372 B1
 SBF/HAD SS7 ....298 F5
 SBN/FI SS3 ....303 L1
 SUD CO10 ....45 M8
Chapel Rd BOC CM0 ....390 K2
 COLN CO4 ....87 K2
 COLW CO3 ....105 M7
 EPP CM16 ....220 A8
 HSTD CO9 ....345 N6
 IL IG1 ....286 D7
 K/T/MI CO5 ....174 B1
 KIR/NAC IP10 ....57 K6
 MAL CM9 ....173 G7
 MAL CM9 ....384 F4
 RCOLE CO7 ....130 E5
 RCOLE CO7 ....106 C4
 RCOS CO16 ....113 G6
 SBN/FI SS3 ....303 J7
Chapel Rw RCOLE CO7 * 110 D7
Chapel St BCAYW CM12 ....258 D3
 CBS CB2 ....22 B8
 HSTD CO9 ....81 H1
 HSTD CO9 ....345 N6
 HVHL CB9 ....344 B6
 RCOS CO16 ....130 L5
Chapel St North COL CO1 ....8 B8
Chapel South COLS CO2 ....8 B8
Chaplaincy Gdns EMPK RM11 ...290 B6
Chaplains Cl HVHL CB9 ....34 C6
Chaplemount Rd WFD IG8 * ...268 A1
Chaplin Cl CHLM/GWD CM2 ...225 L3
 LAIN SS15 ....276 F7
Chaplin Dr COLN CO4 ....9 M2
Chaplin Rd RCOLE CO7 ....363 H6
 SRTFD E15 ....307 H6
Chaplins FOS CO13 ....137 J2
Chapman Rd BELV DA17 ....326 C4
 COS CO15 ....159 J5
 CVI SS8 ....321 K2
 HOM E9 ....306 D3
Chapmans Cl LOS SS9 ....299 L4
Chapmans La K/T/MI CO5 ....178 C4
Chapmans Wk LOS SS9 ....299 L4
Chappel Hl RCOLW CO6 ....83 M8
Chappel Rd RCOLW CO6 ....84 B2
 RCOLW CO6 ....85 G6
 RCOLW CO6 ....106 D3
Chapple Dr HVHL CB9 ....34 D4
Charcroft Gdns PEND EN3 ....248 A4
Chardia Ter CHES/WCR EN8 ...216 B2
Chardwell Cl EHAM E6 ....324 B2
Charfinch Crs BCAYE CM11 ...258 F4
Charfleets Cl CVI SS8 ....320 A2
Charfleets Rd CVI SS8 ....319 M2
Charfleets Service Rd CVI SS8 ...319 L2
Charford Rd CAN/RD E16 ....323 K4
Chargeable La PLSTW E13 ....307 K8
Chargeable St CAN/RD E16 ...307 K8
Chariot Cl BOW E3 ....306 D5
Charity Farm Cha
 BCAYW CM12 ....258 C2
Charlbury Cl HARH RM3 ....271 M5
Charlbury Crs HARH RM3 ....271 M5
Charlbury Gdns
 GDMY/SEVK IG3 ....287 J7
Charlecote Rd BCTR RM8 ....288 B1
 BRTR CM77 ....120 D5
Charlemont Rd EHAM E6 ....308 C4
Charles Cl WOS/PRIT SS0 ....282 C6
Charles Flemwell Ms
 CAN/RD E16 ....323 K4
Charles Grinling Wk
 WOOL/PLUM SE18 ....324 D4
Charles Pell Rd COLN CO4 ...108 D7
Charles Rd CHDH RM6 ....288 A4
 DAGE RM10 ....311 G3
 FSTGT E7 ....307 M4

FX IP11 .....11 H4
RCOLE CO7 .....156 C7
...arles St CAN/RD E16 .....323 M4
COL CO1 .....8 C1
EPP CM16 .....236 B2
GRAYS RM17 .....330 C5
GRH DA9 .....335 J7
IP IP1 .....16 A3
...harlotte Av PIT SS13 .....278 F4
...harlotte St PIT SS13 .....278 F4
...harlotte Av WICKW SS12 .....260 F5
...harlotte Ct RCHLM CM3 .....245 C7
...harlotte Dr FOS CO13 .....137 H3
...harlotte Gdns CRW RM5 .....270 A6
...harlotte Ms SOSN SS2 * 18 F3
...harlotte Pl WTHK RM20 .....335 L1
...harlotte Wy WIT CM8 .....171 L8
...harlton Av IP1 .....47 J3
...harlton Church La
CHARL SE7 .....323 M8
PIT SS13 .....278 F6
...harlton Crs BARK IG11 .....309 J6
...harlton La CHARL SE7 .....324 A8
...harlton Mead La HOD EN11 .....201 K4
...harlton St WTHK RM20 .....335 L1
...harnock Cl FOS CO13 .....137 J3
...harnwood Av CHLM/WR CM1 .....4 B6
...harnwood Dr SWFD E18 .....285 L1
...harnwood Gdns
POP/IOD E14 .....322 D7
...harnwood Rd EN EN1 .....232 C2
...harnwood Vls SWFD E18 .....285 L1
...harter Av GNTH/NBYPK IG2 .....287 G6
...harter Cl COLN CO4 * 87 M7
...harteris Rd WFD IG8 .....267 H5
...harter Rd WFD IG8 .....267 H5
The Charter Rd WFD IG8 .....267 H5
...harters Cl WICKE SS11 .....261 J5
...harters Cross HLWS CM18 .....203 L4
The Charters GTDUN CM6 .....117 G3
...harter Wy BRTR CM77 .....121 M4
COLN CO4 .....107 H1
...hartfield Dr FOS CO13 .....137 G1
Chart Hills Cl THMD SE28 .....326 B2
Chartwell Cl BRTR CM7 .....99 H6
IPNE IP4 .....48 F3
WAB EN9 .....233 M3
...hartwell North SOSN SS2 * 19 G4
...hartwell Sq SOSN SS2 * 19 G4
...hartwell West SOSN SS1 * 19 G4
Chase Av HVHL CB9 .....34 A6
SBF/HAD SS7 .....280 C8
Chase Ct COLN CO4 .....9 M8
Chase Cross Rd CRW RM5 .....270 A6
Chase Dr RCHLM CM3 .....244 F5
Chase End RAYL SS6 .....281 J4
Chase Gdns CHING E4 .....266 D3
WOS/PRIT SS0 .....301 G2
Chase House Gdns
EMPK RM11 .....290 C3
Chase La BARK/HLT IG6 .....287 G3
CHIG IG7 .....269 K2
HAR CO12 .....70 D8
Chaseley St POP/IOD E14 .....322 B2
Chase Rd BRW CM14 .....273 K2
SLH/COR SS17 .....317 K2
SOS SS1 .....19 H4
Chase Rd East RCOLE CO7 .....110 F6
Chase Rd West RCOLE CO7 .....110 D7
Chaseside RAYL SS6 .....281 H5
Chaseside Cl ROM RM1 * 271 H5
Chase Sq GVE DA12 * 337 L3
The Chase BCAYE CM11 .....258 F3
BOC CM0 .....393 N6
BRTR CM7 .....99 K6
BRTR CM7 .....120 D8
BRW CM14 .....256 A6
BRW CM14 * 256 A6
BRW CM14 .....273 L3
BSF CM23 .....139 G3
CHIG IG7 .....268 E3
CHLM/GWD CM2 .....9 L7
COLW CO3 * 106 C7
COS CO15 .....160 C4
DAGE RM10 .....289 G8
GTDUN CM6 .....141 L1
HERT/BAY SG13 .....184 A5
HLWE CM17 .....188 D8
HVHL CB9 .....344 A6
K/T/MI CO5 .....148 D3
K/T/MI CO5 .....177 M7
KESG IP5 .....50 F8
LAIN SS15 .....276 B3
LOU IG10 .....249 M7
MAL CM9 .....384 C11
MAL CM9 .....384 G1
MAL CM9 .....385 N4
MGTR CO11 .....65 J8
MGTR CO11 .....91 G2
MNPK E12 .....308 A1
RAYL SS6 .....281 J4
RBRW/HUT CM13 .....256 F8
RBSF CM22 .....372 C11
RCFD SS4 .....264 F6
RCHLM CM3 .....195 M6
RCHLM CM3 .....229 L2
RCOLE CO7 .....89 K1
RCOLE CO7 .....109 J7
RCOLW CO6 .....103 M5
ROM RM1 .....289 M1
SBF/HAD SS7 .....280 C8
SBN/FI SS3 .....399 J3
SOSN SS2 * 39 M1
SUD CO10 .....21 H2
UPMR RM14 .....291 H2
VGE SS16 .....296 C6
WARE SG12 .....185 L2
WICKW SS12 .....261 J5
WICKW SS12 .....279 H1
WTHK RM20 .....330 A8
Chaseway VGE SS16 .....296 C1
Chaseways SBW CM21 .....188 C1
The Chaseway BRTR CM7 .....121 M4
The Chase Wy COLW CO3 .....106 A5
Chaters Hl SAFWS CB10 * 28 B7
Chatham Hall La RCHLM CM3 .....167 K4
Chatham Rd SWFD E18 .....267 J3
WALTH E17 .....284 F1
Chatham St
WOOL/PLUM SE18 .....324 A8
Chatham Wy BRW CM14 .....273 M3
Chatley Rd RCHLM CM3 .....144 F3
Chatsworth Av BRTR CM77 .....120 D4
Chatsworth Cl BSF CM23 .....138 D2
Chatsworth Crs CHTY IP2 .....53 N5
FX IP11 .....62 B5
Chatsworth Dr IPNE IP4 .....49 H8
Chatsworth Est CLPT E5 .....306 A1
Chatsworth Gdns COS CO15 .....6 C5
HOC/HUL SS5 .....264 D3
SRTFD E15 .....307 J2

Chatterford End BSDN SS14 .....2 F4
Chatteris Av HARH RM3 .....271 M5
Chattisham Rd RIPW IP8 .....52 A5
Chatton Cl WICKW SS12 .....261 H8
Chaucer Cl COS CO15 .....182 D4
MAL CM9 .....214 D5
TIL RM18 .....331 M8
Chaucer Dr BRTR CM7 .....121 K5
Chaucer Rd CHLM/GWD CM2 .....5 M3
FSTGT E7 .....307 H3
FX IP11 .....11 J3
GVW DA11 .....337 G8
HARH RM3 .....271 L6
IP IP1 .....43 G7
SUD CO10 .....20 C1
WALTH E17 .....266 F7
WAN E11 .....285 L4
Chaucer Wk WICKW SS12 .....260 F8
Chaucer Wy COLW CO3 .....106 C3
DART DA1 .....334 D6
HOD EN11 .....185 H7
Chauntler Rd CAN/RD E16 .....323 L2
Chauntry Rd HVHL CB9 .....34 C6
Cheapside East RAYL SS6 .....280 F1
Cheapside West RAYL SS6 .....280 D1
Cheddar Rd WOS/PRIT SS0 .....300 D1
Chedington SBN/FI SS3 .....302 F4
Cheeslon Rd SOCK/AV RM15 .....313 M6
Cheffins Rd HOD EN11 .....185 H4
Cheldon Barton SBN/FI SS3 .....302 F5
Chelmer Av RAYL SS6 .....280 F4
RCHLM CM3 .....167 L8
Chelmer Cl FOS CO13 .....137 H2
MAL CM9 .....199 L1
Chelmer Crs BARK IG11 .....309 L6
Chelmer Dr GTDUN CM6 .....117 H5
RBRW/HUT CM13 .....257 H2
SOCK/AV RM15 .....329 M8
Chelmer Lea CHLM/GWD CM2 .....210 B6
Chelmer Pl CHLM/WR CM1 * 5 L2
Chelmer Rd BRTR CM7 .....121 M4
CDW/CHF RM16 .....331 J4
CHLM/GWD CM2 .....5 M6
HOM E9 .....306 A2
HVHL CB9 .....34 E5
UPMR RM14 .....291 J4
WIT CM8 .....171 J3
Chelmer Ter MAL CM9 .....214 E3
Chelmerton Av
CHLM/GWD CM2 .....210 B6
Chelmer Valley Rd
CHLM/WR CM1 .....193 M7
Chelmer Village Wy
CHLM/GWD CM2 .....210 C3
Chelmer Wy BOC CM0 .....393 N2
SBN/FI SS3 .....303 G6
SOSN SS2 .....18 E2
Chelmsford Av CRW RM5 .....271 J1
Chelmsford Cl EHAM E6 .....324 C1
Chelmsford Dr UPMR RM14 .....291 G2
Chelmsford Gdns IL IG1 .....286 B5
Chelmsford Rd BRWN CM15 .....256 D1
CHLM/WR CM1 .....208 F4
CHONG CM5 .....383 J1
COS CO15 .....159 M7
GTDUN CM6 .....117 G5
GTDUN CM6 .....141 L1
GTDUN CM6 .....164 C1
GTDUN CM6 .....190 C1
ING CM4 .....222 F3
MAL CM9 .....212 F6
RBSF CM22 .....378 C3
RCHLM CM3 .....167 K6
RCHLM CM3 .....229 L2
SWFD E18 .....267 J7
WALTH E17 .....284 E4
WAN E11 .....285 L3
WICKE SS11 .....262 B6
Chelsea Av SOS SS1 .....302 A4
Chelsea Cl IP IP1 .....47 L3
Chelsea Ct SUD CO10 .....20 D1
Chelsea Flds WARE SG12 .....185 J1
Chelsea Gdns HLWE CM17 .....204 F2
Chelsea Rd SUD CO10 .....21 G1
Chelsfield Av ED N9 .....248 A1
Chelsworth Av IPNE IP4 * 48 F3
SUD CO10 .....21 G1
Chelsworth Cl SOS SS1 .....302 A3
Chelsworth Dr HARH RM3 .....272 A5
Chelsworth Rd FX IP11 .....10 E3
Cheltenham Av IP IP1 .....48 A3
Cheltenham Dr LOS SS9 .....300 C3
SBF/HAD SS7 .....280 C6
Cheltenham Gdns EHAM E6 .....308 A8
LEY E10 .....250 D6
Cheltenham Rd HOC/HUL SS5 .....264 C4
LEY E10 .....284 F4
SOS SS1 .....19 L4
Chelwater CHLM/GWD CM2 .....5 M8
Chelwood Rd CHING E4 .....248 A3
Chemsford Rd WICKE SS11 .....262 B4
Chenappa Cl PLSTW E13 .....307 K3
Cheney Rw WALTH E17 .....266 C3
Cheneys Av WAN E11 .....285 H4
Chenies Dr LAIN SS15 .....276 B4
Chepstow Av HCH RM12 .....290 B8
Chepstow Cl BCAYE CM11 .....241 J6
Chepstow Crs
GDMY/SEVK IG3 .....287 J2
IP IP1 .....48 C1
Chepstow Rd FX IP11 .....62 B5
Chequers BKHH IG9 .....249 L8
BSF CM23 .....138 D1
Chequers Ct RCFD SS4 * 392 A12
Chequers La DAGW RM9 .....310 F8
GTDUN CM6 .....117 G5
MAL CM9 .....213 G8
Chequers Rd ABR/ST RM4 .....272 A5
CHLM/WR CM1 .....208 A2
LOU IG10 .....250 A2
MGTR CO11 .....90 F2
The Chequers ING CM4 * 239 L4
RCOLE CO7 .....131 K6
Cherbury Cl THMD SE28 .....326 B4
Cheriton Av CLAY IG5 .....268 A5
Cheriton Rd BRTR CM7 .....121 M5
The Cherries CVI SS8 .....320 C3
Cherry Blossom Cl RIPW IP8 .....53 J3
Cherry Blossom La
RCHLM CM3 .....230 A3
Cherrybrook SS4 SOS SS1 .....302 A4
Cherry Cha K/T/MI CO5 .....174 A1
Cherry Cl CBE/LIN CB1 .....24 C1
CVI SS8 .....320 D1
HOC/HUL SS5 .....264 D6
Cherrydene Cl HOC/HUL SS5 .....263 H7
Cherrydown CDW/CHF RM16 .....315 G1
RAYL SS6 .....281 G1
Cherrydown Av CHING E4 .....265 K1
Cherrydown Cl CHING E4 .....266 A1
Cherrydown East VGE SS16 .....296 C2
Cherrydown Wk
ROMW/RG RM7 .....270 D2
Cherrygarden La
RCHLM CM3 .....212 C4
Cherry Garden La RCHLM CM3 .....212 D4

SAFWS CB11 .....372 A1
RCHLM CM3 .....167 H6
Cherry Garden Rd MAL CM9 .....214 A5
Cherry Gdns BCAYW CM12 .....258 C5
BRTR CM77 .....121 J7
BSF CM23 .....139 H1
DAGW RM9 .....310 F5
SBW CM21 .....162 F5
Cherry Gardens La IPNE IP4 .....49 J5
Cherry La HSTD CO9 .....356 H1
WICKE SS11 .....261 J4
Cherrymeade SBF/HAD SS7 .....298 D1
Cherry Orch BOC CM0 .....393 N2
Cherry Orchard La RCFD SS4 .....282 E5
Cherry Orchard Wy RCFD SS4 .....282 E5
Cherry Rd PEND EN3 .....232 E3
Cherry Rw COLW CO3 .....106 C6
Cherry St ROMW/RG RM7 .....289 G3
Cherry Tree Av HAR CO12 .....70 K3
HSTD CO9 .....81 K3
RAIN RM13 .....311 H6
Cherry Tree Cha SBN/FI SS3 .....303 M4
Cherry Tree Dr
SOCK/AV RM15 .....314 A4
Cherry Tree La COLS CO2 .....129 K7
RAIN RM13 .....311 J7
Cherry Tree Ri BKHH IG9 .....267 K3
Cherry Tree Rd HOD EN11 .....201 M2
SRTFD E15 .....307 K1
Cherrytree Rd SUD CO10 .....21 J7
Cherrytrees BCAYW CM12 .....258 C5
Cherry Trees ING CM4 .....239 L1
Cherry Wk CDW/CHF RM16 .....331 J6
RIPW IP8 * 52 B3
Cherrywood Av COLW CO3 .....127 M1
Cherrywood Dr COLW CO3 .....106 C6
Cherrywoods RCOLE CO7 .....133 C5
Cherston Gdns LOU IG10 .....250 D5
Cherston Rd LOU IG10 .....250 D5
Chertsey Cl SBN/FI SS3 .....303 L4
Chertsey Rd IL IG1 .....309 G1
WAN E11 .....285 G7
Chervil Cl K/T/MI CO5 .....173 M1
Chervil Ms THMD SE28 .....326 A4
Cherwell Dr CHLM/WR CM1 .....192 F3
Cherwell Gv SOCK/AV RM15 .....329 L1
Chesapeake Rd IPSE IP3 .....54 C1
Chesfield Cl BSF CM23 .....139 G1
Chesham Cl ROMW/RG RM7 .....289 C2
Chesham Dr LAIN SS15 .....276 A3
Chesham Rd CHTY IP2 .....16 D2
Cheshire Cl CHLM/GWD CM2 .....5 G6
WALTH E17 .....266 F7
Cheshunt Rd BELV DA17 .....327 J1
FSTGT E7 .....307 J3
Cheshunt Wash
CHES/WCR EN8 .....216 C4
Chesley Gdns EHAM E6 .....308 A2
Chesnut Av North WALTH E17 .....284 F2
Chessington Gdns IP IP1 .....47 L5
Chess La WIT CM8 .....171 L5
Chester Av SOS SS1 .....302 A7
UPMR RM14 .....291 H7
Chester Cl CDW/CHF RM16 .....330 D2
Chesterfield Crs LOS SS9 .....282 A7
Chesterfield Dr IP IP1 .....47 L3
Chesterfield Rd LEY E10 .....284 F1
PEND EN3 .....232 F7
Chesterford Gdns BSDN SS14 .....278 C5
Chesterford Rd MNPK E12 .....308 C2
Chester Hall La BSDN SS14 .....2 E1
Chester Pl CHLM/WR CM1 .....193 M6
Chester Rd CAN/RD E16 .....307 H5
CHIG IG7 .....268 A2
FSTGT E7 .....307 L4
GDMY/SEVK IG3 .....287 J1
LOU IG10 .....250 F1
WALTH E17 .....284 L4
WAN E11 .....285 L4
Chesterton Cl CHTY IP2 .....53 L1
Chesterton Rd PLSTW E13 .....307 K7
Chesterton Rd PLSTW E13 .....307 K7
Chestnut Av BCAYW CM12 .....258 C3
BKHH IG9 .....268 A5
CDW/CHF RM16 .....330 E4
COLS CO2 .....129 K5
COS CO15 .....6 C5
COS CO15 .....160 C5
FOS CO13 .....136 F3
FSTGT E7 .....307 L1
HCH RM12 .....289 J7
HSTD CO9 .....198 F7
MAL CM9 .....196 D2
RCHLM CM3 .....196 D5
SAFWS CB11 .....351 K4
Chestnut Av South
WALTH E17 .....284 F3
Chestnut Cl BKHH IG9 .....268 A5
BOC CM0 .....393 N6
CBS CB2 .....22 K2
GVW DA11 .....337 J2
HCH RM12 .....311 M1
HOC/HUL SS5 .....264 C5
HVHL CB9 .....34 C5
KESG IP5 .....49 K4
Chestnut Ct SAFWS CB11 .....372 B1
VGE SS16 .....296 H1
Chestnut Dr RBSF CM22 .....378 A2
WAN E11 .....285 K4
Chestnut Farm Dr
RCHLM CM3 .....392 B3
Chestnut Gln HCH RM12 .....289 J7
Chestnut Gv BARK/HLT IG6 .....269 H5
BRTR CM7 .....121 K5
BRW CM14 .....273 M1
SBF/HAD SS7 .....297 L2
SOSN SS2 .....301 L2
Chestnut Ms SUD CO10 * 21 K2
WFD IG8 .....267 K4
Chestnut Ri
WOOL/PLUM SE18 .....325 H1
Chestnut Rd PEND EN3 .....232 F6
RCOLE CO7 * 131 L2
VGE SS16 .....296 H1
Chestnuts RBRW/HUT CM13 .....256 E5
The Chestnuts CHTY IP2 * 53 H3
RAYL SS6 .....281 H4
Chestnut Ter SUD CO10 * 42 F7
Chestnut Wk CHLM/WR CM1 .....193 M1
EPP CM16 .....219 J4
GTDUN CM6 .....118 F7
RCHLM CM3 .....230 A3

Chevening Rd GNWCH SE10 .....323 J8
Chevers Pawen PIT SS13 .....278 D8
Chevet St HOM E9 .....306 D2
Chevington Wy HCH RM12 .....312 A1
Cheviot Av COS CO15 .....159 M4
Cheviot Dr CHLM/WR CM1 .....193 G8
Cheviot Rd EMPK RM11 .....289 K5
Cheviot Wy GNTH/NBYPK IG2 .....287 H2
Chevron Cl CAN/RD E16 .....323 K2
Chevy Ct HAR CO12 .....70 A2
Chewton Rd WALTH E17 .....284 D2
Cheyne Av SWFD E18 .....284 C1
Cheyne Cl SUD CO10 .....20 C1
Cheyne Ct SUD CO10 .....279 G1
Chichester Cl BSDN SS14 .....278 C5
CDW/CHF RM16 .....330 A3
CVI SS8 .....320 D3
EHAM E6 .....324 B2
SOCK/AV RM15 .....328 F4
Chichester Gdns IL IG1 .....286 B5
Chichester Rd GRH DA9 .....335 J7
SAFWS CB11 .....30 B1
SOS SS1 .....19 H4
WAN E11 .....285 H8
Chichester Wy MAL CM9 .....214 E5
POP/IOD E14 .....323 G7
Chichester Whf ERITH DA8 .....327 H8
Chickney Rd RBSF CM22 .....373 K11
Chieftan Dr PUR RM19 .....328 D2
Chiffinch Gdns GVW DA11 .....337 H8
Chigborough Rd MAL CM9 .....199 J6
Chignall Rd CHLM/WR CM1 .....193 G6
The Chignalls LAIN SS15 .....276 D7
Chigwell La LOU IG10 .....250 D2
Chigwell Park Dr CHIG IG7 .....268 C3
Chigwell Ri CHIG IG7 .....268 D1
Chigwell Rd SWFD E18 .....285 L1
WFD IG8 .....268 C5
Chilburn Rd COS CO15 .....159 J6
Childerditch Hall Dr
RBRW/HUT CM13 .....274 C4
Childerditch La
RBRW/HUT CM13 .....274 B2
Childerditch St
RBRW/HUT CM13 .....274 D5
Childers Cl FX IP11 .....62 C8
The Childers WFD IG8 .....268 C4
Childs Cl EMPK RM11 .....289 M4
Childs Crs SWCM DA10 .....336 A4
Childwell Aly COL CO1 .....8 E8
Chilham Cl PIT SS13 .....278 E8
Chiltern Cl COL CO1 .....8 A3
RAYL SS6 .....281 G2
Chiltern Gdns HCH RM12 .....288 M8
Chiltern Rd BOW E3 .....306 B8
GNTH/NBYPK IG2 .....287 H2
GVW DA11 .....337 H8
The Chilterns CVI SS8 .....320 C1
Chiltern Wy WFD IG8 .....267 K2
Chilton Cl CHLM/GWD CM2 .....5 C8
RCOLW CO6 .....86 E6
Chilton Gv DEPT SE8 .....322 A7
SUD CO10 * 43 L6
Chilton Lodge Rd SUD CO10 .....21 G7
Chilton Rd CDW/CHF RM16 .....331 K2
IPSE IP5 .....55 H1
Chilver St GNWCH SE10 .....323 H8
Chilworth Ga BROX EN10 .....201 G8
The Chimes SBF/HAD SS7 .....298 B1
Chimney Pot La RCHLM CM3 .....229 H2
Chimswell Wy HVHL CB9 .....33 M5
China La UPMR RM14 .....293 G5
Chinchilla Rd SOS SS1 .....302 A4
Chindit Cl BROX EN10 .....200 E6
Chindits La RBRW/HUT CM13 .....273 H2
Chingdale Rd CHING E4 .....267 H2
Chingford Av CHING E4 .....266 D4
CHING E4 .....34 B4
Chingford La WFD IG8 .....267 J4
Chingford Mount Rd
CHING E4 .....266 D6
Ching Wy CHING E4 .....266 C6
Chinnel La SAFWS CB11 .....351 L8
Chinnery Cl EN EN1 .....232 A1
Chinnery Hl BSF CM23 .....139 C4
Chinook COLN CO4 .....322 F5
Chipka St POP/IOD E14 .....322 E2
Chippenham Gdns HARH RM3 .....272 A5
Chippenham Rd HARH RM3 .....272 A5
Chipperfield Cl UPMR RM14 .....291 J4
Chippetts La COLW CO3 .....104 F6
Chippingdell WIT CM8 .....171 J1
Chippingfield HLWE CM17 .....188 D6
Chipping Hl HSTD CO9 .....81 J3
Chipping Hl WIT CM8 .....171 J2
WIT CM8 .....171 J2
Chipstead Wk RCOS CO16 .....158 C7
Chisenhale Rd BOW E3 .....306 B6
Chisholm Ct WICKW SS12 .....261 H8
Chislett Rw CHLM/GWD CM2 * 5 K8
Chittenden Cl HOD EN11 .....185 J4
Chittock Cl RCOS CO16 .....182 C1
Chittock Ga BSDN SS14 .....278 B7
Chitts Hl COLW CO3 .....106 A4
Chitty's La BCTR RM8 .....288 A7
Chivers Rd BRWN CM15 .....383 N9
CHING E4 .....266 C5
HVHL CB9 .....34 A6

Chudleigh Crs
GDMY/SEVK IG3 .....309 H1
Chudleigh Rd HARH RM3 .....272 B3
Chudleigh St WCHPL E1 .....321 K2
Churchacre MAL CM9 * 385 N4
Church Aly GVE DA12 .....337 K5
Church Av CHING E4 .....267 G5
CHLM/WR CM1 .....193 K5
Church Cha RCHLM CM3 .....245 M8
MAL CM9 .....172 C2
Church Cl BRW CM14 .....383 L11
BRWN CM14 .....239 H1
CBE/LIN CB1 .....23 M2
CVI SS8 .....320 C2
KESG IP5 .....56 F4
RCOLW CO6 .....106 B1
SBN/FI SS3 .....303 G2
SLH/COR SS17 .....316 C2
SUD CO10 .....20 C2
Church Cnr RCOLE CO7 * 110 B4
RCOLW CO6 .....104 E5
SBF/HAD SS7 .....298 A4
Church Ct BROX EN10 * 201 H6
Church Crs BRWN CM15 .....239 H5
COS CO15 .....7 H7
HOM E9 .....306 A4
RIPW IP8 .....46 F7
SOCK/AV RM15 .....313 M1
Church Dr BSF CM23 .....139 C1
Church Elm La DAGE RM10 .....310 C3
Church End BRTR CM7 .....98 E6
GTDUN CM6 .....117 G3
HLWW/ROY CM19 .....203 H3
ROY SG8 .....348 F10
WALTH E17 .....284 E2
Church End Av WICKE SS11 .....261 H3
Church End La WICKE SS11 .....261 G3
Church Farm Wy COLN CO4 .....107 H1
Church Fld EPP CM16 .....220 B7
Church Field Pth
CHES/WCR EN8 .....216 D7
Church Field Rd SUD CO10 .....21 J7
Churchfield Rd RCOLW CO6 .....124 D2
WOTN CO14 .....137 M1
Church Flds HSTD CO9 .....346 A11
K/T/MI CO5 .....250 B4
SBN/FI SS3 .....303 H3
STSD CM24 .....377 K7
SWFD E18 .....267 K7
Churchfields BROX EN10 * 177 L1
K/T/MI CO5 .....250 B4
SBN/FI SS3 .....303 H3
Churchfields Dr HVHL CB9 .....344 A11
Churchfields La BROX EN10 * 201 H6
Church Gdns GTDUN CM6 .....117 G3
Churchgate CHES/WCR EN8 .....216 C7
Churchgate Rd
CHES/WCR EN8 .....216 C7
Churchgate St HLWE CM17 .....188 C8
Church Gn CHLM/WR CM1 .....191 L8
HSTD CO9 .....392 A12
RCFD SS4 .....392 A12
RCOLW CO6 .....104 D3
RIPW IP8 .....47 L8
SAFWN CB10 .....341 J2
Church Gv RCOLW CO6 .....104 D3
Church Hl BRTR CM7 .....354 C11
EPP CM16 .....220 B7
GRH DA9 .....335 H7
HAR CO12 .....367 R8
HERT/BAY SG13 .....343 M5
HVHL CB9 .....34 C4
K/T/MI CO5 .....130 C5
LAIN SS15 .....250 G6
LOU IG10 .....250 C3
MAL CM9 .....90 C2
RCHLM CM3 .....230 A4
RCOLW CO6 .....82 C7
RIPW IP8 .....46 F7
SAFWN CB10 .....29 K1
SLH/COR SS17 .....316 F4
WALTH E17 .....284 C5
WIT CM8 .....146 C5
WOOL/PLUM SE18 .....324 C5
Church Hill Rd HLWE CM17 .....284 E2
Church Hollow PUR RM19 .....328 B8
Churchill Av HSTD CO9 .....81 K2
HVHL CB9 .....34 E4
IPNE IP4 .....49 H6
Churchill Cl CHONG CM5 .....382 H1
RCOLE CO7 .....156 F5
SUD CO10 .....37 J5
Churchill Crs SLH/COR SS17 .....317 G4
Churchill Dr SUD CO10 .....20 C1
Churchill Pl POP/IOD E14 .....322 E3
Churchill Ri CHLM/WR CM1 .....194 B6
Churchill Rd BRTR CM7 .....99 H6
CAN/RD E16 .....323 M2
GRAYS RM17 .....331 G5
GVW DA11 .....337 J6
K/T/MI CO5 .....148 D3
Churchill South SOS SS1 * 19 G4
Churchill Sq SOSN SS2 * 19 G4
Churchill Ter CHING E4 .....266 D4
Churchill Wy COLS CO2 .....129 L2
Church La ABR/ST RM4 .....252 A4
ABR/ST RM4 .....252 F4
BCAYE CM11 .....200 C3
BROX EN10 .....99 J4
BRTR CM7 .....99 J4
BRWN CM15 .....138 B2
BSF CM23 .....23 L7
CBE/LIN CB1 .....24 F7
CBS CB2 .....22 C2
CHES/WCR EN8 .....216 A4
CHLM/WR CM1 .....208 A4
CHLM/WR CM1 .....210 A1
COLW CO3 .....380 H10
DAGE RM10 .....310 F4
EPP CM16 .....221 H4
FOS CO13 .....136 A5
FX IP11 .....62 D1
GTDUN CM6 .....377 Q2
GTDUN CM6 .....379 R6
GVE DA12 .....338 F8
HAR CO12 .....345 N1
HSTD CO9 .....355 N2
HSTD CO9 .....356 F1
ING CM4 .....224 D2
K/T/MI CO5 .....173 M1
KIR/NAC IP10 .....56 F1
KIR/NAC IP10 .....60 F1
LOU IG10 .....250 D2
MAL CM9 19

Cold Hall Cha *RCOLE CO7* 110 B7
Coldham Gv *PEND EN3* 232 F7
Coldharbour La *RAIN RM13* 322 F4
Coldharbour La *RAIN RM13* 327 J1
Coldharbour Pl *GVW DA11* 337 J2
HLWW/ROY 12 B7
Coldnailhurst Av *BRTR CM7* 99 J8
Cold Norton Rd *RCHLM CM3* 231 G8
Cold Store Rd *FX IP11* 10 D1
Cole Av *CDW/CHF RM16* 331 M8
Colebrooke Dr *WAN E11* 285 M8
Colebrook Gdns *LOU IG10* 250 E2
Colebrook La *LOU IG10* 250 E2
Cole Cl *THMD SE28* 325 L4
Cole End La *SAFWN CB10* 30 F4
Colegrave Rd *SRTFD E15* 307 G2
Colehills Cl *SAFWS CB11* 72 C5
Coleman Rd *BELV DA17* 326 D6
Colemans Av *WOS/PRIT SS0* 301 G1
Colemans La *RCHLM CM3* 212 A6
WAB EN9 ....217 L4
Coleman St *SOSN SS2* 19 H3
Cole Ness Rd *IPSE IP3* 54 F1
Colenso Rd *GNTH/NBYPK IG2* 287 H1
Coleridge Av *MNPK E12* 308 E4
Coleridge Cl *CHESW EN7* 216 A1
Coleridge Rd *DART DA1* 334 A5
HARH RM3 ....271 L6
IP IP1 ....47 J3
MAL CM9 ....214 D4
TIL RM18 ....331 M8
WALTH E17 ....284 C2
Coleridge Wk
RBRW/HUT CM13 ....256 F3
Coles Cl *CHONG CM5* 380 H12
Coles Gn *LOU IG10* 250 E3
Coles La *CBE/LIN CB1* 24 F7
WOTN CO14 ....369 K10
Coles Oak La *RCOLE CO7* 363 K11
Colet Rd *RBRW/HUT CM13* 256 F1
Colgate Pl *PEND EN3 *....233 J7
Colin Cl *RDART DA2* 334 E8
Colinton Rd *BCTR RM8* 287 J1
Collard Av *LOU IG10* 250 F2
College Av *GRAYS RM17* 330 A4
College Cl *CHES/WCR EN8* 216 E1
WARE SG12 ....184 E1
College Gdns *CHING E4* 248 A4
REDBR IG4 ....286 B3
College Ga *HLW CM20* 12 F6
College Pl *GRH DA9* 335 M6
WALTH E17 ....285 H1
College Rd *BRTR CM7* 121 J2
CHES/WCR EN8 ....216 C2
COS CO15 ....7 J5
GRAYS RM17 ....330 A4
GVW DA11 ....336 E3
HERT/BAY SG13 ....184 E3
HOD EN11 ....201 G1
WALTH E17 ....284 F1
College Sq *HLW CM20* 12 F6
College St *IPSE IP3* 16 F6
College Wy *SOS SS1* 19 L4
Coller Rd *HAR CO12* 14 A4
Colies Brook Rd *RCOLE CO7* 133 J3
Collett Cl *CHES/WCR EN8* 216 E6
Colletts Cha *RCOLW CO6* 85 J3
Colley Rd *CHLM/GWD CM2* 240 E3
Collier Cl *EHAM E6* 324 E4
Collier Row La *CRW RM5* 270 F7
Collier Row Rd *CRW RM5* 270 D4
The Colliers *MAL CM9* 215 H2
Collimer Cl *RIPS/CAP IP9* 365 F5
Collindale Cl *CI SS8* 321 C1
Collindale Gdns *COS CO15* 159 M8
Collington Cl *GVW DA11* 337 H5
Collington St *GNWCH SE10 *....323 G8
Collingwood *SBF/HAD SS7* 298 D1
Collingwood Av *IPSE IP3* 55 H3
Collingwood Cl *BRTR CM7* 99 M8
Collingwood Flds *RCOLE CO7* 363 Q5
COS CO15 ....183 G4
RAIN RM13 ....311 G4
RCHLM CM3 ....245 J7
VGE SS16 ....3 L9
WIT CM8 ....171 J3
Collingwood Ter *VGE SS16* 3 L9
Collingwood Wk *SBN/FI SS3* 303 H4
Collins Cl *BRTR CM7* 121 J3
SLH/COR SS17 ....317 H3
Collins Cross *BSF CM23* 115 H3
Collins La *WIT CM8 *....171 K3
Collins Meadow
HLWW/ROY CM19 ....12 E3
Collinson's Cfty *IP IP2* 47 M8
Collins Rd *HSTD CO9* 358 F3
Collins Wy *LOS SS9* 282 D7
RBRW/HUT CM13 ....257 H1
Collinwood Gdns
GNTH/NBYPK IG2 ....286 C3
Colman Cl *SLH/COR SS17* 317 G2
Colman Rd *CAN/RD E16* 323 M1
Colmar Cl *WCHPL E1* 306 A8
Colne TIL RM18 ....332 F3
Colne Bank Av *ROY SC8* 349 K9
Colne Cavey *COLN CO4* 108 A4
Colne Cha *WIT CM8* 171 M4
Colne Cl *RCHLM CM3* 245 J7
SOCK/AV RM15 ....329 M3
Colne Ford Rd *RCOLW CO6* 3 H3
Coleis Rd *FX IP11* 62 F7
Colne Park Rd *RCOLW CO6* 3 G7
Colne Pl *VGE SS16* 3 J8
Colne Ri *K/T/MI CO5* 130 C5
Colne Rd *BURES CO8* 359 P9
CLPT E5 ....306 A1
COS CO15 ....7 G7
HSTD CO9 ....81 J3
HSTD CO9 ....356 F9
RCOLE CO7 ....156 F3
RCOLW CO6 ....102 D6
RCOLW CO6 ....124 D2
Colne Springs *HSTD CO9* 345 N6
Colne St *PLSTW E13* 307 H4
Colne Va *UPMR RM14* 291 H4
Colne Valley Cl *HSTD CO9* 81 G3
Colne Valley Rd *HVHL CB9* 34 C6
Colne Vw *RCOS CO16* 180 C3
Colne Wy *RCOS CO16* 180 C1
Coln Rd *DART DA1* 334 C8
Coleys Cl *SUD CO10* 20 A1
Colombo Rd *IL IG1* 286 F6
Colomb St *GNWCH SE10* 323 H8
The Colonnade
CHES/WCR EN8 ....216 E6
DRPT SE8 * 322 C7
Colson Pth *LOU IG10* 250 A4
Colson Rd *LOU IG10* 250 A4
Colsterworth Rd *COS CO15* 159 G3
Colthorpe Rd *HOD EN11* 201 K2

Coltishall Cl *WICKE SS11* 261 L7
Coltishall Rd *HCH RM12* 311 M3
Coltness Crs *ABYW SE2* 325 L8
Coltsfield *STSD CM24* 115 M2
Coltsfoot Ct *COLN CO4* 106 C4
Coltsfoot Pth *HARH RM3* 272 A6
Coltsfoot Rd *CHTY IP2* 53 K1
The Colts *BSF CM23* 138 F6
Colts Yd *WAN E11* 285 J6
Columbia Av *WALTH E17* 49 M6
Columbia Rd *PLSTW E13* 307 J3
Columbia Whf *PEND EN3 *....248 B1
Columbia Wharf Rd
GRAYS RM17 ....330 D7
Columbine Av *EHAM E6* 324 B1
Columbine Gdns *CHTY IP2* 47 K8
WOTN CO14 ....137 L2
Columbine Ms *COLW CO3* 105 M6
The Columbines *SUD CO10* 39 H5
Columbine Wy *HARH RM3* 272 B7
Colvers *HLWE CM17* 378 D11
Colville Av *BRTR CM7* 120 F7
SLH/COR SS17 ....295 J3
Colville Ms *BCAYW CM12* 240 C8
Colville Rd *WALTH E17* 266 C2
WAN E11 ....284 D1
Colvin Cha *CHLM/GWD CM2* 225 L4
Colvin Cl *COLW CO3* 106 C7
Colvin Gdns *BARK/HLT IG6* 268 F6
CHES/WCR EN8 ....232 E5
CHING E4 ....266 F2
SWFD E18 ....285 L2
Colvin Rd *EHAM E6* 308 B4
Colwall Gdns *WFD IG8* 267 K4
Colworth Cl *SBF/HAD SS7* 299 H2
Colworth Rd *WAN E11* 285 H4
Colyer Rd *GVW DA11* 337 G7
Colyers Reach
CHLM/GWD CM2 ....210 D3
HVHL CB9 ....34 A4
RAYL SS6 ....281 L4
SUD CO10 ....20 A1
Constable Rw *RCOLE CO7 *....363 P11
Constable St *CHLM/WR CM1 *....194 D7
Constable Wy *CHLM/WR CM77* 121 L8
Constance Cl *CHLM/WR CM1* 193 K2
WIT CM8 ....171 K5
Constance St *CAN/RD E16* 324 A1
Constantine Rd *COLW CO3* 107 G8
WIT CM8 ....171 M5
Constitution Hl *GVE DA12* 337 M6
IP IP1 ....48 A5
SBF/HAD SS7 ....298 A2
SUD CO10 ....20 E5
Convalescent Av *FX IP11* 11 L4
Convent Cl *LAIN SS15* 276 F1
Convent Hl *IPSE IP3* 99 K8
Convent La *BRTR CM7* 99 K8
Convent Rd *CVI SS8* 320 E2
Con Wy *SBF/HAD SS7* 298 A2
Conway Av *SBN/FI SS3* 303 L2
Conway Cl *CHTY IP2* 54 A5
Conway Rd
WOOL/PLUM SE18 ....325 G7
Conway's Rd *CDW/CHF RM16* 315 K1
Conyburry Cl *WAB EN9* 234 B2
Conyer Cl *MAL CM9* 214 C5
Conyer Rd *IP EN9* 12 E2
Conyer St *BOW E3 *....306 B6
Conyers Wy *LOU IG10* 250 E5
Cook Cl *GRH DA9* 335 L6
HAR CO12 ....70 E2
Cook Crs *COLN CO4* 108 B4
Cooke Cl *CDW/CHF RM16* 330 B2
Cookes Cl *WAN E11* 285 J7
Cookham Ct *SBN/FI SS3* 303 H3
Cookhill Rd *ABYW SE2* 325 L5
Cook La *CRW RM5* 270 F7
Cooks Ferry Rbt *UED N18* 266 B4
Cooks Gn *PIT SS13* 278 E4
Cook's Hall Rd *RCOLW CO6* 105 M2
Cook's La *BRTR CM7* 76 B1
COLW CO3 ....106 B1
Cook's Rd *SRTFD E15* 306 E6
Cooks Spinney *HLW CM20* 188 B3
Coolfin Rd *CAN/RD E16* 323 K2
Coolgardie Av *CHIG IG7* 268 D2
CHING E4 ....267 M4
Coolynne Wy *COS CO15* 159 L6
Coombe Dr *VGE SS16* 294 F4
Coombe Ri *BRWN CM15* 256 C4
CHLM/GWD CM2 ....193 L6
SLH/COR SS17 ....317 H3
Coombe Rd *BOC CMO* 393 N1
GVE DA12 ....337 M2
HARH RM3 ....290 C1
Coombers La *EPP CM16* 236 B2
Coombes Rd *HOM E9* 306 C5
Coombes Gv *RCFD SS4* 283 K3
Coombewood Dr *CHDH RM6* 288 C4
SBF/HAD SS7 ....280 B8
Cooper Av *WALTH E17* 266 A7
Cooper Cl *GRH DA9* 335 M7
Cooperdale Cl *BRTR CM7* 121 M6
Cooper Dr *BRTR CM7* 121 M6
Coopersale Common
EPP CM16 ....220 E6
Coopersale La *EPP CM16* 236 B7
Coopersale Rd *HOM E9* 306 C5
Coopersales *LAIN SS15* 276 C7
Coopers Av *MAL CM9* 198 A5
Coopers Cl *BSF CM23* 138 C5
CHIG IG7 ....269 L1
DAGE RM10 ....310 A5
Coopers Crs *RCOLW CO6* 106 C1
Coopers Dr *BCAYE CM11* 258 F7
Coopers End *RD RBSF CM22* 375 H10
Coopers End Rbt *RBSF CM22* 375 J11
Coopers Shaw Rd *TIL RM18* 332 A6
Coopers Hl *CHONG CM5* 382 H3
Coopers La *COS CO15* 7 H7
LEY E10 ....284 E6
RCHLM CM3 ....144 A4
RCOLE CO7 ....363 N12
Coopers Pk *BRTR CM7 *....121 J9
Coopers Rd *BCTR RM8* 288 C6
Copdock *BSDN SS14 *....3 J4
Copeland Rd *WALTH E17* 284 D1
Copelands *RCFD SS4* 302 F7
Copelis Cl *HVHL CB9* 34 D3

Connaught Gdns East
COS CO15 ....7 L4
Connaught Gdns West
COS CO15 ....7 L4
Connaught La *IL IG1* 286 F7
Connaught Ms
WOOL/PLUM SE18 ....324 D8
Connaught Rd *CAN/RD E16* 249 L4
HCH RM12 ....290 A8
HVHL CB9 ....34 B6
IL IG1 ....287 H1
RAYL SS6 ....281 L5
RCOS CO16 ....134 E8
WALTH E17 ....284 D3
WAN E11 ....285 L6
WOOL/PLUM SE18 ....324 D8
Connaught Wy *BCAYW CM12* 240 C8
Connington Crs *CHING E4* 267 G2
Connop Rd *PEND EN3* 232 E8
Connor Rd *BARK/HLT IG6* 268 F7
WAN E11 ....285 H6
Connor St *HOM E9 *....306 A5
Conqueror's Cl *RCHLM CM3* 196 G3
Conrad Cl *CDW/CHF RM16* 330 E1
Conrad Gdns *CDW/CHF RM16* 330 E1
Conrad Rd *SLH/COR SS17* 337 H3
Consort Cl *BRW CM14* 273 M4
Constable Av *CAN/RD E16* 323 L4
Constable Cl *COLN CO4* 107 H1
K/T/MI CO5 ....178 A6
MGTR 90 E1
Constable Ms *BCTR RM8* 309 L2
Constable Rw *RCOLE CO7 *....363 P11
Constable St *CHLM/WR CM1 *....194 D7
Constable Wy *CHLM/WR CM77* 121 L8
Constance Cl *CHLM/WR CM1* 193 K2
WIT CM8 ....171 K5
Constance St *CAN/RD E16* 324 A1
Constantine Rd *COLW CO3* 107 G8
WIT CM8 ....171 M5
Constitution Hl *GVE DA12* 337 M6
IP IP1 ....48 A5
SBF/HAD SS7 ....298 A2
SUD CO10 ....20 E5
Convalescent Av *FX IP11* 11 L4
Convent Cl *LAIN SS15* 276 F1
Convent Hl *IPSE IP3* 99 K8
Convent La *BRTR CM7* 99 K8
Convent Rd *CVI SS8* 320 E2
Con Wy *SBF/HAD SS7* 298 A2
Conway Av *SBN/FI SS3* 303 L2
Conway Cl *CHTY IP2* 54 A5
Conway Rd
WOOL/PLUM SE18 ....325 G7
Conway's Rd *CDW/CHF RM16* 315 K1
Conyburry Cl *WAB EN9* 234 B2
Conyer Cl *MAL CM9* 214 C5
Conyer Rd *IP EN9* 12 E2
Conyer St *BOW E3 *....306 B6
Conyers Wy *LOU IG10* 250 E5
Cook Cl *GRH DA9* 335 L6
HAR CO12 ....70 E2
Cook Crs *COLN CO4* 108 B4
Cooke Cl *CDW/CHF RM16* 330 B2
Cookes Cl *WAN E11* 285 J7
Cookham Ct *SBN/FI SS3* 303 H3
Cookhill Rd *ABYW SE2* 325 L5
Cook La *CRW RM5* 270 F7
Cooks Ferry Rbt *UED N18* 266 B4
Cooks Gn *PIT SS13* 278 E4
Cook's Hall Rd *RCOLW CO6* 105 M2
Cook's La *BRTR CM7* 76 B1
COLW CO3 ....106 B1
Cook's Rd *SRTFD E15* 306 E6
Cooks Spinney *HLW CM20* 188 B3
Coolfin Rd *CAN/RD E16* 323 K2
Coolgardie Av *CHIG IG7* 268 D2
CHING E4 ....267 M4
Coolynne Wy *COS CO15* 159 L6
Coombe Dr *VGE SS16* 294 F4
Coombe Ri *BRWN CM15* 256 C4
CHLM/GWD CM2 ....193 L6
SLH/COR SS17 ....317 H3
Coombe Rd *BOC CMO* 393 N1
GVE DA12 ....337 M2
HARH RM3 ....290 C1
Coombers La *EPP CM16* 236 B2
Coombes Rd *HOM E9* 306 C5
Coombes Gv *RCFD SS4* 283 K3
Coombewood Dr *CHDH RM6* 288 C4
SBF/HAD SS7 ....280 B8
Cooper Av *WALTH E17* 266 A7
Cooper Cl *GRH DA9* 335 M7
Cooperdale Cl *BRTR CM7* 121 M6
Cooper Dr *BRTR CM7* 121 M6
Coopersale Common
EPP CM16 ....220 E6
Coopersale La *EPP CM16* 236 B7
Coopersale Rd *HOM E9* 306 C5
Coopersales *LAIN SS15* 276 C7
Coopers Av *MAL CM9* 198 A5
Coopers Cl *BSF CM23* 138 C5
CHIG IG7 ....269 L1
DAGE RM10 ....310 A5
Coopers Crs *RCOLW CO6* 106 C1
Coopers Dr *BCAYE CM11* 258 F7
Coopers End *RD RBSF CM22* 375 H10
Coopers End Rbt *RBSF CM22* 375 J11
Coopers Shaw Rd *TIL RM18* 332 A6
Coopers Hl *CHONG CM5* 382 H3
Coopers La *COS CO15* 7 H7
LEY E10 ....284 E6
RCHLM CM3 ....144 A4
RCOLE CO7 ....363 N12
Coopers Pk *BRTR CM7 *....121 J9
Coopers Rd *BCTR RM8* 288 C6
Copdock *BSDN SS14 *....3 J4
Copeland Rd *WALTH E17* 284 D1
Copelands *RCFD SS4* 302 F7
Copelis Cl *HVHL CB9* 34 D3

Copeman Rd
RBRW/HUT CM13 ....257 G3
Copenhagen Pl *POP/IOD E14* 322 C2
Cope St *BERM/RHTH SE16* 322 A7
Copford Rd *RAYL SS6* 281 J4
Copland Cl *CHLM/GWD CM2* 210 C5
CHLM/WR CM1 ....193 C5
Copleston Rd *IPNE IP4* 49 G9
Coploe Rd *SAFWN CB10* 540 H6
Coppen Rd *BCTR RM8* 288 C6
Copperas Rd *RCOLE CO7* 156 C5
GVE DA12 ....338 C7
Copper Beech Cl *CLAY IG5* 268 D7
Copper Beeches *COLW CO3* 106 A8
Copper Beech Rd
SOCK/AV RM15 ....313 M7
Copperfield *BCAYE CM11* 259 G5
CHIG IG7 ....269 G5
Copperfield Gdns *BRW CM14* 255 J4
Copperfield Rd *BOW E3* 306 B8
CHLM/WR CM1 ....193 G6
CHTY IP2 ....49 J8
THMD SE28 ....325 M2
Copperfields *LAIN SS15* 276 F5
SAFWN CB10 ....351 R5
Copperfields Wy *HARH RM3* 290 A7
Copper Gv *RIPS/CAP IP9* 365 J4
Copperwood *HERT/BAY SG13* 184 A3
Coppice Cl *GTDUN CM6* 117 G4
Coppice End *COLN CO4* 107 J2
Coppice Hatch *HLWS CM18* 203 J3
LAIN SS15 ....277 J4
Coppice Pth *CHIG IG7* 269 L3
Coppice Rw *EPP CM16* 235 L6
The Coppice *COS CO15* 181 L5
Coppice Wy *SWFD E18* 285 J2
Coppins Cl *CHLM/WR CM1* 210 B1
The Coppings *HOD EN11* 185 M8
Coppins Rd *COS CO15* 6 A4
Coprolite St *IPSE IP3* 17 J4
Copse Hl *HLWW/ROY CM19* 203 J2
The Copse *BCAYW CM12* 258 D1
BSF CM23 ....139 K1
CHING E4 ....249 J8
COLN CO4 ....107 J2
GTDUN CM6 ....117 G4
HERT/BAY SG13 ....184 A3
IPSE IP3 ....159 G7
RCOS CO16 ....159 G7
Cotswold Av *IP IP1* 48 A4
RAYL SS6 ....281 G2
Cotswold Ct *COLN CO4* 107 H1
Cotswold Crs *CHLM/WR CM1* 193 G6
Cotswold Dr *SUD CO10* 42 F1
Cotswold Gdns *EHAM E6* 308 A4
GNTH/NBYPK IG2 ....287 G5
RBRW/HUT CM13 ....257 H3
Cotswold Rd *COS CO15* 7 G7
GVW DA11 ....337 J6
HARH RM3 ....272 C8
WOS/PRIT SS0 ....18 A4
Cottage Dr *COLS CO2* 129 M2
Cottage Gv *CHES/WCR EN8 *....216 E7
Cottage Gn *RCOS CO16* 158 F7
Cottage Pl *RCOS CO16* 158 F7
MGTR 366 H2
Cottage Wk *VGE SS16* 3 M8
Cottesmore Av *CLAY IG5* 268 C8
Cottesmore Ct *COLN CO4* 320 D3
Cottesmore Gdns *LOS SS9* 299 K4
Cottingham Rd *RIPW IP9* 53 L8
Cottis Cl *VGE SS16* 294 D2
Cotton Cl *DAGW RM9* 309 M4
WAN E11 ....285 H5
Cotton Dr *HERT/BAY SG13* 184 C2
Cotton La *GRH DA9* 334 F7
Cottons Ap *ROMW/RG RM7* 289 G3
Cotton St *POP/IOD E14* 322 F3
Cottonwood Ct *COS CO15* 129 H8
Couchmore Av *CLAY IG5* 268 A6
Coulde Dennis *RCHLM CM3* 227 L6
Coulsdon Pl *RCOS CO16* 158 F7
Coulson Cl *BCTR RM8* 287 M6
Coulter Ms *BCAYE CM11* 258 D1
Coulton Av *GVW DA11* 337 H5
Council Av *GVW DA11* 336 G4
Counting House La
GTDUN CM6 ....117 G4
County Cl *CHLM/GWD CM2* 324 G5
Coupals Cl *HVHL CB9* 34 F1
Coupals Crt *HVHL CB9 *....34 F1
Coupals Rd *HVHL CB9* 34 F1
Courage Cl *EMPK RM11* 289 M4
Courier Rd *DAGW RM9* 310 A6
Courtauld Cl *HSTD CO9* 81 J4
Courtauld Rd *BRTR CM7* 121 J4
PIT SS13 ....278 E3
Courtaulds Cl *THMD SE28* 325 K4
Court Av *BELV DA17* 326 B5
HARH RM3 ....272 D6
Courtenay Rd *SUD CO10* 20 D1
Courtenay Dr *CDW/CHF RM16* 330 C2
Courtenay Gdns *UPMR RM14* 290 F1
Courtenay Ms *WALTH E17* 284 B3
Courtenay Rd *WALTH E17* 284 B3
WAN E11 ....285 J8
Courtfield Cl *BROX EN10* 201 L1
Courtland Av *CHING E4* 248 C7
IL IG1 ....286 F5
Courtland Dr *CHIG IG7* 268 F2
Courtland Gv *THMD SE28* 325 A3
Courtland Ms *MAL CM9* 214 C5
Courtland Pl *MAL CM9* 214 C5
Courtland Rd *EHAM E6* 308 B2
Courtlands *BCAYW CM12* 258 B3
CHLM/WR CM1 ....193 K3
Courtney Park Rd *VGE SS16* 276 D8
Courtney Rd *CDW/CHF RM16* 331 N4
Court Rd *CHLM/WR CM1* 193 K2
The Courts *FX IP11* 69 J1
RAYL SS6 ....281 H2
Court St *HAR CO12* 361 M8
Court Wy *ING CM4* 239 J4
Court Wy *BARK/HLT IG6* 286 D1
HARH RM3 ....272 C6
The Courtyards *FX IP11 *....87 M7
The Courtyard *BRTR CM7 *....121 K1
Coval Av *CHLM/WR CM1* 4 C5
Coval La *CHLM/WR CM1* 4 C5
Coval Wls *CHLM/WR CM1* 4 C5
Covelees Wall *EHAM E6* 324 D1
Coveleys
RBRW/HUT CM13 ....256 D5
Coventry Cl *COL CO1* 8 D5
EHAM E6 ....324 C3
HOC/HUL SS5 ....263 J4

Coventry Cross Est *BOW* E3 .....306 F8
Coventry Hill Lower Rd
  HOC/HUL SS5 .....263 H6
Coverdale *WIT* CM8 * 171 H1
Coverley Cl *RBRW/HUT* CM13 .....273 M5
Covert Cl *HVHL* CB9 .....34 D4
Covert Rd *BARK/HLT* IG6 .....269 J5
The Coverts *CHLM/WR* CM1 .....5 D4
  K/T/MI CO5 .....178 A7
  RBRW/HUT CM13 .....256 D4
Covesfield *GVW* DA11 .....337 J4
Cowbridge La *BARK* IG11 .....308 E4
Cowdray Av *COL* CO1 .....8 C3
Cowdray Crs *COL* CO1 .....8 C3
Cowdrie Wy *CHLM/GWD* CM2 .....210 L1
Cowell St *WIT* CM8 * 54 B2
Coweis Farm La *GTDUN* CM6 .....75 H8
Cow La *RCOS* CO16 .....180 F2
  SAFWN CB10 .....341 N6
Cow Leaze *EHAM* E6 .....324 D2
Cowles *CHESW* CM7 .....216 A5
Cowley Av *GRH* DA9 .....335 J3
Cowley Ct *WAN* E11 .....285 H8
Cowley Rd *FX* IP11 .....11 L1
  HARH RM3 .....271 L6
  IL IG1 .....286 C5
  WAN E11 .....285 L3
Cowlins *HLWE* CM17 .....188 E5
Cowpar Ms *BRTR* CM7 .....171 K5
Cowper Av *EHAM* E6 .....308 H4
  TIL RM18 .....331 L7
Cowper Rd *BELV* DA17 .....326 C2
  RAIN RM13 .....311 H3
Cowper St *IPNE* IP4 .....49 J2
Cowslip Cl *CHTY* IP2 .....47 K8
Cowslip Ct *COL* CO5 .....105 M6
Cowslip Md *BSDN* SS14 .....3 J4
Cowslip Rd *SWFD* E18 .....267 L8
Cow Watering La
  CBAYW CM12 .....208 C2
Coxbridge Ct *BCAYW* CM12 .....258 D3
Cox Cl *KESG* IP5 .....50 D4
Coxes Cl *SLH/COR* SS17 .....317 CO2
Coxhall Rd *RIPS/CAP* IP9 .....364 C4
Cox La *IPNE* IP4 .....17 C1
Cox Ley *RBSF* CM22 .....378 B2
Coxmount Rd *CHARL* SE7 .....324 A8
Coxon Dr *CDW/CHF* RM16 .....330 B2
Cox Rd *RCOLE* CO7 .....131 H7
Cox's Cl *HVHL* CB9 .....33 M6
  RCHLM CM3 .....245 H5
Cox's Hi *MGTR* CM7 .....90 D2
Coxtie Green Rd *BRW* CM14 .....254 D6
Coxwell Rd *WOOL/PLUM* SE18 .....325 G6
Coytes Gdns *IP* IP1 .....16 E5
Cozens La East *BROX* EN10 .....201 G6
Cozens La West *BROX* EN10 .....200 F8
Crabbe St *IPNE* IP4 .....48 F7
Crabb's Hi *RCHLM* CM3 .....196 C4
Crabs Cft *BRTR* CM7 .....121 M2
Crabtree *FOS* CO13 .....136 F1
Crabtree Av *CHDH* RM6 .....288 A2
Crabtree Cft *CBE/LIN* CB1 .....24 E6
Crabtree La *RCOLW* CO6 .....85 H2
Crabtree Manorway North
  BELV DA17 .....326 F5
Crabtree Manorway South
  BELV DA17 .....326 F6
Crabtree Wk *BROX* EN10 .....200 H1
Cracknell La *EN* EN1 .....232 C6
  RCOLE CO7 .....130 E3
Crafton Gn *STSD* CM24 .....115 M2
Craftsmans Sq *SOSN* SS2 .....289 L1
Craig Cl *FX* IP11 .....62 A3
Craigdale Rd *ROM* RM1 .....289 J4
Craigfield Av *COS* CO15 .....159 J7
Craig Gdns *SWFD* E18 .....267 J8
Craig's La *BURES* CO8 .....359 P11
Craigs Wk *WAN* EN8 .....216 K6
Craiston Wy *CHLM/GWD* CM2 .....210 C8
Crammavill St
  CDW/CHF RM16 .....314 D8
Cramphorn Wk *CHLM/WR* CM1 .....4 H2
Cramswell Cl *HVHL* CB9 .....34 B4
Cranberry La *CAN/RD* E16 .....307 H8
Cranborne Cha *IPNE* IP4 .....4 E1
Cranborne Cl *COLN* CO4 .....107 J3
Cranborne Gdns *UPMR* RM14 .....290 E5
Cranborne Rd *BARK* IG11 .....309 G5
  CHES/WCR EN8 .....232 E2
  HOD EN11 .....201 J2
Cranbourne Gdns
  BARK/HLT IG6 .....286 F1
  SRTFD E15 .....306 F1
Cranbrook Av *MNPK* E12 .....308 F1
Cranbrook Dr *GPK* RM2 .....289 L2
Cranbrook La *SUD* CO10 .....40 C8
Cranbrook Ms *WALTH* E17 .....284 C3
Cranbrook Ri *IL* IG1 .....286 C3
Cranbrook Rd *IL* IG1 .....286 D5
Cranbrook St *BETH* E2 .....306 A6
Crane Av *COLW* CO3 .....127 L1
Crane Ct *DAGE* RM10 .....310 D3
Crane Md *BERM/RHTH* SE16 .....322 A8
  WARE SG12 .....184 F1
Cranes Cl *BSDN* SS14 .....278 C4
Cranes Farm Rd *BSDN* SS14 .....3 J1
Cranes La *BSDN* SS14 .....3 J1
  K/T/MI CO5 .....148 C4
Cranfield Pk RIPW* IP8 .....46 C8
Cranfield Park Av
  WICKW SS12 .....279 H3
Cranfield Park Rd
  WICKW SS12 .....279 H4
Cranford Cl *FOS* CO13 .....137 H4
Cranford St *WAP* E1W 322 A3
Cranham Gdns *UPMR* RM14 .....291 J5
Cranham Rd *EMPK* RM11 .....289 L4
  GTDUN CM6 .....375 N3
Cranleigh *CHESW* CM7 .....216 B6
Cranleigh Cl *RCOS* CO16 .....158 D3
Cranleigh Dr *LOS* SS9 .....300 B3
Cranleigh Gdns *BARK* IG11 .....309 G5
  HOC/HUL SS5 .....263 H6
  LOU IG10 .....250 A3
Cranley Av *WOS/PRIT* SSO 18 A6
Cranley Dr *GNTH/NBYPK* IG2 .....286 F5
Cranley Gdns *SBN/FI* SS3 .....302 F7
Cranley Rd *GNTH/NBYPK* IG2 .....286 F5
  PLSTW E13 .....323 L1
  WOS/PRIT SSO 18 A4
Cranmer Cl *BCAYW* CM12 .....240 A1
Cranmer Gdns *DAGE* RM10 .....310 D2
Cranmer Rd *FSTGT* E7 .....307 L1
Cranmer's La *RCOLE* CO7 .....103 H1
Cranmore Cl *RBSF* CM22 .....374 D3
Cranmoregreen La *SUD* CO10 .....40 C4
Cranston Av *WOS/PRIT* SSO 283 C5
Cranston Gdns *CHING* E4 .....266 C5
Cranston Park Av
  UPMR RM14 .....312 F1

Cranwell Cl *BOW* E3 .....306 E8
Cranwell Crs *IPSE* IP3 .....55 H4
Cranwell Gdns *BSF* CM23 .....115 K8
Cranwell Gv *KESG* IP5 .....50 B6
Cranworth Crs *CHING* E4 .....249 G8
Craven Av *CVI* SS8 .....320 D2
Craven Cl *RCFD* SS4 .....265 G3
Craven Dr *COLN* CO4 .....107 H2
Craven Gdns *BARK* IG11 .....309 H6
  BARK/HLT IG6 .....286 D1
  CRW RM5 .....270 D4
  HARH RM3 .....271 F5
Crawford Av *CDW/CHF* RM16 .....314 D8
Crawford Cha *WICKW* SS12 .....261 H8
Crawford Cl *BCAYW* CM12 .....240 F8
Crawford La *KESG* IP5 .....50 B6
Crawley Cl *SLH/COR* SS17 .....295 K8
Crawley End *ROY* SG8 .....349 Q7
Crayfields *GTDUN* CM6 .....117 C4
Crayford Cl *MAL* CM9 .....214 B5
Crayford Rd *SUD* CO10 .....40 A1
Craylands *BSDN* SS14 .....278 C6
Craylands La *SWCM* DA10 .....336 B4
Craylands Sq *SWCM* DA10 .....336 A3
Crays Hi *BCAYE* CM11 .....277 L1
Crays Hill Rd *BCAYE* CM11 .....259 H8
Crays Vw *BCAYW* CM12 .....258 E5
Crealock Wk *WIT* IG8 .....267 J4
Creasen Butt Cl *MAL* CM9 .....214 D1
Creasey Cl *EMPK* RM11 .....289 J7
Credon Cl *COS* CO15 .....159 J6
Credon Dr *COS* CO15 .....159 J6
Credon Rd *PLSTW* E13 .....307 M6
Credo Wy *WTHK* RM20 .....335 L1
Creekhurst Cl *RCOLE* CO7 .....156 D7
Creek Rd *BARK* IG11 .....309 J7
  CVI SS8 .....320 D2
Creeksea Ferry Rd *RCFD* SS4 .....396 C1
Creeksea La *BOC* CMO 393 J7
Creekside *RAIN* RM13 .....311 J8
The Creek *GVW* DA11 .....337 J8
Creek View *RHCLM* CM3 .....245 H4
Creekview Rd *RCHLM* CM3 .....245 A4
Creek Wy *RAIN* RM13 .....327 H1
Creephedge La *RCHLM* CM3 .....228 A8
Cree Wy *ROM* RM1 .....271 J1
Creffield Rd *COL* CO1 .....107 G7
Creighton Av *EHAM* E6 .....308 A6
Cremorne Rd *DAGW* DA11 .....337 J5
Crepping Hall Dr
  RIPS/CAP IP9 .....364 C11
Crescent Av *GRAYS* RM17 .....331 G4
  HCH RM12 .....289 J7
Crescent Cl *BCAYW* CM12 .....258 C1
Crescent Gv *GRAYS* RM17 * 331 C5
Crescent Dr *BRWN* CM15 .....256 B4
Crescent Gdns *BCAYW* CM12 .....258 C1
Crescent Rd *BCAYW* CM12 .....258 C1
  BRW CM14 .....273 L3
  BSF CM23 .....139 H3
  CHING E4 .....249 H7
  CHLM/GWD CM2 .....210 D6
  CVI SS8 .....321 G3
  DAGE RM10 .....310 E1
  FX IP11 .....11 C3
  IP IP1 .....16 C3
  LEY E10 .....284 E7
  LOS SS9 .....299 L4
  MAL CM9 .....198 C8
  MAL CM9 .....385 P4
  PLSTW E13 .....307 K5
  SBF/HAD SS7 .....298 A3
  SOCK/AV RM15 .....328 F5
  SWFD E18 .....267 M8
  WOOL/PLUM SE18 .....324 E8
  WOTN CM14 .....
The Crescent *COLN* CO4 .....87 M6
  COS CO15 .....159 L6
  EPP CM16 .....236 A2
  FOS CO13 .....137 J4
  GRH DA9 .....335 M8
  GVW DA11 .....337 J7
  HLWE CM17 .....188 D3
  HSTD CO9 * 347 N11
  LOS SS9 .....282 A7
  LOU IG10 .....250 A6
  RCHLM CM3 .....144 B8
  RCOLW CO6 .....86 A4
  RCOLW CO6 .....86 E4
  RCOLW CO6 .....126 D2
  RCOS CO16 .....135 J3
  SBF/HAD SS7 .....299 J3
  UPMR RM14 .....291 H5
  WALTH E17 .....284 B3
Cressells *LAIN* SS15 .....2 D7
Cresset Cl *WARE* SG12 .....185 K6
Cressing Rd *BRTR* CM7 .....121 J7
  WIT CM8 .....147 G5
Crest Av *GRAYS* RM17 .....330 E6
  PIT SS13 .....278 F7
Crest Dr *PEND* EN3 .....232 D8
Cresthill Av *GRAYS* RM17 .....330 F4
Crestlands *RCOLE* CO7 .....156 C7
The Crest *SBW* CM21 .....162 E7
Crest Vw *GRH* DA9 .....335 K6
Creswick Av *RAYL* SS6 .....280 D4
Crete Hall Rd *GVW* DA11 .....337 G4
Crews St *POP/IOD* E14 .....322 B8
Cricketers Cl *CHLM/WR* CM1 .....193 L7
  ERITH DA8 .....327 H4
  SUD CO10 .....20 D7
Cricketers La
  RBRW/HUT CM13 .....275 G2
Cricketers Rw
  RBRW/HUT CM13 .....275 G2
Cricketers Wy *PIT* SS13 .....278 E3
Cricketfield Gv *LOS* SS9 .....300 E3
Cricketfield La *BSF* CM23 .....138 E1
Cricket Hill La *FX* IP11 .....62 E1
Crickhollow *RCHLM* CM3 .....244 F8
Cricklade Av *HARH* RM3 .....272 A5
Cridland St *SRTFD* E15 .....307 J3
Cringle Lock *RCHLM* CM3 .....245 J4
Cripplegate *BOC* CMO 389 P12
Cripsey Av *CHONG* CM5 .....380 G12
Crispin Cl *HVHL* CB9 .....34 A6
Crittal Cl *BRTR* CM7 * 121 G1
Crittall Cl *WIT* CM8 .....147 H1
  *Crittall Dr *BRTR* CM7 .....121 G1
  *Crittall Dr *WIT* CM8 .....171 L2
Croasdaile Rd *STSD* CM24 .....115 M4
Croasdale Rd *STSD* CM24 .....115 M1
Crocus Cl *CHTY* IP2 .....53 J1
Crocus Fids *SAFWN* CB10 .....28 B6
Croft Cl *BELV* DA17 .....326 C2
  CHLM/WR CM1 .....194 B5
Croft Ct *CHLM/WR* CM1 .....194 B5
  GTDUN CM6 * 117 H5

Crofters *SBW* CM21 .....162 F6
Crofters Ct *DEPT* SE8 .....322 B7
Crofters End *SBW* CM21 .....162 F6
Croft La *HVHL* CB9 .....34 E1
  KIR/NAC CO15 .....61 L2
  RCHLM CM3 .....166 D2
Croft Lodge Cl *WFD* IG8 .....267 C4
Crofton Av *SLH/COR* SS17 .....317 H1
Crofton Cl *CHONG* CM5 .....267 C3
Crofton Rd *CDW/CHF* RM16 .....331 H4
  IPNE IP4 .....49 G6
  PLSTW E13 .....307 L2
Croft Rd *COS* CO15 .....6 D4
  K/T/MI CO5 .....178 E3
  PEND EN3 .....248 B8
  SBF/HAD SS7 .....298 C8
  SUD CO10 .....20 L5
The Crofts *SBN/FI* SS3 .....303 H1
Croft St *CHTY* IP2 .....16 E9
The Croft *BROX* EN10 .....216 F1
  BURES CO8 .....359 Q8
  CHING E4 .....267 H1
  HSTD CO9 .....346 B11
  LOU IG10 .....250 D2
  RAYL SS6 .....281 H5
  RBSF CM22 .....374 D4
  RCOLW CO6 .....82 D7
  SUD CO10 .....5 C5
  SUD CO10 .....39 L1
Croft Wy *WIT* CM8 .....171 H1
Cromarty Rd *IPNE* IP4 .....49 G5
Crombie Cl *REDBR* IG4 .....286 C3
Crome Cl *COLW* CO3 .....106 D8
Cromer Av *LAIN* SS15 .....276 E5
Cromer Cl *LAIN* SS15 .....276 E5
Cromer Rd *RCOS* CO16 .....159 G5
Cromer Rd *CHDH* RM6 .....288 A5
  EMPK RM11 .....290 B4
  IP IP11 .....47 L5
  LEY E10 .....285 L5
  ROMW/RG RM7 .....288 F4
  SOS SS1 .....19 G5
Crompton Cl *BSDN* SS14 .....278 A1
Crompton Pl *PEND* EN3 .....233 H4
Crompton Rd *CHTY* IP2 .....47 K6
Crompton St *CHLM/WR* CM1 .....4 D4
  CHESW EN7 .....216 C8
Cromwell Av *BCAYW* CM12 .....258 D2
Cromwell Cl *BSF* CM23 .....138 C2
Cromwell La *MAL* CM9 .....214 C2
Cromwell Pk *GTDUN* CM6 .....118 D8
Cromwell Rd *BRW* CM14 .....273 L5
  COL CO1 .....8 D9
  FSTGT E7 .....307 M4
  GRAYS RM17 .....330 D5
  HERT/BAY SG13 .....184 A2
  HOC/HUL SS5 .....264 D1
  SAFWS CB11 .....30 B2
  SOSN SS2 .....301 J1
  WALTH E17 .....284 F5
Cromwell Sq *IP* IP1 .....16 E5
Cromwell Wy *WIT* CM8 .....171 H1
Crondon Park La *ING* CM4 .....241 H4
Crooked Billet Rbt *CHING* E4 .....266 H6
Crooked Elms *HAR* CO12 .....4 D4
Crooked La *GVE* DA12 .....337 L4
Crooked Mile *WAB* EN9 .....217 K8
Crooked Wy *WAB* EN9 .....201 M8
Crooke Rd *DEPT* SE8 .....322 B8
Coombs Rd *CAN/RD* E16 .....323 D4
Cropenburg Wk *CVI* SS8 .....298 D1
Croppath Rd *DAGE* RM10 .....310 D1
Croquet Gdns *RCOLE* CO7 .....150 F4
Crosby Rd *DAGE* RM10 .....310 D6
Cross Av *CHTY* IP2 .....53 G1
  FSTGT E7 .....307 H3
  WOS/PRIT SSO 300 F7
Crossbrook St
  CHES/WCR EN8 .....216 E8
Crossby Rd *BRWN* CM15 .....239 H5
Cross Cl *HVHL* CB9 .....34 D4
Cross Cottages *COLN* CO4 .....362 C11
Crossfell Rd *SBF/HAD* SS7 .....280 C6
Crossfield Rd *COS* CO15 .....6 D7
  HOD EN11 .....201 J1
  SOSN SS2 .....302 A3
Crossfields *RCOLW* CO6 .....361 P4
Cross Field Wy *COLN* CO4 .....362 C12
Crossfield Wy *FOS* CO13 .....136 F1
Crossgate Fld *FX* IP11 .....62 B3
Cross Gn *VGE* SS16 .....2 E4
Cross Hi *HAR* CO12 .....113 M4
Crossing La *K/T/MI* CO5 .....178 C7
Cross La East *GVE* DA12 .....337 L7
Cross La West *DAW* DA11 .....337 K7
Crossley Av *COS* CO15 .....182 B6
Crossley Gdns *IP* IP1 .....47 H5
Crossness Rd *BARK* IG11 .....309 J7
Crosspath *HSTD* CO9 * 356 E7
  CHES/WCR EN8 .....232 E4
  CHING E4 .....249 M6
  GVW DA11 .....337 J7
  MAL CM9 .....279 J6
  ROMW/RG RM7 .....288 D1
  SBF/HAD SS7 .....298 E1
  WFD IG8 .....268 G5
  WIT CM8 .....171 J3
Cross Roads *LOU* IG10 .....249 G1
Cross St *FX* IP11 .....62 D2
  SAFWN CB10 .....28 A4
  SUD CO10 .....20 D5
Crosstree Wk *COLS* CO2 .....129 M2
Cross Wy *K/T/MI* CO5 .....178 A6
Crossway *BCTR* RM8 .....287 M7
Crossways *BRWN* CM15 .....256 D2
  CBE/LIN CB1 .....25 G7
  CHLM/GWD CM2 .....209 M6
  COS CO15 .....182 C5
  GPK RM2 .....289 L1
  RCOLW CO6 .....82 D7
Crossways Bvd *GRH* DA9 .....334 F6
The Crossways *WOS/PRIT* SS0 .....300 D5
Crotchets Cl *RIPS/CAP* IP9 .....58 D2
Crouch Av *BARK* IG11 .....309 J7
  HOC/HUL SS5 .....263 H4
Crouch Beck *RCHLM* CM3 .....245 H5
Crouchman Cl
  CDW/CHF RM16 .....330 F1
Crouchman's Av *SBN/FI* SS3 .....303 M5
Crouchman's Farm Rd
  MAL CM9 .....196 F7
Crouch Meadow
  HOC/HUL SS5 .....263 H1
Crouch Rd *BOC* CMO 393 L8
  GRAYS RM17 .....331 K4
Crouch Va *UPMR* RM14 .....291 H5
Crouchview Cl *WICKE* SS11 .....261 L6

Crouch View Crs
  HOC/HUL SS5 .....264 C5
Crouch View Gv
  HOC/HUL SS5 .....263 C8
Croutel Rd *FX* IP11 .....63 G2
Crowborough Rd *SOSN* SS2 .....19 G1
Crowden Wy *THMD* SE28 .....325 M3
Crowe Hall *RIPS/CAP* IP9 .....364 D11
Crowfoot Cl *HOM* E9 .....307 J2
  THMD SE28 .....325 H4
Crow Gn *BRWN* CM15 .....255 K4
Crow Green La *BRWN* CM15 .....255 K5
Crow Green Rd *BRWN* CM15 .....255 J5
Crowhall La *MGTR* CM7 .....366 A10
Crowhurst Rd *COLW* CO3 .....8 A7
Crowland Cl *CHTY* IP2 .....53 M5
Crowland Rd *HVHL* CB9 .....34 D4
Crowlands Av
  ROMW/RG RM7 .....288 E4
Crow La *RCOS* CO16 .....134 C3
  ROMW/RG RM7 .....288 C5
Crown & Anchor Ms *IP* IP1 * 16 E5
Crown Av *PIT* SS13 .....278 E6
Crown Bays Rd *COLN* CO4 .....9 A4
Crown Buildings *CHING* E4 * 249 G8
Crown Cl *BOW* E3 .....306 D5
  PIT SS13 .....278 F7
  RBSF CM22 .....189 K1
  WDBR IP12 .....51 G3
Crown Ct *COLN* CO4 * 87 H7
Crownfield *BROX* EN10 .....201 H7
Crownfield Av
  GNTH/NBYPK IG2 .....287 H3
Crownfield Rd *SRTFD* E15 .....307 G2
Crown Gdns *RAYL* SS6 .....280 E5
Crown Ga *COLN* CO4 .....88 A7
  HLW CM20 .....13 D1
Crown Hi *RAYL* SS6 .....280 F3
  WAB EN9 .....235 G3
Crownhill Rd *WFD* IG8 .....268 B3
Crown La *HAR* CO12 .....15 D1
  RCOS CO16 .....134 A2
Crown La North *RCOLE* CO7 .....108 D1
Crown La South *RCOLE* CO7 .....108 D1
Crown Meadow *BRTR* CM7 .....122 A1
Crown Rd *BARK/HLT* IG6 .....287 G2
  BCAYE CM11 .....258 A5
  BRW CM14 .....255 L5
  COS CO15 .....6 B7
  GRAYS RM17 .....330 E5
  HOC/HUL SS5 .....263 L8
  RCHLM CM3 .....230 C7
Crown St *BRTR* CM7 .....76 B3
  BCAYE CM11 .....258 A5
  BRW CM14 .....255 L5
  COS CO15 .....6 B7
  GRAYS RM17 .....330 E5
  HOC/HUL SS5 .....263 L8
  RCHLM CM3 .....230 C7
Crown St *BRTR* CM7 .....76 B3
  DAGE RM10 .....310 A7
  FX IP11 .....62 D2
  HSTD CO9 .....356 F5
  IP IP1 .....16 E3
  RCOLE CO7 .....363 N11
Crown Ter *BSF* CM23 .....139 H2
Crown Wy *BOC* CMO 393 L1
Crown Yd *BCAYW* CM12 * 258 D3
Crow Pond Rd *RCHLM* CM3 .....169 H1
Crowsheath La *BCAYE* CM11 .....242 B7
Crows La *RCHLM* CM3 .....228 E2
Crows Rd *BARK* IG11 .....308 B1
  EPP CM16 .....220 A8
  SRTFD E15 .....307 G7
Crowstone Av *WOS/PRIT* SSO 300 E5
Crowstone Cl *WOS/PRIT* SSO 300 E5
Crowstone Rd *WOS/PRIT* SSO * 18 A5
Crowstone Rd
  CDW/CHF RM16 .....330 F1
  WOS/PRIT SSO 300 E5
Crow St *RBSF* CM22 .....372 C12
Crowswell Ct *FX* IP11 .....62 A3
Croxford Wy *ROMW/RG* RM7 .....289 G6
Croxon Wy *BOC* CMO 393 L6
Croydon Rd *PLSTW* E13 .....307 H3
Crozier Av *BSF* CM23 .....138 D1
Crozier Ter *HOM* E9 .....306 D2
Cruce Wy *RCOS* CO16 .....180 C2
Crucible Cl *CHDH* RM6 .....287 M5
Cruden Rd *GVE* DA12 .....338 C8
Cruick Av *SOCK/AV* RM15 .....329 K3
Cruikshank Rd *SRTFD* E15 .....307 H1
Crummock Cl *BRTR* CM77 .....120 F7
Crumpsall St *ABYW* SE2 .....325 H1
Crunch Cft *HVHL* CB9 .....35 H6
Crusader Dr *PUR* RM19 .....328 D2
Crusader Wy *BRTR* CM7 .....122 A1
Crushes Cl *RBRW/HUT* CM13 .....257 H7
Crushton Pl *CHLM/WR* CM1 .....193 L7
Crusoe Rd *ERITH* DA8 .....327 G4
Crystal Av *HCH* RM12 .....312 B1
Crystal Wy *BCTR* RM8 .....287 M5
Cuba St *POP/IOD* E14 .....322 C7
Cublands *HERT/BAY* SG13 .....184 D1
Cuckfield Av *IPSE* IP3 .....55 K2
Cuckoo Hi *BURES* CO8 .....359 M6
Cuckoo La *CDW/CHF* RM16 .....330 C1
  HSTD CO9 .....356 C9
Cuckoos Cl *CDW/CHF* RM16 .....330 C1
Cuckoo Wy *BRTR* CM7 .....120 F7
Culford Cl *CDW/CHF* RM16 .....330 D1
Culford Wk *FX* IP11 .....10 D5
Cullen Sq *SOCK/AV* RM15 .....329 K3
Cullingham Rd *IP* IP1 .....16 A4
Cullings Ct *WAB* EN9 .....234 F1
Culloden St *POP/IOD* E14 .....322 F2
Culpepper Cl *CHIG* IG7 .....268 E5
Culverdown *BSDN* SS14 .....278 A4
Culver Ri *RCHLM* CM3 .....245 H6
Culver Sq *COL* CO1 * 8 C4
Culver East Col CO1 * 8 D5
Culver St West *COL* CO1 .....8 C4
Culver Wk *COL* CO1 * 8 C4
Cumberland Av *GVE* DA12 .....337 M8
  HCH RM12 .....290 D4
  MAL CM9 .....214 D4
  SBF/HAD SS7 .....297 M2
  SOSN SS2 .....301 M2
Cumberland Cl
  BARK/HLT IG6 * 268 C7
  BRTR CM7 .....121 J7
  FX IP11 .....63 D7
Cumberland Crs
  CHLM/WR CM1 .....193 K6
Cumberland Dr *LAIN* SS15 .....276 D7
Cumberland Rd
  CDW/CHF RM16 .....330 B1
  MNPK E12 .....308 A1
  PLSTW E13 .....323 L1
  WFD IG8 .....268 G5
Cumberland St *IP* IP1 .....16 C2
Cumbrae Ms *WICKW* SS12 .....261 L8
Cumley Rd *CHONG* CM5 .....221 M9
Cumming Av *PEND* EN3 .....232 D8
Cumming St *IP* IP1 .....16 C2
Cumminga Hall La
  ABR/ST RM4 .....271 M2
Cundy Rd *CAN/RD* E16 .....323 M2
Cunningham Av *PEND* EN3 .....232 F4
Cunningham Cl *CHDH* RM6 .....287 M3
  SBN/FI SS3 .....303 J1
Cunningham Rd
  CHES/WCR EN8 .....216 F5
Cunningham Ri *EPP* CM16 .....221 K3
Cunnington Rd *BRTR* CM7 .....121 M2

Cunobelin Wy *COLS* CO2 .....128 C5
Cupids Cha *SBN/FI* SS3 .....303 M5
Cuppers Ct *MAL* CM9 .....171 H4
Curds Rd *RCOLW* CO6 .....102 D2
Curlew Av *RCHLM* CM3 .....388 C5
Curlew Cl *COS* CO15 .....159 J7
  K/T/MI CO5 .....149 G3
  MAL CM9 .....
  THMD SE28 .....326 A3
Curlew Cres *VGE* SS16 .....295 G2
Curlew Cft *COLN* CO4 .....108 C5
Curlew Dr *BROX* EN10 * 217 G1
Curlew Rd *CHTY* IP2 .....53 J2
The Curlews *GVE* DA12 .....338 A7
Curling La *GRAYS* RM17 .....330 C4
Curling Tye *BSDN* SS14 .....3 M4
Curling Tye La *MAL* CM9 .....213 J2
Curling Wk *BSDN* SS14 .....3 M4
Currants Farm Rd *BRTR* CM7 .....99 H8
Currants La *HAR* CO12 .....15 K3
Curriers La *IP* IP1 .....16 C5
Curteys *HLWE* CM17 .....188 E4
Curtis Cl *RCOS* CO16 .....182 E2
  RIPW IP8 .....53 H4
Curtis Mill La *ABR/ST* RM4 .....253 H4
Curtis Rd *EMPK* RM11 .....290 C6
Curtisway *RAYL* SS6 .....281 H1
Curwen Av *FSTGT* E7 .....307 L1
Curzon Av *PEND* EN3 .....248 A5
Curzon Crs *BARK* IG11 .....309 J7
Curzon Dr *GRAYS* RM17 .....330 F6
Curzon Rd *SUD* CO10 .....21 J5
Curzon Wy *CHLM/GWD* CM2 .....210 C8
Cusak Rd *CHLM/GWD* CM2 .....210 C3
Cussons Cl *CHESW* EN7 .....216 B7
Custerson Dr *BRTR* CM77 .....121 L8
Custom House Reach
  BERM/RHTH SE16 * 322 C6
Cut-a-Thwart La *MAL* CM9 .....213 J2
Cutforth Rd *SBW* CM21 .....162 F6
Cuthberga Cl *BARK* IG11 .....308 F4
Cuthbert Cl *CHESW* EN7 .....216 A7
Cuthbert Rd *WALTH* E17 .....284 F1
Cut Hedge *BRTR* CM7 .....120 F7
Cuthedge La *RCOLW* CO6 .....123 L6
Cutlers Cl *RCOLW* CO6 .....58 A8
Cutlers Rd *RCHLM* CM3 .....245 H5
Cutler St *IP* IP1 .....16 D4
Cutmore Pl *CHLM/GWD* CM2 .....4 D8
Cutmore St *GVW* DA11 .....337 L5
Cuton Hall La
  CHLM/GWD CM2 .....194 D8
The Cut *K/T/MI* CO5 .....149 M8
Cut Throat La *WIT* CM8 .....171 K2
Cutting Dr *PIT* SS13 .....81 K4
Cutty Sark Ct *GRH* DA9 .....335 K7
Cygnet Cl *BSF* CM23 .....139 G3
  HSTD CO9 .....356 E9
Cygnet Vw *WTHK* RM20 .....329 H4
Cygnet Wk *RCOLW* CO6 * 127 L5
Cymbeline Wy (Colchester
  By-Pass) *COLW* CO3 .....106 C6
Cypress Cl *COS* CO15 .....159 H6
  WAB EN9 * 253 L4
Cypress Dr *CTDUN* CM6 .....116 E4
Cypress Gdns *BARK/HLT* IG6 .....269 H5
  COLN CO4 .....108 B5
Cypress Ms *K/T/MI* CO5 .....177 L6
Cypress Rd *WIT* CM8 .....171 K4
Cyprus Pl *EHAM* E6 .....324 C1
Cyril Child Cl *COLN* CO4 .....108 A5
Czarina Ri *LAIN* SS15 .....2 A2

D

Daarle Av *CVI* SS8 .....320 D2
Dace Rd *BOW* E3 .....306 D5
Dacre Av *CLAY* IG5 .....268 A3
  SOCK/AV RM15 .....329 G4
Dacre Cl *CHIG* IG7 .....268 F3
Dacre Crs *SOCK/AV* RM15 .....329 G4
Dacre Gdns *CHIG* IG7 .....268 F3
Dacre Rd *PLSTW* E13 .....307 L5
  WAN E11 .....285 L5
Dads Wd *HLWW/ROY* CM19 .....12 F7
Daen Ingas *RCHLM* CM3 .....211 M6
Daffodil Cl *CHTY* IP2 .....53 G2
Daffodil Av *BRWN* CM15 .....255 L5
Daffodil Gdns *IL* IG1 .....308 G2
Daffodil Wy *CHLM/WR* CM1 .....194 C6
Dagenham Av *DAGW* RM9 .....310 C5
Dagenham Rd *DAGE* RM10 .....310 F2
  LEY E10 .....284 C5
  RAIN RM13 .....311 G4
  ROMW/RG RM7 .....289 C5
Dagmar Rd *DAGE* RM10 .....310 F4
Dagnam Park Dr *HARH* RM3 .....272 B4
Dagnam Park Gdns
  HARH RM3 .....272 D5
Dagnam Park Sq *HARH* RM3 .....272 D5
Dagnets La *BRTR* CM77 .....144 F1
Dagwood La *BRWN* CM15 .....383 Q12
Dahlia Cl *CHLM/WR* CM1 .....194 C6
  RCOS CO16 .....6 A3
Dahlia Gdns *IL* IG1 .....308 E3
Dahlia Rd *ABYW* SE2 .....326 A3
Dahlia Wk *COLN* CO4 .....108 B5
Daiglen Dr *SOCK/AV* RM15 .....329 K3
Daimler Av *COS* CO15 .....182 A6
Daimler Rd *IP* IP1 .....47 J1
Daines Cl *MNPK* E12 .....286 C1
  SOCK/AV RM15 .....313 K8
  SOS SS2 .....302 C4
Daines Rd *BCAYE* CM11 .....258 A4
Daines Wy *SOS* SS1 .....302 E4
Dains Pl *FX* IP11 .....62 B6
Dairy Farm Rd *RCHLM* CM3 .....392 C12
Dairyglen Av *CHES/WCR* EN8 .....232 E1
Dairyhouse La *MGTR* CM7 .....366 B9
Dairy La *WOOL/PLUM* SE18 .....324 C7
Dairy Rd *CHLM/GWD* CM2 .....210 C3
Daisleys La *RCHLM* CM3 .....168 C3
Daisy Green Rd *COLW* CO3 .....105 G5
Daisyley Rd *GTDUN* CM6 .....95 K2
Daisy Rd *SWFD* E18 .....267 L8
Dakin Pl *WCHPL* E1 .....322 D2
Dakota Gdns *EHAM* E6 .....308 B8
  MNPK E12 .....286 D2
Dalberg Wy *ABYW* SE2 .....326 A3
Dale Cl *COLW* CO3 .....105 L6
  SBW CM21 .....162 E6
Dale Ct *HAR* CO12 .....14 B8
  SBW CM21 .....162 E6
Dale Gdns *WFD* IG8 .....267 G4
Dale Hall La *IP* IP1 .....48 A3
Dalen Av *CVI* SS8 .....320 D2
Dales Rd *IP* IP1 .....47 M2
The Dales *HAR* CO12 .....113 M4
  RCFD SS4 .....283 C9
Dales Vw *RIPW* IP8 .....53 H4
Dales View Rd *IP* IP1 .....47 M2

The Dale RCOLE CO7 ...130 F5
  SBF/HAD SS7 ...298 D1
  WAB EN9 ...233 M4
Dale View Av CHING E4 ...266 F1
Daleview Av ROC CO11 ...366 KO1
Dale View Crs CHING E4 ...266 F1
Dale View Gdns EMPK RM11 ...267 G2
Dale Wy CBS CB2 ...22 F5
Dalewood CI EMPK RM11 ...290 C5
Dalewood Gdns SBF/HAD SS7 ...298 E1
Dalkeith Rd IL IG1 ...286 F8
Dallwood Wy BRW CM14 ...255 J5
Dalmatia Rd SOS SS1 ...302 A4
Dalmeney VGE SS16 ...294 K2
Dalroy CI SOCK/AV RM15 ...329 K2
Dalrymple CI CHLM/GWD CM2 ...5 M1
Daltes La RCOS CO16 ...181 L2
Dalton Gdns BSF CM23 ...138 F6
Daltons Fen PIT SS13 ...278 F5
Dalwood BRW CM14 ...255 H5
Dalwood Gdns SBF/HAD SS7 ...298 E2
Days Rd RCFD SS4 ...283 H3
Damant's Farm La FOS CO13 ...136 A1
Damases La RCHLM CM3 ...195 L3
Damask Crs CAN/RD E16 ...307 G3
Damask Ms BRTR CM7 * ...121 L2
Damask Rd COLW CO3 ...105 L6
Dames Rd FSTGT E7 ...307 K1
Damigos Rd GVE DA12 ...338 C7
Dampier Rd RCOLW CO6 ...124 C2
Damselfly Rd IPSE IP3 ...47 K6
Danacre LAIN SS15 ...276 B6
Danbury CI BRW CM14 ...255 J5
  CHDH RM6 ...288 A1
  LOS SS9 ...300 C1
Danbury Crs SOCK/AV RM15 ...329 K2
Danbury Down BSDN SS14 ...3 J7
  RAIN RM13 ...311 J3
  RAYL SS6 ...280 C1
Danbury V RCHLM CM3 ...212 D1
Danbury Vale WFD IG8 ...267 M8
Dancing Dicks La WIT CM8 ...170 D3
Dandalan CI IP IP1 ...47 K6
Dandelion CI ROMW/RG RM7 ...289 H7
Dandies Cha LOS SS9 ...282 A6
Dandies CI LOS SS9 ...282 A6
Dandies Dr LOS SS9 ...282 A6
Dandridge CI GNWCH SE10 ...323 J8
Dane Acres BSF CM23 ...138 C6
Dane Common HVHL CB9 ...35 K4
Danehurst Gdns REDBR IG4 ...286 D1
Danemead HOD EN11 ...185 H6
Dane O'Coys Rd BSF CM23 ...114 F8
Dane Pk BSF CM23 ...138 C5
Dane PI BOW E3 ...306 B6
Dane Rd CHLM/WR CM1 ...4 B4
  IL IG1 ...308 F2
Dane's Av SBN/FI SS3 ...303 J7
Danes CI GVE DA11 ...336 F8
Danes Ct SUD CO10 ...45 M4
Danescroft Dr LOS SS9 ...300 A1
Danesfield SBF/HAD SS7 ...297 L3
Danesleigh Gdns LOS SS9 ...300 A1
Danes Rd ROMW/RG RM7 ...288 F6
Dane St BSF CM23 ...139 H3
  SBN/FI SS3 ...303 K7
Danes Wy BRWN CM15 ...255 K5
Danette Gdns DAGE RM10 ...288 C7
Dangan Rd WAN E11 ...285 K4
Daniel Bolt CI POP/IOD E14 ...322 E1
Daniel CI CDW/CHF RM16 ...330 D4
  CDW/CHF RM16 ...331 L2
Daniel Cole Rd COLS CO2 ...129 J1
Daniell CI RCOS CO16 ...158 F7
Daniell Dr COLS CO2 ...128 C3
Daniels CI SUD CO10 ...43 M1
Daniel Wy WIT CM8 ...147 H1
Danyon CI RAIN RM13 ...311 M6
Daphne CI BRTR CM7 ...120 F6
Daphne Gdns CHING E4 ...266 F1
Dapifer Dr BRTR CM7 ...122 A4
Darby Dr WAB EN9 ...233 L4
D'Arcy Av BOC CM0 ...393 M7
D'Arcy CI BOC CM0 ...393 M7
  FOS CO13 ...137 J3
Darcy CI CHES/WCR EN8 ...232 F1
  RBRW/HUT CM13 ...256 F3
D'Arcy Gdns DAGW RM9 ...310 C3
D'Arcy Hts COLS CO2 ...129 K2
Darcy Ri RCHLM CM3 ...212 B4
D'Arcy Rd COLS CO2 ...129 K2
  K/T/MI CO5 ...174 C2
  RCOS CO16 ...157 L8
D'Arcy Wy MAL CM9 ...384 A1
  RCOLE CO7 ...156 B6
Darell Wy BCAYE CM11 ...259 G4
Darenth Dr DAGE RM10 ...338 E6
Darenth La SOCK/AV RM15 ...329 K2
Darenth Rd LOS SS9 ...299 L4
Darent Valley Pth DART DA1 ...334 A3
Darina Ct COLW CO3 * ...105 L6
Darkhouse La K/T/MI CO5 ...130 D7
Dark La BRW CM14 ...273 K6
  CHESW EN7 ...216 B8
  SBF/HAD SS7 ...280 C1
Darlinghurst Gv LOS SS9 ...300 A1
Darlington Ct BRWN CM15 ...255 K6
Darlington Gdns HARH RM3 ...272 A4
Darndale CI WALTH E17 ...266 C8
Darnel Wy COLS CO2 ...105 L6
Darnet Rd MAL CM9 ...385 H4
Darnley Rd GRAYS RM17 * ...330 C3
  GVW DA11 ...337 H5
  WFD IG8 ...267 K4
Darnley St GVW DA11 ...337 H5
Darrell CI CHLM/WR CM1 ...193 M7
Darrell Rd FX IP11 ...10 E8
Darsham CI FX IP11 ...10 E8
  WIT CM8 ...171 G3
Darter CI UPMR RM14 ...291 J3
  WIT CM8 ...171 G3
Dartfields HARH RM3 ...272 A4
Dart Gn SOSN SS2 ...263 G8
Dartmoor Wk POP/IOD E14 * ...322 E1
Dartmouth CI RAYL SS6 ...263 G8
Dartmouth Rd CHLM/WR CM1 ...194 A7
Dartview CI GRAYS RM17 ...331 H3
Darwell CI EHAM E6 ...308 D1
Darwin CI BRTR CM7 ...129 L4
  COLS CO2 ...129 L4
Darwin Rd IPNE IP4 ...17 M7
  TIL RM18 ...331 J3
Dash End HVHL CB9 ...35 L4
Dash End La HVHL CB9 ...35 L4
The Dashes HLW CM20 ...13 M4
Dashwood CI RIPW IP8 ...53 M1
Dashwood Rd GVW DA11 ...337 K6
Datchet Dr SBN/FI SS3 ...303 H3
Daubeney Ct CLPT E5 ...306 B2
Daundy CI CHTY IP2 ...47 J8
Davall CI HAR CO12 ...70 A4
Davenants PIT SS13 ...278 E5
Davenport HLWE CM17 ...204 F2

Daventry Av WALTH E17 ...284 D4
Daventry Gdns HARH RM3 ...271 M4
Daventry Rd HARH RM3 ...271 M4
Davern CI GNWCH SE10 ...323 J7
Davey CI COL CO1 ...9 K8
  IPSE IP3 ...54 H1
Davey Rd HOM E9 ...306 G2
David Av WICKE SS11 ...261 K3
David Dr HARH RM3 ...272 C5
David Rd BCTR RM8 ...288 B5
Davidson CI SUD CO10 ...45 M5
Davidson Gdns WICKW SS12 ...261 H8
David St BCAYE CM11 ...258 F3
David's Wk BCAYE CM11 ...258 F3
Davids Wy BARK/HLT IG6 ...269 H4
Davies CI RAIN RM13 ...311 M7
Davies La WAN E11 ...285 H7
Davington Gdns BCTR RM8 ...309 L2
Davington Rd BCTR RM8 ...309 L3
Davinia CI WFD IG8 ...268 C5
Davis Av GVW DA11 ...337 H6
Davison Dr CHES/WCR EN8 ...216 E6
Davis Rd CDW/CHF RM16 ...330 D2
  SOCK/AV RM15 ...329 K2
Davis St PLSTW E13 ...307 L6
Davy Rd COS CO15 ...159 H6
Dawes Av HCH RM12 ...290 A4
Dawes CI GRH DA9 ...335 J7
  RIPS/CAP IP9 ...58 C4
Dawes La K/T/MI CO5 ...178 B4
Dawley CI SOCK/AV RM15 ...329 K2
Dawlish Crs RAYL SS6 ...263 G8
Dawlish Dr GDMY/SEVK IG3 ...309 J1
  LOS SS9 ...300 B4
Dawlish Rd COS CO15 ...182 F5
  LEY E10 ...284 F1
Dawn CI MAL CM9 ...214 A3
Dawn Crs SRTFD E15 ...307 G1
Dawnford CI COLW CO3 ...105 M7
Daws CI CHLM/WR CM1 ...208 C4
Daws Heath Rd RAYL SS6 ...281 H5
  SBF/HAD SS7 ...280 F2
Daws HI CHING E4 ...248 F3
Dawson Av BARK IG11 ...309 J4
Dawson CI SAFWN CB10 ...28 C7
  WOOL/PLUM SE18 ...324 C7
Dawson Drift IPSE IP5 ...50 B6
Dawson Gdns BARK IG11 ...309 J4
Dawson Ms BCAYE CM11 ...258 F3
Daw St BRTR CM7 ...77 H1
Daylop Dr CHIG IG7 ...344 A8
Days CI CHLM/WR CM1 ...193 L5
Days Gn RIPS/CAP IP9 ...58 C4
Days La BRWN CM15 ...255 K4
Days Rd RIPS/CAP IP9 ...58 C4
Dayton Dr ERITH DA8 ...334 A3
Dazeley's La RCOLE CO7 * ...64 C5
Deacon CI CAN/RD E16 ...63 J7
Deacon Dr LAIN SS15 ...276 A7
The Deacon Est CHING E4 * ...266 D6
Deacon Wy WFD IG8 ...268 C6
Dead La BURES CO8 ...360 D2
  MGTR CO5 ...90 E3
  RCOLE CO7 ...88 D7
  RCOS CO16 ...157 J3
  RCOS CO16 ...158 E2
Deadman's La CHLM/GWD CM2 ...225 M1
  COS CO15 ...182 F5
Dealtree CI BRWN CM15 ...383 Q9
Deal Wy RCOLE CO7 ...156 B4
Deanery Gdns BRTR CM7 ...99 J6
Deanery Rd SRTFD E15 ...307 H3
Deane's CI HAR CO12 ...70 A4
Deane's Cha HAR CO12 ...70 A4
Dean Gdns WALTH E17 ...285 G2
Deanhall Av SUD CO10 ...7 M2
Dean Rd CBE/LIN CB1 ...27 M2
  THMD SE28 ...325 K3
Dean Rogers PI BRTR CM7 ...99 J6
Deans CI HVHL CB9 ...34 C4
Deans Rd BRW CM14 ...273 L2
Dean St FSTGT E7 ...307 K2
  RCOLE CO7 ...156 B6
Dean Wy CHLM/WR CM1 ...4 B1
Deason St SRTFD E15 * ...306 F1
Debden CI WFD IG8 ...268 A6
Debden Dr SAFWN CB10 ...31 H7
Debden Gn VGE SS16 ...294 B1
Debden La LOU IG10 ...235 J8
Debden Rd LOU IG10 ...235 J8
  SAFWS CB11 ...30 A1
Debden Wy BOC CM0 * ...393 K7
De Beauvoir Cha BCAYE CM11 ...260 A1
De Beauvoir Rd IS N1 ...364 C1
Deben Av WOS/PRIT SS0 ...300 F1
Deben Dr SUD CO10 ...21 G4
Debenham Rd CHESW EN7 ...216 C5
Deben La COLN CO4 ...108 D5
  HVHL CB9 ...34 E5
  IP IP1 ...47 L3
Deben Valley Dr KESG IP5 ...50 D6
Deben Wk RCOS CO16 ...158 F7
Deben Wy FX IP11 ...11 H1
De Bohun Ct SAFWN CB10 ...28 D7
De Brink-on-the-Green KESG IP5 * ...50 F6
De Burgh Dr SUD CO10 ...37 J1
De Burgh Rd COLW CO3 ...106 B7
Deck Rd BERM/RHTH SE16 ...322 C5
Dedham Av BCAYE CM11 ...258 F3
Dedham Meade RCOLE CO7 ...89 J2
Dedham MI RCOLE CO7 ...363 N10
Dedham PI IPNE IP4 * ...17 C5
Dedham Rd BCAYE CM11 ...258 F3
  COLN CO4 ...362 D11
  RCOLE CO7 ...89 J2
  RCOLE CO7 ...363 N9
Dee CI UPMR RM14 ...291 J3
Deepdale SBF/HAD SS7 ...280 C1
Deepdale Av HAR CO12 ...14 C3
Deepdene ING CM4 ...239 H8
  VGE SS16 ...3 H8
Deepdene Av RAYL SS6 ...262 C1
Deepdene CI WAN E11 ...285 H4
Deepdene Rd LOU IG10 ...250 E4
The Deeping COS CO15 ...19 G4
Deepwater Rd CVI SS8 ...320 B3
Deerbank Rd BCAYE CM11 ...258 F3
Deere Av RAIN RM13 ...311 M5
Deerhurst Cha RCHLM CM3 ...228 C2
Deerhurst CI SBF/HAD SS7 ...280 E6
Deerhurst Rd GVW DA11 ...337 H6
  VGE SS16 ...3 H8
Deer Pk HLWW/ROY CM19 ...203 M4
Deer Park Wy WAB EN9 ...233 J6
Dee St POP/IOD E14 ...322 F1

Dee Wy ROM RM1 ...271 H7
Defoe Crs COLN CO4 ...87 H8
Defoe Pde CDW/CHF RM16 ...322 C5
Defoe Wy CRW RM5 ...270 D5
Deford Rd WIT CM8 ...171 G5
De Greys Rd SUD CO10 ...45 M4
Deirdre Av WICKW SS12 ...260 H6
Deirdre CI WICKW SS12 ...260 H6
Delafield Rd CHARL SE7 ...323 L8
  GRAYS RM17 ...331 L8
Delamare Rd CHES/WCR EN8 ...217 H8
Delamere Rd CHLM/WR CM1 ...4 B6
  COLN CO4 ...108 A2
Delargy CI CDW/CHF RM16 ...331 L2
Delaware Rd SBN/FI SS3 ...303 G6
Delder Av CVI SS8 ...321 G3
Delfzul Rd CVI SS8 ...321 G3
Delft Rd CVI SS8 ...320 D1
Delgada Rd CVI SS8 ...321 G2
Delhi Rd EN EN1 ...288 F7
Delimands LAIN SS15 ...276 C7
Delisle Rd THMD SE28 ...325 H5
Della Ct COLW CO3 * ...107 H5
Dell CI SRTFD E15 ...307 G2
  WFD IG8 ...267 L2
Dell La BSF CM23 ...139 H2
  BRKF CM22 ...163 H1
Dellow CI GNTH/NBYPK IG2 ...287 G5
Dellows La RBSF CM22 ...374 C3
Dell Rd GRAYS RM17 ...330 D2
  PEND EN3 ...232 D8
Dells CI CHING E4 ...248 F3
Dells Wood CI HOD EN11 ...185 H6
The Dell ABYW SE2 ...325 K8
  BRW CM14 ...273 L6
  CHLM/GWD CM2 ...210 C7
  COL CO1 ...9 H4
  GRH DA9 ...335 J7
  GNTH/NBYPK IG2 ...287 G5
  GVW DA11 ...337 L6
  HCH RM12 ...290 A7
  IPSE IP3 ...17 G2
  LAIN SS15 ...276 C7
  WALTH E17 ...284 C4
Devon Rd COS CO15 ...160 B2
  CVI SS8 ...298 C7
  HAR CO12 ...70 C4
Dewar La KESG IP5 ...50 B6
Dewberry CI GNWCH SE10 ...323 J7
Dewberry Gdns EHAM E6 ...324 B2
Dewberry St POP/IOD E14 ...322 F1
Dewes Green Rd BSF CM23 ...72 A8
Dewey Rd DAGE RM10 ...310 D3
Dewgrass Gv CHES/WCR EN8 ...232 E5
Dewhurst Rd CHES/WCR EN8 ...216 D7
Dewlands BRTR CM7 ...121 H7
  BSDN SS14 ...2 D8
Dewsbury Gdns HARH RM3 ...272 A5
Dewsbury Rd HARH RM3 ...272 A4
Dewsgreen VGE SS16 ...294 B1
Dewyk Rd CVI SS8 ...298 C8
Dexter CI GRAYS RM17 ...330 D2
Deyncourt Gdns UPMR RM14 ...290 F6
Deyncourt Rd WAN E11 ...285 M2
Deynes Rd SAFWS CB11 ...373 L2
Dhobi PI IP IP1 ...47 L6
Dial CI GRH DA9 ...335 M7
Dial La IP IP1 ...16 F6
Dial Rd RCOLE CO7 ...157 H2
Diamond CI BCTR RM8 ...287 M7
  GVW DA11 ...336 D5
  IP IP1 ...47 M7
Diana CI CDW/CHF RM16 ...330 D2
  SWFD E18 ...267 J2
Diana Rd WALTH E17 ...284 C4
Diana Wy COS CO15 ...6 B8
Dianthus CI ABYW SE2 ...325 K8
Diban Av HCH RM12 ...311 H1
Dickens Av DART DA1 ...334 A3
  TIL RM18 ...331 J3
Dickens CI BRTR CM7 ...121 L2
  EHAM E6 ...308 B8
  GVE DA12 ...338 B8
  RCHLM CM3 ...169 K4
Dickens Ri CHIG IG7 ...268 F1
Dickens Wy ROM RM1 ...289 J1
Dickins CI CHESW EN7 ...216 B6
Dickinson Ter KESG IP5 ...50 E6
Dickson CHESW EN7 ...216 B6
Dicky Moors RCHLM CM3 ...167 G2
Didsbury CI EHAM E6 ...308 C8
Digby CI KESG IP5 ...50 E6
Digby Gdns DAGE RM10 ...310 B4
Digby Rd BARK IG11 ...309 K6
  HOM E9 ...306 D2
  IPNE IP4 ...49 J1
  SLH/COR SS17 ...295 J5
Dig Dag HI CHESW EN7 ...216 A6
Diggon St WCHPL E1 ...322 E1
Dilbridge Rd East COLN CO4 ...9 K2
Dilbridge Rd West COLN CO4 ...9 K2
Dillwyn St IP IP1 ...16 C7
Dillwyn St West IP IP1 ...16 C7
Dilston RCHLM CM3 ...212 D3
Dimond CI FSTGT E7 ...307 K1
Dimsdale Dr EN EN1 ...232 A3
Dimson Crs BOW E3 ...306 D6
Dinant Av CVI SS8 ...298 E7
Dinant Link Rd CVI SS8 ...201 H4
Dinants RCOLW CO6 ...126 B2
Dingle Gdns POP/IOD E14 * ...322 E2
Dinsdale CI COS CO15 ...19 J4
Direton Rd SRTFD E15 ...307 G1
The Dismals RCHLM CM3 ...169 K4
Disney CI ING CM4 ...239 H8
Dison CI PEND EN3 ...248 E8
Disraeli CI THMD SE28 ...325 K5
Disraeli Rd FSTGT E7 ...307 K3
  RAYL SS6 ...280 C1
Distillery La COLS CO2 ...129 L2
Ditchburn St POP/IOD E14 ...322 F2
Ditchfield Rd HOD EN11 ...185 J6
Ditchingham Gv IPNE IP4 ...49 K4
Ditton Court Rd WOS/PRIT SS0 ...184 C3
Divot PI RMIT/BAY SG13 ...184 C3
Dixon Av CHLM/WR CM1 ...209 K1
  RCOS CO16 ...158 B4
Dixon CI EHAM E6 ...324 B2
Dixon Wy RCOLW CO6 ...126 C6
Dobbies La KIR/NAC IP10 ...50 E8
Dobbins Drift IPSE IP5 ...50 B6
Dobbs Drift KIR/NAC IP10 ...50 E8
Dobbs La RCOLS CO5 ...281 H4
Dobb's Weir Rd HOD EN11 ...201 M3
Dock Approach Rd CDW/CHF RM16 ...315 J8
  GRAYS RM17 ...331 H4

Delius CI COLN CO4 ...108 B7
Delius Wy BARK/HLT IG6 ...269 H4
Delmar Gdns CLAY IG5 ...286 D1
Delmores VGE SS16 ...294 F2
Delta Rd RBRW/HUT CM13 ...257 G2
De Lucy Rd ABYW SE2 ...325 L7
De Lucy St ABYW SE2 ...325 L7
Delvers Md DAGE RM10 ...310 D1
Delview CVI SS8 ...298 C8
Delvins PIT SS13 ...278 D5
Delvyn's La HSTD CO9 ...357 K4
De Mandeville Rd RBSF CM22 ...374 C3
De-Marci St BRTR CM7 ...122 A2
Demesne Rd KESG IP5 ...50 D6
Denbigh CI EMPK RM11 ...290 C2
Denbigh Rd EHAM E6 ...308 A7
  LAIN SS15 ...276 C7
Denby Gra HLWE CM17 ...204 F2
Dencourt Crs BSDN SS14 ...278 B2
Dendridge CI EN EN1 ...232 C2
Dene CI RAYL SS6 ...281 G1
Dene Ct CHLM/WR CM1 ...193 M7
Denecroft Gdns GRAYS RM17 ...331 J2
Dene Gdns RAYL SS6 ...281 G1
Dene Holm Rd GVW DA11 ...337 G7
Denehurst Gdns VGE SS16 ...294 B1
  WFD IG8 ...267 L3
Dene Pth SOCK/AV RM15 ...329 K2
Denesmere SBF/HAD SS7 ...280 E6
Deneway VGE SS16 ...296 A3
Dengayne BSDN SS14 ...3 M6
Dengie CI WIT CM8 ...171 G5
Denham CI COLN CO4 ...87 F5
Denham Dr GNTH/NBYPK IG2 ...286 F5
Denham Rd CHIG IG7 ...269 M1
Denham V RAYL SS6 ...280 D2
Denham Wy BARK IG11 ...309 H5
Denholm Wk RAIN RM13 ...311 M6
Denholme Wk RAIN RM13 ...311 M6
Denmark Rd BRW CM14 ...273 L2
  SBN/FI SS3 ...303 L1
  WAN E11 ...285 J5
Denner Rd CHING E4 ...266 D4
Dennises La UPMR RM14 ...313 J4
Dennis Rd GVW DA11 ...337 K8
  UPMR RM14 ...313 K5
Denny Av WAB EN9 ...233 L5
Denny Ct SRTFD E15 * ...307 H3
Denny Ga CHES/WCR EN8 ...217 J7
Densham Rd SRTFD E15 ...307 H5
Dent CI SOCK/AV RM15 ...329 K2
Denton Ap WOS/PRIT SS0 ...300 F1
Denton Av WOS/PRIT SS0 ...300 F1
Denton CI CHTY IP2 ...53 J3
Denton Court Rd GVE DA12 ...338 D7
Denton Crs GVE DA12 ...338 D7
Denton St GVE DA12 ...338 D7
Denton Ter KESG IP5 ...50 D6
Denton Wf CLPT E5 ...284 D1
Denton Wharf GVE DA12 * ...338 D7
Denys Dr BSDN SS14 ...3 M5
De Quincey Ms CAN/RD E16 ...322 C1
Derby Av ROMW/RG RM7 ...288 C7
  UPMR RM14 ...291 J3
Derby CI BCAYE CM11 ...241 G5
  IPNE IP4 ...17 M5
  RCHLM CM3 ...388 E8
  VGE SS16 ...294 C1
Derbydale RCFD SS4 ...264 D1
Derby Gdns FSTGT E7 ...308 B1
Derby Rd FSTGT E7 ...307 K3
  HOD EN11 ...201 L5
  HOM E9 ...306 D4
  IPNE IP4 ...17 L6
  IPSE IP3 ...48 D8
  SWFD E18 ...267 J2
Derby Road Br GRAYS RM17 ...330 D1
Dereham Av IPSE IP3 ...54 D2
Dereham CI COLS CO2 ...128 E2
Dereham PI CRW RM5 ...270 B5
Dereham Rd BARK IG11 ...309 L3
Derek Gdns SOSN SS2 ...283 H7
Deri Av RAIN RM13 ...311 M7
Derifall CI EHAM E6 ...324 C1
Dering CI LOS SS9 ...300 C1
Dering Wy GVE DA12 ...338 F7
Derrick Gdns CHARL SE7 ...323 L8
Derry Av SOCK/AV RM15 ...329 K1
Dersingham Av MNPK E12 ...308 C1
Derventer Av CVI SS8 ...298 D7
Derwent Av RAYL SS6 ...262 C1
Derwent CI COLN CO4 ...108 A3
Derwent Gdns REDBR IG4 ...286 C1
Derwent Pde SOCK/AV RM15 ...329 K3
Derwent Rd COLN CO4 ...108 A3
  IPSE IP3 ...54 D2
Derwent St GNWCH SE10 ...323 J7
Derwent Wy BRTR CM7 ...120 E6
  HCH RM12 ...311 H2

Desford Rd CAN/RD E16 ...307 H8
Dessons Ct SLH/COR SS17 * ...317 J1
De Staunton CI RCOLE CO7 ...131 L6
Detling CI HCH RM12 ...311 M2
Detling Rd GVW DA11 ...337 G6
Devalls CI EHAM E6 ...324 D1
Devas St BOW E3 ...306 D4
Devenay Rd SRTFD E15 ...307 J4
Devenish Rd ABYW SE2 ...325 K5
Devereaux CI WOTN CO14 ...137 J1
De Vere Av MAL CM9 ...214 A4
De Vere CI RCHLM CM3 ...196 B2
De Vere Gdns IL IG1 ...286 C4
De Vere La RCOLE CO7 ...130 C5
De Vere Rd COLW CO3 ...106 C5
  RCOLW CO6 ...82 C5
De Veres Rd HSTD CO9 * ...81 H5
Devereux Rd CDW/CHF RM16 ...330 D4
  SOS SS1 ...10 C7
Devereux Wy BCAYW SE2 ...240 C7
De Vere Wy HAR CO12 ...70 A4
Deverill Rd CHLM/WR CM1 ...193 L5
Deveron Gdns SOCK/AV RM15 ...329 K2
Deveron Wy ROM RM1 ...271 J7
De Vigier Av SAFWN CB10 ...28 D7
Devlin Rd RIPW IP8 ...53 M1
Devon CI BKHH IG9 ...267 L1
Devon Gdns RCFD SS4 ...264 D1
Devonport Gdns IL IG1 ...286 C4
Devon Rd BARK IG11 ...309 H5
  COLS CO2 ...128 E2
  FX IP11 ...62 F2
Devons Est BOW E3 ...306 D4
Devonshire CI LAIN SS15 ...276 D5
  SRTFD E15 ...307 H1
Devonshire Gdns CHING E4 ...121 L2
  SLH/COR SS17 ...332 C7
Devonshire Rd BOC CM0 ...393 K6
  BOC CM0 ...393 L6
  CAN/RD E16 ...323 J2
  CDW/CHF RM16 ...330 D5
  GNTH/NBYPK IG2 ...287 G5
  GVW DA11 ...337 L6
  HCH RM12 ...290 A7
  IPSE IP3 ...17 G7
  LAIN SS15 ...276 D5
  WALTH E17 ...284 D4

Dock Basin FX IP11 * ...10 C9
Dockers Tanner Rd POP/IOD E14 ...322 D7
Dockfield Av HAR CO12 ...14 A7
Dock Hill Av BERM/RHTH SE16 ...322 A5
Dockland St CAN/RD E16 ...324 C4
Docklands St CAN/RD E16 ...324 B3
Dock La HAR CO12 ...568 E8
Dock Rd CAN/RD E16 ...323 K4
  FX IP11 ...10 D8
  GRAYS RM17 ...331 E8
  RCHLM CM3 ...388 E8
Dockside Rd CAN/RD E16 ...324 A3
The Docks FX IP11 ...10 D8
Dock St CHTY IP2 ...16 F7
Dockwra La RCHLM CM3 ...212 C6
Doctor's La SUD CO10 ...345 Q3
Doctor Watson's La KESG IP5 ...49 M4
Docwra Rd K/T/MI CO5 ...148 C3
Docwra's Rd K/T/MI CO5 ...148 C3
Doddenhill CI SAFWN CB10 ...28 D8
Doddinghurst Rd BRWN CM15 ...255 M7
Dodmans RIPS/CAP IP9 ...58 C4
Dodson V KESG IP5 ...50 B6
Dod St POP/IOD E14 ...322 D2
Doesgate La UPMR RM14 ...293 H4
Doeshill Dr WICKW SS12 ...261 H6
Dogden La BSF CM23 ...92 F7
Doggetts Cha RCFD SS4 ...265 J2
Doggetts CI RCFD SS4 ...265 J2
Doggetts La RCOLW CO6 ...126 C3
Doghouse Rd BRTR CM7 ...101 H7
  RCOLW CO6 ...123 M6
Dog Kennel La ING CM4 ...223 G5
Dogs Head St IPNE IP4 ...16 F7
Doherty Rd PLSTW E13 ...307 K6
Dolben Ct DEPT SE8 * ...322 F8
Dolby Ri CHLM/GWD CM2 ...210 C8
Dollant Av CVI SS8 ...320 D1
Dolphin Ap ROM RM1 ...289 J2
Dolphin CI CBE/LIN CB1 ...25 G2
  THMD SE28 ...325 L4
Dolphin La BCAYW CM12 ...240 C1
  POP/IOD E14 ...322 E3
Dolphins WOS/PRIT SS0 ...283 G8
Dolphin Wy RCFD SS4 ...139 H1
  WTHK RM20 ...329 L4
Domanco Ldg LOS SS9 * ...299 L4
Dombey CI CHLM/WR CM1 ...193 K8
Dombey Dr CHTY IP2 ...47 K8
Dominica CI PLSTW E13 ...308 A7
Dominic Ct WAB EN9 ...233 A7
Dominion Dr CRW RM5 ...270 B3
Dominion Wy RAIN RM13 ...311 K7
Domitian CI COLN CO4 ...87 K7
Domsey Bank RCOLW CO6 ...126 B2
Domsey Cha RCFD SS4 ...265 J2
Domsey La K/T/MI CO5 ...125 L5
Domsey La RCHLM CM3 ...194 B2
Doms La RCHLM CM3 ...169 K3
Donald Biggs Dr GVE DA12 ...337 M8
Donald Dr CHDH RM6 ...287 M3
Donald Thorn CI WICKW SS12 * ...261 J7
Donald Wy CHLM/GWD CM2 ...210 B6
Doncaster Wy UPMR RM14 ...290 C8
Doncella CI CDW/CHF RM16 ...329 M9
Don Ct WIT CM8 ...171 G3
Donegal Rd IP IP1 ...47 L6
Dongola Rd PLSTW E13 * ...307 L4
  WCHPL E1 ...322 D1
Dongola Rd West PLSTW E13 ...307 L4
Donington Av BARK/HLT IG6 ...286 F1
Donne Dr COS CO15 ...182 C5
Donne CI CDW/CHF RM16 ...330 D4
Donnison Av BCTR RM8 ...287 M7
Donovan's Gdn RBRW/HUT CM13 ...275 L2
Don Wy ROM RM1 ...271 J7
Donyland Wy COS CO15 ...130 C5
Dooley Rd FX IP11 ...10 E8
  HSTD CO9 ...81 K3
Dora St POP/IOD E14 ...322 D2
Dorchester End COLS CO2 ...129 L2
Dorchester Gdns CHING E4 ...266 C1
Dorchester Rd BCAYW CM12 ...240 A8
  GVE DA12 ...338 A8
  IPSE IP3 ...55 J2
Dordells LAIN SS15 ...2 E8
Dore Av MNPK E12 ...308 F2
Dorewards Av BRTR CM7 ...99 H6
Dorian Rd HCH RM12 ...289 M5
Doric Av RCFD SS4 ...265 G4
Doris Rd FSTGT E7 ...307 J4
Dorking Crs RCOS CO16 ...158 B4
Dorking Ri HARH RM3 ...272 A4
Dorking Wk HARH RM3 ...272 A4
Dorkins Wy UPMR RM14 ...291 J4
Dormer CI SRTFD E15 ...307 J4
Dorothy Curtice Ct RCOLW CO6 ...105 H8
Dorothy Farm Rd RAYL SS6 ...281 K4
Dorothy Gdns BCTR RM8 ...309 J1
Dorothy Sayers Dr WIT CM8 ...147 H1
Dorrington Gdns HCH RM12 ...290 A6
Dorset Av CHLM/GWD CM2 ...210 C8
  ROM RM1 ...289 J1
Dorset CI CDW/CHF RM16 ...330 D4
  IPNE IP4 ...48 E1
Dorset Gdns RCFD SS4 ...264 D1
Dorset PI SRTFD E15 ...307 H2
Dorset Rd BOC CM0 ...393 M9
  FSTGT E7 ...307 M1
  MAL CM9 ...214 C4
Dorset Wy BCAYW CM12 ...240 A8
Dorvis La SAFWN CB10 ...27 L2
Doubleday Dr MAL CM9 ...198 C8
Doubleday Gdns BRTR CM7 ...99 L8
Doubleday La WICKE SS11 ...261 J8
  WICKW SS12 ...279 L1
Doublet Ms BCAYE CM11 ...241 G5
Douglas Av HARH RM3 ...272 A5
  WALTH E17 ...266 C8
Douglas CI CDW/CHF RM16 ...330 D4
  CHLM/GWD CM2 ...226 C2
Douglas Dr WICKW SS12 ...325 G1
Douglas Gdns BRTR CM7 ...99 L8
Douglas Ms HARH RM3 ...272 A5
Douglas PI POP/IOD E14 * ...322 E7
Douglas Rd CAN/RD E16 ...323 G1
  CHING E4 ...249 J7
  GDMY/SEVK IG3 ...287 K5
  HAR CO12 ...14 C2
  ROM RM1 ...289 J1
  SOS SS1 ...299 M8
Douglas Ter WALTH E17 ...266 C8
Doug Siddons Ct GRAYS RM17 * ...330 D2
Doulton CI HLWE CM17 ...204 E2
Doulton Wy RCFD SS4 ...264 D1
Douro St BOW E3 ...306 D5

Dove Ap EHAM E6 ....324 B1
Dove Cl BSF CM23 ....138 F6
  CDW/CHF RM16 ....330 E2
  STSD CM24 ....115 M2
Dovecote SBN/FI SS3 ....303 H4
Dove Crs HAR CO12 ....70 C3
Dovedale CVI SS8 ....299 C8
  FX IP11 ....10 F4
Dovedale Av CLAY IG5 ....268 C8
Dovedale Gdns BCAYE CM11 ....259 M1
  VGE SS16 ....294 D1
Dovedale Gdns COS CO15 ....159 M7
Dovehouse Cft HLW CM20 ....188 B7
Dovehouse Md BSF CM23 ....309 D1
Dove House Gdns CHING E4 ....266 D1
Dove House Rd HVIL CB9 ....34 C4
Dove La CHLM/GWD CM2 ....210 A7
Dovercliff Rd CVI SS8 ....321 H2
Dover Cl BRTR CM7 ....99 J1
  COS CO15 ....183 G5
  ROMW/RG RM7 ....270 F8
Dover Rd GVW DA11 ....337 G5
  IPSE IP3 ....55 G1
  MNPK E12 ....285 M7
  RCOLE CO7 ....156 C5
Dover Rd East GVW DA11 ....337 H5
Dovervelt Rd CVI SS8 ....298 C8
Dover Wy PIT SS13 ....278 E7
Dovesgate SBF/HAD SS7 ....298 B7
Doves La GTDUN CM6 ....140 D3
Doves Ms LAIN SS15 * 277 C4
Dove St IPNE IP4 ....17 J4
Dowches BOC CM4 ....393 H4
Dowches Cl K/T/MI CO5 ....148 F2
Dowches Gdns K/T/MI CO5 ....148 F2
Dow Ct BOC CM4 ....393 H4
Dowding Cl HCH RM12 ....311 L4
Dowland Cl SLH/COR SS17 ....316 F2
Dowling Cl HCH RM12 ....311 L4
The Downage HLW CM20 ....188 B7
Downer Rd SBF/HAD SS7 ....298 A4
Downer Rd North
  SBF/HAD SS7 ....280 B8
Downesway SBF/HAD SS7 ....298 A4
Downey Cl BSDN SS14 ....3 J1
Downfield CI HERT/BAY SG13 ....184 D5
Downfield Rd CHES/WCR EN8 ....232 F1
  HERT/BAY SG13 ....184 D5
Downhall Cl BSF CM23 ....281 G1
Downhall Park Wy RAYL SS6 ....262 F8
Down Hall Rd RAYL SS6 ....280 F2
Downhall Rd RBSF CM22 ....378 C7
Downham Bvd IPSE IP3 ....55 H6
Downham Ct CRW RM5 ....270 D6
Downham Rd BCAYE CM11 ....242 A8
  CVI SS8 ....320 C1
  ING CM4 ....241 K1
  WICKE SS11 ....260 F3
Downing Cl CHTY IP2 ....53 L3
Downing Rd DAGW RM9 ....310 C5
Downings EHAM E6 ....324 D5
Downlands WAB EN9 ....233 M4
Downleaze RCHLM CM3 ....245 H5
Downs Crs GTDUN CM6 ....116 F4
  HVIL CB9 ....34 C5
Downsell Rd WAN E11 ....307 G1
Downsfield Rd WALTH E17 ....284 B4
Downs Gv VGE SS16 ....296 B2
Downshall Av
  GDMY/SEVK IG3 ....287 H4
Downside Cl CHTY IP2 ....53 L3
Downsland Dr BRW CM14 ....273 M2
Downs Rd MAL CM9 ....214 D2
Downs Ter GTDUN CM6 * 96 A4
The Downs FX IP11 ....61 M5
  GTDUN CM6 ....116 F4
  HLW CM20 ....13 K6
Downsway CHLM/WR CM1 ....194 A3
Downton Dr HVIL CB9 ....34 B7
Downtown Rd
  BERM/RHTH SE16 ....322 B5
Dowsett La BCAYE CM10 ....241 J4
Dragon Cl BOC CM4 ....393 K8
Dragonfly Cl PLSTW E13 ....307 L2
Dragon's Gn SAFWN CB10 ....29 G8
Dragoon Rd DEPT SE8 ....322 C8
Drake Av PIT SS13 ....278 E7
  RCHLM CM3 ....388 D9
Drake Cl BERM/RHTH SE16 ....322 A4
  BRW CM14 ....256 A8
  SBF/HAD SS7 ....298 F1
Drake Crs THMD SE28 ....325 M2
Drake Gdns BRTR CM7 ....121 J4
Drake Ms HCH RM12 ....311 K4
Drake Rd CDW/CHF RM16 ....330 B1
  LAIN SS15 ....277 C3
  WOS/PRIT SS0 ....300 C1
Drakes Ap COS CO15 ....182 D4
Drakes Cl CHES/WCR EN8 ....216 E4
Drakes La RCHLM CM3 ....168 C6
Drake Sq North IPSE IP3 ....55 G3
Drake Sq South IPSE IP3 ....55 G3
The Drakes SBN/FI SS3 ....303 H5
Drakes Wy RAYL SS6 ....281 H1
Draper Cl BELV DA17 ....326 C2
Drapers Cha BRTR CM77 ....120 A4
Drapers Ct HVIL CB9 ....34 A7
Draper La HVIL CB9 ....34 B3
Drapers Rd RCHLM CM3 ....245 H5
  SRTFD E15 ....306 F1
Drapery Common SUD CO10 ....39 L1
Drawell Cl WOOL/PLUM SE18 ....325 H8
Draycot Av WAN E11 ....285 L4
Drayman's Cl BSF CM23 ....138 C4
Draymans Gv BRTR CM77 ....120 F5
Draymans Wy IPSE IP3 ....54 D7
Drayson Cl WAB EN9 ....233 L2
The Drays SUD CO10 ....42 E4
Drayton Av LOU IG10 ....250 C3
Drayton Cl IL IG1 ....287 G6
  MAL CM9 ....214 D4
Drayton Rd WAN E11 ....285 K6
Dreadnought St GNWCH SE10 ....323 H6
Drew Rd CAN/RD E16 ....324 D1
Drewsteignton SRTFD E15 ....303 G5
The Dreys SAFWN CB10 ....31 L1
Driberg Wy BRTR CM7 ....121 K4
Driffield Cl K/T/MI CO5 ....149 C7
Driffield Rd BOW E3 ....306 B1
The Drift FX IP11 * 61 M5
  IPNE IP4 ....48 J7
  IPSE IP3 ....55 H4
  KESG IP5 ....50 F6
  MGTR CO11 ....64 F3
  RIPS/CAP IP9 ....364 F11
  SUD CO10 ....45 M4
Driftway VGE SS16 ....296 C2
The Driftway IPNE IP4 ....49 C6
The Driftway BARK IG11 ....309 J4
  BKHH IG9 ....249 M7
  CHESW EN7 ....216 D4
  CHING E4 ....249 G7
  CHLM/WR CM1 ....249 G7
  COS CO15 ....159 L6
  CRW RM5 ....271 G7
  GTDUN CM6 ....74 D3
  HAR CO12 ....71 G3
  HARH RM3 ....272 B7

HLW CM20 ....13 K4
HOC/HUL SS5 ....263 G2
IL IG1 ....201 H1
LOU EN11 ....201 M1
RAYL SS6 ....281 L5
RBRW/HUT CM13 ....273 M5
RCFD SS4 ....220 B3
RCHLM CM3 ....388 C9
SBW CM21 ....162 F7
SWFD E18 ....285 K1
WALTH E17 ....284 E1
WIT CM8 ....148 B7
WOS/PRIT SS0 ....300 E3
The Driveway CVI SS8 ....320 E3
Droitwich Av SOSN SS2 ....302 B4
Dronfield Gdns BCTR RM8 ....309 M2
Drood Cl CHLM/WR CM1 ....193 J6
Drover's Ct FX IP11 ....62 A5
Drovers Md BRW CM14 ....273 L3
Drovers Wy BSF CM23 ....138 D5
The Druce SAFWS CB11 ....72 A5
Drum Fld RCOLE CO7 ....363 L8
Drummond Av
  ROMW/RG RM7 ....289 G2
Drummond Pl WICKW SS12 ....261 H8
Drummond Rd
  ROMW/RG RM7 ....288 F2
  WAN E11 ....285 L4
The Drummonds EPP CM16 ....239 C8
Drury Dr SUD CO10 ....43 J7
Drury La BRTR CM7 ....121 J2
  GTDUN CM6 ....379 Q3
  HSTD CO9 ....345 M7
Drury Rd COLS CO2 ....106 C4
Dryden Av HCH RM12 ....311 K4
Dryden Cl BARK/HLT IG6 ....269 J5
  MAL CM9 ....214 D5
Dryden Pl TIL RM18 ....331 L7
Dryden Rd IP IP1 ....47 M2
Dry Dock RCOLE CO7 ....130 C5
Drysdale Av CHING E4 ....248 E6
Dry St VGE SS16 ....294 F3
  VGE SS16 ....295 K3
Drywoods RCHLM CM3 ....245 C8
Duarte Pl CDW/CHF RM16 ....330 C2
Dubarry Cl SBF/HAD SS7 ....298 C1
Du Cane Pl WIT CM8 * 171 K3
Duchess Cl BSF CM23 ....138 C2
Duchess Gv BKHH IG9 * 267 L1
Duckamere RIPW IP8 ....46 F4
Duckend Farm La
   CHLM/WR CM1 ....75 J7
Ducker's La CHLM/WR CM1 ....165 M6
Ducketts Md
  HLWW/ROY CM19 ....186 C8
  RCFD SS4 ....392 A11
Duckett St WCHPL E1 ....322 A1
Ducking Stool Ct ROM RM1 ....289 H2
Duck La EPP CM16 ....220 D4
Duck Lees La PEND EN3 ....248 B4
Duckling La SBW CM21 ....162 F7
Duck St GTDUN CM6 ....119 J4
Dudbrook Rd BRW CM14 ....382 H12
Duddery Hl HVIL CB9 ....34 C4
Duddery Rd HVIL CB9 ....34 D6
Dudely Cl GVW DA11 ....337 C5
Dudley Av CHES/WCR EN8 ....232 E2
  RCHLM CM3 ....195 H4
Dudley Rd COS CO15 ....6 C7
  HARH RM3 ....272 A5
  IL IG1 ....308 E1
  K/T/MI CO5 ....149 C5
  RCOLW CO6 ....182 G2
  WALTH E17 ....266 D8
Duffield Cl CDW/CHF RM16 ....330 D1
Duffield Dr COLN CO4 ....108 D6
Duffield Rd CHLM/GWD CM2 ....210 A7
Duffries Cl RAIN RM13 ....167 H6
Duff St POP/IOD E14 ....322 E1
Dugard Av COLN CO3 ....128 B1
Dugmore Av RCOS CO16 ....136 F1
Duke Cl LAIN SS15 ....2 A1
  CDW/CHF RM16 ....330 C2
  COS CO15 ....235 M5
Dukes Av BOC CM4 ....393 N2
  CDW/CHF RM16 ....330 D2
Dukes Cl EPP CM16 ....221 J5
  FX IP11 ....63 J7
Dukes Farm Cl BCAYW CM12 ....240 F8
Dukes Farm Rd BCAYW CM12 ....258 F1
Dukes La CHLM/GWD CM2 ....210 C1
  CHONG CM5 ....381 R3
Dukes Orch RBSF CM22 ....376 D1
Duke's Pk WDBR IP12 ....51 J1
Dukes Ride BSF CM23 ....138 D2
Duke's Rd BCAYE CM11 ....258 F1
  BRTR CM7 ....99 H8
  EHAM E6 ....308 D5
Duke St CHLM/WR CM1 ....7 H2
  HOD EN11 ....201 M1
  IPSE IP3 ....17 J7
  RCOLE CO7 ....156 B7
Dulverton Av WOS/PRIT SS0 ....300 D1
Dulverton Ct WOS/PRIT SS0 ....300 D1
Dulverton Rd HARH RM3 ....272 A5
Dulwich Rd COS CO15 ....183 M1
Dumbarton Av
  CHES/WCR EN8 ....232 E4
Dumbarton Dr IPNE IP4 ....49 C5
Dumney La RCHLM CM3 ....143 L2
  RCHLM CM3 ....144 B3
Dumont Av RCOS CO16 ....180 G3
Dunbar Av DAGE RM10 ....288 D8
Dunbar Gdns DAGE RM10 ....310 D2
Dunbar Pl WICKW SS12 ....261 K8
Dunbar Rd FSTGT E7 ....307 K5
Duncan Cl WICKW SS12 ....261 J8
Duncan Ri HSTD CO9 ....346 A11
Duncan Rd COLS CO2 ....128 E1
Dundee Av LOS SS9 ....299 M3
Dundee Cl LOS SS9 ....299 M3
Dundee Rd BSDN SS14 ....278 C4
Dundee Wy PLSTW E13 ....307 L6
Dundee Wy PEND EN3 ....248 B6
Dundonald Cl EHAM E6 ....324 D2
Dundonald Dr LOS SS9 ....300 C4
Dunedin Rd IL IG1 ....288 D5
  LEY E10 ....284 E8
  RAIN RM13 ....311 J7
Dunelm St WCHPL E1 ....322 A1
Dunfane BCAYW CM12 ....240 F7
Dungannon Cha SOS SS1 ....302 C3
Dungannon Dr SOS SS1 ....302 C3
Dunkeld Rd BCTR RM8 ....287 L7
Dunkellin Gv SOCK/AV RM15 ....329 J5
Dunkellin Wy SOCK/AV RM15 ....329 J5
Dunkin Rd DART DA1 ....334 D6
Dunlin Cl BOC CM4 ....393 N6
Dunlin Cl MAL CM9 ....199 F8
  RCHLM CM3 ....245 G4
Dunlin Ct K/T/MI CO5 ....148 F3
Dunlin Rd CHTY IP2 ....53 K3
Dunlop Rd CHTY IP2 ....47 J1
  TIL RM18 ....331 J7

Dunmore Rd CHLM/GWD CM2 ....210 D2
Eastbourne Gv
  WOS/PRIT SS0 ....300 D7
Eastbourne Rd EHAM E6 ....308 D7
  SRTFD E15 ....307 H5
East Bridge Rd RCHLM CM3 ....245 E5
Eastbrook Av DAGE RM10 ....310 F1
Eastbrook Dr DAGE RM10 ....233 M6
Eastbrook Rd WAB EN9 ....233 M6
Eastbrooks PIT SS13 ....278 E6
Eastbury Av BARK IG11 ....309 H5
  RCFD SS4 ....283 C1
Eastbury Rd EHAM E6 ....308 D8
  ROMW/RG RM7 ....289 G4
Eastbury Sq BARK IG11 ....309 J5
Eastbury Ter WCHPL E1 ....306 F2
Eastcheap RAYL SS6 ....280 F1
Eastcliff FX IP11 ....63 K5
Eastcliff Av LOS SS9 ....7 M3
East Cl RAIN RM13 ....311 L8
Eastcote Gv SOSN SS2 ....302 A2
East Crs CVI SS8 ....320 C1
East Cross Route HOM E9 ....306 C1
East Dene Dr HARH RM3 ....272 A4
East Dock Rd CAN/RD E16 ....14 D7
East Dr SBW CM21 ....162 F8
East Duck Lees La PEND EN3 ....248 B6
Eastend La RBSF CM22 ....375 J4
East End La RCOLE CO7 ....64 C7
Eastend Rd COS CM0 ....386 C11
East End Rd RCOLE CO7 ....64 D5
East Entrance DAGE RM10 ....310 E6
Easterford Rd K/T/MI CO5 ....148 E3
Easterling Cl HAR CO12 ....14 D7
Eastern Av CHES/WCR EN8 ....233 C3
  GNTH/NBYPK IG2 ....286 D1
  HVIL CB9 ....34 C5
  REDBR IG4 ....286 A4
  SBF/HAD SS7 ....279 M8
  SOCK/AV RM15 ....328 F5
  SOSN SS2 ....301 M2
  WAN E11 ....285 M4
  WTHK RM20 ....329 J8
Eastern Av East ROM RM1 ....289 C1
Eastern Av West CHDH RM6 ....288 D7
Eastern Cl IPNE IP4 ....55 L1
  SOSN SS2 ....301 K4
Eastern Crs CHLM/WR CM1 ....193 J3
Eastern Esp CVI SS8 ....321 G1
  SOS SS1 ....19 J4
Eastern Gtwy CAN/RD E16 ....323 G1
Eastern Rd BOC CM4 ....393 M4
  PLSTW E13 ....307 J1
  RAYL SS6 ....280 F4
  RCOLE CO7 ....156 B7
  ROM RM1 ....289 J1
  WALTH E17 ....284 F3
Easternville Gdns
  GNTH/NBYPK IG2 ....286 F4
Eastern Wy GRAYS RM17 ....330 E6
  THMD SE28 ....325 K5
East Ferry Rd POP/IOD E14 ....322 E4
Eastfield Gdns DAGE RM10 ....310 D1
Eastfield Rd BRW CM14 ....256 A5
  CHES/WCR EN8 ....233 C2
  CVI SS8 ....299 C8
  DAGE RM10 ....310 D1
  LAIN SS15 ....277 J3
  PEND EN3 ....232 B4
  WALTH E17 ....284 F2
Eastfield St POP/IOD E14 ....322 E1
East Ga HLW CM20 ....13 G5
Eastgate BSDN SS14 ....3 M1
Eastgate St HAR CO12 ....75 K2
East Glebe Dr RAYL SS6 ....280 F2
East Gores Rd RCOLW CO6 ....125 J3
East Hall La RAIN RM13 ....328 A2
East Ham Crs
  RBRW/HUT CM13 ....256 D7
East Ham Manor Wy
  EHAM E6 ....324 D2
East Hanningfield Rd
  CHLM/GWD CM2 ....227 H2
  RCHLM CM3 ....243 L4
Easthaven COS CO15 ....6 C6
East Hl COL CO1 ....8 A3
Easthorpe St HAR CO12 ....75 K2
East India Dock Rd
  POP/IOD E14 ....322 D2
East Kent Av GVW DA11 ....336 C4
Eastland Ct FX IP11 ....62 C6
East La RCOLE CO7 ....363 P12
East Lawn IPNE IP4 ....49 H5
Eastlea Ms CAN/RD E16 ....307 H5
Eastleigh Rd SBF/HAD SS7 ....266 C8
  WALTH E17 * 266 C8
Eastly VGE SS16 ....2 D9
East Mayne PIT SS13 ....278 C6
East Mersea Rd K/T/MI CO5 ....178 G3
East Ml GVW DA11 ....337 J4
East Mill Gn RIPS/CAP IP9 ....59 J7
East Milton Rd GVE DA12 ....338 A2
Eastmoor Pl
  WOOL/PLUM SE18 ....324 A6
Eastmoor St CHARL SE7 ....324 A7
East Rd GNWCH SE10 ....323 G8
Easton End LAIN SS15 ....276 D7
Easton Rd WIT CM8 ....171 M1
Easton Wy FOS CO13 ....137 L3
East Pk HLWE CM17 ....188 F4
East Park Cl CHDH RM6 ....288 A3
East Philbrick Crs RAYL SS6 ....280 F2
East Rd BSF CM23 ....139 J2
  CHDH RM6 ....288 B5
  HLW CM20 ....188 C5
  K/T/MI CO5 ....178 A6
  LOS SS9 ....300 A5
  MAL CM9 ....385 N4
  RCFD SS4 ....283 C5
  RCOLE CO7 ....130 C6
  SAFWN CB10 ....28 C7
  SOSN SS2 ....301 J2
  SUD CO10 ....20 D5
  WTHK RM20 ....330 A5
East Rw RIPS/CAP IP9 * 364 F11
  WAN E11 ....285 K4
East Side COLN CO4 ....87 L1
East Sq BSDN SS14 ....3 M1
East Stockwell St COL CO1 ....8 A3
East St BARK IG11 ....308 F4
  BRTR CM7 ....121 J4
  COL CO1 ....15 M1
  HAR CO12 ....71 G5
  LOS SS9 ....300 B5
  MAL CM9 ....385 N4
  RCFD SS4 ....283 C1
  RCOLE CO7 ....130 C6
  SAFWN CB10 ....28 C7
  SOSN SS2 ....301 J2
  SUD CO10 ....20 C5
  WTHK RM20 ....330 A5
East Ter GVE DA12 ....337 M4
  WOTN CO14 ....369 N12
East Thorpe BSDN SS14 ....3 M1
East Thurrock Rd
  GRAYS RM17 ....330 E5
East Tilbury Rd
  SLH/COR SS17 ....332 D1
East Vw CHING E4 ....266 D1

Dunmow Rd CHLM/GWD CM2 ....210 D2
Eastwood Gv
  WOS/PRIT SS0 ....300 F2
Dunmow Rd CHDH RM6 ....287 M3
  LOU IG10 ....250 B6
Dunmow Dr RAIN RM13 ....311 J3
Dunmow Gdns
  RBRW/HUT CM13 ....275 C8
  BRTR CM77 ....76 B6
  BSF CM23 ....139 K2
  CHONG CM5 ....379 N12
  CHONG CM5 ....381 M6
  GTDUN CM6 ....74 D4
  GTDUN CM6 ....119 D4
  GTDUN CM6 ....140 C5
  GTDUN CM6 ....379 R2
  RBSF CM22 ....376 B2
  RBSF CM22 ....377 J2
  SRTFD E15 ....307 C1
Dunning Ct MGTR CO11 ....329 K2
Dunningford Cl HARH RM3 ....311 J2
Dunnings La UPMR RM14 ....292 E3
Dunnock Cl ED N9 ....248 A8
Dunnock Rd EHAM E6 ....324 D1
Dunnock Wy COLN CO4 ....108 A6
Dunoon Cl BRTR CM7 ....122 A1
Dunsey Wood CVI SS8 ....34 A4
Dunspring La CLAY IG5 ....268 C8
Dunstable Rd HARH RM3 ....272 A5
  SLH/COR SS17 ....316 F2
Dunstalls HLWW/ROY CM19 ....203 H5
Dunster Av WOS/PRIT SS0 ....288 D8
Dunster Rd ROMW/RG RM7 ....270 F8
Dunster Crs UPMR RM14 ....290 D7
Dunster Dr HVIL CB9 ....34 B5
Dunthorne Rd COLN CO4 ....108 B3
Dunthorpe Rd RCOS CO16 ....159 C3
Dunton Rd LEY E10 ....284 E5
  RBRW/HUT CM13 ....275 C5
  ROM RM1 ....289 H2
Dupont Cl BRTR CM7 ....76 D4
Dupree Rd CHARL SE7 ....323 L8
Durants Park Av PEND EN3 ....248 A4
Durban Gdns DAGE RM10 ....310 F4
Durban La LAIN SS15 ....277 J3
Durban Rd GNTH/NBYPK IG2 ....287 H8
  SRTFD E15 ....306 F3
  WALTH E17 ....266 C7
The Durdans VGE SS16 ....294 E1
Durell Gdns DAGW RM9 ....310 A2
Durell Rd DAGW RM9 ....310 A2
Durham Av GPK RM2 ....289 M2
  WFD IG8 ....268 A4
Durham Cl BRTR CM7 ....76 D4
  SBW CM21 ....162 D8
  WARE SG12 ....185 J4
Durham Ri WOOL/PLUM SE18 ....324 F8
Durham Rd CAN/RD E16 ....307 H8
  DAGE RM10 ....310 A2
  LAIN SS15 ....276 C8
  MNPK E12 ....308 A1
  RCFD SS4 ....264 E8
  SOSN SS2 ....302 A3
Durham Wy WCHPL E1 ....322 A1
Durham Sq COL CO1 ....8 B6
Durham Sr RAYL SS6 ....263 C8
Durley Av WICKW SS12 ....260 C5
Durley Rd SBF/HAD SS7 ....298 B1
Durnell Wy LOU IG10 ....250 D2
Durrants Cl RAIN RM13 ....311 M6
Durrant Wy SWCM DA10 ....336 E5
Durrington Ct VGE SS16 ....3 J7
Durrington Rd CLPT E5 ....306 B1
Dury Falls Cl EMPK RM11 ....290 C6
Dutch St HSTD CO9 * 346 A12
Duxford WICKE SS11 ....261 K7
Duxford Cl HCH RM12 ....311 L3
Duxford Rd CBS CB2 ....22 A4
  SAFWN CB10 ....340 C4
Dye House La BOW E3 ....306 D5
Dyers Hall Rd WAN E11 ....285 D5
Dyer's Rd COLW CO3 ....127 M2
  HSTD CO9 ....345 K12
  MAL CM9 ....214 D3
Dyers Wy HARH RM3 ....271 K6
Dyke Crs CVI SS8 ....320 A1
Dykes Cha MAL CM9 ....214 B2
Dykes St IP IP1 ....16 E2
Dylan Rd BELV DA17 ....326 D6
Dymchurch Cl CLAY IG5 ....286 D1
Dymoke Rd ROM RM1 ....289 J3
Dymokes Wy HOD EN11 ....185 J1
Dyne's Hall Rd HSTD CO9 ....345 K9
Dynevor Gdns LOS SS9 ....299 L4
Dyson Rd FSTGT E7 ....307 J3
  WAN E11 ....285 H4
Dysons Cl CHES/WCR EN8 ....232 C2
Dytchleys Rd BRW CM14 ....254 C4

E

Eagle Av CHDH RM6 ....288 B4
Eagle Cl HCH RM12 ....311 L4
  WAB EN9 ....234 B4
Eaglegate COL CO1 * 8 B3
Eagle Ct BRTR CM7 ....99 J8
  BRWN CM15 ....383 M11
  WAN E11 ....284 F2
Eagles FX IP11 ....11 K1
Eagles Rd GRH EA3 ....335 L6
Eagle St IPNE IP4 ....17 C5
Eagle Ter WFD IG8 ....268 D4
Eagle Wy GVW DA11 ....336 D3
  KESG IP5 ....50 F5
  RBRW/HUT CM13 ....273 M5
  SBN/FI SS3 ....303 H5
Ealing Rd BOW E3 ....306 E2
Eardley Rd BELV DA17 ....326 D6
Earlham Gv FSTGT E7 ....307 J2
Earlhams Cl HAR CO12 ....70 E3
Earl Mountbatten Dr
  BCAYW CM12 ....258 C2
Earl Ri WOOL/PLUM SE18 ....325 C8
Earl Rd GVW DA11 ....337 H4
Earls Cl BSF CM23 ....138 C3
  FX IP11 ....63 J7
Earls Colne Rd RCOLW CO6 ....103 J3
Earlsfield Dr CHLM/GWD CM2 ....210 C2
Earls Hall Av SOSN SS2 ....301 H1
Earls Hall Rd RCOS CO16 ....301 J1
Earls Hall Pde SOSN SS2 ....301 H1
Earlsmead WIT CM8 ....171 M1
Earl's Pth LOU IG10 ....249 M3
Earls Wk BCTR RM8 ....309 J1
Earlswood SBF/HAD SS7 ....298 A1
Earlswood Gdns CLAY IG5 ....286 D1
Earlswood St GNWCH SE10 ....323 H6
Earlswood Wy COLS CO2 ....160 B7
Easdale Dr HCH RM12 ....311 L3
Easdale Dr HCH RM12 ....311 L3
Easington Wy RAIN RM15 ....329 K1
East Arbour St WCHPL E1 ....322 A1
East Av MNPK E12 ....308 B4
  WALTH E17 ....284 E2

CHLM/WR CM1 ....208 C4
RCOLE CO7 * 363 N11
East View Cl SAFWN CB10 ....352 C2
Eastview Dr RAYL SS6 ....263 C8
East Wk BSDN SS14 ....13 G5
  HLW CM20 ....13 C5
East Ward Ms COL CO1 ....8 C4
East Wy WAB EN9 ....233 L6
Eastway HLW CM20 ....306 D5
  WAN E11 ....285 L3
  WIT CM8 ....171 K2
Eastwick Hall La HLW CM20 ....187 H5
Eastwick Rd HLW CM20 ....187 H5
  WARE SG12 ....186 C6
Eastwood Back La
  SBF/HAD SS7 ....281 K6
Eastwood Bvd WOS/PRIT SS0 ....300 D3
Eastwoodbury Cl SOSN SS2 ....283 C7
Eastwoodbury La SOSN SS2 ....283 C7
Eastwood Cl SWFD E18 ....267 K8
  RAIN RM13 ....327 L2
Eastwood La South
  WOS/PRIT SS0 ....300 E3
Eastwood Old Rd LOS SS9 ....281 M8
Eastwood Park Dr LOS SS9 ....282 F8
Eastwood Ri LOS SS9 ....281 M7
Eastwood Rd GDMY/SEVK IG3 ....287 K5
  LOS SS9 ....300 A2
  RAYL SS6 ....281 J5
  SWFD E18 ....267 K8
Eastwood Rd North LOS SS9 ....300 B1
Eatington Rd LEY E10 ....285 C3
Eaton Dr CRW RM5 ....270 E6
Eaton Gdns DAGW RM9 ....310 B4
  RAIN RM13 ....311 H1
Eaton Ms COLS CO2 ....129 J2
Eaton Rd IL WAN E11 ....285 M3
Eaton Rd LOS SS9 ....299 M3
  UPMR RM14 ....291 H7
Eatons Md CHING E4 ....266 D7
Eaton Ter BOW E3 * 306 B7
Eaton Wy MAL CM9 ....173 G6
Ebenezer Cl WIT CM8 ....147 M8
Ebony Cl COLS CO2 ....129 C5
Eccles Rd CHTY IP2 ....53 J3
Eccleston Gdns CHDH RM6 ....287 L5
Eccleston Gdns BCAYW CM12 ....240 D8
Echo Ct GVE DA12 ....337 M7
Echo Hts CHING E4 * 248 E8
Eckersley Rd CHLM/WR CM1 ....193 L2
Eclipse Rd PLSTW E13 ....323 L1
Eddy Cl ROMW/RG RM7 ....288 C2
Edenbridge Rd HOM E9 * 306 A4
  WIT CM8 ....171 M1
Eden Cl PEND EN3 ....233 H1
  WIT CM8 ....171 M1
Eden Gn SOCK/AV RM15 ....329 L1
Edenhall Rd HARH RM3 ....271 M4
Eden Pl GVE DA12 ....337 J5
Eden Rd HVIL CB9 ....34 B5
  IPNE IP4 ....49 C8
  WALTH E17 ....284 E3
Edens Cl BSF CM23 ....139 J2
Edenside FOS CO13 ....137 J2
Edenvale CHESW EN7 ....216 C7
Edgar Rd BOW E3 ....306 E7
Edgecotts VGE SS16 ....3 J4
Edgefield Av BARK IG11 ....309 J4
  MGTR CO11 ....90 E2
Edgehill Gdns DAGE RM10 ....310 D1
Edgeworth Rd CHTY IP2 ....53 K3
Edgware Rd RCOS CO16 ....180 G3
Edinburgh Av SUD CO10 ....20 D5
Edies La RCOLW CO6 ....360 H4
Edinburgh Cl CBS CB2 ....22 C1
  LOS SS9 ....299 C3
  SLH/COR SS17 ....317 J1
Edinburgh Cl RAYL SS6 ....262 E8
  WIT CM8 ....171 K5
Edinburgh Crs
  CHES/WCR EN8 ....232 F1
Edinburgh Gdns BRTR CM7 ....121 L1
Edinburgh Pl TIL RM18 ....331 L8
Edinburgh Pl HLW CM20 ....188 B5
Edinburgh Rd PLSTW E13 ....307 L2
  WALTH E17 ....284 D3
Edinburgh's Dr
  ROMW/RG RM7 ....288 C2
Edinburgh Wy HLW CM20 ....13 G1
  PIT SS13 ....278 E7
Edison Av HCH RM12 ....325 L6
  HCH RM12 ....289 J6
Edison Cl BRTR CM7 ....121 J4
  HCH RM12 ....289 J6
Edison Rd COLN CO4 ....108 A6
Edison Rd COLN CO4 ....160 B3
  PEND EN3 ....248 C2
Edith Cavell Wy HVIL CB9 ....344 A7
Edith Cl CVI SS8 ....320 E1
Edith Rd CHDH RM6 ....288 A5
  COS CO15 ....6 F8
  CVI SS8 ....320 E1
  EHAM E6 ....308 A4
  FOS CO13 ....137 C1
  SOSN SS2 ....302 A3
  SRTFD E15 ....307 C2
  WALTH E17 ....283 L4
Edith Wy SLH/COR SS17 ....295 K8
Edison Cl WALTH E17 ....284 D3
Edmeston Cl HOM E9 ....306 B3
Edmonton Cl KESG IP5 ....49 M6
Edmonton Rd KESG IP5 ....49 M6
Edmund Cl HVIL CB9 ....34 C4
Edmund Gn HSTD CO9 ....80 B7
Edmund Halley Wy
  GNWCH SE10 ....323 H5
Edmund Hurst Dr EHAM E6 ....324 E1
Edmund Rd CDW/CHF RM16 ....311 H7
  RAIN RM13 ....311 H7
  WIT CM8 ....171 H5
Edridge Cl HCH RM12 ....312 A2
Edward Av CHING E4 ....266 E3
  RCOS CO16 ....156 C6
Edward Bright Cl MAL CM9 ....214 D3
Edward Cl CHLM/GWD CM2 ....240 C8
  CDW/CHF RM16 ....330 A1
  GPK RM2 ....289 M7
Edward Dr CHLM/GWD CM2 ....209 M6
Edward Gdns WICKE SS11 ....47 L3
Edward Mann Cl East
  WCHPL E1 ....322 A1
Edward Mann Cl West
  WCHPL E1 ....322 A1
Edward Marke Dr
  K/T/MI CO5 ....153 L2
Edward Rd CHDH RM6 ....288 B4
  RCOS CO16 ....135 J3
  WALTH E17 ....266 E5
Edwards Cl RBRW/HUT CM13 ....257 H7
Edwards Rd BELV DA17 ....326 D2
Edward St CAN/RD E16 ....307 H4

HAR CO12 ...66 D8
Edwards Wy RBRW/HUT CM15 ...257 H2
Edward Temme Av SRTFD E15 ...307 J4
Edwina Gdns REDBR IG4 ...286 D2
Edwin Av EHAM E6 ...308 D6
Edwin Cl RAIN RM13 ...311 J7
Edwin Hall Wy RCHLM CM3 ...244 A4
Edwin's Hall Rd RCHLM CM3 ...244 F2
Edwin's Md HOM E9 ...306 F1
Edwin St CAN/RD E16 ...323 K1
GVE DA12 ...337 K5
Egbert Crs COLN
Egbert Gdns WICKE SS11 ...261 G4
Egerton Dr VGE SS16 ...276 D3
Egerton Gdns GDMY/SEVK IG3 ...287 J8
Egerton Green Rd COLS CO2 ...128 D2
Egg Hall EPP CM16 ...220 B7
Egglestone Cl CHTY IP2 ...53 L4
Eggshell La HSTD CO9 ...344 D10
Eglantine Wy RCOLW CO6 ...360 G4
Eglington Rd CHING E4 ...249 K6
Eglinton Dr CHLM/GWD CM2 ...210 A4
Eglinton Rd SWCM DA10 ...336 F4
Egremont St COL CO10 ...39 L2
Egremont Wy COLW CO3 ...127 M1
Egret Crs COLN ...108 C5
Eider Cl FSTGT E7 ...307 J2
Eight Acre La COLS CO2 ...128 E3
Eighth Av MNPK E12 ...308 C1
Eisenhower Rd EHAM E6 ...324 B1
Eisenhower Rd LAIN SS15 ...276 B1
Elan Rd SOCK/AV RM15 ...329 K1
Elbow La HERT/BAY SG13 ...184 C8
Elbury Dr CAN/RD E16 ...323 L4
Eldbert Cl SOSN SS2 ...302 B3
Eldeland LAIN SS15 ...2
Elder Av WICKW SS12 ...260 F7
Elderberry Cl CHESW EN7 ...216 B6
Elderberry Cl VGE SS16 ...276 E8
WFD IG8 ...268 G6
Elderberry Gdns WIT CM8 ...171 J4
Elder Cl CBS CB2 ...22 A1
Elderfield HLWE CM17 ...188 E5
Elderfield Wk CLPT E5 ...306 A1
Elderflower Wy SRTFD E15 ...307 H4
Elderstep Av CVI SS8 ...321 H2
Elderton Rd WOS/PRIT SS0 ...18 A4
Elder Wy RAIN RM13 ...312 A1
WICKW SS12 ...260 F7
Eld La COL CO1 ...8 C7
Eldon Cl COLN CO4 ...108 A4
Eldon Rd HOD EN11 ...201 L5
WALTH E17 ...284 C1
Eldon Wy HOC/HUL SS5 ...264 A7
Eldred Av CVI SS8 ...128 G2
Eldred Dr SUD CO10 ...45 M5
Eleanor Cha WICKW SS12 ...260 H5
Eleanor Cl K/T/MI CO5 ...150 A7
Eleanor Cross Rd CHES EN8 ...232 A4
Eleanor Gdns BCTR RM8 ...288 C7
Eleanor Rd CHES/WCR EN8 ...232 A7
SRTFD E15 ...307 J3
Eleanor St BOW E3 ...306 D7
Eleanor Wy BRW CM14 ...256 A6
CHES/WCR EN8 ...233 G4
Electric Av HERT/BAY SG13 ...233 G6
WOS/PRIT SS0 ...300 F3
Eleven Acre Ri LOU IG10 ...250 C9
Eleventh Av STSD CM24 ...374 C11
Eley Rd UED N18 ...266 A4
Elgar Cl BKHH IG9 ...268 A1
LAIN SS15 ...277 G5
PLSTW E13 ...307 M6
SBF/HAD SS7 ...279 G5
Elgar Dr WIT CM8 ...171 J3
Elgar Gdns TIL RM18 ...331 K7
Elgin Av CHLM/WR CM1 ...4 E3
HARH RM3 ...272 A4
Elgin Rd BROX EN10 ...217 G2
CHES/WCR EN8 ...216 D8
GDMY/SEVK IG3 ...287 H6
Elham Dr PIT SS13 ...278 D7
Elianore Rd COLW CO3 ...106 C6
Elim Wy PLSTW E13 ...307 J7
Eliot Cl DAGW RM9 ...310 A4
DART DA1 ...334 E7
Eliot Wy MAL CM9 ...214 D4
Elizabeth Av IL IG1 ...287 G7
RAYL SS6 ...280 F5
WIT CM8 ...171 K6
Elizabeth Cl COLN CO4 ...107 M1
HOC/HUL SS5 ...282 B1
ROMW/RG RM7 ...270 E1
SAFWN CB10 ...28 C7
TIL RM18 ...331 L8
WAB EN9 ...201 L8
Elizabeth Dr EPP CM16 ...235 M6
Elizabeth Rd BRWN CM15 ...255 G6
BSF CM23 ...138 E4
CDW/CHF RM16 ...330 C2
EHAM E6 ...308 A5
HAR CO12 ...14 D9
RAIN RM13 ...327 L1
Elizabeth Sq POP/IOD E14 ...322 B2
Elizabeth St GRH DA9 ...335 H7
Elizabeth Vls MAL CM9 * ...174 D3
Elizabeth Wy FX IP11 ...10 D4
HLWW/ROY CM19 ...12 A4
HSTD CO9 ...81 H3
LAIN SS15 ...277 G8
MAL CM9 ...214 D8
RCHLM CM3 ...196 D7
RCOLE CO7 ...130 F2
RCOLE CO7 ...156 C7
SAFWN CB10 ...341 M4
SBF/HAD SS7 ...298 F1
SUD CO10 ...44 D8
Elkington Rd PLSTW E13 ...307 L8
The Elkins ROM RM1 ...271 H4
Ellenborough Cl BSF CM23 ...138 E4
Ellenbrook Cl LOS SS9 ...300 B2
Ellenbrook Rd CHTY IP2 ...53 L4
Ellen Wy BRTR CM77 ...120 F6
Ellerman Rd TIL RM18 ...331 L8
Ellerton Gdns DAGW RM9 ...309 M4
Ellerton Rd WAN E11 ...285 J3
Ellesmere Cl WAN E11 ...285 J3
Ellesmere Gdns REDBR IG4 ...286 A3
Ellesmere Rd BOW E3 ...306 B6
CVI SS8 ...320 B2
Ellesmere St POP/IOD E14 ...322 E2
Ellingham Rd WAN E11 ...304 F1
Ellie Cl SLH/COR SS17 ...316 F3
Ellington Rd RCHLM CM3 ...245 J7
Elliot Cl RCHLM CM3 ...245 J7
SRTFD E15 ...307 H4
WFD IG8 ...268 A5
Elliot Ms SOSN SS2 ...301 L2
Elliots Dr WOTN CO14 ...137 L1

Elliott Gdns HARH RM3 ...271 L7
Elliott St GVE DA12 ...338 A5
IP IP1 ...16
Elliotts Yd SUD CO10 * ...20 B8
Ellis Av RAIN RM13 ...327 K1
Ellis Cl CDW/CHF RM16 ...316 A5
Elliscombe Rd CHARL SE7 ...323 M8
Ellis Rd COLN CO4 ...87 J1
COS CO15 ...6
MGTR CO11 * ...366 A9
Ellistons Yd SUD CO10 * ...44 B8
Elmore Ln HARH RM3 ...271 L7
Elm Av MAL CM9 ...198 A8
UPMR RM14 ...290 F8
Elm Bank Pl SLH/COR SS17 * ...316 D3
Elmbourne Dr BELV DA17 ...326 E1
Elmbridge HLWE CM17 ...189 H5
Elmbridge Rd BARK/HLT IG6 ...269 K5
Elmbrook Dr BSF CM23 ...138 F6
Elm Bungalows BRTR CM77 * ...121 L5
Elm Cl BKHH IG9 ...268 A1
CHLM/GWD CM2 ...210 B3
EPP CM16 ...219 J2
HSTD CO9 ...356 C11
HVHL CB9 ...34 C5
K/T/MI CO5 ...149 M6
MGTR CO11 ...65 J3
RAYL SS6 ...281 G2
RBSF CM22 ...374 D3
RBSF CM22 ...377 K2
RCOLE CO7 ...131 L5
ROMW/RG RM7 ...270 F7
SBN/FI SS3 ...303 H6
WAB EN9 ...233 L4
WAN E11 ...285 L4
Elm Ct HVHL CB9 ...35 H8
SAFWN CB11 ...350 A1
Elm Crs COLN CO4 ...9
Elmcroft RCOLE CO7 ...109 J7
Elmcroft Av WAN E11 ...285 L3
Elmcroft La FX IP11 ...63 H6
Elmcroft Rd IP IP1 ...47 M3
Elmdale Dr MGTR CO11 ...91 C1
Elmden Ct COLN CO4 ...9
Elmdene Av EMPK RM11 ...290 C1
Elmdene Rd WOOL/PLUM SE18 ...324 D8
Elmdon Rd SOCK/AV RM15 ...329 K1
Elm Dr CHES/WCR EN8 ...216 F6
HAR CO12 ...14 E1
HSTD CO9 ...81 J4
RAYL SS6 ...281 G2
RCOLE CO7 ...156 A6
Elmer Ap SOS SS1 ...19 G5
Elmer Av ABRCST RM4 ...271 H2
SOS SS1 ...19 G5
Elmer Cl RAIN RM13 ...311 K4
Elmer Gdns RAIN RM13 ...311 K4
Elmers La KESC IP5 ...50
Elmfield Cl COS CO15 ...160 B2
GVW DA11 ...337 G6
Elmfield Rd CHING E4 ...266 F1
WALTH E17 ...284 C1
Elm Gdns EPP CM16 ...221 J4
Elmgreen Cl SRTFD E15 ...307 H6
Elm Green La RCHLM CM3 ...211 M5
Elm Gv BSF CM23 ...139 J2
COS CO15 ...159 H7
COS CO15 ...182 B5
EMPK RM11 ...290 B4
FOS CO13 ...136 F3
HOC/HUL SS5 ...263 J8
RCOLE CO7 ...130 E4
RCOLW CO6 ...361 G8
SAFWN CB10 ...28 C7
SOS SS1 ...302 D5
Elm Hall Gdns WAN E11 ...285 L4
Elmham Dr KIR/NAC IP7 ...56 A5
Elmhurst Cl BSF CM23 ...138 F2
Elmhurst Cl HVHL CB9 ...34 E6
Elmhurst Dr EMPK RM11 ...289 M9
IPSE IP3 ...17 M9
SWFD E18 ...267 K8
Elmhurst Rd FSTGT E7 ...307 L4
HAR CO12 ...15 L4
PEND EN3 ...232 D7
Elmhurst Wy LOU IG10 ...250 D7
Elm La K/T/MI CO5 ...125 K4
RIPS/CAP IP9 ...58 A5
RIPW IP8 ...52 B5
Elmley Cl WOOL/PLUM SE18 ...325 H5
Elmore Rd PEND EN3 ...248 A1
WAN E11 ...284 E4
Elmores LOU IG10 ...250 D3
Elm Park Av HCH RM12 ...311 L1
Elm Park Rd LEY E10 ...284 D6
Elm Ri WIT CM8 ...147 J6
Elm Rd BSF CM23 ...138 F1
CHLM/GWD CM2 ...4 B6
CVI SS8 ...320 D3
FSTGT E7 ...307 J3
GRAYS RM17 ...330 A3
GRH DA9 ...335 H8
GVE DA12 ...337 M3
KESC IP5 ...49 L4
LOS SS9 ...300 C2
PIT SS13 ...279 H4
RCHLM CM3 ...244 F5
RCOLE CO7 ...363 Q6
RCOS CO16 ...158 F2
ROMW/RG RM7 ...270 D3
SBF/HAD SS7 ...299 G5
SBN/FI SS3 ...303 M3
SOCK/AV RM15 ...329 K1
SUD CO10 ...21 G7
WALTH E17 ...284 D1
WAN E11 ...285 G1
WICKE SS11 ...261 L5
Elms Cl CBS CB2 ...22
Elmsdale Rd WALTH E17 ...284 C2
Elms Dr CHLM/WR CM1 ...209 K1
Elms Farm Rd HCH RM12 ...311 M2
Elms Gdns DAGW RM9 ...310 C1
Elms Hall Rd RCOLW CO6 ...82 B5
Elmsleigh Dr LOS SS9 ...300 B3
Elms Rd HVHL CB9 ...34 E6
Elmslie Cl WFD IG8 ...268 A5
Elms St WFD IG8 ...268 A5
Elmstead Cl SLH/COR SS17 ...295 H4
Elmstead Rd COLN CO4 ...9 M7
GDMY/SEVK IG3 ...287 H7
The Elms CHONG CM5 ...382 H4
FOS CO13 ...137 G2
HERT/BAY SG13 ...184 B3
LOU IG10 ...249 L2
SAFWN CB10 ...341 M4
Elm St IP IP1 ...16
Elm Ter MGTR CO11 * ...91 C1
WTHK RM20 ...335 L1
Elmtree Av BRWN CM15 ...255 H3
Elm Tree Av FOS CO13 ...137 J3
Elm Tree Cl RCOLW CO6 * ...360 G4
Elmtree Rd VGE SS16 ...296 C1
Elm View Rd SBF/HAD SS7 ...297 M2
Elm Vls RCOS CO16 * ...135 K3

Elm Wk BRTR CM77 ...120 C3
GPK RM2 ...289 K1
Elm Wy BRW CM14 ...273 K3
RCHLM CM3 ...195 H4
Elmway CDW/CHF RM16 ...314 F1
Elmwood SBW CM21 ...163 G8
Elmwood Av COLS CO2 ...128 G3
HOC/HUL SS5 ...262 F2
Elmwood Dr K/T/MI CO5 ...178 A7
Elm Wych COLS CO2 ...128 F1
Elounda St CBF/HAD SS7 ...298 A7
Elphinstone Rd WALTH E17 ...266 D8
Elrington Rd WFD IG8 ...267 K4
Elronds Rest RCHLM CM3 ...244 F5
Elsa St WCHPL E1 ...322 B1
Elsden Cha BOC CM0 ...393 H4
Elsenham Ct RAYL SS6 ...280 E2
Elsenham Crs BSDN SS14 ...278 C7
Elsenham Ms BSDN SS14 ...278 C7
Elsham Rd WAN E11 ...285 H8
Elsinge Rd EN EN1 ...232 C6
Elsinor Av CVI SS8 ...298 D7
Elsmere Rd IP IP1 ...48 B5
Elstow Gdns DAGW RM9 ...310 B5
Elstow Rd DAGW RM9 ...310 B4
Elstree Gdns BELV DA17 ...326 A1
IL IG1 ...308 F2
Elthorne Pk RCOS CO16 ...6 C3
Eltisley Rd IL IG1 ...308 E1
Elton Pk CHTY IP2 ...47 J7
Elvaston Rd LAIN SS15 ...277 C5
Elvet Av EMPK RM11 ...289 M2
Elwes Cl COLN CO4 ...9 L2
Elwick Rd SOCK/AV RM15 ...329 K1
Elwin Rd K/T/MI CO5 ...150 A8
Elwood HLWE CM17 ...204 F2
Ely Cl BOC CM0 ...393 N1
RAYL SS6 ...280 F1
Ely Gdns DAGE RM10 ...288 F8
Ely Pl WFD IG8 ...268 D4
Elyd Rd IPNE IP4 ...48 E4
LEY E10 ...284 F4
SOSN SS2 ...19 K1
Elysian Gdns MAL CM9 ...385 M4
Ely Wy RAYL SS6 ...280 F1
Emanuel Dr VGE SS16 ...294 E1
Emberson Ct CHLM/GWD CM2 ...210 C1
Emberson Vw EPP CM16 ...221 J3
Emblems GTDUN CM6 ...116 F3
Emerald Cl CAN/RD E16 ...324 B2
KESC IP5 ...50 B6
Emerald Gdns BCTR RM8 ...288 D5
Emerson Dr EMPK RM11 ...290 A5
Emerson Rd IL IG1 ...286 D5
Emily St CAN/RD E16 ...323 J2
Emlen St IP IP1 ...16 B4
Emmanuel Cl CHTY IP2 ...53 L4
Emma Rd PLSTW E13 ...307 J6
Emma's Crs WARE SG12 ...185 J5
Emmaus Wy CHIG IG7 ...268 D4
Emmett Av BARK/HLT IG6 ...286 F3
Emmott Cl WCHPL E1 ...306 B8
Empire Rd K/T/MI CO5 ...178 A7
Empire Wharf Rd POP/IOD E14 ...323 G7
Empress Av CHING E4 ...266 E6
IL IG1 ...286 E4
K/T/MI CO5 ...178 A6
MNPK E12 ...285 M7
WFD IG8 ...267 J6
Empress Dr K/T/MI CO5 ...178 A7
Empress Pde CHING E4 * ...266 C6
Empress Rd GVE DA12 ...338 A5
Emsom St BOW E3 ...306 E8
Emson Cl CBE/LIN CB11 ...25 C7
Emsworth Rd BARK/HLT IG6 ...268 E8
Enborne Gn SOCK/AV RM15 ...329 K1
Endean Ct RCOLE CO7 ...130 D3
Endeavour Cl MAL CM9 ...385 N4
Endeavour Dr BSDN SS14 ...277 L4
Endeavour Rd CHES/WCR EN8 ...216 F5
Endeavour St GNWCH SE10 ...323 H6
Enderby St GNWCH SE10 ...323 K6
Enderley Rd WIT CM4 ...171 K1
Endsleigh Ct COLW CO3 ...106 F6
Endsleigh Gdns IL IG1 ...286 C5
Endway SBF/HAD SS7 ...299 H3
The Endway GTDUN CM6 ...94 C2
HVHL CB9 ...344 B5
RCHLM CM3 ...392 A1
Enfield Rd WICKE SS11 ...261 M6
Engayne Gdns UPMR RM14 ...290 F8
Englands La LOU IG10 ...250 D3
Englefield Cl HOC/HUL SS5 ...282 D1
Englefields BOC CM0 ...390 D6
Engleric ROY SG8 ...349 Q7
English St BOW E3 ...306 C8
Enid Wy COLN CO4 ...107 G3
Ennerdale Av CHING E4 ...266 C6
Ennismore Cl SOSN SS2 ...301 K2
Ensign N LOS SS9 ...300 C2
Enstone Rd PEND EN3 ...248 B3
Enterprise Ct BRTR CM77 ...121 J2
WIT CM8 ...171 K1
Enterprise Rd WICKW SS12 ...261 H4
Enterprize Wy DEPT SE8 ...322 C7
Enville Wy COLN CO4 ...107 L1
Epping Cl CHLM/WR CM1 ...4 B6
COS CO15 ...159 J5
LOS SS9 ...282 C6
POP/IOD E14 ...322 D7
ROMW/RG RM7 ...288 E1
Epping Gld CHING E4 ...248 G6
Epping La ABR/ST RM4 ...251 J2
Epping New Rd BKHH IG9 ...249 L8
LOU IG10 ...234 A10
Epping Rd CHONG CM5 ...380 A10
EPP CM16 ...219 L8
EPP CM16 ...220 B6
HLWW/ROY CM19 ...202 C3
LOU IG10 ...235 G5
Epping Wy CHING E4 ...248 G6
WIT CM8 ...171 H5
Epsom Cl RCOS CO16 ...158 F2
Epsom Dr IP IP1 ...48 C5
Epsom Rd GDMY/SEVK IG3 ...287 J4
LEY E10 ...284 A5
Epsom Wy HCH RM12 ...312 A1
Epstein Rd THMD SE28 ...325 J1
Erbury Rd SUD CO10 ...20 E5
Erebus Dr WOOL/PLUM SE18 ...324 C7
Erica Wk COLN CO4 ...9 L2
Eric Clarke La BARK IG11 ...308 E8
Eric Est BOW E3 ...306 D8
Erick Av CHLM/WR CM1 ...193 M3
Erica Rd CHDH RM6 ...288 A3
Erith Cl PUR RM19 ...328 D7

Erith Crs CRW RM5 ...270 F7
Erith High St ERITH DA8 ...327 H8
Erith Rd BELV DA17 ...326 F5
Erle Havard Rd RCOLW CO6 ...106 B1
Ermine Cl CHESW EN7 ...216 E3
Ernald Av EHAM E6 ...308 B6
Ernan Cl SOCK/AV RM15 ...329 K1
Ernan Rd SOCK/AV RM15 ...329 K1
Ernest Rd EMPK RM11 ...290 D4
RCOLE CO7 ...130 F4
Ernest St WCHPL E1 ...306 F4
Ernleigh Rd IPNE IP4 ...49 J5
Erriff Dr SOCK/AV RM15 ...329 K1
Errington Cl CDW/CHF RM16 ...331 G2
Errington Rd COLW CO3 ...107 G8
Erroll Rd ROM RM1 ...289 J2
Erskine Pl WICKW SS12 ...261 G1
Erskine Rd MGTR CO11 ...91 C1
WALTH E17 ...284 C2
Erwarton Wk RIPS/CAP IP9 ...58 A6
Erwood Rd CHARL SE7 ...324 B8
Escreet Gv WOOL/PLUM SE18 ...324 D7
Esdaile Gdns UPMR RM14 ...290 F8
Esdaile La HOD EN11 ...201 H4
Esher Av ROMW/RG RM7 ...288 F4
Esher Rd CHLM/WR CM1 ...4 E6
Eskley Gdns SOCK/AV RM15 ...329 K1
Esk Rd PLSTW E13 ...307 L8
Esk Wy ROM RM1 ...271 H6
Esmond Cl RAIN RM13 ...311 L6
Esplanade Cl CHLM/WR CM1 ...4 B2
Esplanade Gdns WOS/PRIT SS0 ...300 E5
The Esplanade COS CO15 ...160 D3
HOC/HUL SS5 ...262 F2
RCHLM CM3 ...388 D6
Essenden Rd BELV DA17 ...326 D8
Essex Av CHLM/WR CM1 ...193 K6
COS CO15 ...182 B5
SUD CO10 ...20 D5
Essex Cl CVI SS8 ...320 D3
LAIN SS15 ...276 E2
RAYL SS6 ...280 F5
ROMW/RG RM7 ...288 E2
WALTH E17 ...284 C2
Essex Gdns EMPK RM11 ...290 D4
LOS SS9 ...300 D3
SLH/COR SS17 ...332 D1
Essex Hall Rd COL CO1 ...8 A2
Essex HI SAFWN CB11 ...350 A1
Essex Regiment Wy RCHLM CM3 ...167 K3
RCHLM CM3 ...196 A1
Essex Rd BARK IG11 ...309 G6
BOC CM0 ...393 M8
BRTR CM7 ...121 L1
CHDH RM6 ...288 A6
CHING E4 ...249 H8
CVI SS8 ...320 C1
DAGE RM10 ...310 F2
DART DA1 ...334 A8
GVW DA11 ...337 K6
HOD EN11 ...201 J2
MAL CM9 ...214 C4
MNPK E12 ...308 B2
ROMW/RG RM7 ...288 E2
SWFD E18 ...267 J8
WALTH E17 ...284 B4
WTHK RM20 ...335 M1
Essex Rd South LEY E10 ...285 G5
Essex St FSTGT E7 ...307 K2
SOSN SS2 ...19 H4
Essex Wy BRTR CM77 ...122 D8
CHLM/WR CM1 ...165 G4
CHONG CM5 ...206 B2
CHONG CM5 ...382 A3
COLN CO4 ...361 Q12
EMPK RM11 ...290 D4
HAR CO12 ...70 A5
HAR CO12 ...367 P7
IPSE IP3 ...55 K4
MGTR CO11 ...90 C1
RBRW/HUT CM13 ...273 M5
RCHLM CM3 ...165 L2
RCOLW CO6 ...103 L6
SBN/FI SS3 ...303 L6
WTHK RM20 ...335 M1
Essex Whf CLPT E5 * ...284 A7
Essex Yeomanry Wy COLW CO3 ...105 L6
Essian St WCHPL E1 ...322 E1
Estate Rd SBF/HAD SS7 ...299 J2
Estate Wy LEY E10 ...284 C6
The Estate Yd RCHLM CM3 ...196 H4
Estella Md CHLM/WR CM1 ...193 M3
Estfeld Cl HOD EN11 * ...185 J3
Esther Rd WAN E11 ...285 H5
Estuary Cl BARK IG11 ...309 L7
COLN CO4 ...107 J3
Estuary Ct MAL CM9 * ...385 N3
Estuary Crs COS CO15 ...67 G5
RIPS/CAP IP9 ...67 G5
Estuary Dr FX IP11 ...11 J4
Estuary Gdns SBN/FI SS3 ...303 M3
Estuary Ms MAL CM9 ...385 M4
Estuary Park Rd K/T/MI CO5 ...178 B7
Estuary Rd RIPS/CAP IP9 ...67 G5
Etchingham Rd SRTFD E15 ...306 F1
Ethelbert Gdns GNTH/NBYPK IG2 ...286 C3
Ethelburga Rd HARH RM3 ...272 C7
Etheldore Av HOC/HUL SS5 ...264 C2
Ethelred Gdns WICKE SS11 ...261 H4
Ethel Rd CAN/RD E16 ...323 L3
RAYL SS6 ...281 G2
Etheridge Rd LOU IG10 ...250 F3
Etloe Rd LEY E10 ...284 D7
Eton Cl CVI SS8 ...298 C5
Eton Ct COS CO15 ...7 G4
FOS CO13 ...137 K4
IL IG1 ...308 F3
Eton Wk SBN/FI SS3 ...303 H4
Etton Cl HCH RM12 ...290 F2
Ettrick St POP/IOD E14 ...322 F2
Euclid Wy WTHK RM20 ...335 J1
Eudo Rd COLS CO2 ...128 C5
Eugene Cl GPK RM2 ...289 M2
Europa Pk WTHK RM20 ...335 M1
Europa Wy HAR CO12 ...47 J5
Europe Rd WOOL/PLUM SE18 ...324 D7
Eustace Pl WOOL/PLUM SE18 ...324 C7
Eustace Rd CHDH RM6 ...288 A7
EHAM E6 ...308 B2
Euston Av IPNE IP4 ...49 L1
Euston Ct FX IP11 ...10 D2
Evabrook Cl CHTY IP2 ...53 L4
Evandale Rd RAIN RM13 ...311 J3
Evans Cl GRH DA9 ...335 K7
Evanston Av CHING E4 ...266 C7
Evanston Gdns REDBR IG4 ...286 A4
Evans Wy CBS CB2 ...22 A1
Evelyn Denington Rd EHAM E6 ...308 B8
Evelyn Pl CHLM/WR CM1 * ...4 D2
Evelyn Rd CAN/RD E16 ...323 K4
HOC/HUL SS5 ...264 B8
RCHLM CM3 ...144 A1

WALTH E17 ...284 F2
Evelyn Sharp Cl GPK RM2 * ...290 A1
Evelyn St DEPT SE8 ...322 B8
Evelyn Ter MAL CM9 * ...199 J8
Evelyn Wood Rd BRTR CM77 ...122 B8
Everard Rd BSDN SS14 ...278 C5
Everest RAYL SS6 ...263 G8
Everest Cl GVW DA11 ...337 H5
Everest Gdns BSF CM23 ...138 A5
Everest Ri POP/IOD E14 ...322 F1
Everest Wy HAR CO12 ...14 E4
Everest Wy MAL CM9 ...198 G8
Evergreen Ct WICKW SS12 * ...260 F7
Evergreen Dr COLN CO4 ...108 A1
The Evergreens SBN/FI SS3 * ...396 H11
Everitt Rd SAFWN CB10 ...28 C7
Everitt Wy HSTD CO9 ...356 F7
Eve Rd WAN E11 ...307 H1
Eversleigh Gdns UPMR RM14 ...291 G6
Eversley Cl EHAM E6 ...308 A5
Eversley Cl LOU IG10 ...250 F5
Eversley Rd PIT SS13 ...279 G8
SBF/HAD SS7 ...279 M6
Everton Crs IP IP1 ...47 L4
Eves Cnr RCHLM CM3 ...212 B6
Eves Cl HAR CO12 ...70 C4
Evesham Cl CHLM/WR CM1 ...193 K6
Evesham Rd WALTH E17 ...266 D8
Evesham Rd GVE DA12 ...337 J4
SRTFD E15 ...307 J4
Evesham Wy CLAY IG5 ...286 D1
Ewan Cl COLW CO3 ...105 K2
LOS SS9 ...299 K2
Ewanrigg Ter WFD IG8 ...267 M4
Ewan Wy HARH RM3 ...272 A5
Ewan Wy COLW CO3 ...105 M1
SBF/HAD SS7 ...299 M5
Ewart Pl BOW E3 ...306 C6
Ewell Hall Cha K/T/MI CO5 ...148 F1
Ewellhurst Rd CLAY IG5 ...268 D5
Excel Marina CAN/RD E16 ...323 H4
Excel Waterfront CAN/RD E16 ...323 L2
Exchange St ROM RM1 ...289 H4
Exchange Wy CHLM/WR CM1 ...5 H1
Exeter Cl BRTR CM7 ...121 J1
BSDN SS14 ...278 C6
EHAM E6 ...324 C1
RCOLW CO6 ...86 C6
SBN/FI SS3 ...303 J4
Exeter Dr COL CO1 ...8 A1
Exeter Gdns IL IG1 ...308 B2
Exeter Rd CAN/RD E16 ...323 K1
CHLM/WR CM1 ...194 B8
DAGE RM10 ...310 G3
FX IP11 ...62 G8
GVE DA12 ...338 A4
IPSE IP3 ...55 G1
PEND EN3 ...248 A3
WALTH E17 ...284 D3
Exford Av WOS/PRIT SS0 ...282 C5
Exhibition La SBN/FI SS3 ...303 J4
Exley Cl ING SM4 ...239 L1
Exmoor Cl BARK/HLT IG6 ...268 F7
Exmoor Rd FX IP11 ...62 G6
Exmouth Dr RAYL SS6 ...263 G8
Exmouth Rd GRAYS RM17 ...330 E5
WALTH E17 ...284 C3
Exning Rd CAN/RD E16 ...307 L3
Express Dr GDMY/SEVK IG3 ...287 L6
Extension Dr HERT/BAY SG13 ...184 B4
Exton Gdns BCTR RM8 ...310 A2
Eyhurst Av HCH RM12 ...289 M6
Eynsford Cl GDMY/SEVK IG3 ...287 H7
GRH DA9 ...335 M7
Eynsham Dr ABYW SE2 ...325 D1
Eyre Cl GPK RM2 ...289 L2

F
Fabians Cl RCOLW CO6 ...124 D2
Fabian St EHAM E6 ...308 C8
Factory HI K/T/MI CO5 ...174 D2
Factory La BARK IG11 ...64 F6
Factory La East HSTD CO9 ...81 H4
Factory La West HSTD CO9 ...81 H4
Factory Pl POP/IOD E14 ...322 F4
Factory Rd CAN/RD E16 ...324 A4
GVW DA11 ...336 F4
Fagbury Rd FX IP11 ...47 M3
Faggotters La HLWE CM17 ...189 M8
Faggot Yd BRTR CM7 * ...99 J3
Faggus La RAIN RM13 ...312 A1
Faints Cl CHESW EN7 ...216 A7
Fairbairn Av KESC IP5 ...50 C6
Fairbank Cl CHONG CM5 ...382 C5
Fairburn Cl SOS SS1 ...19 K4
Fair Cl RCOLE CO7 ...156 B2
Fairclough Av RCOS CO16 ...182 E2
Faircross Av BARK IG11 ...308 F3
CRW RM5 ...271 G6
Fairfax Av PIT SS13 ...278 D7
Fairfax Dr WOS/PRIT SS0 ...300 B3
Fairfax Md CHLM/GWD CM2 ...210 A3
Fairfax Ms CAN/RD E16 ...323 L4
Fairfax Rd COL CO1 ...9 M2
GRAYS RM17 ...330 E4
HERT/BAY SG13 ...184 A2
TIL RM18 ...331 L7
Fairfield INC CM4 ...239 M1
SBN/FI SS3 ...303 M3
FX IP11 ...62 G6
UPMR RM14 ...290 F8
Fairfield Av CDW/CHF RM16 ...314 F6
HCH RM12 ...289 M6
PEND EN3 ...248 A4
RCOLE CO7 ...110 D6
Fairfield Cl BRTR CM7 ...121 J1
Fairfield Crs LOS SS9 ...282 C6
Fairfield Gdns BCAYW CM12 ...258 C5
LOS SS9 ...282 C6
Fairfield Ri BROX EN10 ...217 G2
Fairfield Rd BOW E3 ...306 F6
BRTR CM7 ...121 J1
BRW CM14 ...273 L4
CHLM/WR CM1 ...4 C3
CHONG CM5 ...382 C5
COS CO15 ...6 F5
EPP CM16 ...220 B6
HOD EN11 ...201 H1
IL IG1 ...308 B4
IPSE IP3 ...54 E3
LOS SS9 ...282 C6
WALTH E17 ...266 A4
Fairfields RCHLM CM3 ...230 A8
Fairfield Wy CBE/LIN CB11 ...25 C1
Fairfoot Rd BOW E3 ...306 E8
Fairford Cl HARH RM3 ...272 E5
Fairford Wy HARH RM3 ...272 E5
Fairham Av SOCK/AV RM15 ...329 K1

Fairhaven Av K/T/MI CO5 ...178 B6
Fairhead Rd North COLN CO4 ...9 J4
Fairhead Rd South COLN CO4 ...9 J4
Fairholme Av GPK RM2 ...289 K3
Fairholme Dr UPMR RM14 ...291 J1
Fairholme Rd IL IG1 ...286 C5
Fairkytes Av RAIN RM11 ...290 C4
Fairland Cl RAYL SS6 ...263 H8
Fairland Rd SRTFD E15 ...307 J3
Fairlands Av BKHH IG9 ...267 A5
Fairlawn Dr WFD IG8 ...267 A5
Fairlawn Gdns CHONG CM5 ...283 H8
Fairlawns RAIN RM13 ...290 C5
Fairleads RCHLM CM3 ...212 C6
Fair Leas SAFWS CB10 ...28 B8
Fairleigh Av PIT SS13 ...279 L8
Fairleigh Dr LOS SS9 ...300 A4
Fairleigh Ms LOS SS9 * ...300 A4
Fairleigh Rd PIT SS13 ...279 L8
Fairley Wy CHESW CM7 ...216 C6
Fairlight CHING E4 ...267 G1
Fairlight WFD IG8 ...267 K5
Fairlight Cl CHING E4 ...267 G1
Fairlight Rd SBF/HAD SS7 ...298 D2
Fairlop Av CVI SS8 ...320 D1
Fairlop Cl COS CO15 ...159 J5
  HCH RM12 ...311 L3
Fairlop Gdns BARK/HLT IG6 ...268 B3
  BSDN SS14 ...3 F5
Fairlop Rd BARK/HLT IG6 ...268 F8
  WAN E11 ...285 G5
Fair Md BSDN SS14 ...3 J2
Fairmead RAYL SS6 ...263 E1
Fairmead Av SBF/HAD SS7 ...281 H8
  WOS/PRIT SS0 ...300 A3
Fairmead Gdns REDBR IG4 ...286 A3
Fairmead Rd LOU IG10 ...249 L4
Fairmeads LOU IG10 ...250 C2
Fairmont Cl BELV DA17 ...326 A5
Fairoak Gdns RAIN RM11 ...271 M8
Fair Oak Pl BARK/HLT IG6 ...268 C1
Fairoaks Gv EN3 ...232 E7
Fairstead Hall Rd
  RCHLM CM3 ...145 K7
Fairstead Rd RCHLM CM3 ...145 F5
Fairsted BSDN SS14 ...2 F7
Fairthorn Rd CHARL SE7 ...323 K4
Fairview BCAYW CM12 ...258 D4
  CVI SS8 ...298 C8
Fairview Av RAIN RM13 ...312 A6
  RBRW/HUT RM13 ...257 H3
  SLH/COR SS17 ...316 F4
Fairview Cha SLH/COR SS17 ...316 F5
Fairview Cl CHIG IG7 ...269 M6
  SBF/HAD SS7 ...279 M6
Fair View Cl WALTH E17 ...266 F7
Fairview Crs SBF/HAD SS7 ...279 M6
Fairview Dr CHIG IG7 ...269 H4
  WOS/PRIT SS0 ...300 F1
Fairview Gdns LOS SS9 ...299 M3
  WFD IG8 ...267 G5
Fairview Rd BSDN SS14 ...3 L6
  CHIG IG7 ...269 L5
Fairview Vls CHING E4 * ...266 D5
Fairway BSF CM23 ...139 K3
  CDW/CHF RM16 ...314 E8
  CHLM/GWD CM2 ...210 A6
  WARE SG12 ...163 C7
  WFD IG8 ...267 M4
  WICKW SS12 ...279 H2
Fairway Dr BOC CM0 ...393 L8
  THMD SE28 ...326 A2
Fairway Gdns IL IG1 ...308 C2
  LOS SS9 ...281 M8
Fairway Gardens Cl LOS SS9 ...281 M8
Fairways CHES/WCR EN8 ...216 A4
  COLN CO6 ...106 C3
  SOS SS1 ...302 C5
  WALTH E17 * ...284 C2
The Fairways
  CHES/WCR EN8 * ...216 L4
  IPSE IP4 ...49 K8
  RCHLM CM3 ...230 C8
The Fairway GVW DA11 ...337 K7
  HLWS CM18 ...204 A4
  LOS SS9 ...281 M8
  SBF/HAD SS7 ...279 M6
  UPMR RM14 ...290 F5
Fairycroft Rd SAFWN CB10 ...28 A8
Fairy Hall La BRTR CM77 ...120 D4
Falaize Av IL IG1 ...308 E1
Falbro Crs SBF/HAD SS7 ...299 G4
Falcon Av GRAYS RM17 ...330 C1
Falcon Cl DART DA1 ...334 C7
  HVHL CB9 ...34 C7
  LOS SS9 ...282 B8
  RAYL SS6 ...280 C2
  SBW CM21 ...162 D8
Falcon Crs COL CO1 ...107 C5
  PEND EN3 ...248 A5
Falconer Rd BARK/HLT IG6 ...54 F8
  HVHL CB9 ...34 F8
Falconers Pk SBW CM21 ...162 E8
Falconer St BSF CM23 ...138 C3
Falcon Flds MAL CM9 ...214 D5
Falcon Ms GVW DA11 ...337 L1
  MAL CM9 ...214 C5
Falcon Pk BSDN SS14 ...2 J5
Falcon Rd BOC CM0 ...393 M4
  PEND EN3 ...248 A5
Falcons Md CHLM/GWD CM2 ...4 D7
Falcon St FX IP11 ...62 G7
  IP IP1 ...16 C7
  PLSTW E13 ...307 K8
Falcon Wy CHLM/GWD CM2 ...209 M8
  COS CO15 ...159 J2
  VGE SS16 ...3 M4
  WAN E11 ...285 K2
Falcon Yd RCOLE CO7 ...130 F3
Fal Dr WIT CM8 ...171 H7
Falkenham End BSDN SS14 ...3 H5
Falkenham Pth BSDN SS14 ...3 J4
Falkenham Rd BSDN SS14 ...3 H5
Falkenham Rw EMPK RM11 ...290 D6
Falkirk Cl EMPK RM11 ...290 D6
Falkland Cl RCHLM CM3 ...195 H5
Falkland Dr MAL CM9 * ...213 H7
Falklands Dr MGTR SG12 ...91 G7
Falklands Rd BOC CM0 ...393 M4
  HVHL CB9 ...34 D5
Falkner St ING CM4 ...241 J7
Fallow Cl CHIG IG7 ...269 J4
Fallowden La SAFWN CB10 ...29 J1
Fallowfield SBN/FI SS3 ...303 G4
Fallowfield Cl HAR CO12 ...114 B8
Fallowfield Rd COLS CO2 ...128 F3
Fallow Flds LOU IG10 ...249 M7
The Fallows CVI SS8 ...298 D7
Falmer Rd WALTH E17 ...284 C1
Falmouth Av CHING E4 ...267 L4
Falmouth Cl KESG IP5 ...50 F5
Falmouth Gdns REDBR IG4 ...286 A3
Falmouth Rd CHLM/WR CM1 ...194 D8
Falmouth St SRTFD E15 ...307 G2
Falstaff Pl VGE SS16 * ...276 D7
Falstones LAIN SS15 ...277 G7
Fambridge Cha WIT CM8 ...146 F3

Fambridge Cl MAL CM9 ...214 D4
Fambridge Dr WICKW SS12 ...261 H7
Fambridge Rd BCTR RM8 ...288 D7
  MAL CM9 ...214 D4
  RCFD SS4 ...264 C2
  RCHLM CM3 ...246 B6
  RCHLM CM3 ...392 C3
Fane Rd SBF/HAD SS7 ...280 D7
Fanns Ri PUR RM19 ...328 D2
Fanny's La RCOS CO16 ...158 A3
Fanshawe Av BARK IG11 ...308 B2
Fanshawe Crs DAGW RM9 ...310 B2
  EMPK RM11 ...290 A4
Fanshawe Rd
  CDW/CHF RM16 * ...331 K2
Fantail Cl THMD SE28 ...325 M2
Fanton Av WICKW SS12 ...279 J2
Fanton Cha WICKE SS11 ...261 K7
Fanton Gdns WICKE SS11 ...261 K7
Fanton Wk WICKE SS11 ...261 L8
Faraday Av COS CO15 ...159 K5
Faraday Rd CHLM/WR CM1 ...191 D2
  LOS SS9 ...281 M7
  SRTFD E15 ...307 J3
Faraday Wy
  WOOL/PLUM SE18 ...324 D4
Farford Fld SUD CO10 ...45 M4
Farina Cl IP IP3 ...47 L6
Faringdon Av HARH RM3 ...271 M7
Faringford Rd SRTFD E15 ...307 H4
Farley Cl CHLM/WR CM1 ...4 A9
Farley Rd GDMY/SEVK IG3 ...287 H6
Farley Rd CVI SS8 ...320 B1
Farm Cl GVW DA11 ...337 J8
Farmadine SAFWS CB11 ...28 B8
Farmadine Gv SAFWS CB11 ...28 B8
Farm Cl BKHH IG9 ...267 M2
  CHES/WCR EN8 ...216 D1
  DAGE RM10 ...310 F4
  RBRW/HUT CM13 ...256 F3
Farm Crs RCHLM CM3 ...262 B1
Farmcroft GVW DA11 ...337 L1
Farmadine Rd GNWCH SE10 ...323 K8
Farm End CHING E4 ...249 H5
Farm Ct WAB EN9 ...234 B8
Farm Gv LEY E10 ...284 C6
Farmhill Rd WALTH E17 ...284 C1
Farm La HOD EN11 ...201 K1
  WTHK RM20 ...330 B5
Farmington Av COS CO15 ...159 J5
Farm Rd CDW/CHF RM16 ...331 J1
  CVI SS8 ...298 D8
  HAR CO12 ...113 M1
  TIL RM18 ...332 F1
Farman Av WALTH E17 ...266 D8
Farnborough Av WALTH E17 * ...284 B1
Farne Dr W WICKW SS12 ...261 J8
Farnes Av WICKW SS12 ...260 F7
Farnes Dr GPK RM2 ...271 M8
Farnham Cl SBW CM21 ...162 D8
Farnham Rd GDMY/SEVK IG3 ...287 J4
  HARH RM3 ...272 A4
Farnley Rd CHING E4 ...249 H7
Farnol Rd DART DA1 ...334 D7
Farrance Rd CHDH RM6 ...288 B4
Farrance St POP/IOD E14 ...322 C2
  BROX EN10 * ...217 C1
Farr Av BARK IG11 ...309 K6
Farriers WARE SG12 ...185 H3
Farriers Cha GVE DA12 ...338 C6
  KESG IP5 ...50 F5
Farriers Dr BCAYW CM12 * ...240 D8
Farriers End BROX EN10 ...217 C8
  COLW CO3 ...106 A8
Farriers Wy BRTR CM77 ...120 E8
  SOSN SS2 ...283 J8
Farriers Went FX IP11 ...62 G6
Farrington Service Rd
  SOS SS1 * ...19 C5
Farrins Rents
  BERM/RHTH SE16 ...322 B4
Farrow Gdns CDW/CHF RM16 ...314 D8
Farrow Pl BERM/RHTH SE16 ...322 B6
Farrow Rd CHLM/WR CM1 ...4 A9
Farthingale La WAB EN9 ...234 A4
Farthingale Wk SRTFD E15 ...307 C4
Farthing Cl DART DA1 ...334 E1
Farthing Rd IP IP1 ...47 H1
Farthings K/T/MI CO5 * ...178 B6
Farthings Cha K/T/MI CO5 * ...178 B6
Farthings Went RIPS/CAP IP9 ...58 H2
Fastnet SOSN SS2 ...282 D6
Fastnet Cl HVHL CB9 ...35 C5
Faulkbourne Rd WIT CM8 ...170 F1
Faulkeners Wy FX IP11 ...62 B5
Faulkner Cl BCTR RM8 ...288 A4
Faulkner Rd CHDH RM6 ...287 M4
Fauners VGE SS16 ...16 E8
Faverolle Gn CHES/WCR EN8 ...216 E6
Faversham Av CHING E4 ...249 H8
Faversham Cl CHING E4 ...269 L1
Fawe St POP/IOD E14 ...322 C1
Fawkner Cl CHLM/GWD CM2 ...210 A3
Fawley Cl IPNE IP4 ...49 H6
Fawn Rd CHIG IG7 ...269 M4
  PLSTW E13 ...307 M6
Fawters Ct RBRW/HUT CM13 ...257 G2
Faymore Gdns
  SOCK/AV RM15 ...329 K3
Fearon St GNWCH SE10 ...323 K4
Featherby Wy RCFD SS4 ...283 K4
Feathers Fld FX IP11 ...62 B5
Feathers Hl RBSF CM22 ...376 F11
Federation Rd ABYW SE2 ...325 M7
Feeches Rd SOSN SS2 ...283 G8
Feedhams Cl RCOLE CO7 ...130 F2
Feenan Hwy TIL RM18 ...331 M8
Feering Dr BSDN SS14 ...278 C8
Feering HI K/T/MI CO5 ...149 G2
Feering Rd BCAYE CM11 ...258 B3
Feering Rw BSDN SS14 ...278 C8
Felbrig Cl BRTR CM77 ...120 E6
Felbridge Rd GDMY/SEVK IG3 ...287 L3
Felbrigg Cl CDW/CHF RM16 ...331 L3
Felipe Rd CDW/CHF RM16 ...329 M1
Felix Rd KESG IP5 ...50 A6
Felix St IP IP3 ...55 H3
  IPSE IP3 ...55 H3
  WDBR IP12 ...51 L4

Fellbrigg Av KESG IP5 ...49 L7
Fell Christy CHLM/WR CM1 ...193 L8
Fellowes Cl COLN CO4 ...107 J3
Fell Rd HSTD CO9 ...344 G4
Felltram Wy CHARL SE7 ...323 K4
Felmongers HLW CM20 ...188 C7
Felmores PIT SS13 ...278 C5
Felnor Wk FX IP11 ...63 M2
Fels Cl DAGE RM10 ...288 E6
Fels Farm Av DAGE RM10 ...288 E6
Felspar Cl WOOL/PLUM SE18 ...325 J8
Felstead Av CLAY IG5 ...268 D7
Felstead Cl COLS CO2 ...129 K5
  RBRW/HUT CM13 ...256 F2
  SBF/HAD SS7 ...298 A1
Felstead St HOM E9 ...306 C3
Felsted Rd BCAYE CM11 ...258 F3
  CAN/RD E16 ...324 A2
Felton Cl BROX EN10 ...217 G3
Felton Rd BARK IG11 ...309 H6
Fen Br RCOLE CO7 ...363 Q9
Fenbridge La RCOLE CO7 ...363 Q9
Fencepiece Rd BARK/HLT IG6 ...268 F8
Fen Cl BRWN CM15 ...238 F8
  UPMR RM14 ...293 J5
Fendyke Rd ABYW SE2 ...326 A7
Fengates Rd CAN/RD E16 ...323 J2
Fen La CDW/CHF RM16 ...315 M8
  RCOLE CO7 ...89 C4
  UPMR RM14 ...292 A6
Fenman Gdns
  GDMY/SEVK IG3 ...287 L6
Fen Meadow FX IP11 ...62 B5
Fen Cl RCHLM CM3 ...244 F5
Fenn Rd RCOLE CO7 ...132 D2
Fennel Cl CAN/RD E16 ...323 J1
  RCHLM CM3 ...244 E5
Fennel Cl CAN/RD E16 ...149 M8
Fennells HLWW/ROY CM19 ...203 H5
Fennells Cl HVHL CB9 ...34 C6
Fenner Rd CDW/CHF RM16 ...329 M6
Fenners Wy PIT SS13 ...278 D3
Fennings Rd RCHLM CM3 ...244 E5
Fenswood Av WDBR IP12 ...57 M2
Fenton Av RCOLE CO7 ...298 D7
Fenton Cl BROX EN10 ...217 G3
Fentons Av PLSTW E13 ...307 L7
Fentons Wy LAIN SS15 ...276 C6
Fenton Gra HLWE CM17 ...204 D2
Fenton Rd CDW/CHF RM16 ...330 B2
  HVHL CB9 ...34 D5
Fenton's Av PLSTW E13 ...307 L7
Fenwick Cl CVI SS8 ...298 D7
Ferguson Av GPK RM2 ...271 M8
Ferguson Cl SAFWS CB11 ...28 D8
Ferguson Ct GPK RM2 ...272 A8
Ferguson Gv
  CHES/WCR EN8 * ...216 E7
Ferguson's Cl POP/IOD E14 ...322 E7
Fermoy Rd SOS SS1 ...302 E6
Fernbank BCAYW CM12 ...258 C4
  BKHH IG9 ...249 L8
Fernbank Av HCH RM12 ...311 M1
Fernbrook Av SOS SS1 ...302 A5
Fern Cl BCAYW CM12 ...258 E7
  BROX EN10 ...217 C1
Ferndale Av WALTH E17 ...285 G3
  LAIN SS15 ...276 E7
Ferndale Cl COS CO15 ...159 J6
Ferndale Crs CVI SS8 ...320 B1
Ferndale Rd CRW RM5 ...270 F5
  FSTGT E7 ...307 L4
  GVE DA12 ...337 L7
  HAR CO12 ...15 K5
  PEND EN3 ...232 F7
  RAYL SS6 ...280 C2
  WAN E11 ...285 J7
Ferndale St EHAM E6 ...324 D1
Fernden Wy ROMW/RG RM7 ...288 C4
Ferndown EMPK RM11 ...290 D6
Ferndown Rd FOS CO13 ...137 H4
  FX IP11 ...63 H8
Ferndown Wy RCHLM CM3 ...216 H5
Fern Gv HVHL CB9 ...34 B5
Fernhall Dr REDBR IG4 ...286 A3
Fernhall La WAB EN9 ...234 E1
Fernhayes Cl CHTY IP2 ...53 M3
Fernhill HLWS CM18 ...294 M5
Fernhill Cl WALTH E17 ...267 G8
Fern Hill La HLWS CM18 ...204 A5
Fernhill St CAN/RD E16 ...324 C5
Fernlea COLN CO4 ...106 F3
Fernlea Rd BOC CM0 ...393 K6
  HAR CO12 ...15 K6
  SBF/HAD SS7 ...298 B2
Fernleigh Dr LOS SS9 ...300 D4
Ferns Cl PEND EN3 ...232 F6
Fernside BKHH IG9 ...248 B8
Fernside Cl SLH/COR SS17 ...295 L6
Ferns Rd SRTFD E15 ...307 K3
Fern St BOW E3 ...306 D6
Fern Wk VGE SS16 ...294 B1
Fern Wy COS CO15 ...182 G6
Fernways IL IG1 ...308 B1
Fernwood SBF/HAD SS7 ...299 H1
Ferranti Cl WOOL/PLUM SE18 ...324 D4
Ferrers Av RCHLM CM3 ...230 C8
  RCHLM CM3 ...244 F5
Ferris Av RCHLM CM3 ...230 D8
Ferro Rd RAIN RM13 ...311 K8
Ferry La FX IP11 ...10 C7
  RAIN RM13 ...311 J8
Ferrymead CVI SS8 ...298 C8
Ferry Rd BOC CM0 ...392 H4
  FX IP11 ...63 H6
  HOC/HUL SS5 ...263 J3
  K/T/MI CO5 ...130 D7
  RCHLM CM3 ...246 B6
  SBF/HAD SS7 * ...280 D7
  SLH/COR SS17 ...317 G1
  TIL RM18 ...331 K8
Ferry St POP/IOD E14 ...322 E7
Feryby Rd CDW/CHF RM16 ...331 L3
Fesants Cft HLW CM20 ...188 C6
Festival Gdns MAL CM9 ...384 G1
Festival Link BSDN SS14 ...3 L6
Festoon Wy CAN/RD E16 ...324 A3
Fetherston Rd SLH/COR SS17 ...317 G1
Fiat Av COS CO15 ...182 A7
Fiddlers Cl GRH DA9 ...335 L4
Fiddlers Folly COLW CO3 ...105 H3
Fiddlers Hl COLW CO3 ...105 H3

Fiddlers La RCOLE CO7 ...363 R6
Field Cl ABR/ST RM4 ...251 L3
  BKHH IG9 ...267 M2
  CHING E4 ...266 D5
The Fielders CVI SS8 ...320 B1
Fieldfare BCAYW CM12 ...258 C5
Fieldfare Rd THMD SE28 ...325 M3
Field Gdns CHONG CM5 ...382 G9
Field Gate La RBSF CM22 ...374 F1
Fieldhouse Cl SWFD E18 ...267 C1
Fielding Av TIL RM18 ...331 L7
Fieldings Rd CHES/WCR EN8 ...217 G7
Field Rd FSTGT E7 ...307 K1
  SOCK/AV RM15 ...328 C6
Fields Cl RCOS CO16 ...134 C6
Fieldside SAFWS CB11 * ...30 B7
Fields Park Crs CHDH RM6 ...288 C3
Field Vw SUD CO10 ...20 C4
Field Vw KIR/NAC IP10 ...56 C5
Fieldview Cl COLN CO4 ...107 J1
Field View Dr MAL CM9 ...173 M8
Field Wy HOD EN11 ...185 J7
  RCOLE CO7 ...130 F3
Fieldway RCOS CO16 ...134 C6
  CDW/CHF RM16 ...314 D8
  PIT SS13 ...296 F5
  WARE SG12 ...185 J5
  WICKW SS12 ...279 G5
Fiennes Cl BCTR RM8 ...287 M6
Fiesta Dr DAGW RM9 ...310 F6
Fifth Av CAN/RD E16 ...323 K1
  IPNE IP4 ...49 G4
Fifth Av CHLM/WR CM1 ...193 L8
  CVI SS8 ...320 B1
  FOS CO13 ...137 H4
  HLW CM20 ...13 G2
  HSTD CO9 ...81 M3
  MNPK E12 ...288 C1
  WICKE SS11 ...261 K7
  WTHK RM20 ...335 K1
Fifth Avenue Allende Av
  HLW CM20 ...13 G2
Filborough Wy GVE DA12 ...338 C6
Filey Rd BOC CM0 ...393 L8
Fillebrook Av LOS SS9 ...300 C3
Fillebrook Rd WAN E11 ...285 C6
Finbars Wk IPNE IP4 ...17 L5
Finborough Cl KESG IP5 ...49 L8
Finchale Rd ABYW SE2 ...325 L6
Fincham's Cl CBE/LIN CB1 ...25 L7
Finchdale COS CO15 ...159 J7
Finch Dr BRTR CM7 ...99 C8
Finches Cl SLH/COR SS17 ...295 M8
The Finches HERT/BAY SG13 ...184 C5
  SBF/HAD SS7 ...280 D6
Finchfield RAYL SS6 ...281 C4
Finch Gdns CHING E4 ...266 D4
Finch Hl SUD CO10 ...44 F7
Finchingfield Av WFD IG8 ...267 M6
Finchingfield Rd HSTD CO9 ...354 D3
  HVHL CB9 ...344 B7
The Finchingfields
  BRWN CM15 ...383 M11
Finchingfield Wy COLS CO2 ...129 K5
  WICKW SS12 * ...260 E4
Finchland Vw RCHLM CM3 ...245 G2
Finchley Av CHLM/GWD CM2 ...4 C8
Finchley Cl DART DA1 ...334 D3
Finchley Rd GRAYS RM17 ...330 C5
  IPNE IP4 ...17 J3
  WOS/PRIT SS0 ...18 A4
Finchmoor HLWS CM18 ...203 L4
Finch's WIT CM8 ...172 C7
Findhorn St POP/IOD E14 ...322 F2
Findhorn Av RCOS CO16 ...285 G3
Findley Cl RIPS/CAP IP9 ...364 C11
Findon Gdns RAIN RM13 ...327 K1
Finer Cl RCOS CO16 ...6 F7
Fingal St GNWCH SE10 ...323 L4
Fingringhoe Rd K/T/MI CO5 ...153 L2
Fingrith Hall La ING CM4 ...222 H1
Finham Cl COLN CO4 ...108 C1
Finland St BERM/RHTH SE16 ...322 B6
Finnymore Rd DAGW RM9 ...310 B2
Finsbury Rd RCOS CO16 * ...81 J1
Fincuane Gdns RAIN RM13 ...311 K5
Firbank Cl CAN/RD E16 ...324 A1
Firbank Rd CRW RM5 ...270 F5
Fir Ct LAIN SS15 ...276 F1
Fircroft Rd IP IP1 ...47 L6
Firebronds Rd RIPS/CAP IP9 ...364 E9
Firecrest Rd CHLM/GWD CM2 ...209 M8
Firefly Gdns EHAM E6 ...308 D8
Firefly Wy IPSE IP3 ...55 G4
Firfield Rd SBF/HAD SS7 ...298 C1
Firham Park Av HARH RM3 ...272 D6
Firlands BSF CM23 ...138 F5
The Firle VGE SS16 ...294 F2
Firle Wk COLS CO2 ...129 K3
Firmans VGE SS16 ...294 E5
Firmins Ct RCOLW CO6 ...106 A8
Fir Pk HLWW/ROY CM19 ...203 L4
Firs Cha K/T/MI CO5 ...177 M6
Firs Dr CHLM/WR CM1 ...208 A4
  LOU IG10 ...250 D7
Firsgrove Crs BRW CM14 ...273 L3
Firs Hamlet K/T/MI CO5 ...177 M7
Firs Rd K/T/MI CO5 ...174 M1
  K/T/MI CO5 ...177 M7
First Av BCAYW CM12 ...258 C6
  BRWN CM15 ...383 M6
  CHDH RM6 ...287 M4
  CHLM/WR CM1 ...193 L8
  COS CO15 ...7 M4
  CVI SS8 ...320 A2
  DAGE RM10 ...310 E6
  FOS CO13 ...137 H5
  GVW DA11 ...337 L1
  HOC/HUL SS5 ...263 J4
  HSTD CO9 ...81 M3
  MNPK E12 ...288 C1
  PLSTW E13 ...307 K7
  RCOS CO16 ...134 C4
  SBF/HAD SS7 * ...280 D7
  SLH/COR SS17 ...317 G1
  STSD CM24 ...374 C11
  SUD CO10 ...20 C4
  WICKE SS11 ...261 K7
  WOS/PRIT SS0 ...300 B5
  WOTN CO14 ...369 M10
  WTHK RM20 ...335 K1

Fir Tree La RCHLM CM3 ...212 B6
Fir Tree Ri CHLM/GWD CM2 ...209 H7
  RIPW IP8 ...53 L5
Fir Trees ABR/ST RM4 ...251 L3
Fir Trees Cl BERM/RHTH SE16 ...322 B4
Fir Tree Wk MAL CM9 * ...198 G1
Fir Wy COS CO15 ...182 D7
Firwood's Rd HSTD CO9 ...81 H5
Fishbane Cl IPSE IP3 ...55 K8
Fisher Cl CBS CB2 ...340 F5
  HVHL CB9 ...35 G5
  PEND EN3 ...233 H7
Fishermans Dr
  BERM/RHTH SE16 ...322 A6
Fishermans Wy HOD EN11 ...201 L1
Fishermen's HI GVW DA11 ...336 E3
Fishers Cl CHES/WCR EN8 ...233 H4
Fishers Hatch HLW CM20 ...13 K5
Fisher's La RCOLE CO7 ...64 F2
Fisher's Wy BELV DA17 ...326 F6
Fisher Wy BRTR CM7 ...121 M1
Fishguard Wy CAN/RD E16 ...324 E4
Fishmarket St GTDUN CM6 ...74 F5
Fish Pond Hl RIPS/CAP IP9 ...365 M10
Fishponds HI RCOLW CO6 ...361 K12
Fishponds La RIPS/CAP IP9 ...364 F5
Fish St MAL CM9 ...384 F1
Fisin Wk COLW CO3 ...128 B2
Fisons Cl CAN/RD E16 ...323 K4
Fitches Crs MAL CM9 ...214 G4
Fitchett Cl MGTR CO11 ...90 C5
Fitzgerald Rd RIPW IP8 ...46 F5
  WAN E11 ...285 K3
Fitzgilbert Rd COLS CO2 ...128 F3
Fitzilian Av HARH RM3 ...272 C2
Fitzmaurice Rd IPSE IP3 ...55 J3
Fitzpiers SAFWN CB10 ...28 B7
Fitzroy Ct BCAYW CM12 ...258 C4
Fitzroy St IP IP1 ...16 M1
Fitzstephen Rd BCTR RM8 ...309 L1
Fitzwalter La CHLM/WR CM1 ...4 A7
Fitzwalter Pl CHLM/WR CM1 ...4 A7
Fitzwalter Rd COLW CO3 ...106 E7
  GTDUN CM6 ...118 B6
  RCHLM CM3 ...195 J5
Fitzwarren SBN/FI SS3 ...303 G4
Fitzwilliam Cl CHTY IP2 ...53 L3
Fitzwilliam Ms CAN/RD E16 ...323 K4
Fitzwilliam Rd COLS CO2 ...106 E1
Fitzwilliams Ct HLWE CM17 ...188 F5
Five Acres HLWS CM18 ...203 M4
  RCHLM CM3 ...228 C2
  RIPS/CAP IP9 ...364 F5
  STSD CM24 ...15 M1
  WOTN CO14 ...137 L3
Fiveash La BRTR CM77 ...123 H4
Fiveash Rd GVW DA11 ...337 H8
Five Elms Rd DAGW RM9 ...288 C6
Fivefields Ct COLN CO4 ...108 A6
Five Oaks SBF/HAD SS7 ...298 E1
Five Oaks La CHIG IG7 ...270 B5
Fladgate Rd WAN E11 ...285 H4
Flag Hl RCOLE CO7 ...157 J4
Flagstaff Gdns
  BRWN CM15 ...233 J3
  WAB EN9 ...233 J2
Flail Cl RCOLE CO7 ...109 J1
Flambird's Cha RCHLM CM3 ...229 J6
Flamboro Cl LOS SS9 ...282 K7
Flamborough St
  POP/IOD E14 ...322 B2
Flamborough Wk
  POP/IOD E14 ...322 B2
Flamingo Wk HCH RM12 ...311 K4
Flamstead End Rd
  CHES/WCR EN8 ...216 C6
Flamstead Gdns DAGW RM9 ...309 M4
Flamsteed Rd DAGW RM9 ...309 M4
Flamsteed Rd CHARL SE7 ...324 B8
Flanders Cl BRTR CM7 ...99 C8
Flanders Fld COLS CO2 ...129 L2
Flanders Rd EHAM E6 ...308 C4
Flanders Wy HOM E9 ...306 A4
Flandrian Cl CHING E4 ...248 D1
Flatford Dr RCOS CO16 ...182 C1
Flatford Rd HVHL CB9 ...33 M8
  RCOLE CO7 ...363 R8
Flavell Ms GNWCH SE10 ...323 K5
Flavian Cl HVHL CB9 ...35 G6
Flaxen Cl CHING E4 ...266 C2
Flaxen Rd CHING E4 ...266 C2
Flaxfields CBE/LIN CB1 ...25 M4
Flax La SUD CO10 ...39 M1
Fleeming Cl WALTH E17 ...266 C8
Fleeming Rd WALTH E17 ...266 C8
Fleet Av UPMR RM14 ...291 C4
Fleet Av UPMR RM14 ...291 C4
Fleethall Gv CDW/CHF RM16 ...314 D8
Fleethall Rd RCFD SS4 ...283 K5
Fleet Rd GVW DA11 ...336 F8
  SBF/HAD SS7 ...298 A3
Fleetwood Av COS CO15 ...160 B5
  FX IP11 ...62 G7
  WOS/PRIT SS0 ...300 C5
Fleetwood Cl CAN/RD E16 ...324 A1
  COS CO15 ...160 B5
Fleetwood Rd FX IP11 ...63 G8
Fleming Cl BRTR CM7 ...121 M1
  CHESW E7 ...216 D4
Fleming Gdns TIL RM18 ...332 F1
Fleming Rd CDW/CHF RM16 ...329 M1
  RBRW/HUT CM13 ...273 M5
Flemings Farm Rd LOS SS9 ...282 A3
Flemming Av THMD SE28 ...326 A3
Flemish Ct COL CO1 ...8 C2
Flemming Crs LOS SS9 ...300 A4
Flempton Rd LEY E10 ...284 B6
Fletcher Cl EHAM E6 ...324 D4
Fletcher Dr WICKW SS12 ...261 G7
Fletcher La LEY E10 ...284 C5
Fletcher Rd CHING E4 ...269 J4
  IPSE IP3 ...55 J3
Fletchers VGE SS16 ...295 H4
Fletchers La RIPS/CAP IP9 ...50 E5
Fletchers Sq SOSN SS2 ...283 J8
Flex Meadow
  HLWW/ROY CM19 ...202 F7
Flindell Dr RIPW IP8 ...46 F5
Flint Cl CHTY IP2 ...54 A3
  SRTFD E15 ...307 J3
  VGE SS16 ...276 D1
Flint St WTHK RM20 ...335 L1
Flintwich Mnr
  CHLM/WR CM1 ...193 M1
Flitch Cl GTDUN CM6 ...117 H6
Flitch Wy BRTR CM77 ...119 K7
  GTDUN CM6 ...94 B3
  RBSF CM22 ...376 A1
Flixton Cl RCOS CO16 ...182 C1
Floathaven Cl THMD SE28 ...325 K4
Flora Cl POP/IOD E14 ...322 C2
Flora Gdns CHDH RM6 ...287 M4
Flora Rd WIT CM8 ...148 E1
Flora St BELV DA17 ...326 C5
Florence Cl HCH RM12 ...290 B4
  HLWE CM17 ...204 D3
  SBF/HAD SS7 ...298 C1

WTHK RM20 ....330 B5
Florence Ct WAN E11 ....285 L2
Florence Gdns SBF/HAD SS7 ..298 F2
Florence Rd ABYW SE2 ....325 M6
Florence St IP1 ....320 F7
  PLSTW E13 ....307 K6
  WOTN CO14 ....369 N11
Florence St CHLM/WR CO11 ...307 J8
Florence Vls MGTR CO11 * ...316 H3
Florence Wy VGE SS16 ....276 E8
Florie's RCOLW CO6 ....103 J3
Flowers Wy COS CO15 ....182 D6
Flowmere Rd ROY SG8 ....349 L2
Flux's La EPP CM16 ....236 B3
Fobbing Farm Cl VGE SS16 ...295 K2
Fobbing Rd SLH/COR SS17 ....317 M1
Fodderwick BSDN SS14 2
Foden Cl IP1 ....47 H3
Fogerty Cl PEND EN3 ....233 J7
Foksville Rd CVI SS8 ....320 F6
Fold Cl CBE/LIN CB1 ....24 E7
Fold Cft HLW CM20 ....12 C5
The Fold COLS CO2 ....128 D7
  K/T/MI CO5 ....174 C3
  RCOLE CO7 ....130 E6
Folly Vw WARE SG12 ....185 J4
Folly Wall POP/IOD E14 .....322 F5
Fonnereau Rd IP IP1 ....16 E2
Fontayne Av CHIG IG7 ....268 A3
  RAIN RM13 ....311 H4
  ROM RM1 ....271 H8
Font Cl CO5 ....276 F7
Fonteyn Cl LAIN SS15 ....276 F5
Fonteyn Gdns WFD IG8 * 268 A4
Fontwell Park Gdns
  HCH RM12 ....312 B1
Forbes Cl EMPK RM11 ....289 L4
Ford Cl LAIN SS15 ....276 D7
  RAIN RM13 ....311 J4
Ford End WFD IG8 ....267 L4
Fordham Cl EMPK RM11 ....290 D5
Fordham Pl IPNE IP4 ....49 J1
Fordham Rd RCOLW CO6 ....84 C3
  RCOLW CO6 ....85 G2
Fordhams Rw
  CDW/CHF RM16 ....315 L5
Ford La COLN CO4 ....86 F8
  RAIN RM13 ....311 J4
Ford Rd BOW E3 ....155 K2
  COS CO15 ....6 D6
  DAGE RM10 ....310 D4
  GVW DA11 ....336 E3
Fords La RCOLW CO4 ....87 G8
Fordson Rd CHLM/GWD CM2....194 E7
Fords Park Rd CAN/RD E16 ...323 K2
Ford St BOW E3 ....306 B6
  CAN/RD E16 ....323 J2
  RCOLW CO6 ....104 D1
Fordstreet Hl RCOLW CO6 ....104 A1
Fordwater Cl HSTD CO9 ......344 C4
Fordwich Rd RCOLE CO7 ......156 B4
Fordyce Cl UPMR RM14 ....290 D5
Fordyke Rd BCTR RM8 ....288 B7
Forebury Av SBW CM21 ....163 G7
The Forebury SBW CM21 ......163 G7
Fore Fld BRTR CM7 ....122 A2
Forefield Gn CHLM/WR CM1 ...194 C6
Fore Hamlet IP IP3 ....17 H3
Foreland St
  WOOL/PLUM SE18 ....325 G7
Foremark Cl BARK/HLT IG6 ...269 G3
Foresight Rd COLS CO2 ......130 A3
Forest Ap CHING E4 ....249 H7
  WFD IG8 ....267 K6
Forest Av CHIG IG7 ....268 D4
  CHING E4 ....249 H7
Forest Cl WAB EN9 ....234 C4
  WAN E11 ....285 J3
  WFD IG8 ....267 L3
Forest Ct CHING E4 ....249 J8
  WAN E11 ....285 H2
Forest Dr CHLM/WR CM1 4
  CHONG CM5 ....381 K8
  EPP CM16 ....235 M6
  MNPK E12 ....286 A8
  WFD IG8 ....267 G6
Forest Dr East WAN E11 .....285 G5
Forest Dr West WAN E11 .....284 F5
Forest Edge BKHH IG9 ....267 M2
Forester Cl WALTH E17 ......285 G2
Foresters Ct RCOLE CO7 * ...130 A3
Foresters Dr WALTH E17 .....285 G2
Forest Gld CHING E4 ....267 H1
  EPP CM16 ....220 F5
  HVHL CB9 ....34 C3
  VGE SS16 ....294 C1
  WAN E11 ....285 H4
Foresthall Rd STSD CM24 ....115 J1
Forest La CHIG IG7 ....268 D4
  FSTGT E7 ....307 K2
  KESG IP5 ....50 F7
Forest Mount Rd WFD IG8 ....267 G6
Forest Park Av COS CO15 ....159 H6
The Forest WALTH E17 ....285 H2
  IPNE IP4 ....17 H6
  LAIN SS15 ....276 F4
Forest Ri WALTH E17 ....285 G2
Forest Rd BARK/HLT IG6 .....269 H7
  CHES/WCR EN8 ....216 A1
  COLN CO4 ....9 J1
  FSTGT E7 ....307 K1
  LOU IG10 ....250 A4
  PEND EN3 ....232 F6
  ROMW/RG RM7 ....288 E1
  WALTH E17 ....267 H8
  WAN E11 ....285 G5
  WFD IG8 ....267 H8
  WIT CM8 ....147 K7
Forest Side CHING E4 ....249 J7
  EPP CM16 ....235 L4
  FSTGT E7 ....307 L1
Forest St FSTGT E7 ....307 K2
The Forest WALTH E17 ....285 H2
Forest Vw CHING E4 ....249 J7
  WAN E11 ....285 G3
Forest View Av WAN E11 .....285 G3
Forest View Dr LOU SS9 .....299 K2
Forest View Rd LOU IG10 ....234 D8
  MNPK E12 ....286 B1
  WALTH E17 ....267 J7
Forest Wy HLWE CM17 ....189 K7
  HLWE CM17 ....204 C5
  LOU IG10 ....234 D8
  LOU IG10 ....250 B3
  RBSF CM22 ....376 B10

WFD IG8 ....267 L3
WAN SS9 ....299 L3
Forge Cl KIR/NAC IP10 ......56 F1
Forge Cft BRTR CM77 ....122 F2
Forge La GVE DA12 ....338 C2
Forge Pl GVE DA12 * 338 C2
Forge St RCOLE CO7 ....363 N11
Formont CAN/RD E16 ....323 J1
Forres Cl HOD EN11 ....201 H4
Forrest Cl RCHLM CM3 ....244 A4
Forster Cl CHING E4 ....267 G6
Forster Rd WALTH E17 ....284 E2
Forsters CHDH RM6 ....288 C4
Forsyth Dr BRTR CM7 ....121 K3
Forsythia CHLM/WR CM1 ......208 A1
  IL IG1 ....308 C1
Forterie Gdns
  GDMY/SEVK IG3 ....287 K8
Fortescue Cha SOS SS1 ......302 C4
Forth Rd UPMR RM14 ....291 G4
Forties Cl HVHL CB9 ....35 G4
Fortinbras Wy
  CHLM/GWD CM2 ....5 C9
Fortin Cl RCOLE CO7 ....329 K4
Fortin Wy SOCK/AV RM15 .....329 K3
Fortis Cl CAN/RD E16 ....323 M2
Fort Rd TIL RM18 ....337 L2
Fortrose Cl POP/IOD E14 ....323 G2
Fortrye Cl GVW DA11 ....337 H3
Fort St CAN/RD E16 ....323 L4
Fortune Cl RCHLM CM3 ....144 C6
The Fortunes HLWS CM18 .....204 A3
Fort William Rd
  SLH/COR SS17 ....295 L3
Forty Acre La CAN/RD E16 ...323 K1
Forty Hl EN1 ....232 B4
Forum Cl BOW E3 ....306 C5
Fossdene Rd CHARL SE7 ......323 J4
Fossetts La RCOLW CO6 ......85 G8
Fossetts Wy SOSN SS2 ....301 L4
Fossington Rd BELV DA17 ....326 A7
Fossway BCTR RM8 ....287 M7
Fostal Cl LOS SS9 ....282 C7
Foster Cl CHES/WCR EN8 .....216 A1
  SRTFD E15 ....307 H2
Foster Rd CVI SS8 ....320 F4
  HAR CO12 ....68 D8
  MAL CM9 ....198 A4
  PLSTW E13 ....306 F2
Fosters Cl CHLM/WR CM1 .....208 A1
  SWFD E18 ....267 J1
Foster St HLWE CM17 ....205 G5
Fothergill Cl PLSTW E13 ....307 H1
Foulgar Cl RCHLM CM3 ....245 H5
Foundation St IPNE IP4 .....17 G3
Founders Rd HOD EN11 ....185 J4
Foundry Cl BERM/RHTH SE16 ..322 A5
Foundry La BOC CM0 ....393 L4
  IPSE IP3 ....16 F1
  RCOLW CO6 ....82 C7
  RCOLW CO6 ....105 G6
Fountain Cl POP/IOD E14 ....323 G2
Fountain Farm HLWS CM18 ....204 A4
Fountain La HOC/HUL SS5 ....263 L8
  RCOLW CO6 ....127 C5
Fountain Pl WAB EN9 ....233 K4
Fountain Rd CHLM/WR CM1 ....190 G2
Fountains Cl CHTY IP2 ......53 M2
Fountain Wk GVW DA11 ....337 J4
Fouracres PEND EN3 ....248 B1
  SAFWS CB11 ....28 A1
Four Acres SBW CM21 ....163 H1
Four Ash Hl HSTD CO9 ....345 K4
Four Oaks BRW CM14 * 256 B6
Four Seasons Cl BOW E3 .....306 D6
Four Sisters Cl LOS SS9 ....282 C7
Four Sisters Wy LOS SS9 ....282 C7
Fourth Av CHLM/WR CM1 ......193 M1
  COS CO15 ....183 M1
  FOS CO13 ....137 G7
  HLW CM20 ....13 G5
  HSTD CO9 ....81 J4
  MNPK E12 ....308 C1
  RCOS CO16 ....181 J7
  ROMW/RG RM7 ....288 F6
  SLH/COR SS17 ....295 H4
  WICKE SS11 ....261 K4
  WTHK RM20 ....335 K1
Fourways RBSF CM22 ....374 D7
The Four Wents CHING E4 ....267 G1
Fowe's La SUD CO10 ....347 J6
Fowey Av REDBR IG4 ....269 A3
Fowler Cl SOS SS1 ....19 L4
Fowler Rd BARK/HLT IG6 .....269 M4
  FSTGT E7 ....307 H1
Fowley Cl CHES/WCR EN8 .....233 G4
Fowley Mead Pk
  CHES/WCR EN8 * 233 G4
Foxborough Cha ING CM4 .....225 K4
Foxburrow Cl HVHL CB9 ......34 C4
Fox Burrows La
  CHLM/WR CM1 ....193 E3
Fox Cl CAN/RD E16 ....323 K1
  CRW RM5 ....270 E4
  SBF/HAD SS7 ....280 C4
Foxcroft Rd UPMR RM14 ......209 J1
Foxdells La BSF CM23 ....115 G2
Foxden WIT CM8 ....148 A7
Foxendale Folly COLW CO3 * .105 M6
Foxes Cl CAN/RD E16 ....323 K1
Foxes Dr CHESW EN7 ....216 A5
Foxes Gn CDW/CHF RM16 ......331 K1
Foxes Gv RBRW/HUT CM13 ....257 L3
Foxes La RCOLW CO6 ....105 G4
  SUD CO10 ....345 G4
Foxes Pde WAB EN9 * 233 K4
Foxfield Cl HOC/HUL SS5 ....264 D7
Foxfield Dr SLH/COR SS17 ...295 H6
Foxglove Cl BSF CM23 ....138 D3
  COS CO15 ....159 J6
  HOD EN11 ....185 K8
  WIT CM8 ....171 J4
Foxglove Crs IPSE IP3 ......53 M5
Foxglove Dr WAN E11 ....285 M2
Foxglove Pth THMD SE28 .....325 H5
Foxglove Rd ROMW/RG RM7 ....289 G1
  SOCK/AV RM15 ....329 J3
Foxglove Wk COLN CO4 ....108 A8
Foxglove Wy CHLM/WR CM1 ....194 C6
Foxgrove Gdns FX IP11 ......63 J3
Foxgrove La FX IP11 ....63 J3
Foxhall Rd RCOLE CO7 * 363 R5
Fox Hall Farm SOSN SS2 * ...302 B1
Foxhall Flds RCOLE CO7 .....363 R5
Foxhall Rd BOC CM0 ....389 L10
  IPNE IP4 ....17 J1
  IL IG1 ....287 G2
  RCOLE CO7 ....364 C6
  RCOS CO16 ....159 H1
Friars Ct COLS CO2 * 129 M2
Friarscroft BROX EN10 ......201 H4
Friars Gate Cl WFD IG8 .....267 K3
Friars La BRTR CM7 ....121 J7
  MAL CM9 ....214 C3

Fox House Rd BELV DA17 .....326 E7
Foxlands Crs DAGE RM10 .....310 D5
Foxlands Rd DAGE RM10 ......310 D5
Fox Lea KESG IP5 ....50 F7
Foxleigh BCAYW CM12 ....258 G5
Foxleigh Cl BCAYW CM12 .....259 G5
Foxley Dr BSF CM23 ....139 H1
Fox Manor Wy WTHK RM20 .....335 L1
Foxmeadows SBF/HAD SS7 .....280 C5
Fox Rd CAN/RD E16 ....323 J1
Foxtail Rd IPSE IP3 ....55 L5
Foxton Rd HOD EN11 ....201 H4
  WTHK RM20 ....330 A5
Foxwood Cl CHLM/WR CM1 .....267 H1
Foxwood Cl RCOLW CO11 ......89 G3
Foxwood Crs IPNE IP4 ....49 G8
Foxwood Gv GVW DA11 ....337 H6
Foxwood Pl LOS SS9 ....300 A3
Foyle Dr SOCK/AV RM15 ......329 K2
Foys Wk SOCK CM11 ....258 F6
Frambury La SAFWS CB11 .....372 A1
The Frame IP1 ....47 A4
Framlingham Wy BRTR CM77 ...120 F5
Frampton Rd BSDN SS14 .....278 C4
  EPP CM16 ....220 B5
Frances Cl RCOLE CO7 ....130 C5
Frances Gdns SOCK/AV RM15 .329 J2
Frances Ga CHLM/WR CM1 .....194 D6
Frances Rd CHING E4 ....266 D5
Francis Av IL IG1 ....287 G2
Franciscan Wy IP IP1 ....16 C5
Francis Cl HVHL CB9 ....34 C5
  K/T/MI CO5 ....173 M1
  KESG IP5 ....50 D5
Francis Ct WIT CM8 ....122 F8
Francis Ms MAL CM9 ....214 E5
Francis Rd BRTR CM7 ....121 C5
  DART DA1 ....334 C2
  LEY E10 ....284 F7
  SUD CO10 ....20 C7
  WAN E11 ....285 G2
Francis St RCOLE CO7 ....156 C5
  SRTFD E15 ....307 H2
Francis Wk RAYL SS6 ....280 F2
Frances Wy COLN CO4 ....146 A1
Francombe Gdns ROM RM1 ....289 A4
Frank Burton Cl CHARL SE7 .323 J4
Frank Clater Cl COLN CO4 ...107 J3
Frankland Cl WFD IG8 ....267 M4
Frankland Rd CHING E4 ......266 D4
Franklin Av CHESW EN7 .....216 A5
Franmil Rd EMPK RM11 ....289 J5
  IPSE IP3 ....55 H8
  RCHLM CM3 ....246 E5
Franklin St BOW E3 ....306 E7
Franklins Wy WICKE SS11 ....261 M6
Franklyn Gdns BARK/HLT IG6 .269 G5
Frank Martin Ct CHESW EN7 .216 A4
Franmil Rd EMPK RM11 ....289 J5
Fraser Cl CHLM/GWD CM2 .....276 J3
  LAIN SS15 ....276 J3
  SBN/FI SS3 ....303 J4
Fraser Rd CHES/WCR EN8 ....216 A6
  ERITH DA8 ....326 F8
  IP IP1 ....47 A2
  RIPW IP8 ....47 A2
  WALTH E17 ....284 C7
Frating Abbey Farm Rd
  RCOLE CO7 ....132 F7
Frating Crs WFD IG8 ....267 K5
Frating Hl RCOLE CO7 ....132 A2
Frating Rd RCOLE CO7 ....89 J3
  RCOLE CO7 ....110 B6
Frayes Cha CHONG CM5 ....379 P10
Frazer Cl ROMW/RG RM7 .....289 J3
Frederica Rd CHING E4 ......249 G7
Frederick Pl
  WOOL/PLUM SE18 ....324 D4
Frederick Rd RAIN RM13 .....311 G6
Frederick Sq POP/IOD E14 ...322 F3
Frederic St WALTH E17 ......307 J2
Fredricks Cl MGTR CO11 * ...366 F7
Freeborne Gdns RAIN RM13 ...311 K3
Freebournes Rd WIT CM8 ....171 J2
Freehold Rd IPNE IP4 ....48 C7
Freeland Rd COS CO15 ......6 C4
Freelands Rd RCOLE CO7 ....156 F7
Freeman Cl SLH/COR SS17 ...317 J1
Freeman Rd GVW DA12 ....338 E8
Freemantle Av PEND EN3 ....248 A5
Freeman Wy EMPK RM11 ....290 B4
Freemasons Rd CAN/RD E16 ..323 L2
Freewood La SAFWS CB11 ....350 B4
Freezes Barns CHLM/GWD CM2 344 A6
Freightmaster Est
  RAIN RM13 ....327 K7
The Fremnells BSDN SS14 ....3 L4
French's Cl WARE SG12 .....185 H4
Frensham Cl COS CO15 ......6 D4
Frensham Cl COLN CO4 ......106 A4
Frere Wy K/T/MI CO5 ....130 G3
Frerichs Cl WICKW SS12 ....261 G6
Freshfields HAR CO12 ....70 C4
Freshfields Av UPMR RM14 ..312 C2
Freshfields Rd HAR CO12 ....14 C1
Freshwater Crs MAL CM9 ....214 E1
Freshwater Dr VGE SS16 ....296 C3
Freshwater La COS CO15 ....159 J5
Freshwater Rd BCTR RM8 ....288 A6
Freshwaters HLW CM20 ......13 M4
Freshwell Av CHDH RM6 .....287 M2
Freshwell Gdns
  RBRW/HUT CM13 ....275 G8
  SAFWN CB10 ....351 R3
Freshwell St SAFWN CB10 ....28 A1
Fresh Wharf Rd BARK IG11 ..308 C5
Fresian Cl BRW CM14 ....274 C5
Freston Hl RIPS/CAP IP9 ....364 F5
Freston Rd IPSE IP3 ....55 H5
Freston St BRWN CM15 * 255 H1
Frettons BSDN SS14 ....278 B4
Friar Cl HVHL CB9 ....34 C4
Friar's Av BRWN CM15 ......256 C5
  WALTH E17 ....284 E7
  WFD IG8 ....267 M6
Friar's Bridge Rd IP IP1 ...16 D5
Friar's Cl BRWN CM15 ....256 C5
  CHING E4 ....266 D4
  FX IP11 ....63 J7
  HSTD CO9 ....356 D7
  IL IG1 ....287 G2
  RCOLE CO7 ....110 A7
  RCOS CO16 ....159 H1
Friars Ct COLS CO2 * 129 M2
Friarscroft BROX EN10 ......201 H4
Friars Gate Cl WFD IG8 .....267 K3
Friars La BRTR CM7 ....121 J7
  MAL CM9 ....214 C3

RBSF CM22 ....378 C4
Friars Md HVHL CB9 ....344 E1
  POP/IOD E14 ....322 F6
Friar's Rd EHAM E6 ....308 A5
Friars St IP IP1 ....16 E7
  SUD CO10 ....20 C7
The Friars CHIG IG7 ....269 H3
  HLWW/ROY CM19 ....203 J3
Friars Wd ABYW SE2 ....326 A8
  CHLM/GWD SEVK IG3 ....5 H5
Friars Wd BSF CM23 ....139 K1
Friary Cl CHLM/WR CM1 .....267 H3
Friary Flds MAL CM9 ....214 D3
Friary La WFD IG8 ....267 K3
The Friary CHES/WCR EN8 ...233 G3
Friday Hl CHING E4 ....267 H1
Friday Hl East CHING E4 ....267 H1
Friday Hl West CHING E4 ....267 H1
Friday Rd ERITH DA8 ....327 G8
Friday Wood Gn COLS CO2 ...129 K5
Friedberg Av BCAYE CM12 ...258 C4
Friends Cl CHES/WCR EN8 ...232 A3
Friends Fld BURES CO8 .....359 G8
Friendship Wy SRTFD E15 ...306 F5
Friends Wk KESG IP5 ....50 C5
  SAFWS CB11 ....30 A2
Friern Gdns WICKW SS12 ....260 E6
Friern Pl WICKW SS12 ......260 E6
Frietuna Rd COS CO15 ......159 H3
Frimley Cl EMPK RM11 ......290 D6
Frimley Rd GDMY/SEVK IG3 ..287 H8
Frimley Wy WCHPL E1 * 306 A8
Frinton Dr WFD IG8 ....267 G6
Frinton Ms IL IG1 ....286 D4
Frinton Rd COS CO15 ....160 A4
  CRW RM5 ....270 D6
  EHAM E6 ....308 A7
  FOS CO13 ....136 F3
  RCOS CO16 ....135 L4
Frith Rd WAN E11 ....306 A1
Frithwood Cl BCAYW CM12 ...258 F6
Frithwood La BCAYW CM12 ...258 C6
Fritton Cl CHTY IP2 ....53 M4
Frizlands La DAGE RM10 ....288 C4
Frobisher Dr COS CO15 .....182 G4
Frobisher Gdns LEY E10 * ..284 C4
  HAR CO12 ....70 C4
  IPSE IP3 ....54 D4
Frobisher Wy BRTR CM7 .....121 M1
  GRH DA9 ....335 L6
  SBN/FI SS3 ....303 H4
Froden Brook BCAYW CM11 ...258 F6
Froden Cl BCAYE CM11 ......258 F7
Frogge St SAFWN CB10 ......340 H5
Frog La DAGW RM9 ....327 G1
Frogs Aly RIPS/CAP IP9 ....60 E8
Frog St BRWN CM15 ....255 H1
Frome TIL RM18 ....332 F3
Fronk's Av HAR CO12 ....71 H1
Fronk's Rd HAR CO12 ....71 H1
Front La UPMR RM14 ....291 H7
Front Rd IPSE IP3 ....55 L5
Frowick La RCOS CO16 ......157 K4
Fryatt Av HAR CO12 ....14 C7
Fryerning La ING CM4 ......223 H4
Fry Rd EHAM E6 ....308 A4
Fryth Cl HVHL CB9 ....34 D4
Fuchsia La IPNE IP4 ....48 F3
Fuchsia St ABYW SE2 ....325 L6
Fuchsia Wy RCOS CO16 ......6 A2
Fulbourne Rd WALTH E17 ....266 F6
Fulcher Av CHLM/GWD CM2 ...210 C2
Fulfen Wy SAFWS CB11 ......30 A2
Fulford Dr LOS SS9 ....282 D7
Fullarton Crs SOCK/AV RM15 329 J2
Fullbridge MAL CM9 ....214 D2
Fuller Cl BSF CM23 ....139 H2
  BCTR RM8 ....287 M8
Fuller's Rd WFD IG8 ....267 G6
Fuller's Wy SWFD E18 ......267 J7
Fullers Cl CRW RM5 ....270 E5
  K/T/MI CO5 ....148 E5
  WAB EN9 ....234 B3
Fullers Fld NHMKT IP6 * ...48 E3
Fullers Md HLWE CM17 ......204 D3
Fullers Rd COLS CO2 ....130 L3
  SWFD E18 ....267 J7
Fullers Yd HLWE CM17 * 34 C4
Fullwell Av CLAY IG5 ......268 A4
Fulmar Cl COLN CO4 ....108 A5
Fulmar Rd HCH RM12 ....311 L3
Fulmar Wy WICKE SS11 .....261 K4
Fulmer Rd CAN/RD E16 ......323 L2
Fulready Rd LEY E10 ....285 G3
Fulton Crs BSF CM23 ......115 K8
Fulwich Rd DART DA1 ....334 C2
Furlongs VGE SS16 ....3 L9
The Furlongs ING CM4 ......239 L2
Furlong Wy WARE SG12 .....185 H2
Furneaux La K/T/MI CO5 ....130 C8
Furness Cl CDW/CHF RM16 ...331 L4
Furness Rd
  CHTY IP2 ....53 L5
Furness Wy HCH RM12 ....311 L2
The Furrells CBE/LIN CB1 ..24 C1
Furriers Cl BSF CM23 ......138 D2
Furrow Rd COLW CO3 ....106 B8
Furrowfelde VGE SS16 ......295 K1
Further Meadow
  CHLM/WR CM1 ....208 D5
Further St RCOLW CO6 ......360 F1
Furtherwick Rd CVI SS8 ....320 E4
Furze Crs RCOLE CO7 ....131 K6
Furze Farm Cl CHDH RM6 ...270 B8
Furzefield CHESW EN7 ......216 C6
Furze Gld VGE SS16 ....295 K1
Furze La ING CM4 ....241 K5
  RCOLE CO7 ....110 D8
Furze St BOW E3 * 322 D1
Fusedale Wy SOCK/AV RM15 ..329 J3
Fyefields PIT SS13 ....278 F5
Fyfield Av WICKW SS12 .....260 F8
Fyfield Cl RBRW/HUT CM13 ..275 G8
Fyfield Rd SOCK/AV RM15 ...329 J3
Fyfield Rd CHONG CM5 ......380 H12
  CHONG CM5 ....381 K6
  RAIN RM13 ....311 J5
  WALTH E17 ....284 C1
  WFD IG8 ....267 M6
Fynn Valley Wk NHMKT IP6 ..49 L1

SBF/HAD SS7 ....281 K6
Gaces Acre SAFWS CB11 .....351 P12
Gad Cl PLSTW E13 ....307 H2
Gadsden Cl CAN/RD E16 .....291 H4
Gadwall Cl CAN/RD E16 .....323 K2
Gadwall Reach K/T/MI CO5 ..130 G3
Gafzelle Dr SUD CO10 ......321 H3
Gager Dr K/T/MI CO5 ....150 B8
Gage Rd CAN/RD E16 ....150 J2
Gage's Rd SUD CO10 ....346 D2
Gaiger Cl CHLM/WR CM1 .....194 A6
Gainsborough Av CVI SS8 ...321 H3
  MNPK E12 ....308 D2
  TIL RM18 ....331 K7
Gainsborough Cl
  BCAYW CM12 ....258 E4
  RCOS CO15 ....178 A7
  RCOS CO15 ....158 A7
Gainsborough Crs
  CHLM/GWD CM2 ....210 B2
Gainsborough Dr
  GVW DA11 ....337 G8
  MGTR CO11 ....90 F1
  WOS/PRIT SS0 ....300 F1
Gainsborough La IPSE IP3 ..54 E5
Gainsborough Pl
  RBRW/HUT CM13 ....257 G4
Gainsborough Rd BRTR CM7 ..309 L8
  COLW CO3 ....106 E8
  FX IP11 ....11 M1
  HVHL CB9 ....34 A4
  IPNE IP4 ....48 G5
  RAIN RM13 ....311 K5
  SRTFD E15 ....307 H2
  SUD CO10 ....20 C7
  WAN E11 ....285 H5
  WFD IG8 ....268 A3
Gainsborough St SUD CO10 ..20 C7
Gainsborough Yd SUD CO10 * 20 C7
Gains Cl CVI SS8 ....321 C1
Gainsford Av COS CO15 ....7 M3
Gainsford End Rd HSTD CO9 .345 N3
Gainsford Rd WALTH E17 ....284 C2
Gainsthorpe Rd CHONG CM5 ..380 F2
Galadriel RCHLM CM3 ....244 A4
Galahad Cl BOC CM0 ....393 L8
Galbraith St POP/IOD E14 ..322 H4
Galeborough Av WFD IG8 ....267 G6
Gale St BOW E3 ....322 D1
  DAGW RM9 ....310 A3
Gales Wy WFD IG8 ....268 B6
Galey Gn SOCK/AV RM15 .....329 L1
Gall End La STSD CM24 .....374 A6
Galleon Bvd GRH DA9 ......335 M6
Galleon Cl ERITH DA8 ......327 G7
Galleon Rd CDW/CHF RM16 ...329 C5
Galleons Dr BARK IG11 .....309 H5
Galleons Hl CHLM/WR CM1 ...191 L8
Galleydene SBF/HAD SS7 ....298 F2
Galley Gn HERT/BAY SG13 ...185 H7
Galley Hill Rd GVW DA11 ...336 C3
Galleyhill Rd WAB EN9 .....233 M3
Galleys Cnr BRTR CM77 * ...122 A8
Galleywood Crs CRW RM5 ...271 G5
Galleywood Rd
  CHLM/GWD CM2 ....225 K1
Galliford Rd MAL CM9 .....214 E3
Gallions Cl BARK IG11 ....309 K7
Gallions Rd CAN/RD E16 ....324 C3
  CHARL SE7 ....323 H4
Gallions View Rd THMD SE28 325 H5
Gallon Cl CHARL SE7 ......323 H4
The Gallops SBW CM21 * 276 E8
Galloson Rd
  WOOL/PLUM SE18 ....325 H7
Galloway Cl BROX EN10 ....217 G4
  BSF CM23 ....139 G1
Galloway Dr RCOS CO16 ....158 F2
Galloway Rd BSF CM23 .....138 G1
Gallows Green Rd GTDUN CM6 95 H2
Gallows Hl SAFWS CB11 ....351 R6
Galsworthy Av CHDH RM6 ...287 L5
  POP/IOD E14 ....322 E2
Galsworthy Cl THMD SE28 ...325 L4
Galton Rd WOS/PRIT SS0 ....300 E5
Galway Av IP IP1 ....47 M3
Gambleside VGE SS16 ......296 B2
Gamuel Cl WALTH E17 ....284 C4
Gandalf's Ride RCHLM CM3 ..244 F7
Gandhi Cl WALTH E17 ......284 C4
Gandish Cl RCOLE CO7 * 64 B5
Gandish Rd RCOLE CO7 .....64 B3
Ganels Cl BCAYE CM11 .....258 F6
Ganels Rd BCAYE CM11 .....258 F6
Ganges Rd RIPS/CAP IP9 ...66 F5
Ganges Hl SBW CM21 ....163 H6
Gannet Cl HVHL CB9 ....34 F5
Gannet Rd CHTY IP2 ....53 M4
Gant Ct WAB EN9 ....234 A4
Gantshill Crs
  GNTH/NBYPK IG2 ....286 D3
Ganwick Cl HVHL CB9 ......34 C4
Gaol La SUD CO10 ....20 D6
The Gap COS CO15 ....160 D3
  SAFWS CB11 ....350 G12
Garbutt Rd UPMR RM14 .....290 F7
Garden Cl CHING E4 ....266 D4
  CHLM CM3 ....392 C1
  RIPS/CAP IP9 ....66 D2
Garden Ct FOS CO13 * 137 G3
  RCOLW CO6 ....82 C7
Garden Dr COLW CO3 ....106 B7
Garden End ING CM4 ....239 L2
Gardeners CHLM/GWD CM2 ....210 A8
Gardeners La RCFD SS4 ....283 B12
Gardeners Rw RCOLW CO6 ....124 D3
Garden Farm K/T/MI CO5 ...176 A6
Garden Fld FX IP11 ....62 D8
  RCHLM CM3 ....244 C1
Garden Flds BOC CM0 ......389 M1
  GTDUN CM6 ....103 M5
  RCOLW CO6 ....103 M5
Gardenia Rd RCOS CO16 .....108 A3
Gardenia Wk COLN CO4 .....108 B6
Gardenia Wy WFD IG8 ......267 K5
Garden Pl SUD CO10 ....20 D7
  WOTN CO14 ....355 K1
Garden Rd GVW DA11 ....337 G8
Garden Side SUD CO10 .....20 C5
The Gardens BRWN CM15 ....383 Q10
Garden St WCHPL E1 * 322 A1
Garden Terrace Rd
  HLWE CM17 ....188 D7
Garden Wy LOU IG10 ....235 H2
Garden Yd HSTD CO9 * 81 J3
Gardiner Cl BCTR RM8 .....310 A1
  PEND EN3 ....248 A6
Gardiners Cl BSDN SS14 ...278 A4
Gardiners La
  North BSDN SS14 ....260 A8
Gardiner's La
  South BSDN SS14 ....278 B3
Gardiners Link BSDN SS14 ..278 A3
The Gardiners HLWE CM17 ..204 C2
Gardiners Wy BSDN SS14 ...278 A3

Gabion Av PUR RM19 ....329 G7
Gablefields CHLM/GWD CM2 ..210 G7
The Gables GRAYS RM17 * ...330 C3
  HAR CO12 ....15 J4
  PIT SS13 ....278 E5
  SAFWS CB11 * 351 N11

Gardner Av SLH/COR SS17 ...295 K8
Gardner Cl WAN E11 ...285 L4
Gardner Rd PLSTW E13 ...307 L3
Garfield Cl FX IP11 ...11 K3
Garfield Rd CHING E4 ...249 G8
FX IP11 ...11 K3
PLSTW E13 ...307 L3
Garford St POP/IOD E14 ...322 C3
Garganey Wk THMD SE28 ...325 M3
Gargery Cl GVE DA12 ...338 C5
Garibaldi St
  WOOL/PLUM SE18 ...325 H7
Garland Cl CHES/WCR EN8 ...232 F1
Garland Rd HAR CO12 ...14 B5
Garnault Rd EN EN1 ...232 A8
Garner Cl BCTR RM8 ...288 A7
Garner Dr BROX EN10 ...216 H4
Garner Rd WALTH E17 ...266 F7
Garnetts RBSF CM22 ...377 J1
Garnetts La GTDUN CM6 ...118 F7
Garnon Md EPP CM16 ...220 E6
Garnons Cha RCFD ...360 F12
Garrettlands CHLM/GWD CM2 ...211 J7
Garrick Dr WOOL/PLUM SE18 ...325 G6
Garrick St GVW DA11 ...337 L4
Garrick Wy FX IP11 ...47 M2
Garrison La FX IP11 ...11 J4
Garrison Rd BOW E3 ...306 D5
Garrod Ct COLS CO2 ...129 L6
Garrods RIPS/CAP IP9 ...58 E4
Garron La SOCK/AV RM15 ...329 J2
Garry Cl ROM RM1 ...271 H6
Garry Wy ROM RM1 ...271 H6
Garside Rd WOOL/PLUM SE18 ...325 C6
Garth Rd SOCK/AV RM15 ...313 M8
Garthwood Rd RCOLW CO6 ...106 B1
Gartmore Rd GDMY/SEVK IG3 ...287 G3
Garvary Rd CAN/RD E16 ...323 C2
Gascoigne Gdns WFD IG8 ...268 L6
Gascoigne Rd BARK IG11 ...308 C5
  COLN CO4 ...9 J4
Gascoigne Wy BCAYE CM11 ...259 G3
Gascoyne La HARH RM3 ...272 A4
Gascoyne Rd HOM E9 ...306 A4
Gaselee St POP/IOD E14 ...322 F3
Gas La ROY SG8 ...370 B4
Gasson Rd SWCM DA10 ...336 B4
Gaston End RCOLE CO7 ...363 R6
Gaston St RCOLE CO7 ...363 R7
Gatacre Rd IP IP1 ...16 A7
Gate Farm Rd RIPS/CAP IP9 ...67 C4
Gatefield Cl WOTN CO14 ...137 J2
Gatehope Dr SOCK/AV RM15 ...329 J2
Gatehouse Ms ING IG4 ...239 L2
Gatekeeper Cl BRTR CM7 ...121 L4
Gate Lodge Sq LAIN SS15 ...277 J3
Gate Lodge Wk LAIN SS15 ...277 J3
Gate St MAL CM9 ...214 C2
Gate Street Ms MAL CM9 ...214 C2
Gateway BSDN SS14 ...278 A5
Gathorne St BETH E2 ...306 A6
Gatling Rd ABYW SE2 ...325 K8
Gatscombe Rd HOC/HUL SS5 ...264 A7
The Gattens RAYL SS6 ...281 J1
Gatwick Cl BSF CM23 ...115 J8
Gatwick Rd GVE DA12 ...337 L5
Gatwick Vw BCAYW CM12 ...258 E5
Gauden Rd BRTR CM7 ...99 A6
Gavenny Pth SOCK/AV RM15 ...329 J2
Gaverick St POP/IOD E14 ...322 D7
Gavin Wy COLN CO4 ...87 L8
Gawsworth Cl WFD IG8 ...307 J2
Gay Bowers BSDN SS14 ...263 M3
  HOC/HUL SS5 ...263 L4
Gay Bowers La RCHLM CM3 ...212 C7
Gay Bowers Rd RCHLM CM3 ...228 B1
Gay Bowers Wy WIT CM8 ...171 K6
Gaye St IP IP1 ...16 A7
Gayfer Av KESG IG5 ...50 F5
Gayfere Rd CLAY IG5 ...286 C1
Gay Gdns DAGE RM10 ...310 F1
Gayleighs RAYL SS6 ...281 G1
Gay Links BSDN SS14 ...3 G4
Gaylor Rd TIL RM18 ...331 H7
Gaymers La FX IP11 ...62 A5
Gaynes Ct UPMR RM14 ...312 E1
Gaynesford VGE SS16 ...295 H1
Gaynes Hill Rd WFD IG8 ...268 B6
Gaynes Park Rd UPMR RM14 ...312 E1
Gaynes Rd UPMR RM14 ...290 E7
Gay Rd SRTFD E15 ...307 C6
Gaysham Av
  GNTH/NBYPK IG2 ...286 D3
Gays La RCFD SS4 ...392 B11
Gayton Rd SOSN SS2 ...19 H1
Gaywood LAIN SS15 ...276 D6
Gaywood Av CHES/WCR EN8 ...216 A8
Gaywood Rd WALTH E17 ...284 D1
Gazelle Cl COLN CO4 ...107 M1
Geariesville Gdns
  BARK/HLT IG6 ...286 D2
Geary Dr BRW CM14 ...255 M8
Geddings Rd HOD EN11 ...201 J3
Geere Rd SRTFD E15 ...307 H5
The Geerings FX IP11 ...63 J8
Geesh Rd CVI SS8 ...298 F8
Geisthorp Ct WAB EN9 ...234 B5
Gelsthorpe Rd CRW RM5 ...270 G6
Generals La RCHLM CM3 ...194 E3
Generals Ms FX IP11 ...62 C8
The Generals Wk PEND EN3 ...232 F7
Genesta Cl MAL CM9 ...385 N3
Genesta Rd WOS/PRIT SS0 ...300 F1
Geneva Av WDBR IP12 ...51 H5
Geneva Gdns CHDH RM6 ...288 D8
Geneva Rd IP IP1 ...16 D3
Genever Cl CHING E4 ...266 D4
Genk Cl CVI SS8 ...298 F3
Gennep Rd CVI SS8 ...298 F3
Gentian Ct COLN CO4 ...106 F3
Gentry Cl SLH/COR SS17 ...316 F3
Geoffrey Av HARH RM3 ...272 D5
Geoffrey Gdns EHAM E6 ...308 A6
Geoff Seaden Cl COL CO1 ...9 K8
George Av RCOLE CO7 ...156 C6
George Avey Cft EPP CM16 ...221 J4
George Beard Rd DEPT SE8 ...322 C7
George Cardnell Wy
  RCHLM CM3 ...388 B8
George Cl CO015 ...287 B7
  CVI SS8 ...298 C7
George Cut RCOLE CO7 ...156 C7
George Frost Cl IPNE IP4 ...17 C7
George Gent Cl HVHL CB9 ...344 A7
George La SUD CO10 ...39 A7
  SWFD E18 ...267 A8
George Lovell Dr PEND EN3 ...233 H7
George Rd BRTR CM7 ...121 J4
  CHING E4 ...266 A8
Georges Dr BRW CM15 ...255 J3
George St BARK IG11 ...308 C4
  CAN/RD E16 ...306 F5
  CHLM/GWD CM2 ...5 D6
  COL CO1 ...8 D6
  GRAYS RM17 ...330 D5
  HAR CO12 ...15 L4
  ROM RM1 ...289 J4
  SAFWN CB10 ...28 A8
SBN/FI SS3 ...303 J7
Georgeville Gdns
  BARK/HLT IG6 ...286 D2
George Williams Wy COL CO1 ...8
Gepp Pl CHLM/GWD CM2 ...210 E1
Gepps Cl CHLM/WR CM1 ...165 G3
Gerald Rd BCTR RM8 ...288 C7
  CAN/RD E16 ...307 J8
GVE DA12 ...338 B5
Geralds Av IPNE IP4 ...48 H8
Geranium Cl RCOS CO16 ...6 B3
Geranium Wk COLN CO4 ...L6
Gerard Av BSF CM23 ...138 C5
Gerard Gdns RAIN RM13 ...311 H6
Gerard Rd RCOS CO16 ...158 F7
Gernon Cl CHLM/WR CM1 ...193 L2
  RAIN RM13 ...312 A6
Gernon Rd BOW E3 ...306 D6
  RCOLE CO7 ...89 H6
Gerpins La UPMR RM14 ...312 C5
Gerrard Crs BRW CM14 ...273 M2
Gertrude Rd BELV DA17 ...326 D7
Gestingthorpe Rd SUD CO10 ...347 N8
Geylen Rd CVI SS8 ...322 J1
Ghyllgrove BSDN SS14 ...3 J5
Ghyllgrove Cl BSDN SS14 ...3 H2
Gibb Cft HLWS CM18 ...203 M5
Gibbfield Cl CHDH RM6 ...288 B1
Gibbins Rd SRTFD E15 ...306 F4
Gibbons Ct GTDUN CM6 ...117 G4
Gibbs St IP IP1 ...16 B3
Gibbs Cl CHES/WCR EN8 ...216 E7
Gibbs Fld BSF CM23 ...138 E4
Gibb Ter BOW E3 ...306 E2
Gibralter Cl RBRW/HUT CM13 ...273 M5
Gibson Cl BSF CM23 ...139 J1
  GVW DA11 ...337 J8
  SAFWN CB10 ...28 A8
Gibson Gdns SAFWN CB10 ...28 A8
Gibson Rd BCTR RM8 ...287 M6
  HSTD CO9 ...356 E9
Gibson St GNWCH SE10 ...323 H8
Gibson V CHLM/WR CM1 ...193 L5
Gibson Wy SAFWN CB10 ...28 A8
Gideons Wy SLH/COR SS17 ...317 G2
Giffins Cl BRTR CM7 ...121 H4
Gifford Cl RIPS/CAP IP9 ...364 C3
Gifford Gn PIT SS13 ...278 E3
Gifford Rd SBF/HAD SS7 ...280 A8
Giffords Cross Av
  SLH/COR SS17 ...317 K1
Giffords Cross Rd
  SLH/COR SS17 ...317 K2
Giffordside CDW/CHF RM16 ...331 L4
Giffords Pl IPNE IP4 ...48 L7
Gifhorn Rd CVI SS8 ...321 J1
Gift La SRTFD E15 ...307 H5
Gilbert Dr VGE SS16 ...276 D8
Gilbert Rd COL CO1 ...129 L1
  RAYL SS6 ...281 J3
  SWCM DA10 ...336 A4
Gilbert St VGE SS16 ...276 D8
Gilbert Rd BELV DA17 ...326 D6
  CDW/CHF RM16 ...329 M6
  ROM RM1 ...289 J2
  SUD CO10 ...39 H6
Gilbert Ter GVW DA11 ...337 J7
Gilbey Av BSF CM23 ...139 J3
Gilbey Crs STSD CM24 ...115 M1
Gilchrist Wy BRTR CM7 ...121 H1
Gilda Av PEND EN3 ...248 B5
Gilda Ter BRTR CM7 ...121 H4
Gildborne Cl SLH/COR SS17 ...296 A8
Gilden Cl HLWE CM17 ...188 E6
Gilden Wy HLWE CM17 ...188 E6
Gilderdale Cl COLN CO4 ...108 A2
Gilders SBW CM21 ...162 F1
Gilders Wy RCOS CO16 ...B1
Giles Cl RAIN RM13 ...312 A6
Gillam Wy RAIN RM13 ...311 K3
Gillards Ms WALTH E17 ...284 D2
Gillards Wy WALTH E17 ...284 D2
Gill Av CAN/RD E16 ...323 K2
Gill Cl MAL CM9 ...198 C7
Gill Crs GVW DA11 ...337 J8
Gillcrest Dr BOW E3 ...306 E3
Gillett Av EHAM E6 ...308 B6
Gillian Crs GPK RM2 ...271 M8
Gillman Dr SRTFD E15 ...307 H5
Gill St POP/IOD E14 ...322 C3
The Gill SBF/HAD SS7 ...281 G8
Gilman Dr SBN/FI SS3 ...302 F6
Gilmore Wy CHLM/GWD CM2 ...210 D2
Gilmour Cl ENC/FH EN2 ...232 B5
Gilmour Rd BCAYW CM12 ...258 C4
Gilpin Cl BLPT CM5 ...M8
Gilpin's Gallop WARE SG12 ...185 J5
Gippeswyk Av IPS IP2 ...16 A8
Gippeswyk Rd CHTY IP2 ...16 B8
Gipping Cl HVHL CB9 ...344 B7
Gippingstone Rd RIPW IP8 ...46 F2
Gipping Valley River Pth
  RIPW IP8 ...46 F2
Gipping Wy RIPW IP8 ...46 F2
Gipson Park Cl LOS SS9 ...282 A7
Gipsy La BSF CM23 ...115 K5
  GRAYS RM17 ...330 D5
Giralda Cl CAN/RD E16 ...324 A2
Giraud St POP/IOD E14 ...322 D4
Girling Rd SUD CO10 ...20 D7
Girton Ct CHES/WCR EN8 ...216 A8
Girton Rd HVHL CB9 ...34 H6
Girton Wy CHTY IP2 ...53 H6
Gladden Rd HLWS CM18 ...203 M5
Gladden Flds RCHLM CM3 ...244 H4
Gladding Rd MNPK E12 ...308 A1
The Glade CLAY IG5 ...268 C8
  COLN CO4 ...108 A3
  UPMR RM14 ...256 D2
  VGE SS16 ...295 M1
  WFD IG8 ...267 M1
Gladeview COS CO015 ...159 J6
The Gladeway WAB EN9 ...233 J4
Gladiator Wy COLS CO2 ...128 D3
Gladstone Av MNPK E12 ...308 B4
Gladstone Gdns CHLM/GWD CM2 ...5 H6
Gladstone Gdns RAYL SS6 ...280 E4
Gladstone Rd BKHH IG9 ...249 M8
  COL CO1 ...107 G8
  DART DA1 ...334 C8
  HOC/HUL SS5 ...264 B8
  HOD EN11 ...201 J2
  IPSE IP5 ...17 G1
  K/T/MI CO5 ...174 A1
Gladwin Rd COLS CO2 ...128 D3
Gladwyns LAIN SS15 ...2 C1
Glamis Cl CHESW EN7 ...216 B6
Glamis Dr EMPK RM11 ...290 D8
Glamorgan Rd CHTY IP2 ...54 A6
Glandford Wy CHDH RM6 ...287 L3
Glanmead BRWN CM15 ...256 F8
Glanmire BCAYE CM11 ...241 G7
Glanthams Rd BRWN CM15 ...256 D5
Glanville Dr EMPK RM11 ...290 C6
Glanville Pl KESG IP5 ...50 A7
Glasgow Rd PLSTW E13 ...307 H1
Glasseys La RAYL SS6 ...280 F5
Glasshouse Flds WAP E1W ...322 A3
Glass Yd WOOL/PLUM SE18 ...324 F4
Glastonbury Av WFD IG8 ...268 A6
Glastonbury Cha
  WOS/PRIT SS0 ...282 E8
Glastonbury Cl CHTY IP2 ...53 L4
Glaucus St BOW E3 ...322 E1
Glebe Av BRTR CM7 ...99 H6
  WFD IG8 ...267 K5
Glebe BSDN SS14 ...3 J1
Glebe Cl BSF CM23 ...159 J1
Glebe Crs CBS CB2 ...22 E3
  CHLM/WR CM1 ...193 L4
  WIT CM8 ...171 H1
Glebe Dr RAYL SS6 ...280 F2
Glebe End RBSF CM22 ...374 F4
Glebe Fld BSDN SS14 ...3 K8
Glebefield RCHLM CM3 ...196 B1
Glebe Gdns K/T/MI CO5 ...125 C8
  RBRW/HUT CM13 ...275 H2
Glebelands CHIG IG7 ...269 G2
  HLW CM20 ...13 M1
  RCOLW CO6 ...86 E4
  SBF/HAD SS7 ...279 J2
Glebe La BOC CM0 ...390 F6
  GTDUN CM6 ...94 C8
  RIPS/CAP IP9 ...365 C8
Glebe Meadow RCHLM CM3 ...167 H6
Glebe Rd BCAYE CM11 ...260 C5
  CHLM/WR CM1 ...382 G3
  CHOMC CM5 ...L4
  COLS CO2 ...128 F3
  DAGE RM10 ...310 E3
  GVW DA11 ...337 J3
  K/T/MI CO5 ...149 M8
  MAL CM9 ...198 F8
  RAIN RM13 ...311 L7
  WICKE SS11 ...261 H6
Glebe Ter BOW E3 ...306 E2
The Glebe HLW CM20 ...13 M4
  HVHL CB9 ...34 B4
  RCHLM CM3 ...230 D4
  SAFWS SN11 ...30 B2
Glebe Wy BOC CM0 ...393 N6
  COS CO015 ...182 D6
  EMPK RM11 ...290 D6
  FOS CO13 ...183 G4
  SBF/HAD SS7 ...299 J2
Glebeway WFD IG8 ...267 M4
Glemham Dr IPNE IP4 ...55 L1
Glemsford Cl SLH/COR SS17 ...296 A8
Glen Cl SBF/HAD SS7 ...298 E4
Glencree BCAYE CM11 ...241 G7
Glen Crs WFD IG8 ...267 M3
Glen Cft HOC/HUL SS5 ...264 C6
Glendale RCHLM CM3 ...245 H4
Glendale Av CHDH RM6 ...287 M5
  BRWN CM15 ...256 A8
Glendale Gdns LOS SS9 ...300 A1
Glendale Gv COLN CO4 ...107 M2
Glendale Rd BOC CM0 ...393 M7
  ERITH DA8 ...326 F7
Glendale Wy THMD SE28 ...325 M4
Glendower Rd CHING E4 ...249 G8
Glendown Rd ABYW SE2 ...325 H8
Gleneagles SBF/HAD SS7 ...279 G8
Gleneagles Cl FX IP11 ...63 J8
  HARH RM3 ...272 C6
Gleneagles Dr IPNE IP4 ...49 H8
Gleneagles Rd LOS SS9 ...281 M8
Gleneagles Wy RCHLM CM3 ...196 B1
Glenester Cl HOD EN11 ...185 H8
Glen Faba Rd
  HLWW/ROY CM19 ...202 A1
Glenfield Av SUD CO10 ...62 F7
Glenfield Rd SLH/COR SS17 ...295 L8
Glenforth St GNWCH SE10 ...323 J8
Glengall Br POP/IOD E14 ...322 D6
Glengall Gv POP/IOD E14 ...322 D6
Glengall Rd WFD IG8 ...267 K4
Glengarnock Av POP/IOD E14 ...322 F7
Glenham Dr GNTH/NBYPK IG2 ...286 D3
Glen Hazel BRWN CM15 ...238 A1
Glenhurst Av IPNE IP4 ...49 G5
Glenhurst Rd SOSN SS2 ...19 J3
Glenister Rd GNWCH SE10 ...323 J8
Glenmere VGE SS16 ...296 A1
Glenmere Park Av
  SBF/HAD SS7 ...298 C4
Glenmore St SOSN SS2 ...302 A4
Glenmore Wy BARK IG11 ...308 F8
Glenny Rd BARK IG11 ...308 B5
Glenparke Rd FSTGT E7 ...307 J2
Glenridding SBF/HAD SS7 ...280 B8
Glen Ri WFD IG8 ...267 M3
Glen Rd LOS SS9 ...300 D1
  PLSTW E13 ...307 H2
  SBF/HAD SS7 ...298 D4
  WALTH E17 ...284 C1
Glenside BCAYE CM11 ...259 F4
  CHIG IG7 ...268 A4
  SUD CO10 ...21 G7
Glen Ter POP/IOD E14 ...322 D6
The Glen HOC/HUL SS5 * ...263 M8
RAIN RM13 ...311 M8
RAYL SS6 ...281 H5
SLH/COR SS17 ...317 G2
WOS/PRIT SS0 ...296 D1
Glenthorne Gdns
  BARK/HLT IG6 ...286 D1
Glenthorne Rd WALTH E17 ...284 B3
Glenton Cl ROM RM1 ...271 H6
Glenton Wy ROM RM1 ...271 H6
Glentress Cl CAN/RD E16 ...308 A2
Glen Vw GVE DA12 ...337 M6
Glenwood BROX EN10 ...201 G5
Glenwood Av HOC/HUL SS5 ...264 C6
  LOS SS9 ...281 L6
  RAIN RM13 ...311 K8
  WOS/PRIT SS0 ...18 D1
Glenwood Gdns
  GNTH/NBYPK IG2 ...286 D3
  VGE SS16 ...294 B3
Glenworth Av POP/IOD E14 ...323 G2
Gleten Rd CVI SS8 ...321 G1
Glimpsing Gn ERITH DA18 ...326 B6
Glisson Sq COLS CO2 ...128 D3
Globe Cl K/T/MI CO5 ...150 A7
Globe Crs BSF CM23 ...114 E3
Globe Pond Rd
  BERM/RHTH SE16 ...322 B4
Globe Rd EMPK RM11 ...289 K4
  SRTFD E15 ...307 J2
  WFD IG8 ...267 M5
Globe Yd SUD CO10 ...20 D5
Gloster Pk KESG IP5 ...51 H1
Gloster Ter RCFD SS4 * ...283 L1
Gloucester Av
  CDW/CHF RM16 ...330 F6
  CHES/WCR EN8 ...232 F1
  COLS CO2 ...128 E2
  EMPK RM11 ...290 D3
  MAL CM9 ...214 C5
  RAYL SS6 ...281 K5
  TIL RM18 ...332 F4
Gloucester Crs
  CHLM/WR CM1 ...193 G8
Gloucester Gdns BRTR CM7 ...121 L2
  IL IG1 ...286 B5
Gloucester Pl BCAYW CM12 ...240 C8
Gloucester Rd BELV DA17 ...326 C8
  BRWN CM15 ...255 L5
  BRTR CM7 ...99 A6
  HVHL CB9 ...34 A6
  IPSE IP5 ...54 F3
  LEY E10 ...284 D5
  MNPK E12 ...286 D2
  ROM RM1 ...289 H4
  WALTH E17 ...266 A6
  WAN E11 ...285 K4
Gloucester Ter SOS SS1 ...302 C7
Gloucester Wy SUD CO10 ...20 C7
Glover Cl ABYW SE2 ...325 K7
  CBS CB2 ...22 A3
  CHESW EN7 * ...216 A5
Glovers RCHLM CM3 ...144 C6
Glovers Fld BRWN CM15 ...383 N11
Glovers La HLWE CM17 ...204 F6
Glynde Wy SOSN SS2 ...302 C4
Glyndon Rd
  WOOL/PLUM SE18 ...324 F4
Glynn Rd CLPT E5 ...306 A1
Glyn Rd CLPT E5 ...306 A1
Goat Hall La CHLM/GWD CM2 ...225 D2
Goat House La RCHLM CM3 ...229 H2
Goat La EN EN1 ...231 L4
Goat Lodge Rd MAL CM9 ...172 G8
Goatsmoor La BCAYE CM11 ...241 G8
Goatswood La ABR/ST RM4 ...253 L7
Gobions VGE SS16 ...2 D6
Gobions Av CRW RM5 ...271 G6
Goda Cl WIT CM8 ...171 G3
Godalming Rd POP/IOD E14 ...322 E1
Godbold Cl KESG IP5 ...50 F5
Godbold Rd SRTFD E15 ...307 H6
Goddard Rd CDW/CHF RM16 ...314 D8
Goddard Rd East IP IP1 ...47 L2
Goddards Wy IL IG1 ...287 G3
Godfrey Hl WOOL/PLUM SE18 ...324 E4
Godfrey Rd
  WOOL/PLUM SE18 ...324 C7
Godfrey St SRTFD E15 ...306 F6
Godings Wy BRTR CM7 ...121 H1
Godman Rd CHLM/GWD CM2 ...331 J2
Godmans La RCOLW CO6 ...126 B2
Godric Pl BRTR CM7 ...121 H1
Godric Rd WIT CM8 ...171 H1
Godstow Rd ABYW SE2 ...325 K6
Godwin Cl CHING E4 ...233 N6
  HSTD CO9 ...81 G4
Godwin Rd FSTGT E7 ...307 L1
Goffs La CHESW EN7 ...216 B7
  RCOS CO16 ...113 J5
Goings La K/T/MI CO5 ...177 M7
Goirle Av CVI SS8 ...321 H1
Goldace GRAYS RM17 ...330 C5
Goldberry Md RCHLM CM3 ...244 F7
Gold Cl BROX EN10 ...200 F5
Goldcrest Cl CAN/RD E16 ...324 A1
  COLN CO4 ...108 C2
  THMD SE28 ...325 M1
Goldcrest Dr BCAYW CM11 ...258 F4
Goldcrest Rd CHTY IP2 ...53 J5
Goldenacres Ms RCFD SS4 ...265 G4
Golden Cross Ms RCFD SS4 * ...265 G3
Golden Cross Rd RCFD SS4 * ...265 G3
Golden Dawn Wy COLN CO4 ...107 J3
Golden Hind Pl DEPT SE8 * ...322 C7
Golden La RCOS CO16 ...135 G2
  SAFWN CB10 ...342 C11
Golden Lion La HAR CO12 ...15 L4
Goldenlond RCOLW CO6 ...361 F4
Golden Manor Dr SBF/HAD SS7 ...280 C8
Golden Noble Hl COL CO1 ...8 E7
Golden Pde WALTH E17 * ...284 E1
Golden Plover Cl CAN/RD E16 ...323 K2
Goldfinch Cl COLN CO4 ...108 C2
Goldfinch La SBF/HAD SS7 ...280 C5
Goldfinch Rd THMD SE28 ...325 M2
Goldhanger Cl RAYL SS6 ...280 C5
Goldhanger Cross BSDN SS14 ...278 B6
Goldhanger Rd MAL CM9 ...214 F6
Goldhaze Cl WFD IG8 ...268 B6
Golding Crs SLH/COR SS17 ...317 H2
Goldingham Av LOU IG10 ...250 F6
Golding Rd BRTR CM7 ...121 J4
Goldings Cl HVHL CB9 ...344 B7
Goldings Crs SOS SS16 ...296 B2
Golding's Ri LOU IG10 ...235 G8
Goldings Rd LOU IG10 ...250 F6
Golding Thoroughfare
  CHLM/GWD CM2 ...210 D2
Goldington Av HOD EN11 ...185 G8
Goldington Crs BCAYW CM12 ...240 C8
Golding Wy RCOS CO16 ...157 G5
  SUD CO10 ...39 L1
Goldlay Av CHLM/GWD CM2 ...5 J8
Goldlay Gdns CHLM/GWD CM2 ...5 J8
Goldlay Rd CHLM/GWD CM2 ...5 J8
Goldmer Cl SBN/FI SS3 ...302 E5
Goldsands Rd BOC CM0 ...393 P3
Goldsborough Crs CHING E4 ...266 D5
Goldsdown Cl PEND EN3 ...248 B2
Goldsdown Rd PEND EN3 ...248 A2
Goldsmid St
  WOOL/PLUM SE18 ...325 H8
Goldsmith GRAYS RM17 ...330 C5
Goldsmith Av MNPK E12 ...308 B3
  ROM RM7 ...289 M5
Goldsmith Dr RAYL SS6 ...262 F6
Goldsmith Rd IP IP1 ...47 K1
  LEY E10 ...284 E6
  WALTH E17 ...266 A6
Goldsmiths Av SLH/COR SS16 * ...317 K2
Goldwing Cl CAN/RD E16 ...323 K2
Golf Course Rd
  CDW/CHF RM16 ...316 A7
Golfe Rd IL IG1 ...287 G8
Golf Green Rd COS CO15 ...182 D5
Golf Ride SBF/HAD SS7 ...298 A2
Golf Rd FX IP11 ...63 J8
Gollogly Ter CHARL SE7 ...323 H8
Goodall Rd WAN E11 ...284 F8
Goodchild Wy HSTD CO9 ...346 B11
Goodey Cl COL CO1 ...107 K9
Goodey Rd BARK IG11 ...309 G4
Goodier Rd CHLM/WR CM1 ...209 J1
Goodlake Cl HAR CO12 ...70 D3
Goodliffe Pk BSF CM23 ...115 J7
Goodman Gv KESG IP5 ...50 D6
Goodman Rd LEY E10 ...284 F5
Goodmans SBN/FI SS3 * ...303 L2
Goodmans Rd
  CHLM/WR CM1 ...144 D3
Goodmayes Av
  GDMY/SEVK IG3 ...287 K6
Goodmayes La
  GDMY/SEVK IG3 ...309 K1
Goodmayes Rd
  GDMY/SEVK IG3 ...287 K6
Goodview Rd LAIN SS15 ...295 K3
Goodway Gdns POP/IOD E14 ...323 H2
Goodwins Ct CHES/WCR EN8 ...216 F6
Goodwins Rd SAFWS CB11 ...351 M2
Goodwin Stile BSF CM23 ...138 C4
Goodwood Av HCH RM12 ...290 C4
  PEND EN3 ...232 F7
  RBRW/HUT CM13 ...257 J3
Goodwood Cl HOD EN11 ...201 G2
  IP IP1 ...48 H1
  SBF/HAD SS7 ...107 G8
Goosander Wy
  THMD SE28 ...325 G6
Goose La RBSF CM22 ...163 G5
Gooseley La EHAM E6 ...308 D2
Gooshays Dr HARH RM3 ...272 B5
Gooshays Gdns HARH RM3 ...272 B5
Gordon Av CHING E4 ...267 H5
  HCH RM12 ...289 J7
Gordon Cl BCAYW CM12 ...258 C2
Gordon Dr COLN CO4 ...87 L8
Gordon Pl GVE DA12 ...337 M4
  SOS SS1 ...18 F5
Gordon Prom East GVE DA12 ...338 A4
Gordon Rd BARK IG11 ...309 H5
  BELV DA17 ...327 G8
  BRWN CM15 ...256 D4
  BSDN SS14 ...3 M7
  CDW/CHF RM16 ...331 H4
  CHES/WCR EN8 ...233 H4
  CHING E4 ...249 H7
  CHLM/GWD CM2 ...209 K7
  GVW DA11 ...337 K5
  HAR CO12 ...71 G3
  IL IG1 ...287 G8
  IPNE IP4 ...48 H3
  LOS SS9 ...299 L3
  SLH/COR SS17 ...316 C7
  SLH/COR SS17 * ...317 J7
  SRTFD E15 ...307 H4
  SWFD E18 ...267 M1
  WAN E11 ...285 K4
Gordons PIT SS13 ...278 D4
Gordon St PLSTW E13 ...307 K3
Gordon Wy HAR CO12 ...71 G3
Gorefield Rd RBSF CM22 ...162 F3
Gore Rd BRTR CM7 ...120 D5
  GVE DA12 ...338 D7
  RCFD SS4 ...396 B5
Gorebrook BCAYW CM11 ...259 G3
The Gore BSDN SS14 ...3 K8
Goring Cl CRW RM5 ...270 F7
Goring Gdns BCTR RM8 ...309 M1
  DAGE RM10 ...310 A2
  IPNE IP4 ...49 J3
Gorman Rd
  WOOL/PLUM SE18 ...324 D4
Gorse Cl CAN/RD E16 ...323 H2
Gorsehayes CHTY IP2 ...16 C8
Gorse La COS CO15 ...159 K4
  K/T/MI CO5 ...174 A1
Gorse Rd IPSE IP5 ...49 J3
Gorse Wk COLN CO4 ...108 A2
Gorse Wy COLW CO3 ...128 A4
  COS CO015 ...159 M5
Gorseway ROMW/RG RM7 ...289 L4
Gosbecks Vw COLS CO2 ...128 B5
Gosbecks Rd COLS CO2 ...128 A5
Gosfield Rd BCTR RM8 ...288 B4
  BRTR CM7 ...100 A3
  COLS CO2 ...129 J7
Gosford Cl SUD CO10 ...39 G7
Gosford Gdns REDBR IG4 ...286 C2
Gosford Wy FX IP11 ...63 H8
Goshawk Dr CHLM/GWD CM2 ...5 J8
Goslings SBN/FI SS3 * ...303 L2
The Goslings SBN/FI SS3 * ...303 L2
  WIT CM8 ...171 G3
Gosport Dr HCH RM12 ...311 K8
Gosport Rd WALTH E17 ...284 A1
Gossage Rd
  WOOL/PLUM SE18 ...325 G6
The Gossetts GTDUN CM6 ...190 D8
Gossling Pl KESG IP5 ...50 D6
Gotsfield Cl SUD CO10 ...43 M7
Gouge Av GVW DA11 ...337 J8
Gould Cl CHONG CM5 ...380 C4
Gouldings Av WOTN CO14 ...137 L4
Goulds Rd BURES CO8 ...358 F5
Coulton Rd CHLM/WR CM1 ...193 G6
Gourney Gv CDW/CHF RM16 ...314 D7

Government Rw PEND EN3 233 H7
Govier Cl SRTFD E15 307 H4
Gowan Brae SBF/HAD SS7 * 279 L8
Gowan Cl SBF/HAD SS7 279 L8
Gower Rd FSTGT E7 307 K3
Gowers Av CHLM/GWD CM2 210 B7
Gowers Cl KESG IP5 50 D6
Gowers La CDW/CHF RM16 331 J1
The Gowers HLW CM20 188 B7
Gower St CHTY IP2 16 F7
Goya Ri SBN/FI SS3 303 K5
Goyfield Av FX IP11 11 J2
Grace Cl BARK/HLT IG6 269 J5
Grace Gdns BSF CM23 139 G5
Grace Pl BOW E3 306 E7
Graces Cl WIT CM8 171 K6
Graces La RCHLM CM3 211 L4
Grace St BOW E3 306 E7
Graces Wk FOS CO13 137 K3
RCHLM CM3 211 J3
Grafton Gdns BCTR RM8 288 B7
Grafton Pl CHLM/GWD CM2 210 D1
Grafton Rd BCTR RM8 288 B7
CVI SS8 320 F3
HAR CO12 15 K6
Grafton Wy IP IP1 16 E6
Graham Av BROX EN10 200 F6
IP IP1 48 A5
Graham Cl BCAYW CM12 240 E8
HOC/HUL SS5 264 B6
RBRW/HUT CM13 256 F1
SLH/COR SS17 317 G1
Grahame Ct WICKW SS12 261 G8
Graham Rd FX IP11 62 E8
IP IP1 16 C1
PLSTW E13 307 K8
Grailands BSF CM23 138 E1
Grainger Cl SOSN SS2 19 H2
Grainger Rd SOSN SS2 19 H2
Gramer Cl WAN E11 285 G7
Grammar School Pl SUD CO10 20 C7
Grampian Gv CHLM/WR CM1 193 G7
The Granaries WAB EN9 233 M4
Granary Cl RCHLM CM3 231 L8
Granary Rw SAFWS CB11 * 28 B8
The Granary
HLWW/ROY CM19 186 C8
SUD CO10 37 L7
WARE SG12 185 K6
Granby Park Rd CHESW EN7 216 A6
Granby Rd GVW DA11 337 G4
WOOL/PLUM SE18 324 E6
Grand Ct West LOS SS9 * 300 C5
Grand Depot Rd
WOOL/PLUM SE18 324 D8
Grand Dr LOS SS9 300 C5
Grand Pde LOS SS9 300 C5
Grandview Rd SBF/HAD SS7 280 C6
Grand Wk WCHPL E1 * 306 B8
Grange Av LOS SS9 281 K8
RCHLM CM3 388 E10
WFD IG8 267 K5
WICKW SS12 260 E7
Grange Cl FX IP11 62 D8
HSTD CO9 81 H6
KESG IP5 50 D5
LOS SS9 300 B2
RBRW/HUT CM13 256 F8
WFD IG8 267 K6
WOTN CO14 137 K2
Grange Ct WAB EN9 233 K4
Grange Crs CHIG IG7 269 G4
RDART DA2 334 E8
THMD SE28 325 M2
Grange Farm Av FX IP11 10 E1
Grange Gdns RAYL SS6 280 E2
SOS SS1 19 J5
WARE SG12 184 F1
Grange La GTDUN CM6 117 L6
HLWW/ROY CM19 202 D1
KESG IP5 50 D5
Grange Pde BCAYE CM11 * 258 F6
Grange Pk BSF CM23 115 G8
Grange Park Dr LOS SS9 300 C3
Grange Park Rd LEY E10 284 E7
Granger Av MAL CM9 214 C4
Grange Rd BCAYE CM11 258 F6
BOC CM0 390 E6
BSF CM23 139 H2
FX IP11 10 F3
GRAYS RM17 330 E5
GVW DA11 337 K5
HAR CO12 70 F3
HARH RM3 271 L5
IL IG1 308 F1
IPNE IP4 17 K5
K/T/MI CO5 149 K8
LEY E10 284 D6
LOS SS9 300 A4
MGTR CO11 90 A7
MGTR CO11 90 C4
PIT SS13 279 H5
PLSTW E13 307 K7
RCHLM CM3 166 B3
RCOLW CO6 86 E6
SAFWN CB10 340 B9
SBF/HAD SS7 280 C6
SOCK/AV RM15 328 F4
WALTH E17 284 B3
WICKE SS11 260 F3
WIT CM8 198 B1
Granger Rw CHLM/WR CM1 193 J7
Granger Wy ROM RM1 289 K4
Grangeside BSF CM23 115 G7
The Grange HOD EN11 * 201 H4
Grange Wk BSF CM23 139 H2
Grange Wy COLS CO2 130 A1
Grangeway SBF/HAD SS7 280 D7
WFD IG8 267 M3
Grangeway Gdns
REDBR IG4 286 B3
Grangewood SBF/HAD SS7 * 280 A8
Grangewood Av
CDW/CHF RM16 331 H2
RAIN RM13 311 M8
Grangewood Cl
RBRW/HUT CM13 256 D6
Grangewood St EHAM E6 308 A5
Granites Cha BCAYE CM11 259 J7
Granite St WOOL/PLUM SE18 325 J8
Granleigh Rd WAN E11 285 H7
Granta Cl SAFWN CB10 341 L8
Granta Leys CBE/LIN CB1 24 E6
Granta Rd CBS CB2 22 B4
Granta V CBE/LIN CB1 25 G7
Grantchester Pl KESG IP5 49 M6
Grant Cl WICKW SS12 261 H8
Grantham Av BRTR CM77 120 E6
Grantham Ct COL CO1 8 E6
Grantham Crs CHTY IP2 16 B8
Grantham Gdns CHDH RM6 288 C4
Grantham Rd MNPK E12 308 D8
RCOLW CO6 86 E7
Grantham Wy
CDW/CHF RM16 314 D8
Grantley Cl RCOLW CO6 105 G8
Grantley St WCHPL E1 306 A7
Grantock Rd WALTH E17 267 G7
Granton Av HCH RM12 290 C7
Granton Rd GDMY/SEVK IG3 287 K6
Grant St PLSTW E13 307 K7
Granville Cl BCAYW CM12 240 C8
RCOLW CO6 106 B2
SBF/HAD SS7 298 B1
Granville Gdns HOD EN11 185 H7
Granville Rd COL CO1 107 L8
COS CO15 7 H6
EPP CM16 220 C7
FX IP11 11 K4
GVW DA11 337 J5
IL IG1 286 E6
SWFD E18 267 L8
WALTH E17 284 E4
Granville St IP IP1 16 C3
Granville Wy RCOLE CO7 156 D6
Grapnells VGE SS16 296 C1
Grasby Cl RCOLE CO7 130 E3
Grasmead Av LOS SS9 300 C3
Grasmere Av FX IP11 63 J7
HOC/HUL SS5 263 G2
Grasmere Cl BRTR CM77 120 F7
IPSE IP3 55 G5
LOU IG10 250 C2
Grasmere Gdns FOS CO13 137 H2
REDBR IG4 286 B3
Grasmere Rd CVI SS8 320 B2
PLSTW E13 307 K6
SBF/HAD SS7 280 B7
Grassfields FOS CO13 137 H3
Grasshaven Wy THMD SE28 325 J4
Grassmere COLN CO4 * 107 L1
Grassmere Rd EMPK RM11 290 C2
Gratmore Gn VGE SS16 296 B2
Gravel Cl CHIG IG7 269 K1
Gravel Hl RCOLW CO6 361 M7
Gravel Hill Wy HAR CO12 70 D4
Gravel La CHIG IG7 251 K6
Gravelly La CHLM/WR CM1 207 L2
Gravelpit La MGTR CO11 65 H2
Gravel Pit La MGTR CO11 65 H3
Gravel Rd LOS SS9 281 L5
The Gravel RCOLW CO6 124 C3
Gray Av BCTR RM8 288 C6
Gray Gdns HCH RM12 311 K3
Graylands GRAYS RM17 * 330 B5
Grayling Cl BRTR CM7 121 H4
CAN/RD E16 307 H8
Grayling Dr COLN CO4 108 C4
Gray Rd COLW CO3 107 G7
Grays Av VGE SS16 294 F4
Grays Cl K/T/MI CO5 177 M7
Grays Ct BSF CM23 138 F1
Grays End Cl CDW/CHF RM16 330 D2
Gray's La BRTR CM7 78 B1
Grays Md HSTD CO9 356 E7
Graysons Cl RAYL SS6 281 H3
Grays Wk RBRW/HUT CM13 257 G3
Great Bentley Rd RCOLE CO7 132 D2
Great Berry Farm Cha
VGE SS16 294 D1
Great Berry La VGE SS16 294 D1
Great Brays HLWS CM18 204 B2
Great Burches Rd
SBF/HAD SS7 280 D6
Great Cambridge Rd
CHES/WCR EN8 232 D1
Great Canfield Rd RBSF CM22 377 L2
Great Cob CHLM/WR CM1 194 B8
Great Colman St IPNE IP4 16 F4
Great Cullings
ROMW/RG RM7 289 H7
Great Eastern Av SOSN SS2 19 G2
Great Eastern Cl BSF CM23 139 H3
Great Eastern Rd BRW CM14 273 M3
HOC/HUL SS5 264 B8
SRTFD E15 307 G4
SUD CO10 20 E7
Great Eastern Sq FX IP11 62 F8
Great Fld FX IP11 62 B5
Greatfield Av EHAM E6 308 C8
Greatfields Rd BARK IG11 309 G5
Great Fox Meadow
BRWN CM15 383 N11
Great Galley Cl BARK IG11 309 L7
Great Gardens Rd
EMPK RM11 289 L4
Great Gibcracks Cha
RCHLM CM3 227 K3
Great Gipping St IP IP1 16 D5
Great Godfreys
CHLM/WR CM1 208 C4
Great Gregorie VGE SS16 2 B8
Great Gregories La EPP CM16 235 M3
Great Hadham Rd BSF CM23 138 A4
Great Harlings RIPS/CAP IP9 66 F4
Great Harrods WOTN CO14 137 K2
Great Hays LOS SS9 281 M8
Great Holland Common Rd
COS CO15 136 A7
Greathouse Cha
SLH/COR SS17 295 M7
Great House Farm Rd
COLS CO2 128 D8
Great Knightleys LAIN SS15 2 A6
Great Lawn CHONG CM5 382 H1
Great Leighs Wy PIT SS13 278 F4
Great Leylands HLWS CM18 204 B2
Great Meadow BROX EN10 201 H8
Great Mistley VGE SS16 3 K8
Great Nelmes Cha
EMPK RM11 290 C3
Great Notley Av BRTR CM77 120 E8
Great Oak Ct HSTD CO9 346 B12
Great Oaks BSDN SS14 2 F6
CHIG IG7 268 F3
RBRW/HUT CM13 256 E2
Great Owl Rd CHIG IG7 268 D2
Great Plumtree HLW CM20 13 M2
Great Queen St DART DA1 334 C8
Great Ranton PIT SS13 278 F5
Great Ropers La BRW CM14 273 K5
Great Saling WICKE SS11 261 K7
Great Smials RCHLM CM3 244 F7
Great Spenders BSDN SS14 3 L2
Great Sq BRTR CM7 121 J2
Great Tey Rd RCOLW CO6 103 M8
Great Totham Rd WIT CM8 172 C8
Great Tufts RIPS/CAP IP9 58 E4
Great Warley St
RBRW/HUT CM13 273 K7
Great Wheatley Rd RAYL SS6 280 D4
Great Whip St CHTY IP2 16 F7
Great Yeldham Rd HSTD CO9 355 N3
Greaves Cl BARK IG11 309 H4
Grebe Cl BARK IG11 309 K8
CHTY IP2 53 K3
FSTGT E7 307 J2
RCHLM CM3 388 D9
WALTH E17 266 B6
Grebe Crest WTHK RM20 329 K7
Greding Wk RBRW/HUT CM13 256 E5
Greenacre Gdns WALTH E17 284 F2
Greenacre La ING CM4 241 H5
Greenacre Ms LOS SS9 300 B3
Greenacres CBS CB2 22 A8
COLN CO4 107 H2
COS CO15 7 K2
EPP CM16 220 A6
RCOLW CO6 124 C4
SBF/HAD SS7 299 H2
Greenacres Cl RAIN RM13 312 B7
Greenacre Sq
BERM/RHTH SE16 * 322 A5
Green Acres Rd COLS CO2 128 C8
Greenall Cl CHES/WCR EN8 216 F8
Green Av CVI SS8 320 B2
Greenaway Av UED N18 * 266 A4
Greenbank CHESW EN7 216 C6
Greenbank Cl CHING E4 266 F1
HARH RM3 272 A2
Greenbanks LOS SS9 300 D3
UPMR RM14 291 H7
Greenbury Cl ROY SG8 348 E10
Green Butts CBS CB2 22 A4
Green Chain Wk CHARL SE7 324 A7
THMD SE28 326 A4
Green Cl CHES/WCR EN8 232 F2
CHLM/WR CM1 210 A1
EPP CM16 219 J2
RCHLM CM3 196 F2
Green Cnr GTDUN CM6 * 96 C8
Green Crs KIR/NAC IP10 56 F5
Greendale Wk GVW DA11 337 H8
Greendyke CVI SS8 298 C8
Green End La FOS CO13 136 D4
Greene Vw BRTR CM7 121 L5
Green Farm La GVE DA12 339 H8
Green Farm Rd RCOLW CO6 82 E3
Greenfell Man DEPT SE8 * 322 C8
Greenfield WIT CM8 171 K4
Greenfield Dr RCOLW CO6 103 L4
Greenfield Gdns DAGW RM9 309 M5
Greenfield Rd DAGW RM9 309 M5
Greenfields BCAYW CM12 258 D5
HSTD CO9 80 B6
LOU IG10 250 D4
STSD CM24 115 M2
WOTN CO14 * 137 J2
Greenfields Cl BCAYW CM12 258 C5
Greenfield St WAB EN9 233 K4
Greenfields Wy HVHL CB9 34 B7
Greenfinch Av CHTY IP2 53 J2
Greenfinch End COLN CO4 108 C5
Greenford Rd COS CO15 6 B6
Greengate St PLSTW E13 307 L6
Green Gld EPP CM16 235 M7
Green Glades EMPK RM11 290 C4
Greenham Crs CHING E4 266 C5
Greenhaven Dr THMD SE28 325 L2
Greenheys Dr SWFD E18 285 J1
Greenhill BKHH IG9 249 M8
Green Hl WOOL/PLUM SE18 324 C8
Greenhill Gv MNPK E12 308 B1
Greenhill Pk BSF CM23 138 E4
Greenhill Rd GVW DA11 337 J7
Greenhills HLW CM20 13 K6
Greenhurst Rd RCOLE CO7 156 D7
Greening St ABYW SE2 325 M7
Greenland Ms DEPT SE8 322 A8
Greenland Quay
BERM/RHTH SE16 322 A7
Greenlands RCFD SS4 283 G1
Green La BCAYW CM12 276 D2
BCTR RM8 288 C7
BOC CM0 393 J6
BROX EN10 217 J1
BRW CM14 255 G1
BRW CM14 255 K8
BRW CM14 273 K6
BRWN CM15 255 M6
CBE/LIN CB1 24 F7
CDW/CHF RM16 314 F5
CHIG IG7 250 F8
CHIG IG7 269 H2
CHING E4 * 249 H3
CHLM/WR CM1 207 L1
COLN CO4 108 B2
COLN CO4 361 Q12
CVI SS8 320 C2
GTDUN CM6 116 F4
HLWE CM17 205 J2
IL IG1 287 G7
K/T/MI CO5 150 A7
K/T/MI CO5 174 B4
LOS SS9 282 A6
MAL CM9 199 M1
NHMKT IP6 49 H1
RCHLM CM3 388 D11
RCOLE CO7 89 G7
RCOLE CO7 108 F4
RCOLE CO7 363 K6
RCOLW CO6 86 F7
RCOLW CO6 104 E5
RCOS CO16 134 D8
RIPS/CAP IP9 59 M6
SUD CO10 36 D1
VGE SS16 295 G1
WAB EN9 234 E5
WDBR IP12 51 G3
WIT CM8 145 K3
WOTN CO14 369 N11
Greenlaw St
WOOL/PLUM SE18 324 D6
Greenleafe Dr BARK/HLT IG6 286 E1
Greenleaf Rd EHAM E6 307 M5
WALTH E17 284 C1
Greenleas SBF/HAD SS7 280 E7
Green Man La WIT CM8 172 C7
Green Md RCHLM CM3 244 F6
Green Oak Gld RIPW IP8 53 J5
Greenoaks SBF/HAD SS7 298 B2
Greenock Wy ROM RM1 271 H6
Green Pond Cl WALTH E17 284 B1
Green Pond Rd WALTH E17 284 B1
Green Ride LOU IG10 249 K6
Green Rd SBF/HAD SS7 298 A4
The Green Rd CBS CB2 22 D1
The Greens Cl LOU IG10 250 D2
Greens End
WOOL/PLUM SE18 324 E7
Greens Farm La BCAYE CM11 258 F4
Greenshank Cl WALTH E17 266 B6
Greenshaw BRW CM14 255 L8
Greenside BCTR RM8 287 M7
Greenslade Rd BARK IG11 309 G4
Green Sleeves Dr BRW CM14 273 L4
Greensmill MGTR CO11 64 F8
Greenspire Gv RIPW IP8 53 G3
Greenstead SBW CM21 162 F8
Greenstead Av WFD IG8 267 M5
Greenstead Cl
RBRW/HUT CM13 257 H3
Greenstead Gdns WFD IG8 267 M5
Greenstead Rd COL CO1 9 J6
Greensted Cl BSDN SS14 278 C8
Greensted Rd CHONG CM5 382 B2
LOU IG10 250 B7
The Greenstead BSDN SS14 278 C8
The Greens IPNE IP4 55 L1
Greenstone Ms WAN E11 285 K4
Green St CBS CB2 22 A8
FSTGT E7 307 H5
GTDUN CM6 377 M6
HLWE CM17 188 E8
ING CM4 222 F7
PEND EN3 248 A3
Greensward La HOC/HUL SS5 264 C7
The Green BKHH IG9 * 249 L8
BSF CM23 * 139 G5
CDW/CHF RM16 315 K5
CHES/WCR EN8 216 D6
CHLM/WR CM1 208 E4
CHLM/WR CM1 209 J1
COS CO15 182 E3
EPP CM16 235 M7
FOS CO13 * 136 D5
HAR CO12 * 70 E3
ING CM4 222 B5
LOS SS9 282 B6
MGTR CO11 91 J1
RAIN RM13 328 B3
RCOS CO16 * 181 L7
SLH/COR SS17 317 G4
SRTFD E15 307 J3
WAN E11 285 L4
Green Trees EPP CM16 236 B1
Green Trees Av RCHLM CM3 230 C8
Greenview Pk COS CO15 159 K6
Green Wk CHONG CM5 382 G4
WFD IG8 268 B5
The Green Wk CHING E4 248 F8
Greenway BCAYE CM11 259 G4
BCTR RM8 287 M7
BSF CM23 139 K3
COS CO15 137 J4
HARH RM3 272 E5
HLWW/ROY CM19 202 F1
RBRW/HUT CM13 256 D3
Green Wy RCOLW CO6 82 D3
Greenway Av WALTH E17 285 G2
Greenway Ct IL IG1 286 D6
SRTFD E15 307 H6
Greenway Gdns BRTR CM77 121 G6
Greenways CHLM/WR CM1 193 L7
CVI SS8 298 C8
HSTD CO9 80 C6
K/T/MI CO5 149 G2
MAL CM9 214 C3
RCFD SS4 283 J3
SAFWS CB11 30 B2
SBF/HAD SS7 297 L3
SOS SS1 302 B6
Greenways Cl IP IP1 48 A5
The Greenways RCOLW CO6 124 D2
The Greenway COS CO15 159 L6
PEND EN3 232 E5
WICKE SS11 260 F2
Greenwich Cl IPSE IP3 54 D3
Greenwich Crs EHAM E6 324 B1
Greenwich Foot Tnl
POP/IOD E14 322 F8
Greenwich Rd IPSE IP3 54 C3
Greenwich Vw POP/IOD E14 322 E6
Greenwich Wy WAB EN9 233 K6
Greenwood Av CHESW EN7 232 C1
DAGE RM10 310 E1
PEND EN3 248 B1
SBF/HAD SS7 298 A4
Greenwood Cl CHESW EN7 232 C1
HVHL CB9 34 B5
Greenwood Dr CHING E4 266 F4
Greenwood Gdns
BARK/HLT IG6 268 F6
Greenwood Gv COLN CO4 107 M2
Greenwood Rd CHIG IG7 269 L3
PLSTW E13 307 J6
Greenyard WAB EN9 233 K3
Greg Cl LEY E10 284 F4
Gregory Cl HOC/HUL SS5 282 C1
Gregory Ms WAB EN9 233 J2
Gregory Rd CHDH RM6 288 A2
Gregory St SUD CO10 20 C6
Grenade St POP/IOD E14 322 C3
Grenadier Rd HVHL CB9 33 M5
Grenadier St CAN/RD E16 324 D4
Grenadine Cl CHESW EN7 216 A5
Grendel Wy COS CO15 160 C3
Grenfell Av COS CO15 160 B2
HCH RM12 289 J6
Grenfell Cl COLN CO4 9 J3
Grennan Cl RBRW/HUT CM13 275 G1
Grenville Av BROX EN10 201 G7
Grenville Cl CHES/WCR EN8 232 E2
Grenville Gdns WFD IG8 267 M6
Grenville Rd BRTR CM7 121 H2
CDW/CHF RM16 329 L8
SUD CO10 20 F1
Gresham Ct BRW CM14 273 M2
Gresham Dr CHDH RM6 287 L3
Gresham Rd BRW CM14 273 M2
CAN/RD E16 323 L2
EHAM E6 308 C6
Gresley Cl COLN CO4 8 D1
WALTH E17 284 B4
Gresley Gdns CHTY IP2 16 F9
Grevatt Ldg PIT SS13 * 278 F8
Greville Cl WOTN CO14 369 P11
Greville Rd WALTH E17 284 F2
Greyfriars IP IP1 16 D5
RBRW/HUT CM13 256 E3
Grey Friars Rd IP IP1 16 E6
Greygoose Pk
HLWW/ROY CM19 203 H4
Greyhound Hl COLN CO4 88 B1
Greyhound La
CDW/CHF RM16 331 K1
Greyhound Rd SUD CO10 39 L2
Greyhound Wy SOSN SS2 19 H2
Grey Lady Pl BCAYE CM11 258 E2
Grey Ladys CHLM/GWD CM2 225 L2
Greys Cl SUD CO10 38 F4
Greys Hollow SAFWS CB11 93 L1
Greystone Gdns
BARK/HLT IG6 268 F8
Greystones Cl COLW CO3 128 D2
Greyswood Av UED N18 * 266 A4
Grey Towers Av EMPK RM11 290 A6
Grey Towers Gdns
EMPK RM11 289 M6
Gridiron Pl UPMR RM14 290 E7
Grieves Ct COLW CO3 127 M1
Grieves Rd GVW DA11 337 J8
Griffin Av CVI SS8 298 F8
UPMR RM14 291 H4
Griffin Ct CHTY IP2 * 17 G9
Griffin Manor Wy THMD SE28 325 G6
Griffin Rd WOOL/PLUM SE18 325 G8
The Griffins CDW/CHF RM16 330 E1
Griffin Wk GRH DA9 335 J7
Griffith Cl CHDH RM6 287 M5
Grifon Cl CDW/CHF RM16 329 M6
Grifon Rd CDW/CHF RM16 329 M6
Griggs Ap IL IG1 286 F7
Griggs Gdns HCH RM12 311 M2
Griggs Rd LEY E10 284 F4
Grimsby Gv CAN/RD E16 324 E5
Grimshaw Wy ROM RM1 289 H3
Grimston La FX IP11 61 L7
Grimston Rd BSDN SS14 278 C4
COLS CO2 129 K1
Grimston Wy WOTN CO14 137 L2
Grimwade Cl MGTR CO11 65 G6
Grimwade St IPNE IP4 17 H6
The Grindle RIPW IP8 46 E6
Grinstead La RBSF CM22 163 K3
Grinstead Rd DEPT SE8 322 B8
The Grip CBE/LIN CB1 24 E8
Groombridge Rd HOM E9 306 A4
Groom Pk COS CO15 6 F3
Groom Rd BROX EN10 217 G4
Groomside BRTR CM7 121 K3
Grooms La WIT CM8 147 H1
Grosmont Rd
WOOL/PLUM SE18 325 J8
Grosvenor Cl BSF CM23 138 E6
CHLM/GWD CM2 5 L9
IPNE IP4 48 D5
K/T/MI CO5 150 A8
LOU IG10 250 E1
Grosvenor Ct WOS/PRIT SS0 * 300 F6
Grosvenor Crs DART DA1 334 A7
Grosvenor Dr EMPK RM11 289 M6
LOU IG10 250 E2
Grosvenor Gdns
BCAYW CM12 258 D1
UPMR RM14 291 G7
WFD IG8 267 K5
Grosvenor Ms WOS/PRIT SS0 300 F6
Grosvenor Park Rd
WALTH E17 284 D3
Grosvenor Ri East WALTH E17 284 E3
Grosvenor Rd BCTR RM8 288 C6
BROX EN10 201 G6
CDW/CHF RM16 316 A6
EHAM E6 308 A5
FSTGT E7 307 L3
IL IG1 286 F8
LEY E10 284 F6
RAYL SS6 262 D8
ROMW/RG RM7 289 G5
SBF/HAD SS7 298 B4
SUD CO10 43 G7
WAN E11 285 L3
WOS/PRIT SS0 300 F6
Grosvenor Wharf Rd
POP/IOD E14 323 G7
The Grotto WARE SG12 184 E1
Grove Av K/T/MI CO5 177 M8
VGE SS16 294 E2
WOTN CO14 137 L1
Grovebury Rd THMD SE28 325 L5
Grove Cl RAYL SS6 281 J3
Grove Ct RAYL SS6 281 K4
WAB EN9 233 J3
WOS/PRIT SS0 * 300 E2
Grove Crs SWFD E18 267 J8
Grove Crescent Rd
SRTFD E15 307 G3
Grovedale Cl CHESW EN7 216 A8
Grove End LOS SS9 * 300 B5
SWFD E18 267 J8
Grove Farm Rd WIT CM8 173 J4
Grove Fld BRTR CM7 99 M3
Grove Gdns PEND EN3 248 A1
Grove Green Rd LEY E10 284 F8
WAN E11 285 G7
Groveherst Rd DART DA1 334 C5
Grove Hl COLN CO4 88 C1
LOS SS9 281 L6
RCOLE CO7 89 G1
RIPW IP8 53 H6
STSD CM24 115 M2
SWFD E18 267 J8
Grovelands SOSN SS2 19 M1
Grovelands Rd WICKW SS12 261 G7
Grovelands Wy GRAYS RM17 330 C4
Grove La CHIG IG7 269 J2
EPP CM16 220 B8
IPNE IP4 17 K5
RIPS/CAP IP9 365 N8
Grove Orch BRTR CM7 99 M4
Grove Pk WAN E11 285 L3
Grove Park Av CHING E4 266 E6
Grove Park Rd RAIN RM13 311 K5
Grove Rd BCAYW CM12 258 C3
CHDH RM6 287 M5
CHING E4 266 F2
CHLM/GWD CM2 5 H6
CVI SS8 320 F1
FX IP11 62 F7
GRAYS RM17 330 F5
GVW DA11 336 E3
HOM E9 306 A5
K/T/MI CO5 150 B8
MGTR CO11 65 G5
RAYL SS6 281 J3
RCOS CO16 135 G8
RIPS/CAP IP9 59 H7
SBF/HAD SS7 298 A3
SLH/COR SS17 317 G5
SWFD E18 267 J8
WALTH E17 284 E3
WAN E11 285 J5
Grove Rd West PEND EN3 232 D7
Grover St SOS SS1 19 H6
Groves Cl SOCK/AV RM15 329 J3
Groveside Rd CHING E4 267 H2
Grove St BERM/RHTH SE16 322 C7
The Grove BCAYE CM11 240 F8
BRW CM14 273 J3
CBE/LIN CB1 24 E6
CHLM/GWD CM2 210 E8
COS CO15 7 G7
GVE DA12 337 L5
IP IP1 48 B3
KESG IP5 50 F5
RBSF CM22 376 A5
RCHLM CM3 228 C4
SLH/COR SS17 * 317 G5
SOSN SS2 19 L1
SRTFD E15 307 H4
SWCM DA10 336 B3
UPMR RM14 312 D1
WIT CM8 171 K3
Grove Wk SBN/FI SS3 303 H7
Groveway BCTR RM8 310 A1
Grovewood Av LOS SS9 281 L6
Grovewood Cl LOS SS9 281 L6
Grovewood Pl WFD IG8 268 C5
Grundy St POP/IOD E14 322 E2
Grymes Dyke Ct COLW CO3 * 106 A7
Gryme's Dyke Wy COLW CO3 128 A2
Guardian Av CDW/CHF RM16 330 A1
Guardian Cl EMPK RM11 289 L7
Guardsman Cl BRW CM14 256 A8
Gubbins La HARH RM3 272 C7
Guelph's La GTDUN CM6 74 D2
Guernsey Gdns WICKE SS11 260 F4
Guernsey Rd LEY E10 285 G6
Guernsey Wy BRTR CM7 121 G3
Guildford Rd COL CO1 8 F5
EHAM E6 324 B2
GDMY/SEVK IG3 287 H7
HARH RM3 272 B5
SOSN SS2 19 H3
WALTH E17 266 F7
Guildhall Wy SAFWN CB10 29 K2
Guild Rd CHARL SE7 324 A8
Guildsway WALTH E17 266 C7
The Guilfords HLWE CM17 188 E4
Guinea Cl BRTR CM7 122 A1
Guinevere Gdns
CHES/WCR EN8 216 E8
Guinness Cl HOM E9 306 B4

Guinness Trust Est
  SRTFD E15 * 307 J5
Guithavon Ri WIT CM8 ....171 J3
Guithavon St WIT CM8 ....171 J3
Guithavon Sq WIT CM8 ....171 J3
Guithavon Va WIT CM8 ....171 J3
Gulliver St BERM/RHTH SE16 ..322 C6
Gulls Cft BRTR CM7 ......121 M2
Gull's La RCOLE CO7 ......89 K2
Gulpher Rd FXI IP1 ......62 D7
Gumley Rd WTHK WM20 ....330 A5
Gunfleet Ct GVE DA12 ....338 B5
  K/T/MI CO5 ....177 L6
Gun Hill COLN CO4 ......363 J10
  TIL RM18 ....332 A5
Gun Hill Pl VGE SS16 ......3 J8
Gunmakers La HOM E9 ....306 B5
Gunner Dr PEND EN3 ......233 H7
Gunner La WOOL/PLUM SE18 ..324 D8
Gunners Gv CHING E4 ....266 F2
Gunners Rd SBN/FI SS3 ....303 K6
Gunning Ms GRAYS RM17 ..330 F4
Gunning St WOOL/PLUM SE18 ..325 H7
Gunn Rd SWCM DA10 ......336 B6
Gunson Ga CHLM/GWD CM2 ....5 L9
Gunwhale Cl
  BERM/RHTH SE16 ....322 A4
Gurdon Rd CHARL SE7 ....323 K8
  COLS CO2 ....129 J2
Gurlings Cl HVHL CB9 ....34 D3
Gurney Benham Cl COLS CO2 ..128 E1
Gurney Cl BARK IG11 ....308 E3
  SRTFD E15 ....307 H2
  WALTH E17 ....266 A7
Gurney Rd SRTFD E15 ....307 H2
Gurton Rd RCOLW CO6 ....124 D2
Gustedhall La HOC/HUL SS5 ..282 B3
Gutteridge La
  RCOS CO16 ....134 B6
Gutteridge La ABR/ST RM4 ..252 F6
Gutters La CHLM/WR CM1 ..193 L6
Guy Cook Cl SUD CO10 ....45 M4
Guys Farm Rd RCHLM CM3 ..245 J4
Guysfield Cl RAIN RM13 ..311 K5
Guysfield Dr RAIN RM13 ..311 K5
Gwendalen Av CVI SS8 ....321 G1
Gwendoline Av PLSTW E13 ..307 L6
Gwendoline Rd IPNE IP4 ..55 N1
Gwyn Cl RCHLM CM3 ......195 H4
Gwynne Park Av WFD IG8 ..268 C5
Gwynne Rd HAR CO12 ......15 J6
Gwynn Rd GVW DA11 ......336 F7
Gyllyngdune Gdns
  GDMY/SEVK IG3 ......287 J8
Gymnasium St IP IP1 ....16 C3
Gypsy Cl WARE SG12 ....185 G5
Gypsy La K/T/MI CO5 ....125 L6
  WARE SG12 ....185 G5

H

Haarlem Rd CVI SS8 ......320 A1
Haarle Rd CVI SS8 ......321 G3
Habgood Rd LOU IG10 ....250 B3
Hackamore Rd SBF/HAD SS7 ..280 E8
Hackmans La RCHLM CM3 ..229 H2
Hacton Dr RM RM12 ......312 D1
Hacton La HCH RM12 ....290 C7
  UPMR RM14 ....312 C2
Hadden Rd THMD SE28 ..325 H6
Haddestoke Ga BROX EN10 ..217 G4
Haddon Cl RAYL SS6 ....280 C2
Haddon Md RCHLM CM3 ..245 C8
Hadton Pk COL CO1 ......9 K8
Hadfield Dr BRTR CM77 ..121 L1
Hadfield Rd SLH/COR SS17 ..317 L4
Hadham Cl BSF CM23 ....138 E1
Hadham Gv BSF CM23 ....138 D1
Hadham Rd BSF CM23 ....114 A8
Hadleigh Ct BROX EN10 ..201 J3
Hadleigh Park Av
  SBF/HAD SS7 ....298 F2
  LOS SS9 ....299 M4
  RCOLE CO7 ....362 H4
  RCOS CO16 ....158 E8
  RIPW IP8 ....53 H1
  WOS/PRIT SS0 ....18 C6
Hadley Cl BRTR CM7 ....99 L4
Hadley Gra HLWE CM17 ..204 D2
Hadley Rd BELV DA17 ....326 C7
Hadrian Cl BOW E3 ......306 D5
  COLN CO4 ....87 L7
  HVHL CB9 ....34 B6
Hadrians Cl WIT CM8 ....171 H5
Hadrian St GNWCH SE10 ..323 H8
Hadrians Wy MAL CM9 ..214 D1
Hadstock Rd CBE/LIN CB1 ..24 E8
Haggars La RCOLE CO7 ..132 C2
Hagger Ct WALTH E17 * ..285 C1
Hagg Hl RCHLM CM3 ....229 H8
Haig Ct CHLM/GWD CM2 ....4 E6
Haig Gdns GVE DA12 ....337 M5
Haig Rd CDW/CHF RM16 ..331 K2
Haig Rd East PLSTW E13 ..307 M7
Haig Rd West PLSTW E13 ..307 M7
Haigville Gdns BARK/HLT IG6 ..286 F2
Hailes Wd RBSF CM22 ....174 E3
Hailey Cl HOD EN11 ....185 H1
Hailey La HOD EN11 ....184 H1
Hailsham Cl HARH RM3 ..271 M4
Hailsham Rd HARH RM3 ..271 M4
Hainault Av RCFD SS4 ..282 A1
  WOS/PRIT SS0 ....18 B1
Hainault Buildings LEY E10 * ..284 F6
Hainault Cl SBF/HAD SS7 ..299 H6
Hainault Gore CHDH RM6 ..288 B3
Hainault Gv CHIG IG7 ....269 G4
Hainault Rd CHLM/GWD CM1 ..4 A5
  CHDH RM6 ....269 L8
  CHDH RM6 ....287 L1
  CHDH RM6 ....288 C4
  CHIG IG7 ....268 F3
  RCHLM CM3 ....246 D4
  ROM RM1 ....289 G1
  ROMW/RG RM7 ....288 F7
  WAN E11 ....284 F6
Hainault St IL IG1 ......286 E1
Hainault St DAGW RM9 ..310 C1
Halcyon Wy EMPK RM11 ..290 C6
Haldane Cl PEND EN3 ....233 J7
Haldane Gdns GVW DA11 ..336 F6
Haldane Rd EHAM E6 ....308 C4
  THMD SE28 ....326 A3
Haldan Rd CHING E4 ....266 C4
  CHTY IP2 ....53 J3
Hale Cl CHING E4 ......266 C4
Hale End HARH RM3 ......271 M5
Hale End Rd CHING E4 ..266 E4
Halesowen Cl CHTY IP2 ..53 L5
Hale St POP/IOD E14 ....322 E3
Halesworth Cl HARH RM3 ..272 B5

Halesworth Rd HARH RM3 ..272 B5
The Hale CHING E4 ......267 C6
Half Acres BSF CM23 ....139 C1
Halfacres WIT CM8 ......171 K6
Halfhides WAB EN9 ......233 L3
Half Moon La EPP CM16 ..236 A1
Halford Ct RIPW IP8 ....55 H3
Halford Rd WALTH E17 ....285 G5
Halfway Ct PUR RM19 ....328 D7
Halidon Ri HARH RM3 ....272 E5
Halifax Rd CHTY IP2 ....54 A3
Halifield Dr BELV DA17 ..326 B6
Hall Cl BRWN CM15 ......383 Q11
Hallam Ct BCAYW CM12 ..258 C1
Hall La BRWN CM15 ......328 F4
Hall Bridge Ri MAL CM9 ..214 F1
Hall Cha CHLM/GWD CM2 ..210 D7
  COS CO15 ....126 E2
  RBSF CM22 ....372 Q12
Hall Crs CBS CB2 ......22 H1
  SBF/HAD SS7 ....299 G2
  SOCK/AV RM15 ......328 F5
Hallcroft Cha COLN CO4 ..107 M1
Hall Cut RCOLE CO7 ......156 D5
Hallet Rd GTDUN CM6 ....80 A5
Hallet Rd CVI SS8 ......321 H2
Hallett Rd GTDUN CM6 ..118 B7
Halley Rd FSTGT E7 ......308 A3
  MNPK E12 ....308 A3
Hall Farm Cl K/T/MI CO5 ..149 H1
  SBF/HAD SS7 ....298 A4
Hall Farm Gn BRTR CM7 * ..97 J5
Hall Farm Rd SBF/HAD SS7 ..298 A3
Hall Fld FX IP11 ......62 C8
Hall Green La
  RBRW/HUT CM13 ......257 G3
Hallingbury Cl RBSF CM22 ..139 J5
Hallingbury Rd BSF CM23 ..139 J5
  SBW CM21 ....163 H5
Halling Hl HLW CM20 ....13 L3
Halliwell Rd IPNE IP4 ....49 G7
Hall La BRWN CM15 ......256 C2
  CHING E4 ....266 C4
  CHLM/GWD CM2 ......210 F7
  CHLM/GWD CM2 ......226 A8
  CHLM/WR CM1 ....209 L1
  HAR CO12 ....70 F3
  HARH RM3 ....272 F5
  HSTD CO9 ....345 N7
  INC CM4 ....239 L5
  RCOS CO16 ....135 K5
  ROY SG8 ....349 L9
  UPMR RM14 ....290 F1
  WALTH E17 ....369 N12
Hallmores BROX EN10 ....201 H5
Hallowell Down RCHLM CM3 ..245 H7
Hall Park Av WOS/PRIT SS0 ..300 E5
Hall Pond Wy FX IP11 ....62 C8
Hall Ri SUD CO10 ......44 F4
Hall Rd BOC CM0 ......393 P1
  BRTR CM7 ....98 C6
  BURES CO8 ....359 P12
  CHDH RM6 ....287 M4
  DART DA1 ....334 C6
  EHAM E6 ....308 C5
  GPK RM2 ....289 L1
  GVW DA11 ....336 F8
  HOC/HUL SS5 ....282 D3
  HVHL CB9 ....35 L2
  K/T/MI CO5 ....173 M2
  MAL CM9 ....198 E2
  MAL CM9 ....214 E1
  MAL CM9 ....385 N4
  RBSF CM22 ....374 C6
  RCFD SS4 ....283 C4
  RCOLE CO7 ....109 M3
  RCOLW CO6 ....85 G8
  RCOLW CO6 ....86 A8
  RCOLW CO6 ....127 H1
  SOCK/AV RM15 ......328 F4
  SUD CO10 ....42 D7
  SUD CO10 ....347 P7
  WAN E11 ....307 H2
Hallside Rd EN EN1 ......232 M8
Halls Rw SLH/COR SS17 * ..316 E2
Hall St CHLM/GWD CM2 ....5 H5
  SUD CO10 ....42 D7
Hall Ter SOCK/AV RM15 ..329 G5
Hall Vw RCOLE CO7 ......133 H6
Hall Wik FX IP11 ......62 C8
Hallwood Crs BRWN CM15 ..256 B3
Hallywell Crs EHAM E6 ..324 C1
Halsham Crs BARK IG11 ..309 J3
Halstead Ct WICKW SS12 ..260 F8
Halstead Rd BRTR CM7 ....100 B2
  FOS CO13 ....136 F1
  HSTD CO9 ....80 F1
  RCOLW CO6 ....82 C6
  RCOLW CO6 ....104 D1
  RCOLW CO6 ....105 K6
  WAN E11 ....285 L3
Halstead Wy
  RBRW/HUT CM13 ......256 F2
Halston Cl SLH/COR SS17 * ..317 L1
Halston Pl MAL CM9 ......214 C5
Halstow Rd GNWCH SE10 ..323 K8
Halt Dr TIL RM18 ......332 D3
Halton Crs IPSE IP3 ....55 H4
Halton Rd CDW/CHF RM16 ..331 J5
Halt Robin Rd BELV DA17 ..326 E1
Haltwhistle Rd RCHLM CM3 ..244 F5
Halyard Reach RCHLM CM3 ..245 G6
Hamberts Rd RCHLM CM5 ..245 G4
Hamble Cl WIT CM8 ......171 H5
Hamble La SLH/COR SS17 ..329 J1
Hamble Wy BOC CM0 * 393 K7
Hamboro Gdns LOS SS9 ..299 L4
Hambro' Av RAYL SS6 ....281 G5
Hambro Cl RAYL SS6 ......281 H1
Hambro HI RAYL SS6 ......263 H8
Hambro Pde RAYL SS6 ....263 G8
Hambro Rd BRW CM14 ....256 A5
Hamburgh Ct CHES/WCR EN8 ..216 E6
Hamden Crs DAGE RM10 ..288 E8
Hamel Wy SAFWS CB11 ..372 E5
Hamerton Rd GVW DA11 ..336 F5
Hameway EHAM E6 ....308 D8
Hamford Ct CHING E4 ....266 D4
Hamford Dr HAR CO12 ....113 M2
Hamfrith Rd SRTFD E15 ..307 J1
Hamilton Av BARK/HLT IG6 ..286 E2
  HOD EN11 ....201 H1
Hamilton Cl
  BERM/RHTH SE16 ....322 B5
  LOS SS9 ....299 K3
Hamilton Ct RCHLM CM3 * ..245 H7

Hamilton Crs BRW CM14 ..273 M4
Hamilton Dr EMPK RM11 ..272 B8
Hamilton Gdns FX IP11 ....11 M3
  HOC/HUL SS5 ....264 C8
Hamilton Ms RAYL SS6 ....281 J2
  SAFWS CB11 ....28 C7
Hamilton Rd COLW CO3 ..107 G8
  FOS CO13 ....136 C1
  FXI IP11 ....11 M2
  GPK RM2 ....289 L3
  IL IG1 ....308 E1
  IPSE IP3 ....55 G7
  RBSF CM22 ....377 N1
  RCOLE CO7 ....130 E5
  SRTFD E15 ....307 H7
  SUD CO10 ....20 D7
  WALTH E17 ....266 B8
Hamilton St FX IP11 ....62 D7
  HAR CO12 ....14 B4
Hamlet Cl CRW RM5 ......270 D6
Hamlet Ct BURES CO8 ....359 P9
Hamlet Court Ms
  WOS/PRIT SS0 ....18 C3
Hamlet Court Rd
  WOS/PRIT SS0 ....18 C3
Hamlet Dr COLN CO4 ....108 C8
Hamlet HI HLWW/ROY CM19 ..202 B1
Hamlet Pk HVHL CB9 * 34 E7
Hamlet Rd CHLM/GWD CM2 ..5 G6
  CRW RM5 ....270 D6
  HVHL CB9 ....34 D6
  SWF/PRIT SS0 ....18 E6
Hamlets Wy BOW E3 ......306 C9
Hamley Cl SBF/HAD SS7 ..299 L7
Hammarskjold Rd HLW CM20 ..12 F4
Hammond Cl CBS CB2 ....22 A4
  CHESW EN7 ....216 A4
Hammonds Cl BCTR RM8 ..287 M8
Hammonds La RBAYE CM11 ..258 F4
  RBRW/HUT CM13 ......273 L5
Hammonds Rd
  CHLM/GWD CM2 ......211 G4
  RBSF CM22 ....376 H11
Ham Park Rd FSTGT E7 ....307 K4
Hampden Cl EPP CM16 ....221 H5
Hampden Crs BRW CM14 ..273 M4
  CHESW EN7 ....216 C3
Hampden Rd GRAYS RM17 ..330 C1
Hampit Rd SAFWS CB11 ..28 C7
Hampshire Rd EMPK RM11 ..290 D2
Hampstead Av RCOS CO16 ..6 C7
  WFD IG8 ....268 D6
Hampstead Rd THMD SE28 ..325 L4
Hampstead Gdns
  HOC/HUL SS5 ....264 C6
Hampton Cl SOSN SS2 ....301 H1
Hampton Ct HOC/HUL SS5 ..264 A7
Hampton Crs GVE DA12 ..338 B7
Hampton Gdns SBW CM21 ..188 C2
Hampton Rd CHING E4 ....266 C4
  CHLM/GWD CM2 ......210 B7
  FSTGT E7 ....307 L2
  IL IG1 ....308 F1
  WAN E11 ....285 G6
Hamstel Ms SOSN SS2 * ..302 A3
Hamstel Rd HLW CM20 ....12 A4
  SOSN SS2 ....302 A3
Hamsters Cl HSTD CO9 ..358 C9
Hanameel St BARK IG11 ..323 J4
Hanaper Dr ROY SG8 ....348 E10
Hanbury Cl CHES/WCR EN8 ..216 E8
Hanbury Gdns COLN CO4 ..87 G8
Hanbury Rd CHLM/WR CM1 ..4 A8
Hance La BRTR CM77 ....120 C3
Hanchet End HVHL CB9 ....33 L4
Hanchetts Orch GTDUN CM6 ..74 D2
Hancock Rd BOW E3 ......306 F7
Handel Crs TIL RM18 ....332 D4
Handel Cl CVI SS8 ......321 K6
Handel Wk COLN CO4 * ..108 B7
Handford Ct IP IP1 ......16 B4
Handford Rd IP IP1 ......16 B4
Handforth Rd IL IG1 ....286 E1
Hand La SBW CM21 ......162 D6
Handleys Cha LAIN SS15 ..277 J1
Handleys La WIT CM8 ....172 C6
Handsworth Av CHING E4 ..267 G5
Handtrough Wy BARK IG11 ..308 E6
Hanford Rd SOCK/AV RM15 ..328 F4
Hanging Hill La
  RBRW/HUT CM13 ......256 E6
Haning Hill La
  RBRW/HUT CM13 ......256 E6
Hankin Av HAR CO12 ....70 B4
Hanlee Brook
  CHLM/GWD CM2 ......210 C8
Hannah Cl CVI SS8 ......298 D7
Hannards Wy CHIG IG7 ..269 H5
Hannett Rd CVI SS8 ......321 K4
Hanningfield Cl RAYL SS6 ..280 D2
Hanningfield Wy COLN CO4 ..87 H7
Hanover Av K/T/MI CO5 ..125 K4
Hanover Br K/T/MI CO5 ..125 J2
Hanover Cl BSDN SS14 ..278 B8
Hanover Ct SUD CO10 ....278 B8
Hanover Dr BSDN SS14 ..278 B8
Hanover Gdns BARK/HLT IG6 ..268 C8
Hanover Ms HOC/HUL SS5 ..264 A7
Hanover PI BRW CM14 ....273 L4
  SAFWN CB10 ....351 K4
Hansells Md
  HLWW/ROY CM19 ......202 B1
Hanson Dr LOU IG10 ....250 F2
Hanwell Cl RCOS CO16 ....6 C7
Ha'Penny Fld RIPS/CAP IP9 ..364 C5
Harberson Rd SRTFD E15 ..307 J5
Harberts Rd HLWW/ROY CM19 ..12 B3
Harbet Rd UED N18 ......266 E7
Harbinger Rd POP/IOD E14 ..322 E7
Harborough Hall Rd
  K/T/MI CO5 ....150 A3
Harbour Crs HAR CO12 ....15 M5
Harbourer Rd BARK/HLT IG6 ..269 L4
Harbour Wy RCOLE CO7 ..130 C5
Harcamlow Wy GTDUN CM6 ..74 D7
  GTDUN CM6 ....94 A5
  RBSF CM22 ....93 K1
  RBSF CM22 ....375 K12
  ROY SG8 ....349 N7
Harcourt Av HAR CO12 ..14 C7
  MNPK E12 ....308 C1
  SOSN SS2 ....18 C2
Harcourt Ms ROM RM1 ..289 J3
Harcourt Rd SRTFD E15 ..307 J3
Harden Rd GVW DA11 ....336 F7
Hardens Manorway
  CHARL SE7 ....323 H4
Hardie Rd DAGE RM10 ..288 F8
Harding St
  SLH/COR SS17 ....317 G3
Hardinge St
  WOOL/PLUM SE18 ....324 E6

Harding Rd CDW/CHF RM16 ..331 K2
Hardings Cl RCOLW CO6 ..104 E5
Harding's Elms Rd
  BCAYE CM11 ....277 L1
Harding's La ING CM4 ....223 J2
Hardley Crs EMPK RM11 ..290 A2
Hardman Rd CHARL SE7 ..323 J8
Hardwick Cl BRTR CM77 ..120 E6
  IPNE IP4 ....49 M7
  RAYL SS6 ....281 G4
Hardwick Crs DART DA1 ..334 E8
Hardwicke St BARK IG11 ..308 E5
Hardwick Rd HVHL CB9 ..34 A1
Hardy Av CAN/RD E16 ....323 K4
  GVW DA11 ....337 J3
Hardy Cl BERM/RHTH SE16 ..322 A5
  BRTR CM7 ....121 K5
  MGTR CO11 ....64 F6
Hardy Ct SUD CO10 ......20 F1
Hardy Dr HAR CO12 ......14 B4
Hardy Gv DART DA1 ......334 D6
Hardy Rd CHING E4 ......266 A7
Hardys Wy CVI SS8 ......298 D7
Harebell Av BCAYW CM12 ..258 C1
  COLN CO4 ....107 L2
  HERT/BAY SG13 ......184 C1
Harebell Rd EHAM E6 ....324 D1
  WIT CM8 ....171 H2
Harebell Wy HARH RM3 ..272 F5
Harefield Cl BCE/LIN CB1 ..25 H7
Hare La GPK RM2 ....289 L2
Haresfield Rd DAGE RM10 ..310 D3
Haresland Cl SBF/HAD SS7 ..281 J8
Hare St HLWW/ROY CM19 ..12 D7
  WOOL/PLUM SE18 ....324 D6
Hares Wk Springs
  HLWW/ROY CM19 ......12 D7
Hare Wk SUD CO10 ......20 F4
Hare Ter WTHK RM20 * ..330 A4
Harewood Av RCFD SS4 ..264 C8
Harewood Dr CLAY IG5 ..268 C8
Harewood HI EPP CM16 ..235 M5
Harewood Rd BRWN CM15 ..255 K6
  CHLM/WR CM1 ....4 D3
Harford Cl CHING E4 ....248 A7
Harforde Ct HERT/BAY SG13 * ..184 C1
Harford Rd CHING E4 ....248 A7
Harford St WCHPL E1 ....306 C9
Harfred Av MAL CM9 ....215 H2
Hargrave Cl STSD CM24 ..88 A1
Hargreaves Av CHESW EN7 ..232 C1
Hargreaves Cl CHESW EN7 ..232 C1
Harkilees Wy BRTR CM7 ..99 J4
Harkness CHESW EN7 ....216 C7
Harkness Rd HARH RM3 ..272 A5
Harkstead La RIPS/CAP IP9 ..365 K1
Harkstead Rd RIPS/CAP IP9 ..365 K1
Harlech Rd PIT SS13 ....278 E3
Harlesden Cl HARH RM3 ..272 C5
Harlesden Rd HARH RM3 ..272 C5
Harley Cl BOW E3 ......306 C7
Harley St LOS SS9 ......299 M4
Harlinger St
  WOOL/PLUM SE18 ....324 B6
Harlings Gv CHLM/WR CM1 ..5 H2
The Harlings HERT/BAY SG13 * ..184 C1
Harlow Common HLWE CM17 ..204 A4
Harlow Gdns CRW RM5 ..270 C6
Harlow Rd CHONG CM5 ..380 D6
  HLWE CM17 ....189 J7
  HLWW/ROY CM19 ......186 D6
  RAIN RM13 ....311 J5
Harman Av WFD IG8 ....267 K6
Harman Cl CHING E4 ....267 K6
Harman Wk RCOS CO16 ....6 A2
Harmer St GVE DA12 ....337 M4
Harness Cl CHLM/WR CM1 ..194 A4
Harness Rd THMD SE28 ..325 K5
Harnham Dr BRTR CM77 ..120 E7
Harold Av BELV DA17 ....326 E4
Harold Cl HLWW/ROY CM19 ..203 G2
Harold Crs WAB EN9 ....233 H2
Harold Court Rd HARH RM3 ..272 F5
Harold Gdns WICKE SS11 ..261 G4
Harold Gv CHING E4 ......266 C7
  FOS CO13 ....137 G4
Harold HI Rd HARH RM3 ..272 D5
Harold Rd BRTR CM7 ....121 H7
  CHING E4 ....266 D7
  COS CO15 ....7 J4
  FOS CO13 ....137 G4
  PLSTW E13 ....307 L2
  WAN E11 ....285 G6
  WFD IG8 ....267 H7
Harolds Rd HLWW/ROY CM19 ..203 G2
Haroldstone Rd WALTH E17 ..285 G2
Harold Vw HARH RM3 ....272 E6
Harold Wy FOS CO13 ....137 G4
Haron Cl CVI SS8 ......320 E2
Harpclose Rd SUD CO10 ..20 C7
Harpenden Rd MNPK E12 ..287 M2
Harper Cl CDW/CHF RM16 ..329 M8
Harper Rd EHAM E6 ......324 C2
Harper's Est RCOLW CO6 ..361 G6
Harper's HI RCOLW CO6 ..361 K7
Harper's La BRWN CM15 ..256 A5
Harper's wy RAYL SS6 ....280 F2
Harp Meadow La COLS CO2 ..129 G2
Harpour Rd BARK IG11 ..308 C5
Harpur's Rd SUD CO10 ....39 L1
Harrap Cha GRAYS RM17 ..330 C1
Harridge Cl LOS SS9 ....300 D2
Harridge Rd LOS SS9 ....300 D2
Harrier Cl HCH RM12 ....311 L1
  IPSE IP3 ....55 L5
Harrier Ms THMD SE28 ..325 G5
Harrier Wy EHAM E6 ....324 C1
  WAB EN9 ....234 B4
Harriescourt WAB EN9 ..234 B2
Harrington Cl K/T/MI CO5 ..149 G1
  WAN E11 * 285 L1
Harrington Wy
  WOOL/PLUM SE18 ....324 A6
Harriott Cl GNWCH SE10 ..323 K7
Harris Cl GVW DA11 ......337 J8
Harris Gdns
  HARH RM3 ....272 B5
  SLH/COR SS17 ....317 L1
  WICKW SS12 ....261 H1
Harrison Cl RBRW/HUT CM13 ..257 J3
  CHLM/WR CM1 ....4 A3
Harrison Dr BRTR CM7 ..121 K4
Harrison Gdns HOC/HUL SS5 ..263 M8
Harrison Gv KESG IP5 ....50 D6
Harrison Rd COLS CO2 ..129 J7
  DAGE RM10 ....310 D3
  WAB EN9 ....233 J7
Harrisons BSF CM23 ....115 G7
Harrisons Whf PUR RM19 ..328 B8
Harris Rd CVI SS8 ......321 K4
Harris Rd DAGE RM10 ....310 C2
Harris St WALTH E17 ....284 C1
Harrods Ct BCAYE CM11 ..259 H3
Harrogate Dr HOC/HUL SS5 ..264 C5

Harrogate Rd HOC/HUL SS5 ..264 C5
Harrold Rd BCTR RM8 ....309 E4
Harrowby Gdns GVW DA11 ..337 H7
Harrow Cl IG1 ....308 F1
  IPNE IP4 ....48 F8
Harrow Crs HARH RM3 ..271 F5
Harrow Dr EMPK RM11 ..289 M5
Harrow Gdns HOC/HUL SS5 ..264 C5
Harrowgate Rd HOM E9 ..306 H8
Harrow Gn WAN E11 ....285 H8
Harrow HI HSTD CO9 ....355 F5
Harrow La POP/IOD E14 ..322 F4
Harrow Manor Wy
  THMD SE28 ....325 M4
  BARK IG11 ....309 H5
  COS CO15 ....7 G4
  CVI SS8 ....298 E5
  HVHL CB9 ....34 B6
  IL IG1 ....308 F1
  UPMR RM14 ....292 F6
  WAN E11 ....285 H6
  WICKW SS12 ....279 K3
Harrow St RCOLW CO6 ..361 J2
Harrow Ter HAR CO12 ....14 A4
Harrow Vw CHLM/GWD CM2 ..210 B3
Harsnett Rd COL CO1 ....107 L6
Harston Dr PEND EN3 ..233 H8
Hart Cl HVHL CB9 ......34 C5
Hart Cnr WTHK RM20 * ..330 A4
Hart Crs CHIG IG7 ......269 J4
Hartest Wy SUD CO10 ....21 K9
Hartfield Dr UPMR RM14 ..337 G5
Hartfield Ter BOW E3 ....306 D6
Hartford Cl HAYL SS6 ....280 D2
Hartford End PIT SS13 ..278 D4
Hartington Pl SOS SS1 ....19 K2
Hartington Rd CAN/RD E16 ..323 J2
  SOS SS1 ....19 K2
  WALTH E17 ....284 C1
Hartlake Rd HOM E9 ....306 A3
Hartland Rd LOS SS9 ....282 A6
Hart La CHES/WCR EN8 ..216 E8
  EPP CM16 ....221 H7
  HCH RM12 ....289 K7
  SRTFD E15 ....307 J4
Hartley Av EHAM E6 ....308 C8
Hartley Cl CHLM/GWD CM2 ..210 D3
Hartley Rd WAN E11 ....285 L3
Hartley St CHTY IP2 ....54 A3
Hartmann Rd CAN/RD E16 ..324 A4
Hartmoor Ms PEND EN3 ..232 E7
Hart Rd HLWE CM17 ....188 D4
  SBF/HAD SS7 ....280 C8
Harts Gv WFD IG8 ......267 K4
Hartshill Rd GVW DA11 ..337 G7
Hartshorn Gdns EHAM E6 ..308 D8
Harts La BARK IG11 ....308 C4
  RCOLE CO7 ....88 C1
Hartslock Dr ABYW SE2 ..326 A3
Hart St BRW CM14 ......273 M1
  CHLM/GWD CM2 ....4 E6
Hartswood Cl BRW CM14 ..256 B5
Hartsworth Cl PLSTW E13 ..307 J6
Hartville Rd
  WOOL/PLUM SE18 ....325 H7
Hartwell Dr CHING E4 ..266 H7
Harty Cl CDW/CHF RM16 ..314 G8
Harvard Cl COLN CO4 ..107 J8
Harvel Crs ABYW SE2 ..326 A4
Harvest Cl RCHLM CM3 ..245 G6
Harvest Ct FX IP11 * 69 J2
  K/T/MI CO5 ....149 H1
Harvest End COLW CO3 ..106 A8
Harvest La SUD CO10 ....44 E7
Harvesters MAL CM9 * ..384 C11
Harvesters Wy KESG IP5 ..50 C8
  RCOLW CO6 ....103 L5
Harvest La LOU IG10 ....250 A7
Harvest Rd CVI SS8 ......298 E8
Harvest Wy MAL CM9 ....198 G4
  RCOLE CO7 ....109 J7
Harvey CDW/CHF RM16 ..330 A4
  PIT SS13 ....278 E4
Harvey Crs COLS CO2 ....105 M8
Harvey Gdns CHARL SE7 ..323 M8
Harvey Gdns CHARL SE7 ..323 M8
Harvey Rd COLS CO2 ....128 E3
  IL IG1 ....308 C1
  MAL CM9 ....198 D1
  PIT SS13 ....278 E4
  RCOLE CO7 ....130 E4
  WAN E11 ....285 H6
Harvey's La ROMW/RG RM7 ..289 L3
Harvey St HSTD CO9 ......81 J3
Harwater Dr LOU IG10 ..250 C2
Harwell Cl BRTR CM7 ....122 A1
Harwich Rd COLN CO4 ....6 A1
  HAR CO12 ....368 A4
  MGTR CO11 ....91 K7
  MGTR CO11 ....366 F2
  RCOLE CO7 ....110 C7
  RCOLE CO7 ....111 J3
  RCOLE CO7 ....113 K7
  RCOS CO16 ....113 K7
Harwood Av EMPK RM11 ..290 B1
Harwood Cl COLS CO2 * ..129 K1
Harwood Hall La UPMR RM14 ..312 G1
Hascombe Rd COS CO15 ..183 G5
Haselfoot Rd RCHLM CM3 ..195 H4
Haselmere Gdns FOS CO13 ..137 J2
Haskard Rd DAGW RM9 ..310 A3
Haskell Ms BRTR CM7 ..121 K5
Haskins SLH/COR SS17 ..317 H3
Haskins Wk KESG IP5 ....50 C8
Haslemere BSF CM23 ....139 L5
Haslemere Dr IPNE IP4 ..17 K2
Haslemere Rd
  GDMY/SEVK IG3 ......287 J3
  WICKE SS11 ....260 F3
Hasler Cl THMD SE28 ....325 H1
Hasler Rd MAL CM9 ....385 N3
Haslers La GTDUN CM6 ..117 G2
Haslewood Av HOD EN11 ..201 H2
Hassell Rd CVI SS8 ....321 G4
Hassenbrook Rd
  SLH/COR SS17 ....317 G3
Hassett Rd HOM E9 ......306 A3
Hasted Cl CRH DA9 ......335 M8
Hasted Rd CHARL SE7 ..324 A8
Hastings Av BARK/HLT IG6 ..269 J6
  COS CO15 ....183 G5
Hastings Pl RCOLE CO7 ..156 G6
Hastings Rd COLW CO3 ..289 G3
  GPK RM2 ....289 G3
The Hastings WICKE SS11 ..261 G4
Hastingwood Rd HLWE CM17 ..204 H6
Hastings St
  WOOL/PLUM SE18 ....324 D5
Hatchcroft Gdns RCOLE CO7 ..109 K7
Hatcher Crs COL CO1 ....107 M6
Hatches Farm Rd
  BCAYW CM12 ....258 A8

Hatchfields RCHLM CM3....167 J6
Hatch Gn RBSF CM22....163 J1
Hatch Gv CHDH RM6....288 D2
Hatch La CHING E4....267 G3
Hatch Rd BRWN CM15....255 H6
Hatch Side CHIG IG7....268 D4
The Hatch PEND EN3....248 A1
Hatchwoods WFD IG8....323 J8
Hatcliffe St GNWCH SE10....323 J8
Hatfield CI BARK/HLT IG6....286 E1
  HCH RM12....312 A2
  RBRW/HUT CM13....257 G3
Hatfield Dr BCAYE CM11....259 G3
Hatfield Rd CDW/CHF RM16....330 A4
  IPSE IP3....54 F1
  MAL CM9....197 L6
  RAYL SS6....280 E2
  RCHLM CM3....169 M2
  RCHLM CM3....197 J1
  SRTFD E15....307 H2
  WIT CM8....171 H7
Hatfields LOU IG10....250 E3
Hathaway CI CHIG IG7....268 E5
Hathaway Crs MNPK E12....308 C3
Hathaway Gdns CHDH RM6....288 A3
Hathaway Rd HARH RM3....330 E3
Hatherleigh Wy HARH RM3....272 A7
Hatherley Gdns EHAM E6....308 A4
Hatherley Rd WALTH E17....284 C2
The Hatherley BSDN SS14....3
Hatley Av BARK/HLT IG6....286 E2
Hatley Gdns SBF/HAD SS7....279 M8
Hatterill LAIN SS15....5
Hattersfield CI BELV DA17....326 C7
Hatton CI CDW/CHF RM16....330 A2
  GVW DA11....337 H8
Hatton Rd CHES/WCR EN8....216 E7
  CVI SS8....320 A3
Haubourdin CI HSTD CO9....81 K3
Haughley Dr IPNE IP4....49 L7
Hauliers Rd FX IP11....10 E6
Havalon CI BSDN SS14....3
Havana CI ROM RM1....289 H4
Havana Dr RAYL SS6....262 C4
Havannah St POP/IOD E14....322 D5
Havant Rd WALTH E17....284 F1
Havelock Rd BELV DA17 *....326 C7
  GVW DA11....337 J6
Havelock St IL IG1....286 E7
Haven Av COS CO15....160 C3
Haven CI CVI SS8....320 A2
  FX IP11....10 F2
  VGE SS16....296 B2
Haven Ex FX IP11 *....10
Havengore Av GVE DA12....338 B5
Haven PI CDW/CHF RM16....330 F1
Haven Ri BCAYE CM11....259 F4
Haven Rd COLS CO2....130 B2
  CVI SS8....320 A3
Havenside SBF/FI SS3....396 H12
The Havens SBF/NAC RM17....55 K6
The Haven GRAYS RM17....331 J3
  HAV CO12....138 B8
Haverfield Rd BOW E3....306 A7
Haverhill Rd CBE/LIN CB1....32 C2
  CBE/LIN CB1....33 H8
  CHING E4....248 E8
  HVHL CB9....34 E1
  HVHL CB9....343 M5
Havering CI COLN CO4....108 A7
  COS CO15....159 H6
  SBN/FI SS3....303 L1
Havering Dr ROM RM1....289 H4
Havering Gdns CHDH RM6....287 M5
Havering Rd ROM RM1....271 G2
Havering St WCHPL E1....322 K2
Havering Wy BARK IG11....309 L7
Havers La BSF CM23....139 L7
Havisham Rd GVE DA12....338 D6
Havisham Wy CHLM/WR CM1....193 G3
Havis Rd SLH/COR SS17....317 H1
Hawarden Rd WALTH E17....284 C2
Haward Rd HOD EN11....201 K1
Hawbridge RIPS/CAP IP9....58 D2
Hawbridge Rd WAN E11....285 G6
Hawes La WAB EN9....233 K8
Hawes St CHTY IP2....17 L9
Hawfinch Rd COLS CO2....128 D8
Hawgood St BOW E3....322 D1
Hawk CI WAB EN9....234 B4
Hawk Cnr ROM RM20 *....330 A4
Hawkdene CHING E4....248 E6
Hawkenbury
  HLWW/ROY CM19....203 H3
Hawkendon Rd RCOS CO16....182 D1
Hawke PI BERM/RHTH SE16 *....322 A5
Hawker CI KESG IP5....51 L5
Hawke Rd IPSE IP3....54
Hawkesbury Bush La
  VGE SS16....295 K3
Hawkesbury CI BARK/HLT IG6....269
  CVI SS8....320 C3
Hawkesbury Rd CVI SS8....320 B2
Hawkes CI GRAYS RM17....330 K5
Hawkes La FX IP11....62 C7
Hawkes Rd RCOLW CO6....124 C2
Hawkesway COS CO15....159 J2
Hawk HI WICKE SS11....261 M1
Hawkhurst CI CHLM/WR CM1....193 A3
Hawkhurst Gdns CRW RM5....271 J6
Hawkinge Wy HCH RM12....311 M3
Hawkins CI WICKE SS11....261 J6
  WICKE SS11....20 C1
Hawkins Dr CDW/CHF RM16....330 A1
Hawkins Rd COL CO1....9 L7
  RCOLE CO7....131 L9
  SUD CO10....21 G1
Hawkins Ter CHARL SE7....324
Hawkins Wy BRTR CM7....121 M1
Hawk La SUD CO10 *....20 A8
  WICKE SS11....262 A3
Hawkridge SBN/FI SS3....302 F5
Hawkridge CI CHDH RM6....287 M4
Hawkridge Dr GRAYS RM17....331 G4
Hawks CI RCHLM CM3....212 D8
Hawks HI EPP CM16....221 H5
Hawksmead CI PEND EN3....232 K6
Hawksmoor CI EHAM E6....324
  WOOL/PLUM SE18....325 H8
Hawksmoor Gn
  RBRW/HUT CM13....257 G1
Hawksmouth CHING E4....248 E7
Hawksway VGE SS16....295 L1
Hawkswood Rd HOC/HUL SS5....242 C6
Hawkwell Cha BCAYE CM11....282 B1
Hawkwell Park Dr
  HOC/HUL SS5....264 C8
Hawkwell Rd HOC/HUL SS5....264 B8
Hawkwell CI RCHLM CM3....245 H4
Hawkwood Crs CHING E4....248 D8
Hawkwood Rd HSTD CO9....81 H3
Hawley Rd UED N18....266 A4
Hawlmark End RCOLW CO6....126 B2
Hawsted BKHH IG9....249 L7

Hawthorn Av CBS CB2....22 C3
  COLN CO4....108 B6
  RAIN RM13....311 L8
  RBRW/HUT CM13....256 D3
Hawthorn CI CHLM/GWD CM2....209 H4
  HOC/HUL SS5....264 C8
  HSTD CO9....81 K3
  RBSF CM22....377
Hawthorn Dr CHTY IP2....53 J3
Hawthorne Av CHESW EN7....216 D8
  HOM E9....306 C1
Hawthorne CI CHESW EN7....232 C1
Hawthorne Gdns
  HOC/HUL SS5....263 L8
Hawthorne Rd SLH/COR SS17....317 J1
  WALTH E17....284 D1
Hawthornes RCHLM CM3....230 H4
Hawthorn PI ERITH DA8....326 F8
Hawthorn Ri BSF CM23....139 L8
Hawthorn Rd BKHH IG9....267 M3
  COS CO15....159 H6
  CVI SS8....320 F2
  HOD EN11....201 J1
  HVHL CB9....34 D1
  MAL CM9....174 D3
  RCHLM CM3....170 D8
  SUD CO10....21 J7
The Hawthorns BOC CM0....393 M6
  RCHLM CM3....212 D6
  SLH/COR SS17....317 H1
  SUD CO10 *....21 J1
Hawthorn Wk RCHLM CM3....145 H4
Hawthorn Wy RAYL SS6....281 H5
Hawtree CI SOS SS1....19 L7
Hayburn Wy HCH RM12....289 H1
Hay CI SRTFD E15....307 H4
Haycocks La K/T/MI CO5....178 C4
Haycocks Rd HVHL CB9....33 M4
Haycroft BSF CM23....139 K3
Hay Currie St POP/IOD E14....322 F1
Hayday Rd CAN/RD E16....307 K4
Haydens Rd HLWW/ROY CM19....12 F7
Haydock CI HAR RM12....312 C1
Haydon CI HARH RM3....271 L6
Haydon Rd BCTR RM8....287 M7
Haye La K/T/MI CO5....153 M1
Hayes Barton SOS SS1....302 F5
Hayes Cha RCHLM CM3....244 C8
  WICKE SS11....262 C1
Hayes CI CHLM/GWD CM2....5 H3
  WTHK RM20....335 M4
Hay De RAIN RM13....311 L4
Hayes CI CVI SS8....320 C4
Hayes Rd COS CO15....6 C1
Hayfield Av CBS CB2....22 C8
Hay Gn RCHLM CM3....212 C5
Hayhill Rd IPNE IP4....17 J2
Hayhouse Rd RCOLW CO6....82 D8
Hay La North BRTR CM7....121 M2
Hay La South BRTR CM7....121 M2
Hayle TIL RM18....332 F2
Hayley Bell Gdns BSF CM23....139 G8
Hayling Gv WICKE SS11....261 M3
Hayman Rd IPSE IP3....54 E1
Haymeads La BSF CM23....139 K3
Haynes Green Rd K/T/MI CO5....150 E5
Haynes Rd EMPK RM11....290 A3
Havron's La CHLM/WR CM1....165 G5
Haysoms CI ROM RM1....289 H2
Haytor CI BRTR CM7....121 M1
The Haywain COLW CO3....106 A8
Haywards CI CHDH RM6....287 M3
Hayward Ct WAB EN9....234 A4
Haywood PI
  CDW/CHF RM16 *....331 M1
Hayword Ct WAB EN9....234
Hazelbrouck Gdns
  BARK/HLT IG6....269 G6
Hazel CI HCH RM12....289 L8
  HVHL CB9....34 E1
  LAIN SS15....277 J3
  LOS SS9....299 M4
  RCOLE CO7....132 D8
  SBF/HAD SS7....299 C8
Hazeldene CHES/WCR EN8....232 F2
Hazeldene Rd BCTR RM8....287 L1
Hazeldon CI RCHLM CM3....167 M7
Hazel Dr IPSE IP3....55 K4
  SOCK/AV RM15....313 M7
Hazel End RBRW/HUT CM13....256 D3
Hazeleigh Gdns WFD IG8....323 J8
Hazeleigh Hall La MAL CM9....213 M8
Hazelend Rd BSF CM23....115 G3
Hazel Gdns CDW/CHF RM16....331 J8
Hazel Gv BRTR CM7....121 H4
  CHDH RM6....288 B1
Hazel La WFD IG8....268 B6
Hazel Av COS CO2....128 D2
Hazel Rd ROMW/RG RM7....270 E7
Hazelmere PIT SS13....296 C1
Hazelmere Gdns EMPK RM11....289 L3
Hazel Ms RCOLE CO7....156 B6
Hazel Rd SRTFD E15 *....307 H2
Hazelton Rd COLN CO4....9 L2
Hazelville CI HAR CO12....70 D4
Hazel Wy CHING E4....266 C6
Hazelwood HOC/HUL SS5....282 C1
Hazelwood Ct
  SBF/HAD SS7....279 L6
  TIL RM18....332 D3
Hazelwood CI CLPT E5....284 D8
Hazelwood Ct MAL CM9....198 E4
Hazelwood Crs RCOS CO16....158 F4
Hazelwood Gdns
  BRWN CM15....255 K5
Hazelwood Gv LOS SS9....282 K6
Hazelwood Park CI
  BARK/HLT IG6....269 H4
Hazelwood Rd WALTH E17....266 A4
Hazlemere Rd COS CO15....183 M3
  SBF/HAD SS7....280 A8
Hazlitt Rd IP IP1....48 M2
Headcorn CI PIT SS13....278 F9
Headgate COL CO1....8 B8
Headingham CI CHTY IP2....53 M3
Headingley CI CHESW EN7....278 D3
  PIT SS13....278
Headland CI AVHL CB9....34 E1
Headley Cha BRW CM14....273 M3
Headley Common
  RBRW/HUT CM13....273
Headley Dr GNTH/NBYPK IG2....286 A4
Headley Rd BCAYE CM11....258 F1
Head St COL CO1....8 B8

HSTD CO9....81 J3
K/T/MI CO5....130 C5
MAL CM9....384 B2
WCHPL E1....322 A7
Heard's La BRTR CM7....354 C4
  BRWN CM15....238 C7
Hearn Rd ROM RM1....289 H4
Hearsall Av CHLM/WR CM1....193 L5
  SLH/COR SS17....317 H3
Heath CI BCAYW CM12....258 C8
  GPK RM2....289 K1
  RCOLE CO7....64 A2
Heathcote Av CLAY IG5....268 C8
Heathcote Gdns HLWE CM17....204 F5
Heathcote Gv CHING E4....266 F2
Heath Ct FX IP11....62 A3
Heathcroft Gdns WALTH E17....267 G8
Heathdene Dr BELV DA17....326 E7
Heath Dr CHLM/GWD CM2....209 H4
  ROM RM1....271 G8
  SBF/HAD SS7....299 J3
Heather Av IPSE IP3....55 H2
  ROM RM1....271 G8
Heather Bank BCAYE CM11....258 A2
Heather CI BRWN CM15....255 H5
  BSF CM23....138 C2
  COLS CO2....128 C2
  COS CO15....159 J2
  CVI SS8....320 C3
  EHAM E6....324 D2
  KIR/NAC RM1....50 A8
  ROM RM1....271 G8
Heather Ct CHLM/WR CM1....271
  WICKE SS11....261 K7
Heather Dr COLW CO3....106 C8
  ROM RM1....271 G8
  SBF/HAD SS7....299 J3
Heather Gdns ROM RM1....271 G8
  WAB EN9....233 K6
Heather Gln ROM RM1....271 G8
Heatherhayes CHTY IP2....53 M3
Heatherley Dr CLAY IG5....286 C2
Heather Rd CHING E4....266 E4
Heather Wy HARH RM3....271 G2
Heatherwood CI MNPK E12....285 M7
Heathfield CHING E4....266 F2
  KESG IP5....50 E1
  SBF/HAD SS7....280 B7
Heathfield CI CAN/RD E16....324 A1
Heathfield Ms KIR/NAC RM1....50 A8
Heathfield Park Dr
  CHDH RM6....287 L3
Heathfield Rd CHLM/WR CM1....193 L5
  RIPS/CAP IP9....364 C3
Heathfields FX IP11....105 L5
  RCOLW CO6....105 L5
Heathgate HERT/BAY SG13....184 C6
  WIT CM8....172 A7
Heathgate Piece FX IP11....62 B7
Heathlands RCOLE CO7....132 D2
Heathlands Pk IPNE IP4....55 L4
Heath La HERT/BAY SG13....184 E1
  IPNE IP4....49 L8
Heathleigh Dr VGE SS16....294 E2
Heath Park Rd GPK RM2....289 K3
Heath Rd BCAYE CM11....259 H4
  CDW/CHF RM16....315 J8
  CHDH RM6....288 A6
  COLW CO3....105 J4
  IPNE IP4....49 L8
  K/T/MI CO5....130 C5
  MGTR CO11....91 G7
  RCOLE CO7....64 A2
  RCOS CO16....112 A4
  RCOS CO16....158 B4
  WD8R IP12....115
Heath Rw BSF CM23....115 K8
Heathside RCOLW CO6....106 B1
Heathside CI
  GNTH/NBYPK IG2....287 G3
Heath Ter MGTR CO11 *....91 L3
The Heath COLS CO2....128 C2
  RCOLE CO7....89 J1
Heath Vw KESG IP5....49 M7
Heath View Gdns
  CDW/CHF RM16....330 F1
Heath View Rd
  CDW/CHF RM16....330 F1
Heath Vls WOOL/PLUM SE18....325 G8
Heathway DAGW RM9....310 C1
  WFD IG8....267 M4
Heathwood Gdns CHARL SE7....324 B7
Heatley Wy COLN CO4....108 A7
Heaton Av HARH RM3....271 L6
Heaton CI CHING E4....266 F2
  HARH RM3....271 M6
Heaton Grange Rd GPK RM2....271 G8
Heaton Wy HARH RM3....271 M6
  K/T/MI CO5....150 A7
Heavitree CI
  WOOL/PLUM SE18....325 G8
Heavitree Rd
  WOOL/PLUM SE18....325 G8
Hecham CI WALTH E17....266 C6
Heckford's Rd RCOLE CO7....133 H5
Heckford St WAP E1W....322 C1
Heckworth CI COLN CO4....87 M7
Hector CI COLS CO2....128 D2
Hector St WOOL/PLUM SE18 *....325 J8
Hedgecoe Av RAYL SS6....281 G5
Hedgelands COLW CO3....105 J4
Hedge La SBF/HAD SS7....299 C1
Hedgemans Rd DAGW RM9....310 A4
Hedgemans Wy DAGW RM9....310 A4
Hedge Place Rd GRH DA9....335 J8
Hedgerows COLW CO3....106 A7
  SBW CM21....163 G7
The Hedgerows BSF CM23....139 J5
The Hedgerow Rd HOM E9 *....306 D1
Hedger's Av HOM E9 *....306
Hedingham Dr WICKW SS12....261 J1
Hedingham PI RCFD SS4 *....283 C1
Hedingham Rd BCTR RM8....309 L1
  CDW/CHF RM16....329 M8
  EMPK RM11....290 A3
  HSTD CO9....80 D1
  HSTD CO9....81 G1
  RCOLE CO7....357
Hedley Av WTHK RM20....335 M1
Hedworth Av CHES/WCR EN8....232 F3
Heenan CI BARK IG11....308 F5
Heeswyk Rd CVI SS8....299 J3
Heideburg Rd CVI SS8....298 D2
Heigham Rd EHAM E6....308 D1
Heighams HLWW/ROY CM19....203 G4
Heilsbury Rd CVI SS8....299
Heiden Av CVI SS8....298 E8
Heron Ct BKHH IG9....249 K8
Helena CI HOC/HUL SS5....264 C8
Helena Ct RCHLM CM3....245 G4

Helena Rd IPSE IP3....17 J8
  PLSTW E13....307 J6
  RAYL SS6....281 D5
  WALTH E17....284 D3
Helena Sq POP/IOD E14....322 D5
Helen How RCHLM CM3....144 C6
Helen Rd EMPK RM11....290 A1
Helens Ga CHES/WCR EN8....217 G4
Helen St WOOL/PLUM SE18 *....324 E7
Helford Ct WIT CM8....171 J7
Helford Wy UPMR RM14....291 J2
Helions Bumpstead Rd
  HVHL CB9....34 D8
Helions Park Av HVHL CB9....34 D6
Helions Park Gdns HVHL CB9....34 D6
Helions Park Gv HVHL CB9....34 D6
Helions Service Rd HVHL CB9....34 C7
  HVHL CB9....343 R7
Helions Wk HVHL CB9....34 D6
Helleborine GRAYS RM17....330 C3
Hellendoorn Rd CVI SS8....320 C6
Helm CI RCOLW CO6....105 J4
Helmons La CHLM/GWD CM2....242 D1
Helmore Ct LAIN SS15 *....276 C7
Helmore Rd BARK IG11....309 J4
Helmores LAIN SS15....276 C7
Helmsdale CVI SS8....298 C8
Helmsdale CI ROM RM1....271 H6
Helmsdale Rd ROM RM1....271 H6
Helpeston BSDN SS14....2
Helsinki Sq BERM/RHTH SE16....322 C6
Helston CI KESG IP5....50 A7
Helston Rd CDW/CHF RM16....316 A6
Hemingway Rd WIT CM8....147 M8
Hemley Rd CDW/CHF RM16....316 A6
Hemmells LAIN SS15....276 E5
Hemmings CI MAL CM9....214 B5
Hemnall St EPP CM16....236 A1
Hempstalls LAIN SS15....2
Hempstead CI BKHH IG9....267 K1
Hempstead Rd HVHL CB9....33 M4
  WALTH E17....285 G1
Hemsdale CI EMPK RM11....289 L3
  HVHL CB9....33 M4
  RIPW IP8....46 F8
Henderson Dr DART DA1....334 D6
Henderson CI RCHLM CM3....230 H4
Henderson Rd WICKW SS12....261 H8
  WICKW SS11....261 G8
Hendon Gdns CRW RM5....270 F5
Hengist Av WICKE SS11....261 M3
Hengrave CI CHTY IP2....53 M3
Henham CI RCHLM CM3....230 H4
Henham Rd RBSF CM22....373 F4
  SAFWS CB11....373 F4
Henley Av IP IP1....48 A2
Henley CI COLW CO3....106 B7
Henley Crs WOS/PRIT SS0....301 C5
Henley Gdns CHDH RM6....288 B3
Henley Rd CAN/RD E16....324 C5
  IL IG1....308 F1
  IPSE IP3....48 A1
Henney CI RCHLM CM3....230 H4
Henniker Gdns EHAM E6....308 A4
Henniker Ga CHLM/GWD CM2....210 D2
Henniker Rd IP IP1....47 J3
  SRTFD E15....307 G2
Henny Back Rd BURES CO8....358 H5
Henny Rd BURES CO8....359 J1
Henny Vw SUD CO10 *....45 L5
Henrietta CI RCOLE CO7....130 C2
Henrietta St SRTFD E15....306 F2
Henry Addlington CI
  EHAM E6....324
Henry CI COS CO15....369 N6
  HVHL CB9....34 A1
Henry Dixon Rd WIT CM8....148 A7
Henry Dr LOS SS9....299 L3
Henry Laver Ct COLW CO3....8 A6
Henry Morris Rd CBS CB2....22 C1
Henry Rd CHLM/WR CM1....209 L1
  EHAM E6....308 B6
  IPSE IP3....55
Henry's Av WFD IG8....267 J4
Henry St GRAYS RM17....330 J4
Henshawe Rd BCTR RM8....288 A8
Henslow Rd IPNE IP4....49 J7
Henson Av CVI SS8....321 J1
Henstead Gdns IPSE IP3....54 E3
Henwood Side WFD IG8....268 A5
Hepburn CI CDW/CHF RM16....330 A4
Hepscott Rd HOM E9 *....306 D1
Herald CI BSF CM23....138 C2
Herbage Park Rd MAL CM9....212 F4
Herbert CI SUD CO10....21 G1
Herbert Gdns CHDH RM6....288 A6
Herbert Gv SOS SS1....19 L6
Herbert Rd COS CO15....320 F1
  CVI SS8....320 F1
  EMPK RM11....290 B5
  GDMY/SEVK IG3....287 H7
  KESG IP5....50 E1
  MNPK E12....308 B2
  SBN/FI SS3....302 C1
  SWCM DA10....336 C4
  WALTH E17....284 C1
Herbert St PLSTW E13....307 K5
Herd La SLH/COR SS17....317 H1
Hereford Ct CHLM/WR CM1....210 C8
  COS CO15....160 B3
  WAN E11....285 L3
Herent Dr CLAY IG5....286 C1
Hereward CI RCOLE CO7....130 C2
  WAB EN9....233 K2
Hereward Gdns WICKE SS11....261 G4
Hereward Gn LOU IG10....250 F1
Hereward Wy BRTR CM7....77 M2
Herga Hyll CDW/CHF RM16....315 K8
Herington Gv
  RBRW/HUT CM13....256 D3
Heriot Av CHING E4....266 D2
Heriot Wy MAL CM9....198 E1
Heritage Rd RCFD SS4....283 H1
  RCHLM CM3....231 L8
Hermes Wy SBN/FI SS3....303 H1
Hermitage Av SBF/HAD SS7....298 D3
  SWFD E18....285 G1
Hermitage Dr SBF/HAD SS7....298 D3
Hermitage Mdw SUD CO10....37 L4
Hermitage Wk SWFD E18....285 L1
Hermit Rd CAN/RD E16....307 H3
Hermon HI WAN E11....285 L3
Hermon Av RCFD SS4....283 H1
Heron Av WICKE SS11....261 J6
Heron Cha RBRW/HUT CM13....275 J2
Heron CI BKHH IG9....249 K8
  RAYL SS6....280 E3
  SBW CM21....162 B1

WALTH E17....266 C8
Heron Ct BSF CM23....139 H2
Heron Di BSDN SS14....3 M5
Heron Dr WARE SG12....185 M6
Heron Flight Av HCH RM12....311 K4
Heron Gdns RAYL SS6....280 E3
Herongate SBF/HAD SS7....297 L1
  SBN/FI SS3....303 H5
Herongate
  CHES/WCR EN8....217
  MNPK E12....285 M7
Heron Gdns COS CO15....159 J6
Heron HI BELV DA17....326 C7
Heron Md PEND EN3....233 H8
Heron Ms IL IG1....286 E7
Heron Quays POP/IOD E14....322 D4
Heron Rd CHTY IP2....53 C2
  K/T/MI CO5....149 G2
Heronsgate FOS CO13....137 J3
Herons La CHONC CM5....381 K8
Herons Wd HLW CM20....7 D3
Heron Wy FOS CO13....137 H2
  MAL CM9....198 F8
  RCHLM CM3....388 D7
  UPMR RM14....291 H6
  WTHK RM20....329 H6
Heronway RBRW/HUT CM13....256 D3
Herrick CI COLW CO3....106 D7
Herringham Rd CHARL SE7....323 M6
Herring's Wy FOS CO13....85 C7
Herschell Rd LOS SS9....299 M4
Hertford Dr SLH/COR SS17....295 M4
Hertford Rd BCTR RM8....349 G8
  SAFWS CB11....373 A1
Hertford Rd BARK IG11....308 D4
  CVI SS8....320 C2
  GNTH/NBYPK IG2....287 H4
  HOD EN11....200 F1
  PEND EN3....232 D2
  SUD CO10....37 L4
  WARE SG12....184 E1
Hertfordshire Wy BSF CM23....138 F6
Hertfordshire way ROY SG8....370 A3
Hertsmere Rd POP/IOD E14....322 C2
Hervey CI RIPS/CAP IP9....66 F4
Hervey Park Rd WALTH E17....284 B1
Hervey St IPNE IP4....17 H2
Hervilly Wy WOTN CO14....137 L2
Hesketh Rd FSTGT E7....285 K8
Hesper CI COL CO1....107 M8
Hesperus Crs POP/IOD E14....322 E7
Hesselyn Dr RAIN RM13....311 L4
Hester PI BOC CM0....393 M8
Hetherington CI COLS CO2....129 K5
Hetzand Rd CVI SS8....321 J2
Heveron CI GNWCH SE10....323 J8
Hever CI HOC/HUL SS5....264 C8
Heverham Rd
  WOOL/PLUM SE18....325 H7
Hevingham Dr CHDH RM6....287 L4
Hewes CI COLN CO4....108 C6
Hewison St BOW E3....306 B4
Hewitt Rd HAR CO12....70 D4
Hewlett Rd BOW E3....306 B4
Heybridge Ap MAL CM9....198 C6
Heybridge Dr BARK/HLT IG6....287 G1
  IL IG1....287 G1
Heybridge Rd ING CM4....239 J4
Heybridge St MAL CM9....198 D8
Heybridge Wy WALTH E17....284 B5
Heycroft Dr BRTR CM7....122 A7
Heycroft Rd HOC/HUL SS5....264 C8
  LOS SS9....299 M4
Heycroft Wy CHLM/GWD CM2....210 D2
  K/T/MI CO5....150 A7
  RCOLW CO6....361 L4
Heydon La ROY SG8....349 N6
  SAFWS CB11....349
Heydon Rd ROY SG8....349 K9
Heygate Av SOS SS1....19 L7
Heynes Rd BCTR RM8....309 M1
The Heythrop CHLM/WR CM1....194 A1
  ING CM4....239 K2
Heywood Ct CHTY IP2....53 J4
Heywood Ct MAL CM9....198 E7
Heywood La GTDUN CM6....117 G6
Heywood Wy MAL CM9....198 E7
Heywood Rd SRTFD E15....307 J2
Hibbard Rd RIPW IP8....47 J5
Hibberd Rd WALTH E17....284 C5
Hibernia Dr GVE DA12....338 C8
Hickford HI SUD CO10....38 A7
Hickin CI CHARL SE7....324 A7
Hickin St POP/IOD E14....322 F6
Hickling CI LOS SS9....281 L7
Hickling Rd IL IG1....308 C1
Hickman Av CHING E4....266 F6
Hickman CI BROX EN10....200 F6
  CAN/RD E16....324 A1
Hickman Rd CHDH RM6....287 M5
Hickory Av CHING E4....266 F2
Hicks St DEPT SE8....322 B8
Hickstars La BCAYE CM11....258 F6
Hicks Wy HVHL CB9....35 H8
Hidcote Wy BRTR CM7....120 E6
Hide CI CBS CB2....22 C3
Higgins Rd KESG IP5 *....50 E1
Higham HI RCOLE CO7....362 H2
Higham Hill Rd WALTH E17....266 C6
Higham PI WALTH E17....284 B1
Higham Rd RCOLE CO7....362 H2
  WFD IG8....267 K5
Highams Cha MAL CM9....384 C5
Highams Rd HOC/HUL SS5....264 B8
Higham Station Av CHING E4....266 E6
The Highams WALTH E17 *....284 B1
Higham St WALTH E17....284 B1
High Ash CI TIL RM18....332 D2
Highbank VGE SS16....294 C1
Highbank CI LOS SS9....281 L7
High Beach Dr FX IP11....62 C7
High Beeches SBF/HAD SS7....297 L2
High Beech Rd LOU IG10....250 B4
Highbirch RCOS CO16....134 A8
Highbridge Rd BARK IG11....308 B5
High Bridge Rd
  CHLM/GWD CM2....5 J3
Highbridge St WAB EN9....233 J3
Highbury Av HOD EN11....201 H1
Highbury Gdns
  GDMY/SEVK IG3....287 H7
Highbury Wy SUD CO10....21 K9
Highclere Rd WICKE SS11....261 J6
  COLN CO4....108 C6
Highcliff Crs RCFD SS4....264 C8
High Cliff Dr LOS SS9....300 C5
Highcliffe CI WICKE SS11....261 J6
Highcliffe Gdns REDBR IG4....286 B3
Highcliffe Rd WICKE SS11....261 J6
Highcliff Rd SBF/HAD SS7....298 C5
High Cliff Wy WICKE SS11....261 J6
Highcliff Wd SBF/HAD SS7....298 C5
High Cloister BCAYE CM11....259 G4
High CI ROY SG8....349 M6
High Cross La GTDUN CM6....377 Q5
Highcross La GTDUN CM6....377 R4

High Cross La East
  GTDUN CM6 ...116 B8
High Easter Rd GTDUN CM6 ...141 J3
  GTDUN CM6 ...164 C7
High Elms CHIG IG7 ...269 K5
  UPMR RM14 ...291 H6
  WFD IG8 ...267 K4
High Elms Rd HOC/HUL SS5 ...263 H4
Highfield HLWS CM18 ...204 B2
  HOC/HUL SS5 * ...263 H2
  SUD CO10 ...37 M6
Highfield Ap BCAYE CM11 ...259 G5
  IP IP1 ...47 L4
Highfield Av BSF CM23 ...139 K3
  HAR CO12 ...14 E8
  SBF/HAD SS7 ...298 E1
Highfield CI BRTR CM7 ...99 K7
  CBS CB2 ...340 E1
  CRW RM5 ...270 F5
  RCHLM CM3 ...212 A4
  WOS/PRIT SS0 ...301 G2
Highfield Crs HCH RM12 ...290 C2
  RAYL SS6 ...281 G3
  WOS/PRIT SS0 ...301 G2
Highfield Dr BROX EN10 ...200 F7
  COLW CO3 ...106 F7
  WOS/PRIT SS0 ...301 G2
Highfield Gdns
  CDW/CHF RM16 ...331 G5
  EPP CM16 ...235 M1
  WOS/PRIT SS0 ...301 G2
Highfield Gv WOS/PRIT SS0 ...301 G2
Highfield Link CRW RM5 ...270 F5
Highfield PI EPP CM16 ...235 M1
Highfield Ri RCHLM CM3 ...392 D1
Highfield Rd BCAYE CM11 ...259 G6
  CHLM/WR CM1 ...209 H1
  CRW RM5 ...270 F5
  FX IP11 ...11 M2
  HCH RM12 ...290 C2
  IP IP1 ...47 K3
  SUD CO10 ...21 J3
  WFD IG8 ...268 B6
Highfield Rd North DART DA1 ...334 D4
High Flds GTDUN CM6 ...117 C5
Highfields HSTD CO9 ...81 H5
  HSTD CO9 ...346 B11
  RBSF CM22 ...372 G11
  RIPS/CAP IP9 ...58 B7
  SAFWN CB10 ...28 B7
  SAFWS CB11 ...373 J2
Highfields La K/T/MI CO5 ...149 G6
Highfields Md RCHLM CM3 ...227 L5
Highfield Stile RD WIT CM8 ...171 H8
Highfield Stile Rd BRTR CM7 * ...99 K7
High Garrett BRTR CM7 ...99 M4
Highgate Gv SBW CM21 ...162 C7
Highgrove Rd BCTR RM8 ...309 M2
High Hall FI FX IP11 ...61 M5
High House La
  CDW/CHF RM16 ...332 A2
Highland Av BRW CM14 ...255 M8
  DAGE RM10 ...288 C9
  LOU IG10 ...250 C6
Highland Gv BCAYE CM11 ...258 G2
  SLH/COR SS17 ...295 L4
  WAB EN9 ...201 M8
Highland Rd BSF CM23 ...139 G6
Highlands HSTD CO9 ...80 B4
Highlands Av WGE SS16 * ...3 M9
Highlands Bvd LOS SS9 ...299 L3
Highlands Crs PIT SS13 ...279 J7
Highlands Dr MAL CM9 ...214 B3
Highlands Gdns IL IG1 ...286 C6
Highlands HI RCHLM CM3 ...388 G11
Highlands PIT SS13 ...279 J7
  WICKE SS11 ...262 E3
High La RBSF CM22 ...189 M3
  STSD CM24 ...115 M1
High Md CHIG IG7 ...268 F4
  HOC/HUL SS5 ...263 K8
Highmead RAYL SS6 ...280 F3
  STSD CM24 ...115 M1
High Meadow BCAYE CM11 ...258 F3
  GTDUN CM6 ...116 F5
High Mdw CHIG IG7 ...269 G4
High Meads Rd CAN/RD E16 ...324 C2
High Oaks VGE SS16 ...294 E2
High Pastures RBSF CM22 ...189 L1
High Rdg WIT CM8 * ...172 F5
High Rd BKHH IG9 ...249 G6
  BROX EN10 ...201 G6
  CDW/CHF RM16 ...314 D8
  CDW/CHF RM16 ...315 J5
  CHDH RM6 ...288 C4
  CHIG IG7 ...268 E2
  COLS CO2 ...128 C8
  EPP CM16 ...220 C2
  EPP CM16 ...221 H5
  EPP CM16 ...235 K3
  FX IP11 ...62 A4
  GDMY/SEVK IG3 ...287 K6
  HOC/HUL SS5 ...263 K8
  IL IG1 ...286 F7
  LAIN SS15 ...276 E5
  LEY E10 ...284 E4
  RAYL SS6 ...280 F5
  RCOLW CO6 ...360 H4
  SBF/HAD SS7 ...279 L8
  SLH/COR SS17 ...295 M4
  SLH/COR SS17 ...316 C3
  SLH/COR SS17 ...317 K4
  VGE SS16 ...294 E4
  VGE SS16 ...296 C1
High Rd Broxbourne
  BROX EN10 ...201 G2
High Rd East FX IP11 ...63 G8
High Rd Leyton LEY E10 ...284 F4
High Rd Leytonstone
  WAN E11 ...285 H4
High Rd North LAIN SS15 ...276 F4
High Rd Ongar (Chelmsford Rd)
  CHONG CM5 ...383 J1
High Rd Turnford BROX EN10 ...216 F4
High Rd West FX IP11 ...62 F8
High Rd Woodford Gn
  WFD IG8 ...267 K2
High Row Fld FX IP11 ...63 H8
High Silver LOU IG10 ...250 A4
High Stile GTDUN CM6 ...116 F5
Highstone Av WAN E11 ...285 K4
High St BARK/HLT IG6 ...268 F4
  BCAYW CM12 ...258 D3
  BOC CM0 ...386 F10
  BOC CM0 ...393 N1
  BRTR CM7 ...76 E3
  BRTR CM7 ...77 M2
  BRTR CM7 ...121 J2
  BRW CM14 ...273 M1
  BSF CM23 ...139 G2
  BURES CO8 ...359 Q8
  CBE/LIN CB1 ...23 M4
  CBE/LIN CB1 ...24 B4
  CBE/LIN CB1 ...24 C8
  CBE/LIN CB1 ...25 G7
  CBE/LIN CB1 ...342 H2

CBS CB2 ...22 C3
CBS CB2 ...22 E4
CBS CB2 ...23 G1
CHES/WCR EN8 ...216 E7
CHES/WCR EN8 ...232 E2
CHLM/GWD CM2 ...210 C6
CHLM/WR CM1 ...193 L8
CHONG CM5 ...382 H1
COL CO1 ...8 D7
COLN CO4 ...88 A1
COS CO15 ...320 F1
CVI SS8 ...334 B8
DART DA1 ...334 B8
EMPK RM11 ...290 A6
EPP CM16 ...236 A1
FX IP11 ...62 D7
GRAYS RM17 ...330 D5
GRH DA9 ...335 L6
GTDUN CM6 ...96 A8
GTDUN CM6 ...117 G5
GVE DA12 ...337 L4
GVW DA11 ...336 E4
HAR CO12 ...15 J7
HLWE CM17 ...188 D5
HLWW/ROY CM19 ...186 C8
HOD EN11 ...201 H3
HSTD CO9 ...81 H3
HSTD CO9 ...346 B12
HVHL CB9 ...34 D6
ING CM4 ...223 M8
ING CM4 ...239 L2
ING CM4 ...241 H3
IP IP1 ...46 E5
K/T/MI CO5 ...130 D5
K/T/MI CO5 ...148 F3
K/T/MI CO5 ...177 L7
LOS SS9 ...299 M5
MAL CM9 ...214 C3
MAL CM9 ...385 M4
MGTR CO11 ...91 G1
PLSTW E13 ...307 K6
PUR RM19 ...328 C2
RAYL SS6 ...280 F4
RBSF CM22 ...372 G12
RBSF CM22 ...374 E4
RBSF CM22 ...378 H1
RCFD SS4 ...392 B11
RCOLE CO7 ...130 E5
RCOLE CO7 ...156 C7
RCOLE CO7 ...363 M11
RCOLW CO6 ...82 D7
RCOLW CO6 ...361 N8
RCOS CO16 ...135 J3
RIPW IP8 ...46 F7
ROM RM1 ...289 H3
ROY SG8 ...348 E9
ROY SG8 ...349 Q8
ROY SG8 ...370 B4
SAFWN CB10 ...28 A8
SAFWS CB11 ...340 H1
SAFWN CB10 ...341 M7
SAFWN CB10 ...341 N9
SAFWN CB10 ...342 H12
SAFWS CB11 ...72 D5
SAFWS CB11 ...351 N1
SAFWS CB11 ...372 B1
SAFWS CB11 ...372 E5
SAFWS CB11 ...373 J2
SBF/HAD SS7 ...280 A5
SBF/HAD SS7 ...299 G2
SBN/FI SS3 ...303 J1
SBN/FI SS3 ...303 K6
SLH/COR SS17 ...316 F4
SOCK/AV RM15 ...328 F4
SOS SS1 ...19 G5
SRTFD E15 ...306 F6
SUD CO10 ...37 L6
SUD CO10 ...39 G4
SUD CO10 ...43 M5
SWCM DA10 ...336 C3
WALTH E17 ...284 C2
WAN E11 ...285 L4
WARE SG12 ...185 K5
WICKW SS12 ...261 G6
WOTN CO14 ...137 M1
High St North K/T/MI CO5 ...177 M7
  MNPK E12 ...308 B3
High St South EHAM E6 ...308 C6
The High HLW CM20 ...6 C4
High Tree La WOTN CO14 ...369 N11
Hightrees ING CM4 ...241 G3
High Vw BOC CM0 ...389 M1
  BSF CM23 ...115 K6
  MGTR CO11 * ...64 E7
Highview HOC/HUL SS5 * ...263 H4
  GRAYS RM17 ...330 F4
Highview Av VGE SS16 ...294 B1
High View CI COS CO15 ...159 H7
  LOU IG10 ...249 M5
Highview Crs
  RBRW/HUT CM13 ...256 F2
High View Gdns GRAYS RM17 ...330 F4
Highview Gdns UPMR RM14 ...290 F4
High View Rd BCAYE CM11 ...259 M8
High View Rd IP IP1 ...47 J5
  SWFD E18 ...267 J3
Highview Ter DA1 * ...334 A7
Highwood CI BRW CM14 ...255 L7
  LOS SS9 ...300 C1
Highwood Gdns CLAY IG5 ...286 B1
Highwood La RCHLM CM1 ...250 J1
High Wood Rd HOD EN11 ...185 G9
Highwoods Ap COLN CO4 ...107 L1
Highwoods Sq COLN CO4 ...107 L1
High Wych La SBW CM21 ...162 B7
High Wych Rd HLW CM20 ...187 M3
  SWM CM21 ...162 B8
Hilary CI HCH RM12 ...312 A2
  RCFD SS4 ...265 H4
Hilary Crs RAYL SS6 ...281 H3
Hilbery Rd CVI SS8 ...320 F2
Hildabrook CI CHTY IP2 ...53 K4
Hilda Rd CAN/RD E16 ...307 H3
  EHAM E6 ...308 A4
Hildaville Dr WOS/PRIT SS0 ...300 F3
Hildersham Rd CBE/LIN CB1 ...24 A2
Hilderstone Rd PIT SS13 ...278 F5
Hill Av WICKE SS11 ...261 J3
Hillborough Rd
  WOS/PRIT SS0 ...301 G2
Hill Bunker's BELV DA17 ...326 D4
Hill CI SBF/HAD SS7 ...298 B2
Hill Crs CHLM/GWD CM2 ...5 L4
  EMPK RM11 ...289 M4
  HVHL CB9 ...34 D4
Hillcrest COS CO15 ...159 J7
  FOS CO13 ...137 G1
  RCHLM CM3 ...388 A5

Hillcrest Ap RIPW IP8 ...47 G3
Hillcrest Av HOC/HUL SS5 ...263 K1
  WTHK RM20 ...335 K1
Hillcrest CI SLH/COR SS17 ...316 C1
Hillcrest Ct HAR CO12 ...15 M8
  SLH/COR SS17 * ...316 C2
Hillcrest Dr GRH DA9 ...335 K7
Hillcrest Rd EMPK RM11 ...289 K5
  HOC/HUL SS5 ...264 B8
  LOU IG10 ...250 A6
  RCHLM CM3 ...244 F6
  SLH/COR SS17 ...316 B2
  SOS SS3 ...19 J5
  SUD CO10 ...20 D1
  WALTH E17 ...267 J2
Hillcrest Vw VGE SS16 ...296 A2
Hillcrest Wy EPP CM16 ...236 B1
Hillcroft LOU IG10 ...250 D2
Hillcroft Rd EHAM E6 ...324 E1
Hildene Av HARH RM3 ...271 M5
Hildene CI HARH RM3 ...272 A4
Hill Farm La RIPS/CAP IP9 ...565 Q6
Hill Farm Rd HMNKT IP6 ...50 H1
Hillfoot Av CRW RM5 ...270 F5
Hillfoot Rd CRW RM5 ...270 F5
Hill Gv ROM RM1 ...289 H1
Hillhouse WAB EN9 ...234 B4
Hillhouse CI BCAYW CM12 ...258 E1
Hillhouse Ct BCAYW CM12 * ...258 E1
Hill House CI RCOLE CO7 ...156 D6
Hill House Dr BCAYW CM12 ...258 E1
Hill House Dr CDW/CHF RM16 ...331 L4
Hill House La INE IP4 ...17 J6
Hillards Rd RCOLE CO7 ...110 F5
Hillie Bunnies RCOLW CO6 ...82 E6
Hillingdon Rd GVW DA11 ...337 L3
Hill La HOC/HUL SS5 ...264 C8
  HVHL CB9 ...344 F1
Hillman Av COS CO15 ...182 B7
Hillman CI EMPK RM11 ...290 A1
Hillreach WOOL/PLUM SE18 ...324 C6
Hillridge COLN CO4 ...107 L2
Hill Ri UPMR RM14 ...290 F1
Hill Rd CRW RM5 ...270 F5
Hill Rd BRW CM14 ...273 K2
  CHLM/GWD CM2 ...5 L8
  COS CO15 ...159 H7
  EPP CM16 ...235 H7
  HAR CO12 ...15 H7
  RCOLW CO6 ...124 C2
  SAFWN CB10 ...352 G1
  SBF/HAD SS7 ...298 G1
  SOSN SS2 ...301 J2
Hill Rd South CHLM/GWD CM2 ...5 L8
Hill's Chace BRW CM14 ...273 M3
Hills CI DART DA1 ...121 J1
Hills Crs COLW CO3 ...106 D8
Hillside CBS CB2 ...22 B1
  FOS CO13 ...137 H5
  GRAYS RM17 ...331 G3
  HLWE CM17 ...204 E8
  HOD EN11 ...201 G2
  LOS SS9 ...300 B5
  MAL CM9 ...214 D2
  WARE SG12 ...184 E1
Hillside Av BSF CM23 ...139 H2
  CHES/WCR EN8 ...232 E1
  GVE DA12 ...338 A7
  HOC/HUL SS5 ...264 B8
  WFD IG8 ...267 M4
Hillside CI BCAYE CM11 ...258 E4
  WFD IG8 ...267 M4
Hillside Crs CHES/WCR EN8 ...232 E1
  COS CO15 ...159 M8
  IPSE IP3 ...55 G2
  LOS SS9 ...300 D5
  WARE SG12 ...185 J5
Hillside Dr GVE DA12 ...338 A7
Hillside Gdns BRTR CM7 ...121 J4
  WALTH E17 ...285 G1
Hillside Gv CHLM/GWD CM2 ...209 M8
Hillside La WARE SG12 ...185 H4
Hillside Ms CHLM/GWD CM2 ...4 C1
Hillside Rd BCAYW CM12 ...258 E4
  BOC CM0 ...393 M1
  BOC CM0 ...393 M1
  GTDUN CM6 ...118 D7
  HOC/HUL SS5 ...263 J8
  LOS SS9 ...281 L8
  SBF/HAD SS7 ...298 A4
  SUD CO10 ...21 M8
Hillside Ter GVE DA12 * ...337 L6
Hillside Wk BRW CM14 ...273 K2
Hill's Rd BKHH IG9 ...249 L8
  HSTD CO9 ...356 F9
Hill St SAFWN CB10 ...28 A8
Hill Ter SLH/COR SS17 ...295 M8
  SUD CO10 * ...37 M6
The Hill GVW DA11 ...336 F4
  HLWE CM17 ...188 D5
Hill Top LOU IG10 ...250 D5
Hilltop WALTH E17 * ...284 E1
Hilltop Av HOC/HUL SS5 ...263 H4
Hill Top Av SBF/HAD SS7 ...298 C3
Hill Top CI LOU IG10 ...250 D5
Hilltop Ri RCOS CO16 ...134 E4
Hill Top Rd WFD IG8 ...268 A3
Hilltop Rd WICKE SS11 ...261 G6
Hilltop Vw WFD IG8 ...268 A3
Hill Tree CI SBW CM21 ...162 B8
Hill Vw HVHL CB9 ...344 E3
Hillview Av EMPK RM11 ...289 M4
Hill View CI K/T/MI CO5 ...130 C5
Hill View Crs IL IG1 ...286 C6
Hill View Rd RAYL SS6 ...280 F3
Hillway BCAYE CM11 ...259 G3
  CBE/LIN CB1 ...24 D7
  WOS/PRIT SS0 ...300 D6
The Hillway BRWN CM15 ...239 H5
The Hill Wy BRWN CM15 ...239 J5
Hillwood CI RBRW/HUT CM13 ...256 F4
Hillwood Gv
  RBRW/HUT CM13 ...256 F2
Hillyroom Gdns K/T/MI CO5 ...178 A2
Hilly Fld HLWS CM18 ...204 A3
Hillyfield WALTH E17 ...266 E2
Hillyfields LOU IG10 ...250 D2
Hilton CI MGTR CO11 ...91 G1
Hilton Rd CVI SS8 ...298 D8
  IPSE IP3 ...55 H1
  KESG IP5 ...51 M5
Hilton Wk CVI SS8 ...298 D8
Hilversum Wy CVI SS8 ...298 D8
Hind CI CHIG IG7 ...269 J4

Hind Gv POP/IOD E14 ...322 D2
Hindles Rd CVI SS8 ...321 G1
Hindmans Wy DAGW RM9 ...310 C6
Hind Ter WTHK RM20 ...330 A5
Hines CI RCOLW CO6 ...104 C5
Hines Rd IPSE IP3 ...54 A1
Hinguar St SLH/COR SS17 ...303 J7
Hinksey Pth ABYW SE2 ...326 A6
Hintesham CI IPNE IP4 ...49 L8
Hintlesham Dr FX IP11 ...62 C8
Hinxton Rd CBS CB2 ...340 F1
Hipkins BSF CM23 ...138 F5
Hipkins PI BROX EN10 ...216 C7
Histon CI KESG IP5 ...49 L6
Hitcham Rd RCOLW CO6 ...124 C2
  WALTH E17 ...284 C5
Hitch Common Rd
  SAFWS CB11 ...372 A1
Hitchin CI HARH RM3 ...271 M3
Hitchin Ms BRTR CM7 ...121 L5
Hither Blakers SBW CM21 ...162 B8
Hitherfield Rd BCTR RM8 ...288 D7
Hitherwood CI HCH RM12 ...312 A3
Hitherwood Rd COLS CO2 ...128 C3
Hive CI GVW DA11 ...336 E4
Hobart CI CHLM/WR CM1 ...193 H8
Hobart Rd BARK/HLT IG6 ...268 A3
  DAGW RM9 ...310 A1
  TIL RM18 ...331 K7
Hobbiton HI RCHLM CM3 ...244 F7
Hobbs CI CHES/WCR EN8 ...216 E1
Hobbs Cross Rd EPP CM16 ...236 D4
  HLWE CM17 ...169 G6
Hobday St POP/IOD E14 ...322 E2
Hobhouse Rd SLH/COR SS17 ...317 G1
Hobleythick La SOSN SS2 ...301 G2
Hobsons CI HOD EN11 ...185 G9
Hobtoe Rd HLWW/ROY CM19 ...186 C6
Hockerill St BSF CM23 ...139 G3
Hockley Av EHAM E6 ...308 B6
Hockley Ct BOC CM0 ...386 H11
  BSDN SS14 ...278 B7
  CBE/LIN CB1 ...32 E8
Hockley Dr GPK RM2 ...271 L8
Hockley La BOC CM0 ...386 H10
Hockley Ms BARK IG11 ...309 H6
Hockley Ri HOC/HUL SS5 ...264 B8
Hockley Rd COS CO15 ...3 M1
  RAYL SS6 ...281 H2
Hockney Gdns IPSE IP3 ...54 F5
Hoddesdon Rd BELV DA17 ...326 D5
  WARE SG12 ...184 E1
Hodges CI CDW/CHF RM16 ...330 A4
Hodges Holt WIT CM8 ...171 K6
Hodgkins CI THMD SE28 ...326 A3
Hodgkinson Rd FX IP11 ...10 A7
Hodgson Ct WICKW SS12 ...261 K8
Hodgson Wy WICKW SS12 ...261 K8
Hodings Rd HLW CM20 ...12 C5
Hodson PI PEND EN3 * ...233 M8
Hoecroft WAB EN9 ...202 A8
Hoe Dr COLW CO3 ...106 D3
Hoe La ABR/ST RM4 ...251 L3
  EN EN1 ...232 D7
  RCHLM CM3 ...167 H7
  SUD CO10 ...39 J5
  WAB EN9 ...202 A8
  WARE SG12 ...184 E1
Hoe Mill Rd MAL CM9 ...213 G1
Hoestock Rd SBW CM21 ...162 A7
The Hoe BCAYW CM12 ...276 E1
Hoffmanns Wy
  CHLM/WR CM1 ...209 L1
Hogarth Av BRW CM14 ...256 B6
Hogarth CI CAN/RD E16 ...324 A1
  K/T/MI CO5 ...178 A7
Hogarth Dr SBN/FI SS3 ...303 K5
Hogarth End FOS CO13 ...137 H2
Hogarth Reach LOU IG10 ...250 C5
Hogarth Rd BCTR RM8 ...309 L2
  CDW/CHF RM16 ...314 D8
  IPSE IP3 ...54 E4
Hogarth Sq IPSE IP3 * ...54 E4
Hogarth Wy RCFD SS4 ...264 F7
Hogg La CDW/CHF RM16 ...330 D2
Hog Hill Rd CRW RM5 ...270 D4
Hogsdell La HERT/BAY SG13 ...184 C5
Hog's La ROY SG8 ...349 G9
Hogwell Cha RCHLM CM3 ...245 J4
Holbech CI BSDN SS14 ...278 A8
Holbeck La CHESW EN7 ...216 A4
Holbek Rd CVI SS8 ...321 G1
Holborn PI PLSTW E13 ...323 L1
Holborough CI COLN CO4 ...108 C2
Holbrook CI BCAYE CM11 ...245 G4
  RCHLM CM3 ...245 G4
  RCOS CO16 ...182 C1
Holbrook Crs FX IP11 ...10 F1
  IPSE IP3 ...54 D4
  RIPS/CAP IP9 ...364 D11
  RIPS/CAP IP9 ...365 K11
  SRTFD E15 ...307 G2
Holbys Rw RCOS CO16 ...135 J3
Holcombe Crs CHTY IP2 ...53 J9
Holcombe Rd IL IG1 ...286 B3
Holcote CI BELV DA17 ...326 B6
Holdbrook RCOLW CO6 ...85 G4
Holden CI BCTR RM8 ...287 J1
  CHTY IP2 ...17 H8
Holden Gdns BRW CM14 ...256 A6
  BSDN SS14 ...278 A4
Holden Rd BSDN SS14 ...278 A4
  COLN CO4 ...107 J2
Holden Wy UPMR RM14 ...291 G6
Holdsworth CI SUD CO10 ...39 G4
Holecroft WAB EN9 ...233 M4
Holen CI WDBR IP12 ...44 F8
Holford Rd CDW/CHF RM16 ...316 D8
  TIL RM18 ...332 A3
Holgate PIT SS13 ...278 E7
Holgate Rd DAGE RM10 ...310 D2
Holgate St CHARL SE7 ...324 D6
Holkham Av RCHLM CM3 ...245 J4
Holkham CI IPNE IP4 ...49 L8
Holland Av CVI SS8 ...298 A8
Holland Rd ROMW/RG RM7 ...288 D7
Holland Park Av
  GDMY/SEVK IG3 ...287 K6
Holland Rd COS CO15 ......
  EHAM E6 ...308 C5
  FOS CO13 ...136 E4
  FOS CO13 ...137 G5
  FX IP11 ...11 M1
  IPNE IP4 ...17 M7
  RCOS CO16 ...159 A3
  SRTFD E15 ...307 H1
  WOS/PRIT SS0 ...18 D2
Hollands Rd HVHL CB9 ...34 D1
Hollands Wk VGE SS16 ...296 A3

Holland Vls FOS CO13 * ...136 D5
Holledge Crs FOS CO13 ...137 H5
Hollesley Av HVHL CB9 ...33 M4
Holliday HI CHLM/GWD CM2 ...242 B5
Holliday Wy DAGE RM10 ...310 G4
Hollies Rd BRTR CM7 ...122 A6
The Hollies SLH/COR SS17 ...316 E4
Holliland Cft RCOLW CO6 ...103 H4
Hollington Rd EHAM E6 ...308 C7
Hollingtons Gv COLS CO2 ...151 K2
Hollis Lock CHLM/GWD CM2 ...243 H8
Hollis PI GRAYS RM17 ...330 D2
Holliwel CI COLW CO3 ...106 A7
Holloway Crs GTDUN CM6 ...379 B6
Holloway Rd EHAM E6 ...308 C7
  MAL CM9 ...198 C5
  WAN E11 ...285 G5
Hollowfield Av GRAYS RM17 ...331 G5
Hollow HI HVHL CB9 ...33 M4
Hollow La BURES CO8 ...359 Q6
  CHLM/WR CM1 ...193 G5
  RIPS/CAP IP9 ...365 Q5
Hollow Rd GTDUN CM6 ...52 C5
  K/T/MI CO5 ...148 C5
  RIPW IP8 ...52 C5
  ROY SG8 ...349 Q10
  SAFWS CB11 ...350 C5
  SAFWS CB11 ...372 D3
  SUD CO10 ...345 A3
The Hollow WFD IG8 ...267 L8
Hollybank WIT CM8 ...171 J4
Holly Blue CI RIPW IP8 ...53 H5
Hollybush CI WAN E11 ...285 K3
Holly Bush Cnr RCOLE CO7 ...363 K4
Hollybush La EPP CM16 ...236 A1
Hollybush HI RCOLE CO7 ...157 G5
  WAN E11 ...285 K3
Hollybush St PLSTW E13 ...307 K1
Hollybush Wy CBE/LIN CB1 ...25 G5
  CHESW EN7 ...216 A3
Holly CI BKHH IG9 ...268 A2
  BOC CM0 ...393 K4
  COLS CO2 ...128 F3
  IL IG1 ...287 G5
Holly Crs WFD IG8 ...267 G6
Hollycroft CI IP IP1 ...47 M2
Hollycross Rd WARE SG12 ...185 G4
Hollydown Wy WAN E11 ...285 K6
Holly Dr CHING E4 ...248 E5
  SOCK/AV RM15 ...314 A5
Holly End KESG IP5 ...50 C5
Holly Fld HLWW/ROY CM19 ...203 K5
Hollyfield BCAYE CM11 ...240 F8
Holly Gv VGE SS16 ...296 A2
Holly Hill Rd BELV DA17 ...326 E5
Hollyhock Rd SAFWN CB10 ...28 E8
Holly La KESG IP5 ...49 M5
  RCOLW CO6 ...85 G2
  RIPW IP8 ...53 G5
Hollymead SLH/COR SS17 ...317 G1
Hollymead CI COLN CO4 ...107 J2
Hollyon CI RCOS CO16 ...112 C3
Holly Rd CHLM/GWD CM2 ...209 M8
  K/T/MI CO5 ...149 M8
Hollytree Ct COLS CO2 * ...128 C3
Hollytree Gdns RAYL SS6 ...280 E2
Hollyview CI RCOS CO16 ...112 C3
  K/T/MI CO5 ...149 M8
Hollywood CI
  CHLM/GWD CM2 ...210 A3
Hollywood Rd CHING E4 ...266 D6
Holly La Wd WDBR IG8 ...267 G8
Holman CI RCOLW CO6 ...85 G2
Holman Crs COLW CO3 ...127 K5
Holman Rd HSTD CO9 ...81 H5
Holmans RCHLM CM3 ...195 H5
Holmbridge Gdns PEND EN3 ...248 A4
Holmbrook Wy FOS CO13 ...137 H4
Holm Ct KESG IP5 * ...50 C5
Holmes CI CHES/WCR EN8 ...232 C7
Holme Rd EHAM E6 ...308 A4
Holmesdale CHES/WCR EN8 ...232 C6
Holmes Meadow EPP CM16 ...203 J3
Holme Rd HSTD CO9 ...81 H4
Holme Wy WICKW SS12 ...261 G6
Holme Wy CBS CB2 ...22 C4
Holmhurst Rd BELV DA17 ...326 E5
Holmsdale CI WOS/PRIT SS0 ...300 F3
Holmwood CVI SS8 ...299 H8
Holmwood Av BRWN CM15 ...256 C5
Holmwood CI RCOS CO16 ...158 C4
Holmwood Rd
  GDMY/SEVK IG3 ...287 K6
  PEND EN3 ...232 D5
Holness Rd SRTFD E15 ...307 H1
Holst Av LAIN SS15 ...276 B3
Holst CI SLH/COR SS17 ...316 F4
Holstein Wy ERITHM DA18 ...326 A6
Holstock Rd IL IG1 ...286 C6
Holt CI CHIG IG7 ...269 J4
  THMD SE28 ...325 G2
Holt Dr COLS CO2 ...129 G4
Holton Rd CVI SS8 ...321 G1
  RAYL SS6 ...281 K4
Holton St WCHPL E1 ...307 K6
Holt Farm Wy RCFD SS4 ...283 G4
Holton Rd CVI SS8 ...321 G1
  RAYL SS6 ...281 K4
Holt Rd CAN/RD E16 ...324 A1
  HARH RM3 ...271 M3
Holt's Rd RCOLW CO6 ...85 G4
The Holt BARK/HLT IG6 ...268 F4
Holt Wy CHIG IG7 ...269 J4
Holtynge SBF/HAD SS7 ...297 M8
Holybread La RCHLM CM3 ...211 M4
Holy Cross HI BROX EN10 ...217 G4
Holyfield Rd WAB EN9 ...217 K5
Holyhead CI BOW E3 ...307 K6
Holyoake Ct
  BERM/RHTH SE16 ...322 F3
Holyoak La HOC/HUL SS5 ...282 C1
Holyrood HAR CO12 ...70 E1
Holyrood CI WOS/PRIT SS0 ...300 C1
Holyrood Dr WOS/PRIT SS0 ...300 C1
Holyrood Gdns
  CDW/CHF RM16 ...331 M4
Holywells CI IPSE IP3 ...17 K7
Holy Wells Rd IPSE IP3 ...17 K7
Homebridge SAFWN CB10 ...353 J4
Home CI BROX EN10 ...201 G2
  HLW CM20 ...13 L1
  SBW CM21 ...344 D8
Homecroft Gdns LOU IG10 ...250 D4
Home Farm La RCOLE CO7 ...89 G5
Home Farm Rd
  RBRW/HUT CM13 ...274 D3
Homefield BOC CM0 ...389 P1
  RIPS/CAP IP9 ...58 C7
  WAB EN9 ...234 D4

Homefield Av
  GNTH/NBYPK IG2 ....287 H3
Homefield Cl BCAYE CM11 ...259 C8
  CHLM/WR CM1 ....193 G8
  EPP CM16 ....220 B8
Homefield Rd COLS CO2 ....128 F4
  HVHL CB9 ....34 C8
  WIT CM8 ....171 K1
Homefields Wy SBF/HAD SS7 ...279 G3
  RCOLW CO6 ....82 E8
Home Gdns DAGE RM10 ....288 F8
  DART DA1 ....334 M1
Homelands Cl BCAYE CM11 .....259 M1
Homeleigh Ct CHES/WCR EN8 ..216 B8
Homelye Cha CHLM CM6 ....117 L4
  CHLM/WR CM1 ....208 D4
  LAIN SS15......................276 E5
Home Mead Cl GVE DA12 ....337 H3
Home Mdw BCAYW CM12 ....258 D3
Home Pastures RBSF CM22 ......378 A2
Homer Cl IP IP1 ....47 L1
Homer Dr POP/IOD E14 ....322 D7
Homer Rd HOM E9 ....306 B3
Homerton Cl COS CO15 ....159 J5
Homerton Gv BCAYE CM11 ....259 M1
Homerton High St HOM E9 ......306 A2
Homerton Rd HOM E9 ....306 C2
Homesdale Cl WAN E11 ....285 K3
Homesdale Rd RIPS/CAP IP9 * ..66 D2
Homestead CHLM/WR CM1 ....193 L4
Homestead Dr VGE SS16 ....294 F3
Homestead Gdns
  SBF/HAD SS7 ....299 G2
  BCTR RM8 ....288 C7
  PIT SS13 ....279 M6
  SBF/HAD SS7 ....299 G3
Homestead Rd BCAYE CM11 .....260 A5
Homeway HARH RM3 ....272 A5
Homing Rd RCOS CO16 ....158 F1
Honeybourne BSF CM23 ....138 C5
Honey Brook WAB EN9 ....233 M5
Honey Cl BRWN CM15 ....238 A1
  CHLM/GWD CM2 ....210 A7
  DAGE RM10 ....310 D3
Honeycroft LOU IG10 ....250 D4
  MGTR CO11 * 90 E2
Honey La CHES/WCR EN8........233 C4
  RCOLW CO6 ....361 J5
  SAFWS CB11 ....72 A5
  WAB EN9 ....233 M4
Honeymeade HLW CM20 ....188 D2
Honey Pot La RCHLM CM3 ....246 B2
Honeypot La BRW CM14 ....273 K1
  BSDN SS14 ....45 H5
  ING CM4 ....240 F4
  MAL CM9 ....174 E4
  MGTR CO11 ....112 C1
  RCOS CO16 ....158 F1
Honeypots CHLM/GWD CM2 ....209 M7
Honeysuckle Cl BRWN CM15 ...255 G5
  BSF CM23 ....138 D3
  HARH RM3 ....271 M5
  HERT/BAY SG13 ....144 E6
  WIT CM8 ....34 H4
Honeysuckle Gdns CHTY IP2 ....53 K1
Honeysuckle Wy COLN CO4 ....108 B3
  RCOLW CO7 ....132 D8
  WIT CM8 ....171 L1
Honeywood Rd RCOLW CO6 ....124 D2
Honiley Av WICKW SS12 ....279 H3
Honington Cl WICKE SS11 ....261 L7
Honiton Rd ROMW/RG RM7 ....289 L8
  SOS SS1 ....19 L5
Honorius Dr COLN CO4...........87 J3
Honor Link CHLM/WR CM1.....194 D6
Honywood Cl RCOLW CO6 .....126 B2
  COLW CO3 ....107 G3
Honywood Wy FOS CO13........137 J2
Hood Cl WICKE SS11 ....261 H7
Hood Gdns BRTR CM7 ....121 M4
Hood Rd IPSE IP3 ....54 D4
  RAIN RM13 ....311 H5
Hood Wk ROMW/RG RM7 ....270 E7
Hook End La BRWN CM15 ......383 B8
Hook End Rd BRWN CM15 ......383 G9
Hooker's Rd WALTH E17 ....284 A1
Hook La ABR/ST RM4 ....252 C6
Hooks Hall Dr DAGE RM10 .....288 F8
The Hopgrounds BRTR CM7 ....556 C11
Hopkins Cl CHLM/GWD CM2 ...210 C2
  FOS CO13 ....137 J3
  GPK RM2 ....289 H1
Hopkins Md BRTR CM7 ....121 C4
Hopkins Ms SRTFD E15 ....307 C5
Hopkins Rd LEY E10 ....284 F1
Hopkirk Cl RCHLM CM3 ....212 D6
Hop Meadow RCOLE CO7 ....363 Q7
The Hoppet ING CM4 ....239 M4
Hoppett Rd CHING E4 ....267 J2
Hopping Jacks La
  RCHLM CM3 ....212 D6
Hoppit Md BRTR CM7 ....121 C4
The Hoppitt CHONG CM5 ....380 D6
Hopton Cl HVHL CB9 ....35 M5
Hopton Rd WOOL/PLUM SE18 .324 C5
Horace Av SLH/COR SS17 ....295 H4
Horace Rd BARK/HLT IG6 ......286 E4
  BCAYE CM11 ....258 E1
  FSTGT E7 ....307 L1
  SOS SS1 ....19 J6
Horatio Pl POP/IOD E14 ....322 F6
Hordle Hl HAR CO12 ....15 J7
Hordle St HAR CO12 ....15 J7
Horkesley Hl RCOLN CO4 ......361 M9
Horkesley Rd COLN CO4 ....87 D5
  RCOLW CO6 ....361 L9
Horkesley Wy WICKW SS12 ....261 H7
Horkesley Gdns
  RBRW/HUT CM13 ....256 F2
Horley Cl RCOS CO16 ....158 F1
Hornbeam Av UPMR RM14 .....312 D1
Hornbeam Cha
  SOCK/AV RM15 ....314 A3

Hornbeam Cl
  CHLM/GWD CM2 ....209 K7
  COLS CO2 ....129 G3
  EPP CM16 ....235 M3
  IL IG1 ....309 G2
  RBRW/HUT CM13 ....256 E6
Hornbeam Gv WICKE SS11 .....267 H4
  RCOS CO16 ....159 H2
Hornbeam La CHING E4 ....249 H5
Hornbeam Rd BKHH IG9 ....268 A2
  EPP CM16 ....235 L2
Hornbeams SBF/HAD SS7 ....279 C5
Hornbeams Av EN EN1 ....232 D5
Hornbeam Sq BOW E3 ....306 C5
The Hornbeams HAR CO12 .....70 A6
  HLW CM20 ....12 D1
Hornbeam Wy CHESW EN7 ....216 A7
  LAIN SS15 ....277 L8
Horn Book SAFWS CB11 ....28 C8
Hornby Av WOS/PRIT SS0 .....282 B8
Hornby Cl SOSN SS2............283 C8
Hornchurch Rd WICKE SS11 ...261 L6
Horndon Cl CRW RM5 ....270 F7
Horndon Gn CRW RM5 ....270 F7
Horndon Rd CRW RM5 ....270 F7
  SLH/COR SS17 ....316 D10
Horne Rw RCHLM CM3 ....212 A8
Horner Pl WIT CM8 ....171 H6
Hornet Wy BOC CM0 ....393 H4
Hornford Wy ROMW/RG RM7 ..289 H5
Horn Hl HSTD CO9 ....356 D12
Horn La CBE/LIN CB1 ....24 E7
  GNWCH SE10 ....323 J5
  WAB EN9 ....267 K5
Horn Link Wy GNWCH SE10 ...323 K7
Hornminster Gln EMPK RM11 ..290 D7
Hornsby Av CDW/CHF RM16 ...315 D5
Hornsby Sq LAIN SS15 ....276 B6
Hornsby Wy LAIN SS15 ....276 B6
Hornsland Rd CVI SS8 ....321 H2
Horns Rd BARK/HLT IG6 ....286 F5
Horrocks Cl COLS CO2 ....129 K1
Horsebridges Cl DAGW RM9 ...310 B5
Horsecroft Rd
  HLWW/ROY CM19 ....202 F2
Horseferry Rd POP/IOD E14 ....322 B5
Horse & Groom La
  CHLM/GWD CM2 ....225 K2
Horseheath Gn CBE/LIN CB1 ...32 F4
Horseheath Rd CBE/LIN CB1 ...25 J7
  HVHL CB9 ....33 K1
Horse Leaze EHAM E6 ....324 C2
Horseman Ct BCAYW CM12 ....240 D8
Horseman Side BRW CM14 .....254 B2
Horseshoe Cl BCAYW CM12 ...240 D8
  POP/IOD E14 ....322 F8
  ROY SG8 * 37 J4
  SAFWS CB11 ....350 C1
Horseshoe Crs SBN/FI SS3 .....303 J7
Horseshoe Hl WAB EN9 ....234 D3
Horseshoe La HVHL CB9 ....34 B1
Horseshoe Lawns
  HOC/HUL SS5 ....263 H2
Horsey Rd FOS CO13 ....136 F1
Horsham Av IPSE IP3 ....55 J2
Horsham Cl HVHL CB9 ....33 M4
Horsley Cross BSDN SS14 ....3 H4
Horsley Rd CHING E4 ....250 B8
Hoskin's Cl CAN/RD E16 ....323 M2
Hoskins Cl GNWCH SE10 ....323 G8
Hospital Ap CHLM/WR CM1 ...193 L2
Hospital La COLW CO3 ....107 G3
Hospital Rd COLW CO3 ....107 G3
  SBN/FI SS3 ....303 J7
Hossack Rd IPSE IP3 ....54 F5
Hotham St SRTFD E15 ....307 H5
Houblons Hl EPP CM16 ....236 E1
Houchin Dr CHONG CM5 ....381 L7
Houchin's La RCHLM CM3 ......125 H2
Houghton Pl IPNE IP4 ....49 J4
Hove Av WALTH E17 ....284 C3
Hove Cl GRAYS RM17 ....330 F5
  RBRW/HUT CM13 ....256 F5
Hovefields Av PIT SS13 ....279 H3
Hovefields Dr WICKW SS12 ....279 G3
  SOS SS1 ....302 A5
Hoveton Pd THMD SE28 ....325 M2
Hoveton Wy WFD IG8 ....268 E3
Howard Av HAR CO12 ....70 E3
Howard Cha BSDN SS14 ....2 C1
Howard Cl BRTR CM7 ....121 L2
  HVHL CB9 ....34 A6
  LOU IG10 ....250 B6
  WAB EN9 ....233 M4
Howard Crs PIT SS13 ....278 F3
Howard Dr CHLM/GWD CM2 ...210 D3
Howard Pl CVI SS8 ....320 E3
Howard Rd BARK IG11 ....309 H1
  CDW/CHF RM16 ....329 M6
  COS CO15 ....183 M1
  DART DA1 ....334 D8
  EHAM E6 ....308 C6
  IL IG1 ....308 E1
  SAFWS CB10 ....28 B7
  UPMR RM14 ....290 F7
  WAN E11 ....285 H3
Howards Cha SOSN SS2 ....18 D1
Howards Cl RCHLM CM3 ....195 H5
Howards Cft COLS CO2..........87 C3
Howard's La CBE/LIN CB1 .....32 C5
Howard's Rd PLSTW E13 ....307 K7
Howard St IPNE IP4 ....49 G4
Howards Wy KESG IP5 ....55 J4
Howard Vyse Ct COS CO15 ......9 F1
Howarth Rd ABYW SE2 ....325 K8
Howbridge Hall Rd WIT CM8 ..171 K8
Howbridge Rd WIT CM8 ....171 K8
Howden Cl THMD SE28 ....325 M3
Howe Av IPSE IP3 ....55 H2
Howe Cha HSTD CO9 ....81 H6
Howe Cl COLN CO4 ....9 C7
  ROMW/RG RM7 ....289 L8
  SAFWS CB11 * 350 D1
Howe Green Rd RCHLM CM3 ..230 B7
Howe La SAFWN CB10 ....353 K5
Howell Cl CHDH RM6 ....288 A4
Howe Rd HVHL CB9 ....34 B7
Howfield Gn HOD EN11 ....185 L8
Howland Wy
  BERM/RHTH SE16 ....322 B5
Howlett Cl KESG IP5 ....50 D4
Howse Rd WAB EN9 ....233 M5
Hows Md EPP CM16 ....220 B7
Hoxter Wy SUD CO10 ....20 D7
Hoxton St RCOS CO16 ....6 C1
Hoylake Gdns HARH RM3 ......272 D5
Hoynors RCHLM CM3............212 D6
Hoy St CAN/RD E16 ....323 J2
Hoy Ter WTHK RM20 ....330 E4
Hubbards Cha EMPK RM11 ....290 D3
  WOTN CM8 ....369 L12
Hubbards Cl EMPK RM11 ......290 D3
Hubbard St SRTFD E15 ....307 H5
Hubert Rd BRW CM14 ....273 K1
  COLW CO3 ....106 E5
  EHAM E6 ....308 A3

  RAIN RM13 ....311 J7
Hucklesbury Av COS CO15 .....160 B3
Hucknall Cl HARH RM3 ....272 C5
Huddart St BOW E3 ....322 C1
Huddleston Wy CBS CB2 ....22 D1
Hudson Cl HAR CO12 ....70 F4
  HVHL CB9 ....34 C8
  RCOS CO16 ....6 A3
Hudson Crs LOS SS9 ....282 B8
Hudson Rd WOOL/PLUM SE18 .324 F8
Hudson Rd LOS SS9 ....282 A7
Hudsons Cl SLH/COR SS17 * ...317 G2
Hudson's Hl BRTR CM7 ....78 C1
Hudsons La RCOLW CO6 ....362 D5
Hudson Wy CVI SS8 ....298 D7
Hughan Rd SRTFD E15 ....307 H4
Hugh Dickson Rd COL CO1.....107 H3
Hughes Rd CDW/CHF RM16 ...331 K2
  RCOLE CO7 ....363 P5
Hughes Ter CAN/RD E16 * 323 J2
Hugo Gdns RAIN RM13 ....311 G7
Hullbridge Rd RAYL SS6 ....263 G5
  RCHLM CM3 ....244 F5
Hull Cl BERM/RHTH SE16 * 322 A4
Hullett's La BRWN CM15 ....255 J4
Hull Gv HLW CM17 ....378 E11
Hull Gv HLWW/ROY CM19 .....203 A8
Hull La RCHLM CM3 ....169 A3
Hull's La CHLM/GWD CM2 .....211 M8
  WIT CM8 ....171 A3
Hulse Av BARK IG11 ....309 H1
  ROMW/RG RM7 ....270 C7
Hulton Cl RCHLM CM3 ....195 H5
Humber Av COS CO15 ....182 D7
  SOCK/AV RM15 ....329 J2
Humber Cl RAYL SS6 ....280 F4
Humber Doucy La IPNE IP4 ....48 F3
Humber Dr UPMR RM14 ....291 G4
Humber Rd CHLM/WR CM1 ....193 M8
  WIT CM8 ....171 A3
Humberstone Rd PLSTW E13 ..307 M1
Hume Cl TIL RM18 ....337 L1
Humes Av IL IG1 ....308 E1
Humphry Cl CLAY IG5 * 268 C5
Humphry's Farm La
  RCHLM CM3 ....166 F6
Humphries Cl DAGW RM9 .....310 A5
Humphry Rd SUD CO10 ....20 A4
Hundon Cl HVHL CB9 ....35 M3
Hundred Acres
  CHES/WCR EN8 * 233 C4
Hundred La COLN CO4 ....87 L1
Hungerdown CHING E4 ....248 B1
Hungerdown La MGTR CO11 ....90 B3
  RCOLE CO7 ....89 M6
Hunnable Rd BRTR CM7 ......121 J2
Hunsdon Cl DAGW RM9 ....310 B3
Hunsdon Rd WARE SG12 ......185 M5
Hunt Cl K/T/MI CO5 ....149 C1
Hunt Dr RCOS CO16 ....6 C1
Hunter Av BRWN CM15 ....256 D2
Hunter Dr BRTR CM7 ....121 M3
  HCH RM12 ....311 H1
  MGTR CO11 ....90 E2
  WICKW SS12 ....261 H4
Hunter Rd IPSE IP3 ....55 H5
Hunters Av BCAYW CM12 ......258 E6
Hunters Cha CHONG CM5 .....382 H4
  RBRW/HUT CM13 ....257 H3
Hunters Cnr RCOLS CO2 * 106 C3
Hunters End FX IP11 ....62 B6
Hunter's Gv CRW RM5 ....270 E4
Hunters Hall Rd DAGE RM10 ..310 D1
Hunters Reach CHESW EN7 ...216 A7
Hunters Ride KESG IP5 ....55 J4
Hunters Rdg COLN CO4 ....107 L1
Hunters Rd IL IG1 ....308 E2
Hunters Sq DAGE RM10 ....310 D1
Hunters Wy CHLM/WR CM1 ...194 C6
  SAFWS CB11 ....30 C6
Huntingdon Cl BROX EN10 ...216 F2
Huntingdon Rd CBS CB2 ....22 A7
  SOS SS1 ....302 A5
Huntingdon St CAN/RD E16 ...323 J2
  COS CO15 ....159 H7
Hunting Ga COL CO1 ....9 K7
Huntings Rd DAGE RM10 ......310 D3
Huntland Cl RAIN RM13 ....311 J7
Huntley Av GVW DA11 ....336 F1
Hunt Rd GVW DA11 ....337 H8
  RCOLW CO6 ....82 D7
Hunt's Cl CHLM/WR CM1 ......208 E5
Hunt's Dr CHLM/WR CM1 .....208 E5
Hunts Farm Cl MAL CM9 ......385 N3
Hunts Hl SUD CO10 ....39 G4
Hunts La SAFWN CB10 ....341 J2
Huntsman Rd BARK/HLT IG6 ..269 J1
Huntsmans Dr UPMR RM14 ...312 F2
Huntsmans Gt BCAYW CM12 ..258 E6
Hunts Md BCAYW CM12 ....248 A3
  PEND EN3 ....232 D4
Hunts Rd CBS CB2 ....340 E1
Hunt Wy FOS CO13 ....137 J2
Hunwicke Rd COLN CO4 ....108 B7
Hurdle Makers Hl RIPW IP8 ...52 L7
Hurlock Rd BCAYE CM11 ......258 E1
Hurnard Dr COLN CO4 ....106 D4
Hurrell Down COLN CO4 ....107 K1
  RCHLM CM3 ....195 J4
Hurrells La BCHLM CM3 ....211 K2
Hurricane Cl WICKE SS11 .....261 K3
Hurricane Rd IPSE IP3 ....55 H4
Hurricane Wy EPP CM16 ......221 G5
  WICKE SS11 ....261 K3
Hurry Rd SRTFD E15 ....307 H5
Hurrys Cl CBS CB2 ....22 D2
Hursley Rd CHIG IG7 ....269 J4
Hurst Av HVHL CB9 ....266 F1
Hurst Dr CHES/WCR EN8 ......232 A4
Hurstlands Cl EMPK RM11 ....289 M5
Hurst La ABYW SE2 ....326 A1
Hurstleigh Gdns CLAY IG5 ....268 C5
Hurst Park Av HCH RM12 .....312 B1
Hurst Pl ABYW SE2 ....325 M8
Hurst Pl BKHH IG9 ....250 A8
  WALTH E17 ....284 H1
Hurst Wy CHLM/GWD CM2 ....210 A8
Hutchings St POP/IOD E14 ....322 D5
Hutchins Cl HCH RM12 ....311 M1
  SRTFD E15 ....306 F4
Hutchins Rd THMD SE28 ......325 L3
Hutland Rd IPNE IP4 ....17 D7
Hutton Cl WFD IG8 ....267 J5
Hutton Dr CT RBRW/HUT CM13 * ..257 H2
Hutton Dr RBRW/HUT CM13 ..257 H2
Hutton Ga RBRW/HUT CM13 ..256 E3
Hutton Rd RBRW/HUT CM13 ..256 E2
  SOSN SS2 ....283 G1
Hutton Village
  RBRW/HUT CM13 ....257 H1

Huxley Dr CHDH RM6 ....287 L5
Huxley Rd LEY E10 ....284 F7
  RCOS CO16 ....6 A3
Hyam's La RIPS/CAP IP9 ......364 D11
Hycliffe Gdns CHIG IG7 ....268 C5
Hyde Cha RCHLM CM3 ....228 A4
Hyde Cl PLSTW E13 ....307 K6
Hyde Gn RCHLM CM3 ....212 C6
Hyde Md WAB EN9 ....217 M1
Hyde Rd BRTR CM7 ....78 E4
  RCHLM CM3 ....228 A4
Hyderabad Wy SRTFD E15 ....307 H4
Hyde Rd SUD CO10 ....20 D7
Hyder Rd CDW/CHF RM16 ....331 K2
The Hyde VGE SS16 ....294 F1
Hydeway SBF/HAD SS7 ....280 C8
Hyde Wy WICKW SS12 ....261 G7
Hyde Wood La HSTD CO9 ......346 C10
Hydewood Rd HSTD CO9 ......346 C10
Hyland Cl EMPK RM11 ....289 L5
Hyland Rd EMPK RM11 ....289 L5
Hylands Cl GTDUN CM6 ....141 K1
Hylands Rd WALTH E17 ....267 G8
The Hylands HOC/HUL SS5 ...264 A8
Hyland Wy EMPK RM11 ....289 L5
Hyll Cl SAFWN CB10 ....341 L6
Hylton St WOOL/PLUM SE18 .324 F7
Hyntle Cl CHTY IP2 ....47 K8
Hynton Rd BCTR RM8 ....287 M7
Hythe Cl BRTR CM7 ....99 J1
  COS CO15 ....183 G5
Hythe Gv RCOLE CO7 ....156 B4
Hythe Hl COL CO1 ....9 H9
Hythe Quay COL CO1 ....9 K9
Hythe Station Rd COL CO1 .....9 J9
Hythe St DART DA1 ....334 E3
The Hythe MAL CM9 ....214 E3

Ian Rd BCAYW CM12 ....258 C1
Ibbetson Pth LOU IG10 ....250 F3
Ibbotson Av CAN/RD E16 .....323 J2
Ibscott Cl DAGE RM10 ....310 F3
I Butts SBN/FI SS3 ....303 M4
Iceland Rd BOW E3 ....306 D5
Iceni Wy COLS CO2 ....128 D5
Ickleton Rd CBS CB2 ....340 E1
  SAFWN CB10 ....341 K7
  SAFWS CB11 ....350 B1
Icknield Cl SAFWN CB10 ......341 K6
Icknield Rd GNTH/NBYPK IG2 .286 B5
Icknield Wy ROY SG8 ....350 B1
  SAFWS CB11 ....350 A1
Icknield Way Pth ROY SG8 ....348 E4
Ickworth Ct FX IP11 ....10 D3
Ickworth Ct FX IP11 ....10 D3
Ickworth Crs IPNE IP4 ....286 B5
Ickworth Park Rd WALTH E17 .284 B2
Iconfield Pk HAR CO12 * 14 C6
Idonia St DEPT SE8 ....322 E6
Idmiston Rd SRTFD E15 ......307 J2
Idmiston Sq WPK KT4 ....290 B5
Ilchester Rd BCTR RM8 ....287 K1
Ilex Cl COLS CO2 ....129 G3
Ilford Hl IL IG1 ....286 D8
Ilford La IL IG1 ....308 E1
Ilfracombe Av RCHLM CM3 ...388 E4
  WOS/PRIT SS0 ....300 E4
Imperial Cl WOS/PRIT SS0 * ..18 D5
Imperial Dr GPK RM2 ....289 L1
Imperial Pk RAYL SS6 * 262 F5
Imperial St BOW E3 ....306 F7
Imphal Cl COLS CO2 ....128 D7
Inchbonnie Rd RCHLM CM3 ...244 F8
Indescon Ct POP/IOD E14 ....322 D5
Indigo Ms POP/IOD E14 * 322 F5
Ingal Rd PLSTW E13 ....307 K8
Ingarfield Rd COS CO15 ....160 B3
Ingatestone By-Pass
  ING CM4 ....223 L8

Ingatestone Rd
  CHLM/WR CM1 ....223 H3
  ING CM4 ....222 C6
  ING CM4 ....240 C4
  MNPK E12 ....285 M6
  WFD IG8 ....267 K5
Ingaway VGE SS16 ....294 F1
Ingelrica Av RCHLM CM3 ......196 E2
Ingersoll Rd PEND EN3 ....232 D4
Ingestre St HAR CO12 ....15 K5
Ingestre St FSTGT E7 ....307 K1
Ingham Rd HVHL CB9 ....34 C8
Ingleby Gdns CHIG IG7 ....269 L2
Ingleby Rd CDW/CHF RM16 ...331 L2
  DAGE RM10 ....310 E3
  IL IG1 ....286 E6
Ingledew Rd
  WOOL/PLUM SE18 ....324 G8
Ingleglen EMPK RM11 ....289 L3
Inglehurst Gdns REDBR IG4 ..286 C3
Inglenook COS CO15 ....159 L6
Ingleside Cl SAFWS CB11 .....28 B7
Inglewood Cl BARK/HLT IG6 ..269 K2
Inglewood Cl BARK/HLT IG6 ..269 K2
  HCH RM12 ....312 A1
  POP/IOD E14 ....322 D7
Inglis Rd COLW CO3 ....107 G3
Ingoldsby Rd GVE DA12 ....338 A6
Ingram Av EMPK RM11 ....289 L3
Ingram Ms BRTR CM7 ....121 L5
Ingram Rd GRAYS RM17 ......330 D3
Ingram's Piece RCOLE CO7 ....89 H5
Ingram's Well Rd SUD CO10 ...20 C6
Ingrave Cl WICKW SS12 ......261 L1
Ingrave Rd BRW CM14 ....256 B6
  ROM SM1 ....289 G2
Ingrebourne Gdns
  UPMR RM14 ....290 F7
Ingrebourne Rd RAIN RM13 ..311 L8
Ingress Park Av GRH DA9 ....335 M7
Ingreway HARH RM3 ....272 C5
Inkerman Rw LOU IG10 ....250 F3
Inkerpole Pl CHLM/GWD CM2 .210 C2
Inks Gn CHING E4 ....266 J7
Inmans Rw WFD IG8 ....267 H8
Innes Cl WICKW SS12 ....261 G8
Innham Hl HSTD CO9 ....356 D12
Inniskilling Rd PLSTW E13 ....307 M1
Innova Wy PEND EN3 ....233 H8
Inskip Cl LEY E10 ....284 F1
Inskip Dr EMPK RM11 ....290 B6
Inskip Rd BCTR RM8 ....288 A4
Institute Rd EHAM E6 ....308 C2
Integer Gdns WAN E11 * 285 G5
Invergine Rd CHARL SE7 .....323 L8

Invermore Pl
  WOOL/PLUM SE18 ....324 F7
Inverness Av WOS/PRIT SS0 ..18 A5
Inverness Cl COL CO1 ....8 C5
Inverness Dr BARK/HLT IG6 ..269 K5
Inverness Rd IPNE IP4 ....48 F5
Invicta Cl BCAYW CM12 ....258 B1
Invicta Rd RDART DA2 ....334 C4
Inworth La RCOLW CO6 ....84 A3
Inworth Wk COLS CO2 * 149 H1
Iona Wy WICKW SS12 ....261 J9
Ionia Wk GVE DA12 ....338 C2
Ipswich Ms VGE SS16 ....276 C8
Ipswich Rd COL CO1 ....9 H5
  COLN CO4 ....9 J1
  COLN CO4 ....88 G3
  COLN CO4 ....363 J11
  COS CO15 ....160 A3
  KIR/NAC IP10 ....55 L7
  MGTR CO11 ....65 G4
  RCOLE CO7 ....363 K9
  RIPS/CAP IP9 ....364 G6
  WDBR IP12 ....57 H2
Ireland Cl EHAM E6 ....324 C1
Ireland Rd IPSE IP3 ....54 E4
Ireton Pl GRAYS RM17 ....330 D3
Ireton Rd COLW CO3 ....107 G5
Ireton St BOW E3 ....306 D8
Iris Cl BRWN CM15 ....255 G5
  CHLM/WR CM1 ....194 C8
  CHTY IP2 ....47 L8
Iris La CHING E4 ....324 E1
Iris Wy CHING E4 ....266 C5
Irlam Rd CHTY IP2 ....53 J3
Iron Dr HERT/BAY SG13 ......184 C2
Iron Latch La COLW CO3 .....105 M5
Ironside Cl BERM/RHTH SE16 .322 A5
Irons Wy CRW RM5 ....270 F6
Ironwell La HOC/HUL SS5 ....282 D2
  RCFD SS4 ....283 D2
Irvine Gdns SOCK/AV RM15 ..329 J3
Irvine Pl WICKW SS12 ....261 J9
Irvine Rd WDBR IP12 ....57 M3
Irvine Wy BCAYW CM12 ......258 D4
Irving Cl BSF CM23 ....138 E5
Irvington Cl LOS SS9 ....300 A1
Irvon Hill Rd WICKW SS12 ...294 F1
Irye Md CRW RM5 ....270 F6
Isaac Sq CHLM/GWD CM2 ....210 A2
Isabel Ga CHES/WCR EN8 ....217 G4
Isambard Ms POP/IOD E14 ...322 F6
Isbourne Rd COLN CO4 ....129 K1
Ishams Cha WIT CM8 ....171 M6
Isis Dr UPMR RM14 ....291 H4
Island La FOS CO13 ....368 H12
  FOS CO13 ....368 H10
Island Rd BERM/RHTH SE16 ..322 A7
  FOS CO13 ....368 H10
The Island RCOLE CO7 * 363 K9
Islay Whf POP/IOD E14 * 322 F5
Ismailia Rd FSTGT E7 ....307 L4
Isom Cl PLSTW E13 ....307 M3
Ivan Clark's Cnr CBE/LIN CB1 .32 M2
Iveagh Cl HOM E9 ....306 A1
Ive Farm Cl LEY E10 ....284 D7
Ive Farm La LEY E10 ....284 D7
Iveley Rd CLPH SW4 ....322 H8
Ives Gdns ROM RM1 ....289 H5
Ives Rd CAN/RD E16 ....323 H1
Ivinghoe Rd BCTR RM8 ......309 L2
Ivry St IP IP1 ....16 D7
Ivy Barns La ING CM4 ....223 K4
Ivy Bower Cl GRH DA9 ....335 L7
Ivybridge BROX EN10 ....201 H5
Ivy Chimneys Rd EPP CM16 ..235 M2
Ivy Cl DART DA1 ....334 D8
Ivyhouse Rd DAGW RM9 .....310 A3
Ivy La K/T/MI CO5 ....179 L2
Ivy Lodge La HARH RM3 ......272 C5
Ivy Lodge Rd RCOLW CO6 ....86 F5
Ivy Rd CAN/RD E16 ....323 K2
  SBF/HAD SS7 ....299 K8
  WALTH E17 ....284 C4
Ivy Ter COS CO15 * 180 K1
  HOD EN11 ....201 K1
Ivy Todd Hl SAFWS CB11 * ...372 H1
Ivy Vls MGTR CO11 * 65 G4
Ivy Wk DAGW RM9 ....310 A3
Ixworth Rd HVHL CB9 ....34 B7

Jacaranda Cl CHLM/WR CM1 ..194 C7
Jack Andrews Dr COLN CO4 ...87 J3
Jack Clow Rd SRTFD E15 .....307 H6
Jack Cornwell St MNPK E12 ..308 D1
Jackdaw Cl BCAYE CM11 .....258 F5
  SBN/FI SS3 ....303 J7
Jack Evans St SOCK/AV RM15 .329 K2
Jack Hatch Wy RCOLE CO7 ...130 D2
Jacks Cl WICKE SS11 ....261 J6
Jack's La CHLM/GWD CM2 ...210 A2
Jack Stevens Cl HLWE CM17 *..204 D3
Jackson Cl EMPK RM11 ....290 C2
  GRH DA9 ....335 K7
  HOM E9 ....50 A4
  KESG IP5 ....50 D4
Jackson Pl CHLM/GWD CM2 ..210 A2
Jackson Rd BARK IG11 ....309 G1
  COS CO15 ....6 D1
  WDBR IP12 ....57 H4
Jacksons Cl CHONG CM5 * 382 H4
Jacksons Dr CHESW EN7 .....216 B6
Jacksons La BCAYE CM11 ....258 E2
  SAFWN CB10 ....341 H4
Jacksons Ms BCAYE CM11 ...258 F3
Jackson Wy KESG IP5 ....50 D4
Jack Stevens Cl HLWE CM17 *..204 D3
Jacobs Av HARH RM3 ....272 A5
Jacobs Cl DAGE RM10 ....310 F1
Jacquard Wy BRTR CM7 ......121 K3
Jacqueline Gdns
  BCAYW CM12 ....258 C1
Jacqueline Vls WALTH E17 * ..284 C3
Jade Cl BCTR RM8 ....287 M6
  CAN/RD E16 ....324 C1
Jaffe Rd IL IG1 ....286 F6
Jaggard's Rd RCOLW CO6 ....124 C3
James Av BCTR RM8 ....288 A4
James Boden Cl FX IP11 * 62 B6
James Carter Rd COLW CO3 ..105 J3
James Cl GPK RM2 ....289 K3
  PLSTW E15 ....307 K6
  RCOLE CO7 ....130 C2
James Cft CHLM/GWD CM2 ...210 C3
James Gdns TOTM N17 ....267 G8
James La LEY E10 ....285 G6
James Lee Sq PEND EN3 ......233 H8
Jameson Pl SUD CO10 ....20 B5
Jameson Rd COS CO15 ....6 B5
James Rd BARK IG11 ....308 F4
  COS CO15 ....160 A3
  EPP CM16 ....220 B7
Jamestown Wy POP/IOD E14 .323 G5
James Yd CHING E4 * 267 G2

Jamuna Cl POP/IOD E14 ...322 B1
Janebrook Rd CHTY IP2 ...53 K3
Janet St POP/IOD E14 ...322 D6
Janson Cl SRTFD E15 ...307 H2
Janson Rd SRTFD E15 ...307 H2
Janus Cl HCH CB9 ...35 G7
Japan Rd CHDH RM6 ...288 A4
  WAP E1 ...322 A3
Jardine Rd PIT SS13 ...278 A5
Jarmin Rd COL CO1 ...8 C4
Jarndyce CHLM/WR CM1 ...193 J7
Jarrow Rd CHDH RM6 ...287 M4
Jarrow Wy HOM E9 ...306 F1
Jarvis Cleys CHESW EN7 ...216 A4
Jarvis Fld RCHLM CM3 ...196 A6
Jarvis Rd CVI SS8 ...298 D7
  SBF/HAD SS7 ...298 B1
Jarvis Wy HARH RM3 ...272 B8
Jasmin Cl BSF CM23 ...138 C3
Jasmine Cl CHTY IP2 ...53
  COLN CO4 ...9 M5
  CVI SS8 ...320 C3
  FX IP11 ...62 A3
  IL IG1 ...308 E2
  VGE SS16 ...294 C1
Jasmine Dr HERT/BAY SG13 ...184 B3
Jasmine Rd ROMW/RG RM7 ...289 H7
Jasmine Wy COS CO15 ...182 D6
Jason Cl CDW/CHF CM16 ...316 B6
  CVI SS8 ...298 E8
Jasons Cl BRW CM14 ...273 J5
Jasper Cl PEND EN3 ...232 D8
Jasper Rd CAN/RD E16 ...324 A2
Jay Cl BRTR CM77 ...121 C5
  HVHL CB9 ...34 F7
Jays La RCOLW CO6 ...126 C2
The Jays RCOL CO6 ...107 L2
Jaywick La RCOS CO16 ...182 D3
Jaywick Rd HVHL CB9 ...34 F7
Jeans La BSF CM23 ...138 F2
Jebb St BOW E3 ...306 D6
Jedburgh Rd PLSTW E13 ...307 M7
Jefferies Rd HVHL IP4 ...17 J1
Jefferson Av LAIN SS15 ...276 D7
Jefferson Cl COLN CO4 ...106 D6
  GNTH/NBYPK IG2 ...286 E3
Jeffery Rd CHLM/GWD CM2 ...210 D6
Jeffrey Cl COLW CO3 ...106 A6
Jeffrey's Rd BRTR CM77 ...122 A4
  PEND EN3 ...248 C4
Jekylls La BRTR CM7 ...354 C5
Jellicoe Av CVI SS8 * ...337 M8
Jellicoe Wy BRTR CM7 ...121 M1
Jena Cl SBN/FI SS3 ...303 H6
Jenkins La RBSF CM22 ...374 D2
Jenkins La BARK IG11 ...308 F7
  BSF CM23 ...139 K4
Jenkins Rd PLSTW E13 ...307 L8
Jenner Cl BRTR CM7 ...121 J4
Jenner Md CHLM/GWD CM2 ...210 D7
Jenningham Dr
  CDW/CHF RM16 ...314 D8
Jennings Pl ING CM4 ...224 D5
Jenningtree Wy BELV DA17 ...326 F5
Jenny Hammond Cl WAN E11 ...285 J8
Jephson Rd FSTGT E7 ...307 M4
Jeremiah St POP/IOD E14 ...322 E2
Jericho Pl ING CM4 ...222 B5
Jermayns LAIN SS15 ...2 E3
Jerningham Av CLAY IG5 ...268 C4
Jerounds HLWW/ROY CM19 ...203 J3
Jersey Cl HOD EN11 ...201 H2
Jersey Gdns WICKE SS11 ...261 G5
Jersey Rd BRTR CM7 ...121 G8
  IL IG1 ...285 E1
  LEY E10 ...285 L2
  MAL CM9 ...214 D1
  RAIN RM13 ...311 K4
Jervis Av PEND EN3 ...232 F5
Jervis Cl RIPS/CAP IP9 ...364 G8
Jervis Cl BSF CM23 ...139 C5
Jesmond Rd CDW/CHF CM16 ...315 G8
  CVI SS8 ...320 C8
Jessel Dr LOU IG10 ...250 F2
Jesse Rd LEY E10 ...284 F6
Jessett Cl ERITH DA8 ...327 G4
Jessica Cl COLN CO4 ...108 C6
Jessop Cl COS CO15 ...159 K5
Jessup Cl WOOL/PLUM SE18 ...324 F1
Jetty Wk GRAYS RM17 ...330 D5
Jewell Vw KESC SS9 ...50 C6
Jewel Rd WALTH E17 ...284 D1
Jim Bradley Cl
  WOOL/PLUM SE18 ...324 D7
Jimmy's La MCTR CO11 ...65 J1
Joan Gdns BCTR RM8 ...288 B7
Joan Rd BCTR RM8 ...288 B7
Jocelyns HLWE CM17 ...188 D5
Jodane Rd DEPT SE8 ...322 C1
Jodrell Rd HOM E9 ...306 C5
Jodrell Wy WTHK RM20 ...329 J8
John Ball Wk COL CO1 ...8 A4
John Burns Dr BARK IG11 ...309 H5
Johnby Cl PEND EN3 ...232 F7
John Childs Wy RAYL SS6 ...281 H3
John Eliot Cl WAB EN9 ...201 M8
John English Av BRTR CM7 ...121 G1
John Harper St COL CO1 * ...8 A4
John Harrison Wy
  BERM/RHTH SE16 ...322 A6
  GNWCH SE10 ...323 J6
John Kent Av COLS CO2 ...128 C3
John Raven Ct K/T/MI CO5 ...149 G2
John Ray St BRTR CM7 ...121 K2
John Silkin La DEPT SE8 ...322 J6
Johnson Cl BRTR CM7 ...121 J6
  CHTY IP2 ...54 B2
  GVW DA11 ...337 G8
  RCFD SS4 ...265 G8
  WICKW SS12 ...261 G8
Johnson Rd CHLM/GWD CM2 ...210 C8
  RCOS CO16 ...181 L8
Johnson's Dr RCOLE CO7 ...109 K7
Johnsons Wy GRH DA9 ...335 M8
Johnsons Whf GRH DA9 * ...335 K6
Johns Rd BSF CM23 ...115 H8
The Johns CHONG CM5 ...382 H1
Johnston Cl COS CO15 ...160 A4
  HSTD CO9 ...81 J5
Johnstone Rd EHAM E6 ...308 C7
  SOS SS1 ...5 J3
Johnston Rd WFD IG8 ...267 K6
Johnston Wy MAL CM9 ...214 D5
John St GRAYS RM17 ...330 C5
  RCOLE CO7 ...156 C6
  SBN/FI SS3 ...303 K7
  SRTFD E15 ...307 K5
John Tate Rd HERT/BAY SG13 ...184 A3
John Tibauld Ct HVHL CB9 ...344 A4
John William Cl WTHK RM20 ...330 A4
John Wilson St
  WOOL/PLUM SE18 ...324 D7
Joiner's Ct CBE/LIN CB1 ...24 E7

Joiner's Rd CBE/LIN CB1 ...24 E7
Jollyboys La North
  GTDUN CM6 ...118 F7
Jollyboys La South
  GTDUN CM6 ...142 F1
Jones Cl SOSN SS2 ...301 H2
Jones Rd PLSTW E13 ...307 L8
Jonquil Wy COLN CO4 ...106 E3
Jordans Cl DAGE RM10 ...310 L1
Jordans Wy RAIN RM13 ...312 A6
Joseph Gdns WIT CM8 ...147 H1
Joseph Ray Rd WAN E11 ...285 J7
Joseph St BOW E3 ...322 C1
Joshua St POP/IOD E14 ...322 F2
Josling Cl GRAYS RM17 ...330 C5
Joslin Rd PUR RM19 ...328 F8
Joslyn Cl PEND EN3 ...233 H8
Josselin Cl RCOLW CO6 ...82 E6
Josselin Ct PIT SS13 ...278 F3
Josselin Rd PIT SS13 ...278 F3
The Josselyns FX IP11 ...62 A1
Jotmans La SBF/HAD SS7 ...297 K2
Journeymans Wy SOSN SS2 ...283 K8
Jovian Wy COLN CO4 ...87 J7
Joyce Cl WAB EN9 ...233 L4
Joyce Green Wy DART DA1 ...334 A3
Joyce's Cha MAL CM9 ...384 D5
Joyce's Cl CBS CB2 ...22 C7
Joydon Dr CHDH RM6 ...287 L4
Joyners Cl DAGW RM9 ...310 C1
Joyners Fld HLWS CM18 ...203 K5
Joy Rd GVE DA12 ...337 M6
Jubilee Av CHING E4 ...266 F5
  LAIN SS15 ...153 L3
  COS CO15 ...159 H6
  ROMW/RG RM7 ...288 C3
Jubilee Cl COLW CO3 ...106 A6
  FX IP11 ...62 A3
  GRH DA9 ...335 M8
  HAR CO12 ...70 D3
  HOC/HUL SS5 ...264 B8
  ROMW/RG RM7 ...288 C3
Jubilee Ct GTDUN CM6 ...116 F4
  HSTD CO9 ...356 F9
Jubilee Crs GVE DA12 ...338 B7
Jubilee Dr WICKW SS12 ...260 F5
Jubilee End MGTR CO11 ...64 F8
Jubilee La RCOLE CO7 ...108 F2
Jubilee Ri RCHLM CM3 ...212 C7
Jubilee Rd BCAYE CM11 ...277 M1
  RAYL SS6 ...281 H3
  SUD CO10 ...20 L4
  WTHK RM20 ...335 L1
Jubilee Vls RIPS/CAP IP9 * ...66 C2
Jubilee Wy FOS CO15 ...133 J3
Jude St CAN/RD E16 ...323 J2
Judge Rd CHLM/GWD CM2 ...210 L1
Judith Av CRW RM5 ...270 E5
Julia Gdns BARK IG11 ...310 A6
Julian Cl COLN CO4 ...87 L7
Julian Cl CHLM/WR CM1 ...193 L4
  HVHL CB9 ...35 G6
Julian Pl POP/IOD E14 ...322 E8
Julien Court Rd BRTR CM7 ...121 K1
Juliers Cl CVI SS8 ...321 G2
Juliers Rd CVI SS8 ...321 G2
Juliette Rd PLSTW E13 ...307 K6
Juliette Wy PUR RM19 ...328 C5
Junction Rd BRW CM14 ...273 M3
  DART DA1 ...334 A8
  PLSTW E13 ...307 L5
  RCHLM CM3 ...230 D7
  ROM RM1 ...289 J2
  VGE SS16 ...294 C1
Junction Rd East CHDH RM6 ...288 B5
Junction Rd West CHDH RM6 ...288 B5
June Av IP IP1 ...48 A3
Juniper Cl BCAYE CM11 ...258 F1
  BROX EN10 ...217 G3
  HSTD CO9 ...81 L5
Juniper Ct CHDH RM6 ...287 L4
  GTDUN CM6 ...116 E4
  RBRW/HUT CM13 * ...256 C6
Juniper Crs WIT CM8 ...171 K1
Juniper Dr CHLM/GWD CM2 ...209 L3
  SOCK/AV RM15 ...314 B3
Juniper La EHAM E6 ...324 B1
Juniper Rd COLW CO3 ...105 M8
  IL IG1 ...300 C1
  LOS SS9 ...300 C1
  RCHLM CM3 ...195 H5
Juniper Wy COLN CO4 ...105 M8
  HARH RM3 ...272 A5
Jupes Hl RCOLE CO7 ...363 R12
  RCOLW CO6 ...84 A7
Jupiter Cl HVHL CB9 ...34 F7
Jupiter Dr IPNE IP4 ...49 G6
Jupp Rd SRTFD E15 ...307 G4
Jupp Rd West SRTFD E15 ...307 G4
Jurgens Rd PUR RM19 * ...328 F7
Jury St GVE DA12 ...337 L4
Justinian Cl HVHL CB9 ...35 G6
Justin Rd CHING E4 ...266 C1
Jute La PEND EN3 ...248 B2
Jutland Rd PLSTW E13 ...307 K8
Jutsums Av ROMW/RG RM7 ...288 C5
Jutsums La ROMW/RG RM7 ...288 C5
Juvina St WIT CM8 ...171 J6

K

Kale Cft COLW CO3 ...106 A8
Kale Rd ERITHM DA18 ...326 A5
  SBF/HAD SS7 ...298 B1
Kamerwyk Av CVI SS8 ...321 F1
Kandlewood
  RBRW/HUT CM13 ...256 C3
Kane Ms COL CO1 * ...8 B6
Karen Cl BRWN CM15 ...255 M7
  IP IP1 ...48 D1
  RAIN RM13 ...311 H6
  SBF/HAD SS7 ...298 A5
  SLH/COR SS17 ...316 H6
  WICKW SS12 ...261 H7
Karina Cl CHIG IG7 ...269 H4
Kashgar Rd
  WOOL/PLUM SE18 ...325 J8
Kate's La SAFWN SB10 ...29 H7
Katherine Cl
  BERM/RHTH SE16 ...322 A4
  RAYL SS6 ...281 K4
Katherine Gdns BARK/HLT IG6 ...268 A4
Katherine Rd EHAM E6 ...308 A4
  PIT SS13 ...279 G7
Katherine's Wy
  HLWW/ROY CM19 ...203 H4
Kathleen Cl SLH/COR SS17 ...317 G7
Kathleen Dr COS SS9 ...300 C3
Kathleen Ferrier Crs
  LAIN SS15 ...276 F5
Katonia Av RCHLM CM3 ...388 C4
Kavanaghs Rd BRW CM14 ...273 L2
Kavanaghs Ter BRW CM14 ...273 L2
Kay Cl RCHLM CM3 ...144 D6
Kays Ter SWFD E18 * ...267 J8

Kay St SRTFD E15 ...307 G4
Keable Rd RCOLW CO6 ...126 B2
Keary Rd SWCM DA10 ...336 C5
Keating Cl MGTR CO11 ...90 F7
Keatley Gn CHING E4 ...266 C5
Keats Av BRTR CM7 ...121 J5
  CAN/RD E16 ...323 L4
  HARH RM3 ...271 J4
Keats Cl CHIG IG7 ...268 F5
  MAL CM9 ...214 D5
  PEND EN3 ...248 A3
  WAN E11 ...285 J2
Keats Crs IP IP1 ...47 L2
Keats Gdns TIL RM18 ...331 H8
Keats Rd BELV DA17 ...326 F5
  COLW CO3 ...106 C7
Keats Wk CHING E4 ...266 C5
Keats Wy WICKW SS12 ...260 G5
Keble Cl COLW CO3 ...107 H5
Kecksy's SBW CM21 ...163 G5
Kedington Hl SUD CO10 ...45 L7
Kedleston Cl K/T/MI CO5 ...150 B3
Keeble Cl RCOLE CO7 ...155 H6
Keeble Pk MAL CM9 ...214 D6
Keeble Wy BRTR CM7 * ...121 K2
Keegan Pl CVI SS8 * ...320 C1
Keelars La RCOLE CO7 ...131 H3
Keel Rd BARK IG11 ...309 M6
  BERM/RHTH SE16 ...322 A4
Keelers Wy RCOLW CO6 ...86 C5
Keelings La BOC CMO ...390 D9
Keelings Rd BOC CMO ...390 C9
Keepers Gn CHLM/GWD CM2 ...225 L2
Keepers On COLN CO4 ...106 E2
Keeper's La FX IP11 * ...61 M8
  RCOLW CO6 ...361 L2
Keer Av CVI SS8 ...321 G3
Keighley Ms SBN/FI SS3 ...303 G3
Keir Hardie Wy BARK IG11 ...309 H4
  K/T/MI CO5 ...150 B4
Keith Cl COS CO15 ...159 L5
Keith Rd BARK IG11 ...309 G3
  WALTH E17 ...266 C7
Keith Wy EMPK RM11 ...290 D5
  SOS SS1 ...283 H8
Kelburn Wy RAIN RM13 ...311 K7
Kelland Rd PLSTW E13 ...307 K8
Keller Crs MNPK E12 ...308 A1
Kellington Rd CVI SS8 ...298 D5
Kellner Rd THMD SE28 ...325 J6
Kelly Rd CHTY IP2 ...47 K8
  PIT SS13 ...279 G7
Kelly Wy CHDH RM6 ...288 B3
Kelman Cl CHES/WCR ENB ...232 C5
Kelmscott Cl WALTH E17 ...266 C1
Kelsie Wy BARK/HLT IG6 ...269 K5
Kelso Cl RAYL SS6 ...262 F7
  RCOLW CO6 ...86 C2
Kelston Rd BARK/HLT IG6 ...268 C2
Kelvedon Rd CHLM/WR CM1 ...193 K4
  RAYL SS6 ...280 D2
  RBRW/HUT CM3 ...257 H2
Kelvedon Dr IPNE IP4 ...49 J3
Kelvedon Gn BRWN CM15 ...383 N11
Kelvedon Hall La BRW CM14 ...383 J10
Kelvedon Rd BCAYE CM11 ...258 F3
  K/T/MI CO5 ...149 G8
  MAL CM9 ...174 F7
  WIT CM8 ...172 C8
Kelvedon Wy WFD IG8 ...268 C5
Kelvin Ct FOS CO13 * ...137 J4
Kelvin Rd IP IP1 ...47 L4
  SBF/HAD SS7 ...280 A4
  TIL RM18 ...331 K8
Kelvinside SLH/COR SS17 ...295 L8
Kemball St IPNE IP4 ...48 F8
Kembles RAYL SS6 ...263 H6
Kemley Rd IP IP1 ...48 A5
Kemp Rd BCTR RM8 ...306 B2
Kempe Rd BRTR CM7 ...354 C11
  EN EN1 ...232 C6
Kemps Dr POP/IOD E14 ...322 D3
Kemps Farm COLW CO3 * ...105 J2
Kempson Dr SUD CO10 ...45 M4
The Kempsters FX IP11 ...62 C1
Kempthorne Rd DEPT SE8 ...322 B7
Kempthorne St HARH RM3 ...272 F5
Kempton Av HCH RM12 ...312 C1
Kempton Cl IP IP1 ...47 M2
Kempton Pk RCOS CO16 ...134 E4
Kempton Rd EHAM E6 ...308 C1
  IP IP1 ...47 M2
Kemsing Rd GNWCH SE10 ...323 M4
Kemsley Cl GRH DA9 ...335 L8
Kemsley Cl FX IP11 ...62 B4
  RCOLW CO6 ...82 C7
Kendal Av BARK IG11 ...309 H5
  EPP CM16 ...220 B8
Kendal Cl HOC/HUL SS5 ...263 H4
  RAYL SS6 ...281 H3
  WFD IG8 ...268 C1
Kendal Ct WICKE SS11 ...261 K4
Kendal Cft HARH RM3 ...311 K2
Kendale CDW/CHF RM16 ...331 L4
Kendall Rd COL CO1 ...8 C7
Kendal Rd WAB EN9 ...233 K5
Kendal Wy LOS SS9 ...300 C3
Kendon Cl WAN E11 ...285 L3
Kenholme LOS SS9 ...300 C5
Kenilworth Av HARH RM3 ...272 A4
  WALTH E17 ...266 D1
Kenilworth Gdns
  GDMY/SEVK IG3 ...287 J7
  HCH RM12 ...289 M8
  LOU IG10 ...250 D2
  RAYL SS6 ...281 H3
  WOS/PRIT SS0 ...300 D2
Kenilworth Pl LAIN SS15 ...277 H4
Kenilworth Rd BOW E3 ...306 F6
  COS CO15 ...160 A4
Kenley Cl WICKE SS11 ...261 K7
Kenley Gdns HCH RM12 ...290 C7
Kenmore Cl CVI SS8 ...321 H3
Kennard Rd SRTFD E15 ...307 G4
Kennard St CAN/RD E16 ...324 D3
Kennedy Av HOD EN11 ...201 J2
Kennedy Cl CHES/WCR EN8 ...216 E6
  IPNE IP4 ...48 F5
  PLSTW E13 ...307 K6
  RAYL SS6 ...281 K4
Kennedy Rd BARK IG11 ...309 G5
Kennedy Wy COS CO15 ...7 K5
Kennel La BCAYE CM11 ...258 G1
Kennel Rd KIR/NAC IP10 ...56 A7
Kennet Ct UPMR RM14 ...291 H5
Kenneth Av IL IG1 ...308 B1
Kenneth Gdns SLH/COR SS17 ...295 L7
Kenneth Moor Rd IL IG1 * ...286 D7
Kenneth Rd CHDH RM6 ...288 A7
  SBF/HAD SS7 ...278 C8
Kenney Cl RIPW IP8 ...46 A7
Kenning Rd HOD EN11 ...201 H3

Kennington Av SBF/HAD SS7 ...279 M8
Kennylands Rd BARK/HLT IG6 ...269 K6
Kensington Av MNPK E12 ...308 C2
Kensington Ct GRAYS RM17 * ...330 A8
Kensington Gdns
  BCAYW CM12 ...258 D1
  IL IG1 ...286 D6
Kensington Rd BRWN CM15 ...255 K6
  IP IP1 ...47 M8
  ROMW/RG RM7 ...288 D1
  SOS SS1 ...302 A6
Kent Av CVI SS8 ...298 C8
  DAGW RM9 ...310 D8
  LOS SS9 ...300 C3
Kent Cl LAIN SS15 ...276 C7
  RCOLE CO7 ...156 C6
Kent Crs BSF CM23 ...138 C5
Kent Dr HCH RM12 ...312 A1
Kent Elms Cl SOSN SS2 ...282 C8
Kentford Rd FX IP11 ...10 E2
Kent Green Cl HAC/HUL SS5 ...264 C8
The Kentings BRTR CM7 ...121 H5
Kentish Rd BELV DA17 ...326 F4
Kentlea Rd THMD SE28 ...325 H6
Kentmere Rd
  WOOL/PLUM SE18 ...325 H7
Kenton Av HOM E9 ...306 A3
Kenton Wy VGE SS16 ...276 C8
Kent Rd DAGE RM10 ...310 C2
  GRAYS RM17 ...330 F5
  GVW DA11 ...337 H5
Kent's Av COS CO15 ...160 C3
Kent St BETH E2 ...306 D8
Kent Yd SAFWS CB11 ...331 N1
Kent Vw SOCK/AV RM15 ...328 E5
Kent Vw Gdns
  GDMY/SEVK IG3 ...287 H7
Kent View Rd VGE SS16 ...278 C8
Kent Vls SOS SS1 * ...18 F3
Kent Wy RAYL SS6 ...281 K5
Kentwell Cl IPNE IP4 ...55 L1
Kenway RAIN RM13 ...311 M7
  ROMW/RG RM7 ...270 F8
  SOSN SS2 ...302 A1
Kenway Cl RAIN RM13 ...311 M7
Kenway Wk RAIN RM13 ...312 A1
Kenwood Gdns CBE/LIN CB1 ...25 C6
  CLAY IG5 ...286 D2
  SWFD E18 ...285 L1
Kenwood Rd SLH/COR SS17 ...317 L6
Kenworthy Cl CHES/WCR EN8 ...232 C5
Kenworthy Rd BRTR CM7 ...121 H3
  HOM E9 ...306 D2
Kenwyn Rd DART DA1 ...334 A7
Kenyon Rd RCOLE CO7 ...363 L8
Kenyon St CHTY IP2 ...16 F8
Keogh Rd SRTFD E15 ...307 H3
Keppel Rd DAGW RM9 ...310 B1
  EHAM E6 ...308 C2
Kerbey St POP/IOD E14 ...322 E2
Kerby Rd CHLM/GWD CM2 ...210 D2
Kerridge's Cut MGTR CO11 ...91 K1
Kerril Cft HLW CM20 ...12 B4
Kerrison Rd SRTFD E15 ...307 G5
Kerry Av IP IP1 ...47 L4
  PUR RM19 ...328 C5
Kerry Cl CAN/RD E16 ...323 L2
  UPMR RM14 ...291 J5
Kerry Rd CDW/CHF RM16 ...315 G8
Kersbrooke Wy
  SLH/COR SS17 ...295 L8
Kersey Cl SUD CO10 ...21 K8
Kersey Dr RCOS CO16 ...158 C3
Kersey Gdns HARH RM3 ...272 A4
Kersey Rd FX IP11 ...10 E3
Kershaw Cl CDW/CHF RM16 ...329 M6
  EMPK RM11 ...290 D4
Kershaw Rd DAGE RM10 ...288 B3
Kershaws Cl WICKW SS12 ...260 F6
Kessler Av BRTR CM7 ...355 J10
Kesteven Cl BARK/HLT IG6 ...269 K5
Kesteven Rd CHTY IP2 ...16 D5
Kestrel Av EHAM E6 ...324 E1
Kestrel Cl BARK/HLT IG6 ...269 L5
  HCH RM12 ...311 L4
Kestrel Gdns BSF CM23 ...138 D5
Kestrel Ms MAL CM9 ...280 C2
Kestrel Pk RBRW/HUT CM13 * ...257 H1
Kestrel Ri HSTD CO9 ...81 J2
Kestrel Rd CHTY IP2 ...53 J2
  HVHL CB9 ...34 F6
  WAB EN9 ...234 B6
Kestrel Wy COS CO15 ...159 K5
  EMPK RM11 ...290 A4
  HOC/HUL SS5 ...263 H4
Keswick Av COS CO15 ...159 M7
  EMPK RM11 ...290 A4
  HOC/HUL SS5 ...263 H4
Keswick Cl FX IP11 ...63 H7
  RAYL SS6 ...281 H3
Keswick Dr PEND EN3 ...232 E6
Keswick Gdns RAYL SS6 ...281 H3
  REDBR IG4 ...286 B2
Ketley Cl K/T/MI CO5 ...150 B4
Ketleys CHLM/GWD CM2 ...225 M2
Ketleys Vw BRTR CM7 ...98 G3
Kettering Rd HARH RM3 ...272 A4
  PEND EN3 ...232 F5
Kettlebaston Rd LEY E10 ...284 C7
Kettlebaston Wy IP IP1 ...48 B2
Kettlebury Wy CHONG CM5 ...382 G6
Kevin Cl BCAYE CM11 ...258 G3
Kew La FOS CO15 ...136 C5
Keyes Cl SBN/FI SS3 ...303 H3
Keyes Rd DART DA1 ...334 C2
Keyes Wy BRTR CM7 ...121 K1
Keymer Wy COLW CO3 ...128 D3
Keynes Cl HAR CO12 ...70 E3
Keynsham Av WFD IG8 ...267 J2
Key Rd COS CO15 ...17 G6
Keysers Rd BROX EN10 ...201 H3
Keysland SBF/HAD SS7 ...298 B1
Kezia St DEPT SE8 ...322 B6
Khartoum Pl GVE DA12 ...337 M4
Khartoum Rd IL IG1 ...308 C1
  PLSTW E13 ...307 L2
Kibcaps VGE SS16 ...276 C6
Kidder Rd BRTR CM77 ...120 C7
Kidd Pl CHARL SE7 ...324 B3
Kielder Cl BARK/HLT IG6 ...269 K5
Kildare Av IP IP1 ...47 J5
Kildare Rd CAN/RD E16 ...323 K1

Kildermorie Cl COLN CO4 ...108 A8
Kildowan Rd GDMY/SEVK IG3 ...287 K7
Killip Cl CAN/RD E16 ...323 J2
Killowen Rd HOM E9 * ...306 C1
Kilmaine Rd HAR CO12 ...71 H5
Kilmarnock Gdns BCTR RM8 ...287 K8
Kilmartin Rd GDMY/SEVK IG3 ...287 K7
Kilmartin Wy HCH RM12 ...311 L1
Kilmington Cl
  RBRW/HUT CM13 ...256 B2
Kiln Barn Av COS CO15 ...159 M7
Kiln Dr SUD CO10 ...20 C3
Kilner St POP/IOD E14 ...322 D2
Kilnfield BRWN CM15 ...238 A3
  CHONG CM5 ...382 H2
Kiln Fld FX IP11 ...62 C2
Kiln La HLWE CM17 ...204 D1
  MGTR CO11 ...91 G7
Kiln Rd EPP CM16 ...221 J3
  SBF/HAD SS7 ...298 A2
Kiln Wy GRAYS RM17 ...330 E5
Kilnwood Av HOC/HUL SS5 ...264 C8
Kiln Wood La CRW RM5 ...256 A8
Kilowan Cl VGE SS16 ...294 C1
Kilsmore La CHES/WCR EN8 ...216 E6
Kiltie Rd K/T/MI CO5 ...150 B3
Kilworth Av BRWN CM15 ...256 A7
  SOS SS1 ...19 G3
Kimberley Av EHAM E6 ...308 B2
  GNTH/NBYPK IG2 ...287 G2
  ROMW/RG RM7 ...288 C5
Kimberley Cl BSF CM23 ...139 K4
  CHING E4 ...249 K8
  SBF/HAD SS7 ...297 M1
  SBN/FI SS3 ...396 H11
  WALTH E17 ...266 D1
  WAN E11 ...285 L4
Kimberley Wy CHING E4 ...249 K8
Kimberly Dr LAIN SS15 ...277 G4
Kimpton Av BRWN CM15 ...255 L6
Kimpton Cl CHONG CM5 ...380 C12
Kinburn St
  BERM/RHTH SE16 * ...322 A5
Kincaid Rd RCOS CO16 ...181 L6
Kinder Ct THMD SE28 ...325 J6
Kinfauns Av EMPK RM11 ...289 M6
Kinfauns Rd GDMY/SEVK IG3 ...287 L6
Kingaby Gdns RAIN RM13 ...311 K4
King Alfred Rd HARH RM3 ...272 A4
King Arthur Ct
  CHES/WCR EN8 ...232 C5
King Charles Rd K/T/MI CO5 ...178 A2
King Coel Rd COLW CO3 ...106 D6
King Edgar Yd ROY SG8 * ...348 F8
King Edward Av ROY SG8 * ...393 L2
  DART DA1 ...334 A8
  RAIN RM13 ...312 A2
King Edward Dr
  CDW/CHF RM16 ...331 L4
King Edward Quay COLS CO2 ...108 C8
King Edward Rd BRW CM14 ...273 M3
  CHES/WCR EN8 ...232 C5
  GRH DA9 ...335 K7
  IPSE IP3 ...55 H5
  LAIN SS15 ...276 E4
  ROM RM1 ...289 J4
  WALTH E17 ...266 E4
King Edward's Rd BARK IG11 ...309 G5
  PEND EN3 ...248 C4
  RCHLM CM3 ...245 J7
  SLH/COR SS17 ...317 G7
King Edward Ter LAIN SS15 ...276 E4
King Edward VII Dr
  RIPS/CAP IP9 ...67 H5
King Edward Wy WIT CM8 ...171 H1
Kingfield St POP/IOD E14 ...322 F4
Kingfisher Cl CBS CB2 ...22 C7
  COLN CO4 ...108 C6
  HVHL CB9 ...34 F6
  MAL CM9 ...198 D3
  RBRW/HUT CM13 ...256 C6
  SBN/FI SS3 ...303 H3
  THMD SE28 ...28 B1
  WARE SG12 ...185 G1
Kingfisher Crs RAYL SS6 ...280 E2
Kingfisher Dr GRH DA9 ...335 L8
Kingfisher Ga BRTR CM7 ...99 G3
  SBF/HAD SS7 ...297 M1
Kingfisher Mdw HSTD CO9 ...81 J2
Kingfisher Rd UPMR RM14 ...291 H4
Kingfishers COS CO15 ...159 K5
  VGE SS16 ...3 J3
Kingfisher St EHAM E6 ...324 E1
Kingfisher Wy BSF CM23 ...139 D5
  K/T/MI CO5 ...150 B3
King George Av CAN/RD E16 ...324 B2
  GNTH/NBYPK IG2 ...287 G2
King George Cl
  ROMW/RG RM7 ...288 C3
  WAB EN9 ...233 L4
King George Rd COLS CO2 ...129 G1
  WARE SG12 ...185 G1
King George's Av COL CO12 ...114 D2
King George's Cl RAYL SS6 ...281 H3
King George's Rd
  BRWN CM15 ...255 L6
King George VI Av TIL RM18 ...332 A3
King Harold Rd COLW CO3 ...128 D3
King Henry Cl WAB EN9 ...233 L4
King Henry's Dr RCFD SS4 ...283 H4
King Henry's Ms PEND EN3 ...233 H7
Kinglet Cl FSTGT E7 ...307 K3
Kingley Cl WICKW SS12 ...260 F5
Kingley Dr WICKW SS12 ...260 F5
King & Queen Whf
  BERM/RHTH SE16 ...322 A5
Kings Acre RCOLW CO6 ...124 C4
Kings Cl CHDH RM6 ...288 A5
  COS CO15 ...159 M7
  IPNE IP4 ...48 F5
  WFD IG8 ...267 K6
Kingsbridge Cl BRTR CM7 ...120 C7
Kingsbridge Rd POP/IOD E14 ...322 D4
Kingsbridge Rd BARK IG11 ...309 G7
  BSF CM23 ...139 K4
  HARH RM3 ...272 A4
Kingsbury Cl RCOLW CO6 ...126 B2
Kingsbury Rd FX IP11 ...63 H7
Kingsbury Wk SUD CO10 ...45 L4
King's Cha BRW CM14 ...273 M3
  HVHL CB9 ...34 F7
Kings Ct BSF CM23 ...139 K4
  K/T/MI CO5 ...149 G2
  PLSTW E13 ...307 L2
Kings Crs COS SS15 ...276 C7
Kings Cft BOC CMO ...393 L2
Kingsdon La HLWE CM17 ...204 D1
Kingsdown Cl GVE DA12 ...338 B7

PIT SS13 ...278 F7
Kingsdown Rd WAN E11 ...285 H8
Kings Dr GVE DA12 ...337 F8
Kings Farm RAYL SS6 ...263 K6
WALTH E17 * ...266 E7
Kingsfield HOD EN11 ...201 H4
Kingsfield Av CRW RM5 ...270 C4
Kingsfield Dr PEND EN3 ...232 E5
Kingsfield Ct IPNE IP4 ...48 C4
Kingsfield Ter DART DA1 * ...334 K8
Kingsfield Wy PEND EN3 ...232 E5
Kings Fleet Rd FX IP11 ...11 G3
Kingsford Dr
  CHLM/GWD CM2 ...210 E2
Kingsford Wy EHAM E6 ...324 C1
Kings Gdns IL IG1 ...287 G6
UPMR RM14 ...291 K5
Kingsgate Dr IPNE IP4 ...48 C4
King's Gn LOU IG10 ...250 E5
Kings Gv ROM RM1 * ...289 K3
Kings Hvn CVI SS8 * ...320 A2
Kingshawes SBF/HAD SS7 ...280 E5
Kings Head Ct COL CO1 ...8 A3
Kings Head HI CHIG IG7 ...248 E7
King's Head St HAR CO12 ...15 G1
Kings Head Wk
  CHLM/GWD CM2 ...5 J5
King's HI HVHL CB9 ...35 K4
SUD CO10 ...21 G7
Kingshill Av CRW RM5 ...270 C4
Kingsland HLWS CM18 ...203 K3
  RIPS/CAP IP9 ...66 D3
Kingsland Beach K/T/MI CO5 *...177 H6
Kingsland K/T/MI CO5 * ...177 K5
Kingsland Hts K/T/MI CO5 * ...178 M6
Kingsland La CLCW CO6 ...360 C4
Kingsland Rd K/T/MI CO5 ...177 M6
  PLSTW E13 ...307 M7
Kings La BRTR CM77 ...122 B1
  SUD CO10 ...43 J3
Kingsley Av CHES/WCR EN8...216 A1
  DART DA1 ...334 D7
Kingsley CI DAGE RM10 ...310 H6
  IP IP1 ...47 M2
Kingsley Ct GPK RM2 ...289 L4
Kingsley Gdns CHING E4 ...266 D2
  EMPK RM11 ...290 A4
Kingsley La SBF/HAD SS7 ...280 E5
Kingsley Ms IG1 IG1 ...286 F7
Kingsley Rd BARK/HLT IG6 ...268 F7
  FSTGT E7 ...307 K4
  LOU IG10 ...251 G3
  RBRW/HUT CM13 ...257 G5
  WALTH E17 ...266 C8
Kingsley Wk CDW/CHF RM16..351 K5
Kings Lynn Dr HARH RM3...272 K3
Kingsman Dr CDW/CHF RM16 ...314 E7
  RCOS CO16 ...6 C7
Kingsman St SLH/COR SS17 ...316 E4
Kingsmans Farm Rd
  HOC/HUL SS5 ...263 J1
Kingsman St
  WOOL/PLUM SE18 ...324 C7
Kingsmead CHES/WCR EN8 ...216 F8
  SBW CM21 ...162 F8
  WAB EN9 * ...201 K8
Kingsmead Rd ROM RM1 ...289 H4
Kingsmead CI
  HLWW/ROY CM19 ...202 C2
Kings Meadow HVHL CB9 ...35 K4
  SUD CO10 ...21 G8
Kings Meadow Ct
  K/T/MI CO5 * ...148 F2
Kingsmead Rd COL CO1 ...8 C4
Kingsmead Pk BRTR CM7 * ...121 M1
Kingsmead Wy HOM E9 ...306 D1
Kingsmere SBF/HAD SS7 ...280 E5
Kingsmere CI K/T/MI CO5 ...178 A4
Kings Ms CHIG IG7 * ...268 F7
  RCOLE CO7 ...130 C1
Kings MI SAFWN CB10 * ...341 J7
Kingsmill Gdns DAGW RM9 ...310 C2
Kingsmill Rd DAGW RM9 ...310 C2
Kingsmoor Rd
  HLWW/ROY CM19 ...203 J4
Kings Oak ROMW/RG RM7 ...288 D4
Kings Pde COS CO15 ...160 D4
  SLH/COR SS17 ...316 F4
Kings Pk CVI SS8 * ...321 G1
  SBF/HAD SS7 ...280 E5
Kingspark Ct WAN E11 * ...285 K1
Kings Pas WAN E11 * ...285 H8
Kings PI BKHH IG9 ...268 A1
  LOU IG10 ...250 F7
King's Quay St HAR CO12 ...15 L2
Kingsridge Gdns DART DA1 ...334 D7
King's Rd BARK IG11 ...308 F4
  BOC CM0 ...393 N2
  BOC CM0 ...99 N7
  BRTR CM7 * ...99 H7
  BRW CM14 ...273 M2
  CHES/WCR EN8 ...232 F4
  CHING E4 ...249 G8
  CHLM/WR CM1 ...231 J1
  COS CO15 ...183 G4
  CVI SS8 ...319 N2
  EHAM E6 ...307 K1
  HAR CO12 ...15 L2
  HERT/BAY SG13 ...184 B2
  HSTD CO9 ...81 H4
  LAIN SS15 ...276 E4
  MAL CM9 ...173 H6
  RAYL SS6 ...281 H3
  ROM RM1 ...289 K3
  SBF/HAD SS7 ...298 B3
  WAN E11 ...285 H8
  WOS/PRIT SS0 ...300 D3
Kingsteignton SBN/FI SS3 ...302 A1
King Stephen Rd COL CO1 ...9 J3
Kingston Av CHLM/GWD CM2 ...210 D7
  SBN/FI SS3 ...303 G3
Kingston Cha MAL CM9 ...198 D1
Kingston Ct CHDH RM6 ...288 B4
Kingston Ct GVW DA11 ...336 A3
Kingston Crs CHLM/GWD CM2...210 D7
Kingston HI VGE SS16 ...295 G3
Kingston Hill Av CHDH RM6 ...288 B4
Kingston Pde GRAYS RM17 * ...330 F4
Kingston Rdg VGE SS16 ...295 G3
Kingston Rd IL IG1 ...308 F1
  IP IP1 ...47 L5
  ROM RM1 ...289 K3
Kingston Wy SBF/HAD SS7 ...280 C5
  CHONG CM5 ...383 D5
  FX IP11 ...07 D8
  GVE DA12 ...337 G3
  IP IP1 ...16 A4
  MAL CM9 ...214 D4
  MGTR CO11 ...91 M5
  PLSTW E13 ...307 L6
  SLH/COR SS17 ...316 F4
  SUD CO10 ...20 C6
Kings Wk MAL CM9 ...385 D6
Kings Wy BCAYE CM11 ...259 G7
IPSE IP3 ...55 G3

RCHLM CM3 ...244 F4
Kingsway HAR CO12 ...15 J7
  HOC/HUL SS5 ...263 G4
  K/T/MI CO5 ...149 M7
  WOS/PRIT SS0 ...300 D3
Kingsway Ms WOS/PRIT SS0 ...300 D3
Kingswood Cha LOS SS9 ...300 A2
Kingswood CI BCAYW CM12 ...258 E2
Kingswood CI BOC CM0 ...386 F10
Kingswood Crs RAYL SS6 ...280 E4
Kingswood Rd COLN CO4 ...107 J1
  GDMY/SEVK IG3 ...287 K6
  VGE SS16 ...3 L1
  WAN E11 ...285 H5
Kings Yd SRTFD E15 * ...306 D3
Kingwell Av COS CO15 ...6 F2
King William Ct WAB EN9 * ...233 K5
King William La GNWCH SE10 ...323 H8
Kinlett CI CLVDN CO4 ...107 L1
Kinloch Cha WIT CM8 ...171 H5
Kinnaird Wy WFD IG8 ...268 F1
Kinross Rd IPNE IP4 ...49 G4
Kinross Ter WALTH E17 ...266 C8
Kintbury CBS CB2 ...340 E1
Kinveachy Gdns CHARL SE7 ...324 F5
Kipling Av TIL RM18 ...331 K5
Kipling CI CHLM/WR CM1 ...193 K8
Kipling Ms SOSN SS2 ...301 K2
Kipling Rd DART DA1 ...334 K1
  IP IP1 ...47 L2
Kipling Wy BRTR CM7 ...121 H5
Kirby CI BARK/HLT IG6 ...269 H5
  HARH RM5 ...272 A4
  IPNE IP4 ...48 F6
  LOU IG10 ...250 F7
Kirby Hall Rd HSTD CO9 ...356 F6
Kirby Rd BSDN SS14 ...278 D5
  FOS CO13 ...136 D5
  WOTN CO6 ...137 K1
Kirby St IPNE IP4 ...48 G4
Kirkbare FOS CO13 ...137 L3
Kirkdale Rd WAN E11 ...285 H5
Kirkham Av BARK/HLT IG6...269 K3
Kirkham CI CHTY IP2 ...53 M5
Kirkham Rd EHAM E6 ...324 C1
  SLH/COR SS17 ...294 C6
Kirkham Shaw SLH/COR SS17 ...294 C6
Kirkhurst CI RCFD SS4 ...156 D7
Kirkland Av CLAY IG5 ...268 A3
Kirklees Rd BCTR RM8 ...309 H4
Kirkmans Rd CHLM/GWD CM2...226 A2
Kirkmichael Rd POP/IOD E14 *...322 C2
Kirk PI CHLM/GWD CM2 ...210 C2
Kirk Rd WALTH E17 ...284 C1
Kirkton CI RIPS/CAP IP9 ...66 H4
Kirton CI KIR/NAC IP10 ...311 M3
Kirton Rd KIR/NAC IP10 ...57 K1
  KIR/NAC IP10 ...62 A1
  PLSTW E13 ...307 M6
Kitcat Ter BOW E3 ...306 C1
Kitchener Rd FSTGT E7 ...307 L3
  IP IP1 ...47 L5
  RCHLM CM3 ...246 D4
  WALTH E17 ...266 C7
Kitchener Wy RIPS/CAP IP9...66 F3
Kitchen Fld BRTR CM77 ...122 D1
Kitchen HI SUD CO10 ...44 C3
Kitkatts Rd CVI SS8 ...320 D2
Kitson Wy HLW E20 ...12 C1
Kittiwake CI CHTY IP2 ...53 L2
Kittiwake Dr MAL CM9 ...198 F6
Kiwi Ter EHAM E6 ...308 D2
Knapp Rd BOW E3 ...306 C1
Knapton CI CHLM/WR CM1 ...194 A6
The Knares VGE SS16 ...2 B9
Knebworth Av WALTH E17 ...266 D7
Knee HI ABYW SE2 ...325 M8
Knee Hill Crs ABYW SE2 ...325 M8
Knightbridge Wk
  BCAYW CM12 ...258 D2
Knight CI BCTR RM8 ...287 M3
Knighthead Point
  POP/IOD E14 * ...322 D4
Knighton CI ROMW/RG RM7 ...289 G4
  WFD IG8 ...267 L3
Knighton Dr WFD IG8 ...267 L1
Knighton La BRKH RM13 ...267 L1
Knighton Rd FSTGT E7 ...285 K8
  ROMW/RG RM7 ...289 G4
Knights LAIN SS15 ...277 G6
Knightsbridge CI COLS CO2 *...128 C7
Knightsbridge Gdns
  ROMW/RG RM7 ...289 G4
Knights CI BSF CM23 ...138 C1
  FX IP11 ...63 G1
  K/T/MI CO5 ...174 C2
  MGTR CO11 ...90 D7
Knights La KESG IP5 ...51 M4
Knights Manor Wy DART DA1 *..334 C4
Knights Rd EHAM E6 ...323 H4
  ROMW/RG RM7 ...289 G4
Knight St RCHLM CM3 ...245 H6
Knights Wk ABRY/ST RM4 ...251 L1
Knights Wy BARK/HLT IG6 ...268 F7
  GTDUN CM6 ...117 G4
  RBRW/HUT CM13 ...257 G5
Knightswood CI RAIN RM13 ...311 J6
Knightswood CI BOC CM0 *...389 L12
Knivet CI RAYL SS6 ...281 J4
Knobs Hill Rd SRTFD E15 ...306 B3
Knockhall Cha GRH DA9 ...335 M7
Knockhall Rd GRH DA9 ...335 M8
Knole La SAFWS CB11 ...350 B6
Knollcroft SBN/FI SS3 ...303 G3
The Knoll BCAYW CM12 ...258 E2
  HERT/BAY SG13 ...184 A2
  RAYL SS6 ...281 G6
Knottisford St BETH E2 ...306 A7
Knotts Green Ms LEY E10 ...284 E4
Knotts Green Rd LEY E10 ...284 E4
Knowles CI HSTD CO9 ...81 H4
The Knowle HOD EN11 ...201 H4
  VGE SS16 ...3 K9
Knox CI CHLM/WR CM1 ...214 A6
Knox Ct WICKW SS12 ...261 G8
Knox Gdns COS CO15 ...6 C5
Knox Rd COS CO15 ...6 C5
  FSTGT E7 ...307 K4
Knutsford CI RUP IP8 ...55 L5
Kohima Rd COLS CO2 ...128 C3
Kolburg Rd CVI SS8 ...321 G3
Kollum Rd CVI SS8 ...321 G3
Koln CI CVI SS8 ...319 N2
Komberg Crs CVI SS8 ...298 C5
Konnybrook SBF/HAD SS7 ...298 D2
Korndyk Av CVI SS8 ...320 C4
Kossuth St GNWCH SE10 ...323 H8
Kreswell Gv HAR CO12 ...71 G3
Kursaal Wy SOS SS1 ...15 J6
Kylemore CI EHAM E6 ...308 A6
Kyme Rd ROM RM1 ...289 H4
Kynance CI HARH RM3 ...271 M2
Kynaston PI WIT CM8 ...171 H1

Kynaston Rd BRTR CM7 ...98 C5
Kynoch Ct SLH/COR SS17 ...317 H4
Kynoch Rd UED N18 ...266 A3

L

Laars Av CVI SS8 ...320 F1
Laburnham CI UPMR RM14 ...291 K5
Laburnham Gdns
  UPMR RM14 ...291 J5
Laburnum Av HCH RM12 ...289 K7
  WICKW SS12 ...260 F5
Laburnum CI CHES/WCR EN8...260 C5
  CHING E4 ...266 C5
  COS CO15 ...6 A5
  HOC/HUL SS5 ...263 L7
  IPSE IP3 ...55 H5
  POP/IOD E14 ...323 H5
  RIPW IP8 ...53 H5
  WICKW SS12 ...260 F6
Laburnum Crs FOS CO13 ...137 G5
Laburnum Dr
  CHLM/GWD CM2 ...209 L7
  SLH/COR SS17 ...317 K2
Laburnum Gdns KESG IP5 ...49 K4
Laburnum Gv COLN CO4 ...108 B5
  CVI SS8 ...320 A2
  GVW DA11 ...337 G5
  HOC/HUL SS5 ...263 L7
  RAIN RM13 ...311 J4
  SOCK/AV RM15 ...314 A4
Laburnum Rd EPP CM16 ...220 D7
  HOD EN11 ...201 J1
Laburnum Wk HCH RM12 ...311 M2
  RAYL SS6 ...262 F4
  RCHLM CM3 ...196 D2
  RCOLW CO6 ...361 L7
  WAB EN9 ...147 M8
Labworth Rd CVI SS8 ...320 F3
Lacewing CI PLSTW E13 ...307 K7
  RIPS/CAP IP9 ...53 K5
Lacey Dr BCTR RM8 ...287 M8
Lacey St BETH E2 ...17 J5
Lacey's Wy CBS CB2 ...22 C4
Lackmore Rd EN EN1 ...232 D5
Lacon Rd RIPW IP8 ...46 F3
Ladbroke Dr COLS CO2 ...129 K2
Ladbrooke Rd RCOS CO16 ...159 G7
Ladell CI COLW CO3 ...128 D2
Ladram CI SOS SS1 ...302 F5
Ladram Rd SOS SS1 ...302 E5
Ladram Wy SOS SS1 ...302 E4
Ladyfields LOU IG10 ...250 E4
Lady La CHLM/GWD CM2 ...5 J7
  IP IP1 ...16 C4
Ladyshot HLW CM20 ...188 C3
Ladysmith Av EHAM E6 ...308 B6
  GNTH/NBYPK IG2...287 G5
  RCOLE CO7 ...156 B6
Ladysmith Wy LAIN SS15 *...277 J4
Ladywell La CHLM/GWD CM2 ...210 A4
Ladywell Prospect
  SBF/HAD SS7 ...279 G5
Ladywell St SRTFD E15 ...307 J3
Ladywood Rd IPNE IP4 ...49 H6
Lagado Ms BERM/RHTH SE16...322 A4
Lagonda Av BARK/HLT IG6 ...269 L1
Lagonda Drive IP IP1 ...47 H3
Laindon Common Rd
  BCAYW CM12 ...258 C6
Laindon Link LAIN SS15 ...2 B8
Laindon Rd BCAYW CM12 ...258 D5
Laindon West LAIN SS15 ...276 B5
Laird Av CDW/CHF RM16 ...331 G1
Lake Av BCAYW CM12 ...258 D2
  COS CO15 ...6 A5
  RAIN RM13 ...312 A6
Lake CI BCTR RM8 ...288 A8
Lakedale Rd
  WOOL/PLUM SE18 ...325 H8
Lake Dr HOO/HM ME3 ...339 M7
  SBF/HAD SS7 ...280 B7
Lakefields CI RAIN RM13 ...312 A6
Lake Gdns DAGE RM10 ...310 H1
Lake House Rd WAN E11 ...285 K8
Lakeland CI CHIG IG7 ...254 B7
Lake Ri ROM RM1 ...289 J1
  WTHM RM20 ...317 K7
Lake Rd CHDH RM6 ...288 A4
  DAGW RM9 ...310 E2
  LEY E10 ...284 E5
  WAB EN9 ...201 M7
Lakeside BCAYW CM12 ...258 D1
  RAIN RM13 ...311 B6
  SBN/FI SS3 ...303 G1
Lakeside Av REDBR IG4 ...286 A2
  THMD SE28 ...325 K4
Lakeside CI CHIG IG7 ...269 D1
Lakeside Crs BRW CM14 ...256 A6
  CVI SS8 * ...299 G8
  CHTY IP2 ...53 K3
Lakeside Rd CHES/WCR EN8 ...216 D6
Lake Vw BCAYW CM12 ...258 D1
Lake Vw BOW E3 ...306 A6
Lake View Est BOW E3 * ...306 A6
Lake Wk COS CO15 ...6 A5
Lake Wy COS CO15 ...182 G1
Lakforth SUD CO10 ...43 G1
Lakin CI CHLM/GWD CM2 ...210 G1
Lamarsh HI BURES CO8 ...359 L2
Lamarsh Rd BURES CO8 ...359 K6
Lamb La TIL RM18 ...331 K5
Lamberhurst Rd BCTR RM8 ...288 B8
Lambert Cross SAFWN CB10 ...28 B6
Lambert Rd CAN/RD E16 ...323 L2
Lamberts La KESG IP5 ...49 H3
Lambert's Rd RCOLW CO6 ...103 G3
Lambeth CI IP IP1 ...47 L2
Lambeth Ms HOC/HUL SS5 *...263 M7
Lambeth Rd LOS SS9 ...282 B7
  SBF/HAD SS7 ...279 B7
Lambkins Wy WALTH E17 ...284 C2
Lamb La HSTD CO9 ...356 E10
Lambley Rd DAGW RM9 ...309 L3
Lambourn CI SBN/FI SS3 ...303 G3
Lambourne CVI SS8 * ...321 H6
Lambourne CI CHIG IG7 ...255 M5
  COLW CO3 ...128 A1
  COS CO15 ...6 C5
Lambourne Crs BSDN SS14 ...278 D4
  CHING E4 ...249 G5
  HCH RM12 ...266 A7
Lambourne Dr
  RBRW/HUT CM13 ...257 H2
Lambourne Gdns BARK IG11 ...309 G4
  CHING E4 ...249 G5
  HCH RM12 ...266 A7
Lambourne Hall Rd RCFD SS4 ...392 C12
Lambourne Rd BARK IG11 ...309 H4

CHIG IG7 ...269 J3
  GDMY/SEVK IG3 ...287 H7
  IP IP1 ...48 A1
  WAN E11 ...284 C1
Lamb's La North RAIN RM13 ...312 A3
Lamb's La South RAIN RM13 ...327 M1
Lambs Meadow WFD IG8 ...268 A3
  LEY E10 ...284 B7
Lammas Dr BRTR CM7 ...122 A1
Lammasmead BROX EN10 ...217 G3
Lammas Rd HOM E9 ...306 A4
  LEY E10 ...284 B7
Lammas Wy RCOLE CO7 ...130 C1
Lamont CI CHLM/GWD CM2 ...210 G1
Lamorna Av GVE DA12 ...338 E7
Lamorna CI WALTH E17 ...266 E7
Lampern CI BCAYW CM12 ...240 E4
Lampern Crs BCAYW CM12 ...240 E4
Lampern Ms BCAYW CM12 ...240 E4
Lampits HOD EN11 ...201 J4
Lampits HI SLH/COR SS17 ...295 J4
Lampits Hill Av SLH/COR SS17 ...295 K4
Lampits Rd SLH/COR SS17 ...295 K4
Lamplighters CI DART DA1 ...334 F4
  WAB EN9 ...234 B7
Lamport CI WOOL/PLUM SE18..324 C7
Lamson Rd RAIN RM13 ...135 K4
Lanark Rd IPNE IP4 ...49 G4
Lancaster Av BARK IG11 ...309 H4
  WAN E11 ...285 L2
Lancaster CI BRWN CM15 ...255 H5
Lancaster Crs SOS SS1 ...19 L5
Lancaster Dr HCH RM12 ...311 M2
  KESG IP5 ...51 L2
  LOU IG10 ...250 E7
  POP/IOD E14 ...322 F4
  VGE SS16 ...276 C8
Lancaster Gdns RAYL SS6 ...281 H3
  BSF CM23 ...138 C2
  RCOLW CO6 ...102 C3
Lancaster Gdns East COS CO15 ...7 L5
Lancaster Gdns West COS CO15 ...7 K5
Lancaster Rd BRWN CM15 ...255 H5
  EPP CM16 ...221 H4
  FSTGT E7 ...307 J4
  IPNE IP4 ...17 J5
  RAYL SS6 ...281 H4
  SUD CO10 ...43 G7
  WALTH E17 ...266 A8
  WAN E11 ...285 H5
Lancaster Wy BRTR CM7 ...121 H1
  BSF CM23 ...138 C2
  RCOLW CO6 ...102 C3
Lancelot Rd BARK/HLT IG6 ...269 H5
Lancer Wy BCAYW CM12 ...258 E2
Lancey CI CHARL SE7 ...324 F5
Lanchester Av COS CO15 ...182 C4
Lancing Av IPNE IP4 ...48 F6
Lancing Rd GNTH/NBYPK IG2...287 G5
  HARH RM3 ...272 A4
Landau Wy BROX EN10 ...217 G4
  ERITH DA8 ...328 A1
Land CI RCOS CO16 ...6 A1
Landermere BSDN SS14 ...278 A5
Landermere Rd RCOS CO16 ...135 K4
Landermere Vw RCOS CO16 *...135 K4
Lander Rd GRAYS RM17 ...331 G4
Landguard Rd FX IP11 ...11 G4
Landisdale RCHLM CM3 ...212 B6
Land La COL CO1 ...8 C3
Landmead CHES/WCR EN8 ...216 A1
Landons POP/IOD E14 ...322 D4
Landridge Dr EN EN1 ...232 C1
Landsburg Rd CVI SS8 ...299 G8
Landscape Rd WFD IG8 ...267 L6
Landsdown Rd SUD CO10 ...21 J8
Landseer Av CHING E4 ...266 B2
  IPSE IP3 ...54 F4
Landseer Av GVW DA11 ...337 G5
  MNPK E12 ...308 B2
Landseer Rd COLW CO3 ...106 B8
  IPSE IP3 ...54 F4
Landview Gdns CHONG CM5 ...382 K6
Landwick La BOC CM0 ...390 E10
Lane Av GRH DA9 ...335 M8
Lane End HLWE CM17 ...204 C7
Lanecroft Wy CHTY IP2 ...53 M4
Lane Rd RCOLW CO6 ...83 G7
Lanes Av GVW DA11 ...337 G5
Laneside Av RBRW RM8 ...288 C4
The Lane K/T/MI CO5 ...177 K6
  MGTR CO11 ...91 M7
Lanfranc Rd BOW E3 ...306 B6
Langdale BRTR CM77 ...120 D6
Langdale BCTR RM8 ...287 M6
  FX IP11 ...63 J1
Langdale Dr COLN CO4 ...107 L1
Langdale Gdns
  CHLM/GWD CM2 ...5 K2
  HCH RM12 ...311 K2
  PEND EN3 ...232 E5
Langdon Crs EHAM E6 ...308 D6
Langdon Rd EHAM E6 ...308 D6
  RAYL SS6 ...281 L6
Langdon Wy SLH/COR SS17 ...295 L8
Langemore Wy BCAYE CM11 ...258 G7
Langenhoe WICKW SS12 ...261 H1
Langenhoe Hall La
  K/T/MI CO5 ...153 K9
Langenhoe Pk K/T/MI CO5 ...153 L9
Langer Rd FX IP11 ...11 G6
Langfield CI WAB EN9 ...201 M8
Langford Br CHONG CM5 ...383 M9
Langford Rd SBF/HAD SS7 ...280 C5
Langford Gn
  RBRW/HUT CM13 ...256 F2
Langford Gv MAL CM9 ...198 D1
Langford Rd MAL CM9 ...198 C1
  WFD IG8 ...268 E5
  WIT CM8 ...197 M2
Langham CI BKHH IG9 ...268 A1
Langham Crs EMPK RM11 ...290 A4
Langham Dr GDMY/SEVK IG3...309 J1
Langham La COLN CO4 ...87 G5
Langham PI COLN CO4 ...107 L1
Langham Rd COLN CO4 ...87 G5
Langhorne Dr DAGE RM10 ...310 C2
Langland Gv SLH/COR SS17 ...317 L8
Langland Av BRTR CM7 ...355 D7
Langley Av BRTR CM7 ...11 G5
  HAR CO12 ...62 D8
  HARH RM3 ...272 A4
  LOS SS9 ...281 L6
  SOS SS1 ...19 M6
Langley Crs DAGW RM9 ...309 L3
Langley Dr BRW CM14 ...273 M2
  WAN E11 ...285 L2
Langley Gdns DAGW RM9 ...310 A4
Langley Gn WAB EN9 * ...201 M8
Langley HI BURES CO8 ...359 M6
Langleys VGE SS16 * ...3 G9

Langport Dr WOS/PRIT SS0 ...300 D1
Langside CI LAIN SS15 ...276 D5
Langston Rd LOU IG10 ...251 G4
Langstons FX IP11 ...62 C1
Langthorne Crs GRAYS RM17 ...330 F5
Langthorne Rd WAN E11 ...285 G6
Langton Av CHLM/WR CM1 ...193 H6
  EHAM E6 ...308 D7
Langton Rd HOD EN11 ...201 J1
Langton Wy CDW/CHF RM16...331 G1
Languidic CI SUD CO10 ...21 M9
Langwood FX IP11 ...62 C1
Langwood CI RAYL SS6 ...177 M6
Lanham Farm Rd BRTR CM77 ...122 A1
Lanham Green Rd
  BRTR CM77 ...122 D6
Lanhams PIT SS13 ...278 F5
Lanhams Ct PIT SS13 ...278 F5
Lanrick Rd POP/IOD E14 ...323 G2
Lanridge Rd ABYW SE2 ...326 A6
Lansbury Av BARK IG11 ...309 K4
  CHDH RM6 ...288 B5
Lansbury Crs GRAYS RM17 ...334 G7
Lansbury Gdns
  POP/IOD E14 * ...323 G2
Lansbury Rd PEND EN3 ...248 A1
Lansdown Av SBF/HAD SS7 ...281 G8
Lansdowne Av LOS SS9 ...300 C4
  K/T/MI CO5 ...149 M7
Lansdowne Dr RAYL SS6 ...280 F2
Lansdowne Ms CHARL SE7 ...324 A8
Lansdowne Rd CHING E4 ...266 D1
  FX IP11 ...63 G3
  GDMY/SEVK IG3 ...287 J6
  IPNE IP4 ...48 F8
  SWFD E18 ...285 K1
  WALTH E17 ...284 D4
  WAN E11 ...285 H5
Lansdowne Sq GVW DA11 ...337 J4
Lansdowne PI GVW DA11 ...337 G5
Lansdown Rd FSTGT E7 ...307 H4
  TIL RM18 ...331 J6
Lanterns P POP/IOD E14 ...322 D4
Lantern Ter SOS SS1 * ...19 L7
Lanthorn CI BROX EN10 ...200 A5
Lanvalley Rd COLW CO3 ...106 D7
Lapis CI GVE DA12 ...338 C6
Lappmark Rd CVI SS8 ...321 G1
Lapwater CI LOS SS9 ...299 M3
Lapwing Dr K/T/MI CO5 ...148 F2
  MAL CM9 ...198 F6
Lapwing Rd CHTY IP2 ...53 J2
Lapwing Ter FSTGT E7 ...308 K2
  WICKE SS11 ...259 H4
Larch CI COLN CO4 ...9 M4
  LAIN SS15 ...276 F4
Larchcroft CI IP IP1 ...48 A1
Larchcroft Rd IP IP1 ...47 M3
Larches Av EN EN1 ...232 C4
The Larches RCHLM CM3 ...195 H5
  SBF/HAD SS7 ...279 G5
Larch Gv CHLM/GWD CM2 ...209 M7
  RCOLW CO6 ...361 L8
  WIT CM8 ...171 H1
Larch Rd LEY E11 ...284 D7
Larch Wk MAL CM9 ...198 F6
Larch Wy GTDUN CM6 ...116 D4
Larchwood BSF CM23 ...138 C2
Larchwood Av CRW RM5 ...270 C5
Larchwood CI CHTY IP2 ...47 M1
  CRW RM5 ...270 C5
  LOS SS9 ...281 L6
Larchwood Gdns
  BRWN CM15 ...255 K6
Larke Ri WOS/PRIT SS0 ...301 G1
Larkfield CHIG IG7 ...269 J3
Larkfield RCFD SS4 ...283 G1
Larkfield Rd RCOLE CO7 ...133 G4
Larkfields GVW DA11 ...337 G5
Larkhill Av RCFD SS4 ...265 K3
Larkhill Ri IPNE IP4 ...49 H6
Lark Hill Rd RCFD SS4 ...265 J4
Larkhill Wy FX IP11 ...62 D8
Lark Ri RBRW/HUT CM13 ...256 F5
Lark Ri SUD CO10 ...21 J6
Larks CI HVHL CB9 ...34 F1
Larksfield Crs HAR CO12 ...14 E7
Larkshall Crs CHING E4 ...266 F3
Larkshall Rd CHING E4 ...266 F3
Lark's La RCHLM CM3 ...167 J3
Larkspur CI BSF CM23 ...138 C3
  SOCK/AV RM15 ...313 M1
  WIT CM8 ...171 H1
Larkspur Rd CHTY IP2 ...53 L2
Larks Ri HSTD CO9 ...12 K4
Larkswood CI RBRW/HUT CM13 ...256 F4
Larkswood HLWE CM17 ...204 B6
Larkswood Rd CHING E4 ...266 D2
  SLH/COR SS17 ...317 L8
Larkway FOS CO13 ...137 G2
Larmans Rd PEND EN3 ...232 E4
The Larneys FOS CO13 ...137 H2
Larsen Dr WAB EN9 ...233 J4
Larup Av CVI SS8 ...298 F8
La Salle CI CHTY IP2 ...16 A4
Lascelles CI BRWN CM15 ...255 H5
  WAN E11 ...285 G7
Lascelles Gdns RCFD SS4 ...264 E5
Lassell St GNWCH SE10 ...323 G8
Latchett Rd SWFD E18 ...267 K7
Latchetts Shaw VGE SS16 ...3 G9
Latchford PI CHIG IG7 ...269 J3
Latchingdon CI RAYL SS6 ...280 C2
Latchingdon Gdns WFD IG8 ...268 A3
Latchingdon Rd RCHLM CM3 ...230 C8
Latchmore Bank RBSF CM22 ...139 J2
Latham CI EHAM E6 ...324 A2
Lathcoates Crs
  CHLM/GWD CM2 ...210 B5
Lathom Rd EHAM E6 ...308 C4
Latimer Av EHAM E6 ...308 C4
Latimer Dr HCH RM12 ...290 A4
  LAIN SS15 ...276 C4
Latimer Rd FSTGT E7 ...307 L1
Lattice Av IPNE IP4 ...49 H6
Lattinford Br RIPS/CAP IP9 *...79 L4
Latton Gn HLWS CM18 ...204 A5
Latton Hall CI HLW CM20 ...188 C2
Latton House HLWS CM18 ...204 A5
Latton St HLW CM20 ...204 C1
Laud's CI FX IP11 ...62 D8
Launceston CI COLS CO2 ...129 H2
Launceston Rd COLS CO2 ...129 H2
Launch St POP/IOD E14 ...322 F4
Launder's La RAIN RM13 ...328 D1
Laundry Gdns SUD CO10 ...20 D5
Laundry La BRWN CM15 ...239 G5
  WAB EN9 ...218 A3
Laura CI WAN E11 ...285 L1
Laurel Av GVE DA12 ...337 M7
  HAR CO12 ...14 D7
  KESG IP5 ...49 M6
  WICKW SS12 ...260 F6

Laurel Cl BARK/HLT IG6 .....268 F5
COS CO15 .....159 L6
HVHL CB9 .....34 A4
LOS SS9 .....300 A5
RBRW/HUT CM13 .....256 F1
Laurel Ct RBRW/HUT CM13 * 256 F1
Laurel Crs ROMW/RG RM7 .....289 H4
Laurel Dr GTDUN CM6 .....116 E4
SOCK/AV RM15 .....314 A4
SUD CO10 .....42 M1
Laurel Gdns CHING E4 .....248 G1
Laurel Gv CHLM/GWD CM2 .....210 D4
Laurel-Hayes CHTY IP2 .....53 M2
The Laurels BRTR CM7 * 121 K2
RAYL SS6 .....281 J5
RCHLM CM3 .....245 G5
Laurel Wy SWFD E18 .....285 J2
Laurence Av WIT CM8 .....171 K5
Laurence Cl RCOLE CO7 .....109 J7
Laurie Ct RBRW/HUT CM1 .....208 A5
Lauriston Rd HOM E9 .....306 A1
Lavender Av MKCM15 .....255 L5
Lavender Cl BSF CM23 .....139 K7
CHESW EN7 .....216 A5
HARH RM3 .....272 A6
HLW CM20 .....13 K4
K/T/MI CO5 .....173 M1
SOCK/AV RM15 .....314 B3
WIT CM8 .....171 H4
Lavender Ct CHLM/WR CM1 .....194 C8
Lavender Dr BOC CM7 .....393 M2
Lavender Fld HVHL CB9 .....34 C8
Lavender Gv CHLM/GWD CM2 .....210 D4
Lavender Hl CHTY IP2 .....53 L7
Lavender Ms WOS/PRIT SS0 .....301 C2
Lavender Pl IG1 IG1 .....308 E2
Lavender Rd
BERM/RHTH SE16 .....322 B4
Lavender St SRTFD E15 .....307 H3
Lavender Wk COS CO15 .....182 D6
WICKW SS12 .....260 F6
Lavenham Cl RCOS CO16 .....182 E1
Lavenham Rd CHTY IP2 .....41 K8
The Lavers RAYL SS6 * 281 H2
Lavington St HOM E9 .....306 A1
Lavinia Rd DART DA1 .....334 E6
Lawford Cl HCH RM12 .....311 H4
Lawford La CHLM/WR CM1 .....208 A7
Lawless St POP/IOD E14 * 322 E3
Lawling Av MAL CM9 .....198 F4
Lawlinge Rd RCHLM CM5 .....231 L8
Lawn Av SOSN SS2 .....301 J4
Lawn Cha WIT CM8 .....171 J4
Lawn Farm Gv CHDH RM6 .....288 C1
Lawn House Cl POP/IOD E14 .....322 F1
Lawn La CHLM/WR CM1 .....194 A8
Lawn Rd GVW DA11 .....336 F4
Lawns Cl K/T/MI CO5 .....177 M6
Lawnscourt SBF/HAD SS7 .....279 K5
Lawns Crs HART RM17 .....331 G5
The Lawns Dr BROX EN10 .....201 L1
Lawns Pl HART RM17 * 331 G5
The Lawns BRW CM14 * 256 D4
CHING E4 .....266 D6
CHLM/WR CM1 .....194 C8
IPNE IP4 .....49 M5
SBF/HAD SS7 .....279 M6
Lawns Wy CRW RM5 .....270 F6
Lawn Wy FX IP11 .....62 D8
Lawrance Gdns
CHESW/CR EN8 .....216 A6
Lawrance Sq GVW DA11 * 337 G5
SBW CM21 .....162 F4
WALTH E17 .....266 A4
WARE SG12 .....185 K6
Lawrence Crs DAGE RM10 .....288 D2
Lawrence Gdns TIL RM18 .....331 L6
Lawrence Hl CHING E4 .....266 D1
Lawrence Moorings
SBW CM21 .....163 G8
Lawrence Rd EHAM E6 .....308 B5
GPK RM2 .....289 L1
PIT SS13 .....279 J3
PLSTW E13 .....307 H1
Lawrence St CAN/RD E16 .....323 J1
IL IG1 .....309 G2
Laws Cl SAFWS CB11 .....30 A2
Law's Drift KIR/NAC IP10 .....61 K1
Lawshall Hl RCOLW CO6 .....126 F2
Lawson Cl CAN/RD E16 .....323 M2
IL IG1 .....309 G2
Lawson Gdns DART DA1 .....334 A6
Lawson Rd DART DA1 .....334 A6
Lawton Rd BOW E3 .....306 B7
LEY E10 .....284 F6
LOU IG10 .....250 E3
Laxton Gv FOS SS13 * 136 D4
Laxton Rd RCOLE CO7 .....131 J4
Laxtons SLH/COR SS17 .....317 G2
The Laxtons RCFD SS4 .....283 L3
Layer Breton Hl COLS CO2 .....151 K4
Layer Rd COLS CO2 .....128 E3
HVHL CB9 .....34 B6
K/T/MI CO5 .....153 H1
K/T/MI CO5 .....176 A5
Laymarsh Cl BELV DA17 .....326 C6
Layzell Cft SUD CO10 .....45 M5
Leabank Sq HOM E9 .....306 A2
Lea Bridge Rd CLPT E5 .....284 A7
Leach Cl CHLM/GWD CM2 .....210 E6
Lea Cl BRTR CM7 .....122 B8
BSF CM23 .....115 J8
Leadale Av CHING E4 .....266 D7
Leader Av MNPK E12 .....308 D2
Leaforis Rd CHESW EN7 .....216 A5
Leafy Wy RBRW/HUT CM13 .....257 G4
Lea Gv BSF CM23 .....115 J8
MAL CM9 .....197 G4
Lea Hall Gdns LEY E10 * 284 F6
Lea Hall Rd LEY E10 .....284 D6
Lea La WIT CM8 .....172 C4
Lea Main Cl COLN CO4 .....108 C6
Leamington Av WALTH E17 .....284 D6
Leamington Gdns
GDMY/SEVK IG3 .....287 H3
Leamington Rd HARH RM3 .....272 A6
HOC/HUL SS5 .....264 C6
SOS SS1 .....19 L2
Leamouth Rd EHAM E6 .....324 C1
POP/IOD E14 .....323 G2
Leapingwell Cl
CHLM/GWD CM2 .....210 D2
Lea Rd CDW/CHF RM16 .....331 K4
HOM E9 .....201 K4
SBF/HAD SS7 .....279 M8
WAB EN9 .....284 F3
Learoyd Gdns EHAM E6 .....324 D4
Leas Cl WOS/PRIT SS0 .....300 A5
Leas Gdns WOS/PRIT SS0 .....300 A5
Lea Side K/T/MI CO5 .....178 A7
Leas La COLS CO2 .....127 M7
Leasowes Rd LEY E10 .....284 E6
Lea Rd COLS CO2 .....128 C4
COS CO15 .....6 C6
The Leas BOC CM0 .....393 M7
FOS SS13 .....137 G4

ING CM4 .....239 K3
UPMR RM14 .....291 G5
WOS/PRIT SS0 .....300 F6
The Leasway BRW CM14 .....256 C4
CDW/CHF RM16 .....314 F8
RAYL SS6 .....280 E5
UPMR RM14 .....290 F3
WICKW SS12 .....260 F6
The Leasway WOS/PRIT SS0 .....300 C1
Leat Cl SBW CM21 .....163 G6
Leathart Cl HCH RM12 .....311 L4
Leatherbottle Gn
ERITHM SE18 .....326 C6
Leatherbottle Hi ING CM4 .....241 K2
Leatherdale St WCHPL E1 * 306 H5
Leather Gdns SRTFD E15 .....307 H5
Leather La EMPK RM11 .....290 H4
HSTD CO9 .....346 B12
HVHL CB9 .....34 B6
Leather Rd BERM/RHTH SE16 .....322 B4
Leather St WAP E1W 322 A7
Lea Valley Rd EN EN3 .....248 D7
Lea Valley Wk WAB EN9 .....217 H4
WARE SG12 .....185 H3
Leaview WAB EN9 .....233 J3
Lea Wy BCAYW CM12 .....258 E5
Le Cateau Barracks COLS CO2 * 8 A7
Le Cateau Rd COLS CO2 .....8 B7
Lechmere Av WFD IG8 .....267 M8
Lechmere Av CHIG IG7 .....268 A8
Leda Av PEND EN3 .....248 A1
Lede Rd CVI SS8 .....320 E1
Lee Av CHDH RM6 .....288 B4
Lee Chapel La VGE SS16 .....294 F2
Leech's La RCOLE CO7 .....107 L1
Lee Cl WALTH E17 .....266 A7
WARE SG12 .....185 K5
Lee Conservancy Rd HOM E9 .....306 C2
Leecon Wy RCFD SS4 .....283 C2
Leeds Cl IL IG1 .....287 C6
Leeford Cl CHLM/WR CM1 .....193 J7
Lee Gardens Av EMPK RM11 .....290 F4
Lee Cl WALTH E17 .....268 F1
Lee Lotts SBN/FI SS3 .....303 K1
Lee Park Wy UED N18 .....60 B1
Lee Rd HAR CO12 .....15 G9
IPSE IP3 .....54 E2
PIT SS13 .....279 J7
Lee Vls SOS SS1 * 19 K7
Lee Wk VGE SS16 .....2 F8
Leeward Ct FX IP11 * 62 F8
Leeward Rd RCHLM CM3 .....245 H6
Leeway DEPT SE8 .....322 C8
The Leeway RCHLM CM3 .....212 C6
Lee Woottens La VGE SS16 * 2 F5
Lee Lea La CHLM/WR CM1 .....143 G4
Lefevre Wk BOW E3 .....306 C5
Leggatt Dr RIPW IP8 .....46 F3
Leggatt Rd SRTFD E15 .....306 F1
Legg St CHLM/WR CM1 .....5 H2
Leghorn Rd
WOOL/PLUM SE18 .....325 G8
Legions Wy BSF CM23 .....139 M1
Legion Ter BOW E3 .....306 D5
Legon Av ROMW/RG RM7 .....288 F6
Legra Av HOD EN11 .....201 J3
Leicester Av CHTY IP2 .....53 L4
Leicester Cl
COL CO1 .....8 A6
COS CO15 .....182 C4
Leicester Ct WIT CM8 * 147 G1
Leicester Gdns
GDMY/SEVK IG3 .....287 H5
WAN E11 .....285 L3
Leige Av VGE SS16 .....298 D7
Leigham Court Dr LOS SS9 .....300 C1
Leighams Rd RCHLM CM3 .....228 B8
Leigh Av REDBR IG4 .....286 A2
Leigh Beck La CVI SS8 .....321 H3
Leigh Beck Rd CVI SS8 .....321 J2
Leigh Cliff Rd LOS SS9 .....300 C5
Leighcroft Gdns LOS SS9 .....300 F1
Leigh Dr HARH RM3 .....272 A4
Leigh Fells PIT SS13 .....278 F7
Leighfields Av SBF/HAD SS7 .....280 B2
Leighfields Av LOS SS9 .....282 A7
Leighfields Rd LOS SS9 .....282 A7
Leigh Gdns LOS SS9 .....299 M4
Leigh Hall Rd LOS SS9 .....300 C4
Leigh Hts SBF/HAD SS7 .....299 J6
Leigh Hill Cl LOS SS9 .....300 B5
Leigh Hill LOS SS9 .....300 B5
Leighlands Rd RCHLM CM3 .....245 H6
Leigh Park Cl LOS SS9 .....299 M4
Leigh Park Rd LOS SS9 .....300 A5
Leigh Rd CVI SS8 .....320 E3
EHAM E6 .....308 D4
GVW DA11 .....337 J8
LEY E10 .....284 C5
LOS SS9 .....300 D4
Leighs Rd RCHLM CM3 .....168 D3
Leighton Av LOS SS9 .....300 C3
Leighton Rd IPSE IP3 .....54 F5
Leighton Gdns TIL RM18 .....331 L5
Leighton Rd IPSE IP3 .....54 F5
SBF/HAD SS7 .....279 M6
Leighton Sq IPSE IP3 .....54 F5
Leigh View Dr LOS SS9 .....300 C1
Leighville Gv LOS SS9 .....300 A4
Leighwood Av LOS SS9 .....300 A8
Leinster Rd LOS SS9 .....300 H6
Leiston Rd HVHL CB9 .....34 B6
Leith Park Rd GVW DA11 .....337 H6
Leitrim Av SBN/FI SS3 .....302 F7
Lekoe Rd CVI SS8 .....298 C2
Lely Rd IPSE IP3 .....54 E5
Lemna Rd WAN E11 .....285 H1
Lemons Hi RIPS/CAP IP9 .....364 A4
Lena Kennedy Cl CHING E4 .....266 C5
Lenham Wy PIT SS13 .....278 F7
Lennard Av SOCK/AV RM15 .....329 J2
Lennox Cl ROM RM1 .....289 J6
Lennox Dr WICKW SS12 .....261 J8
Lennox Gdns IL IG1 .....286 C6
Lennox Rd GVW DA11 .....337 J5
WALTH E17 .....284 D1
Lennox Rd East GVW DA11 .....337 K5
Lensbury Wy ABYW SE2 .....326 C4
Lensbury Cl CHESW/CR EN8 .....216 C6
Lens Rd FSTGT E7 .....307 K1
Lenthall Av GRAYS RM17 .....330 E2
Lenthall Rd LOU IG10 .....251 J4
Lenthorp Rd GNWCH SE10 .....323 J8
Lenton St WOOL/PLUM SE18 .....325 J7
Leonard Av ROMW/RG RM7 .....289 H4
SWCM DA10 .....336 F5
Leonard Cl CHING E4 .....266 C5
FSTGT E7 * 307 K1
VGE SS16 .....295 G1
WOS/PRIT SS0 .....18 D1
Leonard St CAN/RD E16 .....324 C1

Leonard Wy BRW CM14 .....273 H3
Leon Dr VGE SS16 .....296 A3
Leopold Cl COS CO15 * 99 H4
Leopold Rd FX IP11 .....11 L5
IPNE IP4 .....48 E3
WALTH E17 .....284 D3
Leopold St BOW E3 .....322 C1
Les Bois COLS CO2 .....128 D8
Leslie Ct COLN CO4 .....9 M3
Leslie Dr LOS SS9 .....282 A7
Leslie Gdns RAYL SS6 .....281 J5
Leslie Pk BOC CM0 .....299 H8
Leslie Rd CAN/RD E16 .....323 L2
IPSE IP3 .....55 J4
RAYL SS6 .....281 H4
WAN E11 .....307 G2
Lesney Gdns RCFD SS4 .....283 G2
Lessington Av
ROMW/RG RM7 .....288 F4
Lessness Pk BELV DA17 .....326 C8
Lester Av SRTFD E15 .....307 H8
Leston Cl RAIN RM13 .....311 J7
Lettice Martin Cft CBS CB2 .....22 A4
Letton Cl RIPS/CAP IP9 .....58 D4
Lettons Cha RCHLM CM3 .....245 G1
Leucha Rd WALTH E17 .....284 A3
Leven Cl CHES/WCR EN8 .....232 E3
Leven Dr CHES/WCR EN8 .....232 E3
Leven Rd POP/IOD E14 .....322 F1
Levens Wy BRTR CM7 .....120 F7
Lever La RCFD SS4 .....283 H3
Lever Sq CDW/CHF RM16 .....331 K5
Leverton Wy WAB EN9 .....233 K4
Leveson Rd CDW/CHF RM16 .....331 J1
Levett Gdns IG11 .....309 J1
Levett Rd BARK IG11 .....309 H1
SLH/COR SS17 .....317 H3
Levine Gdns BARK IG11 .....310 A6
Levington La KIR/NAC IP10 .....56 G1
Levington Rd FX IP11 .....11 L6
IPSE IP3 .....54 F1
KIR/NAC IP10 .....60 B1
Lewes Cl GRAYS RM17 .....330 D5
SOSN SS2 .....301 K2
Lewes Rd HARH RM3 .....272 A3
SOSN SS2 .....301 K2
Lewes Wy RBRW/HUT CM13 .....256 E6
Lewin Pl RCHLM CM3 .....195 H5
Lewis Av WALTH E17 .....266 D7
Lewis Cl BRWN CM15 .....256 C5
Lewis Crs CBE/LIN CB1 .....23 M4
Lewis Dr CHLM/GWD CM2 .....209 L7
Lewis La RIPS/CAP IP9 .....364 A1
Lewis Rd EMPK RM11 .....290 F4
SWCM DA10 .....336 M4
Lewis Wy DAGE RM10 .....310 E3
Lexden Rd CHDH RM6 .....287 L4
Lexden Gv COLW CO3 .....106 C7
Lexden Ms COLW CO3 .....106 C6
Lexden Rd COLW CO3 .....106 D6
RCOLW CO6 .....106 A1
Lexden Ter WAB EN9 * 233 K4
Lexington Wy UPMR RM14 .....291 H4
Leybourne Dr CHLM/WR CM1 .....194 A5
Leybourne Rd WAN E11 .....285 J6
Leyburn Cl WALTH E17 .....284 D1
Leyburn Crs HARH RM3 .....272 B6
Leyburn Rd HARH RM3 .....272 B6
Leyes Rd CAN/RD E16 .....323 M3
Ley Fld RBSF CM22 .....377 K2
Leyfields PIT SS13 .....278 F7
Leyfields RCFD SS4 .....283 H3
Leyland Av CHES/WCR EN8 .....216 D7
Leyland Gdns WFD IG8 .....267 J3
Leys Av DAGE RM10 .....310 E3
Leys Dr RCOS CO16 .....158 F4
Leyside BRTR CM7 .....120 F5
Leysings VGE SS16 .....2 A9
Leyspring Rd WAN E11 .....285 J6
Leys Rd RCOLE CO7 .....130 F2
Leys Rd East PEND EN3 .....248 B1
The Leys CHLM/GWD CM2 .....194 C8
VGE SS16 .....276 F7
Leyton Ct LOS SS9 * 159 J5
Leyton Gra LEY E10 .....284 D7
Leyton Green Rd LEY E10 .....284 F6
Leyton Park Rd LEY E10 .....284 F7
Leyton Rd SRTFD E15 .....306 F2
Leywick St SRTFD E15 .....307 H6
Leywood Cl BRTR CM7 .....121 J8
Libra Rd BOW E3 .....306 C3
PLSTW E13 .....307 K6
Lichfield Cl CHLM/WR CM1 * 209 H1
COL CO1 .....8 A5
Lichfield Rd BCTR RM8 .....309 L1
BOW E3 .....306 D3
EHAM E6 .....308 A7
WFD IG8 .....267 H3
The Lichfields BSDN SS14 .....278 C6
Lichfield Ter UPMR RM14 .....291 H7
Lichfield Wy BROX EN10 .....201 H7
Liddington Rd SRTFD E15 .....307 J3
Liddon Rd PLSTW E13 .....307 K5
Liden Cl WALTH E17 .....284 D1
Lidgate Ct FX IP11 .....10 D7
Lie Field CI BRTR CM7 * 122 A2
Lieutenant Ellis Wy
CHESW EN7 .....232 A1
Lifchild Cl WIT CM8 .....171 K6
Liffler Rd WOOL/PLUM SE18 .....325 J5
Lifstan Wy SOS SS1 .....302 B6
Lighterman Ms WCHPL E1 .....322 A2
Lighterman's Rd
POP/IOD E14 .....322 D5
Lilac Av CVI SS8 .....298 C4
EN EN1 .....60 B1
RCOS CO16 .....181 C7
WICKW SS12 .....260 F7
Lilac Cl BRWN CM15 .....255 L5
CHESW EN7 .....232 C4
CHING E4 .....266 C5
CHLM/GWD CM2 .....209 M7
Lilac Ct RCOLE CO7 .....130 D3
Lilac Rd HOD EN11 .....201 J2
The Lilacs SOSN SS2 * 19 G1
Lilbourne Dr BCAYE CM11 .....258 F4
Lilford Cl CHLM/WR CM13 .....209 H1
IP IP1 .....48 A1

The Lillies BRTR CM7 .....99 L4
Lilliput Rd ROMW/RG RM7 .....289 G5
Lillyville Wk RAYL SS6 .....281 K4
Lily Cl CHLM/WR CM1 .....194 C7
Lily Rd LEY E10 .....284 D6
Limbourne Av BCTR RM8 .....288 A5
Limbourne Dr MAL CM9 .....198 F4
Limburg Rd CVI SS8 .....320 A1
Lime Av COLN CO4 .....9 M1
GVW DA11 .....337 G5
HAR CO12 .....14 F8
RBRW/HUT CM13 .....256 C6
UPMR RM14 .....312 D1
Limebrook Wy MAL CM9 .....214 B6
Lime Cl BKHH IG9 .....268 A5
COS CO15 .....6 A6
ROMW/RG RM7 .....288 F5
SOCK/AV RM15 .....313 M7
WIT CM8 .....147 K5
Limecroft Cl IP IP1 .....47 L3
Limefields SAFWN CB10 .....29 K8
Lime Gv BARK/HLT IG6 .....269 J5
BRWN CM15 .....383 B12
SUD CO10 .....44 F8
Limeharbour POP/IOD E14 .....322 E6
Limehouse POP/IOD E14 * 322 D3
Limehouse Cswy
POP/IOD E14 .....322 C3
Limehouse Link POP/IOD E14 .....322 B3
Limehouse Link (Tunnel)
POP/IOD E14 .....322 C3
Limekiln La STSD SG24 .....115 K3
Lime Pl LAIN SS15 .....276 F4
Limerick Gdns UPMR RM14 .....291 J5
Lime Rd SBF/HAD SS7 .....298 C5
Limes Av CHIG IG7 .....268 A5
RIPW IP8 .....47 L7
WAN E11 .....285 L2
Limes Ct BSF CM23 .....139 J4
Limes Dr CHLM/GWD CM2 .....225 J3
Limeslade Cl SLH/COR SS17 * 295 H4
Limes Rd CHES/WCR EN8 .....232 E2
The Limes CBS CB2 .....22 A4
CHLM/GWD CM2 .....225 J3
COS CO15 * 7 G7
EMPK RM11 .....290 G4
HSTD CO9 .....80 B6
ING CM4 .....239 M1
KESG IP5 .....49 J4
PUR RM19 .....328 J5
RAYL SS6 .....262 A4
RBRW/HUT CM13 .....256 F5
RCOLE CO7 .....89 J7
SUD CO10 .....42 F6
Limestone Wk ABYW SE2 .....326 A3
Lime St RCOLE CO7 .....156 C6
WALTH E17 .....284 D1
Limetree Av SBF/HAD SS7 .....297 L3
Limetree Rd CVI SS8 .....321 G2
Lime Wk CHLM/GWD CM2 .....209 M7
SRTFD E15 * 307 H3
Lime Wy BOC CM0 .....393 M7
Limewood Cl WALTH E17 .....284 D1
Lincefield VGE SS16 .....294 E2
Lincoln Av COS CO15 .....182 A5
ROMW/RG RM7 .....289 H7
Lincoln Cha SOSN SS2 .....302 A2
Lincoln Cl BSF CM23 .....138 A2
EMPK RM11 .....290 D3
IP IP1 .....48 A2
Lincoln Est BOW E3 .....306 D4
Lincoln Gdns IL IG1 .....286 A6
Lincoln La RCOLW CO6 .....86 F4
Lincoln Rd BSDN SS14 .....278 D6
FSTGT E7 .....307 H3
PLSTW E13 .....307 J4
RCFD SS4 .....283 J5
SWFD E18 .....267 J3
Lincolns Fld EPP CM16 .....220 F7
Lincolns La BRW CM14 .....254 F6
Lincoln St WAN E11 .....285 H1
Lincoln Ter FX IP11 .....11 J4
Lincoln Wy COL CO1 .....8 A5
CVI SS8 .....320 B1
RAYL SS6 .....262 A4
Linda Gdns BCAYW CM12 .....258 E5
Lindbergh Rd IPSE IP3 .....55 J4
Linden Cl CHESW EN7 .....216 C5
CHLM/GWD CM2 .....209 M6
MCTR CO11 .....90 F2
PUR RM19 .....334 F1
RAYL SS6 .....262 A5
SBF/HAD SS7 .....279 M6
Linden Dr COS CO15 .....181 L7
Linden Leas SBF/HAD SS7 .....279 M8
Linden Ri BRW CM14 .....256 A4
Linden Rd SBF/HAD SS7 .....279 M8
The Lindens BRTR CM7 .....121 K2
CBS CB2 .....22 A4
COLW CO3 .....106 C6
ING CM4 .....241 M1
LOU IG10 .....250 C5
VGE SS16 .....276 F7
WAB EN9 * 233 K4
WALTH E17 * 284 D3
Linden St ROMW/RG RM7 .....289 G4
Linden Wy CVI SS8 .....320 B1
Linde Rd CVI SS8 .....320 E1
Lindfield Rd HARH RM3 .....272 A3
Lindisfield St POP/IOD E14 .....322 D2
Lindhill Cl PEND EN3 .....248 B1
Lindhurst Dr BCAYE CM11 .....259 H4
Lindisfarne Av SOS SS9 .....300 D8
GVE DA12 .....338 C1
Lindisfarne Ct WICKW SS12 .....261 K8
Lindisfarne Md BCTR RM8 .....306 B1
Lindisfarne Rd BCTR RM8 .....287 B1
Lindley Rd LEY E10 .....284 F7
Lindon Rd WICKE SS11 .....260 F7
Lindsay Pl CHESW EN7 .....216 A2
Lindsell La BSDN SS14 .....278 B5
GTDUN CM6 .....95 J2
Lindsey Av SUD CO10 .....21 L7
Lindsey Cl BRW CM14 .....256 C4
Lindsey Gn PIT SS13 .....278 D5
Lindsey Rd BCTR RM8 .....287 M8
Lindsey St EPP CM16 .....205 L5
IPNE IP4 .....49 H6
SBN/FI SS3 .....303 K1
Lindsey St BRW CM14 .....254 D8
BSF CM23 .....115 J8
IPNE IP4 .....49 H6
Linford Cl HLWW/ROY CM19 .....203 G5
Linford Dr BSDN SS14 .....278 C6
Linford Ms MAL CM9 .....214 B6
Linford Rd HLWW/ROY CM19 .....203 G5
WALTH E17 .....266 F5
Lingcroft VGE SS16 .....276 F7
Lingfield Av UPMR RM14 .....290 K2
Lingfield Cl RCFD SS4 .....283 J3
Lingfield Rd GVW DA11 .....337 H5
IP IP1 .....48 A1

Lingmere Cl CHIG IG7 .....268 F5
Ling Rd CAN/RD E16 .....323 K6
Lingside KESG IP5 .....50 E7
Ling's La RIPS/CAP IP9 .....365 M10
Lingwood Cl RCHLM CM3 .....212 B6
Link Av BSF CM23 .....139 G1
CBS CB2 .....22 C1
COS CO15 .....6 D8
CVI SS8 .....320 B1
DAGW RM9 .....310 G6
HSTD CO9 .....80 B6
RAYL SS6 .....281 G2
RCOS CO16 * 181 L7
RIPS/CAP IP9 .....58 D4
RIPS/CAP IP9 .....66 E1
SLH/COR SS17 .....317 G2
Links Av FX IP11 .....62 F7
GPK RM2 .....271 L8
HERT/BAY SG13 .....184 C2
Links Dr CHLM/GWD CM2 .....209 H8
Links KESG IP5 .....49 K6
Linkside CHIG IG7 .....268 F4
Links Rd BSF CM23 .....139 K3
RCOS CO16 .....181 L7
WFD IG8 .....267 K4
The Links BCAYW CM12 .....258 E5
CHES/WCR EN8 .....216 E4
WALTH E17 .....284 B2
Linksway LOS SS9 .....299 M1
Links Wy SBF/HAD SS7 .....299 J5
The Link PEND EN3 .....248 B1
RIPS/CAP IP9 .....66 E1
Linkway BCTR RM8 .....309 M1
BSDN SS14 .....276 E6
Link Wy BSF CM23 .....138 E3
EMPK RM11 .....290 B6
Linkway Rd BRW CM14 .....273 G6
Linley Cl FX IP11 .....333 G6
Linley Gdns COS CO15 .....16 E7
Linnet Cl ED N9 .....248 A8
SBN/FI SS3 .....303 H4
SEE28 .....325 M4
Linnet Dr CHLM/GWD CM2 .....209 M7
SBF/HAD SS7 .....297 M3
Linnet Rd CHTY IP2 .....53 J1
Linnets COS CO15 .....159 J7
VGE SS16 .....295 G2
Linnett Cl CHING E4 .....266 F3
Linnetts La HVHL CB9 .....344 A1
Linnet Wy PUR RM19 .....328 J8
RCOLE CO7 .....133 G5
Linropping Av CVI SS8 .....320 J1
Linsdell Rd BARK IG11 .....308 F5
Linstead Cl RCOS CO16 .....182 D1
Linton Cl CHARL SE7 .....323 H4
SAFWS CB11 .....30 A1
Linton Ct ROM RM1 .....271 H8
Linton Gdns EHAM E6 .....324 B2
Linton Rd BARK IG11 .....308 F4
CBE/LIN CB1 .....23 M3
CBE/LIN CB1 .....26 E1
CBE/LIN CB1 .....32 C2
IPNE IP4 .....49 J7
The Lintons CHLM/GWD CM2 .....210 F1
Linwood SBW CM21 * 162 F2
Lionel Hurst Cl SUD CO10 .....45 M4
Lionel Rd CVI SS8 .....320 D2
Lionfield Ter CHLM/WR CM1 .....5 H1
Lion Hl SLH/COR SS17 .....318 A1
Lion La BCAYW CM12 .....258 D5
Lion Meadow HVHL CB9 .....344 B6
Lion St IP IP1 .....16 E4
Lion Wk COL CO1 * 8 A5
Liphook Cl HCH RM12 .....311 J1
Lippits Hi VGE SS16 .....294 F2
Lippitts Hl LOU IG10 .....249 H2
Lisa Cl BCAYW CM12 .....240 F1
Lisbon Cl WALTH E17 .....266 C8
Lisle Cl GVE DA12 .....338 C2
Lisle Pl GRAYS RM17 .....330 D2
Lisle Rd COLS CO2 .....107 G4
Lister Av HARH RM3 .....272 A4
Lister Rd BRTR CM7 .....121 J1
IP IP1 .....47 L4
TIL RM18 .....331 M6
WAN E11 .....285 H6
Lister Tye CHLM/GWD CM2 .....5 K9
Listonhall Cha HSTD CO9 .....356 C12
Liston La SUD CO10 .....42 E2
Liston Wy WFD IG8 .....267 M6
Listowel Rd DAGE RM10 .....288 D8
Litchborough Pk RCHLM CM3 .....212 C5
Litchfield Rd SUD CO10 .....42 F7
Litchfield Av SRTFD E15 * 307 H3
Little Acres WARE SG12 .....184 C1
Little Aston Rd HARH RM3 .....272 A3
Little Baddow Rd MAL CM9 .....212 F2
RCHLM CM3 .....212 B6
Little Bakers WOTN CO14 .....137 K2
Little Belhus Cl
SOCK/AV RM15 .....313 K4
Little Bentley BSDN SS14 .....3 H4
Little Bentley Rd RCOLE CO7 .....111 L4
Little Berry La VGE SS16 .....294 D1
Little Braxted La WIT CM8 .....148 A8
Little Brays HLWS CM18 .....204 B3
Little Bromley Rd RCOLE CO7 .....89 C7
RCOLE CO7 .....110 B2
RCOLE CO7 .....111 G4
Littlebrook Gdns
CHES/WCR EN8 .....216 A6
Littlebrook Manor Wy
DART DA1 .....334 D7
Little Brook Rd
HLWW/ROY CM19 .....202 D1
PIT SS13 .....278 D5
Littlebury Gdns COLS CO2 .....129 H1
Littlebury Gn PIT SS13 .....278 D5
Littlebury Green Rd
SAFWS CB11 .....351 K2
Little Cattins
HLWW/ROY CM19 .....203 G5
Little Charlton PIT SS13 .....278 H4
Little Chishill Rd ROY SG8 .....348 H11
Little Chittock BSDN SS14 .....278 C6
Little Clacton Rd ROS CO13 .....136 D2
RCOS CO16 .....159 G3
Littlecotes COLN CO4 .....107 G4
Littlecroft RCHLM CM3 .....245 G7
Little Croft St CHTY IP2 .....16 E7
Littlefield Rd COLS CO2 .....128 F4
Little Flds RCHLM CM3 .....245 J5
Little Foxes HERT/BAY SG13 .....200 D3
Little Fretches LOS SS9 .....300 D8
Little Friday Rd CHING E4 .....267 G1

Little Garth PIT SS13 .....278 D8
Little Gaynes Gdns
  UPMR RM14 .....312 E1
Little Gaynes La UPMR RM14 .....312 D1
Little Gearies BARK/HLT IG6 .....312 D2
Little Gerpins Rd UPMR RM14 .....312 C5
Little Gipping St IP IP1 .....16 D4
Little & Great Sir Hughes La
  CHLM/GWD CM2 .....226 D3
Little Gregories La EPP CM16 .....235 L5
Little Grove Fld
  HLWW/ROY CM19 .....12 E7
Little Gulls RIPS/CAP IP9 .....58 C4
Little Gypps Cl CVI SS8 .....320 C5
Little Gypps Rd CVI SS8 .....320 C2
Little Harrods WOTN CO14 .....137 K2
Little Hayes Cha
  RCHLM CM3 .....245 M4
Little Hays LOS SS9 .....281 L7
Little Heath CHDH RM6 .....287 L2
  RBSF CM22 .....378 A4
Little Horkesley Rd
  RCOLW CO6 .....85 K1
Littlehurst La LAIN SS15 .....277 L3
Little Hyde Cl HSTD CO9 .....346 B11
Little Hyde La CM4 .....223 M1
Little Hyde Rd HSTD CO9 .....346 B11
Little Ilford La MNPK E12 .....308 C1
Little Kingston VGE SS16 .....295 G3
Little Larchmount
  SAFWS CB11 .....30 A1
Little Laver Rd CHONG CM5 .....380 G6
  HLWE CM17 .....378 F11
Little London Hi BRTR CM7 .....354 C9
Little London La MAL CM9 .....196 F8
Little Lullaway LAIN SS15 .....2 B4
Little Meadow
  CHLM/WR CM1 .....208 D4
Little Mdw MAL CM9 .....213 H7
Littlemoor Rd IL IG1 .....287 G8
Littlemore Rd ABYW SE2 .....325 K5
Little Nell CHLM/WR CM1 .....193 H6
Little Norsey Rd BCAYW CM12 .....258 F1
Little Oaks BSDN SS14 .....2 H5
  HAR CO12 * 70 D4
Little Oxcroft LAIN SS15 .....276 F11
Little Paddocks BRTR CM77 * 123 L5
Little Pluckett's Wy BKHH IG9 .....250 A8
Little Pynchons HLWS CM18 .....204 A4
Little Russels
  RBRW/HUT CM13 .....257 H3
Little St Mary's SUD CO10 .....42 F3
Little's Crs CHTY IP2 .....16 F1
Little Searles PIT SS13 .....278 E6
Little Spenders BSDN SS14 .....3 L2
Little Stambridge Hall Rd
  RCFD SS4 .....183 L3
Little Stile CHLM/WR CM1 .....208 D5
Little Stone Ct COS CO15 .....182 C5
Little St WAB E9 .....233 K6
Little Tey Rd K/T/MI CO5 .....125 J6
Little Thorpe SOS SS1 .....302 D4
Littlethorpe VGE SS16 .....296 C1
Littleton Av CHING E4 .....249 J8
Little Totham Rd MAL CM9 .....199 M4
Little Tufts RIPS/CAP IP9 .....58 E4
Little Wakering Hall La
  SBN/FI SS3 .....397 K12
Little Wakering Rd
  SBN/FI SS3 .....396 H10
Little Walden Rd SAFWN CB10 .....28 C1
Little Wlk HLW CM20 .....13 G5
Little Waltham Rd
  CHLM/WR CM1 .....194 A4
Little Warley Hall La
  RBRW/HUT CM13 .....274 B4
Little Wheatley Cha RAYL SS6 .....280 D2
Little Whip St CHTY 16 F1
Little Wd FOS CO13 .....137 H3
Little Yeldham Rd HSTD CO9 .....346 C11
Liverpool Rd CAN/RD E16 .....323 H1
  LEY E10 .....284 F4
Livesey Cl WOOL/PLUM SE18 .....324 F6
Livingstone Rd SRTFD E15 .....306 F5
  WALTH E17 .....284 F4
Llewellin Cl CHLM/GWD CM2 .....210 A1
Llewellyn Drift KESG 50 A4
Lloyd Ms PEND EN3 .....233 H8
Lloyd Rd DAGW RM9 .....310 C3
  EHAM E6 .....308 C5
  RIPS/CAP IP9 .....66 C1
  WALTH E17 .....284 F4
Lloyds Av IP IP1 .....16 F4
The Lloyds KESG IP5 .....50 B6
Lloyd Wise Cl SOSN SS2 .....302 A2
Loamy Hill Rd WIT CM8 .....173 J4
Lobelia Cl CHLM/WR CM1 .....194 C1
Locarno Av WICKE SS11 .....261 K4
Locarno Rd IPSE IP3 .....55 G2
Lochnagar St POP/IOD E14 .....322 D1
Locke Cl RAIN RM13 .....311 J3
  SLH/COR SS17 .....316 F7
Lockfield Av PEND EN3 .....248 B2
Lockgate Ct HOM E9 .....306 C2
Lockhart Av CCLW CO3 .....106 F6
Lockhart St BOW E3 .....306 A3
Lockhurst St CLPT E5 .....306 F1
Lockram La WIT CM8 .....171 K3
Lock Rd HSTD CO9 .....81 H5
Locks Hi HSTD SS4 .....283 J4
Lock's La RCOLW CO6 .....360 F4
Locksley Cl SOSN SS2 .....302 C3
Locksley Est POP/IOD E14 .....322 C1
Locksley St POP/IOD E14 .....322 C1
Lockwood Pl CHING E4 .....266 B7
Lockwood Wy WALTH E17 .....266 A8
Lock Wy RAIN RM19 .....328 F6
Locton Gn BOW E3 * 306 C5
Lodge Av CHLM/GWD CM2 .....210 C6
  DAGW RM9 .....309 H7
  GPK RM2 .....289 K3
Lodge Cl CHIG IG7 .....269 K4
  COS CO15 .....66 E4
  RAYL SS6 .....281 H4
  RBRW/HUT CM13 .....257 H3
  SBF/HAD SS7 .....280 E8
Lodge Ct RCOLW CO6 .....106 C1
Lodge Crs CHES/WCR EN8 .....232 C4
  RCHLM CM3 .....195 H5
Lodge Farm Cl LOS SS9 * 282 A8
Lodge Farm Dr FX IP11 .....63 H8
Lodge Farm Rd SUD CO10 .....39 M2
Lodge Hall HLWS CM18 .....203 M5
Lodge Hi REDBR IG4 .....286 E2
Lodgelands Cl RAYL SS6 .....281 J4
Lodge La CDW/CHF RM16 .....330 E2
  COLN CO4 .....88 A5
  CRW RM5 .....270 D6
  K/T/MI CO5 .....153 G5
  K/T/MI CO5 .....153 M4
  RCHLM CM3 .....229 L1
  RCOLE CO7 .....112 D5
  WAB EN9 .....233 L5
Lodge Rd BRTR CM7 .....121 K4
Lodge Rd CHLM/WR CM1 .....194 C5
  EPP CM16 .....235 H4

HAR CO12 .....70 B5
K/T/MI CO5 .....150 A2
MAL CM9 .....213 L6
MAL CM9 .....214 C2
BCAYW CM12 .....228 B7
RCHLM CM3 .....228 K1
RCOLE CO7 .....156 B5
  RCOS CO15 .....135 J7
Lodge Vls WFD IG8 .....267 J6
Lodore St POP/IOD E14 .....322 F2
Lodwick SBN/FI SS3 .....302 B1
Loewen Rd CDW/CHF RM16 .....331 K2
Loftin Wy CHLM/GWD CM2 .....5 J7
Logan Cl PEND EN3 .....248 A1
Logan Link WICKW SS12 .....261 J8
Logan Ms ROM RM1 .....289 H1
Loman Pth SOCK/AV RM15 .....329 J2
Lombard Av IPNE IP4 .....17 M2
Lombards Cha
  RBRW/HUT CM13 .....275 G8
The Lombards EMPK RM11 .....290 C5
Lombard Wall CHARL SE7 .....323 L6
Lombardy Pl CHLM/WR CM1 .....5 G1
Lombardy Rd SUD CO10 .....43 G7
Lonbarn Hl MGTR CO11 .....366 D7
London City Airport Link
  CAN/RD E16 .....323 J3
London Hi CHLM/GWD CM2 .....225 K3
  RAYL SS6 .....280 F2
London Rd ABR/ST RM4 .....252 F1
  BARK IG11 .....308 E4
  BCAYE CM11 .....260 B7
  BCAYW CM12 .....257 M3
  BRTR CM77 .....120 E8
  BSF CM23 .....139 G6
  CBS CC2 .....22 C4
  CHDH RM6 .....288 D4
  CHLM/GWD CM2 .....5 G4
  CHONG CM5 .....382 E8
  COLW CO3 .....105 J2
  COS CO15 .....6 C8
  EPP CM16 .....204 C8
  GRAYS RM17 .....330 F5
  GRH DA9 .....335 H8
  GVW DA11 .....337 G4
  HERT/BAY SG13 .....184 H5
  HLWE CM17 .....188 D6
  HLWE CM17 .....204 D1
  IP IP1 .....16 A4
  K/T/MI CO5 .....125 M5
  K/T/MI CO5 .....148 E5
  K/T/MI CO5 .....149 H1
  MAL CM9 .....213 J6
  PIT SS13 .....279 G8
  PLSTW E13 .....307 K6
  PUR RM19 .....328 D6
  RAYL SS6 .....280 D1
  RCHLM CM3 .....144 E3
  RCOLW CO6 .....86 B5
  RCOS CO15 .....126 D2
  RCOS CO15 .....159 G5
  ROMW/RG RM7 .....288 F4
  ROY SG8 .....348 E10
  ROY SG8 .....370 C6
  SAFWN CB10 .....341 K7
  SAFWS CB11 .....30 A1
  SAFWS CB11 .....351 N10
  SBF/HAD SS7 .....279 G4
  SBF/HAD SS7 .....298 F2
  SBW CM21 .....162 F7
  SLH/COR SS17 .....316 A4
  SOCK/AV RM15 .....328 E5
  SOSN SS2 .....18 F4
  SWCM DA10 .....336 B3
  TIL RM18 .....331 L8
  VGE SS16 .....296 A4
  WARE SG12 .....184 F2
  WICKE SS11 .....261 M7
  WTHK RM20 .....330 A5
London Rd Purfleet
  PUR RM19 .....334 F1
London Rd West Thurrock
  WTHK RM20 .....335 J1
Londons Cl UPMR RM14 .....312 F2
Lone Barn Ct IP IP1 .....47 J3
Longacre BSDN SS14 .....3 H4
  CHLM/WR CM1 .....209 G5
  COLN CO4 .....88 A5
Long Acre HLWE CM17 .....188 C5
Long Acre Ct BRTR CM77 .....122 B7
  WALTH E17 .....267 G7
Longacres BRTR CM7 .....121 K4
Long Acres K/T/MI CO5 .....125 J7
Longaford Wy
  RBRW/HUT CM13 .....256 F4
Long Banks HLWS CM18 .....203 L6
Long Border Rd RBSF CM22 .....374 F12
Long Brandocks
  CHLM/WR CM1 .....208 C4
Long Common MAL CM9 .....198 D4
Long Ct PUR RM19 .....328 D2
Long Croft Dr CHES/WCR EN8 .....233 H4
Longcroft Ri LOU IG10 .....250 D5
Longcroft Rd COLN CO4 .....9 K5
Long Deacon Rd CHING E4 .....249 H8
Longdryve COLS CO2 * 129 G1
Longfellow Dr
  RBRW/HUT CM13 .....256 F3
Longfellow Rd BOW E3 * 306 B7
  MAL CM9 .....214 D4
  WALTH E17 .....284 E4
Long Fld FX IP11 .....62 D7
Longfield HLWS CM18 .....204 B6
  LOU IG10 .....249 M5
  WIT CM8 .....147 M5
Longfield Av EMPK RM11 .....289 J1
  PEND EN3 .....232 D2
  WALTH E17 .....284 E4
Longfield Cl WICKE SS11 .....261 K6
Longfield La CHESW EN7 .....216 A5
Longfield Rd CHLM/GWD CM2 .....210 A5
  RCHLM CM3 .....245 G8
  RIPS/CAP IP9 .....58 D2
  WICKE SS11 .....261 K6
Long Flds CHONG CM5 .....382 H4
Longfields RCOS CO16 .....181 L1
Long Gages BSDN SS14 .....2 H5
Long Gv BRTR CM7 .....122 B5
  CHIG IG7 .....269 H3
Long Grove Cl BROX EN10 .....200 F5
Longhams Dr HARH RM3 .....272 A1
Longhayes Av CHDH RM6 .....288 A4
Longhedges SAFWS CB11 .....28 D1

Long Horse Cft SAFWS CB11 .....30 B2
Longhouse Rd
  CDW/CHF RM16 .....331 L2
Longlands CHES/WCR EN8 .....232 E2
Long La BRTR CM77 .....120 E8
  CBE/LIN CB1 .....24 D1
  CDW/CHF RM16 .....330 E1
  FOS CO13 .....136 F6
  HOC/HUL SS5 .....263 J2
  SAFWS CB11 .....350 G8
Longleaf Dr BRTR CM7 .....121 J5
Longleat Cl CHLM/WR CM1 .....193 J6
Long Ley HLW CM20 .....13 M6
Long Leys CHING E4 .....266 E5
Long Lyndersood LAIN SS15 .....2 C6
Long Mark Rd CAN/RD E16 .....324 A2
Longmarsh La THMD SE28 .....325 H4
Longmead Av
  CHLM/GWD CM2 .....210 C5
Longmead Cl BRWN CM15 .....256 B4
Longmeade GVE DA12 .....338 C6
Long Meadow BRTR CM7 .....120 E8
  BSF CM23 .....138 C3
  RBRW/HUT CM13 .....256 F5
Long Meadow Dr WICKE SS11 .....261 H5
Longmeads WIT CM8 .....172 B8
Longmead Ms CHLM/WR CM1 .....208 C4
Long Moor CHES/WCR EN8 .....216 F7
Longmore Av
  CHLM/GWD CM2 .....210 B5
Longnor Rd WCHPL E1 .....306 A7
Long Pastures SUD CO10 .....39 A7
Long Perry RIPS/CAP IP9 .....58 E4
Longport St BARK/HLT IG6 .....269 K5
Long Reach Rd BARK IG11 .....309 J8
Long Riding BSDN SS14 .....3 J8
Long Ridings Av
  RBRW/HUT CM13 .....256 E1
Longrise BCAYW CM12 .....258 C5
Long Rd CVI SS8 .....320 C2
  MGTR CO11 * 90 C7
Long Rd East RCOLE CO7 .....89 K2
Long Rd West RCOLE CO7 .....89 H2
Longsands SBN/FI SS3 .....303 G6
Longshaw Rd CHING E4 .....267 G2
Longshipp Wy MAL CM9 .....214 B5
Longshore DEPT SE8 .....322 C7
Longshots Cl CHLM/WR CM1 .....193 K4
Longstomps Av
  CHLM/GWD CM2 .....209 K7
Longstraw Cl COLW CO3 .....106 A7
Long St IPNE IP4 .....17 J6
  WAB EN9 .....218 F8
Longtail BCAYE CM11 .....240 F8
Longtown Rd HARH RM3 .....271 M4
Longview Wy CRW RM5 .....271 G7
Longwick VGE SS16 .....294 F1
Long Wd HLWS CM18 .....203 L6
Longwood Gdns CLAY IG5 .....286 A2
Longwood Cl UPMR RM14 .....312 F2
Longworth Cl THMD SE28 .....326 A2
Long Wyre St COL CO1 .....8 A8
The Loning PEND EN3 .....232 D7
Lonsdale CBE/LIN CB1 .....25 H7
Lonsdale Av EHAM E6 .....308 A8
  RBRW/HUT CM13 .....257 G2
  ROMW/RG RM7 .....288 F4
  IPNE IP4 .....17 M1
Lonsdale Crs
  GNTH/NBYPK IG2 .....286 D5
Lonsdale Rd RCOS CO16 .....135 K3
  SOSN SS2 .....302 A3
  WAN E11 .....285 J5
Looe Gdns BARK/HLT IG6 .....286 E1
Looe Rd FX IP11 .....63 H8
Loompits Wy SAFWS CB11 .....351 R6
Loop Rd WAB EN9 .....233 J7
Lophams Cl HLWS CM18 .....34 C4
Loraine Wy RIPW IP8 .....46 E1
Lord Av CLAY IG5 .....286 C2
Lord Gdns CLAY IG5 .....286 B2
Lord Holland Rd COLS CO2 .....129 J2
Lord Roberts Av LOS SS9 .....300 C4
Lords Av BSF CM23 .....138 C2
Lordship Rd CHES/WCR EN8 .....216 F7
  CHLM/WR CM1 .....208 E3
Lordsland La BRTR CM77 .....100 E3
Lord St CAN/RD E16 .....324 B4
  GVE DA12 .....337 L5
  HOD EN11 .....200 F3
Lordswood Rd COLS CO2 .....128 F3
Lordswood Wy CHLM CM6 .....164 A6
Lord Warwick St
  WOOL/PLUM SE18 .....324 C6
Lorien Gdns RCHLM CM3 .....244 F7
Lorkin's La HSTD CO9 .....358 E6
Lorkin Wy RCOLW CO6 .....106 C1
Lorne Gdns WAN E11 .....285 M2
Lorne Rd BRW CM14 .....273 M3
  FSTGT E7 .....307 H1
  WALTH E17 .....284 D3
Lornes Cl SOSN SS2 .....302 A2
Lorraine Cl BCAYE CM11 .....259 G7
Lorrimore Cl BCAYW CM12 .....240 C8
Lorton Cl GVE DA12 .....338 B7
Loten Rd SBF/HAD SS7 .....297 L3
Lottem Rd SBF/HAD SS7 .....321 L3
Lott's Rd WBPK RM16 .....158 C1
Lotus Cl IP IP1 .....47 H4
Lotus Wy COS CO15 * 182 B7
Loudoun Av GNTH/NBYPK IG2 .....286 D5
Loughton La EPP CM16 .....235 L7
Loughton Wy BKHH IG9 .....250 A8
Louisa Av SBF/HAD SS7 .....297 J2
Louisa St WCHPL E1 .....322 A1
Louis Dr RAYL SS6 .....280 D2
Louis Dr East RAYL SS6 .....280 D1
Louis Dr West RAYL SS6 .....280 D1
Louise Cl WOTN CO14 .....369 P10
Louise Gdns RAIN RM13 .....311 G3
Louise Rd RAYL SS6 .....281 H3
  SRTFD E15 .....307 H3
Louisville Cl WARE SG12 .....185 K5
Louvain La RCOLE CO7 .....89 H2
Louvaine Av WICKW SS12 .....261 H6
Louvain Rd HAR CO12 .....70 D4
Lovage Ap EHAM E6 .....308 B1
Lovel Ri BERM/RHTH SE16 .....322 B6
Lovell Ri LOS SS9 .....282 D7
Lovell Rd EN EN1 .....232 D4
Lovell Wk RAIN RM13 .....311 H5
Lovens Cl CVI SS8 .....320 F3

Lover's La GRH DA9 .....336 A2
  RCOLE CO7 .....133 K6
  RIPS/CAP IP9 .....365 M9
Loves Wk CHLM/WR CM1 .....208 B5
Lovetofts Dr IP IP1 .....47 J2
Lovet Rd HLWW/ROY CM19 .....12 A8
Lovibrook Rd IL IG1 .....308 C1
Low Cl GRH DA9 .....335 H7
Lowe Av CAN/RD E16 .....323 K1
Lowe Cha WOTN CO14 .....369 M7
Lowe Cl CHIG IG7 .....269 K4
Lowefields RCOLW CO6 .....83 G5
Lowell St POP/IOD E14 .....322 B2
Lowen Rd RAIN RM13 .....311 G6
Lower Anchor St
  CHLM/GWD CM2 .....4 B7
Lower Av PIT SS13 .....279 H5
Lower Barn Rd RIPW IP8 .....52 B3
Lower Bedfords Rd
  ROM RM1 .....271 K5
Lower Broad St DAGE RM10 .....310 D3
Lower Brook St IPNE IP4 .....16 A7
Lower Burnham Rd
  RCHLM CM3 .....246 B3
Lower Bury La EPP CM16 .....235 G4
Lower Cha CHING E4 .....392 C1
Lower Church Rd
  SBF/HAD SS7 .....279 L7
Lower Cloister BCAYE CM11 .....258 A6
Lower Dales View Rd IP IP1 .....47 J3
Lower Downs Slade HVHL CB9 .....34 D5
Lower Dunton Rd
  RBRW/HUT CM13 .....276 A3
  UPMR RM14 .....294 A2
Lower Farm Rd COLN CO4 .....362 F6
Lower Gn CHLM/GWD CM2 .....225 L4
  RCOLW CO6 .....83 G4
Lower Hall La CHING E4 .....248 D7
Lower Harlings RIPS/CAP IP9 .....66 F5
Lower Higham Rd GVE DA12 .....338 C6
Lower Holt St RCOLW CO6 .....82 F7
Lower House La WDBR IP12 .....57 K3
Lower Houses Rd
  RIPS/CAP IP9 .....365 N10
Lower Island Wy WAB EN9 .....233 J5
Lower King BRTR CM7 .....122 B4
Lower Lambricks RAYL SS6 .....281 G1
Lower Langley RCOLW CO6 .....103 M4
Lower Lea Crossing
  POP/IOD E14 .....323 H3
Lower Marldyke Av
  RAIN RM13 .....310 F6
Lower Marine Pde HAR CO12 .....71 H3
Lower Meadow
  CHES/WCR EN8 .....216 E5
  HLWS CM18 .....203 M5
Lower Mill GTDUN CM6 .....117 H6
Lower Noke Cl BRW CM14 .....272 K1
Lower Orwell St IPNE IP4 .....17 G6
Lower Park Crs BSF CM23 .....138 A2
Lower Park Rd BELV DA17 .....326 D6
  LOU IG10 .....250 A6
  RCOLE CO7 .....156 F7
  WICKW SS12 .....278 F1
Lower Queen's Rd BKHH IG9 .....268 B1
Lower Range Rd GVE DA12 .....338 F5
Lower Rd BELV DA17 .....326 F6
  BRWN CM15 .....239 G4
  BURES CO8 .....360 A12
  COLS CO2 .....127 G8
  ERITH DA8 .....327 G2
  GVE DA12 .....339 H7
  HOC/HUL SS5 .....263 G4
  K/T/MI CO5 .....151 J4
  K/T/MI CO5 .....153 G8
  KIR/NAC IP10 .....62 G2
  LOU IG10 .....250 D1
  RBSF CM22 .....163 K2
  SUD CO10 .....39 G3
  SUD CO10 .....42 A4
  TIL RM18 .....337 L2
  WARE SG12 .....185 G3
Lower Rochester Rd
  HOO/HM NE13 .....339 M7
Lower Southend Rd
  WICKE SS11 .....261 G5
Lower Stock Rd ING CM4 .....241 L4
Lower St LAIN SS15 .....277 H4
  RCOLE CO7 .....363 K8
  RIPS/CAP IP9 .....364 D11
  RIPW IP8 .....46 F1
  STSD CM24 .....115 M3
  STSD CM24 .....374 A6
  SUD CO10 .....39 G3
  SUD CO10 .....42 A4
Lower Swaines EPP CM16 .....219 M8
The Lowe CHIG IG7 .....269 K4
Lowfield SBW CM21 .....162 F4
Lowfield La HOD EN11 .....200 F2
Low Hall Cl CHING E4 .....248 D7
Low Hall La WALTH E17 .....266 A8
Low Hill Rd HLWW/ROY CM19 .....202 A3
Lowland Gdns
  ROMW/RG RM7 .....288 C4
Lowlands Rd SOCK/AV RM15 .....328 F4
Low Rd HAR CO12 .....71 G3
Lowry Cl HVHL CB9 .....34 A4
  SBN/FI SS3 .....303 H5
Lowry Gdns IPSE IP3 .....54 F5
Lowry Rd BCTR RM8 .....289 H1
Lowshoe La ROMW/RG RM7 .....270 F1
Low Street La TIL RM18 .....332 C4
Lowther Rd WALTH E17 .....266 F3
Loxford Pl PIT SS13 .....278 D5
Loxford Av EHAM E6 .....308 A6
Loxford La IL IG1 .....308 C3
Loxford Rd BARK IG11 .....308 B2
Loxham Rd CHING E4 .....266 E6
Luard Wy COLS CO2 .....151 H2
  WIT CM8 .....171 J4
Lubbards Cl RAYL SS6 .....263 G8
Lubberhedges La GTDUN CM6 .....96 B3
Lucas Av CHLM/GWD CM2 .....210 G8
  PLSTW E13 .....307 L1
  RCOLW CO6 .....106 A7
Lucas Ct WAB EN9 .....234 A3
Lucas Crs DA9 .....289 L2
Lucas La BSDN SS14 .....2 B7
Lucas's La RCOS CO16 .....113 G7
Lucerne Dr WICKE SS11 .....261 K6
Lucerne Gv WALTH E17 .....285 G2
Lucerne Rd RCOLE CO7 .....109 G7
Lucerne Wk WICKE SS11 .....261 K6
Lucerne CHLM/WR CM1 .....208 D4
  HARH RM3 .....272 A5
Lucius St HSTD CO9 .....356 C5
Luck's Cl RCHLM CM3 .....167 J3
Luckyn La BSDN SS14 .....277 J2
Luctons Av BKHH IG9 .....249 M8
Lucy Cl COLW CO3 .....105 M7
Lucy La North COLW CO3 .....105 M7
Lucy La South COLW CO3 .....105 M6
Lucy Rd SOS SS1 .....19 J7

Ludgores La RCHLM CM3 .....212 A8
Ludgrove RCHLM CM3 .....231 K7
Ludham Cl THMD SE28 .....325 M2
  WFD IG8 .....268 D2
Ludham Hall La RBRW/HUT CM77 .....121 G6
Ludlow Cl IP IP1 .....48 A1
Ludlow Pl GRAYS RM17 .....330 G2
Luffield Rd ABYW SE2 .....325 K5
Luff Wy WOTN CO14 .....137 J2
Lufkin Rd COLN CO4 .....107 J2
Lugano Av WDBR IP12 .....51 H5
Lugar Cl COLN CO4 .....108 B7
Lugg Ap MNPK E12 .....286 D6
Luker Rd SOS SS1 .....19 G5
Lukin Crs CHING E4 .....267 G2
Lukin's Dr GTDUN CM6 .....117 G6
Lullington Rd DAGW RM9 .....310 B2
Lulworth Av IPSE IP3 .....55 J2
  COS CO15 .....182 F5
  SLH/COR SS17 .....316 A5
Lulworth Dr CRW RM5 .....270 E4
  HVHL CB9 .....34 A5
Lumber Leys WOTN CO14 .....137 K2
Lummis V KESG IP5 .....50 B6
Luncies Rd BSDN SS14 .....278 B8
Lundy Cl HVHL CB9 .....35 G4
  SOSN SS2 .....282 E6
Lunnish Hi HAR CO12 .....367 K6
Lupin Cl ROMW/RG RM7 .....194 C7
Lupin Dr CHLM/WR CM1 .....194 C7
Lupin Rd CHTY IP2 .....53 K1
Lupin Wy RCOS CO16 .....158 D7
Luppits Cl RBRW/HUT CM13 .....256 D5
Lushes Ct LOU IG10 .....250 E5
Lushes Rd LOU IG10 .....250 E5
Lushington Av RCOS CO13 .....137 G3
Lushington Rd MGTR CO11 .....90 E1
Lutea Cl LAIN SS15 .....277 G4
Luther Dr K/T/MI CO5 .....150 B8
Luther King Cl WALTH E17 .....284 B4
Luther King Rd
  HLWW/ROY CM19 .....12 F7
Luther Rd CHTY IP2 .....16 D8
Luthers Cl BRWN CM15 .....383 M11
Luton Pl PLSTW E13 .....307 H8
  WALTH E17 .....284 E1
Lutus Cl SUD CO10 .....37 K7
Luxborough La CHIG IG7 .....268 C3
Luxembourg Ms SRTFD E15 .....307 H2
Luxford Pl SBW CM21 .....163 G8
Luxford St BERM/RHTH SE16 .....322 A7
lyal Rd BOW E3 .....306 B6
Lych Ga LAIN SS15 .....276 F7
Lydeard Rd EHAM E6 .....308 C4
Lydford St WOS/PRIT SS0 .....301 G4
Lydgate Cl MGTR CO11 .....90 E1
Lydia Dr RCOS CO16 .....180 G3
Lyford St WOOL/PLUM SE18 .....324 C6
Lyle Cl KESG IP5 .....50 B6
Lylt Rd CVI SS8 .....320 D2
Lyme Cl SOSN SS2 .....282 E6
Lymington Av COS CO15 .....159 J5
  LOS SS9 .....300 B3
Lymington Rd BCTR RM8 .....288 A6
Lympstone Cl WOS/PRIT SS0 .....282 D6
Lynbrook Cl RAIN RM13 .....311 G6
Lynceley Gra EPP CM16 .....220 B7
The Lynch HOD EN11 .....201 J3
Lyndale BRWN CM15 .....383 N11
Lyndale Av SOSN SS2 .....301 L2
Lyndene SBF/HAD SS7 .....279 L8
Lyndhurst Av IPNE IP4 .....49 M6
Lyndhurst Dr EMPK RM11 .....289 M6
  LEY E10 .....284 C1
  RCHLM CM3 .....203 L1
Lyndhurst Gdns BARK IG11 .....309 H5
  GNTH/NBYPK IG2 .....287 G4
Lyndhurst Ri CHIG IG7 .....268 D3
Lyndhurst Rd CHING E4 .....266 F6
  COS CO15 .....183 M1
  SLH/COR SS17 .....317 J1
Lyndhurst Wy
  RBRW/HUT CM13 .....256 F4
Lyndon Rd BELV DA17 .....326 D7
Lyndsey Pl CHESW EN7 * 216 C8
Lyne Crs WALTH E17 .....266 F2
Lyneham Wk CLPT E5 * 306 E2
Lynford Gdns GDMY/SEVK IG3 .....287 J3
Lynfords Av WICKE SS11 .....261 J2
Lynfords Dr WICKE SS11 .....261 J3
Lynmouth Av CHLM/GWD CM2 .....5 J6
Lynmouth Gdns
  CHLM/GWD CM2 .....5 J6
Lynmouth Rd WALTH E17 .....284 A6
Lynne Cl FOS CO13 .....137 G3
Lynnett Rd BCTR RM8 .....288 A4
Lynn Ms WAN E11 .....285 H7
Lynn Rd GNTH/NBYPK IG2 .....287 G5
  WAN E11 .....285 H7
Lynn View Cl SBF/HAD SS7 .....279 M8
Lynross Cl HARH RM3 .....272 A6
Lynstede BSDN SS14 .....278 B8
Lynton Av ROMW/RG RM7 .....270 E4
Lynton Cl HAR CO12 .....14 F7
Lynton Crs GNTH/NBYPK IG2 .....286 E5
Lynton Dr CHLM/WR CM1 .....194 B6
Lynton Pde CHES/WCR EN8 * 216 F5
Lynton Rd CHING E4 .....337 K6
  RCHLM CM3 .....289 L1
  SBF/HAD SS7 .....298 F4
  SOS SS1 .....302 C7
Lynton Rd South GVW DA11 .....337 K6
Lynton Wy CBS CB2 .....22 C4
Lynwood Av FX IP11 .....63 G6
Lynwood Cl CRW RM5 .....270 G5
  SWFD E18 .....267 M1
Lynwood Dr CRW RM5 .....270 G5
Lynwood Gn RAYL SS6 .....281 H4
Lyon Cl CHLM/GWD CM2 .....225 G5
  COS CO15 .....7 K4
Lyon Rd ROM RM1 .....289 J2
Lyons Hall Rd BRTR CM7 .....100 D5
Lysander Dr IPSE IP3 .....55 J5
Lyster Av CHLM/GWD CM2 .....210 D6
Lytham Cl THMD SE28 .....326 A2
Lyttelton Rd LEY E10 .....284 D4
Lytton Av PEND EN3 .....232 F4
Lytton Rd CDW/CHF RM16 .....331 K4
  GPK RM2 .....289 J2
  WAN E11 .....285 H5
Lyttons Wy HOD EN11 .....185 J4

M

Mabbitt Wy COLN CO4 .....87 L8
Maberly Ct SAFWN CB10 .....28 A7
Mabey's Wk SBW CM21 .....162 B4
Mabley St HOM E9 .....307 G1
Macarthur Rd FSTGT E7 .....307 K1
Macaulay Rd EHAM E6 .....47 J2
  VGE SS16 .....276 D8
Macbean St
  WOOL/PLUM SE18 .....324 D6
Macbeth Cl COLN CO4 .....108 C3
Macdonald Av DAGE RM10 .....288 E3

EMPK RM11 ...290 B2
WOS/PRIT SS0 ...301 H2
Macdonald Rd *FSTGT* E7 ...307 K1
WALTH E17 ...266 F4
Macdonald Wy *EMPK* RM11 ...290 B2
Macer's La *BROX* EN10 ...217 K4
Mace St *BETH* E2 ...306 A4
Mace Wk *CHLM/WR* CM1 ...4 D1
Macgregor Dr *WICKW* SS12 ...261 H8
Macgregor Rd *CAN/RD* E16 ...323 M1
Macintyres Wk *RCFD* SS4 ...129 L4
Mackay Ct *COLS* CO2 ...129 H7
Mackenzie Cl *WICKW* SS12 ...261 H7
Mackenzie Dr *KESG* IP5 ...50 A5
Mackintosh La *HOM* E9 ...306 A2
Mackley Dr *SLH/COR* SS17 ...295 J8
Maclarens *WIT* CM8 ...172 D7
Maclaren Wy *WICKW* SS12 * ...261 H8
Maclean Ter *GVE* DA12 * ...338 C7
Maclennan Av *RAIN* RM13 ...312 A3
Macleod Cl *GRAYS* RM17 ...331 G5
Macmurdo Cl *LOS* SS9 ...282 A6
Macmurdo Rd *LOS* SS9 ...282 A6
Maconochies Rd
  POP/IOD E14 * ...322 C6
Macon Wy *UPMR* RM14 ...291 J4
Macquarie Wy *POP/IOD* E14 ...322 E7
Maddams St *BOW* E3 ...306 C4
Madden Cl *SWCM* DA10 ...336 B4
Maddox Rd *HLW* CM20 ...13 H4
Madeira Av *LOS* SS9 ...300 B3
Madeira Gv *WFD* IG8 ...267 M5
Madeira Rd *COS* CO15 ...160 A5
  WAN E11 ...285 G1
Madeline Gv *IL* IG1 ...309 G2
Madeline Pl *CHLM/WR* CM1 ...193 H7
Madelis *EPP* CM16 ...236 A1
Madge Gill Wy *EHAM* E6 ...308 B6
Madgements Rd *BRTR* CM77 ...100 F5
Madgeways Cl *WARE* SG12 * ...185 G4
Madgeways La *WARE* SG12 ...185 G4
Madles La *ING* CM4 ...241 J4
Madras Rd *IL* IG1 ...308 E1
Madrid Av *RAYL* SS6 ...262 D6
Mafeking Av *EHAM* E6 ...308 A6
  GNTH/NBYPK IG2 ...287 G5
Mafeking Rd *CAN/RD* E16 ...307 J3
Magazine Farm Wy
  COLW CO3 ...106 D3
Magazine Rd *SBN/FI* SS3 ...303 H7
Magdalen Cl *COS* CO15 ...6 A7
Magdalene Cl *CHTY* IP2 ...53 L2
Magdalene Crs *WIT* CM8 ...147 G2
Magdalene Gdns *EHAM* E6 ...308 B5
Magdalen Gdns
  RBRW/HUT CM13 ...257 H2
Magdalen Gn *COL* CO1 ...9 G8
  GTDUN CM6 ...74 D1
Magdalen Rd *COS* CO15 ...6 B6
Magdalen St *COL* CO1 ...8 E5
Magenta Cl *BCAYW* CM12 ...258 A3
Maginley Crs *KESG* IP5 ...49 L7
Magna Cl *CBE/LIN* CB1 ...23 M3
Magna Rd *SBN/FI* SS3 ...396 C10
Magnaville Rd *BSF* CM23 ...138 F5
Magnet Rd *WTHK* RM20 ...335 M1
Magnet Ter *SLH/COR* SS17 * ...317 H1
Magnolia Cl *CHLM/GWD* CM2 ...209 J7
  COL CO1 * ...320 D3
  HERT/BAY SG13 ...184 B3
  LEY E10 ...284 D7
  SOCK/AV RM15 ...314 A6
  WIT CM8 ...147 K6
Magnolia Dr *VGE* SS16 ...322 B4
Mahonia Dr *VGE* SS16 ...322 C4
  COL CO1 * ...248 E7
Maida Rd *BELV* DA17 ...326 D6
Maida Wy *CHING* E4 ...248 B7
Maidenhall Ap *CHTY* IP2 ...54 A3
Maidenhall Rd *SRTFD* E15 ...307 H6
Maidens Br *EN* EN1 * ...232 B7
Maidment Crs *WIT* CM8 ...171 J4
Maids Head Pde *RCOS* CO16 * ...135 J4
Maidstone Av *CRW* RM5 ...270 F8
Maidstone Rd *FX* IP11 ...62 D8
Mailers La *BSF* CM23 ...93 G7
Main Barracks
  WOOL/PLUM SE18 * ...324 C8
Main Rd *RBRW/HUT* CM13 ...276 A8
Maine Crs *RAYL* SS6 ...280 L1
Main Ga *TIL* RM18 * ...331 H8
Main Rd *BOC* CM0 ...389 M1
  CHLM/WR CM1 ...193 L5
  FOS CO13 ...136 D6
  GPK RM2 ...271 K8
  GPK RM2 ...289 J2
  HAR CO12 ...14 B4
  HOC/HUL SS5 * ...367 H2
  HOC/HUL SS5 ...264 B8
  IPNE IP4 ...48 F2
  KESG IP5 ...49 L8
  KIR/NAC IP10 ...56 E4
  RCHLM CM3 ...144 B1
  RCHLM CM3 ...144 C5
  RCHLM CM3 ...195 G5
  RCHLM CM3 ...211 K6
  RCHLM CM3 ...227 M4
  RCHLM CM3 ...243 K4
  RCHLM CM3 ...243 M1
  RCOLE CO7 ...132 C2
  RCOLW CO6 ...85 J1
  RIPS/CAP IP9 ...60 A7
  RIPS/CAP IP9 ...365 L1
  RIPS/CAP IP9 ...365 P6
  SBF/HAD SS7 * ...280 C2
  WDBR IP12 ...50 F1
Main St *CBE/LIN* CB1 ...2 D2
Maitland Pl *SBN/FI* SS3 ...303 H4
Maitland Rd *SRTFD* E15 ...307 L3
  STSD CM24 ...115 M3
  WICKW SS12 ...261 H8
Maizey St *WCHPL* E1 ...255 K5
Majendie La *HSTD* CO9 ...356 F7
Majendie Rd
  WOOL/PLUM SE18 ...325 G8
Major Rd *SRTFD* E15 ...306 F2
Makemores *BRTR* CM77 ...120 C3
Makepeace Rd *WAN* E11 ...285 K2
Makins Rd *HAR* CO12 ...14 A4
Malabar St *POP/IOD* E14 ...322 D5

Malam Gdns *POP/IOD* E14 ...322 E3
Malan Sq *RAIN* RM13 ...311 L3
Malcolm Wy *WAN* E11 ...285 K3
Maldon Ct *SUD* CO10 ...21 K6
Maldon Rd *BOC* CM0 ...390 B2
  BOC CM0 ...390 D1
  BOC CM0 ...392 H5
  CHLM/GWD CM2 ...210 D6
  COLS CO2 ...127 K7
  COLS CO2 ...151 L2
  COLW CO3 ...106 F8
  ING CM4 ...224 E5
  K/T/MI CO5 ...148 E8
  K/T/MI CO5 ...176 A3
  MAL CM9 ...197 J5
  MAL CM9 ...198 E1
  MAL CM9 ...199 M8
  MAL CM9 ...213 L6
  MAL CM9 ...231 H5
  MAL CM9 ...384 L4
  RCHLM CM3 ...196 F4
  RCHLM CM3 ...212 C6
  RCHLM CM3 ...388 F9
  ROMW/RG RM7 ...288 F5
  SOSN SS2 ...19 J8
  WIT CM8 ...171 J8
Maldon Wk *WFD* IG8 ...267 M5
Malford Gv *SWFD* E18 ...285 J1
Malgraves *PIT* SS13 ...278 E6
Malgraves Pl *PIT* SS13 ...278 E6
Malin Cl *HVHL* CB9 ...35 L1
Malkin Dr *HLWE* CM17 ...204 F3
Mallard Cl *BRTR* CM77 ...120 F8
  COLS CO2 ...128 C4
  DART DA1 ...334 C2
  K/T/MI CO5 ...148 F2
  MAL CM9 ...385 N3
  UPMR RM14 ...291 J7
Mallard Rd *CHLM/GWD* CM2 ...209 J7
  WALTH E17 * ...285 L1
Mallard Wy *CHTY* IP2 ...53 K3
  RBRW/HUT CM13 ...256 D3
  SUD CO10 ...45 M4
Mallinson Cl *HCH* RM12 ...311 M2
Mallion Ct *WAB* EN9 ...234 A3
Mallory Wy *BCAYW* CM12 * ...258 C4
Mallow Ct *GRAYS* RM17 ...331 G5
Mallow Gdns *BCAYW* CM12 ...240 C8
Mallowhayes Cl *CHTY* IP2 ...16 C9
Mallows Fld *HSTD* CO9 ...81 H4
Mallows Gn *HLWW/ROY* CM19 ...205 H6
Mallows Green Rd *BSF* CM23 ...92 D1
Mallows La *HSTD* CO9 ...355 L6
The Mall *EMPK* RM11 ...289 L6
  SRTFD E15 * ...307 L4
Malmesbury Cl *CHTY* IP2 ...53 M3
Malmesbury Rd *BOW* E3 ...306 C2
  CAN/RD E16 ...323 H1
  SWFD E18 ...267 J2
Malmesbury Ter *CAN/RD* E16 * ...323 J1
Malmesbury West End
  BOW E3 ...306 C7
Malmsmead *BOC* CM0 ...302 F5
Malpas Rd *CDW/CHF* RM16 ...331 A2
Malta Rd *LEY* E10 ...284 C6
  TIL RM18 ...331 J8
Maltby Dr *EN* EN1 ...232 B7
Maltese Rd *CHLM/WR* CM1 ...209 K1
Malthouse Rd *MGTR* CO11 ...91 C1
Malting Farm La *RCOLE* CO7 ...88 F3
Malting Green Rd *COLS* CO2 ...128 C8
Malting La *CDW/CHF* RM16 ...315 K4
  FOS CO13 ...368 F12
  SUD CO10 ...45 L8
Maltings Cha *ING* CM4 ...239 L2
Maltings Cl *BURES* CO8 ...359 P8
Maltings Ct *WIT* CM8 ...171 J4
Maltings Hl *CHONG* CM5 ...380 E6
Maltings La *EPP* CM16 ...220 B7
  ROY SG8 ...349 K9
  WIT CM8 ...171 K5
Maltings Pk *RCOLW* CO6 * ...106 C1
Maltings Rd *CHLM/GWD* CM2 ...210 D8
  RCOLE CO7 ...156 D1
  WICKE SS11 ...262 B3
The Maltings *BOC* CM0 ...393 M1
  BRTR CM77 ...120 D3
  GTDUN CM6 ...117 G4
  HAR CO12 ...367 P9
  ROM RM1 ...289 J5
  SAFWS CM11 * ...372 B1
  WICKE SS11 * ...262 B3
Maltings Wk *WBRTR* CM7 ...121 K2
Malting Ter *CHTY* IP2 * ...17 G8
Malting Villas Rd *RCFD* SS4 ...283 J3
Malting Yd *RCOLE* CO7 ...130 C1
Malvern Av *CHING* E4 ...267 G1
  CVI SS8 ...320 A2
Malvern Cl *IPSE* IP3 ...55 G1
  KESG IP5 ...49 L6
  RAYL SS6 ...262 A3
Malvern Dr *GDMY/SEVK* IG3 ...309 J1
  WFD IG8 ...267 M4
Malvern Gdns *LOU* IG10 ...250 C8
Malvern Rd *EHAM* E6 ...308 B5
  GRAYS RM17 ...331 H3
  HOC/HUL SS5 ...264 C5
  PEND EN3 ...232 F7
  WAN E11 ...285 H7
Malvern Wy *RCOLW* CO6 ...86 G6
Malvina Av *GVE* DA12 ...337 J5
Malwood Dr *SBF/HAD* SS7 ...279 J8
Malwood Rd *SBF/HAD* SS7 ...279 L8
Malyon Court Cl *SBF/HAD* SS7 ...298 E1
Malyon Rd *WIT* CM8 ...171 J5
Malyons Cl *PIT* SS13 ...278 D5
Malyons Gn *PIT* SS13 ...278 D5
Malyons La *HOC/HUL* SS5 ...263 J5
Malyons Ms *PIT* SS13 ...278 D5
Malyons Pl *PIT* SS13 ...278 D5
The Malyons *SBF/HAD* SS7 ...298 E1
Managers St *POP/IOD* E14 * ...322 F14
Manbey Gv *SRTFD* E15 ...307 J2
Manbey Park Rd *SRTFD* E15 * ...307 J2
Manbey Rd *SRTFD* E15 ...307 J2
Manbey St *SRTFD* E15 * ...307 J2
Manbrough Av *EHAM* E6 ...308 B4
Manchester Dr *LOS* SS9 ...300 E4
Manchester Gv *POP/IOD* E14 ...322 F8
Manchester Rd *CHTY* IP2 ...53 M7
  COS CO15 ...160 B3
  POP/IOD E14 ...322 F6
Mandela Rd *CAN/RD* E16 ...323 K2
Mandeville Cl *BROX* EN10 ...201 K4

Mandeville Rd *PEND* EN3 ...232 F7
  RCOLW CO6 ...126 B2
  SAFWS CM11 ...30 A1
Mandeville St *CLPT* E5 ...284 B8
Mandeville Wy
  CHLM/WR CM1 ...193 L2
  FOS CO13 ...137 J2
  SBF/HAD SS7 ...279 M6
  VGE SS16 ...322 B5
Mandrake Wy *SRTFD* E15 * ...307 H4
Mandy Cl *IPNE* IP4 ...48 F7
Manfield Gdns *RCOS* CO16 ...157 L8
Manford Cl *CHIG* IG7 ...269 L8
Manford Cross *CHIG* IG7 ...269 K4
Manford Wy *CHIG* IG7 ...269 H4
Mangapp Pde *BOC* CM0 ...393 M5
Mangers La *CBS* CB2 ...22 A8
Manilla Rd *SOS* SS1 ...19 M7
Manilla St *POP/IOD* E14 ...322 D5
Manister Rd *ABYW* SE2 ...325 K6
Manly Dixon Dr *PEND* EN3 ...232 F7
Mannall Wk *KESG* IP5 ...50 A5
Mannering Gdns
  WOS/PRIT SS0 ...300 E2
Manners Cnr *SOSN* SS2 * ...283 H8
Manners Rd *SOSN* SS2 ...283 H8
Manning Gv *WIT* CM8 ...294 F1
Manning Rd *DAGE* RM10 ...310 D4
  FX IP11 ...11 J5
  WALTH E17 ...284 B2
Mannings Cl *SAFWS* CB11 ...30 B2
Mannings La *RIPS/CAP* IP9 ...365 K3
Manning St *SOCK/AV* RM15 ...328 F4
Mannington Cl *IPNE* IP4 ...49 L8
Manningtree Rd *RCOLE* CO7 ...64 C4
  RCOLE CO7 ...111 J5
  RCOLE CO7 ...363 P11
  RIPS/CAP IP9 ...364 B11
Mannin Rd *CHDH* RM6 ...287 J1
Mannock Dr *LOU* IG10 ...250 F2
Mannock Rd *DART* DA1 ...334 C5
Manns Wy *RAYL* SS6 ...262 F8
Mann's La *CHONG* CM5 ...296 M3
Manor Av *WRPK* RM11 ...278 F7
  PIT SS13 ...278 F7
Manor Cl *BCAYE* CM1 ...259 M2
  DAGE RM10 ...311 G3
  GVE DA12 ...338 E7
  RAYL SS6 ...281 G5
  RCOLW CO6 ...86 F6
  ROM RM1 ...289 K3
  SOCK/AV RM15 ...328 F4
  SUD CO10 ...38 F3
  THMD SE28 ...307 M8
Manor Ct *CHES/WCR* EN8 * ...232 E1
  EN EN1 ...232 D6
  SOS SS1 * ...19 M6
Manor Crs *EMPK* RM11 ...289 M3
  RCHLM CM3 ...167 L8
Manor Croft Pde
  CHES/WCR EN8 * ...216 E8
Manordene Rd *THMD* SE28 ...325 M2
Manor Dr *CHLM/GWD* CM2 ...210 D6
Manor Farm Cl *HVHL* CB9 ...34 C6
Manor Farm Dr *CHING* E4 ...267 K2
Manor Farm Rd *EN* EN1 ...232 C5
Manor Gdns *COLW* CO3 ...107 G6
Manor Hall Gdns *LEY* E10 ...284 D6
Manor Hatch *HLWS* CM18 ...204 B3
Manor Hatch Cl *HLWS* CM18 ...204 C2
Manor House Wy *RCOLE* CO7 ...156 B6
Manor La *HAR* CO12 ...70 F3
  RIPS/CAP IP9 ...364 B11
  SAFWN CM16 ...28 A8
Manor Links *BSF* CM23 ...139 K2
Manor Park Rd *MNPK* E12 ...308 A1
Manor Pl *BRTR* CM7 * ...121 K2
Manor Rd *ABR/ST* RM4 ...252 A8
  BARK IG11 ...309 J3
  BOC CM0 ...390 C2
  BSF CM23 ...139 H2
  CAN/RD E16 ...323 H1
  CHDH RM6 ...288 A4
  CHIG IG7 ...268 D5
  CHLM/GWD CM2 ...5 H6
  COLW CO3 ...107 A7
  DAGE RM10 ...310 F3
  DAGE RM10 ...311 G3
  FX IP11 ...11 J5
  GRAYS RM17 ...330 F5
  GTDUN CM6 ...94 C3
  GVE DA12 ...337 L4
  HAR CO12 ...14 D9
  HLWE CM17 ...188 F7
  HOC/HUL SS5 ...263 M7
  HOD EN11 ...201 H1
  HVHL CB9 ...34 C6
  IPNE IP4 ...48 F5
  KESG IP5 ...50 F5
  LAIN SS15 ...276 L8
  LEY E10 ...284 D5
  LOU IG10 ...249 L6
  LOU IG10 ...249 L6
  MAL CM9 ...197 H8
  RCHLM CM3 ...196 F4
  RCHLM CM3 ...244 F5
  RCOLE CO7 ...130 F4
  RCOLW CO6 ...86 E7
  ROM RM1 ...289 K3
  SBF/HAD SS7 ...279 M7
  SLH/COR SS17 ...318 C3
  SUD CO10 ...20 D2
  SWCM DA10 ...336 B5
  TIL RM18 ...331 K8
  WAB EN9 ...233 J4
  WALTH E17 ...266 B8
  WIT CM8 ...171 K1
  WOS/PRIT SS0 ...18 A6
  WTHK RM20 ...335 M1
Manor Sq *BCTR* RM8 ...287 M7
The Manors *WIT* CM8 * ...147 J7
Manor St *BRTR* CM7 ...121 K3
Manors Wy *WIT* CM8 ...146 F1
Manor Ter *FX* IP11 ...68 D1
Manor Wy *BRW* CM14 ...273 K2
  CHING E4 ...267 G3
  COS CO15 ...160 D3
  GRAYS RM17 ...330 F6
  RAIN RM13 ...311 H8
  SWCM DA10 ...336 B2
  WFD IG8 ...267 L4

WAN E11 ...285 L4
Mansfields *CHLM/WR* CM1 ...208 C4
Manstead Gdns *CHDH* RM6 ...287 M5
  RAIN RM13 ...327 G8
Manston Cl *CHES/WCR* EN8 ...216 D8
Manston Dr *BSF* CM23 ...265 C8
Manston Rd *HLW* CM20 ...13 J7
  RCHLM CM12 ...311 L3
Manthorpe Rd
  WOOL/PLUM SE18 ...324 F1
Mantle Wy *SRTFD* E15 ...307 H4
Manton Rd *ABYW* SE2 ...325 K7
  CHING E4 ...248 A7
Manwick Rd *FX* IP11 ...11 H6
Manwood St *CAN/RD* E16 ...324 C4
Maple Av *BRTR* CM7 ...121 G5
  BSF CM23 ...138 E1
  CBS CB2 ...22 A8
  CHING E4 ...266 C5
  LOS SS9 ...300 C5
  WAN E11 ...285 G1
Maple Cl *BARK/HLT* IG6 ...269 H6
  BKHH IG9 ...268 A2
  BSF CM23 ...138 E1
  CBE/LIN CB1 ...24 E6
  CHTY IP2 ...16 A9
  COS CO15 ...6 C5
  HAR CO12 ...14 C4
  HCH RM12 ...289 G3
  RBRW/HUT CM13 ...256 C6
Maple Dr *CHLM/GWD* CM2 ...209 J7
  FOS CO13 ...137 G3
  RAYL SS6 ...262 F6
  SOCK/AV RM15 ...314 A4
  WIT CM8 ...147 K8
Mapleford Sweep *VGE* SS16 ...3 B7
Maple Ga *LOU* IG10 ...250 D7
Maple Gv *BSF* CM23 ...138 E1
  HCSG IP5 ...49 J8
  LOU IG10 ...37 G5
Maple La *SAFWN* CB10 ...31 H7
Mapleleaf Cl *HOC/HUL* SS5 ...264 C6
Mapleleafe Gdns
  BARK/HLT IG6 ...286 E1
Mapleleaf Gdns *WICKW* SS12 ...260 E7
Maple Leaf Sq
  BERM/RHTH SE16 * ...322 A5
Maple Md *BCAYW* CM12 ...258 C5
Maple Rd *GRAYS* RM17 ...330 F5
  RAYL SS6 ...262 F6
  SOCK/AV RM15 ...314 A4
  WIT CM8 ...147 K8
Maplesden *SBF/HAD* SS7 ...299 C4
Maple Spring *BSF* CM23 ...138 D1
Maple Springs *WAB* EN9 ...234 B3
Maplestead *BSDN* SS14 * ...3 J1
Maplestead Rd *DAGW* RM9 ...309 H6
The Maples *HLWW/ROY* CM19 ...203 H6
  KESG IP5 ...49 K5
Maple St *ROMW/RG* RM7 ...288 D2
Mapleton Crs *PEND* EN3 ...232 D6
Mapleton Rd *CHING* E4 ...266 F2
Mapletree La *EPP* CM16 ...223 J4
Maple Tree La *VGE* SS16 ...276 F3
Maple Wy *BOC* CM0 ...393 K7
  COLS CO2 ...129 G8
  CVI SS8 ...320 B2
  RCOLW CO6 ...360 H4
Maplin Cl *SBF/HAD* SS7 ...279 M6
Maplin Gdns *BSDN* SS14 ...278 A5
Maplin Rd *CAN/RD* E16 ...323 K2
Maplin St *BOW* E3 ...306 C7
Maplin Wy *SOS* SS1 ...302 F6
Maplin Wy North *SBN/FI* SS3 ...302 F5
Mapperley Dr *WFD* IG8 ...267 J3
Marabou Cl *MNPK* E12 ...308 B2
Maran Wy *BSF* CM23 ...324 A2
Marascara Cl *DAGE* RM10 ...129 K6
Marathon Wy *THMD* SE28 ...325 J3
Marauder Wy *RCOLW* CO6 ...102 C3
Marbled White Dr *RIPW* IP8 ...53 C5
Marchant Rd *WAN* E11 ...285 G2
Marchmant Cl *HCH* RM12 ...289 H8
March Dr *SUD* CO10 ...37 L4
Marconi Rd *CHLM/WR* CM1 ...5 J6
  GVW DA11 ...337 G8
  LEY E10 ...284 C6
Marcos Rd *CVI* SS8 ...302 C4
Marcus Av *SOS* SS1 ...302 K6
Marcus Cha *SOS* SS1 ...302 K6
Marcus Cl *COLN* CO4 ...87 J7
  HVHL CB9 ...35 G6
Marcus Gdns *SOS* SS1 ...302 K6
Marcus Rd *FX* IP11 ...11 J5
Marcus St *SRTFD* E15 ...307 H5
Marden Ash *LAIN* SS15 ...276 L1
Marden Rd *ROM* RM1 ...289 K4
Mardyke Cl *DAGE* RM10 ...310 F4
Mardyke Rd *HLW* CM20 ...188 B7
Mardyke Vw *SOCK/AV* RM15 * ...329 H4
Marennes Crs *RCOLE* CO7 ...156 B2
Mareth Rd *COLS* CO2 ...129 G8
Margaret Av *BRWN* CM15 * ...248 D3
  CHING E4 ...248 A5
Margaret Bondfield Av
  BARK IG11 ...309 K4
Margaret Cl *GPK* RM2 ...156 C7
  RCOLE CO7 ...156 C7
  WAB EN9 ...233 J4
Margaret Dr *EMPK* RM11 ...290 C6
Margaret Rd *COL* CO1 ...8 C2
  EPP CM16 ...236 B7
  GPK RM2 ...289 J2
Margaret St *FX* IP11 ...62 D7
  GTDUN CM6 ...74 D2
Margaretting Rd
  CHLM/GWD CM2 ...208 D5
  ING CM4 ...225 J4
  MNPK E12 ...285 M7
Margaret Wy *REDBR* IG4 ...286 B8
  SAFWN CM16 ...28 A8
Margarite Wy *WICKW* SS12 ...260 E7
Margate Rd *IPSE* IP3 ...55 G2
Margery Girling House
  FX IP11 * ...63 H7
Margery Park Rd *FSTGT* E7 ...307 H3
Margery Rd *BCTR* RM8 ...288 A8
Margreth Rd *BCAYW* CM12 ...276 F2
Margherita Wy *WAB* EN9 ...234 A4
Margretan Av *CVI* SS8 ...321 G3
Marguerite Dr *LOS* SS9 ...300 E4
Marguerite Wy *BSF* CM23 ...138 D2
Mariam Gdns *HCH* RM12 ...290 D3
Marian Cl *CDW/CHF* RM16 ...314 D6
Maria St *HAR* CO12 ...15 K4
Marie Cl *SLH/COR* SS17 ...295 K4
Marie St *WCHPL* E1 ...255 K5
Marigold Av *CHING* E4 ...248 A5
Marigold Cl *RCOS* CO16 ...6 B2
Marigold La *INC* CM4 ...241 H5

Marigold Pl *HLWE* CM17 * ...188 D5
Marina Av *RAYL* SS6 ...280 C2
Marina Cl *SOSN* SS2 ...301 H1
Marina Dr *GVW* DA11 ...337 G8
Marina Gdns *CHES/WCR* EN8 ...216 D8
  COS CO15 ...159 M8
  FX IP11 ...11 H5
  ROMW/RG RM7 ...289 L3
Marina Ms *WOTN* CO14 ...137 M1
Marina Rd *RCHLM* CM3 ...196 D1
Marine Av *CVI* SS8 ...321 G3
  CVI SS8 ...321 H2
  LOS SS9 ...300 A4
  WOS/PRIT SS0 ...18 D7
Marine Cl *LOS* SS9 ...299 K4
Marine Ct *FOS* CO13 * ...137 J5
  PUR RM19 ...328 C2
Marine Dr *BARK* IG11 ...309 L2
  WOOL/PLUM SE18 ...324 C7
Marine Pde *CVI* SS8 ...321 J3
  HAR CO12 ...15 J8
  LOS SS9 ...299 K4
  RCHLM CM3 ...388 B8
  SOS SS1 ...19 J7
Marine Pde East *COS* CO15 * ...7 G4
Marine Pde West *COS* CO15 ...183 M4
Mariner Rd *MNPK* E12 ...308 C1
Mariners Ct *SBN/FI* SS3 ...303 K7
Mariners Ms *POP/IOD* E14 ...323 C7
Mariners Wy *GVW* DA11 ...337 M6
  MAL CM9 ...214 D5
Marion Av *RCOS* CO16 ...159 K4
Marion Cl *BARK/HLT* IG6 ...269 G6
Marion Gv *WFD* IG8 ...267 H4
Marisco Cl *CDW/CHF* RM16 ...331 L4
Mariskals *PIT* SS13 ...278 C8
Maritime Av *MAL* CM9 ...215 H4
Maritime Cl *GRH* DA9 ...335 L7
Maritime Ga *GVW* DA11 ...337 G6
Maritime Quay *POP/IOD* E14 ...322 D8
Maritime St *BOW* E3 ...306 C4
Marjorams Av *LOU* IG10 ...250 D2
Mark Av *CHING* E4 ...248 A6
Markby Cl *CBS* CB2 ...340 E1
Mark Av *WICKW* SS12 ...260 E7
Market Cl *COL* CO1 ...8 B5
Market End *RCOLW* CO6 ...124 C3
Market Gv *HSTD* CO9 ...346 E4
Market Hl *HVHL* CB9 ...34 D5
  MAL CM9 ...214 D4
  RCOLW CO6 ...124 D3
  SUD CO10 ...20 D7
Market La *CBE/LIN* CB1 ...24 E7
Market Link *ROM* RM1 ...289 K7
Market Pavement *BSDN* SS14 ...2 F7
Market Pl *ABR/ST* RM4 ...251 L3
  BRTR CM7 ...121 J2
  GTDUN CM6 ...117 G4
  ING CM4 ...239 L1
  ROM RM1 ...289 H3
  SOS SS1 ...19 J6
  TIL RM18 * ...331 K8
Market Rd *CHLM/WR* CM1 ...5 G5
  IP IP1 ...16 D3
  WICKW SS12 ...260 E7
Market Rw *SAFWN* CB10 ...28 A8
Market Sq *BSDN* SS14 ...2 F7
  BSF CM23 ...139 G2
  HLW CM20 ...13 G5
Market St *EHAM* E6 ...308 C4
  HAR CO12 ...15 J3
  HLWE CM17 ...188 D5
  SAFWN CB10 ...28 A7
  WOOL/PLUM SE18 ...324 D9
Markfield Gdns *CHING* E4 ...248 C7
Mark Hall Moors *HLW* CM20 ...188 D1
Markhams *SLH/COR* SS17 ...317 J3
Markhams Cha *LAIN* SS15 ...277 G6
Markhams Cl *HVHL* CB9 ...34 C4
Markhouse Av *WALTH* E17 ...284 B4
Markhouse Rd *WALTH* E17 ...284 B4
Marking's Fld *SAFWN* CB10 ...28 B7
Markland Dr *CMS* ...214 D4
Mark La *GVE* DA12 ...338 B5
Marklay Dr *RCHLM* CM3 ...244 F5
Markmanor Av *WALTH* E17 ...284 B5
Mark Rd *BOC* CM0 ...390 A4
Marks Av *CHONG* CM5 ...296 M3
Marks Cl *BCAYW* CM12 ...258 B4
  ING CM4 ...239 J4
Marks Ct *SOS* SS1 ...19 J6
Marks Gdns *BRTR* CM7 ...121 J4
Marks Hall La *GTDUN* CM6 ...190 B2
Marks Hall Rd *RCOLW* CO6 ...102 C4
Marks La *HSTD* CO9 ...243 J5
Mark St *SRTFD* E15 ...307 H4
Markwell Wd *EPP* CM16 ...236 A3
Markyate Rd *BCTR* RM8 ...309 L2
Marlands Rd *CLAY* IG5 ...286 A1
Marlborough Av *BOC* CM0 ...390 D6
Marlborough Ct *BSF* CM23 ...139 G4
  CDW/CHF RM16 ...330 F1
  COS CO15 ...6 B6
  SBF/HAD SS7 ...280 A6
  UPMR RM14 ...291 J4
Marlborough Gdns
  UPMR RM14 ...291 J4
Marlborough Rd *BCTR* RM8 ...309 H1
  BRTR CM7 ...121 K1
  BRWN CM15 ...255 G6
  CHING E4 ...266 C5
  CHLM/GWD CM2 ...4 D3
  FSTGT E7 ...307 M4
  IPNE IP4 ...17 M7
  ROMW/RG RM7 ...288 D2
  SOS SS1 ...302 A5
  SRTFD E15 * ...307 H1
  SWFD E18 ...285 L1
  WOOL/PLUM SE18 ...324 E6
Marlborough Wk
  HOC/HUL SS5 ...263 M7
Marlborough Wy
  BCAYW CM12 ...240 D8
Marle Gdns *WAB* EN9 ...233 K2
Marlescroft Wy *LOU* IG10 ...250 F3
Marley Rd
  BERM/RHTH SE16 * ...322 A7
Marlin Cl *SBF/HAD* SS7 ...281 H1
Marloes Cl *PUR* RM19 ...328 D2
Marlowe Cl *BARK/HLT* IG6 ...268 F7
  BCAYW CM12 ...258 A3
  BRTR CM7 ...121 K5
  MAL CM9 ...214 D5
Marlowe Rd *COS* CO15 ...182 D4
  WALTH E17 ...284 C3
Marlow Gdns *COLW* CO3 ...106 C7
Marlow Gdns *SOSN* SS2 ...301 H1
Marlow Ct *EHAM* E6 ...308 C7
Marlow Wy *BERM/RHTH* SE16 ...322 A5
Marlpits Rd *MAL* CM9 ...229 H1
Marlton St *GNWCH* SE10 ...323 J4
Marlyon Rd *BARK/HLT* IG6 ...270 F7

Marmadon Rd WOOL/PLUM SE18 .... 325 J7
Marmion Ap CHING E4 .... 266 * C3
Marmion Av CHING E4 .... 266 C3
Marmion Cl CHING E4 .... 266 C3
Marne Rd COLS CO2 .... 129 H1
Marney Cl CHLM/GWD CM2 .... 210 C3
Marney Dr BSDN SS14 .... 278 C6
Marney Wy FOS SO13 .... 137 H3
Maroon St POP/IOD E14 .... 322 B1
Marquis Cl COLW CO3 .... 105 L7
Marram Cl COLW CO3 .... 105 L7
Marrilyne Av PEND EN3 .... 233 J1
Marriott Rd SRTFD E15 .... 307 H5
Mar Rd SOCK/AV RM15 .... 313 M8
Marryat Rd EN EN1 .... 232 C5
Marshall Cl K/T/MI CO5 .... 149 G1
 KESG IP5 .... 50 B5
 SLH SS9 .... 299 K2
Marshall Rd LEY E10 .... 306 C4
Marshalls RCFD SS4 .... 283 C1
Marshalls Cl RAYL SS6 .... 281 J3
Marshalls Gv ROM RM1 .... 289 H1
 WOOL/PLUM SE18 .... 324 C1
Marshalls Piece GTDUN CM6 .... 96 A7
Marshalls Rd BRTR CM7 .... 121 L8
 ROMW/RG RM7 .... 289 G2
Marshbarns BSF CM23 .... 138 C1
Marsh Cl CHES/WCR EN8 .... 233 D1
Marsh Crs K/T/MI CO5 .... 130 C5
Marshcroft Dr CHES/WCR EN8 .... 216 F8
Marsh Farm La RCOLE CO7 .... 157 G3
Marsh Farm Rd RCHLM CM3 .... 245 D4
Marshfield St POP/IOD E14 .... 322 H6
Marshfoot La GRAYS RM17 .... 331 H1
Marshgate La SRTFD E15 .... 306 E5
Marsh Green Rd DAGE RM10 .... 310 D8
Marsh HI HOM E9 .... 306 B2
 WAB EN9 .... 217 M5
Marsh La FX IP11 .... 63 J4
 HLWE CM17 .... 188 F4
 LEY E10 .... 284 C7
 RBRW/HUT CM13 .... 239 K6
 SLH/COR SS17 .... 296 A7
 WARE SG12 .... 184 J1
 WARE SG12 .... 185 L6
Marsh Rd BOC CM0 .... 390 F4
 BOC CM0 .... 393 M7
 RCOLW CO6 .... 362 C5
Marsh St DART DA1 .... 334 C7
 POP/IOD E14 * 322 L7
Marsh Vw CVI SS8 .... 320 A1
Marsh View Ct VGE SS16 .... 296 B2
Marsh Wall POP/IOD E14 .... 322 B2
Marsh Wy DAGW RM9 .... 311 L9
 RCOLE CO7 .... 156 A7
Marshy La SUD CO10 .... 346 D6
Marston Beck CHLM/GWD CM2 .... 210 D3
Marston Cl DAGE RM10 .... 288 D8
Marston Rd CLAY IG5 .... 268 B8
 HOD EN11 .... 201 J2
Martello La FX IP11 .... 63 J8
Martello Rd WOTN CO4 .... 137 M1
Marten Rd WALTH E17 .... 266 C6
Marten's La RCOLW CO6 .... 361 K4
Martens Meadow BRTR CM7 .... 122 A4
Martham Cl BARK/HLT IG6 .... 268 C3
 THMD SE28 .... 326 A3
Martha Rd SRTFD E15 .... 307 H3
Martin Cl BCAYE CM11 .... 258 C4
 ED N18 .... 248 A8
Martindale Av CAN/RD E16 .... 323 K5
 LAIN SS15 .... 277 C5
Martindale Rd RAIN RM13 .... 311 L8
Martin Dr RAIN RM13 .... 311 L8
Martin End COLS CO2 .... 128 D8
Martinet Gn IPSE IP3 .... 55 L7
Martingale SBF/HAD SS7 .... 280 C8
Martingale Cl BCAYE CM11 .... 241 G8
Martingale Dr CHLM/WR CM1 .... 194 C6
Martingale Rd BCAYE CM11 .... 241 G8
Martin Gdns DAGW RM9 .... 309 H1
Martini Dr PEND EN3 .... 233 M7
Martin Rd BCTR RM8 .... 309 H1
 CHTY IP2 .... 16 B8
 SOCK/AV RM15 .... 329 G4
Martins Cl SLH/COR SS17 .... 317 G2
Martinsdale COS CO15 .... 159 J7
Martins Dr CHES/WCR EN8 .... 216 C6
 HERT/BAY SG13 .... 184 C3
Martins La CBE/LIN CB1 .... 25 H7
Martins Ms SBF/HAD SS7 .... 297 M1
Martins Pl THMD SE28 .... 325 H4
Martin Rd HSTD CO9 * 81 H4
 SUD CO10 .... 21 K3
Martin St THMD SE28 .... 325 H4
Martins Wk THMD SE28 .... 325 H4
Martinsyde IP5 .... 51 G5
Martins Wk HOC/HUL SS5 .... 282 C1
Martlesham Cl HCH RM12 .... 311 M2
Martlesham Rd FRAM/WMKT IP13 .... 50 E2
Martley Dr IL IG1 .... 286 C9
Martock Av WOS/PRIT SS0 .... 282 D8
Martyns Gv WOS/PRIT SS0 .... 300 E3
Martyns Ri SUD CO10 .... 42 H4
Marvens CHLM/GWD CM2 .... 226 A4
Marwell R ROM RM1 .... 289 K4
Marybank WOOL/PLUM SE18 .... 324 C7
Maryborough Gv COLS CO2 .... 129 L3
Maryland Pk SRTFD E15 .... 307 G2
Maryland Rd SRTFD E15 .... 307 G1
Marylands Av HOC/HUL SS5 .... 264 A2
Maryland Sq SRTFD E15 .... 307 G1
Maryland St SRTFD E15 .... 307 G1
Mary La North RCOLE CO7 .... 110 C5
Mary La South RCOLE CO7 .... 110 C6
Mary McArthur Dr STSD CM24 .... 115 M1
Maryon Rd WOOL/PLUM SE18 .... 324 A7
Maryon CHARL SE7 .... 324 B7
 IPSE IP3 .... 55 L4
Mary Park Gdns BSF CM23 .... 139 G5
Mary Rose Cl CDW/CHF RM16 .... 329 M7
 DART DA1 .... 334 C7
Mary Ruck Wy BRTR CM77 .... 121 L8
Mary St CAN/RD E16 .... 323 G5
Mary Warner Rd RCOLE CO7 .... 89 H6
Mascalls Gdns BRW CM14 .... 273 J3
Mascalls La BRW CM14 .... 273 J3
Mascalls Wy CHLM/GWD CM2 .... 210 C3
Mascot Sq CAN/RD E16 * 323 G5

Mashiters HI ROM RM1 .... 271 G7
Mashiters Wk ROM RM1 .... 289 H1
Mason Cl COLS CO2 .... 128 C2
Mason Dr HARH RM3 .... 272 B8
Mason Rd COL CO1 .... 6 C3
 RCOS CO16 .... 182 G2
Masons Cl WF IG8 .... 267 H1
 IPSE IP4 .... 17 M4
Masons Ct BSF CM23 .... 138 F2
Masons HI WOOL/PLUM SE18 .... 324 F1
Mason St EN EN1 .... 232 C5
Mason Wy WAB EN9 .... 233 M8
Massingham St WCHPL E1 .... 306 A10
Masterman Rd EHAM E6 .... 308 B7
Master's St WCHPL E1 .... 322 A1
Masthead Cl GRH DA9 .... 334 F6
Masthouse Ter POP/IOD E14 * 322 D7
Mast House Ter POP/IOD E14 .... 322 D7
Mastmaker Rd POP/IOD E14 .... 322 D5
Matcham Rd WAN E11 .... 285 H8
Matching Fld BRWN CM15 .... 383 N11
Matching Gn BSDN SS14 .... 3 M1
Matching La BSF CM23 .... 138 C1
 GTDUN CM6 .... 379 K8
Matching Rd HLWE CM17 .... 189 H5
 RBSF CM22 .... 378 C4
Matfield Cl CHLM/WR CM1 .... 194 A6
Mathams Dr BSF CM23 .... 138 C1
Mather Wy CHTY IP2 .... 17 C8
Mathews Av EHAM E6 .... 308 C1
Mathews Cl HSTD CO9 .... 81 K2
 RCOLE CO7 .... 363 K8
Mathews Md BARK/HLT IG6 .... 259 L8
Mathews Park Av SRTFD E15 .... 307 J4
Matlock Cl RIPW IP8 .... 53 H8
Matlock Gdns HCH RM12 .... 290 B1
Matlock Rd CVI SS8 .... 320 C2
 LEY E10 .... 284 C1
Matlock St WCHPL E1 .... 322 B1
Matson Rd IP IP1 .... 47 J1
Maud Cashmore Wy WOOL/PLUM SE18 .... 324 C1
Maude Rd WALTH E17 .... 284 B2
Maude Ter WALTH E17 .... 284 B2
Maud Gdns BARK IG11 .... 309 L1
 PLSTW E13 .... 307 J4
Maudlyn Rd COL CO1 .... 9 J2
Maud Rd LEY E10 .... 284 F8
 PLSTW E13 .... 307 H1
Maudslay Rd IP IP1 .... 47 J1
Maud St CAN/RD E16 .... 323 J1
Maugham Cl WICKW SS12 .... 261 J1
Maunder Cl CDW/CHF RM16 .... 330 A5
Mounds Hatch HLWS CM18 .... 203 M5
Maurice Rd CVI SS8 .... 321 G5
Mauritius Rd GNWCH SE10 .... 323 K1
Maverton Rd BOW E3 * 306 C5
Mavis Gv HCH RM12 .... 290 B1
Mawney Cl ROMW/RG RM7 .... 288 E1
Mawney Rd ROMW/RG RM7 .... 270 E8
Maxey Gdns DAGW RM9 .... 310 B1
Maxey Rd DAGW RM9 .... 310 B1
Maximfeldt Rd ERITH DA8 .... 327 H8
Maxim Rd ERITH DA8 .... 327 H8
Maximus Dr COLN CO4 .... 87 K7
Maya Cl SBN/FI SS3 .... 303 K4
Mayall Cl PEND EN3 .... 233 M8
May Av CVI SS8 .... 320 A1
 GVW DA11 .... 337 J6
Maybank Av HCH RM12 .... 311 L2
 SWFD E18 .... 267 M7
Maybank Rd SWFD E18 .... 267 M7
Mayberry Wk COLS CO2 .... 129 K2
Maybrick Rd EMPK RM11 .... 289 M3
Maybury Av CHES/WCR EN8 .... 216 C6
Maybury Cl EN EN1 .... 232 C5
 RCOLW CO6 .... 126 C2
Maybury Rd BARK IG11 .... 309 K6
 IPSE IP3 .... 55 K8
 PLSTW E13 .... 307 M8
Maybush Cl FX IP11 .... 63 J6
Maybush Rd EMPK RM11 .... 290 B5
Maycock Av COLS CO2 .... 129 M1
Maycroft Gdns GRAYS RM17 .... 331 G4
Mayda Cl HSTD CO9 .... 81 J1
Maydells IP SS13 .... 278 E8
Maydells Ct PIT SS13 * 278 E8
Mayes Cl BSF CM23 .... 139 L1
Mayesbrook Rd BARK IG11 .... 309 L3
Mayes Pl GTDUN CM6 .... 74 D7
Mayfair Av CHDH RM6 .... 287 M5
 IL IG1 .... 286 C7
 PIT SS13 .... 278 E7
Mayfair Ct COLS CO2 * 129 M1
Mayfair Gdns WFD IG8 .... 267 K6
Mayfair Rd DART DA1 .... 334 A7
Mayfield BCAYE CM11 .... 258 B3
 ING CM4 .... 222 B6
Mayfield Av HOC/HUL SS5 .... 263 H3
 SOSN SS2 .... 301 H1
 WFD IG8 .... 267 K5
Mayfield Cl COLN CO4 .... 110 F6
 HLWE CM17 .... 189 G5
Mayfield Gdns BRW CM14 .... 255 M8
Mayfield La KESG IP5 .... 50 F7
Mayfield Pk BSF CM23 .... 138 E6
Mayfield Rd BCTR RM8 .... 287 M6
 BELV DA17 .... 326 F4
 CHING E4 .... 266 C1
 CHLM/WR CM1 .... 208 D3
 GVW DA11 .... 337 H6
 IPNE IP4 .... 49 H6
 PEND EN3 .... 233 H7
 PLSTW E13 .... 307 J8
 WALTH E17 .... 266 B8
Mayfields CDW/CHF RM16 .... 330 D1
 KESG IP5 .... 50 F7
Mayflower Av HAR CO12 .... 15 L5
Mayflower Cl BERM/RHTH SE16 .... 322 A7
 COLW CO3 .... 106 A7
 SOCK/AV RM15 .... 313 M8
 SOSN SS2 .... 282 E7
 WAB EN9 .... 233 M4
Mayflower Gdns BSF CM23 .... 138 G5
Mayflower Rd BCAYE CM11 .... 258 C4
 CDW/CHF RM16 .... 329 M8
Mayflowers SBF/HAD SS7 .... 279 G6
 VGE SS16 .... 294 B1
 SUD CO10 .... 20 D7
Mayfly Cl RIPW IP8 .... 53 K5
Mayford Wy RCOS CO16 .... 158 F7
Maygreen Crs EMPK RM11 .... 289 K5
Mayhew Cl CHING E4 .... 266 D2
 SWFD E18 .... 267 D3
Mayland Av CVI SS8 .... 320 C3
Mayland Cl MAL CM9 .... 215 G9
 RCHLM CM3 .... 388 D10
Mayland Gn RCHLM CM3 .... 388 F1
Mayland HI RCHLM CM3 .... 388 F1
Mayland Rd WIT CM8 .... 171 K3

Maylands Av HCH RM12 .... 311 L1
Maylands Dr BRTR CM77 .... 121 G5
Maylands Rd HARH RM3 .... 272 F5
Maylins Dr SBW CM21 .... 162 E7
Maynard Cl GTDUN CM6 .... 117 G2
Maynards EMPK RM11 .... 284 F3
The Maynards SAFWN CB10 * 28 A7
Mayo Cl CHES/WCR EN8 .... 216 D3
Maypole Cl SAFWS CB11 .... 351 R6
 ERITH DA8 .... 334 A1
Maypole Green Rd COLS CO2 .... 181 K1
 RCOS CO16 .... 181 K1
Maypole Rd GVE DA12 .... 338 C6
 K/T/MI CO5 .... 149 M7
 MAL CM9 .... 213 C8
 WIT CM8 .... 172 C4
The Maypole GTDUN CM6 .... 116 F3
 IPSE IP3 .... 55 H3
 PLSTW E13 .... 307 K6
Maysent Av BRTR CM7 .... 99 J3
May's La RCOLE CO7 .... 89 H1
May St ST ROY SG8 .... 349 K9
Mayswood Gdns DAGE RM10 .... 310 D5
Maytree Cl RAIN RM13 .... 311 H6
Mayville Rd IL IG1 .... 286 H8
 WAN E11 .... 285 H8
May Wk CHLM/GWD CM2 .... 209 M6
 STSD CM24 .... 374 B4
Maywin Dr EMPK RM11 .... 290 D2
Maze Green Hts BSF CM23 .... 138 E2
Maze Green Rd BSF CM23 .... 138 G4
The Maze LOS SS9 .... 282 A6
Mazoe Cl BSF CM23 .... 139 G4
Mazoe Rd BSF CM23 .... 139 G4
McAdam Cl HOD EN11 .... 201 H1
McCall Crs CHARL SE7 .... 324 C4
McCalmont Dr RAYL SS6 .... 262 F6
McCudden Rd DART DA1 .... 334 C5
McCullum Rd BOW E3 .... 306 C5
McDivitt Wk LOS SS9 .... 282 D7
McDowall Cl CAN/RD E16 .... 323 K1
McEntee Av WALTH E17 .... 266 A7
McEwan Wy SRTFD E15 * 307 G5
McGrath Rd FSTGT E7 .... 307 J3
McIntosh Cl ROM RM1 .... 289 H1
McKenzie Rd BROX EN10 .... 201 H1
McLeod Rd ABYW SE2 .... 325 M7
Mead Barn EPP CM16 .... 235 M6
Mead Cl CDW/CHF RM16 .... 330 E1
 GPK RM2 .... 271 K8
 LOU IG10 .... 250 A3
Mead Ct WAB EN9 .... 233 J4
Mead Crs CHING E4 .... 266 F3
 DART DA1 .... 334 C5
Meade Rd HOD EN11 .... 201 H1
Meadgate PIT SS13 .... 278 F5
 WFD IG8 .... 268 B4
Meadgate Ter CHLM/GWD CM2 .... 5 L8
Mead Gv CHDH RM6 .... 268 A7
Mead Monks RCHLM CM3 .... 228 C3
Meadow Clays SAFWS CB11 .... 351 N1
Mead Ct BRTR CM7 .... 98 D6
 CHING E4 .... 248 D6
 COS CO15 .... 159 L6
 FX IP11 .... 62 A3
 HERT/BAY SG13 .... 184 A2
 HOM E9 .... 306 C2
 IL IG1 .... 81 J5
 PEND EN3 .... 232 B1
 RCOLE CO7 .... 110 D7
 SBF/HAD SS7 .... 280 E7
 SLH/COR SS17 .... 332 D2
Meadow Cl BCAYE CM11 * 258 F3
 WICKE SS11 .... 261 H5
Meadow Crs IPSE IP3 .... 55 L4
Meadowcroft SLH/COR SS17 * 316 C2
Meadowcroft Wy FOS CO13 .... 137 J2
Meadowcross WAB EN9 .... 233 M4
Meadow Dr SOS SS1 .... 302 B5
 VGE SS16 .... 294 F5
Meadowfield CBS CB2 .... 22 B3
Meadowford Cl THMD SE28 .... 325 H4
Meadowgate ING CM4 .... 241 D2
Meadow Grass Cl COLW CO3 .... 105 L7
Meadowland RD WICKE SS11 .... 261 K7
Meadowlands BSF CM23 .... 115 K3
 EMPK RM11 .... 290 B5
Meadow La CBE/LIN CB1 .... 24 E7
 K/T/MI CO5 .... 177 M9
 SUD CO10 .... 20 D7
 WICKE SS11 .... 261 H2
Meadow Ms BCAYE CM11 .... 258 F3
 ING CM4 .... 222 B6
Meadow Rd BARK IG11 .... 309 L3
 CDW/CHF RM16 .... 314 F8
 COLS CO2 .... 129 G8
 DAGW RM9 .... 310 C3
 EPP CM16 .... 234 F7
 GVW DA11 .... 337 K2
 HOC/HUL SS5 .... 263 H3
 LOU IG10 .... 250 B5
 RCHLM CM3 .... 243 H1
 ROMW/RG RM7 .... 288 D2
 SAFWN CB10 .... 341 L6
 SBF/HAD SS7 .... 299 H3
Meadows Cl RCHLM CM3 .... 212 D7
Meadow Side CHLM/WR CM1 .... 5 G1
Meadowside BRTR CM7 .... 99 H3
 CHLM/GWD CM2 .... 5 K2
 RAYL SS6 .... 281 J3
Meadowside Gdns IPNE IP4 .... 49 J4
Meadowside Rd UPMR RM14 .... 312 F5
The Meadows BSF CM23 .... 138 F4
 RBRW/HUT CM13 .... 274 F1
 WAB EN9 .... 233 M6
Meadowsweet Cl BSF CM23 .... 138 D3
 CAN/RD E16 .... 323 M4
 HVHL CB9 .... 35 A4
Meadowvale IPNE IP4 .... 49 M1
Meadow Vw EPP CM16 .... 220 D1
 SWFD E18 .... 267 M7
Meadow Wy BOC CM0 .... 393 K6
 BRTR CM77 .... 121 H8
 CHIG IG7 .... 268 F1
 COS CO15 .... 182 C6
 HOC/HUL SS5 .... 264 B8

K/T/MI CO5 .... 153 L3
 RCHLM CM3 .... 231 K7
 SBW CM21 .... 163 H8
 UPMR RM14 .... 290 F7
 The Wickw SS11 .... 261 G2
The Meadow Wy BCAYE CM11 .... 258 F2
Mead Pastures MAL CM9 .... 213 G8
Mead Pth CHLM/GWD CM2 .... 209 D8
Mead Rd GVW DA11 .... 337 J2
Meads Cl ING CM4 .... 239 C7
Meads La GDMY/SEVK IG3 .... 287 H8
Meads Rd PEND EN3 .... 248 B1
The Meads CHLM/GWD CM2 .... 4 F5
 ING CM4 .... 239 C7
 UPMR RM14 .... 291 H7
 VGE SS16 .... 296 D2
Meadsway RBRW/HUT CM13 .... 273 L5
 BROX EN10 * 201 J7
 CHES/WCR EN8 .... 74 D7
 GTDUN CM6 .... 116 F3
 LAIN SS15 .... 276 E7
 SUD CO10 .... 42 E8
Meadview Rd WARE SG12 .... 184 D1
Mead Wk DAGW CM5 .... 382 G4
Meadway CVI SS8 .... 320 A1
 GDMY/SEVK IG3 .... 309 H1
 GPK RM2 .... 271 K8
 GRAYS RM17 .... 331 G5
 HOD EN11 .... 201 H1
 HSTD CO9 .... 80 B1
 MAL CM9 .... 213 C8
 MGTR CO11 .... 90 E2
 PEND EN3 .... 232 B1
 RAYL SS6 .... 281 J4
 SBF/HAD SS7 .... 279 M6
 WFD IG8 .... 267 M6
The Meadway BKHH IG9 .... 267 A8
 WOS/PRIT SS0 .... 300 A5
Meakins Cl LOS SS9 * 282 C7
Mealand Rd MNPK E12 .... 308 F2
Mearns Pl CHLM/GWD CM2 .... 210 C1
Meath Rd IL IG1 .... 286 D6
 SRTFD E15 .... 307 J6
Medbury Rd GVE DA12 .... 338 F6
Medcalfe Ter SUD CO10 * 20 D6
Medcalf Rd PEND EN3 .... 233 J7
Medebridge Rd CDW/CHF RM16 .... 314 C6
Mede Wy RCOLE CO7 .... 130 F2
Medhurst Cl BOW E3 .... 306 B6
Medhurst Crs GVE DA12 .... 338 C6
Medick Ct GRAYS RM17 .... 331 H5
Medina Cl GRAYS RM17 .... 331 H5
Medlar Dr GVW DA11 .... 337 G5
Medlar Rd GRAYS RM17 .... 331 G5
Medlars Md RBSF CM22 .... 376 C12
Medley Rd BRTR CM77 .... 120 C3
Medoc Cl PIT SS13 .... 278 F5
Medora Rd ROMW/RG RM7 .... 289 G2
Medusa Ct HAR CO12 .... 71 G3
Medway Cl CHLM/GWD CM2 .... 209 C1
 IL IG1 .... 308 F2
Medway Crs LOS SS9 .... 299 L3
Medway Rd BOW E3 .... 306 A6
 IPSE IP3 .... 54 C7
Meekings Rd SUD CO10 .... 21 J3
The Meers FOS CO13 .... 137 H3
Meesden Mdw MAL CM9 .... 214 B5
Meeson Rd SRTFD E15 .... 307 J4
Meeson's La GRAYS RM17 .... 330 C3
Meeson Ms RCFD SS4 .... 283 G2
Meeson St CLPT E5 .... 306 F1
Meesons Whf SRTFD E15 * 306 F4
Meeting Fld SUD CO10 .... 42 A2
Meeting La HSTD CO9 .... 345 N6
 K/T/MI CO5 .... 178 F5
Meggison Wy SBF/HAD SS7 .... 297 M2
Megs Wy BRTR CM7 .... 121 M2
Meister Cl IL IG1 .... 287 G8
Melba Ct CHLM/GWD CM2 .... 5 G4
Melba Gdns TIL RM18 .... 331 L8
Melbourne Av CHLM/WR CM1 .... 193 G8
Melbourne Cha COLS CO2 .... 129 L4
Melbourne Gdns CHDH RM6 .... 288 B3
Melbourne Rd COS CO15 .... 6 A7
 EHAM E6 .... 308 C1
 IL IG1 .... 286 H1
 IPNE IP4 .... 49 H6
 LEY E10 .... 284 C1
 TIL RM18 .... 331 L8
 WALTH E17 .... 284 B2
Melcombe Rd SBF/HAD SS7 .... 297 M2
Meldrum Rd GDMY/SEVK IG3 .... 287 J1
Melford Av BARK IG11 .... 309 H3
Melford Cl IPNE IP4 .... 49 J6
Melford Gv BRTR CM77 .... 120 C3
Melford Rd EHAM E6 .... 308 C1
 IL IG1 .... 287 G1
 SUD CO10 .... 42 C6
 SUD CO10 .... 42 C7
 WALTH E17 .... 284 D1
 WAN E11 .... 285 H7
Melford Wy FX IP11 .... 10 D4
Melksham Cl HARH RM3 .... 272 C5
Melksham Gdns HARH RM3 .... 272 C5
Mellis Cl HVHL CB9 .... 35 A4
Mellis Ct FX IP11 .... 62 C8
Mellish Cl BARK IG11 .... 309 L3
Mellish Rd WALTH E17 .... 267 K4
Mellish St POP/IOD E14 .... 322 D6
Mellor Cha COLW CO3 .... 106 B5
Mellor Cl COLW CO3 .... 106 B5
Mellow Purgess Cl LAIN SS15 .... 276 F7
Mellow Purgess End LAIN SS15 .... 276 F7
Mellows Rd CLAY IG5 .... 286 C1
 IL IG1 .... 286 C1
Mell Rd MAL CM9 .... 385 G9
Mell St GNWCH SE10 .... 323 K1
Melon Rd WAN E11 .... 285 H8
Melplash Cl IPSE IP3 .... 55 K1
Melplash Rd IPSE IP3 .... 55 K1
Melrose Gdns COS CO15 .... 159 M8
 IPNE IP4 .... 49 M8
Melrose Rd K/T/MI CO5 .... 177 J9
Melstock Av UPMR RM14 .... 312 F1
Melton Cl RCOS CO16 .... 182 C5
Melton Gdns ROM RM1 .... 289 D1
Melville Ct DEPT SE8 .... 322 F4
Melville Dr WICKW SS12 .... 261 G3
Melville Heath RCHLM CM3 .... 149 A1
Melville Rd IPNE IP4 .... 17 L5
 RAIN RM13 .... 311 H6
 ROMW/RG RM7 .... 270 D2
 WALTH E17 .... 266 C7
Memorial Av SRTFD E15 .... 307 H8
Memory Cl MAL CM9 .... 213 G5
Mendham Cl RAYL SS6 .... 281 G5
Mendip Crs WOS/PRIT SS0 .... 18 A5
Mendip Cl CHLM/WR CM1 .... 193 G5
Mendip Dr KESG IP5 .... 49 G5
Mendip Rd CHLM/WR CM1 .... 193 K5
 EMPK RM11 .... 289 K5
 HOC/HUL SS5 .... 264 B8

GNTH/NBYPK IG2 .... 287 H3
 LOS SS9 .... 300 D1
The Mendips WOS/PRIT SS0 * 282 D3
Mendlesham Cl RCOS CO16 .... 182 C5
Mendoza Cl EMPK RM11 .... 290 F7
Menin Rd COLS CO2 .... 129 G1
Mentmore VGE SS16 .... 294 F5
Menzies Av LAIN SS15 .... 276 C7
Meon Cl CHLM/WR CM1 .... 194 A6
Meopel Av CVI SS8 .... 298 D2
Merbury Rd THMD SE28 .... 325 G4
Merbury St WOOL/PLUM SE18 .... 324 E6
Mercator Pl POP/IOD E14 .... 322 D8
Mercer Av SBN/FI SS3 .... 303 K1
Mercer Rd BCAYE CM11 .... 241 G8
Mercers HLWW/ROY CM19 .... 203 H4
Mercers Cl GNWCH SE10 .... 323 K1
Mercers Wy COL CO1 .... 8 B4
Merchant St BOW E3 * 306 C5
 RCHLM CM3 * 245 H6
Mercia Cl CHLM/GWD CM2 .... 210 D8
Mercury Cl CDW/CHF RM16 .... 331 H5
Mercury Gdns ROM RM1 .... 289 J3
Meredene BSDN SS14 .... 278 D8
Meredith Rd CDW/CHF RM16 .... 331 J5
 COS CO15 .... 6 A7
 IP IP1 .... 47 J3
Meredith SBW CM21 .... 162 E7
Mere Gdns IPNE IP4 .... 55 L5
Meres St WIT CM8 .... 171 H4
Mereworth Rd PLSTW E13 .... 307 K7
Meriadoc Dr RCHLM CM3 .... 245 H6
Meriden Cl BARK/HLT IG6 .... 268 C3
Meridian Sq SRTFD E15 .... 307 G5
Meridian Wy WARE SG12 .... 185 J4
 RBRW/HUT CM13 .... 274 A1
Merilies Cl WOS/PRIT SS0 .... 300 E2
Merilies Gdns WOS/PRIT SS0 .... 300 E2
Merino Cl WAN E11 .... 285 L6
Merivale Cl MGTR CO11 .... 90 E2
Merivale Rd BARK/HLT IG6 .... 269 G3
Merlin Cl CHLM/GWD CM2 .... 210 C8
 CRW RM5 .... 271 G5
 WAB EN9 .... 234 D1
Merlin Ct CVI SS8 .... 320 C1
Merlin End COLN CO4 .... 108 C4
Merlin Gdns ROM RM1 .... 271 G5
Merlin Gv BARK/HLT IG6 .... 268 C3
Merlin Pl CHLM/WR CM1 .... 193 G5
Merlin Rd CHTY IP2 .... 53 H7
 CRW RM5 .... 271 G5
 MNPK E12 .... 286 A7
Merlin Wy EPP CM16 .... 221 H4
 WICKE SS11 .... 261 G4
Merlin Vw EPP CM16 .... 221 H4
Mermagen Dr RAIN RM13 .... 311 J3
Mermaid Cl GVW DA11 .... 337 G5
Mermaid Wy MAL CM9 .... 214 B5
Merriam Av HOM E9 .... 306 C2
Merriam Cl CHING E4 .... 266 F4
 MGTR CO11 .... 65 G5
Merricks La VGE SS16 .... 296 B3
Merrielands Crs DAGW RM9 .... 310 C5
Merrilees Crs COS CO15 .... 160 A4
Merring Wy WAB EN9 .... 203 G3
Merrion Cl RIPW IP8 .... 53 H3
Merrivale SBF/HAD SS7 .... 297 M3
Merrivale Av REDBR IG4 .... 286 A2
Merryfield Ap LOS SS9 .... 300 E5
Merryfields Av HOC/HUL SS5 .... 264 B8
Merryhill Cl CHING E4 .... 248 E4
Merrylands LAIN SS15 .... 276 D6
Merrymount Gdns COS CO15 .... 7 J5
Merryweather Cl DART DA1 .... 334 D6
Mersea Av K/T/MI CO5 .... 177 J2
Mersea Crs WICKW SS12 .... 261 K8
Mersea Fleet Wy BRTR CM7 .... 121 H4
Mersea Rd COLS CO2 .... 129 K4
 K/T/MI CO5 .... 153 H8
 K/T/MI CO5 .... 153 L3
Mersea Vw RCOS CO16 .... 180 D2
Mersey Rd UPMR RM14 .... 290 C4
Mersey Wy UPMR RM14 .... 54 E2
 WALTH E17 .... 284 D1
 WIT CM8 .... 172 C4
Merstham Dr RCOS CO16 .... 158 F7
Merten Rd CHDH RM6 .... 288 B6
Merton Ct COLS CO2 .... 129 K6
 RCHLM CM3 .... 245 J7
Merton Pl CDW/CHF RM16 .... 331 H5
 RCHLM CM3 .... 245 J7
Merton Rd BARK IG11 .... 309 L3
 GDMY/SEVK IG3 .... 287 G3
 HOC/HUL SS5 .... 263 K5
 SBF/HAD SS7 .... 297 M1
 WALTH E17 .... 284 D1
Messant Cl GPK RM2 .... 272 C8
Messines Rd COLS CO2 .... 129 G1
Messing Gn K/T/MI CO5 .... 150 A3
Mess Rd SBN/FI SS3 .... 303 J8
Meteor Rd WOS/PRIT SS0 .... 18 A5
Meteor Wy CHLM/WR CM1 .... 4 C5
Metford Crs PEND EN3 .... 233 M7
Methersgate BSDN SS14 .... 3 J4
Methuen Rd BELV DA17 .... 326 F4
Metropolitan Cl POP/IOD E14 .... 322 C1
Metsons La CHLM/WR CM1 .... 223 G3
Metz Av CVI SS8 .... 320 D1
Meux Cl CHESW EN7 .... 232 C5
Mews Ct BSF CM23 .... 115 K3
Mews Pl WFD IG8 .... 267 K3
The Mews BSF CM23 .... 139 H6
 HOC/HUL SS5 .... 263 H3
 REDBR IG4 .... 286 A3
 ROM RM1 .... 289 H2
 SBW CM21 .... 162 E7
 SUD CO10 * 45 K1
Meyel Av CVI SS8 .... 298 D2
Meyer Gn EN EN1 .... 232 B8
Meynell Av CVI SS8 .... 320 F3
Meynell Gdns HOM E9 .... 306 C2
Meynell Rd HARH RM3 .... 271 L5
 HOM E9 .... 306 A4
Meyrick Crs COLS CO2 .... 107 J8
Mey Wk HOC/HUL SS5 .... 263 M7
Micawber Wy CHLM/WR CM1 .... 193 G6
Michael Gdns EMPK RM11 .... 290 A3
Michael Rd WAN E11 .... 285 H6
Michaels Rd BSF CM23 .... 115 M3
Michaelstowe Cl HAR CO12 .... 70 D1
Michaelstowe Dr HAR CO12 .... 70 D1
Michel Wk WOOL/PLUM SE18 .... 324 E1
Michigan Av MNPK E12 .... 308 D1
Michigan Cl KESG IP5 .... 50 A5
Mickfield Ms FX IP11 * 62 C8
Micklegate Rd FX IP11 .... 11 H7
Mid Colne VGE SS16 .... 3 M9
Middleborough COL CO1 .... 8 M8
Middle Boy ABR/ST RM4 .... 251 D7
Middle Dr SLH/COR SS17 .... 295 L4
Middlefield HSTD CO9 .... 80 E3
Middlefield Av HOD EN11 .... 201 H1
Middlefield Rd HOD EN11 .... 201 H1
 MGTR CO11 .... 91 K2
Middle Gn BRWN CM15 .... 383 R11
 RCOLW CO6 .... 83 H4

Middle King *BRTR* CM7 ....122 A4
Middle Md *RCFD* SS4 ....283 J3
Middlemead *CHLM/GWD* CM2 ...242 C1
  RCHLM CM3 ...242 F3
Middle Mead Cl
  CHLM/GWD CM2 ...242 C1
Middle Mi *COL* CO1 ...9 H7
Middle Rd *PLSTW* E13 ...307 K8
  RBRW/HUT CM13 ...256 F7
  WAB EN9 ...233 J2
Middle St *SAFWS* CB11 ...72 C5
  WAB EN9 ...218 B1
Middleton Av *CHING* E4 ...266 C3
Middleton Cl *CHING* E4 ...266 C2
  CHTY IP2 ...53 J3
  RCOS CO16 ...159 G7
Middleton Dr
  BERM/RHTH SE16 ...322 A5
Middleton Gdns
  GNTH/NBYPK IG2 ...286 E4
Middleton Hall La
  BRWN CM15 ...256 B5
Middleton Rd *BRWN* CM15 ...256 B4
  SUD CO10 ...20 B4
Middleton Rw *RCHLM* CM3 ...245 H7
Middle Wy *SUD* CO10 ...43 G1
Middlewick Cl *COLS* CO2 ...128 C4
Midguard Wy *MAL* CM9 ...214 B5
Midhurst Av *WOS/PRIT* SS0 ...201 C1
Midhurst Cl *HCH* RM12 ...311 J1
Midland Cl *COLS* CO2 ...129 J1
Midland Rd *LEY* E10 ...284 F5
Midlothian Rd *BOW* E3 ...306 C4
Midship
  BERM/RHTH SE16 ...322 A4
Midship Point *POP/IOD* E14 * ...322 D5
Midsummer Meadow
  SBN/FI SS3 ...303 H4
Midway *COS* CO15 ...182 A7
Midway Rd *COLS* CO2 ...128 F3
Mighell Av *REDBR* IG4 ...286 A3
Milano Av *WDBR* IP12 ...51 H5
Milbank *CHLM/GWD* CM2 ...210 E1
Milbanke Cl *SBN/FI* SS3 ...303 H4
Milburn Crs *CHLM/WR* CM1 ...209 G4
Milch La *RCHLM* CM3 ...120 D8
Milden Rd *CHTY* IP2 ...47 K8
Mildmayes *VGE* SS16 ...294 F1
Mildmay *CHLM/GWD* CM2 ...210 H7
  IL IG1 ...286 E8
  IPSE IP3 ...54 F4
  ROMW/RG RM7 ...288 F3
Mildmays *RCHLM* CM3 ...211 M5
Mildred Cl *DART* DA1 ...334 D8
Mildred Rd *ERITH* DA8 ...327 H8
Mile Cl *WAB* EN9 ...233 K3
Mile End Pl *WCHPL* E1 ...306 C7
Mile End Rd *BOW* E3 ...306 C7
  COLN CO4 ...107 H5
The Mile End *WALTH* E17 ...266 A7
Miles Cl *COLW* CO5 ...105 M7
  HLWW/ROY CM19 ...12 C9
Miles Dr *THMD* SE28 ...325 H4
Miles Gray Rd *BSDN* SS14 ...277 H4
Mile Stone Rd *RDART* DA2 ...334 E4
Milford Cl *RCOLE* CO7 ...130 F4
Milford Rd *CDW/CHF* RM16 ...315 G4
Military Rd *COL* CO1 ...8 E9
Military Wy *HAR* CO12 ...70 A1
Milk St *CAN/RD* E16 ...324 E4
Milkwell Rd *WFD* IG8 ...267 L6
Millais Av *MNPK* E12 ...308 D2
Millais Pl *TIL* RM18 ...331 K6
Millais Rd *WAN* E11 ...306 F1
Millars Cl *RCHLM* CM3 ...245 H5
The Millars *CHLM/WR* CM1 ...193 K2
Millbank Av *CHONG* CM5 ...382 G3
Millbridge Rd *WAB* EN9 ...171 J8
Millbrook Gdns *CHDH* RM6 ...288 B4
  GPK RM2 ...271 H4
Mill Cswy *ROY* SG8 ...349 P6
Mill Cha *HSTD* CO9 ...81 H3
  HVHL CB9 ...344 B8
Mill Ct *BOC* CO10 ...76 E3
  BRTR CM7 ...76 B3
  CHLM/WR CM1 ...191 K8
  FX IP11 ...10 F2
  K/T/MI CO5 ...149 M7
  RBSF CM22 ...374 D4
  RIPS/CAP IP9 ...58 B4
Mill Ct *GTDUN* CM6 ...377 Q2
Mill End *RCOLW* CO6 ...74 D3
Millennium Cl *CAN/RD* E16 ...323 K2
Millennium Ct *POP/IOD* E14 ...323 G6
Millennium Wy *GNWCH* SE10 ...323 H6
Mill Wharf *POP/IOD* E14 ...323 G7
Miller Av *PEND* EN3 ...23 H8
Miller Rd *GVE* DA12 ...338 C2
Miller's Barn Rd *COS* CO15 ...182 D4
Millers Cl ...99 K5
  BSF CM23 ...138 D4
  CBE/LIN CB1 ...25 G6
  CHIG IG7 ...269 L1
  COLW CO3 ...105 M7
  RCOLW CO6 ...141 E6
Millers Cft *CHLM/GWD* CM2 ...210 C7
  GTDUN CM6 ...117 H4
Millersdale *HLWW/ROY* CM19 ...203 J5
Millers Green Rd *CHONG* CM5 ...381 Q5
Miller's La *CHIG* IG7 ...251 J8
  COLW CO3 ...106 A4
  WARE SG12 ...185 K5
Millers Md *K/T/MI* CO5 ...149 H1
Millers Rd *BRTR* CM7 ...354 B3
Millers Vw *IP* IP1 ...41 L6
Mill Fld *GTDUN* CM6 ...141 K1
  HLWE CM17 ...188 F1
  RIPW IP8 ...47 G3
Millfield *CHONG* CM5 ...383 K2
  RIPS/CAP IP9 * ...365 P6
Millfield Av *WALTH* E17 ...266 C4
Millfield Cl *RAYL* SS6 ...281 K2
Millfield Dr *GVW* DA11 ...337 H7
Millfield Gdns *IPNE* IP4 ...48 H7
Mill Fids *RCHLM* CM3 ...212 D7
Millfields *BOC* CM0 * ...393 L8
  CHLM/WR CM1 ...209 L3
  COLS CO2 ...128 D8
  K/T/MI CO5 ...149 M7
  SBW CM21 ...163 L3
  STSD CM24 ...115 M3
Millfields Wy *HVHL* CB9 ...34 E5
Mill Gra *BOC* CM0 ...393 L6
Mill Gn *BOC* CM0 ...393 L9
  PIT SS13 ...278 D3
Mill Green Ct *PIT* SS13 * ...278 D3
Mill Green Rd *ING* CM4 ...323 F7
Mill Gv *CHONG* CM5 ...383 L1
Millharbour *POP/IOD* E14 ...322 E6
Millhaven Cl *CHDH* RM6 ...287 L4
Millhead Wy *RCFD* SS4 ...283 L3
Mill Hl *BRTR* CM7 ...121 L3

BRWN CM15 ...256 B3
BSF CM23 ...114 F4
CHLM/GWD CM2 ...225 J3
HVHL CB9 ...34 C6
MGTR CO11 ...90 A1
MGTR CO11 ...90 F1
RCHLM CM3 ...229 M5
RIPS/CAP IP9 ...58 N3
SBF/HAD SS7 ...298 A4
STSD CM24 ...115 L3
SUD CO10 ...20 D7
Mill Hill Dr *BCAYW* CM12 ...240 E8
Millhurst Ms *HLWE* CM17 ...188 F5
Millicent Rd *LEY* E10 ...284 C6
Milligans Cha
  CHLM/GWD CM2 ...225 L4
Milligan St *POP/IOD* E14 ...322 C5
Milliners Wy *BSF* CM23 ...138 F5
Millman Rd RM4 ...253 M2
BCAYE CM11 ...241 L8
BROX EN10 ...201 G7
BRTR CM77 ...120 B5
BRTR CM77 ...122 A7
BRTR CM7 ...354 E6
BRWN CM15 ...238 A1
BRWN CM15 ...383 M11
BUNT SG9 ...371 M10
CBE/LIN CB1 ...24 F7
CBS CB2 ...22 B8
CDW/CHF RM16 ...315 K6
CHDH RM6 ...288 B4
CHES/WCR EN8 ...216 F6
CHING E4 ...248 E3
CHLM/WR CM1 ...193 L4
CHONG CM5 ...221 M7
CHONG CM5 ...380 C4
CHONG CM5 ...383 K3
COLS CO2 ...128 E8
COLS CO2 ...151 J2
FOS CO15 ...136 B6
FX IP11 ...11 H2
GTDUN CM6 ...96 A8
GTDUN CM6 ...117 G5
HAR CO12 ...15 J7
HLWE CM17 ...188 F5
HSTD CO9 ...346 B10
HSTD CO9 ...357 M9
HSTD CO9 ...358 D10
ING CM4 ...223 K7
ING CM4 ...241 J3
K/T/MI CO5 ...125 L3
MAL CM9 ...214 D5
MAL CM9 ...214 C2
MAL CM9 ...384 B2
MGTR CO11 ...91 G1
MGTR CO11 ...366 A8
RBSF CM22 ...378 A1
RCFD SS4 ...283 L4
RCHLM CM3 ...143 G6
RCHLM CM3 ...144 E6
RCHLM CM3 ...169 K2
RCHLM CM3 ...212 B2
RCHLM CM3 ...229 M4
RCOLE CO7 ...109 L1
RCOLE CO7 ...363 N10
RCOLW CO6 ...82 C8
RCOLW CO6 ...361 Q1
RCOLW CO6 ...362 D5
RCOS CO16 ...134 C7
RCOS CO16 ...135 J4
RIPS/CAP IP9 ...365 P6
RIPW IP8 ...47 G4
RIPW IP8 ...53 H6
SAFWN CB10 ...28 B7
SAFWN CB10 ...340 H2
SAFWS CB11 ...351 N2
SBW CM21 ...163 G6
SLH/COR SS17 ...295 M7
SLH/COR SS17 ...295 M7
SUD CO10 ...20 B7
SUD CO10 ...38 L5
WFD IG8 ...267 J4
WIT CM8 ...171 J3
WOOL/PLUM SE18 ...324 D8
WOTN CO14 ...369 M12
Mill Lane Cl *BROX* EN10 ...201 G7
  RCOS CO16 ...134 D7
Millmarsh La *PEND* EN3 ...248 B1
Mill Park Rd *HCH* RM12 ...311 J1
Mill Park Dr *BRTR* CM7 ...121 L4
Mill Piece *POP/IOD* E14 ...322 B2
Mill Pl *POP/IOD* E14 ...322 B2
Mill Pond Rd *DART* DA1 ...334 E5
Mill Race *WARE* SG12 ...185 L5
Mill Ri *RIPS/CAP* IP9 ...364 G8
Mill Rd *BCAYE* CM11 ...259 G2
BOC CM0 ...390 D5
BOC CM0 ...393 L6
BRTR CM7 ...76 E1
BRTR CM7 ...354 C12
CAN/RD E16 ...323 L4
CHLM/WR CM1 ...165 G8
COLN CO4 ...87 J1
COLN CO4 ...107 H1
GTDUN CM6 ...118 D8
GVW DA11 ...337 H5
HSTD CO9 ...344 H10
HSTD CO9 ...345 K3
HVHL CB9 ...34 D6
HVHL CB9 ...343 M5
IL IG1 ...79 J3
ING CM4 ...241 H3
IPSE IP3 ...17 H9
K/T/MI CO5 ...177 M3
MAL CM9 ...175 G6
PUR RM19 ...334 E1
RBSF CM22 ...374 D7
RCHLM CM3 ...388 D8
RCOLE CO7 ...64 D7
RCOLW CO6 ...105 Q1
RCOLW CO6 ...361 Q1
SAFWN CB10 ...31 K7
SAFWS CB11 ...372 H1
SOCK/AV RM15 ...328 F3
Mills Ct *PIT* SS13 ...278 F4
Mills Gv *POP/IOD* E14 ...322 F5
Mill Side *STSD* CM24 ...115 L3
Mills La *SOCK/AV* RM15 ...314 D4
Millsmead Wy *LOU* IG10 ...250 D7
Mills Rd *SUD* CO10 ...21 H5
The Mills *IPNE* IP4 ...48 F5
Mill St *BSF* CM23 ...139 H4
COL CO1 ...8 E6
HLWE CM17 ...188 F4
RCOLE CO7 ...156 D7
RCOLW CO6 ...361 M8
RCOLW CO6 ...361 Q1
RCOS CO16 ...134 C5
Mills Wy *RBRW/HUT* CM13 ...256 F4

Mill Tye *SUD* CO10 ...45 K5
Millview *HSTD* CO9 * ...81 K8
Mill Vw *SAFWN* CB10 ...341 K7
Millview Ct *RCFD* SS4 * ...283 J4
Millview Mdw *RCFD* SS4 ...283 J4
Mill Vue Rd *CHLM/GWD* CM2 ...210 C3
Mill Wk *K/T/MI* CO5 ...149 M7
Millwall Dock Rd
  POP/IOD E14 ...322 D6
Millways *MAL* CM9 ...198 E1
Millwell Crs *CHIG* IG7 ...269 G4
Millwrights *K/T/MI* CO5 ...149 M7
Milner Pl *CBS* CB2 ...22 B2
Milner Rd *BCTR* RM8 ...287 H7
SRTFD E15 ...307 H7
SUD CO10 ...21 L4
Milner St *WCHPL* E1 ...17 H7
Milnrow *RIPW* IP8 ...53 H5
Milroy Av *GVW* DA11 ...357 H7
Milton Av *BRTR* CM7 ...121 K5
EHAM E6 ...308 A4
GVE DA12 ...338 A6
HCH RM12 ...289 H7
VGE SS16 ...294 B1
WOS/PRIT SS0 ...18 C6
Milton Cl *COLW* CO3 ...105 J3
Milton Crs *CHONG* CM5 ...380 C12
GNTH/NBYPK IG2 ...286 F5
Milton Gdns *TIL* RM18 ...331 L7
Milton Hall Cl *HPLS* SS3 ...303 A6
Milton Hall Rd *GVE* DA12 ...338 A6
Milton Pl *CHLM/WR* CM1 ...193 M4
GVE DA12 ...337 M4
SOS SS1 ...18 D7
Milton Rd *BELV* DA17 ...326 D7
BRW CM14 ...273 L2
GRAYS RM17 ...330 D3
GVE DA12 ...357 J4
HAR CO12 ...15 J7
MAL CM9 ...214 D5
MGTR CO11 ...90 E3
ROM RM1 ...289 K4
SLH/COR SS17 ...295 J7
SWCM DA10 ...336 B4
WALTH E17 ...284 D2
WIT CM8 ...147 J4
WOS/PRIT SS0 ...18 C6
Milton St *IPNE* IP4 ...48 H7
SOSN SS2 ...19 H3
SWCM DA10 ...336 B4
Miltsin Av *CVI* SS8 ...298 F8
Milverton Gdns
  GDMY/SEVK IG3 ...287 J7
Milwards *HLWW/ROY* CM19 ...203 H5
Mimosa Cl *BRWN* CM15 ...255 L5
CHLM/WR CM1 ...194 C7
HARH RM3 ...271 M6
VGE SS16 ...294 C1
Minchen Rd *HLW* CM20 ...13 M1
Minden Rd *SUD* CO10 ...20 D7
Mineral St *WOOL/PLUM* SE18 ...325 H7
Minerva Cl *HAR* CO12 ...35 G7
HVHL CB9 ...34 D8
Minerva Rd *CHING* E4 ...266 D7
Ming St *POP/IOD* E14 ...322 D3
Minos Wy *IP* IP1 ...47 J5
Minsmere Dr *RCOS* CO16 ...158 F7
Minsmere Wy *SUD* CO10 ...21 J5
Minson Rd *HOM* E9 ...306 F1
Minster Rd *HVHL* CB9 ...34 C8
LAIN SS15 ...276 F7
Minster Wy *EMPK* RM11 ...290 F6
Minton Hts *RCFD* SS4 ...264 F7
Minton La *HLWE* CM17 ...204 A5
Miramar Av *CVI* SS8 ...320 B2
Miramar Wy *HCH* RM12 ...312 A2
Miranda Wk *COLN* CO4 ...108 B6
Mirfield St *CHARL* SE7 ...324 A6
Miriam Rd *WOOL/PLUM* SE18 ...325 H4
Mirosa Dr *MAL* CM9 ...214 A6
Mirosa Reach *MAL* CM9 ...214 A6
Mission Gv *WALTH* E17 ...284 C2
Mission La *RCOLE* CO7 ...3 H1
Mistley End *VGE* SS16 ...294 F2
Mistley Pth *VGE* SS16 ...3 H1
Mistley Rd *HLW* CM20 ...188 B4
Mistley Side *VGE* SS16 ...3 H1
Mitcham Rd *EHAM* E6 ...308 A2
GDMY/SEVK IG3 ...287 K2
Mitchell Av *GVW* DA11 ...337 G2
HSTD CO9 ...81 H2
Mitchell Cir *BRTR* CM7 ...354 F11
Mitchell Cl *ABYW* SE2 ...325 M4
BELV DA17 ...326 F6
RAIN RM13 ...311 M6
Mitchells Av *CVI* SS8 ...321 C1
Mitchell Wy *RCHLM* CM3 ...245 G5
Mitford Cl *IP* IP1 ...47 M1
Mitre Gdns *BSF* CM23 ...139 H5
Mitre Rd *SRTFD* E15 ...307 H1
The Mitre *POP/IOD* E14 ...322 C3
Mitre Wy *IPSE* IP3 ...17 K7
Mitton V *BCAYE* CM11 ...259 H4
Moat Edge Gdns
  BCAYW CM12 ...258 D1
Moat Farm Cha *WIT* CM8 ...171 J4
Moat Farm Rd *IPNE* IP4 ...48 J1
Moat Fld *RCOLW* CO6 ...3 H1
Moat Flds *RCOLW* CO6 ...85 Q7
Moat House Ldg *BSDN* SS14 * ...3 H1
Moat La *BURES* CO8 ...359 A5
Moat Ri *RAYL* SS6 ...281 G4
Moat Rd *HSTD* CO9 ...344 H6
RCOLW CO6 ...85 Q7
Moatside *BUNT* SG9 ...371 F8
Moden Rd *WOTN* CO14 ...137 K2
Moffat Av *IPNE* IP4 ...49 G4
Mohmmad Khan Rd
  WAN E11 * ...285 J2
Moiety Rd *POP/IOD* E14 ...322 C4
Mole Hall La *SAFWS* CB11 ...372 G6
Molehill Green Rbt
  RBSF CM22 ...375 K8
Molesworth *HOD* EN11 ...185 H4
Mollands Cl *COLW* CO3 ...296 C4
Mollands La *SOCK/AV* RM15 ...314 D4
Mollison Av *PEND* EN3 ...232 C5
PEND EN3 ...248 B1
Molrams La *HLW* CM20 ...210 A2
Momples Rd *HLW* CM20 ...188 B4
Monarch Cl *HVHL* CB9 ...34 D6
RAIN RM13 ...311 H5
TIL RM18 ...331 L8
Monarch Dr *CAN/RD* E16 ...324 A1
Monarch Pl *BKHH* IG9 ...267 M1
Monarch Rd *BELV* DA17 ...326 D6
Monarch's Wy
  CHES/WCR EN8 ...232 A7
Monastery Rd *LAIN* SS15 ...276 F7
Mona St *CAN/RD* E16 ...323 J1
Monega Rd *FSTGT* E7 ...307 M3

MNPK E12 ...308 A3
Moneypiece Cl *HVHL* CB9 ...34 D3
Monier Rd *BOW* E3 ...306 D4
Monkchester Cl *LOU* IG10 ...250 D1
Monkdowns Rd *RCOLW* CO6 ...124 E2
Monk Dr *CAN/RD* E16 ...323 J7
Monkham's Av *WFD* IG8 ...267 L4
Monkham's Dr *WFD* IG8 ...267 L4
Monkham's La *WFD* IG8 ...267 L3
Monklands Ct *HSTD* CO9 ...81 L4
Monks Cha *RBRW/HUT* CM13 ...256 F6
Monks Cl *ABYW* SE2 ...326 A7
BROX EN10 ...201 H6
FX IP11 ...63 J7
Monks Ga *RIPW* IP8 ...46 F7
Monksgrove *LOU* IG10 ...250 D5
Monks Hvn *SLH/COR* SS17 ...317 G2
Monks HI *SAFWS* CB11 ...30 C1
Monkside *BSDN* SS14 ...3 M3
Monks La *COLW* CO3 ...89 G1
Monks Lodge Rd *HSTD* CO9 ...357 J1
Monkswick Rd *HLW* CM20 ...13 L1
Monkswood Av *WAB* EN9 ...233 L3
Monkswood Dr *BSF* CM23 ...138 E3
Monkswood Gdns *CLAY* IG5 ...286 A1
Monkwick Av *COLS* CO2 ...129 K4
Monkwood Cl *ROM* RM1 ...289 K3
Monmouth Cl *CHTY* IP2 ...54 L2
Monmouth Ms *WFD* IG8 ...267 L4
Monmouth Ms *SUD* CO10 ...276 D3
Monmouth Rd *DAGW* RM9 ...310 C2
Monnow Rd *SOCK/AV* RM15 ...328 C1
Monoux Cl *BCAYE* CM11 ...259 G4
Monoux Gv *WALTH* E17 ...266 D7
Mons Av *BCAYE* CM11 ...259 G3
Monson Rd *BROX* EN10 ...201 G6
Mons Rd *COLS* CO2 ...129 C1
Montague Av *SLH/COR* SS17 ...299 L3
Montague Pl *CVI* SS8 ...320 B2
Montague Wy *BCAYW* CM12 ...240 D1
Montague Rd *FX* IP11 ...11 J2
WAN E11 ...285 J7
Montagu Gdns
  CHLM/GWD CM2 ...194 C6
  HLWW/ROY CM19 ...203 K6
Montalt Rd *WFD* IG8 ...267 J5
Montana Rd *KESC* IP5 ...49 M6
Montayne Rd *CHES/WCR* EN8 ...232 C2
Montbretia Cl *COLW* CO3 ...106 A7
Monteagle Av *BARK* IG11 ...308 F5
Montefiore Av *RAYL* SS6 ...262 F5
Montesquieu Ter
  CAN/RD E16 ...323 J2
Montfort Av *SLH/COR* SS17 ...317 K1
Montfort Gdns *BARK/HLT* IG6 ...268 F1
Montgomery Cl
  CHLM/WR CM1 ...194 B6
  COLS CO2 ...129 L1
Montgomery Ct *SBN/FI* SS3 ...303 H4
Montgomery Crs *HARH* RM3 ...272 A4
Montgomery Dr
  CHES/WCR EN8 ...216 F6
Montgomery Rd *CHTY* IP2 ...54 A4
Monton Ri *CHTY* IP2 ...53 J3
Montpelier Cl *BCAYW* CM12 ...240 D8
Montpelier Gdns *CHDH* RM6 ...287 M5
EHAM E6 ...308 A7
WAN E11 ...285 J7
Montreal Rd *IL* IG1 ...286 C9
TIL RM18 ...337 J1
Montrose Av *GPK* RM2 ...271 M8
Montrose Cl *WFD* IG8 ...267 K3
Montrose Rd
  CHLM/GWD CM2 ...210 C1
Montsale *PIT* SS13 ...278 F5
Monument Farm Rd
  KIR/NAC IP10 ...56 B1
Moody St *WCHPL* E1 ...306 A7
Moon Hall La *HVHL* CB9 ...34 L8
Moons Cl *RCFD* SS4 ...265 G6
Moorcroft *RCFD* SS4 ...264 F7
Moorcroft Av *SBF/HAD* SS7 ...288 H7
Moore Av *TIL* RM18 ...331 L8
WTHK RM20 ...330 F4
Moore Cl *BCAYE* CM11 ...241 G8
SWCM DA10 ...336 B4
Moore Crs *DAGW* RM9 ...309 H1
Moore Rd *IP* IP1 ...47 L2
BELV DA17 ...326 F5
Moores La *RCOLW* CO6 ...103 M5
Moore St *BRTR* CM7 ...122 A7
Moorend *RCOLW* CO6 ...85 L7
Moorfield *RCFD* SS4 ...264 F7
Moorfield Cl *KESC* IP5 ...50 B6
Moorfield Rd *CBS* CB2 ...22 A8
Moorfields *HLWS* CM18 ...203 K6
Moor Hall La *BSF* CM23 ...138 D6
RCHLM CM3 ...228 D2
Moor Hall Rd *HLWE* CM17 ...189 H1
Moorhen Av *BOC* CM0 ...389 M1
Moorhouse Gn *RCOLE* CO7 ...89 K5
The Moorings *BSF* CM23 ...139 H3
Moorland Cl *ROMW/RG* RM7 ...270 C2
Moor La *UPMR* RM14 ...291 J6
Moor Park Cl *LOS* SS9 ...281 M6
Moor Park Gdns *LOS* SS9 ...281 M6
Moor Pasture Wy *HVHL* CB9 ...34 E1
Moor Rd *COLN* CO4 ...88 A2
RCOLW CO6 ...103 M5
Moors Cl *RCOLE* CO7 ...133 G4
Moors Cft *BRTR* CM7 ...122 A6
Moor's Farm Cha *MAL* CM9 ...199 H4
Moorsfield *SUD* CO10 ...45 L2
Moorside *COL* CO1 ...9 J3
Moors La *BRTR* CM77 ...120 D6
GTDUN CM6 ...118 D6
WIT CM8 ...147 J4
Mope La *WIT* CM8 ...172 A8
Mopsies Rd *BSDN* SS14 ...278 B7
Moran Av *K/T/MI* CO5 ...193 L6
Morant Gdns *CRW* RM5 ...270 C4
Morant Rd *CDW/CHF* RM16 ...331 L2
COL CO1 ...107 L8
Morant St *POP/IOD* E14 ...322 D3
Moray Cl *ROM* RM1 ...271 H6
Moray Wy *ROM* RM1 ...271 H6
Mordaunt Gdns *DAGW* RM9 ...310 B4
Mordaunt St *BKHH* IG9 ...267 M1
Morden Wharf Rd
  GNWCH SE10 ...323 H6

Mordon Rd *GDMY/SEVK* IG3 ...287 J5
Morebarn Rd *RCOLE* CO7 ...110 D3
Morecambe Cl *HCH* RM12 ...311 J2
  WCHPL E1 * ...322 A1
Morecambe St *POP/IOD* E14 ...322 D4
More Cl *CAN/RD* E16 ...323 J2
More La *RCOLE* CO7 ...133 G4
Moreland Av *CDW/CHF* RM16 ...330 F1
Moreland Wy *CHING* E4 ...266 E2
Morella Cl *RCOLE* CO7 ...133 G4
Morello Cl *COLS* CO2 ...129 K6
Moremead *WAB* EN9 ...233 J3
Mores La *BRW* CM14 ...255 J5
Moreton Br *RCFD* SS4 ...283 C5
Moreton Cl *CHESW* CN7 ...216 A1
Moreton Gdns *WFD* IG8 ...268 A2
Moreton Rd *CHONG* CM5 ...380 C7
CHONG CM5 ...381 J7
Moretons Ct *CHLM/GWD* CM2 ...242 D1
PIT SS13 ...278 D3
Moretons Ct *PIT* SS13 ...278 A4
Moretons Ms *PIT* SS13 ...278 A4
Morgan Av *WALTH* E17 ...285 G1
Morgan Cl *DAGE* RM10 ...310 A2
Morgan Crs *EPP* CM16 ...235 J4
Morgan Dr *IP* IP1 ...47 K3
Morgan St *BOW* E3 ...306 C5
CAN/RD E16 ...323 K1
Morgan Wy *RAIN* RM13 ...311 K5
WFD IG8 ...268 A2
Morice Rd *HOD* EN11 ...201 L1
Morieux Rd *LEY* E10 ...284 C4
Morland Rd *DAGE* RM10 ...310 B5
IL IG1 ...286 C7
IPSE IP3 ...17 K6
WALTH E17 ...284 C3
Morland Wy *CHES/WCR* EN8 ...216 C4
Morley Av *CHING* E4 ...267 G4
Morley Gv *HLW* CM20 ...12 C1
Morley HI *SLH/COR* SS17 ...295 L3
Morley Link *SLH/COR* SS17 ...295 M3
Morley Rd *BARK* IG11 ...309 G3
CHDH RM6 ...288 B5
HSTD CO9 ...81 J4
K/T/MI CO5 ...174 C7
LEY E10 ...284 C1
SRTFD E15 ...307 J1
Morleys Pl *CBS* CB2 * ...22 C7
Morleys Sq *CDW/CHF* RM16 ...331 L2
Morleys Rd *RCOLW* CO6 ...82 G7
Mornington Av *IL* IG1 ...286 E8
IP IP1 ...47 L3
RCFD SS4 ...283 J3
Mornington Crs *CVI* SS8 ...320 B2
SBF/HAD SS7 ...299 J3
Mornington Gv *BOW* E3 ...306 C2
Mornington Rd *CHING* E4 ...249 G2
CVI SS8 ...298 C8
WAN E11 ...285 H5
WFD IG8 ...267 G4
Mornings
  HLWW/ROY CM19 ...203 K6
Morpeth Gv *HOM* E9 ...306 A1
Morpeth St *BETH* E2 ...306 B1
Morrab Gdns *GDMY/SEVK* IG3 ...287 K3
Morrells *VGE* SS16 ...294 F1
Morrin's Cha *SBN/FI* SS3 ...304 A3
Morris Av *CBE/LIN* CB1 ...25 G5
COS CO15 ...182 E4
MNPK E12 ...308 C2
Morris Cl *CHING* E4 ...249 G5
LAIN SS15 ...276 F4
Morris Gdns *DART* DA1 ...334 E8
Morris Harp *SAFWN* CB10 ...28 B7
Morrison Av *CHING* E4 ...266 E6
Morris Rd *BCTR* RM8 ...288 C2
CHLM/GWD CM2 ...5 M1
HARH RM3 ...271 M2
POP/IOD E14 ...322 E2
WAN E11 ...285 J4
Morrow La *RCOLE* CO7 ...89 K5
Morse Cl *PLSTW* E13 ...307 K2
Mors End *RCOLE* CO7 ...156 C5
Morson Rd *PEND* EN3 ...248 B3
Morston Hall Rd *FX* IP11 ...61 J7
Morten Rd *COL* CO1 ...9 H2
Mortham St *SRTFD* E15 ...307 H1
Mortimer Ga *CBE/LIN* CB1 ...25 H5
Mortimer Pl *SUD* CO10 ...37 L4
Mortimer Rd *EHAM* E6 ...308 C3
RAYL SS6 ...263 H5
RCHLM CM3 ...159 G1
Mortlake Rd *CAN/RD* E16 ...323 K4
IL IG1 ...308 F1
Mortlock Gdns *CBE/LIN* CB1 ...25 K6
Morton Cl *MAL* CM9 ...198 C4
SRTFD E15 ...307 K2
Morton Wy *HSTD* CO9 ...81 K3
Morvaie Cl *BELV* DA17 ...326 C2
Morville St *BOW* E3 ...306 C4
Mosbach Gdns
  RBRW/HUT CM13 ...256 F6
Moseley St *SOSN* SS2 ...302 B4
Moss Bank *GRAYS* RM17 ...330 B2
Mossdale Cl *COLW* CO3 ...296 B6
Mossdown Cl *BELV* DA17 ...326 F4
Moss Dr *VGE* SS16 ...296 F1
Mossfield Cl *COLW* CO3 ...106 A7
Mossford Gn *BARK/HLT* IG6 ...286 C1
Mossford La *BARK/HLT* IG6 ...268 C8
Mossford St *BOW* E3 ...306 C4
Moss La *NHMKT* IP6 ...288 H7
ROM RM1 ...289 G4
Moss Rd *COLW* CO3 ...128 A2
DAGE RM10 ...310 D2
SOCK/AV RM15 ...328 C1
WIT CM8 ...147 M4
Moss Wy *RCOLW* CO6 ...106 A7
Mostyn Gv *BOW* E3 ...306 C2
Motehill *VGE* SS16 ...294 F1
Motherwell Wy *WTHK* RM20 ...330 F4
Mottingham Rd *ED* N9 ...248 A3
Mottisfont Rd *ABYW* SE2 ...325 M4
Mottram Cl *RIPW* IP8 ...53 H6
Mott's Cl *BRTR* CM7 ...121 L5
Mott St *CHING* E4 ...250 A6
Mott's Yd *GTDUN* CM6 ...96 A8
Moules La *CBE/LIN* CB1 ...26 A4
Moulsham Cha *CHLM/GWD* CM2 ...5 L9
Moulsham Dr *CHLM/GWD* CM2 ...5 L9
Moulsham Hall La
  RCHLM CM3 ...144 B8
Moulsham St *CHLM/GWD* CM2 ...4 F7
Moulsham Thrift
  CHLM/GWD CM2 ...209 K2
Moulton Wy *UPMR* RM14 ...291 J6
Mountague Pl *POP/IOD* E14 ...322 E3
Mountain Ash Av *LOS* SS9 ...281 G2
Mountain Ash Cl *COLN* CO4 ...107 J4
SBF/HAD SS7 ...281 K6
Mountain's Farm Rd
  GTDUN CM6 ...140 A7
Mountains Cl *MAL* CM9 ...172 A7
Mount Av *CHING* E4 ...266 D4
HARH RM3 ...272 A4
HOC/HUL SS5 ...264 C5
RAYL SS6 ...281 M6
RBRW/HUT CM13 ...256 F6
WOS/PRIT SS0 ...300 C3
Mountbatten Cl *HVHL* CB9 ...34 A6
Mountbatten Ct *BKHH* IG9 ...268 B2
IP IP1 ...16 D6
Mountbatten Dr *COLS* CO2 ...129 J1

Mountbatten Rd BRTR CM7 ...121 L1
SUD CO10 ...20 F1
Mountbatten Wy
CHLM/WR CM1 ...194 A6
Mount Cl RAYL SS6 ...280 E4
WICKE SS11 ...261 H5
Mount Crs BRW CM14 ...256 A7
HOC/HUL SS5 ...264 B7
SBF/HAD SS7 ...298 E7
Mountdale Gdns LOS SS9 ...300 C1
Mount Dr IPSE IP3 ...55 L4
STSD CM24 ...115 M4
Mount Echo Av CHING E4 ...70 E4
Mount Echo Dr CHING E4 ...248 E8
Mountfield Cl SLH/COR SS17 ...317 K2
Mountfield Rd EHAM E6 ...308 D6
Mountfields PIT SS13 ...296 F1
Mountfitchet Rd STSD CM24 ...115 H4
Mounthill Av IPSE IP3 ...81 G4
Mountjoy Cl THMD SE28 ...325 J1
Mount Lield Ct East
WOS/PRIT SS0 * ...300 F6
Mount Lield Ct West
WOS/PRIT SS0 * ...300 F6
Mount Lodge Cha MAL CM9 ...173 G2
Mountnessing SBF/HAD SS7 ...299 G3
Mountnessing La
BRWN CM15 ...238 B4
Mountnessing Rd
BCAYW CM12 ...240 A6
BCAYW CM12 ...258 A6
BRWN CM15 ...238 D2
Mountney Cl ING CM4 ...239 H7
Mount Pleasant HSTD CO9 ...81 H4
MAL CM9 ...214 C4
MGTR CO11 * ...366 A9
Mount Pleasant Av
RBRW/HUT CM13 ...257 F3
Mount Pleasant Est MAL CM9 ...173 H7
Mount Pleasant Ms
HSTD CO9 * ...81 H4
Mount Pleasant Pl
WOOL/PLUM SE18 ...325 C7
Mount Pleasant Rd CHIG IG7 ...269 G3
CRW RM5 ...271 G5
DART DA1 ...334 C8
RCHLM CM3 ...245 C6
SAFWS CB11 ...30 A1
WALTH E17 ...266 B8
Mount Ri HSTD CO9 ...81 G4
Mount Rd BCTR RM8 ...288 C6
BRTR CM7 ...121 K2
EPP CM16 ...236 F2
HVHL CB9 ...34 E6
IL IG1 ...308 E2
RCOLW CO6 ...124 E3
SBF/HAD SS7 ...298 E7
WICKE SS11 ...261 H5
Mountsorrel HERT/BAY SG13 ...184 A3
Mounts Rd GRH DA9 ...335 L8
The Mount BCAYE CM11 ...259 H2
BRW CM14 ...273 M2
COLW CO6 ...106 C7
HARH RM3 ...271 J4
MAL CM9 ...385 N4
ROY SG8 ...348 D10
SLH/COR SS17 ...317 J2
Mount Vw BCAYE CM11 ...259 H3
Mountview VGE SS16 ...296 B2
Mountview Crs BOC CM0 ...385 M12
Mount View Rd CHING E4 ...248 F1
Mountview Rd COS CO15 ...7 K1
Mount Wy WICKE SS11 ...261 H5
Mount Zion SBF/HAD SS7 * ...299 G4
Moverons La RCOLE CO5 ...155 L3
Movers La BARK IG11 ...309 G5
Mowbray Rd HLW CM20 ...13 M1
Mowbrays Cl CRW RM5 ...270 F2
Mowbrays Rd CRW RM5 ...270 F8
Mowbrey Gdns LOU IG10 ...250 F2
Mowden Hall La
RCHLM CM3 ...196 B4
Mowlands RIPS/CAP IP9 ...58 L4
Moxom Av CHES/WCR EN8 ...216 A1
Moxon Cl PLSTW E13 ...307 J6
Moyers Rd LEY E10 ...284 F1
Moy Rd COLS CO2 ...129 K4
Muckingford Rd TIL RM18 ...332 C1
Mucking Hall Rd SBN/FI SS3 ...303 F9
Mucking Wharf Rd
SLH/COR SS17 ...316 F0
Muggeridge Rd DAGE RM10 ...310 E1
Muirfield Crs POP/IOD E14 ...322 C3
Muir Pl WALTH E17 * ...266 C8
Muir Cl CAN/RD E16 ...324 C4
Muirway SBF/HAD SS7 ...279 L6
Mulberry Av COLS CO2 ...129 K1
Mulberry Cl BSF CM23 ...139 H4
CHING E4 ...266 D1
GPK RM2 ...289 L2
Mulberry Ct BSF CM23 ...139 G4
Mulberry Dr PUR RM19 ...328 C2
Mulberry Gdns WIT CM8 ...171 K1
Mulberry Gn HLWE CM17 ...188 B5
Mulberry Hl BRWN CM15 ...256 F5
Mulberry Rd CVI SS8 ...319 M2
Mulberry Wk K/T/MI CO5 * ...174 A2
BELV DA17 ...326 F5
CHLM/WR CM1 ...194 A8
SWFD E18 ...267 L8
Mulgrave Rd
WOOL/PLUM SE18 ...324 C7
Mulberry Gdns VGE SS16 ...296 C5
Mullein Ct GRAYS RM17 ...331 C5
Mullins Rd BNTY CM ...99 J7
The Mullions BCAYW CM12 ...258 C2
Multon Lea CHLM/WR CM1 ...194 D4
Mumford Cl RCOLW CO6 ...106 A1
Mumford Rd IP IP1 ...47 K5
RCOLW CO6 ...106 A1
Mumfords La FOS CO13 ...136 D2
Munday Rd CAN/RD E16 ...323 K2
Mundells CHESW EN7 ...216 B3
Mundon Gdns IL IG1 ...308 C3
Mundon Rd BRTR CM7 ...122 A5
MAL CM9 ...214 E5
Munford Dr SWCM DA10 ...336 B7
Mungo Park Rd RAIN RM13 ...311 K4
Munnings Cl HVHL CB9 ...34 A4
IPSE IP3 ...55 J4
Munnings Dr RCOS CO16 ...159 G7
Munnings Rd COLW CO6 ...106 D8
Munnings Wy MGTR CO11 ...64 C7
Munro Av WICKE SS11 ...261 H8
Munro Rd WIT CM8 ...147 J8
Munsons Aly SOC CM0 ...393 N1
Munsterburg Rd CVI SS8 ...320 C3
Munster Ct BCAYW CM12 ...240 C4
Murchison Cl CHLM/WR CM1 ...194 E1
LEY E10 ...284 F7
Murdock Cl CAN/RD E16 ...323 J2
Mufitt Wy UPMR RM14 ...312 D1
Murray Cl BRTR CM7 * ...99 J3

Murray Rd IPSE IP3 ...54 F2
Murray Sq CAN/RD E16 ...323 K2
Murray Wy WICKE SS12 ...261 G8
Murrell Lock
CHLM/GWD CM2 ...210 D1
Murrells La HOC/HUL SS5 ...263 K6
Murrills Rd IPSE IP3 ...55 L4
Murthering La ABR/ST RM4 ...253 L4
Murton Slade HVHL CB9 ...34 D5
Murtwell Dr CHIG IG7 ...268 F5
Muscade Cl K/T/MI CO5 ...150 A7
Museum St COL CO1 ...8 C7
IP IP1 ...16 F3
SAFWN CB10 ...28 A7
Musgrave Cl CHESW EN7 ...216 A5
HAR CO12 ...70 E4
Muskalls Cl CHESW EN7 ...216 B5
Musk Cl COLW CO5 ...106 A6
Musket Gv LOS SS9 ...281 L6
Muskham Rd HLW CM20 ...188 B6
Muswell Wk RCOS CO16 ...6 C1
Mutlow Hill London Rd
SAFWS CB11 ...351 N8
Mutton Rw CHONG CM5 ...382 D4
Mychett Cl RCOS CO16 ...158 E7
Myddleton Rd WARE SG12 ...184 E1
Mygrove Cl RAIN RM13 ...312 A6
Mygrove Gdns RAIN RM13 ...312 A6
Mygrove Rd RAIN RM13 ...312 A6
Myland Hall Cha COLN CO4 ...107 M2
Mylne Cl CHES/WCR EN8 ...216 D5
Myln Meadow ING CM4 ...241 J3
Mynchens LAIN SS15 ...2 C8
Myneer Pk RCOLW CO6 ...124 E3
Mynott Ct K/T/MI CO5 * ...174 A1
Myra St ABYW SE2 ...325 K6
Myrtle Aly WOOL/PLUM SE18 ...324 D6
Myrtledene Rd ABYW SE2 ...325 K6
Myrtle Gv CVI SS8 * ...107 L8
SOCK/AV RM15 ...328 F5
Myrtle Rd BRW CM14 ...273 M5
EHAM E6 ...308 B1
HARH RM3 ...271 M5
IL IG1 ...286 C1
IPSE IP3 ...17 K8
WALTH E17 ...284 C3
Myson Wy BSF CM23 ...139 K2

N

Nabbott Rd CHLM/WR CM1 ...4 M7
Nacton Crs IPSE IP3 ...55 G3
Nacton Rd FX IP11 ...11 G7
IPSE IP3 ...17 L8
IPSE IP3 ...54 F2
IPSE IP3 ...55 J5
Nadine St CHARL SE7 ...323 M8
Naffenton St LOU IG10 ...250 A6
Nagle Cl WALTH E17 ...266 A1
Nag's Head La UPMR RM14 ...272 F7
Nails La BSF CM23 ...139 G2
Nairn Ct TIL RM18 * ...331 J8
Nairn St POP/IOD E14 ...322 F1
Nalla Gdns BELV DA17 ...193 M7
Namur Rd CVI SS8 ...298 D1
Nancy Smith Ms COLS CO2 ...107 J3
Nankin St POP/IOD E14 ...322 F1
Nansen Av RCFD SS4 ...265 G7
Nansen Rd COS CO15 ...160 A3
IPSE IP3 ...55 G3
Napier Av COS CO15 ...182 A7
POP/IOD E14 ...322 D6
SOS SS1 ...18 D5
Napier Cl BSDN SS14 ...3 J1
EMPK RM11 ...289 G1
Napier Crs WICKE SS12 ...261 H3
Napier Gdns SBF/HAD SS7 ...280 F2
Napier Rd BELV DA17 ...326 E2
COLS CO2 ...8 C2
EHAM E6 ...308 D1
GVW DA11 ...337 J6
PEND EN3 ...248 A5
RAYL SS6 ...281 J2
SRTFD E15 ...307 H6
WAN E11 ...285 M1
Narboro Ct EHAM E6 * ...289 K4
Nare Rd SOCK/AV RM15 ...328 F5
Narrow Boat Cl THMD SE28 ...325 G5
Narrow St POP/IOD E14 ...322 A2
Narvik Cl MAL CM9 ...214 B6
Naseby Rd CLAY IG5 ...268 C1
DAGE RM10 ...310 E2
Nash Cl SCOLW CO3 ...106 E8
MGTR CO11 ...64 E8
Nash Dr CHLM/WR CM1 ...193 M2
Nash Rd CHDH RM6 ...288 A2
Nassau Rd RCOS CO16 ...181 L1
Natal Rd IL IG1 ...308 C1
Nathan Cl UPMR RM14 ...291 H6
Nathan Ct COLS CO2 ...129 L5
Nathan's La CHLM/WR CM1 ...208 A3
Nathan Wy THMD SE28 ...325 H5
Nation Wy CHING E4 ...248 F8
Nats La SAFWS CB11 ...351 M7
Naunton Wy HCH RM12 ...290 M8
Naval Rw POP/IOD E14 ...322 F5
Navarre Gdns CRW RM5 ...270 A5
Navarre Rd EHAM E6 ...308 B6
Navarre St IP IP1 ...16 F5
Navestock Cl CHING E4 * ...266 F2
RAYL SS6 ...280 C5
Navestock Crs WFD IG8 ...267 K7
Navestock Gdns SOS SS1 ...302 C4
Navestock Side BRW CM14 ...254 F2
Navestock Ter WFD IG8 ...267 M6
Navigation Rd
CHLM/GWD CM2 ...5 K3
Nayland Cl WICKE SS12 ...261 K6
Nayland Dr RCOS CO16 ...182 K1
Nayland Rd BURES CO8 ...359 C4
COLN CO4 ...87 G3
FX IP11 ...10 D3
HVHL CB9 ...34 B7
RCOLW CO6 ...86 A7
RCOLW CO6 ...85 L10
Nayling Rd BRTR CM7 ...120 F3
Naylor Gv PEND EN3 ...248 A5
Naze Ct WOTN CO14 * ...369 P10
Nazeing Cl WLAB EN9 ...201 L8
Nazeingbury Pde
WAB EN9 * ...201 L8
Nazeing Common WAB EN9 ...218 D1
Nazeing New Rd BROX EN10 ...201 J3
The Nazeing BSDN SS14 ...3 M2
Naze Park Rd WOTN CO14 ...369 N11
Neal Ct WAB EN9 ...234 A3
Neale St WT CM8 ...171 M3
Neasden Av RCOS CO16 ...6 B1
Neasham Rd BCTR RM8 ...309 L2
Neath Dr CHTY IP2 ...53 M4
Neatscourt Rd EHAM E6 ...324 A1
Neave Crs HARH RM3 ...271 M7
Needham Cl BCAYE CM11 ...258 C2
Needleman St
BERM/RHTH SE16 ...322 A5

Need more space SAFWS CB11 ...28 B8
Neil Armstrong Wy LOS SS9 ...282 D7
Nelmes Cl EMPK RM11 ...290 C5
Nelmes Crs EMPK RM11 ...290 B3
Nelmes Rd EMPK RM11 ...290 B3
Nelmes Wy EMPK RM11 ...290 B2
Nelson Cl BRW CM14 ...256 A8
RAYL SS6 ...281 J1
ROMW/RG RM7 ...270 E7
Nelson Dr LOS SS9 ...300 C4
Nelson Gdns EMPK RM7 ...121 M1
RAYL SS6 ...281 J1
Nelson Gv CHLM/WR CM1 ...4 D5
Nelson Ms SOS SS1 ...19 G6
Nelson Pl RCHLM CM3 ...245 L7
Nelson Rd BELV DA17 ...326 C5
BSDN SS14 ...3 M6
BSF CM23 ...139 H4
CDW/CHF RM16 ...316 A6
CHING E4 ...248 E8
COLW CO3 ...106 B6
COS CO15 ...6 C5
GVW DA11 ...337 J7
HAR CO12 ...15 H7
IPNE IP4 ...48 F6
PEND EN3 ...248 A6
RAIN RM13 ...311 J2
RAYL SS6 ...281 J2
RCFD SS4 ...265 C7
SOCK/AV RM15 ...313 M6
SUD CO10 ...21 H2
WAN E11 ...285 K2
WOS/PRIT SS0 ...300 D3
Nelson St CAN/RD E16 ...323 J3
EHAM E6 ...308 C0
RCOLE CO7 ...156 B8
SOS SS1 ...19 G6
Nelwyn Av EMPK RM11 ...290 C3
Neptune Cl RAIN RM13 ...311 J6
Neptune Ct CC CO10 ...9 J7
Neptune Quay IPSE IP3 ...17 H6
Neptune Sq IPSE IP3 ...17 H6
Nesbit Cl WICKW SS12 ...260 F8
Ness Rd ERITH DA8 ...334 A1
RIPS/CAP IP9 ...365 R12
SBN/FI SS3 ...303 G6
Nesta Rd WFD IG8 ...267 J5
Nestle Wy WOS/PRIT SS0 ...345 P1
The Nesters SUD CO10 ...345 P1
Nethan Rd SOCK/AV RM15 ...328 F3
Nether Ct HSTD CO9 ...81 K4
Netherfield Gdns BARK IG11 ...309 D1
Netherfield La WARE SG12 ...185 M6
Nethergate St SUD CO10 ...37 L7
Netherhall Rd
HLWW/ROY CM19 ...202 A3
Nether Hl HSTD CO9 ...347 L10
Nether Mayne LAIN SS15 ...2 F1
Netherpark Dr GPK RM2 ...271 J8
Nether Priors BSDN SS14 ...3 J8
Nether Rd SUD CO10 ...38 F5
Netley Cl CHTY IP2 ...53 F5
Netley Rd GNTH/NBYPK IG2 ...287 C3
WALTH E17 ...284 C3
Nettesbury Farm
HLWS CM18 ...13 L8
Netteswell Orch HLW CM20 ...13 J2
Netteswell Rd HLW CM20 ...13 J2
Nevell Rd CDW/CHF RM16 ...331 C4
Nevendon Ms PIT SS13 ...278 D3
Nevendon Rd PIT SS13 ...278 D3
WICKW SS12 ...260 F8
Nevern Cl RAYL SS6 ...281 H5
Nevern Rd RAYL SS6 ...281 H5
Neville Cl WAN E11 ...285 L4
Neville Gdns BCTR RM8 ...288 A8
Neville Rd BARK/HLT IG6 ...268 A7
BCTR RM8 ...288 A7
GVW DA11 ...337 J6
SRTFD E15 ...307 K4
SWFD E18 ...267 K4
Neville Shaw BSDN SS14 ...3 G4
Nevill Wy LOU IG10 ...250 B6
Nevin Dr CHING E4 ...248 E5
Nevis Cl ROM RM1 ...271 H5
New Acres THMD SE28 ...325 L4
Newark Cl CHTY IP2 ...53 L4
Newark Knok EHAM E6 ...324 C4
New Av VGE SS16 ...294 D1
New Barn La RBSF CM22 ...139 K8
Newbarn Rd RCOLW CO6 ...103 L4
New Barn St PLSTW E13 ...307 K6
New Barns Wy CHIG IG7 ...268 C2
Newbiggen St GTDUN CM6 ...74 C2
Newbourne Gdns FX IP11 ...10 E3
Newbourn Rd KIR/NAC IP10 ...57 J2
KIR/NAC IP10 ...57 L5
New Bowers Wy
CHLM/WR CM1 ...194 B6
New Br CHLM/GWD CM2 ...5 H4
Newbridge Hl RCOLW CO6 ...106 C8
Newbridge Rd K/T/MI CO5 ...150 C8
Newburgh Rd GRAYS RM17 ...331 C4
Newbury Av PEND EN3 ...233 C7
Newbury Cl BSF CM23 ...138 F1
HARH RM3 ...271 M5
Newbury Gdns HARH RM3 ...272 A4
UPMR RM14 ...290 C8
Newbury Rd BCAYW CM12 ...240 E4
GNTH/NBYPK IG2 ...287 G4
HARH RM3 ...271 M4
IG1 ...286 E4
IPNE IP4 ...49 G3
Newby Dr IPNE IP4 ...49 G3
Newby Pl POP/IOD E14 ...322 F3
New Captains Rd
K/T/MI CO5 ...177 J1
New Cardinal St IP IP1 ...16 D2
Newcastle Av BARK/HLT IG6 ...269 K5
COLW CO3 ...128 B1
New Century Rd LAIN SS15 ...276 A1
New Church Rd RCOLW CO6 ...106 A1
New City Rd PLSTW E13 ...307 M7
Newcomen Rd WAN E11 ...285 J4
Newcomen Wy COLN CO4 ...87 M7
Newcourt Rd CHLM/GWD CM2 ...5 M4
Newcourt SAFWN CB10 * ...28 B8
New Cut BURES CO8 ...359 D4
COLS CO2 ...128 C3
RCOLE CO7 ...133 L7
SUD CO10 ...20 C5
New Rw CBE/LIN CB11 * ...342 H1
RCFD SS4 ...397 K4
Newry Av FX IP11 ...11 J3
Newson St IP IP1 ...16 D2
Newstead Rd SBN/FI SS3 ...303 L1
New St BRTR CM7 ...121 J3
CHLM/WR CM1 ...4 E6
GTDUN CM6 ...117 H1
HSTD CO9 ...80 B8
RCOLE CO7 ...156 C0
ROY SG8 ...349 K7
SAFWN CB10 ...28 C3
SBF/HAD SS7 ...299 C3
SUD CO10 ...20 D5
New St Flds GTDUN CM6 ...117 H1
Newsum Gdns RAYL SS6 ...280 C4
New Swan Ct WAB EN9 * ...201 L8
Newteswell Dr WAB EN9 ...233 L2

New Thorpe Av RCOS CO16 ...135 K3
Newton Abbot Rd GVW DA11 ...337 J7
Newton Cl BRTR CM7 ...185 J4
HOD EN11 ...185 M7
WALTH E17 ...284 B4
Newton Cft COS CO10 ...21 G6
Newton Dr SBW CM22 ...99 J4
Newton Gdns RCOS CO16 ...6 E7
Newton Gn GTDUN CM6 ...116 F8
Newton Hall Gdns RCFD SS4 ...265 G7
Newton Pl POP/IOD E14 ...322 E6
Newton Rd HAR CO12 ...14 C9
IPSE IP3 ...54 F1
SRTFD E15 * ...307 G2
SUD CO10 ...20 F8
TIL RM18 ...331 K8
Newtons Cl RAIN RM13 ...311 H4
Newton's Ct GRH DA9 ...335 G6
Newton St IPNE IP4 ...17 H4
Newton Vls GTDUN CM6 ...116 E4
Newton Wy RCOS CO16 ...157 K8
Newtown Rd BSF CM23 ...139 G5
New Town St COL CO1 ...8 E6
RCOS CO16 ...135 J3
New Union Cl POP/IOD E14 ...322 F6
New Wanstead WAN E11 ...285 J1
New Waverley Rd LAIN SS15 ...277 H4
New Wy CHTY IP2 ...47 L2
RCOS CO16 ...180 C2
New Way La HLWE CM17 ...189 G4
HLWE CM17 ...205 J2
New Writtle St CHLM/GWD CM2 ...4 F7
New Zealand Wy RAIN RM13 ...311 J3
Niagara Cl CHES/WCR EN8 ...216 E2
Nicholas Cl CHLM/WR CM1 ...213 G7
SOCK/AV RM15 ...313 M7
Nicholas St COL CO1 ...8 C4
Nicholas Rd BCTR RM8 ...288 C7
FX IP11 ...10 C7
Nicholl Rd EPP CM16 ...236 A1
LAIN SS15 ...276 A1
Nicholls Fld HLWS CM18 ...204 C2
Nichols Cl MGTR CO11 ...90 D2
Nichols Gv BRTR CM7 ...121 L3
Nicholson Crs SBF/HAD SS7 ...298 E1
Nicholson Gv WICKW SS12 ...261 H8
Nicholson Pl RCHLM CM3 ...245 L7
Nicholsons Gv COL CO1 ...8 D2
Nickleby Cl THMD SE28 ...325 M2
Nickleby Rd CHLM/WR CM1 ...193 L7
GVE DA12 ...338 D6
Nicola Ms BARK/HLT IG6 ...268 A6
Nien-oord RCOS CO16 ...182 K1
Nigel Ms IL IG1 ...308 M1
Nigel Rd FSTGT E7 ...307 M2
Nightingale Av CHING E4 ...291 H4
UPMR RM14 ...291 H4
Nightingale Cl CHING E4 ...267 H4
COLN CO4 ...108 C5
COS CO15 ...7 H1
HAR CO12 ...70 E4
RAYL SS6 ...281 H7
SOSN SS2 ...302 A3
WIT CM8 ...171 H5
Nightingale Hi COLN CO4 ...362 G11
Nightingale La WAN E11 ...285 M3
Nightingale Ms SAFWN CB10 ...28 A7
Nightingale Pl WOOL/PLUM SE18 ...127 M1
Nightingale Rd CVI SS8 ...320 C2
IPSE IP3 ...54 F2
Nightingales VGE SS16 ...296 C5
Nightingale Sq IPSE IP3 ...54 F5
Nightingale Wy COS CO15 ...7 H1
EHAM E6 ...324 B1
Nile Rd PLSTW E13 ...307 M6
Nina Mackay Cl SRTFD E15 * ...307 H5
Nineacres BRTR CM7 ...121 J8
Nine Acres CHTY IP2 ...47 J7
Nine Acres Cl MNPK E12 ...308 B2
Nine Ashes Rd BRWN CM15 ...244 B4
ING CM4 ...383 R3
Nine Elms Gv GVW DA11 ...337 K5
Ninefields WAB EN9 ...234 B3
Ninth Av STSD CM24 ...374 C10
Nipsells Cha RCHLM CM3 ...388 C7
Nita Rd BRW CM14 ...273 M4
Niven Cl WICKW SS12 ...261 H4
No1 St WOOL/PLUM SE18 ...324 G6
No2 St WOOL/PLUM SE18 ...324 G6
Noakes Av CHLM/GWD CM2 ...276 D2
Noak Hill Cl BCAYW CM12 ...276 D2
Noak Hill Rd HARH RM3 ...271 L4
HARH RM3 ...272 A2
LAIN SS15 ...276 D1
Noaks Rd HADL IP7 ...52 L1
Nobel Cl UED N18 ...266 A5
Nobel Sq PIT SS13 ...278 F3
Nobles Green Cl LOS SS9 ...282 A5
Nobles Green Rd LOS SS9 ...282 B6
The Nobles BSF CM23 ...138 C2
Nock Gdns KESG IP5 ...50 A7
Noel Rd EHAM E6 ...308 B8
Nonsuch Cl BARK/HLT IG6 ...268 C5
Nonsuch Meadow SUD CO10 ...20 C5
The Nook RCOLE CO7 ...130 F4
WARE SG12 ...185 J5
Norbiton Rd POP/IOD E14 ...322 C3
Norbury Cl RCOLW CO6 ...106 A1
Norbury Gdns CHDH RM6 ...288 C3
Norbury Rd CHING E4 ...266 D2
IPNE IP4 ...49 G4
Nordenfeldt Rd ERITH DA8 ...327 G3
Nordland Rd CVI SS8 ...321 G1
Nordmann Pl SOCK/AV RM15 ...314 A4
Nordale SBN/FI SS3 ...313 M3
Nore Rd LOS SS9 ...281 M5
Nore Vw VGE SS16 ...294 C1
Norfolk Cl CVI SS8 ...298 C8
DART DA1 ...334 C4
LAIN SS15 ...276 A1
MAL CM9 ...214 B4
Norfolk Crs COLN CO4 ...198 C1
Norfolk Dr CHLM/WR CM1 ...193 M6
Norfolk Gdns BRTR CM7 ...121 L1
Norfolk Pl CDW/CHF RM16 ...316 M8
Norfolk Rd BARK IG11 ...309 H4
DAGE RM10 ...310 C4
EHAM E6 ...308 C5
GDMY/SEVK IG3 ...338 C4
GVE DA12 ...338 C4
IPNE IP4 ...49 G4
MAL CM9 ...214 B4
ROMW/RG RM7 ...288 C4
UPMR RM14 ...291 L3
WALTH E17 ...266 B7
Norfolk Sq SOS SS1 ...307 K2
Norfolk Wy BSF CM23 ...139 G2
CVI SS8 ...298 C8
Norlington Rd WAN E11 ...284 C1
Norman Av BSF CM23 ...138 D3
Norman Cl FX IP11 ...63 J7

RCOLW CO6 ...126 B2
RCOS CO16 ...181 K1
ROMW/RG RM7 ...270 G2
WAB EN9 ...54 F3
Norman Crs IPSE IP3 ...263 H6
RBRW/HUT CM13 ...256 D6
Normandie Av BURES CO8 ...359 F9
COLS CO2 ...129 K2
Normandy Av BOC CM0 ...393 M8
Normandy Ter CAN/RD E16 ...323 J4
Normandy Wy HOD EN11 ...201 L1
Norman Gv BOW E3 ...306 E6
Norman HI RCHLM CM3 ...169 L3
Normanhurst
  RBRW/HUT CM13 ...256 F2
Norman PI LOS SS9 * ...300 B5
Norman Rd BELV DA17 ...326 E5
COS CO15 ...160 A3
EHAM E6 ...308 C6
EMPK RM11 ...289 K5
IL IG1 ...308 E2
MGTR CO11 ...91 G1
WAN E11 ...285 H1
Normans CI BRTR CM7 ...99 M8
BSF CM23 ...139 G4
Norris Gv BROX EN10 ...201 H2
Norris La HOD EN11 ...201 L2
Norris Ri HOD EN11 ...201 L1
Norris Rd HOD EN11 ...201 H2
Norseman CI GDMY/SEVK IG3 ...287 L3
Norsey CI BCAYE CM11 ...258 E2
Norsey Dr BCAYE CM11 ...258 F2
Norsey Rd BCAYE CM11 ...258 E2
Norsey View Dr
  BCAYW CM12 ...240 E7
Northallerton Wy HARH RM3 ...272 A4
Northampton Rd PEND EN3 ...248 A1
Northampton Gv VGE SS16 ...294 C1
Northampton Meadow
  BRTR CM7 ...76 D3
Northampton Rd PEND EN3 ...248 J8
North Av CHLM/WR CM1 ...193 J8
CVI SS8 ...320 C1
HVHL CB9 ...34 G5
SOSN SS2 ...19 L2
Northbank Rd WALTH E17 ...266 E1
North Barn BROX EN10 ...201 J8
North Benfleet Hall Rd
  WICKW SS12 ...279 J4
North Birkbeck Rd WAN E11 ...285 L4
Northbourne Rd COS CO15 ...7 H5
North Cir CO1 ...8 B5
Northbrook Rd IL IG1 ...286 D7
Northbrooks
  HLWW/ROY CM19 ...12 F8
North Circular WALTH E17 ...266 E2
North Circular Rd BARK IG11 ...308 D4
CHING E4 * ...266 B5
SWFD E18 ...285 M1
North CI CHIG IG7 ...269 K4
DAGE RM10 ...310 D3
IPNE IP4 ...48 D5
North Colne VGE SS16 ...3 L9
North Colonnade
  POP/IOD E14 ...322 E4
Northcote Rd GVW DA11 ...337 J6
WALTH E17 ...284 B2
North Countess Rd
  WALTH E17 ...266 C8
North Ct ING CM4 * ...239 M2
North Crs CAN/RD E16 ...307 G5
HVHL CB9 ...344 A6
SOSN SS2 ...282 F8
WICKW SS12 ...261 G6
North Crockerford VGE SS16 ...278 B8
Northcroft SUD CO10 ...20 C8
North Cross Rd BARK/HLT IG6 ...286 F7
North Dell CHLM/WR CM1 ...194 A6
Northdene CHIG IG7 ...269 J8
Northdown Gdns
  GNTH/NBYPK IG2 ...287 H3
Northdown Rd EMPK RM11 ...289 L5
GPK RM2 ...289 M1
RBRW/HUT CM13 ...257 G2
RCHLM CM3 ...388 C7
North End BKHH IG9 ...249 M7
BOC CM0 ...389 N12
North End RBRW/HUT CM13 ...273 M4
North End HSTD CO9 ...346 F10
SAFWN CB10 ...341 J7
Northern Ap COLN CO4 ...87 G8
Northern Av SBF/HAD SS7 ...279 M8
Northern Quays IPSE IP3 ...17 L1
Northern Relief Rd BARK IG11 ...308 F4
Northey St POP/IOD E14 ...322 E3
Northfalls Rd CVI SS8 ...321 J2
North Farm LOU IG10 ...249 M6
Northfield BRTR CM7 ...76 F4
Northfield CI BCAYE CM11 ...258 C1
Northfield Crs SBN/FI SS3 ...303 K1
Northfield Gdns COLN CO4 ...107 K5
Northfield Rd
  CHES/WCR EN8 ...232 F2
DAGW RM9 ...310 C4
EHAM E6 ...308 B1
SAFWS CB11 ...30 B1
SBW CM21 ...162 F5
Northfields BRTR CM7 ...76 F4
North Ga HLW CM20 ...12 F2
Northgate End BSF CM23 ...139 G1
Northgate St COL CO1 ...8 B6
  IP IP1 ...16 C6
North Gv WAB EN9 ...234 E7
North Gunnels BSDN SS14 ...3 H8
North Hall Rd SAFWS CB11 ...372 D7
North HI COL CO1 ...8 A7
RCHLM CM3 ...196 A4
North Hill Rd HARH RM3 ...272 A3
North Hill Gdns IPNE IP4 ...17 K3
North Kent GVW DA11 ...336 F4
North Kent Aveune
  GVW DA11 ...336 F4
Northlands Ap VGE SS16 ...294 F4
Northlands CI CHES/WCR EN8 ...295 F4
Northlands Farm Cha
  SLH/COR SS17 ...295 H6
Northlands Pavement
  PIT SS13 ...278 E8
North La RCOLW CO6 ...126 E1
North Lawn IPNE IP4 ...49 G5
Northolme CI
  CDW/CHF RM16 * ...330 F2
Northolt Av BSF CM23 ...115 J8

Northolt Wy HCH RM12 ...311 M2
North PI HLW CM20 ...188 B4
North Quay FX IP11 * ...10 C8
Northridge Rd GVE DA12 ...337 M8
North Ri SUD CO10 ...21 H9
North Rd ABR/ST RM4 ...271 H1
BCAYE CM11 ...260 A8
BELV DA17 ...326 E6
BRW CM14 ...255 M8
CBE/LIN CB1 ...23 K4
CHDH RM6 ...289 B3
CHES/WCR EN8 ...232 F3
COS CO15 ...287 H7
GDMY/SEVK IG3 ...287 H1
HOD EN11 ...201 H2
HSTD CO9 ...346 A11
MAL CM9 ...385 M3
PUR RM19 ...328 F7
RBSF CM22 ...377 K1
RCOLE CO7 ...156 C6
SOCK/AV RM15 ...292 A3
SUD CO10 ...347 N7
WOOL/PLUM SE18 ...325 H7
North Sea Vw HAR CO12 ...70 E5
North Shoebury Rd
  SBN/FI SS3 ...303 G4
North Side BRTR CM7 * ...99 K4
North Station Rd COL CO1 ...8 B2
North St BARK IG11 ...308 F4
BOC CM0 ...390 D4
BOC CM0 ...393 N1
BSF CM23 ...139 G1
EMPK RM11 ...290 A5
GTDUN CM6 ...117 G4
GVE DA12 ...337 L5
HVHL CB9 ...344 A6
LOS SS9 ...300 B5
MAL CM9 ...175 Q8
MGTR CO11 ...91 G1
PLSTW E13 ...307 H2
RCFD SS4 ...283 J3
ROM RM1 ...289 G2
SBN/FI SS3 ...303 L1
SUD CO10 ...20 D5
WAB EN9 ...234 B4
WOTN CO14 ...369 M12
North Street Pde
  SUD CO10 ...20 D5
North Ter BSF CM23 * ...139 G1
  CBS CB2 * ...22 C7
Northumberland Av
  EMPK RM11 ...289 M3
EN EN1 ...232 C8
LAIN SS15 ...276 F8
MNPK E12 ...285 M6
SOS SS1 ...19 M7
Northumberland CI
  BRTR CM7 ...121 L1
Northumberland Ct
  CHLM/GWD CM2 ...210 C1
Northumberland Crs SOS SS1 ...302 A6
Northumberland Rd
  EHAM E6 ...324 B2
SLH/COR SS17 ...332 C1
WALTH E17 ...284 D5
Northumbria St POP/IOD E14 ...322 D2
North View Av TIL RM18 ...331 K7
Northview Dr WFD IG8 ...268 A8
Northville Dr WOS/PRIT SS0 ...300 F1
North Wall RCOS CO16 ...180 C2
North Weald CI WICKE SS11 * ...261 L7
Northwick Rd CVI SS8 ...319 K10
Northwood CDW/CHF RM16 ...331 G4
Northwood Av HCH RM12 ...311 K1
Northwood CI CHESW EN7 ...216 A5
Northwood Gdns CLAY IG5 ...286 D2
Northwood Rd PIT SS13 ...286 C6
North Woolwich Rd
  CAN/RD E16 ...323 L4
North Gv CVI SS8 ...321 J1
Norton CI CHING E4 ...266 C4
  SLH/COR SS17 ...317 J1
Norton Heath Rd
  CHONG CM5 ...206 B5
Norton La CHONG CM5 ...381 L11
Norton Rd CHLM/WR CM1 * ...4 E2
DAGE RM10 ...311 G3
HVHL CB9 ...34 G1
ING CM4 ...239 L1
LEY E10 ...306 B1
Norway Crs HAR CO12 ...14 B8
Norway Ga BERM/RHTH SE16 ...322 B6
Norway PI POP/IOD E14 ...322 E3
Norway Rd CAN/RD E16 ...307 G2
Norwich CI COL CO1 ...8 D2
RCOS CO16 ...159 G7
SOSN SS2 ...301 M3
Norwich Crs CHDH RM6 ...289 F8
RAYL SS6 ...262 F5
Norwich Rd IP IP1 ...16 B2
Norwood Av COS CO15 ...289 M2
ROMW/RG RM7 ...289 G5
Norwood Rd SBF/HAD SS7 ...298 B4
Norwood End BSDN SS14 ...3 M3
  CHONG CM5 ...381 K3
Norwood Rd CHES/WCR EN8 ...216 A6
Norwood Wy WOTN CO14 ...137 K2
Notcutts RCOLE CO7 ...64 C1
Notley Dr HVHL CB9 ...33 L4
Notley Rd BRTR CM7 ...120 F3
RBRW/HUT CM13 ...121 J4
Nottage CI SLH/COR SS17 ...317 J4
Nottidge Rd IPNE IP4 ...17 K4
Nottingham Av CAN/RD E16 ...323 H1
Nottingham CI COS CO15 ...160 B3
LEY E10 ...284 F4
Nottingham Wy VGE SS16 ...276 C8
Nounsley Rd RCHLM CM3 ...196 F6
Nuneaton Rd DAGW RM9 ...310 A4
Nunn CI WDBR IP21 ...51 H5
Nunnery St HSTD CO9 ...356 F5
Nunns CI RCOLW CO6 ...124 D3
Nunn's CI COL CO1 ...8 A6
Nunns Gv GRAYS RM17 ...331 G3
Nunsbury Dr BROX EN10 ...216 F3
Nun's Meadow VGE SS16 ...3 B5
Nuns Wk HSTD CO9 ...346 A12
Nunty's La BRTR CM77 ...101 J3
Nursery CI CHDH RM6 ...288 A4
  COLW CO3 ...105 M8
  PEND EN3 ...248 A1
  RAYL SS6 ...281 G4
  SOCK/AV RM15 ...313 M8
  WFD IG8 ...267 J4
Nursery Wk FX IP11 ...11 L4
Nursery Flds SBW CM21 ...162 E7
Nursery Gdns LAIN SS15 ...276 F5
  PEND EN3 ...248 A1
Nursery La FSTGT E7 ...307 K3
Nursery Rd BROX EN10 * ...216 F3
  BRWN CM15 ...383 R8
  BSF CM23 ...139 G4
  CHLM/GWD CM2 ...5 G7

HOD EN11 ...185 J8
LOU IG10 ...250 A4
SLH/COR SS17 ...317 J2
SUD CO10 ...45 L4
WAB EN9 ...201 L8
Nursery Wk IP IP11 ...11 L4
Nutberry Av CDW/CHF RM16 ...330 D1
Nutberry CI CDW/CHF RM16 ...330 D1
Nutberry Rd DAGW RM9 ...310 D1
Nutcombe Crs RCFD SS4 ...285 C1
Nutfield Gdns
  GDMY/SEVK IG3 ...287 J7
Nutfield Rd SRTFD E15 ...306 F1
Nuthampstead Rd ROY SG8 ...370 D1
Nuthatch CI BCAYE CM11 ...258 F5
Nuthatch Gdns THMD SE28 ...325 C5
Nutmeg CI CAN/RD E16 ...307 H8
Nutmeg La POP/IOD E14 ...323 G2
Nutter La WAN E11 ...285 M3
Nyssa CI WFD IG8 ...268 A4
Nyth CI UPMR RM14 ...291 G4

O

Oakapple CI COLS CO2 ...129 G4
Oak Av BCAYE CM11 ...277 M1
  COS CO15 ...182 D3
  UPMR RM14 ...290 E8
  WICKE SS11 ...261 M6
Oakbank RBRW/HUT CM13 ...257 F1
Oak Bungalows BRTR CM7 ...121 M2
Oak Cha WICKW SS12 ...261 D6
Oak CI FX IP11 ...11 G2
  MAL CM9 ...214 C5
  RCOLW CO6 ...106 B2
  RCOS CO16 ...135 K4
  WAB EN9 ...233 L4
Oak Crs CAN/RD E16 ...323 H1
Oakdale Gdns CHING E4 ...266 E3
Oakdene BCAYW CM12 ...240 A6
Oak Dene CI ROM RM1 ...289 F8
Oakdene Rd PIT SS13 ...278 E5
Oak Dr SBW CM21 ...188 D1
Oak End HLWS CM18 * ...204 A3
Oak Fall WIT CM8 ...147 K8
Oak Farm Rd MAL CM9 ...213 G3
Oakfield CHING E4 ...266 E4
Oakfield La RCHLM CM3 ...169 K5
Oakfield Rd EHAM E6 ...308 D5
  HOC/HUL SS5 ...264 D5
  IL IG1 ...286 E8
  RIPW IP9 ...52 E7
  SBF/HAD SS7 ...297 M2
  WALTH E17 ...266 B8
Oak Gld EPP CM16 ...220 E7
Oak Gln EMPK RM11 ...290 B1
Oak Gv RIPW IP9 ...46 F7
Oak Hall Rd WAN E11 ...285 L4
Oak Hill CI WFD IG8 ...267 H6
Oak Hill Gdns WALTH E17 ...267 H1
Oak Hill La CHTY IP2 ...16 C9
Oak Hill Rd ABR/ST RM4 ...253 C2
Oak Holm COLS CO2 ...129 K2
Oakhurst CI BARK/HLT IG6 ...268 F7
  WALTH E17 ...285 H2
  WICKW SS12 ...260 F6
Oakhurst Dr WICKW SS12 ...260 E7
Oakhurst Gdns CHING E4 ...249 J8
  WALTH E17 ...285 H2
Oakhurst Rd PEND EN3 ...232 E6
  RAYL SS6 ...281 H3
  SOSN SS2 ...301 K3
Oakland Gdns
  RBRW/HUT CM13 ...256 F1
Oakland PI BKHH IG9 ...267 K1
Oakland Rd HAR CO12 ...15 H4
  SRTFD E15 ...307 H1
Oaklands RCOLW CO6 ...361 J2
Oaklands Av COLW CO3 ...105 M8
  ROM RM1 ...289 H1
Oaklands CI BRTR CM77 ...121 G5
  BSF CM23 ...115 J7
Oaklands Crs CHLM/GWD CM2 ...210 C8
Oaklands Dr BSF CM23 ...115 J7
  HLWE CM17 ...204 D2
  SOCK/AV RM15 ...329 A1
Oaklands Gv BROX EN10 ...216 F2
Oaklands Ms RCFD SS4 ...282 F1
Oaklands Pk BSF CM23 ...115 J7
Oaklands Park Av IL IG1 ...286 F7
Oaklands Wy RCHLM CM3 ...277 M2
Oak La BARK IG11 ...280 D1
  RAYL SS6 ...280 C2
Oakley CI CHING E4 ...266 E4
  WTHK RM20 ...335 J4
Oakley Dr BCAYW CM12 ...258 E2
  HARH RM3 ...272 A4
Oakley Rd BRTR CM7 ...70 J6
  HAR CO12 ...70 E5
  MGTR CO11 ...367 J12
Oak Lodge Av CHIG IG7 ...269 G4
Oak Lodge Tye
  CHLM/WR CM1 ...194 D7
Oakmead Rd RCOS CO16 ...180 D7
Oakmoor Wy CHIG IG7 ...269 H4
Oak Piece EPP CM16 ...221 H3
Oak Rdg HAR CO12 ...70 A4
Oak Rd BKHH IG9 ...268 A7
Oak Rd BCAYE CM11 ...242 C5
  BCAYE CM11 ...277 M1
  CVI SS8 ...320 A8
  EPP CM16 ...220 A4
  GRAYS RM17 ...331 G3
  GVE DA12 ...337 M5
  HARH RM3 ...272 A4
  HSTD CO9 ...81 G8
  HSTD CO9 ...358 C5
  K/T/MI CO5 ...149 M6
  MAL CM9 ...198 A2
  RCFD SS4 ...283 J3
  RCOLW CO6 ...103 H3
  SUD CO10 ...45 M6
  WIT CM8 ...147 M6

Oak Rd North SBF/HAD SS7 ...299 H3
Oak Rd South SBF/HAD SS7 ...299 H3
Oakroyd Av GTDUN CM6 ...117 H5
Oaks Av CRW RM5 ...270 C8
Oaks Dr COLW CO3 ...107 C6
Oaks Gv CHING E4 ...267 H1
Oaks La GNTH/NBYPK IG2 ...287 H3
Oaksmere Gdns CHTY IP2 ...53 L8
Oaks PI COLN CO4 ...107 H2
Oakstead CI IPNE IP4 ...17 M3
The Oaks BCAYE CM11 ...258 F7
  FOS CO13 ...137 J3
  KESG IP5 ...50 E7
  RDART DA2 ...334 E8
  WFD IG8 ...267 H6
  WOOL/PLUM SE18 ...324 F8
Oak St BSF CM23 ...139 G3
  ROMW/RG RM7 ...288 F3
Oak Tree CI HERT/BAY SG13 ...184 C6
  LOU IG10 ...250 F1
Oaktree CI BSF CM23 ...139 C6
Oaktree Gv IL IG1 ...309 G2
Oak Tree Rd RCOLE CO7 ...131 G5
Oaktrees MAL CM9 ...173 L5
Oakview HAR CO12 ...70 C4
Oakview CI CHESW EN7 ...216 C6
Oak Wk HOC/HUL SS5 ...264 D6
  HSTD CO9 ...356 E7
  SBF/HAD SS7 ...279 M5
Oakway CDW/CHF RM16 ...314 C6
Oakway Av COS CO15 ...160 B3
  K/T/MI CO5 ...178 A6
  LOS SS9 ...300 B3
  RBRW/HUT CM13 ...257 H2
Oakwood Cha EMPK RM11 ...290 C6
Oakwood CI FOS CO13 ...137 H3
  WFD IG8 ...268 B5
Oakwood Ct RCHLM CM3 ...392 D2
  SBF/HAD SS7 ...279 H3
  WFD IG8 ...268 B5
Oakwood Dr BCAYW CM12 ...240 F8
  K/T/MI CO5 ...178 A6
Oakwood Gdns
  GDMY/SEVK IG3 ...287 J7
  K/T/MI CO5 ...178 A6
Oakwood Gv PIT SS13 ...278 C8
Oakwood HI LOU IG10 ...250 D6
Oakwood Hill Industrial Est
  LOU IG10 ...250 E5
Oakwood Rd RAYL SS6 ...281 F1
  SLH/COR SS17 ...317 G1
Oak Yd HSTD CO9 * ...81 H3
Oasthouse Ct SAFWN CB10 ...28 A3
Oasthouse Spinney
  BRTR CM7 * ...99 J3
Oast Wy RCFD SS4 ...283 J3
Oates Rd CRW RM5 ...270 A4
Oatfield CI COLW CO3 ...106 A4
Oatland Ri WALTH E17 ...266 B8
Oatlands RCOLE CO7 ...109 J1
Oban CI PLSTW E13 ...307 M8
Oban PI PLSTW E13 ...307 M8
  SOSN SS2 ...19 L6
Oban St IP IP1 ...16 C2
  POP/IOD E14 ...323 G2
Oberon CI BCAYW CM12 ...258 A2
Obrey CI COLN CO4 ...108 C6
Observer Wy K/T/MI CO5 ...148 C1
Ocean Est WCHPL E1 ...306 A1
Ocean St WCHPL E1 ...322 A1
Ockelford Av CHLM/WR CM1 ...193 J4
Ockendon Rd UPMR RM14 ...313 G5
Ockendon Wy WOTN CO14 ...137 K2
Octavia Dr WIT CM8 ...171 H4
Oddcroft RCOLW CO6 ...82 C4
Odeon Rbt CHLM/GWD CM2 ...5 G5
Odessa Rd CVI SS8 ...307 J7
  FSTGT E7 ...307 J1
Odessa St BERM/RHTH SE16 ...322 C5
Offa's Md HOM E9 ...306 B1
Office La MAL CM9 ...173 L5
Ogard Rd HOD EN11 ...201 K3
Ogilby St WOOL/PLUM SE18 ...324 C5
Ogilvie Ct WICKW SS12 ...261 H6
Oglethorpe Rbt DAGE RM10 ...288 C7
Ohio Rd PLSTW E13 ...307 J3
Okehampton Sq HARH RM3 ...271 M1
Old Barn La RCHLM CM3 ...243 L4
Old Barn Rd BURES CO8 ...359 G11
Old Barns La ING CM4 ...206 D1
Old Bell CI STSD CM24 ...115 L3
Old Bell La RCHLM CM3 ...243 F4
Oldbury Av CHLM/GWD CM2 ...210 C6
Old Buryelode La STSD CM24 ...374 E5
Old Cattle Market IPNE IP4 ...16 E7
Old Church La
  RBRW/HUT CM13 ...239 H8
  SUD CO10 ...44 D7
Oldchurch Ri ROMW/RG RM7 ...289 H4
Old Church Rd CHING E4 ...266 D2
  PIT SS13 ...279 J8
  RBRW/HUT CM13 ...239 J7
  RCHLM CM3 ...227 L8
  WCHPL E1 * ...322 A2
Oldchurch Rd ROMW/RG RM7 ...289 H4
Old Coach Rd COL CO1 ...9 H5
Old Coach Yd CBS CB2 * ...22 C7
Old Ct CHLM/WR CM1 ...5 L1
Old Court Rd CHLM/WR CM1 ...5 L1
Old Crown La BRW CM14 ...255 J7
Old Dairy PI SUD CO10 * ...20 E5
Old Farm Rd BCAYW CM12 * ...258 C2
Old Ferry Rd RCOLE CO7 ...130 C4
Oldfield Gv DEPT SE8 ...322 A4
Oldfield Rd RIPW IP9 ...53 G8
Old Ford Lock SRTFD E15 * ...306 C2
Old Ford Rd BOW E3 ...306 C6
Old Forge Rd COLS CO2 ...128 C2
  EN EN1 ...232 A4
  RCHLM CM3 ...195 H5
Old Forge Rw
  HERT/BAY SG13 * ...184 C6
Old Foundry Rd IPNE IP4 ...17 H4
Old Hall CI SBN/FI SS3 * ...303 L1
Old Hall La MAL CM9 ...385 M4
  RIPS/CAP IP9 ...59 J2
  WOTN CO14 ...369 M2
Old Hall Ri HLWE CM17 ...204 F1
Oldhall Rd RIPS/CAP IP9 ...66 D1
Old Haverhill Rd HVHL CB9 ...35 C1
Old Heath Rd BOC CM0 ...393 M4
  COLS CO2 ...129 M1
Old Hill HOD EN11 ...201 L1
Old Hill Av VGE SS16 ...294 C8
Oldhouse Cft CHLM/WR CM20 ...11 F4
Old House La COLN CO4 ...87 H4
  HLWW/ROY CM19 ...202 A4
Old House Rd RCOLW CO6 ...86 D4
Old Ipswich Rd RCOLE CO7 ...89 J1
Old Jenkins CI SLH/COR SS17 ...316 D4
Old Kirton Rd FX IP11 ...61 M1
Old Leigh Rd LOS SS9 ...300 F5
Old London Rd HAD SS7 ...298 B2
  RIPS/CAP IP9 ...58 C6
  WICKE SS11 ...261 M6
The Old Maltings BSF CM23 ...139 H4

Old Market Ct SUD CO10 * ...20 D6
Old Market Pl SUD CO10 ...20 D6
Old Md SOSN SS2 ...282 D8
Old Mead Rd RBSF CM22 ...374 D1
Old Mill CI MAL CM9 * ...214 C5
Old Mill Ct SWFD E18 ...285 M1
Old Mill La BSF CM23 ...163 J3
  COS CO15 ...125 G6
Old Mill Rd COLN CO4 ...362 D12
  SAFWS CB11 ...30 D7
Old Nazeing Rd BROX EN10 ...201 N7
Old Oaks WAB EN9 ...233 M4
Old Orch HLWS CM18 ...203 L3
Old Park Rd ABYW SE2 ...325 K8
Old Parsonage Wy
  FOS CO13 ...137 J3
Old Perry St GVW DA11 ...337 H7
Old Pier St WOTN CO14 ...137 M1
Old Post Office Rw SUD CO10 * ...382 C7
Old Rectory Rd CHONG CM5 ...43 M5
  River La BSF CM23 ...139 G2
Old Rd ABR/ST RM4 ...254 A2
  BRTR CM77 ...101 M1
  COS CO15 ...137 J3
  FOS CO13 ...188 D3
  HLWE CM17 ...204 F1
  HSTD CO9 ...358 A4
  K/T/MI CO5 ...125 J6
  RCOLW CO6 ...125 G3
Old East GVE DA12 ...338 A4
The Old Rd RCOLW CO6 ...360 H2
Old West CI WFD IG8 ...43 M5
Old Rope Wk HVHL CB9 ...34 B6
Old Rose Gdns COLN CO4 * ...107 K5
Old School CI RCOS CO16 ...181 K2
Old School Crs FSTGT E7 ...307 K3
Old School Fld
  CHLM/WR CM1 ...210 B1
Old School La RCOLE CO7 ...109 K1
Old School Meadow
  SBN/FI SS3 ...303 G1
Old School Yd SAFWS CB11 * ...30 C7
Old Ship la RCFD SS4 ...283 J3
Old Shire La WAB EN9 ...234 B4
Old Southend Rd
  CHLM/GWD CM2 ...227 G4
  SOS SS1 ...19 K6
Old Station Rd LOU IG10 ...250 D4
The Old Station Yard
  WALTH E17 ...284 F2
Old St WCHPL E1 ...307 L6
Old Street Hl RBSF CM22 ...376 D7
Old Tramyard
  WOOL/PLUM SE18 ...325 H7
Old Vicarage CI
  CHLM/WR CM1 ...164 F3
Old Vicarage Rd HAR CO12 ...14 A7
Old Wy FOS CO13 ...137 J5
Old Wickford Rd RCHLM CM3 ...244 C6
Old Worlds End RCFD SS4 * ...396 C2
Oldwyk VGE SS16 ...296 B6
Olga St BOW E3 ...306 B6
Olive Av LOS SS9 ...299 K3
Olive Gv COLS CO2 ...160 A4
Olive CI WTHK RM20 ...335 J2
Oliver Gdns EHAM E6 ...324 B4
Oliver PI WIT CM8 ...171 H5
Oliver Rd BRWN CM15 ...256 C7
  LEY E10 ...284 F1
  RAIN RM13 ...311 J5
  WALTH E17 ...284 F3
  WTHK RM20 ...335 K2
Olivers CI COS CO15 ...6 E8
  SUD CO10 ...43 G2
Olivers Ct COS CO15 * ...6 E8
Olivers Crs SBN/FI SS3 ...303 K1
Olivers Dr WIT CM8 ...171 K6
Olivers La COLS CO2 ...128 C2
Olivers Rd COS CO15 ...6 E8
Oliver Wy CHLM/WR CM1 ...193 J4
Olive St ROMW/RG RM7 ...289 C3
Oliveswood Rd GTDUN CM6 ...117 G6
Olivia Dr SLH/COR SS17 ...300 C3
Ollard's Gv LOU IG10 ...250 A4
Ollerton Gn BOW E3 ...306 C5
Olley Wk K/T/MI CO5 ...148 C1
Olympia CI POP/IOD E14 ...322 F6
Olympus CI IP IP1 ...47 H9
Omnibus Wy WALTH E17 ...266 C8
Onega Ga BERM/RHTH SE16 ...322 B6
Onehouse Ga IP IP1 ...48 A4
One Tree HI SLH/COR SS17 ...295 J5
Ongar CI CHDH RM6 ...287 M3
  RCOS CO16 ...182 E1
Ongar Pk BRW CM14 ...256 A5
Ongar Rd ABR/ST RM4 ...208 A4
  BRWN CM15 ...255 K6
  BRWN CM15 ...383 J7
  BRWN CM15 ...383 M12
  CHLM/WR CM1 ...207 A5
  CHLM/WR CM1 ...208 A4
  CHONG CM5 ...381 J10
  GTDUN CM6 ...117 M7
  RBRW/HUT CM13 ...190 A3
Ongar Wy RAIN RM13 ...311 H5
Onra Rd WALTH E17 ...284 D5
Onslow CI CHING E4 ...267 C1
Onslow Crs COLS CO2 ...129 J2
Onslow Gdns CHONG CM5 ...382 H1
  SWFD E18 ...285 L1
Ontario CI BROX EN10 ...216 F5
Ontario Wy POP/IOD E14 ...322 F3
Onyx Ms SRTFD E15 ...307 H3
Opal Av IP IP1 ...47 J9
Opal CI CAN/RD E16 ...324 A2
Openshaw Rd ABYW SE2 ...325 C5
Ophir Rd RCOLE CO7 ...156 C6
Orange Gv CHIG IG7 ...268 F5
Orange St GTDUN CM6 ...74 D2
Orange Tree CI
  CHLM/GWD CM2 ...209 M7
Orange Tree HI ROM RM1 ...271 G4
Orchard Av BCAYE CM11 ...260 A8
  BCAYW CM12 ...240 F8
  HOC/HUL SS5 ...264 B6
  HSTD CO9 ...81 G8
  RAIN RM13 ...311 M8
  RAYL SS6 ...263 C6
  RBRW/HUT CM13 ...256 C6
Orchard CI BCAYW CM12 ...258 C1
  CHING E4 ...266 D2
  CHLM/GWD CM2 ...209 M7
  CHLM/WR CM1 ...74 D2
  GTDUN CM6 ...74 D2
  HAR CO12 ...113 M2
  HAR CO12 ...367 J12
  HOC/HUL SS5 ...264 C6
  HSTD CO9 ...81 G8
  HVHL CB9 ...34 C6
  MAL CM9 ...214 C5
  MAL CM9 ...385 M4
  RBSF CM22 ...189 K1
  RCHLM CM3 ...196 A4
  RCOLE CO7 ...109 J1

RCOLW CO6 .....127 G3
RCOS CO16 .....6 A1
SAFWS CB11 .....30 A1
SAFWS CB11 .....372 A1
SBN/FI SS3 .....303 K1
SOCK/AV RM15 .....313 M8
WARE SC12 .....K5
Orchard Cft HLW CM20 .....188 D7
Orchard Dr BRTR CM7 .....121 F8
  EPP CM16 .....235 M6
  FOS CO13 .....136 D5
  GRAYS RM17 .....330 D1
  WAB EN9 .....253 J4
Orchard Ga CHTY IP2 .....47 H8
Orchard Gv KESG SS7 .....49 M6
  LOS SS9 .....282 C5
Orchard La BRWN CM15 .....255 J5
  WFD IG8 .....267 K3
Orchard Ldr K/T/MI CO5 * 174 A1
Orchard Md LOS SS9 .....282 B8
Orchard Ms K/T/MI CO5 * 173 M7
Orchard Piece ING CM4 .....222 C5
Orchard Pightle CBE/LIN CB1 .....26 E1
Orchard Pl CHES/WCR EN8 .....216 C7
  POP/IOD E14 .....323 H3
  SUD CO10 .....20 E1
Orchard Rd BELV DA17 .....326 D7
  BOC CM0 .....393 M9
  BOC CM0 .....393 N1
  BSF CM23 .....139 H2
  CBS CB2 .....22 C2
  COL CO1 .....8 A2
  DAGE RM10 .....310 D5
  GVW DA11 .....336 F9
  K/T/MI CO5 .....148 D7
  MAL CM9 .....214 C3
  RCHLM CM3 .....388 D8
  RCOLE CO7 .....131 L5
  RIPW IP8 .....46 E2
  ROMW/RG RM7 .....270 C8
  SBF/HAD SS7 .....279 L7
  SOCK/AV RM15 .....336 M1
  SWCM DA10 .....336 B3
Orchard Rw FX IP11 * 62 D8
Orchards WIT CM8 .....171 J4
Orchard Side LOS SS9 .....282 C7
Orchard Sq BROX EN10 .....217 G2
The Orchards EPP CM16 .....236 B9
  SBW CM21 .....162 F6
Orchard St CHLM/GWD CM2 5
  DART DA1 .....334 A6
  IPNE IP4 .....17 H4
  WALTH E17 .....284 B2
Orchard Ter GRH DA9 * 335 H7
The Orchard BROX EN10 * 201 H6
  GTDUN CM6 .....118 F3
  WICKW SS12 .....260 G6
Orchard Wy RBRW/HUT CM13 .....276 A6
Orchard Wy RCOLE CO7 .....269 K2
  SUD CO10 .....39 L2
Orchid Av WIT CM8 .....171 H1
Orchid Cl CHTY IP2 .....53 K1
Orchid Pl RCHLM CM3 .....245 G5
Orchill Dr SBF/HAD SS7 .....299 H1
Orchis Gv GRAYS RM17 .....330 C3
Orchis Wy HARH RM3 .....272 C5
Ordell Rd BOW E3 .....306 C6
Ordnance Crs GNWCH SE10 .....323 H5
Ordnance Rd CAN/RD E16 .....323 J1
  GVE DA12 .....337 M6
  PEND EN3 .....232 E7
Oregon Av MNPK E12 .....308 C4
Oregon Rd KESG SS7 .....49 M6
Oreston Rd RAIN RM13 .....312 H1
Orford Crs CHLM/WR CM1 .....193 M3
  HVHL CB9 .....34 C7
  SWFD E18 .....285 L1
  WALTH E17 .....284 E8
Orford St IP IP1 * 16 C2
Oriel Cl SUD CO10 .....21 J3
Oriel Gdns CLAY IG5 .....286 C1
Oriel Rd HOM E9 .....306 H4
Oriental Rd CAN/RD E16 .....324 C1
Orient Wy CLPT E5 .....284 A4
Oriole Cl BSF CM23 .....138 C3
  THMD SE28 .....325 L3
Orion Cl BSDN SS14 * 278 C4
Orion Wy BRTR CM7 .....121 L1
Orissa Rd WOOL/PLUM SE18 .....325 H8
Orkney Cl HVHL CB9 .....35 G6
Orkney Gdns WICKW SS12 .....260 H7
Orkney Rd FX IP11 .....48 F4
Orlando Ct WOTN CO14 .....137 M7
Orlando Dr PIT SS13 .....278 F4
Orlick Rd GVE DA12 .....338 D7
Ormesby Chine RCHLM CM3 .....245 G6
Ormesby Cl THMD SE28 .....326 A3
Ormiston Rd GNWCH SE10 .....323 K6
Ormonde Av RCFD SS4 .....283 H7
  SBF/HAD SS7 .....299 H5
Ormonde Cl RCOLW CO6 .....106 B1
Ormonde Gdns LOS SS9 .....299 K8
Ormonde Ri BKHH IG9 .....249 M6
Ormonds Crs GNWCH SE10 .....244 E1
Ormsby Rd CVI SS8 .....320 A3
Orpen Cl RCOLW CO6 .....106 B1
Orpen's Hl COLS CO2 .....127 K7
Orrmo Rd CVI SS8 .....321 G2
Orsett Av LOS SS9 .....281 M6
Orsett End BSDN SS14 .....3 M1
Orsett Heath Crs
  CDW/CHF RM16 .....331 J4
Orsett Rd CDW/CHF RM16 .....316 K4
  GRAYS RM17 .....330 E4
Orsett Ter WFD IG8 .....267 M7
Orton Cl ING CM4 .....224 C8
Orvis La RCOLE CO7 .....64 D6
Orwell Br IPSE IP3 .....53 D6
Orwell Cl COLN CO4 .....108 A4
Orwell Ct WICKE SS11 .....261 L8
Orwell Pl IPNE IP4 .....17 G5
Orwell Ri RIPS/CAP IP9 .....365 K3
Orwell Rd COS CO15 .....7 C5
  FX IP11 .....11 H1
  HAR CO12 .....15 K7
  IPSE IP3 .....54 F1
  PLSTW E13 .....307 H6
Orwell View Rd RIPS/CAP IP9 .....66 F2
Orwell Wy RCOS CO16 .....6 A1
Osbert Rd WIT CM8 .....171 H1
Osborne Cl COS CO15 .....159 K6
  EMPK RM11 289
Osborne Gv WALTH E17 .....284 C1
Osborne Rd BELV DA17 .....326 A8
  BKHH IG9 .....249 L6
  BROX EN10 .....201 H6
  BRWN CM15 .....255 H6
  CHES/WCR EN8 .....216 F5
  EMPK RM11 .....289 L7
  FSTGT E7 .....307 C2
  HOM E9 .....306 C3
  IPSE IP3 .....53 F1
  K/T/MI CO5 .....178 D5
  LEY E10 .....284 B1
  PEND EN3 .....248 A2
  PIT SS13 .....279 H5
  VGE SS16 .....3 K7

WOS/PRIT SS0 .....18 C3
Osbornes Ct RCOLE CO7 * 156 C7
Osborne Sq DAGW RM9 .....310 C1
Osborne St COL CO1 .....8 C3
Osbourne Av HOC/HUL SS5 .....263 M7
Osea Rd MAL CM9 .....215 L2
Osea Wy RCHLM CM3 * 194 C8
O'Shea Gv BOW E3 .....306 C5
Osier Dr LAIN SS15 .....276 E8
Osier Wy LEY E10 .....284 E8
Osmond Cl BARTH CM77 .....121 L8
Osney Wy GVE DA12 .....338 D7
Osprey Cl EHAM E6 .....324 E1
  SBN/FI SS3 .....303 H4
  SWFD E18 .....285 L1
  WALTH E17 .....266 E8
Osprey Est BERM/RHTH SE16 .....322 A7
Osprey Rd HVHL CB9 .....34 E6
  WAB EN9 .....234 B3
Ospreys COS CO15 .....159 J7
Ostell Crs PEND EN3 .....233 H8
Osterberg Rd DART DA1 .....334 C6
Osterley Dr VGE SS16 .....276 C8
Osterley Rt RCHLM CM3 .....245 G8
Ostler Cl BSF CM23 .....138 D5
Ostler's Gn SAFWS CB11 .....350 A5
Oswald's Md CLPT E5 .....306 B1
Oswald St CLPT E5 .....284 A5
Othello Cl COLN CO4 .....108 C5
Otis St BOW E3 .....306 F7
Otley Ct FX IP11 .....62 C8
Otley Dr CAN/RD E16 .....286 A1
Otley Rd CAN/RD E16 .....323 C4
Ottawa Gdns DAGE RM10 .....311 C6
Ottawa Rd TIL RM18 .....337 M7
Otten Cl SUD CO10 .....347 J4
Otterbourne Rd CHING E4 .....267 G2
Ottershaw Wy RCOS CO16 .....158 C7
Ottley Pl ING CM4 * 241 J7
Ouida St CVI SS8 .....321 G2
Oulton Cl HAR CO12 .....14 F9
Oulton Crs BARK IG11 .....309 J3
Oulton Rd IPSE IP3 .....54 B3
Ousden Cl CHES/WCR EN8 .....216 F8
Ousden Dr CHES/WCR EN8 .....216 F8
Ouse Cha WIT CM8 .....171 C3
Outing Cl SOS SS1 .....19 L6
Outing's La BRWN CM15 .....383 Q10
Outpart Eastward HAR CO12 * 15 L3
Outram Rd EHAM E6 .....308 C4
Outwood Common Rd
  BCAYE CM11 .....258 F6
Outwood Farm Cl
  BCAYE CM11 .....259 H5
Outwood Farm Rd
  BCAYE CM11 .....259 H5
Oval Gdns GRAYS RM17 .....330 E6
Oval Rd North DAGE RM10 .....310 F5
Oval Rd South DAGE RM10 .....310 F5
The Oval BROX EN10 .....216 F3
Overbury Rd CLPT E5 .....306 C1
Overcliff WOS/PRIT SS0 * 18 A4
Overcliffe GVW DA11 .....337 G4
Overcliff Rd GRAYS RM17 .....331 G4
Overhall Hl RCOLW CO6 .....82 F3
Over Hall La SAFWN CB11 .....342 A3
Overlord Cl BROX EN10 .....200 F6
Overmead Dr RCHLM CM3 .....245 H5
Overshot Rd RCHLM CM3 .....228 B1
Overton Cl SBF/HAD SS7 .....279 M7
Overton Dr CHDH RM6 .....287 H5
  SBF/HAD SS7 .....279 M7
Overton Rd ABYW SE2 .....325 M6
  LEY E10 .....284 E6
  SBF/HAD SS7 .....279 L7
Overton Wy SBF/HAD SS7 .....279 M7
Overy St DART DA1 .....334 C8
Ovex Cl POP/IOD E14 .....322 F6
Ovington Gdns BCAYW CM12 .....240 C8
Owen Cl CRW RM5 .....270 D5
  THMD SE28 .....325 M4
Owen Gdns WFD IG8 .....268 B5
Owenite St ABYW SE2 .....325 L7
Owens Ms WAN E11 .....285 H1
Owen Ward Cl COLS CO2 .....128 D2
Owlets Hall La HARH RM3 .....290 F1
Owl Pk LOU IG10 * 249 J2
Owl's Hl RCHLM CM3 .....169 L2
Owl's Retreat COLN CO4 .....108 D3
Oxborrow Cl FOS CO13 .....136 D5
Oxcroft BSF CM23 .....139 H4
Oxendon Dr HOD EN11 .....201 H4
Oxenford Cl BROX EN10 .....200 F6
Oxestalls Rd DEPT SE8 .....322 C9
Oxford Av CDW/CHF RM16 .....331 K3
  EMPK RM11 .....290 C4
Oxford Cl CHES/WCR EN8 .....216 F7
  GVE DA12 .....338 C7
  SUD CO10 .....21 H9
Oxford Ct BRW CM14 .....276 B7
  CHLM/GWD CM2 .....210 A1
  COLW CO3 * 107 C7
  RCOLW CO6 .....82 F5
Oxford Crs COS CO15 .....6 F7
Oxford La HSTD CO9 .....356 J7
Oxford Meadow HSTD CO9 .....356 H7
Oxford Pl RCOLW CO6 * 82 F5
Oxford Rd CHLM/GWD CM2 * 107 D7
  COS CO15 .....7 C5
  SOS SS1 .....320 F1
  FOS CO13 .....132 K5
  HARH RM3 .....81 G4
  IL IG1 .....308 F1
  IPNE IP4 .....17 J4
  KESG SS7 .....49 M6
  MGTR CO11 .....91 G1
  RCFD SS4 .....283 H1
  SLH/COR SS17 .....316 E5
  SLH/COR SS17 .....316 E5
  WFD IG8 .....307 C3
Oxleas EHAM E6 .....324 E2
Oxley Cl GPK RM2 .....271 M8
Oxley Gdns SLH/COR SS17 .....317 G5
Oxley Hl K/T/MI CO5 .....153 K2
  MAL CM9 .....174 A5
Oxney Parker Dr COLN CO4 .....87 K2
Oxleys Rd WAB EN9 .....234 B3
The Oxleys HLWE CM17 .....188 C5
Oxlip Rd WIT CM8 .....171 H1
Oxlow La DAGE RM10 .....310 D1
Oxney Cl CHLM/WR CM1 .....208 E5
Oxton Cl K/T/MI CO5 .....130 D5
Oxwich Cl SLH/COR SS17 .....317 G5
Oysterbed Rd FX IP11 .....67 K6
Oyster Catchers Cl
  CAN/RD E16 .....323 J2
Oyster Pl CHLM/GWD CM2 .....210 A1
Oyster Tank Rd RCOLE CO7 .....156 F7
Ozier Ct SAFWS CB11 .....30 A1
Ozier Fld HSTD CO9 .....81 J3
Oziers RBSF CM22 .....374 E7

Ozolins Wy CAN/RD E16 .....323 J2
Ozonia Cl WICKW SS12 .....260 F8
Ozonia Cl WICKW SS12 .....260 F8
Ozonia Wy WICKW SS12 .....260 F8

P

Paarl Rd CVI SS8 .....320 D1
Paceheath Cl CRW RM5 .....271 G5
Pacific Cl SWCM DA10 .....336 B5
Pacific Rd CAN/RD E16 .....323 K2
Packard Av IPSE IP5 .....55 C3
Packard Pl RIPW IP8 .....47 J5
Packards La RCOLW CO6 .....85 H3
Packe Cl K/T/MI CO5 .....149 L5
Packham Rd GVW DA11 .....337 J8
Paddick Cl BCAYE CM11 .....258 F6
  HAR CO12 .....15 H1
  LOS SS9 .....282 B5
Paddock Dr CHLM/WR CM1 .....194 B3
Paddock Md HLWS CM18 .....203 K6
The Paddocks ABR/ST RM4 .....253 J6
  BURES CO8 .....359 P9
  CDW/CHF RM16 .....315 L5
  GTDUN CM6 .....140 B6
  HERT/BAY SG13 .....184 C3
  ING CM4 .....241 H3
  KESG IP5 .....50 F5
  MAL CM9 .....198 D1
  RAYL SS6 .....281 J3
  RCOLE CO7 .....345 G4
  SRTFD E15 .....307 K5
  SUD CO10 .....21 K4
  WIT CM8 .....171 K3
Paddock Wy CBS CB2 .....22 C2
  RCOLE CO7 .....130 F2
The Paddock BROX EN10 .....201 H6
  BSF CM23 .....138 C4
  ING CM4 .....241 H3
Padgetts Wy HOC/HUL SS5 .....263 G2
Padham's Green Rd ING CM4 .....239 M5
Padnall Rd CHDH RM6 .....288 A3
Padstow Rd KESG IP5 .....49 M8
Pageant Cl TIL RM18 .....331 M7
Pageant Crs
  BERM/RHTH SE16 .....322 C4
Page Cl DAGW RM9 .....310 C5
Page Gdns KESG IP5 .....50 D5
Page Md BSDN SS14 2
Page Rd COS CO15 .....6 E6
  HERT/BAY SG13 .....184 B3
  PIT SS13 .....279 J6
Pages Cl BSF CM23 .....138 C4
  BSF CM23 .....139 H4
Pages Ct MAL CM9 .....385 J5
Paget Cl RBSF CM22 .....374 E4
Paget Gdns CHLM/WR CM1 .....240 D8
Paget Rd IL IG1 .....308 E1
  IP IP1 .....16 C1
  K/T/MI CO5 .....130 C6
Pagets Gdns CHLM/WR CM9 * 384 A2
Pagette Wy GRAYS RM17 .....330 D4
Paglesfield RBRW/HUT CM13 .....256 F2
Paglesham Rd RCFD SS4 .....396 G3
Paignton Av CHLM/WR CM1 .....194 B3
Paignton Cl RAYL SS6 .....263 G8
Palace Gdns BKHH IG9 .....250 A8
Palace Gv LAIN SS15 .....2 A1
Palace Pde WALTH E17 * 284 C2
Palace View Rd CHING E4 .....268 F4
Palamos Rd LEY E10 .....284 D6
Palatine Av LAIN SS15 .....276 D7
Paley Gdns LOU IG10 .....250 A5
Palfrey Hts MGTR CO11 .....65 C5
Palins Wy CDW/CHF RM16 .....314 D5
Pallett Ct HOD EN11 .....201 J5
Palliser Dr RAIN RM13 .....327 K1
Palliser Rd COLS CO2 * 7 J2
Pall Ml LOS SS9 .....300 C5
Palm Cl CHLM/GWD CM2 .....209 M7
  LEY E10 .....284 E8
  WAB EN9 .....147 M9
Palmcroft Cl IP IP1 .....47 M2
Palmcroft Wy IP IP1 .....47 M2
Palmeira Av WOS/PRIT SS0 .....18 B7
Palmeira Pde WOS/PRIT SS0 .....18 B7
Palmer Cl LAIN SS15 * 277 G7
Palmer Rd BCTR RM8 .....288 A6
  PLSTW E13 .....307 L8
Palmers SLH/COR SS17 .....317 J2
Palmer's Av GRAYS RM17 .....330 F4
Palmers Cl CBE/LIN CB1 .....24 E4
Palmers Cft CHLM/GWD CM2 .....210 F3
Palmers Dr GRAYS RM17 .....330 F3
Palmers Gv WAB EN9 .....202 A8
Palmers Hl EPP CM16 .....220 B7
Palmers La ROY SG8 .....349 P7
Palmerston Rd CVI SS8 .....320 A2
  RAIN RM13 .....311 M6
Palmerston Gdns
  WTHK RM20 .....330 A4
Palmerston Ldg
  CHLM/GWD CM2 .....210 C6
Palmerston Rd BKHH IG9 .....267 M1
  IPNE IP4 .....17 J4
  RCOS CO16 .....135 K3
  WALTH E17 .....284 C2
  WOS/PRIT SS0 .....18 A6
  WTHK RM20 .....330 A4
Palmers Wy CHES/WCR EN8 .....216 F7
Palm Ms LAIN SS15 .....277 G1
Palmerswent Cl SUD CO10 .....43 G1
Palm Rd ROMW/RG RM7 .....288 F3
Pamela Gdns BSF CM23 .....139 J6
Pampas Cl COLN CO4 .....107 K1
Pampisford Rd CBE/LIN CB1 .....23 C4
Pamplins LAIN SS15 .....276 C1
Panadown LAIN SS15 .....276 D2
Pancroft ABR/ST RM4 .....251 J6
Panfield La BARTH CM7 .....99 H8
Panfield Ms
  GNTH/NBYPK IG2 .....286 D7
Panfield Rd ABYW SE2 .....325 K6
  CHESW EN7 .....216 B2
  COLN CO4 .....88 B2
Pankhurst Av CAN/RD E16 .....323 K4
Pannin Ms BRTR CM7 .....121 K8
Pannells Cl FX IP11 .....67 J5
Pantile Av SOSN SS2 .....301 M2
Pantile Cl BOC CM0 .....393 M6
Pantile Hl BOC CM0 .....393 M6
Pantlings La K/T/MI CO5 .....124 C8
Panton Crs COLN CO4 .....108 B5
Panton Ms BRTR CM7 .....121 K8
Papenburg Rd CVI SS8 .....298 D7
Paper Mill Br RCHLM CM3 .....2 B9
Paprills VGE SS16 .....3 H3

Parade Dr HAR CO12 .....70 B4
Parade Rd IPNE IP4 .....17 J2
The Parade BRW CM14 .....273 M2
  COLS CO2 * 129 K4
  GVE DA12 * 338 F7
  HARH RM3 * 272 E5
  PIT SS13 * 278 E8
  SOCK/AV RM15 * 328 E1
  SWCM DA10 * 336 B5
  WOTN CO14 .....137 M2
Paradise Cl CHESW EN7 .....216 C2
Paradise Rd CHLM/WR CM1 .....208 A3
  WAB EN9 .....233 A4
Paradise Rd CAN/RD E16 .....323 G1
Par Cl HERT/BAY SG13 .....184 C2
Pardoe Pl IPNE IP4 .....49 K8
Pardoe Rd LEY E10 .....284 F5
Pargat Dr LOS SS9 .....281 M6
Pargetters Hyam
  HOC/HUL SS5 .....264 C5
Parham Dr GNTH/NBYPK IG2 .....286 C7
Paringdon Rd
  HLWW/ROY CM19 .....203 J5
Parish Cl EMPK RM11 .....289 L7
  LAIN SS15 .....276 F6
Parish Whf WOOL/PLUM SE18 .....324 D2
Parkanaur Av SOS SS1 .....302 E3
Park Av BARK IG11 .....308 F3
  BSF CM23 .....139 G6
  CHLM/WR CM1 .....4 B3
  CVI SS8 .....321 H3
  EHAM E6 .....308 D5
  FX IP11 .....63 D7
  GVE DA12 .....337 M6
  GVW DA11 .....337 H6
  HLWE CM17 .....204 D4
  IL IG1 .....286 D7
  LOS SS9 .....282 B5
  RBRW/HUT CM13 .....256 F7
  SRTFD E15 .....307 H3
  STSD CM24 .....115 M3
  SUD CO10 .....21 J7
  SWCM DA10 .....336 B4
  UPMR RM14 .....312 D1
  WALTH E17 .....284 C3
  WAN E11 .....285 L6
  WIT CM8 .....147 K2
  WOS/PRIT SS0 .....18 A6
Park Av Ingress GRH DA9 .....335 L8
Park Bvd COS CO15 .....160 B3
Park Cha GPK RM2 .....271 J7
Park Cha RCOS CO16 .....157 M8
  SBF/HAD SS7 .....299 H3
Park Cl EPP CM16 .....221 H5
  KESG IP5 .....50 F5
  SUD CO10 .....21 J7
  WICKW SS12 .....260 F7
Park Corner Rd MEO DA13 .....336 D9
Park Ct HLW CM20 .....13 H4
  HSTD CO9 .....356 F8
Park Crs EMPK RM11 .....289 K5
  WOS/PRIT SS0 .....18 A5
Parkdale Rd
  WOOL/PLUM SE18 .....325 H8
Parkdale Rd
  WOOL/PLUM SE18 .....325 H8
Park Dr BCAYE CM11 .....259 H8
  CHARL SE7 .....324 D7
  DAGE RM10 .....288 F7
  HSTD CO9 .....81 H7
  ING CM4 .....222 C5
  MAL CM9 .....214 C4
  RBSF CM22 .....378 C5
  ROM RM1 .....289 G2
  UPMR RM14 .....312 F1
  WICKW SS12 .....261 G7
Park End Rd ROM RM1 .....289 H5
Parker Cl CAN/RD E16 .....324 C1
Parker Rd CHLM/GWD CM2 .....5 J6
  GRAYS RM17 .....330 C4
Parker's Farm Rd
  UPMR RM14 .....293 J3
Parker St CAN/RD E16 .....324 C1
Parker Wy HSTD CO9 .....81 J6
Parkes Rd CHIG IG7 .....269 J4
Parkeston By-Pass HAR CO12 .....14 C5
Parkeston Quay HAR CO12 .....66 F1
Parkeston Rd FX IP11 .....10 F1
  HAR CO12 .....14 A6
Parkeston Rbt HAR CO12 .....14 A6
Parkfield BETH E2 * 306 A6
Parkfield St K/T/MI CO5 .....130 C6
Park Gdns ERITH DA8 .....264 C7
  HOC/HUL SS5 .....264 C7
Parkgate WOS/PRIT SS0 .....18 A5
Park Gate Rd SLH/COR SS17 .....295 K2
  WIT CM8 .....147 K2
Park Gv SRTFD E15 .....307 H3
Park Grove Rd WAN E11 .....285 J2
Parkhall Rd BRTR CM7 .....79 G6
Park Hl CBE/LIN CB1 .....33 C5
  HLWE CM17 .....188 C6
  LOU IG10 .....250 A5
Parkhill Cl HCH RM12 .....289 M7
Parkhill Rd CHING E4 .....248 F1
Parkhurst Rd DAYL SS6 .....262 F7
  MNPK E12 .....308 C1
  PIT SS13 .....278 E8
  WALTH E17 .....284 C2
Parkland Av ROM RM1 .....271 G6
Parkland Cl HOD EN11 .....185 J8
Parkland Rd WFD IG8 .....267 H6
Parklands BCAYE CM11 .....259 M1
  BRTR CM7 .....121 K6
  CHIG IG7 .....270 B2
  CVI SS8 .....298 D7
  RCFD SS4 .....283 G1
  RCOLW CO6 .....124 D3
Parklands Av RAYL SS6 .....281 H4
Parklands Cl
  GNTH/NBYPK IG2 .....286 D7
Parklands Dr CHLM/WR CM1 .....5 L8
  CHONG CM5 .....382 G4
Park La BCAYE CM11 .....259 M1
  BROX EN10 .....200 F5
  BSF CM23 .....139 G5
  CBE/LIN CB1 .....342 A4
  CHDH RM6 .....288 A2
  CHES/WCR EN8 .....216 B3
  CHESW EN7 .....216 B3
  COLN CO4 .....88 B2
  CVI SS8 .....321 H3
  EMPK RM11 .....289 L7
  HCH RM12 .....311 L3
  HLW CM20 .....13 H4
  HSTD CO9 .....355 N2
  MAL CM9 .....199 G4
  RBRW/HUT CM13 .....275 G2
  RCHLM CM3 .....166 C1
  RCOLW CO6 .....82 C7
Park Lane Cl RCOLW CO6 .....82 C7
Park La Paradise BROX EN10 .....216 F3
Park Ldg BCAYW CM12 * 258 D2
Park Md HLW CM20 .....13 G4
Parkmead LOU IG10 .....250 D5
Park Meadow BRWN CM15 .....238 G4
Park Ms GNWCH SE10 .....323 G8
Parkmill Cl SLH/COR SS17 .....317 K1
Park North IP IP1 .....48 B2
  POP/IOD E14 .....322 C4
Park Rd BOC CM0 .....393 M7
  BRW CM14 .....255 L8
  CBS CB2 .....22 C2
  CHES/WCR EN8 .....232 E4
  CHLM/WR CM1 .....130 H3
  COLN CO4 .....130 H3
  COS CO15 .....6 E7
  EHAM E6 .....321 L3
  GTDUN CM6 .....116 D3
  HAR CO12 .....15 K6
  HOD EN11 .....201 H4
  HVHL CB9 .....34 C6
  IL IG1 .....287 G8
  IP IP1 .....48 B2
  LEY E10 .....284 D6
  LOS SS9 .....299 L1
  MNPK E12 .....308 A1
  MNPK E12 .....308 A1
  PEND EN3 .....232 F6
  RBSF CM22 .....374 E3
  RCOLE CO7 .....64 E5
  RCOLE CO7 .....109 J1
  RCOLE CO7 .....110 F5
  RCOLE CO7 .....130 D5
  RCOLW CO6 .....361 N10
  RCOLW CO6 .....361 K4
  SBF/HAD SS7 .....299 H3
  SLH/COR SS17 .....316 G4
  SLH/COR SS17 .....317 K2
  SRTFD E15 .....307 K5
  STSD CM24 .....115 M3
  SUD CO10 .....21 J7
  SWCM DA10 .....336 B4
  UPMR RM14 .....312 F1
  WALTH E17 .....284 C3
  WAN E11 .....285 L6
  WIT CM8 .....147 K2
  WOS/PRIT SS0 .....18 A6
Park Side BCAYE CM11 .....259 H8
  BKHH IG9 .....267 L1
  GTDUN CM6 .....96 F3
  PIT SS13 .....278 D6
  WOS/PRIT SS0 .....300 D7
Parkside CDW/CHF RM16 .....331 G2
  CHES/WCR EN8 .....232 E4
  CHLM/WR CM1 .....5 L8
Parkside Av IPNE IP4 .....17 G1
  ROM RM1 .....271 G6
  TIL RM18 .....331 L8
Parkside Est HOM E9 * 306 A5
Parkside Quarter COLS CO2 * 7 K1
Parkside Rd HAR CO12 .....326 E7
Park Sq East COS CO15 .....182 G5
Park Sq West COS CO15 .....182 G4
Parkstone Av EMPK RM11 .....290 B4
  SBF/HAD SS7 .....298 E1
  WICKW SS12 .....260 G3
Parkstone Dr SOSN SS2 .....301 J4
Parkstone Rd WALTH E17 .....284 E4
Park St GTDUN CM6 .....74 D4
  RCOLW CO6 .....361 N10
Park Ter GRH DA9 .....335 M3
  HAR CO12 .....15 K6
  PEND EN3 .....232 F8
  WOS/PRIT SS0 .....18 A6
Park Vale Cl HSTD CO9 .....356 F9
Park Vw CVI SS8 .....321 G3
  HOD EN11 .....201 H4
  SOCK/AV RM15 .....329 G4
Park View Crs
  GRAYS RM17 .....330 E4
Park View Dr LOS SS9 .....281 L8
Park View Gdns CLAY IG5 .....286 C2
Park View Rd IP IP11 .....47 M4

Parsloe Rd EPP CM16 203 J6
Parsloes Av DAGW RM9 310 B2
Parsonage Cha MAL CM9 231 C5
Parsonage Cl CBS CB2 340 F1
CHLM/WR CM1 193 K4
FX IP11 10 F2
Parsonage Farm La
SAFWN CB10 353 L5
Parsonage Fld BRWN CM15 238 A3
Parsonage Gv BURES CO8 359 P9
Parsonage La BSF CM23 139 J1
GTDUN CM6 142 A2
ING CM4 224 D6
LAIN SS15 276 F7
RCHLM CM3 167 K3
RCHLM CM3 212 A3
RCOS CO16 112 A5
SAFWN CB10 31 J7
SAFWS CB11 72 C6
STSD CM24 374 A9
Parsonage Rd RAIN RM13 311 M6
RBSF CM22 377 J1
WTHK RM20 335 M1
Parsonage St HSTD CO9 81 J4
POP/IOD E14 322 F7
Parsonage Wy CBE/LIN CB1 25 G7
Parsons Cnr SBN/FI SS3 * 303 G4
Parson's Fld RCOLE CO7 363 P11
Parson's Heath COLN CO4 108 B3
Parson's Hl COLW CO3 106 D7
RCOLE CO7 110 B5
Parsons La COL CO1 9 J9
Parsons Lawn SBN/FI SS3 303 G4
Parsons Rd PLSTW E13 307 M6
SBF/HAD SS7 280 A6
Parsons Yd MGTR CO11 * 91 G1
Partridge Av CHLM/WR CM1 193 J7
Partridge Cl CAN/RD E16 324 A1
HAR CO12 368 A1
Partridge Ct HLWS CM18 203 M3
Partridge Dr RCOLW CO6 85 G8
Partridge Rd CHTY IP2 53 J2
HLWS CM18 203 L3
Partridge Sq EHAM E6 324 B1
Parvills WAB EN9 233 L2
Paschal Wy CHLM/GWD CM2 210 B5
Pasfield WAB EN9 233 L3
Paske Av HVHL CB9 34 C6
Paslowes VGE SS16 296 C1
Pasquier Rd WALTH E17 284 B1
Passfield Dr POP/IOD E14 322 E1
Passingham Av BCAYE CM11 258 F7
Passingham Cl BCAYE CM11 258 F6
Pasteur Dr HARH RM3 272 A8
Paston Cl RCHLM CM3 245 H4
Pastoral Wy BRW CM14 273 M4
Pasture High RCHLM CM3 212 A2
Pasture Loates STSD CM24 115 L1
Pasture Rd DAGW RM9 310 C2
The Pastures IPNE IP4 49 L8
Patching Hall La
CHLM/WR CM1 193 J5
Paternoster Cl WAB EN9 234 A3
Paternoster Hl WAB EN9 234 A2
Paternoster Rw ABR/ST RM4 253 M8
WOTN CO14 * 137 M1
Pathfields Rd COS CO15 6 D4
The Path RCOLE CO7 133 H5
Pathways BSDN SS14 278 B8
Patmore Cl BSF CM23 138 D1
Patmore Flds RBSF CM22 93 M3
Patmore Rd COLN CO4 9 M4
WAB EN9 233 M4
Patmore Wy CRW RM5 270 E4
Paton Cl BOW E3 306 D7
Patricia Dr EMPK RM11 290 B6
SLH/COR SS17 295 M7
Patricia Gdns BCAYE CM11 259 G6
BSF CM23 138 F4
Patrick Gv WAB EN9 233 J3
Patrick Rd PLSTW E13 307 M7
Patten Cl RCOLW CO6 126 B2
Patterdale SBF/HAD SS7 279 L6
Pattern Bush Cl MGTR CO11 65 G5
Patteson Rd IPSE IP3 17 J8
Pattina Wk BERM/RHTH SE16 322 B4
Pattison Cl WIT CM8 171 K5
Pattiswick Cnr BSDN SS14 278 B6
Pattiswick Sq BSDN SS14 278 B6
Pattocks BSDN SS14 3 M6
Pattocks La RCOLW CO6 103 M3
Pattrick's La HAR CO12 15 H7
Paul Cl SRTFD E15 307 H4
Pauline Cl COS CO15 159 L7
Pauline Gdns BCAYW CM12 258 C1
Pauline St CHTY IP2 16 F9
Paul Julius Cl POP/IOD E14 323 G3
Paul Robeson Cl EHAM E6 308 D7
Pauls Ct HOD EN11 * 201 H3
Pauls Crs RCOLE CO7 109 J7
Pauls La HOD EN11 201 H3
Paul Spendlove Ct
COLN CO4 * 108 B4
Paul's Rd CHTY IP2 47 L8
LAIN SS15 276 F5
Paul St SRTFD E15 307 H5
The Pavement WAN E11 * 284 F6
Pavet Cl DAGE RM10 310 E3
Pavilion Cl SOSN SS2 302 B4
Pavilion Dr LOS SS9 300 C5
Pavilion Rd IL IG1 286 C8
The Pavilions EPP CM16 221 K3
The Pavilion CHES/WCR EN8 232 F4
Pavillion Pl BCAYW CM12 258 C1
Pavitt Meadow
CHLM/GWD CM2 225 M3
Pawle Cl CHLM/GWD CM2 210 D6
Pawsey Cl PLSTW E13 307 K5
Paxfords LAIN SS15 276 C7
Paxman Av COLS CO2 128 D2
Pax Ter MGTR CO11 * 65 G4
Paxton Rd COS CO15 159 L5
Paxwood WIT CM8 * 172 A8
Paycocke Cl BSDN SS14 278 C3
Paycocke Rd BSDN SS14 278 C3
Paycocke Wy RCOLW CO6 124 D2
Paycock Rd
HLWW/ROY CM19 203 H3
Payne Cl BARK IG11 309 J4
Payne Pl RCHLM CM3 227 L7
Payne Rd BOW E3 306 E6
Payne's La RCOLE CO7 110 F2
WAB EN9 217 K2
Paynes Meadow CBE/LIN CB1 24 F4
Paynters Md VGE SS16 296 B2
Paynters Ter HSTD CO9 * 81 J3
Payzes Gdns WFD IG8 * 267 J5
Peacehaven FOS CO13 137 K4
Peace Rd COLW CO3 105 M7
Peach Av HOC/HUL SS5 264 B6
Peach Cft GVW DA11 337 H8
Peacock Cl BRTR CM7 121 J4
EMPK RM11 290 B2
WALTH E17 266 C6
Peacocks HLWW/ROY CM19 203 G3
Peacocks Cl SUD CO10 38 F3
Peacocks Rd SUD CO10 38 F3
Peacock St GVE DA12 337 M5
KESG IP5 50 D6
Peake Av FOS CO13 136 D3
Peakes Cl K/T/MI CO5 173 L1
Peakes La CHESW EN7 216 A5
Peakes Wy CHESW EN7 216 A5
Peaketon Av REDBR IG4 286 A3
Pea La UPMR RM14 313 K3
Peal Rd SAFWS CB11 30 B2
Pearce Mnr CHLM/GWD CM2 4 D8
Pearce Rd IPSE IP3 48 F8
Pearcroft Rd IP IP1 48 A2
WAN E11 285 G7
Pearcy Cl HARH RM3 272 B6
Pearl Cl EHAM E6 324 D2
Pearl Rd IP IP1 47 H5
WALTH E17 284 D1
Pearmain Cl WICKE SS11 261 G4
Pearmains RCHLM CM3 144 C6
Pearmain Wy COLW CO3 127 M1
Pear Rd WAN E11 285 G8
Pearse Wy IPSE IP3 55 K4
Pearson Rd IPNE IP4 49 H8
Pearsons SLH/COR SS17 317 K2
Pearsons Av RAYL SS6 280 E1
Pearsons Wy RIPW IP8 52 E4
Peartree Cl BRTR CM7 121 K4
BRWN CM15 238 A4
MAL CM9 384 B7
SOCK/AV RM15 313 M7
SOSN SS2 301 M2
Peartree Gdns BCTR RM8 309 L2
ROMW/RG RM7 270 E8
Peartree Hl BURES CO8 84 E1
Peartree La BRWN CM15 383 R11
RCHLM CM3 228 C2
UPMR RM14 293 J4
Pear Tree Md HLWS CM18 204 B3
Peartree Rd COLW CO3 128 A1
Peartrees RBRW/HUT CM13 274 F1
Pear Trees SBF/HAD SS7 298 C1
Peartree Wy GNWCH SE10 323 K7
RCOS CO16 158 F3
Pease Cl HCH RM12 311 L4
Pease Pl RCHLM CM3 227 L7
Peasey La KESG IP5 50 B7
Peaslands Rd SAFWS CB11 30 B1
Peasmead Ter CHING E4 * 266 F3
Pebmarsh Cl COLS CO2 129 K5
Pebmarsh Dr WICKW SS12 261 H7
Pebmarsh Rd HSTD CO9 358 F9
RCOLW CO6 82 C3
Peck's Hl WAB EN9 201 M7
Pecockes Cl SUD CO10 45 M4
Pedder's Cl COLW CO3 128 C2
Pedlars Cl RCHLM CM3 212 D7
Pedlars End CHONG CM5 380 C7
Pedlars Pth RCHLM CM3 212 D7
Pedley Rd BCTR RM8 287 M6
Pedro St CLPT E5 284 A8
Peel Av SBN/FI SS3 303 K6
Peel Cl CHING E4 266 E1
Peel Crs BRTR CM7 121 H2
Peel Dr CLAY IG5 286 B1
Peel Pl CLAY IG5 268 B8
Peel Rd CHLM/GWD CM2 210 C1
SWFD E18 267 J7
Peel St IP IP1 16 E3
Peel Wy HARH RM3 272 C8
Peel Yd KESG IP5 50 F5
Peerage Wy EMPK RM11 290 B5
Peers Sq CHLM/GWD CM2 210 D1
Peerswood Rd COLS CO2 129 G3
Peewit Ct FX IP11 * 10 F3
Peewit Hl FX IP11 10 F5
Peewit Rd CHTY IP2 53 H2
Pegasus Ct GVE DA12 337 M8
Pegasus Wy BRTR CM7 99 H8
COLN CO4 9 K2
Pegelm Gdns EMPK RM11 290 C5
Peggotty Cl CHLM/WR CM1 193 J7
Peggy's Wk SAFWS CB11 351 M2
Peg Millar's La RCHLM CM3 145 M7
Pegrams Rd HLWS CM18 203 K4
Pekin St POP/IOD E14 322 D2
Peldon Pavement BSDN SS14 3 M2
Peldon Rd HLWW/ROY CM19 203 H3
K/T/MI CO5 153 K5
K/T/MI CO5 176 D2
Pelham Av BARK IG11 309 J5
Pelham Cl HAR CO12 70 E3
Pelham Pl SLH/COR SS17 317 H1
Pelham Rd GVW DA11 337 J5
IL IG1 287 G7
SAFWS CB11 72 C5
SOSN SS2 302 B4
SWFD E18 285 L1
Pelham Rd South GVW DA11 337 J6
Pelhams La COL CO1 8 C7
Pelican Cl CHTY IP2 53 K2
Pelling St POP/IOD E14 322 C2
Pellipar Rd WOOL/PLUM SE18 324 C8
Pelly Av WIT CM8 171 K5
Pelly Ct EPP CM16 236 A1
Pelly Rd PLSTW E13 307 K6
Pelton Rd GNWCH SE10 323 H8
Pembar Av WALTH E17 * 284 B1
Pemberton Av GPK RM2 289 L1
ING CM4 239 L1
Pemberton Ct ING CM4 * 239 L1
Pemberton Fld RCFD SS4 264 E1
Pemberton Gdns CHDH RM6 288 B3
Pembrey Wy HCH RM12 311 M3
Pembridge La BROX EN10 200 A7
Pembroke Av MAL CM9 214 C4
SLH/COR SS17 317 K1
Pembroke Cl BCAYW CM12 240 D8
BROX EN10 216 F2
CHTY IP2 54 A2
COLS CO2 129 M2
EMPK RM11 290 D2
ERITH DA8 326 F7
Pembroke Gdns COS CO15 160 B3
DAGE RM10 288 E8
Pembroke La CBE/LIN CB1 25 H7
Pembroke Ms PIT SS13 278 F5
Pembroke Pde ERITH DA8 * 326 F8
Pembroke Pl CHLM/WR CM1 193 K6
SUD CO10 43 G7
Pembroke Rd EHAM E6 324 C1
ERITH DA8 326 F8
GDMY/SEVK IG3 287 J6
WALTH E17 284 E3
Pembury Rd WOS/PRIT SS0 300 F6
Penda's Md HOM E9 306 B1
Pendle Cl BSDN SS14 278 D4
Pendle Dr BSDN SS14 278 C4
Pendlestone Rd WALTH E17 284 E3
Pendleton Rd CHTY IP2 53 J4
Pendower RAYL SS6 280 E5
Penerley Rd RAIN RM13 327 L1
Penfold Rd COS CO15 6 F8
ED N9 248 A8
FX IP11 11 M1
Pengelly Cl CHESW EN7 216 C8
Penge Rd PLSTW E13 307 M4
Penhall Rd CHARL SE7 324 A7
Penhurst Av SOSN SS2 301 J2
Penhurst Dr RCHLM CM3 245 G8
Penhurst Rd BARK/HLT IG6 268 E6
Peninsular Park Rd
CHARL SE7 323 K8
Penlan Hall La RCOLW CO6 84 E7
Penlow Rd HLWS CM18 203 K4
Penmon Rd ABYW SE2 325 K6
Pennant Ter WALTH E17 266 C8
Penn Cl CDW/CHF RM16 315 L4
RIPS/CAP IP9 58 E3
Penn Gdns CRW RM5 270 D6
Pennial Rd CVI SS8 320 D1
Pennine Rd CHLM/WR CM1 193 G7
Pennine Wy GVW DA11 337 H8
Pennington Cl CRW RM5 270 D5
Pennington La STSD CM24 115 L1
Penningtons BSF CM23 138 D4
Penn Ms BRTR CM7 121 K5
Pennsylvania La K/T/MI CO5 149 L8
Penny Cl RAIN RM13 311 L7
Penny Flds BRW CM14 273 M3
Pennyfields POP/IOD E14 322 D3
Penny La IPSE IP3 55 L4
Pennymead HLW CM20 204 B1
Penny Meadow RIPS/CAP IP9 58 D4
Pennyroyal Av EHAM E6 324 D2
Pennyroyal Crs WIT CM8 171 H1
Pennyroyal Gdns CHTY IP2 53 K1
Penny Royal Rd RCHLM CM3 212 A7
Penny's La ING CM4 224 C5
Pennystone Rd SAFWS CB11 30 B1
Penrhyn Av WALTH E17 266 D7
Penrhyn Crs WALTH E17 266 D7
Penrhyn Gv WALTH E17 266 D7
Penrice Cl COLN CO4 108 B7
Penrith Crs HCH RM12 311 K2
Penrith Rd BARK/HLT IG6 269 J5
HARH RM3 272 D5
Penrose Md CHLM/WR CM1 208 E5
Penryn Rd KESG IP5 49 L6
Penshurst HLWE CM17 188 C6
Penshurst Pl BRTR CM77 120 E7
Penshurst Rd HOM E9 306 A4
IPSE IP3 55 J1
Penson's La CHONG CM5 382 B2
Penticton Rd BRTR CM7 121 G3
Pentire Cl UPMR RM14 291 H4
Pentire Rd WALTH E17 267 G7
Pentland Av CHLM/WR CM1 193 K7
SBN/FI SS3 302 F7
Pentlow Dr SUD CO10 39 H4
Pentlow Hawke Cl HVHL CB9 34 E6
Pentlow Hl SUD CO10 39 K5
Pentlow Wy BKHH IG9 250 B7
Pentney Rd CHING E4 249 G8
Penton Dr CHES/WCR EN8 216 E7
Pentrich Av EN EN1 232 B8
Pentstemon Dr SWCM DA10 336 B3
Penventon Ct TIL RM18 * 331 K8
Penwood Cl BCAYE CM11 241 G7
Penzance Cl CHLM/WR CM1 194 B8
COS CO15 182 F5
Penzance Gdns HARH RM3 272 D5
Penzance Rd HARH RM3 272 D5
KESG IP5 49 M7
Pepper Cl EHAM E6 324 C1
Peppercorn Cl COLN CO4 8 C1
Peppercorn Wy CHTY IP2 16 F9
Pepper Hl GVW DA11 336 F8
WARE SG12 185 G4
Peppermint Pl WAN E11 285 H8
Pepper's Rd COLN CO4 87 H4
Pepper St POP/IOD E14 322 E6
Pepples La SAFWN CB10 31 K8
Pepys Cl GVW DA11 337 G8
TIL RM18 331 M7
Pepys Est DEPT SE8 322 C8
Pepys Park Est DEPT SE8 322 C7
Pepys St HAR CO12 15 K4
Percival Gdns CHDH RM6 287 M4
Percival Rd EMPK RM11 289 M4
FOS CO13 368 G12
WOTN CO14 369 N11
Percy Cottis Rd RCFD SS4 283 H2
Percy Gdns PEND EN3 248 A5
Percy Rd CAN/RD E16 323 H1
GDMY/SEVK IG3 287 K5
LOS SS9 300 A3
ROMW/RG RM7 288 F1
WAN E11 285 H5
Percy Ruse Cl SUD CO10 21 J6
Percy St GRAYS RM17 330 F5
Peregrine Cl BSF CM23 138 E3
COS CO15 159 J7
SBN/FI SS3 303 H4
VGE SS16 3 H9
Peregrine Ct COLN CO4 108 C5
Peregrine Dr
CHLM/GWD CM2 209 K8
SBF/HAD SS7 297 M3
Peregrine Gdns RAYL SS6 280 E2
Peregrine Rd BARK/HLT IG6 269 L4
Peregrin Rd WAB EN9 234 B4
Peridot St EHAM E6 324 B1
Periwinkle Cl ROY SG8 370 B2
Perkins Cl GRH DA9 335 J7
Perkins Rd BARK/HLT IG6 287 G3
Perkins Wy IPSE IP3 54 E4
Perram Cl BROX EN10 216 F4
Perriclose CHLM/WR CM1 194 A6
Perrin Pl CHLM/GWD CM2 4 E6
Perriors Cl CHESW EN7 216 B5
Perry Cl RAIN RM13 311 G6
Perryfield HLWE CM17 378 D11
Perry Gn BSDN SS14 3 G3
Perry Gv DART DA1 334 D6
Perry Hl CHLM/WR CM1 5 L1
WAB EN9 218 A1
Perry La COLN CO4 88 C1
Perrymans Farm Rd
GNTH/NBYPK IG2 287 G4
Perry Rd HLWS CM18 203 K4
K/T/MI CO5 149 L8
SBF/HAD SS7 297 L2
WIT CM8 171 L4
Perrysfield Rd
CHES/WCR EN8 216 F5
Perry Spring HLWE CM17 204 D3
VGE SS16 3 L8
Perry St BCAYW CM12 258 D1
GVW DA11 337 H6
Perry Wy SOCK/AV RM15 328 F3
WIT CM8 171 L4
Persardi Ct COLS CO2 129 K6
Pershore Cl GNTH/NBYPK IG2 286 E3
Pershore End COLW CO3 106 B8
Perth Cl COLS CO2 129 K4
Perth Rd BARK IG11 309 G6
GNTH/NBYPK IG2 286 E4
LEY E10 284 B6
PLSTW E13 307 L6
Perth Ter GNTH/NBYPK IG2 286 F5
Pertwee Cl RCOLE CO7 156 B5
Pertwee Dr CHLM/GWD CM2 210 C7
RCHLM CM3 244 F6
Pertwees Ct COL CO1 9 K9
Pertwee Wy K/T/MI CO5 153 L3
Pesthouse La HAR CO12 113 M2
Peterboat Cl GNWCH SE10 323 H7
Peterborough Av
UPMR RM14 291 H6
Peterborough Rd LEY E10 284 F3
Peterborough Wy BSDN SS14 278 C5
Peter Bruff Av RCOS CO16 6 B1
Peterfield's La HSTD CO9 80 B8
Peterhouse Cl CHTY IP2 53 K3
Peters Cl BCTR RM8 288 A6
Petersfield CHLM/WR CM1 193 L7
Petersfield Av HARH RM3 272 B5
Petersfield Cl HARH RM3 272 D5
Petersfield Rd CBS CB2 340 E1
Peter's Gv RIPS/CAP IP9 58 D4
Peterstone Rd ABYW SE2 325 L5
Peter St ING CM4 241 J4
Peterswood HLWS CM18 203 L5
Peters Wood Hl WARE SG12 184 E2
Peto Av COLN CO4 8 C1
Peto St North CAN/RD E16 323 J2
Petrebrook CHLM/GWD CM2 210 D2
Petre Cl ING CM4 239 K3
RBRW/HUT CM13 274 F8
Petrel Wy CHLM/GWD CM2 209 M7
Petresfield Wy
RBRW/HUT CM13 274 F8
Petrolea Cl COL CO1 8 C2
Petronius Wy COLN CO4 87 L8
Petro St South CAN/RD E16 323 J3
Pett Cl EMPK RM11 289 L7
Pett La BRTR CM77 146 D1
Pettits Bvd ROM RM1 271 H8
Pettits Cl ROM RM1 271 H8
Pettits La BRWN CM15 238 B3
ROM RM1 271 H8
Pettits La North ROM RM1 271 G7
Pettit's Pl DAGE RM10 310 D2
Pettit's Rd DAGE RM10 310 D2
Pettley Gdns ROMW/RG RM7 289 G3
Pettman Crs THMD SE28 325 G7
Petts La SAFWN CB10 26 B8
Pett St WOOL/PLUM SE18 324 B7
Pettys Cl CHES/WCR EN8 216 E7
Petunia Crs CHLM/WR CM1 194 C7
Petworth Cl BRTR CM77 120 E6
RCOLE CO7 130 F5
Petworth Gdns SOSN SS2 302 C3
Petworth Wy HCH RM12 311 J1
Pevensey Dr COS CO15 182 F5
Pevensey Gdns HOC/HUL SS5 263 J5
Pevensey Rd FSTGT E7 307 K1
Pevensey Wy PIT SS13 278 E7
Peverel Av RCHLM CM3 196 F4
Pewsey Cl CHING E4 266 D4
Pewterers Av BSF CM23 138 D5
Pharos La K/T/MI CO5 177 M7
Pheasant Cl CAN/RD E16 323 L2
Pheasant Ri RIPW IP8 52 E5
Pheasant Rd CHTY IP2 53 K2
Phelips Rd EPP CM16 203 H6
Philan Wy CRW RM5 271 G5
Philbrick Crs West RAYL SS6 280 E2
Philmore Cl
WOOL/PLUM SE18 325 H8
Philip Av FX IP11 10 F4
ROMW/RG RM7 289 G6
Philip Cl BRWN CM15 255 L6
WOTN CO14 137 K1
Philip Rd CHTY IP2 16 E8
RAIN RM13 311 H7
WIT CM8 171 H5
Philips Cl BRTR CM77 120 C3
Philips Rd BRTR CM77 120 C3
Philip St PLSTW E13 307 K8
Philip Sydney Rd WTHK RM20 330 A4
Phillida Rd HARH RM3 272 D8
Phillip Rd RCOLE CO7 130 E5
Phillips Cha BRTR CM7 99 K8
Phillips Field Rd SUD CO10 45 K4
Philmead Rd SBF/HAD SS7 297 L3
Philpot End La GTDUN CM6 140 E2
Philpott Av SOSN SS2 302 A3
Phoenix Cl WALTH E17 266 C8
Phoenix Ct POP/IOD E14 322 D7
Phoenix Gv CHLM/GWD CM2 4 D7
Phoenix Rd IPNE IP4 48 F6
Phoenix Wy SBF/HAD SS7 280 F6
Picardy Manorway
BELV DA17 326 E6
Picardy Rd BELV DA17 326 D8
Picardy St BELV DA17 326 D6
Picasso Wy SBN/FI SS3 303 K4
Piccotts La BRTR CM7 97 K5
Pickering Av EHAM E6 308 D6
Pickers Wy COS CO15 160 B2
Picketts CVI SS8 320 A1
Picketts Av LOS SS9 300 B1
Picketts Cl LOS SS9 300 B1
Pickett's Lock La ED N9 266 A1
Picketts Rd FX IP11 63 H8
Pick Hl WAB EN9 234 D2
Picknage Rd ROY SG8 348 F9
Pickpocket La BRTR CM77 121 G7
Pickwick Av CHLM/WR CM1 193 G7
Pickwick Cl LAIN SS15 277 G6
Pickwick Gdns GVW DA11 337 G8
Pickwick Rd CHTY IP2 47 K7
Picton Av IP IP1 48 C4
Picton Cl RAYL SS6 281 H4
Picton Gdns RAYL SS6 281 G4
Piedmont Rd
WOOL/PLUM SE18 325 G8
Pier Ap WOTN CO14 137 M2
Pier Av COS CO15 6 F7
Pierce Gld K/T/MI CO5 149 M8
Piercing Hl EPP CM16 235 L5
Piercys PIT SS13 278 D8
Pier Gap COS CO15 7 G8
Pier Hl SOS SS1 19 H7
Pierrefitte Wy BRTR CM7 121 H2
Pier Rd CAN/RD E16 324 D5
FX IP11 10 C9
GRH DA9 335 L6
GVW DA11 337 J4
Pier St POP/IOD E14 322 F7
Pier Wy WOOL/PLUM SE18 325 G6
Pier Whf GRAYS RM17 * 330 D6
Pigeon's La RIPW IP8 52 C3
Piggotts Wy BSF CM23 138 F4
Piggs Cnr GRAYS RM17 * 330 F2
The Pightle BRTR CM7 354 C11
HVHL CB9 34 D5
RIPS/CAP IP9 58 E3
Pightle Wy WOTN CO14 137 K2
Pig La BSF CM23 139 H6
Pigott St POP/IOD E14 322 D2
Pigstye Green Rd
CHONG CM5 206 C5
Pike La UPMR RM14 313 J2
Pike Wy EPP CM16 221 H5
Pilborough Wy COLW CO3 128 B2
Pilcox Hall La RCOS CO16 111 M6
Pilgrim Cl BRTR CM7 99 J8
Pilgrims Cl BCAYE CM11 258 E3
BRWN CM15 255 J5
SAFWN CB10 341 L7
SOS SS1 302 B4
Pilgrims Ct DART DA1 334 D7
Pilgrim's La BRW CM14 255 H4
CDW/CHF RM16 329 M4
Pilgrims Ms POP/IOD E14 323 G3
Pilgrims' Rd SWCM DA10 336 B2
Pilgrims Vw GRH DA9 335 M8
Pilgrims Wy SBF/HAD SS7 299 J2
Pilgrim Wy LAIN SS15 276 F7
Pilkingtons HLWE CM17 204 E1
Pilot Cl WICKE SS11 * 261 K8
Pilots Pl GVE DA12 337 M4
Pimblett Rw RBSF CM22 372 G12
Pimpernel Rd CHTY IP2 53 L2
Pinceybrook Rd HLWS CM18 203 K5
Pincey Rd STSD CM24 374 G10
Pinchpools Rd BSF CM23 93 H6
Pindar Rd HOD EN11 201 K2
Pine Av GTDUN CM6 116 E4
GVE DA12 338 A6
IP IP1 48 A4
SRTFD E15 307 G2
Pine Bank KESG IP5 50 E7
Pine Cl CHES/WCR EN8 216 D6
CVI SS8 320 B2
ING CM4 239 M1
LEY E10 284 D7
LOS SS9 281 L8
MGTR CO11 65 G5
RCOLE CO7 133 J5
Pine Ct UPMR RM14 312 D1
Pine Crs RBRW/HUT CM13 257 G1
Pinecroft GPK RM2 289 M2
RBRW/HUT CM13 256 E3
Pinecroft Gdns COLN CO4 107 L2
Pinecroft Ri SUD CO10 44 F4
Pinecroft Rd IP IP1 47 M3
Pine Dr ING CM4 239 M1
Pinefield Cl POP/IOD E14 * 322 D3
Pine Gv BSF CM23 139 J3
K/T/MI CO5 177 L6
WIT CM8 147 K8
Pinelands BSF CM23 115 G8
Pine Rd SBF/HAD SS7 299 G3
Pines Av EN EN1 232 D6
Pines Hl STSD CM24 115 L4
Pines Rd CHLM/WR CM1 193 G8
The Pines BRTR CM7 * 121 J3
CDW/CHF RM16 314 E8
FX IP11 63 K7
LAIN SS15 276 F4
RCHLM CM3 170 D8
WFD IG8 267 K2
Pinetree Cl KESG IP5 49 L6
Pinetrees SBF/HAD SS7 298 F2
Pine View Rd IP IP1 47 M5
Pinewood Av LOS SS9 282 A8
RAIN RM13 311 L8
Pinewood Cl COS CO15 159 H6
FOS CO13 137 G3
HLWE CM17 204 D3
HOC/HUL SS5 263 H3
TIL RM18 332 E2
Pinewood Rd ABR/ST RM4 270 F3
Pinewood Wy
RBRW/HUT CM13 257 G1
Pinkeneys ROY SG8 349 Q6
Pinkham Dr WIT CM8 171 J5
Pink La WIT CM8 146 A6
Pinkney Cl SAFWN CB10 31 H7
Pinkuah La SUD CO10 39 J7
Pinley Gdns DAGW RM9 309 L5
Pin Ml BSDN SS14 3 H5
Pin Mill Cl RIPW IP8 53 H4
Pinmill Rd RIPS/CAP IP9 365 Q5
Pinnacles WAB EN9 233 M4
Pinners Cl BOC CM0 393 J6
Pinnock's Av GVW DA11 337 L6
Pintail Cl CHTY IP2 53 K3
EHAM E6 324 B1
Pintail Crs BRTR CM77 120 F7
Pintail Rd WFD IG8 267 L6
Pintolls RCHLM CM3 245 G7
Pioneer Pl COL CO1 8 E9
Pipchin Rd CHLM/WR CM1 193 H7
Piperell Wy HVHL CB9 34 D8
Piper Rd COLW CO3 106 E6
Pipers Cl HVHL CB9 34 F7
Piper's Tye CHLM/GWD CM2 226 A2
Pipers Vale Cl IPSE IP3 54 D4
Piper Way IL IG1 287 G6
Pippins Rd BOC CM0 393 M7
The Pippins HSTD CO9 81 G3
SUD CO10 39 M1
Pipps Hill Rd BSDN SS14 277 L4
Pipps Hill Rd North
BCAYE CM11 277 L2
Pipps Hill Rd South BSDN SS14 3 G1
Pirie Rd RCOLW CO6 106 B1
Pirie St CAN/RD E16 323 L4
Pirrip Cl GVE DA12 338 C6
Pishiobury Dr SBW CM21 188 E1
Pitcairn Cl ROMW/RG RM7 288 D2
Pitcairn Rd IP IP1 47 K5
Pitchford St SRTFD E15 307 G4
Pitfield Cl CHLM/GWD CM2 5 M8
Pitfield Crs THMD SE28 325 K4
Pit La K/T/MI CO5 149 M7
Pitmans Cl SOS SS1 19 H5
Pitmire La BURES CO8 359 L3
Pitsea Hall La VGE SS16 296 E2
Pitsea Pl WCHPL E1 322 A2
Pitsea Rd PIT SS13 278 D7
Pitsea St WCHPL E1 322 A2
Pitsea View Rd BCAYE CM11 278 A1
Pitseaville Gv VGE SS16 278 B8
Pitt Av WIT CM8 171 K5
Pitt Cha CHLM/GWD CM2 210 B8
Pittfields VGE SS16 276 D8
Pittman Cl RBRW/HUT CM13 256 F8
Pittman Gdns IL IG1 308 F2
Pittman's Fld HLW CM20 13 L5
Pitts End RCOLE CO7 64 A2
Pixley St POP/IOD E14 322 C2
Place Farm La BRWN CM15 383 P11
Pladda Ms WICKW SS12 261 J8
Plains Farm Cl RCOLE CO7 88 A8
Plains Fld BRTR CM7 122 A4
Plains Rd MAL CM9 173 J7
The Plain EPP CM16 220 C7
Plaistow Cl SLH/COR SS17 317 G3
Plaistow Green Rd HSTD CO9 80 F8
Plaistow Gv SRTFD E15 307 J5
Plaistow Park Rd PLSTW E13 307 L6
Plaistow Rd PLSTW E13 307 K6
Plaistow Wy ROY SG8 349 K9
Plane Av GVW DA11 337 G5
Plane Tree Cl BOC CM0 393 L7
CHLM/GWD CM2 209 L7
Plane View Cl COS CO15 182 E3
Plantaganet Pl WAB EN9 233 J3
Plantagenet Gdns CHDH RM6 288 A5
Plantagenet Pl CHDH RM6 288 A5
Plantain Gdns WAN E11 * 285 G8
Plantation Cl GRH DA9 335 J8
SAFWS CB11 30 B3
Plantation Rd CBS CB2 22 D2
RCHLM CM3 195 J4
Planton Wy RCOLE CO7 156 A6
Plashet Gdns
RBRW/HUT CM13 256 D7
Plashet Gv EHAM E6 307 M5
Plashet Rd PLSTW E13 307 K5
Plashets RBSF CM22 163 K8
The Plashets RBSF CM22 189 K1

Plashetts BSDN SS14 .....3 M4
Plas Newydd SOS SS1 .....302 B7
Platford Gn EMPK RM11 .....290 E2
Platters Cl IPSE IP3 .....54 F6
Platters Rd FX IP11 .....11 H6
Plaw Hatch Cl BSF CM23 .....139 K1
Players Ct GTDUN CM6 .....118 C4
Playfield Rd RIPS/CAP IP9 .....58 E4
Playford La KESG IP5 .....49 K4
Playford Rd IPNE IP4 .....49 K6
Playhouse Sq MAL CM20 .....12 F6
Plaza Wy SOS SS1 * 302 A5
Pleasant Dr CHLM/GWD CM12 .....258 A3
Pleasant Ms SOS SS1 .....19 K7
Pleasant Mt MGTR CO11 * 91 K1
Pleasant Rd BSF CM23 .....138 F1
  SOS SS1 .....19 K6
Pleasant Ter LOS SS9 * 300 B5
Pleasant Va SAFWS CB11 .....30 A2
Pleasant Vw ERITH DA8 .....327 H8
Pleshey Cl SOS SS1 .....302 C5
  WICKW SS12 .....261 H1
Pleshey Rd RCHLM CM3 .....166 D1
Plevna St POP/IOD E14 .....322 F6
Plimsoll Cl POP/IOD E14 .....322 E2
Plough Dr COLW CO3 .....106 D8
Plough La RCOLW CO6 .....361 J4
  SUD CO10 .....20 D7
Ploughmans Cl BSF CM23 .....138 D4
Ploughmans Headland
  COLW CO3 .....106 A8
Plough Ri CHLM/WR CM14 .....291 H5
Plough Rd RCOLE CO7 .....133 H5
  RIPS/CAP IP9 .....58 C4
Plough St IPSE IP3 .....7 J6
Plover La FOS CO13 .....137 H3
Plover Gdns UPMR RM14 .....291 J6
Plover Rd IP2 .....53 K3
The Plovers BOC CM0 .....389 K7
Plover Wy BERM/RHTH SE16 .....322 B6
Plowmans RAYL SS6 .....281 H1
Plowman Rd HLWW/ROY RM19 .....203 K5
Plumberow LAIN SS15 * 2
Plumberow Av HOC/HUL SS5 .....264 B6
Plumberow Mount Av
  HOC/HUL SS5 .....264 B5
Plume Av COLW CO3 .....128 D1
  MAL CM9 .....214 C4
Plumleys PIT SS13 .....278 E6
Plummers Rd RCOLW CO6 .....85 H7
Plumpton Av HCH CM12 .....290 C8
Plumpton Rd HOD EN11 .....201 K1
Plum Tree La RCHLM CM3 .....212 A8
Plumptre La RCHLM CM3 .....212 A8
Plums La COLW CO3 * 97 H1
Plumstead High St
  WOOL/PLUM SE18 .....325 G7
Plumstead Rd
  WOOL/PLUM SE18 .....324 F7
Plumtree Av CHLM/GWD CM2 .....210 E3
Plumtree Cl DAGE RM10 .....310 E3
Plymouth Rd CAN/RD E16 .....323 K1
  CDW/CHF RM16 .....329 M8
  CHLM/WR CM1 .....4 B9
  FX IP11 .....62 E7
Plymouth Whf POP/IOD E14 .....323 G4
Plympton Cl BELV DA17 .....326 B8
Plymtree SOS SS1 * 302 C5
Pochard Wy CHLM/GWD CM77 .....120 F7
Pocklington Cl
  CHLM/GWD CM2 .....210 D1
Pod's Brook Rd BRTR CM7 .....121 D1
Pods La BRTR CM7 .....120 A3
Point Clear Rd RCOS CO16 .....191 G3
Point Ct CVI SS8 .....321 J2
Pointer Cl THMD SE28 .....325 A2
Pointers Cl POP/IOD E14 .....322 E8
Point Rd CVI SS8 .....321 J2
Pointwell La RCOLW CO6 .....124 D6
Pole Barn La FOS CO13 .....137 L4
Polecat Rd BRTR CM7 .....122 C7
Pole Hill Rd CHING E4 .....248 F7
Pole La WIT CM8 .....145 M2
Polesworth Rd DAGW RM9 .....310 C6
Poley Rd SLH/COR SS17 .....316 F4
Polford Cl CAN/RD E16 .....323 K3
  CHIC IG7 .....269 K4
Pollard Hatch
  HLWW/ROY RM19 .....203 J4
Pollards Cl LOU IG10 .....249 M5
  RCFD SS4 .....283 J4
Pollard's Gn CHLM/GWD CM2 .....210 C3
Pollard Wk RCOS CO16 .....6 C8
Polstead Br RCOLW CO6 .....361 Q2
Polstead La RAYL SS6 .....280 C2
Polsteads VGE SS16 .....296 B2
Polstead St RCOS CO16 .....361 Q3
Polstead Wy RCOS CO16 .....182 E1
Polthorne Gv
  WOOL/PLUM SE18 .....324 F7
Polytechnic St
  WOOL/PLUM SE18 .....324 D7
Pomfret Md BSDN SS14 .....2 F5
Pompadour Cl BRW CM14 .....273 M4
Pond Cha COLW CO3 .....128 D1
Pond Cl FX IP11 .....62 C9
  HOC/HUL SS5 * 263 H2
Pond Cross Farm
  SAFWS CB11 .....B1
Pond Cross Wy SAFWS CB11 .....372 A1
Ponders Rd RCOLW CO6 .....104 F2
Pondfield La
  RBRW/HUT CM13 .....256 D7
Pondfield Rd COLN CO4 .....9 J3
  DAGE RM10 .....310 E2
Pondholton Dr WIT CM8 .....171 J6
Pond La RBSF CM22 .....378 B2
Pond Rd SRTFD E15 .....307 H6
  CHLM/GWD CM2 .....225 L3
Pond Wk UPMR RM14 .....291 H7
Honey Cha WIT CM8 .....172 C8
Poole Cl IPSE IP3 * 55 J2
Poolehurst Wk
  HOC/HUL SS5 * 263 H2
Poole Rd EMPK RM11 .....290 H2
  HOM E9 .....306 A3
Pooles La HOC/HUL SS5 .....263 H2
  SUD CO10 .....38 F4
Poolmans St
  BERM/RHTH SE16 .....322 A5
Pool's La CHLM/WR CM1 * 73 G1
Poore St SBF/HAD SS7 .....299 H1
Poors La SBF/HAD SS7 .....287 H8
Poors La North LAIN SS15 .....287 H7
Poperinghe Rd COLS CO2 .....129 J1
Popes Ct HVHL CB9 .....35 H8
Popes Crs PIT SS13 .....278 D8
Pope's Rd RCOLW CO6 .....103 M1
Popes Wk RAYL SS6 .....281 J3
Poplar Av RCOS CO15 .....182 D3

Poplar Bath St POP/IOD E14 .....322 E3
Poplar Cl CHLM/GWD CM2 .....209 M7
  RCOS CO15 .....182 E5
  HOM E3 .....306 C2
  HSTD CO9 .....81 J7
HVHL CB9 .....34 A4
ING CM4 .....222 A4
  ING CM4 .....239 K3
  RCHLM CM3 .....244 A4
  SOCK/AV RM15 .....314 A4
  WIT CM8 .....147 J3
Poplar Dr RBRW/HUT CM13 .....256 F7
Poplar Gv BOC CM0 .....393 G4
Poplar Grove Cha MAL CM9 .....198 G6
Poplar High St POP/IOD E14 .....322 F3
Poplar La RIPW IP8 .....53 D8
Poplar Mt BELV DA17 .....326 A7
Poplar Pl THMD SE28 .....325 H1
Poplar Rd CVI SS8 .....320 F2
  RAYL SS6 .....281 H4
  SUD CO10 .....21 J7
Poplar Rw EPP CM16 .....235 J4
Poplars Cl HOC/HUL SS5 .....198 B1
Poplar Shaw WAB E17 .....284 F4
Poplars Rd WALTH E17 .....284 E4
The Poplars ABR/ST RM4 .....251 L3
  GTDUN CM6 .....116 F3
  MGTR CO11 .....65 J3
Poplar St ROMW/RG RM7 .....288 D2
Poplar Wy BARK/HLT IG6 .....286 F5
  FOS CO13 .....137 G3
Poppleton Rd WAN E11 .....285 H1
Poppy Cl BELV DA17 .....326 B6
  CHTY IP2 .....47 J5
Poppyfield Cl LOS SS9 .....282 A7
Poppy Gdns COLS CO2 .....129 M2
Porchester Cl EMPK RM11 .....290 D4
Porchester Rd CHLM/GWD CM12 .....240 G5
Porchfield Cl GVE DA12 .....337 H6
Pork La FOS CO13 .....137 L7
Porlock Av WOS/PRIT SS0 .....300 D1
Portal Av KESG IP5 .....50 F4
Port Av GRH DA9 .....335 G6
Portelet Rd WCHPL E1 .....306 F4
Porter Cl WTHK RM20 .....335 K4
Porter Rd EHAM E6 .....324 C2
  IPSE IP3 .....55 L4
Porters PIT SS13 .....278 F5
Porters Av DAGW RM9 .....309 L5
Porters Brook Wk COLN CO4 * 9 K8
  COLW CO3 .....105 J3
Porter's La COLN CO4 .....105 J3
Porters Pk RCHLM CM3 .....195 K5
Porter Wy RCOS CO16 .....182 E1
Portia Wy BOW E3 .....306 C8
Portland Av GVE DA12 .....337 H1
  SOS SS1 .....19 J6
Portland Cl BRTR CM7 .....121 J7
  CHDH RM6 .....288 A7
Portland Crs HAR CO12 .....15 J3
Portland Ms CHESW EN7 .....232 A3
Portland Pl BSF CM23 .....139 L4
  HERT/BAY SG13 .....184 D5
Portland Rd BSF CM23 .....139 L4
  COL CO1 .....8 C4
  GVW DA11 .....337 G3
  GVW DA11 .....337 G6
Port La COL CO1 .....8 C4
  RBSF CM22 .....139 J1
Portlight St MGTR CO11 * 91 K1
Portman Dr HERT/BAY SG13 .....184 C6
Portman Rd IP IP1 .....16 A4
Portmeers Wk WALTH E17 * 284 C4
Portmore Gdns CRW RM5 .....270 F4
Portnoi Cl ROM RM1 .....271 K4
Portobello La CBS CB2 .....22 B2
Portobello Rd WOTN CO14 .....137 M1
Port of Felixstowe Rd FX IP11 .....10 D5
Portreath Pl CHLM/WR CM1 .....193 K6
Portree La POP/IOD E14 .....323 G4
Portsea Rd TIL RM18 .....331 M7
Portsmouth Rd COS CO15 .....182 F5
Portway CHLM/GWD CM2 .....210 A2
  RAIN RM13 .....311 J5
  SRTFD E15 .....307 K5
Portway Ct HSTD CO9 .....81 G4
Posford Ct COLN CO4 .....87 J4
Postman's La RCHLM CM3 .....212 B2
Post Meadow BCAYE CM11 .....259 D2
Post Mill Cl IPNE IP4 .....17 L3
Post Office Ap FSTGT E7 .....307 J2
Post Office La MAL CM9 .....199 J4
Post Office Rd
  CHLM/WR CM1 .....193 L5
  HLW CM20 .....13 H5
  ING CM4 .....239 L2
  MAL CM9 .....213 M8
Post Office Rw RCFD SS4 * 396 G2
  SUD CO10 * 43 M8
Postway Ms IL IG1 .....17 L7
Postwood Gn HERT/BAY SG13 .....184 D1
Post Wood Rd WARE SG12 .....184 J2
Potash Cl RIPS/CAP IP9 .....59 J5
Potash Rd BCAYE CM11 .....241 D7
HLWE CM17 .....378 E10
Potiphar Pl BRW CM14 .....273 L3
Pot Kiln Cha HSTD CO9 .....347 N11
Pot Kiln Rd SUD CO10 .....21 J9
The Pot Kilns SUD CO10 .....21 L8
Potters Cl LOU IG10 .....250 B2
  RCHLM CM3 .....212 D7
Potters Fld HLWE CM17 .....244 A3
Potter St BSF CM23 .....139 L4
  HLWE CM17 .....356 F10
  HSTD CO9 .....356 F10
Potters Wy SOSN SS2 .....283 J8
Pottery La CHLM/WR CM1 .....193 K8
  HSTD CO9 .....356 F6
Potton Dr WICKW SS12 .....261 G6
Pouch Ml FX IP11 .....286 C6
Poulett Rd EHAM E6 .....307 G2
Poulk Hall La RCHLM CM3 .....144 D7
Poulteney Rd STSD CM24 .....177 K8
Poulton Cl MAL CM9 .....214 A5
Pound Cl WAB IG11 .....217 M1
Pound Farm Dr HAR CO12 .....14 B8
Poundfield Cl RCOLE CO7 * 131 L6
Poundfield Rd LOU IG10 .....250 A2
Pound Flds CHLM/WR CM1 .....166 D8
Pound Ga GTDUN CM6 .....96 A7
Pound La CDW/CHF RM16 .....315 K4
  LAIN SS15 .....277 G4
  RIPS/CAP IP9 .....58 G2
  RIPW IP8 .....52 F6
  WICKW SS12 .....279 J4
Pound La Central LAIN SS15 .....277 J7
Pound La North LAIN SS15 .....277 G4
Pound Park Rd CHARL SE7 .....324 A7
Pound Wk SAFWN CB10 .....28 A7
Powdermill La WAB EN9 .....216 D5
Powdermill Ms WAB EN9 .....233 J3

Powdermill Wy WAB EN9 .....233 J3
Powell Gdns DAGE RM10 .....310 D1
Powell Rd BKHH IG9 .....249 M7
LAIN SS15 .....276 B6
Power Dr PEND EN3 .....233 J3
Powers Hall End WIT CM8 .....171 H2
Powis Rd BOW E3 .....306 C2
Powis St WOOL/PLUM SE18 .....324 C6
Pownall Crs COLS CO2 .....129 J1
Pownsett Ter IL IG1 .....308 F2
Poynder Rd TIL RM18 .....331 L7
Poynings Av SOSN SS2 .....302 A3
Poynings Wy HARH RM3 .....272 B2
Poynters RAYL SS6 .....280 F4
Poynter Pl FOS CO13 .....137 H2
Poynters La SBN/FI SS3 .....303 C3
Pragel St PLSTW E13 .....307 L6
Pratts Farm La RCHLM CM3 .....193 M1
Pratt's La RIPS/CAP IP9 .....365 J5
Premier Av CDW/CHF RM16 .....330 F1
Premiere Pl POP/IOD E14 .....322 F3
Prentice Cl BSF CM23 .....283 J3
Prentice Hall La MAL CM9 .....385 K4
Prentiss Ct CHARL SE7 .....324 A7
Prescott VGE SS16 .....296 C2
Prescott Cl EMPK RM11 .....289 L6
Prescott Gn LOU IG10 .....250 F5
Prescott Rd CHES/WCR EN8 .....216 F5
Presdales Dr WARE SG12 .....184 F1
President Rd COLW CO3 .....106 B8
Prestage Wy POP/IOD E14 .....322 F3
Prestbury Rd FSTGT E7 .....307 H1
Preston Av CHING E4 .....267 J5
Preston Dr IP IP1 .....47 J1
  WAN E11 .....285 M3
Preston Gdns IL IG1 .....308 C1
  PEND EN3 .....232 F7
  RAYL SS6 .....281 G1
Preston Rd COS CO15 .....160 A4
  GVW DA11 .....337 H6
  HARH RM3 .....272 A4
  WAN E11 .....285 H4
  WOS/PRIT SS0 .....18 A4
Preston's Rd POP/IOD E14 .....322 F4
Prestwick Av FX IP11 .....63 H7
Prestwick Dr BSF CM23 .....115 J8
Prestwood Cl SBF/HAD SS7 .....280 E1
Prestwood Dr CRW RM5 .....280 D6
  SBF/HAD SS7 .....280 D6
Pretoria Av WALTH E17 .....284 B4
Pretoria Cl LAIN SS15 * 277 L4
Pretoria Crs CHING E4 .....248 F2
Pretoria Rd CAN/RD E16 .....307 J7
  CHING E4 .....248 F2
  HSTD CO9 .....81 J3
  IL IG1 .....308 C1
  ROMW/RG RM7 .....288 F2
  WAN E11 .....285 G6
Prettygate Rd COLW CO3 .....106 C8
Prettyman Rd FX IP11 .....55 J3
  IPSE IP3 .....55 L4
Priestley Gdns CHDH RM6 .....287 L4
Priestley Wy WALTH E17 .....284 A1
Priests Av ROM RM1 .....271 J3
Priests Fld RBRW/HUT CM13 .....256 D7
Priest's La BRWN CM15 .....256 B5
Primley La RBSF CM22 .....163 J3
Primrose Av GDMY/SEVK IG3 .....287 K3
Primrose Cl BOW E3 .....306 C2
  BSF CM23 .....138 D3
  CVI SS8 .....298 E1
  VGE SS16 .....296 F2
Primrose Fld HLWS SG13 .....184 A3
Primrose Gln EMPK RM11 .....290 D2
Primrose HI BRW CM14 .....273 K8
  CHLM/WR CM1 .....194 B3
  CHTY IP2 .....53 L4
  HVHL CB9 .....34 C1
  RIPS/CAP IP9 .....364 D4
Primrose La K/T/MI CO5 .....149 M7
  MGTR CO11 .....91 J8
Primrose Pth CHESW EN7 .....232 B1
Primrose Pl WIT CM8 .....171 H1
Primrose Rd COS CO15 .....160 A4
  LEY E10 .....284 C6
  SWFD E18 .....267 J3
Primrose Ter GVE DA12 * 337 H6
Primrose Wk BOC CM0 .....393 G6
  COLN CO4 .....108 B5
Primula Wy CHLM/WR CM1 .....194 B3
Prince Albert Rd K/T/MI CO5 .....177 M7
  WOS/PRIT SS0 .....282 C7
Prince Charles Av
  CDW/CHF RM16 .....315 L4
Prince Charles Cl COS CO15 .....6 B9
  SUD CO10 .....20 E4
Prince Charles Rd COLS CO2 .....129 L3
Prince Cl WOS/PRIT SS0 .....282 F8
Princedale Cl IP IP1 .....47 M4
Prince Edward Rd
  BCAYE CM11 .....258 D2
  HOM E9 .....306 C3
Princel La RCOLE CO7 .....363 N10
Prince of Wales Dr CHTY IP2 .....53 M3
Prince of Wales Rd
  CAN/RD E16 .....323 M2
  WIT CM8 .....198 D1
Prince Philip Av
  CDW/CHF RM16 .....314 C9
  COS CO15 .....182 F4
Prince Philip Rd COLS CO2 .....129 J4
Prince Regent La
  CAN/RD E16 .....323 K3
  PLSTW E13 .....307 M3
Princes Av BOC CM0 .....393 N14
  PEND EN3 .....232 F6
  RCHLM CM3 .....388 D4
  SBF/HAD SS7 .....280 C7
  SLH/COR SS17 .....317 H4
  WFD IG8 .....267 L3
Princes Cl BCAYW CM12 .....240 F7
  EPP CM16 .....221 K3
  LAIN SS15 2
Princes Ct BCAYW CM12 .....240 F7
  BSF CM23 .....138 D3
Princes Gdns IL IG1 * 308 C1
  WAB IG11 .....234 D3
Princes Ga FX IP11 .....11 L7
Princes Pk RAIN RM13 .....311 J4
Princes Riverside Rd
  BERM/RHTH SE16 .....322 A5
Princes Rd BARK/HLT IG6 .....287 G2
  BKHH IG9 .....267 M1
  BOC CM0 .....393 N14
  BRW CM14 .....254 D8
  CHLM/GWD CM2 .....225 L3
  CVI SS8 .....320 D4
Princess Alice Wy THMD SE28 .....325 G5
Princess Anne Cl COS CO15 .....182 F4
Princess Av RCFD SS4 .....318 M3
Princess Gdns RCFD SS4 .....264 D1

Princess Margaret Rd
  TIL RM18 .....332 E3
Princess Rd RAYL SS6 .....281 C7
Princes St HAR CO12 .....14 B4
Princes St CHLM/WR CM1 .....16 C7
  GVE DA12 .....337 L4
  WOS/PRIT SS0 .....18 F4
Prince's Ter PLSTW E13 .....307 L1
Prince St SUD CO10 .....20 C5
Prince Wy BKHH IG9 .....267 M1
  RBRW/HUT CM13 .....256 D5
Princethorpe Rd IPSE IP3 .....55 H1
Princeton Ms COLN CO4 .....107 L1
Prince William Av CVI SS8 .....298 E1
Printers Wy HLW CM20 .....188 B4
Priolo Rd CHARL SE7 .....323 M8
Prior Cha GRAYS RM17 .....330 C3
Prior Cl HSTD CO9 .....81 G5
The Priories HOC/HUL SS5 .....263 H4
Prior Rd IL IG1 .....286 D8
Priors Cl BSDN SS14 .....3 J5
  HERT/BAY SG13 .....184 D6
Priors Cft WALTH E17 .....266 F8
Priors East BSDN SS14 .....3 J6
Priors Pk HCH RM12 .....289 M8
Prior's Wy BOC CM0 .....393 P9
  RCOLW CO6 .....124 D2
Priors Wood Rd
  HERT/BAY SG13 .....184 D6
  RBSF CM22 .....377 K1
Prior Wy COLN CO4 .....107 J3
Priory Av CHING E4 .....266 C2
  HLWE CM17 .....188 D4
  HVHL CB9 .....34 C5
  SOSN SS2 .....301 J2
  WALTH E17 .....284 D3
Priory Cl BROX EN10 .....216 F2
  BRWN CM15 .....255 K5
  CHING E4 .....266 C2
  CHLM/WR CM1 .....4 B4
  HOD EN11 .....201 H4
  RCHLM CM3 .....196 A4
  RCOS CO16 .....181 K7
Priory Crs SOSN SS2 .....301 J2
Priory Dr ABYW SE2 .....326 A8
  STSD CM24 .....115 M4
Priory Farm Rd RCHLM CM3 .....196 A4
Priory Gdns DART DA1 .....334 A7
  CHES/WCR EN8 .....217 G5
Priory Gv HARH RM3 .....272 B3
Priory HI DART DA1 .....334 A7
Priory La RCHLM CM3 .....228 C4
Priory Ms EMPK RM11 .....289 M8
  RCHLM CM3 .....196 F5
Priory Pk RCOS CO16 .....181 K1
Priory Pth HARH RM3 .....272 B3
Priory Rd BARK IG11 .....309 G4
  COS CO15 .....6 C5
  DART DA1 .....334 A6
  EHAM E6 .....308 A3
  FX IP11 .....63 J8
  HARH RM3 .....272 B2
  IP IP1 .....16 A1
  RCHLM CM3 .....228 B4
  RCOLW CO6 .....103 J2
  SLH/COR SS17 .....317 H2
  SUD CO10 .....20 D2
  WIT CM8 .....173 J2
Priory St BOW E3 .....306 E2
  COL CO1 .....8 E7
  RCOLW CO6 .....82 E6
The Priory BCAYW CM12 .....240 F7
Priory View Rd LOS SS9 * 282 B8
Priory Wk COL CO1 .....8 D7
  SUD CO10 .....20 C7
Priory Wd HSTD CO9 .....356 F5
Priory Wood Crs LOS SS9 .....282 B8
Priory Wood Rbt RBSF CM22 .....376 B1
Pritchett Cl PEND EN3 .....233 J7
Prittle Cl SBF/HAD SS7 .....280 E1
Prittlewell Cha WOS/PRIT SS0 .....300 D1
Prittlewell Sq SOS SS1 .....18 E7
Prittlewell St SOSN SS2 .....19 J3
Proctor Cl K/T/MI CO5 .....153 L3
Proctors Wy BSF CM23 .....139 H5
Proctor Wy RCOLW CO6 .....126 A3
Professional Pl WICKW SS12 * 261 K8
Progress Ct BRTR CM7 .....121 J7
Progress Rd RCOS CO9 .....281 M7
Progress Wy RCOS CO16 .....158 F4
Promenade COS CO15 .....182 A7
Promenade HAR CO12 .....71 H3
The Promenade FX IP11 * 62 D7
Prospect Av BSF CM23 .....138 A4
Prospect Av SLH/COR SS17 .....316 E4
Prospect Cl BELV DA17 .....326 D7
  RCHLM CM3 .....196 A2
  SOS SS1 .....19 M7
Prospect Gv GVE DA12 .....338 C2
Prospect HI WALTH E17 .....284 E2
Prospect Pl DART DA1 .....334 F6
  GRAYS RM17 .....330 E5
  ROMW/RG RM7 .....270 F8
  TIL RM18 .....28 C9
Prospect Rd CHES/WCR EN8 .....216 D1
  EMPK RM11 .....290 D1
  IP IP1 .....16 B7
  WFD IG8 .....267 M4
Prospect St IP IP1 .....16 B7
Prospect V WOOL/PLUM SE18 .....324 D7
Prospect Wy
  RBRW/HUT CM13 .....239 G8
Prospero Cl COLN CO4 .....108 C4
Protea Cl CAN/RD E16 .....307 J3
Protea Wy CVI SS8 .....320 D1
Provence Cl COLW CO3 .....105 M6
Providence BOC CM0 .....393 M9
Providence La HOM E9 * 306 C4
Providence Pl COL CO1 .....8 D3
Providence St GRH DA9 .....335 K7
  IP IP1 .....16 C3
Provident Sq BCAYE CM11 .....258 E4
Prower Cl BCAYE CM11 * 258 E4
Prunus Cl COS CO15 .....160 A4
Prykes Dr CHLM/WR CM1 * 4 C4
Pryor Cl WIT CM8 .....171 K4
Pryors Cl BSF CM23 .....139 L1
Puck La VGE SS16 .....3 K8
Puckleside VGE SS16 .....296 F1
Pudding La CHIG IG7 .....251 H6
  COS CO15 * 6 C8
  ROY SG8 .....151 L2
Pudding Mill La SRTFD E15 .....306 E6
The Pudgell ROY SG8 .....349 K9

Pudsey Hall La RCFD SS4 .....265 K3
  BARK IG11 .....309 L7
  WICKW SS12 .....261 J8
Puffin Pl SBN/FI SS3 .....303 H4
Puffinsdale Cl FSTGT E7 .....7 H1
Puffin Cl SLH/COR SS17 .....316 C7
Pulham Av BROX EN10 .....200 F6
Pulleyns Av EHAM E6 .....308 B7
Pullman Ct WICKE SS11 .....261 L6
Pulpitfield Cl WOTN CO14 .....137 K1
Pulteney Cl BOW E3 .....306 D6
Pulteney Rd SWFD E18 .....285 L3
Pump HI CHLM/GWD CM2 .....210 C2
  LOU IG10 .....250 C2
  SOS SS1 .....181 M1
Pump La CHLM/WR CM1 .....181 B5
  EPP CM16 .....219 J2
  RCHLM CM3 .....166 B4
  RCHLM CM3 .....230 A4
Pump Mead Cl BOC CM0 .....393 N1
Pump St SLH/COR SS17 .....316 A9
Punchard Wy FX IP11 .....62 E8
Purbeck Rd EMPK RM11 .....289 K5
Purcell Cl CHLM/WR CM1 .....208 D4
  COLN CO4 .....108 B7
Purcell La COLS CO2 .....277 C5
  SLH/COR SS17 .....316 F2
Purdeys Wy RCFD SS4 .....283 K5
Purdis Av IPSE IP3 .....55 L3
Purdis Farm La IPSE IP3 .....55 L3
  KIR/NAC IP10 .....56 C3
Purdis Rd KIR/NAC IP10 .....56 C3
Purdy St BOW E3 .....306 F2
Purfleet By-Pass PUR RM19 .....328 F8
Purfleet Deep Whf
  PUR RM19 * 334 F1
Purfleet Rd SOCK/AV RM15 .....328 E4
Purford Gn HLWS CM18 .....206 B2
Purland Cl BCTR RM8 .....288 C6
Purland Rd THMD SE28 .....325 J5
Purleigh Av WFD IG8 .....268 A5
Purleigh Cl PIT SS13 .....278 A1
Purleigh Gv RCHLM CM3 .....230 E4
Purleigh Rd RAYL SS6 .....280 B4
Purleigh St RCHLM CM3 .....230 C4
Purley Cl CLAY IG5 .....268 A1
Purley Rd RCOS CO16 .....158 E7
  WOS/PRIT SS0 .....282 F8
Purley Wy EPP CM16 .....235 M5
Purplett St CHTY IP2 .....17 G8
Purrett Rd WOOL/PLUM SE18 .....325 K8
Purvis Wy COLN CO4 .....87 J3
Putney Rd PEND EN3 .....232 B1
Putticks La RCOLE CO7 .....64 B2
Pyefleet Cl K/T/MI CO5 .....153 L2
  RCOLE CO7 .....156 B6
Pyefleet Vw K/T/MI CO5 .....153 L2
Pyenest Rd HLWW/ROY RM19 .....203 J4
Pyesand FOS CO13 .....136 F1
Pygot Pl BRTR CM7 .....121 L4
Pyms Pl GRAYS RM17 .....330 D3
Pyms Rd CHLM/GWD CM2 .....225 L2
Pynchbek BSF CM23 .....138 F6
Pynchon Ms CHLM/WR CM1 .....5 L2
Pynchon Paddocks
  RBSF CM22 .....163 L2
Pyne Ga CHLM/GWD CM2 .....225 L4
Pynest Green La WAB EN9 .....234 B7
Pynham Cl ABYW SE2 .....325 K6
Pyrles Gn LOU IG10 .....250 E2
Pyrles La LOU IG10 .....250 E2
Pytt Fld HLWE CM17 .....204 C2

Q

Quadling St IP IP1 .....16 F7
The Quadrant PUR RM19 .....328 F7
Quaker La WAB EN9 .....233 K4
Quaker's La HVHL CB9 .....34 D6
Quakers Pl FSTGT E7 .....308 A2
Quale Rd CHLM/GWD CM2 .....210 E1
Quantock Cl KESG IP5 .....49 L6
Quarles Cl CRW RM5 .....270 D6
Quarles Park Rd CHDH RM6 .....287 L4
Quarry HI GRAYS RM17 .....330 D4
Quarry Ms PUR RM19 .....328 D7
Quarry Springs HLW CM20 .....204 B3
Quarry Wy WTHK RM20 .....335 J1
Quarter Ga RCHLM CM3 .....245 H8
Quartermile La LEY E10 .....306 E1
Quatre Ports CHING E4 .....267 G4
Quay House POP/IOD E14 * 322 F2
Quay La FOS CO13 .....368 G12
  GRH DA9 .....335 L6
  RCOS CO16 .....135 L1
Quay St MGTR CO11 .....91 G7
  RCOLE CO7 .....130 E6
Quay Wy SOS SS1 .....19 H5
Quebec Cl SOS SS1 .....19 H5
Quebec Dr KESG IP5 .....50 A8
  TIL RM18 .....332 E2
Quebec Wy BERM/RHTH SE16 .....322 A5
Queech La RIPS/CAP IP9 .....58 E3
The Queech RIPS/CAP IP9 .....58 E3
Queen Anne Dr K/T/MI CO5 .....153 L3
Queen Anne Gdns
  K/T/MI CO5 .....178 A7
Queen Anne Rd HOM E9 .....306 A3
  K/T/MI CO5 .....178 A7
Queen Anne's Dr
  WOS/PRIT SS0 .....300 F1
Queen Anns Gv
  HOC/HUL SS5 .....263 G5
Queenborough Gdns
  GNTH/NBYPK IG2 .....286 D2
Queenborough La
  BRTR CM77 .....120 D4
Queenborough Rd BOC CM0 .....393 N1
Queenbury Cl K/T/MI CO5 .....178 A7
Queen Edith Dr HVHL CB9 .....344 A7
Queen Elizabeth Av
  COS CO15 .....182 F4
  TIL RM18 .....332 C3
Queen Elizabeth Cha
  RCFD SS4 .....283 J6
Queen Elizabeth Ct
  WAB IG11 * 185 L5
Queen Elizabeth Dr
  SLH/COR SS17 .....295 J8
Queen Elizabeth II Br
  WTHK RM20 .....335 H4
Queen Elizabeth Rd
  WALTH E17 .....284 B1
Queen Mary Av COLS CO2 .....129 K4
  TIL RM18 .....332 C3
Queen Mary Ct WAB EN9 .....233 H4
Queen Marys Cl WAB EN9 .....233 K5

Queens Av HOC/HUL SS5 * ...263 H2
  LOS SS9 ...300 B4
  MAL CM9 ...214 D4
  WFD IG8 ...267 L8
Queensberry Pl FSTGT E7 ...308 A2
Queensbury Rd IPSE IP3 ...54 F4
Queensbury Av RCOLW CO6 ...105 H8
Queenscliffe Rd CHTY IP2 ...16 B1
Queen's Cl SBW CM21 ...163 G5
  STSD CM24 ...115 M1
  SUD CO10 ...20 E5
Queens Crs BSF CM23 ...138 F4
Queensdale Cl IP IP1 ...48 A4
Queen's Dr CHES/WCR EN8 ...233 H4
  LEY E10 ...284 D5
Queen's Farm Rd GVE DA12 ...339 H7
Queen's Gdns BRTR CM7 ...98 D6
  RAIN RM13 ...311 J3
  UPMR RM14 ...291 J4
Queensgate Dr IPNE IP4 ...48 E5
Queen's Gate Ms
  BCAYW CM12 * ...240 C8
Queen's Grove Rd CHING E4 ...249 G8
Queensland Rd RIPS/CAP IP9 ...66 G3
Queensland Av RCFD SS4 ...283 J6
Queensland Cl WALTH E17 ...266 C4
Queensland Crs
  CHLM/WR CM1 ...193 G8
Queensland Dr COLS CO2 ...129 K4
Queensmere SBF/HAD SS7 ...280 F8
Queens Park Av BCAYW CM12 ...240 D8
Queens Park Rd HARH RM5 ...272 C7
Queen's Rd BARK IG11 ...308 F4
  BCAYE ...277 L1
  BKHH IG9 ...267 L1
  BOC CM0 ...393 L8
  BRTR CM7 ...99 J8
  BRW CM14 ...273 M2
  CHES/WCR EN8 ...232 F4
  CHLM/GWD CM2 ...5 L4
  COLW CO3 ...106 F7
  COS CO15 ...6 B9
  EPP CM16 ...221 K3
  FOS CO13 ...137 J5
  FX IP11 ...11 L3
  GVE DA12 ...337 M8
  HAR CO12 ...70 F5
  LAIN SS15 ...276 D4
  LOS SS9 ...300 B5
  LOU IG10 ...250 C3
  PLSTW E13 ...307 L5
  RAYL SS6 ...281 G4
  RCOLE CO7 ...130 E5
  RCOLW CO6 ...82 E6
  RCOLW CO6 ...106 A2
  SBF/HAD SS7 ...298 A3
  SUD CO10 ...20 C4
  WALTH E17 ...284 C4
  WAN E11 ...285 L6
  WOS/PRIT SS0 ...18 F5
Queen's Rd West PLSTW E13...307 K6
Queen's Sq IPSE IP3 ...55 G3
Queens Ter SHVHL CB9 ...33 M1
Queens Ter PLSTW E13 ...307 L5
Queens Town Gdns
  RAIN RM13 ...311 J7
Queen St BOC CM0 ...393 L8
  BRW CM14 ...273 M4
  CHLM/GWD CM2 ...4 F6
  CHONG CM5 ...381 M7
  COL CO1 ...8 D7
  FX IP11 ...62 D7
  GVE DA12 ...337 L4
  HSTD CO9 ...356 F6
  HSTD CO9 ...356 G10
  HVHL CB9 ...34 D5
  IP IP1 ...16 E5
  MAL CM9 ...214 D3
  RCOLE CO7 ...156 C7
  RCOLW CO6 ...124 D3
  ROMW/RG RM7 ...289 G4
Queens Wk CHING E4 ...249 G8
Queens Wy CHES/WCR EN8 ...233 G4
  IPSE IP3 ...55 L5
Queensway CBS CB2 ...22 C1
  CHONG CM5 ...380 C12
  COS CO15 ...160 A4
  HVHL CB9 ...34 B5
  K/T/MI CO5 ...149 M7
  MGTR CO11 ...90 F1
  SOSN SS2 ...18 F1
  SUD CO10 ...45 L4
Queenswood Av
  RBRW/HUT CM13 ...257 C1
  WALTH E17 ...266 C4
Queenswood Gdns WAN E11...285 L6
Queen Victoria Dr
  RIPS/CAP IP9 ...67 G5
Quendon Dr WAB EN9 ...233 L3
Quendon Rd BSDN SS14 ...278 B5
Quendon Wy FOS CO13 ...137 K3
Quennell Wy
  RBRW/HUT CM13 ...256 F3
Quentin Cl IP IP1 ...47 K5
Quickset Rd SAFWS CB11 ...340 C12
Quilp Dr CHLM/WR CM1 ...193 J6
Quilter Dr RIPW IP8 ...53 H4
Quilter Rd FX IP11 ...69 G1
Quilters Cl BSDN SS14 ...3 M2
  COS CO15 ...160 C3
Quilters Dr BCAYW CM12 ...258 D5
Quilters Straight BSDN SS14 ...3 M2
Quilter Rd WOOL/PLUM SE18 ...325 J8
Quince Cl MGTR CO11 ...65 G4
Quince Tree Cl SOCK/AV RM15...313 M8
Quinion Cl CHLM/WR CM1 ...193 G6
Quinton's La FX IP11 ...62 H6
Quintons Dr RCOLE CO7 ...363 R6
Quinton Wy WAB EN9 ...233 K5
Quixley St POP/IOD E14 ...323 G2
Quorn Gdns LOS SS9 ...299 K4
The Quorn ING CM4 ...239 K3

R

Rabbits Rd MNPK E12 ...308 B1
Raby St POP/IOD E14 * ...322 B2
Rachael Clarke Cl
  SLH/COR SS17 ...317 H1
Rachael Gdns WIT CM8 ...147 H1
Rachel Cl BARK/HLT IG6 ...287 G2
Rackenford Dr CHTY IP2 ...53 J6
Rackford Dr CHTY IP2 ...53 J6
Radbourne Cl CHTY IP2 ...53 J6
Radbourne Rd IPSE IP3 ...54 F4
Radcliffe Dr CHTY IP2 ...53 J3
Radford Cl BCAYW CM12 ...258 G3
Radford Crs BCAYW CM12 ...258 D2
Radford Wy BARK IG11 ...309 J7
  BCAYW CM12 ...258 D5
Radiator Rd SUD CO10 * ...45 K4
Radland Rd CAN/RD E16 ...323 K2
Radlett Cl FSTGT E7 ...307 J3
Radley Av GDMY/SEVK IG3 ...289 J3
Radley Ct BERM/RHTH SE16 ...322 A5

Radley Green Rd ING CM4 ...206 F7
Radleys La RCOLW CO6 ...360 H5
Radley St WFD E18 * ...267 H3
Radleys Md DAGE RM10 ...310 C5
Radley Ter RCOLE CO7 ...156 E1
Radlix Rd LEY E10 ...284 D6
Radnor Crs REDBR IG4 ...286 A3
Radstocks BCAYW CM12 ...258 E2
Radwinter Rd SAFWN CB10 ...29 L1
  SAFWN CB10 ...29 L1
  SAFWS CB11 ...28 D8
Raeburn Cl FOS CO13 ...137 J2
Raeburn Rd IPSE IP3 ...54 F4
Raeburn Rd South IPSE IP3 ...54 F4
Raglan Av CHES/WCR EN8 ...232 C4
Raglan Ms COS CO15 ...6 A6
Raglan Rd BELV DA17 ...326 A5
  FOS CO13 ...137 J4
  WALTH E17 ...284 C4
  WOOL/PLUM SE18 ...324 F8
Raglan Vls WALTH E17 * ...284 C4
Ragley Cl BRTR CM77 ...121 H8
Rags La CHESW EN7 ...216 A5
Rahn Rd EPP CM16 ...236 B1
Raider Cl ROMW/RG RM7 ...270 C7
Raile Wk SUD CO10 * ...43 L3
Railey Rd SAFWS CB11 ...30 B1
Railway Cottages COS CO15 ...7
Railway Pl BELV DA17 ...326 B5
Railway Rd CHES/WCR EN8 ...233 J1
Railway Sq CHLM/WR CM1 * ...4 F5
Railway Station Whf
  LEY E10 ...284 B6
Railway St BCTR RM8 ...287 M6
  BRTR CM7 ...121 J5
  CHLM/WR CM1 ...4 D3
  GVW DA11 ...336 D3
  MGTR CO11 ...91 G1
Railway Ter MGTR CO11 * ...91 G1
  SOSN SS2 ...301 G2
  WALTH E17 ...266 F7
Rainbow Av CVI SS8 ...320 F1
  POP/IOD E14 ...322 E4
Rainbow La SLH/COR SS17 ...317 K5
Rainbow Rd CHLM/WR CM3 ...170 C3
Rainbow Ms MAL CM9 ...198 C4
Rainbow Rd CDW/CHF RM16 ...329 N7
  CVI SS8 ...320 F1
  HLWE CM17 ...189 M6
  K/T/MI CO5 ...178 A7
  PUR RM19 ...329 J1
Rainbow Wy RCOLW CO6 ...82 C4
Raine Av HVHL CB9 ...34 M1
Rainer Cl CHES/WCR EN8 ...216 E7
Rainham Rd RAIN RM13 ...311 J4
Rainham Rd North
  DAGE RM10 ...288 E7
Rainham Rd South
  DAGE RM10 ...310 F1
Rainham Wy FOS CO13 ...137 F1
Rainhill Wy BOW E3 ...306 D2
Rainsborough Av DEPT SE8 ...322 F7
Rainsborowe Rd COLS CO2 ...128 C1
Rainsford Av CHLM/WR CM1 ...4 C1
Rainsford La CHLM/WR CM1 ...4 C3
Rainsford Rd CHLM/WR CM1 ...4 C1
Rainsford Wy HCH RM12 ...289 M4
Rainton Rd CHARL SE7 ...323 K4
Raleana Rd POP/IOD E14 ...322 F4
Raleigh Cl SUD CO10 ...21 G1
Raleigh Dr LAIN SS15 ...277 G2
Raleigh Rd SUD CO10 ...21 G1
Ramac Wy CHARL SE7 ...323 L7
Rambler Cl COLW CO3 ...106 A6
Ramblers Wy BOC CM0 ...393 N9
Ram Gorse HLW CM20 ...6 E2
Ramney Dr PEND EN3 ...232 F6
Ramparts Cl RCOLW CO6 ...82 E6
Ramparts Ct COLW CO3 ...106 C6
The Ramparts RAYL SS6 ...281 H3
Rampart St SBN/FI SS3 ...303 G12
Rampart Ter SBN/FI SS3 ...303 G12
Ramplings Av COS CO15 ...6
Rampton Cl CHING E4 ...266 D2
Ramsay Rd CHES/WCR EN8 ...216 D2
Ramsay Dr VGE SS16 ...296 D2
Ramsay Gdns GPK RM2 ...271 L7
Ramsay Rd FSTGT E7 ...307 J1
  MAL CM9 ...215 J4
Ramsey Rd HAR CO12 ...70 C1
  HSTD CO9 ...81 D7
Ramsgate Dr IPSE IP3 ...55 L5
Ramsgill Ap GNTH/NBYPK IG2 ...287 J2
Ramsgill Dr GNTH/NBYPK IG2 ...287 J2
Rams Gv CHDH RM6 ...288 B2
Ramshaw Dr
  CHLM/GWD CM2 ...5 L4
Ramuz Dr WOS/PRIT SS0 ...18 A2
Rana Ct BRTR CM7 ...121 J1
Rana Rd BRTR CM7 ...121 J1
Rancliffe Rd EHAM E6 ...308 B6
Randall Cl GTDUN CM6 ...117 C4
Randall Dr HCH RM12 ...311 M1
Randalls Dr RBRW/HUT CM13 ...257 H2
Randolph Ap CAN/RD E16 ...324 A2
Randolph Cl LOS SS9 ...300 B2
  MAL CM9 ...214 A7
Randolph Rd WALTH E17 * ...284 E3
Rands Rd CHLM/GWD CM6 ...140 D4
Rands Wy IPSE IP3 ...55 L5
Randulph Ter CHLM/WR CM1 * ...5 H5
Randway RAYL SS6 ...281 L4
Randwell Cl IP IP1 ...49 G8
Ranelagh Gdns GVW DA11 ...337 J5
  EHAM E6 ...308 M2
  FX IP11 ...11 ...
  WAN E11 ...307 ...
Range Rd GVE DA12 ...338 A5
Rangers Rd BKHH IG9 ...249 K7
Ranger Wk COLS CO2 ...129 K7
Ransome Cl COLS CO2 ...128 C1
Ransome Cr IP IP3 ...46 F7
Ransome Crs IPSE IP3 ...55 G5
Ransome Rd IPSE IP3 ...55 L5
Ransome Wy CHLM/WR CM1 ...209 L1
Ransom Rd CHARL SE7 * ...323 J5
Rantree Fold VGE SS16 ...296 E2
Ranulf Cl HLWE CM17 ...188 D3
Ranulph Wy RCHLM CM3 ...196 E2

Ranwell Cl BOW E3 * ...306 C5
Ranworth Av HOD EN11 ...185 J7
Raphael Av ROM RM1 ...289 J1
  TIL RM18 ...351 K7
Raphael Dr CHLM/WR CM1 ...194 C6
  SBN/FI SS3 ...303 K5
Raphael Rd GVE DA12 ...338 A5
Raphaels LAIN SS15 ...2 B7
Rapier Cl PUR RM19 ...328 C2
Ratcliffe Ct K/T/MI CO5 ...148 E3
Ratcliffe Cross St WCHPL E1 * ...322 A2
Ratcliffe La POP/IOD E14 ...322 B2
Ratcliff Rd COLW CO3 ...106 D3
Ratcliff Rd FSTGT E7 ...307 M2
Rat Hi RIPS/CAP IP9 ...365 P12
Rathmore Rd CHARL SE7 ...323 L8
  GVW DA11 ...337 K5
Rat La SBF/HAD SS7 ...280 F5
Ratsborough Cha BOC CM0 ...393 M3
Rat's La LOU IG10 ...234 C8
Rattwick Dr CVI SS8 ...321 K7
Ratty's La HOD EN11 ...201 L3
Ravel Gdns SOCK/AV RM15 ...328 G2
Ravel Rd SOCK/AV RM15 ...329 G2
Raven Cl BCAYW CM12 ...258 C4
Raven Crs BCAYW CM12 ...258 C4
Ravencroft CDW/CHF RM16 ...331 L1
Ravendale Wy SBN/FI SS3 ...303 L1
Raven Dr SBF/HAD SS7 ...297 L3
Ravenhill Rd PLSTW E13 ...307 M5
Raven La BCAYW CM12 ...258 C1
Ravenoak Wy CHIG IG7 ...269 H4
Ravensbourne Crs HARH RM3 ...290 C1
Ravensbourne Dr
  RCHLM CM1 ...4 A5
Ravensbourne Gdns CLAY IG5 ...268 D2
Ravens Ct WOS/PRIT SS0 * ...18 E6
Ravenscourt WOS/PRIT SS0 * ...300 C1
Ravenscourt Cl HCH RM12 ...290 B8
Ravenscourt Dr HCH RM12 ...290 B8
  VGE SS16 ...278 C8
Ravenscourt Rd HCH RM12 ...290 B8
Ravens Crs GTDUN CM6 ...119 H6
Ravenscroft BROX EN10 * ...201 L6
Ravenscroft Cl CAN/RD E16 ...323 K1
Ravenscroft Rd CAN/RD E16 ...323 K1
Ravensdale COS CO15 ...295 L1
  VGE SS16 ...295 L1
Ravensfield BSDN SS14 ...278 C7
  DAGW RM9 ...310 A3
Ravensfield Rd IP IP1 ...47 K3
Ravenside Cl UED N18 ...266 C1
Ravens La RIPW IP8 ...46 F3
Ravensmere EPP CM16 ...220 B8
Ravenswood Av IPSE IP3 ...55 G5
Ravenswood Cha RCFD SS4 ...283 J6
Ravenswood Cl CRW RM5 ...270 E4
Ravenswood Rd WALTH E17 ...284 C4
Raven Wy COLN CO4 ...107 H1
Rawden Cl HAR CO12 ...14 E4
Rawdon Dr HOD EN11 ...201 H4
Rawlings Crs COLN CO4 ...87 L8
Rawlyn Cl CDW/CHF RM16 ...329 N8
Rawreth Gdns WICKE SS11 * ...262 A4
Rawreth La WICKE SS11 ...262 G6
Rawsthorne Rd CAN/RD E16 ...324 C1
Rawstorn Rd COLW CO3 ...8 A3
Ray Av HAR CO12 ...14 D1
Rayburn Rd EMPK RM11 ...290 D5
Raycliff Av RCOS CO16 ...159 H6
Ray Cl CVI SS8 ...320 D3
  LOS SS9 ...299 L4
Raydons Gdns DAGW RM9 ...310 L1
Raydons Rd DAGW RM9 ...310 A2
Raydon Wy SUD CO10 ...21 L1
Rayfield EPP CM16 ...220 B8
Rayfield Cl GTDUN CM6 ...141 K1
Ray Gdns BARK IG11 ...309 K6
Rayhaven HAR CO12 ...70 D1
Ray La HAR CO12 ...66 D1
Rayleigh Av LOS SS9 ...281 G5
  WOS/PRIT SS0 ...18 C2
Rayleigh Cl BRTR CM7 ...121 J1
  COLN CO4 ...9 D1
  RBRW/HUT CM13 ...256 D3
Rayleigh Downs Rd RAYL SS6 ...281 K6
Rayleigh Dr LOS SS9 ...300 D3
Rayleigh Pde
  RBRW/HUT CM13 * ...256 F3
Rayleigh Rd CAN/RD E16 ...323 L4
  IP IP1 ...47 K4
  LOS SS9 ...281 G6
  LOS SS9 ...282 C2
  RBRW/HUT CM13 ...256 F3
  SBF/HAD SS7 ...280 D6
  SLH/COR SS17 ...316 F4
  WFD IG8 ...267 M6
The Rayleighs COLW CO3 * ...106 D3
Rayley La EPP CM16 ...221 L4
Ray Lodge Rd WFD IG8 ...267 M5
Ray Md RCHLM CM3 ...167 J6
Rayment Av CVI SS8 ...321 G2
Rayment Drift KESG IP5 ...55 J1
Raymond Av SWFD E18 ...285 J1
Raymond Gdns CHIG IG7 ...269 L2
Raymond Rd
  GNTH/NBYPK IG2 ...287 G5
  PLSTW E13 ...307 L1
Raymonds Cl RCHLM CM3 ...244 F6
Raymonds Dr SBF/HAD SS7 ...280 D6
Rayne Ct SWFD E18 ...285 J2
Rayner Rd COLS CO2 ...128 E1
Rayner Wy HSTD CO9 ...81 H4
Raynes Av WAN E11 ...285 L1
Raynham Rd BSF CM23 ...139 K1
Raynhams SAFWN CB10 * ...28 D7
Raynton Rd PEND EN3 ...232 E2
Ray Rd CRW RM5 ...270 F4
Rayside BSDN SS14 ...3 K7
The Ray CHLM/WR CM1 ...194 A5
Ray Wk LOS SS9 ...299 L4
Read Rd HOC/HUL SS5 ...282 D4
Read St WAB EN9 ...234 B3
Reade Rd RIPS/CAP IP9 ...364 D2
Readers Ct CHLM/GWD CM2 ...5 J4
Reading Cl VGE SS16 ...276 D3
Reading Rd IPNE IP4 ...49 M2
The Readings HLWS CM18 ...204 D4
Reads Cl IL IG1 ...286 A6
Reaper Rd COLS CO2 ...128 C1
Rebecca Gdns WIT CM8 ...147 H1
Rebecca Meade GTDUN CM6 ...94 A1
Rebels La SBN/FI SS3 ...302 L1
Rebow Rd HAR CO12 ...70 E1
  RCOLE CO7 ...130 C5
Rebow St COL CO1 ...9 D3
Recketts Ct COS CO15 ...7
Recreation Av HARH RM3 ...272 C8
  LOS SS9 ...300 C3
  ROMW/RG RM7 ...288 D7
  SLH/COR SS17 ...295 L5
Recreation Cl FX IP11 ...62 D7
Recreation Gnd STSD CM24 ...115 H2
Recreation La FX IP11 ...62 E2

Recreation Rd COL CO1 ...107 L8
  COS CO15 ...7 H5
  HVHL CB9 ...356 D9
  SUD CO10 ...20 C4
Recreation Wk BCAYE CM11 ...241 M8
  SUD CO10 ...45 H1
Recreation Wy IPSE IP3 ...55 G3
Rectory Av RCFD SS4 ...264 F7
Rectory Cha BRWN CM15 ...383 R11
  RBRW/HUT CM13 ...274 B6
  SOS SS1 ...302 B4
Rectory Cl CHING E4 ...266 D2
  COLN CO4 ...107 H3
  ING CM4 ...241 G3
  RCHLM CM3 ...167 M7
  SAFWS CB11 ...351 N1
  SBF/HAD SS7 ...299 G1
  WARE SG12 ...186 E1
Rectory Ct PIT SS13 * ...278 C7
Rectory Fld HLWW/ROY CM19...203 J3
  RIPS/CAP IP9 ...365 P6
Rectory Gdns PIT SS13 ...278 E7
  UPMR RM14 ...291 G7
Rectory Garth RAYL SS6 ...281 G2
Rectory Gv LOS SS9 ...300 A5
  WICKE SS11 ...261 G1
Rectory Hi RCOLE CO7 ...130 F4
  RCOLE CO7 ...363 R8
  RCOLW CO6 ...361 G2
Rectory La BSF CM23 ...114 D3
  CHLM/WR CM1 ...209 L1
  HAR CO12 ...367 R8
  HLWW/ROY CM19 ...203 J3
  K/T/MI CO5 ...153 G2
  LOU IG10 ...250 D2
  MAL CM9 ...209 L1
  MGTR CO11 ...65 H4
  RBRW/HUT CM13 ...275 H2
  RCHLM CM3 ...144 A6
  RCHLM CM3 ...247 L1
  SAFWN CB10 ...27 K8
  WIT CM8 ...147 K7
Rectory Meadow BRTR CM77 ...122 A7
Rectory Mdw HSTD CO9 ...356 E8
Rectory Park Dr PIT SS13 ...278 E8
Rectory Pl WOOL/PLUM SE18 ...324 D7
Rectory Rd BCAYW CM12 ...276 C1
  BRTR CM7 ...100 E6
  CBS CB2 ...340 E4
  CDW/CHF RM16 ...315 L5
  CHLM/WR CM1 ...208 L5
  CHTY IP2 ...16 G9
  COLN CO4 ...362 G11
  DAGE RM10 ...310 D3
  FOS CO13 ...136 D6
  GRAYS RM17 ...331 G2
  HAR CO12 ...367 R10
  HOC/HUL SS5 ...282 D2
  HSTD CO9 ...356 E8
  HVHL CB9 ...35 L3
  K/T/MI CO5 ...130 B6
  K/T/MI CO5 ...149 M8
  MAL CM9 ...174 E4
  MGTR CO11 ...367 K6
  MNPK E12 ...308 C2
  PIT SS13 ...278 F6
  RCHLM CM3 ...246 C5
  RCOLE CO7 ...111 G5
  RCOLE CO7 ...130 F3
  RCOLE CO7 ...132 C5
  RCOLW CO6 ...104 C5
  RCOLW CO6 ...126 F4
  RCOS CO16 ...134 D8
  RCOS CO16 ...158 C2
  RIPS/CAP IP9 ...365 M10
  SBF/HAD SS7 ...299 H3
  SLH/COR SS17 ...316 F4
  SUD CO10 ...45 H5
  SWCM DA10 ...336 B5
  TIL RM18 ...332 A5
  WALTH E17 ...284 E2
Rectory Ter SLH/COR SS17 * ...317 H1
Rectory Wd HLW CM20 ...12 E4
Reculver Rd
  BERM/RHTH SE16 ...322 A7
Redan St IP IP1 ...16 C7
Red Barn Dr RCOLW CO6 ...360 G4
Red Barn La HAR CO12 ...113 G2
Red Barn Rd RCOLE CO7 ...156 C5
Red Barracks Rd
  WOOL/PLUM SE18 ...324 C7
Redbourne Dr THMD SE28 ...326 A2
Redbridge La East REDBR IG4 ...286 A4
Redbridge La West WAN E11 ...285 L4
Redbury Cl RAIN RM13 ...311 L3
Redcar Rd HARH RM3 ...272 C3
Redcliff Dr CHLM/GWD CM2 ...5 L6
Redcliffe Gdns IL IG1 ...286 D6
Redcliff Rd CHLM/GWD CM2 ...5 M6
Redcliffe Rd EHAM E6 ...308 B5
Reddells Cl SUD CO10 ...20 F6
Redden Court Rd HARH RM3 ...290 D1
Reddings La BOC CM0 ...390 B6
Rede Wy SUD CO10 ...21 L9
Redfern Gdns GPK RM2 ...272 A8
Redgate La RIPS/CAP IP9 ...54 F2
Redgates Pl RCHLM CM3 ...244 F6
Redgates Pl CHLM/WR CM1 ...210 A1
Redgrave Rd VGE SS16 ...296 E5
Redhills Rd RCHLM CM3 ...245 H5
Red House Cl FX IP11 ...61 M5
  WARE SG12 ...184 F1
Redhouse La COLN CO4 ...87 G3
  SUD CO10 ...20 D7
Red House Wk KIR/NAC IP10 ...60 C1
The Redinge BCAYE CM11 ...259 G6
Redlands Pl PEND EN3 ...248 C1
Red La SLH/COR SS17 ...317 G2
Red Lion Crs HLWE CM17 ...204 D3
Red Lion La HLWE CM17 ...204 D3
Red Lion Yd COL CO1 * ...8 C7
Redmayne Dr CHLM/GWD CM2...128 A7
Redmill COLW CO3 ...128 A7
Redpoll Wy ERITHM DA18 ...326 A6
Redricks La HLW CM20 ...188 A5
Rediffe Rd PLSTW E13 ...307 L5
Redriff Rd BERM/RHTH SE16 ...322 A5
  ROMW/RG RM7 ...270 B6
Red Rd BRW CM14 ...273 L4
Redrose La HSTD CO9 ...356 B4
Redrose Wk RCOS CO16 ...158 D2
Redruth Cl CHLM/WR CM1 ...194 B8
Redruth Rd HARH RM3 ...272 C3
Redshank Cl HVHL CB9 ...34 F6
Redshank Dr MAL CM9 ...198 G4
Red Sleeve RIPS/CAP IP9 ...58 G2
Redstart Cl EHAM E6 ...324 B1

Redstock Rd SOSN SS2 ...19 H1
Redvers Cl BSF CM23 ...115 G5
Redwald Rd CLPT E5 ...306 A1
Red White & Blue Rd
  BSF CM23 ...115 J3
Red Willow HLWW/ROY CM19 ...203 G5
Redwing Dr CHTY IP2 ...16 H1
Redwing Rd BCAYE CM11 ...258 C6
Redwold Dr WDBR IP12 ...51 H3
Redwood Cha SOCK/AV RM15 ...313 M
Redwood Cl
  BERM/RHTH SE16 ...322 B
  BOW E3 ...306 D
  COLN CO4 ...108 B
  WIT CM8 ...147 K
Redwood Gdns CHING E4 * ...248 E
  LAIN SS15 ...277 G
The Redwoods CVI SS8 ...320 E
Reed Cl CAN/RD E16 ...323 K
  RCOS CO16 ...6 B
Reede Rd DAGE RM10 ...310 E
Reede Wy DAGE RM10 ...310 E
Reed Hall Av COLS CO2 ...128 E
Reedings Wy SBW CM21 ...163 G
Reedland Wy FX IP11 ...62 G
Reed Pond Wk GPK RM2 ...271 J
  VGE SS16 ...294 E
Reeds La HVHL CB9 ...34 D
Reeds Wy WICKW SS12 ...260 F
Reesland Cl MNPK E12 ...308 D
Reeve Gdns KESG IP5 ...50 B
Reeve Ldg FX IP11 * ...62 G
Reeves Cl BRWN CM15 ...383 Q
  VGE SS16 ...294 C
Reeves La HLWW/ROY CM19 ...202 D
Reeves Pightle ROY SG8 ...349 G
Reeves Rd BOW E3 ...306 E
Reeves Wy RCHLM CM3 ...245 H
Refinery Rd HAR CO12 ...66 E
Reform Ter MGTR CO11 * ...91 G
Regal Cl CHLM/GWD CM2 ...5 L
Regan Cl SLH/COR SS17 ...317 H
Regarder Rd CHIG IG7 ...269 L
Regarth Av ROM RM1 ...289 H
Regency Cl BSF CM23 ...138 E
  CHIG IG7 ...268 F
  CHLM/GWD CM2 ...5 M
  RCFD SS4 ...283 H
  WICKE SS11 ...261 G
Regency Ct BRW CM14 ...273 M
  COLS CO2 ...129 M
  HLWS CM18 ...204 B
  MAL CM9 ...198 D
Regency Gdns EMPK RM11 ...289 H
Regency Gn COLW CO3 ...128 C
  SOSN SS2 ...301 J
Regency Ldg COS CO15 * ...6
Regeneration Rd
  BERM/RHTH SE16 ...322 A
Regent Cl CDW/CHF RM16 ...323 L
  RAYL SS6 ...280 E
  RCOLE CO7 ...156 C
Regent Ct LAIN SS15 ...2
Regent Dr BCAYW CM12 ...240 C
Regent Gdns
  GDMY/SEVK IG3 ...289 K
Regent Rd EPP CM16 ...220 A
  RCOLE CO7 ...156 C
Regents Cl BOC CM0 ...393 N
  COLN CO4 ...87 M
Regents Dr WFD IG8 ...268 D
Regents Pl LOU IG10 ...250 A
Regent Sq BELV DA17 ...326 E
  BOW E3 ...306 E
Regent St IPNE IP4 ...17 J
  K/T/MI CO5 ...130 C
  MGTR CO11 ...91 G
Regimental Wy HAR CO12 ...70 E
Regina Cl IPNE IP4 ...49 G
Reginald Ms HLWE CM17 ...188 D
Reginald Rd FSTGT E7 ...307 K
  HARH RM3 ...272 D
Reichaven Rd
  WOOL/PLUM SE18 ...325 J
Reigate Av RCOS CO16 ...159 G
Reigate Cl IPSE IP3 ...55 G
Reigate Rd GDMY/SEVK IG3 ...287 G
Rembrandt Cl CVI SS8 ...320 D
  POP/IOD E14 ...323 G
  SBN/FI SS3 ...303 K
Rembrandt Dr GVW DA11 ...337
Rembrandt Gv
  CHLM/WR CM1 ...194 B
Rembrandt Wy COLW CO3 ...106 A
Rembrow Rd RIPS/CAP IP9 ...58 D
Remembrance Av BOC CM0 ...393 N
  RCHLM CM3 ...196 G
Remercie Rd MGTR CO11 ...91 G
Remington Rd EHAM E6 ...324 A
Remus Rd BOW E3 ...306 D
Renacres VGE SS16 ...294 E
Rendlesham Rd FX IP11 ...62
  IP IP1 ...16
Renfrew Cl EHAM E6 ...324 D
Renfrew Rd IPNE IP4 ...49 G
Renness Rd WALTH E17 ...284 D
Rennie Pl CHLM/GWD CM2 ...210 B
Rennison Cl CHESW EN7 ...216 A
Renoir Pl CHLM/WR CM1 ...194 B
Renown Cl ROMW/RG RM7 ...270 C
Rensburg Rd WALTH E17 ...284
Rensburg Vls WALTH E17 * ...284
Renwick Rd BARK IG11 ...309 M
Repton Av GPK RM2 ...289 K
Repton Cl PIT SS13 ...278 D
Repton Ct PIT SS13 ...278 D
Repton Dr GPK RM2 ...289 K
Repton Gdns GPK RM2 ...289 K
Repton Gv CLAY IG5 ...268 C
  SOSN SS2 ...301 J
Repton St POP/IOD E14 ...322 B
Repulse Cl ROMW/RG RM7 ...270 B
Reservoir Cl GRH DA9 ...335 M
Reston Wy CAN/RD E16 ...324 C
Retford Cl HARH RM3 ...272 C
Retford Pth HARH RM3 ...272 C
Retford Rd HARH RM3 ...272 C
Retingham Wy CHING E4 ...266
Retreat Rd HOC/HUL SS5 ...264 D
  WOS/PRIT SS0 ...18 C
The Retreat BRTR CM7 * ...121 J
  BRW CM14 ...255
  GRAYS RM17 ...330
  RBRW/HUT CM13 ...256
  RCOLW CO6 ...106
  WIT CM8 ...171
Retreat Wy CHIG IG7 ...269 M
Rettendon Cl RAYL SS6 ...280
Rettendon Gdns WICKE SS11...261
Rettendon Vw WICKE SS11 ...261
Reubens Rd RBRW/HUT CM13...256
Reveley Sq BERM/RHTH SE16 ...322
Review Rd DAGE RM10 ...310
Reydon Av WAN E11 ...285
Reymead Cl K/T/MI CO5 ...177
Reynard Copse BSF CM23 ...115
Reynards Cl FOS CO13 ...137

Reynards Copse COLN CO4 ... 107 K2
Reynards Ct SUD CO10 * ... 39 M7
Reynard Wy HERT/BAY SG13 ... 184 M5
Reynard CI CHDH RM6 ... 287 M5
COLW CO3 ... 106 E8
IPSE IP13 ... 54 F8
MNPK E12 ... 308 D2
Reynolds CI HVHL CB9 ... 34 A4
Reynolds Ct FX IP11 ... 62 C8
Reynolds Flds HOO/HM ME3 ... 339 M7
Reynolds Gdns RCFD SS4 ... 264 F8
Reynolds Ga RCHLM CM3 ... 245 J6
Reynolds Rd IPSE IP3 ... 54 F5
Reynolds Wy COS CO15 ... 43 K7
Rhapsody Crs BRW CM14 ... 273 L2
Rhoda Rd SBF/HAD SS7 ... 298 A4
Rhoda Rd HAD SS7 ... 288 B8
Rhodes Av BSF CM23 ... 139 C4
Rhodesia Rd WAN E11 ... 285 C7
Rhodeswell Rd BOW E3 ... 322 B1
Rhondda Gv BOW E3 ... 306 B2
Rhugarve Gdns CBE/LIN CB1 ... 25 J7
Rhum Ms WLSV SS12 ... 261 K8
Ribble CI WFD IG8 ... 267 M5
Riby Rd FX IP11 ... 11 J3
Ricardo St POP/IOD E14 ... 322 E2
Richard Av RCOLE CO7 ... 156 C7
RCOLE CO7 ... 156 C7
Richard Burn Wy SUD CO10 ... 20 D1
Richard CI WOOL/PLUM SE18 ... 324 B7
Richard House Dr
CAN/RD E16 ... 323 M2
Richards Av ROMW/RG RM7 ... 288 A2
Richardson CI GRH DA9 ... 335 J2
Richardson PI CHLM/GWD CM1 ... 4 D1
Richardson Rd RCOLE CO7 ... 64 A2
SRTFD E15 * ... 307 H6
Richardson La RIPS/CAP IP9 ... 365 K1
Richardson Wk COLW CO3 ... 105 H4
Richards PI WALTH E17 ... 284 D1
Richards Wk RCOS CO16 ... 159 H7
Rich CI RCHLM CM3 ... 144 C6
Riche CI GTDUN CM6 ... 118 F3
Riches Rd IL IG1 ... 286 F7
Richford Rd SRTFD E15 ... 307 J5
Richmond Av CHING E4 ... 267 M3
SBF/HAD SS7 ... 297 M3
SBN/FI SS3 ... 303 K1
Richmond CI BSF CM23 ... 138 G2
WALTH E17 ... 284 C4
Richmond Ct BROX EN10 ... 201 O6
Richmond Crs CHING E4 ... 267 C4
HAR CO12 ... 71 G3
Richmond Dr COS CO15 ... 182 C4
RAYL SS6 ... 281 G5
WFD IG8 ... 268 D6
WOS/PRIT SSO ... 300 F1
Richmond PI
WOOL/PLUM SE18 ... 324 F7
Richmond Rd CHING E4 * ... 208 D8
CHLM/GWD CM2 ... 210 D1
FSTGT E7 ... 307 L2
GRAYS RM17 ... 330 F5
IL IG1 ... 286 F8
IP IP1 ... 47 L6
K/T/MI CO5 ... 178 A7
ROM RM1 ... 289 J4
WAN E11 ... 285 G7
WICKE SS11 ... 260 F3
Richmond PI PLSTW E13 ... 307 K6
SOSN SS2 ... 302 A4
Richmond Vls WALTH E17 * ... 266 F7
Richmond Wy WAN E11 ... 285 K7
Rich St POP/IOD E14 ... 322 C4
Ricketts Dr BCAYW CM12 ... 258 C2
Rickling VGE SS16 ... 296 C5
Rickling Green Rd SAFWS CB11 ... 73 M8
Rickling Rd SAFWS CB11 ... 73 L8
Rick Roberts Wy SRTFD E15 ... 307 F7
Rickstones Rd WIT CM8 ... 147 K6
Riddiford Dr CHLM/GWD CM1 ... 209 J1
Riddings La HLWS CM18 ... 204 B3
Riddles Dr COLW CO3 ... 8 D1
Rideout St WOOL/PLUM SE18 ... 324 E7
Ridgdale St BOW E3 ... 306 F1
Ridge CI THMD SE28 ... 309 B1
Ridgemount SBF/HAD SS7 ... 298 B1
The Ridge RCHLM CM3 ... 212 B8
WOTN CO14 ... 137 L1
Ridgeway BCAYW CM12 ... 258 D5
COLN CO4 ... 107 K3
GRAYS RM17 ... 331 H5
HOC/HUL SS5 * ... 263 H2
ING CM4 ... 239 K4
MAL CM9 ... 214 D5
RAYL SS6 ... 280 F4
RBRW/HUT CM13 ... 256 E4
WFD IG8 ... 267 M3
Ridgeway Av GVE DA12 ... 337 L8
Ridgeway Gdns REDBR IG4 ... 286 D3
WOS/PRIT SSO ... 300 F1
Ridgeways HLWS CM17 ... 204 F5
The Ridgeway BRTR CM7 ... 121 K4
CBE/LIN CB1 ... 25 J7
CHING E4 ... 248 F8
GPK RM2 ... 289 K2
HAR CO12 ... 14 D1
HARH RM3 ... 272 D7
LOS SS9 ... 300 D5
Ridgewell CI CHLM/GWD CM1 ... 209 J1
Ridgewell CI DAGE RM10 ... 310 D2
Ridgewell Rd HSTD CO9 ... 345 K3
HSTD CO9 ... 345 Q10
SUD CO10 ... 345 P4
Ridgewell Wy COLS CO2 ... 129 J2
Ridgwell Rd CAN/RD E16 ... 315 K4
Ridings Av BRTR CM7 ... 120 E6
The Ridings BSF CM23 ... 138 E5
CHLM/GWD CM2 ... 210 A6
CVI SS8 * ... 298 D8
RCFD SS4 ... 283 J4
RCOLW CO7 ... 361 J2
Ridlands CI BRTR CM77 ... 122 B7
Ridley CI HARH RM3 ... 271 J7
Ridley Gdns RBSF CM22 ... 374 D3
Ridley Rd CHLM/WR CM1 ... 193 L5
FSTGT E7 ... 307 M1
PIT SS13 ... 278 F4
Riffams Ct PIT SS13 ... 278 F5
Riffams Dr PIT SS13 ... 278 F5
Riffhams Cha RCHLM CM3 ... 212 A4
Riffhams Dr CHLM/GWD CM2 ... 211 M5
Riffhams La RCHLM CM3 ... 211 M5
Rifle Rd BRTR CM7 ... 121 L4
Rifle St POP/IOD E14 ... 322 F1
Rigby Gdns MGTR CO11 ... 91 L1
Rigby CI CDW/CHF RM16 ... 331 L3
Rigby Ms IL IG1 ... 286 D7
Rigby Rd PEND EN3 ... 202 D8
Rigden St POP/IOD E14 ... 322 F2
Rigg Ap LEY E10 ... 285 J1
Rignals La CHLM/GWD CM2 ... 226 A2
Riley Av LOS SS9 ... 300 E5
Riley CI IP IP1 ... 47 H4
Riley Rd PEND EN3 ... 202 D8
Rimini CI COLS CO2 ... 128 D3

Rimmer CI SUD CO10 ... 43 K7
Ringham Rd IPNE IP4 ... 48 F7
Ringlet CI GPK RM2 ... 323 L1
Ringwood Av HCH RM12 ... 280 A2
Ringwood Dr LOS SS9 ... 300 L6
Ringwood Rd WALTH E17 ... 284 C4
Ripley CI RCOS CO16 ... 158 E7
Ripley Ms WAN E11 ... 285 H4
Ripley Rd BELV DA17 ... 326 D7
CAN/RD E16 ... 323 M2
GDMY/SEVK IG3 ... 287 J7
Ripley Vw COLW CO10 ... 235 J8
Ripon Gdns IL IG1 ... 286 B4
Ripple Rd BARK IG11 ... 308 F4
BARK IG11 ... 310 B6
Rippleside BSDN SS14 ... 278 C8
Ripple Wy COLN CO4 ... 9 J7
Rippolson Rd
WOOL/PLUM SE18 ... 325 J8
Risbridge Dr HVHL CB9 ... 35 K3
Risbridge Rd GPK RM2 ... 271 J8
Rise Pk LAIN SS15 ... 277 J7
Rise Park Bvd ROM RM1 ... 271 J7
Rise Park Pde ROM RM1 ... 271 J7
The Rise BKHH IG9 ... 250 A8
RCOLW CO7 ... 105 K5
WAN E11 ... 285 X3
Riseway BRWN CM15 ... 256 B6
The Risings WALTH E17 ... 285 L2
The Rising BCAYE CM11 ... 258 A4
Ritabrook Rd CRW IP2 ... 53 K4
Ritchings Av WALTH E17 ... 284 B2
Rivendell N RCHLM CM3 ... 244 F7
Rivenhall SBF/HAD SS7 ... 280 E5
WICKE SS11 ... 261 K4
Rivenhall Flds WIT CM8 * ... 147 J2
Rivenhall Gdns SWFD E18 ... 285 J2
River Av ROM RM1 ... 290 F4
River Bank CI SUD CO10 ... 37 M4
River Barge CI POP/IOD E14 ... 322 F3
River CI CHES/WCR EN8 ... 233 H4
HSTD CO9 ... 81 J4
RAIN RM13 ... 327 L1
WAN E11 ... 285 M4
Riverdale LOS SS9 ... 282 A6
Riverdale Rd ERITH DA8 ... 326 A1
WOOL/PLUM SE18 ... 325 J8
Riverdene Rd IL IG1 ... 286 C7
River Dr UPMR RM14 ... 290 F4
Riverfield La SBW CM21 ... 162 F8
Riverhead Rd WALTH E17 ... 266 A8
River HI RCHLM CM3 ... 169 G2
River Md BRTR CM7 ... 121 K1
Rivermead Rd UED N18 ... 266 H4
River Meads WARE SG12 ... 185 K4
Rivermill HLW CM20 ... 5 G5
River Rd BARK IG11 ... 309 H6
BKHH IG9 ... 250 B8
BRW CM14 ... 273 H5
Riversdale GVW DA11 ... 337 H7
Riversdale Rd CRW RM5 ... 270 F4
Riverside BRTR CM77 ... 123 G2
BSF CM23 ... 139 G2
CHARL SE7 ... 323 L6
CHLM/WR CM1 ... 5 J7
Riverside Av BROX EN10 ... 201 H8
Riverside East MGTR CO11 ... 64 F7
Riverside West MGTR CO11 ... 64 F7
Riverside Ct CHING E4 ... 248 E8
HLW CM20 ... 188 D3
Riverside Ms BROX EN10 * ... 216 H1
Riverside Rd BOC CM0 ... 393 M4
IL IG1 ... 286 B8
IP IP1 ... 47 J6
SRTFD E15 ... 306 F1
Riverside Wk COL CO1 * ... 9 J3
Riverside Wy DART DA1 ... 334 F7
K/T/MI CO5 ... 148 F4
Riversmead HOD EN11 ... 201 H7
Rivers St IPNE IP4 ... 17 L2
Riverton Dr BOC CM0 ... 385 L12
Rivertons VGE SS16 ... 296 C5
Riverview WFD IG8 ... 268 D6
Riverview VGE SS16 ... 296 C5
Riverview Vw WIT CM8 ... 171 K5
River View CI LAIN SS15 ... 276 F4
Riverview Gdns HOC/HUL SS5 ... 262 F2
River View Rd GRH DA9 ... 335 K7
River View Rd RIPS/CAP IP9 ... 365 L11
SBF/HAD SS7 ... 298 A3
Riverview Ter PUR RM19 * ... 328 E3
River View Ter RCHLM CM3 ... 392 F7
River Wy GNWCH SE10 ... 323 J6
HLW CM20 ... 188 D3
LOU IG10 ... 250 D6
River Whf BELV DA17 * ... 327 L1
Rivey CI CBE/LIN CB1 ... 25 G6
Rivey Wy CBE/LIN CB1 ... 25 G5
Riviera Dr SOS SS1 ... 19 M4
Rivington Av WFD IG8 ... 268 A4
Rivish La SUD CO10 ... 42 F2
Rixsen Rd MNPK E12 ... 308 B2
Roach Av RAYL SS6 ... 280 A6
Roach Rd BOW E3 ... 306 G4
Roach V COLN CO4 ... 108 A5
LOS SS9 ... 282 C6
Roach Valley Wy
HOC/HUL SS5 ... 281 M7
RCFD SS4 ... 282 B6
RCFD SS4 ... 396 F5
Robeck Rd IPSE IP3 ... 54 D7
Robert CI BCAYW CM12 ... 258 C2
CHIG IG7 ... 269 J4
CHLM/GWD CM2 ... 210 D1
HARH RM3 ... 271 J8
Robert's HI BURES CO8 ... 84 C2
Robertson CI BROX EN10 ... 216 H6
Robertson Dr WICKW SS12 ... 261 J8
Robertson Rd SRTFD E15 ... 306 F1
Roberts Rd BELV DA17 ... 326 D8
COLS CO2 ... 107 J8
LAIN SS15 ... 276 E3
RCHLM CM3 ... 246 D6
WALTH E17 ... 266 F7
Robert St WOOL/PLUM SE18 ... 325 G8
Robert Wallace CI BSF CM23 ... 115 G4
Robeson St BOW E3 ... 322 C1
Robin CI BCAYW CM12 ... 240 F4
CRW RM5 ... 271 G4
RCOLE CO7 ... 133 C5
WARE SG12 ... 185 K4
Robin Crs COLS CO15 ... 127 L1
Robin Dr CHTY IP2 ... 53 J1
Robin Hood Gdns
POP/IOD E14 * ... 322 F2
Robin Hood La POP/IOD E14 ... 322 F2
Robin Hood Rd BRWN CM15 ... 255 L7
RBSF CM22 ... 374 G4
Robinia Av GVW DA11 ... 337 H5
Robinia CI BARK/HLT IG6 ... 269 J1
LAIN SS15 ... 277 L1

Robinia Crs LEY E10 ... 284 E7
Robinsbridge Rd RCOLW CO6 ... 124 C3
Robinsdale CI COS CO15 ... 159 J7
Robinson CI BSF CM23 ... 139 G4
HCH RM12 ... 311 L4
WAN E11 ... 285 H6
Robinson Rd CDW/CHF RM16 ... 316 A1
DAGE RM10 ... 310 D1
RCOLE CO7 ... 156 D6
Robinsons CI BOC CM0 ... 393 M2
Robin Wy CHLM/GWD CM2 ... 209 M1
SUD CO10 ... 44 F4
Robjohns Rd CHLM/WR CM1 ... 4 A8
Robletts Wy RCOLW CO6 ... 85 H1
Robson CI EHAM E6 ... 324 D2
Robsons CI CHES/WCR EN8 ... 216 D7
Robyns Cft GVW DA11 ... 337 H8
Rochdale Rd ABYW SE2 ... 325 L8
WALTH E17 ... 284 D5
Rochdale Wy COLN CO4 ... 108 D3
Roche Av RCFD SS4 ... 283 H3
Rochefort Dr RCFD SS4 ... 283 J5
Rochehall Wy RCFD SS4 ... 283 L5
Rochelle CI GTDUN CM6 ... 74 D2
Rochester Av PLSTW E13 ... 307 M5
Rochester CI BRTR CM7 ... 121 G2
Rochester Dr WOS/PRIT SSO ... 300 F1
Rochester Gdns IL IG1 ... 286 C5
Rochester Ms WOS/PRIT SSO ... 300 F1
Rochester Wy SUD CO10 ... 20 C1
Rocheway RCFD SS4 ... 283 K3
Rochford Av BRWN CM15 ... 256 D1
CHDH RM6 ... 287 M3
WAB EN9 ... 233 L4
WOS/PRIT SSO ... 300 F1
Rochford CI BROX EN10 ... 216 F4
EHAM E6 ... 308 H4
HCH RM12 ... 311 J3
WICKE SS11 ... 261 H1
Rochford Garden Wy
RCFD SS4 ... 283 H2
Rochford Gn LOU IG10 ... 250 F4
Rochford Hall CI RCFD SS4 ... 283 H4
Rochford Rd BSF CM23 ... 115 J8
CHLM/GWD CM2 ... 5 H2
CVI SS8 ... 321 G2
SOSN SS2 ... 283 H8
Rochford Wy WOTN CO14 ... 137 H2
Rockall CI SOSN SS2 ... 282 D6
Rockall CI HVHL CB9 ... 35 G6
Rockchase Gdns EMPK RM11 ... 290 F4
Rockingham Av EMPK RM11 ... 289 L4
Rockingham CI COLN CO4 ... 108 A2
Rockleigh Av LOS SS9 ... 300 A4
Rockleigh Ct BRWN CM15 ... 256 D3
Rockmount Rd
WOOL/PLUM SE18 ... 325 J8
Rockwell Rd DAGE RM10 ... 310 E2
Rockwood Gdns LOU IG10 ... 250 F3
Rodbridge Dr SOS SS1 ... 302 G5
Rodbridge HI SUD CO10 ... 42 F5
Roddam CI COLW CO3 ... 106 F7
Roden CI HLWE CM17 ... 189 G7
Roden St IL IG1 ... 286 B8
Roding CI CHONG CM5 ... 381 L7
Roding Gdns LOU IG10 ... 250 B6
Roding La BKHH IG9 ... 250 B8
Roding La North WFD IG8 ... 268 B8
Roding La South REDBR IG4 ... 286 A3
Roding Leigh RCHLM CM3 ... 245 H6
Roding Rd CLPT E5 ... 306 A1
EHAM E6 ... 324 E1
LOU IG10 ... 250 C5
Rodings Av SLH/COR SS17 ... 317 G1
The Rodings LOS SS9 ... 282 A6
UPMR RM14 ... 291 G4
Roding Vw BKHH IG9 ... 250 A8
CHONG CM5 ... 381 L1
RAIN RM13 ... 312 A6
WICKW SS12 ... 261 H7
Rodmere St GNWCH SE10 ... 323 H8
Rodney Crs HOD EN11 ... 201 H1
Rodney Gdns BRTR CM7 ... 121 M1
Rodney PI WALTH E17 ... 266 B8
Rodney Rd CHONG CM5 ... 382 F7
WAN E11 ... 285 L2
Rodney Wy CHLM/WR CM1 ... 4 B9
ROMW/RG RM7 ... 270 C7
Roebuck CI HERT/BAY SG13 ... 184 M8
Roebuck La BKHH IG9 ... 249 M8
Roebuck Rd BARK/HLT IG6 ... 269 L5
Roedean CI SOSN SS2 ... 302 L4
Roedean Gdns SOSN SS2 ... 302 C3
Roehampton Av GVE DA12 ... 338 B5
Roe's CI CBS CB2 ... 22 C1
Roffey St POP/IOD E14 ... 322 F1
Rogation CI COLW CO3 ... 106 A8
Rogers CI FX IP11 ... 62 B7
Rogers Gdns DAGE RM10 ... 310 D2
Rogers Rd CAN/RD E16 ... 323 J2
DAGE RM10 ... 310 D2
GRAYS RM17 ... 331 F3
Roggel Rd CVI SS8 ... 321 G3
Rokeby Gdns WFD IG8 ... 267 K7
Rokeby St SRTFD E15 ... 307 H1
Rokells BSDN SS14 ... 2 L1
Rokell Wy FOS CO13 ... 137 J3
Rokescroft PIT SS13 ... 278 D3
Roland La CVI SS8 ... 320 E1
Roland Ms WCHPL E1 * ... 322 A1
Roland Rd WALTH E17 ... 285 J1
Rollason Gdns CHDH RM6 ... 288 D2
Rollesby Gv HTHMD SE28 ... 309 M3
Rollestons CHLM/WR CM1 ... 208 A3
Rolley La K/T/MI CO5 ... 148 F3
Roll Gdns BARK/HLT IG6 ... 269 G2
Rolls Park Av CHING E4 ... 266 D1
Rolls Park Rd CHING E4 ... 266 D1
Rolph CI RCOS CO16 ... 135 K3
Roma Av WDBR IP12 ... 51 J3
Romagne CI UPMR RM14 ... 316 C2
Romainville Wy CVI SS8 ... 319 M1
Roman CI BRWN CM15 ... 239 H5
RAIN RM13 ... 311 L6
Roman Ct BRTR CM7 ... 121 M4
Romanhurst MAL CM9 ... 214 F1
Roman Ri SBW CM21 ... 162 E7
Romans CI CHLM/WR CM1 ... 208 E4
Roman V HLWE CM17 ... 188 F1
Roman Wy BCAYW CM12 ... 258 D5
BOC CM0 ... 393 M5
FX IP11 ... 63 J7

RVHL CB9 ... 35 G7
RCOS CO16 ... 180 D2
SAFWS CB11 ... 351 N1
WAB EN9 ... 233 G3
Roma Rd WALTH E17 ... 284 D5
Rom Crs ROMW/RG RM7 ... 289 H5
Romeland WAB EN9 ... 233 G4
Romford CI COLN CO4 ... 9 H4
Romford Rd CHDH RM6 ... 270 A5
CHIG IG7 ... 269 L3
CHONG CM5 ... 382 F7
MNPK E12 ... 286 D8
SOCK/AV RM15 ... 328 E3
Romney Cha EMPK RM11 ... 290 C4
Romney CI BRTR CM7 ... 159 J1
FOS CO13 ... 137 H2
RCOLE CO7 ... 156 B4
RCOS CO16 ... 159 B1
Romney Dr HCH RM12 ... 311 C4
GVW DA11 ... 337 H8
IPSE IP3 ... 54 F6
WOOL/PLUM SE18 ... 324 F6
Romney Rd BCAYW CM12 ... 258 C4
GVW DA11 ... 337 H8
IPSE IP3 ... 54 F6
WOOL/PLUM SE18 ... 324 F6
Romsey CI HOC/HUL SS5 ... 264 A7
SLH/COR SS17 ... 279 L8
Romsey Crs SBF/HAD SS7 ... 279 L8
Romsey Rd DAGW RM9 ... 310 A3
Romsey Wy SBF/HAD SS7 ... 279 K8
SBF/HAD SS7 ... 279 L8
Romulus CI COLN CO4 ... 87 J8
Rom Valley Wy
ROMW/RG RM7 ... 289 H4
Ronald Av SRTFD E15 ... 307 H7
Ronald Dr RAYL SS6 ... 280 D1
Ronald Hill Gv LOS SS9 ... 300 A4
Ronald Park Av
WOS/PRIT SSO ... 300 F3
Ronald Rd HARH RM3 ... 272 D7
HSTD CO9 ... 81 H5
Roneo Cnr ROMW/RG RM7 ... 289 H4
Roneo Link HCH RM12 ... 289 J6
Ron Green Ct ERITH DA8 ... 327 G8
Ron Leighton Wy EHAM E6 ... 308 B5
Ronnie La MNPK E12 ... 287 M7
Roodegate BSDN SS14 ... 2 B1
Rook End La SAFWS CB11 ... 373 J5
The Rookeries RCOLW CO6 ... 126 E1
Rookery CI RAYL SS6 ... 89 H1
RCHLM CM3 ... 170 D8
SAFWN CB10 ... 341 L7
Rookery HI SLH/COR SS17 ... 317 H1
Rookery La K/T/MI CO5 ... 149 M6
MAL CM9 ... 173 H6
Rookery Ms FOS CO13 ... 246 B5
SAFWS CB11 ... 351 M9
Rookery Md RCHLM CM3 ... 245 H1
SAFWN CB10 ... 341 L7
Rookery Wy WGRAYS RM17 ... 331 C4
Rookes CI SAFWN CB10 ... 341 K1
Rookes Crs SLH/COR SS17 ... 317 G1
Rookwood Av LOU IG10 ... 250 F3
RCOS CO16 ... 159 H7
Rookwood Gdns CHING E4 ... 267 J2
Rookwood Wy HVHL CB9 ... 34 D7
Rookyards VGE SS16 ... 278 B8
Roosevel Av CVI SS8 ... 320 D1
Roosevelt Rd LAIN SS15 ... 276 D7
Roosevelt Wy COLS CO2 ... 129 L1
DAGE RM10 ... 311 G3
Roos Hill Debden Rd
SAFWS CB11 ... 30 B4
Roots Hall Av SOSN SS2 ... 301 J2
Roots Hall Dr SOSN SS2 ... 18 J3
Roots La WIT CM8 ... 198 L2
Ropemaker Rd
BERM/RHTH SE16 ... 322 B5
Ropemaker's Flds
POP/IOD E14 ... 322 C3
Ropers La SUD CO10 ... 42 F5
Ropery St BOW E3 ... 306 C4
Rope St BERM/RHTH SE16 ... 322 B5
Rope Wk IPNE IP4 ... 17 L2
Rope Yd Rails
WOOL/PLUM SE18 ... 324 E6
Rosabelle Av RCOLE CO7 ... 130 E4
Rosalind CI COLN CO4 ... 108 C6
Rosary Gdns WOS/PRIT SSO ... 300 F1
Rosbach P CVI SS8 ... 321 G2
Rosberg Rd CVI SS8 ... 321 H2
Roscommon Wy CVI SS8 ... 319 M1
Rose Acre BSDN SS14 ... 278 C1
RCOLE CO7 ... 156 N3
Roseacre Ct EMPK RM11 ... 290 C4
Roseacres RBSF CM22 ... 377 K2
Rose Av COLW CO3 ... 106 B6
GVE DA12 ... 338 B6
SWFD E18 ... 267 L8
Rosebank BRW CM14 ... 256 A6
Rosebank HAR CO12 ... 14 C8
Rosebank Av HCH RM12 ... 311 M4
Rosebank Est BOW E3 ... 306 C6
Rosebank Gdns BOW E3 ... 306 C6
GVW DA11 ... 337 H6
Rosebank Gv WALTH E17 ... 284 C1
Rosebank Rd K/T/MI CO5 ... 177 K7
WALTH E17 ... 284 D1
Rosebay Av BCAYW CM12 ... 258 D5
Rosebay CI WIT CM8 ... 171 G2
Roseberry Av SBF/HAD SS7 ... 298 C1
VGE SS16 ... 294 E1
Roseberry CI UPMR RM14 ... 291 J5
Roseberry Gdns UPMR RM14 ... 291 J5
Roseberry Rd COL CO1 ... 8 F7
Rosebery Ct GVW DA11 ... 337 H7
Rosebery Rd CHLM/GWD CM2 ... 5 H7
FX IP11 ... 63 G7
GRAYS RM17 ... 330 D2
IPNE IP4 ... 17 L2
Rosebury Sq WFD IG8 ... 268 E5
Rose Ct WICKW SS12 ... 261 H8
Rose Ct CHESW EN7 ... 216 B4
COLS CO2 ... 107 J8
Rose Crs COLN CO4 ... 107 G5
Rosecroft CI COS CO15 ... 159 J7
VGE SS16 ... 294 D1
Rosecroft Wy HOD EN11 ... 201 M1
Rosedale Av CHESW EN7 ... 216 A7
Rosedale CI ABYW SE2 ... 325 L7
Rosedale Gdns DAGW RM9 ... 309 M4
Rosedale Rd DAGW RM9 ... 309 M5
FSTGT E7 ... 307 M2

GRAYS RM17 ... 331 G4
ROM RM1 ... 288 G1
Rosedale Wy CHESW EN7 ... 216 B5
Rosedene Gdns
GNTH/NBYPK IG2 ... 286 D2
Rosedene Ter LEY E10 ... 284 E7
Rose Dr BOC CM0 ... 393 M2
Rosefield POP/IOD E14 ... 322 D3
Rosefield Gdns POP/IOD E14 ... 322 C3
Rosefinch CI HVHL CB9 ... 34 F4
Rose Gdns BRTR CM7 ... 121 G1
RCOS CO16 ... 181 L7
Rose Gln CHLM/GWD CM2 ... 209 M6
ROM RM1 ... 289 H6
Rose on SUD CO10 ... 360 D2
Rosehatch Av CHDH RM6 ... 288 A1
Rose HI BRTR CM7 ... 121 K3
Rosehill CI HOD EN11 ... 201 G3
Rosehill Crs IPSE IP3 ... 17 L7
Rosehill Rd IPSE IP3 ... 17 L7
Roselaine BSDN SS14 ... 3 G4
Rose La BCAYW CM12 ... 258 D3
CHDH RM6 ... 288 B2
IPNE IP4 ... 17 L4
MAL CM9 ... 175 L5
RCOLE CO7 ... 130 E6
SAFWN CB10 ... 341 M7
Roselawn Flds
CHLM/WR CM1 ... 193 L5
Rosemary Av BRTR CM7 ... 121 J1
FX IP11 ... 63 G7
ROM RM1 ... 289 J1
Rosemary CI COS CO15 ... 7 H3
CTDUN CM6 ... 116 F4
K/T/MI CO5 ... 149 M8
Rosemary Crs COS CO15 ... 7 H3
CTDUN CM6 ... 116 F4
K/T/MI CO5 ... 149 M8
Rosemary Dr POP/IOD E14 ... 323 G2
REDBR IG4 ... 286 A3
Rosemary Gdns BCTR RM8 ... 288 D3
SUD CO10 ... 20 E1
Rosemary La GTDUN CM6 ... 95 M6
CTDUN CM6 ... 116 F4
HSTD CO9 ... 81 H3
HSTD CO9 ... 81 G4
RCOLE CO7 ... 132 C6
Rosemary Rd COS CO15 ... 6 E3
Rosemary West COS CO15 ... 6 E7
Rosemead SBF/HAD SS7 ... 279 M6
Rosemead Gdns
RBRW/HUT CM13 ... 239 G8
Rosemount HLWW/ROY CM19 ... 203 J4
Rosemount CI WFD IG8 ... 268 E5
Roserna Rd CVI SS8 ... 321 G2
Rose Rd CVI SS8 ... 320 D2
Roserton St POP/IOD E14 ... 322 F1
The Roses WFD IG8 ... 267 J6
Rose St COLW DA11 ... 336 F4
Rose V HOD EN11 ... 201 H3
Rose Va BRW CM14 ... 273 M2
Rose Valley Crs SLH/COR SS17 ... 317 G1
Rose Wy RCFD SS4 ... 283 K5
Rose Vls MGTR CO11 * ... 65 G5
Rosewood Av HCH RM12 ... 311 K2
Rosewood CI COLN CO4 ... 107 K1
SOCK/AV RM15 ... 314 B3
Rose Yd HSTD CO9 * ... 81 J3
Rosher CI SRTFD E15 ... 307 G4
Rosherville Wy GVW DA11 ... 337 H5
Rosilian Dr HOC/HUL SS5 ... 263 H4
Rosina St HOM E9 ... 306 A1
Roslings CI CHLM/WR CM1 ... 193 G7
Roslyn CI BROX EN10 ... 200 F7
Roslyn Gdns GPK RM2 ... 271 J3
Rossall CI EMPK RM11 ... 289 K4
Ross Av BCTR RM8 ... 288 C3
Ross CI HVHL CB9 ... 34 F6
SAFWS CB11 ... 30 B3
Rossdene Gdns GTDUN CM6 ... 164 A6
Rossell Rd TIL RM18 ... 331 G8
Rossendale CHLM/WR CM1 ... 4 B6
Rossendale CI COLN CO4 ... 108 M2
Rossetta CI RCOLE CO7 ... 130 E3
Rossington CI IP IP1 ... 47 L1
Rossiter Rd SBN/FI SS3 ... 303 G1
Rosslyn Av BCTR RM8 ... 288 C5
CHING E4 ... 267 J1
HARH RM3 ... 272 E8
HOC/HUL SS5 ... 264 B7
WALTH E17 ... 284 F2
Ross Rd IPNE IP4 ... 49 G4
Ross Wy VGE SS16 ... 294 E2
Roswell CI CHES/WCR EN8 ... 216 D7
Rothbury Av RAIN RM13 ... 327 L1
Rothbury Cottages
GNWCH SE10 ... 323 H7
Rothbury Rd CHLM/WR CM1 ... 209 G4
HOM E9 ... 306 C4
Roth Dr RBRW/HUT CM13 ... 256 F6
Rotherfield Rd PEND EN3 ... 232 E7
Rotherhithe Old Rd
BERM/RHTH SE16 ... 322 A7
Rotherhithe St
BERM/RHTH SE16 ... 322 A4
Rothesay Av CHLM/GWD CM2 ... 4 F7
Rothmans Av
CHLM/GWD CM2 ... 210 D3
Rothsay Pl FSTGT E7 ... 307 M4
Rothwell CI LOS SS9 ... 281 M7
Rothwell Gdns DAGW RM9 ... 309 M4
Rothwell Rd DAGW RM9 ... 309 M5
Rotterdam Dr POP/IOD E14 ... 322 F2
Rouge La GVE DA12 ... 337 L8
Roughtallys EPP CM16 ... 221 G5
Roughtons CHLM/GWD CM2 ... 225 M2
Roundacre HSTD CO9 ... 81 H5
LAIN SS15 ... 2 H5
Roundaway Rd CLAY IG5 ... 268 G3
Roundbush Rd K/T/MI CO5 ... 151 L4
Round CI COLW CO3 ... 106 D3
Round Coppice Rd
STSD CM24 ... 376 B1
Round Hill Rd SBF/HAD SS7 ... 298 D3
Roundhills WAB EN9 ... 233 M4
The Roundings
HERT/BAY SG13 ... 184 D7
Roundmead CI LOU IG10 ... 250 D3
Roundmoor Dr
CHES/WCR EN8 ... 216 D7
Roundridge Rd RIPS/CAP IP9 ... 58 D3
Roundwood Av
RBRW/HUT CM13 ... 256 E3
Roundwood Gv
RBRW/HUT CM13 ... 256 E3
Roundwood Gv IPNE IP4 ... 48 F6
Rounton Rd BOW E3 ... 306 D4
WAB EN9 ... 233 M5
Rous Cha CHLM/GWD CM2 ... 225 L4

Rous Rd BKHH IG9 250 B8
Routemaster Cl PLSTW E13 307 L7
Routh Av IPSE IP3 55 L4
Routh St EHAM E6 324 C1
Rover Av BARK/HLT IG6 269 J5
COS CO15 182 B6
Rowallan Cl COLW CO3 128 D2
Rowan Av CBS CB2 22 C3
CHING E4 266 C5
Rowan Cl COLW CO3 128 A1
COS CO15 6 A6
HAR CO12 14 F8
IL IG1 309 G2
RAYL SS6 262 E7
RCOLE CO7 133 J5
Rowan Dr BROX EN10 217 G2
MAL CM9 198 F8
Rowan Gn East
RBRW/HUT CM13 256 C7
Rowan Gn West
RBRW/HUT CM13 256 C7
Rowan Gv SOCK/AV RM15 328 F3
Rowanhayes Cl CHTY IP2 54 A2
Rowan Pl COL CO1 8 B3
The Rowans BCAYE CM11 259 G5
BROX EN10 200 F5
SOCK/AV RM15 328 F4
Rowans Waw RCOLW CO6 360 G3
Rowans Wy LOU IG10 250 C4
WICKE SS11 261 H5
Rowan Wk EMPK RM11 290 A2
LOS SS9 282 A7
SBW CM21 162 F7
Rowan Wy CHDH RM6 287 M1
RCFD SS4 392 B12
RCHLM CM3 196 D2
SOCK/AV RM15 314 A4
WIT CM8 147 K8
Rowarth Av KESG IP5 50 B6
Rowden Pde CHING E4 * 266 D5
Rowden Rd CHING E4 266 E5
Rowdowns Rd DAGW RM9 310 C5
Rowe Gdns BARK IG11 309 J6
Rowell Cl HVHL CB9 34 D3
Rowenhall LAIN SS15 276 C7
Rowhedge RBRW/HUT CM13 256 D6
Rowhedge Cl PIT SS13 279 G3
Rowhedge Rd COLS CO2 130 A3
Rowherns La RCOLE CO7 133 J1
Rowland Crs CHIG IG7 269 H3
Rowlands Cl CHES/WCR EN8 216 E8
HAR CO12 * 70 D3
Rowlandsfields
CHES/WCR EN8 * 216 E8
Rowlands Rd BCTR RM8 288 C7
The Rowlands SBF/HAD SS7 298 B1
Rowland's Yd HAR CO12 70 D3
Rowland Vls MGTR CO11 * 64 D6
Rowley Cl MGTR CO11 65 G5
Rowley Ct HVHL CB9 35 H8
Rowley Hl HVHL CB9 35 H8
Rowley Md EPP CM16 220 D3
Rowley Rd CDW/CHF RM16 315 K5
Rowley's Rd HERT/BAY SG13 184 A2
Rowney Av SAFWN CB10 31 H7
Rowney Gdns DAGW RM9 309 M3
SBW CM21 188 D1
Rowney Rd DAGW RM9 309 L3
Rowney Wd SBW CM21 162 D8
Rowntree Cl PLSTW E13 307 L8
Rowntree Wy SAFWS CB11 30 A2
Rowse Cl SRTFD E15 306 F5
The Rows HLW CM20 12 F5
The Row RCOLE CO7 363 K7
RCOS CO16 * 112 C8
Roxborough Gdns VGE SS16 * 3 L7
Roxburgh Av UPMR RM14 290 F8
Roxburghe Rd RCOS CO16 134 C7
Roxburgh Rd IPNE IP4 49 G4
Roxwell Av CHLM/WR CM1 209 G2
Roxwell Gdns
RBRW/HUT CM13 256 F1
Roxwell Rd BARK IG11 309 K6
CHLM/WR CM1 191 J5
CHLM/WR CM1 208 C1
Roxwell Wy WFD IG8 267 M6
Roxy Av CHDH RM6 287 M5
Royal Albert Rd EHAM E6 324 D3
Royal Albert Wy CAN/RD E16 324 B3
Royal Arsenal West
WOOL/PLUM SE18 * 324 D8
Royal Artillery Wy SOSN SS2 302 B2
Royal Av CHES/WCR EN8 232 F3
Royal Cl CDMY/SEVK IG3 287 K5
RCFD SS4 265 G8
Royal Ct COLN CO4 108 B4
MAL CM9 214 D4
Royal Crescent Monarch Wy
GNTH/NBYPK IG2 287 G4
Royal Docks Rd EHAM E6 324 E1
Royal Ms SOS SS1 19 G7
Royal Oak Cha LAIN SS15 2 A2
Royal Oak Dr WICKE SS11 261 K5
Royal Oak Gdns BSF CM23 138 F3
Royal Pier Rd GVE DA12 337 L4
Royal Rd CAN/RD E16 323 M2
The Royals SOS SS1 * 19 H7
Royal Ter SOS SS1 19 G7
Royal Terrace Pier
GVE DA12 * 337 M4
Royal Victor Pl BOW E3 306 A6
Roy Av IPNE IP4 49 G8
Royce Cl BROX EN10 201 G7
Roy Cl KESG IP5 50 A6
Roycraft Av BARK IG11 309 J6
Roycroft Cl SWFD E18 267 L7
Roydon Br BSDN SS14 3 M2
Roydon Cl LOU IG10 250 B7
Roydon Rd HLWW/ROY CM19 186 F8
WARE SG12 185 L5
Roydon Wy FOS CO13 137 J3
Royer Cl HOC/HUL SS5 282 D1
Roy Gdns GNTH/NBYPK IG2 287 H2
Royle Cl GPK RM2 289 L3
Roy Sq POP/IOD E14 322 B3
Royston Av CHING E4 266 D4
LAIN SS15 277 G4
SOSN SS2 301 L2
Royston Dr CHTY IP2 53 J3
Royston Gdns IL IG1 286 A4
Royston La SAFWN CB10 340 B9
Royston Rd CBS CB2 22 A6
HARH RM3 272 D6
ROY SG8 348 E8
ROY SG8 370 B2
SAFWS CB11 350 H8
Ruaton Dr RCOS CO16 6 A3
Rubens Cl SBN/FI SS3 303 K5
Rubens Ga CHLM/WR CM1 194 C6
Rubens Rd IPSE IP3 54 F4
Rubens Wk SUD CO10 21 G1
Rubicon Av WICKE SS11 261 J5
Ruby Ms WALTH E17 * 284 D1
Ruby Rd WALTH E17 284 D1
Ruckholt Cl LEY E10 284 E8
Ruckholt Rd LEY E10 306 E1
Ruddington Cl CLPT E5 306 B1
Ruddstreet Cl
WOOL/PLUM SE18 324 E7
Rudkin Rd COLN CO4 87 J8
Rudlands RIPW IP8 53 H4
Rudolph Rd PLSTW E13 307 K6
Rudsdale Wy COLW CO3 106 C8
Rue De St Lawrence
WAB EN9 233 K4
Rue's La FX IP11 63 H5
Ruffels Fld GTDUN CM6 118 B1
Ruffles Cl RAYL SS6 281 H2
Ruffles Rd HVHL CB9 34 E6
Rugby Gdns DAGW RM9 309 M3
Rugby Rd DAGW RM9 309 L4
SUD CO10 45 L5
Rugg St POP/IOD E14 322 D3
Rugosa Cl COLW CO3 105 M6
Rumballs Ct BSF CM23 138 D5
Rumbold Rd HOD EN11 201 K1
Rumbullion Dr BCAYW CM12 258 C2
Rumsey Flds RCHLM CM3 212 C6
Rumsley CHESW EN7 216 B5
Rundells HLWS CM18 204 B5
Rundells Wk BSDN SS14 278 B6
The Rundels SBF/HAD SS7 280 D8
Runnacles St WIT CM8 122 F8
Runnacles Wy FX IP11 62 C8
Runnemede WOS/PRIT SS0 * 300 F6
Running Mare La
CHLM/GWD CM2 225 K2
Running Waters
RBRW/HUT CM13 256 D7
Runnymede Cha
SBF/HAD SS7 298 D1
Runnymede Rd CVI SS8 320 E2
SLH/COR SS17 316 F4
Runsell Cl RCHLM CM3 212 C6
Runsell La RCHLM CM3 212 C5
Runsell Vw RCHLM CM3 212 C5
Runwell Cha WICKE SS11 261 K3
Runwell Gdns WICKE SS11 261 G3
Runwell Rd WICKE SS11 261 H4
Runwell Ter SOS SS1 18 F6
Runwood Rd CVI SS8 319 M2
Rupert Rd BOC CM0 393 M1
Rural Cl EMPK RM11 289 L6
Rural V GVW DA11 337 H5
Rurik Ct MAL CM9 214 B5
Ruscoe Rd CAN/RD E16 323 J2
Rushbottom La SBF/HAD SS7 279 L7
Rushbrook Crs WALTH E17 266 C7
Rushbury Cl IPNE IP4 49 G5
Rush Cl SBF/HAD SS7 279 L7
WARE SG12 185 K5
Rushcroft Rd CHING E4 266 E6
Rushdene ABYW SE2 325 M6
Rushdene Rd BCAYW CM12 258 C5
BRWN CM15 255 M7
Rushden Gdns CLAY IG5 286 D1
Rushdon Cl CDW/CHF RM16 330 D2
ROM RM1 289 K3
Rush Dr WAB EN9 233 K6
Rushen Dr HERT/BAY SG13 184 D6
Rushes La BOC CM0 389 R8
Rushes Md HLWS CM18 203 M3
Rushfield SBW CM21 162 F7
Rush Green Gdns
ROMW/RG RM7 288 F6
Rush Green Rd RCOS CO16 182 E2
ROMW/RG RM7 288 F6
Rushgrove St
WOOL/PLUM SE18 324 C7
Rush La RBSF CM22 374 D5
Rushleigh Av CHES/WCR EN8 216 E8
Rushleigh Gn BSF CM23 138 E6
Rushley PIT SS13 279 G5
Rushley Cl CDW/CHF RM16 315 G8
SBN/FI SS3 303 K1
Rushleydale CHLM/WR CM1 194 B8
Rushmeadow Wy FX IP11 63 J6
Rushmere Av UPMR RM14 290 F8
Rushmere Cl K/T/MI CO5 177 M7
Rushmere Rd IPNE IP4 48 F6
Rushmere St KESG IP5 49 K4
Rusholme Av DAGE RM10 288 D8
Rushton Gv HLWE CM17 204 E1
Ruskin Av MNPK E12 308 C3
SOSN SS2 301 K2
UPMR RM14 290 F5
WAB EN9 233 M4
Ruskin Cl FOS CO13 137 H2
HVHL CB9 34 A4
Ruskin Dene BCAYW CM12 258 D2
Ruskin Gdns HARH RM3 271 L7
Ruskin Gv DART DA1 334 D7
Ruskin Rd BELV DA17 326 D7
CDW/CHF RM16 331 K3
CHLM/GWD CM2 210 B3
IPSE IP3 17 M6
SLH/COR SS17 316 F4
The Ruskins BRTR CM77 120 C4
Ruskoi Rd CVI SS8 298 C8
Rusper Rd DAGW RM9 309 M3
Russell Cl BRWN CM15 255 L7
LAIN SS15 276 E7
Russell Gdns CHLM/GWD CM2 225 K1
WICKE SS11 261 H6
Russell Gv RCFD SS4 283 K3
Russell Rd BKHH IG9 249 M8
CAN/RD E16 323 K2
CHING E4 266 C3
COS CO15 7 K5
EN EN1 232 A8
FX IP11 11 J5
GVE DA12 338 A4
IP IP1 16 C6
LEY E10 284 E4
RCHLM CM3 246 E4
TIL RM18 331 H7
WALTH E17 284 C1
Russell Rw RCFD SS4 * 392 B11
Russell's Dr CHES/WCR EN8 216 F8
Russell's Ride CHES/WCR EN8 232 E1
Russell's Rd HSTD CO9 80 D4
Russell Wy CHLM/WR CM1 4 A9
Russel Rd GRAYS RM17 330 D3
Russet Cl BRTR CM7 121 K4
SLH/COR SS17 317 G2
Russets Cl CHING E4 267 G3
The Russets RCFD SS4 265 G8
Russett Cl HVHL CB9 33 M5
Russetts EMPK RM11 290 B2
VGE SS16 276 D8
Russet Wy BOC CM0 393 M7
HOC/HUL SS5 264 B5
Russia Dock Rd
BERM/RHTH SE16 * 322 B4
Rustic Cl UPMR RM14 291 H6
Ruston Rd WOOL/PLUM SE18 324 B6
The Rustons CBS CB2 22 A8
Ruston St BOW E3 306 C5
Rutherford Cl BCAYW CM12 240 D8
LOS SS9 281 M7
Rutherfords CHLM/WR CM1 193 L4
Ruthven Av CHES/WCR EN8 232 E3
Ruthven Cl WICKW SS12 261 G7
Ruthven St HOM E9 306 A5
Rutland Ap EMPK RM11 290 D3
Rutland Av COLS CO2 128 E2
SOS SS1 302 B5
Rutland Cl LAIN SS15 276 D7
Rutland Dr EMPK RM11 290 D3
RAYL SS6 262 E6
Rutland Gdns BCTR RM8 309 M2
BRTR CM7 121 K1
RCFD SS4 264 F8
Rutland Ga BELV DA17 326 E8
Rutland Pl BRTR CM7 * 76 E3
Rutland Rd CHLM/WR CM1 193 K7
FSTGT E7 308 A4
HOM E9 306 A5
IL IG1 308 E1
WALTH E17 284 D4
WAN E11 285 L3
Rydal Av FX IP11 63 J6
Rydal Cl HOC/HUL SS5 263 G3
RAYL SS6 281 H3
Rydal Dr MAL CM9 214 E5
Rydal Wk IPSE IP3 55 H3
Rydal Wy BRTR CM77 120 F7
Ryde Av COS CO15 159 K6
Ryde Cl LOS SS9 281 L8
Ryde Dr SLH/COR SS17 316 F5
Ryder Cl HERT/BAY SG13 184 C2
Ryder Gdns RAIN RM13 311 J3
Ryder Wy PIT SS13 279 G3
The Ryde LOS SS9 281 L8
Rye Cl COLW CO3 106 A8
IPSE IP3 55 J1
RCHLM CM3 196 D2
RCOLE CO7 156 B4
Ryecroft HLWW/ROY CM19 12 D7
Ryecroft Av CLAY IG5 268 E8
Ryedene VGE SS16 296 B2
Ryedene Cl VGE SS16 296 B2
Ryedene Pl VGE SS16 296 B2
Ryefeld Cl HOD EN11 185 J7
The Rye Fld RCHLM CM3 212 A2
Ryegate Rd COL CO1 8 D5
Rye Grass Wy BRTR CM7 121 L4
Rye Hill Rd HLWS CM18 203 L6
Rye Hills HSTD CO9 81 J5
Rye La COLS CO2 152 D1
Rye Mill La K/T/MI CO5 149 G1
Rye Rd HOD EN11 201 J2
Ryes La RBSF CM22 376 C10
SUD CO10 44 D7
Rye St BSF CM23 115 G8
Rye Wk ING CM4 239 K3
Rykhill CDW/CHF RM16 331 L2
Rylands RIPS/CAP IP9 58 D3
Rylands Rd SOSN SS2 301 M2
The Ryle CHLM/WR CM1 208 D5
Rylstone Wy SAFWS CB11 30 C1
Rymill St CAN/RD E16 324 D4
Rysley RCHLM CM3 212 A1

S

Sabbarton St CAN/RD E16 323 J2
Sabina Rd CDW/CHF RM16 331 M3
Sabines Rd ABR/ST RM4 254 C3
Sackville Cl CHLM/WR CM1 4 A1
Sackville Crs HARH RM3 272 B7
Sackville Gdns IL IG1 286 C6
Sackville Rd SOSN SS2 302 B4
Sackville Wy RCOLW CO6 106 A1
Saddington St GVE DA12 337 L5
Saddle Ri CHLM/WR CM1 194 B5
Saddlers Cl BRTR CM77 120 E6
Saddlers Pl KESG IP5 50 F6
Sadler Cl COL CO1 129 L1
Sadlers SBF/HAD SS7 279 L7
Sadlers Cl BCAYE CM11 241 G8
FOS CO13 136 F3
Sadlers Md HLWS CM18 204 B2
Saffory Cl LOS SS9 281 M6
Saffron Av POP/IOD E14 323 G3
Saffron Cl BRTR CM7 77 M2
HOD EN11 201 G2
RBRW/HUT CM13 275 G8
SLH/COR SS17 316 D2
Saffron Ct SAFWS CB11 30 A1
Saffron Gdns BRTR CM7 77 L2
SLH/COR SS17 316 C4
Saffron Rd CBS CB2 22 D1
CDW/CHF RM16 329 M7
CRW RM5 271 G8
Saffron Wk BCAYE CM11 258 E3
BRTR CM7 77 L2
Saffron Wy K/T/MI CO5 173 M1
Sage Cl EHAM E6 324 C1
Sagehayes CHTY IP2 54 A2
Sage Rd COLS CO2 129 K3
Sages RBSF CM22 372 G12
Sages End Rd HVHL CB9 343 K5
Salgasso Cl CAN/RD E16 324 A2
Sainfoin Cl CBS CB2 22 D1
St Agnes Dr CVI SS8 320 A2
St Agnes Rd BCAYW CM12 276 F2
St Agnes Wy KESG IP5 49 L6
St Aidan's Wy GVE DA12 338 B8
St Alban's Av EHAM E6 308 C7
UPMR RM14 291 H7
St Alban's Cl GVE DA12 338 A8
St Alban's Gdns GVE DA12 338 A8
St Alban's Rd COLW CO3 107 G6
COS CO15 7 J5
DART DA1 334 C8
EPP CM16 220 E7
GDMY/SEVK IG3 287 J6
WFD IG8 267 K6
St Andrew's Av COLN CO4 9 J6
HCH RM12 311 J2
St Andrews Cl CVI SS8 320 A1
EPP CM16 221 K2
IPNE IP4 49 J8
RCOLE CO7 131 L6
THMD SE28 326 A2
St Andrews Dr BCAYW CM12 258 E2
RIPS/CAP IP9 365 P6
St Andrews Gdns COLN CO4 9 H5
St Andrews La LAIN SS15 276 F6
St Andrew's Meadow
HLWS CM18 13 L8
St Andrews Pl BRWN CM15 256 C5
RCOLE CO7 156 B4
St Andrew's Ri SUD CO10 44 B4
St Andrew's Rd COS CO15 6 E5
FX IP11 62 F8
GVE DA12 * 337 L5
HSTD CO9 81 H3
IL IG1 286 C5
PLSTW E13 307 L7
RCFD SS4 283 H3
RCHLM CM3 195 J4
RCHLM CM3 196 D1
RCOS CO16 134 C4
ROMW/RG RM7 289 G4
SBN/FI SS3 302 F7
SUD CO10 21 H9
TIL RM18 331 H8
WALTH E17 266 A8
WAN E11 285 H4
St Andrews Wy BOW E3 306 E8
St Annes Cl CDW/CHF RM16 * 314 E8
CHESW EN7 * 216 B6
RCOLW CO6 124 E3
St Annes Ct CHLM/WR CM1 5 K2
St Anne's Pk BROX EN10 201 H6
St Anne's Pas POP/IOD E14 * 322 C2
St Anne's Rd BRWN CM15 238 F5
COLN CO4 9 J4
CVI SS8 321 G2
LEY E10 285 G7
St Anne's Rw POP/IOD E14 322 C2
St Anne St POP/IOD E14 322 C2
St Ann's BARK IG11 308 F5
St Ann's Rd BARK IG11 308 F5
COS CO15 6 E3
SOSN SS2 19 H3
St Anthony's Av WFD IG8 267 M5
St Anthony's Dr
CHLM/GWD CM2 209 M7
St Antony's Rd FSTGT E7 307 L4
St Aubyns Rd IPNE IP4 48 F8
St Augustine Ms COL CO1 8 F7
St Augustine Rd
CDW/CHF RM16 331 L3
IPSE IP3 55 J1
St Augustine's Av SOS SS1 302 E7
St Augustines Cl BROX EN10 201 G6
St Augustines Ct HAR CO12 * 15 H7
St Augustines Dr BROX EN10 201 G6
St Augustine's Gdn IPSE IP3 55 H2
St Augustine's Rd BELV DA17 326 C7
St Augustines Wy
CHLM/WR CM1 194 B7
St Austell Cl KESG IP5 49 M7
St Austell Rd COLN CO4 108 A2
St Austin's La HAR CO12 15 L3
St Awdry's Rd BARK IG11 309 G4
St Barbara's Rd COLS CO2 129 G1
St Barnabas Rd SWFD E18 267 L7
WALTH E17 284 D4
St Barnabas Ter HOM E9 306 A2
St Bartholomew Cl COLN CO4 107 M2
St Bartholomews La
SUD CO10 20 B2
St Bartholomew's Rd
EHAM E6 308 B5
St Benedict's Av GVE DA12 338 B8
St Benet's Rd SOSN SS2 301 J2
St Bernard Rd COLN CO4 108 A3
St Bernard's Rd EHAM E6 308 A5
St Botolph Rd GVW DA11 337 G8
St Botolph's Church Wk
COL CO1 * 8 D8
St Botolph's St COL CO1 8 D7
St Botolph's Ter
WOTN CO14 * 137 M1
St Botolph's Wy HVHL CB9 34 C5
St Bride Ct COLN CO4 9 L1
St Brides Cl ERITHM DA18 326 A5
St Catharine's Rd BROX EN10 201 H5
St Catherines Cl COLS CO2 129 G4
WICKE SS11 261 J5
St Catherine's Ct CHTY IP2 53 K4
St Catherines Rd CHING E4 266 D1
CHLM/WR CM1 4 A4
SUD CO10 42 F2
St Cecilia Rd CDW/CHF RM16 331 L3
St Chads Cl LAIN SS15 276 F6
St Chad's Dr GVE DA12 338 B8
St Chad's Gdns CHDH RM6 288 B5
St Chad's Rd CHDH RM6 288 B4
TIL RM18 331 K7
St Charles Dr WICKE SS11 261 H6
St Charles Rd BRW CM14 273 L1
St Christopher Rd COLN CO4 9 L1
St Christophers Cl CVI SS8 320 A1
St Christophers Wy COS CO15 182 C6
St Clair Cl CLAY IG5 268 C8
COS CO15 159 J5
St Clair Rd PLSTW E13 307 L6
St Clair's Dr RCOS CO16 157 L8
St Clair's Rd RCOS CO16 157 L8
St Clare Dr COLW CO3 106 D6
St Clare Meadow RCFD SS4 283 J2
St Clare Rd COLW CO3 106 D7
St Clement Rd COLN CO4 108 A3
St Clements GTDUN CM6 74 D3
St Clement's Av LOS SS9 300 B3
WTHK RM20 335 K1
St Clements Church La
IPNE IP4 * 17 H6
St Clements Cl GVW DA11 * 337 J8
HOC/HUL SS5 282 D1
SBF/HAD SS7 * 279 M8
St Clements Ct PUR RM19 328 D7
St Clement's Crs
SBF/HAD SS7 280 A8
St Clement's Dr LOS SS9 300 B2
St Clement's Rd SBF/HAD SS7 279 M8
WTHK RM20 335 M2
St Cleres Crs WICKE SS11 261 J6
St Cleres Hall La RCOS CO16 181 L3
St Cleres Wy RCHLM CM3 212 A7
St Columba's Cl GVE DA12 338 B8
St Columb Ct COLN CO4 107 M3
St Cross Ct HOD EN11 201 H5
St Cuthberts Rd HOD EN11 185 K8
St Cyrus Rd COLN CO4 108 A3
St Davids Cl COLN CO4 9 K6
St David's Dr BROX EN10 201 G5
SBF/HAD SS7 299 K2
St Davids Ms BOW E3 306 B7
St David's Rd IPSE IP3 55 G2
VGE SS16 294 E1
St Davids Sq POP/IOD E14 322 E8
St Davids Ter LOS SS9 299 K2
St David's Wy WICKE SS11 261 H6
St Denis Cl HAR CO12 70 F4
St Dominic Rd COLN CO4 9 L1
St Dunstan's Dr GVE DA12 338 B8
St Dunstans Rd FSTGT E7 307 L3
WARE SG12 186 E1
St Edith's Cl BCAYW CM12 258 D4
St Ediths La BCAYW CM12 258 D4
St Edmunds Cl ABYW SE2 326 A5
HAR CO12 70 F4
SOSN SS2 301 M2
St Edmund's Ct COLN CO4 9 J5
St Edmund's Flds GTDUN CM6 117 H3
St Edmund's Hl SUD CO10 359 N3
St Edmunds La BURES CO8 359 Q8
GTDUN CM6 117 H3
St Edmund's Pl IP IP1 48 B5
St Edmunds Rd DART DA1 334 C6
FX IP11 11 H6
IL IG1 286 C4
IP IP1 48 A5
St Edmund's Wy HLWE CM17 188 D5
St Edmund Wy BURES CO8 359 R8
RCOLE CO7 64 A6
SUD CO10 41 G6
St Edwards Wy ROM RM1 289 H2
St Egberts Wy CHING E4 248 F8
St Elmos Rd
BERM/RHTH SE16 322 B5
St Erkenwald Ms BARK IG11 309 G5
St Erkenwald Rd BARK IG11 309 G5
St Fabian's Dr CHLM/WR CM1 209 H1
St Faith Rd COLN CO4 9 L1
St Fidelis' Rd ERITH DA8 327 G7
St Fillan Rd COLN CO4 9 L2
St Francis Ct IP IP1 * 16 E5
St Francis Wy
CDW/CHF RM16 331 M3
IL IG1 309 G1
St Gabriel's Cl WAN E11 285 L6
St Gabriels Ct PIT SS13 278 E8
St George's Av EMPK RM11 290 C5
FSTGT E7 307 L4
GRAYS RM17 330 F3
HAR CO12 15 G9
St Georges Cl BRWN CM15 383 Q9
MAL CM9 215 H2
RCOLE CO7 110 B4
THMD SE28 326 A2
St George's Dr WOS/PRIT SS0 301 H2
St George's La SBN/FI SS3 303 J7
St Georges Ms
BERM/RHTH SE16 322 C7
St George's Park Av
WOS/PRIT SS0 300 E3
St Georges Rd DAGW RM9 310 C1
EN EN1 232 A8
FSTGT E7 307 L4
FX IP11 63 H7
IL IG1 286 C5
LEY E10 284 F8
St George's Sq FSTGT E7 307 L4
GVW DA11 * 337 L4
St George's St IP IP1 16 E3
St Georges Ter FX IP11 * 63 H7
St Georges Wk SBF/HAD SS7 * 279 L7
St Giles Av DAGE RM10 310 E4
St Giles Cl CDW/CHF RM16 315 K5
DAGE RM10 310 E4
HSTD CO9 357 L7
MAL CM9 214 B3
St Giles Crs MAL CM9 214 B3
St Gotthards Av KESG IP5 51 H5
St Gregory's Ct SUD CO10 20 C5
St Gregory's Crs GVE DA12 338 B7
St Guiberts Rd CVI SS8 298 B8
St Helena Ms COLW CO3 107 G8
St Helena Rd
BERM/RHTH SE16 322 A7
COLW CO3 107 G8
St Helens Av COS CO15 159 K6
St Helen's Gn HAR CO12 15 L3
St Helen's La COL CO1 8 C6
St Helens Rd ERITHM DA18 326 A5
IL IG1 286 C4
WOS/PRIT SS0 18 C5
St Helen's St IPNE IP4 17 J4
St Helens Wk BCAYW CM12 258 C1
St Helier's Rd LEY E10 284 E4
St Hilda's Wy GVE DA12 338 B8
St Isidores KESG IP5 50 D6
St Ives Cl HARH RM3 272 C6
KESG IP5 49 M7
RCOS CO16 182 E2
St Ives Rd K/T/MI CO5 153 H7
St Ivians Dr GPK RM2 289 K1
St James' Av CHONG CM5 382 G4
SOS SS1 302 E7
St James Av East
SLH/COR SS17 317 H2
St James Av West
SLH/COR SS17 317 H2
St James Cl CVI SS8 320 A1
WOS/PRIT SS0 300 D2
St James Gdns
GNTH/NBYPK IG2 287 L2
WOS/PRIT SS0 300 D2
St James Ms BCAYW CM12 258 D3
POP/IOD E14 * 322 F6
St James Oaks GVW DA11 * 337 K5
St James Pk CHLM/WR CM1 209 G1
St James Pl DART DA1 334 A8
St James Rd BRTR CM7 99 J8
FSTGT E7 307 J2
VGE SS16 3 M7
St James's Av GVW DA11 337 K5
St James's Cl
WOOL/PLUM SE18 324 F8
St James's Ms WALTH E17 284 B3
St James's Rd BRW CM14 273 M2
GVW DA11 337 K5
St James's St GVW DA11 337 K4
HSTD CO9 356 G5
WALTH E17 284 B3
St James's Wk HOC/HUL SS5 * 263 M7
St James Wy BSF CM23 138 C4
St John Gdns COS CO15 159 H7
St Johns Av BRTR CM7 121 J3
BRW CM14 256 A7
CHLM/GWD CM2 5 G8
COL CO1 8 C8
HLWE CM17 188 D5
St John's Cl COLN CO4 108 A4
LAIN SS15 * 276 F6
RAIN RM13 311 K4
SAFWS CB11 30 A2
St John's Ct BKHH IG9 249 L8
FX IP11 11 K2
MAL CM9 385 M4
RCHLM CM3 * 388 D9
WOS/PRIT SS0 * 18 E7
St Johns Crs CVI SS8 320 A1
STSD CM24 115 M2
St Johns Dr RAYL SS6 280 C1
St John's Gn CHLM/WR CM1 208 E4
COLS CO2 8 C8
St John's La STSD CM24 115 M2
WARE SG12 185 H3
St Johns Ms SLH/COR SS17 317 J1
St Johns Pl BCAYE CM11 259 L1
St John's Rd BARK IG11 309 H5
BCAYE CM11 258 E2
CAN/RD E16 323 K2
CDW/CHF RM16 331 L4
CHING E4 266 E2
CHLM/GWD CM2 5 G7
CHLM/WR CM1 208 E4
COLN CO4 108 A2
COS CO15 6 F1
CRW RM5 270 F4
EHAM E6 308 B5
EPP CM16 220 A8
ERITH DA8 327 G8
GNTH/NBYPK IG2 287 H5
GVE DA12 338 A5
IPNE IP4 48 F7
LOU IG10 250 C2
RCOLE CO7 130 F6
RCOS CO16 158 E8
RCOS CO16 182 A1
SBF/HAD SS7 298 F2
SBN/FI SS3 303 L2
STSD CM24 115 M2
WALTH E17 266 E8
WOS/PRIT SS0 18 C4
St John's St CBS CB2 22 A8
COL CO1 8 B8
MAL CM9 385 M4
St Johns Ter BRTR CM7 * 76 E3
FSTGT E7 307 L3
St Johns Wk HLWE CM17 188 D5
St John's Wy SLH/COR SS17 317 J1
St Joseph Rd COLN CO4 107 M2
St Jude Gdns COLN CO4 108 A3

St Judes Cl COLN CO4 9 M1
St Julian Gv COL CO1 8 E8
St Katherines Rd
ERITHM DA18 326 A5
St Kilda's Rd BRWN CM15 255 L7
St Laurence Dr BROX EN10 216 F1
St Lawrence Dr BOC CM0 389 L1
St Lawrence Gdns ING CM4 * 222 B5
LOS SS9 282 B7
St Lawrence Hl BOC CM0 389 P4
St Lawrence Rd BOC CM0 390 A4
COLN CO4 108 A3
UPMR RM14 290 F7
St Lawrence St POP/IOD E14 322 F4
St Lawrence Wy KESG IP5 50 A5
St Leonards Av CHING E4 267 G5
St Leonards Cl GRAYS RM17 330 C5
SAFWS CB11 351 P10
St Leonards Gdns IL IG1 308 F2
St Leonard's Rd COL CO1 9 J9
IPSE IP3 55 G2
POP/IOD E14 322 F2
SOS SS1 19 J6
WAB EN9 217 L2
St Leonard's St BOW E3 306 E7
St Leonards Ter COL CO1 * 9 J9
St Leonards Wy EMPK RM11 289 L6
St Lucia Dr SRTFD E15 307 J5
St Luke's Av IL IG1 308 E2
St Luke's Cha K/T/MI CO5 174 A1
St Luke's Cl COLN CO4 108 A3
CVI SS8 320 A1
LAIN SS15 276 F6
St Luke's Rd SOSN SS2 301 M2
St Luke's Sq CAN/RD E16 323 J2
St Margarets BARK IG11 309 G5
St Margaret's Av
SLH/COR SS17 316 F5
St Margaret's Crs GVE DA12 338 B8
St Margaret's Gv WAN E11 285 J8
St Margarets Pln IP IP1 16 F3
St Margaret's Rd
CHLM/GWD CM2 210 B2
MNPK E12 285 M7
WARE SG12 185 H7
St Margaret's St IPNE IP4 17 G3
St Margaret's Ter
WOOL/PLUM SE18 324 F8
St Mark Dr COLN CO4 108 A3
St Mark's Av GVW DA11 337 H5
St Mark's Fld RCFD SS4 283 J3
St Marks Ga HOM E9 306 C4
St Marks Rd COS CO15 6 E3
CVI SS8 320 A1
SBF/HAD SS7 298 F2
St Martin's Av EHAM E6 308 A6
St Martins Cl COS CO15 6 E4
ERITHM DA18 326 A5
GTDUN CM6 379 K6
RAYL SS6 280 F5
RBRW/HUT CM13 * 256 F4
SBF/HAD SS7 279 L6
St Martins Ct KESG IP5 50 D6
St Martins Gn FX IP11 61 M5
St Martin's Rd DART DA1 334 C8
St Martins Sq BSDN SS14 2 E6
St Mary Rd WALTH E17 284 E2
St Marys BARK IG11 309 G6
St Mary's Ap MNPK E12 308 C2
St Mary's Av BCAYW CM12 258 D3
BRWN CM15 256 D1
WAN E11 285 L4
St Mary's Cl BRTR CM7 98 E6
CHLM/GWD CM2 210 C7
FX IP11 62 A6
GRAYS RM17 331 G5
GVE DA12 337 M7
RIPW IP8 46 F4
SBF/HAD SS7 * 298 A4
SBN/FI SS3 303 G4
SUD CO10 21 J1
St Mary's Crs FX IP11 62 D7
PIT SS13 278 F6
St Mary's Dr SBF/HAD SS7 298 B4
STSD CM24 374 A7
St Mary's Flds COLW CO3 8 A6
St Mary's La MAL CM9 214 E3
UPMR RM14 290 D7
UPMR RM14 291 K7
UPMR RM14 292 C1
St Marys Md CHLM/WR CM1 * 193 K4
St Marys Ms MAL CM9 * 385 N3
St Marys Pk KIR/NAC IP10 56 F5
St Mary's Pl GTDUN CM6 118 A6
St Mary's Rd BOC CM0 393 L7
BRTR CM7 121 L2
CBS CB2 22 C2
CDW/CHF RM16 331 L3
CHES/WCR EN8 216 D7
COS CO15 6 E4
FOS CO13 137 K4
GRH DA9 335 H7
IL IG1 286 F7
IPNE IP4 17 L3
K/T/MI CO5 148 F3
LEY E10 284 F8
PLSTW E13 307 L6
RCOLE CO7 133 J8
SBF/HAD SS7 298 A5
SOSN SS2 301 J2
WICKW SS12 260 E8
WIT CM8 147 L6
St Mary St WOOL/PLUM SE18 324 C7
St Marys Vw SAFWN CB10 28 B5
St Mary's Wk HVHL CB9 344 A7
St Marys Wy CHIG IG7 268 D4
NHMKT IP6 48 E1
St Matthew's Cl RAIN RM13 311 K4
St Matthews Ct SRTFD E15 307 J4
St Matthew's St IP IP1 16 D3
St Mellion Cl THMD SE28 326 A2
St Michaels Av PIT SS13 296 E1
St Michael's Cha RCOLW CO6 127 G3
St Michaels Cl CAN/RD E16 324 A1
ERITHM DA18 * 326 A5
HLW CM20 13 K5
KESG IP5 49 M7
RCHLM CM3 231 K8
SOCK/AV RM15 328 F3
St Michaels Ct BRTR CM7 * 121 J3
MGTR CO11 91 G1
St Michael's Dr
CHLM/WR CM1 191 K8
St Michael's La BRTR CM7 121 J3
St Michael's Rd BROX EN10 201 G6
BRTR CM7 121 J3
CDW/CHF RM16 331 L4
CHLM/GWD CM2 5 G8
COLS CO2 128 F4
CVI SS8 320 A2
HAR CO12 71 G3
RCOS CO16 135 J3
SBF/HAD SS7 281 J7
St Mildreds Rd CHLM/GWD CM2 5 G8
St Monance Wy COLN CO4 9 L1
St Nazaire Rd CHLM/WR CM1 193 H7
St Neots Cl COLN CO4 9 M1
St Neot's Rd HARH RM3 272 C6
St Nicholas Av HCH RM12 289 K8
St Nicholas Cl WIT CM8 171 J1
St Nicholas Fld BSF CM23 92 C1
St Nicholas Gv
RBRW/HUT CM13 256 F8
St Nicholas La LAIN SS15 277 G6
St Nicholas Pl LOU IG10 250 D4
St Nicholas Rd BOC CM0 390 D5
WIT CM8 171 J1
WOOL/PLUM SE18 325 J8
St Nicholas Rbt HAR CO12 14 C6
St Nicholas St COL CO1 8 D7
IP IP1 16 E5
St Nicholas Wy RCOLW CO6 124 D2
St Olave's Rd EHAM E6 308 D5
KESG IP5 50 B5
St Omar Cl WICKW SS12 261 G7
St Osyth Cl CHTY IP2 53 L5
St Osyth Rd COS CO15 6 A5
RCOLE CO7 132 A6
RCOS CO16 158 E5
St Osyth Rd East RCOS CO16 158 F4
St Osyth Rd West RCOS CO16 158 E4
St Patrick's Pl
CDW/CHF RM16 331 L3
St Paul's Av
BERM/RHTH SE16 * 322 A4
St Paul's Cl CHARL SE7 324 A8
SOCK/AV RM15 328 F3
SWCM DA10 336 B5
St Paul's Dr SRTFD E15 307 G2
St Pauls Gdns BCAYW CM12 258 D1
St Paul's Pl SOCK/AV RM15 328 F3
St Pauls Rd BARK IG11 308 F5
COL CO1 8 A4
COS CO15 7 J6
CVI SS8 320 A1
St Paul's Wy POP/IOD E14 322 C1
WAB EN9 * 233 L3
St Peter's Av CHONG CM5 380 G12
MAL CM9 214 C3
WALTH E17 285 H2
St Peter's Cl BRTR CM7 121 J2
GNTH/NBYPK IG2 287 H2
MAL CM9 384 B7
SWCM DA10 336 C5
St Peter's Ct BOC CM0 390 D1
COL CO1 * 8 B5
SUD CO10 * 20 C7
St Peters Fld BOC CM0 393 K6
St Peter's-in-the-Fields
BRTR CM7 121 J1
St Peter's Pavement
BSDN SS14 278 C4
St Peter's Rd BRTR CM7 121 J1
BRW CM14 273 L3
CDW/CHF RM16 331 L3
CHLM/WR CM1 4 A4
CVI SS8 320 A1
HOC/HUL SS5 263 L6
K/T/MI CO5 177 L7
RCOLW CO6 124 E2
St Peter's St CBS CB2 340 E1
COL CO1 8 B5
IPNE IP4 16 F5
St Peters Ter WICKW SS12 260 F6
St Peters Vw HSTD CO9 356 E8
St Peters Wk BCAYW CM12 258 C1
BRTR CM7 121 J2
St Peter's Wy BOC CM0 390 F4
CHLM/GWD CM2 226 D8
CHONG CM5 383 J2
ING CM4 222 B5
ING CM4 240 F1
ING CM4 241 K3
RCHLM CM3 229 H4
RCHLM CM3 388 D5
St Quintin Rd PLSTW E13 307 L7
St Ronans Crs WFD IG8 267 K6
St Runwald St COL CO1 8 C6
St Saviour Cl COLN CO4 9 M1
Saints Dr FSTGT E7 308 A2
St Stephen's Av WALTH E17 284 F3
St Stephen's Cl WALTH E17 284 E3
St Stephens Crs
RBRW/HUT CM13 256 D7
St Stephen's Rd BOW E3 306 C6
EHAM E6 307 M4
PEND EN3 232 E7
RCHLM CM3 246 C1
WALTH E17 284 E3
Saint's Wk CDW/CHF RM16 331 M3
St Teresa's Cl BSDN SS14 278 C7
St Teresa Wk CDW/CHF RM16 331 L3
St Thomas Cl COLN CO4 108 B3
St Thomas Gdns IL IG1 308 F3
St Thomas Rd BELV DA17 326 F5
BRW CM14 256 A5
CAN/RD E16 323 K2
GVW DA11 * 337 H6
RCFD SS4 264 D1
St Thomas's Av GVW DA11 337 L7
St Thomas's Cl WAB EN9 234 C3
St Thomas's Pl GRAYS RM17 330 F5
St Valery RBSF CM22 377 K2
St Vincent Cha BRTR CM7 99 L8
St Vincent Rd COS CO15 183 G4
St Vincents Av DART DA1 334 D7
St Vincents Rd CHLM/GWD CM2 5 G8
DART DA1 334 D8
WOS/PRIT SS0 18 D6
St Winefride's Av MNPK E12 308 C2
St Winifred's Cl CHIG IG7 268 F4
Sainty Cl RCOLE CO7 * 130 F5
Sairard Cl LOS SS9 282 A6
Sairard Gdns LOS SS9 282 A6
Sakins Cft HLWS CM18 204 A4
Saladin Dr PUR RM19 328 D7
Salamons Wy RAIN RM13 327 H2
Salary Cl COLN CO4 108 B4
Salcombe Dr CHDH RM6 288 C4
Salcombe Rd BRTR CM7 121 M4
WALTH E17 284 C5
Salcott Crs WICKW SS12 261 H6
Salcott St MAL CM9 175 L5
Salehurst Rd IPSE IP3 55 K2
Salem Pl GVW DA11 337 G5
Salerno Crs COLS CO2 128 F3
Salerno Wy CHLM/WR CM1 193 H7
Salesbury Dr BCAYE CM11 259 G3
Salforal Cl RCHLM CM3 243 L4
Salhouse Cl THMD SE28 325 M2
Saling Gn LAIN SS15 277 J3
Salisbury Av BARK IG11 309 G4
COLW CO3 107 G7
SLH/COR SS17 317 G4
WOS/PRIT SS0 18 D3
Salisbury Cl BSF CM23 139 G4
Salisbury Crs CHES/WCR EN8 232 E2
Salisbury Rd CHING E4 266 D2
COS CO15 160 A4
DAGE RM10 310 E3
FSTGT E7 307 K3
GDMY/SEVK IG3 287 H7
GPK RM2 289 L3
GRAYS RM17 330 F5
GVW DA11 337 J6
HOD EN11 201 K2
IPSE IP3 54 F2
LEY E10 284 F7
LOS SS9 299 M4
MNPK E12 308 A2
PEND EN3 233 G7
WALTH E17 284 F3
Salisbury Vls RIPS/CAP IP9 * 66 D2
Salix Rd GRAYS RM17 331 G5
Sallows Cl IP IP1 47 L6
Sally Murray Cl MNPK E12 308 D1
Salmen Rd PLSTW E13 307 J6
Salmon Cl COLW CO3 128 C1
Salmond's Gv
RBRW/HUT CM13 256 F8
Salmon La POP/IOD E14 322 B2
Salmon Rd BELV DA17 326 D8
DART DA1 334 C5
Salmon's La RCOLW CO6 125 K1
Salmon St POP/IOD E14 * 322 C2
Salomons Rd PLSTW E13 323 M1
Salop Rd WALTH E17 284 A4
Saltash Rd BARK/HLT IG6 269 G6
Saltcoats RCHLM CM3 245 G5
Saltcote Maltings MAL CM9 215 H1
Salter Hall Ms SUD CO10 20 B7
Salter Pl CHLM/GWD CM2 210 C3
Salter Rd BERM/RHTH SE16 322 B5
Salters BSF CM23 138 D5
Salter's Meadow MAL CM9 384 G1
Salters Rd WALTH E17 285 G2
Salter St POP/IOD E14 322 D3
Saltford Cl ERITH DA8 327 H8
Salthouse La IPNE IP4 17 G6
The Saltings SBF/HAD SS7 299 G2
Saltley Cl EHAM E6 324 B2
Salt's Gn CHLM/WR CM1 191 G3
Saltwell St POP/IOD E14 322 D3
Salvia Cl RCOS CO16 6 B3
Salway Cl WFD IG8 267 K6
Salway Pl SRTFD E15 307 G3
Salway Rd SRTFD E15 307 G3
Salwey Crs BROX EN10 201 G6
Samantha Cl WALTH E17 284 C5
Sam Bartram Cl CHARL SE7 323 M8
Samford Cl RIPS/CAP IP9 364 G6
Samford Pl RIPW IP8 47 G7
Samian Cl MAL CM9 198 C8
Samphire Cl WIT CM8 171 G2
Samphire Ct GRAYS RM17 331 H5
Sampson Cl BELV DA17 326 A6
Sampson Dr SUD CO10 43 G1
Sampson's La K/T/MI CO5 177 H1
Samsons Cl RCOLE CO7 156 B5
Samson's Rd RCOLE CO7 156 B4
Samson St PLSTW E13 307 M6
Samuel Cl WOOL/PLUM SE18 324 B7
Samuel Ct IPNE IP4 17 H4
Samuel Mnr CHLM/GWD CM2 210 C2
Samuel Rd VGE SS16 294 E1
Samuels Dr SOS SS1 302 E5
Samuel St WOOL/PLUM SE18 324 C7
Sanctuary Gdn SLH/COR SS17 317 H3
Sanctuary Rd LOS SS9 299 K2
Sandal St SRTFD E15 307 H5
Sandalwood Cl WCHPL E1 306 B8
Sandbach Pl
WOOL/PLUM SE18 324 F8
Sandbanks SBF/HAD SS7 299 G3
Sandcliff Rd ERITH DA8 327 G7
Sanderling Gdns MAL CM9 198 F8
Sanderlings SBF/HAD SS7 297 M3
Sanderling Wy GRH DA9 335 K7
Sanders Dr COLW CO3 106 E6
Sanderson Cl
RBRW/HUT CM13 * 274 F8
Sanderson Ms COL CO1 * 8 C6
K/T/MI CO5 130 C5
Sanders Rd CVI SS8 298 D7
Sanderstead Rd LEY E10 284 B6
Sandford Av LOU IG10 250 F3
Sandford Cl RCOLE CO7 130 F5
Sandford Mill Rd
CHLM/GWD CM2 210 D3
Sandford Rd CHLM/GWD CM2 5 M2
EHAM E6 308 C7
Sandgate Cl ROMW/RG RM7 288 F5
Sandhill Rd LOS SS9 281 L5
Sandhurst CVI SS8 319 M2
Sandhurst Av IPSE IP3 17 M8
Sandhurst Cl LOS SS9 300 C1
Sandhurst Crs LOS SS9 300 C1
Sandhurst Dr GDMY/SEVK IG3 309 J1
Sandhurst Rd TIL RM18 331 M8
Sandleigh Rd LOS SS9 300 D4
Sandle Rd BSF CM23 139 H2
Sandling Crs IPNE IP4 49 K8
Sandmartin Crs COLW CO3 127 M1
Sandon Br CHLM/GWD CM2 211 J6
Sandon Brook Pl
CHLM/GWD CM2 211 H5
Sandon Cl BSDN SS14 278 C8
RCFD SS4 283 G2
RCOLW CO6 86 F6
Sandon Ct BSDN SS14 * 278 C8
Sandon Hall Bridleway
CHLM/GWD CM2 227 G2
Sandon Hl RCHLM CM3 142 D6
Sandon Pl CHONG CM5 382 H4
Sandon Rd BSDN SS14 278 C8
CHES/WCR EN8 216 D8
Sandown Av DAGE RM10 310 F3
HCH RM12 290 A7
WOS/PRIT SS0 300 E3
Sandown Cl COS CO15 159 K5
WICKE SS11 261 K6
Sandown Ct DAGE RM10 310 F3
Sandown Rd CDW/CHF RM16 316 B5
IP IP1 47 M2
SBF/HAD SS7 280 E6
WICKE SS11 261 K6
Sandpiper Cl
BERM/RHTH SE16 322 C5
COLN CO4 108 D6
GRH DA9 335 K7
HVHL CB9 34 E6
MAL CM9 198 F8
SBN/FI SS3 303 H5
WALTH E17 266 A6
Sandpiper Rd CHTY IP2 53 K3
The Sandpipers GVE DA12 338 A7
Sandpiper Ter CLAY IG5 * 286 E1
Sandpit Cl IPNE IP4 49 L8
Sandpit La BOC CM0 393 M8
BRW CM14 255 J6
Sandpit Pl CHARL SE7 324 B8
Sandpit Rd SBN/FI SS3 303 L5
Sandringham Av
HLWW/ROY CM19 202 F1
HOC/HUL SS5 263 M7
Sandringham Cl CHTY IP2 53 L3
SLH/COR SS17 317 H2
Sandringham Dr COLS CO2 129 K1
Sandringham Gdns
BARK/HLT IG6 286 F1
Sandringham Pl
CHLM/GWD CM2 5 K3
Sandringham Rd BARK IG11 309 J3
BRWN CM15 255 L5
FSTGT E7 307 M2
LAIN SS15 2 A1
LEY E10 285 G5
SOS SS1 302 A5
Sandringham Wy
CHES/WCR EN8 232 D4
Sandstone La CAN/RD E16 323 M3
Sands Wy WFD IG8 268 C5
Sandwich Cl BRTR CM7 99 H7
Sandwich Rd COS CO15 182 F5
RCOLE CO7 156 C5
Sandy Bank Rd GVE DA12 337 L6
Sandy Cl FX IP11 62 A3
Sandy Hl RCOLW CO6 85 G1
Sandy Hill Av
WOOL/PLUM SE18 324 E8
Sandyhill La IPSE IP3 54 D4
Sandy Hill La
WOOL/PLUM SE18 324 E7
Sandyhill Rd IL IG1 308 E1
Sandy Hill Rd
WOOL/PLUM SE18 324 E8
Sandy La CDW/CHF RM16 331 L5
FRAM/WMKT IP13 50 C1
RDART DA2 336 A8
SOCK/AV RM15 328 D3
SUD CO10 44 C4
WDBR IP12 51 K1
WTHK RM20 335 L1
San Juan Dr CDW/CHF RM16 329 M7
San Marcos Dr
CDW/CHF RM16 329 M8
San Remo Pde WOS/PRIT SS0 18 C7
San Remo Rd CVI SS8 321 G2
Sansom Rd WAN E11 * 285 J7
Santiago Wy WTHK RM20 330 A4
Sapling Pl IPNE IP4 49 K8
Sappers Cl SBW CM21 163 G7
Sapphire Cl BCTR RM8 287 M6
Sapphire Rd DEPT SE8 322 B7
Saracen St POP/IOD E14 322 D2
Sara Crs GRH DA9 335 K6
Saran Ct RCOLE CO7 130 D3
Sarcel BRTR CM77 100 F7
Sargeant Cl COLS CO2 129 L2
Sark Gv WICKW SS12 261 J8
Sarre Av HCH RM12 311 M3
Sarre Wy RCOLE CO7 156 B5
Sarum Ter BOW E3 * 306 C8
Sassoon Wy MAL CM9 214 D4
Satanita Cl CAN/RD E16 324 A2
Satanita Rd WOS/PRIT SS0 300 F5
Saul's Av WIT CM8 171 K5
Sauls Bridge Cl WIT CM8 171 K5
Sauls Gn WAN E11 285 H8
Saunders Av BRTR CM7 121 G1
Saunders Cl CHES/WCR EN8 216 D6
GVW DA11 337 H7
IL IG1 287 G6
POP/IOD E14 * 322 C3
Saunders Ness Rd
POP/IOD E14 323 G7
Saunders Rd
WOOL/PLUM SE18 325 J8
Saunders Wy THMD SE28 325 L3
Saunton Rd HCH RM12 289 K7
Savage Gdns EHAM E6 324 C2
Savernake Rd CHLM/WR CM1 4 B6
Saville Cl SAFWS CB11 72 C5
Saville Rd CAN/RD E16 324 B4
CHDH RM6 288 C4
The Savilles SUD CO10 * 346 H4
Saville St WOTN CO14 369 M12
Savill Rd COLS CO2 129 M3
Savill Rw WFD IG8 267 J5
Savoy Cl SRTFD E15 307 H5
VGE SS16 276 D8
Savoy Wd EPP CM16 203 H7
Sawbridgeworth Rd
SBW CM21 163 K6
Sawells BROX EN10 201 G7
Sawkins Av CHLM/GWD CM2 210 A7
Sawkins Cl CHLM/GWD CM2 210 A7
Sawkins Gdns
CHLM/GWD CM2 210 A7
Sawmill La KIR/NAC IP10 56 A7
Sawney Brook
CHLM/WR CM1 208 D4
Sawpit La BSF CM23 92 E2
Sawston Cl CHTY IP2 53 M3
Sawston Rd CBS CB2 22 F1
Sawyers Cl RIPS/CAP IP9 58 D4
Sawyers Gv BRWN CM15 256 A4
Sawyer's Hall La BRWN CM15 255 M7
Sawyer's Rd MAL CM9 199 M1
Saxham Rd BARK IG11 309 H5
Saxlingham Rd CHING E4 267 G2
Saxmundham Wy RCOS CO16 182 D2
Saxon Bank BRTR CM7 121 L3
Saxon Cl COLW CO3 128 C1
FX IP11 63 J7
GVW DA11 336 F8
HARH RM3 272 C8
HSTD CO9 81 J3
RAYL SS6 263 H8
RBRW/HUT CM13 256 D6
WALTH E17 284 D5
WICKE SS11 261 H4
Saxon Ct MAL CM9 * 214 D2
Saxon Dr WIT CM8 171 H2
Saxon Gdns SBN/FI SS3 302 F6
Saxon La RIPW IP8 52 C5
Saxon Rd BOW E3 306 C6
EHAM E6 308 C8
IL IG1 308 E3
Saxon Shore Wy GVE DA12 337 M4
HOO/HM ME3 339 K2
Saxonville SBF/HAD SS7 297 L1
Saxon Wy CHLM/WR CM1 193 L6
COS CO15 160 C3
MAL CM9 214 E4
SAFWN CB10 351 R4
SBF/HAD SS7 297 M3
Sayer Cl GRH DA9 335 K7
Sayers SBF/HAD SS7 280 D7
Sayesbury Av SBW CM21 162 F7
Sayesbury Rd SBW CM21 162 F7
Sayes Court St DEPT SE8 322 C8
Sayes Gdns SBW CM21 163 G7
Saywell Brook
CHLM/GWD CM2 210 D3
Scalby Rd BOC CM0 393 K3
Scaldhurst PIT SS13 278 F5
Scarborough Rd BOC CM0 393 K3
LOS SS9 300 B3
WAN E11 285 G6
Scarfe Wy COLN CO4 108 B7
Scarletts BSDN SS14 3 J2
Scarletts Cl WIT CM8 171 K6
Scarletts Rd COL CO1 107 M8
Scawen Rd DEPT SE8 322 B8
Sceptre Cl MAL CM9 385 N3
Schneider Cl FX IP11 10 E9
Scholars Rd CHING E4 248 F8
School Cha HSTD CO9 81 H5
School Cl RIPS/CAP IP9 58 D4
School Crs HVHL CB9 35 K3
Schoolfield Rd WTHK RM20 335 K1
School Green La EPP CM16 221 K3
School Hl COLS CO2 151 K1
RIPW IP8 52 E5
Schoolhouse La WAP E1W * 322 A3
School Houses
CDW/CHF RM16 * 315 K5
School La CDW/CHF RM16 315 K5
CHIG IG7 269 J3
CHLM/WR CM1 164 E2
CHLM/WR CM1 193 K4
CHONG CM5 205 L3
CHONG CM5 379 N12
COLS CO2 151 K2
GTDUN CM6 375 L7
HLW CM20 13 J1
HOO/HM ME3 339 M7
HVHL CB9 34 A5
ING CM4 241 G3
K/T/MI CO5 176 B1
MGTR CO11 65 G4
MGTR CO11 90 D3
MGTR CO11 91 J1
RBRW/HUT CM13 274 F1
RBSF CM22 372 G12
RCHLM CM3 144 B5
RCOLE CO7 132 D5
RCOLE CO7 363 L7
RCOLE CO7 363 N10
RCOLE CO7 363 Q6
RCOLW CO6 86 D3
RCOLW CO6 106 B1
RCOLW CO6 361 J12
ROY SG8 348 F10
SAFWS CB11 350 B6
SAFWS CB11 351 N12
SBF/HAD SS7 298 A5
SUD CO10 40 F8
WDBR IP12 51 H2
WICKW SS12 279 K3
School Rd BCAYE CM11 242 C8
BCAYW CM12 258 E5
BRTR CM77 120 B6
BRWN CM15 383 M11
CHLM/WR CM1 164 F8
CHONG CM5 382 A4
COLN CO4 88 B1
COLS CO2 129 K3
DAGE RM10 310 D5
FOS CO13 137 H4
GVE DA12 337 M8
HAR CO12 113 M2
HSTD CO9 346 E10
HSTD CO9 356 D10
HSTD CO9 356 E9
HSTD CO9 357 Q4
HSTD CO9 357 Q9
HVHL CB9 35 K3
K/T/MI CO5 149 M4
MAL CM9 198 E2
MAL CM9 199 L3
MNPK E12 308 C1
RCOLE CO7 109 K8
RCOLW CO6 127 G1
RCOLW CO6 127 G3
RCOLW CO6 361 J12
RCOS CO16 112 B8
RIPS/CAP IP9 67 G5
RIPS/CAP IP9 364 A4
SUD CO10 39 H7
WIT CM8 147 H2
WIT CM8 172 C8
School St RCOLW CO6 361 Q4
SAFWN CB10 341 L7
SUD CO10 20 C7
SUD CO10 42 A3
School Vw BRTR CM7 121 H3
School View Rd CHLM/WR CM1 4 D1
School Wk BRTR CM7 121 J2
School Wy BCTR RM8 287 L8
LOS SS9 300 C2
Schooner Cl BARK IG11 309 L7
POP/IOD E14 323 G6
Schooner Ct GRH DA9 334 F6
Schreiber Rd IPNE IP4 49 G6
Scimitar Pk PIT SS13 279 G3
Scofield Ct SUD CO10 21 H8
Scopes Rd KESG IP5 50 B5
Scotland Green Rd PEND EN3 248 A5
Scotland Green Rd
North PEND EN3 248 A4
Scotland Rd BKHH IG9 249 M8
Scotland St RCOLW CO6 361 R4
Scott Av BRTR CM7 354 H12
WARE SG12 185 J5
Scott Cl BRTR CM7 121 K5
Scott Dr COLW CO3 106 C7
WICKW SS12 261 G8
Scottes La BCTR RM8 288 A6
Scott Rd BSF CM23 138 F3
CDW/CHF RM16 331 K3
IPSE IP3 55 G4
Scotts Cl HCH RM12 311 M2
WARE SG12 184 E1
Scotts Hall Rd RCFD SS4 396 A1
Scotts Pas
WOOL/PLUM SE18 * 324 E7
Scott's Rd LEY E10 284 F6
WARE SG12 184 E1
Scoulding Rd CAN/RD E16 323 J2
Scouler St POP/IOD E14 323 G3
Scraley Rd MAL CM9 198 F7
Scratton Rd SLH/COR SS17 317 G3
SOS SS1 18 F6
Scrattons Ter BARK IG11 310 A6
Scrip's Rd RCOLW CO6 124 D6
Scrivener Dr RIPW IP8 53 H3
Scrub La SBF/HAD SS7 299 H2
Scrub Ri BCAYW CM12 258 C5
Scurvy Hall La RCHLM CM3 167 L4
Scylla Cl MAL CM9 198 F7
Scythe Wy COLW CO3 128 C1
Seaborough Rd
CDW/CHF RM16 331 M2
Seabrooke Ri GRAYS RM17 330 F5
Seabrook Gdns RCHLM CM3 195 J4
ROMW/RG RM7 288 D5
Seabrook Rd BCTR RM8 288 A8
CHLM/GWD CM2 210 D7
The Seabrooks SUD CO10 * 39 L2
Seaburn Cl RAIN RM13 311 H7
Sea Cornflower Wy
COS CO15 182 D6
Seacourt Rd ABYW SE2 326 A5
Sea Crs COS CO15 182 C7
Seafield Av MGTR CO11 91 L1
Seafield Rd HAR CO12 71 G3
Seafields Gdns COS CO15 159 M8
Seafields Rd COS CO15 159 M8
Sea Flowers Wy COS CO15 182 D6
Seaford Rd WALTH E17 284 E1
Seaforth Av SOSN SS2 301 M2
Seaforth Cl ROM RM1 271 H6
Seaforth Dr CHES/WCR EN8 232 E4
Seaforth Gdns WFD IG8 267 M4
Seaforth Gv SOSN SS2 302 A3
Seaforth Rd WOS/PRIT SS0 18 A6
Seager Pl BOW E3 322 C1
Seagers MAL CM9 198 E1
Sea Glebe Wy COS CO15 182 D6
Seagrave Cl WCHPL E1 * 322 A1
Seagry Rd WAN E11 285 K4
Seagull La CAN/RD E16 323 K3
Sea Holly Wy COS CO15 182 D7

Slough House Cl BRTR CM7 ...122 A4
Slough La RCOLE CO7 ...108 E7
  RCOLE CO7 ...109 G1
Slough Rd CHLM/WR CM1 ...164 E3
  MGTR CO11 ...64 F3
  RCHLM CM3 ...228 F3
Slushy La RIPS/CAP IP9 ...365 L10
Smaley La SUD CO10 ...42 F1
Smallbridge Entry
  BURES CO8 ...360 C9
Smallgains Av CVI SS8 ...321 C1
Small Gains La INC CM4 ...241 G5
Smallgains La INC CM4 ...241 G5
Smallholdings K/T/MI CO5 * ...148 F4
Smarden Cl BELV DA17 ...326 D8
Smart Cl HARH RM3 ...271 L7
Smarts Gn CHESW EN7 ...216 A4
Smarts Rd GVE DA12 ...337 L8
Smart St BETH E2 ...306 A7
  IPNE IP4 ...17 G6
Smart Av CVI SS8 ...320 D1
Smeaton Cl COLN CO4 ...87 M8
  WAB EN9 ...233 M8
Smeaton Rd PEND EN3 ...233 H7
  WFD IG8 ...268 C4
Smeed Rd BOW E3 ...306 D4
Smeetham Hall La SUD CO10 ...44 B3
Smith Cl BERM/RHTH SE16 ...322 A4
Smithers Cha RIPS/CAP IP9 ...58 D4
Smithers Dr CHLM/GWD CM2 ...210 D7
Smithies Rd ABYW SE2 ...325 L1
Smiths Av RCHLM CM3 ...388 D9
Smith's End La ROY SG8 ...348 E10
  COLS CO2 ...107 M8
Smiths Fld BRTR CM7 ...120 F3
Smiths Pl KESC IP5 ...50 C6
Smith St SBN/FI SS3 ...303 L1
Smugglers Whf GRH ...335 L7
Smyatts Cl BOC CM0 ...393 N2
Smythe Cl RCOS CO16 ...158 D1
Smythe Rd SUD CO10 ...241 G8
Smythe St POP/IOD E14 ...322 E6
Smythies Av COL CO1 ...8 F7
Snakes Hl BRW CM14 ...254 F5
Snakes La RBSF CM22 ...374 B3
  SOSN SS2 ...282 D8
Snakes La East WFD IG8 ...267 M5
Snakes La West WFD IG8 ...267 K5
Snape Cl RCOS CO16 ...182 D1
Snape Wy FOS CO13 * ...137 J2
Snaresbrook Rd WAN E11 ...285 J2
Sneating Hall La FOS CO13 ...136 B1
Snelling Av GVW DA11 ...337 J7
Snelling Gv CHLM/GWD CM2 ...210 C7
Sniveller's La K/T/MI CO5 * ...148 F6
Snoreham Gdns RCHLM CM3 ...231 K8
Snowberry Cl BRTR CM7 ...122 A1
Snowberry Gv COLS CO2 ...129 K2
Snowcroft RIPS/CAP IP9 ...58 D4
Snowdonia Cl PIT SS13 ...278 F5
Snowdon Rd CHTY IP2 ...54 A3
Snowdrop Cl BSF CM23 ...138 D3
  CHLM/WR CM1 ...194 B6
  WIT CM8 ...171 K1
Snow Hl SUD CO10 ...37 L4
Snow Hill La RCOLW CO6 ...362 L4
Snowshill Rd MNPK E12 ...308 B2
Soames Ms BRWN CM15 ...383 G7
Soane St IPNE IP4 ...17 H3
  PIT SS13 ...278 E5
Softwater La SBF/HAD SS7 ...299 G2
Soham Rd HAR CO10 * ...367 P12
The Soils HAR CO10 ...367 P12
Solar Wy PEND EN3 ...233 J4
Solebay St WCHPL E1 ...306 B6
Solent Rd PLSTW E13 ...307 K7
Solid La BRWN CM15 ...255 J1
Solway TIL RM18 ...332 F2
Somerby Cl BROX EN10 ...201 H7
Somerby Rd IG11 ...309 G4
Somerfield St
  BERM/RHTH SE16 ...322 A8
Somerford Wy
  BERM/RHTH SE16 ...322 B6
Somersby Gdns REDBR IG4 ...286 C3
Somerset Av RCFD SS4 ...283 H2
  WOS/PRIT SS0 ...300 E1
Somerset Cl COLS CO2 ...128 E2
  WFD IG8 ...267 K7
Somerset Crs WOS/PRIT SS0 ...300 F1
Somerset Gdns EMPK RM11 ...290 D6
  PIT SS13 ...278 E7
Somerset Pl CHLM/WR CM1 ...193 K6
Somerset Rd IPNE IP4 ...48 B7
  LAIN SS15 ...276 E7
  PEND EN3 ...233 H8
  SLH/COR SS17 ...332 D1
  WALTH E17 ...287 H3
Somerset Wy COS CO15 ...182 C4
Somersham Rd RIPW IP8 ...46 D1
Somers Rd COLW CO3 ...128 D1
  WALTH E17 ...287 H3
Somerton Av WOS/PRIT SS0 ...300 F1
Somerville Gdns LOS SS9 ...300 C5
Somerville Rd CHDH RM6 ...287 M3
  DART DA1 ...334 C4
Somme Rd COLS CO2 ...129 H1
Sommers Ct WARE SG12 * ...184 F1
Somnes Av CVI SS8 ...320 B7
Sonning Wy SBN/FI SS3 ...303 G4
Sonters Down RCHLM CM3 ...243 M8
Soper Cl CHING E4 ...266 C4
Soper Ms PEND EN3 ...233 H8
Sophia Rd CAN/RD E16 ...323 J3
  LEY E10 ...284 E6
Sophia Sq POP/IOD E14 ...322 B3
Sopwith Crs WICKE SS11 ...261 L2
Sorrel Cl CHTY IP2 ...53 L2
  COLN CO4 ...106 F3
  THMD SE28 ...325 K4
Sorrel Gdns EHAM E6 ...324 B1
Sorrel Gv BRTR CM77 ...121 K6
Sorrel Rd POP/IOD E14 ...323 G2
Sorrell Cl MAL CM9 ...384 B6
  RCHLM CM3 ...167 G2
The Sorrells SBF/HAD SS7 ...317 G4
The Sorrels SBF/HAD SS7 ...280 A6
Sorrel Wk ROM RM1 ...289 J1
South Access Rd LEY E10 ...284 A5
Southall Av BRW CM14 ...273 J4
Southborough Dr
  WOS/PRIT SS0 ...300 E3
Southborough Rd
  CHLM/GWD CM2 ...4 E7
Southbourne Gdns IL IG1 ...308 C1
  WOS/PRIT SS0 ...300 E1

Southbourne Gv
  HOC/HUL SS5 ...264 C7
  WICKW SS12 ...261 D5
  WOS/PRIT SS0 ...300 E1
Southbrook SBW CM21 ...162 F8
Southbrook Dr
  CHES/WCR EN8 ...216 A3
Southbury Cl HCH RM12 ...312 D1
South Charlton Mead La
  HOD EN11 ...201 K4
Southchurch Av SBN/FI SS3 ...303 K6
  SOS SS1 ...19 K5
Southchurch Bvd SOS SS1 ...302 B6
Southchurch Hall Cl SOS SS1 ...19 H5
Southchurch Rd EHAM E6 ...308 D4
  SOS SS1 ...19 H4
Southcliff SBF/HAD SS7 ...297 M1
  WOTN CO14 ...137 M2
Southcliff Pk COS CO15 ...7 M1
Southcliff Prom WOTN CO14 ...137 M2
South Cl DAGE RM10 ...310 D5
  HSTD CO9 ...81 H6
  IPNE IP4 ...48 D5
  RCOS CO16 ...181 J1
South Colne VGE SS16 ...3 M9
The South Colonnade
  POP/IOD E14 ...322 D4
Southcote Crs BSDN SS14 ...278 B5
Southcote Rd WALTH E17 ...284 A1
  WIT CM8 ...171 J1
Southcote Rw BSDN SS14 ...278 C5
South Countess Rd
  WALTH E17 ...284 C1
South Ct INC CM4 * ...239 M2
South Crs CAN/RD E16 ...307 C8
  SOSN SS2 ...283 G8
South Crockerford VGE SS16 ...296 B1
Southcroft Cl FOS CO13 ...136 F3
South Cross Rd BARK/HLT IG6 ...286 B1
Southdale CHIG IG7 ...269 G5
Southdown Crs
  GNTH/NBYPK IG2 ...287 H6
Southdown Rd EMPK RM11 ...289 L5
South Dr BRW CM14 ...256 A7
  GPK RM2 ...289 H1
Southend Arterial Rd
  EMPK RM11 ...290 B1
  LAIN SS15 ...276 A1
  RAYL SS6 ...280 D5
  RBRW/HUT CM13 ...291 G3
  WICKW SS12 ...279 M3
Southend La WAB EN9 ...234 C4
South End Rd RAIN RM13 ...311 K5
Southend Rd BCAYW CM12 ...258 A4
  CHLM/GWD CM2 ...210 A8
  EHAM E6 ...308 L4
  GRAYS RM17 ...350 F5
  MAL CM9 ...212 F8
  RCFD SS4 ...283 J6
  RCHLM CM3 ...227 G2
  REDBR IG4 ...286 B1
  SBN/FI SS3 ...302 F2
  SLH/COR SS17 ...317 G8
  WICKE SS11 ...261 L6
Southend Rd Main Rd
  HOC/HUL SS5 ...264 A8
Southend Rd North Circular
  WALTH E17 ...267 G7
Souther Cross Rd
  CHLM/WR CM1 ...165 G8
Southern Dr LOU IG10 ...250 C6
  RCHLM CM3 ...244 F6
Southern La BRW CM14 ...254 F5
Southernhay BSDN SS14 ...2 F7
  LOS SS9 ...282 A8
  LOU IG10 ...250 A5
South Esk Rd FSTGT E7 ...307 M3
Southey Cl MAL CM9 ...214 F7
Southey Wk TIL RM18 ...331 M5
Southfalls Rd CVI SS8 ...321 J2
Southfield Cha RCAYW CM12 * ...276 B4
Southfield Cl CDW/CHF RM16 ...329 M8
Southfield Dr SBF/HAD SS7 ...281 M8
Southfield Rd CHES/WCR EN8 ...232 F2
  HOD EN11 ...201 H1
Southfields RCOLE CO7 ...363 N11
Southfield Wy BOC CM0 ...393 L1
Southfleet Rd GVW DA11 ...337 A6
  SWCM DA10 ...336 C3
South Ga HLW CM20 ...13 G6
  PUR RM19 ...328 E2
Southgate Crs K/T/MI CO5 ...150 A7
Southgate Gdns SUD CO10 ...42 F1
Southgate St SUD CO10 ...42 F1
Southgreen Gdns RCOS CO16 ...6 A1
South Green Rd K/T/MI CO5 ...154 D2
South Gv WALTH E17 ...284 C3
South Gunnells BSDN SS14 ...3 G1
South Hall Dr RAIN RM13 ...327 L1
South Hanningfield Rd
  RCHLM CM3 ...242 F5
South Hanningfield Wy
  WICKE SS11 ...261 G2
South Heath Rd RCOLE CO7 ...157 M7
South Hl FX IP11 ...11 K4
  SLH/COR SS17 ...294 D7
South Hill Crs SLH/COR SS17 ...316 D2
South Hill Rd GVE DA12 ...337 L6
South House Cha MAL CM9 ...214 B6
Southill St POP/IOD E14 ...322 E2
South Kent Av GVW DA11 ...336 F4
Southland Cl COLN CO4 ...9 K2
Southlands Cha
  CHLM/GWD CM2 ...227 H3
Southlands Rd BCAYE CM11 ...260 A4
Southland Ter PUR RM19 * ...328 E2
South Mayne PIT SS13 ...278 D7
Southmead Crs
  CHES/WCR EN8 ...216 A3
Southmill Rd BSF CM23 ...139 H5
Southminster Rd BOC CM0 ...389 K7
  BOC CM0 ...393 K6
Southminster Rd Button's Hl
  RCHLM CM3 ...392 D1
Southminster Rd Scotts Hl
  BOC CM0 ...393 L1
South Molton Rd
  CAN/RD E16 ...306 G3
Southmoor Wy HOM E9 ...306 C3
South Ordnance Rd
  PEND EN3 ...233 J7
South Pde CVI SS8 ...321 H4
South Park Crs IL IG1 ...287 G8
South Park Dr
  GDMY/SEVK IG3 ...309 H2
  IL IG1 ...287 G8
South Park Rd IL IG1 ...287 H8
South Park Ter IL IG1 ...287 H8
Southport Rd
  WOOL/PLUM SE18 ...325 J2
South Primrose Hl
  CHLM/WR CM1 ...4 D1

South Rdg BCAYE CM11 ...258 F4
South Riding BSDN SS14 ...278 B7
South Rd BCAYE CM11 ...260 A8
  BSF CM23 ...139 H4
  CBE/LIN CB1 ...23 J1
  CHDH RM6 ...287 M3
  EHAM E6 ...308 C4
  HLW CM20 ...188 B6
  RBSF CM22 ...377 K1
  SBN/FI SS3 ...28 D8
  SOCK/AV RM15 ...329 M3
Southsea Av LOS SS9 ...300 A3
South Sea St
  BERM/RHTH SE16 ...322 C6
South Strd BOC CM0 ...386 F11
  BOC CM0 ...390 D6
  BRTR CM7 ...121 K3
  BRW CM14 ...273 M1
  BSF CM23 ...139 G3
  COLS CO2 ...8 B3
  GVE DA12 ...337 L5
  IP IP1 ...16 D3
  MAL CM9 ...394 C1
  MGTR CO11 ...91 G2
  PEND EN3 ...248 A5
  RAIN RM13 ...310 F6
  RCFD SS4 ...283 J4
  RCHLM CM3 ...167 H6
  ROM RM1 ...289 H1
  SAFWN CB10 ...341 L4
South Ter CBS CB2 ...22 C4
South Vw CDW/CHF RM16 ...315 L5
  GTDUN CM6 ...74 D2
  GTDUN CM6 ...116 F9
  RCOLE CO7 ...363 N11
South View Av TIL RM18 ...331 K6
South View Cl RAYL SS6 ...281 J5
Southview Cl RCHLM CM3 ...245 G5
South View Crs
  GNTH/NBYPK IG2 ...286 E4
  WICKE SS11 ...261 J6
South View Dr UPMR RM14 ...290 D8
Southview Dr COS CO15 ...160 C3
  SWFD E18 ...285 L1
  WOS/PRIT SS0 ...300 C5
  WOTN CO14 ...137 M2
South View Gn RIPS/CAP IP9 ...59 H7
South View Hts WTHK W20 * ...335 H4
South View Rd LOU IG10 ...250 C6
  RCHLM CM3 ...243 M8
  SBF/HAD SS7 ...297 M2
  WTHK W20 ...335 M1
Southview Rd HOC/HUL SS5 ...264 C6
  RCHLM CM3 ...212 A7
South Wk BSDN SS14 ...2 F7
Southwalters CVI SS8 ...320 C1
South Wash Rd LAIN SS15 ...277 H3
Southway COL CO1 ...8 A4
South Wy PUR RM19 ...329 H6
  WAB EN9 ...233 J7
South Weald Dr WAB EN9 ...233 L3
South Weald Rd BRW CM14 ...273 K2
Southwell Cl CDW/CHF RM16 ...329 M8
Southwell Grove Rd WAN E11 ...285 H7
Southwest Rd WAN E11 ...285 G6
South Wharf Rd CRAYS RM17 ...330 C5
Southwick Gdns CVI SS8 ...320 C2
Southwick Rd CVI SS8 ...320 C2
Southwold Crs SBF/HAD SS7 ...279 M8
Southwold Rd BARK IG11 ...309 K2
Southwold Wy RCOS CO16 ...158 D8
Southwood Cha RCHLM CM3 ...228 D1
Southwood Gdns
  BARK/HLT IG6 ...286 E2
  RAYL SS6 ...281 L5
Southwood Rd THMD SE28 ...325 L4
Southy Ms CAN/RD E16 ...323 K4
Southy Cl BRTR CM7 ...122 A1
  RCFD SS4 ...283 H3
Sovereign Ct
  HLWW/ROY CM19 ...203 J4
Sovereign Crs COLW CO3 * ...106 C7
  POP/IOD E14 ...322 D3
Sovereign Rd BARK IG11 ...309 M7
Sowerberry Cl
  CHLM/WR CM1 ...193 J6
Sowrey Av RAIN RM13 ...311 J3
Spa Cl HOC/HUL SS5 ...264 B7
Spa Dr BOC CM0 ...385 L12
Spains Hall Pl VGE SS16 ...3 J8
Spains Hall Rd CHONG CM5 ...206 B3
Spalding Av CHLM/WR CM1 ...193 H6
Spalding Rd BRTR CM7 ...121 H1
Spalding Wy CHLM/GWD CM2 ...210 C5
Spalt Cl RBRW/HUT CM13 ...256 D7
Spanbeek Rd K/T/MI CO5 * ...298 E8
Spanbies Rd RCOLE CO7 * ...363 J3
Spanby Rd BOW E3 ...306 D8
Spareleaze Hl LOU IG10 ...250 C4
Sparepenny La North
  SAFWN CB10 ...353 K5
Sparepenny La South
  SAFWN CB10 ...353 L5
Spar-Hawks Rd MAL CM9 * ...213 L2
Sparkbridge LAIN SS15 ...276 D2
Sparke Ter CAN/RD E16 * ...323 J2
Sparkey Cl WIT CM8 ...171 K6
Sparks Cl BCTR RM8 ...288 C2
Sparks Cl IPSE IP3 ...55 K3
Spar La RCHLM CM3 ...229 M2
Sparling Cl COLS CO2 ...128 E3
The Sparlings FOS CO13 ...136 F1
Spa Rd HOC/HUL SS5 ...264 A7
  K/T/MI CO5 ...149 M1
  WIT CM8 ...171 H1
Sparrow Gn DAGE RM10 ...288 E2
Sparrows Cl ING CM4 ...207 K9
Sparrows Rd ING CM4 ...207 K9
Sparrowsend Hl SAFWS CB11 ...351 P8
Sparrows Herne COS CO15 ...159 J7
  VGE SS16 ...295 K2
Sparrow's La RBSF CM22 ...378 F6
Sparsholt Rd BARK IG11 ...309 H5
Speckled Wood Ct BRTR CM7 ...121 H5
Speedwell Cl WIT CM8 ...171 G2
Speedwell Rd CHTY IP2 ...53 L1
  COLS CO2 ...130 A1
Speldhurst Rd HOM E9 ...306 F1
Spellbrook La East
  RBSF CM22 ...163 C1
Spellbrook La West BSF CM23 ...162 F1
Spells Cl BOC CM0 ...393 N1
Spencer Cl BERM/RHTH SE16 ...322 C7
Spencer Dr BCAYW CM12 ...240 C8
  MAL CM9 ...214 A6
  RBSF CM22 ...374 D2
  STSD CM24 ...115 M3
  WFD IG8 ...267 M4
Spencer Gdns HCH RM12 ...311 J1
  RAYL SS6 ...280 E5
  ROMW/RG RM7 ...288 D2
  SUD CO10 ...20 D3
  WFD IG8 ...267 M6
Spring Gardens Rd
  RCOLW CO6 ...84 A6
Spring Gv GVE DA12 ...337 L6
  LOU IG10 ...250 A6
Springhall La SBW CM21 ...162 F8

WALTH E17 ...266 F8
Spencers Cft HLWS CM18 ...204 C3
Spencers Piece COLN CO4 * ...88 C2
Spencer St GVW DA11 ...337 K5
Spencer Wk TIL RM18 ...331 M5
Spendells Cl WOTN CO14 ...369 N11
Spenders Cl BSDN SS14 ...3 H1
The Spennells RCOS CO16 ...135 G3
Spenser Crs UPMR RM14 ...290 F1
Spenser Ms IP IP1 ...47 L2
Spenser Wy COS CO15 ...182 C4
Speranza St
  WOOL/PLUM SE18 ...325 J8
Spert St POP/IOD E14 ...322 B3
Spey St POP/IOD E14 ...322 F1
Spey Wy ROM RM1 ...271 H6
Spicersfield CHESW EN7 ...216 B3
Spicers La SUD CO10 ...42 F1
Spielman Rd DART DA1 ...334 C6
The Spike SAFWS CB11 ...3 J8
Spillbutters BRWN CM15 ...383 Q10
Spilsby Rd HARH RM3 ...272 B6
Spindle Beams RCFD SS4 ...283 J1
Spindle Cl WOOL/PLUM SE18 ...324 B6
Spindle Rd HVHL CB9 ...34 A5
Spindles TIL RM18 ...331 K6
Spindle Wd COLN CO4 ...107 K1
Spindrift Av WOOL/PLUM SE18 ...322 E7
Spinel Cl HCH RM12 ...311 M2
Spinks La WIT CM8 ...171 H4
Spinnaker Cl BARK IG11 ...309 L7
  COS CO15 ...156 C6
Spinnaker Dr MAL CM9 ...215 H2
The Spinnakers SBF/HAD SS7 ...279 L8
Spinnel's Hl RCHLM CM3 ...245 H8
Spinnel's La MGTR CO11 ...366 F11
Spinner Cl IP IP1 ...47 J1
Spinney Cl RAIN RM13 ...311 H6
  WICKE SS11 ...261 J6
Spinney St HERT/BAY SG13 ...184 F4
The Spinney BCAYW CM12 ...258 C1
  BRTR CM7 ...121 M4
  CDW/CHF RM16 ...315 K4
  CHONG CM5 ...382 C4
  HERT/BAY SG13 ...184 A3
  HLW CM20 ...188 B8
  HOD EN11 ...201 G5
  IPNE IP4 ...48 L1
  RBRW/HUT CM13 ...256 F2
  SAFWS CB11 ...372 B2
  STSD CM24 ...115 M4
Spinneyfields K/T/MI CO5 ...150 A7
Spinneywood LAIN SS15 * ...276 D5
Spinning Wheel Md
  CHLM/GWD CM2 ...227 J1
Spire Cha SUD CO10 ...21 H1
Spire Cl GVE DA12 ...337 L6
The Spire Green Centre
  HLWW/ROY CM19 ...202 F2
Spire Rd LAIN SS15 ...276 F6
The Spires CHLM/GWD CM2 ...210 C7
Spital La BRW CM14 ...273 J2
Spital St DART DA1 ...334 A6
Spitfire Cl IPSE IP3 ...55 G4
Sporehams La
  CHLM/GWD CM2 ...227 J1
Sporhams VGE SS16 ...295 J1
Sportsmans La RCHLM CM3 ...196 D3
Sportsway COL CO1 ...8 B3
Spout La SUD CO10 ...358 N2
Spratt Hall Rd WAN E11 ...285 K4
Spratts La BARK/HLT IG6 ...270 A3
Spray St WOOL/PLUM SE18 ...324 E7
Spreadeagle Pl ING CM4 * ...239 M1
Spriggs La ING CM4 ...222 J1
Springbank Av HCH RM12 ...311 M2
  MGTR CO11 ...90 E2
Spring Cha RCOLE CO7 ...130 C3
  RCOLE CO7 ...156 B6
Spring Cl BCTR RM8 ...288 A6
  COLN CO4 ...107 M2
  RCHLM CM3 ...196 A8
  RCOS CO16 ...158 A1
Spring Elms La RCHLM CM3 ...212 C2
Springett's Hl BURES CO8 ...359 N7
Springfarm Cl RAIN RM13 ...312 A2
Springfield EPP CM16 ...236 A2
Springfield Cl RCHLM CM3 ...380 C2
  SBF/HAD SS7 ...299 G1
Springfield Dr
  GNTH/NBYPK IG2 ...286 F3
  WOS/PRIT SS0 ...300 F1
Springfield Gdns UPMR RM14 ...290 F1
  WFD IG8 ...267 M6
Springfield Gn
  CHLM/WR CM1 ...210 B1
Springfield La IP IP1 ...47 L5
Springfield Lyons Ap
  CHLM/GWD CM2 ...194 D7
Springfield Park Av
  CHLM/GWD CM2 ...5 M3
Springfield Park Hl
  CHLM/GWD CM2 ...5 M3
Springfield Park La
  CHLM/GWD CM2 ...210 B2
Springfield Park Pde
  CHLM/GWD CM2 ...5 M3
Springfield Park Rd
  CHLM/GWD CM2 ...5 M3
Springfield Pl CHLM/WR CM1 ...194 A8
Springfield Rd BCAYW CM12 ...240 C8
  BOC CM0 ...393 K7
  CBS CB2 ...22 C4
  CDW/CHF RM16 ...331 H1
  CHES/WCR EN8 ...232 F2
  CHING E4 ...249 H8
  CHLM/WR CM1 ...5 K3
  CVI SS8 ...321 J2
  EHAM E6 ...308 C4
  SRTFD E15 * ...307 H7
  SUD CO10 ...284 C4
  WALTH E17 ...284 C4
  WICKE SS11 ...261 J5
Springfields BROX EN10 ...201 G5
  BRTR CM7 ...120 F5
  CHLM/GWD CM2 ...116 F5
  RCOLE CO7 ...110 C7
  VGE SS16 ...296 C2
Springfield Ter SUD CO10 * ...20 C2
Spring Gdns HCH RM12 ...311 J1
  RAYL SS6 ...280 E5
  ROMW/RG RM7 ...288 D2
  SUD CO10 ...20 D3
  WFD IG8 ...267 M6

Springhall Rd SBW CM21 ...162 F7
Springhead Rd GVW DA11 ...336 F6
Spring Hl SAFWS CB11 ...351 P4
Springhill Cl RCOLE CO7 ...110 E3
Springhill Rd SAFWS CB11 ...30 A1
Springhouse La
  SLH/COR SS17 ...317 K2
Springhouse Rd
  SLH/COR SS17 ...317 H1
Springhurst Cl IPNE IP4 ...17 H1
Springland Cl IPNE IP4 ...48 F1
Springlands Wy SUD CO10 ...20 F1
Spring La COLW CO3 ...173 D6
  MAL CM9 ...173 G6
  MAL CM9 ...214 E1
  RCHLM CM3 ...197 D3
  RCOLE CO7 ...110 C8
  RCOLW CO6 ...105 K5
  RCOLW CO6 ...106 A1
  WIT CM8 ...171 K6
Spring La Hert/Bay SG13 ...185 G6
Springmead BRTR CM77 ...121 C6
Spring Meadow NHMKT IP6 ...50 A1
Spring Pond Cl
  CHLM/GWD CM2 ...210 B2
Spring Pond Meadow
  BRWN CM15 ...383 R8
Springpond Rd DAGW RM9 ...310 B2
Spring Rd IPNE IP4 ...17 K4
  K/T/MI CO7 ...173 M1
  RCOLE CO7 ...156 C6
  RCOS CO16 ...181 K1
  RIPW IP8 ...52 C3
Spring Sedge Cl COLW CO3 ...105 M6
The Springs BROX EN10 ...216 F3
  HERT/BAY SG13 ...184 A3
Springtail Rd RIPW IP8 ...53 H8
Spring V GRH DA9 ...335 M8
Springvale Ct GVW DA11 * ...336 F7
Springvalley Rd RCOLE CO7 ...108 F2
Spring View Rd WARE SG12 ...184 D1
Springwater Cl LOS SS9 ...281 M6
Springwater Gv LOS SS9 ...281 M5
Springwater Rd LOS SS9 ...281 L5
Spring Wy HSTD CO9 ...356 F9
Springwell BSDN SS14 ...3 Q10
Springwell Rd SAFWN CB10 ...341 P12
Springwell CHESW EN7 ...216 B3
Springwood Dr BRTR CM7 ...120 F1
Springwood Wy ROM RM1 ...289 G3
Sprites End FX IP11 ...62 C6
Spriteshall La FX IP11 ...62 C5
Sprites La RIPW IP8 ...53 H2
Sproughton Rd RIPW IP8 ...47 G6
Sprowston Ms FSTGT E7 ...307 K3
Sprowston Rd FSTGT E7 ...307 K3
Spruce Av COLN CO4 ...9 M5
  GTDUN CM6 ...116 E4
Spruce Cl K/T/MI CO5 ...177 G6
  LAIN SS15 ...276 F4
  WIT CM8 ...171 K1
Spruce Hl HLWS CM18 ...203 M6
Spruce Hills Rd WALTH E17 ...266 F8
Sprundel Av CVI SS8 ...321 C3
Spurgate RBRW/HUT CM13 ...256 D5
Spurgeon Cl HSTD CO9 ...356 F9
Spurgeon St COL CO1 ...9 K8
Spurling Rd DAGW RM9 ...310 C3
Spur Rd BARK IG11 ...308 F7
The Spur CHES/WCR EN8 * ...216 B4
Squadrons Ap HCH RM12 ...311 M3
The Square BOC CM0 ...390 D5
  BROX EN10 ...216 F1
  BRTR CM77 ...120 E7
  COLS CO2 * ...128 E2
  IL IG1 ...286 D5
  ING CM4 ...221 H5
  K/T/MI CO5 * ...177 L7
  MAL CM9 ...198 D8
  SBW CM21 ...162 F7
  SLH/COR SS17 * ...316 K2
  WFD IG8 ...267 K4
Squires La KESG IP5 ...50 F5
Squire St RCHLM CM3 ...245 H6
Squirrels Ct CHLM/WR CM1 ...193 J8
Squirrels La BSF CM23 ...294 E2
Squirrel's Cha
  CDW/CHF RM16 ...331 K1
Squirrels Cl BSF CM23 ...139 G1
Squirrels Fld COLN CO4 ...87 G4
Squirrel's Heath Av
  GPK RM2 ...289 L1
Squirrels Heath La
  EMPK RM11 ...289 M2
Squirrels Heath Rd
  HARH RM3 ...272 B8
The Squirrels
  HERT/BAY SG13 ...184 B3
  RIPS/CAP IP9 ...58 D3
Stable Cl COLW CO3 ...106 A7
  K/T/MI CO5 ...178 B6
Stable Ct KESG IP5 ...50 F5
Stablecroft CHLM/WR CM1 ...194 B7
Stablefield Rd WOTN CO14 ...137 K2
Stable Ms K/T/MI CO5 ...178 B5
Stacey Cl LEY E10 ...285 G3
Stacey Dr VGE SS16 ...294 F3
Stacey's Mt BCAYE CM11 ...258 M2
Stackfield HLW CM20 ...188 C6
The Stackyard SAFWN CB10 ...340 H6
Staddles RBSF CM22 ...139 J8
Stadium Rd SOSN SS2 ...19 H1
Stadium Wy
  HLWW/ROY CM19 ...187 G8
  SBF/HAD SS7 ...298 F6
Staffa Cl WICKW SS12 ...261 J4
Staffa Rd LEY E10 ...284 B6
Staffhouse Rd WICKE SS11 ...261 K2
Stafford Av EMPK RM11 ...290 A1
Stafford Cl CDW/CHF RM16 ...329 M7
  CHES/WCR EN8 ...216 C7
  FOS CO13 ...137 H3
  GRH DA9 ...335 J7
  LOS SS9 ...300 C3
  SLH/COR SS17 ...332 D2
  WALTH E17 ...284 C4
Stafford Crs BRTR CM7 ...122 A1
Stafford Dr BROX EN10 ...201 H6
Stafford Gn VGE SS16 ...294 G3
Stafford Rd BOW E3 ...306 C6
  FSTGT E7 ...307 M4
Staffords HLWE CM17 ...188 F5
Stagden Cross BSDN SS14 ...3 K4
Staggart Gn BARK/HLT IG6 ...269 J4
Stag La BKHH IG9 ...268 B1
Stainers BSF CM23 ...138 D4
Staines Rd IL IG1 ...309 G1
Stainforth Rd
  GNTH/NBYPK IG2 ...287 G5
  WALTH E17 ...284 D2
Stainsby Rd POP/IOD E14 * ...322 D2
Stainsby Rd POP/IOD E14 ...322 D2
Stains Cl CHES/WCR EN8 ...216 F6
Stairs Rd SBN/FI SS3 ...304 B1
The Stakings CBS CB2 ...22 C4

Stalham Wy WFD IG8 .....268 E7
Stalin Rd COLS CO2 .....129 L1
Stallards Crs FOS CO13 .....137 L5
Stambourne Rd HSTD CO9 .....345 L8
Stambridge Rd COS CO15 .....6 D7
  RCFD SS4 .....283 J3
Stamford Cl CHTY IP2 .....53 L5
Stamford Gdns DAGW RM9 .....309 M4
Stamford Rd DAGW RM9 .....309 L4
  EHAM E6 .....308 B3
Stammers Pl KESG IP5 .....50 D6
Stammers Rd COLN CO4 .....107 J1
Stanbrook Rd ABYW SE2 .....325 L5
  GVW DA11 .....337 J8
Standard Av COS CO15 .....182 A6
Standard Rd BELV DA17 .....326 D8
  PEND EN3 .....232 F8
Standen Av HCH RM12 .....290 A8
  RCHLM CM3 .....245 C8
Standfield Rd DAGE RM10 .....310 D2
Standley Rd WOTN CO14 .....369 N12
Standrums GTDUN CM6 .....117 G5
Stane Cl BSF CM23 .....139 J4
Stane Fld RCOLW CO6 .....126 B2
Stanes Rd BRTR CM7 .....99 H7
Staneway VGE SS16 .....2 A9
Stanfield Cl COLW CO3 .....128 B5
Stanfield Rd BOW E3 .....306 H6
  SOSN SS2 .....19 H1
Stanfields Ct HLW CM20 .....13 J5
Stanford Cl ROMW/RG RM7 .....288 E4
  WFD IG8 .....268 A8
Stanford Ct WAB EN9 .....234 B3
Stanford Gdns
  SOCK/AV RM15 .....329 H4
Stanford Hall SLH/COR SS17 * 317 J2
Stanford-le-Hope By-Pass
  CHONG CM5 .....382 D5
Stanford Rivers Rd
  CHONG CM5 .....382 D5
Stanford Rd CDW/CHF RM16 .....316 B5
  CDW/CHF RM16 .....331 H1
  CVI SS8 .....320 D2
Stanhope Cl
  BERM/RHTH SE16 * 322 A5
  IL IG1 .....286 C6
Stanhope Gdns BCTR RM8 .....288 C7
Stanhope Rd BCTR RM8 .....288 C7
  CHES/WCR EN8 .....232 F3
  RAIN RM13 .....311 K6
  SWCM DA10 .....336 C3
  WALTH E17 .....284 E3
Stanier Cl SOS SS1 .....19 L4
Stanley Av BARK IG11 .....309 J7
  BCTR RM8 .....288 C6
  GPK RM2 .....289 K2
  IPSE IP3 .....54 F1
  RCOLE CO7 .....156 D5
Stanley Cl GPK RM2 .....289 K2
  GRH DA9 .....335 H4
  HCH RM12 .....289 M7
Stanley Pl CHONG CM5 .....382 H3
Stanley Ri CHLM/GWD CM2 .....210 D2
Stanley Rd CHING E4 .....249 G8
  COS CO15 .....6 A7
  CVI SS8 .....320 F1
  FX IP11 .....11 M5
  GRAYS RM17 .....330 F4
  HCH RM12 .....289 M7
  HSTD CO9 .....81 G3
  IL IG1 .....287 C7
  MNPK E12 .....308 B2
  RCFD SS4 .....264 F6
  RCOLE CO7 .....130 F4
  SAFWN SB10 .....341 M6
  SBF/HAD SS7 .....280 A4
  SOS SS1 .....19 K6
  SRTFD E15 .....307 C5
  SUD CO10 .....20 D4
  SWCM DA10 .....336 C4
  SWFD E18 .....267 J7
  UPMR RM14 .....293 J7
  WALTH E17 .....284 E4
Stanley Rd South RAIN RM13 .....311 H5
Stanley Rd South RAIN RM13 .....311 J6
Stanleys Farm Rd SAFWS CB11 .....30 L1
Stanley Ter BCAYW CM12 .....258 D4
Stanley Vls SLH/COR SS17 * 316 H4
Stanley Wood Av SUD CO10 .....20 F2
Stanley Wooster Wy
  COLN CO4 .....108 B6
Stanmore Cl RCOS CO16 .....6 D1
Stanmore Rd BELV DA17 .....326 E6
  WAN E11 .....285 J6
  WICKE SS11 .....261 L6
Stanmore Wy LOU IG10 .....250 D1
  RCOS CO16 .....181 L1
Stannard Wy SUD CO10 .....21 H9
Stanners LAIN SS15 .....276 L5
Stansfield Rd CAN/RD E16 .....306 H2
Stansfield Rd SBF/HAD SS7 .....279 L6
Stansgate Rd BOC CM0 .....389 J4
  DAGE RM10 .....288 D7
Stanstead Dr HOD EN11 .....201 J1
Stanstead Rd HERT/BAY SG13 .....184 D3
  HOD EN11 .....185 J8
  HSTD CO9 .....81 J5
  WAN E11 .....285 L3
Stansted Cl BCAYE CM11 * 259 G3
  CHLM/WR CM1 .....4 A9
  HCH RM12 .....311 L5
Stansted Rd BSF CM23 .....139 L4
  COLS CO2 .....129 K4
  RBSF CM22 .....374 D4
Stansted Wy FOS CO13 .....137 K3
Stanstrete Fld BRTR CM77 .....120 E8
Stanton Hughes Wy
  MGTR CO11 .....90 E1
Stanway Cl CHIG IG7 .....269 H4
Stanway Rd SBF/HAD SS7 .....279 M8
  WAB EN9 .....234 B9
Stanwell St COL CO1 .....8 D4
Stanwyck Gdns HARH RM3 .....271 L4
Stanwyn Av COS CO15 .....6 F5
Stapleford Av
  GNTH/NBYPK IG2 .....287 H3
Stapleford Cl CHING E4 .....266 F2
  CHLM/GWD CM2 .....4 C1
Stapleford End WICKE SS11 .....261 L8
Stapleford Gdns CRW RM5 .....270 D5
Stapleford Rd ABR/ST RM4 .....252 E4
Stapleford Wy BARK IG11 .....309 L1
Staplegrove SBN/FI SS3 .....302 F5
Staplers Cl MAL CM9 .....198 L1
Staplers Heath MAL CM9 .....198 L2
Staplers Wk MAL CM9 .....172 E1
Staples Cl BERM/RHTH SE16 .....322 A1
Staples Rd LOU IG10 .....250 B3
Stapleton Crs RAIN RM13 .....311 K3
Stapley Rd BELV DA17 .....326 D8
Starboard Av GRH DA9 .....335 L8
Starboard Vw RCHLM CM3 .....245 H8
Starboard Wy POP/IOD E14 .....322 D4
Starch House La
  BARK/HLT IG6 .....269 G8
Starfield Cl IPNE IP4 .....49 G7
Star La CAN/RD E16 .....307 H8

  EPP CM16 .....220 B8
  GTDUN CM6 .....117 G4
  ING CM4 .....239 M1
  IPNE IP4 .....16 F6
  SOSN SS2 .....303 H2
Starling Cl BKHH IG9 .....249 K8
Starmans Cl DAGW RM9 .....310 B5
Star Md GTDUN CM6 .....74 D3
Starr Rd RBSF CM22 .....372 G12
Station Ap BKHH IG9 * 268 A8
  BOC CM0 .....393 L8
  BRTR CM7 .....121 K3
  CHES/WCR EN8 .....232 F4
  CHING E4 * 249 H7
  CHING E4 * 267 G3
  CVI SS8 .....298 C7
  DART DA1 .....334 B8
  FOS CO13 .....137 J4
  FSTGT E7 * 307 L1
  HOC/HUL SS5 .....264 B7
  LAIN CM3 .....244 F5
  RCHLM CM3 .....246 E5
  SOS SS1 .....19 G5
  SOSN SS2 .....301 J2
  SWFD E18 * 267 L8
  VGE SS16 .....296 E1
  WALTH E17 .....284 D3
  WAN E11 .....285 K3
  WAN E11 * 307 H1
  WFD IG8 * 267 M5
  WICKW SS12 * 261 L5
Station Av RAYL SS6 .....280 E2
  SOSN SS2 .....301 K2
  WICKE SS11 .....260 C8
Station Crs BKHTH/KID SE3 .....323 K8
  RAYL SS6 .....281 C2
  RAYL SS6 .....230 C8
Station Pde BARK IG11 .....308 F4
  EHAM E6 * 307 M5
  EHAM E6 * 308 B3
  HCH RM12 .....311 L1
  ROM RM1 .....289 H4
Station Pas SWFD E18 .....267 L8
Station Rd BARK/HLT IG6 .....287 G1
  BCAYW CM12 .....258 C3
  BCTR RM8 .....288 A6
  BELV DA17 .....326 D6
  BOC CM0 .....393 N1
  BROX EN10 .....201 G6
  BRTR CM77 .....120 C6
  BSF CM23 .....139 H3
  CBE/LIN CB1 .....24 E7
  CBS CB2 .....23 J3
  CHIG IG7 .....268 C2
  CHING E4 .....249 G8
  COS CO15 .....175 J7
  CVI SS8 .....321 H3
  EPP CM16 .....221 J5
  EPP CM16 .....236 E1
  FOS CO13 .....136 F3
  FX IP11 .....62 B9
  GPK RM2 .....289 L2
  GRH DA9 .....335 K2
  GTDUN CM6 .....117 H5
  GTDUN CM6 .....118 C7
  GVW DA11 .....336 E4
  HAR CO12 .....14 A4
  HAR CO12 .....15 G3
  HAR CO12 .....15 K4
  HARH RM3 .....272 C7
  HLWE CM17 .....188 D5
  HOC/HUL SS5 .....264 B7
  HSTD CO9 .....345 J5
  HSTD CO9 .....356 E7
  HVHL CB9 .....34 D5
  IL IG1 .....286 E8
  K/T/MI CO5 .....173 M1
  LOS SS9 .....300 B3
  LOU IG10 .....250 C1
  MAL CM9 .....198 A4
  MAL CM9 .....175 J7
  MAL CM9 .....214 D2
  MAL CM9 .....385 N3
  MGTR CO11 .....64 B7
  MGTR CO11 .....366 B7
  MGTR CO11 .....367 J6
  MNPK E12 .....308 A1
  RAYL SS6 .....280 F2
  RBRW/HUT CM13 .....275 H8
  RBSF CM22 .....374 D3
  RBSF CM22 .....377 K2
  RCHLM CM3 .....170 C8
  RCHLM CM3 .....230 D8
  RCHLM CM3 .....392 C10
  RCOLE CO7 .....89 H7
  RCOLE CO7 .....130 D5
  RCOLE CO7 .....131 K5
  RCOLE CO7 .....132 C7
  RCOLE CO7 .....156 D7
  RCOLW CO6 .....82 C4
  RCOLW CO6 .....82 D6
  RCOLW CO6 .....85 H1
  RCOLW CO6 .....108 A7
  RCOS CO16 .....126 D1
  RIPS/CAP IP9 .....59 J5
  SAFWS CB11 .....30 A1
  SAFWS CB11 .....351 M8
  SAFWS CB11 .....372 B1
  SBF/HAD SS7 .....298 A5
  SBW CM21 .....163 G6
  SOS SS1 .....302 C5
  STSD CM24 .....115 M5
  SUD CO10 .....20 E7
  SUD CO10 .....37 M6
  SUD CO10 .....51 K6
  TIL RM18 .....332 E6
  UPMR RM14 .....290 F7
  WAB EN9 .....217 M5
  WALTH E17 .....284 B4
  WARE SG12 .....185 K5
  WICKE SS11 .....261 L6
  WIT CM8 .....146 C3
  WIT CM8 .....171 K2
  WOS/PRIT SS0 .....18 A6
Station Rd East CBS CB2 .....23 J3
Station Rd North BELV DA17 .....326 E6
Station Rd West CBS CB2 .....23 J3
  CHTY IP2 .....16 B6
  SAFWS CB11 .....30 A1
  SRTFD E15 .....307 G4
  WOTN CO14 .....137 M2
Station Wy BKHH IG9 .....268 A8
Staveley Cl POP/IOD E14 .....322 D4
Staverton Rd EMPK RM11 .....290 A4
Stayne Yard Rd
  BERM/RHTH SE16 .....322 B4
Stayner's Rd WCHPL E1 .....306 A2

Stays La CHONG CM5 .....206 D2
Steadman Cl HOO/HM ME3 .....339 M8
Steamer Ter CHLM/WR CM1 .....4 D7
Steam Mill Rd MGTR CO11 .....91 M5
Stebbing Dr GTDUN CM6 .....118 C7
Stebbings VGE SS16 .....294 F1
Stebbing Wy BARK IG11 .....309 K6
Stebondale St POP/IOD E14 .....322 D6
Steed Cl EMPK RM11 .....289 L7
Steeds Meadow SUD CO10 .....42 M1
Steele Av SBF/HAD SS7 .....250 B4
Steel Ap BARK IG11 .....309 L6
Steele Av GRH DA9 .....335 M7
Steele Cl RCOLW CO6 * 126 C2
Steele Rd WAN E11 .....307 H1
Steen Cl ING CM4 .....239 L1
Steeple Bumpstead Rd
  HVHL CB9 .....343 N5
Steeple Cl MAL CM9 .....215 G8
  RCFD SS4 .....283 G2
Steeplefield LOS SS9 .....282 B5
Steeplehall PIT SS13 .....278 E5
Steeple Hts SBF/HAD SS7 .....279 M7
Steeple Mdw BOC CM0 .....393 L11
  BOC CM0 .....389 L11
  RCHLM CM3 .....231 G2
  RCHLM CM3 .....388 C10
Steeple Vw BSF CM23 .....139 G1
Steeple Wy BRWN CM15 .....383 Q10
Steerforth St CHLM/WR CM1 .....193 G6
Steers Wy BERM/RHTH SE16 .....322 B5
Stell Av CVI SS8 .....298 C8
Stella Maris Cl CHTY IP2 .....47 J8
Stella Maris Ct CVI SS8 .....321 J2
Sten Cl PEND EN3 .....233 H7
Stennetts Cl FX IP11 .....62 E1
Stenning Av TIL RM18 .....332 E3
Stepfield WIT CM8 .....171 J5
Stephen Av RAIN RM13 .....311 H3
Stephen Cl HVHL CB9 .....34 E5
  SUD CO10 .....42 M4
Stephen Cranfield Cl
  K/T/MI CO5 .....130 D6
Stephen Marshall Av
  BRTR CM7 .....354 B11
Stephen Rd KESG IP5 .....50 D5
Stephens Cl HARH RM3 .....271 M4
Stephen's Ct IPNE IP4 .....49 G7
Stephens Crs SLH/COR SS17 .....316 C2
Stephenson Av TIL RM18 .....331 K4
Stephenson Rd BRTR CM7 .....121 K4
  COLN CO4 .....88 A7
  COS CO15 .....159 G7
  LOS SS9 .....281 M7
  RCHLM CM3 .....246 D5
  WALTH E17 * 284 B1
Stephenson Rd West
  COS CO15 .....159 K4
Stephenson St CAN/RD E16 .....323 H1
Stephen's Rd SRTFD E15 .....307 H5
Stepney Cswy WCHPL E1 .....322 A1
Stepney Gn WCHPL E1 .....322 A1
Stepney High St WCHPL E1 .....322 A1
Sterling Av CHES/WCR EN8 .....232 E4
Sterling Cl CHLM/WR CM1 .....106 B8
Stern Cl BARK IG11 .....309 M1
Sterry Crs DAGE RM10 .....310 D1
Sterry Gdns DAGE RM10 .....310 D3
Sterry Rd BARK IG11 .....309 L1
  DAGE RM10 .....310 D1
Stevenage Rd EHAM E6 .....308 D3
Stevens Cl CVI SS8 .....321 G1
Stevens La GTDUN CM6 .....119 M3
Stevenson Rd IP IP1 .....16 C5
Stevenson Wy WICKW SS12 .....260 C5
Stevens Rd BCTR RM8 .....287 L7
  WIT CM8 .....171 H4
Stevens Wy CHIG IG7 .....269 H8
Steward Cl CHES/WCR EN8 .....216 F3
Stewards Cl EPP CM16 .....236 D7
  FOS CO13 .....137 J2
Stewards Elm Farm La
  RCFD SS4 .....396 A5
Stewards Green Rd
  EPP CM16 .....236 C3
Stewart Av UPMR RM14 .....290 F7
Stewart Pl WICKW SS12 .....261 J3
Stewart Rd CHLM/GWD CM2 .....209 M3
  WAN E11 .....307 G1
The Stewarts BSF CM23 .....138 F2
Stewart St POP/IOD E14 .....322 D4
Stewarts Wy BSF CM23 .....93 J3
Stewart Young Gv KESG IP5 .....50 D6
Steyning Av SOSN SS2 .....302 B3
Stickland Rd BELV DA17 .....326 D7
Stifford Clays Rd
  CDW/CHF RM16 .....314 C8
Stifford Hl CDW/CHF RM16 .....314 A8
  SOCK/AV RM15 .....329 H1
Stifford Rd SOCK/AV RM15 .....313 M4
Stile Cft HLWS CM18 .....204 B3
Stile La RAYL SS6 .....281 C3
Stilemans WICKE SS11 .....261 G5
Stilemans Wd BRTR CM77 .....122 D4
Stiles Cl ERITH DA8 .....326 E8
The Stiles MAL CM9 .....215 H4
Stirling Av LOS SS9 .....299 L3
Stirling Pl HVHL CB9 .....34 E1
Stirling Pl PIT SS13 .....278 E5
Stirling Rd PLSTW E13 .....307 H1
  WALTH E17 .....284 A2
Stirrup Cl CHLM/WR CM1 .....194 B6
Stivvy's Rd MAL CM9 .....212 F3
Stoat Cl HERT/BAY SG13 .....184 B3
Stock Cha MAL CM9 .....198 A4
Stock Cl SOSN SS2 .....301 J1
Stockdale Rd BCTR RM8 .....288 C7
Stocker Gdns DAGW RM9 .....309 M4
Stockfield Av HOD EN11 .....201 H4
Stockhouse Cl MAL CM9 .....198 A4
Stockhouse Rd MGTR CO11 .....150 D6
Stocking La ROY SG8 .....370 H6
Stockingswater La PEND EN3 .....248 B3
Stockland Rd ROMW/RG RM7 .....289 L4
Stock La ING CM4 .....240 D2
Stockley Cl HVHL CB9 .....34 D1
Stockmen Fld BSF CM23 .....138 D1
Stockmers End RIPS/CAP IP9 .....58 B7
Stock Rd BCAYW CM12 .....258 C4
  CHLM/GWD CM2 .....225 K2
  ING CM4 .....241 G4
Stocksfield BRWN CM15 .....383 N11
Stocksfield Rd WALTH E17 * 284 B1
Stocks La BRWN CM15 .....383 N11
Stocks Pl POP/IOD E14 .....322 C3
Stock St PLSTW E13 .....307 H1
Stockwell Rd CSTN CB10 * 28 L4
Stockwell Cl DART DA1 * 259 G6
  CHESW EN7 .....216 B6
Stockwood SBF/HAD SS7 .....298 D6
Stokeash Cl RCOS CO16 .....182 D2
Stoke Av BARK/HLT IG6 .....269 K5
Stoke Br IP IP1 .....16 E7

Stokebridge Maltings
  IPSE IP3 * 16 F7
Stokefelde PIT SS13 .....278 E6
Stoke Hall Rd CHTY IP2 .....16 E7
Stoke Park Dr CHTY IP2 .....53 K5
Stoke Quay IPSE IP5 .....17 G7
Stoke Rd RAIN RM13 .....312 A6
  RCOLW CO6 .....361 K1
  RCOLW CO6 .....361 J1
  SUD CO10 .....37 M7
Stokes Rd EHAM E6 .....308 B3
The Stokes WOTN CO14 .....369 L2
Stokon Rd CHONG CM5 .....383 D4
Stonebridge Hl RCOLW CO6 .....82 A6
Stonebridge Rd GVW DA11 .....336 E5
Stonechat Rd BCAYW CM12 .....258 F5
  CHTY IP2 .....53 H2
Stone Cl BCTR RM8 .....288 C6
  BRTR CM7 .....121 J3
Stonecrop COLN CO4 .....106 B3
Stonegrove Rd IP11 .....10 C3
Stonehall Av IL IG1 .....286 B4
Stonehall La RCOS CO16 .....159 C4
Stoneham Av COS CO15 .....158 D8
Stoneham St RCOLW CO6 .....124 C7
Stonehill Cl LOS SS9 .....300 A5
Stonehill Rd CHLM/WR CM1 .....207 L1
  LOS SS9 .....300 C1
Stonehouse La PUR RM19 .....329 H8
Stonehouse La K/T/MI CO5 .....177 K6
Stone La K/T/MI CO5 .....173 J3
  MGTR CO11 .....367 J2
Stoneleigh SBW CM21 .....162 F6
Stoneleigh Av EN EN1 .....232 L8
Stoneleigh Cl CHES/WCR EN8 .....232 L8
Stoneleigh Dr HOD EN11 .....185 J8
Stoneleigh Pk RCOLW CO6 .....128 C2
Stoneleigh Rd CLAY IG5 .....286 C1
Stoneleighs SBF/HAD SS7 .....280 C2
Stone Lodge La CHTY IP2 .....16 A2
Stone Lodge La West CHTY IP2 .....53 L2
Stone Lodge Wk CHTY IP2 .....16 G7
Stoneness Rd WTHK RM20 .....335 L1
Stone Path Dr RCHLM CM3 .....196 C1
Stone Place Rd GRH DA9 .....335 K2
Stones Green Rd HAR CO12 .....113 J5
Stone St GVE SS4 .....337 L4
Stonewall EHAM E6 .....308 D3
Stonewood Rd ERITH DA8 .....327 H1
Stoneyard La POP/IOD E14 .....322 C3
Stoney Common STSD CM24 .....115 M4
Stoney Common Rd
  STSD CM24 .....115 L4
Stoney Hills BCAYE CM11 .....241 L8
Stoneycroft Wy WFD IG8 .....268 B2
Stoneydown WALTH E17 .....284 B2
Stoneydown Av WALTH E17 .....284 B2
Stoney Hills BCAYE CM11 .....241 L8
Stonyshotts WAB EN9 .....233 M4
Stopford Ct IP IP1 .....16 B3
Stopford Rd PLSTW E13 .....307 H1
Store Rd CAN/RD E16 .....324 D5
Storers Quay POP/IOD E14 .....323 C7
Stores Rd K/T/MI CO5 .....149 M7
Store St SRTFD E15 .....307 J4
Storey Rd WALTH E17 .....284 C2
Stork Rd FSTGT E7 .....307 J3
Stormonts Wy VGE SS16 .....295 C3
Stornoway Rd SOSN SS2 .....19 M2
Storr Gdns RBRW/HUT CM13 .....257 C1
Stortford Hall Pk BSF CM23 .....139 J3
Stortford Hall Rd BSF CM23 .....139 J3
Stortford Rd GTDUN CM6 .....116 B6
  GTDUN CM6 .....379 P7
  HOD EN11 .....201 J2
  RBSF CM22 .....163 M5
  RBSF CM22 .....376 G12
  SAFWS CB11 .....72 E1
Stort Ldg BSF CM23 .....138 C1
Stort Ml HLW CM20 .....188 C2
Stort Rd BSF CM23 .....139 G3
Stort Valley Wy HLW CM20 .....188 C2
  HLWE CM17 .....189 M7
  HLWE CM17 .....205 K8
  HLWW/ROY CM19 .....186 B8
  SBW CM21 .....162 F8
Stour Av FX IP11 .....11 H3
Stour Cl HAR CO12 .....70 C3
  SBN/FI SS3 .....303 H1
Stourdale Cl MGTR CO11 .....90 D2
Stour Gdns SUD CO10 .....45 L2
Stourmead Cl HVHL CB9 .....35 G1
Stour Rd BOW E3 .....306 D4
  CDW/CHF RM16 .....331 H1
  DAGE RM10 .....288 D2
  HAR CO12 .....15 H1
Stourside RIPS/CAP IP9 .....66 C1
Stour St MGTR CO11 .....92 B7
  SUD CO10 .....20 D4
Stour Ter MGTR CO11 * 91 K1
Stourton Rd WIT CM8 .....171 J2
Stour V HSTD CO9 .....345 J2
Stour Valley Pth BURES CO8 .....359 P9
  HVHL CB9 .....35 G1
  RCOLW CO6 .....360 F1
  RCOLW CO6 .....362 F1
  SUD CO10 .....38 C5
  SUD CO10 .....45 L3
  SUD CO10 .....345 K2
  SUD CO10 .....359 J2
Stour Valley Wk SUD CO10 .....20 D4
Stour Vw MGTR CO11 * 65 M2
  MGTR CO11 * 367 K2
Stourview Av MGTR CO11 .....91 L1
Stourview Cl MGTR CO11 .....91 L1
Stour Wk MGTR CO11 * 366 E8
Stour Wy UPMR RM14 .....290 B3
Stowe Cl RCHLM CM3 .....246 A4
Stowe's La BOC CM0 .....390 B5
Stow Rd RCHLM CM3 .....246 A4
The Stow HLW CM20 .....13 M6
Stow Vls RCHLM CM3 * 245 M1
Stradbroke Gv BKHH IG9 .....250 B8
  CLAY IG5 .....286 C1
Stradbroke Pk CHIG IG7 .....268 E8
Stradbroke Rd IPNE IP4 .....48 F6
Strafford Av CLAY IG5 .....268 D6
Strafford Rd POP/IOD E14 .....322 D4

Strahan Rd BOW E3 .....306 D2
Straight Rd COLN CO4 .....87 G6
  COLW CO3 .....128 C5
  HARH RM3 .....271 J4
  KIR/NAC IP10 .....56 B9
  MGTR CO11 .....91 M4
  RCOLE CO7 .....157 K2
Straight Wy COLS CO2 .....151 K3
Strait Rd EHAM E6 .....324 B3
The Straits WAB EN9 .....233 L4
Strandfield Cl
  WOOL/PLUM SE18 .....325 H8
The Strand CHTY IP2 * 54 A1
Strangman Av SBF/HAD SS7 .....298 C1
Strasbourg Rd CVI SS8 .....299 J1
Stratfield Dr BROX EN10 .....200 F3
Stratford Cl BARK IG11 .....309 K4
  DAGE RM10 .....310 D3
Stratford Gdns SLH/COR SS17 .....317 K3
Stratford Rd COS CO15 .....160 A3
  IP IP1 .....47 L3
  PLSTW E13 .....307 K1
  RCOLE CO7 .....363 K10
Strathfield Gdns BARK IG11 .....309 K4
Strathmore TIL RM18 .....332 F3
Strathmore Gdns HCH RM12 .....289 M7
Strathmore Rd RCHLM CM3 .....246 E6
Strattondale St POP/IOD E14 .....322 D4
Stratton Dr BARK IG11 .....309 K4
Strattonhall Drift
  KIR/NAC IP10 .....60 D9
Stratton Rd HARH RM3 .....272 A4
  Stratton Wk HARH RM3 .....272 A4
Strawberry Ct BRTR CM7 .....121 L4
Strawberry Flds HVHL CB9 .....34 A6
Strawberry La K/T/MI CO5 .....174 A6
Strawbrook Hl RCHLM CM3 .....168 B5
Straw La K/T/MI CO5 .....177 J4
Streatfeild Av EHAM E6 .....308 A1
The Street BOC CM0 .....388 G4
  BRTR CM77 .....100 C5
  BRTR CM77 .....120 C6
  BRTR CM77 .....122 D4
  BRTR CM77 .....123 G3
  BSF CM23 .....93 G7
  BSF CM23 .....93 G7
  CHLM/GWD CM1 .....225 L3
  CHLM/WR CM1 .....164 A4
  CHLM/WR CM1 .....165 G3
  CHLM/WR CM1 .....191 K6
  CHONG CM5 .....206 A2
  CHONG CM5 .....383 J1
  FOS CO13 .....368 F12
  FRAM/WMKT IP13 .....50 C1
  GTDUN CM6 .....118 A5
  GTDUN CM6 .....206 A1
  HAR CO12 .....367 J6
  HSTD CO9 .....80 E3
  HSTD CO9 .....344 D1
  HSTD CO9 .....355 N2
  HSTD CO9 .....358 D13
  K/T/MI CO5 .....150 A3
  K/T/MI CO5 .....177 L5
  KIR/NAC IP10 .....60 D9
  MAL CM9 .....173 J8
  MAL CM9 .....175 K7
  MAL CM9 .....213 G3
  MGTR CO11 .....63 K4
  MGTR CO11 .....366 E8
  RBSF CM22 .....189 C5
  RBSF CM22 .....163 M5
  RCHLM CM3 .....165 K4
  RCHLM CM3 .....169 M4
  RCHLM CM3 .....196 C5
  RCHLM CM3 .....230 B5
  RCHLM CM3 .....231 J8
  RCHLM CM3 .....246 E6
  RCOLE CO7 .....89 H7
  RCOLE CO7 .....363 K10
  RCOLW CO6 .....83 H6
  RCOLW CO6 .....103 L5
  RCOS CO16 .....112 B6
  RCOS CO16 .....134 C1
  RCOS CO16 .....158 A3
  RIPS/CAP IP9 .....58 C4
  RIPS/CAP IP9 .....66 C1
  RIPS/CAP IP9 .....66 C3
  RIPS/CAP IP9 .....364 G12
  RIPW IP8 .....365 L19
  RIPW IP8 .....52 E3
  RIPW IP8 .....52 E3
  SUD CO10 .....39 G5
  SUD CO10 .....39 L4
  SUD CO10 .....45 G2
  SUD CO10 .....345 K2
  SUD CO10 .....345 Q4
  SUD CO10 .....347 K2
  WDBR IP12 .....51 N1
  WIT CM8 .....146 B2
  WIT CM8 .....172 A4
Streimer Rd SRTFD E15 .....306 F1
Stretford Ct WIT CM8 * 147 J2
Strethall Rd SAFWS CB11 .....340 H1
Strickland Av DART DA1 .....334 C4
Strickmere RCOLE CO7 .....363 K10
Stride Rd PLSTW E13 .....307 G1
Strode Rd FSTGT E7 .....307 L1
Stroma Gdns SBN/FI SS3 .....303 L1
Stromburg Rd CVI SS8 .....298 C9
Stromness Rd SOSN SS2 .....19 L3
Strone Rd FSTGT E7 .....307 M2
  MNPK E12 .....308 A2
Strood Av ROMW/RG RM7 .....289 J2
Strood Cl K/T/MI CO5 .....177 H6
The Strood K/T/MI CO5 .....177 K8
Strouds CLOTN IP8 .....295 H4
Struan Av SLH/COR SS17 .....295 Q4
Strudwick Cl BRTR CM7 .....121 G3
Strutt Cl RCHLM CM3 .....196 D3
Struttons Av GVW DA11 .....337 J8
Stuart Cl BRWN CM15 .....255 M1
  CHLM/GWD CM2 .....4 C8
  CVI SS8 .....320 E2
  FX IP11 .....63 J1
  IPNE IP4 .....17 L1
  SBN/FI SS3 .....303 J2
  SOSN SS2 .....301 J1
Stuart Pawsey Ct
  RCOLE CO7 * 130 F4
Stuart Rd BARK IG11 .....309 M1
  GRAYS RM17 .....330 B3
  GVW DA11 .....337 K6
  SOSN SS2 .....301 J1
Stuart St BRTR CM7 .....121 K3
Stuart Wy BCAYE CM11 .....259 G4
Stubbers La UPMR RM14 .....313 H6
Stubbs Cl FOS CO13 .....137 J1
  HVHL CB9 .....34 A4
  IPSE IP3 .....54 E1

MGTR CO11 ....90 E1
Stubbs La BRTR CM7 ....121 F3
Stublands BSDN SS14 ....278 C7
Studd's La COLN CO4 ....107 G5
Studland Av WICKW SS12 ....260 C5
Studley Av CHING E4 ....267 G6
Studley Cl CLPT E5 ....306 B2
Studley Dr REDBR IG4 ....286 A4
Studley Rd DAGW RM9 ....310 A4
FSTGT E7 ....307 L3
Stukeley Rd FSTGT E7 ....307 L4
Stump La IPSE IP3 ....55 G2
Sturdee Av IPSE IP3 ....55 G2
Sturge Av WALTH E17 ....266 E7
Sturlas Wy CHES/WCR EN8 ....232 E3
Sturmer Rd HVHL CB9 ....34 F7
HVHL CB9 ....35 K5
Sturrick La RCOLE CO7 ....133 G4
Sturrocks VGE SS16 ....296 B2
Sturry St POP/IOD E14 ....322 E2
Stutton Cl RIPS/CAP IP9 ....364 D11
Stutton La RIPS/CAP IP9 ....364 F12
Stutton Gn RIPS/CAP IP9 ....59 M8
Stutton Rd MGTR CO11 ....65 K3
Styles BRTR CM7 ....
Sub-Station Rd FX IP11 ....10 F6
Sudbourne Av RCOS CO16 ....182 D1
Sudbourne Rd FX IP11 ....62 C8
Sudbrook Cl WICKW SS12 ....261 G7
Sudbury EHAM E6 ....324 D2
Sudbury Rd BARK IG11 ....309 G2
BCAYE CM11 ....242 C5
BURES CO8 ....359 Q8
FX IP11 ....10 J2
HSTD CO9 ....81 L3
HSTD CO9 ....347 N11
HSTD CO9 ....356 H5
HSTD CO9 ....357 K4
HSTD CO9 ....357 R8
SUD CO10 ....42 E5
SUD CO10 ....43 M3
SUD CO10 ....44 C7
Sudburys Farm Rd
BCAYW CM12 ....257 M7
Sudeley Gdns HOC/HUL SS5 ....264 A7
Sudicamps Ct WAB EN9 ....234 B3
Suez Rd PEND EN3 ....248 B4
Suffield Rd CHING E4 ....266 E2
LOS SS9 ....300 C1
COS CO15 ....160 E3
Suffolk Av K/T/MI CO5 ....178 A6
Suffolk Cl COLN CO4 ....9 H3
Suffolk Coast & Heaths Pth
FX IP11 ....69 G2
IPSE IP3 ....54 F7
KIR/NAC IP10 ....60 B2
RIPS/CAP IP9 ....364 F11
RIPS/CAP IP9 ....365 P14
RIPS/CAP IP9 ....367 Q2
Suffolk Crs MAL CM9 ....214 B4
Suffolk Dr CHLM/GWD CM2 ....210 D1
LAIN SS15 ....276 B3
Suffolk Park Rd WALTH E17 ....284 D2
Suffolk Rd BARK IG11 ....309 G4
DAGE RM10 ....310 E2
DART DA1 ....334 A4
GDMY/SEVK IG3 ....287 H4
CVE DA12 ....338 A4
IPNE IP4 ....
MAL CM9 ....214 B4
PLSTW E13 ....307 J7
SUD CO10 ....20 D5
Suffolk Sq SUD CO10 ....20 D5
Suffolk St FSTGT E7 ....307 K2
WOTN CO14 ....137 M1
Suffolk Wy CVI SS8 ....320 B1
EMPK RM11 ....290 D2
Sugar House La SRTFD E15 ....306 F6
Sugar La HOD EN11 ....355 Q10
Sugden Av WICKW SS12 ....260 D6
Sugden Wy BARK IG11 ....309 J6
Sulleys HI HADL IP7 ....363 J9
Sullivan Av CAN/RD E16 ....324 A1
Sullivan Rd TIL RM18 ....331 K1
Sullivan Wy VGE SS16 ....276 D8
Sultan Rd WAN E11 ....285 L2
Summercourt Rd
WOS/PRIT SS0 ....18 D4
Summerdale BCAYW CM12 ....258 D3
RCHLM CM3 ....389 D2
Summerfield Cl IPNE IP4 ....49 J5
Summerfield Rd LOU IG10 ....250 A6
Summerfields HSTD CO9 ....356 H8
ING CM4 ....239 M7
Summerhill RCHLM CM3 ....392 C2
Summerlands CVI SS8 ....298 C8
Summer Pl WOTN CO14 *........369 P10
Summerton Wy THMD SE28 ....326 A3
Summerwood Cl
SBF/HAD SS7 ....298 F2
Summit Dr WFD IG8 ....268 A8
Summit Rd WALTH E17 ....284 E2
The Summit LOU IG10 ....250 C1
Sumners Farm Cl EPP CM16 ....203 J7
Sumpters Wy SOSN SS2 ....283 J7
Sunbank GTDUN CM6 ....117 G9
Sunbeam Av COS CO15 ....182 B7
Sunbeam Cl K/T/MI CO5 ....130 C1
Sunbury St SBN/FI SS3 ....303 H3
Sunbury St WOOL/PLUM SE18 ....324 C6
Sunbury Rd MAL CM9 ....214 C5
Sundale Cl COS CO15 ....160 C3
Sundal RCOLE CO7 * 89 G6
Sunderland Av CBS CB2 ....22 C1
Sunderland Rd FX IP11 ....10 F5
Sunderland Wy MNPK E12 ....286 A1
Sundorne Rd CHARL SE7 ....323 L8
Sundridge Ct DART DA1 ....334 D6
Sunfield Cl IPNE IP4 ....49 L8
Sunflower Wy HARH RM3 ....272 A2
Sun La GVE DA12 ....337 M7
Sun Lido Square Gdns
BRTR CM7 * 120 F3
Sunnedon VGE SS16 * 3 M8
Sunningdale BSF CM23 ....138 E3
CVI SS8 ....320 F1
Sunningdale Av BARK IG11 ....309 G5
IPNE IP4 ....49 J8
LOS SS9 ....300 D4
RAIN RM13 ....311 G3
Sunningdale Ct SOS SS1 * 19 L5
Sunningdale Dr FX IP11 ....63 C7
Sunningdale Fall RCHLM CM3 ....196 F3
Sunningdale Rd
CHLM/WR CM1 ....209 H1
RAIN RM13 ....311 K4
RCHLM CM3 ....392 B4
Sunningdale Wy FOS CO13 ....137 H2
Sunninghill GVW DA11 ....337 H7
Sunnings La UPMR RM14 ....313 J2
Sunnybank Cl LOS SS9 ....282 C9
Sunny Cft HLWS CM18 ....204 A4
Sunnycroft Gdns
UPMR RM14 ....291 J5

Sunnydene Av CHING E4 ....267 G4
Sunnyfield Cl HARH RM3 ....272 C6
Sunnyfield Gdns
HOC/HUL SS5 ....263 L7
Sunnyfields Rd BRTR CM7 ....100 A3
Sunnyhill Cl CLPT E5 ....306 B1
Sunnymede CHIG IG7 ....269 B1
Sunnymede Cl SBF/HAD SS7 ....280 D7
Sunnymede Dr BARK/HLT IG6 ....286 C5
Sunny Ms CRW RM5 ....270 F6
Sunny Point WOTN RM4 ....369 P10
Sunnyside BRTR CM7 ....121 J2
Sunnyside Dr CHING E4 ....248 F7
Sunnyside Gdns UPMR RM14 ....290 F8
Sunnyside Rd EPP CM16 ....236 F2
IL IG1 ....286 F8
LEY E10 ....284 E2
RCOLW CO6 ....85 G3
Sunnyside Wy RCOS CO16 ....158 F3
Sun Ray Av RBRW/HUT CM13 ....257 H2
Sunrise Av CHLM/WR CM1 ....193 M8
HCH RM12 ....289 M8
Sun Rd SWCM DA10 ....336 C4
WFD IG8 ....267 K4
Sunset Av CHING E4 ....248 F9
Sunset Rd THMD SE28 ....325 K5
Sunshine Cl HOC/HUL SS5 * 263 H2
Sun St BCAYW CM12 ....258 D4
SWCM DA11 ....163 G8
WAB EN9 ....234 B3
Surbiton Av SOS SS1 ....302 A5
Surbiton Rd IP IP1 ....47 L6
SOSN SS2 ....302 A4
Surig Rd CVI SS8 ....320 D1
Surlingham Cl THMD SE28 ....326 A3
Surman Crs RBRW/HUT CM13 ....256 F7
Surmans Cl DAGW RM9 ....309 M5
Surrey Av LGS SS9 ....300 C2
Surrey Dr EMPK RM11 ....290 D3
Surrey La K/T/MI CO5 ....173 M1
Surrey Rd BARK IG11 ....309 H4
DAGE RM10 ....310 F2
FX IP11 ....11 J2
IP IP1 ....16 A4
Surrey St PLSTW E13 ....307 L7
Surrey Water Rd
BERM/RHTH SE16 ....322 A4
Surrey Wy LAIN SS15 ....276 D7
Surridge Cl RAIN RM13 ....311 M7
Susan Rd ROMW/RG RM7 ....288 D7
Susannah St POP/IOD E14 ....322 E2
Sussex Av HARH RM3 ....272 C6
Sussex Cl CHLM/WR CM1 ....209 K1
IL IG1 ....
Sussex Gdns COS CO15 ....160 A5
WFD IG8 ....
Sussex Ct BRW CM14 ....273 L3
COLW CO3 ....106 F6
EHAM E6 ....308 D6
Sussex St PLSTW E13 ....307 L7
Sussex Ter PUR RM19 * 328 E8
Sussex Wy BCAYW CM12 ....242 E8
Sutcliffe Cl WICKW SS12 ....261 G6
Sutherland Bvd LOS SS9 ....299 L3
Sutherland Cl GVE DA12 ....338 D3
Sutherland House
WALTH E17 * 284 B1
Sutherland Pl WICKW SS12 ....261 G8
Sutherland Rd BELV DA17 ....326 D6
BOW E3 ....306 C6
PEND EN3 ....248 A6
WALTH E17 ....266 A8
Sutton Acres RBSF CM22 ....163 L2
Sutton Cl BROX EN10 ....200 F6
LOU IG10 ....250 B7
Sutton Ct WARE SG12 * 184 F1
Sutton Court Dr RCFD SS4 ....283 J4
Sutton Court Rd PLSTW E13 ....307 K7
Sutton Md CHLM/GWD CM2 ....210 D1
Sutton Park Av COLW CO3 ....128 G2
Sutton Rd BARK IG11 ....309 H4
PLSTW E13 ....307 L6
RCFD SS4 ....283 K5
SOSN SS2 ....19 J4
WALTH E17 ....
Suttons Av HCH RM12 ....289 M8
Suttons Gdns HCH RM12 ....290 A8
Suttons La HCH RM12 ....312 A2
Swale Cl SOCK/AV RM15 ....328 F2
Swale Rd SBF/HAD SS7 ....280 D5
Swallowcliffe SBN/FI SS3 ....303 G4
Swallow Cl CDW/CHF RM16 ....329 M2
CLPT E5 ....
FX IP11 ....
GRH DA9 ....335 J7
RAYL SS6 ....280 E2
Swallowdale COLS CO2 ....129 M2
Swallow Di VGE SS16 ....295 L1
Swallow Dr SBF/HAD SS7 ....297 L3
Swallow Fld RCOLW CO6 ....82 F9
Swallowfield Rd CHARL SE7 ....323 L8
Swallow Rd CHTY IP2 ....53 G7
WICKE SS11 ....260 E3
Swallows HI WICKW SS12 ....188 D5
Swallow's Rw RCOLE CO7 * 193 L4
The Swallows BCAYE CM11 ....258 F5
Swallow St EHAM E6 ....324 D1
Swallowtail Cl RIPW IP8 ....53 K5
Swallow Wk HSTD CO9 ....81 J4
Swanage Rd CHING E4 ....266 F6
SOSN SS2 ....19 J1
Swan Ap EHAM E6 ....324 D1
Swanbourne Dr HCH RM12 ....312 A1
Swan Cha HSTD CO9 ....356 F9
Swan Cl COLN CO4 ....108 D7
KESG IP5 ....
RCHLM CM3 ....196 C1
WALTH E17 ....266 E7
Swan Ct BSF CM23 ....139 G3
HSTD CO9 ....356 F9
MAL CM9 ....214 A1
MGTR CO11 ....91 J4
Swan Di COS CO15 ....159 J2
Swanfield Rd CHES/WCR EN8 ....232 F3
Swan Gv RCOLW CO6 ....63 M8
Swan HI RIPW IP8 ....53 G5
Swan La BRWN CM15 ....383 M11
HVHL CB9 ....34 B3
ING CM4 ....225 G2
LOU IG10 ....249 M7
NHMKT IP6 ....48 D1
SUD CO10 ....42 D7
WICKE SS11 ....261 G4
Swan Md VGE SS16 ....3 M8

Swan Meadow RCOLE CO7 ....363 K8
Swan Pas COL CO1 * 8 D6
Swan & Pike Rd PEND EN3 ....233 H6
Swan Rd RCOS CO16 ....124 D3
WOOL/PLUM SE18 ....324 D4
Swanscombe St SWCM DA10 ....336 C4
Swanscomb Rd RCOLW CO6 ....83 G1
Swansea Av CHTY IP2 ....54 A4
Swans Green Cl SBF/HAD SS7 ....280 D7
Swanshope LOU IG10 ....250 D2
Swan Side BRTR CM7 ....121 J2
Swans Pasture
CHLM/WR CM1 ....194 A7
Swans Rd CHES/WCR EN8 ....232 E4
Swanstead VGE SS16 ....296 B2
Swan St HSTD CO9 ....356 F8
K/T/MI CO5 ....149 G2
RCOLW CO6 ....103 M2
Swan Wy PEND EN3 ....248 A2
Swan Yd RCOLW CO6 ....124 D3
Swatchway Cl IPSE IP3 ....55 G5
Swaton Rd BOW E3 ....306 D8
Swaynes Rd COLS CO2 ....129 K3
Sweden Cl HAR CO12 ....14 B7
Sweden Ga BERM/RHTH SE16 ....322 A8
Swedish Est MGTR CO11 * 66 E12
Sweet Briar BSF CM23 ....138 E3
Sweet Briar Av SBF/HAD SS7 ....298 A3
Sweet Briar Cl RCOLW CO6 ....360 C4
Sweet Briar Dr LAIN SS15 ....277 G4
Sweet Briar Rd COLW CO3 ....105 M6
Sweet Md SAFWN SS10 ....28 B4
Swete Ct PLSTW E13 ....307 K6
Sweyne Av HLWE CM17 ....204 D4
SOSN SS2 ....18 E3
Sweyne Cl RAYL SS6 ....280 F2
Sweyne Rd SWCM DA10 ....336 B4
Swift Av COLW CO3 ....127 M1
COS CO15 ....182 C7
Swift Cl BRTR CM7 ....121 K5
THMD SE28 ....325 L2
UPMR RM14 ....291 H4
WALTH E17 ....266 B6
WARE SG12 ....184 B1
Swiftsure Rd CDW/CHF RM16 ....329 M7
Swinborne Ct PIT SS13 * 278 E4
Swinborne Dr PIT SS13 ....278 E4
Swinbourne Dr BRTR CM7 ....121 G2
Swinbournes Cft
RCOLW CO6 * 126 B2
Swinburne Gdns TIL RM18 ....331 L8
Swinburne Rd IP IP1 ....47 L8
Swindon Cl GDMY/SEVK IG3 ....287 H7
Swindon Gdns HARH RM3 ....272 C4
Swindon La HARH RM3 ....272 C4
Swinnerton St HOM E9 ....306 F1
Swinton Cl CHTY IP2 ....53 J4
Swiss Av CHLM/WR CM1 ....209 K1
Sworders VB HAR CO12 ....14 C3
Sybil Phoenix Cl DEPT SE8 ....322 A8
Sybourn St WALTH E17 ....284 C3
UPMR RM14 ....290 D8
Sycamore Av BOW E3 ....306 C5
CHESW EN7 ....216 A5
CVI SS8 ....320 C2
GVE DA12 ....338 A5
RAYL SS6 ....262 E7
RBSF CM22 ....377 K2
RIPW IP8 ....53 H4
TIL RM18 ....331 K7
WIT CM8 ....147 K3
Sycamore Dr BRW CM14 ....255 M8
Sycamore Fld
HLWW/ROY CM19 ....203 H5
Sycamore Gv BRTR CM7 ....121 H5
Sycamore Ms ERITH DA8 * 327 J1
Sycamore Pl RCOLE CO7 ....133 H5
Sycamore Wy
CHLM/GWD CM2 ....209 M7
COS CO15 ....A6
FOS CO13 ....137 G2
MGTR CO11 ....65 G5
RCFD SS4 ....392 A12
SOCK/AV RM15 ....314 A4
Sydenham Cl ROM RM1 ....289 J2
Sydervelt Rd CVI SS8 ....320 D1
Sydner Cl CHLM/GWD CM2 ....210 D1
Sydney Av ABYW SE2 ....326 A6
BARK/HLT IG6 ....268 F8
LOS SS9 ....299 L5
SBF/HAD SS7 ....297 M1
TIL RM18 ....331 L6
WAN E11 ....285 L4
WFD IG8 ....267 G4
Sydney St COLS CO2 ....129 L4
RCOLE CO7 ....156 C7
Sykes Md RAYL SS6 ....281 G4
Sylvan Av CHDH RM6 ....288 C4
EMPK RM11 ....290 C4
Sylvan Cl CDW/CHF RM16 ....330 B5
CHLM/GWD CM2 ....209 J1
CVI SS8 ....320 E3
LAIN SS15 ....276 B3
Sylvan Ct PLSTW E13 * 276 C6
Sylvan Ms GRH DA9 ....335 L6
Sylvan Rd WALTH E17 ....284 C5
WAN E11 ....285 K3
Sylvan Tryst BCAYW CM12 ....258 E4
Sylvan Wy BCTR RM8 ....287 L2
CHIG IG7 ....269 L2
LAIN SS15 ....276 C6
LOS SS9 ....299 K1
Sylvesters Rd WALTH E17 * 284 C5
Sylvia Av RBRW/HUT CM13 ....256 F7
Symington Ms HOM E9 * 306 F1
Symmons Ct BRTR CM7 ....120 C6
Symonds Ct CHES/WCR EN8 ....216 E6
Symonds La CBE/LIN CB1 ....24 C1
Symons Av LOS SS9 ....282 B6
Syracuse Av RAIN RM13 ....312 A7

T

Tabernacle Av PLSTW E13 ....307 K8
Taber Pl WIT CM8 * 171 L2
Tabora Av CVI SS8 ....298 C8
Tabor Av BRTR CM7 ....121 H4
Tabor Cl RCOLE CO7 ....156 B5
Tabor Rd COLN CO4 ....9 K7
Tabors Av CHLM/GWD CM2 ....210 A3
Tabrum's La RCHLM CM3 ....244 F6
The Tabrums RCHLM CM3 ....244 F4
Tabrums Wy UPMR RM14 ....291 H5
Tacket St IPNE IP4 ....16 F5
Tacon Rd FX IP11 ....11 H3
Tadlows Cl UPMR RM14 ....312 E2

Tadworth Pde HCH RM12 ....311 L1
Taeping St POP/IOD E14 ....322 E3
Taffrail Gdns HLWE CM17 ....245 L7
Tailors BSF CM23 ....138 C4
Tailors Ct SOSN SS2 ....283 G8
Tailors Wy SOSN SS2 ....283 G8
Tait Ms MAL CM9 ....214 D2
Taits SLH/COR SS17 ....317 J3
Takeley Cl CRW RM5 ....271 G5
WAB EN9 ....233 J2
Takely End VGE SS16 ....2 F8
Takely Ride VGE SS16 ....2 F8
Talbot Av COS CO15 ....182 C7
RAYL SS6 ....280 F2
Talbot Gdns GDMY/SEVK IG3 ....287 J4
Talbot Rd DAGW RM9 ....310 C4
EHAM E6 ....308 C6
FSTGT E7 ....307 H1
RCOS CO16 ....158 F7
SUD CO10 ....20 C7
Talbot St HAR CO12 ....15 J6
Talbrook BRW CM14 ....273 L3
Talcott Rd COLS CO2 ....129 K3
Talisman Cl GDMY/SEVK IG3 ....287 K3
Tallack Rd LEY E10 ....284 C1
Talleys Cl KESG IP5 ....50 B5
Tallis Cl CAN/RD E16 ....323 L2
SLH/COR SS17 ....316 F2
Tallis Wy BRW CM14 ....273 L3
Tallon Rd RBRW/HUT CM13 ....257 H1
Tallow Ga RCHLM CM3 ....245 G2
Tall Trees COLN CO4 ....107 L6
Tall Trees Cl EMPK RM11 ....290 B4
Tallyho Cnr RCOLE CO7 ....363 K7
Tally-Ho Dr RBRW/HUT CM13 ....257 H4
Talus Cl PUR RM19 ....329 G7
Talwin St BOW E3 ....306 F2
Talza Wy SOSN SS2 ....283 J5
Tamage Rd SUD CO10 ....43 M3
Tamar Cl BOW E3 * 306 C4
UPMR RM14 ....291 H4
Tamar Dr SOCK/AV RM15 ....328 F2
Tamarisk SBF/HAD SS7 ....297 M1
Tamarisk Rd SOCK/AV RM15 ....313 M1
Tamarisk Wy COLN CO4 ....108 B5
COS CO15 ....182 C7
Tamar Ri CHLM/WR CM1 ....193 L4
Tamar St WOOL/PLUM SE18 ....324 D7
Tambour Cl RCOLW CO6 * 103 M4
Tamdown Wy HLWE CM17 ....120 F1
Tamworth Av WFD IG8 ....267 H6
Tamworth Cha COLS CO2 ....129 K3
Tamworth Rd HERT/BAY SG13 ....184 D4
Tanfield Cl CHESW EN7 ....216 B5
Tanfield Dr BCAYW CM12 ....258 D7
Tangent Link HARH RM3 ....272 A2
Tangent Rd HARH RM3 ....272 A2
Tangerine Cl COLN CO4 ....9 J8
Tangham Rd WICKE SS11 ....261 L3
Tangmere Ct WICKE SS11 ....261 L3
Tan House La BRW CM14 ....254 F1
Tankerville Dr LOS SS9 ....300 A1
Tank Hill Rd PUR RM19 ....328 C7
Tank La PUR RM19 ....328 D7
Tan La RCOS CO16 ....135 G2
Tanner Cl RCOS CO16 ....182 E2
Tanners La BARK/HLT IG6 ....286 C1
Tanners Meadow BRTR CM7 ....122 A3
Tanners Rd BARK IG11 ....308 F5
Tanners Vw IP IP1 ....47 L6
Tanners Wy RCHLM CM3 ....244 F5
SAFWN CB10 ....28 A2
Tannery Cl DAGE RM10 ....288 D8
Tannery Rd CBS CB2 ....22 C7
Tanswell Cl PIT SS13 ....278 E4
Tanswell Ct PIT SS13 ....278 E4
Tansy Cl EHAM E6 ....308 B4
HARH RM3 ....272 A2
Tant Av CAN/RD E16 ....323 J2
Tantony Gv CHDH RM6 ....288 A1
The Tanyard CTDUN CM6 ....74 D5
Tanys Dell HLWW/ROY CM20 ....188 B6
Tapestry St RCOLW CO6 * 82 D7
Tapley Rd CHLM/WR CM1 ....193 L2
Tapsworth Cl RCOS CO16 ....6 C5
Tapwoods COLW CO3 ....106 D6
Tara Cl COLN CO4 ....M3
Taranto Rd SOCK/AV RM15 ....314 A4
Tarling Rd CAN/RD E16 ....323 G2
Tarn Hows Cl FX IP11 ....63 D7
Tarnworth Rd HARH RM3 ....272 D4
Tarpan Wy BROX EN10 ....217 G4
Tarragona Ms COLS CO2 ....129 K3
Tarragon Cl K/T/MI CO5 ....149 M1
Tarriff Crs DEPT SE8 ....322 C7
Tasker Rd CDW/CHF RM16 ....331 G4
Tasman Cl SLH/COR SS17 ....317 J1
Tasmania Rd IPNE IP4 ....49 J7
Tasman Rd HVHL CB9 ....34 A4
Tate Rd CAN/RD E16 ....324 C4
Tatsfield Av WAB EN9 ....217 J1
Tattenham Rd LAIN SS15 ....276 C5
Tattersall Gdns LOS SS9 ....299 L3
Tattersalls Cha BCC CM0 ....393 P1
Tattersall Wy CHLM/WR CM1 ....209 H6
Tatton St HLWE CM17 ....188 D8
Taunton Cl BARK/HLT IG6 ....269 J5
IP IP1 ....48 C1
Taunton Dr WOS/PRIT SS0 ....300 C1
Taunton Rd CHLM/WR CM1 ....193 J4
FX IP11 ....62 B8
GVW DA11 ....336 D3
HARH RM3 ....271 M4
Taunton V GVE DA12 ....338 A3
Taverners Green Cl
WICKW SS12 ....261 H7
Taverners Wk WIT CM8 ....171 H1
Taverners Wy CHING E4 ....249 H8
HOD EN11 ....201 H3
Tavern St IP IP1 ....16 C3
Tavistock Av WALTH E17 ....284 A1
Tavistock Cl HARH RM3 ....272 A2
Tavistock Dr CHLM/GWD CM2 ....210 C8
Tavistock Gdns
GDMY/SEVK IG3 ....309 H1
Tavistock Rd CHLM/WR CM1 ....194 B8
WAN E11 ....285 K3
Tavistock Sq
LAIN SS15 ....276 F6
SWFD E18 ....267 M3
WAN E11 ....307 L2
Tavy Br ABYW SE2 ....325 L7
Tawell Ms K/T/MI CO5 ....150 F7
Tawney La ABR/ST RM4 ....237 L2
EPP CM16 ....237 K2
Tawney Rd THMD SE28 ....325 L3
Tawneys Ride BURES CO8 ....359 Q8
Tawny Av UPMR RM14 ....291 M5
Tawny Wy BERM/RHTH SE16 ....322 A8
Tayburn Cl POP/IOD E14 ....322 F2
Taylifers HLWW/ROY CM19 ....203 H6
Taylor Av CHLM/WR CM1 ....193 L2
Taylor Cl CRW RM5 ....270 D6
Taylor Ct COL CO1 ....
Taylor Dr MGTR CO11 ....90 F1

Taylors Av HOD EN11 ....201 H4
Taylor's Buildings
WOOL/PLUM SE18 ....324 E7
Taylors End Rd RBSF CM22 ....374 F12
Taylors Farm Rd HLWS CM18 ....35 L2
Taylors La HOO/HM ME3 ....339 L8
Taylor's Rd K/T/MI CO5 ....130 C5
Tay Wy ROM RM1 ....271 J2
Teagles LAIN SS15 2
Teak Cl BERM/RHTH SE16 ....322 B4
Teal Av RCHLM CM3 ....388 D9
CAN/RD E16 ....324 A1
CHTY IP2 ....53 J2
RCOLE CO7 ....108 D7
Teal Wy K/T/MI CO5 ....149 C3
Teasel Crs THMD SE28 ....325 H4
Teasel Wy SRTFD E15 ....307 H7
Tedder Cl COLS CO2 * 129 K1
Teddington Vls SOSN SS2 * 18 C1
Tees Cl UPMR RM14 ....291 G5
Teesdale Rd WAN E11 ....285 J4
Tees Dr HARH RM3 ....272 A2
Tee Side HERT/BAY SG13 ....184 C2
Tees Rd CHLM/WR CM1 ....193 M7
Teign Dr WIT CM8 ....171 J3
Teigngrace SBN/FI SS3 ....303 G5
Teignmouth Dr RAYL SS6 ....263 G8
Telegraph Ms GDMY/SEVK IG3 ....287 J6
Telegraph Pl POP/IOD E14 ....322 E7
Telese Av CVI SS8 ....321 G1
Telford Cl WALTH E17 ....284 B5
Telham Rd EHAM E6 ....308 D6
Tempest Md EPP CM16 ....221 J5
Tempest Wy RAIN RM13 ....311 K3
Templar Dr THMD SE28 ....326 A2
Templar Rd BRTR CM7 ....122 A3
Templars Cl WIT CM8 ....171 H4
Templars Ct DART DA1 * 334 C7
Temple Av BCTR RM8 ....288 A4
Temple Bank HLWW/ROY 188 C4
Temple Cl CBS CB2 ....22 B8
CHESW EN7 ....232 B1
FOS CO13 ....137 K3
SBF/HAD SS7 ....299 J2
WAN E11 ....285 H5
WOOL/PLUM SE18 ....324 F6
Temple Ct COLN CO4 ....9 M1
Temple Gdns BCTR RM8 ....288 A4
Temple HI DART DA1 ....334 C7
Temple Hill Sq DART DA1 ....334 C7
Temple La BRTR CM7 ....146 E3
Temple Md HLWW/ROY CM19 ....202 C1
Templemead WIT CM8 ....171 J2
Temple Mills La LEY E10 ....306 E1
Temple Pattle MGTR CO11 ....64 F6
Templer Av CDW/CHF RM16 ....330 F1
Temple Rd RCOLS CO2 ....128 D3
EHAM E6 ....308 D6
IPSE IP3 ....55 H1
Templeton Av CHING E4 ....266 C5
Temple Wy MAL CM9 ....198 C6
Templewood Ct SBF/HAD SS7 ....299 H2
Templewood Rd COLN CO4 ....108 B4
PIT SS13 ....278 E4
SBF/HAD SS7 ....299 G2
Temptin Av CVI SS8 ....321 G1
Ten Acre Ap MAL CM9 ....198 C8
Tenbury Cl FSTGT E7 ....308 A2
Tenby Cl CHDH RM6 ....288 B4
Tenby Rd CHDH RM6 ....288 B4
CHTY IP2 ....54 A4
WALTH E17 ....284 B3
Tendring Av RAYL SS6 ....280 C2
Tendring Rd HLWS CM18 ....13 J3
RCOLE CO7 ....111 G5
RCOS CO16 ....112 C3
RCOS CO16 ....135 G1
Tenison Wy CHDH RM6 ....287 M3
Tennand Cl CHESW EN7 ....216 A4
Tennants Rw TIL RM18 ....331 H8
Tennyson Av GRAYS RM17 ....330 E2
MNPK E12 ....308 B4
SOSN SS2 ....301 L2
WAB EN9 ....233 H4
WAN E11 ....285 K5
Tennyson Cl BRTR CM7 ....121 J5
LOS SS9 ....299 K3
PEND EN3 ....248 A5
Tennyson Dr PIT SS13 ....278 A6
Tennyson Rd CHLM/WR CM1 ....193 J3
DART DA1 ....334 D7
HARH RM3 ....271 M4
IPNE IP4 ....17 M1
MAL CM9 ....214 D4
RBRW/HUT CM13 ....256 F7
SRTFD E15 ....307 H4
WALTH E17 ....284 C4
Tennyson Wk GVW DA11 ....337 G8
TIL RM18 ....331 H8
Tenpenny HI RCOLE CO7 ....132 B7
Tensing Av GVW DA11 * 337 H8
Tensing Gdns BCAYW CM12 ....258 C4
Tenterden Rd BCTR RM8 ....288 C4
Tenterfield CTDUN CM6 ....117 H4
Tenter Fld RCOLE CO7 ....363 G4
Tenterfield Rd MAL CM9 ....214 D3
Tenterfields PIT SS13 ....278 E5
SAFWS CB11 ....33 N12
Tenth Av STSD CM24 ....374 D11
Tenth Rd KIR/NAC IP10 ....57 G7
Tercel Pth CHIC IG7 ....269 L3
Terence Cl GVE DA12 ....338 C7
Terence Webster Rd
WICKW SS12 ....261 G7
Teresa Gdns CHES/WCR EN8 ....232 D4
Terling VGE SS16 ....3 H8
Terling Cl COLS CO2 ....129 K4
WAN E11 ....285 J8
Terling Hall Rd RCHLM CM3 ....169 J4
Terling Rd BCTR RM8 ....288 D7
RCHLM CM3 ....170 C7
WIT CM8 ....170 D7
The Terlings BRW CM14 ....273 K2
Terminal Cl SBN/FI SS3 ....303 L3
Terminal Rd North
RBSF CM22 ....375 J10
Terminal Rd South
RBSF CM22 ....375 J10
Terminus Dr VGE SS16 ....296 F3
Terminus St HLW CM20 ....13 D5
Termitts Cha RCHLM CM3 ....170 D6
Terms Av CVI SS8 ....298 C8
Tern Cl HVHL CB9 ....34 C1
K/T/MI CO5 ....149 G2
RCHLM CM3 ....388 D9
Terndale COS CO15 ....159 J7
Tern Gdns UPMR RM14 ....291 H4
Terni Rd CVI SS8 ....321 G2
Tern Ms RCOLE CO7 ....130 C1
Tern Rd CHTY IP2 ....53 K3
Tern Wy BRW CM14 ....273 H3

Terrace Hall Cha RCOLW CO6....86 F7
Terrace Rd HOM E9....306 A4
  PLSTW E13....307 K5
Terrace St GVE DA12....337 L4
The Terrace CHING E4 *....267 H2
  DEPT SE8 *....322 C7
  GTDUN CM6 *....118 G8
  GVE DA12....337 M4
  K/T/MI CO5 *....153 K2
  LOS SS9 *....300 B5
  RAYL SS6 *....262 F6
  RCOLE CO7 *....89 H6
  SBN/FI SS3....303 J7
Terrace Wk DAGW RM9....310 B8
Terry Gdns KESG IP5....50 D6
Teviot Av SOCK/AV RM15....328 F2
Teviot St POP/IOD E14....322 F1
Tew CI K/T/MI CO5....150 A7
Tewkesbury CI LOU IG10....250 D6
Tewkesbury Pde COS CO15 *....6 F2
Tewkesbury Rd COS CO15 *....6 F3
Tewkes Rd CVI SS8....299 G8
Tewson Rd WOOL/PLUM SE18....325 H8
Tey Rd RCOLW CO6....102 F5
  RCOLW CO6....103 H3
  RCOLW CO6....104 A3
  RCOLW CO6....124 F2
Tey Road CI RCOLW CO6....82 F7
Thackeray Av TIL RM18....331 L7
Thackeray CI BRTR CM7....121 K5
Thackeray Dr CHDH RM6....153 L5
Thackeray Rd EHAM E6....308 A6
  IP IP1 *....47 L3
Thackerey Rw WICKW SS12....261 G7
Thai Massing CI
  RBRW/HUT CM13....256 C5
Thame Rd BERM/RHTH SE16....322 E5
Thames Av CHLM/WR CM1....193 G8
  DAGW RM9....310 B8
Thamesbank PI THMD SE28....325 M2
Thames Cir POP/IOD E14....322 F2
Thames CI BRTR CM7....122 A4
  LOS SS9....300 A5
  RAIN RM13....327 L2
  RAYL SS6....280 F4
  SLH/COR SS17....317 K2
Thames Crs CDW/CHF RM16....295 L8
Thames Dr CDW/CHF RM16....331 H4
  LOS SS9....299 G4
Thames Ga DART DA1....334 D7
Thames Haven Rd
  SLH/COR SS17....317 K2
Thameside Crs CVI SS8....320 C2
Thamesmere Dr THMD SE28....325 K3
Thames Pth
  BERM/RHTH SE16....322 C6
  BOW E3....306 F6
  CLPT E5....284 A4
  GNWCH SE10....323 K6
Thames Rd BARK IG11....309 K7
  CAN/RD E16....324 D4
  CVI SS8....320 C3
Thames Vw GRAYS RM17....331 H4
  VGE SS16....294 F4
Thames Wy BOC CM0....393 K7
  GVW DA11....337 H5
  GVW DA11....337 H5
Thamley PUR RM19....328 F2
Thanet Gra WOS/PRIT SS0....282 F3
Thanet Rd IPNE IP4....49 G7
Thant CI LEY E10....306 E1
Thatchers CI LOU IG10....250 F2
Thatchers Cft RCHLM CM3....231 H7
Thatchers Dr RCOLE CO7....109 J7
The Thatchers BSF CM23....138 D5
Thatches Gv CHDH RM6....288 D2
Thaxted on RBRW/HUT CM13....256 F1
Thaxted Rd BKHH IG9....250 B7
  SAFWN CB10....30 C2
  SAFWN CB10....352 A9
Thaxted Wk COLS CO2....129 K5
Thaxted Wy WARE EN9....233 L8
Thear CI WOS/PRIT SS0....300 F1
Theatre Sq SRTFD E15....307 G3
Theberton Rd IPSE IP3....55 H1
Thele Av WARE SG12....185 L5
Theleway CI HOD EN11....185 J8
Thelma Av CVI SS8....320 D1
Theobald Rd WALTH E17....284 C5
Theobalds Av GRAYS RM17....330 F4
Theobald's Gv
  CHES/WCR EN8 *....232 E2
Theobald's La CHES/WCR EN8....232 E2
Theobalds Rd LOS SS9....299 M4
Thermopylae Ga
  POP/IOD E14....322 E7
Thetford PI LAIN SS15....277 G4
Thetford Rd DAGW RM9....310 B8
  IP IP1....47 L6
Theydon Av WAB EN9....234 C3
Theydon Crs BSDN SS14....278 E1
Theydon Gdns RAIN RM13....311 H4
Theydon Gv EPP CM16 *....235 M6
Theydon Gv EPP CM16....220 B8
  WFD IG8....267 M5
Theydon Park Rd EPP CM16....251 H1
Theydon PI EPP CM16....236 A1
Theydon Rd EPP CM16....235 L4
Theydon St WALTH E17....284 C5
Thicket Rd DAGW RM9....309 M3
Thielen Rd CVI SS8....298 D8
Thieves Cnr CHLM/WR CM1....208 C1
Third Av CHDH RM6....287 M4
  CHLM/WR CM1....193 J8
  COS CO15....7 M4
  CVI SS8....320 B1
  DAGE RM10....310 H6
  FOS CO13....137 H5
  GVW DA11 *....337 J4
  HAR CO12....15 C9
  HLWS CM18....13 G7
  HLWW/ROY CM19....203 M4
  HSTD CO9....81 L4
  MNPK E12....308 B1
  PLSTW E13....307 K1
  RCOS CO16....181 L7
  SBF/HAD SS7 *....280 D7
  SLH/COR SS17....317 H1
  STSD CM24....374 C11
  WALTH E17....284 D3
  WICKE SS11....261 K7
  WOTN RM20....369 H10
Thirlmere CI BRTR CM77....121 C6
Thirlmere Rd SBF/HAD SS7....280 B6
Thirslet Dr MAL CM9....214 H4
Thirtieth St STSD CM24....374 C10
Thirtle CI RCOS CO16....159 G3
Thirza Rd DART DA1....334 C4
Thisselt Rd CVI SS8....298 D8
Thistlebrook ABYW SE2....325 N6
Thistle CI CHTY IP2....53 L1
  LAIN SS15....277 J4
Thistledene Av CRW RM5....270 C4
Thistledown BRTR CM7....98 D6
  BSDN SS16....13 J5
  COLN CO4....107 L2
Thistledown Ct BSDN SS14....3 K5
Thistle Md LOU IG10....250 D8

Thistle Rd GVE DA12....338 B5
Thistley CI LOS SS9....300 C1
  MAL CM9....384 B2
Thistley Crs SAFWS CB11....73 M8
Thistley Green Rd BRTR CM7....96 A9
Thoby La BRWN CM15....238 D3
Thomas Av FX IP11....62 B5
Thomas Bata Av TIL RM18....332 E3
Thomas Bell Rd RCOLW CO6....82 D7
Thomas CI BRWN CM15....256 B5
  CHLM/GWD CM2....210 D3
Thomas Cribb Ms EHAM E6....324 C2
Thomas Dr CVI SS8....298 B8
  GVE DA12....338 A7
Thomasin Rd PIT SS13....278 F4
Thomas North Ter
  CAN/RD E16 *....323 J1
  PIT SS13....279 H6
  POP/IOD E14....322 C2
Thomas Rochford Wy
  CHES/WCR EN8....217 G5
Thomas St RCOLE CO7....156 C7
  WOOL/PLUM SE18....324 D7
Thomas Wakley CI COLN CO4....87 J8
Thomas Wk SAFWS CB11....350 A5
Thompson Av COLW CO3....106 C7
  CVI SS8....321 J2
Thompson CI IL IG1....286 F7
Thompson Rd DAGW RM9....288 D7
Thompsons CI CHESW EN7....216 A7
Thong La GVE DA12....338 D7
Thorington Av SBF/HAD SS7....281 G7
Thorington Rd BRTR CM77....120 F7
Thorington Rd RAYL SS6....281 K4
Thorin's Ga RCHLM CM3....244 F4
Thorley Hi BSF CM23....139 C4
Thorley La BSF CM23....138 C5
Thorley Park Rd BSF CM23....138 B6
Thornbera CI BSF CM23....139 G5
Thornbera Gdns BSF CM23....139 F5
Thornbera Rd BSF CM23....139 G5
Thornberry Av RCOS CO16....134 C5
Thornborough Av
  RCHLM CM3....245 H6
Thornbury Rd HOD EN11....185 H1
Thornbury Rd COS CO15 *....7 G3
Thornbush LAIN SS15....2 A5
Thornbush La RIPW IP8....46 B5
Thorncroft EMPK RM11....289 L4
  SAFWN CB10....28 C7
Thorndale SBF/HAD SS7....280 E6
Thorndales BRW CM14....256 A7
Thorndon Ap
  RBRW/HUT CM13....274 F2
Thorndon Av
  RBRW/HUT CM13....274 F7
Thorndon CI RCOS CO16....182 D1
Thorndon Ga
  RBRW/HUT CM13....274 F7
Thorndon Park CI LOS SS9....281 M8
Thorndon Park Crs LOS SS9....281 L8
Thorndon Park Dr LOS SS9....281 L8
Thorne CI CAN/RD E16....323 K2
  WAN E11 *....307 H1
Thorne Rd K/T/MI CO5....148 E3
Thorney Bay Rd CVI SS8....320 C3
Thorney Rd RIPS/CAP IP9....58 D3
Thornfield Rd BSF CM23....138 F1
Thornford Gdns SOSN SS2....283 J8
Thorn Gv BSF CM23....139 J3
Thornham Gv SRTFD E15....307 K4
Thornhayes CI IP2 *....53 M2
Thornhill EPP CM16....221 K4
  LOS SS9....300 B1
  RCHLM CM3....230 A4
Thornhill CI FOS CO13....137 J2
Thornhill Gdns BARK IG11....309 H4
  LEY E10....284 E7
Thornhill Rd LEY E10....284 E7
Thorn La RAIN RM13....312 A6
Thornley Dr IPNE IP4....49 H5
Thornley Rd FX IP11....62 B5
Thornridge BRW CM14....255 L7
Thorns Wy WOTN CO14....137 K2
Thornton Dr COLN CO4....87 J3
Thornton PI ING CM4....241 H3
Thornton Rd BELV DA17 *....326 F7
  IL IG1....308 L1
  RBSF CM22....377 N1
  WAN E11....285 G7
Thorntons Farm Av
  ROMW RM7....288 F7
Thornton Wy LAIN SS15....276 D8
Thorntree Rd CHARL SE7....324 A8
Thorn Wy FX IP11....62 H2
Thornwood COLN CO4....107 J1
Thornwood CI K/T/MI CO5....178 A7
  SWFD E18....267 K5
Thornwood Rd EPP CM16....220 D6
Thorogood Gdns SRTFD E15....307 H2
Thorogood Wy RAIN RM13....311 H5
Thorold Rd IL IG1....286 H1
Thorolds VGE SS16....296 B2
Thoroughfare IP IP1....16 E4
Thoroughgood Rd COS CO15 *....7 H6
Thorpe Bay Gdns SOS SS1....302 D7
Thorpe CI HOC/HUL SS5....302 A2
Thorpe Ct WALTH E17....266 C5
Thorpedale Gdns
  GNTH/NBYPK IG2....286 D2
Thorpedene Av HOC/HUL SS5....263 H3
Thorpedene Gdns SBN/FI SS3....303 G6
Thorpe Esp SOS SS1....302 E6
Thorpe Gn SBN/FI SS3 *....303 J6
Thorpe Hall Av SOS SS1....302 E5
Thorpe Hall CI SOS SS1....302 D5
Thorpe Hall Rd WALTH E17....266 A4
Thorpe La FX IP11....61 L5
Thorpe Park Rd RCOS CO16....135 K6
Thorpe Rd BARK IG11....309 G6
  EHAM E6....308 C5
  FOS CO13....136 C2
  FSTGT E7....288 C4
  HOC/HUL SS5....282 E3
  RCOS CO16....112 D8
  RCOS CO16....159 J3
  WALTH E17....266 A4
Thorpe's Hi RIPW IP8....46 B2
Thorpe Leas CVI SS8....320 E3
Thorrington Cross BSDN SS14....3 J5
Thorrington Rd RCOLE CO7....132 F5
Thors CI RCOS CO16....158 F1
Thors Oak SLH/COR SS17....317 H3
Thoydon Rd BOW E3....306 B6
Thracian CI COLS CO2....128 D7
Threadneedle St RCOLE CO7....363 N10
Three Acres RCOS CO16....181 K4
Three Colt St POP/IOD E14....322 C3
Three Crowns Rd COLN CO4....8 A1
Three Forests Wy
  ABR/STK RM4....237 L2
  CHONG CM5....381 L1
  CHONG CM5....381 L5
  HLWW/ROY CM19....202 A1
  LOU IG10....250 A1
  RBSF CM22....376 B8
  RBSF CM22....376 C4
  SBW CM21....162 A5
  SBW CM21....189 G1
  WAB EN9....202 B1
  WAB EN9....234 D6
Three Gates CI HSTD CO9....81 J6
Three Horseshoes Rd
  HLWW/ROY CM19....203 A3
Three Mile HI ING CM4....224 F5
Three Mill La BOW E3....306 F7
Tremhall Av RBSF CM22....374 G12
  RBSF CM22....376 A1
Threshelford VGE SS16....2 D9
Thresher CI BSF CM23....138 D4
Threshers End COLW CO3....106 A8
Thrifts Md EPP CM16....235 M7
Thrift Wd RCHLM CM3....228 B4
Throckmorten Rd
  CAN/RD E16....323 J2
Through Jollys KESG IP5....50 C5
Throwley CI ABYW SE2....325 N6
  PIT SS13....278 F3
Thrushdale COS CO15....159 J7
Thunder Rd DAGW RM9....310 B8
Thundersley Church Rd
  SBF/HAD SS7....280 A8
Thundersley Gv SBF/HAD SS7....280 C8
Thundersley Park Rd
  SBF/HAD SS7....298 A2
Thurgood Rd HOD EN11....201 H1
Thurlby CI WFD IG8....268 A3
Thurlestone Av
  GDMY/SEVK IG3....309 J1
Thurloe Gdns ROM RM1....289 H4
Thurloe Wk GRAYS RM17....330 F5
Thurlow CI CHING E4....266 K5
Thurlow Dr SOS SS1....302 C5
Thurlow Gdns CHIG IG7....269 G5
Thurlston CI COLN CO4....9 M7
Thurlstone SBF/HAD SS7....280 E6
Thurmans La FX IP11....62 A5
Thurrock Park Wy
  GRAYS RM17....331 G6
Thurso St HARH RM3....272 E5
Thurstable CI MAL CM9....385 F4
Thurstable Rd MAL CM9....385 H4
Thurstable Wy MAL CM9....385 H5
Thurstans HLWW/ROY CM19....203 J6
Thurston Av SOSN SS2....302 B4
Thurston Ct FX IP11....10 D2
Thyme Rd K/T/MI CO5....149 M8
Thynne Rd BCAYE CM11....258 F3
Tibalds Rd BOW E3....306 E8
Tiberius CI COLN CO4....87 L8
  HVHL CB9....35 L6
Tiberius Gdns WIT CM8....171 H5
Tickenhall Dr HLWE CM17....204 F1
Tickfield Av SOSN SS2....18 F1
Tickford Rd ABYW SE2....325 N6
Tidal Basin Rd CAN/RD E16....323 J3
Tideswell CI BRTR CM7....122 A1
Tideway Md WALTH E17....214 E5
Tidey St BOW E3....322 E1
Tidings Hi HSTD CO9....81 L8
Tidworth Av WICKW SS11....261 H5
Tidworth Rd BOW E3....306 D8
Tidy's La EPP CM16....220 B7
Tiffin Dr K/T/MI CO5....150 B7
Tighfield Wk RCHLM CM3....244 F8
Tilburg Rd CVI SS8....320 D1
Tilbury Md HLWS CM18....203 B3
Tilbury Rd EHAM E6....308 C6
  HSTD CO9....345 P6
  HSTD CO9....346 B10
  LEY E10....284 F5
  RBRW/HUT CM13....275 H6
Tildesley CI FOS CO13....136 C3
Tile Barn La WIT CM8....89 M3
Tilegate Rd CHONG CM5....205 K5
  HLWS CM18....204 A3
Tile House Rd RCOLW CO6....86 C5
Tilekiln CI CHESW EN7....216 A7
Tilkey Rd RCOLW CO6....124 C5
Tiller Rd POP/IOD E14....322 D6
Tillingham Ct WAB EN9....234 D2
Tillingham Rd BOC CM0....189 G12
Tillingham Wy RAYL SS6....280 D2
Tillotson Rd IL IG1....286 D5
Tilney Dr DAGW RM9....310 A3
Tilney Turn VGE SS16....296 C1
Tilsit PI RCOLE CO7 *....89 G2
Tilston CI WAN E11....285 G7
Timberden Av BARK/HLT IG6....268 F7
Timber Hi COL CO1 *....9 J7
Timberlog CI BSDN SS14....278 B3
Timberlog La BSDN SS14....278 B3
Timmermans Vw VGE SS16....296 C2
Timber Pond Rd
  BERM/RHTH SE16....322 A5
Timbers BRTR CM77....120 F7
Timothy Rd POP/IOD E14....322 C1
Timsons La CHLM/GWD CM2....210 D3
Tinabrook CI CHTY IP2....53 K4
Tindall CI HARH RM3....272 C3
Tindal St CHLM/WR CM1....5 H3
Tindon End Rd SAFWN CB10....352 C7
Tine Rd CHIG IG7....269 H4
Tinker's CI RCFD SS4....283 J4
Tinker St HAR CO12....367 M8
Tinker Side BSDN SS14....3 H5
Tinnocks La BOC CM0....385 L12
Tintagel Wy MAL CM9....214 A5
Tintern Av WOS/PRIT SS0....18 B3
Tintern CI CHTY IP2....53 M3
Tinto Rd CAN/RD E16....323 K1
Tiplers Br BCAYE CM11....241 J4
Tippersfield SBF/HAD SS7....298 B3
Tippett CI COLN CO4....108 B7
Tipps Cross La BRWN CM15....383 Q9
Tips Cross Md BRWN CM15....383 Q9
Tiptree CI CHING E4....266 D6
  LOS SS9....300 C1
Tiptree Crs CLAY IG5....268 B2
Tiptree Gv WICKW SS12....261 G6
Tiptree Hall La K/T/MI CO5....173 L6
Tiptree Rd WIT CM8....171 H2
Tiree Cha WICKW SS12....261 J8
Tirrell Rd GRAYS RM17....330 F3
Titan Rd GRAYS RM17....330 F4
Titchfield Rd PEND EN3....232 F7
Titchwell Dr IPSE IP3....55 H3
Tithe CI WIT CM8....171 H2
Tithelands WICKW SS12....260 G4
The Tithe WICKW SS12....260 D2
Titley CI CHING E4....266 B6
Titmuss Av THMD SE28....325 L3
Titus Wy COLN CO4....286 D1
Tiverton Av CLAY IG5....268 C2
Tivoli Gdns WOOL/PLUM SE18....324 B7
Tobago St POP/IOD E14....322 D5
Tobruk Rd CHLM/WR CM1....193 J7
  COLS CO2....129 G2
Toddbrook HLWW/ROY CM19....12 D8
Todd CI RAIN RM13....312 A8
Toft Av GRAYS RM17....331 G3
Tofts Cha RCHLM CM3....196 B8
Tofts Wk BRTR CM7....121 J2
Toga CI COLS CO2....128 D3
Tog La RCOLW CO6....86 D2
Tokely Rd RCOLE CO7....132 D2
Tokio Rd IPNE IP4....17 M4
Toledo Rd IPNE IP4....17 M4
Toledo CI COLS CO2....19 J5
Toledo Rd SOS SS1....19 J5
Toll GRH DA9....334 F6
Toller Rd IPSE IP3....17 J9
Tollesbury CI WICKW SS12....261 H7
Tollesbury Gdns
  BARK/HLT IG6....287 G1
Tollesbury Rd MAL CM9....384 F1
Tolleshunt D'Arcy Rd
  COS CO15....384 C2
Tollgate St WCHPL E1 *....306 E8
Tollgate SBF/HAD SS7....280 F7
Tollgate Dr COLS CO3....105 L2
Tollgate East COLW CO3....105 M7
Tollgate Rd CHES/WCR EN8....232 G5
  COLW CO3....105 M8
  EHAM E6....324 B1
Toll Gate Rd RIPS/CAP IP9....58 D4
Tollgate West COLW CO3....105 M8
Tolliday CI RCOLE CO7....130 D3
Tolpuddle Wy PLSTW E13....307 H5
Tolworth Gdns CHDH RM6....288 B3
Tolworth Rd IPNE IP4....48 F7
Tom Cribb Rd
  WOOL/PLUM SE18....324 F6
Tom Jenkinson Rd
  CAN/RD E16....323 J4
Tomkins CI SLH/COR SS17....316 F3
Tomkyns La UPMR RM14....291 G3
Tomline Ct KIR/NAC IP10....56 A9
Tomline Rd FX IP11....11 L3
  IPSE IP3....48 F9
Tomlins CI ROY SC8....348 E10
Tomlins Orch BARK IG11....308 F5
Tomlin's Ter POP/IOD E14....322 B2
Tomlyns CI RBRW/HUT CM13....257 H2
Tom Mann CI BARK IG11....309 H5
Tom Nolan CI SRTFD E15....307 H6
Tom's La BRTR CM7....353 R11
Tomswood HI BARK/HLT IG6....268 C7
Tomswood Rd CHIG IG7....268 D5
Tom Tit La MAL CM9....213 M5
Tonbridge Rd HARH RM3....272 A6
  HOC/HUL SS5....264 C6
Tongres Rd CVI SS8....320 D1
Tony Webb CI COLN CO4....107 L1
Took Ct RCHLM CM3....244 F7
Tooley St GVW DA11....337 G5
Toot Hill Rd RCHLM CM5....382 A4
Top House Ri CHING E4....248 F7
Toplands Av SOCK/AV RM15....328 E4
Topmast Point
  POP/IOD E14 *....322 E5
Toppesfield Av WICKW SS12....260 F3
Toppesfield Rd HSTD CO9....356 A1
Top Rd MAL CM9....174 D3
  MAL CM9....213 M1
  SAFWN CB10....352 B6
Top St WDBR IP12....51 H7
Tor Bryan ING CM4....239 L3
Tor Gv THMD SE28....325 M3
Torney CI VGE SS16....294 C1
Toronto Av MNPK E12....308 C1
Toronto Rd IL IG1....286 E6
  TIL RM18....331 K8
Torquay CI RAYL SS6....263 G8
Torquay Gdns REDBR IG4....286 A2
Torquay Rd CHLM/WR CM1....194 A8
Torrance CI EMPK RM11....289 M6
Torrens Rd SRTFD E15....307 J3
Torrens Sq SRTFD E15....307 J3
Torrington SBN/FI SS3....303 G5
Torrington CI SLH/COR SS17....316 D3
Torrington Dr LOU IG10....250 F2
Torrington Gdns LOU IG10....250 F2
Torrington Rd BCTR RM8....288 B1
Torsi Rd CVI SS8....321 G2
Tortoiseshell CI CHTY IP2....53 K5
Tortoiseshell Wy BRTR CM7....121 J4
Tortosa CI COLS CO2....129 L1
Torver CI BRTR CM77....120 F7
Torver Gv IP IP1 *....47 L3
Totham Hill Gn MAL CM9....173 M7
Totlands Dr COS CO15....159 J7
Tot La BSF CM23....115 G6
Totman CI RAYL SS6....280 F5
Totman Crs RAYL SS6....280 F5
Totnes Wk CHLM/WR CM1....194 M4
Totteridge CI RCOS CO16....159 J8
Totteridge Rd PEND EN3....232 F7
Toucan CI SBN/FI SS3....303 G4
Toucan Wy COS CO15....159 J7
  VGE SS16....295 K2
Toulmin Rd RCHLM CM3....196 D1
Tovell's Rd IPNE IP4....17 M3
Tovey Av HOD EN11....201 H1
Tovey CI WAB EN9....217 M1
Towcester Rd BOW E3....306 F8
Tower Av CHLM/WR CM1....4 C1
Tower CI CHIG IG7....268 E5
  EPP CM16....221 L2
Tower Ct EMPK RM14....273 M1
  WOS/PRIT SS0 *....18 A5
Tower Court Ms WOS/PRIT SS0....18 A5
Tower Cut RCOLE CO7....156 C7
Towerfield CI SBN/FI SS3....303 H6
Towerfield Rd SBN/FI SS3....303 H6
Tower Hamlets Rd FSTGT E7....288 C1
  WALTH E17....284 C1
Tower Hi BRW CM14....273 M1
  WOS/PRIT SS0 *....18 D6
Tower Ms CLPT E5 *....306 E1
Tower Mill Rd IP IP1....47 L6
Tower Rd BELV DA17....326 F7
  CBS CB2....22 F1
  CHLM/WR CM1....208 C4
  COS CO15....6 D5
  EPP CM16....219 M8
  FX IP11....11 L1
  RCOLE CO7....130 C7
Tower Side HOC/HUL SS5 *....263 H3
Towers Rd GRAYS RM17....331 G2
  MAL CM9....198 F8
Tower St IP IP1....16 D4
  RCOLE CO7....156 C7
Tower Vw CBE/LIN CB3....22 F1
Town CI CBS CB2....22 F1
Town Cft CHLM/WR CM1....193 K8
Town End Fld WIT CM8....171 H6
Townfield Cnr GVE DA12....337 M6
Townfield Rd CHLM/WR CM1....193 K8
Townfield St COLS CO2....129 M1
Townfield Wk SBN/FI SS3....303 H6
Towngate BSDN SS14....2 E6

Town La CBS CB2....22 F1
Townley Ct SRTFD E15....307 G7
Town Mead Rd WAB EN9....233 K6
Town Quay BARK IG11....308 F7
Townsend Rd K/T/MI CO5....149 M7
  WOOL/PLUM SE18....325 G9
Town Sq BSDN SS14....2 C5
Town St GTDUN CM6....74 D7
Towpath Rd UED N18 *....266 A4
Towse CI RCOS CO16....181 K7
Tracyes Rd HLWS CM18....204 C3
Traddles Ct CHLM/WR CM1....193 J7
Trader Rd EHAM E6....324 E2
Trafalgar Av BROX EN10....201 G7
Trafalgar CI
  BARK/HLT IG6....287 G1
Trafalgar Gdns WCHPL E1....322 A1
Trafalgar PI WAN E11....285 K3
Trafalgar Rd COLW CO3....106 B7
  COS CO15....21 H2
  GNWCH SE10....323 K5
  RAIN RM13....311 G3
  SBN/FI SS3....303 G6
  SUD CO10....21 H2
Trafalgar Wy BCAYW CM12....240 D2
  BRTR CM7....121 L1
  POP/IOD E14....322 F3
Trafalgar Yd HAR CO12 *....14 A9
Trafford Rd SRTFD E15....306 F2
Trajan CI COLN CO4....87 L2
Tramway Av SRTFD E15....307 G4
Tranmere Gv IP IP1....47 L3
Tranquil Ri ERITH DA8....327 H8
Transom Sq POP/IOD E14....322 E6
Trap's HI LOU IG10....250 C4
Travers Av WALTH E17....266 A7
Travers Wy PIT SS13....278 D2
Trebble Rd SWCM DA10....336 B4
Treby St BOW E3....306 C6
Tredegar Rd BOW E3....306 C6
  DART DA1....334 E6
Tredegar Sq BOW E3....306 C6
Treebeard Copse
  ABRM CM3 *....244 F5
Tree CI ABR/ST RM4....251 L3
  COS CO15....159 L6
Treecot Dr LOS SS9....300 D1
Treelawn Dr LOS SS9....300 C1
Treelawn Gdns LOS SS9....300 C1
Tree Rd CAN/RD E16....323 M2
Tree Tops BRWN CM15....255 M6
Treetops FX IP11....62 D6
Treetops CI ABYW SE2....325 P6
Treetops Vw LOU IG10....250 A6
Trefgarne Rd DAGE RM10....288 D7
Trefoil CI CHTY IP2....53 L1
Tregelles Rd HOD EN11....185 H1
Trego Rd HOM E9....306 D4
Trehearn Rd BARK/HLT IG6....269 G4
Trehurst St CLPT E5....306 E1
Trelawney Rd BARK/HLT IG6....269 G4
Trelawn Rd WAN E11....284 F4
Trelawny CI WALTH E17....284 C4
Trenance Gdns
  GDMY/SEVK IG3....287 K8
Trenchard Crs CHLM/WR CM1....194 A6
Trench St GNWCH SE10....323 G3
Trenders Av RAYL SS6....262 F2
Trenham Av PIT SS13....279 G6
Trent CI TIL RM18....332 F3
Trent Av UPMR RM14....291 K6
Trentbridge CI BARK/HLT IG6....269 J5
Trent CI BOC CM0....189 Q12
  WICKW SS12....261 G7
Trent Ct WAN E11....285 K3
Trent Rd BKHH IG9....249 J1
  CHLM/WR CM1....192 F8
  IPSE IP3....55 H3
  WIT CM8....171 H3
Trescoe Gdns CRW RM5....270 F4
Tresco Rd SRTFD E15....287 J7
Tresco Wy WICKW SS12....261 K8
Tresham Rd BARK IG11....309 J4
Treswell Rd DAGW RM9....310 B8
Trevelyan Av MNPK E12....308 C1
Trevelyan Ct DART DA1....334 D2
Trevelyan Rd SRTFD E15....307 H1
Trevera Ct CHES/WCR EN8 *....232 F3
  HOD EN11 *....201 H7
Trevithick Dr DART DA1....334 C6
Trevor CI BARK/HLT IG6....286 F1
Trevor CI BCAYW CM12....358 C6
Trevose Rd WALTH E17....267 G1
Trews Gdns K/T/MI CO5....148 F2
Trianon Ct PIT SS13....278 F2
Trident St BERM/RHTH SE16....322 A4
Trimble CI ING CM4....239 L1
Trimley CI BSDN SS14....3 E1
  RCOS CO16....182 E1
Trindehay LAIN SS15....2 A4
Tring Av WICKW SS12....260 D3
Tring CI BARK/HLT IG6....286 F1
  HARH RM3....272 A3
Tring Gdns HARH RM3....272 B3
Trinidad Gdns DAGE RM10....311 G3
Trinidad St POP/IOD E14....322 C3
Trinity Av FX IP11....10 A7
  WOS/PRIT SS0....18 D6
Trinity CI BCAYE CM11....258 F2
  BSF CM23....139 G3
  K/T/MI CO5....177 M6
  KESG IP5....49 H6
  LAIN SS15....276 F7
  MGTR CO11....91 G2
  RAYL SS6....281 H4
  RCOLE CO7....130 F5
  WAN E11....285 H7
Trinity Gdns CAN/RD E16....323 J1
  DART DA1....334 A8
Trinity La CHES/WCR EN8....232 G2
Trinity Link HVHL CB9....34 D4
Trinity Ms HSTD CO9 *....81 M1
  K/T/MI CO5....177 M6
Trinity Pk CHING E4....266 C5
Trinity Rd BARK/HLT IG6....286 F1
  BCAYE CM11....258 F2
  CHLM/GWD CM2....5 L3
  GVE DA12....337 M6
  HERT/BAY SG13....184 D2
  HSTD CO9....81 M1
  MGTR CO11....91 G2
  RAYL SS6....281 H4
  RCOLE CO7....130 F5
  SOSN SS2....18 F4
Trinity Ter HSTD CO9 *....81 M1
Trinity Wd HERT/BAY SG13....184 D2
Trinity Wy BSF CM23....139 G2
  CHING E4....266 C5
Trinity Wood Rd
  HOC/HUL SS5....264 D6
Trinovantian Wy BRTR CM7....121 K3
Tripat CI SLH/COR SS17....317 H1

Tripton Rd HLWS CM18 ....13 K8
Tristram Cl WALTH E17 ....285 G1
Triton Wy SBF/HAD SS7 ....280 C7
Triumph Av COS CO15 ....182 B6
Triumph Cl CDW/CHF RM16 ....329 M7
Triumph Rd EHAM E6 ....324 C2
Trivett Cl GRH DA9 ....335 K7
Troon Gdns IPNE IP4 ....49 G5
Troon St WCHPL E1 ....322 E8
Troopers Dr HARH RM3 ....272 A3
Trosley Av GVW DA11 ....337 L7
Trotters Fld BRTR CM7 ....121 C2
Trotter's Gap WARE SG12 ....185 M5
Trotters Rd HLWS CM18 ....204 B4
Trotwood CHIG IG7 ....269 G5
Trotwood Cl CHLM/WR CM1 ....193 H6
Troubridge Cl RCHLM CM3 ....245 J6
Troughton Rd CHARL SE7 ....323 C8
Trowbridge Rd HARH RM3 ....272 A5
  HOM E9 ....306 C3
Troys Cha RCHLM CM3 ....145 M7
Truelove's La ING CM4 ....239 J3
Truman Cl LAIN SS15 ....276 D7
Trumpington Rd FSTGT E7 ....307 J1
Trundle's Rd DEPT SE8 ....322 A8
Trundley's Ter DEPT SE8 ....322 A7
Trunette Rd COS CO15 ....6 E7
The Trunnions RCFD SS4 ....283 J4
Truro Crs KESG IP5 ....49 H7
  RAYL SS6 ....262 F8
Truro Gdns IL IG1 ....286 B5
Truro Rd GVE DA12 ....338 A8
  WALTH E17 ....284 C2
Trusedale Rd EHAM E6 ....324 C2
Trusses Rd BOC CM0 ....386 E10
Trustons Gdns EMPK RM11 ....193 K5
Trust Rd CHES/WCR EN8 ....232 A6
Tryfan Cl REDBR IG4 ....286 A3
Tucker Dr WIT CM8 ....171 J5
Tucker's Rw BSF CM23 ....139 G3
Tuck Rd RAIN RM13 ....311 K3
Tuddenham Av IPNE IP4 ....17 J2
Tuddenham La KESG IP5 ....49 J7
Tuddenham Rd IPNE IP4 ....17 H2
Tudor Av CHESW EN7 ....232 C1
  CHLM/WR CM1 ....4 E2
  GPK RM2 ....289 K1
  SLH/COR SS17 ....317 H1
Tudor Chambers PIT SS13 * 278 E8
Tudor Cl BRWN CM15 ....256 C2
  CHESW EN7 ....232 C1
  CHIG IG7 ....268 D3
  COS CO15 ....182 D4
  GVW DA11 ....337 H6
  ING CM4 ....239 K3
  LOS SS9 ....281 M5
  RAYL SS6 ....281 J3
  RCOLE CO7 ....156 B5
  RIPS/CAP IP9 ....66 F4
  SBF/HAD SS7 ....280 C8
  SUD CO10 ....20 C4
  WARE SG12 ....186 A1
  WFD IG8 ....267 L4
  WIT CM8 ....171 J5
  WOTN CO14 ....369 N11
Tudor Ct K/T/MI CO5 * 177 M6
  LAIN SS15 ....? J3
  WALTH E17 ....284 C5
Tudor Crs BARK/HLT IG6 ....268 F3
Tudor Dr GPK RM2 ....289 K2
Tudor Gdns GPK RM2 ....289 K2
  LOS SS9 ....300 A2
  SBN/FI SS3 ....303 L4
  UPMR RM14 ....290 F7
Tudor Gn COS CO15 ....182 C4
  SUD CO10 ....20 C1
Tudor Man PIT SS13 * 278 E8
Tudor Ms LOS SS9 ....281 M5
Tudor Pde BROX EN10 ....200 F7
Tudor Rd BARK IG11 ....309 J4
  CHING E4 ....266 C5
  CVI SS8 ....320 A2
  EHAM E6 ....307 M5
  LOS SS9 ....281 M5
  SUD CO10 ....20 C2
  WOS/PRIT SS0 ....18 D1
Tudor Rose Cl COLW CO3 ....105 M6
Tudor Wy HOC/HUL SS5 ....282 C1
  WAB EN9 ....
  WICKW SS12 ....260 D8
Tudwick Rd MAL CM9 ....174 B8
Tufnail Rd DART DA1 ....334 C8
Tufnell Wy COLN CO4 ....106 F3
Tufted Cl BRTR CM77 ....120 F8
Tufter Rd CHIG IG7 ....269 J4
Tufton Rd CHING E4 ....266 D3
Tugboat St THMD SE28 ....325 H6
Tukes Wy SAFWS CB11 ....30 C1
Tulip Cl BRWN CM15 ....255 L5
  CHLM/WR CM1 ....194 B6
  EHAM E6 ....307 M6
  HARH RM3 ....271 M5
Tulip Gdns CHING E4 ....267 G2
  IL IG1 ....308 E3
Tulip Wk COLN CO4 ....9 J5
Tulip Wy RCOS CO16 ....6 A4
Tumbler Rd HLWS CM18 ....204 B2
Tumulus Wy COLS CO2 ....128 C3
Tunbridge Rd WDBR SG12 ....18 F1
Tunfield Rd HOD EN11 ....185 J1
Tunley Gn POP/IOD E14 ....322 C1
Tunmarsh La PLSTW E13 ....307 M7
Tunnan Leys EHAM E6 ....324 D2
Tunnel Av GNWCH SE10 ....323 H6
Tunnmeade HLW CM20 ....188 C3
Tunstall Av GNWCH SE10 ....323 H6
Tunstall Cl PIT SS13 ....278 E8
  RCOS CO16 ....157 J3
Tunstock Wy BELV DA17 ....326 A6
Tupelo Rd LEY E10 ....284 E7
Tuppy St WOOL/PLUM SE18 ....324 F6
Turino Av WDBR WD12 ....51 H5
Turin St CHTY IP2 ....16 F7
Turkey Cock La COLW CO3 ....105 H1
Turkey Oaks CHLM/WR CM1 ....5 M7
Turkey St EN EN1 ....232 A5
Turley Cl SRTFD E15 ....307 G5
Turnage Rd BCTR RM8 ....288 C6
Turnbury Cl THMD SE28 ....326 A2
Turner Av MGTR CO11 ....64 C7
Turner Cl BRTR CM77 ....145 J4
  HVHL CB9 ....34 A1
  RCOLE CO7 ....130 F4
  SBN/FI SS3 ....303 J5
  SUD CO10 ....21 G1
Turner Gv KESG IP5 ....50 E3
  IPSE IP3 ....54 C7
  WALTH E17 ....284 F2
Turners Cl CHONG CM5 ....382 C9
Turners Crs BSF CM23 ....138 D5
Turner's Hl CHES/WCR EN8 ....216 D4
Turners Rd POP/IOD E14 ....322 C1
Turnford Pk BROX EN10 ....216 F4
Turnford Vis BROX EN10 * 217 G4
Turnpike Cl RCOLE CO7 ....88 B5

Turnpike HI HVHL CB9 ....33 M1
Turnpike La CDW/CHF RM16 ....332 A4
Turnpike Pl BRTR CM7 ....121 C2
Turnstone Rd PLSTW E13 ....307 H5
Turnstone End COLN CO4 ....108 C5
The Turnstones GVE DA12 ....338 A7
Turold Rd SLH/COR SS17 ....317 H1
Turp Av CDW/CHF RM16 ....330 F1
Turpin Av CRW RM5 ....270 B6
Turpin Cl PEND EN3 ....233 H7
  WAP E1W 322 A4
Turpins Av COS CO15 ....159 M8
Turpins Cl COS CO15 ....159 M8
Turpins La FOS CO13 ....137 H2
  WFD IG8 ....268 C4
The Turpins BSDN SS14 ....3 K3
Turret La IPNE IP4 ....16 F6
Turstan Rd WIT CM8 ....171 H5
Tuscan Rd WOOL/PLUM SE18 ....323 H8
Tuskar St GNWCH SE10 ....323 H8
Tusser Cl WIT CM8 ....147 L5
Tusser Ct CHLM/GWD CM2 * 5 M7
Tusset Ms COS CO15 ....106 B6
Tutors Wy RCHLM CM5 ....245 H6
Tweed TIL RM18 ....332 F3
Tweed St HSTD CO9 ....81 G1
Tweedmouth Rd PLSTW E13 ....307 L6
Tweed Wy ROM RM1 ....271 G6
Twelve Acre Ap KESG IP5 ....50 A6
Twelve Acres BRTR CM7 ....122 A2
Twelvetrees Crs BOW E3 ....306 F6
  CAN/RD E16 ....307 G8
TwentyFirst St STSD CM24 ....374 G11
Twentyman Cl WFD IG8 ....267 K4
Twickenham Rd WAN E11 ....285 L4
Twig Folly Cl BOW E3 ....306 A6
Twig Folly Whf BETH E2 * 306 A6
Twine Cl BARK IG11 ....309 L7
Twine Ter BOW E3 * 306 A6
Twining Rd COLW CO3 ....128 B1
Twin Oaks CHLM/GWD CM2 ....210 B1
Twinstead WICKW SS12 ....? L1
Twin Tumps Wy THMD SE28 ....325 K5
Twisleton Ct DART DA1 ....334 A4
Twitten La CHLM/GWD CM2 ....225 L3
Twitty Fee RCHLM CM3 ....212 D6
Twizzlefoot Br BOC CM0 ....394 A6
Two Acres RIPS/CAP IP9 ....58 E3
Twyford Av SBN/FI SS3 ....303 K1
Twyford Bury La BSF CM23 ....139 H4
Twyford Gdns BSF CM23 ....139 H4
Twyford Rd BSF CM23 ....139 H4
  IL IG1 ....308 F2
Twyzel Rd CVI SS8 ....320 F1
Tyas Rd CAN/RD E16 ....307 H3
Tyburn HI RCOLW CO6 ....83 K7
The Tyburns
  RBRW/HUT CM13 ....256 F5
Tycehurst HI LOU IG10 ....250 C4
Tydeman Cl COLW CO3 ....127 M1
Tye Common Rd
  BCAYW CM12 ....258 B8
Tyefields PIT SS13 ....278 F6
Tye Green Rd RBSF CM22 ....374 D4
Tye Green Village
  HLWS CM18 * 204 A4
Tyehurst Crs COLN CO4 ....107 M3
Tyelands BCAYW CM12 ....258 C5
Tye La RCOLE CO7 ....131 H2
  RIPW IP8 ....46 A3
Tye Rd RCOLE CO7 ....109 H6
The Tye Rd RCOLE CO7 ....133 L5
Tyeshurst Cl ABYW SE2 ....326 A6
The Tye RCHLM CM3 ....227 M6
Tyfield Cl CHES/WCR EN8 ....216 B1
Tylehurst Dr IL IG1 ....308 F2
Tyler Av LAIN SS15 ....276 F1
  RCOS CO16 ....182 L2
Tylers SAFWN CB10 ....29 H5
  SOS SS1 ....19 H5
Tylers Cl CHLM/GWD CM2 ....209 L2
Tylers Crs HCH RM12 ....311 M2
Tylers Gn FX IP11 ....62 B6
Tylers Ride RCHLM CM3 ....245 H6
Tylers Rd HLWW/ROY CM19 ....203 E6
Tyler St GNWCH SE10 ....323 J7
  HAR CO12 ....14 A4
Tyler Wy BRW CM14 ....255 J5
Tylewood SBF/HAD SS7 ....298 F5
Tylney Av RCFD SS4 ....283 G4
Tylney Cft HLWW/ROY CM19 ....203 J3
Tylney Rd FSTGT E7 ....307 M1
Tylneys Rd HLWS CM18 ....81 K2
Tyms Wy RAYL SS6 * 281 J3
Tyndale Cl HOC/HUL SS5 ....263 G2
Tyndale Dr COS CO15 ....182 D4
Tyndales La RCHLM CM3 ....? G3
Tyndall Rd LEY E10 ....284 F7
Tyne Cl UPMR RM14 ....291 G4
Tynedale Sq COLN CO4 ....107 L4
Tyne Gdns SOCK/AV RM15 ....328 E3
Tynemouth Cl EHAM E6 ....324 E2
Tynemouth Dr EN EN1 ....232 B1
Tynemouth Rd
  WOOL/PLUM SE18 ....325 H8
Type St BETH E2 ....306 A6
Tyrell Pl BRWW CM15 * 256 C6
Tyrell Rd RBRW/HUT CM13 ....273 M4
Tyrells HOC/HUL SS5 ....282 A1
Tyrells Cl CHLM/WR CM1 ....210 B1
  UPMR RM14 ....290 F7
Tyrells Wy CHLM/GWD CM2 ....210 C6
Tyrone Cl BCAYE CM11 ....258 F7
  IP IP1 ....47 J3
Tyrone Rd BCAYE CM11 ....258 F7
  EHAM E6 ....308 C6
  SOS SS1 ....302 D7
Tyrrel Dr SOS SS1 ....19 J4
Tyrrells Hall Cl GRAYS RM17 ....331 G5
Tyrrells Rd BCAYE CM11 ....259 G7
Tysea Cl HLWS CM18 ....204 A4
Tysea Hl ABR/ST RM4 ....253 J8
Tysea Rd HLWS CM18 ....204 A4
Tysoe Av PEND EN3 ....233 L5
Tyssen Rd HLWS CM18 ....195 H5
Tyssen Pl SOCK/AV RM15 ....313 M6
Tythe Barn Wy RCHLM CM3 * 244 A3
Tythe Rd CHLM/WR CM1 ....194 B1
The Tythings HSTD CO9 ....81 G1

U
Uamvar St POP/IOD E14 ....322 E1
Uckfield Rd PEND EN3 ....232 E7
Udall Gdns CRW RM5 ....270 D5
Uffen Wy CBS CB2 ....22 B1
Uist Cl LAIN SS15 ....276 E?
Ullswater Av FX IP11 ....62 B6
Ullswater Cl BRTR CM77 ....120 F7
Ullswater Rd SBF/HAD SS7 ....280 C8
Ullswater Wy HCH RM12 ....311 K2
Ulster Av IP IP1 ....47 J4
  SBN/FI SS3 ....302 D7
Ulting Hall Rd MAL CM9 ....197 H6
Ulting La MAL CM9 ....197 J6
Ulting Rd RCHLM CM3 ....196 F2
Ulting Wy WICKE SS11 ....261 M6
Ulverston Rd WALTH E17 ....267 G?
Una Rd HAR CO12 ....? D1
  PIT SS13 ....279 J1
Undercliff Gdns LOS SS9 ....300 C5
Undercliff Rd East FX IP11 ....69 H1
Undercliff Rd West FX IP11 ....11 J4
Underhill SBF/HAD SS7 ....298 D?
Underwood Rd CHING E4 ....266 A4
  WFD IG8 ....268 C4
Underwood Sq LOS SS9 ....299 M3
Undine Av POP/IOD E14 ....322 E4
Unicorn Wk GRH DA9 ....335 J7
Union Cl WAN E11 ....307 C1
  LAIN SS15 ....276 B8
Union La RCFD SS4 ....283 H5
Union Pk GNWCH SE10 ....323 J8
Union Rd COS CO15 ....182 D5
Union St IPNE IP4 * 17 H4
  SRTFD E15 ....307 G5
Unity Cl COLS CO2 ....129 L1
Unity Rd PEND EN3 ....232 D7
Unity St IPSE IP3 ....17 M8
Unity Wy WOOL/PLUM SE18 ....324 A6
University Wy DART DA1 ....334 A5
  EHAM E6 ....324 D3
Uphall Rd IL IG1 ....308 E2
Upland Rd BCAYW CM12 ....258 C8
Upland Court Rd HARH RM3 ....272 C8
Upland Dr COLN CO4 ....9 K1
Upland Rd K/T/MI CO5 ....177 M6
  COLN CO4 ....9 K1
  SBF/HAD SS7 ....297 L1
Uplands Av WALTH E17 ....284 A1
Uplands Cl SUD CO10 ....20 D2
Uplands Crs SUD CO10 ....20 D2
Uplands Dr WALTH E17 ....194 A6
Uplands Park Rd RAYL SS6 ....281 L2
Uplands Rd CHDH RM6 ....288 A1
  COS CO15 ....6 D?
  HOC/HUL SS5 ....264 C8
  RAYL SS6 ....281 L2
  SUD CO10 ....20 D2
  WFD IG8 ....268 B6
The Uplands LOU IG10 ....250 C3
Upminster Rd RCHLM CM3 ....290 C7
Upminster Rd North
  RAIN RM13 ....311 M7
Upminster Rd South
  RAIN RM13 ....311 K8
Upney La HCH RM12 ....311 M2
Upney La BARK IG11 ....309 J4
Uppark Dr GNTH/NBYPK IG2 ....286 F4
Upper Abbey Rd BELV DA17 ....326 C4
Upper Acres WIT CM8 ....147 J8
Upper Bank St POP/IOD E14 ....322 E4
Upper Barclay St IPNE IP4 ....17 G5
Upper Branston Rd COS CO15 ....6 C7
Upper Brentwood Rd
  GPK RM2 ....289 M2
Upper Bridge Rd
  CHLM/GWD CM2 ....4 E5
Upper Brook St IPNE IP4 ....16 F5
Upper Cavendish St ISPE IP3 * 48 F8
Upper Chapel St HSTD CO9 ....81 H3
Upper Cha CHLM/GWD CM2 ....4 D5
  RCHLM CM3 ....392 C2
Upper Cornsland BRW CM14 ....256 A6
Upper East St SUD CO10 ....20 C5
Upper Farm Rd SUD CO10 ....345 Q5
Upper Fenn Rd HSTD CO9 ....81 K3
Upper Fourth Av FOS CO13 ....137 J4
Upperfield Dr FX IP11 ....63 H1
Upper High St IP IP1 ....16 F5
Upper Holly Hill Rd
  BELV DA17 ....326 C5
Upper Holt St RCOLW CO6 ....82 F7
Upper Hook RCHLM CM3 ....204 A3
Upper Lambricks RAYL SS6 ....281 H1
Upper Market Rd
  WICKW SS12 * ....260 F?
Upper Marsh La HOD EN11 ....201 H4
Upper Mayne LAIN SS15 2
Upper Mealines HLWS CM18 ....204 B4
Upper Mill Fld GTDUN CM6 ....117 H6
Upper Moors RCHLM CM3 ....167 J5
Upper North St POP/IOD E14 ....322 D2
Upper Orwell St IPNE IP4 ....17 G5
Upper Pk HLW CM20 ....12 C5
  LOU IG10 ....250 A5
Upper Park Rd BELV DA17 ....326 D6
  COS CO15 ....6 D6
  RCOLE CO7 ....156 C6
  WICKW SS12 ....279 G1
Upper Rainham Rd
  HCH RM12 ....289 M3
Upper Raypits RCFD SS4 * 265 M3
Upper Red BCAYE CM11 ....260 A8
  PLSTW E13 ....307 K7
  SUD CO10 ....359 N1
Upper Roman Rd
  CHLM/GWD CM2 ....5 H6
Upper Ryle BRW CM14 ....255 J4
Upper Second Av FOS CO13 ....137 H4
Upper Sheridan Rd
  BELV DA17 ....326 C4
Upper Shott CHESW EN7 ....216 A4
Upper Stonyfield
  HLWW/ROY CM19 ....12 B6
Upper St RCOLE CO7 ....363 K8
  SUD CO10 ....40 B1
Upper Swaines EPP CM16 ....220 A4
Upper Third Av FOS CO13 ....137 H4
Upperton Rd East PLSTW E13 ....307 M7
Upperton Rd West
  PLSTW E13 ....307 M7
Upper Trinity Rd HSTD CO9 ....81 H4
Upper Walthamstow Rd
  WALTH E17 ....285 G2
Upshers SAFWS CB11 ....30 C1
Upshire Rd WAB EN9 ....234 B5
Upsons Wy KESG IP5 ....50 A6
Upton Av FSTGT E7 ....307 K4
Upton Cl IPNE IP4 ....106 A1
  RCOLW CO6 ....106 A1
  SLH/COR SS17 ....317 L3
Upton La FSTGT E7 ....307 L3
Upton Park Rd FSTGT E7 ....307 L4
Upway RAYL SS6 ....281 L1
The Upway BSDN SS14 ....3 H2
Urban Av HCH RM12 ....289 M8
Urmond Rd CVI SS8 ....320 D1
Urswick Rd DAGW RM9 ....310 A3
Usher Rd BOW E3 ....306 C6
Usk Rd SOCK/AV RM15 ....328 F2

Usk St BETH E2 ....306 A7
Usterdale Rd SAFWN CB10 ....28 B6
Uttons Av LOS SS9 ....300 A5
Uvedale Rd DAGE RM10 ....288 D8
Uxbridge Cl WICKE SS11 ....261 J2
Uxbridge Crs IPSE IP3 ....55 H4

V
Vaagen Rd CVI SS8 ....320 E1
Vadsoe Rd CVI SS8 ....320 E1
Valance Av CHING E4 ....249 J8
Valance Rd SAFWS CB11 ....72 B2
Valance Wy VGE SS16 ....294 F1
Valdoe Rd WALTH E17 ....?
Vale Av SOSN SS2 ....302 B2
Vale Cl BRWN CM15 ....255 J5
  COLN CO4 ....108 B3
Vale End CHLM/GWD CM2 ....225 M2
Vale La RIPS/CAP IP9 ....65 L1
Vale Rd BCTR RM8 ....288 A6
Valence Circ BCTR RM8 ....288 A6
Valence Dr CHESW EN7 ....216 B6
Valence Wood Rd BCTR RM8 ....288 A6
Valenta Cl COL CO1 ....9 K9
Valentine Dr HCH RM12 ....289 H7
Valentines ING CM4 ....241 J3
Valentines Rd IL IG1 ....286 E6
Valentine Wy WIT CM8 ....147 G1
Valerian Wy SRTFD E15 ....307 H7
Vale Rd FSTGT E7 ....307 L3
  GVW DA11 ....337 H6
The Vale BRW CM14 ....255 M8
  ING CM4 ....241 G6
  VGE SS16 ....296 A2
  WFD IG8 ....267 L5
Valetta Gv PLSTW E13 ....307 K6
Valfreda Wy RCOLE CO7 ....130 E4
Valiant Cl ROMW/RG RM7 ....270 D8
Valiant Rd KESG IP5 ....50 F6
Valiant Wy EHAM E6 ....324 C1
Valkyrie Cl WAN E11 ....385 N3
Valkyrie Rd WOS/PRIT SS0 ....18 C5
Vallance Cl CAN/RD E16 ....324 A1
Vallentin Rd WALTH E17 ....284 F2
Valletta Cl CHLM/WR CM1 ....4 B2
Valleybridge Rd COS CO15 ....7 J1
Valley Cl COLW CO3 ....128 B2
  IP IP1 ....48 A5
  LOU IG10 ....250 C6
  MGTR CO11 ....65 G4
  WAB EN9 ....233 K2
Valley Crs RCHLM CM3 ....196 C1
Valley Dr GVE DA12 ....338 A8
Valley Gdns GRH DA9 ....335 L8
Valley Gv CHARL SE7 ....323 M8
Valley Hl LOU IG10 ....250 C7
Valley Rd BCAYE CM11 ....258 E3
  BRTR CM7 ....121 K4
  COS CO15 ....7 J1
  ERITH DA8 ....326 F1
  HAR CO12 ....70 C3
  IP IP1 ....48 A5
  RCOLE CO7 ....130 F5
Valley Side CHING E4 ....248 D8
Valley Vw BRTR CM7 ....354 C11
  GRH DA9 ....335 L8
  RCOLW CO6 ....106 B2
  SUD CO10 ....20 D2
Valley View Cl COLN CO4 ....107 K1
Valleyview Dr SBW CM21 ....161 M4
Valmar Av SLH/COR SS17 ....316 E1
Valognes Av WALTH E17 ....266 B7
Vanbrugh Hl GNWCH SE10 ....323 M8
Vanburgh Cl CAN/RD E16 ....324 A1
Vancouver Rd BROX EN10 ....216 F3
Vandenburg Cir BRTR CM77 ....355 J12
Vanderbilt Av RAYL SS6 ....262 F4
Vanderwalt Av CVI SS8 ....321 G2
Van Dieman's La
  CHLM/GWD CM2 ....5 K7
Van Diemen's Rd
  CHLM/GWD CM2 ....5 K7
Van Diemens Pass CVI SS8 ....321 J2
Vandome Cl CAN/RD E16 ....323 L2
Van Dyck Rd COLW CO3 ....106 D8
Vandyck Cl IPSE IP3 ....54 F5
Vane La RCOLW CO6 ....124 C5
Vanessa Cl BELV DA17 ....326 D4
Vanessa Dr RCOLE CO7 ....130 E4
Vange Corner Dr
  SLH/COR SS17 ....295 L4
Vange Hill Dr VGE SS16 ....3 M9
Vange Park Rd SLH/COR SS17 ....295 L4
Vanguard Cl CAN/RD E16 ....323 K1
  ROMW/RG RM7 ....270 C7
The Vanguards BRTR CM7 ....121 J6
Vanguard Wy BRTR CM7 ....121 J6
  SBN/FI SS3 ....303 J5
Vanners Rd HVHL CB9 ....34 D6
Vanquisher Wk GVE DA12 ....338 C8
Vansittart Rd FSTGT E7 ....307 K1
Vansittart St FSTGT E7 ....307 K5
Vantorts Cl SBW CM21 ....162 A1
Vantorts Rd SBW CM21 ....162 A1
Varden Cl CHLM/WR CM1 ....193 J7
Vardon Dr LOS SS9 ....299 L5
Varley Rd CAN/RD E16 ....323 L2
Varney Cl CHESW EN7 ....216 B5
Vaughan Av HCH RM12 ....312 A1
  SOSN SS2 ....302 B4
Vaughan Cl BRTR CM77 ....120 C3
  RCFD SS4 ....265 H8
Vaughan Gdns IL IG1 ....286 C5
Vaughan Rd SRTFD E15 ....307 J3
Vaughan St
  BERM/RHTH SE16 ....322 C5
  CHTY IP2 ....16 F7
Vaughan Williams Rd
  LAIN SS15 ....276 F5
Vaughan Williams Wy
  BRW CM14 ....273 L4
Vauxhall Av CHLM/WR CM1 ....8 E4
Vauxhall Cl GVW DA11 ....337 L8
Vauxhall Dr BRTR CM7 ....121 C2
Vaux Av HAR CO12 ....70 C2
Vega Cl COL CO1 ....9 J9
Vellacotts CHLM/WR CM1 ....193 K5
Venables Cl CVI SS8 ....321 G2
  DAGE RM10 ....310 D2
Venlo Rd CVI SS8 ....298 F8
Venmore St GTDUN CM6 ....117 J6
Ventnor Dr MAL CM9 ....214 C5
Ventnor Gdns BARK IG11 ....309 H3
Ventris Cl CHTY IP2 ....47 G8
Ventura Dr COL CO1 ....9 K9
Venue St POP/IOD E14 ....322 E1

Venus Rd WOOL/PLUM SE18 ....324 C6
Veny Crs HCH RM12 ....312 A2
Vera Lynn Cl FSTGT E7 ....307 K1
Vera Rd BCAYE CM11 ....260 C5
Verbena Cl CAN/RD E16 ....307 G8
  SOCK/AV RM15 ....329 M2
Verderers Rd CHIG IG7 ....269 K2
Vere Gdns IP IP1 ....48 B3
Vere Rd LOU IG10 ....250 A6
Vermeer Cl CVI SS8 ....303 K5
Vermont Cl COS CO15 ....7 K5
  PIT SS13 ....278 D3
Vermont Crs IPNE IP4 ....17 H1
Vermont Rd IPNE IP4 ....17 H1
Verney Gdns DAGW RM9 ....310 B1
Verney Rd DAGW RM9 ....310 B1
Vernon Av MNPK E12 ....308 C1
  PEND EN3 ....232 F6
  RAYL SS6 ....280 E2
  WFD IG8 ....267 L5
Vernon's Cl RBSF CM22 ....372 G12
Vernon Crs RBRW/HUT CM13 ....256 D6
Vernon St CHTY IP2 ....16 F7
Vernon St BOW E3 ....306 C2
  CRW RM5 ....?
  GDMY/SEVK IG3 ....287 J2
  LOS SS9 ....299 M4
  SRTFD E15 ....307 H4
  SWCM DA10 ....336 C4
  WALTH E17 ....284 C2
  WAN E11 ....285 H6
Vernon's Cl RBSF CM22 ....372 G12
Veronica Cl HARH RM3 ....271 M6
Veronica Wk COLN CO4 ....9 M6
Veronique Gdns
  GNTH/NBYPK IG2 ....286 F3
Verulam Av WALTH E17 ....284 C5
Vesta Cl RCOLW CO6 ....124 C3
Vestry Cl LAIN SS15 ....276 F6
Vestry Rd WALTH E17 ....284 E3
Vexil Cl PUR RM19 ....329 G7
Veyses End RCOLE CO7 ....363 F7
Viaduct Rd CHLM/WR CM1 ....4 F7
  WARE SG12 ....?
The Viaduct SWFD E18 ....267 K8
Vian Av EN EN1 ....232 F5
Via Romana GVE DA12 ....338 G6
Viborg Gdns MAL CM9 ....214 B5
Vicarage Av CBS CB2 ....22 B1
  WIT CM8 ....146 C4
Vicarage Cswy
  HERT/BAY SG13 ....184 A3
Vicarage Cl BRTR CM7 ....97 K6
  BRW CM14 ....273 H4
  CVI SS8 ....320 A2
  LAIN SS15 ....276 F7
  MAL CM9 ....231 H2
  RIPW IP8 ....47 G4
Vicarage Crs RCHLM CM3 ....196 C1
Vicarage Dr BARK IG11 ....308 F4
  MAL CM9 ....231 H3
Vicarage Fld COS CO15 ....45 L4
Vicarage Gdns COS CO15 ....6 D7
Vicarage Hl SBF/HAD SS7 ....298 A4
Vicarage La BOC CM0 ....390 F5
  BSF CM23 ....92 C1
  CHIG IG7 ....269 G2
  CHLM/GWD CM2 ....226 C2
  EHAM E6 ....308 A2
  EPP CM16 ....221 K2
  GTDUN CM6 ....74 D2
  GVE DA12 ....338 D7
  LOS SS9 ....287 G6
  MAL CM9 ....231 H2
  RBSF CM22 ....352 A12
  RCOS CO16 ....135 J3
  RIPS/CAP IP9 ....54 A8
  RIPW IP8 ....47 G4
  SRTFD E15 ....307 H3
  SUD CO10 ....43 L5
  WOTN CO14 ....177 N1
Vicarage Meadow BOC CM0 ....393 N5
  HSTD CO9 ....81 H4
Vicarage Ms CHLM/GWD CM2 ....210 C7
Vicarage Pk
  WOOL/PLUM SE18 ....324 F8
Vicarage Rd BRTR CM7 ....354 C11
  CHLM/GWD CM2 ....4 M8
  CHLM/WR CM1 ....191 M8
  DAGE RM10 ....289 K6
  EMPK RM11 ....289 K6
  EPP CM16 ....220 D7
  FX IP11 ....10 D7
  LEY E10 ....284 E6
  RCHLM CM3 ....166 B3
  SRTFD E15 ....307 J4
  SUD CO10 ....346 H4
  WFD IG8 ....268 B6
  WOOL/PLUM SE18 ....324 F8
Vicarage Sq GRAYS RM17 ....330 D5
Vicarage Wd HLW CM20 ....188 B8
Vicar's Cl SRTFD E15 ....307 G5
Vicars Orch SUD CO10 ....44 B4
Viceroy Cl COLS CO2 ....129 L2
Viceroy Crs SLH/COR SS17 * 316 C2
Vickers Rd ERITH DA8 ....327 G8
Vickery's Wy SOSN SS2 ....283 G11
Victor Ap HCH RM12 ....290 A6
Victor Av PIT SS13 ....279 G7
Victor Cl HCH RM12 ....290 A6
Victor Dr LOS SS9 ....299 M5
Victor Gdns HCH RM12 ....290 A6
  HOC/HUL SS5 ....264 C4
Victoria Cha COL CO1 ....8 C2
Victoria Cl CDW/CHF RM16 ....330 F1
  CRW RM5 ....?
  EHAM E6 ....308 A5
  FOS CO13 ....137 G1
  RAYL SS6 ....262 F8
  SAFWS CB11 ....30 B1
  SOSN SS2 ....18 F2
  VGE SS16 ....294 F2
  WICKW SS12 ....260 G6
Victoria Crs CHLM/WR CM1 ....4 C3
  LAIN SS15 ....276 F5
  MGTR CO11 ....90 A1
  WICKW SS12 ....260 G6
Victoria Dock Rd CAN/RD E16 ....323 G6
  SBN/FI SS3 ....303 M3
Victoria Dr LOS SS9 ....300 B4
Victoria Esp K/T/MI CO5 ....178 A2
Victoria Gdns COLN CO4 ....107 L1
  SAFWS CB11 ....30 B1
Victoria Gv HLWE CM17 ....204 C4
Victoria Park Rd HOM E9 ....306 B4
Victoria Pl COL CO1 * 8 C9
  COL CO1 ....9 G7
  RCOLE CO7 ....156 C7
Victoria Plaza SOSN SS2 ....19 G4

Victoria Rd BARK IG11 ....308 E3
BKHH IG9 ....268 A1
BRW CM14 ....273 H3
CHING E4 ....249 H8
CHLM/WR CM1 ....5 C3
COLW CO3 ....106 F8
COS CO15 ....7 K5
DAGE RM10 ....310 C2
DART DA1 ....334 A7
FX IP11 ....11 K3
GVW DA11 ....337 J6
HVHL CB9 ....34 A6
LAIN SS15 ....276 D6
LOS SS9 ....300 B5
MAL CM9 ....214 A3
PLSTW E13 ....307 K6
RAYL SS6 ....281 H2
RCHLM CM3 ....245 G7
RCHLM CM3 ....245 G7
RCOS CO16 ....134 E8
ROM RM1 ....289 J3
SLH/COR SS17 ....316 C2
SOS SS1 ....19 M5
SWFD E18 ....285 L1
UPMR RM14 ....293 J3
VGE SS16 ....296 A3
WAB EN9 ....233 K4
WALTH E17 ....266 E4
WAN E11 ....307 C3
WOTN CO14 ....137 M1
Victoria Rd South
CHLM/WR CM1 ....5 C3
Victoria St BELV DA17 ....326 C6
BRTR CM7 ....121 J3
FX IP11 ....11 M2
HAR CO12 ....15 A8
IP IP1 ....16 B3
SRTFD E15 ....307 H4
Victoria Wy CHARL SE7 ....323 L8
Victor Mew St WICKW SS12 ....261 G8
Victor Rd COL CO1 ....9 H9
Victor's Crs RBRW/HUT CM13 ....256 F5
Victor Vls MGTR CO11 * 64 D5
Victory Cl CDW/CHF RM16 ....329 M7
Victory La RCFD SS4 ....265 C2
Victory Rd COS CO15 ....6 F5
IPNE IP4 ....48 F6
K/T/MI CO5 ....177 K7
RAIN RM13 ....311 K6
WAN E11 ....285 K2
Victory Wy BERM/RHTH SE16 ....322 B5
GRH DA9 ....337 J3
ROMW/RG RM7 ....270 E8
Vienna Cl CLAY IG5 ....268 A8
HAR CO12 ....70 F4
View Cl CHIG IG7 ....269 L4
Viewland Rd
WOOL/PLUM SE18 ....325 J8
View Point Rd FX IP11 ....68 J2
The View ABYW SE2 ....326 B8
Vigorous Wy CDW/CHF RM16 ....331 L3
Vignoles Rd ROMW/RG RM7 ....288 C5
Viking Cl WDBR IP12 ....51 H9
Viking Gdns EHAM E6 ....324 B1
Viking Hts WDBR IP12 ....51 H3
Viking Pl LEY E10 ....284 C6
Viking Rd GVW DA11 ....336 F8
MAL CM9 ....214 B6
Vikings Wy CVI SS8 ....320 A4
Viking Wy BELV DA17 ....326 F6
BRWN CM15 ....255 L4
COS CO15 ....160 D4
WICKE SS11 ....261 C3
Villa Cl GVE DA12 ....338 E7
Village Ar CHING E4 * 249 G8
Village Cl CHING E4 ....266 H4
FOS CO13 ....137 G3
HOD EN11 ....201 L4
Village Dr CVI SS8 ....320 D1
Village Ga CHLM/GWD CM2 ....210 D2
Village Hall CVI SS8 * 320 A2
Village Wy BARK/HLT IG6 ....286 F1
FOS CO13 ....137 G3
Villa Rd COLW CO15 ....105 M8
SBF/HAD SS7 ....297 M1
Villiers Pl RCHLM CM3 ....195 H4
Villiers-sur-Marne Av
BSF CM23 ....138 C5
Villiers Wy SBF/HAD SS7 ....280 C8
Vince Cl K/T/MI CO5 ....177 M7
Vincent Av CHING E4 ....266 H4
DAGW RM9 ....310 D4
RAIN RM13 ....311 M8
WOOL/PLUM SE18 * 324 D7
Vincents Cl BERM/RHTH SE16 ....322 B5
CHES/WCR EN8 ....216 F6
IP IP1 ....47 K5
SBN/FI SS3 ....303 H6
SLH/COR SS17 ....317 G2
Vincent Rd CHING E4 ....76 D3
DAGW RM9 ....310 D4
RAIN RM13 ....311 M8
WOOL/PLUM SE18 * 324 D7
Vincent St CAN/RD E16 ....323 H4
Vincent Wy BCAYW CM12 ....240 C8
Vine Cl BSDN SS14 ....278 C7
Vine Dr RCOLE CO7 ....130 F2
Vine Farm Rd RCOLE CO7 ....130 F2
Vine Gdns IL IG1 ....308 F2
Vine Gv HLW CM20 ....149 L7
Vine Rd K/T/MI CO5 ....149 L7
SRTFD E15 ....307 J4
Vinesse Rd RCOLW CO6 ....86 A4
Vine St BRTR CM7 ....76 D3
ROMW/RG RM7 ....288 C5
Vineway BRW CM14 ....255 M8
The Vineway HAR CO12 ....14 D7
Vineyard Ga CHLM/GWD CM2 *
....5
Vineyard St COL CO1 ....8 D8
Vint Crs CHING E4 ....106 F7
The Vintners SOSN SS2 ....283 J8
Vintry Ms WALTH E17 ....284 D2
Viola Av ABYW SE2 ....325 L7
Viola Cl SOCK/AV RM15 ....313 M7
Violet Cl CAN/RD E16 ....307 H8
CHLM/WR CM1 ....194 H6
CHTY IP2 ....53 L1
Violet Rd BOW E3 ....306 C1
SWFD E18 ....267 L8
WALTH E17 ....284 D4
Virgil Dr BROX EN10 ....217 G1
Virgil Rd WIT CM8 ....147 J8
Virginia Cl COS CO15 ....7 G4
CRW RM5 ....270 F6
SBF/HAD SS7 ....279 L4
Virginia Gdns BARK/HLT IG6 ....269 G8
Virley Cl MAL CM9 ....215 G1
Viscount Dr COLN CO4 ....87 M8
EHAM E6 ....324 C1
Vista Av PEND EN3 ....248 D2
Vista Dr REDBR IG4 ....286 A4
Vista Rd COS CO15 ....7 H4
WICKE SS11 ....261 J6
The Vista EHAM E6 ....249 G7
Vitulus Cl COLN CO4 ....87 L7
Vivian Cl WOTN CO14 ....137 M1
Vivian Rd BOW E3 ....306 H1
Vixen Dr HERT/BAY SG13 ....184 B3
Voluntary Pl WAN E11 ....285 K4

Volwycke Av MAL CM9 ....214 C5
Voorburg Rd CVI SS8 ....321 G2
Vowler Rd VGE SS16 ....294 E1
Voyagers Gdns THMD SE28 ....325 M2
Voysey Gdns PIT SS13 ....278 C3
Vulcan Cl EHAM E6 ....324 D2

W

Waalwyk Dr CVI SS8 ....320 F1
Waarden Rd CVI SS8 ....320 D1
Waarem Av CVI SS8 ....320 D1
Wacketts CHESW EN7 ....216 B5
Waddesdon Rd HAR CO12 ....15 J5
Waddington Rd SRTFD E15 ....307 G2
Waddington St SRTFD E15 ....307 G3
Wade Reach WOTN CO14 ....137 K1
Wade Rd CAN/RD E16 ....323 M2
COS CO15 ....159 L5
Wades Gv WICKW SS12 ....50 D6
Wade's La RIPS/CAP IP9 ....60 C7
Wade's Pl POP/IOD E14 ....322 E3
Wadeville Av CHDH RM6 ....288 B4
Wadeville Cl BELV DA17 ....326 D8
Wadgate Rd FX IP11 ....11 G1
Wadham Av CHING E4 ....266 F6
Wadham Cl ING CM4 ....239 L1
Wadham Park Av
HOC/HUL SS5 ....263 K5
Wadham Rd CHING E4 ....266 E6
Wadhurst Rd IPSE IP3 ....55 J2
Wadley Cl K/T/MI CO5 ....150 B8
Wadley Rd WAN E11 ....285 H5
Wadsworth Cl PEND EN3 ....248 A5
Wager St BOW E3 ....306 C3
Waghorn Rd PLSTW E13 ....307 M5
Wagon Rd BAR EN5 * 232 B2
Wagstaff Gdns DAGW RM9 ....309 M4
Wagtail Dr MAL CM9 ....198 F8
Wagtail Pl K/T/MI CO5 * 148 F3
Waid Cl DART DA1 ....334 F4
Wainfleet Av CRW RM5 ....270 F4
Wainwright Av BRTR CM7 ....120 F5
RBRW/HUT CM13 ....257 G3
Wainwright Wy KESG IP5 50
Wakefield SAFWN CB10 ....341 L6
Wakefield Av BCAYW CM12 ....258 D3
Wakefield Cl COL CO1 8
Wakefield Gdns IL IG1 ....286 B6
Wakefield Rd GRH DA9 ....335 M7
Wakefield St EHAM E6 ....308 B5
GVW DA11 * 337 L4
Wakefields Wk
Wakelin Cha ING CM4 ....239 K2
Wakeling St WCHPL E1 * 322 B2
Wakelin Rd SRTFD E15 ....307 H6
Wakelin Wy WICKW SS12 ....171 K3
Wakerfield Cl EMPK RM11 ....290 C3
Wakering Av SBN/FI SS3 ....303 H3
Wakering Rd BARK IG11 ....308 F4
SBN/FI SS3 ....303 K5
SBN/FI SS3 ....303 K5
Wakerly Cl EHAM E6 ....324 C2
Wakescolne WICKE SS11 ....261 K7
Wakeshall La SUD CO10 ....346 D6
Wakes St RCOLW CO6 ....83 L7
Walcot Rd PEND EN3 ....248 C2
Waldegrave VGE SS16 ....3 C9
Waldegrave Gdns
UPMR RM14 ....290 E7
Waldegrave Rd BCTR RM8 ....287 M7
MGTR CO11 * 90 E7
Waldegraves La K/T/MI CO5 ....178 D6
The Waldegraves BURES CO8 ....359 Q9
Waldegrave Wy MGTR CO11 * 90 E2
Walden Av RAIN RM13 ....311 G6
SAFWN CB10 ....31 H7
Walden Cl BELV DA17 ....326 E6
MAL CM9 ....198 D1
Walden House Rd WIT CM8 ....172 D1
Walden Rd CBE/LIN CB1 * 308 H6
EMPK RM11 ....290 A4
GTDUN CM6 ....352 C12
SAFWN CB10 ....29 G4
SAFWN CB10 ....31 M1
SAFWS CB11 ....351 N1
Walden Wy BARK/HLT IG6 ....269 H6
EMPK RM11 ....290 A4
FOS CO13 ....137 K3
Waldgrooms GTDUN CM6 ....116 F4
Waldingfield Rd SUD CO10 ....20 F4
Waldon TIL RM18 ....332 E5
Waldringfield BSDN SS14 ....3 H3
Waldringfield Rd WDBR IP12 ....51 J3
Waldrist Wy ERITHM DA18 ....326 C5
Waldstock Rd THMD SE28 ....325 K3
Waley St WCHPL E1 * 322 F1
Walford Pl CHLM/GWD CM2 ....210 D2
Walfords Cl HLWE CM17 ....188 D6
Walford Wy RCOLW CO6 ....124 D5
Walfrey Gdns DAGW RM9 ....310 B4
Walker Cl DART DA1 ....334 E4
WOOL/PLUM SE18 ....324 F7
Walker Dr LOS SS9 ....299 K3
Walkers Cl CHLM/WR CM1 ....194 H6
Walkers Sq SLH/COR SS17 ....317 G4
Walkey Wy SBN/FI SS3 ....303 L5
The Walk BCAYW CM12 * 258 D4
EMPK RM11 ....290 D2
FX IP11 ....62 D8
HOC/HUL SS5 ....263 J4
IP IP1 ....16 F4
RCFD SS4 45
RCOLW CO6 ....105 K5
Wallace Binder Cl MAL CM9 ....214 C4
Wallace Binder Gnd
MAL CM9 * 214 F5
Wallace Crs CHLM/GWD CM2 ....5 K8
Wallace Dr WICKW SS12 ....261 H8
Wallace Gdns SWCM DA10 ....336 B4
Wallace La RCHLM CM3 ....142 E6
Wallace Rd GRAYS RM17 ....330 D3
IP IP1 ....47 K5
Wallace's La RCHLM CM3 ....195 J1
Wallace St SBN/FI SS3 ....303 A6
Wallasea Gdns
CHLM/WR CM1 ....194 C6
Wall Cha RCHLM CM3 ....142 C6
Wall End Rd EHAM E6 ....308 D4
Wallenger Av GPK RM2 ....289 L5
Wallers Cl DAGW RM9 ....310 B5
ROY SG8 ....349 G2
Waller's Hoppet LOU IG10 ....250 E1
Wallflower St SHB W12 ....
Wallington Br
GDMY/SEVK IG3 ....287 J5

Wallis Av SOSN SS2 ....18 E1
Wallis Cl EMPK RM11 ....289 L6
Wallis Ct COLW CO3 ....128 B2
Wallis Pk GVW DA11 ....336 B5
Wallis Rd HOM E9 ....306 C3
Wall La MGTR CO11 ....366 G3
Wall Rd FX IP11 ....321 H1
The Walls MGTR CO11 ....91 H1
Wallwood Rd WAN E11 ....285 G5
Wallwood St POP/IOD E14 ....322 C1
Walmer Cl CHING E4 ....266 E2
ROMW/RG RM7 ....270 E8
Walmer Ter
WOOL/PLUM SE18 ....324 F7
Walnut Cl BARK/HLT IG6 ....286 F2
FX IP11 ....63 J6
HOC/HUL SS5 ....264 B6
Walnut Ct BSF CM23 ....138 E6
WIT CM8 ....171 K1
Walnut Gdns SRTFD E15 ....307 H3
Walnut Gv BRTR CM7 ....121 H3
Walnut Rd LEY E10 ....284 C1
Walnut Tree Av SBW CM21 ....162 F5
Walnut Tree Cl
CHES/WCR EN8 ....201 H3
HOD EN11 ....201 H3
Walnut Tree Crs SBW CM21 * 162 F6
Walnut Tree La RIPS/CAP IP9 ....365 L11
SUD CO10 ....20 F5
Walnut Tree Rd BCTR RM8 ....288 A2
ERITH DA8 ....327 H8
GNWCH SE10 * 323 H8
Walnut Tree Wk WARE SG12 ....184 B5
Walnut Tree Wy COLS CO2 ....128 C3
K/T/MI CO5 ....149 M6
Walnut Wy BKHH IG9 ....268 A2
COS CO15 ....6 A6
RCOLE CO7 ....156 D6
Walpole Gv GRAYS RM17 ....330 F5
Walpole Rd EHAM E6 ....307 M4
SWFD E18 ....267 J7
WALTH E17 ....284 D2
Walsham Cl THMD SE28 ....326 A3
Walsingham La LAIN SS15 ....276 D1
SUD CO10 ....45 M4
Walsingham Rd COLS CO2 ....8 C3
SOSN SS2 ....301 L2
Walsingham Wy
BCAYW CM12 ....240 F2
Walter Radcliffe Wy
RCOLE CO7 ....130 F6
Walters Cl CHLM/GWD CM2 ....225 M2
LOS SS9 ....282 B7
Walter St BETH E2 ....306 A7
Walter Yd COL CO1 ....8 C5
Walter Ter WCHPL E1 ....322 A2
Walter Wy WICKW SS12 ....261 G8
Waltham Cl CHTY IP2 ....53 M3
RBRW/HUT CM13 ....256 F2
Waltham Crs SOSN SS2 ....301 L2
Waltham Gdns PEND EN3 ....232 D6
Waltham Ga CHES/WCR EN8 ....216 F4
Waltham Gln CHLM/GWD CM2 ....3 M3
Waltham Pk WALTH E17 ....266 D6
Waltham Rd RAYL SS6 ....216 B5
RCHLM CM3 ....195 J1
WAB EN9 ....217 M4
WFD IG8 ....268 B5
Walthams PIT SS13 ....278 E6
Walthams Pl PIT SS13 ....278 E6
Walthamstow Av North Circular
CHING E4 ....266 C2
Waltham Wy CHING E4 ....266 C2
FOS CO13 ....137 K4
Walton Av FX IP11 ....10 C4
Walton Ct LAIN SS15 ....276 F5
Walton Gdns
RBRW/HUT CM13 ....256 F1
WAB EN9 ....233 J4
Walton Rd COS CO15 ....7 H5
CRW RM5 ....270 C6
FOS CO13 ....368 B11
HOD EN11 ....201 J1
MNPK E12 ....289 K3
PLSTW E13 ....307 M6
RCOS CO16 ....135 L2
SOS SS1 ....302 C1
WARE SG12 ....184 E1
Walton's Hall Rd
SLH/COR SS17 ....332 D1
Wambrook Cl
RBRW/HUT CM13 ....256 F5
Wamburg Rd CVI SS8 ....321 G1
Wanderer Dr BARK IG11 ....308 D7
Wangey Rd CHDH RM6 ....288 A5
Wanlip Rd PLSTW E13 ....307 K3
Wannock Gdns BARK/HLT IG6 ....268 F1
Wansbeck Rd HOM E9 ....306 A1
Wansfell Rds SOS SS1 ....302 C4
Wansford Cl BRW CM14 ....273 J2
Wansford Rd WFD IG8 ....267 M7
Wanstead La IL IG1 ....285 M2
Wanstead Park Av MNPK E12 ....286 A7
Wanstead Park Rd IL IG1 ....286 B6
Wanstead Rd WAN E11 ....285 K4
Wantz Cha MAL CM9 ....214 D3
Wantz Hant MAL CM9 * 214 D3
Wantz La RAIN RM13 ....311 L8
Wantz Rd DAGE RM10 ....310 E1
ING CM4 ....224 D4
MAL CM9 ....214 D3
Wapping La RCOLE CO7 ....155 L3
Warboys Crs CHING E4 ....266 F4
Warburton Av HSTD CO9 ....356 E9
Warburtons SLH/COR SS17 ....317 J2
Warburton Ter WALTH E17 ....266 F1
Ward Av GRAYS RM17 ....330 E5
Ward Cl CHESW EN7 ....216 B5
Warde Av WOTN CO14 ....137 L1
Warden Av CRW RM5 ....270 F4
Ward Hatch HLW CM20 ....188 C6
Wardle St HOM E9 ....306 A1
Wardle Wy CHLM/WR CM1 ....193 H6
Wardley Cl CHTY IP2 ....53 L4
Ward Pth CHLM/GWD CM2 ....210 E1
Ward Rd RIPW IP8 ....53 G3
SRTFD E15 * 307 G5
Wards Cft SAFWS CB11 ....30 A2
Wards Rd GNTH/NBYPK IG2 ....287 J3
Wards Wharf Ap CAN/RD E16 ....324 A4
Wareham Av IPSE IP3 ....55 J2
Warehouse Rd GTDUN CM6 ....96 C8
Waremead Rd
GNTH/NBYPK IG2 ....286 E3
Warepoint Dr THMD SE28 ....325 G5
Ware Rd HERT/BAY SG13 ....184 B2
HOD EN11 ....201 H1
WARE SG12 ....185 H6
Warescot Rd BRWN CM15 ....255 L7
Warescott Rd BRWN CM15 ....255 L7
Wares Rd CHLM/WR CM1 165
Wargrave Rd COS CO15 7
Warham Rd HAR CO12 ....70 D3
Warley Av ROMW/RG RM7 ....288 C3
Warley Cl BRTR CM7 ....121 M2

Warley Gap RBRW/HUT CM13 ....273 L6
Warley Hl RBRW/HUT CM13 ....273 M4
Warley Mt BRW CM14 ....273 M3
Warley Rd CLAY IG5 ....268 D7
RBRW/HUT CM13 ....273 L6
WFD IG8 ....267 L6
Warley St BETH E2 ....306 A7
UPMR RM14 ....292 A1
Warley Wy FOS CO13 ....137 G5
Warlow Cl PEND EN3 ....233 H7
Warming St CLPT E5 * 284 A8
Warmington St PLSTW E13 ....307 G8
Warner Av WALTH E17 ....284 B2
Warner Cl BCAYE CM11 ....259 G4
BRTR CM77 ....120 C4
SRTFD E15 ....307 H2
Warner Dr BRTR CM7 ....120 F1
Warner Rd WALTH E17 ....284 B2
WARE SG12 ....184 E1
Warners GTDUN CM6 ....117 G5
Warners Av HOD EN11 ....201 G5
Warners Bridge Cha
RCFD SS4 ....283 J7
Warners Gdns SOSN SS2 ....283 H7
Warner Ter POP/IOD E14 * 322 D1
Warner Wy SUD CO10 ....21 H5
Warnham Cl RCOS CO16 ....158 D4
Warren Av WAN E11 * 285 G4
Warren Cha KESG IP5 ....50 D7
Warren Ct CHARL SE7 ....323 M8
CHIG IG7 ....269 G5
Warren Dr BSDN SS14 ....278 D7
HCH RM12 ....289 K8
WICKE SS11 ....261 K5
Warren Fld EPP CM16 ....236 B3
Warrenfield Cl CHESW EN7 ....216 F4
Warren Heath Av IPSE IP3 ....55 J3
Warren Heath Rd IPSE IP3 ....55 J3
Warren Hl LOU IG10 ....249 M5
Warren La BRWN CM15 ....255 J5
CDW/CHF RM16 ....330 A3
COLW CO3 ....127 C4
KESG IP5 ....50 F6
RIPS/CAP IP9 ....66 A2
Warren Lingley Wy
K/T/MI CO5 ....150 B8
Warren Pond Rd CHING E4 ....249 J7
Warren Rd BARK/HLT IG6 ....287 G8
BRTR CM7 ....121 M3
CHING E4 ....266 H3
HSTD CO9 ....81 G4
LEY E10 ....284 D5
LOS SS9 ....299 K2
RCHLM CM3 ....242 G7
WAN E11 ....285 M4
Warrenside BRTR CM7 ....121 L5
The Warrens FOS CO13 ....137 K3
WIT CM8 ....172 C5
Warren Ter CDW/CHF RM16 * 330 A4
The Warren BCAYW CM12 ....258 B1
MNPK E12 ....308 B1
SLH/COR SS17 * 317 H6
Warriner Av HCH RM12 ....290 A7
Warrington Gdns
EMPK RM11 ....289 M4
Warrington Pl POP/IOD E14 * 322 F4
Warrington Rd BCTR RM8 ....288 A2
IP IP1 ....16 C2
Warrington Sq
BCAYW CM12 * 258 B1
BCTR RM8 ....288 A2
Warrior Sq MNPK E12 ....308 F1
SOS SS1 ....19 M5
Warrior Sq East SOS SS1 ....19 L5
Warrior Sq North SOS SS1 ....19 L5
Warrior Square Rd
SBN/FI SS3 ....303 J8
Warspite Rd
WOOL/PLUM SE18 ....324 B6
Warton Rd SRTFD E15 ....306 F5
Warwall EHAM E6 ....324 E2
Warwick Bailey Cl COL CO4 ....107 G3
Warwick Cl BRTR CM7 ....121 K1
CVI SS8 ....298 D3
MAL CM9 ....214 D4
RAYL SS6 ....281 J4
SBF/HAD SS7 ....280 C5
Warwick Ct COLS CO2 * 129 M4
Warwick Crs COS CO15 ....6 D4
MAL CM9 ....214 D4
Warwick Dr CHES/WCR EN8 ....216 F4
MAL CM9 ....214 D4
RCFD SS4 ....283 J6
Warwick Gdns GPK RM2 ....289 M1
IL IG1 ....286 E6
RAYL SS6 ....281 K4
Warwick La RAIN RM13 ....312 C3
Warwick Pl BRW CM14 ....254 F4
GVW DA11 ....336 E3
VGE SS16 ....294 C1
Warwick Rd BSF CM23 ....139 G4
CHING E4 ....266 D4
COS CO15 6
FSTGT E7 ....307 J2
IPNE IP4 ....17 K3
MNPK E12 ....308 F1
PEND EN3 ....233 G7
RAIN RM13 ....311 M8
RAYL SS6 ....281 K4
RBSF SC22 ....377 L2
SOS SS1 ....302 C1
WALTH E17 ....266 C1
Warwick Sq CHLM/WR CM1 ....209 G5
Warwick Ter WALTH E17 * 285 G5
Washall Dr BRTR CM7 ....121 G5
Washford Gdns COS CO15 6
Washington Av LAIN SS15 ....276 D7
MNPK E12 ....308 F1
Washington Cl BOW E3 ....306 F1
Washington Rd EHAM E6 ....307 M4
HAR CO12 ....70 D3
MAL CM9 ....214 D4
SWFD E18 ....267 L8
Wash La COS CO15 ....183 C4
MAL CM9 ....199 L4
Wash Rd LAIN SS15 ....276 D1
RBRW/HUT CM13 ....239 H8
Watchfield La RAYL SS6 ....280 F4
Watch House Rd GTDUN CM6 ....96 C8
Watchouse Gn GTDUN CM6 ....119 G6
Watchouse Rd
CHLM/GWD CM2 ....225 M2
Waterbeach Rd DAGW RM9 ....309 M4
Waterdene CVI SS8 ....298 D3
Waterden Rd SRTFD E15 ....306 D7
The Waterfalls VGE SS16 ....294 E2
Waterfield Cl BELV DA17 ....326 C5

THMD SE28 ....325 L4
Waterford Rd IP IP1 47
SBN/FI SS3 303
Waterfront WTHK RM20 * 329
Waterfront Wk BSDN SS14 277
Waterhale COS CO15 302
Waterhall Av CHING E4 267
Waterhall Cl WALTH E17 266
Water Hall La BRTR CM7 78
Waterhouse La CHLM/WR CM1 5
RCOLE CO7 89
Waterhouse Moor HLWS CM18 13
Water La BRTR CM7 98
BRTR CM77 122
BSF CM23 139
BURES CO8 359
COLW CO3 106
GDMY/SEVK IG3 287
GTDUN CM6 375
HLWW/ROY CM19 202
HSTD CO9 358
HVHL CB9 35
HVHL CB9 343
PUR RM19 328
RCOLW CO6 361
SAFWN CB10 352
SAFWS CB11 30
SAFWS CB11 351
SRTFD E15 307
STSD CM24 115
STSD CM24 39
Waterloo Gdns
ROMW/RG RM7 289
Waterloo La CHLM/WR CM1 5
Waterloo Rd BARK/HLT IG6 268
BRW CM14 255
EHAM E6 307
FSTGT E7 307
IP IP1 16
LEY E10 284
ROMW/RG RM7 289
SBN/FI SS3 303
Waterloo St GVE DA12 337
Watermans Wy EPP CM16 221
GRH DA9 335
Watermark Wy
HERT/BAY SG13 184
Water Mdw VGE SS16 296
Watermill Rd K/T/MI CO5 149
WDBR IP12 57
Waterside RCOLE CO7 156
STSD CM24 115
Waterside Cl BARK IG11 309
HARH RM3 272
HOM E9 306
Waterside Rd BOC CM0 386
RCFD SS4 397
Watersmeet
HLWW/ROY CM19 203
Watersmeet Wy THMD SE28 326
Waterson Rd CDW/CHF RM16 331
Waterton Av GVE DA12 338
Waterville Dr VGE SS16 296
Watervale Ms COLS CO2 129
Wavewick Hi SAFWS CB11 371
Waterworks Cl COLS CO2 152
Waterworks Dr RCOS CO16 158
Waterworks La CLPT E5 284
Waterworks St IPNE IP4 17
Watery La BSF CM23 92
CHONG CM5 380
GTDUN CM6 140
RCOLW CO6 123
WICKE SS11 262
Watery Stones
SAFWS CB11 72
Wates Wy BRWN CM15 256
Watford Rd CAN/RD E16 323
Watkins Cl PIT SS13 279
Watkins Wy SBN/FI SS3 303
Watling La GTDUN CM6 74
Watling Dr GTDUN CM6 74
MEO CM9 336
Watlingation Rd HLWE CM17 188
SBF/HAD SS7 297
Watson Av EHAM E6 308
Watson Cl SBN/FI SS3 303
WTHK RM20 335
Watson Rd COS CO15 6
Watts Cl GTDUN CM6 141
Watts Crs PUR RM19 328
Watts Gv BOW E3 322
Watts Rd COLS CO2 152
Wat Tyler Wk COL CO1 4
Wavell Av COLS CO2 128
Wavell Cl CHES/WCR EN8 216
Waveney Dr CHLM/WR CM1 193
Waveney Rd FX IP11 11
IP IP1 47
Waveney Ter HVHL CB9 34
Waverley Av CHING E4 266
WALTH E17 285
Waverley Crs HARH RM3 271
WICKE SS11 260
Waverley Gdns BARK IG11 309
BARK/HLT IG6 268
CDW/CHF RM16 330
EHAM E6 324
Waverley Rd LAIN SS15 277
RAIN RM13 311
SBF/HAD SS7 279
SWFD E18 267
WALTH E17 284
WOOL/PLUM SE18 324
Wavertree Rd SBF/HAD SS7 297
SWFD E18 267
Wavring Av COS CO15 137
Waxwell Rd HOC/HUL SS5 263
The Wayback SAFWN CB10 28
Way Bank La HSTD CO9 36
Waycross Rd UPMR RM14 291
Wayfarer Gdns BOC CM0 393
Wayfaring Gn GRAYS RM17 330
Wayletts LAIN SS15 276
LOS SS9 281
Wayletts Dr BSF CM23 139
Wayre St HLWE CM17 188
Wayside RCHLM CM3 212
Wayside Av HCH RM12 290
Wayside Cl ROM RM1 289
Wayside Gdns DAGE RM10 310
Wayside Ms GNTH/NBYPK IG2 286
Wayside Rd BSF CM23 138
Weald Br EPP CM16 205
Weald Bridge Rd EPP CM16 205
Weald Cl BRW CM14 273
Weald Hall La EPP CM16 220
Weald Park Wy BRW CM14 273
The Weald CVI 254
Weald Wy ROMW/RG RM7 288
Weald Cl RCOLE CO7 267
Wear Dr CHLM/WR CM1 194
Weare Gifford SBN/FI SS3 302
Weaver Cl EHAM E6 324

	IP1 47	J5
Veaverdale SBN/FI SS5 303	H4
Veaverhead CM6 74	D1
Veaverhead La GTDUN CM6 74	D2
Veavers CI SE16 296	C1
COLW CO3 106	C3
GVW DA11 337	K6
Veavers Ct SUD CO10 20	C6
Veavers Ct SUD CO10 39	L1
Veaversfield WIT CM8 122	F8
Veavers CI RCFD SS4 285	K4
Veavers Ct RCOLW CO6 85	G7
Veavers La SUD CO10 20	C7
Veaver Rw HSTD CO9 81	J4
Vebb CI CHLM/GWD CM2 210	B2
Vebbscroft Rd DAGE RM10 310	D4
Vebb St CHTY IP2 16	E1
Vebster PI HCH RM12 * 290	A4
HSTD CO9 356	E9
WAB EN9 204	B3
Vebster Rd SLH/COR SS17 317	H3
WAN E11 284	E8
Vebsters Wy RAYL SS6 281	G3
Veddell Rd WICKE SS11 * 34	F7
Vedds Wy SBN/FI SS3 303	L1
Vedgwood CI EPP CM16 220	B8
Vedgwood Dr COLN CO4 107	H5
HLWE CM17 204	E2
Vedgwood End BRTR CM7 * 76	A3
Vedgwood Wy RCFD SS4 264	E7
Vedhey HLWW/ROY CM19 12	E6
Vedlake CI EMPK RM11 290	A6
Vedmore Av CLAY IG5 268	D7
Vednesbury Gdns HARH RM3 272	C6
Vednesbury Gn HARH RM3 272	C6
Vednesbury Rd HARH RM3 272	C6
Vedow Rd GTDUN CM6 74	D2
Veeley By-Pass Rd	
RCOS CO16 134	A4
Veeley Rd RCOLE CO7 133	H5
RCOS CO16 134	C4
Veelkes Ct SLH/COR SS17 316	F2
Veel Rd CVI SS8 321	J3
Veggs Willow COLN CO4 9	K6
Veight Rd CHLM/GWD CM2 5	J4
Veirbrook SBF/HAD SS7 280	E5
Veir Farm Rd RAYL SS6 280	F5
Veir Gdns RAYL SS6 280	F5
Veir Gate CLAY IG5 129	L6
K/T/MI CO5 130	B5
Veir Pond Rd RCFD SS4 283	J3
Veir Wynd BCAYW CM12 258	D4
Velbeck CI FX IP11 62	E6
HOC/HUL SS5 282	C1
Velbeck Dr VGE SS16 294	B1
Velbeck Ri VGE SS16 294	C1
Velbeck Rd CVI SS8 320	D3
EHAM E6 308	A4
Velch CI SOSN SS2 302	B2
Velfare Rd SRTFD E15 307	H7
Velford CI CLPT E5 284	A8
Velland Av CHLM/WR CM1 192	H4
Velland Rd BOC CM0 393	K7
Vellands WIT CM8 172	M8
Vellands II WIT CM8 172	M8
Vellby Ct PLSTW E13 307	M5
Vellcome Av DART DA1 334	B6
Vell Cottage PI WAN E11 285	M8
Veller Gv CHESW EN7 216	B6
Vellers Gv CHESW EN7 216	B6
Vellesley EPP CM16 203	H6
Vellesley CI CHARL SE7 * 323	M5
Vellesley Rd BRW CM14 255	M6
COLW CO3 106	A9
COS CO15 6	E4
IL IG1 286	E7
IPNE IP4 17	M5
WALTH E17 284	E4
WAN E11 285	K3
Vell Fld CHLM/WR CM1 208	B1
HSTD CO9 81	J4
Vellfields LOU IG10 250	D3
Vellfield Wy FOS CO13 137	G2
Vell-Green CI SAFWS SB11 30	B9
Velling Rd CDW/CHF RM16 316	N6
Vellington Av CHING E4 266	D1
HOC/HUL SS5 263	G4
WOS/PRIT SS0 300	D4
Vellington Dr BRTR CM7 121	M1
CHLM/WR CM1 193	M1
DAGE RM10 310	F4
Vellington Dr DAGE RM10 310	F4
Vellington Gdns CHARL SE7 323	M8
Vellington HI LOU IG10 250	H2
Vellington Ms BCAYW CM12 240	D8
Vellington PI BROX EN10 * 216	D1
BRW CM14 273	M4
Vellington Rd BELV DA17 326	D2
EHAM E6 308	C8
EPP CM16 221	H5
FSTGT E7 307	J1
HAR CO12 15	F1
LEY E10 284	B6
MAL CM9 214	A2
RAYL SS6 281	J2
TIL RM18 331	K8
WALTH E17 284	E1
WAN E11 285	K1
The Wellingtons BOC CM0 393	N2
Vellington St SCOLS CO2 8	B9
GVE DA12 337	M5
IP IP1 16	B7
RCOLE CO7 156	C7
WOOL/PLUM SE18 324	D7
Vellington Wy BOW E3 306	C2
Vell La BRWN CM15 255	J3
CHLM/WR CM16 314	B8
CHLM/GWD CM2 225	L3
HLW CM20 12	B6
ING CM4 241	H4
K/T/MI CO5 126	D7
RCHLM CM3 211	M7
SUD CO10 37	G8
Vell Md BCAYW CM12 258	F6
Vellmeads CHLM/GWD CM2 5	G7
Vells Av SOSN SS2 283	G7
Vells CI IPNE IP4 17	J4
Vells Ct CHLM/WR CM1 4	F8
Vells Gdns IL IG1 286	B5
RAIN RM13 311	J3
Vells Hall Rd SUD CO10 45	M5
Vells Side RCOLW CO6 126	B2
Vell St COL CO1 8	F5
Vells St CHLM/WR CM1 4	D7
Vellstead Gdns	
WOS/PRIT SS0 300	E2
Vellstead Rd EHAM E6 308	D6
Vell St HOM E9 306	A4
RCOLE CO7 156	B6
SRTFD E15 307	H3

Wellstye Gn BSDN SS14 278	B5
Well Ter MAL CM9 * 198	E8
Wellwood Rd	
GDMY/SEVK IG3 287	K6
Welsh CI SLH/COR SS17 307	K7
Welshwood Park Rd	
COLN CO4 108	B3
Welsummer Wy	
CHES/WCR EN8 216	A5
Welton Wy RCFD SS4 283	K4
Welton Av WICKE SS16 296	C1
Wendene VGE SS16 296	C1
Wenden Rd SAFWS SB11 351	Q5
Wendon Ct RCFD SS4 282	F1
Wendon St BOW E3 306	C5
Wendover Gdns	
RBRW/HUT CM13 256	E5
Wendover Wy HCH RM12 311	M2
Wendy CI RIPS/CAP IP9 365	Q6
Wenham Dr WOS/PRIT SS0 18	C1
Wenham La RCOLE CO7 363	R1
Wenham Rd RIPW IP9 52	C6
Wenlock Rd RCOS CO16 134	C7
Wennington Rd BOW E3 306	A4
RAIN RM13 327	L1
Wensley Av WICKE SS11 267	K6
Wensley CI CRW RM5 270	D4
Wensleydale Av CLAY IG5 268	E1
Wensley Rd SBF/HAD SS7 298	E1
Wentford Vw SUD CO10 37	L4
Wents CI RCOLE CO7 133	H3
Wentworth CI CHLM CM3 196	E1
THMD SE28 325	J5
Wentworth Crs BRTR CM7 99	J8
FX IP11 63	H7
RIPW IP9 53	H3
Wentworth Dr BSF CM23 138	E3
Wentworth Mdw MAL CM9 214	C3
Wentworth Ms BOW E3 306	C4
Wentworth PI	
CDW/CHF RM16 331	G2
Wentworth Rd MNPK E12 308	A1
SOS SS2 301	K2
Wentworth Wy RAIN RM13 311	J1
Werneth Hall Rd CLAY IG5 286	C1
Wesel Av FX IP11 10	C1
Wesley Av CAN/RD E16 323	K4
COLN CO4 83	K5
Wesley End Rd HSTD CO9 345	J10
Wesley Gdns BCAYW CM12 * 240	C8
Wesley Rd LEY E10 284	C1
SOS SS1 19	L6
Wesley Wy IP IP1 47	L6
Wessem Rd CVI SS8 * 298	E8
Wessex CI GDMY/SEVK IG3 287	H4
Westall Rd LOU IG10 250	E6
West Arbour St WCHPL E1 322	A2
West Av CHLM/WR CM1 193	J8
COS CO15 6	E8
HOC/HUL SS5 262	F2
RCHLM CM3 388	B8
VGE SS16 294	B1
WALTH E17 284	D1
West Bank BARK IG11 4	F8
West Beech Av WICKE SS11 261	C6
West Beech CI WICKE SS11 261	H4
West Belvedere RCHLM CM3 212	C6
Westborough Rd	
WOS/PRIT SS0 300	C3
Westbourne CI HOC/HUL SS5 264	C6
SBF/HAD SS7 281	C4
Westbourne Dr BRW CM14 273	J3
Westbourne Gdns	
BCAYW CM12 240	E8
Westbourne Gv	
CHLM/GWD CM2 210	A6
WOS/PRIT SS0 300	E3
Westbourne Rd IP IP1 47	L4
West Bowers Rd MAL CM9 212	F1
Westbury CHES/WCR EN8 * 216	B6
RCFD SS4 282	F1
Westbury CI RCOLW CO6 105	G8
Westbury Dr BRW CM14 273	J3
Westbury La BKHH IG9 267	J1
Westbury Ri HLWE CM17 204	E2
Westbury Rd BARK IG11 309	G5
BKHH IG9 249	M8
BRW CM14 273	M4
FOS CO13 116	B1
IPNE IP4 49	L3
SOSN SS2 301	M2
WALTH E17 284	D1
Westbury Ter FSTGT E7 307	L2
UPMR RM14 291	H7
Westbush CI HOD EN11 185	G4
West Cha MAL CM9 214	C2
MAL CM9 231	H4
Westcliff Av WOS/PRIT SS0 18	A2
Westcliff Dr LOS SS9 300	A4
Westcliff Gdns WOS/PRIT SS0 321	H2
Westcliff Pde WOS/PRIT SS0 18	A2
Westcliff Park Dr	
WOS/PRIT SS0 18	A2
West Cloister BCAYE CM11 309	H1
West Ct HOD EN11 201	H1
RAIN RM13 311	L8
Westcott Av GVW DA11 337	K8
Westcott Crs BROX EN10 159	G4
Westcott House	
POP/IOD E14 * 322	D3
West Ct ING CM4 239	M2
West Crs CVI SS8 320	C1
West Crescent Rd GVE DA12 337	L6
West Cft BCAYE CM11 309	J1
Westcroft CI PEND EN3 232	D8
Westcroft Ct BROX EN10 159	H5
West Dene Dr HARH RM3 272	A4
West Dock Rd HAR CO12 66	D8
Westdene Rd SRTFD E15 306	H1
West Dr BRTR CM7 77	J2
West End Av WALTH E17 284	F1
Westend La HVHL SS8 35	L3
West End Ms COLW CO3 * 106	A9
West End Rd BROX EN10 159	A1
IP IP1 16	E2
K/T/MI CO5 173	J2
West Park Av BCAYW CM12 258	C4
West Park CI HARH RM6 288	C4
West Park Crs BCAYW CM12 258	C4
West Park Dr BCAYW CM12 258	D3
West Park HI BRW CM14 273	K2
West Parkside GNWCH SE10 323	H5
West PI EPP CM16 319	G4
West Point PI HLW CM20 * 307	K5
Westport Rd SRTFD E15 307	J3
West Quay RCOLE CO7 130	C6
Westray Wk WICKW SS12 261	K4
West Rdg BCAYW CM12 258	C4
Westridge CI COS CO15 159	J4
West Rd BSF CM23 138	F1
CHDH RM6 288	C4
COS CO15 183	J9
HLW CM20 188	B3
HSTD CO9 81	M1
IPSE IP3 55	L4
ROMW/RG RM7 289	C5

Western Av BRW CM14 255	M8
DAGE RM10 310	F3
EPP CM16 236	A2
FX IP11 63	J7
GPK RM2 271	M8
HVHL CB9 34	M7
WTHK RM20 * 329	J7
Western CI IPNE IP4 55	J1
WIT CM8 147	M2
Western Cross CI GRH DA9 335	M8
Western Esp CVI SS8 320	E3
WOS/PRIT SS0 18	C7
Western Gtwy CAN/RD E16 323	K4
Western La WIT CM8 147	K2
Western Ms BCAYW CM12 258	D3
Western Prom RCOLE CO7 156	A6
Western Rd BOC CM0 393	M1
BRW CM14 273	M1
LOS SS9 299	K4
PLSTW E13 307	L5
RAYL SS6 280	E4
RCOLE CO7 156	B7
ROM RM1 289	J7
SBF/HAD SS7 281	H7
WAB EN9 201	M8
WALTH E17 284	F3
WIT CM8 147	J2
Western's End MGTR CO11 65	C5
Western Ter HOD EN11 * 185	J8
Westernville Gdns	
GNTH/NBYPK IG2 286	F5
Western Wy THMD SE28 325	J5
Westferry Circ POP/IOD E14 322	D4
Westferry Rd POP/IOD E14 322	D6
West Fld CBE/LIN CB11 * 23	L2
SAFWN CB10 * 352	C2
Westfield HLWS CM18 13	K9
LAIN SS15 276	D5
SUD CO10 37	J7
Westfield CI BSF CM23 138	F1
CHES/WCR EN8 233	G1
PEND EN3 248	B5
RAYL SS6 262	E8
WICKE SS11 261	J5
Westfield Dr RCOLW CO6 124	B4
Westfield Gdns CHDH RM6 287	M4
Westfield Park Dr WFD IG8 268	A8
Westfield Rd BSF CM23 138	F1
DAGW RM9 310	A1
HOD EN11 201	G2
West Flds SAFWS SB11 30	A6
Westfield St	
WOOL/PLUM SE18 324	A6
Westfield Wy WCHPL E1 * 306	B7
Westgate BSDN SS14 278	B7
West Ga HLW CM20 12	A1
Westgate St IP IP1 16	F7
SUD CO10 40	F7
West Gn SBF/HAD SS7 279	L8
West Gv WFD IG8 267	K8
West Ham La SRTFD E15 307	H4
West Hanningfield Rd	
RCHLM CM3 226	A7
Chelmerton St WALTH E17 284	C5
West Hayes RBSF CM22 378	B2
West HI DART DA1 334	A4
Westhill CI GVE DA12 337	L6
West Hill Ri DART DA1 334	A4
West Hill Rd HOD EN11 201	L1
Westholme Rd IP IP1 47	M8
West Hook Wy VGE SS16 294	C2
West House Est BOC CM0 393	M4
West India Av POP/IOD E14 322	D4
West India Dock Rd	
POP/IOD E14 322	D4
West Kent Av GVW DA11 336	F4
Westlake Av PIT SS13 279	H7
Westlake Crs RCOLE CO7 130	D3
Westland KESG IP5 50	C5
Westland Av EMPK RM11 290	A6
Westland Vw CDW/CHF RM16 314	D5
West Lawn IPNE IP4 49	G5
Westlea CI BROX EN10 217	G1
Westlea Rd BROX EN10 217	G1
Westleigh Av LOS SS9 300	B4
Westleton Wy FX IP11 62	C8
West Ley BOC CM0 393	M4
Westley La BKHH IG9 267	L1
Westley Rd VGE SS16 294	F3
West Lodge Av COLW CO3 107	G9
Westlyn CI RAIN RM13 311	M7
West Malling Wy HCH RM12 311	M2
Westman Rd CVI SS8 321	H2
Westmarch RCHLM CM3 244	A5
West Mayne LAIN SS15 276	A7
Westmeade CI CHESW EN7 216	C6
West Mdw IP IP1 47	H1
Westmede BARK/HLT IG6 252	B8
VGE SS16 276	F5
West Mill GVW DA11 337	J4
Westminster Ct IPNE IP4 49	G8
Westminster Ct COLS CO2 * 129	H1
Westminster Dr HOC/HUL SS5 263	H7
WOS/PRIT SS0 300	A1
Westminster Gdns BARK IG11 309	H5
BARK/HLT IG6 269	K1
BRTR CM7 77	J2
CHING E4 249	H8
West Moor Av CBS CB2 22	B1
Westmoor Gdns PEND EN3 248	A2
Westmoor Rd PEND EN3 248	A2
Westmoor St CHARL SE7 324	A7
Westmoreland Av	
EMPK RM11 289	M3
Westmorland CI MGTR CO11 91	J7
MNPK E12 286	F3
Westmorland Rd FX IP11 63	J7
WALTH E17 284	C4
Weston Av WTHK RM20 329	H4
Weston Chambers SOS SS1 * 19	H6
Weston CI RBRW/HUT CM13 256	D5
Weston Gn DAGW RM9 310	B9
Weston Rd COS CO15 183	L5
DAGW RM9 310	A9
SOS SS1 19	G6
West Park Av BCAYW CM12 258	C4

SAFWS CB11 30	A1
SBN/FI SS3 303	C6
SBW CM21 162	C6
SOCK/AV RM15 313	L7
SRTFD E15 307	J5
STSD CM24 115	M4
WOS/PRIT SS0 18	B2
Westropps SUD CO10 42	F6
Westrow CI DARK IG11 309	K2
Westrow Gdns	
GDMY/SEVK IG3 287	J7
West Side BROX EN10 216	F3
West Sq HLW CM20 12	F1
MAL CM9 214	C2
West Station Yd MAL CM9 214	B4
West Stockwell St COL CO1 8	B9
West St COLS CO1 8	B9
ERITH DA8 327	G7
GRAYS RM17 330	D5
GVW DA11 337	L4
HAR CO12 15	K3
K/T/MI CO5 130	C5
LOS SS9 300	B5
MAL CM9 385	L4
RCFD SS4 283	A1
RCOLW CO6 124	B4
SOSN SS2 18	G1
WALTH E17 284	E1
WAN E11 285	H8
WOTN CO14 137	M1
West Thorpe BSDN SS14 3	A4
West Thurrock Wy	
WTHK RM20 329	L8
West Vw LOU IG10 250	C5
RCOLE CO7 363	N11
SAFWN CB10 * 352	C2
West View CI COLN CO4 107	J4
RAIN RM13 311	M7
Westview CI RAIN RM13 * 311	M7
West View Rd WFD IG8 268	A8
West View Ri SBF/HAD SS7 280	E4
West View Rd DART DA1 334	C8
Westward Deals SAVHL CB9 35	L3
Westward Rd CHING E4 266	D4
Westwater SBF/HAD SS7 297	L1
West Wy BRW CM14 273	K2
WAB EN9 233	J7
Westway CHLM/WR CM1 4	D5
COL CO1 8	C5
RCHLM CM3 244	F6
West Wickham Rd	
CBE/LIN CB11 32	D2
West Wood Av BRW CM14 273	K4
West Wood CI SBF/HAD SS7 * 298	L1
Westwood Dr K/T/MI CO5 178	B7
Westwood Gdns	
SBF/HAD SS7 299	G1
West Wood HI COLN CO4 106	G1
Westwood Ldg SBF/HAD SS7 280	F8
Westwood Rd CAN/RD E16 323	L4
COS CO15 320	E2
GDMY/SEVK IG3 287	J6
West Yd HSTD CO9 81	H3
Wetherby CI IP IP1 48	A2
Wetherden St WALTH E17 284	C5
Wetherell Rd HOM E9 306	E4
Wetherfield STSD CM24 115	L2
Wetherland VGE SS16 2	D8
Wetherly CI HLWE CM17 188	D4
HLWE CM17 189	G5
Wethersfield CI RAYL SS6 280	D4
Wethersfield Rd BRTR CM7 78	B3
COLS CO2 129	K5
HSTD CO9 356	D8
Wethersfield Wy WICKE SS11 261	J5
West La COLS CO2 361	R11
Wetzlar CI COLS CO2 * 129	L1
Wetzlar Ct COLS CO2 129	L1
Wexford Rd IP IP1 47	J3
Weybourne CI SOSN SS2 301	L2
Weybourne Gdns SOSN SS2 301	L2
Weybridge Wk SBN/FI SS3 303	G4
Weydale SLH/COR SS17 295	G3
Weyland CI BCTR RM8 288	C4
Weymarks LAIN SS15 277	G2
Weymouth CI COS CO15 183	G5
Weymouth Rd	
CHLM/WR CM1 194	B7
IPNE IP4 17	M4
W Francis Vls MGTR CO11 * 64	C1
Whadden La ING CM4 239	K2
Whalebone Av CHDH RM6 288	C4
Whalebone Cnr COLN CO4 362	G10
Whalebone Gv CHDH RM6 288	C4
Whalebone La North	
CHDH RM6 270	B6
Whalebone La South	
BCTR RM8 288	C4
Whales Yd SRTFD E15 * 307	H4
Whaley Rd COLN CO4 107	J4
Wharf CI SLH/COR SS17 317	G4
Wharfedale Rd IP IP1 47	M4
Wharf La BURES CO8 359	Q9
Wharf Rd BROX EN10 217	H2
BRW CM14 273	M2
BSF CM23 139	G4
CHLM/GWD CM2 5	K4
GRAYS RM17 330	C5
GVE DA12 338	B4
MAL CM9 214	J1
PEND EN3 248	B6
SLH/COR SS17 317	H6
SLH/COR SS17 318	A1
SRTFD E15 307	C5
Wharfside Rd CAN/RD E16 323	H2
Wharf St CAN/RD E16 323	H1
WALTH E17 284	C4
Wharley Hook HLWS CM18 204	A4
Wharton Dr CHLM/WR CM1 194	D6
Wheat Cft BSF CM23 138	G5
CBE/LIN CB11 22	B7
Wheatear PI BCAYE CM11 258	F4
Wheatfield CI COLW CO3 106	A3
Wheatfields HLWE CM17 188	D4
PEND EN3 248	A2
RCFD SS4 396	A5
Wheatfield Wy CHLM/WR CM1 4	D7
VGE SS16 294	B1
Wheatlands SBF/HAD SS7 281	L1
Wheatlands Av BRTR CM7 121	M2
Wheatley CI EMPK RM11 290	A4
GRH DA9 335	M8
RCFD SS4 283	G1
SBW CM21 162	B7
Wheatley Rd SLH/COR SS17 295	H3
Wheaton Rd WIT CM8 171	J4
Wheatsheaf CI COLN CO4 108	A3
COS CO15 183	J9
HLW CM20 188	B7
Wheatsheaf La MGTR CO11 366	G1
Wheat Sheaf La POP/IOD E14 322	C2
Wheatsheaf La MGTR CO11 366	G1
Wheatsheaf Wy CBE/LIN CB11 25	J1
Wheelers EPP CM16 220	B7
Wheelers CI WAB EN9 201	M8
Wheelers Cross BARK IG11 309	H1

Wheelers Farm Gdns	
EPP CM16 221	J4
Wheelers Gn WAB EN9 * 202	K8
Wheelers HI RCHLM CM3 167	M7
Wheelers La BRW CM14 254	A4
SLH/COR SS17 296	A8
Wheel Farm Dr DAGE RM10 288	F8
Wheelwrights CI BSF CM23 138	C5
The Wheelwrights FX IP11 63	K8
SOSN SS2 283	A1
Whernside Av CVI SS8 298	F5
Wherry La IPSE IP3 * 17	G6
Wherstead Rd CHTY IP2 16	F9
Whights' Cnr RIPW IP8 52	C7
Whinchat CI CHTY IP2 53	J2
Whinchat Rd THMD SE28 325	J6
Whinfield KESG IP5 50	F6
Whinfield Av HAR CO12 70	E4
Whinfield CI KESG IP5 50	F6
Whinhams Wy BCAYW CM12 258	C2
The Whinneys KESG IP5 50	C5
Whinyard Wy FX IP11 63	J6
Whipps Cross Rd WAN E11 285	H3
Whist Av WICKE SS11 261	K4
Whistler Ri SBN/FI SS3 303	K5
Whitakers Wy LOU IG10 250	C1
Whitbreads Farm La	
RCHLM CM3 168	A1
Whitby Rd RBRW/HUT CM13 275	G1
Whitby CI GRH DA9 335	K7
Whitby Rd BOC CM0 393	L9
IPNE IP4 48	C5
WOOL/PLUM SE18 324	C7
Whitchurch Rd HARH RM3 272	B3
Whitcroft VGE SS16 294	B7
Whitear Wk SRTFD E15 307	G3
White Av GVW DA11 337	J8
Whitebarn La DAGE RM10 310	D6
White Barns RCHLM CM3 142	E7
Whitebeam CI	
CHLM/GWD CM2 209	J6
Whitebeam Dr	
SOCK/AV RM15 313	M7
White Bear STSD CM24 115	M1
Whiteditch La SAFWS CB11 351	N11
White Elm Rd RCHLM CM3 228	C4
White Elm St IPSE IP3 17	K7
Whitefields Rd	
CHES/WCR EN8 216	D6
White Field Wy CBS CB2 22	A1
Whitefriars Wy COLW CO3 106	D8
White Gardens DAGE RM10 310	D5
White Gate RCOLE CO7 156	D5
SOS SS1 19	H5
White Gates HCH RM12 311	M7
Whitegates CI BRTR CM77 120	F3
Whitehall CI CHIG IG7 269	K2
COLS CO2 129	M1
WAB EN9 171	K3
Whitehall Gdns CHING E4 249	H8
Whitehall La BKHH IG9 267	K1
BSF CM23 115	G8
GRAYS RM17 330	F5
RCOS CO16 134	F2
SLH/COR SS17 295	M6
Whitehall Rd BSF CM23 114	F8
CHING E4 267	H1
COLS CO2 129	M2
GRAYS RM17 330	F2
White Hall La SBN/FI SS3 303	L1
White Hart La CHLM/WR CM1 194	D7
HAR CO12 15	K3
HOC/HUL SS5 264	B8
ROM RM1 86	B8
ROMW/RG RM7 270	D7
White Hart Rd	
WOOL/PLUM SE18 325	H7
White Hart Yd GVE DA12 * 337	M4
White Hern Ct	
CHES/WCR EN8 216	D8
Whitehill La MAL CM9 175	K6
Whitehill Pde GVE DA12 337	M8
Whitehill Rd GVE DA12 337	M7
Whitehills Rd LOU IG10 250	F7
White Horse Ct FX IP11 81	G9
White Horse HI RIPS/CAP IP9 364	H4
White Horse La MAL CM9 214	H4
SAFWS CB11 351	P12
WCHPL E1 306	A8
WIT CM8 171	J2
White Horse Rd EHAM E6 308	C7
HVHL CB9 35	K3
RCOLE CO7 64	A4
RIPS/CAP IP9 58	E4
Whitehorse Rd WCHPL E1 322	B1
Whitehouse Crs	
CHLM/GWD CM2 5	M7
Whitehouse HI MAL CM9 175	K6
Whitehouse La RCOLW CO6 106	C9
SUD CO10 347	J4
Whitehouse Mdw LOS SS9 282	D7
White House Rd IP IP1 47	D2
LOS SS9 282	C8
Whitehouse Rd GTDUN CM6 96	C8
Whitelands CBE/LIN CB11 245	G5
Whitelands BRWN CM15 238	A4
Whitelands CI WICKE SS11 261	H4
Whitelands Wy HARH RM3 272	A4
Whitelegg Rd PLSTW E13 307	J6
White Lodge Crs RCOS CO16 135	M4
White Lyons Rd BRW CM14 273	M4
White Md CHLM/WR CM1 193	C3
White Post Fld SBW CM21 162	E7
White Post La HOM E9 306	D4
White Post La HVHL SS8 35	H1
White Rd SRTFD E15 307	H4
Whites Av GNTH/NBYPK IG2 271	G9
Whitesbridge La ING CM4 225	K8
Whites CI GRH DA9 335	M8
Whites Fld RCOLE CO7 363	Q9
Whites HI ING CM4 241	K4
Whiteshott VGE SS16 295	K1
Whites La CHLM/WR CM3 244	E7
Whitesmith Dr BCAYW CM12 258	B2
White St GTDUN CM6 96	B8
White Stubbs La BROX EN10 200	A7
Whitethorn CI COLN CO4 108	A3
Whitethorn Gdns	
CHLM/GWD CM2 209	M6
EMPK RM11 289	M4
Whitethorn Rd IPSE IP3 55	L4
White Tree Ct RCHLM CM3 244	E7
Whitewaits HLW CM20 12	F6
Whiteways BCAYE CM11 259	G5
CVI SS8 298	B7
LOS SS9 282	C7
Whiteways Ct WIT CM8 171	H2
Whitewebbs La ENC/FH EN2 232	N3
Whitewell Rd COL CO1 8	C8
Whitfield Link CHLM/GWD CM2 5	L9
Whitfield Rd EHAM E6 307	H4

Whitfields SLH/COR SS17 ....317 J3
Whit Hern Ct
  CHES/WCR EN8 * 216 C8
Whitings Wy EHAM E6 ....324 D1
Whitland Cl IP2 ....53 M5
Whitley Rd HOD EN11 ....201 J1
Whitlock Dr HSTD CO9 ....346 A12
Whitmore Av CDW/CHF RM16 ....314 E2
  HARH RM3 ....272 B8
Whitmore Cl CDW/CHF RM16 ....316 B6
Whitmore Ct BSDN SS14 ....278 B4
Whitmore Crs
  CHLM/GWD CM2 ....210 E2
Whitney Av REDBR IG4 ....286 A2
Whitney Rd LEY E10 ....284 D5
Whittaker Rd EHAM E6 ....307 H4
Whittaker Wy K/T/MI CO5 ....177 H4
Witta Rd MNPK E12 ....308 A1
Whittingham Av SOSN SS2 ....302 B3
Whittingstall Rd HOD EN11 ....201 J1
Whittington Rd
  RBRW/HUT CM13 ....257 C2
Whittington Wy BSF CM23 ....138 F6
Whittle Cl WALTH E17 ....284 B4
Whittle Rd CHTY IP2 ....47 L2
Whitton-Church La IP IP1 ....47 K1
Whitton Leyer RIPW IP8 ....53 H3
Whitwell Rd PLSTW E13 ....307 K2
Whitworth Cl CHTY IP2 ....53 J3
Whitworth St GNWCH SE10 ....323 H8
Whybrews SLH/COR SS17 ....317 J3
Whybridge Cl RAIN RM13 ....311 H5
Whyteville Rd FSTGT E7 ....307 L3
Whytewaters VGE SS16 ....296 C2
Whyverne Cl CHLM/WR CM1 ....194 B7
Wick Beech Av WICKE SS11 ....261 H6
Wick Cha SOSN SS2 ....302 B4
Wick Crs WICKW SS12 ....261 H8
Wick Dr WICKW SS12 ....261 H8
Wicken Rd SAFWS CB11 ....31 G12
Wickets Wy HAR/BLT IG6 ....269 L5
Wick Farm Rd BOC CM0 ....389 M1
Wickfield Ash CHLM/WR CM1 ....193 C7
Wickford Dr HARH RM3 ....272 C4
Wickford Ms PIT SS13 ....278 C5
Wickford Pl PIT SS13 ....278 D8
Wickford Rd RCHLM CM3 ....244 D5
  WOS/PRIT SS0 ....18 C3
Wickford Wy WALTH E17 ....284 A2
Wick Gln BCAYW CM12 ....258 C1
Wickham Bishop Rd
  RCHLM CM3 ....197 G1
Wickhambrook Ct FX IP11 ....10 D1
Wickham Crs CHLM/WR CM1 ....193 J7
Wickham Hall La WT CM8 ....197 M2
Wickham Pl VGE SS16 ....3 J9
Wickham Rd
  CDW/CHF RM16 ....331 M1
  CHING E4 ....266 F6
  COLW CO3 ....107 G8
  WT CM8 ....171 J5
Wickham's Cha RCHLM CM3 ....228 E3
Wickhay LAIN SS15 ....3 C7
Wick La BOW E3 ....306 D6
  HAR RM11 ....71 G4
  K/T/MI CO5 ....155 G2
  RCOLE CO7 ....88 E5
  RCOS CO16 ....157 M2
  WICKE SS11 ....261 H6
Wicklow Av CHLM/WR CM1 ....193 J3
Wicklow Rd IP IP1 ....47 J3
Wicklow Wk SBN/FI SS3 ....302 F6
Wickmead Cl SOSN SS2 ....302 B2
Wick Rd BOC CM0 ....393 M9
  COLN CO4 ....88 D2
  COLS CO2 ....130 A3
  HOM E9 ....306 D7
  RCOLE CO7 ....133 L8
Wick Ter COLN CO4 * 88 C2
Widbrook BRWN CM15 ....383 R10
Wid Cl RBRW/HUT CM13 ....257 H4
Widdin St SRTFD E15 ....307 H4
Widdington Cl HARH RM3 ....272 A7
Widecombe Gdns
  REDBR IG4 ....286 B2
Widford Cha
  CHLM/GWD CM2 ....209 J6
Widford Cl CHLM/GWD CM2 ....4 C9
Widford Gv CHLM/GWD CM2 ....209 J6
Widford Park Pl
  CHLM/GWD CM2 ....4 C9
Widford Rd CHLM/GWD CM2 ....209 J6
Widgeon Cl CAN/RD E16 ....323 L2
  CHTY IP2 ....53 L2
Widgeon Pl K/T/MI CO5 ....148 C3
Widgeons PIT SS13 ....278 F7
Widleybrook La BRTR CM7 ....78 C2
Widworthy Hayes
  RBRW/HUT CM13 ....256 F1
  K/T/MI CO5 ....176 F1
Wigborough Wick La RCOS CO16 ....181 J3
Wigeon Cl BRTR CM77 ....120 F8
Wiggins La BCAYW CM12 ....258 B7
Wiggins Vw
  CHLM/GWD CM2 ....210 E1
Wigley Bush La BRW CM14 ....273 H1
Wigmore Rd CHTY IP2 ....53 L2
Wignall St MGTR CO11 ....90 C2
Wigram Av WAN E11 ....285 M4
Wigram Sq WALTH E17 ....284 F1
Wigston Rd PLSTW E13 ....307 L8
Wigton Rd HARH RM3 ....272 B3
  WALTH E17 ....266 E2
Wigton Wy HARH RM3 ....272 B3
Wilberforce St IP IP1 ....16 E1
Wilde Cl TIL RM18 ....331 M8
Wilding Cl KESG IP5 ....50 C1
Wilding Rd RIPW IP8 ....53 H4
Wilfred Av RAIN RM13 ....327 K1
Wilfred St GVE DA12 ....337 L4
Wilkes Rd RBRW/HUT CM13 ....257 G1
Wilkin Ct COLW CO3 ....128 D1
Wilkinson Gv KESG IP5 ....50 B7
Wilkinson Rd CAN/RD E16 ....323 M2
Wilkinsons Md
  CHLM/GWD CM2 ....210 D1
Willan Wall CAN/RD E16 ....323 J3
Willenhall Rd
  WOOL/PLUM SE18 ....324 G4
Willett Rd COLS CO2 ....128 E8
Willetts Fld SAFWS CB10 ....353 K6
Willetts Ms HOD EN11 ....201 J1
William Booth Wy FX IP11 ....62 D4
William Boys Cl COLN CO4 ....9 M3
William Crs COLN CO4 ....270 F7
William Or HOC/HUL SS5 * 263 H2
William Groom Av HAR CO12 ....70 F3
William Guy Gdns BOW E3 ....306 E7
William Hunter Wy
  BRW CM14 ....273 M1

William Morley Cl EHAM E6 ....308 A5
William Morris Cl WALTH E17 ....284 C1
William Rd PIT SS13 ....279 H7
Williams Av WALTH E17 ....266 C2
Williamson Cl GNWCH SE10 ....323 J8
Williamsons Wy
  SLH/COR SS17 ....295 J8
William Sparrow Ct
  RCOLE CO7 * 130 F3
William Sq BERM/RHTH SE16 ....322 B4
William St BARK IG11 ....308 F4
  GRAYS 330 F5
  GVE DA12 ....337 L5
  IP IP1 ....16 F3
  LEY E10 ....284 F4
William's Wk COL CO1 ....8 C6
Willingale Av RAYL SS6 ....280 D2
Willingale Rd BRTR CM7 ....122 A5
  CHONG CM5 ....206 A5
  CHONG CM5 ....381 M7
  LOU IG10 ....250 F1
Willis Rd ERITH DA8 ....326 F7
  SRTFD E15 ....307 J6
Willis St POP/IOD E14 ....322 E2
Willmott Rd SOSN SS2 ....283 C7
Willoughby Av K/T/MI CO5 ....178 A7
Willoughby Cl BROX EN10 ....200 F7
Willoughby Dr
  CHLM/GWD CM2 ....210 C3
  RAIN RM13 ....311 H4
Willoughby's La BRTR CM7 ....99 M5
Willoughby Wy CHARL SE7 ....323 L7
Willow Av FOS CO13 ....137 G3
  RCOS CO16 ....181 L7
Willowbank CHLM/GWD CM2 ....225 L2
  BOC CM0 ....393 L4
  BRWN CM15 ....238 A4
  BSF CM23 ....138 F1
  CHLM/WR CM1 ....193 L4
  CVI SS8 ....320 C2
  HCH RM12 ....289 L8
  HOC/HUL SS5 ....264 C7
  HVHL CB9 ....34 B7
  RBRW/HUT CM13 ....256 E2
  RCOLE CO7 ....88 A7
  RCOLE CO7 ....156 A7
  SUD CO10 ....20 D8
Willow Ct FOS CO13 * 137 G3
Willow Crs RCHLM CM3 ....196 D3
Willowcroft Rd IP IP1 ....47 M3
Willowdale BRWN CM15 ....255 J5
  CHES/WCR EN8 ....216 F5
  HSTD CO9 ....356 C7
Willowdene Ct BRW CM14 ....273 M5
Willow Dr RAYL SS6 ....280 F1
Willowfield LAIN SS15 ....276 F5
Willowfields Cl
  WOOL/PLUM SE18 ....325 H8
Willow Gn ING CM4 ....239 L1
Willow Gv RCHLM CM3 ....244 D4
  RCOLW CO6 ....361 L7
Willow Md SBW CM21 ....162 F8
Willow Mdw HSTD CO9 ....356 F9
Willow Pk RCOLW CO6 ....105 H8
Willow Pl HLWE CM17 ....205 G5
Willow Ri WIT CM8 ....147 K8
Willow Rd CHDH RM6 ....288 B4
Willow Springs BSF CM23 ....138 E1
The Willows BCAYE CM11 ....259 G6
  COLS CO2 ....129 K2
  GRAYS RM17 ....331 G5
  RCHLM CM3 ....195 H5
  SAFWN CB11 ....341 L6
  SBF/HAD SS7 ....297 L1
  SOS SS1 ....302 D4
  WARE SS12 * 185 J5
Willow St CHING E4 ....249 G7
  ROMW/RG RM7 ....288 F2
Willow Tree Cl HOM E9 ....306 B5
Willow Tree Wy RCOLW CO6 ....82 E2
Willow Vw WARE SS12 * 184 F1
Willow Wk DART DA1 * 334 B7
  HOC/HUL SS5 ....261 G4
  K/T/MI CO5 ....149 M6
  RCFD SS4 ....392 A12
  SBF/HAD SS7 ....299 C2
  UPMR RM14 ....291 H6
  WALTH E17 ....284 C3
Willow Wy COS CO15 ....182 D6
  HAR RM11 ....70 F3
  HARH RM3 ....272 E5
  HSTD CO9 ....81 G4
Willrose Crs ABYW SE2 ....325 L8
Wil's Ayley La SAFWN CB10 ....29 H7
Wills Hi SLH/COR SS17 ....317 G2
Wilmer Lea Cl SRTFD E15 ....306 F4
Wilmington Gdns BARK IG11 ....309 G4
Wilmington Rd COLN CO4 * 107 M3
Wilmot Gn RBRW/HUT CM13 ....273 M5
Wilmot Rd LEY E10 ....284 E7
Wilmount
  WOOL/PLUM SE18 ....324 E7
Wilmslow Dr RIPW IP8 ....53 H3
Wilmslowe CVI SS8 ....299 G8
Wilrich Av CVI SS8 ....321 G2
Wilshire Av CHLM/GWD CM2 ....210 C2
Wilsman Rd SOCK/AV RM15 ....313 H6
Wilsner PIT SS13 ....278 F6
Wilson Cl BSF CM23 ....139 H5
  RCOLE CO7 ....130 D3
  SLH/COR SS17 ....316 F7
Wilson Ct WICKW SS12 * 260 F7
Wilson Marriage Rd
  COLN CO4 ....9 J2
Wilson Rd IL IG1 ....286 C5
  COLN CO4 ....9 J2
  PLSTW E13 ....308 A2
  RIPW IP8 ....53 L2
  WOS/PRIT SS0 ....18 E7
Wilson's La RCOLW CO6 ....126 B2
Wilson's Pl POP/IOD E14 ....322 C2
Wilson St WALTH E17 ....284 F3
Wilthorne Gdns DAGE RM10 ....310 C6
Wilton Dr CRW RM5 ....239 J2
Wilton Rd ABYW SE2 ....325 M6
Wiltmarc Crs RAYL SS6 ....280 E7
Wimbish End PIT SS13 ....278 E7
Wimbish Ms PIT SS13 * 278 E7
Wimbish Wk SAFWN CB10 ....31 H7
Wimborne Av IPSE IP3 ....55 H5
Wimborne Cl BKHH IG9 ....267 M1
  SBW CM21 ....162 E7
Wimborne Rd SOSN SS2 ....19 J3

Wimbourne LAIN SS15 ....276 D6
Wimbourne Gdns FOS CO13 ....137 G3
Wimhurst Cl CHLM/WR CM1 ....5 J2
Wimpole Cl KESG IP5 ....49 L7
Wimpole Rd COL CO1 ....8 C5
Winbrook Cl RAYL SS6 ....281 H5
Wincanton Cl IPNE IP4 ....48 F4
Wincanton Gdns
  BARK/HLT IG6 ....286 E1
Wincanton Rd HARH RM3 ....272 A4
Wincelow Hall Rd
  SAFWN CB10 ....342 G12
Winchcombe Cl LOS SS9 ....300 B2
Winchelsea Dr
  CHLM/GWD CM2 ....210 A6
Winchelsea Pl RCOLE CO7 ....156 C5
Winchester Av UPMR RM14 ....291 K1
Winchester Cl BSF CM23 ....138 E5
  LOS SS9 ....300 A3
Winchester Crs GVE DA12 ....338 A8
Winchester Gdns LAIN SS15 ....276 F4
Winchester Rd CHING E4 ....266 F6
  COL CO1 ....107 K8
  FOS CO13 ....137 K4
  IL IG1 ....287 C8
Winchester Wy CHTY IP2 ....53 L5
Winch Vw EPP E17 ....220 C7
Wincoat Cl SBF/HAD SS7 ....297 L2
Wincoat Dr SBF/HAD SS7 ....297 L2
Windermere Av HCH RM12 ....311 K2
  HOC/HUL SS5 ....263 G5
Windermere Cl IPSE IP3 ....55 C5
Windermere Dr BRTR CM77 ....120 F7
Windermere Gdns
  REDBR IG4 ....286 B3
Windermere Rd BRTR CM77 ....120 F6
Winding Piece RIPS/CAP IP9 ....58 E7
Winding Wy BCTR RM8 ....287 M8
Windlass Pl DEPT SE8 ....322 B7
Windley Tye CHLM/WR CM1 ....4 A1
Windmill Av CL CBS CB2 ....22 C1
Windmill Cl IL IG1 ....308 J1
  COLN CO4 ....117 H4
  GTDUN CM6 ....117 H4
  HAR CO12 ....367 Q8
  ROY SG8 ....370 B3
  UPMR RM14 ....290 D7
  WAB EN9 ....233 M4
Windmill Ct COLN CO4 * 107 H1
  RCOLW CO6 ....127 G1
Windmill Fld WARE SS12 ....184 E1
Windmill Flds HLWE CM17 ....189 G5
Windmill Gdns BRTR CM7 ....99 K5
Windmill Hts BCAYW CM12 ....258 E5
Windmill Hi RIPS/CAP IP9 ....58 B4
  SAFWN CB10 ....351 G2
  SUD CO10 ....40 E7
Windmill La CHES/WCR EN8 ....216 H1
  SRTFD E15 ....306 F2
Windmill Mdw GTDUN CM6 ....379 R2
Windmill Pk COS CO15 ....7 G2
Windmill Rd HSTD CO9 ....81 C4
  MGTR CO11 ....90 C6
Windmills RCOLW CO6 ....103 M5
The Windmills CHLM/WR CM1 ....193 L2
Windmill St GVE DA12 ....337 L3
Windmill Vw K/T/MI CO5 ....149 M7
Windmill Wy BRWN CM15 ....383 M11
Windrose Cl
  BERM/RHTH SE16 ....322 A5
Windrush Dr CHLM/WR CM1 ....193 H2
Windrush Rd KESG IP5 ....50 B5
Windsor Av CDW/CHF RM16 ....330 C5
  COS CO15 ....6 C7
  SLH/COR SS17 ....295 K8
  WALTH E17 ....266 B8
Windsor Cl CHESW EN7 ....216 A7
  COLS CO2 ....129 K3
  CVI SS8 ....320 E2
  LOS SS9 ....300 B2
Windsor Ct RCOLE CO7 ....156 C7
Windsor Gdns BRTR CM7 ....121 L1
  BSF CM23 ....138 D2
  HOC/HUL SS5 ....282 E1
  SBF/HAD SS7 ....298 F1
  WICKE SS11 ....261 G4
Windsor Ms RAYL SS6 * 280 F4
Windsor Pl SUD CO10 ....21 H6
Windsor Rd BCAYE CM11 ....242 A4
  BCTR RM8 ....288 D2
  BRWN CM15 ....255 L6
  CHING E4 ....249 J8
  COS CO15 ....6 C7
  EMPK RM11 ....289 M5
  FSTGT E7 ....307 L2
  FX IP11 ....11 G4
  IL IG1 ....308 F1
  IP IP1 ....47 L6
  K/T/MI CO5 ....178 A6
  LEY E10 ....284 E7
  PEND EN3 ....231 H8
  PIT SS13 ....279 H5
  WAN E11 ....285 K3
  WOS/PRIT SS0 ....18 D7
The Windsors BKHH IG9 ....268 B1
Windsor Wy CHLM/WR CM1 ....4 A1
  RAYL SS6 ....281 H4
Windsor Wd WAB EN9 ....233 M3
Windy Hl RBRW/HUT CM13 ....256 F6
Windyridge FFND EN3 * 231 J8
Winfard Dr BROX EN10 ....201 G8
Winfrith Rd IPSE IP3 ....55 H6
Wingate Cl BRTR CM7 ....121 H1
Wingate Rd IL IG1 ....308 C2
Wingfield GRAYS 330 C4
Wingfield Cl
  RBRW/HUT CM13 ....256 D6
Wingfield Gdns UPMR RM14 ....291 K1
Wingfield Rd GVW DA11 ....337 L5
  SRTFD E15 ....307 H2
  WALTH E17 ....284 E3
Wingfield St IPNE IP4 ....17 K7
Wingletye La EMPK RM11 ....290 C6
Wingrave Crs BRW CM14 ....273 H5
Wingway BRW CM14 ....273 A1
Winifred Av HCH RM12 ....312 A1
Winifred Rd BCTR RM8 ....288 B1
  ERITH DA8 ....327 H4
  IP IP1 ....16 E3
Winifred St CAN/RD E16 ....324 C4
Winmill Rd BCTR RM8 ....288 C1
Winn Bridge Cl WFD IG8 ....268 C4
Winnington Rd PEND EN3 ....232 D7
Winnock Rd COL CO1 ....8 F9
Winns Av WALTH E17 ....284 C1

Winns Ter WALTH E17 ....266 D8
Winsbeach WALTH E17 ....285 G1
Winsey Cha BRTR CM7 ....354 D15
Winsford Gdns WOS/PRIT SS0 ....300 D1
Winsford Wy
  CHLM/GWD CM2 ....194 E7
Winsley Ap SBF/HAD SS7 ....279 L8
Winsley Sq COL CO1 ....107 L8
Winslow Gv CHING E4 ....267 H1
Winsor Ter EHAM E6 ....324 E1
Winstanley Rd SAFWS CB11 ....30 C2
Winstanley Wy BSDN SS14 ....2 C1
Winstead Gdns DAGE RM10 ....310 D1
Winston Av COLW CO3 ....128 C1
  IPNE IP4 ....49 H5
  K/T/MI CO5 ....150 B8
Winston Churchill Wy
  CHES/WCR EN8 ....232 D3
Winston Cl BRTR CM7 ....99 H7
  FX IP11 ....62 D3
  GRH DA9 ....335 J8
  ROMW/RG RM7 ....288 C2
Winston Wy HSTD CO9 ....81 K2
  IL IG1 ....286 B8
Winstree PIT SS13 ....278 E5
Winstree Rd BOC CM0 ....393 L8
  COLW CO3 ....106 A8
Winstreet Cl COLS CO2 ....128 C8
Winter Av EHAM E6 ....308 A1
Wintercoat Rd BCTR RM8 ....287 M7
Winterbournes WOTN CO14 ....137 K2
Winter Folly LAIN SS15 ....2 B8
Winter Gardens Pth CVI SS8 ....298 D6
Winterscroft Rd HOD EN11 ....201 G3
Winter's Rd K/T/MI CO5 ....151 G4
Winters Wy WAB EN9 ....234 B3
Winterswyk Av CVI SS8 ....321 H2
Winton Av COLW SS12 ....260 D5
  WOS/PRIT SS0 ....18 C5
Winton Cl ED N9 ....248 A7
Winton Dr CHES/WCR EN8 ....216 H7
Wiscombe Hl VGE SS16 ....294 F2
Wisdoms Gn RCOLW CO6 ....124 D2
Wisdons Cl DAGE RM10 ....288 E6
Wiseman Rd LEY E10 * 284 D7
Wisemans Gdns SBW CM21 ....162 E8
Wise Rd SRTFD E15 ....306 F5
Wissington Uplands
  RCOLW CO6 ....360 C8
Wistaria Cl BRWN CM15 ....255 L5
Wistaria Pl RCOS CO16 ....6 B2
Wisteria Cl IL IG1 ....308 C2
Wisteria Rd RCOLW CO6 ....361 J3
Witchards VGE SS16 ....3 J1
Witch Elm HAR CO12 ....70 E3
Witch La ROCLW CO6 ....102 E5
Witchtree La SAFWN CB11 ....343 J10
Witham Cl K/T/MI CO5 ....250 B6
Witham Gdns
  RBRW/HUT CM13 ....275 C8
Witham Ldg WIT CM8 ....171 H4
Witham Rd BRTR CM77 ....121 L8
  BRTR CM77 ....146 D2
  DAGE RM10 ....310 D2
  GPK RM2 ....289 L3
  MAL CM9 ....173 M8
  RCHLM CM3 ....170 B4
  WIT CM8 ....145 M1
  WIT CM8 ....172 A7
The Witherings EMPK RM11 ....290 B3
Withersfield Rd HVHL CB9 ....34 B4
Withipoll St IP IP1 ....17 C5
Withrick Wk RCOS CO16 ....157 K8
Withy Md CHING E4 ....249 G8
Withypool SBN/FI SS3 ....303 G4
The Withywyinde RCHLM CM3 ....244 F7
Witney Rd BOC CM0 ....393 M9
Wittem Rd CVI SS8 ....298 A6
Wittenham Wy CHING E4 ....267 G2
The Witterings CVI SS8 ....298 A6
Witting Cl RCOS CO16 ....6 C1
Witton Wood Rd FOS CO13 ....137 H4
Wivenhoe Cross RCOLE CO7 ....130 E3
Wivenhoe Rd BARK IG11 ....309 K6
  RCOLE CO7 ....108 F4
  RCOLE CO7 ....131 K6
Wix By-Pass MGTR CO11 ....366 E12
Wix Rd DAGW RM9 ....310 A5
Woburn Av BSF CM23 ....138 D2
  EPP CM16 ....235 M4
  FOS CO15 ....137 G2
Woburn Pl BCAYW CM12 ....240 C4
Wodehouse Rd DART DA1 ....334 D6
Wokindon Rd
  CDW/CHF RM16 ....331 L2
Wolfe Crs CHARL SE7 ....324 A8
Wolferton Rd MNPK E12 ....308 C1
Wollaston Crs PIT SS13 ....279 C5
Wollaston Wy PIT SS13 * 278 F4
Wolmers Hey RCHLM CM3 ....167 J6
Wolseley Av COS CO15 ....182 C7
Wolseley Rd CHLM/GWD CM2 ....4 E7
  FSTGT E7 ....307 L4
  ROMW/RG RM7 ....289 C5
Wolsey Av CHESW EN7 ....216 A7
  EHAM E6 ....308 C2
  WALTH E17 ....284 C1
Wolsey Gdns BARK/HLT IG6 ....268 C7
  FX IP11 ....11 G5
Wolsey St IP IP1 ....16 F5
Wolton Rd COLS CO2 ....128 C2
  KESG IP5 ....50 B6
Wolvercote Rd ABYW SE2 ....326 A5
Wombwell Gdns GVW DA11 ....337 H7
Wonston Rd BOC CM0 ....393 M9
Woodall Rd PEND EN3 ....248 A6
Wood Av HOC/HUL SS5 ....264 A5
  PUR RM19 ....328 F2
Wood Barn La MGTR CO11 ....90 A2
Woodberry Cl CVI SS8 ....298 C2
  LOS SS9 ....281 H6
Woodberry Down EPP CM16 ....220 B7
Woodberry Rd WICKE SS11 ....261 K6
Woodberry Wy CHING E4 ....248 F1
  WOTN CO14 ....137 L2
Woodbine Cl
  HLWW/ROY CM19 ....203 K3
Woodbine Pl WAN E11 ....285 K4
Woodbridge Gv RCOS CO16 ....182 D3
Woodbridge La HARH RM3 ....272 A4
Woodbridge Rd BARK IG11 ....309 G4
  IPNE IP4 ....17 J2
  WDBR IP12 ....51 L5
Woodbridge Rd East IPNE IP4 ....49 H2
Woodbrooke Wy
  SLH/COR SS17 ....295 L8
Woodbrook Gdns WAB EN9 ....233 M3
Woodburn Cl SBF/HAD SS7 ....298 C1
Woodbury Cl WAN E11 ....285 L2

Woodbury Hl LOU IG10 ....250 B6
Woodbury Rd WALTH E17 ....284 C3
  HVHL CB9 ....34 B7
Woodcock CAN/RD E16 ....323 M3
Woodcote Av SBF/HAD SS7 ....279 L8
Woodcote Cl CHES/WCR EN8 ....216 C7
Woodcote Crs PIT SS13 ....279 G5
Woodcote Rd LOS SS9 ....300 B3
  WAN E11 ....285 L3
Woodcotes SBN/FI SS3 ....303 G4
Woodcote Wy SBF/HAD SS7 ....279 L8
Woodcroft Av WARE SS12 ....185 J5
Woodcroft Cl SBF/HAD SS7 ....298 E8
Woodcroft Ms DEPT SE8 ....322 B7
Woodcutters Av
  CDW/CHF RM16 ....330 C5
  LOS SS9 ....281 M6
Wood Dl CHLM/GWD CM2 ....210 B2
Woodedge Cl CHING E4 ....249 M1
Wood End SAFWS CB11 ....372 E6
Wood End Av HOC/HUL SS5 ....264 A7
Wooden Cl SBF/HAD SS7 ....298 C8
Wooder Gdns FSTGT E7 ....307 J1
Woodfield Av GVW DA11 ....337 L3
Woodfield Cl STSD CM24 ....115 M1
  WOTN CO14 ....137 K2
Woodfield Dr GPK RM2 ....289 K1
  K/T/MI CO5 ....177 C2
Wood Field End COLS CO2 ....128 D2
Woodfield Gdns LOS SS9 ....300 C4
Woodfield Park Dr LOS SS9 ....300 C4
Woodfield Rd CHLM/WR CM1 ....121 K6
  LOS SS9 ....300 C4
  SBF/HAD SS7 ....199 C5
Woodfields STSD CM24 ....115 M1
Woodfield Ter STSD CM24 ....115 M1
Woodfield Wy HCH RM12 ....290 A4
  RCHLM CM3 ....196 F1
The Woodfines EMPK RM11 ....290 A3
Woodford Av
  GNTH/NBYPK IG2 ....286 C2
Woodford Bridge Rd
  REDBR IG4 ....286 A4
Woodford Cl COS CO15 ....159 J4
Woodford New Rd
  WALTH E17 ....285 H1
  WFD IG8 ....285 H1
Woodford Rd FSTGT E7 ....307 L3
  SWFD E18 ....285 K1
Woodgates Rd RCOLE CO7 ....58 A4
Woodget Cl EHAM E6 ....324 B8
Woodgrange Cl SOS SS1 ....302 E5
Woodgrange Dr SOS SS1 ....19 K8
Woodgrange Rd FSTGT E7 ....307 K2
Woodgreen Rd WAB EN9 ....234 A1
Woodhall Cl SUD CO10 ....20 D8
Woodhall Crs EMPK RM11 ....290 D5
Woodhall Gv BSF CM23 ....138 C4
Woodhall Hl CHLM/WR CM1 ....192 F5
Woodhall Rd CHLM/WR CM1 ....193 G5
  SUD CO10 ....20 D7
Woodham Ct SWFD E18 ....285 J2
Woodham Halt RCHLM CM3 ....244 F7
Woodham Mortimer Rd
  MAL CM9 ....213 H6
Woodham Park Dr
  SBF/HAD SS7 ....297 G2
Woodham Rd RCHLM CM3 ....245 J2
  RCHLM CM3 ....262 A4
  SBF/HAD SS7 ....297 G2
Woodham Wy WARE SS12 ....185 J5
Woodhatch Cl EHAM E6 ....324 B4
Woodhaven Gdns
  BARK/HLT IG6 ....286 F2
Woodhill HLWS CM18 ....203 M4
  WOOL/PLUM SE18 ....324 C4
Woodhill Common Rd
  RCHLM CM3 ....211 G3
Woodhill Rd CHLM/GWD CM2 ....211 G2
  RCHLM CM3 ....211 C4
Woodhouse Gv MNPK E12 ....308 B3
Wood House La BROX EN10 ....200 C4
Woodhouse La
  CHLM/WR CM1 ....193 J1
  KIR/NAC IP10 ....56 B8
Woodhouse Rd WAN E11 ....285 L5
Woodhouse Sq IPNE IP4 * 17 G2
Woodhurst Rd ABYW SE2 ....325 K4
  CVI SS8 ....320 D2
Woodison Gv HLWW/ROY CM19 ....12 E2
Woodison St BOW E3 ....306 D7
Woodland Av
  RBRW/HUT CM13 ....256 F1
Woodland Cha COLW CO3 ....105 J2
Woodland Cl ING CM4 ....239 M1
  RBRW/HUT CM13 ....256 F1
  RCHLM CM3 ....170 D2
  SBF/HAD SS7 ....299 J3
  WFD IG8 ....267 J2
Woodland Dr COLW CO3 ....106 A2
Woodland Gv EPP CM16 ....236 B2
  GNWCH SE10 ....323 H6
Woodland Mt HERT/BAY SG13 ....184 A1
Woodland Park Cha
  RCHLM CM3 ....388 C12
Woodland Rd CHING E4 ....248 F1
  CHLM/WR CM1 ....209 K4
  HERT/BAY SG13 ....184 A1
  LOU IG10 ....250 B2
Woodlands BRTR CM7 ....139 J4
  BSF CM23 ....139 J4
  COLN CO4 ....108 C4
  COS CO15 ....182 C7
  HAR CO12 ....113 G2
  RCHLM CM3 ....392 D4
  RIPS/CAP IP9 ....365 R12
Woodlands Av CHDH RM6 ....288 A4
  EMPK RM11 ....290 A4
  RAYL SS6 ....281 L4
  WAN E11 ....285 M3
Woodlands Cl
  CDW/CHF RM16 ....331 M1
  COS CO15 ....159 K4
  HOC/HUL SS5 ....264 A7
  HOD EN11 * 201 J1
  RAYL SS6 ....281 L4
  VGE SS16 ....3 J4
Woodlands Dr HOD EN11 ....201 J1
  SLH/COR SS17 ....295 M8
Woodlands Gdns
  WALTH E17 ....285 H1
Woodlands Pde
  HOC/HUL SS5 ....264 A7
Woodlands Pk LOS SS9 ....299 K6
Woodlands Park Dr
  GTDUN CM6 ....116 E2
Woodlands Ri RCOS CO16 ....134 C2

Woodlands Rd HARH RM3 ...272 D7
 HERT/BAY SG13 ...184 A3
 HOC/HUL SS5 ...264 F8
 IL IG1 ...286 F8
 RIPS/CAP IP9 ...364 F6
 ROM RM1 ...289 J1
 WALTH E17 ...284 F1
 WAN E11 * ...285 H7
 WICKW SS12 ...261 G6
The Woodlands CBE/LIN CB1 ...24 E6
 RCOLE C07 ...156 B5
 SBN/FI SS3 ...303 B3
Woodlands Wy RIPW IP8 ...47 G1
Woodland Ter CHARL SE7 ...324 B7
Woodland Wy ABYW SE2 ...326 G4
 CHONG CM5 ...382 G4
 EPP CM16 ...235 K7
 GRH DA9 ...235 K7
 HSTD C09 ...80 B5
 RCOLE C07 ...130 E4
 WFD IG8 ...267 L2
Wood La BSF CM23 ...115 M7
 BUNT SG9 ...371 M9
 CHONG CM5 ...206 A2
 COLW C03 ...105 J4
 DAGE RM10 ...288 D7
 GTDUN CM6 ...164 B4
 HCH RM12 ...311 K2
 HOC/HUL SS5 ...164 B5
 MAL CM9 ...198 D8
 MAL CM9 ...231 H4
 WFD IG8 ...267 J4
Woodleigh Av LOS SS9 ...300 A2
Woodley Wk SBN/FI SS3 ...303 H3
Woodlow SBF/HAD SS7 ...280 E7
Woodmanhurst Rd
 SLH/COR SS17 ...295 J8
Woodman La CHING E4 ...249 G5
Woodman Pth
 BARK/HLT IG6 ...269 H4
Woodman Rd BRW CM14 ...273 M4
Woodman St CAN/RD E16 ...324 D5
Wood Meads EPP CM16 ...220 B7
Woodmill Ms HOD EN11 * ...201 J1
Woodpecker CI BSF CM23 ...138 D3
 COLN C04 ...108 C5
Woodpecker Ct CHIG IG7 ...53 J2
 THMD SE28 ...325 M3
Woodpond Av HOC/HUL SS5 ...264 A8
Woodreden CI
 HLWW/ROY CM19 ...202 C2
Woodridden Hl WAB EN9 ...234 E5
Woodriffe Rd WAN E11 ...285 L6
Wood Rd MAL CM9 ...198 E7
Woodroffe CI CHLM/GWD CM2 ...210 C8
Woodroffe Farm La MAL CM9 ...385 P4
Woodrolfe Pk MAL CM9 ...385 Q3
Woodrolfe Rd MAL CM9 ...385 P4
Woodrow WOOL/PLUM SE18 ...324 B7
Woodrows La RCOS CO16 ...158 B8
Woodrow Wy COLN C04 ...108 C5
Woodrush End COLW C03 ...105 L7
Woodrush Rd IPSE IP3 ...55 K3
Woodrush Wy CHDH RM6 ...288 H2
Woods CI HVHL CB9 ...35 H8
Woodshire Rd DAGE RM10 ...288 D7
Woodside BKHH IG9 ...267 M1
 BOC CM0 ...393 M1
 BSF CM23 ...139 L1
 CHESW EN7 ...232 B1
 EPP CM16 ...220 E5
 HERT/BAY SG13 ...184 D6
 LOS SS9 ...281 L8
 MAL CM9 ...198 E2
 RCHLM CM3 ...212 B4
 WOTN CO14 ...137 L3
Woodside Av SBF/HAD SS7 ...279 L5
Woodside Cha HOC/HUL SS5 ...282 B1
Woodside CI COLN C04 ...108 B4
 RAIN RM13 ...311 K6
 RBRW/HUT CM13 ...257 G1
 SBF/HAD SS7 ...281 K7
Woodside Gdns CHING E4 ...266 C4
Woodside Pde LOS SS9 * ...281 L7
Woodside Park Av
 WALTH E17 ...285 G2
Woodside Rd HOC/HUL SS5 ...263 L8
 PLSTW E13 ...307 M8
 WFD IG8 ...267 K3
Woodside Vw SBF/HAD SS7 ...279 M5
Woodside Wy GTDUN CM6 ...116 D4
Woodspring CI CHTY IP2 ...53 M3
Woods Rd RCHLM CM3 ...142 E7
The Woods SBF/HAD SS7 ...299 J2

Woodstock K/T/MI C05 ...177 M6
 LAIN SS15 ...276 C7
Woodstock Av HARH RM3 ...272 E4
Woodstock CI
 HERT/BAY SG13 ...184 C1
Woodstock Crs HOC/HUL SS5 ...264 A7
 LAIN SS15 ...276 C7
Woodstock Gdns
 GDMY/SEVK IG3 ...287 K7
Woodstock Rd BROX EN10 ...200 E5
 FSTGT E7 ...307 M4
 WALTH E17 ...284 F1
Woodstock St CAN/RD E16 ...323 J2
Woodstock Ter POP/IOD E14 ...322 E3
Woodstone Av IP IP1 ...48 D7
Wood Vw GRAYS RM17 ...331 H3
Woodview VGE SS16 ...294 B1
Woodview Av CHING E4 ...266 F3
Woodview CI COLN C04 ...108 A1
Woodview Dr RCHLM CM3 ...144 D6
Woodview Rd GTDUN CM6 ...116 F5
Woodville CI RCFD SS4 ...283 C1
Woodville Gdns BARK/HLT IG6 ...286 F1
Woodville PI GVE DA12 ...337 L5
Woodville Rd CVI SS8 ...321 G2
 IPNE IP9 ...17 L5
 SWFD E18 ...267 L8
 WALTH E17 ...284 E1
 WAN E11 ...285 J6
Woodville St
 WOOL/PLUM SE18 ...324 B7
Woodward CI GRAYS RM17 ...330 J3
Woodward Gdns DAGW RM9 ...309 M4
Woodward Hts GRAYS RM17 ...330 E3
Woodward Rd DAGW RM9 ...309 L5
Woodwards HLWW/ROY CM19 ...203 K5
Woodward Ter GRH DA9 ...335 H8
Wood Wy BRTR CM77 ...120 F7
Woodway RBRW/HUT CM13 ...256 D4
Woodyards BOC CM0 ...386 E10
Woolands Rd WAN E11 ...285 H7
Woolards Wy RCHLM CM3 ...245 C6
Woolf CI THMD SE28 ...325 L2
Woolhampton Wy CHIG IG7 ...269 L2
Woolifers Av SLH/COR SS17 ...317 L1
Woollards CI IP IP1 ...16 A4
Woollards Gdns SUD CO10 ...42 F1
Woollard St WAB EN9 ...233 K4
Woollard Wy ING CM4 ...222 B4
Woolmans CI BRW CM14 ...201 C8
Woolmergreen LAIN SS15 ...2 A4
Woolmers Md RCHLM CM3 ...166 B3
Woolmonger's La ING CM4 ...383 C1
Woolmore St POP/IOD E14 ...322 F3
Woolner Dr RCOS CO16 ...159 C7
Woolnough CI HVHL CB9 ...34 A2
The Woolnoughs KESG IP5 ...50 C6
Woolpack La BRTR CM77 ...99 J8
Woolpit Downs BURES CO8 * ...359 P9
Woolpit's Rd BRTR CM7 ...97 H4
Woolshotts Rd WICKW SS12 ...260 C6
Woolston CI WALTH E17 ...266 A8
Woolverstone CI CHTY IP2 ...53 J4
Woolwich Church St
 CHARL SE7 ...324 A7
Woolwich Foot Tnl
 CAN/RD E16 ...324 D5
Woolwich High St
 WOOL/PLUM SE18 ...324 D6
Woolwich Manor Wy
 CAN/RD E16 ...324 E4
Woolwich Manorway
 CAN/RD E16 ...324 E5
Woolwich Manor Wy
 EHAM E6 ...308 C8
Woolwich New Rd
 WOOL/PLUM SE18 ...324 E7
Woolwich Rd BELV DA17 ...326 C8
 GNWCH SE10 ...323 K8
 RCOS CO16 ...6 A2
Wooster Gdns POP/IOD E14 ...323 G2
Wootton CI EMPK RM11 ...290 A3
Worcester Av UPMR RM14 ...291 J6
Worcester Ct BRTR CM7 ...121 M7
 GRH DA9 ...335 L6
 RCHLM CM3 ...388 D8
 SLH/COR SS17 ...317 G2
 VGE SS16 ...276 B1
Worcester Ct
 CHLM/GWD CM2 ...210 C8

Worcester Crs RCOLE C07 ...131 L5
 WFD IG8 ...267 M3
Worcester Dr RAYL SS6 ...281 J4
Worcester Gdns IL IG1 ...286 B5
Worcester Rd BOC CM0 ...393 M7
 COL CO1 ...8 C3
 IPSE IP3 ...54 F1
 MNPK E12 ...286 C8
 WALTH E17 ...266 A4
Worcesters Av EN EN1 ...232 B8
Worcester La K/T/MI C05 ...149 G2
Wordsworth Av MAL CM9 ...214 D5
 MNPK E12 ...308 B4
 SWFD E18 ...285 L1
Wordsworth CI HARH RM3 ...271 M7
 SOSN SS2 ...301 L2
 TIL RM18 ...331 M8
Wordsworth Crs IP IP1 ...47 K2
Wordsworth Rd BRTR CM7 ...99 J4
 COLW CO3 ...106 C7
Wordsworth Wy DART DA1 ...334 D5
Worgan St BERM/RHTH SE16 ...322 A6
Workhouse Hl COLN C04 ...87 H1
Workhouse La RCHLM CM3 ...244 D3
Workhouse Rd RCOLW C06 ...85 M7
Workshop La KIR/NAC IP10 ...56 A8
Worland Rd SRTFD E15 ...307 H4
Worlds End La K/T/MI C05 ...149 G2
Wormley Ct WAB EN9 ...234 E3
Wormley Lodge CI
 BROX EN10 ...217 G1
Wormyngford Ct WAB EN9 ...234 B8
 EMPK RM11 ...290 A4
Worrin CI BRWN CM15 ...256 C4
Worrin Rd BRWN CM15 ...256 C5
Worsdell Wy COLN C04 ...8 C1
Worsley Ct CHTY IP2 ...53 J7
Worsley Rd WAN E11 ...307 H1
Wortham PI HVHL CB9 ...34 D5
Worthing CI SRTFD E15 ...307 H5
 WTHK RM20 ...330 B5
Worthing Ms COS CO15 ...182 F5
Worthing Rd LAIN SS15 ...276 D7
Worthington Wy COLW CO3 ...128 C5
Wortley Rd EHAM E6 ...308 A4
Wouldham Rd CAN/RD E16 ...323 J2
 WTHK RM20 ...330 B5
Wrabness Rd HAR CO12 ...367 H6
Wragby Rd WAN E11 * ...285 H8
The Wraglins BSF CM23 ...139 L4
Wrangley Ct WAB EN9 ...234 B3
Wratting Rd HVHL CB9 ...34 A6
Wray Av CLAY IG5 ...286 D1
Wray CI EMPK RM11 ...290 A5
Wraysbury Dr LAIN SS15 ...277 G4
Wren Av CHTY IP2 ...53 J2
 LOS SS9 ...281 H6
Wrenbrook Rd BSF CM23 ...139 G4
Wren CI BCAYE CM11 ...258 F4
 CAN/RD E16 ...323 J2
 COLW C03 ...127 H1
 ED N9 ...248 A8
 LOS SS9 ...282 A6
 RCOLE C07 * ...133 G4
 SBF/HAD SS7 ...279 L7
Wrendale COS CO15 ...159 J7
Wren Dr WAB EN9 ...234 B5
Wren Gdns DAGW RM9 ...310 A2
 HCH RM12 ...289 J6
Wren PI BRW CM14 ...256 A6
Wren Rd DAGW RM9 ...310 A2
Wrens Pk FX IP11 ...63 J7
The Wrens HLWW/ROY CM19 ...12 D7
Wren Ter LOU IG10 ...250 C1
Wren Wk TIL RM18 ...331 L6
Wrexham Rd BOW E3 ...306 D6
 HARH RM3 ...272 A3
 LAIN SS15 ...276 E8
Wright La KESG IP5 ...50 C6
Wright Md CHLM/GWD CM2 ...210 C1
Wright Rd IPSE IP3 ...55 H7
Wright's Av WFD IG8 ...277 J2
Wright's Green La RBSF CM22 ...163 K5
Wrights CI DAGE RM10 ...310 C1
Wright's Green La BRWN CM15 ...238 A2
Wright's Piece RBSF CM22 ...372 H11
Wright's Rd BOW E3 ...306 C1
Wrights Wy RCOLW C06 ...360 G4
Wrigley CI CHING E4 * ...267 C4
Writtle CI RCOS CO16 ...182 E1
Writtle Rd CHLM/WR CM1 ...4 D1
 ING CM4 ...224 C2
Wrotham Rd GVW DA11 ...337 K8
Wroths Pth LOU IG10 ...250 C1
Wroxall Rd DAGW RM9 ...309 M3

Wroxham CI COLW C03 ...106 E7
 SBF/HAD SS7 ...281 L1
Wroxham Rd POP/IOD E14 ...322 F4
 THMD SE28 ...326 A3
Wryneck CI COLN C04 ...107 J2
Wyatt CI FSTGT E7 ...307 K3
Wyatts Dr SOS SS1 ...302 C6
Wyatts Green La BRWN CM15 ...238 D4
Wyatt's Green Rd BRWN CM15 ...238 D4
Wyatts La SUD CO10 ...359 N1
 WALTH E17 ...284 E1
Wyburn Rd SBF/HAD SS7 ...281 G7
Wyburns Av RAYL SS6 ...281 H5
Wyburns Av East RAYL SS6 ...281 H5
Wych Elm HLW CM20 ...12 F5
Wych Elm CI EMPK RM11 ...290 D5
Wych Elm Rd EMPK RM11 ...290 D4
Wychford Dr SBW CM21 ...162 D8
Wychwood Gdns CLAY IG5 ...286 C2
Wycke Hl MAL CM9 ...214 D5
Wycke La MAL CM9 ...385 P5
Wycliffe Gv COL CO1 ...8 C3
Wycliffe Rw GVW DA11 ...337 J6
Wycombe Av SBF/HAD SS7 ...279 K7
Wycombe Rd
 GNTH/NBYPK IG2 ...286 C3
Wyedean Gv CHING E4 ...267 H1
Wye Rd CHLM/GWD CM2 ...338 A3
 IPSE IP3 ...54 F2
Wyfields CLAY IG5 ...268 E7
Wykeham Av DAGW RM9 ...309 M3
 EMPK RM11 ...290 A4
Wykeham Gn DAGW RM9 ...309 M3
Wykeham Rd CHLM/WR CM1 ...208 G4
Wyke Rd BOW E3 ...306 D4
Wykes Bishop St IPSE IP3 ...17 J8
Wykes Gn BSDN SS14 ...3 L4
Wyldwood CI HLWE CM17 ...188 D3
Wymark CI RAIN RM13 ...311 J6
Wynan Rd POP/IOD E14 ...322 E8
Wyncolls Rd COLN C04 ...87 M8
Wyndam CI COLS CO2 ...129 L5
Wyndham Crs COS CO15 ...7 J3
Wyndham Rd EHAM E6 ...308 A4
Wynndale Rd SWFD E18 ...267 L1
Wynters VGE SS16 ...295 L1
Wynterton CI IPSE IP3 ...55 G4
Wynyard CI SAFWN CB10 ...28 B6
Wyse's St ING CM4 ...207 J2
Wythefield PIT SS13 ...278 D7
Wythenshawe Rd
 DAGE RM10 ...288 D2
Wythes Rd CAN/RD E16 ...324 D8
Wyvern Rd IPSE IP3 ...55 H4
Wyvis St POP/IOD E14 ...322 E1

Y

Yabsley St POP/IOD E14 ...322 F4
Yale Ms COLN C04 ...107 L1
Yale Wy HCH RM12 ...311 K1
Yamburg Rd CVI SS8 ...321 G2
Yardley LAIN SS15 ...2 A6
Yardley CI CHING E4 ...248 E5
Yardley Hall La GTDUN CM6 ...352 A11
Yardley La CHING E4 ...248 E5
The Yard BRTR CM7 ...121 K3
Yare Av WIT CM8 ...171 G2
Yarmouth CI RCOS CO16 ...6 A2
Yarmouth Rd IP IP1 ...47 L7
Yarnacott SBF/HAD SS7 ...302 F5
Yarnton Wy ABYW SE2 ...325 M5
 ERITHM DA18 ...326 C6
Yarrow Crs EHAM E6 ...324 B1
Yarwood Rd CHLM/GWD CM2 ...210 A1
Yateley St WOOL/PLUM SE18 ...324 A6
Yearling CI WARE SG12 ...185 G3
Yeldham Lock
 CHLM/GWD CM2 ...210 D3
Yeldham PI HVHL CB9 ...34 D5
Yeldham Rd HSTD C09 ...56 D5
Yellowpine Wy CHIG IG7 ...269 L3
Yelverton CI HARH RM3 ...271 M7
Yeoman CI EHAM E6 ...324 E3
Yeoman Dr FX IP11 ...10 E1
Yeomans CI BSF CM23 ...138 E4
Yeoman St BERM/RHTH SE16 ...322 B2
Yeomans Wy BARK/HLT IG6 ...268 F5
Yeo St BOW E3 ...322 E1
Yeovil Cha WOS/PRIT SS0 ...300 E1
Yerril Gdn HVHL CB9 ...34 B6

Yevele Wy EMPK RM11 ...290 B5
Yew CI BKHH IG9 ...268 A5
Yew Ct LAIN SS15 ...277 G4
 WIT CM8 ...147 L3
Yew Ct CHTY IP2 ...53 M2
Yewlands HOD EN11 ...201 H4
 SBW CM21 ...162 F8
Yewlands Dr HOD EN11 ...201 H4
Yews Av EN EN1 ...232 C6
The Yews GVE DA12 ...338 A7
Yew Tree CI COLN C04 ...108 B5
 RBRW/HUT CM13 ...257 G5
 RCHLM CM3 ...170 D8
Yew Tree Gdns CHDH RM6 ...288 B5
 CHLM/GWD CM2 ...209 M7
 ROMW/RG RM7 ...289 ...
Yewtree Gv KESG IP5 ...49 G6
Yew Tree PI BSF CM23 ...139 G1
Yewtree Ri RIPW IP8 ...47 H4
Yew Wk HOD EN11 ...201 H4
Yew Wy COS CO15 ...182 C7
Yonge CI RCHLM CM3 ...195 H4
Yorick Av K/T/MI C05 ...177 M7
Yorick Rd K/T/MI C05 ...177 M7
York Av SLH/COR SS17 ...295 G8
York CI BRWN CM15 ...256 C3
 EHAM E6 ...324 C2
 RAYL SS6 ...281
 SUD CO10 ...20 D3
York Crs LOU IG10 ...250 B3
Yorks HLWS CM18 ...204 A3
York Gdns BRTR CM7 ...121 L1
York Hl LOU IG10 ...250 B3
York PI COL CO1 * ...8 F5
 IL IG1 ...286 D8
York Ri RAYL SS6 ...281 K5
York Rd BCAYW CM12 ...240 D8
 BOC CM0 ...393 M9
 BRWN CM15 ...256 C3
 CHES/WCR EN8 ...232 F4
 CHING E4 ...266 D4
 CHLM/GWD CM2 ...160 A4
 COS CO15 ...160 A4
 EPP CM16 ...221 H5
 FSTGT E7 ...307 K3
 FX IP11 ...11 M1
 GVE DA12 ...337 M6
 GVW DA11 ...337
 HVHL CB9 ...34 B6
 IL IG1 ...286 D8
 IPSE IP3 ...54 F1
 KESG IP5 ...50 F7
 LEY E10 ...
 RAIN RM13 ...311 G4
 RAYL SS6 ...281 K5
 RCFD SS4 ...264 F6
 RCOLE C07 ...156 B7
 RCOLW C06 ...82 C7
 SLH/COR SS17 ...316 C1
 SOS SS1 ...19 J6
 SUD CO10 ...20 D4
 WALTH E17 ...266 D8
York Road Ar SOS SS1 * ...19 H6
Yorkshire Rd POP/IOD E14 ...322 B2
York Sq POP/IOD E14 * ...322 B2
York St BARK IG11 ...308 C5
 MGTR ...91 G1
Young CI LOS SS9 ...282 D7
 RCOS CO16 ...6 B2
Young Rd CAN/RD E16 ...324 B1
Youngs Rd GNTH/NBYPK IG2 ...287 G3
Yoxley Ap GNTH/NBYPK IG2 ...286 F4
Yoxley Dr GNTH/NBYPK IG2 ...286 F4
Ypres Rd COLS CO2 ...129 H2
Yunus Khan CI WALTH E17 ...284 D3

Z

Zambesi Rd BSF CM23 ...139 G4
Zandi Rd CVI SS8 ...321 G3
Zealand Dr CVI SS8 ...321 H2
Zealand Rd BOW E3 ...306 B6
Zelham Dr CVI SS8 ...321 J2
Zenith BSDN SS14 ...278 B3
Zetland St POP/IOD E14 ...322 F1
Zider Pass CVI SS8 ...321 J2
Zion PI GVW DA11 ...337 L5

Index – featured places

Aaron House Clinic
 of Physiotherapy
 WOS/PRIT SS0 ...300 E2
The Abbey Clinic
 BELV DA17 ...326 C8
Abbey Lane Commercial Estate
 SRTFD E15 ...307 G6
Abbey Mead Industrial Park
 WAB EN9 ...233 J4
Abbey Park Industrial Estate
 BARK IG11 ...308 E6
Abbey Primary School
 ABYW SE2 ...325 M6
Abbey Road Health Centre
 SRTFD E15 ...307 H5
Abbey Sports Centre
 BARK IG11 ...308 F5
Abbey Wharf Industrial Estate
 BARK IG11 ...309 C1
Abbey Wood School
 ABYW SE2 ...325 K6
Abbotsweld Primary School
 HLWS CM18 ...203 L3
Abbotts Hall Primary School
 SLH/COR SS17 ...317 H2
ABC Cinema
 BRW CM14 ...273 M1
 GVE DA12 ...337 L4
Abridge Golf & Country Club
 EPP CM16 ...237 G2
Acacia Business Centre
 WAN E11 ...285 H8
Acorn Trading Centre
 ROM RM0 ...330 B5
Acton CE Primary School
 SUD CO10 ...43 M4
Acton Place Industrial Estate
 SUD CO10 ...43 L1
Adams Business Centre
 BSDN SS14 ...278 B4
The Adult College of Barking
 & Dagenham BARK IG11 ...309 H3
Adult Community College
 COL CO1 ...8 E6
Adult Community College
 Chelmsford CHLM/WR CM1 ...4 B3

Adult Education Centre
 POP/IOD E14 ...322 F6
Adventure Island
 SOS SS1 ...19 J7
Ainslie Wood Primary School
 CHING E4 ...266 E4
Airborne Industrial Estate
 LOS SS9 ...282 B8
Airport Business Park
 SOSN SS2 ...283 H7
Albany School (Grant
 Maintained) PEND EN3 ...232 E8
The Albany School
 HCH RM12 ...289 L7
Albright Industrial Estate
 RAIN RM13 ...327 J1
Alderman Blaxill School
 COLS CO2 ...128 C2
Aldersbrook County
 Secondary School
 MNPK E12 ...285 M6
Aldersbrook Primary School
 WAN E11 ...285 L6
The Alderton Primary School
 LOU IG10 ...250 D5
The Alec Hunter High School
 BRTR CM7 ...121 M3
Alexander McLeod
 Primary School ABYW SE2 ...325 L8
Alexandra Business Centre
 PEND EN3 ...248 A4
Alfred Salter Primary School
 BERM/RHTH SE16 ...322 A5
Alfreds Way Industrial Estate
 BARK IG11 ...309 K5
Alleyn Court Preparatory
 School SBN/FI SS3 ...302 D2
Alleyn Court Pre-Preparatory
 School WOS/PRIT SS0 ...300 F4
All Nations Christian College
 WARE SG12 ...185 J2
All Saints Catholic School
 BCTR RM8 ...288 D6
All Saints CE Middle School
 SUD CO10 ...43 K7

All Saints CE Primary School
 HAR CO12 ...14 C9
 WAN E11 ...214 M3
All Saints Primary School
 BSF CM23 ...139 J1
Allum Medical Centre
 WAN E11 ...285 J6
Alma Primary School
 PEND EN3 ...248 B5
Alnesbourne Priory Golf Club
 KIR/NAC IP10 ...55 H8
Al-Noor Primary School
 GDMY/SEVK IG3 ...287 K7
Alpha Business Centre
 WALTH E17 ...284 C3
Alpha Business Park
 IP IP1 ...47 K2
Alpine Business Centre
 EHAM E6 ...324 D1
Alresford Business Centre
 RCOLE C07 ...131 L5
Alresford Primary School
 RCOLE C07 ...131 L6
Alsa Business Park
 STSD CM24 ...374 A4
Altmore Infant School
 EHAM E6 ...308 C4
Alton Park Junior School
 COS CO15 ...6 C7
Alton Water Sports Centre
 RIPS/CAP IP9 ...364 E10
Amberfield School
 KIR/NAC IP10 ...56 D7
Ambresbury Banks Fort
 EPP CM16 ...235 J2
Amwell View Special School
 WARE SG12 ...185 J1
Anchorage Point Industrial
 Estate CHARL SE7 ...323 M6
Anchor Press Social &
 Sports Club K/T/MI C05 ...150 A8
Ancient House
 IP IP1 ...16 F4
Andrewsfield (Saling)
 Aerodrome GTDUN CM6 ...97 G2

Andrews Lane J & I School
 CHESW EN7 ...216 C6
Angel Centre
 DART DA1 ...334 B8
Angerstein Business Park
 GNWCH SE10 ...323 K7
Anglesea Centre
 GVW DA11 ...337 L4
Anglian Industrial Estate
 BARK IG11 ...309 J3
Anglia Polytechnic University
 BRWN CM15 ...256 A4
 CHLM/WR CM1 ...193 K2
Anglia Polytechnic University
 (Central Campus)
 CHLM/GWD CM2 ...4 F3
Anglia Polytechnic University
 (Rivermead Campus)
 CHLM/WR CM1 ...209 L1
Anglia Trading Estate
 COL CO1 ...8 B3
Anglo European School
 ING CM4 ...239 M1
Animal Cemetery
 REDBR IG4 ...286 A1
Annandale Clinic
 WOS/PRIT SS0 ...300 E2
Annwood Lodge Business Park
 WICKW SS12 ...280 B5
Anstey First School
 BUNT SG9 ...370 F9
Antonys RC Primary School
 WFD IG8 ...267 K3
Appleton School
 SBF/HAD SS7 ...279 M8
Ardleigh Green Primary School
 EMPK RM11 ...290 A1
Ardleigh St Marys CE
 Primary School RCOLE C07 ...89 C2
Arena Essex
 WTHK RM20 ...329 K6
Arena Sports & Leisure Club
 COLS CO2 ...107 H8
Arnhem Wharf Primary School
 POP/IOD E14 ...322 C5

Arthur Bugler J & I School
 SLH/COR SS17 ...317 H2
The Arthur Findlay College
 STSD CM24 ...374 B8
Arts Centre
 COL CO1 ...8 F5
 GVE DA12 ...337 L4
Arts Centre Cinema
 HVHL CB9 ...34 D6
Ashdon Primary School
 SAFWN CB10 ...27 L8
Ashgrove College
 WALTH E17 ...284 D1
Ash Industrial Estate
 HLWW/ROY CM19 ...203 G2
Ashingdon Primary School
 RCFD SS4 ...264 E4
Ashleigh Commercial Estate
 CHARL SE7 ...323 M7
Ashton Playing Fields Track
 WFD IG8 ...268 B5
Associated Newspapers
 BERM/RHTH SE16 ...322 A6
Atherton Leisure Centre
 FSTGT E7 ...307 L2
Atlantic Hotel
 CHLM/WR CM1 ...5 J1
Audley End House & Gardens
 SAFWS CB11 ...351 Q4
Aveley FC
 SOCK/AV RM15 ...328 F3
Aveley Medical Centre
 SOCK/AV RM15 ...313 M8
Aveley Primary School
 SOCK/AV RM15 ...329 H4
Aveley School (Foundation)
 SOCK/AV RM15 ...329 H4
The Aveley School
 SOCK/AV RM15 ...329 G4
Aveling Park School
 WALTH E17 ...266 D8
Avenue Industrial Estate
 CHING E4 ...266 C5
 GPK RM2 ...272 A8
Avenue Primary School
 MNPK E12 ...308 B1

Avon House School
WFD IG8 ....267 K3
Axis Business Centre
SRTFD E15 ....306 E5
Aylands School
PEND EN3 ....232 D6
Ayloff Primary School
HCH RM12 ....311 L1
Bacon's College
BERM/RHTH SE16 ....322 B4
Baddow Hall J & I School
CHLM/GWD CM2 ....210 D7
Balaam Leisure Centre
PLSTW E13 ....307 K8
Balfour Medical Centre
GRAYS RM17 ....330 F3
Ballards Gore Golf Club
RCFD SS4 ....396 B5
Ballingdon Hill Industrial Estate
SUD CO10 ....44 A5
Ballingdon Trading Estate
SUD CO10 ....44 A5
Balmoral Hotel
WOS/PRIT SS0 ....18 A4
Balmoral Trading Estate
BARK IG11 ....325 J1
Bancrofts School
WFD IG8 ....267 K2
Bankside Park Industrial Estate
HCH RM12 ....309 K7
Bannockburn Primary School
WOOL/PLUM SE18 ....325 J7
Barbara Castle Health Centre
HLWW/ROY CM19 ....203 H5
Barclay J & I School
LEY E10 ....285 G4
Barkantine Clinic
POP/IOD E14 ....322 D5
Barking Abbey Comprehensive School (Lower)
BARK IG11 ....309 G2
Barking Abbey Comprehensive School (Upper)
BARK IG11 ....309 J3
Barking Abbey Industrial Estate *BARK* IG11 ....308 E3
Barking Abbey Leisure Centre
BARK IG11 ....309 K3
Barking College
ROMW/RG RM7 ....289 G7
Barking FC
BCTR RM8 ....309 L2
Barking Hospital
BARK IG11 ....309 J4
Barking Industrial Park
BARK IG11 ....309 J5
Barking RUFC
DAGW RM9 ....310 A3
Barkingside Cemetery
BARK/HLT IG6 ....286 E1
Barkingside FC
BARK/HLT IG6 ....287 G2
Barkway CE First School
ROY SG8 ....370 A3
Barkway Park Golf Club
ROY SG8 ....370 D5
Barley Lane Primary School
GDMY/SEVK IG3 ....287 K5
Barley VP First School
ROY SG8 ....348 F9
Barling Magna Primary School *SBN/FI* SS3 ....396 G10
Barn Business Centre
RCOLE CO7 ....64 B1
Barn Croft Primary School
WALTH E17 ....284 B4
Barnes Farm J & I School
CHLM/GWD CM2 ....210 D2
Barons Court County Infant School *WOS/PRIT* SS0 ....18 D5
Barratt Industrial Park
BOW E3 ....306 F4
Barstable School
BSDN SS14 ....278 C7
Bartlet Hospital
FX IP11 ....69 G1
The Basildon Centre
BSDN SS14 ....2 E6
Basildon & District Crematorium
PIT SS13 ....297 H1
Basildon Golf Club
VGE SS16 ....295 G1
Basildon Hospital
VGE SS16 ....295 J2
Basildon RFC
BSDN SS14 ....278 A4
Basildon United FC
BSDN SS14 ....278 A4
Bata Medical Centre
TIL RM18 ....332 F3
Bates Industrial Estate
HARH RM3 ....272 D6
Battlesbridge Motorcycle Museum *WICKE* SS11 ....262 A3
Baynards Primary School
K/T/MI CO5 ....149 L6
BBC Radio Suffolk
IP IP1 ....16 D3
Beacon Hill Industrial Estate
PUR RM19 ....328 E2
Beacon Hill Special School
CHTY IP2 ....53 L2
Beal High School
REDBR IG4 ....286 B1
Bealings School
FRAM/WMKT IP13 ....50 C1
Beam Primary School
DAGE RM10 ....310 F6
Bearwalden Business Park
SAFWS CB11 ....351 M8
Beauchamps GM School
WICKE SS11 ....261 K5
Beaumont Primary School
LEY E10 ....284 E5
Beckers Green CP School
BRTR CM7 ....122 A3
Beckingham Business Park
MAL CM9 ....384 A3
Beckton Ski Centre
EHAM E6 ....308 A6
Beckton Special School
EHAM E6 ....324 A1
Beckton Triangle Retail Park
EHAM E6 ....308 E7
Becontree Day Hospital
BCTR RM8 ....288 B7
Becontree Primary School
BCTR RM8 ....287 L8
Bedonwell Medical Centre
BELV DA17 ....326 C8
Beehive Preparatory School
REDBR IG4 ....286 C2
Belchamp St Paul CE Primary School *SUD* CO10 ....346 H4
Belcon Industrial Estate
HOD EN11 ....201 K3
Belfairs Golf Club
LOS SS9 ....299 M1

Belfairs High School
LOS SS9 ....299 M3
Belfairs Sports Ground
LOS SS9 ....300 A1
Belfairs Swimming Pool
LOS SS9 ....299 M3
Belhus Golf Club & Leisure Centre
SOCK/AV RM15 ....329 H2
Belhus Woods Country Park
SOCK/AV RM15 ....313 G7
Bellamy's Wharf
BERM/RHTH SE16 ....322 A4
Belmont Park School
LEY E10 ....284 F4
Belstead School
RIPW IP8 ....53 H3
Belvedere Industrial Estate
BELV DA17 ....327 G4
Belvedere Link Business Park
BELV DA17 ....326 F3
Belvedere Primary School
BELV DA17 ....326 F7
Benbridge Industrial Estate
MAL CM9 ....198 D8
Benfleet Business Centre
SBF/HAD SS7 ....298 A3
Benhurst JMI School
HCH RM12 ....289 L8
Ben Jonson Primary School
WCHPL E1 ....306 B8
Bentalls Industrial Estate
MAL CM9 ....198 D8
Bentalls Shopping Centre
MAL CM9 ....198 D8
Bentfield Primary School
STSD CM24 ....115 L1
Bentley Golf Club
BRWN CM15 ....255 H1
Bentley Primary School
RIPS/CAP IP9 ....59 J6
Bentley Street Industrial Estate *GVE* DA12 ....337 M4
Benton Hall Golf Club
WIT CM8 ....171 L7
Benyon Primary School
SOCK/AV RM15 ....313 M6
Berger Primary School
HOM E9 ....306 A3
The Beth Chatto Gardens
RCOLE CO7 ....109 K8
Bexley College
ERITH DA8 ....326 F7
Billericay IT Learning Centre
BCAYW CM12 ....258 D4
The Billericay School
BCAYW CM12 ....258 D5
Billericay Swimming Pool
BCAYW CM12 ....258 D2
Billericay Town FC
BCAYW CM12 ....258 B4
Billingsgate Fish Market
POP/IOD E14 ....322 E4
Birchanger CE Primary School
BSF CM23 ....115 L6
Birchanger Industrial Estate
BSF CM23 ....115 H7
Birch Business Centre
COLS CO2 ....127 K6
Birch CE Primary School
COLS CO2 ....151 K1
Birch Grove Golf Club
COLS CO2 ....128 E5
Birchmere Business Park
THMD SE28 ....325 J5
Birchwood CP School
KESG IP5 ....50 F6
Birchwood High School
BSF CM23 ....139 K1
The Bishop CE & RC Primary School *CHLM/WR* CM1 ....194 C7
Bishop John Robinson CE Primary School *THMD* SE28 ....325 M3
Bishops Park College
RCOS CO16 ....182 D2
Bishop's Park Health Centre
BSF CM23 ....139 G1
Bishop's Stortford Business Centre *BSF* CM23 ....139 H3
Bishop's Stortford College
BSF CM23 ....138 F2
Bishop's Stortford Golf Club
BSF CM23 ....139 L2
The Bishop's Stortford High School *BSF* CM23 ....139 G5
Bishop's Stortford RFC
BSF CM23 ....114 E8
Bishop William Ward CE Primary School *RCOLW* CO6 ....86 E6
Blackall Industrial Estate
IPNE IP4 ....245 J4
Blackfriars Priory Hall
IPNE IP4 ....17 G5
The Black Lion Hotel
SUD CO10 ....40 F7
Blackmore CP School
ING CM4 ....222 B5
Black Notley Primary School
BRTR CM77 ....123 G3
Blackshots Leisure Centre
CDW/CHF RM16 ....331 G1
Blackwall Trading Estate
POP/IOD E14 ....323 G1
Blackwater Leisure Centre
MAL CM9 ....214 E4
Blackwater Sailing Club
MAL CM9 ....215 J2
Blackwater Trading Estate
MAL CM9 ....214 D1
Blenheim Primary School
LEY E10 ....300 C2
Blessed John Roche Catholic School *POP/IOD* E14 ....322 D2
Blois Meadow Business Centre
HVHL CB9 ....344 B5
Bluebridge Industrial Estate
HSTD CO9 ....77 K3
Blyth's Wharf
POP/IOD E14 ....322 B3
Bocking Church Street Primary School *BRTR* CM7 ....99 J5
Boleyn Cinema
EHAM E6 ....308 A6
Bonner Primary School
BETH E2 ....306 A6
Bonner's Saltings Nature Reserve *K/T/MI* CO5 ....177 L2
Bonney Grove SPLD Base
CHESW CM2 ....216 B8
Bonnygate Primary School
SOCK/AV RM15 ....329 L1
Boomes Industrial Estate
RAIN RM13 ....311 J8
Boreham Airfield
RCHLM CM3 ....194 E1
Boreham Industrial Estate
RCHLM CM3 ....195 J3

Boreham Primary School
RCHLM CM3 ....195 J5
The Boswells School
CHLM/WR CM1 ....194 A7
Bournemouth Park Primary School
SOSN SS2 ....19 J1
Bournes Green Primary School
SOS SS1 ....302 E5
Bow County Court
SRTFD E15 ....307 H3
Bower Hill Industrial Estate
EPP CM16 ....236 B2
Bower Park School
ROM RM1 ....271 H5
Bow Industrial Park
SRTFD E15 ....306 D4
Bow Secondary School
BOW E3 ....306 D6
Bow Triangle Business Centre
BOW E3 ....306 D6
Boxgrove Primary School
ABYW SE2 ....325 M6
Boxted CE Primary School
COLN CO4 ....362 A10
Boyce Hill Golf Club
SBF/HAD SS7 ....298 B3
Boyd School
UPMR RM14 ....291 H7
Boyton Vineyard
SUD CO10 ....345 P1
The Brackenbury Sports Centre
FX IP11 ....63 H8
Bracken Industrial Estate
BARK/HLT IG6 ....269 J6
Bradfield Primary School
MGTR CO11 ....366 B8
Bradwell Quay Yacht Club
BOC CM0 ....386 D9
Brady Primary School
RAIN RM13 ....327 M1
Braeside Senior School
BKHH IG9 ....249 L8
Braintree Athletics Track
BRTR CM7 ....121 G1
Braintree College
BRTR CM7 ....99 K8
Braintree Golf Club
BRTR CM7 ....100 D7
Braintree RFC
BRTR CM7 ....122 A3
Braintree Town FC
BRTR CM7 ....121 M3
Bramford CE Primary School
RIPW IP8 ....46 F4
Brampton Manor School
EHAM E6 ....308 A8
Brampton Primary School
EHAM E6 ....308 B7
Bramston Sports Centre
WIT CM8 ....171 J4
Brandy Hole Yacht Club
HOC/HUL SS5 ....263 K1
Branfil J & I School
UPMR RM14 ....312 D1
Branolls Health Centre
PLSTW E13 ....307 K8
Brantham Athletic & Social Club *MGTR* CO11 ....64 F6
Braxted Park Golf Club
WIT CM8 ....148 D8
Brays Grove School
HLWS CM18 ....204 C3
Brentwood Chiropody Surgery
BRW CM14 ....256 A5
The Brentwood Clinic
BRWN CM15 ....256 A4
Brentwood Community Hospital *BRWN* CM15 ....256 B4
Brentwood County High School *BRW* CM14 ....256 A6
Brentwood IT Learning Centre
BRW CM14 ....273 M1
Brentwood Pre-Preparatory School *BRWN* CM15 ....256 B4
Brentwood RFC
BRW CM14 ....256 B7
Brentwood School
BRWN CM15 ....256 A4
Brentwood Sports Ground
BRWN CM15 ....256 A4
Brentwood Theatre
BRW CM14 ....256 A6
Brentwood Ursuline Convent High School *BRW* CM14 ....256 A6
Brett Vale Golf Club
HADL IP7 ....363 L1
Brewery Museum
IPSE IP5 ....54 D2
Briarswood Clinic
CVI SS8 ....298 C8
Brick Lane Music Hall
CAN/RD E16 ....324 A4
Bridge Hospital
WIT CM8 ....171 J4
Bridge View Industrial Estate
WTHM RM20 ....335 K1
Bridgewick Arts Centre
BOC CM0 ....395 J1
Briggens House Hotel
WARE SG12 ....186 D6
Brightlingsea J & I School
RCOLE CO7 ....156 B7
Brightlingsea Sailing Club
RCOLE CO7 ....156 B8
Brightlingsea United FC
RCOLE CO7 ....156 C6
Brightside Primary School
BCAYW CM12 ....240 B8
Brimsdown Primary School
PEND EN3 ....248 A3
Brinkley Grove Primary School
COLN CO4 ....87 L8
Briscoe Primary School
PIT SS13 ....278 E5
Britannia Business Centre
CHES/WCR EN8 ....233 G4
Britannia Primary School
IPNE IP4 ....49 G8
Britannia Sports Ground
WALTH E17 ....266 D6
Britannia Village Primary School
CAN/RD E16 ....323 L4
Brittania Business Park
CHES/WCR EN8 ....233 G4
Brittons School Technology College *RAIN* RM13 ....311 J4
Broadfields Primary School
HLW CM20 ....13 K5
Brockelbank Industrial Estate
GNWCH SE10 ....323 K7
Brocks Business Park
WICKE SS11 ....261 J7
Broke Hall Primary School
IPNE IP4 ....49 K8

Bromfords School
WICKW SS12 ....260 E7
Bromfords Sports Centre
WICKW SS12 ....260 E8
Bronte School
GVW DA11 ....337 K5
Brook Craft Market
IP IP1 ....16 F4
Brooke Trading Estate
ROM RM1 ....289 G7
Brook Farm Industrial Estate
ABR/ST RM4 ....253 G7
Brookfield Retail Park
CHES/WCR EN8 ....216 E5
Brookhouse Business Park
CHTY IP2 ....47 L7
Brookland J & I School
CHES/WCR EN8 ....216 F6
Brooklands Primary School
MGTR CO11 ....65 G5
Brook Natural Health Centre
CVI SS8 ....320 B2
Brook Road Industrial Estate
RAYL SS6 ....281 G5
Brookside Business Centre
RBSF CM22 ....139 G8
Brookside Primary School
HARH RM3 ....272 B4
Brook Street Business Centre
COL CO1 ....9 G8
Brookweald CC
BRW CM14 ....255 H8
Broomfield FC
CHLM/WR CM1 ....193 L5
Broomfield Hospital
CHLM/WR CM1 ....193 K2
Broomfield Primary School
CHLM/WR CM1 ....193 L4
Broomgrove County J & I School *RCOLE* CO7 ....130 E2
Broomhills Industrial Estate
BRTR CM7 ....121 G3
Broom Hill Swimming Pool
IP IP1 ....47 M5
Brothwick Wharf
DEPT SE8 ....322 D8
Broxbourne Business Centre
CHES/WCR EN8 ....216 E4
Broxbourne Primary School
BROX EN10 ....201 H7
Broxbourne Sailing Club
HOD EN11 ....201 L6
The Broxbourne School
BROX EN10 ....200 F8
Broxbourne Sports Club
BROX EN10 ....201 L6
Brunel Court Industrial Centre
COLN CO4 ....87 M8
Buckhurst Hill FC
BKHH IG9 ....250 B8
Buckhurst Hill Primary School
BKHH IG9 ....268 B1
Buckingham Road Cemetery
IL IG1 ....287 G7
Bucklesham Primary School
KIR/NAC IP10 ....57 G3
Building Crafts College
SRTFD E15 ....306 F4
Bull Hill Industrial Estate
COS CO15 ....7 H2
The Bull Hotel
SUD CO10 ....42 F1
Bull Lane Industrial Estate
SUD CO10 ....43 K1
Bulmer Road Industrial Estate
SUD CO10 ....44 F2
Bulmer St Andrews CE Primary School *SUD* CO10 ....44 B6
Bulphan CE Primary School
UPMR RM14 ....293 J4
Bunsay Downs Golf Club
MAL CM9 ....212 F3
BUPA Roding Hospital
REDBR IG4 ....286 A1
Bures Primary School
BURES CO8 ....359 Q8
Burleigh Primary School
CHES/WCR EN8 ....216 E8
Burlington Road Surgery
IP IP1 ....48 A7
Burnham Business Park
BOC CM0 ....393 J7
Burnham Clinic
BOC CM0 ....393 M8
Burnham Museum
BOC CM0 ....393 L9
Burnham-on-Crouch Golf Club *BOC* CM0 ....392 H7
Burnham-on-Crouch Primary School *BOC* CM0 ....393 N8
Burnham Road Clinic
LOS SS9 ....299 M4
Burnham Trading Estate
DART DA1 ....334 A6
Burnside Industrial Estate
BARK/HLT IG6 ....269 L4
Burnt Mill Industrial Estate
HLW CM20 ....12 E1
Burnt Mill School
HLW CM20 ....13 K2
Burnt Mills Industrial Estate
PIT SS13 ....278 E4
Burrsville County J & I School
COS CO15 ....159 H4
The Burstead Golf Club
BCAYW CM12 ....258 B8
Burton End Community Primary School *HVHL* CB9 ....34 A4
Burwell Industrial Estate
LEY E10 ....284 B6
The Business Academy Bexley
ERITHM DA18 ....326 B5
Business Aviation Terminal
STSD CM24 ....374 C11
Buttermarket Shopping Centre
IP IP1 ....16 F5
Buttsbury Infant School
BCAYW CM12 ....240 C8
Buttsbury Junior School
BCAYW CM12 ....240 B8
Buzzard Creek Industrial Estate
BARK IG11 ....309 J7
Bygrove JMI School
POP/IOD E14 ....322 D1
Cabot Place
POP/IOD E14 ....322 D2
Calverton Primary School
CAN/RD E16 ....324 A2
Cambell Primary School
DAGW RM9 ....310 A4
Camelia Hotel
SOSN SS2 ....302 B7
Campanile Hotel
BSDN SS14 ....277 H4
GRH DA9 ....335 G3
Campion School
EMPK RM11 ....290 C2
Canada Place
POP/IOD E14 ....322 E4

Canada Square
POP/IOD E14 ....322 E4
Canada Water Retail Park
BERM/RHTH SE16 ....322 A6
Canada Wharf Museum
POP/IOD E14 ....322 C4
Canal Industrial Park
GVE DA12 ....338 A4
Canary Riverside
POP/IOD E14 ....322 C4
Canary Wharf Pier
POP/IOD E14 ....322 C4
Canary Wharf Tower
POP/IOD E14 ....322 D4
Canewdon Endowed Primary School *RCFD* SS4 ....392 B12
Canfield CC
GTDUN CM6 ....377 P8
Cann Hall Primary School
RCOS CO16 ....158 C3
Cannon Wharf Business Centre
DEPT SE8 ....322 B7
Canon Palmer RC High School
IL IG1 ....287 H6
Canons Brook Golf Club
HLW CM20 ....12 A4
Canvey Island FC
CVI SS8 ....321 J3
Canvey Primary School
CVI SS8 ....320 C2
Capel Manor College
EN EN1 ....232 C6
Capel St Mary CE Primary School *RIPS/CAP* IP9 ....58 C1
Capital Industrial Estate
BELV DA17 ....326 E1
BELV DA17 ....326 F1
Capitol Industrial Centre
WICKE SS11 ....261 K8
Cardinal Park
IP IP1 ....16 E5
Cardinal Pole RC College
HOM E9 ....306 E1
Cardinal Pole RC Secondary Lower School *HOM* E9 ....306 A4
Cardwell Primary School
WOOL/PLUM SE18 ....324 C7
Car Ferry Terminal
RAR CO12 ....66 D8
Carnarvon Medical Centre
SOSN SS2 ....18 F1
Carpenters Business Park
HOM E9 ....306 D3
Carpenters Primary School
SRTFD E15 ....306 F5
Castilion Primary School
THMD SE28 ....325 M2
Castle Camps CE VC Primary School *CBE/LIN* CB1 ....342 V1
The Castledon Special School
WICKW SS12 ....260 E8
Castle Garden Medical Centre
COL CO1 ....8 F6
Castle Hill J & I School
IP IP1 ....47 M2
Castle Hill Middle School
HVHL CB9 ....34 A5
Castle House
RCOLE CO7 ....363 P12
Castle Manor Upper School
HVHL CB9 ....34 B5
Castle Point Athletics Track
CVI SS8 ....298 A7
Castle Point Golf Club
CVI SS8 ....298 C7
Castlepoint Museum
CVI SS8 ....321 J2
Castle View Secondary School
CVI SS8 ....298 C7
Caterham High School
CLAY IG5 ....268 C8
Cathall Leisure Centre
WAN E11 ....285 G8
Cathedral CE Primary School
CHLM/WR CM1 ....5 J2
Cathedral of St Mary & St Helen *BRWN* CM15 ....256 A5
The Cathedral Primary School
CHLM/WR CM1 ....209 M2
The Causeway Business Centre
BSF CM23 ....139 G2
Causton Industrial Estate
MGTR CO11 ....64 C8
Causton Junior School
FX IP11 ....62 D7
Cavalry Barracks
COLS CO2 ....8 C5
Cavendish CE Primary School
SUD CO10 ....38 C7
Cayley Primary School
POP/IOD E14 ....322 B1
Cecil Jones High School
SOSN SS2 ....302 A4
Cecil Road Primary School
GVW DA11 ....337 G6
Cedar Hall Special School
SBF/HAD SS7 ....280 E7
The Cedar School
FSTGT E7 ....307 H4
Cedarwood Primary School
KESG IP5 ....50 B7
Central Foundation Girls School *BOW* E3 ....306 D7
Central Park Pool
HARH RM3 ....272 A4
Central Park Primary School
EHAM E6 ....308 A4
Chadwell Heath Industrial Park
BCTR RM8 ....288 B6
Chadwell Heath Leisure Centre *CHDH* RM6 ....288 A4
Chadwell Heath School
CHDH RM6 ....287 L3
Chadwell Infant & Primary School *CHDH* RM6 ....287 M5
Chadwell St Mary Primary School *CDW/CHF* RM16 ....331 K2
Chadwell Springs Golf Club
WARE SG12 ....184 D2
Chafford School
RAIN RM13 ....327 M3
Chaffords Sports Complex
RAIN RM13 ....327 M4
Chalkstone Middle School
HVHL CB9 ....34 C5
Chalkwell Hall Primary School
LOS SS9 ....300 C6
Chalvedon School & Sixth Form College *PIT* SS13 ....278 E3
Chancellor Park Primary School *CHLM/GWD* CM2 ....210 G4
Channelsea Business Centre
SRTFD E15 ....307 G4
Channels Golf Club
RCHLM CM3 ....194 B2
Chantry Clinic
CHTY IP2 ....53 H7

Chantry High School *CHTY* IP2 ...53 L2
Chantry J & I School *CHTY* IP2 ...53 K1
Chantry Primary School *CVI* DA12 ...337 M5
Chapel End Infant School *WALTH* E17 ...266 E7
Chapel End Junior School *WALTH* E17 ...266 E7
Chapel High Shopping Centre *BRW* CM14 ...273 M4
Chapel Hill Business & Retail Park *BRTR* CM77 ...121 M1
Chappel Primary School *RCOLW* CO6 ...84 A8
Charfleet Industrial Estate *CVI* SS8 ...319 M2
Charfleets Farm Industrial Estate *CVI* SS8 ...320 A2
Charlton Athletic FC (The Valley) *CHARL* SE7 ...323 M8
Charlton Health & Fitness Centre *CHARL* SE7 ...323 M8
Charter Hall *COL* CO1 ...8 E4
Charterhouse Trading Estate *HVHL* CB9 ...34 F7
Chase Lane Infant & Junior School *CHING* E4 ...266 C3
    HAR CO12 ...70 D3
Chelmer Valley High School *CHLM/WR* CM1 ...193 M1
Chelmer Village Retail Park *CHLM/GWD* CM2 ...210 B3
Chelmondiston CP School *RIPS/CAP* IP9 ...365 P6
Chelmsford Athletics Club *CHLM/WR* CM1 ...193 H7
Chelmsford Cathedral *CHLM/WR* CM1 ...5 H3
Chelmsford College *CHLM/GWD* CM2 ...5 G8
    CHLM/GWD CM2 ...5 J9
Chelmsford County High School *CHLM/WR* CM1 ...209 K1
Chelmsford Crematorium *CHLM/WR* CM1 ...4 C8
Chelmsford & Essex Centre (Hospital) *CHLM/GWD* CM2 ...5 G5
Chelmsford & Essex Museum *CHLM/GWD* CM2 ...4 F8
Chelmsford Golf Club *CHLM/GWD* CM2 ...209 J7
Chelmsford RFC *CHLM/GWD* CM2 ...210 B1
Chelmsford Road Industrial Estate *GTDUN* CM6 ...117 J6
Chelmsford Squash Club *CHLM/GWD* CM2 ...209 L6
Cherry Tree Primary School *COLS* CO2 ...129 K5
    VGE SS16 ...3 L7
Cheshunt Community Hospital *CHES/WCR* EN8 ...232 F1
Cheshunt FC *CHES/WCR* EN8 ...232 D2
Cheshunt Field *COLS* CO3 ...128 C3
Cheshunt Golf Club *CHESW* EN7 ...216 C5
Cheshunt School *CHES/WCR* EN8 ...216 D8
Chesterfield Primary School *PEND* EN3 ...232 F1
Chetwood Primary School *RCHLM* CM3 ...245 G7
Chichester Hotel *WICKE* SS11 ...262 A7
Chief Clerk County Court *COLW* CO3 ...107 H7
Chigwell Golf Club *CHIG* IG7 ...268 D4
Chigwell Junior School *CHIG* IG7 ...268 F1
Chigwell Primary School *CHIG* IG7 ...268 D4
Chigwell Row Infants School *CHIG* IG7 ...269 M1
Childerditch Industrial Park *RBRW/HUT* CM13 ...274 C5
Childs Welfare Clinic *DAGW* RM9 ...309 M2
Chilford Hall Vineyard *CBE/LIN* CB1 ...25 C3
Chilton Industrial Estate *SUD* CO10 ...21 H2
    SUD CO10 ...21 H5
    SUD CO10 ...21 J5
    SUD CO10 ...21 K5
    SUD CO10 ...43 K8
    SUD CO10 ...45 K1
Chimnocks Wharf *POP/IOD* E14 ...322 B6
Chinese Herbal Medical Centre *CHLM/GWD* CM2 ...5 H5
Chingford CE Infant School *CHING* E4 ...249 G8
Chingford CE Junior School *CHING* E4 ...249 G8
Chingford Foundation School *CHING* E4 ...248 E8
Chingford Hall Primary School *CHING* E4 ...266 C3
Chingford Health Centre *CHING* E4 ...266 C3
Chingford Industrial Centre *CHING* E4 ...266 B4
Chingford RFC *CHING* E4 ...248 D8
Chipping Hill School *WIT* CM8 ...171 J2
Chipping Ongar Primary School *CHONG* CM5 ...382 G4
Chirstchurch Mansion *IP* IP1 ...16 F3
Chisenhale Primary School *BOW* E3 ...306 D8
Chishill Windmill *ROY* SG8 ...348 H9
Chrisp Street Health Centre *POP/IOD* E14 ...322 E2
Christ Church Cemetery *BRW* CM14 ...273 M3
The Christian School *RBSF* CM22 ...377 M2
Chudleigh Hotel *COS* CO15 ...6 F8
Churchfield School *WOOL/PLUM* SE18 ...325 J7
Churchfields J & I School *SWFD* E18 ...267 K7
Churchgate CE Primary School *HLWE* CM17 ...188 F6
Church Lane School *UPMR* RM14 ...313 L2
Church Langley Primary School *HLWE* CM17 ...204 D1

Church Mead Infant School *LEY* E10 ...284 D6
Church Mead Junior School *LEY* E10 ...284 D6
Cineplex Movie Starr Cinema ...320 F4
Cineworld Cinema *BRTR* CM77 ...121 M5
    BSF CM23 ...139 G3
City of London Cemetery *MNPK* E12 ...286 A8
City of London Crematorium *MNPK* E12 ...286 A8
Civic Hall Cinema *HOD* EN11 ...201 G4
Civic Industrial Estate *HVHL* CB9 ...34 C8
Civic Theatre *CHLM/WR* CM1 ...4 E2
Civil Service Sports Club *KIR/NAC* IP10 ...56 B4
Clacton Airfield *COS* CO15 ...182 E4
Clacton Covered Market *COS* CO15 ...7 G7
Clacton & District Hospital *COS* CO15 ...6 E1
Clacton Factory Shopping Village *COS* CO15 ...159 K4
Clacton High School Performing Arts College *COS* CO15 ...7 J4
Clacton Leisure Centre *COS* CO15 ...7 J3
Clacton-on-Sea Golf Club *COS* CO15 ...182 F5
Clacton Pier *COS* CO15 ...7 H3
Clacton Police Station *COS* CO15 ...183 H5
Clacton RFC *COS* CO15 ...7 J2
Clara Grant Primary School *BOW* E3 ...306 D8
Clare Castle Country Park *SUD* CO10 ...37 M6
Clare CP School *SUD* CO10 ...37 L5
Clare Middle School *SUD* CO10 ...38 A5
Claremont Clinic *FSTGT* E7 ...307 L2
Clarklands Industrial Estate *SBW* CM21 ...162 E4
Clavering Primary School *SAFWS* CB11 ...72 D5
Clayhall Clinic *CLAY* IG5 ...286 B1
Clement Primary School *HVHL* CB9 ...34 C6
Clements Hall Leisure Centre *HOC/HUL* SS5 ...282 D1
Cleveland Primary School *IL* IG1 ...308 C1
Cleves Primary School *EHAM* E6 ...308 A5
Cliff Hotel *HAR* CO12 ...15 H8
Cliff Lane Primary School *IPSE* IP3 ...54 D2
Clifford Road Primary School *IPNE* IP4 ...17 M5
Cliffs Bandstand *SOS* SS1 ...18 F7
Cliffs Pavilion *WOS/PRIT* SS0 ...18 C7
Clockhouse Primary School *CRW* RM5 ...270 E5
Clock Museum *COL* CO1 ...8 C7
Clore Tikva School *BARK/HLT* IG6 ...268 F8
Coalhouse Fort *TIL* RM18 ...333 H7
Coastal Business Centre *COS* CO15 ...6 C6
Cockridden Farm Industrial Estate *RBRW/HUT* CM13 ...275 J4
Coggeshall Town FC *RCOLW* CO6 ...124 A4
Colbayns High School *RCOS* CO16 ...6 C1
Colchester Business Park *COLN* CO4 ...87 M7
Colchester Camping Caravan Park *COLC* CO3 ...106 C5
Colchester Castle *COL* CO1 ...8 C6
Colchester Cemetery *COLS* CO2 ...129 K2
Colchester County Court *COL* CO1 ...8 B8
Colchester County High School *COLW* CO3 ...106 E7
Colchester Crematorium *COLS* CO2 ...129 J2
Colchester & Essex Museum *COL* CO1 ...8 C6
Colchester Garrison Athletics Stadium *COLS* CO2 ...107 J8
Colchester General Hospital *COLN* CO4 ...107 H2
Colchester Golf Club *COLN* CO4 ...106 F2
Colchester High School *COLW* CO3 ...8 A8
Colchester Institute *COLW* CO3 ...107 G5
Colchester Leisure Centre *COL* CO1 ...8 E3
Colchester Mercury Theatre *COLW* CO3 ...107 G6
Colchester Retail Park *COLW* CO3 ...107 G6
Colchester RFC *COLN* CO4 ...87 K7
Colchester Royal Grammar School *COLW* CO3 ...107 G8
Colchester United FC (Layer Rd) *COLS* CO2 ...128 F1
Colchester Zoo *COLW* CO3 ...127 M5
Cold Norton CP School *RCHLM* CM3 ...230 B8
Colegrave School *SRTFD* E15 ...307 G2
College of Teachers *EPP* CM16 ...235 L6
College St Pierre *LOS* SS9 ...282 C7
Collier Row Clinic *ROMW/RG* RM7 ...270 C7
Collier Row FC *ROMW/RG* RM7 ...270 C7
Collingwood Primary School *RCHLM* CM3 ...245 H7
The Colne Community School *RCOLE* CO7 ...156 B5

Coine Engaine CE Primary School *RCOLW* CO6 ...82 D3
Colneis Junior School *FX* IP11 ...63 G7
Colne Medical Centre *RCOLE* CO7 ...156 B7
Colne Valley Golf Club *RCOLW* CO6 ...82 D6
Colne Valley Railway *HSTD* CO9 ...356 D4
Colne View Retail Park *COL* CO1 ...8 E2
Colne Yacht Club *RCOLE* CO7 ...156 C8
Comelle House Trading Estate *DEPT* SE8 ...322 B8
Commonside School *HLWS* CM18 ...204 A5
Community Centre (Island History Trust) *POP/IOD* E14 ...322 F7
Connaught Girls School & Language College *WAN* E11 ...285 H6
Convent Preparatory School *GVE* DA12 ...337 M7
Convent School *CHLM/WR* CM1 ...194 D7
Conway Medical Centre *WOOL/PLUM* SE18 ...325 G8
Conway Primary School *WOOL/PLUM* SE18 ...325 H7
Coopersale Hall School *EPP* CM16 ...236 C5
Coopersale & Theydon Garnon CE School *EPP* CM16 ...220 B1
Coopers Company & Coburn School *UPMR* RM14 ...291 G8
Co-ordinated Industrial Estate *SBF/HAD* SS7 ...281 G6
Copdock CC *RIPW* IP8 ...52 E6
Copdock Primary School *RIPW* IP8 ...52 E5
Copford CE Primary School *RCOLW* CO6 ...126 F3
Copleston High School *IPNE* IP4 ...49 H8
Coppermill Primary School *WALTH* E17 ...284 A3
Coppice Primary School *CHIG* IG7 ...269 K4
Coppins Green GM Primary School *COS* CO15 ...6 D2
Corbets Tey School *UPMR* RM14 ...312 C2
The Cornelius Vermuyden School *CVI* SS8 ...298 B8
Cornell Estate *CHLM/GWD* CM2 ...5 L4
Corn Exchange & Film Theatre *IP* IP1 ...16 E4
Cornwallis Business Centre *BSDN* SS14 ...2 B1
Corringham Cemetery *SLH/COR* SS17 ...317 L1
Corringham Health Centre *SLH/COR* SS17 ...317 L1
The Corringham Leisure Centre *SLH/COR* SS17 ...317 L1
Corringham Primary School *SLH/COR* SS17 ...317 L1
Corton Trading Estate *SBF/HAD* SS7 ...280 A6
The Cottage Museum *BRTR* CM7 ...76 D4
County Hotel *CHLM/WR* CM1 ...4 E2
    RIPW IP8 ...52 D6
    WFD IG8 ...267 J7
County Junior School *CHLM/WR* CM1 ...208 D5
Coupals Primary School *HVHL* CB9 ...35 G6
Court Industrial Estate *CHLM/GWD* CM2 ...5 K4
Courtyard by Marriott Hotel *KIR/NAC* IP10 ...55 K6
Coward Industrial Estate *CDW/CHF* RM16 ...331 L4
Cramphorn Theatre *CHLM/WR* CM1 ...4 E2
Cranbourne JMI School *HOD* EN11 ...185 J8
Cranbrook College *IL* IG1 ...286 D7
Cranes Industrial Estate *BSDN* SS14 ...278 C3
Cranham Health Centre *UPMR* RM14 ...291 H5
Craylands Clinic *BSDN* SS14 ...278 B6
Craylands Primary School *SWCM* DA10 ...336 A3
Crays Hill Primary School *BCAYE* CM11 ...260 A4
Creekmouth Industrial Estate *BARK* IG11 ...309 H8
Cressing Primary School *BRTR* CM77 ...122 N7
Cricketers Retail Park *PIT* SS13 ...278 C2
Cricklefield Stadium *IL* IG1 ...287 H7
Criton Industrial Estate *CDW/CHF* RM16 ...316 D6
Cromwell Business Centre *BARK* IG11 ...309 H7
Crouch Yacht Club *BCC* CM0 ...393 L9
Crowlands Primary School *ROMW/RG* RM7 ...288 D7
Crown Close Business Centre *BOW* E3 ...306 D5
Crown College *WOS/PRIT* SS0 ...18 D7
Crownfield Primary School *ROMW/RG* RM7 ...270 D7
Crown Hall *RAYL* SS6 ...280 F5
The Crown House Hotel *SAFWN* CB10 ...341 K7
Crown Pools *IP* IP1 ...16 E4
Crowstone Preparatory School *RCFD* SS4 ...283 L2
Crusader Business Park *COS* CO15 ...159 K5
Cubitt Town Primary School *POP/IOD* E14 ...322 F6
Cudmore Grove Country Park *K/T/MI* CO5 ...179 L3
Culloden Primary School *POP/IOD* E14 ...323 G2
Culver Shopping Centre *COL* CO1 ...8 C6
Cumberland Comprehensive School *CAN/RD* E16 ...323 J1

Curwen Primary School *PLSTW* E13 ...307 K6
Cygnet Clinic Beckton *EHAM* E6 ...324 E1
Cygnet Leisure Centre *GVW* DA11 ...337 H6
Cyril Jackson Primary School *POP/IOD* E14 ...322 C3
Dabchicks Sailing Club *K/T/MI* CO5 ...177 K6
Dacre Industrial Estate *CHES/WCR* EN8 ...217 G7
Dagenham Chest Clinic *BCTR* RM8 ...288 C8
Dagenham Civic Centre *DAGE* RM10 ...288 C8
Dagenham Priory Comprehensive School & Performing Arts College *DAGE* RM10 ...310 E4
Dagenham & Redbridge FC *DAGE* RM10 ...310 E2
Dagenham Superbowl *DAGE* RM10 ...310 E6
Dagenham Swimming Pool *BCTR* RM8 ...288 C7
Daiglen School *BKHH* IG9 ...249 M8
Daily Telegraph *POP/IOD* E14 ...322 D6
Dale Hall Primary School *IP* IP1 ...48 A3
Dame Johane Bradburys School *SAFWN* CB10 ...28 C1
Dame Tipping CE Primary School *ABR/ST* RM4 ...271 G2
Danbury Clinic *RCHLM* CM3 ...212 C6
Danbury Country Park *RCHLM* CM3 ...211 L6
Danbury Park Primary School *RCHLM* CM3 ...211 M6
Darent Industrial Park *ERITH* DA8 ...328 A8
Darlinghurst Primary School *LOS* SS9 ...300 C5
Dartford County Court *DART* DA1 ...334 B8
Dartford Magistrates Court *DART* DA1 ...334 A8
Dartford Tunnel *WTHK* RM20 ...335 G3
Datapoint Business Centre *CLPT* E5 ...306 B1
Daubeney Primary School *CLPT* E5 ...306 B1
Davenant Foundation School *LOU* IG10 ...235 K8
Davies Lane Infant School *WAN* E11 ...285 J7
Dawlish Primary School *LEY* E10 ...284 F7
Days Inn *RBSF* CM22 ...139 M1
The Deanes School *SBF/HAD* SS7 ...280 C7
Deans Trading Estate *RAIN* RM13 ...312 A8
Debden CE Primary School *SAFWS* CB11 ...372 H2
Debden Park High School *LOU* IG10 ...251 G3
Debden Sports Club *LOU* IG10 ...250 F5
Deben High School *FX* IP11 ...11 J1
Deben Sports Club *LOU* IG10 ...250 F5
De la Salle School *BSDN* SS14 ...3 H2
Delta Wharf *GNWCH* SE10 ...323 G5
Deneholm Primary School *CDW/CHF* RM16 ...330 F1
Dengie Hundred Sports Centre *BOC* CM0 ...393 K9
Denver Industrial Estate *RAIN* RM13 ...327 J1
Deptford Business Centre *DEPT* SE8 ...322 A8
Deptford Park Business Centre *DEPT* SE8 ...322 B8
Deptford Park Primary School *DEPT* SE8 ...322 B8
Deptford Trading Estate *DEPT* SE8 ...322 B8
Dersingham Infant School *MNPK* E12 ...308 C2
De Vere Arms Hotel *RCOLW* CO6 ...82 D6
De Vere CP School *GNWCH* SE10 ...323 H7
Dewhurst St Mary JMI School *CHES/WCR* EN8 ...216 C7
Diane Matthews Clinic *ROMW/RG* RM7 ...289 G2
Dilkes Primary School *SOCK/AV* RM15 ...329 J2
Dipple Medical Centre *PIT* SS13 ...278 C2
Docklands Medical Centre *POP/IOD* E14 ...322 D7
Docklands Sailing Centre *POP/IOD* E14 ...322 C6
Docklands Sailing & Watersports Centre *POP/IOD* E14 ...322 C6
Dockmaster's House *POP/IOD* E14 ...322 D3
Dockyard Industrial Estate *WOOL/PLUM* SE18 ...324 C6
Doddinghurst Infant School *BRWN* CM15 ...383 Q11
Doddinghurst Junior School *BRWN* CM15 ...383 Q11
Doggetts Primary School *RCFD* SS4 ...283 J2
The Dolphin Leisure Centre *ROM* RM1 ...289 J2
Dome *GNWCH* SE10 ...323 H4
Dominion Business Park *ED* N9 ...266 A1
Dominoes Health Centre *GRAYS* RM17 ...330 D5
Dorma Trading Estate *LEY* E10 ...284 A6
Dorothy Barley Primary School *BCTR* RM8 ...309 L2
Doucecroft School *K/T/MI* CO5 ...148 F2
Dovercourt Swimming Pool *HAR* CO12 ...71 G4
Dover Road Primary School *GVW* DA11 ...337 H6

Dovers Corner Industrial Estate *RAIN* RM13 ...311 J7
Downfield Primary School *CHES/WCR* EN8 ...232 B6
Down Hall Country House Hotel *RBSF* CM22 ...378 B6
Down Hall Primary School *RAYL* SS6 ...262 F8
Downham CE Primary School *BCAYE* CM11 ...259 M1
Downing Primary School *CHTY* IP2 ...53 L3
Downsell Primary School *WAN* E11 ...307 G1
Downshall Primary School *GNTH/NBYPK* IG2 ...287 H5
The Downs Primary School *HLW* CM20 ...13 H6
Drakes Lane Industrial Estate *RCHLM* CM3 ...168 E6
Drapers Sports Club *MAL* CM9 ...199 G8
Drapers Sports Ground *SRTFD* E15 ...306 F1
Drew Primary School *CAN/RD* E16 ...324 B4
Dr Walkers CE Primary School *CHONG* CM5 ...381 L7
Dry Ski Slope *RBRW/HUT* CM13 ...273 M6
Dukes Park Industrial Estate *CHLM/GWD* CM2 ...194 C8
The Dukes Priory Hospital *CHLM/WR* CM1 ...210 A1
Dunbar Wharf *POP/IOD* E14 ...322 C3
Duncan's Gate *COL* CO1 ...8 D5
Dundee Wharf *POP/IOD* E14 ...322 C3
Dunmow St Marys Primary School *GTDUN* CM6 ...116 F5
Dunmow Sports Centre *GTDUN* CM6 ...116 F3
Dunningford Primary School *HCH* RM12 ...311 J2
Durands Wharf *POP/IOD* E14 ...322 C5
Duxford Airfield *CBS* CB2 ...340 B1
Duxford CE CP School *CBS* CB2 ...22 A8
Duxford Chapel *CBS* CB2 ...22 C6
Duxford Lodge Hotel *CBS* CB2 ...340 E1
Dycourts School *HARH* RM3 ...272 D3
Earlham Primary School *FSTGT* E7 ...307 J2
Earls Colne Primary School *RCOLW* CO6 ...82 E7
Earls Hall Primary School *WOS/PRIT* SS0 ...301 G1
East Anglian Railway Museum *RCOLW* CO6 ...84 A7
East Barking Centre *BCTR* RM8 ...309 M2
East Beckton District Centre *EHAM* E6 ...324 C2
East Bergholt CE Primary School *RCOLE* CO7 ...363 Q6
East Bergholt High School *RCOLE* CO7 ...64 A1
Eastbrook Comprehensive School *DAGE* RM10 ...310 F1
Eastbrook End Cemetery *DAGE* RM10 ...289 H8
Eastbrookend Country Park *DAGE* RM10 ...311 G2
Eastbury Comprehensive School *BARK* IG11 ...309 J5
Eastbury Infant School *BARK* IG11 ...309 J4
Eastcourt Independent School *GDMY/SEVK* IG3 ...287 K6
East Essex Adult Community College *MAL* CM9 ...214 C3
East Essex Aviation Society & Museum *K/T/MI* CO5 ...180 B1
Eastfield Primary School *PEND* EN3 ...232 E8
Eastgate Business Park *LEY* E10 ...284 B6
Eastgate Centre *BSDN* SS14 ...3 G6
Eastgate Shopping Centre *IPNE* IP4 ...17 G4
East Gates Industrial Estate *COL* CO1 ...9 H7
East Greenwich Christ Church CE Primary School *GNWCH* SE10 ...323 H7
East Ham Industrial Estate *CAN/RD* E16 ...308 A8
East Ham Jewish Cemetery *EHAM* E6 ...308 B7
East Ham Leisure Centre *EHAM* E6 ...308 C6
East Ham Memorial Hospital *FSTGT* E7 ...308 A4
East Ham Nature Reserve *EHAM* E6 ...308 C8
East Hanningfield CE Primary School *RCHLM* CM3 ...227 L6
East Hanningfield Industrial Estate *RCHLM* CM3 ...227 L7
Eastlea Community Centre *CAN/RD* E16 ...307 J8
Eastlea Community School *CAN/RD* E16 ...307 H8
East London Business College *WAN* E11 ...285 H6
East London Cemetery *PLSTW* E13 ...307 J2
East London Crematorium *PLSTW* E13 ...307 J7
East London RFC *EHAM* E6 ...308 C4
East London RUFC *PLSTW* E13 ...307 G7
East Thamesmead Business Park *ERITHM* DA18 ...326 C5
East Thurrock FC *SLH/COR* SS17 ...317 L2
East Tilbury J & I Schools *TIL* RM18 ...332 F4
Eastwood GM Infant School *LOS* SS9 ...282 C8
Eastwood High School *LOS* SS9 ...282 C8
Eastwood Industrial Estate *LOS* SS9 ...281 M7
Eastwood Primary School *LOS* SS9 ...282 C7
The Eastwood School *LOS* SS9 ...282 B8

Eaton Manor RFC WAN E11 ...285 M3
Ebbsfleet Industrial Estate GVW DA11 ...336 D3
Edinburgh Primary School WALTH E17 ...284 C3
Edith Borthwick School BRTR CM7 ...99 J5
Edward Francis Junior School RAYL SS6 ...281 G2
Edwards Hall Primary School LOS SS9 ...281 M6
Edwin Lambert School EMPK RM11 ...289 K4
Eight Ash Green CE Primary School COLW CO3 ...105 J4
Elbourne Trading Estate BELV DA17 ...326 E6
Eldenwall Industrial Estate BCTR RM8 ...288 B6
Eldon Way Industrial Estate HOC/HUL SS5 ...264 B7
Eleanor Estate CHES/WCR EN8 ...233 G4
Eleanor Smith Special School PLSTW E13 ...307 K6
Electric Palace Cinema CO CO12 ...15 L3
Elizabeth Orwell Hotel FX IP11 ...63 G8
Ellen Wilkinson Primary School EHAM E6 ...324 A1
Elm Green Preparatory School RCHLM CM3 ...212 A2
Elm Hall CP School WIT CM8 ...147 J7
Elmhurst Primary School FSTGT E7 ...307 L4
Elms Business Park WICKW SS12 ...279 H1
Elms Industrial Estate HARH RM3 ...272 E6
Elmstead CP School RCOLE CO7 ...109 K6
Elmwood Primary School RCHLM CM3 ...245 G6
Elsenham Primary School RBSF CM22 ...374 E4
Elton Park Business Centre CHTY IP2 ...47 K7
Elton Park Industrial Estate CHTY IP2 ...47 K7
Embroidery World Business Centre WFD IG8 ...268 A8
Emd Walthamstow Cinema WALTH E17 ...284 D2
Emerson Park School EMPK RM11 ...290 E5
Emery Theatre POP/IOD E14 ...322 E2
Empire Cinema HSTD CO9 ...81 G3
The Endeavour School BRWN CM15 ...256 C5
Enfield Crematorium EN EN1 ...232 C7
Engaines Primary School RCOS CO16 ...158 D3
Engayne Primary School UPMR RM14 ...291 H4
Enterprise Business Park POP/IOD E14 ...322 E2
Enterprise Trading Estate BRTR CM77 ...120 C4
Epping CE Primary School EPP CM16 ...219 H2
Epping County Infant School EPP CM16 ...219 M7
Epping Forest Conservation Centre LOU IG10 ...234 D8
Epping Forest District Museum WAB EN9 ...233 K3
Epping Forest Tertiary College LOU IG10 ...250 E3
The Epping Golf Course EPP CM16 ...236 C3
Epping Junior School EPP CM16 ...220 A8
Epping Ongar Railway CHONG CM5 ...382 F1
  EPP CM16 ...220 C8
Epping Sports Centre EPP CM16 ...236 C4
Erith Library & Museum ERITH DA8 ...327 H8
Erith Playhouse ERITH DA8 ...327 J8
Erlsmere Hotel WOS/PRIT SS0 ...18 A6
Esplanade Hotel COS CO15 ...7 H8
Essex Agricultural Showground RCHLM CM3 ...144 D3
Essex County Council Youth Camp K/T/MI CO5 ...178 F6
Essex CCC (County Ground) CHLM/GWD CM2 ...5 G4
Essex County Hospital COLW CO3 ...107 G7
Essex Cricket School CHLM/GWD CM2 ...4 F4
The Essex Golf & Country Club RCOLW CO6 ...102 C3
The Essex Nuffield Hospital BRWN CM15 ...256 B4
Essex Primary School MNPK E12 ...308 B3
Ethel Davis School CHDH RM6 ...287 L3
Euro Business Centre SRTFD E15 ...307 J5
Europa Trading Estate ERITH DA8 ...327 G8
  WTHK RM20 ...330 A4
Euro Retail Park IPSE IP3 ...55 J4
Everest Sports Club CHES/WCR EN8 ...216 C7
Everik Business Centre RBRW/HUT CM13 ...257 H1
Eversley College SBW CM21 ...162 E7
Eversley Primary School PIT SS13 ...279 G7
ExCeL Exhibition Centre CAN/RD E16 ...323 L3
The Exchange IL IG1 ...286 E7
Express by Holiday Inn BKHH IG9 ...267 L1
  CAN/RD E16 ...323 H2
  CHING E4 ...266 D6
  DART DA1 ...334 E6
  GNWCH SE10 ...323 J6
  RAYL SS6 ...280 F5
  RIPW IP8 ...52 F1
  SRTFD E15 ...306 E6

The Faircross Complementary Medical Centre BARK IG11 ...309 H3
Fairfield Clinic BKHH IG9 ...249 L8
Fairfield Infant School IP IP1 ...62 F8
Fairfields Primary School CHESW EN7 ...216 B5
Fairhouse J & I School BSDN SS14 ...3 L6
  BSDN SS14 ...278 A7
Fairlop Primary School BARK/HLT IG6 ...268 F7
Fairview Industrial Estate DAGW RM9 ...327 G2
Fairway Medical Centre LOS SS9 ...300 A1
Fairways Business Park LEY E10 ...284 B7
Fairways Primary School LOS SS9 ...299 M1
Farnham CE Primary School BSF CM23 ...114 E3
Farnham Green Primary School GDMY/SEVK IG3 ...287 K4
Farthing Road Industrial Estate IP IP1 ...47 J6
Fawbert & Barnards Primary School HLWE CM17 ...188 D6
Feering Primary School K/T/MI CO5 ...149 H1
Felixstowe Leisure Centre FX IP11 ...68 E2
Felixstowe Cemetery FX IP11 ...11 H1
Felixstowe College FX IP11 ...69 H4
Felixstowe Ferry Golf Club FX IP11 ...63 K6
Felixstowe Ferry Sailing Club FX IP11 ...63 L3
Felixstowe General Hospital FX IP11 ...68 F1
Felixstowe International College FX IP11 ...63 H8
Felixstowe Leisure Centre FX IP11 ...11 K4
Felixstowe Pier FX IP11 ...11 L4
Felixstowe RFC FX IP11 ...10 F3
Felixstowe & Walton FC FX IP11 ...62 F7
Felstead Vineyard RCHLM CM3 ...120 A7
Felsted CP School GTDUN CM6 ...119 G6
Felsted Preparatory School GTDUN CM6 ...118 E8
Ferry Lane Industrial Estate RAIN RM13 ...327 K1
Festival Leisure Park BSDN SS14 ...277 L4
Financial Times POP/IOD E14 ...322 F2
Finchingfield CE Primary School BRTR CM7 ...354 C11
Finchingfield Guildhall & Museum BRTR CM7 ...354 C11
Fingringhoe CE Primary School K/T/MI CO5 ...130 C8
Firepower (Museum of Artillery) WOOL/PLUM SE18 ...324 E6
The Firs Junior School BSF CM23 ...138 F3
Fisher Athletic FC BERM/RHTH SE16 ...322 A4
Fitness Unlimited Leisure Centre BOW E3 ...306 D6
The Fitzwimarc School RAYL SS6 ...281 H2
Five Elms Primary School DAGW RM9 ...288 C8
Five Lakes Hotel, Golf, Country Club & Spa MAL CM9 ...175 J5
Flamstead End Primary School CHESW EN7 ...216 B5
Flatford Bridge Cottage (NT) RCOLE CO7 ...64 A6
Fleetway Sports Club GVE DA12 ...337 M6
Flitch Industrial Estate GTDUN CM6 ...117 G6
Flix Cinema RCHLM CM3 ...245 H6
Florence Nightingale Health Centre HLWE CM17 ...204 D1
Fondu Sports Club PUR RM19 ...328 F7
Ford End CE Primary School BELV DA17 ...142 A7
Fordgate Business Park BELV DA17 ...326 F5
Fordham All Saints CE Primary School RCOLW CO6 ...105 G1
Ford Industrial Park DAGW RM9 ...310 E7
Ford Road Industrial Estate COS CO15 ...6 D6
Fordview Industrial Estate RAIN RM13 ...311 G7
Forest Business Park WALTH E17 ...284 A5
Forest Gate Community School FSTGT E7 ...307 K2
Forest House Business Centre WAN E11 ...285 J5
Forest Industrial Park BARK/HLT IG6 ...269 H6
Forest Medical Centre LOU IG10 ...250 B5
Forest Park Cemetery & Crematorium BARK/HLT IG6 ...269 M4
Fore Street Pool IPNE IP4 ...17 H6
Forest Road Medical Centre WALTH E17 ...284 C1
Forest School WALTH E17 ...285 H2
Forest Trading Estate WALTH E17 ...284 A1
The Former Health Centre CHARL SE7 ...324 A1
Forres CP School HOD EN11 ...185 J4
Forrester Park Golf & Tennis Club MAL CM9 ...172 F8
Forty Hall ENC/FH EN2 ...232 A7
Forty Hill CE Primary School EN EN1 ...232 B7
Fossetone Primary School CHARL SE7 ...323 L8
Four Seasons Hotel POP/IOD E14 ...322 C4
Four Swannes Primary School CHES/WCR EN8 ...232 F4

Foxfield Primary School WOOL/PLUM SE18 ...324 F8
Foxhall Heath Stadium IPNE IP4 ...49 M5
Frances Bardsley School for Girls ROM RM1 ...289 K3
Freeport Retail Village BRTR CM7 ...121 L4
Free Trade Wharf WAP E1W ...322 A3
Freight Services Office HAR CO12 ...14 B4
Freshwell Health Centre BRTR CM7 ...354 C11
Fresh Wharf Estate BARK IG11 ...308 C5
Friars Clinic SUD CO10 ...20 C7
Friars Grove Infant School COLN CO4 ...107 M3
Friars Grove Junior School COLN CO4 ...9 J1
Friars Primary School SBN/FI SS3 ...303 J5
Friends School SAFWS CB11 ...30 B1
Frinton Golf Club FOS CO13 ...137 H7
Frinton-on-Sea Lawn Tennis Club FOS CO13 ...137 H6
Frinton-on-Sea Primary School FOS CO13 ...137 H4
Frinton Road Medical Centre COS CO15 ...160 A3
Frinton Summer Theatre FOS CO13 ...137 J4
The Frinton & Walton Heritage Museum WOTN CO14 ...369 N11
Frinton & Walton Swimming Pool WOTN CO14 ...369 N12
Frobisher Primary School COS CO15 ...182 C4
Frost Business Centre BRTR CM77 ...122 F2
The Fryerns Medical Centre BSDN SS14 ...278 B5
Fullmen Industrial Park CVI SS8 ...319 M2
Fullwell Cross Health Centre BARK/HLT IG6 ...268 F8
Fullwell Cross Swimming Pool & Recreation Centre BARK/HLT IG6 ...268 F8
Fullwood Primary School BARK/HLT IG6 ...286 F2
Funland SOS SS1 ...19 K7
Furze Infant School CHDH RM6 ...288 B4
Gable Hall School SLH/COR SS17 ...295 J8
Gainsborough Primary School HOM E9 ...306 C3
  SRTFD E15 ...307 H7
Gainsborough's House SUD CO10 ...20 C6
Gainsborough Sports Centre IPSE IP3 ...55 J5
Galley Hill Industrial Estate SWCM DA10 ...336 G5
Galleywood Infant School CHLM/GWD CM2 ...225 L3
Galliford Road Industrial Estate MAL CM9 ...214 D1
Gallions Mount Primary School WOOL/PLUM SE18 ...325 J8
Gallions Primary School EHAM E6 ...324 E2
Gallions Reach Shopping Park EHAM E6 ...324 E1
Ganges Museum RIPS/CAP IP9 ...67 H5
Gants Hill Medical Centre GNTH IG2 ...286 D4
Garon Park Track SOS SS2 ...302 A1
Gascoigne Primary School BARK IG11 ...308 C5
Gatehouse School BETH ...306 A6
Gateway Business Centre WOOL/PLUM SE18 ...324 F6
Gateway Community College North CDW/CHF RM16 ...331 J1
Gaynes School UPMR RM14 ...312 F2
Gearies Infant School GNTH/NBYPK IG2 ...286 D3
Gearies Junior School GNTH/NBYPK IG2 ...286 E3
Gemini Business Estate NWCR SE14 ...322 A8
The Geoffrey Lloyd Foulkes Clinic IL IG1 ...286 D7
George Green School POP/IOD E14 ...322 F8
George Hotel COL CO1 ...8 C6
George Mitchell School LEY E10 ...284 E6
George Tomlinson Primary School WAN E11 ...285 H6
George Yard Shopping Centre BRTR CM7 ...121 H2
Ghyllgrove Primary School BSDN SS14 ...2 F4
Gidea Park College GPK RM2 ...289 K1
Gidea Park Primary School GPK RM2 ...289 J2
Gidea Park Sports Ground GPK RM2 ...271 M8
Giffards Primary School SLH/COR SS17 ...317 J1
The Gilberd School COLN CO4 ...87 L8
Gilbert Colvin Primary School CLAY IG5 ...268 D7
The Glade Business Centre WTHK RM20 ...329 J8
Glade Primary School CLAY IG5 ...268 C7
Glebe Infant School RAYL SS6 ...280 F2
Glebe Junior School RAYL SS6 ...280 F2
Glenham College IL IG1 ...286 E7
Glenwood Special School SBF/HAD SS7 ...279 K6
Globe Industrial Estate GRAYS RM17 ...330 F5
Globe Wharf BERM/RHTH SE16 ...322 A3
Globe Works Industrial Estate GRAYS RM17 ...330 F4
Gloucester Park Athletic Stadium BSDN SS14 ...2 D2

Gloucester Park Swimming Pool LAIN SS15 ...2 D5
Godwin Junior School FSTGT E7 ...307 L1
Goffs School CHESW EN7 ...216 B7
Goldings Hill Clinic LOU IG10 ...250 D2
Golds Nurseries Business Park RBSF CM22 ...374 D2
Goodmayes Retail Park CHDH RM6 ...287 L5
Gordon Infant School IL IG1 ...287 G8
Goresbrook Leisure Centre DAGW RM9 ...310 A5
Goresbrook Sports Centre DAGW RM9 ...310 A5
Goseland Primary School KESG IP5 ...50 C5
Gorse Lane Industrial Estate COS CO15 ...159 L5
Gosbecks Primary School COLS CO2 ...128 D2
Gosfield Community Primary School HSTD CO9 ...80 B5
Gosfield Lake Golf Club HSTD CO9 ...79 M5
Gosfield School HSTD CO9 ...80 C3
Gosforth Primary School REDBR IG4 ...286 C6
Gove Farm Retail Park CHDH RM6 ...287 M6
Grafton Primary School BCTR RM8 ...288 D7
Grainger Road Industrial Estate SOSN SS2 ...19 G2
Grange Barn (NT) RCOLW CO6 ...124 C4
Grange Infant School GVE DA12 ...337 J4
Grange Paddocks Pool & Gym BSF CM23 ...115 G8
Grange Park Industrial Estate COLS CO2 ...130 A2
Grange Primary School FX IP11 ...10 D1
  WICKW SS12 ...260 E7
Grange Way Business Park COLS CO2 ...130 A2
Grangewood Independent School FSTGT E7 ...308 A4
Gravesend County Court GVE DA12 ...337 L4
Gravesend CC GVW DA11 ...337 K5
Gravesend Grammar School GVE DA12 ...338 A5
Gravesend Grammar School for Girls GVW DA11 ...337 K6
Gravesend Museum GVE DA12 ...337 L4
Gravesend & Northfleet FC GVW DA11 ...336 D3
Gravesend & North Kent Hospital GVW DA11 ...337 K4
Gravesend Rowing Club GVE DA12 ...337 M4
Gravesend Yacht Club GVE DA12 ...338 A4
Grays Athletic FC GRAYS RM17 ...330 E5
Grays Business Centre GRAYS RM17 ...330 E5
Grays Convent School GRAYS RM17 ...330 E5
Grays County Court GRAYS RM17 ...330 D5
Grays Health Centre GRAYS RM17 ...330 D4
The Grays School GRAYS RM17 ...330 E5
Great Abington Primary School CBE/LIN CB1 ...23 M3
Great Baddow High School CHLM/GWD CM2 ...210 A4
Great Bardfield Primary School BRTR CM7 ...76 E3
Great Bentley Primary School RCOLE CO7 ...133 C6
Great Berry Primary School VGE SS16 ...294 C1
Great Bradfords Primary School BRTR CM7 ...121 L1
Great Bromley St Georges CE Primary School RCOLE CO7 ...110 B4
Great Chesterford Primary School SAFWN CB10 ...341 L1
Great Cornard Upper School SUD CO10 ...45 L5
The Great Dunmow Maltings Museum GTDUN CM6 ...117 G3
Great Dunmow Primary School GTDUN CM6 ...116 F4
Great Easton CE Primary School GTDUN CM6 ...94 C3
Great Leighs Primary School RCHLM CM3 ...144 C3
Great Leighs Racecourse (open 2006) RCHLM CM3 ...144 C2
Great Oakley CE Primary School HAR CO12 ...113 L2
Great Oaks Clinic BSDN SS14 ...2 E6
Great Sampford CP School SAFWN CB10 ...353 K5
Great Stony School CHONG CM5 ...382 H1
Great Tey CE Primary School RCOLW CO6 ...103 M4
Great Totham CP School MAL CM9 ...172 D6
The Great Wakering Health Centre SBN/FI SS3 ...303 J1
Great Wakering Primary School SBN/FI SS3 ...303 J1
Great Wakering Sports Centre SBN/FI SS3 ...303 J1
Great Waltham Primary School RCHLM CM3 ...167 H6
Greengate Medical Centre PLSTW E13 ...307 G2
Greenhithe Health Clinic GRH DA9 ...335 L7
Greenland Pier POP/IOD E14 ...322 C6
Greenleaf Primary School WALTH E17 ...284 D1
The Green Man Hotel HLWE CM17 ...188 D5
Greenshields Industrial Estate CAN/RD E16 ...323 K4
Greenstead Clinic COLN CO4 ...108 D5
Greenstead St Andrews Primary School COLN CO4 ...108 B6
Greensted Primary School BSDN SS14 ...278 C4

Greensward College HOC/HUL SS5 ...264 B8
Greenwich Business Park IPSE IP3 ...54 C7
Greenwich Community College WOOL/PLUM SE18 ...324 C4
Greenwich Industrial Estate CHARL SE7 ...323 L7
Greenwich Pier POP/IOD E14 ...322 F6
Greenwood School WAN E11 ...81 J4
Greenwoods Estate Health Spa & Retreat ING CM4 ...241 H4
Greyhound Trading Park SOSN SS2 ...19 H2
The Grip Industrial Estate CBE/LIN CB1 ...23 M2
The Grove Centre WIT CM8 ...171 K8
Grove Medical Centre DEPT SE8 ...322 E7
Grove Primary School CHDH RM6 ...287 L8
  RAYL SS6 ...281 G2
Grove Tennis Club CHLM/GWD CM2 ...5 G5
Grundy Park Leisure Centre CHES/WCR EN8 ...216 F8
Guardian Angels RC Primary School BOW E3 ...306 B8
Guardian Business Centre HARH RM3 ...272 A4
Guardian Newspapers POP/IOD E14 ...322 E2
Gulpher Business Park FX IP11 ...62 F4
Guru Gobind Singh Khalsa College CHIG IG7 ...250 C4
Guru Nanak Sports Club GVE DA12 ...337 H4
Gusford Primary School CHTY IP2 ...53 J4
Gwyn Jones Primary School WAN E11 ...285 G4
GX Superbowl EHAM E6 ...324 B4
Hackney Sports Centre HOM E9 ...306 D2
Hacton Primary School HARH RM12 ...312 B8
Hadleigh Business Centre SBF/HAD SS7 ...299 H3
Hadleigh Castle SBF/HAD SS7 ...299 G5
Hadleigh Castle Country Park SBF/HAD SS7 ...298 E5
Hadleigh Clinic SBF/HAD SS7 ...298 F5
Hadleigh Junior School SBF/HAD SS7 ...299 G5
Hadleigh Road Industrial Estate CHTY IP2 ...47 J5
Haileybury College HERT/BAY SG13 ...184 F5
Haileybury College Track HERT/BAY SG13 ...184 E5
Hailey Hall Special School HOD EN11 ...185 J5
Hailey Road Business Park ERITHM DA18 ...326 D5
Hainault Business Park BARK/HLT IG6 ...269 M4
Hainault Forest Country Park CHIG IG7 ...270 A2
Hainault Forest Golf Club CHIG IG7 ...270 A2
Hainault Forest High School & the Learning Centre BARK/HLT IG6 ...269 K4
Half Moon Theatre WCHPL E1 ...306 C5
Halifax Primary School CHTY IP2 ...54 A3
Halley Primary School POP/IOD E14 ...322 B1
Hallmark Industrial Estate FOS CO13 ...393 P5
Hall Mead School UPMR RM14 ...291 G5
Hall Road Industrial Estate BOC CM0 ...393 P1
Hallsford Bridge Industrial Estate CHONG CM5 ...383 G5
Hallsford Business Centre CHONG CM5 ...383 H5
Hallsville Primary School CAN/RD E16 ...323 H3
Halstead Industrial Estate HSTD CO9 ...81 J2
Halstead Hospital HSTD CO9 ...81 H2
Halstead Town FC HSTD CO9 ...81 H2
Halstow Primary School GNWCH SE10 ...323 H8
Hamer Indoor Market BOW E3 ...306 C5
Hamford CP School FOS CO13 ...137 J2
Hamilton Primary School COLW CO3 ...107 G5
Hamlet International Industrial Estate ERITH DA8 ...327 G5
Hamstel Primary School SOSN SS2 ...302 A5
Handford Hall Primary School IP IP1 ...16 A2
Handsworth Health Clinic CHING E4 ...267 G2
Handsworth Primary School CHING E4 ...267 G2
Harbinger Primary School POP/IOD E14 ...322 C2
Hare Street Primary School HLWW/ROY CM19 ...12 A4
Harlowbury Primary School HLWE CM17 ...188 B5
Harlow Business Park HLWW/ROY CM19 ...12 B4
Harlow College HLW CM20 ...13 G2
  HLW CM20 ...13 J1
Harlow Museum (Passmores House) HLWS CM18 ...12 F5
Harlow RFC HLW CM20 ...13 L4
Harlow Sailing Club RCHLM CM3 ...144 C8
Harlow Sports Centre HLW CM20 ...13 H2
Harlow Swimming Pool HLW CM20 ...13 J1
Harold Court Primary School HARH RM3 ...272 C5
Harold Wood Clinic HARH RM3 ...272 C5
Harold Wood JMI School HARH RM3 ...290 D1

Hartley Primary School
  EHAM E6 ....308 B5
The Hartswood Clinic
  RBRW/HUT CM13 ....273 L5
Hartswood Golf Club
  BRW CM14 ....256 B7
Harvey Centre
  HLW CM20 ....13 G6
Harwich Community
  Primary School
  HAR CO12 ....15 L6
Harwich & District Hospital
  HAR CO12 ....14 D9
Harwich & Dovercourt Golf Club
  HAR CO12 ....70 E1
Harwich Industrial Estate
  HAR CO12 ....14 B5
Harwich & Parkeston FC
  HAR CO12 ....15 G8
Harwich Primary School
  HAR CO12 ....15 L5
Harwich Redoubt Fort
  HAR CO12 ....15 L5
Harwich School
  HAR CO12 ....70 F3
Harwich Sports Centre
  HAR CO12 ....70 F3
Harwich Town Sailing Club
  HAR CO12 ....15 L3
Harwood Equestrian Centre
  UPMR RM14 ....312 E3
Haslemere Industrial Estate
  BSF CB23 ....139 H5
  HLWW/ROY CM19 ....12 A7
Hassenbrook School
  SLH/COR SS17 ....317 H3
Hassengate Medical Centre
  SLH/COR SS17 ....316 C3
Hastingwood Business Centre
  HLWE CM17 ....204 D3
Hastingwood Trading Estate
  UED N18 ....266 B5
Hatfield Forest (NT)
  RBSF CM22 ....376 F4
Hatfield Heath Primary School
  RBSF CM22 ....378 A3
Hatfield Peverel Infant School
  RCHLM CM3 ....196 E2
Hatton School
  REDBR IG4 ....286 A1
Haverhill Golf Club
  HVHL CB9 ....35 H7
Haverhill Leisure Centre
  HVHL CB9 ....34 E6
Haverhill Rovers FC
  HVHL CB9 ....34 D7
Havering College
  HARH RM3 ....272 C3
Havering College of FE & HE
  EMPK RM11 ....289 L5
  EMPK RM11 ....290 B2
Havering Country Park
  ABR/ST RM4 ....271 G3
Havering CC
  ABR/ST RM4 ....253 J2
Havering Hospitals
  HARH RM3 ....272 C3
Havering Magistrates Court
  ROM RM1 ....289 H2
Havering Sixth Form College
  EMPK RM11 ....290 C6
The Havers School
  BSF CB23 ....138 F4
Hawksmoor Primary School
  THMD SE28 ....325 L3
Hawkswood School & Centre
  CHING E4 ....248 F5
The Hayward Special School
  CHLM/WR CM1 ....209 K1
Hazelmere Infant School
  COLN CO4 ....108 B5
Heathcote School
  RCHLM CM3 ....212 B6
Heathcote Secondary School
  CHING E4 ....267 H1
Heathlands CE Primary School
  RCOLW CO6 ....86 B8
Heath Primary School
  KESG IP5 ....50 A6
The Heath School
  COLW CO3 ....106 A8
Heathside Special School
  IPNE IP4 ....49 H4
Heathway Industrial Estate
  DAGE RM10 ....310 E1
Heathway Medical Centre
  DAGW RM9 ....310 C1
Heckford Street
  Business Centre WAP E1W 322 A3
Hedgerows Business Park
  CHLM/WR CM1 ....194 D7
Hedges & Butler Estate
  SRTFD E15 ....306 C1
Hedingham Castle
  HSTD CO9 ....356 G5
Hedingham School
  HSTD CO9 ....356 E6
Helena Romanes School
  GTDUN CM6 ....116 F3
Henham & Ugley
  Primary School RBSF CM22 ..372 G12
Henry Green Primary School
  BCTR RM8 ....288 A6
Henry Maynard Junior School
  WALTH E17 ....284 F1
The Hereward County School
  LOU IG10 ....250 F1
Herington House School
  RBRW/HUT CM13 ....256 F2
Heron Industrial Estate
  SRTFD E15 ....306 E6
Herongate Primary School
  THMD SE28 ....325 G6
Herons Gate Trading Estate
  BSDN SW14 ....278 D3
Herringham Primary School
  CDW/CHF RM16 ....331 L2
Hertford Regional College
  WARE SG12 ....184 E1
Hertford Regional College
  (Northgate Centre)
  BSF CB23 ....139 G1
Hertfordshire & Essex
  Community Hospital
  BSF CB23 ....139 K3
Hertfordshire & Essex
  High School BSF CB23 ....139 J3
Hester House
  HLW CM20 ....12 E3
Heybridge CP School
  MAL CM9 ....198 F8
Heybridge House
  Industrial Estate MAL CM9 ..214 V1
Heybridge Swifts FC
  MAL CM9 ....199 G7
Heydon Grange Golf &
  Country Club ROY SG8 ....349 J2
Higham Primary School
  HOO/HM ME3 ....339 M8

Highams Lodge Business Centre
  WALTH E17 ....284 A1
Highams Park School
  CHING E4 ....267 G5
High Beech CE Primary School
  LOU IG10 ....249 K1
High Beech Golf Club
  LOU IG10 ....234 C7
Highbridge Retail Park
  WAB EN9 ....233 J4
High Chelmer Shopping Centre
  CHLM/WR CM1 ....5 G3
Highfields Primary School
  MGTR CO11 ....90 F1
Highlands J & I School
  IL IG1 ....286 C6
Highlands Primary School
  IL IG1 ....286 C6
High Ongar Primary School
  CHONG CM5 ....383 K1
High Street Business Park
  CHES/WCR EN8 ....232 F2
The Highway Trading Centre
  WCHPL E1 ....322 A3
High Wood Hospital
  BRWN CM15 ....255 L8
Highwood Primary School
  CHLM/WR CM1 ....223 K1
Highwoods Community
  Primary School COLN CO4 ..107 L1
High Woods Country Park
  COLN CO4 ....107 K2
Hilldene Primary School
  HARH RM3 ....271 M5
Hill Farm Industrial Estate
  BSF CM23 ....362 B11
Hillgrove Business Park
  WAB EN9 ....201 K8
Hillmead JMI School
  BSF CM23 ....115 K8
Hillmead Primary School
  BSF CM23 ....138 D2
Hillside Community
  Primary School CHTY IP2 ....16 E9
Hillside Special School
  SUD CO10 ....20 C1
Hilltop Primary School
  WICKE SS11 ....261 K5
Hillyfield Primary School
  WALTH E17 ....284 B1
Hilton Docklands Pier
  POP/IOD E14 ....322 C4
The Hiltongrove
  Business Centre
  WALTH E17 ....284 D2
Hinguar Primary School
  SBN/FI SS3 ....303 J6
HM Prison
  CHLM/GWD CM2 ....5 M2
  THMD SE28 ....325 H6
Hoblongs Industrial Estate
  GTDUN CM6 ....117 H7
Hockerill Anglo European
  College BSF CM23 ....139 H2
Hockerill Sports Club
  BSF CM23 ....139 J4
Hockley Primary School
  HOC/HUL SS5 ....263 M7
Hoddesdon Health Centre
  HOD EN11 ....201 H4
Hoddesdon Industrial Estate
  HOD EN11 ....201 K2
Hoddesdon Lawn Tennis Club
  HOD EN11 ....201 G3
Hogarth Primary School
  BRWN CM15 ....256 B5
Holborn College
  WOOL/PLUM SE18 ....324 A7
Holbrook CP School
  RIPS/CAP IP9 ....364 G7
Holbrook High School
  RIPS/CAP IP9 ....364 G7
Holdbrook Primary School
  CHES/WCR EN8 ....233 G4
Holiday Inn
  BRW CM14 ....273 H3
  COLW CO3 ....105 J4
  RIPW IP8 ....53 G2
Holiday Park
  RCOS CO16 ....181 M6
Holland Haven Primary School
  COS CO15 ....160 B3
Holland Park Primary School
  COS CO15 ....7 L2
Holly House Private Hospital
  BKHH IG9 ....267 L1
Hollytrees Junior School
  BRW CM14 ....273 L3
Hollytrees Museum
  COL CO1 ....8 D6
Holly Trees Primary School
  BRW CM14 ....273 M3
Hollywood Bowl
  BSDN SW14 ....277 L4
Holmwood House School
  COLW CO3 ....106 A5
Holt Farm Infant School
  RCFD SS4 ....283 G2
Holy Cross Catholic
  Primary School HLWS CM18 ..204 B3
Holy Cross RC Primary School
  SOCK/AV RM15 ....329 L1
Holy Family RC Primary School
  POP/IOD E14 ....322 D3
  SBF/HAD SS7 ....298 A1
  WIT CM8 ....171 J4
Holy Family Technology
  College WALTH E17 ....284 E2
Holy Trinity CE Primary School
  GVE DA12 ....337 M5
  HSTD CO9 ....81 C3
Holy Trinity Museum of
  Social History COL CO1 ....8 C7
Holy Trinity Primary School
  CHES/WCR EN8 ....232 E2
Holywells High School
  IPSE IP3 ....55 G1
Home Farm CP School
  COLW CO3 ....106 C3
Home Farm Industrial Estate
  WARE SG12 ....186 A4
Homerton Hospital
  CLPT E5 ....306 A2
Homestead Special School
  COLU CO4 ....88 B1
Homoeopathic Health Centre
  PLSTW E13 ....307 K8
The Honeywood School
  RCOLW CO6 ....124 D2
Honilands Primary School
  EN EN1 ....232 C6
Horizon Business Centre
  ED N9 ....266 A1
Hornchurch Clinic
  EMPK RM11 ....290 B6
Hornchurch Country Park
  HCH RM12 ....311 M3
Hornchurch Sports Centre
  EMPK RM11 ....289 M7

Hornchurch Stadium
  UPMR RM14 ....290 D7
Horndon Industrial Park
  RBRW/HUT CM13 ....274 E8
Horndon on the Hill CE
  Primary School
  SLH/COR SS17 ....316 C1
Horn Stairs
  POP/IOD E14 ....322 C4
Hotel Continental
  HAR CO12 ....15 H9
Hotel Ibis
  BARK IG11 ....308 E5
  POP/IOD E14 ....322 F3
  SRTFD E15 ....307 H3
  WTHK RM20 ....335 J1
House on the Hill Museum
  Adventure STSD CM24 ....374 A6
Howard Business Park
  WAB EN9 ....233 H3
Howard Hall
  BRTR CM7 ....121 J1
Howbridge CE Junior School
  WIT CM8 ....171 J5
Howe Green House School
  RBSE CM22 ....139 J4
Howland Quay
  BERM/RHTH SE16 ....322 A6
HSBC Tower
  POP/IOD E14 ....322 E4
Hubbinet Industrial Estate
  ROMW/RG RM7 ....288 F1
Hullbridge Clinic
  HOC/HUL SS5 ....263 G9
Hullbridge Sports Club
  HOC/HUL SS5 ....263 H4
Hunters Hall Primary School
  DAGE RM10 ....310 E2
Hurst Drive Primary School
  CHES/WCR EN8 ....232 D4
Hutton All Saints CE Primary
  School RBRW/HUT CM13 ....257 G2
Hutton Clinic
  RBRW/HUT CM13 ....257 G1
Hyderabad Barracks
  COLS CO2 ....107 K8
Hyland House School
  WALTH E17 ....267 G3
Hylands Golf Club
  ING CM4 ....224 E3
Hylands House & Park
  CHLM/WR CM1 ....208 F8
Hylands School
  CHLM/WR CM1 ....209 G3
Hyleford Leavers Unit School
  BARK/HLT IG6 ....269 G3
Hyleford School
  IL IG1 ....309 H2
Ian Mikardo High School
  BOW E3 ....306 E7
Icknield Primary School
  CBS CB2 ....22 D1
IKEA Store Lakeside
  WTHK RM20 ....329 L8
Ilford County Court
  IL IG1 ....287 G7
Ilford County High School
  BARK/HLT IG6 ....268 F3
Ilford Golf Club
  IL IG1 ....286 F8
Ilford Jewish Primary School
  BARK/HLT IG6 ....268 D4
Ilford Medical Centre
  IL IG1 ....286 E8
Ilford Preparatory School
  GDMY/SEVK IG3 ....287 J6
Ilford Retail Park
  IL IG1 ....286 F7
Ilford Swimming Pool
  IL IG1 ....287 G7
Ilford Trading Estate
  BSDN SW14 ....278 B3
Immanuel School
  ROM RM1 ....271 H5
Imperial Retail Park
  GVW DA11 ....337 K4
Imperial Trading Estate
  RAIN RM13 ....311 M8
Infant College
  IL IG1 ....286 D7
Ingatestone & Fryerning CE
  Junior School ING CM4 ....239 K1
Ingatestone Infant School
  ING CM4 ....239 K1
Ingrave Johnstone CE Primary
  School RBRW/HUT CM13 ....274 F1
Ingrebourne Primary School
  HARH RM3 ....271 M3
Innkeeper's Lodge
  WICKE SS11 ....261 L2
Innova Business Park
  PEND EN3 ....233 G6
International Business Centre
  CVI SS8 ....320 A2
International Business Park
  CVI SS8 ....319 M2
Invicta Industrial Estate
  SRTFD E15 ....306 F1
Invicta Sports Club
  DART DA1 ....334 A7
Ipswich Airport (disused)
  IPSW IP3 ....55 H5
Ipswich Crematorium
  IPNE IP4 ....48 E5
Ipswich Golf Club
  IPSE IP3 ....55 L3
Ipswich High School GDST
  RIPS/CAP IP9 ....365 M1
Ipswich Hospital
  IPNE IP4 ....49 H1
Ipswich Museums & Galleries
  IP IP1 ....16 E3
Ipswich Regent Theatre
  IPNE IP4 ....16 F2
Ipswich RUFC
  KESG IP5 ....51 L1
Ipswich School
  IP IP1 ....16 E1
Ipswich School Pre-Preparatory
  Department IP IP1 ....16 D2
Ipswich Sports Club
  IP IP1 ....48 B4
Ipswich Town FC (Portman Rd)
  IP IP1 ....16 C5
Ipswich Transport Museum
  IPSE IP3 ....55 H7
Island Clinic
  POP/IOD E14 ....322 C1
Ivanhurst Industrial Estate
  RCHLM CM3 ....262 A1
Ivry Street Medical Practice
  IP IP1 ....16 D1
Ivy Chimneys Primary School
  EPP CM16 ....236 A2
Ivy Street Primary School
  MGTR CO11 ....366 D6
The James Hornsby School
  LAIN SS15 ....277 G6

James Oglethorpe Primary
  School UPMR RM14 ....291 J7
Janet Duke Primary School
  LAIN SS15 ....277 G7
Jenny Hammond
  Primary School WAN E11 ....307 H1
Jerounds J & I School
  HLWW/ROY CM19 ....203 J4
The Joe Richardson Community
  School DAGW RM9 ....310 A5
John Bramston Primary School
  BARK/HLT IG6 ....269 K5
John Bunyan J & I School
  LAIN SS15 ....121 H1
John Falkner Infant School
  CBS CB2 ....22 B2
John F Kennedy
  Special School
  SRTFD E15 ....307 G5
The John Paxton Junior School
  CBS CB2 ....22 C2
John Perry Primary School
  DAGE RM10 ....311 G3
John Ray Junior School
  BRTR CM7 ....121 J5
The John Warner School
  HOD EN11 ....185 J8
Joseph Clarke Special School
  CHING E4 ....267 G5
Jotmans Hall Primary School
  SBF/HAD SS7 ....297 L1
Jubilee Primary School
  THMD SE28 ....325 M3
Jubilee Sports Ground
  CHING E4 ....267 G3
The Junior School
  BSF CB23 ....138 E2
Kaizen Primary School
  PLSTW E13 ....307 L8
Katella Trading Estate
  BARK IG11 ....309 H7
Katherine Road Medical Centre
  FSTGT E7 ....307 M3
Katherine Semar Infant School
  SAFWS CB11 ....30 B3
Katherine Semar Junior School
  SAFWS CB11 ....30 B3
Katherines Primary School
  HLWW/ROY CM19 ....203 G3
Keir Hardie Primary School
  CAN/RD E16 ....323 K1
Keith Davis Cue Sports Club
  DAGW RM9 ....310 A4
Kelmscott Community Centre
  WALTH E17 ....284 C5
Kelmscott Leisure Centre
  WALTH E17 ....284 C5
Kelmscott School
  WALTH E17 ....284 C5
Kelrose Swimming Pool Centre
  RBRW/HUT CM13 ....274 B7
Kelvedon Hatch Primary
  School BRWN CM15 ....383 M10
Kelvedon St Marys CE
  Cont School K/T/MI CO5 ....148 F3
Kendall CE Primary School
  COLS CO2 ....129 M1
Kenneth More Theatre
  IL IG1 ....286 F8
Kenningtons Primary School
  SOCK/AV RM15 ....328 F2
Kensington Primary School
  MNPK E12 ....308 C3
Kent Kraft Industrial Estate
  GVW DA11 ....336 C2
Kents Hill Primary School
  SBF/HAD SS7 ....298 A1
Kentwell Hall
  SUD CO10 ....40 F5
Kesgrave High School
  KESG IP5 ....50 C5
Kestner Industrial Estate
  GRH DA9 ....335 K6
Keys Meadow Primary School
  PEND EN3 ....233 G6
Kimberley Industrial Estate
  WALTH E17 ....266 C6
The King Edmund School
  RCFD SS4 ....265 H8
King Edward Industrial Park
  COLS CO2 ....108 A8
King Edward VI Grammar
  School CHLM/WR CM1 ....209 K2
King Edward VI Grammar
  Sports Ground
  CHLM/WR CM1 ....193 J1
Kingfisher Leisure Park
  SUD CO10 ....20 E7
King George Hospital
  GDMY/SEVK IG3 ....287 K3
King Harold GM School
  WAB EN9 ....233 M3
The King John School
  SBF/HAD SS7 ....298 E2
King & Queen Wharf
  WAP E1W 322 A3
Kingsdale Industrial Estate
  CHLM/WR CM1 ....5 J1
The Kingsdale
  CHLM/WR CM1 ....5 J1
Kingsdown Special School
  LOS SS9 ....282 D7
Kings Estate
  HCH RM12 ....311 K1
Kings Fleet Primary School
  FX IP11 ....63 J7
Kingsford Community School
  PLSTW E13 ....307 M8
Kings Ford Infant School
  COLS CO2 ....128 F2
Kingsland College of
  Business Studies
  SRTFD E15 ....307 G6
Kingsmead Primary School
  CLPT E5 ....306 B1
Kingsmoor Infant School
  HLWW/ROY CM19 ....203 K5
Kingsmoor Recreation Centre
  HLWW/ROY CM19 ....203 J5
King Solomon High School
  BARK/HLT IG6 ....269 G8
Kingston Primary School
  SBF/HAD SS7 ....280 B7
Kingsway Hall
  HAR CO12 ....15 J7
Kingsway Hall Art & Theatre
  HAR CO12 ....71 J1
Kingswode Hoe School
  COLW CO3 ....106 F6
Kingswood Medical Centre
  VGE SS16 ....3 H9
Kingswood Primary School
  VGE SS16 ....3 H8
Kingswood School
  HARH RM3 ....272 G6

Kirby Primary School
  FOS CO13 ....136 E2
Knightsmead Special School
  SOCK/AV RM15 ....329 J3
Knightswick Centre
  CVI SS8 ....320 E1
Knockhall Community
  Primary School GRH DA9 ....335 M7
KP Estate
  RAIN RM13 ....327 H3
The Kursaal Entertainment
  Centre SOS SS1 ....19 L7
Kubrick Business Estate
  FSTGT E7 ....307 L1
Laburnum Health Centre
  DAGE RM10 ....288 D7
Laindon Health Centre
  LAIN SS15 ....276 E7
Laindon Park Primary School
  LAIN SS15 ....277 H5
Laindon Road Clinic
  BCAYW CM12 ....258 D5
Lakeside Retail Park
  WTHK RM20 ....329 K7
Lakeside Shopping Centre
  WTHK RM20 ....329 L6
Lakes Industrial Park
  BRTR CM7 ....121 K3
Lambourne Primary School
  ABR/ST RM4 ....251 L4
Lambs Court
  POP/IOD E14 ....322 B3
Lancaster Ipswich Athletics
  Track & Stadium IPNE IP4 ....48 E3
Lancaster Special School
  WOS/PRIT SS0 ....300 F1
Landguard Fort
  FX IP11 ....68 B7
Langdon Hills Country Park
  VGE SS16 ....294 E4
Langdon Hills Golf Club
  SLH/COR SS17 ....294 B5
Langdon Park School
  POP/IOD E14 ....322 E2
Langdon School
  EHAM E6 ....308 E6
Langenhoe Community
  Primary School K/T/MI CO5 ..153 K3
Langer Park Industrial Estate
  FX IP11 ....11 H4
Langer Primary School
  FX IP11 ....11 H6
Langham Primary School
  COLN CO4 ....88 C1
Langthorne Health Centre
  WAN E11 ....285 G8
Langthorne Hospital
  WAN E11 ....307 G1
Langtons J & I School
  EMPK RM11 ....290 B6
Lansbury Lawrence Primary
  School POP/IOD E14 ....322 E2
Lansdowne Primary School
  TIL RM18 ....331 J8
Larkshall Business Centre
  CHING E4 ....267 G1
La Salette RC Primary School
  RAIN RM13 ....311 K7
Laser Clinic
  CHESW CM7 ....216 C8
Latchingdon Primary School
  RCHLM CM3 ....231 L7
Lathom Junior School
  EHAM E6 ....308 B4
Latton Bush Business Centre
  HLWS CM18 ....204 A4
Latton Bush Recreation Centre
  HLWS CM18 ....203 M4
Laurence Industrial Estate
  SOSN SS2 ....282 E7
Lauriston Primary School
  HOM E9 ....306 A5
Lawford CE Primary School
  MGTR CO11 ....90 D2
Lawford Mead Primary School
  CHLM/WR CM1 ....193 G8
Lawn Cemetery
  CHLM/GWD CM2 ....226 C1
Lawn Primary School
  GVW DA11 ....336 A1
Lawrence Trading Estate
  GNWCH SE10 ....323 H7
  GRAYS RM17 ....330 F3
Lawrence Wharf
  POP/IOD E14 ....322 C5
Layer Marney Tower
  K/T/MI CO5 ....151 G5
Leah Manning Centre
  HLW CM20 ....13 H3
Lea Park Trading Estate
  LEY E10 ....284 C5
Lea Road Industrial Park
  CHES/WCR EN8 ....233 H4
Leaside Business Centre
  PEND EN3 ....248 C2
The Leas Special School
  COS CO15 ....6 C7
Lea Valley High School
  PEND EN3 ....232 D5
Lea Valley Trading Estate
  UED N18 ....266 A5
Lea Valley Campsite
  CHING E4 ....248 E2
Lee Valley Caravan Park
  HOD EN11 ....201 K5
Lee Valley Leisure Centre
  Camping & Caravan
  ED N9 ....248 A8
Lee Valley Leisure Golf Club
  ED N9 ....248 B7
Lee Valley Park
  WAB EN9 ....217 J6
Lee Valley Park Farms
  WAB EN9 ....217 K6
Lee Valley Watersports Centre
  CHING E4 ....248 E2
Leigh Beck Primary School
  CVI SS8 ....321 H2
Leigh Cemetery
  LOS SS9 ....300 A3
Leigh North Street
  Primary School LOS SS9 ....300 B5
Leopold Street Clinic
  BOW E3 ....322 C1
Lesnes Abbey
  ABYW SE2 ....326 A7
Lessness Heath Primary School
  BELV DA17 ....326 D8
The Leventhorpe School
  WARE SG12 ....162 F5
The Leverton Infant School
  WAB EN9 ....234 A4
Lexden Primary School
  COLW CO3 ....106 B7

Lexden Springs Special School COLW CO3 .....106 B6
Lexden Squash Club COLW CO3 .....106 A6
Lexden Wood Golf Club COLW CO3 .....106 D5
Ley Park CP School BROX EN10 .....201 G8
The Leys Primary School DAGE RM10 .....310 F4
Leyton Business Centre LEY E10 .....284 C7
Leyton FC LEY E10 .....284 C6
Leyton Industrial Village LEY E10 .....284 A5
Leyton Leisure Centre LEY E10 .....284 E6
Leyton Orient FC (Matchroom Stadium) LEY E10 .....284 E8
Leytonstone School WAN E11 .....285 H4
Leyton VI Form College LEY E10 .....285 G4
Leyton Youth Sports Ground LEY E10 .....284 E6
Liberty II Centre ROM RM1 .....289 H2
The Liberty ROM RM1 .....289 H3
Lime Grove Estate HVHL CB9 .....34 F8
Limehouse Hole Stairs POP/IOD E14 .....322 C4
Limes Farm Primary School CHIG IG7 .....269 G5
The Limes Medical Centre EPP CM16 .....220 C2
    EPP CM16 .....221 J4
Lincewood Primary School VGE SS16 .....294 E2
Lingwood Clinic SLH/COR SS17 .....316 F4
Links Business Centre BSF CM23 .....139 K2
Linton CE (Aided) Infant School CBE/LIN CB1 .....24 C7
Linton Health Centre CBE/LIN CB1 .....24 F7
Linton Heights Junior School CBE/LIN CB1 .....25 G7
Linton Mead Primary School THMD SE28 .....325 L3
Linton Village College CBE/LIN CB1 .....24 E7
Linton Zoological Gardens CBE/LIN CB1 .....24 E8
Lionmede Bowling Club & Tennis Courts CHLM/GWD CM2 .....5 M2
Lion Walk Shopping Centre COL CO1 .....8 C7
Lister Community School Performing Arts College PLSTW E15 .....307 L6
Lister Medical Centre HLWS CM18 .....203 K4
Littlebrook Business Centre DART DA1 .....334 F5
Littlegarth School RCOLW CO6 .....361 N10
Little Hallingbury CE Primary School RBSF CM22 .....163 K1
Little Heath School CHDH RM6 .....287 L2
Little Ilford School MNPK E12 .....308 C2
Little Malgraves Industrial Estate UPMR RM14 .....294 C4
Little Oakley CE School HAR CO12 .....70 A6
Little Thurrock Primary School GRAYS RM17 .....331 G2
Little Waltham CE Primary School RCHLM CM3 .....167 L6
Lloyd Park Centre WALTH E17 .....266 D8
Locks View Court POP/IOD E14 .....322 B3
Log Church CHONG CM5 .....382 C7
Lombard Trading Estate CHARL SE7 .....323 L7
London Arena POP/IOD E14 .....322 C6
London City Airport CAN/RD E16 .....324 B4
The London Industrial Estate EHAM E6 .....324 D1
London Industrial Park EHAM E6 .....324 C1
London International Cruise Terminal TIL RM18 .....337 K2
London, Leyton-Lee Valley Ice Centre LEY E10 .....284 A7
London Road Industrial Estate CBS SG8 .....22 C4
London Road Retail Park WOS/PRIT SSO 18 C4
London Stansted Airport RBSF CM22 .....374 H10
Longfield Medical Centre MAL CM9 .....198 E8
Longlands Primary School BROX EN10 .....217 G3
Long Melford CE Primary School SUD CO10 .....42 F2
The Long Melford Practice SUD CO10 .....42 F1
Long Ridings J & I School RBRW/HUT CM13 .....256 C1
Longshaw Primary School CHING E4 .....267 G2
Longview Adolescent Unit COLN CO4 .....107 J2
Lord Butler Leisure Centre SAFWS CB11 .....30 C2
Lord Lister Health Centre FSTGT E7 .....307 K1
Lorimar Business Centre RAIN RM13 .....327 H2
Loughton CC LOU IG10 .....250 C1
Loughton Golf Club LOU IG10 .....250 E1
Loughton Hall Clinic LOU IG10 .....250 C3
Loughton Health Centre LOU IG10 .....250 B3
Loughton Mental Health Centre LOU IG10 .....250 B5
Lovell's Wharf GNWCH SE10 .....323 G8
Lovewood Museum HOD EN11 .....201 H4
Lowfield Sports Ground HOD EN11 .....201 G3
Low Hall Sports Ground WALTH E17 .....284 A4

Low House Touring Caravan Centre KIR/NAC IP10 .....56 B4
Loxford School of Science & Technology IL IG1 .....309 G2
Loyola Preparatory School BKHH IG9 .....249 M8
LPR Sports Club BARK/HLT IG6 .....269 J7
Lubbins Park Primary School CVI SS8 .....320 F3
Lutomer House Business Centre POP/IOD E14 .....322 E4
Lychgate Industrial Estate SBF/HAD SS7 .....280 B4
Lyndean Industrial Estate ABYW SE2 .....325 M6
Lyon Business Park ABYW SE2 .....309 H6
Lyons Hall CP School BRTR CM7 .....121 H1
Madeira Grove Clinic WFD IG8 .....267 L4
Magnet Estate CDW/CHF RM16 .....329 M8
Maidenhall Sports Centre CHTY IP2 .....54 B3
Maidstone County Infant School FX IP11 .....62 D8
Maison Talbooth Hotel RCOLE CO7 .....363 L11
Maldon Agricultural Museum MAL CM9 .....384 B6
Maldon Court Preparatory School MAL CM9 .....214 C2
Maldon Golf Club MAL CM9 .....198 B8
Maldon Museum MAL CM9 .....214 E3
Maldon Primary School MAL CM9 .....214 D3
Mallard House Business Centre FRAM/WMKT IP13 .....50 C2
The Maltings Industrial Estate BOC CM0 .....393 P1
    SBW CM21 .....163 G7
    WARE SG12 .....185 L5
Mandeville Primary School CLPT E5 .....284 B8
Manford Way Health Centre BARK/HLT IG6 .....269 J5
Mangapps Farm Railway Museum BOC CM0 .....393 K5
Manifest Theatre MGTR CO11 .....91 G1
Manningtree High School MGTR CO11 .....90 E2
Manningtree Sports Centre MGTR CO11 .....90 E1
Manorfield Primary School POP/IOD E14 .....322 E1
Manor Fields Primary School BSF CM23 .....138 E4
Manor Infant School BARK IG11 .....309 J3
The Manor of Groves Golf Club SBW CM21 .....162 A7
Manor Park Cemetery FSTGT E7 .....308 A1
Manor Park Crematorium FSTGT E7 .....307 M1
Manor Park Methodist School MNPK E12 .....308 B1
Manor Primary School BSDN SS14 .....3 J2
    SRTFD E15 .....307 H6
The Manor Primary School ROM RM1 .....289 J3
Manor Trading Estate SBF/HAD SS7 .....280 A7
Manor Way Business Centre DAGW RM9 .....327 G1
Manor Way Industrial Estate GRAYS RM17 .....330 F6
Manuden Primary School BSF CM23 .....93 H8
Maple River Industrial Estate HLW CM20 .....188 C3
Margaretting CE Primary School INC CM4 .....224 B5
Marillac Hospital RBRW/HUT CM13 .....274 A1
Marion Richardson Primary School WCHPL E1 .....322 A2
Maritime Industrial Estate CHARL SE7 .....323 L7
Maritime Museum GNWCH SE10 .....323 H7
Market Field School RCOLE CO7 .....109 K8
Mark Hall Comprehensive School HLWE CM17 .....188 D7
Mark Hall Cycle Museum HLW CM20 .....188 C6
Markhams Chase Leisure Centre LAIN SS15 .....277 G7
Marks Gate Junior School CHDH RM6 .....288 B1
Marks Hall Arboretum RCOLW CO6 .....102 B6
Marks Hill (Nature Reserve) VGE SS16 .....294 B1
Marlborough Hotel FX IP11 .....11 J5
Marner Primary School BOW E3 .....306 E8
Marshalls Park School ROM RM1 .....271 H6
Marsh Farm Country Park RCHLM CM3 .....245 J8
Marsh Gate Business Centre SRTFD E15 .....306 F6
Marshgate Trading Estate SRTFD E15 .....306 E4
Marsh Green School DAGW RM9 .....310 D6
Marsh View Industrial Estate RAIN RM13 .....312 C3
Martells Industrial Estate RCOLE CO7 .....89 G8
Martlesham Beacon Hill Primary School WDBR IP12 .....50 F3
Marygreen Manor Hotel BRW CM14 .....273 J3
Maryland Industrial Estate SRTFD E15 .....307 H2
Maryland Primary School SRTFD E15 .....307 H2
Matching Green CE Primary School HLWE CM17 .....378 E11
Matrix Business Centre DART DA1 .....334 B7
Maunds Wood CP School HLW CM18 .....203 L5
The Mawney School ROMW/RG RM7 .....289 G3

May Avenue Industrial Estate GVW DA11 .....337 J6
Mayesbrook Park Arena BCTR RM8 .....309 K2
Mayespark Primary School GDMY/SEVK IG3 .....287 K8
Mayfair Industrial Estate RCHLM CM3 .....231 K4
Mayfield Infant School CHES/WCR EN8 .....216 F5
Mayfield School & College BCTR RM8 .....287 M6
Mayflower High School BCAYW CM12 .....240 F8
Mayflower Primary School HAR CO12 .....14 F7
    POP/IOD E14 .....322 D2
Mayflower Retail Park BSDN SS14 .....278 A3
Maylandsea CP School RCHLM CM3 .....388 C9
Maylandsea Medical Centre RCHLM CM3 .....388 B8
Maylands Golf Club & Country Club HARH RM3 .....272 E4
Maytime School IL IG1 .....286 D8
Mayville J & P School WAN E11 .....285 H8
McEntee School WALTH E17 .....266 C7
Meadgate Primary School CHLM/GWD CM2 .....210 B5
Mead Industrial Park HLW CM20 .....188 C6
Mead JMI School HARH RM3 .....272 C5
The Meadows Shopping Centre CHLM/GWD CM2 .....5 J4
The Mead School HLWS CM18 .....203 M3
Meeanee Barracks COL CO1 .....107 K8
Megaknowl CHLM CM1 .....209 H6
Melbourne Park Athletics Centre CHLM/WR CM1 .....193 H7
Melbourne Park Primary School CHLM/WR CM1 .....193 J7
Mellish Industrial Estate WOOL/PLUM SE18 .....324 A6
Memorial Grounds SOSN SS2 .....283 L8
Menzies Prince Regent Hotel COL CO1 .....8 D7
Meridian Primary School GNWCH SE10 .....323 G8
Meridian Trading Estate CHARL SE7 .....323 L7
Merrielands Retail Park DAGW RM9 .....310 C5
Merrylands Primary School LAIN SS15 .....276 C7
Mersea Community & Sports Centre K/T/MI CO5 .....177 M7
Mersea Island School K/T/MI CO5 .....177 M7
Mersea Island Vineyard K/T/MI CO5 .....178 E6
Messing cum Inworth Community Primary School K/T/MI CO5 .....149 M3
Midas Business Centre DAGE RM10 .....310 D1
Midas Industrial Estate DAGE RM10 .....310 D1
Middle School Team ROM RM1 .....289 J4
Middleton Special School WARE SG12 .....184 E2
Mid Essex Adult Community College RBRW/HUT CM13 .....256 E2
Mid Essex Magistrates Courts CHLM/WR CM1 .....5 H3
Mid Kent Golf Club GVW DA11 .....337 L8
Mildmay Industrial Estate BOC CM0 .....393 L8
Mildmay Infant School CHLM/GWD CM2 .....209 L8
Mile End Hospital WCHPL E1 .....306 A7
Mile End Stadium BOW E3 .....322 B1
Milehams Industrial Estate PUR RM19 .....328 D6
Millbrook School CHES/WCR EN8 .....216 F7
Mildene Primary School K/T/MI CO5 .....150 A7
Millennium Harbour Development POP/IOD E14 .....322 C5
The Millennium Primary School GNWCH SE10 .....323 J6
Millennium Wharf Development POP/IOD E14 .....323 G6
Millfields Primary School RCOLE CO7 .....131 G4
Mill Hall RAYL SS6 .....281 G3
The Mill Hotel SUD CO10 .....20 B6
Millhouse Primary School LAIN SS15 .....276 F5
Mill River Trading Estate PEND EN3 .....248 B4
Millside Industrial Estate DART DA1 .....334 A6
Milsom's Hotel RCOLE CO7 .....363 K10
Milton Hall Primary School WOS/PRIT SSO 18 D4
Milton Road Business Park GVE DA12 .....337 M5
Mint Business Park CAN/RD E16 .....323 K1
Mirravale Trading Estate BCTR RM8 .....288 B5
Mission Grove Primary School WALTH E17 .....284 C3
Mistley Norman CE Primary School MGTR CO11 .....91 K1
Mistley Towers MGTR CO11 .....65 J8
Mole Hall Wildlife Park SAFWS CB11 .....65 J8
Monega Primary School MNPK E12 .....308 A2
Monkwick Primary & Infant School COLS CO2 .....129 J3
Monkwick Sports Centre COLS CO2 .....129 J3
Monro Industrial Estate CHES/WCR EN8 .....232 F4
Monteagle Primary School DAGW RM9 .....309 L5
Montessori School RBSF CM22 .....375 J10

The Montgomerie Primary School SBF/HAD SS7 .....279 L6
Montgomery Infant School COLS CO2 .....128 F3
Moonhall Business Park HVHL CB9 .....34 D8
Moon & Sixpence WDBR IP12 .....51 K5
Moot Hall MAL CM9 .....214 C2
Moreton Bay Industrial Estate GPK RM2 .....272 A8
Moreton CE Primary School CHONG CM5 .....380 D6
Morland Primary School IPSE IP3 .....54 F5
Mossford Green Primary School BARK/HLT IG6 .....268 F8
Moulsham High School CHLM/GWD CM2 .....209 L6
Moulsham Lodge Clinic CHLM/GWD CM2 .....209 L7
Moulsham Primary School CHLM/GWD CM2 .....5 C8
Mountfitchet Castle & Norman Village STSD SG24 .....374 A7
The Mountfitchet High School STSD SG24 .....374 A9
Mountnessing CE Primary School BRWN CM15 .....239 G5
MSF Whitehall College BSF CM23 .....114 F8
Mudchute City Farm POP/IOD E14 .....322 F7
Mudlands Estate RAIN RM13 .....311 H7
Mulberry Business Centre BERM/RHTH SE16 .....322 A5
Mulgrave Primary School WOOL/PLUM SE18 .....324 D7
Murrayfield Pavilion BSDN SS14 .....2 C2
Murrayfield Primary School IPSE IP3 .....54 F1
Museum in Docklands POP/IOD E14 .....322 D3
Myland Primary School COLN CO4 .....107 G1
Nabbotts County Junior School CHLM/WR CM1 .....194 B6
Nacton CE VC Primary School KIR/NAC IP10 .....56 A7
Natural History Museum COL CO1 .....8 D7
Nayland CP School RCOLW CO6 .....361 N6
Nazeing CE School WAB EN9 .....217 M1
Nazeing Golf Club WAB EN9 .....218 D2
Nazeing Park School WAB EN9 .....202 B8
Nelmes Primary School EMPK RM11 .....290 C1
Nelson Dock Museum POP/IOD E14 .....322 C4
Nelson Primary School EHAM E6 .....308 C4
Nether Hall SUD CO10 .....38 F3
Nevendon Trading Estate PIT SS13 .....278 E4
New Atlas Wharf Development POP/IOD E14 .....322 C6
Newbury Park Health Centre GNTH/NBYPK IG2 .....287 G4
New Caledonian Wharf POP/IOD E14 .....322 C6
New Cangle Primary School HVHL CB9 .....34 C4
New Cemetery IPNE IP4 .....48 D5
New City Primary School PLSTW E13 .....307 M7
New England Industrial Estate BARK IG11 .....308 F6
    HOD EN11 .....201 K2
New Hall Preparatory School RCHLM CM3 .....194 D4
New Hall Vineyard RCHLM CM3 .....230 A1
Newham College of Further Education EHAM E6 .....308 C6
    SRTFD E15 .....307 H4
Newham Community College CAN/RD E16 .....307 H1
Newham General Hospital PLSTW E13 .....307 M8
Newham Leisure Centre PLSTW E13 .....323 M1
Newham Medical Centre PLSTW E13 .....307 M6
Newham Sixth Form College PLSTW E13 .....307 L8
Newlands Shopping Centre WIT CM8 .....171 K3
Newlands Spring Primary School CHLM/WR CM1 .....193 G6
Newmans Estate COS CO15 .....6 C6
Newport Free Grammar School SAFWS CB11 .....351 N12
Newport J & I School LEY E10 .....284 F7
Newport Primary School SAFWS CB11 .....372 A1
New River Trading Estate CHES/WCR EN8 .....216 E4
New Rush Hall School IL IG1 .....286 F7
New Spitalfields Market LEY E10 .....284 D8
Newton Industrial Estate BCTR RM8 .....288 A2
Newtons Primary School RAIN RM13 .....311 G6
Nightingale Clinic PLSTW E13 .....307 M6
Nightingale Primary School SWFD E18 .....285 M2
Noak Bridge Medical Centre LAIN SS15 .....277 J4
Noak Bridge Primary School LAIN SS15 .....277 J4
Noak Hill School HARH RM3 .....272 N1
Noor Ul Islam School LEY E10 .....284 F7
Norlington School WAN E11 .....285 G4
Norman Booth Leisure Centre HLWE CM17 .....188 E6
Normanhurst School CHING E4 .....249 N7
Norsey Wood (Nature Reserve) BCAYE CM11 .....259 G5

North Beckton Primary School EHAM E6 .....308 C2
Northbury Primary School BARK IG11 .....308 D1
North Crescent Primary School WICKW SS12 .....261 G4
North Fambridge Yacht Club RCHLM CM3 .....246 A6
Northfleet Cemetery GVW DA11 .....336 E7
Northfleet Industrial Estate GVW DA11 .....336 C6
Northfleet School for Girls GVW DA11 .....337 G5
Northfleet Technology College GVW DA11 .....337 G5
Northgate County High School IPNE IP4 .....48 C1
Northgate Industrial Park ROMW/RG RM7 .....270 C2
Northgate Primary School BSF CM23 .....114 F6
Northgate Sports Centre IPNE IP4 .....48 C2
North Havering College of Adult Education ROM RM1 .....289 J1
North Hill Business Park SLH/COR SS17 .....316 C6
North Primary School COL CO1 .....8 A1
North Weald Airfield EPP CM16 .....221 G6
North Weald Golf Club EPP CM16 .....221 H6
North & West Essex Adult Community College GTDUN CM6 .....74 C4
    HLW CM20 .....12 C3
North West Kent College GVE DA12 .....338 C1
Northwick Park J & I School CVI SS8 .....320 A4
Northwood Primary School ERITHM DA18 .....326 B5
Notley Green Primary School BRTR CM77 .....120 F1
Notley High School BRTR CM7 .....121 J1
Novotel CAN/RD E16 .....323 L2
    IP IP1 .....16 E3
NTGB Sports Ground EHAM E6 .....308 C4
Nuclear Bunker BRW CM14 .....383 K1
Number 10 Bowling ROM RM1 .....289 H4
Number Ten Bowling Centre BRTR CM7 .....121 L4
Nuralite Industrial Centre HOO/HM ME3 .....339 K5
Oakdale Infant School SWFD E18 .....267 L4
Oakdale Junior School SWFD E18 .....267 L4
Oakhill Primary School WFD IG8 .....267 H4
Oak Industrial Park GTDUN CM6 .....117 J4
Oaklands Farm Industrial Estate BCAYE CM11 .....241 L6
Oaklands Infant School CHLM/GWD CM2 .....5 L7
Oaklands School LOU IG10 .....250 A4
Oaks Hospital COLN CO4 .....107 H4
The Oaks Industrial Estate HLW CM20 .....188 A6
Oak Tree Medical Centre GDMY/SEVK IG3 .....287 H2
Oakwood Business Park COS CO15 .....159 G4
Oakwood County Infant School COS CO15 .....6 C7
Oakwood Estate HLW CM20 .....188 B6
Oakwood Hill Industrial Estate LOU IG10 .....250 E6
Oakwood Infant School COS CO15 .....183 G6
Occupational Health Centre HAR CO12 .....66 C8
Ockendon School SOCK/AV RM15 .....329 K3
Odeon Cinema CHLM/GWD CM2 .....5 J4
    COL CO1 .....8 B2
    GNTH/NBYPK IG2 .....286 D4
    HLW CM20 .....12 F3
    IPNE IP4 .....17 G2
    ROM RM1 .....289 J2
    SOS SS1 .....19 G6
    SWFD E18 .....267 K2
Odessa Infant School FSTGT E7 .....307 K2
Old Bancroftians FC BKHH IG9 .....268 A2
Old Bellgate Wharf Development POP/IOD E14 .....322 C6
The Old Brickworks Business Centre HARH RM3 .....272 C4
Old Cemetery IPNE IP4 .....48 E1
Old Chigwellians Sports Club CHIG IG7 .....250 E4
Oldchurch Hospital ROMW/RG RM7 .....289 G4
Old Court Theatre CHLM/WR CM1 .....5 J2
Old Ford Primary School BOW E3 .....306 C4
Old Grammar School RCOLE CO7 .....363 N10
The Old Guild Theatre GVW DA11 .....337 G8
Old Harlow Health Centre HLWE CM17 .....188 D5
Old Heath Primary School COLS CO2 .....129 M3
Old Market Retail Park PIT SS13 .....278 C6
Old Palace Primary School BOW E3 .....306 C4
Old Royal Naval College GNWCH SE10 .....323 G6
Old Station Museum CAN/RD E16 .....324 D3
Old Sun Wharf POP/IOD E14 .....322 B4
Old Westcliffians RFC RCFD SS4 .....282 F5
Olga Primary School BOW E3 .....306 B6
The Olive Branch Hotel RCOS CO16 .....135 J4
Olympic Business Centre BSDN SS14 .....278 C3

...ree Hill Country Park
  .../COR SS17 ....295 H5
...r & District Sports Club
  ...ONG CM5 ....382 B1
...r Health Centre
  ...ONG CM5 ....382 B1
...r Leisure Centre
  ...ONG CM5 ....380 H12
...r Road Trading Estate
  ...DUN CM6 ....117 H6
...r War Memorial Hospital
  ...DUN CM6 ....380 H12
...na Business Park
  ...ED EN11 ....201 K2
...rchard Health Centre
  ...RK IG11 ....308 F6
...ard Shopping Centre
  ...RT DA1 ....334 B8
...ard Theatre
  ...RT DA1 ....334 B8
...t Industrial Park
  ...E10 ....284 D7
...t Business Centre
  ...RM/RHTH SE16 ....322 A8
...t CE Primary School
  ...W/CHF RM16 ....315 K5
...t Golf Club
  ...W/CHF RM16 ....316 B7
...t Hospital
  ...W/CHF RM16 ....315 K5
...t Industrial Estate
  ...W/CHF RM16 ....316 C5
...l Business Centre
  ...RE IP3 ....54 D3
...l Country Park
  ...RE IP3 ....54 E5
...l High School
  ...IP11 ....62 D8
...ll Park School
  ...IP10 ....60 A1
...r/NAC IP10
...ll Retail Park
  ...TY IP2 ....47 L8
...l Yacht Club
  ...RE IP3 ....54 B4
...ady Immaculate RC
  ...mary School
  ...LM/GWD CM2 ....4 F5
...ady of Lourdes Catholic
  ...mary School LOS SS9 ....300 D3
...ady of Lourdes RC
  ...mary School WAN E11 ....285 J4
...ady RC Primary School
  ...P/IOD E14 ....322 C2
...adys Catholic
  ...mary School
  ...RT DA1 ....334 A8
...er House School
  ...LW CO3 ....107 G6
...er Business Centre
  ...CM9 ....385 Q3
...ters Ash Primary School
  ...W DA11 ....337 G8
...e Cinema
  ...IP11 ....11 M1
...e Theatre
  ...OS/PRIT SS0 ....18 B3
...r's College
  ...AYS RM17 ....331 J3
...lise Wildlife Park
  ...OX EN10 ....200 A7
...gdon Primary School
  ...WS CM18 ....203 L5
...hill Primary School
  ...AY IG5 ....286 C1
...Infants School
  ...TFD E15 ....307 J4
...ands Primary School
  ...RM1 ....289 G1
...Medical Centre
  ...RM/RHTH SE16 ....322 A7
...School
  ...YL SS6 ....262 E1
...School for Girls
  ...G1 ....286 D7
...way Middle School
  ...HE CB9 ....34 A8
...way Primary School
  ...ITHM DA18 ....326 B6
...don Wood
  ...WS CM18 ....203 L7
...don Wood Cemetery
  ...WW/ROY CM19 ....203 K7
...don Wood Crematorium
  ...WW/ROY CM19 ....203 K7
...oes Primary School
  ...GW RM9 ....310 C3
...onage Farm Industrial
  ...tate STSD SM24 ....374 A10
...onage Farm Primary
  ...hool RAIN RM13 ....311 M7
...ons Heath Primary School
  ...LN CO4 ....108 B3
...enger Ferry Terminal
  ...AR CO12 ....14 B3
...mores School
  ...WS CM18 ....203 L3
...s Theatre School
  ...MPK RM11 ....290 A5
...ocke's House (NT)
  ...LW CO6 ....124 C4
...A Hospital
  ...DBR IG4 ....286 A1
...tree Business Centre
  ...LW CO3 ....128 B1
...vit Caravan Park
  ...IP11 ....11 G5
...broke Business Centre
  ...DN SS14 ....278 B3
...Peninsula Business Centre
  ...S/CAP IP9 ....54 A8
...y Fields Primary School
  ...LM/WR CM1 ....194 A7
...r Hills Primary School
  ...RM/RHTH SE16 ....322 A4
...Philip Morrant School
  ...LW CO3 ....106 E8
...enix Business Centre
  ...P/IOD E14 ....322 D1
...Phoenix Primary School
  ...IN SS15 ....276 F7
...enix Secondary &
  ...mary School BOW E3 ....306 C7
...re House Cinema
  ...TFD E15 ....307 L6
...Pier at Harwich Hotel
  ...CO12 ....15 K2
...Avenue Cinema
  ...CO15 ....6 E6
...rims Hatch CP School
  ...RWN CM15 ....255 K6
...wood Primary School
  ...RM5 ....270 E4
...wood Special School
  ...ARE SG12 ....184 E2
...eer School
  ...DN SS14 ....3 L3
...r's Vale CP School
  ...SE IP3 ....54 E4

Pipps Hill Retail Park
  LAIN SS15 ....2 B2
Pitsea Health Clinic
  PIT SS13 ....278 D8
Pitsea Leisure Centre
  PIT SS13 ....278 E8
Pitsea Primary School
  PIT SS13 ....278 D8
Pitsea Swimming Pool
  PIT SS13 ....278 E8
Place Farm Community
  Primary School
  HVHL CB9 ....34 C5
Plaistow Hospital
  PLSTW E13 ....307 L6
Plaistow Primary School
  PLSTW E13 ....307 M5
Plashet Jewish Cemetery
  MNPK E12 ....308 A3
Plashet Road Medical Centre
  PLSTW E13 ....307 L4
Plashet School
  EHAM E6 ....308 B4
Playhouse
  HLW CM20 ....203 K1
Playhouse Theatre
  HLW CM20 ....13 G6
Plaza Business Centre
  PEND EN3 ....248 C2
Plume School
  MAL CM9 ....214 C3
Plumstead Leisure Centre
  WOOL/PLUM SE18 ....325 G6
Plumstead Manor School
  WOOL/PLUM SE18 ....325 G8
Police Cadet School
  WAN E11 ....285 K6
Ponders End Industrial Estate
  PEND EN3 ....248 C4
Pontlands Park Country Hotel
  CHLM/GWD CM2 ....210 D8
Poplar Business Park
  POP/IOD E14 ....322 F3
Porters Grange Primary School
  SOS SS1 ....19 K4
Portmans Walk Industrial Centre
  IP IP1 ....16 B5
Portway Primary School
  SRTFD E15 ....307 K5
Pot Kiln Primary School
  SUD CO10 ....21 H8
Potter Street Primary School
  HLWE CM17 ....204 C3
Pound Park Nursery School
  CHARL SE7 ....324 A8
Powers Hall Junior School,
  Speech & Language Unit
  WIT CM8 ....171 G2
Premier Travel Inn
  BARK IG11 ....308 E5
  BRTR CM77 ....122 A5
  BSDN SS14 ....277 K4
  CAN/RD E16 ....324 A3
  CDW/CHF RM16 ....329 M6
  CHDH RM6 ....288 B3
  CHLM/GWD CM2 ....194 B6
  CHTY IP2 ....54 B5
  COLN CO4 ....88 D7
  EHAM E6 ....324 D1
  GVW DA11 ....337 H3
  HLW CM20 ....188 C3
  LOU IG10 ....233 J4
  PEND EN3 ....233 G6
  PIT SS13 ....278 D5
  PUR RM19 ....328 C8
  PUR RM19 ....329 H7
  RAIN RM13 ....328 C2
  RCHM CM3 ....194 F5
  REDBR IG4 ....286 A3
  ROM RM1 ....289 J3
  SLH/COR SS17 ....295 M4
  WOS/PRIT SS0 ....282 E8
Presdales School
  WARE SG12 ....184 E1
Prettygate Primary School
  COLW CO3 ....128 D1
Prince Avenue Primary School
  WOS/PRIT SS0 ....283 G5
Prince of Wales Primary School
  PEND EN3 ....233 G7
Princess Alexandra Hospital
  HLW CM20 ....12 E5
Priory Park
  KIR/NAC IP10 ....55 H7
Priory Park Industrial Estate
  SOSN SS2 ....301 K1
Priory School
  SOSN SS2 ....301 H2
Priory Shopping Centre
  DART DA1 ....334 A8
Prittlebrook Industrial Estate
  SOSN SS2 ....301 J1
Prittlewell Centre
  SOSN SS2 ....18 E3
Prittlewell Priory Museum
  SOSN SS2 ....301 J2
The Prittlewell Technology
  College WOS/PRIT SS0 ....300 F7
Prospect Business Park
  LOU IG10 ....251 G4
Prout Industrial Estate
  CVI SS8 ....321 J2
Pump House
  BERM/RHTH SE16 ....322 B4
Purdeys Industrial Estate
  RCFD SS4 ....283 K4
Purfleet Industrial Park
  PUR RM19 ....328 C4
Purfleet Primary School
  PUR RM19 ....328 D7
Purford Green Primary School
  HLWS CM18 ....204 B3
Purleigh CP School
  RCHLM CM3 ....230 A4
Pylon Trading Estate
  CAN/RD E16 ....307 G8
Quarry Hill Infant School
  GRAYS RM16 ....330 A4
Quarry Hill Junior School
  GRAYS RM16 ....330 A4
Quatro Business Park
  BSDN SS14 ....278 D3
Quayside Industrial Estate
  MAL CM9 ....214 D1
The Quay Theatre
  SUD CO10 ....20 C4
Quebec Industrial Estate
  BERM/RHTH SE16 ....322 B4
Queen Elizabeth Museum
  CHING E4 ....249 J7
Queen Mary & Westfield College
  SWFD E18 ....267 K7
  WCHPL E1 ....306 A4
Queensgate Centre
  ....187 M5
Queensland Preparatory school
  WOS/PRIT SS0 ....300 F5
Queens Theatre
  EMPK RM11 ....290 A5

Quest End Industrial Estate
  RAYL SS6 ....262 F7
Quilters J & I School
  BCAYW CM12 ....258 D4
Quwwat Ul Islam Girls School
  FSTGT E7 ....307 K3
RA Butler J & I School
  SAFWS CB11 ....28 B8
Radford Business Centre
  BCAYW CM12 ....258 C2
Radwinter CE Primary School
  SAFWN CB10 ....352 C2
Rainbow Quay
  BERM/RHTH SE16 ....322 B6
Rainham Cemetery
  RAIN RM13 ....311 M7
Rainham Hall (NT)
  RAIN RM13 ....311 K8
Rainham Trading Estate
  RAIN RM13 ....311 H7
Rainham Village Primary School
  RAIN RM13 ....311 K8
Ramac Industrial Estate
  CHARL SE7 ....323 K8
The Ramsden Hall
  Special School BCAYE CM11 ....259 J2
The Ramsey School
  HSTD CO9 ....81 K3
Ranelagh Primary School
  CHTY IP2 ....47 L8
Ransomes Industrial Park
  IPSE IP3 ....55 J6
Raphael Independent School
  EMPK RM11 ....289 K4
Ravensbourne School
  HARH RM3 ....272 A5
Ravenscroft Primary School
  PLSTW E13 ....307 K8
  RCOS CO16 ....182 E1
Ravenside Retail Park
  UED N18 ....266 A4
Ravenswood Community
  Primary School IPSE IP3 ....55 H5
Ravenswood Industrial Estate
  WALTH E17 ....284 F2
Rawreth Industrial Estate
  RAYL SS6 ....262 D8
Ray Island Nature Reserve
  K/T/MI CO5 ....177 L3
Rayleigh Lanes Indoor Market
  RAYL SS6 ....281 G3
Rayleigh Primary School
  RAYL SS6 ....280 F3
Ray Lodge Primary School
  WFD IG8 ....268 A5
Raynehurst Junior School
  GVE DA12 ....338 C7
Rayne Primary School
  BRTR CM77 ....120 B3
Raynham Road
  Industrial Estate BSF CM23 ....139 J1
Redbridge College
  CHDH RM6 ....287 L3
Redbridge Drama Centre
  SWFD E18 ....267 K7
Redbridge Museum
  IL IG1 ....286 E5
Redbridge Primary School
  REDBR IG4 ....286 B3
Redbridge Sports Centre
  BARK/HLT IG6 ....269 J2
Redbridge Tuition Service
  GNTH/NBYPK IG2 ....286 F1
Redburn Industrial Estate
  PEND EN3 ....248 A6
Redden Court School
  HARH RM3 ....290 C1
Redriff Primary School
  BERM/RHTH SE16 ....322 B5
Regent Leisure Centre
  SLH/COR SS17 ....317 C4
Regional Sports Centre
  TIL RM18 ....331 L4
Renwick Industrial Estate
  BARK IG11 ....309 L6
Research & Engineering Centre
  LAIN SS15 ....276 C5
Rettendon Primary School
  RCHLM CM3 ....243 M8
RHS Garden Hyde Hall
  RCHLM CM3 ....244 B1
Rice Bridge Industrial Estate
  RCOS CO16 ....135 K6
Richard Alibon Primary School
  DAGE RM10 ....310 D2
The Richard De Clare
  Primary School HSTD CO9 ....81 J4
Richard Whittington
  Primary School BSF CM23 ....138 F5
Richmond Avenue
  Primary School SBN/FI SS3 ....303 G3
Rickling CE Primary School
  SAFWS CB11 ....93 M1
Rickstones School
  WIT CM8 ....147 J2
Ridgewell Primary School
  HSTD CO9 ....345 N6
Rio Cinema
  BOC CM0 ....393 M9
Ridleys Brewery
  RCHLM CM3 ....143 G6
Ripple J & I School
  BARK IG11 ....309 J3
Risebridge Golf Club
  ROM RM1 ....271 J6
Rise Park Primary School
  ROM RM1 ....271 J6
Rivenhall CE Primary School
  WIT CM8 ....147 L5
Rivenhall Oaks Golf Club
  WIT CM8 ....147 L8
River Lee Country Park
  CHES/WCR EN8 ....217 J7
  WAB EN9 ....217 J2
Rivermead Industrial Estate
  CHLM/WR CM1 ....209 L1
River Road Business Park
  BARK IG11 ....309 H7
Riverside Business Park
  STSD SM24 ....115 M3
Riverside Golf Club
  THMD SE28 ....326 B2
Riverside Health Centre
  MGTR CO11 ....90 F1
Riverside Ice & Leisure Centre
  CHTY IP2 ....54 C2
Riverside Industrial Estate
  BARK IG11 ....309 K7
  DART DA1 ....334 B7
  ED N9 ....248 B6
  MAL CM9 ....214 C1
  RCOS CO16 ....283 J4
Riverside Industrial Park
  CHTY IP2 ....54 C2
Riverside Primary School
  HOC/HUL SS5 ....263 J4
Riverside Retail Park
  CHLM/WR CM1 ....5 L1

Riverside Swimming Centre
  ERITH DA8 ....327 H8
The RJ Mitchell Primary School
  HCH RM12 ....311 L3
Roach Vale Primary School
  COLN CO4 ....108 B4
Robert Clack School
  BCTR RM8 ....288 C6
Robert Drake Primary School
  SBF/HAD SS7 ....280 A6
Robert Leonard
  Industrial Estate SOSN SS2 ....282 F6
Robert Leonard Industrial Site
  SOSN SS2 ....283 J8
Rochford Adult Community
  College RCFD SS4 ....283 K4
Rochford Hundred Golf Club
  RCFD SS4 ....283 G4
Rochford Primary School
  RCFD SS4 ....283 H3
Rochford Swimming Pool
  RCFD SS4 ....283 K3
Roding Primary School
  BCTR RM8 ....309 M1
  WFD IG8 ....268 B6
Rodings Primary School
  CTDLM CM6 ....379 R5
Roding Valley High School
  LOU IG10 ....250 B5
  LOU IG10 ....250 E4
The Roebuck Hotel
  BKHH IG9 ....249 M7
Roebuck Road Trading Estate
  BARK/HLT IG6 ....269 L5
Roger Ascham Primary School
  WALTH E17 ....266 C7
Rokeby School
  SRTFD E15 ....307 G4
Rolph CE Primary School
  RCOS CO16 ....135 J4
Roman Road Primary School
  EHAM E6 ....308 A8
Romford Cemetery
  ROMW/RG RM7 ....288 F5
Romford Clinic
  ROM RM1 ....289 J2
Romford County Court
  GPK RM2 ....289 K1
Romford Golf Club
  ROMW/RG RM7 ....289 H5
Romford Ice Rink
  ROMW/RG RM7 ....289 H5
Romford IT Learning Centre
  ROM RM1 ....289 H3
Romford Shopping Hall
  ROM RM1 ....289 H2
Ropery Business Park
  CHARL SE7 ....323 M7
The Rose & Crown Hotel
  COLN CO4 ....9 H6
Rosedale Clinic
  CHESW EN7 ....216 B6
Rose Hill Primary School
  IPSE IP3 ....55 J7
Roseland JMI School
  HOD EN11 ....185 G8
Rosetta Primary School
  CAN/RD E16 ....323 L1
Rosewood Medical Centre
  HCH RM12 ....311 L2
Rosherville CE Primary School
  GVW DA11 ....337 H4
Roslin Hotel
  SOS SS1 ....302 C7
Rosshill Industrial Park
  SOSN SS2 ....301 L1
Roxwell CE Primary School
  CHLM/WR CM1 ....191 K7
Roxwell Trading Park
  WALTH E17 ....284 B5
Royal Arsenal
  WOOL/PLUM SE18 ....324 E6
Royal Burnham Yacht Club
  BOC CM0 ....393 M9
Royal Corinthian Yacht Club
  BOC CM0 ....393 M10
The Royal Dock Community
  School CAN/RD E16 ....323 M2
Royal Docks Medical Centre
  EHAM E6 ....324 D2
Royal Epping Forest Golf Club
  CHING E4 ....249 H7
Royal Hospital School
  RIPS/CAP IP9 ....364 G10
Royal Liberty School
  GPK RM2 ....289 M1
Royal London Sports Centre
  COLN CO4 ....87 L7
The Royals Shopping Centre
  SOS SS1 ....19 H6
Royal Terrace Pier
  GVE DA12 ....337 M3
Royal Victoria Docks
  Watersports Centre
  CAN/RD E16 ....323 K3
Roydonbury Industrial Estate
  HLWW/ROY CM19 ....203 G1
Roydon CP School
  HLWW/ROY CM19 ....202 C1
Roydon Mill Leisure Park
  HLWW/ROY CM19 ....186 B8
RSPB Reserve
  HOD EN11 ....185 L8
Runwell Community
  Primary School
  WICKE SS11 ....261 G3
Runwell Hospital
  RCHLM CM3 ....243 J8
Rush Croft School
  CHING E4 ....266 E6
Rush Green Junior School
  IL IG1 ....286 C7
Rush Green Primary School
  ROMW/RG RM7 ....289 G6
Rush Green Sports Centre
  RCOS CO16 ....182 E2
Rushmere Golf Club
  IPNE IP4 ....49 J7
Rushmere Hall Primary School
  IPNE IP4 ....48 F4
Rushmere Sports Club
  KESG IP5 ....49 L4
Ryedene Community School
  VGE SS16 ....296 C2
Rye House Stadium
  HOD EN11 ....201 L1
Ryelands JMI School
  HOD EN11 ....201 J2
Rye Park Industrial Estate
  HOD EN11 ....201 K1
The Ryes School
  SUD CO10 ....44 F7
The Sacred Heart of Mary
  RC School UPMR RM14 ....290 E7
Sacred Heart RC Primary School
  SOS SS1 ....19 L4

Saffron Business Centre
  SAFWN CB10 ....28 D7
Saffron Hotel
  SAFWN CB10 ....28 A7
Saffron Walden County
  High School SAFWS CB11 ....351 R5
Saffron Walden Golf Club
  SAFWN CB10 ....351 R3
Saffron Walden Hospital
  SAFWS CB11 ....28 D7
Saffron Walden Museum
  SAFWS CB11 ....28 D7
Saffron Walden Town FC
  SAFWN CB10 ....28 A6
Sai Medical Centre
  POP/IOD E14 ....322 F4
St Agnes RC Primary School
  BOW E3 ....306 D7
St Aidans RC Primary School
  IL IG1 ....287 G6
St Alban's Catholic High School
  IPNE IP4 ....49 H6
St Albans Primary School
  HLW CM20 ....13 L2
St Albans RC Church & School
  Presbytery
  HCH RM12 ....311 K2
St Albans RC JMI School
  HCH RM12 ....311 L4
St Albans Road Infant School
  DART DA1 ....334 C8
St Andrews BA CE
  Primary School RCOS CO16 ....134 C5
St Andrews CE Junior School
  RCHLM CM3 ....196 E2
St Andrews CE Primary School
  EPP CM16 ....221 K3
  HSTD CO9 ....346 A11
  RCOLW CO6 ....126 B2
  RCOLW CO6 ....360 D12
St Andrews Hospital
  BOW E3 ....306 E8
St Andrews Primary School
  WARE SG12 ....185 L5
St Angelas Ursuline
  Convent School FSTGT E7 ....307 L3
St Anne Line RC Infant School
  LAIN SS15 ....2 C6
St Annes Preparatory School
  CHLM/GWD CM2 ....4 F6
St Annes Primary School
  COLN CO4 ....9 J3
St Anne's Trading Estate
  POP/IOD E14 ....322 C2
St Anselms RC Primary School
  DART DA1 ....334 D7
St Antonys RC Primary School
  FSTGT E7 ....307 K4
St Aubyns School
  WFD IG8 ....267 K3
St Augustines Primary School
  BELV DA17 ....326 C6
St Augustines RC Infant School
  GNTH/NBYPK IG2 ....286 E3
St Augustines RC Primary
  School GNTH/NBYPK IG2 ....286 E3
  HOD EN11 ....201 J4
St Bedes RC Primary School
  CHDH RM6 ....287 M3
St Benedicts College
  COLW CO3 ....106 E7
St Bernards High School
  WOS/PRIT SS0 ....18 C5
St Bonaventures School
  FSTGT E7 ....307 K4
St Botolphs CE Primary School
  GVW DA11 ....337 G5
St Botolphs Priory Ruin
  COL CO1 ....8 E8
St Catherines Hoddesdon CE
  Primary School HOD EN11 ....201 J3
St Cedds CE VA Primary School
  BOC CM0 ....386 G11
St Cedds School
  CHLM/WR CM1 ....4 D1
St Christopher Special School
  LOS SS9 ....300 C1
St Clares RC Primary School
  RCOS CO16 ....182 E1
St Clements Hospital
  BOW E3 ....306 C7
  IPSE IP3 ....55 G1
St Clements Junior School
  CHES/WCR EN8 ....216 F5
St Cleres Hall Golf Club
  SLH/COR SS17 ....316 E5
St Cleres School
  SLH/COR SS17 ....316 E5
St Cross RC Primary School
  HOD EN11 ....201 H5
St Edmunds RC Primary School
  POP/IOD E14 ....322 D7
St Edwards CE Comprehensive
  School CHDH RM6 ....288 D4
St Edwards CE Primary School
  ROM RM1 ....289 J1
St Felix RC Primary School
  HVHL CB9 ....34 A6
St Francis RC Primary School
  BRTR CM77 ....121 J1
  MAL CM9 ....214 C2
  SRTFD E15 ....307 H2
St Georges Centre
  GVW DA11 ....337 L4
St Georges CE School
  GVW DA11 ....337 K7
St Georges Hospital
  HCH RM12 ....312 B1
St Georges New Town
  Junior School COLS CO2 ....107 K8
St Georges Primary School
  COLS CO2 ....129 K1
St Georges RC Primary School
  SBN/FI SS3 ....303 H5
St Giles CE Primary School
  HSTD CO9 ....357 L1
St Gregorys CEVC
  Primary School SUD CO10 ....20 B7
St Helena School
  COLC CO3 ....107 G5
St Helens Catholic
  Infant School WALTH E17 ....284 F1
St Helens Primary School
  IPNE IP4 ....17 H4
St Helens RC Junior School
  BRWN CM15 ....256 A3
St Helens RC Primary School
  PLSTW E13 ....307 J8
St Hildas School
  WOS/PRIT SS0 ....300 F4
St Ignatius College
  EN EN1 ....232 B7
St James CE Primary School
  HLW CM18 ....203 L5
St James CE VA
  Primary School COL CO1 ....8 F6
St James CE Junior School
  FSTGT E7 ....307 J2

St James's Health Centre WALTH E17 ....284 B3
St Joachims RC Primary School CAN/RD E16 ....323 M2
St John Baptist CE Primary School HSTD CO9 ..358 D9
St John Fisher RC Primary School ERITHM DA18 ....326 B6
LOU IG10 ....250 F2
St John Payne RC School CHLM/WR CM1 ....193 J7
St John's Abbey Gateway COLS CO2 ....8 D9
St Johns CE Primary School BKHH IG9 ....249 L8
COLN CO4 ....108 A1
IPNE IP4 ....48 F6
RCHLM CM3 ....212 C8
St Johns Green Primary School COLS CO2 ....8 C8
St John's Hospital CHLM/GWD CM2 ....209 J7
St Johns Industrial Estate RBSF CM22 ....377 M2
St Johns RC Comprehensive School GVE DA12 ....338 A6
St Johns RC Primary School BERM/RHTH SE16 ....322 B5
GVE DA12 ....338 A6
St Johns RC Special School WFD IC8 ....268 D4
St Johns School BCAYW CM12 ....258 E1
EPP CM16 ....219 M8
St John's Walk Shopping Centre COL CO1 ....8 C8
St John the Baptist Primary School WARE SG12 ..185 H4
St Josephs Catholic Infant School LEY E10 ....284 C6
St Josephs College CHTY IP2 ....53 M2
St Josephs Convent School WAN E11 ....285 K4
St Josephs RC Aided Primary School HAR CO12 ....71 G3
St Josephs RC JMI School CHES/WCR EN8 ....232 F3
St Josephs RC Junior School LEY E10 ....284 E6
St Josephs RC Primary School BARK IG11 ....308 F5
BSF CM23 ....138 E3
CVI SS8
DAGW RM9 ....310 E1
GNWCH SE10 ....323 H6
SLH/COR SS17 ....317 G3
SUD CO10 ....20 B5
St Josephs RC School GVW DA11 ....337 G5
St Josephs School UPMR RM14 ....290 E7
St Joseph the Worker RC Primary School RBRW/HUT CM13 ..256 F2
St Katherine School CVI SS8 ....298 D8
St Lawrence CE Primary School K/T/MI CO5 ..130 C5
St Lawrence CE School WAB EN9 ....234 A3
St Leonards CE Junior School BOC CM0 ....393 N1
St Leonards Hospital SUD CO10 ....20 C6
St Lukes Catholic Primary School HLWW/ROY CM19 ..203 K3
St Lukes CE Primary School CAN/RD E16 ....323 J2
POP/IOD E14 ....323 G7
St Lukes Church Primary School K/T/MI CO5 ..150 A8
St Luke's Health Centre CAN/RD E16 ....323 J2
St Lukes Special School LOU IG10 ....250 D4
St Margaret Clitherow RC Primary School THMD SE28 ..325 L4
St Margarets CE Primary School HSTD CO9 ..355 P2
IP IP1 ....17 G3
PIT SS13 ....279 H8
St Margarets Hospital EPP CM16 ....220 C7
St Margarets Preparatory School HSTD CO9 ....80 A5
St Margarets Primary School BARK IG11 ....308 E5
St Marks Industrial Estate CAN/RD E16 ....324 A4
St Marks RC Primary School CHTY IP2 ....53 L2
St Marks West Essex Catholic School HLWS CM18 ..13 J8
St Martins School RBRW/HUT CM13 ..256 F4
St Mary Magdalene CE Primary School WOOL/PLUM SE18 ..324 C7
St Mary's Business Centre COLW CO5 ....8 A8
St Marys Catholic Primary School CHING E4 ..249 G8
HCH RM12 ....289 K6
St Mary's Catholic Primary School IPNE IP4 ....17 G3
St Marys Catholic School BSF CM23 ....138 F2
St Marys CE Primary School BOC CM0 ....393 M7
BRWN CM15 ....256 C2
RBSF CM22 ....376 E1
RCHLM CM3 ....244 E1
SAFWN CB10 ....28 A1
STSD CM24 ....115 M2
WALTH E17 ....284 E2
St Marys Hare Park School GPK RM2 ....289 M1
St Marys High School CHESW EN7 ....216 C9
St Marys Lower School WALTH E17 ....284 F1
St Mary's School COLW CO5 ....105 J8
St Marys RC Junior School WALTH E17 ....284 F1
St Marys RC Primary School PEND EN3 ....248 A4
TIL RM18 ....331 J9
St Marys Upper School COLW CO5 ....106 F6
St Matthew's CE Primary School IP IP1 ....16 C1
St Michaels CE Junior School CHLM/GWD CM2 ..225 M3
St Michaels CE Primary School BRTR CM7 ....121 G2
BSF CM23 ....138 F2
St Michaels Hospital BRTR CM7 ....121 H2

St Michaels Preparatory School LOS SS9 ....299 M4
St Michaels RC Primary School COLS CO2 ....128 F4
St Nicholas CE Primary School EHAM E6 ....308 C6
St Nicholas RC Primary School BOC CM0 ....390 C5
WICKE SS11 ....262 B6
St Nicholas School HLWE CM17 ....189 G6
St Nicholas Special School SOSN SS2 ....302 B3
St Osyth CE Primary School RCOS CO16 ....181 L1
St Pancras Catholic Primary School IP IP1 ....47 L2
St Patricks RC JMI School ROMW/RG RM7 ....270 E7
St Patricks RC Primary School WALTH E17 ....284 B2
WOOL/PLUM SE18 ....325 G7
St Pauls CE Primary School BRWN CM15 ....255 G2
St Pauls RC Primary School CHESW EN7 ....216 C5
St Pauls Way School BOW E3 ....306 D8
St Pauls with St Lukes CE Primary School BOW E3 ..322 C1
St Peters Catholic Primary School ROM RM1 ..289 G1
BRW CM14 ....273 C1
CHLM/GWD CM2 ....242 C1
HSTD CO9 ....356 D9
RCOLW CO6 ....124 D3
St Peters College CHLM/WR CM1 ....209 H1
St Peters High School BOC CM0 ....393 L7
St Peters Hospital MAL CM9 ....214 C3
St Peters RC Primary School BCAYE CM12 ....259 H7
DAGW RM9 ....310 C1
WOOL/PLUM SE18 ....324 E8
St Philomena School FOS CO13 ....137 J4
St Pius X RC Primary School CHLM/WR CM1 ....193 J7
St Saviours CE Primary School POP/IOD E14 ....322 C1
WALTH E17 ....284 C5
St Stephens Primary School EHAM E6 ....307 M4
St Teresa RC Primary School BCTR RM8 ....309 M1
St Teresas Primary School COLW CO5 ....106 B8
St Teresas RC Primary School RCFD SS4 ....283 J7
St Thomas a' Becket RC Primary School ABYW SE2 ..325 K6
St Thomas More High School for Boys WOS/PRIT SS0 ..300 D2
St Thomas More RC Primary School SAFWS CB11 ..30 B1
St Thomas Mores Catholic Primary School COL CO1 ....8 F7
St Thomas of Canterbury CE J & I School BRWN CM15 ..256 A3
St Thomas of Canterbury RC Primary School GRAYS RM17 ..330 E3
St Ursulas RC Infant School HARH RM3 ....271 L5
St Ursulas RC Junior School HARH RM3 ....271 L5
St Vincents RC Primary School BCTR RM8 ....287 M7
St Winefrides Catholic Primary School MNPK E12 ..308 C2
Salisbury Primary School MNPK E12 ....308 A2
Salthouse Harbour Hotel IPSE IP3 ....17 H6
Samuel Ward Upper School & Technology College HVHL CB9 ....34 E4
Sanders Draper School HCH RM12 ....312 A1
Sandon School CHLM/GWD CM2 ....210 E7
Sandringham Primary School FSTGT E7 ....307 M3
Saracens House Business Centre IP IP1 ....16 F3
Sarah Bonnell School SRTFD E15 ....307 H3
Sarbir Industrial Park HLW CM20 ....188 D4
Sawbridge Health Clinic SBW CM21 ....162 F7
Sawston Village College CBS CB2 ....22 B1
Sawyers Hall College of Science & Technology BRWN CM15 ..255 M7
Schooling Licensed Conveyancers GRAYS RM17 ..330 E4
School of Health RDART DA2 ....334 E8
Scimitar Park Industrial Estate PIT SS13 ....279 G3
Scott's Grotto WARE SG12 ....184 E1
Scotts Primary School HCH RM12 ....311 M2
Scott Wilkie Primary School CAN/RD E16 ....323 M2
Sealife Adventure SOSN SS1 ....19 L8
Sealife Aquarium SOS SS1 ....301 M7
Seedbed Business Centre BSF SS3 ....303 J6
Seevic College SBF/HAD SS7 ....280 D8
Selwyn Primary School CHING E4 ....266 F5
PLSTW E13 ....307 K5
Seven Kings Health Centre GDMY/SEVK IG3 ....287 H6
Seven Kings High School Technology College GNTH/NBYPK IG2 ..287 G5
Seven Mills Primary School POP/IOD E14 ....322 D5
Severalls Hospital COLN CO4 ....87 J8
Severalls Park Industrial Estate COLN CO4 ....88 A7
Seymour Gardens Medical Centre IL IG1 ....286 C6
Shadwell Dock Stairs WAP E1W 322 A3
Shaftesbury Primary School FSTGT E7 ....307 M4

Shaw Primary School SOCK/AV RM15 ....329 L2
Shears Green Primary School GVW DA11 ....337 J8
Sheepen Road Retail Park COLW CO3 ....107 G5
Sheering CE Primary School RBSF CM22 ....163 L8
Shelley Primary School CHONG CM5 ....380 G12
Shenfield CC BRWN CM15 ....256 C2
Shenfield High School BRWN CM15 ....256 D1
Shenfield Sports Centre BRWN CM15 ....256 D1
Shenval Industrial Estate HLW CM20 ....188 B5
Sheredes School HOD EN11 ....201 G4
Sheringham Junior School MNPK E12 ....308 C1
Shire Hill Industrial Estate SAFWS CB11 ....28 C8
Shoeburyness High School SBN/FI SS3 ....303 N1
Shotley Primary School RIPS/CAP IP9 ....66 G2
Shotley Sailing Club RIPS/CAP IP9 ....67 G3
Showcase Newham Cinema BARK IG11 ....308 F7
Shrewsbury Road Health Centre FSTGT E7 ....308 A4
Shrub End Clinic COLS CO2 ....128 E2
Sidegate Primary School IPNE IP4 ....48 F5
Sidney Russell School DAGW RM9 ....310 B1
Silkmead Farm Industrial Estate BUNT SG9 ..370 C12
Silver End Primary School WIT CM8 ....147 H2
Sir Charles Lucas Art College COLN CO4 ....108 B5
Sir Charles Lucas School COLN CO4 ....108 B5
Sir Francis Drake Primary School DEPT SE8 ....322 B6
Sir George Monoux College WALTH E17 ....266 E8
Sir John Cass Foundation/Redcoat School WCHPL E1 ..322 A1
Sir William Burrough Primary School POP/IOD E14 ..322 B2
Site of Greenwich Hospital GNWCH SE10 ....323 J8
Ski Centre CHTY IP2 ....54 A6
Skillion Business Centre BSDN SS14 ....2 F1
Skillion Business Park BARK IG11 ....309 J7
Ski Slope HLW CM20 ....13 G2
Skitts Hill Industrial Estate BRTR CM7 ....121 L4
SMA Medical Centre LEY E10 ....284 E5
Smilers Industrial Estate PIT SS13 ....279 J5
Snap Theatre BSF CM23 ....139 G2
Snaresbrook College SWFD E18 ....267 K8
Snaresbrook Crown Court WAN E11 ....285 J3
Snaresbrook Primary School WAN E11 ....285 K2
Social History Museum COL CO1 ....107 J4
Somers Heath Primary School SOCK/AV RM15 ..329 K3
Sorsby Health Centre CLPT E5 ....306 A1
South Benfleet Primary School SBF/HAD SS7 ..297 M3
Southchurch Hall Museum SOS SS1 ....19 M6
South East Essex College SOS SS1 ....18 F4
SOSN SS1 ....18 F2
SOSN SS2 ....301 M7
Southend Adult Community College SOS SS1 ..19 M5
Southend Airport SOSN SS2 ....283 G6
Southend Borough FC WOS/PRIT SS0 ....282 E7
Southend County Court SOS SS1 ....19 H5
Southend High School for Boys SOSN SS2 ....301 H2
Southend Hospital WOS/PRIT SS0 ....300 F2
Southend Museum, Planetarium & Discovery Centre SOSN SS2 ..18 F3
Southend-on-Sea Crematorium SOSN SS2 ....301 L1
Southend Pier SOS SS1 ....19 J8
Southend Pier Railway SOS SS1 ....19 J8
Southend RFC SOSN SS2 ....283 J7
Southend United FC (Roots Hall) SOSN SS2 ....301 H3
Southern Road Primary School PLSTW E13 ..307 L6
South Essex Clinical Trials Centre LOS SS9 ....299 L3
South Essex Crematorium UPMR RM14 ....313 G2
Southfields Business Park LAIN SS15 ....276 C6
South Green Primary School BCAYW CM12 ....258 E6
South Grove Primary School WALTH E17 ....284 B4
Southlake Primary School ABYW SE2 ....326 A5
Southmill Trading Centre BSF CM23 ....139 H3
Southminster Infant School BOC CM0 ....393 N2
Southminster Medical Centre BOC CM0 ....393 N1
South Park Business Centre IL IG1 ....287 H7
South Park Clinic IL IG1 ....309 H1
South Park Primary School GDMY/SEVK IG3 ..287 H8
South Quay Plaza POP/IOD E14 ....322 E5
South Rise Primary School WOOL/PLUM SE18 ..325 G8

South Suffolk Business Centre SUD CO10 ....21 G6
Southview Point WIT CM8 ....147 J7
South West Essex Magistrates Court BSDN SS14 ....2 E5
South Woodford Health Centre SWFD E18 ....267 K7
South Woodham Ferrers Leisure Centre RCHLM CM3 ....245 H6
Southwood Primary School DAGW RM9 ....310 B1
Sovereign Business Centre PEND EN3 ....248 C3
The Space Arts Centre Cinema POP/IOD E14 ....322 C7
Spa Pavillion Theatre FX IP11 ....69 G2
Spellbrook Primary School BSF CM23 ....163 G2
The Spinney J & I School HLW CM20 ....188 B8
Springbank Industrial Estate KIR/NAC IP10 ....56 C2
Springfield CC CHLM/GWD CM2 ....210 B1
Springfield Industrial Estate BOC CM0 ....393 J8
Springfield Junior School IL IG1 ....47 L5
Springfield Medical Centre CHLM/WR CM1 ....193 M7
Springfield School CHONG CM5 ....383 K4
Spring Meadow Primary School HAR CO12 ....14 C8
Springwood Industrial Estate BRTR CM7 ....121 G1
Sprites Junior School CHTY IP2 ....53 H3
Sproughton Business Park IP IP2 ....47 H6
Sproughton CE Primary School GPK RM2 ....47 G7
Squirrels Heath Junior School GPK RM2 ....289 L3
Ss Angelas & Bonaventures Sixth Form FSTGT E7 ..307 L3
Ss Peter & Pauls RC Primary School IL IG1 ..287 G8
Stadium Trading Estate SBF/HAD SS7 ....280 F6
Stafford Industrial Estate EMPK RM11 ....290 A1
Stambridge Primary School RCFD SS4 ....396 A7
Standard Industrial Estate CAN/RD E16 ....324 A5
Stanford Industrial Estate SLH/COR SS17 ....316 F4
Stanford-le-Hope Infant School SLH/COR SS17 ..317 G4
Stanhope Industrial Park SLH/COR SS17 ....317 J6
Stansted Clinic STSD CM24 ....115 M2
Stansted Manor Hotel BSF CM23 ....115 L8
Stanway Fiveways Primary School COLW CO3 ..106 A8
Stanway Primary School COLW CO3 ....105 M8
Stanway School COLW CO3 ....105 J8
Stanway Swimming Centre COLW CO3 ....105 J8
Stapleford Abbotts Golf Club ABR/ST RM4 ....253 K7
Stapleford Abbotts Primary School ABR/ST RM4 ..252 E5
Staples Road J & I School LOU IG10 ....250 B3
Staple Tye Shopping Centre HLWS CM18 ....203 L4
Star Business Centre DAGW RM9 ....327 G1
Star Lane Industrial Estate SBN/FI SS3 ....303 J2
Star Primary School CAN/RD E16 ....307 H8
Starr Hotel & Restaurant GTDUN CM6 ....117 H4
Station Industrial Estate BOC CM0 ....393 K8
Station Road Industrial Estate MAL CM9 ....175 H8
Station Yard Industrial Park GTDUN CM6 ....117 H6
Stebbing Primary School CHLM/GWD CM2 ....96 B7
Stebon Primary School POP/IOD E14 ....322 C1
Steeple Bumpstead Primary School HVHL CB9 ..344 J4
Stephen Hawking Primary School POP/IOD E14 ..322 B2
Stepney Greencoat CE Primary School POP/IOD E14 ..322 C2
Stepney Green School WCHPL E1 ....322 A1
Sterling Industrial Estate DAGE RM10 ....310 E1
Stewards School HLWS CM18 ....203 K5
Stifford Clays Health Centre CDW/CHF RM16 ..314 E4
Stifford Clays Primary School CDW/CHF RM16 ..314 E8
Stifford Primary School GRAYS RM17 ....330 B4
Stisted CE Primary School BRTR CM7 ....100 E6
Stock Brook Golf & Country Club BCAYW CM12 ..240 E6
Stock CE Primary School ING CM4 ....241 D2
Stock Industrial Park SOSN SS2 ....301 K1
Stockwell Lodge Medical Centre CHESW EN7 ..216 B5
Stoke-by-Nayland CEVC Primary School RCOLW CO6 ..361 P4
Stoke-by-Nayland Golf Club & Hotel RCOLW CO6 ..361 L2
Stoke-by-Nayland Middle School RCOLW CO6 ..361 P4
Stoke College SUD CO10 ....345 P2
Stoke County High School CHTY IP2 ....54 B2
Stonehill Business Centre UED N18 ....266 A5
Stonehill Business Park UED N18 ....266 A4
Stone House Hospital RDART DA2 ....334 F8

Stone Lake Retail Park CHARL SE7
Stoneydown Park Primary School WALTH E17
Storey Primary School CAN/RD E16
Stortford Hall Industrial Park BSF CM23
Stort Valley Industrial Estate BSF CM23
Stour Sailing Club MGTR CO11
Stratford College SRTFD E15
Stratford Magistrates Court SRTFD E15
Stratford St Mary Primary School RCOLE CO7
Stratford School FSTGT E7
Stratford Shopping Centre SRTFD E15
The Street Industrial Estate MAL CM9
Strumer End Industrial Estate HVHL CB9
Stuarts Industrial Estate CHLM/GWD CM2
Stubbers (Outdoor Pursuits Centre) UPMR RM14
Stump Cross SAFWN CB10
Stutton CE Primary School RIPS/CAP IP9
Sudbury Bowl SUD CO10
Sudbury Health Centre SUD CO10
Sudbury RUFC SUD CO10
Sudbury Town FC SUD CO040
Sudbury Upper School SUD CO10
Sue Ryder Foundation SUD CO10
Suffolk College SOSN IP4
The Suffolk Nuffield Hospital at Christchurch Park IP IP1
Suffolk Retail Park IP IP1
Suffolk Showground IPSE IP3
Summercroft Infant School BSF CM23
Summercroft Junior School BSF CM23
Sumners Community Recreation Centre HLWW/ROY CM19
Sunnymede Primary School BCAYE CM11
Surrey Docks Farm BERM/RHTH SE16
Surrey Docks Health Centre BERM/RHTH SE16
Surrey Docks Watersports Centre BERM/RHTH SE16
Surrey Quays Leisure Park BERM/RHTH SE16
Surrey Quays Shopping Centre BERM/RHTH SE16
Sutton Road Cemetery SOSN SS2
Suttons Business Park RAIN RM13
Suttons JMI School HCH RM12
Suttons Manor Clinic ABR/ST RM4
Swaines Industrial Estate RCFD SS4
Swan Business Park DART DA1
Swanscombe Business Centre SWCM DA10
Swan Valley Community School SWCM DA10
The Sweyne Junior School RAYL S6
The Sweyne Park School RAYL S6
Sybourn Infant School LEY E10
Sybourn Junior School WALTH E17
Sydney Russell Comprehensive School DAGW RM9
Tabor High School BRTR CM7
Tabor Middle School BRTR CM7
Takeley Business Centre RBSF CM22
Takeley Primary School RBSF CM22
Tanys Dell Primary School HLW CM20
Tattingstone CE Primary School RIPS/CAP IP9
Tavy Clinic ABYW SE2
Taylor Trading Estate HERT/BAY SG13
TCA Leisure Centre TIL RM18
Templars County J & I School WIT CM8
Temple Farm Trading Estate CHLM/GWD CM2
Temple Hill Primary School DART DA1
Temple Sutton Primary School SOSN SS2
Tendring Adult Community College COS CO15
Tendring Primary School RCOS CO16
Tendring Technology College FOS CO13
RCOS CO16
Terence McMillan Stadium PLSTW E13
Terling CE Primary School RCHLM CM3
Thames Barrier CAN/RD E16
Thames Barrier Information & Learning Centre WOOL/PLUM SE18
Thameside Community Health Care VGE SS16
Thameside Industrial Estate CAN/RD E16
Thameside Primary School GRAYS RM17

...hameside Theatre *GRAYS* RM17 ...330 D4
...hames Industrial Park *TIL* RM18 ...332 F3
...hames Magistrates Court *BOW* E3 ...306 D7
...hmead Leisure Centre *THMD* SE28 ...325 K3
...hmead Shopping Centre *THMD* SE28 ...325 K3
...hamesview Business Centre *RAIN* RM13 ...327 H1
...hames View Clinic *BARK* IG11 ...309 J6
...hames View J & I School *BARK* IG11 ...309 K6
...hamesview School *GVE* DA12 ...338 C8
...haxted Hall Hotel *GTDUN* CM6 ...74 C1
...haxted Primary School *GTDUN* CM6 ...74 D3
...heatre Royal *SRTFD* E15 ...307 G5
...heydon Bois Golf Club *EPP* CM16 ...235 L4
...heydon Bois Primary School *EPP* CM16 ...235 M6
...histlebrook Industrial Estate *ABYW* SE2 ...325 M6
...homas Arnold Primary School *DAGW* RM9 ...310 C4
...homas Gamuel Primary School *WALTH* E17 ...284 D4
...homas Lord Audley School & Language College *COLS* CO2 ...129 J3
...homas Rivers Medical Centre *SBW* CM21 ...162 D8
...homas Road Industrial Estate *POP/IOD* E14 ...322 D1
...homas Tallis School *WAB* EN9 ...234 A3
...homas Willingale Primary School *LOU* IG10 ...250 J1
...homas Wolsey Special School *IP* IP1 ...47 K2
...horley Hill Primary School *CM23* ...139 G5
...ndon Country Park *BRW/HUT* CM13 ...274 D2
...ndon Park Golf Club *BRW/HUT* CM13 ...274 E1
...rn Grove Primary School *SF* CM23 ...139 J3
...ntree Primary School *HARL* SE7 ...324 A8
...rpe Bay School *OS* SS1 ...302 C4
...rpe Cross *OS* SS9 ...136 A1
...pedene Primary School *N/FI* SS3 ...302 F6
...pe Hall Golf Club *OS* SS1 ...302 D6
...pe Hall Primary School *ALTH* E17 ...266 F7
...pe Hall School *N/FI* SS3 ...302 D3
...e Mills Heritage Centre *TFD* E15 ...306 F7
...e Rivers Golf & untry Club *RCHLM* CM3 ...230 B8
...shelfords Business Park *T/MI* CO5 ...149 H2
...twood School *LM/GWD* CM2 ...225 K2
...dersley J & I School *F/HAD* SS7 ...280 D7
...eston County h School *IP* IP1 ...47 M1
...ock Athletics Stadium *N/CHF* RM16 ...331 G1
...ock & Basildon College *W/CHF* RM16 ...331 J3
...ock & Basildon College (thermayne Campus) *SS16* ...295 J1
...ock Business Centre *HK* RM20 ...335 J1
...table School */MI* CO5 ...150 A7
...y Fort *RM18* ...337 M2
...Gravesend senger Ferry *M18* ...337 L2
...y Manor Infant School *M18* ...331 L6
...y Manor Junior School *M18* ...331 L6
...entre (Swimming Baths) */IOD* E14 ...322 D6
...eisure Centre */IOD* E14 ...322 D6
...am Medical Centre *CM0* ...390 D6
...e Heath Primary School *MI* CO5 ...173 L2
...e Museum *MI* CO5 ...174 A1
...e Sports Centre *MI* CO5 ...150 A6
...dustrial Estate *S* RM17 ...330 D3
...rn Museum *RM14* ...290 F5
...ary Primary School *CM9* ...385 N4
...ury Sailing Club *CM9* ...385 Q3
...unt D'Arcy CE ary School *MAL* CM9 ...384 G1
...e Primary School *W* E13 ...307 M8
...od School *E17* ...285 J8
...l Golf Club *IC* CO5 ...382 A5
...adow Golf Club *R* RM14 ...292 A7
...usiness Park *MI* CO5 ...149 L6
...amlets College *OD* E14 ...322 E6
...nds Golf Club *CM7* ...99 G6
...amparts ping Centre *IP* IP1 ...16 F4
...nfant School *RM11* ...289 M5
...Junior School *RM11* ...289 M5
...heatre *SS14* ...2 E7
...r Business Centre *G11* ...309 J8

Trafalgar Trading Estate *PEND* EN3 ...248 C4
Tramshed Theatre *WOOL/PLUM* SE18 ...324 E7
Travelodge
BSDN SS14 ...277 L4
CBE/LIN CB1 ...23 K1
EPP CM16 ...221 J7
GRH DA9 ...335 H7
HLW CM20 ...13 C1
K/T/MI CO5 ...150 K7
POP/IOD E14 ...323 G2
RBRW/HUT CM13 ...275 H6
REDBR IG4 ...286 C4
RIPS/CAP IP9 ...59 G1
ROM RM1 ...289 H3
WTHK RM20 ...329 J7
Treetops Special School *GRAYS* RM17 ...330 E3
Triangle Shopping Centre *WOTN* CO14 ...137 J2
Tricor Business Park *CHES/WCR* EN8 ...232 F4
Tricor Trading Estate *CHES/WCR* EN8 ...232 F4
Trident Industrial Estate *HOD* EN11 ...201 K2
Trimley St Martin Primary School *FX* IP11 ...62 A1
Trimley St Mary Primary School *FX* IP11 ...62 B5
Trinity Business Centre *BERM/RHTH* SE16 ...322 C5
Trinity Catholic Lower High School *WFD* IG8 ...267 K3
Trinity Hospital *GNWCH* SE10 ...323 G8
Trinity RC High School (Upper) *WFD* IG8 ...267 K3
Trinity Road Primary School *CHLM/GWD* CM2 ...5 L3
Trinity School *DAGE* RM10 ...288 D8
Trinity School Belvedere *BELV* DA17 ...326 F7
Tripcock Point Development Site *THMD* SE28 ...325 J3
Tudor CE Primary School *SUD* CO10 ...20 E3
Tudor Court Primary School *CDW/CHF* RM16 ...330 C1
Tunnel Avenue Trading Estate *GNWCH* SE10 ...323 G5
Tunnel Industrial Estate *WTHK* RM20 ...329 J7
Turner Rise Retail Park *COLN* CO4 ...8 C1
Turnford School *CHES/WCR* EN8 ...216 B1
Two Village Primary School *HAR* CO14 ...367 Q8
Twyford Business Centre *BSF* CM23 ...139 H4
The Tyrrells Primary School *CHLM/WR* CM1 ...194 B8
UCI Cinema
BERM/RHTH SE16 ...322 A6
BSDN SS14 ...277 L4
ED N9 ...248 A7
WTHK RM20 ...329 J7
UCI Filmworks Cinema *GNWCH* SE10 ...323 J7
UGA Cinema *IP* IP1 ...48 B8
UGC Cinema *HLW* CM20 ...188 A5
IP IP1 ...16 E6
Unity Health Centre *SUD* CO10 ...20 D6
Unity Trading Estate *WFD* IG8 ...286 A1
University of East London
BCTR RM8 ...309 K2
EHAM E6 ...324 D3
PLSTW E13 ...307 F4
SRTFD E15 ...306 F4
SRTFD E15 ...307 H5
University of Essex *COLN* CO4 ...130 C1
University of Greenwich *GNWCH* SE10 ...323 G8
WOOL/PLUM SE18 ...324 D6
University of London *ENC/FH* EN2 ...232 B6
University Yacht Club *RCOLE* CO7 ...156 C8
Uphall Primary School *IL* IG1 ...308 E2
Uplands Business Park *WALTH* E17 ...266 A8
Uplands Middle School *SUD* CO10 ...20 E3
Upminster Cemetery *UPMR* RM14 ...313 G2
Upminster Golf Club *UPMR* RM14 ...290 F5
Upminster Primary School *UPMR* RM14 ...290 F8
Upminster Trading Park *UPMR* RM14 ...292 A1
Upper Clapton RFC *EPP* CM16 ...220 C2
Upshire Primary School *WAB* EN9 ...234 C3
Upton Cross Primary School *PLSTW* E13 ...307 L5
Upton Lane Medical Centre *FSTGT* E7 ...307 L3
Ursuline High School *IL* IG1 ...286 E7
Valence House Museum & Library *BCTR* RM8 ...288 A7
Valence Junior School *BCTR* RM8 ...288 A7
Valentine High School *IL* IG1 ...286 D4
Valentines High Lower School *GNTH/NBYPK* IG2 ...286 E3
Valley Farm Holiday Park *COS* CO15 ...159 L7
Vange Primary School *VGE* SS16 ...295 M2
Vanguard Trading Estate *SRTFD* E15 ...306 F5
Vestry House Museum *WALTH* E17 ...284 E2
Vicarage Fields Health Clinic *BARK* IG11 ...308 F4
The Vicarage Field Shopping Centre *BARK* IG11 ...308 F4
Vicarage Primary School *EHAM* E6 ...308 C7
VI Components Industrial Park *ERITH* DA8 ...327 H8
Victoria Industrial Park *DART* DA1 ...334 A7

Victoria Park Industrial Centre *HOM* E9 ...306 C4
Victoria Plaza Shopping Centre *SOSN* SS2 ...19 G4
Victoria Wharf *POP/IOD* E14 ...322 B3
Victoria Wharf Industrial Estate *DEPT* SE8 ...322 C8
Viking Business Centre *ROMW/RG* RM7 ...288 F5
Village Infant School *DAGE* RM10 ...310 D4
VIP Trading Estate *CHARL* SE7 ...323 M7
VUE Cinema
DAGW RM9 ...310 B5
ROM RM1 ...289 H3
WTHK RM20 ...329 K6
Wadham Lodge Sports Centre *WALTH* E17 ...266 C7
Waldegraves Holiday Park *K/T/MI* CO5 ...178 D7
Wadringfield Heath Golf Club *WDBR* IP12 ...51 L7
Walnut Tree Hospital *SUD* CO10 ...20 B6
Waltham Abbey Gatehouse *WAB* EN9 ...233 K5
Waltham Abbey Marriott Hotel *WAB* EN9 ...234 A4
Waltham Abbey Swimming Pool *WAB* EN9 ...233 L5
Waltham Forest College *WALTH* E17 ...266 A8
WALTH E17 ...284 C1
Waltham Forest Magistrates Court *WALTH* E17 ...284 C1
Waltham Forest Pool & Track *WALTH* E17 ...266 E8
Waltham Forest Theatre *WALTH* E17 ...284 C1
Waltham Holy Cross Junior School *WAB* EN9 ...233 L3
Walthamstow Business Centre *WALTH* E17 ...266 F6
Walthamstow Greyhound Stadium *CHING* E4 ...266 N6
Walthamstow School for Girls *WALTH* E17 ...284 C2
Walton & Frinton Yacht Club *WOTN* CO14 ...369 M12
Walton Primary School *WOTN* CO14 ...369 N12
Wansfell College *EPP* CM16 ...235 L5
Wanstead CC *WAN* E11 ...285 L5
Wanstead CE Primary School *WAN* E11 ...285 K5
Wanstead Golf Club *WAN* E11 ...285 L5
Wanstead High School *WAN* E11 ...285 M5
Wanstead Hospital *WAN* E11 ...285 L5
Wanstead Leisure Centre *WAN* E11 ...285 M5
Wardmaster Infirmary *RIPS/CAP* IP9 ...364 G10
Warley Hill Business Park *RBRW/HUT* CM13 ...273 M5
Warley Hospital *BRW* CM14 ...273 L4
Warley Lodge Hospital *RBRW/HUT* CM13 ...274 A3
Warley Park Golf Club *RBRW/HUT* CM13 ...274 A4
Warley Primary School *BRW* CM14 ...273 M4
Warner Industrial Park *SUD* CO10 ...21 G5
Warren Comprehensive School *CHDH* RM6 ...288 C3
Warren Golf Club *MAL* CM9 ...212 E4
Warren Junior School *CHDH* RM6 ...288 C3
Warren Primary School *CDW/CHF* RM16 ...329 M6
Warren Sports Centre *CHDH* RM6 ...288 C3
Warriors Swim Centre *SOS* SS1 ...19 H5
Warwick School for Boys *WALTH* E17 ...284 F2
Waterfront Leisure Centre *WOOL/PLUM* SE18 ...324 D6
Water Gardens Shopping Centre *HLW* CM20 ...13 G6
Waterglade Retail Park *PEND* EN3 ...248 C2
Watermill Business Centre *PEND* EN3 ...248 C2
Waterside Business Park *WIT* CM8 ...171 L1
Waterside Farm Sports Centre *CVI* SS8 ...298 B7
Waterside Industrial Estate *HOD* EN11 ...201 L4
Waterside Primary School *WOOL/PLUM* SE18 ...325 G8
Waterside School *BSF* CM23 ...114 F2
Waterways Business Centre *PEND* EN3 ...233 G8
Wat Tyler Country Park *VGE* SS16 ...296 E4
Weald Park (Country Park) *BRW* CM14 ...255 H7
Weald Park Hotel (Golf & Country Club) *BRW* CM14 ...254 D4
Wellesley Primary School *SOSN* SS2 ...301 M2
Wellington Primary School *BOW* E3 ...306 D7
Well Lane Industrial Estate *RCHLM* CM3 ...211 M6
Wells Hall Community Primary School *SUD* CO10 ...45 M5
Wells Hall Primary School *SUD* CO10 ...45 L5
Wells Park School *CHIG* IG7 ...269 J3
Wells Primary School *WFD* IG8 ...267 L3
Wennington Hall Farm Business Centre *RAIN* RM13 ...328 B2
Wentworth Primary School *MAL* CM9 ...214 C1
West Beckton Health Centre *CAN/RD* E16 ...323 M1
Westborough Primary School *WOS/PRIT* SS0 ...18 C1
The Westborough Primary School *WOS/PRIT* SS0 ...301 H3
Westbourne High School *IP* IP1 ...47 K4

Westcliff High School for Boys *WOS/PRIT* SS0 ...300 D2
Westcliff High School for Girls *LOS* SS9 ...300 D2
Westcliff Hotel *WOS/PRIT* SS0 ...18 D6
Westcliff Leisure Centre *WOS/PRIT* SS0 ...18 D7
West Cliff Theatre *COS* CO15 ...6 E9
Westcourt Primary School *GVE* DA12 ...338 B7
Westerfield Business Centre *NHMKT* IP6 ...48 B7
Westerings Primary School *HOC/HUL* SS5 ...282 A1
West Essex Golf Club *LOU* IG10 ...249 H4
Westfield Community Primary School *HOD* EN11 ...201 G2
HVHL CB9 ...34 E6
Westfleet Trading Estate *WICKE* SS11 ...261 J7
Westgate Park *SUD* CO10 ...2 E7
West Ham Church Primary School *SRTFD* E15 ...307 J5
West Ham Lane Clinic *SRTFD* E15 ...307 H5
West Ham United FC (Upton Park) *EHAM* E6 ...308 A6
West Hatch High School *CHIG* IG7 ...268 C4
West Horndon Primary School *RBRW/HUT* CM13 ...275 K1
West India Pier *POP/IOD* E14 ...322 C5
West India Shopping Centre *POP/IOD* E14 ...322 D4
Westlands Community Primary School *CHLM/WR* CM1 ...4 B3
Westlands County Secondary School *CHLM/WR* CM1 ...209 G4
West Leigh Primary School *LOS* SS9 ...300 A3
Westley Heights Country Park *VGE* SS16 ...294 E3
Westmayne Industrial Park *BSDN* SS15 ...276 B7
West Mersea Museum *K/T/MI* CO5 ...177 L8
Westminster Industrial Estate *WOOL/PLUM* SE18 ...324 A6
West Station Industrial Estate *MAL* CM9 ...214 B4
West Station Yard *MAL* CM9 ...214 B4
West Thamesmead Business Park *THMD* SE28 ...325 J6
West Thurrock Primary School *WTHK* RM20 ...335 K1
Westwood Primary School *SBF/HAD* SS7 ...299 G1
Wethersfield Airfield *BRTR* CM7 ...355 K10
Wethersfield CE Primary School *BRTR* CM7 ...77 M2
Wheatcroft School *HERT/BAY* SG13 ...184 B2
Wheatear Industrial Estate *WIT* CM8 ...171 L4
Whipps Cross Hospital *LEY* E10 ...285 G4
White Bridge Primary School *LOU* IG10 ...250 B7
White Court CP School *BRTR* CM7 ...120 F7
Whitefield School & Leisure Centre *WALTH* E17 ...267 G6
Whitehall Estate *HLWW/ROY* CM19 ...202 F2
Whitehall Industrial Estate *COLS* CO2 ...130 A1
Whitehall Primary School *CHING* E4 ...267 H1
White Hart Hotel *BRTR* CM7 ...121 J2
CO LC ...124 C3
Whitehill Infant School *GVE* DA12 ...337 M8
Whitehouse Industrial Estate *IP* IP1 ...47 H2
White House J & I School *IP* IP1 ...47 K4
White Notley CE Primary School *WIT* CM8 ...146 C4
Whitmore Primary School *BSDN* SS14 ...278 B5
Whittingham Community Primary School *WALTH* E17 ...266 B7
Whitton Community Primary School *IP* IP1 ...47 K2
Whybridge Infant School *RAIN* RM13 ...311 K5
Whybridge Junior School *RAIN* RM13 ...311 J5
Wickford Business Park *WICKW* SS12 ...261 J7
Wickford Junior School *WICKW* SS12 ...260 F6
Wickford Swimming Pool *WICKW* SS12 ...260 F5
Widford Industrial Estate *CHLM/WR* CM1 ...4 B9
Widford Lodge Preparatory School *CHLM/GWD* CM2 ...4 D9
William Bellamy J & I School *DAGE* RM10 ...288 D7
William Davies Primary School *FSTGT* E7 ...308 A3
William de Ferrers School *RCHLM* CM3 ...245 H6
William Edwards School *CDW/CHF* RM16 ...314 C7
William Ford CE Junior School *DAGE* RM10 ...310 D4
William Julien Courtauld Hospital *BRTR* CM7 ...121 H3
William Morris Gallery *WALTH* E17 ...284 D1
William Morris School *WALTH* E17 ...266 B7
William Read Primary School *CVI* SS8 ...320 C2
William Torbitt J & I School *GNTH/NBYPK* IG2 ...287 H3
William Westley CE Primary School *CBS* CB2 ...22 A4
Willis Corroon Building *IP* IP1 ...16 E5
Willowfield Adult Education Centre *WALTH* E17 ...284 A1
Willowfield School *WALTH* E17 ...284 B1

Willowmere Caravan Park *SUD* CO10 ...45 L6
Wimbish Primary School *SAFWN* CB10 ...31 M5
Windrush Primary School *THMD* SE28 ...325 L4
Windsor Industrial Estate *HERT/BAY* SG13 ...184 C1
Windsor School Clacton *COS* CO15 ...7 M3
Windsor Trading Estate *BCAYE* CM11 ...260 A1
Winns Primary School *WALTH* E17 ...266 C8
Winsor Primary School *EHAM* E6 ...324 D2
Winter Gardens Junior School *CVI* SS8 ...298 C8
Witham Cemetery *WIT* CM8 ...171 K1
The Witham Health Centre *WIT* CM8 ...171 K3
Witham RUFC *WIT* CM8 ...171 H4
Witham Town Football & Social Club *WIT* CM8 ...171 H3
Wivenhoe Business Centre *RCOLE* CO7 ...130 F5
Wivenhoe Family Health Centre *RCOLE* CO7 ...130 E3
Wivenhoe Sailing Club *RCOLE* CO7 ...130 F6
Wivenhoe Town CC *RCOLE* CO7 ...130 E3
Wix & Wrabness Primary School *MGTR* CO11 ...366 F12
Wolsey Art Gallery *IP* IP1 ...16 F3
Wolsey Theatre *IP* IP1 ...16 D3
Woodacre Special School *SOCK/AV* RM15 ...329 J1
Woodbridge High School & Language College *WFD* IG8 ...267 L6
Woodcroft School *LOU* IG10 ...250 C1
Woodford County High School *WFD* IG8 ...267 J5
Woodford Golf Club *WFD* IG8 ...267 J4
Woodford Green Preparatory School *WFD* IG8 ...267 K5
Woodford Green Primary School *WFD* IG8 ...267 J4
Woodford Medical Clinic *RCHLM* CM3 ...211 M6
Woodford Trading Estate *WFD* IG8 ...267 M8
Woodgrange Infant School *FSTGT* E7 ...308 A2
Woodgrange Park Cemetery *FSTGT* E7 ...308 A2
Woodgreen Animal Shelter *ROY* SG8 ...349 M8
Woodhall Business Park *SUD* CO10 ...43 J7
Woodhall CP School *SUD* CO10 ...20 E1
Woodham Ley Primary School *SBF/HAD* SS7 ...279 L7
Woodham Walter CE Primary School *MAL* CM9 ...213 G2
Woodhill Primary School *CHARL* SE7 ...324 B7
Woodlands J & I School *IL* IG1 ...309 G1
Woodlands Preparatory School *RBRW/HUT* CM13 ...274 A6
Woodlands School *VGE* SS16 ...2 F9
Wood Lane Sports Centre *BCTR* RM8 ...288 E6
Woodman Road Cemetery *BRW* CM14 ...256 A8
Woodside Junior School *WALTH* E17 ...284 F1
Woodside Primary School *CDW/CHF* RM16 ...331 J2
Woodside School *BELV* DA17 ...326 E7
Wood Street Health Centre *WALTH* E17 ...284 F1
Woodville Halls *GVW* DA11 ...337 L5
Woodville Primary School *RCHLM* CM3 ...244 F4
Wood Wharf *POP/IOD* E14 ...322 E4
Wood Wharf Business Park *POP/IOD* E14 ...322 F5
Woolmore Primary School *POP/IOD* E14 ...322 F3
Woolwich County Court *WOOL/PLUM* SE18 ...324 D6
Woolwich Crown Court *THMD* SE28 ...325 H5
Woolwich Polytechnic School *THMD* SE28 ...325 K4
Worcesters Primary School *EN* ...232 A8
The Working Silk Museum *BRTR* CM7 ...121 J3
World End *TIL* RM18 ...337 L2
Wormley Primary School *BROX* EN10 ...216 F1
Writtle College *CHLM/WR* CM1 ...208 E2
Writtle Primary School *CHLM/WR* CM1 ...208 D5
Wrotham Road Health Clinic *GVW* DA11 ...337 L6
Wrotham Road Primary School *GVW* DA11 ...337 L5
Wyburns Primary School *RAYL* SS6 ...281 J5
Wycke Hill Business Park *MAL* CM9 ...214 B5
Wykeham Primary School *HCH* RM12 ...311 K6
Yale Business Park *IPSE* IP3 ...55 L5
Yardleys Business Park *BSDN* SS14 ...277 J4
BSDN SS14 ...278 C3
Yardley Primary School *CHING* E4 ...248 E5
Yellow Dot Sports Club *SUD* CO10 ...21 G7

The Post Office is a registered trademark of Post Office Ltd. in the UK and other countries.

Schools address data provided by Education Direct.

Petrol station information supplied by Johnsons

One-way street data provided by © Tele Atlas N.V. Tele Atlas

Garden centre information provided by

Garden Centre Association Britains best garden centres

Wyevale Garden Centres

The statement on the front cover of this atlas is sourced, selected and quoted from a reader comment and feedback form received in 2004